UNIX

FOURTH EDITION

Robin Anderson
Andy Johnston
et al

SAMS

UNIX Unleashed, Fourth Edition

Copyright © 2002 by Sams

International Standard Book Number: 067232251X

Library of Congress Catalog Card Number: 2001093499

Printed in the United States of America

First Printing: December 2001

04   03   02   01   4   3   2   1

Trademarks

Warning and Disclaimer

ASSOCIATE PUBLISHER
Jeff Koch

ACQUISITIONS EDITOR
Kathryn Purdum

DEVELOPMENT EDITOR
Mark Renfrow

MANAGING EDITOR
Matt Purcell

PROJECT EDITOR
Natalie Harris

COPY EDITOR
Krista Hansing

PRODUCTION
D&G Limited, LLC

TECHNICAL EDITORS
Robert Jensen
Scott Orr

TEAM COORDINATOR
Denni Bannister

INTERIOR DESIGNER
Gary Adair

COVER DESIGNER
Aren Howell

Contents at a Glance

Contents

6   Logging   253

15   Basic Web Services   639

20   Advanced Web Services   839

About the Lead Authors

Robin Anderson began her involvement with computers innocently enough with an Amiga, WordPerfect, and Infocom games. In late 1993, she turned her hand to student consulting at the University of Maryland, Baltimore County (UMBC), working with PCs, Macs, VAXen, and, finally, UNIX machines.

After graduating with honors in Computer Science and History, Robin remained at UMBC and is now a UNIX SysAdmin Specialist in OIT (UMBC's Office of Information Technology). She also managed OIT's Operations Support Staff and is a member of the Security Work Group.

Robin developed and taught an undergraduate UNIX SysAdmin course for UMBC's CS/EE department in 2000. She has earned two security certifications from the SANS Institute: the GCUX (UNIX Administrator, with honors) and the GCIH (Incident Handling). She works with SANS to develop online exam materials and presentations, and she recently taught SANS LevelOne security courses for UMBC's Department of Professional Education and Training.

Andy Johnston was born in May of 1958. Most of the rest has been improvisation. After teaching high school math, he became a programmer. He worked for the State of Maryland making population projections and lots of maps, and later for Computer Sciences Corporation, where he worked on spacecraft-tracking software and environmental modeling. One day, the UNIX system in which his virtual fish swam suffered a drive crash, and he (quickly) became a UNIX systems administrator. Andy provided system support for several projects, including the International Ultraviolet Explorer. In 1999, he took his current position at the University of Maryland, Baltimore County (UMBC) Office of Information Technology as a manager of UNIX support staff and IT security. Andy holds a Bachelor's degree in Biology from Princeton University and a Master's degree in Mathematics from UMBC. He has been involved at various times in the Baltimore and Washington, D.C. SAGE groups and has spoken at SANS conferences.

About the Contributing Authors

Robert Banz (banz@membrain.com) is the coordinator of systems engineering for the University of Maryland, Baltimore County (UMBC). He has been involved in UNIX software development and administration since 1992, working as an independent consultant and also working directly for various local organizations. His current focus is primarily on directory services and middleware development. On the side, he enjoys music, home improvement, and burning things. (http://www.calefaction.org)

Jay Beale is the lead developer of the Bastille Linux Project, which creates a wildly popular security-tightening program. As an independent security consultant and trainer, he authored the Center for Internet Security's Linux Security Benchmark and wrote the Center's Security Measurement "tester" program. He formerly served as Security Team Director for the Linux vendor MandrakeSoft and as a system and security administrator for the distance-education–focused University of Maryland, University College.

Jay is a frequent conference speaker and the author of a number of articles on UNIX/Linux security, along with the upcoming book *Securing Linux the Bastille Way*, to be published by Addison Wesley. You can learn more about his articles, talks, and favorite security links at http://www.bastille-linux.org/jay.

Matt Bishop received his Ph.D. in computer science from Purdue University, where he specialized in computer security, in 1984. He was a research scientist at the Research Institute of Advanced Computer Science and was on the faculty at Dartmouth College before joining the Department of Computer Science at the University of California at Davis.

His main research area is the analysis of vulnerabilities in computer systems, including modeling them, building tools to detect vulnerabilities, and ameliorating or eliminating them. This includes detecting and handling all types of malicious logic, especially computer worms and computer viruses. He is also active in the areas of network security, the study of denial-of-service attacks and defenses, policy modeling, software assurance testing, and formal modeling of access control. In addition, he studies the issue of trust as an underpinning for security policies, procedures, and mechanisms, and he is known in part for his work in UNIX security.

He is active in information assurance education, is a charter member of the National Colloquium on Information Systems Security Education, and led a project to gather and make available many unpublished seminal works in computer security.

He also teaches software engineering, machine architecture, operating systems, programming, and (of course) computer security.

Rich Blum has worked for the past 13 years as a network and systems administrator for the U.S. Department of Defense at the Defense Finance and Accounting Service. There he has been using UNIX operating systems as an FTP server, TFTP server, email server, mail list server, and network-monitoring device in a large networking environment. Rich currently serves on the board of directors for Traders Point Christian Schools; he is active on the computer support team at the school, helping to support a Microsoft network in the classrooms and computer lab of a small K–8 school. Rich has a bachelor of science degree in electrical engineering, and a master of science degree in management, specializing in management information systems, both from Purdue University. When Rich is not being a computer nerd, he is either playing electric bass for the church worship band or spending time with his wife, Barbara, and two daughters, Katie Jane and Jessica.

Timothy M. Champ is a student systems administrator for the Office of Information Technology at the University of Maryland, Baltimore County (UMBC). Tim has been working with UNIX systems for more than two years, from Solaris to IRIX to multiple Linux distributions. He will finish his bachelor of science degree in computer science in December 2001 and will be looking for full-time employment while he works on his master's degree in information systems. Tim lives outside Baltimore, Maryland, in a suburb called White Marsh.

David Ennis began programming almost 30 years ago and has been an independent consultant in Southern California for the last 25 years. He first discovered UNIX and C in the late 1970s and began working with them at Hughes Aircraft in the mid-1980s. He has worked as a developer, system administrator, trainer, and consultant for a number of companies, including more than a few Fortune 500 companies. His experience with UNIX has been on a wide variety of systems, ranging from PCs to mainframes, using an equally wide variety of UNIX versions. He previously wrote *Teach Yourself the UNIX C Shell in 14 Days*, and he wrote Chapter 9, "Day-to-Day System Administration," in this book.

Todd Herr has a bachelor of science degree in computer science from Lock Haven University of Pennsylvania. He has been working in the IT industry as both a systems administrator and a software developer since 1989. Although he specializes in Solaris, his experience covers many different flavors of UNIX. He has worked in all sizes of environments in both production and user support roles. In his spare time, when not spending time with his family, he likes to play golf, and he hopes to someday be good enough to play it better. He can be reached at todd@angrysunguy.com.

Sandy Kolstad Antunes is firmly enmeshed within the astrophysical, business startup, and role-playing communities, and there is a surprisingly amount of crossover in these. Currently on leave from NASA satellite work to complete his Ph.D., Sandy is also a proud househusband and, when time allows, able freelance writer. For a full background, just look him up on Google.

Emma Kolstad Antunes wrote her first Web page in vi for Mosaic, but she prefers to use Dreamweaver and BBEdit today. She has been a Web master at NASA's Goddard Space Flight Center since 1994. An experienced Web developer with a background in designing and maintaining complex, database-driven Web sites, these days Emma spends more of her time telling other people how to do good Web design than actually getting to do much of her own.

Jon Lasser lives in Baltimore, Maryland, where he is a consultant specializing in UNIX security, systems administration, and training. He is the lead coordinator for the Bastille Linux Project. He can be reached at jon@cluestickconsulting.com.

Kevin Lyda was fork()ed at 37058400. After spending many years processing stdin in various locations (Brooklyn, New York; Salina, Kansas; Huntington, New York; Buffalo, New York), he began spewing results to stdout, first in Buffalo, then in Boston, Massachusetts, and now in Dublin, Ireland. It is his hope that all his calls to read (STDIN_FILENO,...) will succeed for the lifetime of his process and that the data output is of use.

Andrew R. Senft is a co-founder of Easy Software Products, a small software company specializing in printing and Internet technologies. Previously, Andrew worked for the Navy for 10 years as a software engineer.

Carolyn Sienkiewicz is an ex-professional musician who has been administering UNIX systems since 1986. She has a master of science degree in computer science from Johns Hopkins University. When not managing systems and sysadmins, she and her husband can be hailed on the Chesapeake Bay, where they sail their sailboat *Whiskers*, a Catalina 34.

Kurt Wall has been using and programming Linux and UNIX since 1993. In no particular order, he enjoys coffee, cooking, coding, staying up late, and sleeping even later, the latter of which makes any day job a challenge. When he gets tired of computers, he reads an occasional novel—historical fiction, science fiction, philosophy, political theory, American history—and cookbooks, and he dreams of going to culinary school and becoming a professional chef. He graduated with a bachelor of arts degree, cum laude, in American history from the University of Utah.

Kurt is the author of *Linux Programming Unleashed*, *Linux Programming Unleashed*, *2nd Edition*, and *Linux Programming by Example*. He is the lead author of *Red Hat Linux Network and System Administration*. Kurt also has contributed chapters to *The Informix Handbook*, *The Linux Bible*, as well as forthcoming titles on Linux clustering, Linux performance tuning and capacity planning, and Microsoft Access database development. While working for Caldera Systems, Kurt wrote too many Caldera OpenLinux user guides, manuals, FAQs, READMEs, and whitepapers to count.

Kurt is also the technical editor for all or part of *Practical Linux*; *Red Hat Administrator's Handbook*; *Linux Security Toolkit*; *Teach Yourself KDE 1.1 in 24 Hours*; *Teach Yourself Linux in 24 Hours, 2nd Edition*; *Linux: The Complete Reference, 4th Edition*; *Linux Database Bible*; *KDE 2.0 Development*; *Caldera OpenLinux Secrets*; *Linux Administrator's Bible*; and *Caldera OpenLinux Bible*, as well as upcoming books on Linux performance tuning and capacity planning, Linux clustering, Linux for small business environments, and other titles.

Having survived Marine Corps boot camp, Kurt has an extreme dislike for talking about himself in the third person.

Michael Wessler received his bachelor of science degree in computer technology from Purdue University in West Lafayette, Indiana. He is an Oracle Certified Database Administrator for Oracle 8 and 8i. He has administered Oracle databases on NT and various flavors of UNIX and Linux at several different companies, ranging in size from a handful of employees to IT staffs in the thousands. Included in this experience is working at a true dotcom startup and managing a mission-critical OPS database on a Sun Cluster. Michael also has programmed professionally in COBOL, SQL, and PL/SQL. Currently, he is an Oracle consultant for Perpetual Technologies working at the Department of Defense in Indianapolis, Indiana. Michael is the author of *Oracle DBA on UNIX and Linux*, and he is a co-author of *Oracle Unleashed, Second Edition*; *UNIX Primer Plus, Third Edition*; and *COBOL Unleashed*. Michael can be reached at mwessler@yahoo.com.

Dedications

For my kith and kin—you are all dear and dearly loved. —Robin Anderson

To my grandfathers: H.K. Fleming, Writer and Taylor Johnston, Teacher. —Andy Johnston

We wish to thank Ivy and Max for being patient and giving us the time to write this.
—Emma and Sandy Kolstad Antunes

To Joseph, Gloria, Bill, and Sharon. —Robert Banz

To Shuigen, Eric, and Joan, who gave me my first opportunity, along with a good bit
of mentoring, in this wonderful field. —Jay Beale

To my family. —Matt Bishop

This is dedicated to my wife, Barbara, and daughters, Katie Jane and Jessica.
Thanks, as always, for your love, faith, and support. —Rich Blum

Andy and Robin: You've opened the door to me for so many opportunities—thank you.
Mom and Dad: Thank you for the sacrifices that it took to get me where I am in my life.
I love you both so much. —Timothy M. Champ

To my son and daughters, Craig, Courtney, and Andrea: Thank you for putting up with a dad who
often had to stay behind to work on his writing. I love you all very much. Most of all, thanks to my
wife, Perri, who put up with me during what, at times, seemed like an impossible project.
Thank you for your patience, caring, and support during what were trying times for the
entire family. I couldn't have done it without you. —David Ennis

To my wife, Karen, for encouraging me to reach for things that I thought weren't in my grasp, and
to my daughter, Riley, for reminding me what unfettered joy and wonder look like. —Todd Herr

To my irresistible Tammy, for her endless support and love. —Andrew R. Senft

My portion of this work is dedicated to my husband, Mark, who is my precious soul mate
and my safe harbor. —Carolyn Sienkiewicz

To the victims and heroes of September 11, 2001. —Kurt Wall

I would like to dedicate this work to my parents, Jon and Barb. Thanks for all the
support you've given me over the years! —Michael Wessler

Acknowledgments

My love and thanks go first to my kin. Mom and Dad (known to the rest of the world as Betty and Mark Werner)—we've gone through and grown through a lot over the years. I love you very much and am deeply grateful for your support. Erin and Gary—my favorite sister and brother! Thanks for being there and listening to book-related adventures, even if it was for the hundredth time. Grandma (whom the world knows as Violet Reed)—you have always been and continue to be an inspiration to me. Thank you for your unwavering, patient love.

As for my kith, well, you are quite a numerous tribe that I'm glad I can think of as family. Esme, the wonder-kitty—you are a marvelous consolation and distraction rolled up into one furry, smoke-tabby force of nature. Pam and Guy—you are both amazing holistic practitioners and dear friends who have kept me balanced and healthy in so many ways. Serena and Kelly—though sworn to secrecy on the precise number of years of our friendship, I treasure every one. You are both gems. Toby and Brendan—thanks for putting up with the multi-month radio silence as I worked on the book. Your spur-of-the-moment, help-I-think-I'm-panicking words of encouragement were vital. Andy—you know I could never have made it here without you. To the other authors—thanks for putting up with my opinionated ways. You are all stellar. To Rob Jenson—our work is much more complete and (ahem) correct, thanks to your extensive work. Happily, you have averted much embarrassment. Katie—looks like we all made it through, after all!
—Robin Anderson

I would like to thank my wife, Sherryl, for her eagle-eyed review of my galleys, and for her patience with my irritability, distraction, and frequent late nights in the basement working on this book. I would also like to thank my dog, D'Artagnan, for the long walks through which he listened sympathetically and without interruption to my ideas, complaints, and general whining.

The contributing authors are an amazingly talented collection of sysadmins who produced outstanding work here. It is a privilege to appear here in their company. Rob Jenson, it must be noted, has supported us in writing and in restaurants with excellent, extensive corrections and suggestions. ——Andy Johnston

Special thanks to Patrick Chipman for research help on ASP and CGI.pm. —Emma and Sandy Kolstad Antunes

I would like to thank my cat, Tyler, for keeping me sane by purring constantly in my ear. I would also like to thank Robin and Andy for assisting me in the difficult task of writing this acknowledgment. ——-Robert Banz

First, I would like to thank Andy and Robin for their encouragement and support. It helped to get me over the hump and gave me the final push I needed to get my chapter done. A very special thanks to Katie Purdum for her incredible patience with me. Also, her encouragement helped a great deal when I needed a lift at the end. Thank you to all the editors behind the scenes at Sams who I know put the finishing touches on my work to make it shine. —David Ennis

About the Technical Editor

Rob Jenson has been a computer aficionado since 1984 and a systems administrator, software developer, and sometimes both, since 1988, when he received a bachelor of science degree in Computer Science from Rensselaer Polytechnic Institute. The majority of his recent work is in computer security, including work for NASA and a large ISP. He is also the president of Spotch Consulting, Inc., a miniature consulting company. He fancies himself a computer security curmudgeon.

Tell Us What You Think!

As the reader of this book, *you* are our most important critic and commentator. We value your opinion and want to know what we're doing right, what we could do better, what areas you'd like to see us publish in, and any other words of wisdom you're willing to pass our way.

As an Associate Publisher for Sams, I welcome your comments. You can fax, email, or write me directly to let me know what you did or didn't like about this book—as well as what we can do to make our books stronger.

Please note that I cannot help you with technical problems related to the topic of this book, and that due to the high volume of mail I receive, I might not be able to reply to every message.

When you write, please be sure to include this book's title and author as well as your name and phone or fax number. I will carefully review your comments and share them with the author and editors who worked on the book.

Fax: 317-581-4770

Email: feedback@samspublishing.com

Mail: Jeff Koch
Sams
201 West 103rd Street
Indianapolis, IN 46290 USA

Foreword

This new edition of UNIX UNLEASHED has some significant changes from previous editions. All "new edition" books have a series of updates; but, this time, the changes are a reformation of purpose. The target audience shifts from "UNIX user" to "system administrator." The approach changes from "what is a shell" to "why is paging done into swap space." The book no longer goes into depth in software development tools, but now it covers implementation of host security.

The book isn't a checklist. It isn't for the developer who needs to fix a personal machine. It is a complete guide to the how, the why and the when that a sysadmin does major day-to-day tasks. It turns a regular user into a mid-range sysadmin. Unlike a textbook, it is readable from cover to cover. At the same time, it is reference manual-capable without reading like a reference manual. The book was written by UNIX sysadmins for UNIX sysadmins, and it includes a continual string of tips from people who do this work all the time.

So, why yet another UNIX sysadmin book? True, there are a few good ones out there already. Those books are, in my view, geared toward (and well-geared toward) classroom-style learning. They are good reference manuals if you need to look up a specific item. However, this book can also fit those roles. The difference is, I think, that this book is ideally suited to those of us who have to teach ourselves, on the fly, how to administer a site full of UNIX machines.

Hal Miller

Former President, SAGE

Introduction

The field of UNIX system administration has developed considerably in the nearly three decades since the birth of UNIX. Until the 1990s, many system administrators (known as *sysadmins*) themselves were unaware that they were even in a coherent profession. At the start of that decade, the Internet was a relatively obscure mechanism for communication between research institutions. By 1999, Internet activity was a common topic of news articles and financial speculation, and Internet access had become a basic requirement for business and education. UNIX rapidly proved to provide flexible, reliable platforms for Internet services, database servers, and almost anything else called for in the ensuing explosion of information transactions. The spread of UNIX systems created a demand for people who could install, configure, and maintain those systems in a manner that kept them flexible and reliable. That demand not only still exists, but it has grown rapidly.

Still, there seems to be a shortage of well-trained, reliable sysadmins. Few universities offer courses, let alone degrees, in the subject. Where such courses are offered, they are seldom taught by an experienced sysadmin. (There are some happy exceptions that we hope will become a trend.) People often "drift" into our field from other computer-related activities. Some install a free UNIX, such as Linux, on their PC in lieu of a Microsoft operating system and subsequently learn some of the basics on their own. In other cases, a software developer given root access to fix her own system by an overburdened sysadmin eventually becomes a sysadmin herself. The optimal path, though, is through an informal "apprenticeship" in which the "drifter" learns from one or more experienced sysadmins. There is no official end to this apprenticeship. For practical purposes, it usually ends when the apprentice takes a job and finds no more experienced sysadmins (often no other sysadmins at all) present to help.

This book is intended primarily for this apprentice. We assume that you have a working knowledge of UNIX as a user, although many chapters will review the basics to establish context and some familiarity with the operating system itself. Using the classification system of the System Administrator's Guild (SAGE), we assume that you are preparing to function as a Level 2 sysadmin.[1] For the most part, the chapters reflect the different responsibilities that such a sysadmin might have. Each chapter tries to balance theory and practice so that you will know how to perform tasks now but still have enough background to develop deeper knowledge and to troubleshoot unexpected problems. In addition, extra material has been included that might be of interest to the more experienced sysadmin.

The contributors to this book, including the technical editors who reviewed each chapter, are experienced sysadmins. It is our hope that the final work will capture some of the flavor of the "apprentice" system in that it contains many of the explanations and much of the advice that each author would offer in person. Although all the authors have common guidelines for their writing, we try to retain each individual voice.

There may be inconsistencies between chapters; authors may appear to contradict each other. When this dispute is based on opinion and experience, no attempt has been made to reconcile the contradiction. This is also part of the experience of learning to be a sysadmin.

There are many varieties of UNIX. Rather than try (and fail) to discuss each one of them, we have selected two UNIX variants from which to draw examples: Red Hat Linux 7.1 and Sun Microsystems' Solaris 8. These are, respectively, very popular free and commercial distributions of UNIX in their most recent releases as of the summer of 2001. The underlying concepts presented in this book can be applied to other varieties of UNIX with little or no modification. To provide a practical focus throughout the book, we use current versions of Red Hat Linux and Solaris to provide consistent reference platforms on which to base our discussions.

We hope that new sysadmins will find this book a valuable learning tool and that experienced sysadmins will find it a worthwhile reference.

Endnote

[1] *Level 2 refers to a "Junior" sysadmin in the SAGE classification system. The system is documented at:* `http://www.usenix.org/sage/jobs/jobs-descriptions.html`.

Basic Operation

PART

I

Startup and Shutdown

by Robin Anderson

IN THIS CHAPTER

Introduction

As I'm writing this, I envision you sitting with this book on your desk, with a newly installed Operating System on a nearby machine and a look of anticipation on your face. Or possibly frustration—sometimes it's hard to tell. Of course, if you just have bare hardware in front of you, don't despair. Turn to Appendix A, "High-Level Installation Steps," for a short step-by-step guide to installing Red Hat and Solaris. Then come back here for more details.

So now you've definitely got an installed machine and you might be wondering just how it all works. We're going to start here with the basics: the boot process, without which nothing happens. More than that, the boot process *is* Unix in a nutshell; through it you can see all the various components and design schemata that make Unix what it is. The rest of the book is concerned with *administering* the Operating System, but here we are looking at the OS itself and how it gets started every time you press the power button.

Outlining the Five-Step Boot Process

We can break down the boot process into five major stages:

1. Firmware: hardware self-recognition (PROM/BIOS)
2. Bootloader: loading the OS (LILO/bootblk)
3. Kernel: initialization and control transfer
4. `init` and initialization scripts
5. Over to the admin: miscellaneous wrap-up

We'll be going over each of these in detail in the rest of this chapter. The key to understanding this process is realizing that it boils down to functionality layering. That is, each step layers additional functionality onto the system's current state.

The first step is all hardware-based: turning on the power and letting the machine do self-discovery and testing. Then we add logical layers: the kernel, system processes, and so on. The progression can also be thought of in terms of a transition of system control from hardware to software.

So let's consider the lowest layer: hardware. This is where you plug in the power cord and flip on the power switch. Electricity and power supplies, connectors and contact points are the focus of your concerns here. Getting all of this working is an absolute prerequisite to the following steps.

Step 1: Firmware—Hardware Self-Recognition

Let's assume that you succeeded in connecting the hardware to a functioning outlet and you can toggle the power switch. Now that the machine is turned on and is properly distributing power to its components, you are entering Step 1, the firmware stage.

Firmware is instructions that sit at a level between hardware and software, translating between the two realms. While this may sound like a trivial task, it is anything but: Firmware is not just translating between languages, but between species as well. Hardware understands electrical impulses. Software (at its most fundamental level) understands streams of 1s and 0s. Firmware is where the two merge, embedding software-type routines permanently (or semi-permanently) into the hardware. It represents the most basic level of user interaction with a computer (other than old-style plug-pulling).

Some Instances of Firmware

You are likely to run across the following set of terms at some point in your firmware experiences:

- BIOS
- PROM/EPROM/EEPROM
- NVRAM
- CMOS

Before we discuss the specifics of each, let's look at what they all have in common:

- All are instances of non-volatile memory chips found in PCs or Sun systems.
- All are also non–OS-dependent technologies. Their design and action are independent of what you want to store in them.
- All have similar functions: maintaining essential, simple software, drivers, and related variables. They also provide basic access to the keyboard, display, and fixed disks.

- All are designed to be available and remain undamaged even in the event of disk/peripheral failures; their stored programs are run without accessing either a fixed or removable disk

- All house the bootloader program (see the upcoming section "Step 2: Bootloader")

BIOS

BIOS stands for Basic Input/Output System and is generally found on PC motherboards and PC peripheral cards (such as video and SCSI). BIOS settings are usually viewed and modified through a series of text-based menu screens available for access only at boot-time.

PROM

PROM stands for Programmable Read-Only Memory and comes in three flavors:

> *WORM* (Write-Once, Read Many) is a standard device that retains its information even after a reboot or power-down. Any device that can preserve information this way is referred to as "non-volatile."

> *EPROM* (Erasable Programmable Read-Only Memory) is a modified PROM that can be erased for rewrite by exposing it to ultraviolet light. Once upon a time, Sun and other companies used this type of firmware device. It was the first step in allowing users to upgrade firmware without discarding the hardware that it lived on.

> *EEPROM* (Electrically Erasable Programmable Read-Only Memory) is another modified PROM that can be erased for rewrite by exposing to a low-voltage electrical charge (rather than UV light). Sun currently uses this kind of chip; it is much simpler to recover from bad settings and to upgrade when new firmware revisions are released. It also makes it possible to easily change and store settings: You type in the command, and the system sends a tiny current to make the appropriate changes to the firmware's state.

NVRAM

NVRAM stands for Non-Volatile Random-Access Memory and is really a compound device composed of both EEPROM storage and normal RAM. At power-up, contents stored in the PROM are copied or *shadowed* into RAM for faster access. Any changes made to the settings are written back to EEPROM (thus requiring that particular type of PROM).

CMOS

CMOS stands for Complementary Metal Oxide Semiconductor and is a low–power-consumption semiconductor. It has non-volatile properties when powered by a small battery, allowing settings to be maintained even when the system is powered off. Typical settings include date, time, and configuration parameters (for example, the hardware clock).

The appearance of firmware interfaces varies widely from one type of hardware to another and even between revisions. We remind you to carefully read your system's documentation as well as the firmware's own screen menus.

What Firmware Does

So far, we've discussed a lot of the physical implementations of firmware, but not why it is important for you to be able to differentiate which type you have on your local system. This is an important skill to develop since your system's firmware comes from the hardware manufacturer with a given set of chips; you don't really get a choice about what you receive, you simply need to know how to deal with it.

Various components can have their own BIOS, so please note that in the next sections, we are going to discuss the main system's firmware. In the case of a PC, this is the motherboard's BIOS; for a Sun box, this is the system EEPROM. Firmware is responsible for performing hardware self-discovery and essentially letting the system know what components it has. This means that the firmware must have routines for checking attached devices and controllers built in. Note, however, that some hardware cannot be seen without kernel-loaded drivers and modules.

Reminder

Remember that the kernel has not been loaded yet—that doesn't happen until Step 3.

After the devices are identified, they are tested, often with their own embedded routines, for basic functionality. These steps are collectively referred to as *POST*—Power-On Self-Test.

Note

Many firmware instances are "intelligent," allowing you to scan for new devices, configure basic parameters, and even manually invoke built-in tests on hardware and network connections (as with Sun's `probe-scsi` and `probe-net` commands).

Once the system's hardware is acknowledged and verified, the firmware searches for bootable devices, either from an internal list or from an environment variable.

When a bootable device is found, its boot sector (or boot block) is examined for further information, which is then passed on to the OS Loader (covered in the next section). For more information on boot blocks, see Chapter 3, "Filesystem Administration."

Firmware Settings

Most firmware offers a number of user-configurable settings for security and system management. Again, remember that since the interface and terminology might vary widely between firmware instances, this list presents some of the key *types* of setting, rather than their names within the firmware. Some of the more interesting settings include:

- **Security settings**—Usually this takes the form of password protection for the firmware. Note that it is critical that you don't forget this password; in extreme cases, you might have to replace the firmware chip itself to regain access.

- **Auto-booting**—This tells the system whether it should automatically boot or stop at BIOS/PROM. Turning on autoboot allows the system to restart after power failure (when power is restored) without human intervention.

- **Bootable media list**—This is an internal list telling the system where to look for bootable media.

- **Bootable media search sequence**—This is related to the bootable media list and is the order in which potentially bootable devices are searched, first for existence and second for appropriate OS boot information.

- **Power management**—These are settings to allow the machine to suspend/hibernate when not in active use. Obviously, this is something that you would want to disable on a server, but might be useful for a client machine.

- **Boot verbosity**—This controls the number and depth of status messages that you see at boot-time. The system can run fairly silently or can inundate you with a deluge of informational messages. We recommend the torrent; you can always filter out what you don't need, but you can't generate what the system doesn't tell you initially.

Firmware Mechanisms and Specifics

This section will examine the mechanisms provided by Red Hat and Solaris for managing their respective firmware.

Red Hat: PC Hardware Side

On a PC, the BIOS is generally accessible only at boot time. The key combination required varies among BIOS vendors and even versions. Check your initial boot screen for your particular BIOS's key sequence. These are some of the more common ones:

- Del
- Esc
- F1
- F2
- F10
- Ctrl+Esc
- Alt+Esc
- Ins

Note

PC firmware instances often refer to access to the BIOS as the "SETUP" options.

Some of the newer incarnations allow full BIOS access during run-time with a special key combination; check your hardware documentation.

Regardless, Red Hat offers a more limited kind of command-line access to certain firmware features. A good example of this is the `hwclock` command. With it, you can both directly query and set the system's hardware clock:

```
[linux:5 ~]hwclock —show
Sun 02 Sep 2001 02:47:38 PM EDT  0.900760 seconds

[linux:6 ~]hwclock —set —date="9/22/96 16:45:05"

[linux:7 ~]hwclock —show
Sun 22 Sep 1996 04:46:21 PM EDT  0.746125 seconds
```

From the Red Hat 7.1 `hwclock` Man Page

This clock commonly is called the hardware clock, the real time clock, the RTC, the BIOS clock, and the CMOS clock. Hardware Clock, in its capitalized form, was coined for use by `hwclock` because all of the other names are inappropriate to the point of being misleading.

There are some things that a PC BIOS can do that you won't find in Sun's EEPROM, such as enabling and disabling attached devices. Note that some devices will not appear properly on older systems without this kind of manual intervention.

The POST diagnostics output can be viewed by pressing the Tab key shortly after power-on. The messages are both more voluminous and noteworthy if you have the verbose option enabled. Note that this is not an interactive screen, just an informational one.

Solaris: Sun SPARC Hardware Side

On Solaris, the system's self-test diagnostics and self-recognition routines are run by the EEPROM. You can get to the interactive firmware screen by pressing Stop+A anytime.

Note

Stop+A only works when you are using a Sun keyboard physically attached to your system (no other keyboards actually even have the Stop key).

Also note that on older systems, this key combination is L1+A.

If you are using a VT serial terminal,[1] you use the BREAK key or the DEL key to drop to the firmware level.

Disabling Dropping Into Firmware from the Keyboard or Serial Line

Since a single keystroke at a VT serial terminal can drop Solaris to firmware, systems with such terminals are more prone to accidental service interruption than are systems with a Sun Microsystems console.

If the consequences of such an interruption outweigh the advantages of immediate firmware access, the keystroke-based interrupt mechanism can be disabled with special system parameters.

You can either set the system parameters via a system command or by editing /etc/default/kbd. The system command:

```
kbd -a disable
```

will disable keyboard or serial device abort sequences.

To re-enable the abort sequences, just type the following:

```
kbd -a enable
```

If you edit the /etc/default/kbd file, your changes will survive rebooting. To disable keyboard or serial device abort sequences through this file, uncomment (or add) the following line:

```
#KEYBOARD_ABORT=disable
```

To re-enable the abort sequences, just comment out the line by prepending a "#" mark.

If you stop at firmware during boot-up, you can set various configuration variables that will then take effect when you complete the boot process.

Tip

This is one reason that we recommend attaching some sort of system console to your machine—whether the Sun keyboard and monitor or a VT terminal or even just a serial line. You want to be able to stop the machine at boot-time to tweak settings and troubleshoot. A completely *headless* system impedes this process.

If you drop to PROM while the system is fully operational, you suspend the system's normal functioning. Once you make the desired modifications, you have a choice: to reboot to make the changes take immediate effect, or to issue the go command to restore the system to its interrupted state. Note that if you reboot, you will lose any unsaved system and user data; all processes will be killed gracelessly.

Note

There are actually three possible commands to get your system out of firmware mode and back into normal operation, depending on the firmware version. Check your hardware manual to find out whether you should use go, continue, or resume.

Dropping from Production to Firmware

Using Stop+A / L1+A to halt a functioning system for any reason should always be your last recourse. Use it only if you are unable to get a system prompt and shutdown gracefully, preferably giving your users warning and time to log out.

While it may be tempting to use your awesome powers to cut the system off, it is far better to be responsible and work with your users to accommodate their needs.

Working from the OpenBoot Prompt

Note

Sun's firmware is called OpenBoot and is currently at revision 3. You can see the online manuals at `http://docs.sun.com/ab2/coll.216.2`

When you stop at or drop to PROM, you are presented with a rather spartan prompt:

```
ok _
```

That's it. Of course, knowing what to type next is half the battle. So, to check out your environment settings, try `printenv`:

```
ok printenv
```

Variable Name	Value	Default Value
scsi-initiator-id	7	7
keyboard-click?	false	false
keymap		
ttyb-rts-dtr-off	false	false
ttyb-ignore-cd	true	true
ttya-rts-dtr-off	false	false
ttya-ignore-cd	true	true
ttyb-mode	9600,8,n,1,-	9600,8,n,1,-
ttya-mode	9600,8,n,1,-	9600,8,n,1,-
pcia-probe-list	1,2	1
pcib-probe-list	1,3,2,4,5	1,3,2,4,5
banner-name	Sun Server	
energystar-enabled?	false	

```
mfg-mode                  off                      off
diag-level                min                      min
fcode-debug?              false                    false
output-device             screen                   screen
input-device              keyboard                 keyboard
load-base                 16384                    16384
boot-command              boot                     boot
auto-boot?                true                     true
watchdog-reboot?          false                    false
diag-file
diag-device               net                      net
boot-file
boot-device               disk net                 disk net
local-mac-address?        false                    false
ansi-terminal?            true                     true
screen-#columns           80                       80
screen-#rows              34                       34
silent-mode?              false                    false
use-nvramrc?              false                    false
nvramrc
security-mode             none
security-password
security-#badlogins       0
oem-logo
oem-logo?                 false                    false
oem-banner
oem-banner?               false                    false
hardware-revision
last-hardware-update
diag-switch?              false                    false
```

Notice that the system returns three columns of output: the variable name, the current assigned value, and the system default value. The output is also unsorted, so don't be worried by its ordering. There are two reasons why you occasionally see blank spaces where you would expect a column entry: Either there is no value defined or the value is not to be printed onscreen (for security reasons).

If you already know the particular value name that you are interested in, you can use printenv to examine it specifically:

```
ok printenv security-mode
security-mode =        none
```

Before we go into how to modify variable settings, Table 1.1 will familiarize you with some of the most often used options available to you.[2]

TABLE 1.1   Sun Firmware Settings

Variable Name	Function	Typical Default Setting	Recommended Modification
ansi-terminal?	true: Terminal supports ANSI emulation. false: Terminal does not support ANSI emulation	true	-
auto-boot?	true: Initiate full boot after power-on or reset. false: Stop at PROM after power-on or reset	true	-
boot-command	Command and options used to boot when `auto-boot?` is set to true	boot	-
boot-device	Ordered list of devices to check for bootable media. disk: local hard disk net: network server cd: CD-ROM	disk net	Remove `net` so that rogue servers can't be used to subvert legitimate machines
boot-file	Argument specifying kernel file name; passed to boot program	<no setting>	-
diag-device	Like boot-device; ordered list of devices to check for bootable media when booting in diagnostic mode	disk net	Remove `net` so that rogue servers can't be used to subvert legitimate machines
diag-file	Like boot-file; argument specifying kernel file name; passed to boot program when booting in diagnostic mode	<no setting>	-
diag-level	Diagnostics level. off: POST is not run min: POST is called with minimum diagnostics requested max: POST is called with maximum diagnostics requested	max	-

TABLE 1.1 continued

Variable Name	Function	Typical Default Setting	Recommended Modification
diag-switch?	true: Boot in diagnostic mode. false: Do not boot in diagnostic mode.	false	Only switch to `true` if system is experiencing problems
error-reset-recovery	What to do if system crashes (hits an error reset trap): none: Print error message to screen and wait at PROM. sync: Sync disks, print error message to screen and wait at PROM. boot: Perform full reboot.	boot	-
input-device	Console input device: keyboard: Use device directly connected to back of system. `ttya` or `ttyb`: Serial console ports; accept input from serial console's keyboard.	keyboard	Only switch to `ttya` or `ttyb` if you are using one of those serial console lines
nvramrc	NVRAM contents; when used, usually holds local script	<no setting>	-
oem-banner	String to display when `oem-banner?` is set to true	<no setting>	-
oem-banner?	true: Display custom banner at boot-time. false: No special display.	false	-
output-device	Console output device: screen: Use monitor device directly connected to back of system. `ttya` or `ttyb`: Serial console ports; send output to serial console's display.	screen	Only switch to `ttya` or `ttyb` if you are using one of those serial console lines
screen-#columns	Number of characters displayed per line on screen.	80	(Depends on screen)

TABLE **1.1**   continued

Variable Name	Function	Typical Default Setting	Recommended Modification
screen-#rows	Number of lines displayed on screen before scrolling off the top	34	(Depends on screen)
scsi-initiator-id	SCSI-ID of adapter card Note that number must fall between 0 and 7	7	(Verify SCSI-ID of adapter)
security-#badlogins	Running total of incorrect security-password uses	0	(Automatically incremented by firmware; reset to 0 to track time-localized events)
security-mode= none	Sets PROM security level: none: Never require password. command: Require password for boot with options. full: Require password for all operations.	none	Set to `full` on any machine lacking physical security
security-password	Contains firmware security password; never displayed on-screen.	\<no setting\>	Set a password, especially for any machine lacking physical security
silent-mode?	true: Consult `nvramrc` for commands during boot-up. false: Ignore `nvramrc` contents.	false	-
use-nvramrc?			
tpe-link-test?	true: Test connectivity of on-board Ethernet. false: Skip Ethernet test.	true	(Only change if you will be working off the network for an extended period of time to prevent continuous complaints from the system)

Now, this is indeed a long list of potential settings, but notice that the defaults are generally acceptable ones, so don't panic.

Notice that some of the variables end with a question mark. This is not a query, but a literal part of the variable name. This becomes important when you want to change the variable's value, whether here or from inside the OS.

A Word About Security Modes

When you turn on the firmware security mode, you are simply password-protecting low-level operations. That's all, but it's also a good idea to add as many layers of security as feasible.[3]

It's most critical to protect the firmware when the system is not necessarily in a physically secure location. If anyone other than the admin can walk up to the machine and physically manipulate it, you want a firmware password.

Why protect the EEPROM?

This is where you can tell the system what media to look at for booting. A malicious user could set up a bogus boot server and point your system to it from EEPROM. Or that user could just boot into single-user mode (more on that later) and effectively become root on the system. A malicious user could also set the machine to require human intervention at boot-time before coming up. Basically, if the firmware is vulnerable, the entire system is, too.

So what are your options?

By default, no firmware security is enabled—all commands are honored without first demanding a password.

The "command" mode requires the user to enter the firmware password before executing any command other than `boot` and `go`. Note that `go` simply resumes the interrupted operation (whether booting or performing normal Operating System functions). Also note that if you pass any arguments to `boot`, a password *will* be required. This prevents someone from booting into single-user mode and becoming root without authorization.

The "full" mode is just what you would expect: It requires the user to enter the firmware password before executing any command except `go`. If someone manages to accidentally drop into EEPROM mode, you want them to be capable of resuming normal operations without special privileges. This mode prevents "practical jokes" in the lab or office where a user types Stop+A and `boot` to reboot the machine from under another user.

It's easy to change defaults that are *not* acceptable. Invoke `setenv` on the particular variable name that you are interested in and supply the new value that you want.

Let's look at the `boot-device` variable as an example. Our current setting looks like this:

```
ok printenv boot-device
boot-device=disk net
```

Let's say that we'd like to be able to boot from disk and then CD-ROM, but not the network; the command would look like this:

```
ok setenv boot-device disk cd
ok
```

Notice that a successful command has no output; it just returns you to the firmware prompt. Calling `printenv` again verifies our change, though:

```
ok printenv boot-device
boot-device=disk cd
```

Caution

Remember that you are making permanent changes to your system, even though they might not take effect until the next reboot.

Sun's current firmware also allows you to easily reset everything to factory defaults. Issue the `set-defaults` command at the ok prompt, and all your current settings will be wiped out and replaced with the defaults shown by a full `printenv`. To revert just one setting, run `set-default` (no plural) on the single variable name.

Configuring Firmware Security and Password

Sun cautions that you must set your firmware security password before you set the security mode. That way, in the event of a misplaced reboot, you can still access your system. Otherwise, your system will be demanding a password that does not, in fact, exist. There are only two recovery scenarios from this:

1. If the security mode is set to `command`, boot normally, become root, and use `eeprom` to reset the security password (see the next section for `eeprom` commands).

2. If the security mode is set to `full`, and `autoboot?` is not set to `true` you are doomed to contact the vendor in the case of a lost or mis-set firmware password. In some cases, the firmware itself will have to be replaced.

So here are the steps that you need to set these variables the *correct* way from the EEPROM command line:

```
ok password
New password (only first 8 chars are used): <OUTPUT NOT DISPLAYED>
Retype new password: <OUTPUT NOT DISPLAYED>
ok setenv security-mode command
ok
```

There are a few items worth noting in this example. As before, successful commands produce no output. The password that you type in is also not echoed to the screen (to better protect it from "shoulder surfers" and other observation). The system only recognizes up to eight characters in the password, so don't bother making it longer. Finally, note that these settings take immediate effect, so do not require a reboot.

Working from Within the OS

A better choice that doesn't suspend operations is to use the eeprom system command. Unlike before, none of the new settings takes immediate effect; they all require a reboot. Also note that root has complete power, even over the firmware—no firmware password is required, regardless of the security mode. The following listing shows how to invoke eeprom to first check whether security is turned on and then to enable security and set a PROM password:

```
[sun:17 ~]eeprom security-mode
security-mode=none

[sun:18 ~]eeprom security-mode=full
Changing PROM password:
New password:
Retype new password:
```

Again, you shouldn't be surprised that the password is not echoed to the screen where prying eyes or "shoulder-surfers" can see it. Notice, though, that the order in which you do things from within the OS is unimportant, since root has perpetual full access.

To view all current firmware settings and variables, just invoke eeprom with no arguments:

```
[sun:19 ~]eeprom
scsi-initiator-id=7
keyboard-click?=false
keymap: data not available.
ttyb-rts-dtr-off=false
ttyb-ignore-cd=true
```

```
ttya-rts-dtr-off=false
ttya-ignore-cd=true
ttyb-mode=9600,8,n,1,-
ttya-mode=9600,8,n,1,-
pcia-probe-list=1,2
pcib-probe-list=1,3,2,4,5
banner-name=Sun Server
energystar-enabled?=false
mfg-mode=off
diag-level=min
fcode-debug?=false
output-device=screen
input-device=keyboard
load-base=16384
boot-command=boot
auto-boot?=true
watchdog-reboot?=false
diag-file: data not available.
diag-device=net
boot-file: data not available.
boot-device=disk net
local-mac-address?=false
ansi-terminal?=true
screen-#columns=80
screen-#rows=34
silent-mode?=false
use-nvramrc?=false
nvramrc: data not available.
security-mode=none
security-password: data not available.
security-#badlogins=0
oem-logo: data not available.
oem-logo?=false
oem-banner: data not available.
oem-banner?=false
hardware-revision: data not available.
last-hardware-update: data not available.
diag-switch?=false
```

There are a number of things worth noting here. First, eeprom does not display the variable's default setting, just its current value. Other than output formatting, though, eeprom and the firmware printenv give the same results.

Also note that, in some places, the "data not available." message means that no value has been assigned to the variable. In others, such as security-password, it means that the contents are not directly accessible, usually for security reasons.

Finally, realize that while the settings just discussed are our particular system's defaults, those defaults are platform-dependent. So you might have different settings and even a few additional (or missing) variables out of the box.

After power-on, the Sun BIOS also performs a Power-On Self-Test (POST) unless `diag-level` is set to off. The diagnostics output is displayed on a non-interactive screen.

Step 2: Bootloader—Loading the OS

The system is now metaphorically waking up and has answered the first existential question: "What am I?" The next step in the process is to locate the brain and figure out "Who am I?" For any Unix system, fundamental identity is bound up in the local OS. Enter the *bootloader*.

The term "bootloader" is actually a shortened version of the phrase "bootstrap Operating System loader."

So What Is a Bootstrap, Then?

According to the Merriam-Webster Online Collegiate Dictionary[4] this use of the term dates from about 1926. It really does derive from a literal strap that was looped around the back of a boot to help the wearer pull it on. This is also where the phrase "pull yourself up by your bootstraps" comes from.

Bootstrapping something in general means that you make it work with the least amount of external intervention and resources possible. Bootstrapping a computer in particular means that you use a small, independent, internal function to initialize and transfer control to the main Operating System.

What the Bootloader Does

The bootloader is where Unix really begins on your system. This is the point where you start up the chain of software processes that ultimately transfers system control from the hardware to the OS.

The key to storing the bootloader in firmware is to make it small; it must fit in your disk's boot sector. This, in turn, means that it must also be fairly simple, with just enough logic to load and run the next program in the OS boot sequence.[5] The bootloader's location is either found by sequential searching of devices or examining a list provided by the admin. Note that settings for the bootloader are stored in the system firmware.

This kind of division of labor into small, discrete tasks performed by small, dedicated programs epitomizes the Unix way of doing things.[6]

Bootloader Mechanisms and Specifics

Now let's look at some of the OS-specific mechanisms associated with the bootloader under both Red Hat and Solaris.

The Red Hat Bootloader

As part of the standard installation, Red Hat Linux installs LILO— the *Linux Lo*ader— to handle its boot-time needs. Like all bootloaders, LILO is a small program that can live quite happily in a number of locations. The two most common places are the Master Boot Record (MBR) and the first sector of a partition that contains a bootable Linux kernel.

The MBR is the first sector of any disk, whether it's an IDE hard disk, a SCSI hard disk, or a floppy disk (see Chapter 2, "Managing Disk Hardware," for more about disks). It contains critical information about the disk's organization, including which partitions are bootable (that is, where bootloader programs are known to reside on the disk).[7] See Appendix B, "Anatomy of a Filesystem," for more on the internal layout of a disk drive.

The MBR is a much-contested spot, though. Some Operating Systems, such as Windows NT, automatically and completely overwrite the MBR as part of their installation process. Thus, on a dual-boot machine, LILO would *need* to live elsewhere.

Note

Dual-booting is a whole other sack of ferrets and one we are not going to go into. See the following URL for more on LILO and dual-booting: `http://www.redhat.com/support/manuals/RHL-7.1-Manual/install-guide/s1-guimode-lilo-conf.html`

"Elsewhere" turns out to be the first sector of any *partition* within a disk (again, see Appendix B and Chapter 2 for more details). This allows multiple bootloaders to coexist peacefully and not contest MBR rights.

The Solaris Bootloader

Under Solaris, the bootloader is two-staged. The primary boot program is called `bootblk` and resides in the EEPROM. Its only real purpose is to load the next stage, which, in turn, actually loads the OS.

The secondary boot program is called `ufsboot` and lives in the location identified by the `boot-device` and `boot-file` variables. Because it is not resident in the EEPROM, it can be a larger, more complex program. In fact, `ufsboot` is a microcosm of the OS *kernel*, providing the functions for the OS to actually initialize.

Step 3: Kernel—Initialization and Control Transfer

Now we get to the heart and soul of Unix: the kernel. Although the kernel cannot readily stand alone, it is what defines and differentiates Unix from other Operating Systems and various instances of Unix from each other.

The two great truths of Unix are that everything that exists in Unix is a file and everything that happens in Unix is a process.[8] The kernel is a compiled executable file, apparently no different than any other. But once it is loaded into memory at boot-time, it controls all the other system processes and the process scheduler—meaning that it controls everything that happens.

Controlling everything does not mean *doing* everything, however—that's a crucial distinction. The kernel is actually quite circumscribed in its functions. As hinted at previously, most of what most users think of as being Unix (or at least the look and feel of Unix) is *not* the kernel, but externals.

> **Note**
>
> The discussion of the kernel's control function here is purposely broad. There are entire organizations devoted to arguing about what a kernel should or should not be. Specific kernel tasks will be addressed here to provide some understanding of the kernel's place in the operating system. A complete discussion of the Unix kernel is beyond the scope of this book, and frankly outside the responsibility of *most* sysadmins.

A well-designed kernel is also hardware-independent;[9] this is why you can run the same Solaris kernel on an Enterprise and on an UltraSPARC, and the same Red Hat Linux kernel on an Intel processor system and on an AMD processor system.

There are two basic types of kernel: monolithic and microkernels. As you might guess from the names, they exist on opposite ends of the Unix philosophy spectrum. At a minimum, though, *all* Unix kernels have system control functions built in. Also be aware that kernels are different from other executable files in that they must be present on disk while running in memory.

Micro-kernels add hooks for handling external modules and very little else. As a result, they are quite compact in themselves and are quite speedy at built-in functions.

Monolithic kernels, on the other hand, have everything built into them from the start. This means that they are entirely self-reliant, but also larger and somewhat slower.

Micro-kernels offer more flexibility because you can add various support modules without rebooting, but there is a price to pay. Poisoned modules, or Trojan modules, present a big security risk—if the kernel loads such a module, it runs with all the system control and privileges of the kernel itself.

Monolithic kernels require recompiling and rebooting the system before they can add new features. Although they might be safe from infected modules, they also present an impediment to change without downtime.

Both Red Hat and Solaris use the micro-kernel approach, though the Red Hat kernel can be built as a monolithic kernel.

Now, we mentioned that the kernel is a file. While this is always true, the file's location could vary. In fact, the file might be located on a remote server and not on your system at all. For most practical purposes, it doesn't matter *where* the kernel comes from, as long as the system can be configured to find and load it.

For our discussion, we will consider the most typical case of this next boot-up stage: loading a local kernel stored on a local hard disk.

What The Kernel Does

The kernel provides the context for everything else to occur in a Unix system. It is the framework around which everything from filesystems to commands is layered; it constructs a virtual machine where hardware and software meet and interact.

The kernel handles all system resource allocation, including memory, virtual memory, CPU time-sharing, swapping, and paging (all terms that you will see again later in this book). It also handles intrasystem communication, whether between software processes[10] or in software-to-hardware directives. In managing the latter, the kernel can provide access to persistent storage: hard disks and their constituent files.

Files, including the kernel and its associates, are stored in a random-access medium, structured and governed by a filesystem (see Chapter 3 for more details). Filesystems must be logically *mounted* to be available to the system for file access. Of course, like everything else on the system, the kernel ultimately controls filesystems.

This might seem to be a chicken-and-egg problem: You can't actually load the kernel until you mount its filesystem, but you can't mount filesystems until you have a kernel to do it... The trick is that the bootloader steps up to mount the appropriate filesystem so that the OS can properly load and take over.

The kernel is usually located in the / (otherwise known as "root") filesystem, but it can be specifically set otherwise in the firmware or with options passed to a manual `boot` command.

Apart from the kernel, the root filesystem holds configuration files for services, temporary file storage space, system commands necessary to complete boot-up, and so on. While other local filesystems might house critical components, they are of secondary importance and so are mounted later.

> **Note**
>
> It is important to recognize the distinction between two common uses of the word "kernel." The word is used to refer to a binary file that is searched for by the bootstrap loader. The word "kernel" also is used to refer to a process resident in memory that is instantiating and controlling the Operating System. The binary file in the disk is inert. The kernel *process*, like all processes, is dynamic and thus has state. In addition, a micro-kernel will load modules in memory that are not present in the original kernel binary file.

See Chapter 3 for more on filesystems and their contents.

Kernel Mechanisms and Specifics

As already mentioned, the firmware stores variables specifying the location of the kernel. With PCs, this is indirect, requiring the bootloader to know where to look; with Sun systems, the location is explicitly set in EEPROM variables. Of course, these are just default settings and can be overridden by manual commands issued at boot-time.

> ### Tip
>
> We recommend that you keep a backup kernel on a bootable partition other than the root partition so that you can still boot in an emergency. A bad patch can sometimes prevent your system from coming back up, as can disk failure, graceless shutdowns, and a whole raft of other unpredictable events.
>
> Some commonly used filenames are $KERNELNAME.bak $KERNELNAME.sav and $KERNELNAME.OLD. It doesn't matter what you call the backup kernel file as long as you are consistent among the systems that you administer, and that you document where the "known good" kernel file is stored. It is also possible to store a backup kernel file in a directory on the root partition, such as /SAVED/vmunix, though we strongly recommend that another (bootable) partition be used.

About the Red Hat Kernel

There are currently two possibilities for where your Red Hat kernel may actually reside in your system. More accurately, there are two variants of the kernel that you might encounter: compressed and standard.

If you are using v18 and up of LILO, you can use a type of compressed kernel known as a bzImage. This means that you need to dedicate less space to the kernel, but can still build in everything that you need to run your system. Older versions of LILO can also use a compressed kernel, but only of type zImage. In either case, the compressed kernel image can be found at /boot/vmlinuz, which, in turn, is a pointer to the most current revision. Here is an example listing from our system:

```
[linux:50 ~] ls -la /boot/vmlinuz
lrwxrwxrwx   1 root     root         15 Jun 12 12:43 /boot/vmlinuz ->
vmlinuz-2.4.2-2
```

Note that the final *z* (linuz instead of linux) indicates that this is a compressed kernel. During boot-time, you will know that you're using a compressed kernel when you see the message "Uncompressing linux...".

Standard, or uncompressed, kernels are generally necessary when you are not using LILO as your bootloader. They are also the grist for the compression mill. You don't just create a compressed kernel on its own—you convert and compress an already extant kernel.[11] Standard kernels intended for use at boot-time can be found at /boot/vmlinux, which, in turn, is a pointer to the most current revision. Note that the name of this uncompressed kernel ends in *x*.

Just for reference, the source for the Red Hat kernel lives in /usr/src/linux-<major kernel revision #>. As you probably guessed, this is a symbolic link to the most current minor revision-named directory. On our system, the kernel is version 2.4.2, so the source directory symbolic link is linux-2.4:

```
[linux:51 ~] ls -la /usr/src/linux-2.4
lrwxrwxrwx    1 root      root              11 Jun 12 12:52 /usr/src/linux-2.4 ->
linux-2.4.2
```

> **Note**
>
> Depending on the type of installation you did, this might not be there by default; you might have to download the source RPMs for the kernel (check out http://www.kernel.org/pub), or mount your Red Hat CD and copy the kernel source code into /usr/src.

If you want to specify an alternate kernel or non-default boot parameters, the place to do it is at the LILO: prompt. If you are booting in graphical mode, press Ctrl+X to get to the interactive text mode. If you are booting in console mode, you are ready to proceed.

Once you are at the LILO: prompt, press Tab or ? to see your pre-listed kernel options. For example, you might see something like this:

```
LILO:
linux          old-linux      test-linux
```

Let's suppose that you want to boot the test-linux kernel. You can specify what runlevel you want as well (more on runlevels in the next section):

```
LILO: test-linux 3
```

The system is now on its way to full multi-user mode with the test-linux kernel.

About the Solaris Kernel

You can find the compiled Solaris kernel at /kernel/genunix. With Solaris, you don't get current kernel source without purchasing it from Sun, so there is no associated directory for it on the system.

> **Note**
>
> The Solaris kernel binary is always included in the system media, or will come pre-installed on a new system. For more information, or to download the latest free *binary* version of Solaris 8, go to:
>
> `http://www.sun.com/software/solaris/binaries/get.html`

If you want to boot an alternate kernel from EEPROM, just specify it on the command line (see the man page for `boot` for more details). Here you will load the kernel called /kernel/test-solaris on the disk with SCSI-ID 3 and come up in single-user mode:

```
ok boot disk 3 kernel/test-solaris -s
```

This pre-supposes that all the pieces are already in place and are well-known—the disk, the directory, the alternate kernel's name, and so on.

For more information on Solaris kernel tuning, see Chapter 23, "Requirements Analysis and Performance Monitoring."

Step 4: Init and Initialization Scripts

At this point, the kernel is loaded and any peripherals requiring special kernel modules or routines to come online can be accessed. The system is ready to metaphorically ask, "Now what?" and along comes the `init` process to answer the question. Creating the `init` process is the last direct intervention that the kernel makes in the boot process.[12]

When `init` starts, it continues the boot process by performing various default startup routines (checking and mounting filesystems, starting daemons, and so on). In normal operation, `init` makes sure that `getty` is working (to allow users to log in) and adopts orphan processes (processes whose parent has died—in UNIX, all processes must be in a single tree, so orphans must be adopted).

`init` is the first process that can exist on a running UNIX system. As such, it always has a process ID of 1.

Note

Since computers are good with numbers, not names, they track processes by their assigned identification number. A *process ID*, or *PID*, is generated for every process when it first comes into existence. The kernel's scheduler then manages the process by that number. Use the ps command to view both the PID and associated process name.

Note

You might notice that while init has a PID of 1, most computer folks start counting with 0. Even init must answer to a higher function: the kernel scheduler. Without the scheduler, nothing gets CPU time, but it is a catalyst, a facilitator only. This is why init gets pride of place when we talk about boot-up and master processes.

Note that under Solaris, the ps command explicitly displays the scheduler as PID 0, but that under Red Hat, the ps listing shows *no* PID 0.

What Init Does

The init process is responsible for the orderly startup (and shutdown) of all core system functions (outside the kernel). To do this, it must create, or *spawn*, a whole raft of processes. Note that if init is killed for any reason,[13] most of its child processes will also die, taking the system with them in a horrific, graceless fashion.

Note

A spontaneous process is one that springs, full-grown, from the kernel (like Athena from the head of Zeus). All other processes are created in a more mundane fashion—spawned by fork() from a pre-existing parent process.

Init Mechanisms and Specifics: inittab

Of course, it's not enough for init to spawn processes—they have to be the *right* processes. This is where admins get their first real taste of control: The system behaves differently depending on what *runlevel* it is operating.

Runlevels

So, what's a runlevel, you ask? It's a description of various system states ranging from off to single-user no network mode to fully networked multi-user mode. The behavior of the system depends on the runlevel that the OS is currently in, entering, or leaving.

Red Hat and Solaris have mostly the same definitions for runlevels, with key variations, as shown in Table 1.2.

TABLE 1.2   System Runlevels

Runlevel	Red Hat Purpose	Solaris Purpose
0	Firmware	Firmware
1	Single-user, no networking Also called "S" or "s"	Single-user, no networking Also called "S" or "s"
2	Multi-user, no networking	Multi-user, no networking, X Windows
3	Multi-user, fully networked	Multi-user, fully networked, X Windows
4	Not used	Not used
5	Multi-user, fully networked, X Windows	Shut down for power-off; Executes power-off, if supported by hardware
6	Reboot	Reboot

Red Hat also supports runlevels 7–9, but they are supported as admin-defined, non-standard states.

These runlevel numbers are more than just a useful shorthand: They are used at boot-time to bring the system into a well-defined state, and can also be used as arguments to init for changing the system's runlevel (see the later section called "Shutting Down and Generally Changing Init Levels"). They are used in /etc/inittab to enumerate which system directives are necessary to achieve any given state.

Entries in inittab take the following format:

```
id:run-level:action:process
```

> **Note**
>
> Red Hat and Solaris man pages give these fields different names, but their
> function is the same.

The first field acts as an identifier for the entry. Usually, the id field contains 2 alphanumeric characters, but this is not a requirement. What *is* required is that every id field be unique. Since the most straightforward method is sequential numbering, we recommend that you think of the id field as essentially being an entry number.

The `run-level` field contains a string of *all* runlevels for which the `action` should be taken. Essentially, it describes how often to run an action and in what state to maintain that process. Some examples of valid strings include 013, 5, 0, 23, and so on.

The third field describes what you want the system to do. Some of the more often used values include these:

- **boot**—Run "process" only at system bootup
- **once**—Run "process" once upon entering specified runlevel
- **respawn**—Restart "process" whenever (and for whatever) it is terminated
- **wait**—Like once, but awaits completion of "process" before continuing

The fourth and final field specifies the full path to the executable that should be run, as well as any arguments that should be passed to it (separated by whitespace only).

There are a number of critical things to notice when reading an inittab:

- The entry containing the keyword `initdefault` in its third field defines the state into which the system will boot if left to its own devices. This tends to be the fully networked multiuser mode.
- The default runlevel should *never* be set to 0 or 6. These are halt/drop to firmware and reboot, respectively. Both of these will prevent you from even getting on the system long enough to correct your mistake.
- Any process whose action field contains `respawn` should never entirely disappear from your system. If it does, you've got a serious problem to look into.

> ## Caution
>
> Use extreme care when altering your system's initdefault state. Once the system boots (or crashes), you will have to live with this default. If you corrupt /etc/inittab, you may lose access to the OS, and odds are very good that you'll have to boot from external media such as CD-ROM and replace the inittab file.

> ## Tip
>
> Any application processes that will be maintained by inittab (such as a web server) should be thoroughly tested and designed in a way that they do not "crash" unexpectedly. If the process does not start or restart, init will continue to attempt to respawn the process, using up resources and logging error messages. Console messages about "process respawning too quickly" are often a clue that a process that should have started from /etc/inittab was crashing or exiting immediately upon startup.

Red Hat's inittab File

The following listing shows the default /etc/inittab on our Linux system. Note that comments begin with "#"and some helpful tips are included (such as *not* setting the default runlevel to 0 or 6).

```
#
# inittab      This file describes how the INIT process should set up
#              the system in a certain run-level.
#
# Author:      Miquel van Smoorenburg, <miquels@drinkel.nl.mugnet.org>
#              Modified for RHS Linux by Marc Ewing and Donnie Barnes
#

# Default runlevel. The runlevels used by RHS are:
#   0 - halt (Do NOT set initdefault to this)
#   1 - Single user mode
#   2 - Multiuser, without NFS (The same as 3, if you do not have networking)
#   3 - Full multiuser mode
#   4 - unused
#   5 - X11
#   6 - reboot (Do NOT set initdefault to this)
#
id:5:initdefault:
```

```
# System initialization.
si::sysinit:/etc/rc.d/rc.sysinit

l0:0:wait:/etc/rc.d/rc 0
l1:1:wait:/etc/rc.d/rc 1
l2:2:wait:/etc/rc.d/rc 2
l3:3:wait:/etc/rc.d/rc 3
l4:4:wait:/etc/rc.d/rc 4
l5:5:wait:/etc/rc.d/rc 5
l6:6:wait:/etc/rc.d/rc 6

# Things to run in every runlevel.
ud::once:/sbin/update

# Trap CTRL-ALT-DELETE
ca::ctrlaltdel:/sbin/shutdown -t3 -r now

# When our UPS tells us power has failed, assume we have a few minutes
# of power left.  Schedule a shutdown for 2 minutes from now.
# This does, of course, assume you have powerd installed and your
# UPS connected and working correctly.
pf::powerfail:/sbin/shutdown -f -h +2 "Power Failure; System Shutting Down"


# Run gettys in standard runlevels
1:2345:respawn:/sbin/mingetty tty1
2:2345:respawn:/sbin/mingetty tty2
3:2345:respawn:/sbin/mingetty tty3
4:2345:respawn:/sbin/mingetty tty4
5:2345:respawn:/sbin/mingetty tty5
6:2345:respawn:/sbin/mingetty tty6

# Run xdm in runlevel 5
# xdm is now a separate service
x:5:respawn:/etc/X11/prefdm -nodaemon
```

Red Hat provides an excellent tool called chkconfig to help manage the correct addition
and removal of services and actions to /etc/inittab. Please see the man page for more
usage details.

Solaris's inittab File

While the same commenting and common-sense rules apply to the Solaris inittab as to
the one from Red Hat, the stock Sun file is much more sparse:

```
ap::sysinit:/sbin/autopush -f /etc/iu.ap
ap::sysinit:/sbin/soconfig -f /etc/sock2path
fs::sysinit:/sbin/rcS sysinit           >/dev/msglog 2<>/dev/msglog
</dev/console
is:3:initdefault:
```

```
p3:s1234:powerfail:/usr/sbin/shutdown -y -i5 -g0 >/dev/msglog 2<>/dev/msglog
sS:s:wait:/sbin/rcS                     >/dev/msglog 2<>/dev/msglog
</dev/console
s0:0:wait:/sbin/rc0                     >/dev/msglog 2<>/dev/msglog
</dev/console
s1:1:respawn:/sbin/rc1                  >/dev/msglog 2<>/dev/msglog
</dev/console
s2:23:wait:/sbin/rc2                    >/dev/msglog 2<>/dev/msglog
</dev/console
s3:3:wait:/sbin/rc3                     >/dev/msglog 2<>/dev/msglog
</dev/console
s5:5:wait:/sbin/rc5                     >/dev/msglog 2<>/dev/msglog
</dev/console
s6:6:wait:/sbin/rc6                     >/dev/msglog 2<>/dev/msglog
</dev/console
fw:0:wait:/sbin/uadmin 2 0              >/dev/msglog 2<>/dev/msglog
</dev/console
of:5:wait:/sbin/uadmin 2 6              >/dev/msglog 2<>/dev/msglog
</dev/console
rb:6:wait:/sbin/uadmin 2 1              >/dev/msglog 2<>/dev/msglog
</dev/console
sc:234:respawn:/usr/lib/saf/sac -t 300
co:234:respawn:/usr/lib/saf/ttymon -g -h -p "`uname -n` console login: " -T sun
-d /dev/console -l console -m ldterm,ttcompat
```

Also note that Sun gives semi-meaningful entry identifications (the id field) rather than just numbering the lines.

Init Mechanisms and Specifics: init Scripts

Did you notice that in both the Red Hat and Solaris inittab files, every runlevel had a dedicated entry with a reference to rc# (where # indicates a runlevel) in the process field and wait in the action field? These entries tell init to go to the runcontrol directory specified and run the scripts there, according to a specific set of rules. The run-control directory is generally named after the runlevel that it represents, so you will see directories named rc0.d, rc3.d, rc6.d, and so on.

We recommend that sysadmins read the scripts in the rc#.d directories to learn how the operating system is configured as it enters each run state. In most cases, changes to the behavior of the system can be implemented without editing the scripts directly. In general, each script sets up some default conditions and functions, then executes, in order, all scripts in a corresponding runlevel directory that have a name matching a specific pattern. The order that the scripts will run is generally based on the lexicographic sorting of matching file names in the runlevel directory.

The rc# scripts are responsible for starting services, performing cleanup, and generally putting the finishing touches on the system before the users come in.

Solaris and System V init Scripts

Solaris follows the System V[14] run-control schema. There is a central repository for all process-management scripts: /etc/init.d. The actual rc directories, themselves subdirectories of /etc, only contain precisely-named symbolic links to the scripts in the repository. This means that removing a process from an rc directory will not delete it from the system—the original is still stored in init.d.

Conversely, we recommend that when you add your own rc script, you follow the same scheme: create a uniquely-named shell script in /etc/init.d and then make a symlink to it from the appropriate rc directory.

The rules for the naming scheme are as follows:

- The name parent directory reflects the applicable runlevel.
- The scripts relating to processes that must be stopped upon entering the specified runlevel begin with *K* (note the capital). Each script is assigned an ordinal number.
- The scripts relating to processes that must be started upon entering the specified runlevel begin with *S* (note the capital). Each script is assigned an ordinal number.

The *K* scripts are executed from lowest- to highest-numbered. Then the *S* scripts are handled in the same manner. The critical difference is that *K* scripts are invoked with a `stop` argument, and *S* scripts are invoked with a `start` argument.

Note that you also pass through all the runlevels equal to or greater than your current runlevel. This means that if you switch to runlevel 3 (full multiuser mode) from runlevel 0 (firmware), you will pass through and execute the scripts in /etc/rc1.d and /etc/rc3.d before running those in /etc/rc3.d. This means that you do not need to repeat the same scripts in sequential directories (unless they switch from start to stop, or vice versa). Also note that the sequence of *K* scripts and then *S* scripts is observed for each directory in sequence.

Remember that runlevel 0 takes you down to the firmware level. Accordingly, all processes are stopped, which, in turn, means that all the scripts in /etc/rc0.d begin with *K*:

```
[sun:60 ~]ls /etc/rc0.d
K00ANNOUNCE      K34IIim          K39spc           K41slpd
K06mipagent      K34ncad          K40cron          K42inetsvc
K07dmi           K34ncalogd       K40nscd          K43inet
K07snmpdx        K35volmgt        K40syslog        K50asppp
K10dtlogin       K36loc.ja.cssd   K40xntpd         K52llc2
```

```
K15Wnn6          K36sendmail      K41ab2mgr       K68picld
K16apache        K36utmpd         K41autofs       K83devfsadm
K28nfs.server    K36wbem          K41ldap.client  K90dhcpagent
K33atsv          K37power         K41nfs.client   K98nf_fddidaemon
K33audit         K39lp            K41rpc          K98pf_fddidaemon
```

Runlevel 3, on the other hand, only adds new processes, so it is more limited in both scope and type of script:

```
[sun:61 ~]ls /etc/rc3.d
README           S25mdlogd       S76snmpdx       S80mipagent
S15nfs.server    S50apache       S77dmi          S99sshd
```

Tip

Solaris provides a number of README files in /etc/init.d and the rc directories. They detail script invocation order and recommended numbering schemes. Always check these local system documents before changing or adding scripts.

Red Hat: Combining the System V inittab and BSD-Style rc Scripts

Linux combines the System V–style inittab with some BSD-style concepts. The "BSD Way" is to have one script that is executed by the operating system when it comes up: /etc/rc. That script might, in turn, call some of its friends, like /etc/rc.local and /etc/rc.conf. Those scripts, may, in some cases, look for scripts in a System V-like hierarchy. However, it is very important to note that BSD systems do not use /etc/inittab or run levels. This represents the major distinction between the two schemes.

Now let's look at how Red Hat actually implements this. All the rc directories as well as init.d live under /etc/rc.d:

```
[linux:60 ~] ls /etc/rc.d
init.d  rc0.d  rc2.d  rc4.d  rc6.d     rc.sysinit
rc      rc1.d  rc3.d  rc5.d  rc.local
```

To reduce friction and confusion for admins who operate in both worlds, Red Hat also put in some default symbolic links under /etc:

```
[linux:61 ~] ls -ld /etc/rc?.d /etc/init.d
lrwxrwxrwx   1 root      root          10 Jun 12 12:39 /etc/rc0.d -> rc.d/rc0.d
lrwxrwxrwx   1 root      root          10 Jun 12 12:39 /etc/rc1.d -> rc.d/rc1.d
lrwxrwxrwx   1 root      root          10 Jun 12 12:39 /etc/rc2.d -> rc.d/rc2.d
```

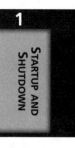

```
lrwxrwxrwx   1 root     root         10 Jun 12 12:39 /etc/rc3.d -> rc.d/rc3.d
lrwxrwxrwx   1 root     root         10 Jun 12 12:39 /etc/rc4.d -> rc.d/rc4.d
lrwxrwxrwx   1 root     root         10 Jun 12 12:39 /etc/rc5.d -> rc.d/rc5.d
lrwxrwxrwx   1 root     root         10 Jun 12 12:39 /etc/rc6.d -> rc.d/rc6.d
lrwxrwxrwx   1 root     root         11 Jun 12 12:39 /etc/init.d ->
rc.d/init.d
```

After completing the progression scheme outline for System V, Linux processes directives stored in rc.local. Be careful, if you add entries to or remove entries from this file, that you don't override it with stray symbolic links from the rc directories to init.d.

Step 5: Over to the Admin— Miscellaneous Wrap-Up

At last the machine is fully functional and ready for action! Remember, though, that your role in the boot process is just beginning when the machine is up and running. This is where administration really starts.

Although the majority of this book is devoted to the administrative tasks that you now face, here are a couple of boot-time tips to get you started:

- Run dmesg to check for boot-time errors that went by too fast to parse on-screen as they appeared (see the later listings for system-specific samples).
- Check the system log to find any stray application errors that dmesg might have "overlooked" (more on reading system logs in Chapter 6, "Logging").

Red Hat's dmesg shows only information from the most recent boot-up. Solaris, on the other hand, does not reset the contents on dmesg upon reboot; you will see old messages in addition to the ones that you are interested in.

Shutting Down and Generally Changing init Levels

You might find shutting down your system quite anti-climactic after all the build-up needed to get running in the first place. Shutting down essentially unwinds the boot-up layering, but with the advantage of running everything with a full kernel and not having to bootstrap.

There are two methods of shutting down a system: removing power and manipulating init. If you lose current, pull the system power cord,[15] or experience some other electric-loss equivalent, your system will surely shut down, although not in any kind of order. You might have to face file corruption, filesystem corruption, and possibly even hardware difficulties[16] in this sort of situation.

It's much cleaner and neater to use `init`, but be sure to use it wisely. All of the following are wrappers for `init` in some fashion: `shutdown`, `reboot`, `halt`, and `sync`. Of all these, `shutdown` is the most preferable, given its feature set:

- It automatically sends a banner notification to all logged-in users of impending shutdown, which is repeated every 30 seconds.
- It has a configurable grace period before invoking `init` to kill processes.
- It can be set to automatically proceed with the shutdown process after the grace period expires.
- It passes a new init level (specified on the command-line) to `init`.

Once `init` is invoked, it goes back through the rc directories, running the *K* scripts and waiting on their return codes to shut down processes as tidily as possible. For the more intransigent, stuck, or unresponsive processes, `init` eventually sends a `kill -TERM` signal, abruptly ending them.

What happens next depends on the runlevel passed on to `init`.

Also note that invoking `init` does not necessarily entail shutting down or even rebooting the machine. In addition to the seven standard runlevels, you can pass the arguments in Table 1.3 to `init`.

TABLE 1.3   init Runlevels

Runlevel	Description
A	Re-execute only those /etc/inittab directives specified with runlevels a, b, or c
B	
C	
Q *or* q	Re-examine /etc/inittab
S *or* s	Single-user, no network mode

Red Hat also supports run-level U or u, which instructs the system to re-execute `init` but *not* to re-examine /etc/inittab.

The Red Hat Boot Sequence as Displayed by dmesg

The following listing is the dmesg output associated with the boot-up of a Dell Optiplex system with Red Hat 7.1 from LILO with a simple kernel selection. Note that these are also the exact contents of /var/log/messages for the same process.

```
Linux version 2.4.2-2 (root@porky.devel.redhat.com) (gcc version 2.96 20000731
➥(Red Hat Linux 7.1 2.96-7
9)) #1 Sun Apr 8 20:41:30 EDT 2001
BIOS-provided physical RAM map:
 BIOS-e820: 00000000000a0000 @ 0000000000000000 (usable)
 BIOS-e820: 0000000000010000 @ 00000000000f0000 (reserved)
 BIOS-e820: 000000000fe07000 @ 0000000000100000 (usable)
 BIOS-e820: 000000000005a000 @ 000000000ff26000 (reserved)
 BIOS-e820: 0000000000080000 @ 000000000ff80000 (reserved)
 BIOS-e820: 0000000000500000 @ 00000000ffb00000 (reserved)
 BIOS-e820: 000000000001f000 @ 000000000ff07000 (ACPI data)
On node 0 totalpages: 65287
zone(0): 4096 pages.
zone DMA has max 32 cached pages.
zone(1): 61191 pages.
zone Normal has max 478 cached pages.
zone(2): 0 pages.
zone HighMem has max 1 cached pages.
Kernel command line: BOOT_IMAGE=linux ro root=304 BOOT_FILE=/boot/vmlinuz-2.4.2
➥-2 hdc=ide-scsi
ide_setup: hdc=ide-scsi
Initializing CPU#0
Detected 996.785 MHz processor.
Console: colour VGA+ 80x25
Calibrating delay loop... 1985.74 BogoMIPS
Memory: 254380k/261148k available (1365k kernel code, 6384k reserved, 92k data,
➥ 236k init, 0k highmem)
Dentry-cache hash table entries: 32768 (order: 6, 262144 bytes)
Buffer-cache hash table entries: 16384 (order: 4, 65536 bytes)
Page-cache hash table entries: 65536 (order: 7, 524288 bytes)
Inode-cache hash table entries: 16384 (order: 5, 131072 bytes)
VFS: Diskquotas version dquot_6.5.0 initialized
CPU: Before vendor init, caps: 0383f9ff 00000000 00000000, vendor = 0
CPU: L1 I cache: 16K, L1 D cache: 16K
CPU: L2 cache: 256K
Intel machine check architecture supported.
Intel machine check reporting enabled on CPU#0.
CPU: After vendor init, caps: 0383f9ff 00000000 00000000 00000000
```

```
CPU: After generic, caps: 0383f9ff 00000000 00000000 00000000
CPU: Common caps: 0383f9ff 00000000 00000000 00000000
CPU: Intel Pentium III (Coppermine) stepping 06
Enabling fast FPU save and restore... done.
Enabling unmasked SIMD FPU exception support... done.
Checking 'hlt' instruction... OK.
POSIX conformance testing by UNIFIX
mtrr: v1.37 (20001109) Richard Gooch (rgooch@atnf.csiro.au)
mtrr: detected mtrr type: Intel
PCI: PCI BIOS revision 2.10 entry at 0xfc08e, last bus=2
PCI: Using configuration type 1
PCI: Probing PCI hardware
Unknown bridge resource 0: assuming transparent
Unknown bridge resource 2: assuming transparent
PCI: Using IRQ router default [8086/2440] at 00:1f.0
isapnp: Scanning for PnP cards...
isapnp: No Plug & Play device found
Linux NET4.0 for Linux 2.4
Based upon Swansea University Computer Society NET3.039
Initializing RT netlink socket
apm: BIOS version 1.2 Flags 0x03 (Driver version 1.14)
Starting kswapd v1.8
pty: 256 Unix98 ptys configured
block: queued sectors max/low 168848kB/56282kB, 512 slots per queue
RAMDISK driver initialized: 16 RAM disks of 4096K size 1024 blocksize
Uniform Multi-Platform E-IDE driver Revision: 6.31
ide: Assuming 33MHz system bus speed for PIO modes; override with idebus=xx
PIIX4: IDE controller on PCI bus 00 dev f9
PIIX4: chipset revision 2
PIIX4: not 100% native mode: will probe irqs later
    ide0: BM-DMA at 0xffa0-0xffa7, BIOS settings: hda:DMA, hdb:pio
    ide1: BM-DMA at 0xffa8-0xffaf, BIOS settings: hdc:DMA, hdd:pio
hda: Maxtor 5T040H4, ATA DISK drive
hdc: SONY CD-RW CRX700E, ATAPI CD/DVD-ROM drive
ide0 at 0x1f0-0x1f7,0x3f6 on irq 14
ide1 at 0x170-0x177,0x376 on irq 15
hda: 78125000 sectors (40000 MB) w/2048KiB Cache, CHS=4863/255/63, UDMA(100)
Partition check:
 hda: hda1 hda2 hda3 hda4
Floppy drive(s): fd0 is 1.44M
FDC 0 is a National Semiconductor PC87306
Serial driver version 5.02 (2000-08-09) with MANY_PORTS MULTIPORT SHARE_IRQ
➥SERIAL_PCI ISAPNP enabled
ttyS00 at 0x03f8 (irq = 4) is a 16550A
ttyS01 at 0x02f8 (irq = 3) is a 16550A
Real Time Clock Driver v1.10d
md driver 0.90.0 MAX_MD_DEVS=256, MD_SB_DISKS=27
md.c: sizeof(mdp_super_t) = 4096
```

```
autodetecting RAID arrays
autorun ...
... autorun DONE.
NET4: Linux TCP/IP 1.0 for NET4.0
IP Protocols: ICMP, UDP, TCP, IGMP
IP: routing cache hash table of 2048 buckets, 16Kbytes
TCP: Hash tables configured (established 16384 bind 16384)
Linux IP multicast router 0.06 plus PIM-SM
NET4: Unix domain sockets 1.0/SMP for Linux NET4.0.
VFS: Mounted root (ext2 filesystem) readonly.
Freeing unused kernel memory: 236k freed
Adding Swap: 2064344k swap-space (priority -1)
usb.c: registered new driver usbdevfs
usb.c: registered new driver hub
usb-uhci.c: $Revision: 1.251 $ time 20:53:29 Apr  8 2001
usb-uhci.c: High bandwidth mode enabled
PCI: Setting latency timer of device 00:1f.2 to 64
usb-uhci.c: USB UHCI at I/O 0xff80, IRQ 11
usb-uhci.c: Detected 2 ports
usb.c: new USB bus registered, assigned bus number 1
hub.c: USB hub found
hub.c: 2 ports detected
PCI: Setting latency timer of device 00:1f.4 to 64
usb-uhci.c: USB UHCI at I/O 0xff60, IRQ 9
usb-uhci.c: Detected 2 ports
usb.c: new USB bus registered, assigned bus number 2
hub.c: USB hub found
hub.c: 2 ports detected
hub.c: USB new device connect on bus2/1, assigned device number 3
usb.c: USB device 3 (vend/prod 0x59b/0x32) is not claimed by any active driver.
SCSI subsystem driver Revision: 1.00
Initializing USB Mass Storage driver...
usb.c: registered new driver usb-storage
scsi0 : SCSI emulation for USB Mass Storage devices
usb-uhci.c: interrupt, status 3, frame# 236
   Vendor: IOMEGA    Model: ZIP 250         Rev: 61.T
   Type:    Direct-Access                   ANSI SCSI revision: 02
WARNING: USB Mass Storage data integrity not assured
USB Mass Storage device found at 3
USB Mass Storage support registered.
scsi1 : SCSI host adapter emulation for IDE ATAPI devices
   Vendor: SONY      Model: CD-RW  CRX700E  Rev: 1.4j
   Type:    CD-ROM                          ANSI SCSI revision: 02
Winbond Super-IO detection, now testing ports 3F0,370,250,4E,2E ...
SMSC Super-IO detection, now testing Ports 2F0, 370 ...
0x378: FIFO is 16 bytes
0x378: writeIntrThreshold is 8
0x378: readIntrThreshold is 8
```

```
0x378: PWord is 8 bits
0x378: Interrupts are ISA-Pulses
0x378: ECP port cfgA=0x14 cfgB=0x40
0x378: ECP settings irq=<none or set by other means> dma=<none or set by other
➥means>
parport0: PC-style at 0x378 (0x778) [PCSPP,TRISTATE,COMPAT,EPP,ECP]
parport0: irq 7 detected
parport0: cpp_daisy: aa5500ff(08)
parport0: assign_addrs: aa5500ff(08)
parport0: cpp_daisy: aa5500ff(08)
parport0: assign_addrs: aa5500ff(08)
ip_conntrack (2040 buckets, 16320 max)
3c59x.c:LK1.1.13 27 Jan 2001  Donald Becker and others.
http://www.scyld.com/network/vortex.html
See Documentation/networking/vortex.txt
eth0: 3Com PCI 3c905C Tornado at 0xec80,  00:b0:d0:f0:f5:76, IRQ 11
  product code 0000 rev 00.3 date 06-10-00
  8K byte-wide RAM 5:3 Rx:Tx split, autoselect/Autonegotiate interface.
  MII transceiver found at address 24, status 782d.
  Enabling bus-master transmits and whole-frame receives.
eth0: scatter/gather disabled. h/w checksums enabled
eth0: using NWAY device table, not 8
usb.c: USB disconnect on device 3
Attached scsi CD-ROM sr0 at scsi1, channel 0, id 0, lun 0
sr0: scsi3-mmc drive: 24x/24x writer cd/rw xa/form2 cdda tray
Uniform CD-ROM driver Revision: 3.12
Intel 810 + AC97 Audio, version 0.02, 20:52:34 Apr  8 2001
PCI: Setting latency timer of device 00:1f.5 to 64
i810: Intel ICH2 found at IO 0xdc40 and 0xd800, IRQ 10
ac97_codec: AC97 Audio codec, id: 0x4144:0x5360 (Unknown)
i810_audio: setting clocking to 41349
i810_audio: ftsodell is now a deprecated option.
```

The Solaris Boot Sequence as Displayed by dmesg

The following listing is the dmesg output associated with the boot-up of a Sun Netra T-1 with Solaris 8 from EEPROM with a simple boot command. Note that these are also the exact contents of /var/adm/messages for the same process.

```
Sep 10 13:32:55 swift pseudo: [ID 129642 kern.info] pseudo-device: tod0
Sep 10 13:32:55 swift genunix: [ID 936769 kern.info] tod0 is /pseudo/tod@0
Sep 10 13:32:55 swift pseudo: [ID 129642 kern.info] pseudo-device: pm0
Sep 10 13:32:55 swift genunix: [ID 936769 kern.info] pm0 is /pseudo/pm@0
Sep 10 13:32:55 swift syslogd: going down on signal 15
Sep 10 13:33:13 swift genunix: [ID 672855 kern.notice] syncing file systems...
```

```
Sep 10 13:33:13 swift genunix: [ID 904073 kern.notice]  done
Sep 10 13:34:34 swift genunix: [ID 540533 kern.notice] ^MSunOS Release 5.8
➡Version Generic_108528-09 64-bit
Sep 10 13:34:34 swift genunix: [ID 913631 kern.notice] Copyright 1983-2001 Sun
➡Microsystems, Inc.  All rights reserved.
Sep 10 13:34:34 swift genunix: [ID 678236 kern.info] Ethernet address =
[ic:ccc}8:0:20:c2:a5:d2
Sep 10 13:34:34 swift unix: [ID 389951 kern.info] mem = 131072K (0x8000000)
Sep 10 13:34:34 swift unix: [ID 930857 kern.info] avail mem = 121421824
Sep 10 13:34:34 swift rootnex: [ID 466748 kern.info] root nexus = Netra t1
➡(UltraSPARC-IIi 360MHz)
Sep 10 13:34:34 swift rootnex: [ID 349649 kern.info] pcipsy0 at root: UPA 0x1f
➡0x0
Sep 10 13:34:34 swift genunix: [ID 936769 kern.info] pcipsy0 is /pci@1f,0
Sep 10 13:34:34 swift pcipsy: [ID 370704 kern.info] PCI-device: pci@1,1, simba0
Sep 10 13:34:34 swift genunix: [ID 936769 kern.info] simba0 is
➡/pci@1f,0/pci@1,1
Sep 10 13:34:34 swift pcipsy: [ID 370704 kern.info] PCI-device: pci@1, simba1
Sep 10 13:34:34 swift genunix: [ID 936769 kern.info] simba1 is /pci@1f,0/pci@1
Sep 10 13:34:34 swift scsi: [ID 365881 kern.info] /pci@1f,0/pci@1,1/scsi@2
➡(glm0):
Sep 10 13:34:34 swift    Rev. 3 Symbios 53c875 found.
Sep 10 13:34:34 swift simba: [ID 370704 kern.info] PCI-device: scsi@2, glm0
Sep 10 13:34:34 swift genunix: [ID 936769 kern.info] glm0 is
➡/pci@1f,0/pci@1,1/scsi@2
Sep 10 13:34:34 swift simba: [ID 370704 kern.info] PCI-device: pci@1, pci_pci0
Sep 10 13:34:34 swift genunix: [ID 936769 kern.info] pci_pci0 is
➡/pci@1f,0/pci@1/pci@1
Sep 10 13:34:47 swift pci_pci: [ID 370704 kern.info] PCI-device: ide@e, uata0
Sep 10 13:34:47 swift genunix: [ID 936769 kern.info] uata0 is
➡/pci@1f,0/pci@1/pci@1/ide@e
Sep 10 13:34:47 swift scsi: [ID 193665 kern.info] sd15 at uata0: target 2 lun 0
Sep 10 13:34:47 swift genunix: [ID 936769 kern.info] sd15 is
/pci@1f,0/pci@1/pci@1/ide@e/sd@2,0
Sep 10 13:34:47 swift scsi: [ID 193665 kern.info] sd0 at glm0: target 0 lun 0
Sep 10 13:34:47 swift genunix: [ID 936769 kern.info] sd0 is
➡/pci@1f,0/pci@1,1/scsi@2/sd@0,0
Sep 10 13:34:47 swift scsi: [ID 365881 kern.info]         <SUN18G cyl 7506 alt 2
➡hd 19 sec 248>
Sep 10 13:34:51 swift swapgeneric: [ID 308332 kern.info] root on
/pci@1f,0/pci@1,1/scsi@2/disk@0,0:a fstype ufs
Sep 10 13:34:51 swift simba: [ID 370704 kern.info] PCI-device: ebus@1, ebus0
Sep 10 13:34:51 swift ebus: [ID 521012 kern.info] su0 at ebus0: offset
➡14,3803f8
Sep 10 13:34:51 swift genunix: [ID 936769 kern.info] su0 is
/pci@1f,0/pci@1,1/ebus@1/su@14,3803f8
Sep 10 13:34:51 swift ebus: [ID 521012 kern.info] su1 at ebus0: offset
➡14,3602f8
```

```
Sep 10 13:34:51 swift genunix: [ID 936769 kern.info] su1 is
/pci@1f,0/pci@1,1/ebus@1/su@14,3602f8
Sep 10 13:34:51 swift unix: [ID 987524 kern.info] cpu0: SUNW,UltraSPARC-IIi
➥(upaid 0 impl 0x12 ver 0x91 clock 360 MHz)
Sep 10 13:34:53 swift hme: [ID 517527 kern.info] SUNW,hme0 : PCI IO 2.0
➥(Rev Id = c1) Found
Sep 10 13:34:53 swift hme: [ID 517527 kern.info] SUNW,hme0 : Local Ethernet
➥address = 8:0:20:c2:a5:d2
Sep 10 13:34:53 swift simba: [ID 370704 kern.info] PCI-device: network@1,1,
➥hme0
Sep 10 13:34:53 swift genunix: [ID 936769 kern.info] hme0 is
➥/pci@1f,0/pci@1,1/network@1,1
Sep 10 13:34:53 swift hme: [ID 517527 kern.info] SUNW,hme1 : PCI IO 2.0
➥(Rev Id = c1) Found
Sep 10 13:34:53 swift hme: [ID 517527 kern.info] SUNW,hme1 : Local Ethernet
➥address = 8:0:20:c2:a5:d3
Sep 10 13:34:53 swift simba: [ID 370704 kern.info] PCI-device: network@3,1,
➥hme1
Sep 10 13:34:53 swift genunix: [ID 936769 kern.info] hme1 is
➥/pci@1f,0/pci@1,1/network@3,1
Sep 10 13:34:54 swift genunix: [ID 454863 kern.info] dump on /dev/dsk/c0t0d0s1
➥size 513 MB
Sep 10 13:34:56 swift hme: [ID 517527 kern.info] SUNW,hme0 : External
➥Transceiver Selected.
Sep 10 13:34:56 swift hme: [ID 517527 kern.info] SUNW,hme0 : Auto-Negotiated
➥100 Mbps Full-Duplex Link Up
Sep 10 13:35:03 swift pseudo: [ID 129642 kern.info] pseudo-device: tod0
Sep 10 13:35:03 swift genunix: [ID 936769 kern.info] tod0 is /pseudo/tod@0
Sep 10 13:35:03 swift pseudo: [ID 129642 kern.info] pseudo-device: pm0
Sep 10 13:35:03 swift genunix: [ID 936769 kern.info] pm0 is /pseudo/pm@0
Sep 10 13:35:03 swift pseudo: [ID 129642 kern.info] pseudo-device: vol0
Sep 10 13:35:03 swift genunix: [ID 936769 kern.info] vol0 is /pseudo/vol@0
```

Sample Output from Shutting Down Solaris

Finally, here is the output generated by a graceful shutdown of the system with a mere
30 seconds' warning:

```
[sun:1 ~]shutdown -g30 -y

Shutdown started.    Mon Sep 10 20:43:09 EDT 2001

Broadcast Message from root (console) on swift Mon Sep 10 20:43:09...
The system swift will be shut down in 30 seconds

Broadcast Message from root (console) on swift Mon Sep 10 20:43:29...
THE SYSTEM swift IS BEING SHUT DOWN NOW ! ! !
Log off now or risk your files being damaged
```

```
Changing to init state s - please wait
[sun:2 ~]
INIT: New run level: S
The system is coming down for administration.  Please wait.
Unmounting remote filesystems: /vol nfs done.
Print services stopped.
Sep 10 20:43:56 swift syslogd: going down on signal 15
Killing user processes: done.

INIT: SINGLE USER MODE

Type control-d to proceed with normal startup,
(or give root password for system maintenance):
```

And here is the more abrupt init 0, also achieving system shutdown:

```
[sun:1 ~] init 0
[sun:2 ~]
INIT: New run level: 0
The system is coming down.  Please wait.
System services are now being stopped.
Print services stopped.
Sep 10 13:32:55 swift syslogd: going down on signal 15

The system is down.

syncing file systems... done
Program terminated
ok
```

Best Practices

Firmware

- Set the firmware to always boot in verbose mode.
- Set the firmware to not boot from the network unless your site requires it.
- Keep your firmware updated.
- Don't disrupt a running multiuser system by dropping directly into firmware.

Kernel

- Keep a spare, known-good kernel available. Having a backup copy on another bootable disk partition or another disk drive will be very useful in case of a disk failure.
- Keep track of your original media, whether CD or floppy; you might need it later.

Init

- Don't set your default runlevel to 0 or 6 (or 5, under Solaris).

Shutdown

- Be kind to your users—use `shutdown` with a decent grace period.
- Be kind to your system—use `shutdown` rather than just `init`.

Follow-Through

- Always check `dmesg` for boot-time errors.
- Always check the system log for boot-time application errors.

Online References

General

- PCGuide—Systems and Components Reference Guide

  `http://www.pcguide.com/ref/`

- Webopedia: Online Computer Dictionary for Internet Terms and Technical Support

  `http://webopedia.internet.com/`

Red Hat Linux 2.4 Kernels Download Site

`http://www.kernel.org/pub/linux/kernel/v2.4/`

Solaris 8 Kernel Download Site

`http://www.sun.com/software/solaris/binaries/get.html`

The Unix Boot Process

- General

  `http://www.eecs.wsu.edu/~cs302/notes/booting.html`

- Red Hat

  - The Official Red Hat Linux Reference Guide: Behind the Scenes of the Boot Process

    `http://www.redhat.com/support/manuals/RHL-7.1-Manual/ref-guide/`
    `s1-boot-init-shutdown-booting.html`

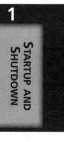

- Boot Prompt & LILO:

  `http://www.linuxdoc.org/HOWTO/BootPrompt-HOWTO-2.html#ss2.2`
  `http://www.redhat.com/support/manuals/RHL-7.1-Manual/install-guide/`
  `s1-guimode-lilo-conf.html`
  `http://www.linuxdoc.org/HOWTO/mini/LILO-2.html#ss2.1`

- Troubleshooting

  `http://www.it.redhat.com/support/docs/faqs/rhl_general_faq/FAQ-5.html`

- Solaris

  - Boot Process Reference

    `http://docs.sun.com/ab2/coll.47.11/SYSADV1/@Ab2PageView/10865`

  - Working from Sun's PROM:

    `http://docs.sun.com/ab2/coll.216.2/OPENBOOTCMDREF_3.x/@Ab2PageView/22`
    `45?Ab2Lang=C&Ab2Enc=iso-8859-1`

  - OpenBoot

    `http://docs.sun.com/ab2/coll.216.2/`

  - rc Boot Progression: `/etc/init.d/README`

Endnotes

[1] *This includes VT100, VT200, VT220, and other Virtual Terminal emulators that have their own monitor and keyboard setup connected to your machine over a serial line.*

[2] *Also see* `http://docs.sun.com/ab2/coll.216.2/OPENBOOTCMDREF_3.x/@Ab2PageView/` `2245?Ab2Lang= C&Ab2Enc=iso-8859-1.`

[3] *This is known as defense-in-depth. See Chapter 21, Security for more.*

[4] *See* `http://www.m-w.com,` *bootstrap, definition 2.*

[5] *See* `http://ase.isu.edu/ase01_07/ase01_07/bookcase/ref_sh/foldoc/24/13.htm.`

[6] *See* `http://www.eecs.wsu.edu/~cs302/notes/booting.html.`

[7] *For more on the MBR, also see* `http://whatis.techtarget.com/definitionsSearchResults/` `1,289878,sid9,00.html?query=mbr.`

[8] *In many modern Unix implementations, there is a shift away from process abstractions and towards the concept of tasks and threads. This differentiation goes beyond the scope of our text.*

[9] *But not completely hardware independent, of course. This is why you occasionally have to recompile a kernel to add device support. More on that in Chapter 2.*

[10] *Also called Inter-Process Communication, or IPC.*

[11] *For a step-by-step conversion guide, see* `http://www.linuxdoc.org/LDP/lki/lki-1.html`.

[12] *See* `http://www.linuxdoc.org/LDP/sag/x100.html#AEN103`.

[13] *Yes, it can be done (`kill -9 -1 1`) but it's not a good idea. In fact, this is a very dangerous command that should never be run on any system that is in production or where you are not the only user. You WILL lose data, crash the system AND have to fix the filesystems! You Have Been Warned!*

[14] *Pronounced "System Five."*

[15] *Or the power cord mysteriously gets knocked loose by Floyd the Clumsy Janitor...*

[16] *Which may have been responsible for the shutdown, too.*

Managing Disk Hardware

by Robin Anderson

IN THIS CHAPTER

Introduction

The first thing an admin looks at when given a new machine is its hardware. After all, if there's no system, there's no admin. And you need to know what's under the hood before you can even think about managing it.

That, of course, is the real goal—the efficient and intelligent management of resources. Time and again, admins are asked to make everything work with what they've already got, so you've got to be ready for whatever shows up on your system.

This chapter begins your journey into the system with a discussion of the various types and communication standards for physical devices. Then we'll show how to both add and remove disks from your system.

Physical Devices

Why start with physical devices? Mainly because they are the most fundamental unit of long-term local storage. Although "thin clients" and other network-dependent devices are becoming popular again,[1] most workstations—and certainly major servers—tend to have their own local storage. It might hold as little as the base Operating System or it might serve a multi-terabyte array of space.

The most common storage medium is the hard disk.[2] The general catalog of hardware parts in a modern hard disk includes arms, heads, and platters. The stored data is logically organized into sectors, tracks, and cylinders. Although the number of sectors per track (see the following note) and tracks per cylinder is fixed for a given drive, they are designed constructs, not actually physical components.

> **Note**
>
> In modern drives, the number of sectors per track can vary between different tracks. The tracks on the outer cylinders of the disk platter, for example, have more writeable surface and thus are assigned more sectors. The number of sectors for a given track is fixed *for that track*, but not all tracks have the same allotment.
>
> Of course, all this is basically hidden from both the user and the admin through the device drivers that translate the disk's cylinders, tracks, and sectors into a linear address space.

Figure 2.1 shows a notional stack of drive platters, each with its own dedicated read/write head supported on a triangular armature.

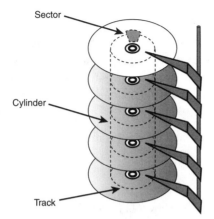

FIGURE 2.1

Basic hard disk schematic.

Sector

Cylinder

Track

The number of actual platters varies based on both the drive and the individual platter's capacity. Remember, though, that these components are mostly hidden, even from admins, except at partitioning time (see Chapter 3, "Filesystem Administration," for information on partitioning).

OS-Independent Hardware Communication Standards

Of course, more devices are available on Unix machines than just hard disks. Many devices came onto the technology field with their own particular cabling, connectors, and interaction methods. The great diversity of vendors and technologies would present a hopeless morass of incompatibilities and babble if not for standards.

Standards are what allow devices to communicate in a meaningful way across platforms and vendor types. The Institute of Electrical and Electronics Engineers Standards Association (IEEE-SA) maintains a large body of these standards.[3] This is why you will often see labels on physical cabling stating IEEE standards compliance, and why wireless communications are referred to as "IEEE 802.11." The American National Standards Institute (ANSI) also maintains a broad array of technological and other standards.[4] Some of these are delegated to working committees and other groups. We will mention which organization has control of the various standards that we discuss.

You are likely to come across these devices in almost any environment now, so we're going to say a few words about the following standards: serial, FireWire, USB, parallel, and ATAPI. Then we'll go into more detail about the most common standards for fixed, or nonremovable, hard disks: IDE and SCSI.

Brief Notes on Serial

Serial communications send successive, individual bits over the wire in a notional single-file queue. Essentially, only one event can be handled at a time. Standard serial-based connections are generally characterized as slow, best suited for one-way communications or applications where time differentials are unimportant.[5] The serial communications standard is known as EIA[6] RS-232C.[7]

Modems, dumb terminals, keyboards, and mice are common serial devices in the Unix world.

Serial Connectors

The most common serial connectors are shown in Figure 2.2.

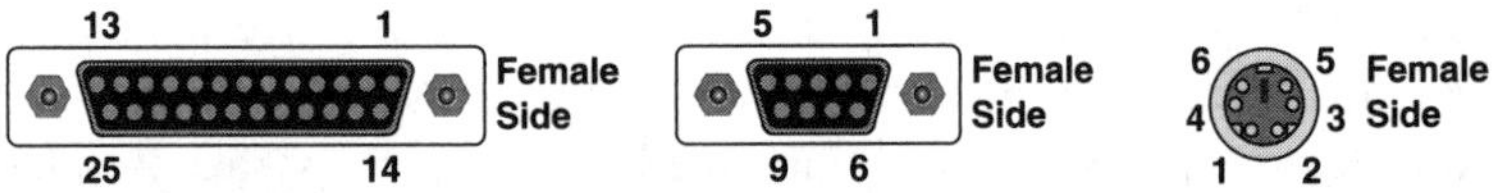

FIGURE 2.2
Common serial connectors.

 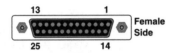 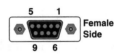

They are, from left to right, DB-25, DB-9, and 6-pin mini-DIN. The mini-DIN connectors are found mainly on keyboards and mice.

Brief Notes on FireWire (IEEE 1394)

FireWire is one of two new innovations on the serial theme. Developed by Apple Computers,[8] FireWire is based on the IEEE 1394 High Performance Serial Bus standard.

FireWire communicates at 400Mbps, supports up to 63 devices and a maximum cable length of 14 feet. These devices are hot-swappable and don't need chain-identification settings or termination (more on these concepts when we discuss SCSI).

Red Hat 7.1, with a 2.4-based kernel, now supports IEEE 1394. Sun Blade systems also currently ship with a built-in FireWire adapter and drivers.

FireWire Connector

Figure 2.3 shows a diagram of a FireWire/IEEE 1394–compliant connector.

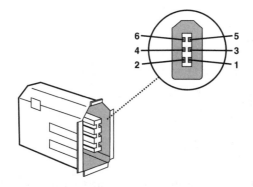

FIGURE 2.3
*FireWire/IEEE
1394–compliant
connector.*

Brief Notes on USB

The other advance in serial communications is the Universal Serial Bus (USB). This
standard was developed and is supported cooperatively by Compaq Computer
Corporation, Hewlett-Packard Company, Intel Corporation, Lucent Technologies,
Microsoft Corporation, NEC Corporation, and Philips Semiconductors.[9] This gave USB
a broad support base even when it was first released.

USB version 1.1 communicates at 12Mbps, supports up to 127 devices[10] and a maximum cable length of 5 meters. USB version 2.0 maintains the same standards but can
communicate at up to 480Mbps.

As with FireWire, all USB devices are hot-swappable and don't need chain-identification
settings or termination (again, more on these concepts when we discuss SCSI later in this
chapter).

Red Hat 7.1, with a 2.4-based kernel, supports USB and true hot-swapping.[11]

Sun Ray and Blade systems also currently ship with built-in USB adapters and drivers.[12]
These systems can support the following types of USB devices: keyboards, mice, mass
storage, printers, and hubs. They *cannot* support third-party controller cards.

USB Connectors

USB cables are not symmetric—they have Type A on one end and Type B on the other,
as Figure 2.4 shows.

FIGURE 2.4
USB Type A and USB Type B connectors.

Type A Slot

Type B Slot

Note that the system's USB port is usually Type A, as are the connectors on external USB hubs. The external peripheral's port is usually a Type B connector.

Brief Notes on ATAPI

ATAPI stands for "AT Attachment Packet Interface" and is actually related to the IDE standard (more on that in a moment). This standard is most often used to communicate with CD-ROM drives, but any device other than hard drives that uses IDE-style communication and connectors is using the ATAPI standard.[13]

Both Red Hat and Solaris support ATAPI devices.

Brief Notes on Parallel

Parallel communications send multiple bits over the wire in a notional multiline set of queues. Essentially, many events can be handled at a time. Although parallel connections are generally characterized as being faster than standard serial, they can't really compare to the new, improved serial standards. IEEE 1284 defines three types of parallel standards:[14]

- Standard Parallel Port (SPP)
- Enhanced Parallel Port (EPP)
- Extended Capabilities Port (ECP)

Parallel ports are intended to support only one device at a time and have a cabling limit of 6 feet.[15] SPP can reach a maximum speed of 150Kbps. EPP and ECP can transfer up to 2Mbps.

The most common parallel device in the Unix world is a printer.

Parallel Connectors

SPP cables are not symmetric—they have DB-25 on one end and male 36-pin Centronics on the other, as Figure 2.5 shows.

FIGURE 2.5

Common parallel connectors.

EPP cables, on the other hand, *are* symmetric and are based on the DB-25 connector. ECP uses the same asymmetric cable as the SPP.

IDE/ATA

Recently, IDE/ATA has become one of the two major hard disk communications standards found in the Unix world.[16] IDE stands for Integrated Drive Electronics and is a parallel standard formally known by ANSI as ATA (Advanced Technology Attachment).[17] IDE/ATA hard disks were the first to have logic boards embedded in their hardware (hence the lasting term "Integrated").[18]

Definitions: IDE/ATA Terms

IDE/ATA is generally considered a PC-oriented standard, but Sun is releasing some of its new platforms (such as the Netra X-1 and Sun Blade) with native IDE/ATA. And although IDE/ATA is generally slower than SCSI, it is also markedly less expensive.

The summary history that you are about to read was greatly informed by the wonderful work available online from PC Guide, created and maintained by Charles Kozierok. (See `http://www.pcguide.com/ref/hdd/if/ide/index.htm`)

IDE/ATA has come a long way since its first introduction in 1990. It has gone through many names and has even switched data transfer models. Some things have remained constant, however.

IDE/ATA is intended to function as an internal device bus. As such, it uses ribbon cables that can only have an official maximum length of 18 inches. Developers have gone out of their way to ensure reasonable backward compatibility between the new bus communications standards and older drives. IDE/ATA buses require no termination (see the later discussion on SCSI for more termination information).

2

MANAGING DISK
HARDWARE

The official standard names and reference numbers are as follows:

- ATA/ATA-1
  - ANSI X3.221-1994
  - Introduced the IDE/ATA standard and 40-conductor cable
  - Supports two devices on one cable
  - Supports disks up to 528Mb
- ATA-2
  - ANSI X3.279-1996
  - Introduced support for up to four devices, two on each of two *channels*
  - Supports disks up to 8.4Gb
- ATA-3
  - ANSI X3.298-1997
  - Revision to ATA-2; improves reliability and robustness
- ATA/ATAPI-4
  - ANSI NCITS 317-1998
  - Standard development moved to NCITS
  - ATAPI merged into ATA standard
  - 80-conductor cable introduced, although it remained 40-conductor–compatible
- ATA/ATAPI-5
  - ANSI NCITS 340-2000
- ATA/ATAPI-6
  - Still under development as ANSI NCITS project 1410

The current disk size limit is 137Gb under ATA/ATAPI-5.

Early IDE/ATA used Programmed Input/Output (PIO) modes to transfer data via the main CPU. Later, Direct Memory Access (DMA) modes bypassed the processor entirely, speeding up transfer times and unburdening the CPU.

IDE bus types are summarized in Table 2.1.

TABLE 2.1 IDE Bus Types, Statistics, and Modes

Official Mode Name	*Aliases*	*PIO Modes[19]*	*PIO Maximum Throughput (Mbps)*	*DMA Modes[20]*	*DMA Maximum Throughput (Mbps)*	*Maximum Number of Devices*
ATA	ATA-1 IDE	0	3.3	Single Word Mode 0	2.1	2
		1	5.2	Single Word Mode 1	4.2	2
		2	8.3	Single Word Mode 2	8.3	2
				Multi Word Mode 0	4.2	2
ATA-2	EIDE Fast IDE Fast ATA Fast ATA-2	3	11.1	Multi Word Mode 1	13.3	4
		4	16.6	Multi Word Mode 2	16.7	4
ATA/ ATAPI-4	Ultra-ATA Ultra-DMA			Ultra-DMA 0	16.7	4
				Ultra-DMA 1	25.0	4
	Ultra-ATA/33 ATA-33 DMA-33			Ultra-DMA 2	33.3	4
ATA/ ATAPI-5				Ultra-DMA 3	44.4	4
	Ultra ATA/66			Ultra-DMA 4	66.7	4
ATA/ ATAPI-6 *proposed*	Ultra ATA/100			Ultra-DMA 5 (?)	100.0	4

IDE/ATA Connectors

IDE/ATA is designed to handle internal devices, so it communicates over ribbon cable with the connector shown in Figure 2.6.

FIGURE 2.6

IDE/ATA connectors.

As mentioned before, all types of IDE/ATA communicate over one of two flavors of ribbon cable, although both have the same 40-pin connector. The original standard called for 40 conductors in the cable. When ATA/ATAPI-4 was developed, it introduced the 80-conductor cable for greater reliability and general robustness. Many devices that expect the new style cable can still communicate over the 40-conductor cable, although with diminished capacity.

Master and Slave on IDE/ATA Buses

Because all IDE/ATA standards support multiple devices on the same bus, there has to be some way to differentiate among them. Without some kind of identification mechanism, there wouldn't be any way to be sure that commands are received and interpreted by their intended target.

Each IDE/ATA *channel*, or independently managed device chain, supports at most two devices. This allows for a very simple labeling scheme: One device is the *master*, and the other, if it exists, is the *slave*. This means that the main controller can send out commands addressed to the intended target's label and although the devices share a common bus, only the one identified in the command will accept and act on the instruction.[21]

The appellations *master* and *slave* are misleading; there is no special function associated with either one. The master can conceptually be considered the "first device," and the slave can be thought of as the "second device," regardless of physical arrangement. In the Unix world, this is only important when considering dynamic device name assignments (as under Red Hat).

The only real difference between master and slave IDE/ATA devices is jumper positioning.[22] There should only be one master and one slave on any given channel. If a device is alone on a channel, set its jumpers to the master device setting.[23]

SCSI

The Small Computer System Interface, better known as SCSI,[24] is the ANSI standard of choice for large disk arrays and high-speed performance. SCSI is based on the parallel interface (which is why you shouldn't be surprised to see DB-25 as one of the standard, though older, connector types).

Definitions: SCSI Terms

As many varieties as exist for IDE/ATA, there are even more types and subtle distinctions to the realm of SCSI transport technology. It's critical to be able to keep them straight, though, because you can actually damage your system with voltage differentials, depending on the kind of controller and devices you are trying to mix.

There are three SCSI bus types: Single-ended (SE), High-voltage differential (HVD), and Low-voltage differential (LVD). All three have different types of controllers and put out different electric currents across the cable.

SE is the oldest and simplest standard. The cable carries a current of 5VDC,[25] and each component wire transmits 1 bit of data at a time. The original bus also relied on passive termination. SE is rather sensitive to line noise and reflection problems, so it supports only short bus lengths.

HVD was developed next and significantly increased bus length and reliability. Cables still carried a current of 5VDC. Each bit was transmitted across *two* wires, with the actual data being represented by the *difference* between their voltages.[26] This, plus active termination, allows a longer bus, higher reliability, and higher data throughput. HVD is the most expensive of the three SCSI standards to implement and is no longer being manufactured or supported.

LVD superceded both SE and HVD with a more flexible standard designed with an eye to improving data throughput. LVD sends only 3.3VDC over the cable, allowing faster cycling through the entire range.[27] Because each bit is still transmitted as the signal differential of two wires, LVD retains the higher signal-to-noise ratio and greater cable lengths that HVD introduced. The lower voltage is not only faster for data transfers, but runs cooler as well[28]—always desirable when dealing with electronics. LVD controllers and devices sport a wide interface that facilitates its high data-transfer rates.

There is also a combination or *multimode* form of LVD, formally referred to as LVD/MSE—Multimode Single-Ended. LVD/MSE devices have built-in logic allowing them to acclimate to SE buses. This means that LVD/MSE devices are quite versatile and can be used in all-LVD, all-SE, or combination chains. What's more, they auto-sense the bus type on which they reside, so the changeover happens automatically, with no admin intervention to set switches or jumpers.

> **Note**
>
> Be warned, however, that when LVD/MSE devices are added to a chain with either an SE controller or an SE device on it, all communication standards and limitations revert to those of SE. The only real benefit is that you can purchase newer devices that support a communication standard likely to still be in the market in a few years that will still work on your old systems.

Although LVD can get along with SE, it does not play well with HVD. Because the HVD mode relies on the differential between two wires at 5VDC, it doesn't have any mechanism to scale back to 3.3VDC.[29] Do *not* mix the two device or controller types. We have seen LVD-only hardware damaged by adding it to the higher-voltage HVD bus.

The official standard names and reference numbers are as follows:[30]

- SCSI/SCSI-1
  - ANSI X3.131-1986
  - Introduced the SCSI standard
  - Supports bus speeds of up to 5MHz
  - Supports what is now called narrow mode
  - Transfers 1 bit at a time
- SCSI-2
  - ANSI X3.131-1994
  - Introduced support for bus speeds up to 10MHz
  - Introduced support for nondisk devices
  - Introduced Fast, Wide, and Fast-Wide modes
  - Introduced capability of devices to discover and negotiate bus type
  - Transfers 2 bits at a time (over wide interface)
- SCSI-3
  - ANSI X3.302-1999
  - Introduced bus speeds of 40MHz, 80MHz, 160MHz, and 320 MHz
  - Introduced CRC error-correction
  - Introduced LVD bus and interface
  - Introduced support for IEEE 1394 Fibre Channel protocols

Note that where words are in square brackets, the enclosed term is optional—you might not see it when reading drive specs and the like.

Narrow/8-bit buses transfer 1 bit of data at a time, whereas Wide/16-bit buses transfer 2 bits of data at a time.

SCSI bus types are summarized in Table 2.2.

TABLE 2.2 SCSI Bus Types, Statistics, and Modes[31]

SE Bus

	Supported Modes	*Maximum Number of Devices*	*Maximum Bus Length (m)*	*Bus Width (bits)*	*Maximum Throughput (Mbps)*
SCSI-1	[Narrow] SCSI-1	8	6	8	5
SCSI-2	[Narrow] Fast SCSI-2	8	3	8	10
	Wide SCSI-2	16	3	16	10
	Fast Wide SCSI-2	16	3	16	20
SCSI-3	[Narrow] Ultra SCSI-3	4	3	8	20
		8	1.5	8	20
		16	1.5	16	40
	Wide Ultra SCSI-3	4	3	16	40
		8	1.5	16	40

HVD Bus

	Supported Modes	*Maximum Number of Devices*	*Maximum Bus Length (m)*	*Bus Width (bits)*	*Maximum Throughput (Mbps)*
SCSI-1	[Narrow] SCSI-1	8	25	8	5
SCSI-2	[Narrow] Fast SCSI-2	8	25	8	10
	Wide SCSI-2	16	25	16	10
	Fast Wide SCSI-2	16	25	16	20
SCSI-3	[Narrow] Ultra SCSI-3	16	25	16	20
	Wide Ultra SCSI	16	25	16	20
	[Narrow] Ultra2 SCSI	8	25	8	40
	Wide Ultra2 SCSI	16	25	16	40

2

MANAGING DISK
HARDWARE

TABLE 2.2   continued

LVD Bus

	Supported Modes	*Maximum Number of Devices*	*Maximum Bus Length (m)*	*Bus Width (bits)*	*Maximum Throughput (Mbps)*
SCSI-1	**[Narrow] SCSI-1**	8	12	8	5
SCSI-2	**[Narrow] Fast SCSI-2**	8	12	8	10
	Wide SCSI-2	16	12	16	10
	Fast Wide SCSI-2	16	12	16	20
SCSI-3	**[Narrow] Ultra SCSI-3**	8	12	8	20
	Wide Ultra SCSI-3	16	12	16	40
	[Narrow] Ultra2 SCSI-3	8	12	8	40
	Wide Ultra2 SCSI-3	16	12	16	80
	[Wide] Ultra3 SCSI or				
	[Wide] Ultra160/m or				
	[Wide] Ultra160 SCSI	16	12	16	160
	[Wide] Ultra320 SCSI	8	12	16	320

Note that, as mentioned before, LVD can support only a 12m bus length for the modes in bold if *all* devices on the bus are LVD. If there are mixed LVD and SE devices on the bus, then the entire bus switches to SE; see Table 2.2.

Also be aware that the controller counts as one of the devices on the chain. So, if you have a SCSI-1 bus, you may add a maximum of seven devices other than the controller.

SCSI Connectors

As if bus types and modes were not enough to juggle, there are also a number of different connector types for SCSI (see Figure 2.7). Happily, you can use conversion cables between disks with different connector types *as long as they support the same mode*. When you start crossing modes, you need to take special steps to adjust voltages and terminate the bus correctly (more on that next).

SCA is a relatively new kind of connector that combines drive power and SCSI communication.[32] As such, it was designed to have the bus controller integrated into the system's backplane and have drives plug in directly to the backplane. If you want to use an SCA drive externally, you must provide it with a special cable/adapter.[33]

FIGURE 2.7
Common SCSI Connectors.

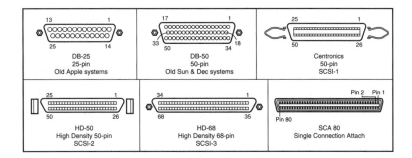

2

MANAGING DISK
HARDWARE

SCSI IDs

Like IDE/ATA buses, SCSI chains must have some way of differentiating among attached devices. But because a SCSI controller can handle as many as 15 additional devices at once, the IDE/ATA *master/slave* nomenclature is insufficient. Instead, SCSI devices have unique numbers, or *SCSI-IDs*, on the local bus.

Note that as with most other computer-related counting, SCSI buses begin with device number 0. One device on the chain must be reserved for the controller itself. By convention, this defaults to the last device number (7 for Narrow, 15 for Wide). Be aware, however, that not all manufacturers adhere to this rubric, so check your documentation.

SCSI-ID is always set via jumpers.[34] External SCSI cases will often have a SCSI-ID selector switch on the case for ease of use, but it must be correctly connected to the device's jumper pins inside.

SCSI devices may be assigned any open ID number on the bus. The most important thing to remember is that you must avoid duplicate SCSI-IDs. Such collisions can cause the bus to stop functioning, give "odd" errors, or, worse yet, appear to work marginally but corrupt data.

Tip

Although SCSI devices do not *have* to be assigned sequential numbers, it's a good idea to do so anyway, to lessen the chance of ID collisions on the chain.

Here's a method for avoiding internal/external collisions: Label your system chassis with the SCSI IDs of all internal devices. Next, label each of your external devices with its assigned SCSI ID.

It also might be useful for you to list the filesystems (slice and name) that reside on SCSI disk.

Countless hours have been lost over the years by admins trying to figure out what device was *really* using which SCSI-ID and what filesystems were stored on it.

SCSI Termination

As we mentioned before, SCSI buses carry voltage and need to be *terminated* to reliably function properly. Unterminated electric signals will reflect from the end of the last device and rebound up the chain again unless they are dampened or absorbed in some manner. Reflected signals make for line noise and corrupted/failed transmissions.

SCSI buses are terminated at the far end (and *only* at the far end) with a device composed of resistors. Terminators come in two types: passive and active. Passive terminators are older and only effectively work with narrow, SCSI-1 buses. Active terminators were developed with the SCSI-2 specification and draw on live power to prevent signal reflection.[35] Diminished reflection noise allows longer bus lengths, higher throughput, and greater reliability. In fact, SCSI-2 strongly recommends active termination and SCSI-3 actually requires it.

We recommend that you use terminators that have indicator lights to show that the terminator is both attached and functioning properly. Generally, only active terminators have indicator lights, but make sure you check that assumption before relying on the terminator's type!

The longer your bus, and the faster its throughput, the more critical it is that you have strong active termination. Most external active terminators will have an imprint of the word "Active" on their cases.[36] Most modern hard disks also come with built-in active terminators that can be enabled with a jumper. If the terminal drive is in an external case, then it is preferable to also use an external terminator. If the terminal drive is internal, though, you will need to verify that the correct jumper is in place. Again, be sure that you are terminating *only* the last device on an internal bus chain.

If you are in doubt about an external terminator's type, especially if you are having SCSI problems,[37] we recommend that you spend the few extra dollars and invest in a new active terminator. Also, older SCSI equipment might have compatibility problems when mixing internal and external termination. Even if it doesn't solve your problem, you know that termination will no longer be a contributing factor.

> **Note**
>
> A lot of variety exists among SCSI terminators, and we can address only the most commonly encountered implementations. The "References" section at the end of this chapter includes a URL for the SCSI Termination FAQ for the reader who wants to find out more.

SCSI Troubleshooting

SCSI troubleshooting can seem somewhat arcane, so we developed a flowchart to help you through the process. There are always new and exciting problems cropping up, so be warned that even this diagram might not ultimately pinpoint the trouble you are having. The following discussion refers to the SCSI Troubleshooting Flowchart poster in the book. You will find it useful to have the flowchart in hand as you read this section.

In a Hurry?

Of course, if you are opening this section in the middle of a crisis, you might not want to spend time going through the flowchart right now. Here's a quick-and-dirty method, recommended by Rob Jensen, for troubleshooting your SCSI chain. Use these steps only if you are fairly sure that the problem is a device or cable.

When troubleshooting problems on a SCSI chain, sometimes there is value in isolating the problem down to the individual component. So, start by disconnecting all external SCSI devices and terminating the bus; see if the problem is with an internal disk unit.

Then add the external disk units, one at a time, rebooting the system and verifying that they can be seen.

After all the disk units are added with no problems, add the other peripherals (tape units, CD units, and so on) one at a time.

Sometimes the problem is total cable length. As a rule of thumb, each cable junction/connection counts as 6 inches on the SCSI chain, and internal cabling inside the enclosure also contributes to the maximum cable length.

If you're not sure where the problem is coming from, you will want to proceed more methodically. You can follow our discussion here based on the flowchart poster in the book. Go ahead and get it—we'll wait.

Important note: If you pass through the same decision point more than twice in your troubleshooting efforts, you might either have a problem not identified by the flowchart, or you might have a faulty device that must be replaced (be it the drive, power provider, or something else).

Now, what does all this mean? It means that SCSI is a fairly intricate standard with lots of pieces that can go wrong—and many of the pieces are not even directly related to the standard itself (like power).

One Step at a Time

The key to successful troubleshooting is to take one step at a time. Like a good scientist, you should change only one variable at each step, if possible. Although this might seem to take more time, in the long run this methodology will allow you to isolate problems faster and more accurately.

Also like a scientist, don't be shy about taking notes while you work. Just because each step is simple doesn't imply that the whole process won't be very involved.

Here's a little commentary to supplement the flowchart:

We are only considering a *hard disk* that is having problems on the SCSI chain. This is because a hard disk has the most possibilities for component failure, especially if it is an external unit. You should be able to troubleshoot most other SCSI devices with a subset of the flowchart provided.

The first, and probably most obvious, question is: Does the system recognize the drive as being attached to an active SCSI bus? If not, then you might just need to re-initialize. Remember, you will always need to re-initialize the SCSI bus when new hardware has been added. With hot-swap–capable buses, this can be done with a simple command while the system is still up. On most PCs, you will have to power down the machine to add the device and then power it back up to initialize the bus with the new device present. Under Solaris, you follow the same basic process, but you also need to issue the command boot -r from eeprom to get the system to perform a device discovery as it reboots (more on this later in this chapter). The key thing to note is that if the device you just added to the chain is not being recognized by the system, it might be because the chain was not properly re-initialized.

Once the system recognizes the disk, you want to check that the disk properly responds to system commands. The most fundamental operation is a partitioning command; its successful operation indicates that the system is aware of the disk and can interact with it. On a Red Hat system, the command is fdisk; on a Solaris box, the command is format (more on these commands in Chapter 3).

The next command to try is mount. The disk's SCSI–ID and filesystem slice determine its device name. Refer to the section "Naming Conventions" for further details on device name specification. A successful mount command indicates that the system recognizes and can interact with the filesystem on a given disk/partition.

An *unsuccessful* mount could just mean that there is no filesystem (or no *valid* filesystem) on the indicated partition. In this case, you might want to try issuing the command `fsck -n`. This invokes a filesystem state check, but in a read-only mode, so as not to damage a working or even mounted filesystem. Note that `fsck -n` is valid on both Red Hat and Solaris. (See Chapter 3 for more details.)

To test that your system can write to both the drive and its constituent filesystem(s), just `cd` to a directory located in the filesystem in question, and `touch` a file into existence. If the command fails because of an I/O error, then you likely have hardware problems. If it fails because of a "permission denied" error, then check the following four items:

1. Are you `root`?
2. Is the disk write-protected (via jumper or read-only mounting)? See the next paragraph for more details.
3. Is the directory write-protected (via Unix permissions or ACLs)?
4. Is the disk full?

Read testing should precede write testing in troubleshooting. If the disk can perform read but not write commands, it might have jumpers configured to write-protect. This is not always a problem, but if you need to write something to the drive, you must first change the jumper settings (which means shutting down the system, unless it is hot-swap–capable). If you were not aware that the drive was set to write-protect, you should do two things: First, make sure that it wasn't an accident, and, second, label the drive (or system chassis) for the future.

A filesystem also can be write-protected by mounting it read-only, whether permanently or temporarily (see Chapter 3 for more details). As with hardware-based write protection, this can be useful, but only when its state is documented and well known.

The next step is to check power: whether the device is receiving power, whether it is responding to power, and so on. It's a very simple thing, but you'd be amazed how often it can be a problem. Also, don't ignore the possibility that you have a bad power cable or power supply. It's easy to look for a deeper technological problem when all that's really happening is that your power cable is frayed or loose.

Every drive has both an internal and an external power vector; remember to check both when troubleshooting power problems.

For drives located inside the system, check the following:

- Internal vector
  - Is the case chassis receiving power?
  - Are the internal power connectors tightly housed?

- External vector
  - Check if the system's UPS (or even room circuit) is turned on and not overloaded

For all external drives, check the following:

- Internal vector
  - Is the external case's power supply functioning correctly?
  - Are the external case's internal connectors tightly housed?
- External vector
  - Check whether the external case's power strip, UPS, or even the room circuit is turned on and not overloaded.
  - Bad power strips can be puzzling and time-consuming, especially if you have only the new case on the bad strip! Get strips with power-on indicator lights, or carry known good plug-on testers or simple items (such as a lamp). Sometimes just one outlet on the strip is bad. Get rid of the whole thing.

> **Note**
>
> *Do not* mess around with electrical equipment, power supplies, or the like if you are not certified to do so. Using the "if you plug it in and it doesn't work, it's broken" maxim should be sufficient for most of your needs. All further exploration of your electric systems should be left to professionals. In case you have not heard, electricity can be dangerous.

Insufficient power capacity is labeled as "defective" in the flowchart. If the fuse/breaker on power strip or UPS is tripped, it is labeled as "defective" as well.

Next, check whether your disk responds as expected at power-on. SCSI disks should spin up on power-on, even if only briefly. If your disk doesn't, there might be a problem (especially if you can't see the device on the chain after re-initialization). What makes this portion of troubleshooting confusing is that the same jumper acts differently on different disks. For some hard disks, having the jumper present indicates "enable auto-spin-up"; on others, it indicates *"disable* auto-spin-up."[38] Check your drive's manuals first, but if the current jumper configuration does not work, it should not harm anything to reverse it.[39]

LEDs are definitely your friend—they are the first indicators of a problem. Most drives have a power indicator as well as an activity light. If you have a power indicator and it doesn't light up, it's a good indication that there's something wrong somewhere along your power path. If it turns out that the LED is broken, then it still might indicate something wrong with your setup (LEDs are generally tucked away and take some work to break). Use them as an early warning system for drives, power strips, UPSes, and other electrical equipment.

The best way to tell if a disk is performing auto–spin-up correctly is to check the LED. If this isn't an option (whether because the LED is broken or because it is not standard on your drive), then try either listening to the sound or feeling the drive vibrate on power-up.

War Story

We were adding a disk to a server and, naïvely enough, expected no problems with such a simple procedure. After going carefully through the process of shutting down and attaching the new disk, we were ready to power up. We flipped the switch and tried to re-initialize the bus. Suddenly there was a spreading silence in the busy computer room. We quickly looked up—not only had our new disk powered down, but so had its host server and sibling disks! Another nearby server was dark and shouts from the next row of racks told us that we weren't the only victims of the power outage.

What had happened? It turned out that there were a *lot* of machines and peripherals running on the same underpowered circuit. Admins had daisy-chained power off the main UPSes on the circuit thereby overloading it. It just so happened that we were trying to add a disk at the same time as another group, so took out a third of our computer room.

Lessons learned:

- Know your power layout.
- Don't chain power off the UPS beyond its intended capacity.
- Don't overdedicate power circuits.
- Have one person in charge of room power management, if possible. *Check with this person before adding new power-consuming equipment.*

When checking that cable connections are tight, remember that loose cables can sometimes indicate damage to either the cable itself or the case/chassis.

Also remember to check *inside* the cable connectors. It's very easy to bend a pin and still get the cable to connect to the device, but, depending on which pin it was, it will *never* work. Troubleshoot by swapping out uncertain cables with known good cables.

> **Tip**
>
> While you are troubleshooting, keep track of cables that you think may be bad and *mark* them. Power cables are cheap and easy to replace. SCSI cables are more costly, so they might be candidates for return to the vendor as defective.
>
> When you have verified that a cable is bad and that it can't be returned, cut off both ends and discard it. Don't leave bad cables lying around where someone else might think they are useable.

Be aware that termination problems can look like something else entirely. Disk I/O timeouts, sense errors, devices "disappearing" from the chain, and others can all arise from bad bus termination. Make sure that your termination is in good (active) order before you spend a lot of time dissecting the chain in other ways.

Some SCSI buses provide service to both internal and external devices. This might present an extra challenge when assigning unique IDs—they must be unique to the whole bus, not just the internal or external portion. This is where labels on the chassis regarding internal devices are very useful.

Even if you set the ID on an external case (or internal sled), it might not appear the way you are expecting to the system. This could be because of errant jumper settings overriding the ID-switch or improper wiring on the ID-switch itself; sometimes even a SCSI-ID conflict will make a device disappear from the system's view of the chain. If fixing these things doesn't correct the problem, then the drive itself might be defective.

When a drive unexpectedly fails to appear to the system, there are three key questions to ask:

1. Is the device really attached to a SCSI bus? Sometimes in all the excitement, the drive doesn't get hooked up or is only hooked up partially.

2. Is the SCSI bus active? Is the controller card properly seated? Is the cable coming out of the controller card fastened properly? Is the card, in fact, working?

3. Is the device on the right SCSI bus? Speaking of missing things in the excitement, have you put the device in the right place? It's easy to hook up to the wrong chain when there are multiple SCSI controllers on a machine.

2

War Story 2

Once upon a time, there was an SGI Crimson that had two external SCSI buses and they both looked exactly alike. One day the admins needed to add a new disk to SCSI bus 1. The cables were labeled 0 and 1, so everything seemed in order, even though (because of odd external case shapes) the disk stacks were intermingled.

We put the new disk on the chain marked 1, rebooted, and were greeted with bus timeouts and other unpleasantness. We knew that we had set the SCSI-ID to an open number, so we started looking at our termination, cables, controller...

An hour later, we had traced the cable back into the desk-side machine to check that the buses were what we thought. Lo and behold, the cable labels did not match the bus numbers. And our disk stack, which looked more a like a haystack, had been less than helpful. We had added the disk to the wrong chain.

Lessons learned:

- Make sure that your labels match reality. Time spent updating labels is well spent, indeed.
- Spot-check the labels when manipulating hardware.
- Keep external disks sorted by controller. Don't intermingle disks from different controllers.

When checking internal (ribbon) cables for possible damage, look for the following things:

- Damaged sockets
- Sharp creases in the cable
- Frayed edges and broken wires

When checking external cables for possible damage, look for the following things:

- Bent, broken, or missing pins
- Sharp creases in the cable
- Damage near the head, showing bare or disconnected wires

Tip

Remember that although marginal cables might work if they are short enough, they can impede performance and cause problems when more devices are added.

In the world of SCSI, some types mix and some don't. HVD devices can *only* work on an HVD controller and with other HVD devices. SE and LVD can cooperate, though bus length, number of devices supported, and so on are limited to the maximums for the SE standard. Putting an LVD device on an HVD bus can damage the disk, so make sure you know what's what.

If you have too many devices for the bus mode, it can sometimes mimic a termination problem. First count the number of devices on the bus. Then check whether the bus is internal, external, or a combination (to make sure you don't miss devices). Finally, verify the bus mode and see if the number of physical devices exceeds the effective bus mode's maximum. Again, don't forget that SE + LVD = SE.

Power-on is a stressful time for any electronic device. The small surge can blow out an already marginal power supply, so be ready with spares.

Old or slow devices on a SCSI chain can cause the whole chain to exceed its timeout limit. If you get consistent timeouts, try moving the slowest disk to end of chain. If the move doesn't ameliorate the problem, the disk should be replaced with a faster one. If the problem persists, then the controller might be failing.

Marginal SCSI bus controllers might successfully manage a small number of devices, but often fail when more are added. Test this by sequentially removing devices from the end of the chain; if functionality is restored, then you should replace the controller in question.

The bus might not be bad; it might just lack drivers. Make sure that all necessary drivers are on your system before declaring the controller bad. If the controller was working before adding the new device, the device might actually be the problem. Full testing means that you should add known working devices to the chain; if the chain is fine, the other device was bad. If the chain breaks and all other parameters are okay, consider the controller marginal.

"Sticktion" refers to times when the drive heads actually get stuck to the platter surfaces after the drive has spun down. Once it happens, it is chronic, so find a way to replace the drive. The most reliable way to free a stuck drive head is to rap the drive *lightly* on a tabletop. Of course, if done at the wrong angle or too hard, this is also the best way to permanently damage the drive. Drives should not be whacked about if they can be replaced under warranty instead.

A final word on warranty: Don't be afraid to exercise it. After a while, you will probably develop an instinct for whether a drive is defective. Although you should still check other possibilities, once you're satisfied that it's the drive, get it replaced. Drive warranties are longer now than ever before, but there's no sense in pushing it to the 11th hour.

SCSI vs. IDE/ATA

The biggest question that most admins come away with from any discussion of IDE/ATA and SCSI standards is, "Which is better?" Once you realize that this is both a loaded and a context-sensitive question, you will be less prone to the religious debates that seem to wrack so many newsgroups and discussion boards.

IDE/ATA was basically designed as an internal communications standard, so is best suited for devices mounted inside a machine. IDE/ATA has the advantage of being inexpensive and widely used. PCs generally come with IDE drives and CD-ROMs built in. Some Suns are also being shipped with IDE as the standard onboard controller.

SCSI, on the other hand, can handle both internal and external devices, but costs a good deal more than its IDE/ATA counterpart. The trade-off is that SCSI tends to have higher data throughput and broader expandability. Many performance-intensive settings will opt for some form of SCSI devices for mass storage. In the PC world, SCSI is generally an added feature. Higher-end non-PC vendor boxes tend to run on SCSI.

The good news is that you can usually combine IDE/ATA *and* SCSI devices on the same machine. It's just a matter of having the right controllers and drivers. Just remember to check that your Operating System supports booting from the bus type that you set up as the boot device and that no file necessary for full boot resides on disks on the secondary chain (which might not be initialized by the time the files are needed in the boot process).

Know Your System

Before you jigger with *anything* on your system, be sure that you understand everything already there. In short, take an inventory. But first, a little terminology....

Naming Conventions

What's in a name? The location of your device! By now, you shouldn't be surprised to hear that there is more than one naming scheme for system devices. (In fact, you should be *really* surprised if there weren't!)

Linux uses letters to differentiate disks and numbers to indicate partitions. This scheme is extremely compact and simple, as shown in Figure 2.8.

FIGURE 2.8

Diagrammed Red Hat device name.

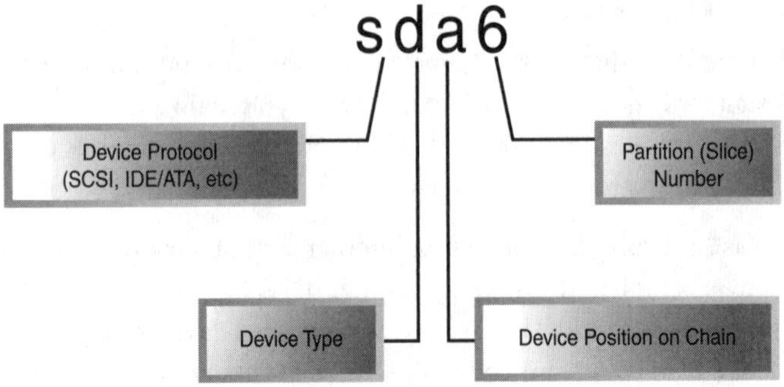

sda6

Device Protocol
(SCSI, IDE/ATA, etc)

Partition (Slice)
Number

Device Type

Device Position on Chain

The diagrammed label refers to partition 6 on the system's first SCSI disk.

Under the 2.4 kernel, Red Hat can support up to 20 IDE/ATA hard disk devices, denoted at the beginning of the device name as "h." The number of supported partitions depends on the *filesystem* type(s) on the drive but cannot exceed 63.[40] (See Chapter 3 for more details.)

Common IDE/ATA devices available by default include:

- Hard drives:
    - Whole device   hd[a–h]
    - Device partitions   hd[a–h][1–16]
- Tape drives: ht0

Under the 2.4 kernel, Red Hat can support up to 128 SCSI hard disk devices, denoted at the beginning of the device name as "s." Again, the number of supported partitions depends on the *filesystem* type(s) on the drive but cannot exceed 15.[41] (See Chapter 3 for more details.)

Common SCSI devices available by default include:

- Hard drives:
    - Whole device   sd[a–p]
    - Device partitions   sd[a–p][0–15}
- Tape drives: st[0–7]
- CD-ROM: scd[0–7]

One of the more unsettling aspects of the Linux-style of naming is its associated method of assignment. Devices are assigned their letter designation in the order in which they are detected on the chain, *not* by SCSI-ID or IDE/ATA master/slave jumpers. This kind of dynamic naming scheme is actually fairly stable, but can lead to unexpected results if you're not careful with new disk placements.

Solaris uses the System V naming convention, which uses numbers to differentiate both disks and their partitions. Every Operating System seems to have its own little variation on the theme, so it's important to get your bearings before moving things around. Although it's not as compact as the Linux naming scheme, Solaris still makes sure that you get all the necessary information, as Figure 2.9 shows.

FIGURE 2.9
*Diagrammed
Solaris device
name.*

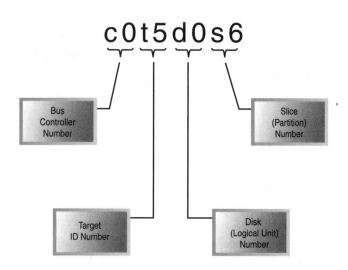

The diagrammed label refers to partition 6 on a disk set to SCSI-ID 5 that sits on the main controller (0 is usually the main internal/external controller).

Notice that we blithely disregarded the "d0" portion of the name. That's because the disk number (or logical unit number, `lun`) is generally 0. If you were addressing a specific device inside a RAID (or similar construct with its own controller responsible for multiple disks), then the `lun` would vary.

As you probably inferred from the inclusion of "target ID" in the naming scheme, Solaris's device name assignment method *is* based on the drive's SCSI-ID or IDE/ATA master/slave status.

Note that Solaris does not differentiate between SCSI and IDE/ATA devices in its high-level naming scheme. We'll see why in the next chapter in the "Devices" section. For now, here are some common device names available by default:

- Hard drives:
  - Whole device   c0t0d0

    c0t1d0
  - Device partitions   c0t0d0s[0–7]

    c0t1d0s[0–7]
- Tape drives: st[0–7]
- CD-ROM: scd[0-7]

Note

More detailed information on devices, their location on the system, and their general purpose is found in the section "Referring to Partitions—Device Files," in Chapter 3.

Getting the OS to Tell You About Its Constituent Hardware

As of the time of this writing, there is no standard, concise hardware-reporting Unix command. Of course, when you think about it, this is not unexpected. The Operating System interacts with but is independent from hardware. But there are still pieces of information that are necessary to sling bits where they belong. Thus, there are several places to look and commands to issue and interpret when you want Red Hat and Solaris to tell you about the current system hardware configuration.

Red Hat

When gathering system information, uname is always a good command to run. It tells you about OS level, basic hardware type, and system name:

```
[linux:25 ~] uname -a
Linux linux.my.site.com 2.4.2-2 #1 Sun Apr 8 20:41:30 EDT 2001 i686 unknown
```

In Red Hat, two key files have a good deal of hardware information: /proc/cpuinfo and /proc/pci.

As the name implies, /proc/cpuinfo provides information about the system's CPU(s). The following shows the contents of a dual-processor system:

```
processor       : 0
vendor_id       : GenuineIntel
cpu family      : 6
model           : 8
model name      : Pentium III (Coppermine)
stepping        : 3
cpu MHz         : 795.907
cache size      : 256 KB
fdiv_bug        : no
hlt_bug         : no
sep_bug         : no
f00f_bug        : no
coma_bug        : no
fpu             : yes
fpu_exception   : yes
cpuid level     : 3
wp              : yes
flags           : fpu vme de pse tsc msr pae mce cx8 apic sep mtrr pge mca
cmov pat pse36 pn mm
x fxsr xmm
bogomips        : 1589.25

processor       : 1
vendor_id       : GenuineIntel
cpu family      : 6
model           : 8
model name      : Pentium III (Coppermine)
stepping        : 3
cpu MHz         : 795.907
cache size      : 256 KB
fdiv_bug        : no
hlt_bug         : no
sep_bug         : no
f00f_bug        : no
coma_bug        : no
fpu             : yes
fpu_exception   : yes
cpuid level     : 3
wp              : yes
flags           : fpu vme de pse tsc msr pae mce cx8 apic sep mtrr pge mca
cmov pat pse36 pn mm
x fxsr xmm
bogomips        : 1589.25
```

The information in /proc/pci is rather more densely packed and tells you all about devices on the PCI[42] bus. The following file listing comes from a machine with 11 devices, including controllers and disks:

```
PCI devices found:
  Bus  0, device   0, function  0:
    Host bridge: Intel Unknown device (rev 0).
```

```
                    Vendor id=8086. Device id=71a0.
                    Medium devsel. Master Capable. Latency=64.
                    Prefetchable 32 bit memory at 0xf8000000 [0xf8000008].
         Bus  0, device  1, function  0:
           PCI bridge: Intel Unknown device (rev 0).
                    Vendor id=8086. Device id=71a1.
                    Medium devsel. Master Capable. Latency=64. Min Gnt=132.
         Bus  0, device 12, function  0:
           SCSI storage controller: Adaptec AIC-7896/7 (rev 0).
                    Medium devsel. Fast back-to-back capable. BIST capable. IRQ 19.
  Master Capable. Latency=64. Min Gnt=39.Max Lat=25.
                    I/O at 0x2000 [0x2001].
                    Non-prefetchable 64 bit memory at 0xf4100000 [0xf4100004].
         Bus  0, device 12, function  1:
           SCSI storage controller: Adaptec AIC-7896/7 (rev 0).
                    Medium devsel. Fast back-to-back capable. BIST capable. IRQ 19.
  Master Capable. Latency=64. Min Gnt=39.Max Lat=25.
                    I/O at 0x2400 [0x2401].
                    Non-prefetchable 64 bit memory at 0xf4101000 [0xf4101004].
         Bus  0, device 14, function  0:
           Ethernet controller: Intel 82557 (rev 8).
                    Medium devsel. Fast back-to-back capable. IRQ 21. Master Capable.
  Latency=64. Min Gnt=8.Max Lat=56.
                    Non-prefetchable 32 bit memory at 0xf4102000 [0xf4102000].
                    I/O at 0x2800 [0x2801].
                    Non-prefetchable 32 bit memory at 0xf4000000 [0xf4000000].
         Bus  0, device 18, function  0:
           ISA bridge: Intel 82371AB PIIX4 ISA (rev 2).
                    Medium devsel. Fast back-to-back capable. Master Capable. No
  bursts.
         Bus  0, device 18, function  1:
           IDE interface: Intel 82371AB PIIX4 IDE (rev 1).
                    Medium devsel. Fast back-to-back capable. Master Capable.
  Latency=64.
                    I/O at 0x2860 [0x2861].
         Bus  0, device 18, function  2:
           USB Controller: Intel 82371AB PIIX4 USB (rev 1).
                    Medium devsel. Fast back-to-back capable. IRQ 21. Master Capable.
  Latency=64.
                    I/O at 0x2840 [0x2841].
         Bus  0, device 18, function  3:
           Bridge: Intel 82371AB PIIX4 ACPI (rev 2).
                    Medium devsel. Fast back-to-back capable.
         Bus  0, device 20, function  0:
           VGA compatible controller: Cirrus Logic GD 5480 (rev 35).
                    Medium devsel. Master Capable. Latency=64. Min Gnt=2.Max Lat=10.
                    Prefetchable 32 bit memory at 0xf6000000 [0xf6000008].
                    Non-prefetchable 32 bit memory at 0xf4103000 [0xf4103000].
         Bus  1, device 15, function  0:
           PCI bridge: DEC Unknown device (rev 6).
```

```
      Vendor id=1011. Device id=23.
      Medium devsel.  Fast back-to-back capable.  Master Capable.
  Latency=240.  Min Gnt=6.
```

Solaris

Running uname on our Solaris reference platform gives us the following output:

```
[sun:4 ~]uname -a
SunOS sun.my.com 5.8 Generic_108528-06 sun4u sparc SUNW,Sun-Blade-100
```

Now we know what the OS thinks our machine's name is (sun.my.com), what version of Solaris it is running (SunOS 5.8 is roughly equivalent to saying Solaris 8), and that it is a Sun Blade 100 (although not all uname hardware identification is this clear).

The fastest way to get a listing of local drives is to run the format command:

```
    [sun:5 ~]format
    Searching for disks...done


    AVAILABLE DISK SELECTIONS:
          0. c0t0d0 <ST315320A cyl 29649 alt 2 hd 16 sec 63>
             /pci@1f,0/ide@d/dad@0,0
    Specify disk (enter its number):
```

Press Ctrl+D to abort format and return to the command prompt.

Caution

The format command is also the easiest and fastest way to irrevocably destroy a disk if you don't know what you are doing. A small error can completely wipe out all the filesystems on the disk.

The print or list commands are generally safe, but use extreme caution with commands that write data to the drive (such as sync, write, save, and so on).

Notice that this machine has only one disk and that format presents a great deal of low-level information about it.

Another Solaris command that gives even more information about disks, including error rates, is iostat -En:

```
    c0t0d0          Soft Errors: 0 Hard Errors: 0 Transport Errors: 0
    Model: ST315320A       Revision: 3.21     Serial No: 3CW0F8C4
    Size: 15.30GB <15302246400 bytes>
    Media Error: 0 Device Not Ready: 0  No Device: 0 Recoverable: 0
```

```
Illegal Request: 0
c0t1d0          Soft Errors: 0 Hard Errors: 2 Transport Errors: 0
Vendor: LITEON   Product: CD-ROM LTN486S   Revision: YSU1 Serial No:
Size: 18446744073.71GB <-1 bytes>
Media Error: 0 Device Not Ready: 2 No Device: 0 Recoverable: 0
Illegal Request: 0 Predictive Failure Analysis: 0
```

This is an extremely useful command if you think that a disk might be giving hardware-related errors or might be failing completely.

Because format and iostat only present information about drives, invoke prtconf -v to get truly detailed information about everything attached to the system. The output is so long that we have not included a sample here; please see the man page for more details and try the command yourself.

Adding/Removing Disks (and Other Devices)

Nothing in sysadmin is ever as simple as it first appears (or as simple as we wish it might be). Adding and removing hardware *seems* as though it should be very simple— just plug it in and off you go. Of course, experienced admins will tell you it's never, never that straightforward. There are many small considerations that can add up to disaster if not properly accounted for. Taking the time to prepare for hardware manipulations will save you frustration and lost sleep, and might even impress your boss.

Adding Devices

Now is the moment of truth—it's time to add a device to your system. Here are two key tips for this endeavor:

1. Don't panic.
2. Make sure that you know your system's pre-addition configuration and can fall back to it in the event of disaster. Even more important, write it all down—the information is useless unless properly documented.

So how do I document the system configuration?

Run the informational commands discussed in this chapter (such as df, uname, and others) and save their output to a file. Don't forget to run format to print your disk partition table(s). Print copies of all this output.

Draw pictures of how all the hardware connects together, both inside and outside the system chassis.

Tag or label all system cables and indicate which ones were used between which devices on the hardware. This is especially important if you are adding internal devices because hard disks look identical, and it might not be trivially obvious from the manufacturer's label which jumper is for SCSI–ID or IDE master/slave. Making a picture of what things looked like before you started tinkering is a really good way to make sure that you can restore the hardware back to the state it was in (that is, the working state) before you tried to add a new device. After you've munged the disk partition table, there is no way to pull the old one off the disk—but you can restore it if it's on paper.

Also, back up and thoroughly test restoration of all data on the system before you add or remove devices. (See Chapter 16, "Backups," for more detailed information on these procedures.)

Before Physical Addition

There are always gotchas when adding new hardware to a system, so we present you with a list of items that you should take into consideration *before* you take down your machine to add new hardware. We are presuming an external SCSI chain for our example:

- Are the device and the bus compatible?

  It won't work to try to add a SCSI device to an IDE chain. Also, an LVD device on an HVD chain *could* damage one or both items.

- Is your bus within specification limits?

  Make sure you aren't overextending your bus length. As your bus increases in length, your cabling should also increase in quality.

  Don't forget to include internal/ribbon cables as well as connection/conversion cables in your length calculations.

- Do you have the right cables and terminators?

  Make sure you've got good quality conversion cables of the right types, as necessary. Many apparently flaky devices can be stabilized with good quality cables.

- Is there kernel support for the device?

  Modern kernels natively support many devices. Other devices come with their own drivers or modules. If support is not built-in, make sure that you have the drivers available and installed on your system.

- Do you have enough power and/or UPS space?

  Many sites require their systems be connected to Uninterruptible Power Supplies (UPS). Make sure that you have enough UPS capacity to support the device and still have enough battery life left to maintain a reasonable lights-out uptime.

  Even if you do not have UPS systems, you need to make sure that you have sufficient power available for the new device. There's nothing worse than the sinking feeling when you flip the switch on a new disk and half the room goes dark because you've just tripped a breaker.[43] Avoid this kind of unplanned downtime by checking power capacity ahead of time.

- Does the device need to sit in a specific physical spot on the chain?

  Some devices need to be attached at the head or tail of a SCSI chain. If your device is sensitive to this, make sure that it will not conflict with any other device with similar requirements already on the chain.

Physical Addition

After all the planning and preparing, the actual hardware addition is somewhat anticlimactic.

More and more systems are being shipped with hot-plug capabilities that allow you to add SCSI devices without shutting down or even rebooting. If you don't have one of these hot-plug/hot-swap–capable systems, though, don't try to do live device additions. You can corrupt the machine's filesystems and cause weird errors and all sorts of other headaches.

Before actually shutting down a machine, it is wise to get management's approval and courteous to warn users about it well ahead of time.

It's also a good idea to make sure you have not only the cable(s) and terminator(s) you *know* you will need, but also have a few spares. This way, if any parts currently in service turn out to be marginal, you won't have to race around desperately looking for a replacement component. Naturally, this is harder to do with the devices themselves, but if you can manage to have an additional hard disk available, you'll be ahead of the curve.

> **Tip**
>
> Correct cable availability is a traditional "gotcha." If you don't know what connectors you have on your system and its peripherals, it might be necessary (and certainly would be advisable) to schedule *two* outages when you want to modify your hardware configuration.

2

The first outage will be very brief; nothing will be changed, but all connectors will be examined to map existing connections and to plan for the new ones. You can then procure the cables required for the new configuration (including alternates—this is especially important with SCSI chains that have all three types of connectors on the devices).

The actual hardware modifications will take place during the second downtime. Before you start, update your system documents so that you *know* what connectors and devices you have. It's also a good idea to map out, in detail, the configuration that you intend to have at the end of the second downtime.

The most graceful way to take a machine offline for hardware maintenance is to use the `shutdown` command (see Chapter 1, "Startup and Shutdown," for more details). Under Red Hat, the syntax to bring the machine to a state where it is safe to power off with two minutes of lead-time without further admin intervention is as follows:

```
/sbin/shutdown -h +2
```

Under Solaris, the syntax to do the same thing is different:

```
/usr/sbin/shutdown -g120 -i5 -y
```

The `shutdown` command invokes `init`, but it also politely sends signals to all running processes, giving them time to exit gracefully before being cut off. It also broadcasts a warning of impending doom to users every 30 seconds (on the minute and half-minute remaining marks).

Once everything reports back as ready, turn off the system's power switch, but leave the system plugged in (for grounding purposes). Now you can physically attach the new device to the correct chain. Physically position the new device on a stable surface near where it will be attached to the system. Attach an appropriate power cable to the new device, and plug the other end into its designated power strip or UPS socket.

If this is an external SCSI device, we're going to assume that it can happily be added to the end of the existing chain, so remove the last device's terminator and transfer it to the new device. Use an appropriate cable to connect the two devices. Power on the new device. If you have an indicator light on the terminator, it should be lit at this point.

After Physical Addition

> **Note**
>
> Many of the items in the following list will be covered in detail in the next chapter, including filesystems. Our discussion of how to add disks would not be complete without these items, so you're getting a brief preview of things to come.

Once the new device is running on your system, there are still a few things that you need to do to integrate it fully.

First, the system must realize that it has new hardware attached. After checking that all peripherals are powered up, turn the system itself back on. If you are using a Solaris box, be sure to issue the break (or Stop-A) command to get into EEPROM, and then enter boot-r to reinitialize the SCSI bus.

> **Note**
>
> Not all Solaris systems offer boot -r anymore, so you will need to check your local system documentation. But all is not lost—there is another, equivalent way to reinitialize your system.
>
> Creating a file named /reconfigure will instruct the system to check for new devices at reboot.[44] Use the touch command to create this file (touch/ reconfigure) because it doesn't need any contents.

Now your new device should be available to the system. If the system does not seem to recognize the new device, you will need to drop back to BIOS/EEPROM level to check why. On a PC, you will probably need to reboot and invoke the SCSI controller card's BIOS. There should be an option within the BIOS menus to scan the bus for new devices. On a Solaris box, after a clean shutdown, you can issue the EEPROM command test-all. This will invoke diagnostics on all devices that have self-testing available, including SCSI, USB, IDE, and network. Note that if you issue this command after a BREAK/STOP-A or a simple halt, your system is likely to hang.

> **Note**
>
> All BIOS- and PROM-based diagnostics will work only from a system console. For some systems, the console is the local monitor and keyboard; for others, it might be a serial line to a central console server box. In the latter case, the sysadmin should verify what keystrokes are necessary to get to the firmware prompt *before* tinkering.

> **Note**
>
> The Solaris diagnostic "test-all" can be very time-consuming, and is somewhat dependent upon diagnostics packages having been installed on the system before shutdown. As a result, be aware that you might not see many informational returns for the amount of time invested. If you need it, then you have to use it. Just consider getting some coffee or something while it runs.

If your device does not correspond to one of the names in the "Naming Conventions" section, you might have to create a new device *node* for it. Details on how to do this are covered in Chapter 3.

To actually put a disk into service, you will need to *partition* it and create *filesystems* there as well. Again, these steps are outlined in Chapter 3.

Removing Devices

At some point, you will need to remove hardware from your system, whether you are replacing a bad disk, transferring devices from one system to another, or simply consolidating multiple disks' contents onto one. In essence, you will be unwinding the processes outlined in the previous sections, starting with file manipulations and ending with removing the device and readjusting the necessary cabling.

As mentioned before, do not try to hot-swap devices on any of your device chains unless you have hardware specifically designed for it (and matching software active on your system). As always, get management's approval for and warn users about any downtime that shutting down the system to remove the device will incur.

When it's time, issue the shutdown command. After everything reports back as ready, turn off the system's power switch, leaving the system plugged in (for grounding purposes). Also power down any peripherals, including the device to be removed.

Now you can physically remove the device. Remember to re-cable the devices that are still on the chain and to reattach the terminator at the end of the chain. Finally, re-initialize the system to recognize that the device is gone.

Do a dry run

There is value, especially on systems with which you might not be not completely familiar, to do a "test uninstall" before actually changing the hardware configuration. There are two basic methods: One relies on hardware manipulation, the other relies on software. Let's consider a dry run of removing an external SCSI device.

The first method requires you to schedule two downtimes. During the first downtime, shut down the system as described earlier. Now simply leave the power switch turned off on the device whose removal you are testing when you restart the system. Let things run for a normal usage cycle (a couple of days, a couple of weeks) and keep a close eye on it to ensure that no special undocumented dependency on that device crops up. Then it is a very safe bet that the device can be removed physically at the second downtime.

To avoid two downtimes, you might want to use the software method instead. Schedule and announce a time when you will unmount all the drive's constituent filesystems and unexport them. As in the previous method, let things run for a while to verify that the filesystem's absence is not a problem. If all seems well, go ahead and schedule downtime to actually remove the device. Note that this method might not point up hardware dependencies, so be ready to deal with any that might crop up during the downtime.

Best Practices

General

- Keep spares of all devices, cables, and terminators available.
- Label everything. If you don't know what it is, you can't use it.
- Mark, destroy, and discard (or return to vendor) bad cables. Above all, keep them away from your systems.
- If even one socket on a power strip is bad, get rid of the whole thing. There could be a short or other more serious problem that will come back to haunt you.

SCSI Devices

- Label all devices with the following information:
  - Host machine name
  - SCSI chain number
  - SCSI-ID number
  - Whether the device's ID is hard-jumpered
  - Filesystems on disk
- Use only active terminators.
- Number new SCSI devices sequentially to avoid conflicts later.

Physical Addition (steps)

1. Get permission and announce downtime.
2. Make sure that you know your system's pre-addition configuration and can fall back to it in case of disaster.
3. Set aside the cable(s) and terminator(s) that you *know* you will need, along with a few spares. Have spare disks, too, if possible.
4. Shut down the system.
5. Power off the system and peripherals.
6. Physically attach a new device—power, bus, termination.
7. Power on the new device.
8. Bring the rest of the system back up.

After Physical Addition (steps)

1. Make the system recognize the new hardware.
2. Add device files as necessary (using mknod).
3. If the new device is a disk:
   - Partition it (see Chapter 3)
   - Create filesystems (see Chapter 3)

Removing a Device (steps)

1. Get permission and announce downtime.
2. Shut down the system.
3. Power off the system and peripherals.

4. Physically remove the device—power, bus, termination.

5. Re-cable remaining devices.

6. Re-initialize the system bus to recognize that the device is gone.

Online References

General Technology Term Definitions

`http://whatis.techtarget.com`

Standards Organizations

ANSI—American National Standards Institute: `http://www.ansi.org`

T10 Committee (I/O interfaces, SCSI): `http://www.t10.org`

T13 Committee (IDE/ATA): `http://www.t13.org`

EIA—Electronic Industries Alliance: `http://www.eia.org/tech`

IEEE—Institute of Electrical and Electronics Engineers: `http://standards.ieee.org`

ISO—International Standards Organization: `http://www.iso.ch`

IDE/ATA

General: `http://www.pcguide.com/ref/hdd/if/ide/conf.htm`

SCSI

Books:

Field, Gary, et al. *The Book of SCSI, 2nd Edition*. No Starch Press, 2000.

General:

`http://www.paralan.com`

`http://www.systemlogic.net/articles/01/2/scsi/index.php`

SCSI Trade Association: `http://www.scsita.org`

FAQs:

`http://www.scsifaq.org`

`http://scsifaq.paralan.com`

`http://www.scsita.org/experts/index01.html`

Connectors:

http://www.cablemakers.com/connector.html

Termination:

http://www.cablemakers.com/scsitermination.htm

Troubleshooting:

Introduction: http://www.wdc.com/service/ftp/scsi/bench.exe

Executable: http://www.wdc.com/service/ftp/scsi/bench.exe

Other Communications Standards

ATAPI: http://www.pcguide.com/ref/hdd/if/ide/stdATAPI-c.html

Fibre Channel:

- http://www.fibrechannel.com
- http://www.fibrechannel.com/technology/index.master.html

USB: http://www.usb.org/

Comparison of USB and FireWire: http://www.techtv.com/screensavers/answerstips/story/0,23008,2406307,00.html

Red Hat

Linux Documentation Project: http://www.linuxdoc.org

Devices:

- http://www.linuxdoc.org/HOWTO/mini/Partition/partition-2.html
- http://www.lanana.org/docs/device-list/devices.txt
- http://www.torque.net/scsi/SCSI-2.4-HOW-TO.html

Solaris

Documentation & FAQs:

- http://docs.sun.com
- http://www.science.uva.nl/pub/solaris/solaris2.html
- http://saturn.tlug.org/suncdfaq/index.html

Endnotes

[1] *Consider mainframe terminals, the original, very thin client.*

[2] *There are many ways to refer to this kind of hardware. It is known variously as a hard disk drive, HDD, hard drive, hard disk, fixed disk, drive, disk, or various epithets, depending on the admin's current level of frustration with it.*

[3] *IEEE/IEEE-SA also offers many other resources and standards information. Its mission statement (from its Web page) is: "The IEEE ('eye-triple-E') helps advance global prosperity by promoting the engineering process of creating, developing, integrating, sharing, and applying knowledge about electrical and information technologies and sciences for the benefit of humanity and the profession." See* `http://standards.ieee.org/`.

[4] *ANSI describes itself as an organization that coordinates the U.S. voluntary standardization and conformity assessment system. See* `http://webstore.ansi.org/ansidocstore/default.asp`.

[5] *But as the definition for serial at* `http://whatis.techtarget.com` *notes, "a serial medium (for example, fiber optic cable) can be much faster than a slower medium that carries multiple signals in parallel."*

[6] *EIA is the Electronic Industries Alliance, a group that "provides a forum for industry to develop standards and publications in our major technical areas: electronic components, consumer electronics, electronic information, and telecommunications." See the Web site* `http:// www.eia.org/tech/index.cfm`.

[7] *There's a nice online summary at* `http://www.ctips.com/rs232.html`.

[8] *See* `http://www.apple.com/firewire/`

[9] *This is an independent standard. See* `http://www.usb.org/`.

[10] *See* `http://www.pcwebopedia.com/TERM/U/USB.html`.

[11] *See* `http://www.redhat.com/support/manuals/RHL-7.1-Manual/release-notes/s1-system.html`.

[12] *For more information on Solaris support of USB, see* `http://docs.sun.com/ab2/coll.736.2/S8ADMINSUPP/@Ab2PageView/5169?DwebQuery=USB&oqt=USB&Ab2Lang=C&Ab2Enc=iso-8859-1`.

[13] *See* `http://www.pcguide.com/ref/hdd/if/ide/stdATAPI-c.html`.

[14] *See* `http://www.beyondlogic.org/spp/parallel.htm` *for a detailed discussion of parallel port standards.*

[15] *See* `http://www.fapo.com/porthist.htm`.

[16] *Although other standards can support hard disks, they are not commonly used for local OS storage and booting.*

[17] *The actual standards are available from the NCITS subcommittee (see* `http://www.ncits.org/`). *To order the standards document, see* `http://www.techstreet.com/cgi-bin/detail?product_id=56120`.

[18] *Though it still requires an external controller.*

[19] *See* `http://webopedia.internet.com/TERM/P/PIO.html`*.*

[20] *See* `http://www.pcguide.com/ref/hdd/if/ide/modes_PIO.htm`*.*

[21] *See Kozierok's page,* `http://www.pcguide.com/ref/hdd/if/ide/conf.htm`*.*

[22] *Some IDE/ATA controllers and devices support* cable select *so that labels are set by position on the cable rather than jumpers. Check the device manuals to see if this option is available on your system.*

[23] *Note that some devices have a* single *mode for this situation. Check the device manuals.*

[24] *And pronounced like "skuzzy."*

[25] *That is, 5 direct current volts.*

[26] *Hence the name "differential." See* `http://whatis.techtarget.com/definition/0,289893,sid9_gci212949,00.html`*.*

[27] *See* `http://www.paralan.com/scsiexpert.html`*.*

[28] *See* `http://www.paralan.com/scsiexpert.html`*.*

[29] *Okay, technically there are step-down cables and expanders, but we can't vouch for their reliability or stability.*

[30] *For a more complete history, see* `http://www.scsifaq.org/scsifaq.html#_Hlk406574300`*.*

[31] *See* `http://www.scsita.org/aboutscsi/index01.html` *and* `http://whatis.techtarget.com/definition/0,289893,sid9_gci212949,00.html`*.*

[32] *Some older Sun workstations had a combined power/SCSI connector.*

[33] *See* `http://www.paralan.com/scsiexpert.html`*.*

[34] *Even sled-based positional internal systems rely on a switch being correctly connected to the jumper pins on the drive.*

[35] *For more details about termination, see* `http://www.scsifaq.org/scsifaq.html#_Hlk413567563`*.*

[36] *Note, though, that the absence of the word* active *does not prove that the terminator is passive.*

[37] *And assuming, of course, that you don't have a SCSI tester.*

[38] *If the drive's auto-spin-up is disabled, a* `START UNIT` *command from the system should get it to spin up. See your SCSI BIOS or management tools.*

[39] *As far as we know—there is, of course, always a risk when twiddling with hardware/jumper settings. Please check with the manufacturer and manuals first.*

[40] *See* `http://www.torque.net/scsi/SCSI-2.4-HOW-TO.html`*.*

[41] *See* `http://www.torque.net/scsi/SCSI-2.4-HOW-TO.html`*.*

[42] *PCI = Peripheral Component Interconnect. See* `http://whatis.techtarget.com/definition/0,,sid9_gci214282,00.html`.

[43] *Okay, maybe there is, but it's still pretty bad.*

[44] *See* `http://docs.sun.com/ab2/coll.47.11/SYSADV1/@Ab2PageView/idmatch (DEVCONFIG2-3)`.

Filesystem Administration

by Robin Anderson

IN THIS CHAPTER

Introduction

Now that you know what hardware is present on your system, it's time to actually do something with it all. It's not enough to simply plug devices into a power source and machine bus—you should be able to guess by now that nothing in UNIX is *that* "automagical."

As always, our philosophy is to present the information that you will need on the spot and then flesh it out with background details. Although we intend for you to be able to do your job as quickly as possible, we'd also like you to be able to understand *why* you are doing these particular tasks and issuing these specific commands.

In this chapter, we examine the logical constructs that UNIX provides for accessing physical drives and other devices. In the next chapter, we will populate the local disks with users and discuss their proper care and feeding.

Dividing Disk Space Wisely

So, now you have a chain of devices on your machine, all properly attached, named, and ready to go. Many of these devices are likely to be hard disks, whether they are internal or external. The next step to make these disks active and accessible from the system is *partitioning*. Because partitioning more or less permanently divides disk space, you will need to know a little bit about the final layer between the hardware and the user—the *filesystem*—so that you can make wise decisions.

Virtual Devices: Partitions

Partitions are the lowest level of disk space organization over which admins have any control. As mentioned before, sectors, tracks, and cylinders all have a preset, fixed size on a given disk. Admins have no way—or real need—to alter these parameters.

The key thing about partitions is that they are independent of any operating system. Every major OS recognizes these low-level disk divisions and addresses each partition as a separate logical device. Information about partitions is kept in a *partition table* stored in the *disk label* or *volume header* of the physical hard disk. This is how disks maintain information about themselves and why they can be transferred from one machine to another without losing the information.

Partitions allow admins to multi-boot systems with various Operating Systems stored on the same hard disk. Only with the release of Red Hat 7.1 could you run an OS out of an existing partition.

Originally, there was a strict one-to-one mapping of partitions to filesystems.[1] Partitions could be considered containers for the filesystems.

Now, you can span one filesystem over multiple partitions with *logical volumes* (see the later section, "Logical Volumes"). Partitions can now be thought of more as building blocks for system storage rather than simple containers.

What you still can't do is assign multiple filesystems to one partition (without redividing the space). Here, partitions are acting as boundaries; regular filesystems cannot extend past the edges of the partition, but neither can the partition be subdivided.

Because partitions are hardware-level divisions that predated filesystem quotas, they can provide low-level overflow protection. With the right kind of schema, certain partitions can fill up without affecting overall system performance. At the very least, one partition filling up will not directly affect space on another partition.

All flavors of UNIX require a minimum of two partitions: / and swap. In this sort of system, / holds the entire operating system, local software, configurations, local accounts, and logs.

Swap Space

Swap space, usually known simply as *swap*, allows the Operating System to access raw disk space directly without the intervention of a filesystem. Swap was designed to act as an extension of the system's main memory (RAM), and it allows the system to surmount that memory's size limitations.

The main OS mechanisms that access this space are *swapping* and *paging*. *Swapping* and *paging* are distinct functions, although the two are often confused—even by more experienced sysadmins.

A computer has one physical linear memory space, some of which is reserved for objects that must remain *resident* (such as the Operating System, paging tables, and some other critical data structures). Resident elements must always remain in memory so that they are quickly available for use.

Of course, many other processes and objects have no residency requirements. When the Operating System detects that a certain threshold of resource usage has been reached, it looks for ways to switch allocations to processes that need it most.

Swapping is one of the mechanisms used by the OS to manage memory allocations. When a process is *swapped*, it is written to the swap space, along with all its currently associated data and other state information. The process's slot in main memory is now free for use by another process.

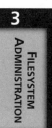

3

FILESYSTEM
ADMINISTRATION

When a process goes into a wait state for a relatively long time, it doesn't actively need CPU time, so it is *swapped*, along with all its concomitant state information, out of main memory and onto a disk. Conversely, if a process has been resource-starved, the process will be swapped out of disk storage and back into main memory, allowing it access to the CPU. Intensive swapping, called *thrashing*, indicates that the entire system is severely starved for resources—usually RAM.

Paging also makes use of the swap disk area. Unlike swapping, which stores an entire process along with all its current state information, paging stores only parts of a process's executable code and discards state information. This is a normal memory-management procedure that takes place even on systems with sufficient resources. The Operating System predetermines the size of segments that can be retrieved and kept in main memory; these segments are called *pages*. So, when a process is paged into memory from disk or swap, or is paged out of memory into swap space, the transfer is done in page-sized increments.

Why Page into Swap Space?

You might be wondering why we don't just set aside space for one page, or a set of pages, for a given process in main memory and then just read new pages from the filesystem into main memory as they are needed. Why put the most recently used page into swap space?

The answer is fairly simple: Navigating the filesystem to reach the executable being paged is an "expensive" operation. It takes far fewer resources to go into raw swap space and retrieve a recently used page than to go to disk space formatted with filesystem structures.

Because swap space is finite, most systems cull pages with what is known as the Least Recently Used (LRU) algorithm: The longer a page has not been requested, the more likely it is to be pushed out of swap storage.

In short, paging is a way to make more memory available to processes than physically exists on the system. Without paging, all parts of a program that might require real memory would have to be accommodated at process initiation. Programs would need to be very tiny (hard to do with complex programs) or would have to run sequentially (inefficient for all concerned).

> **Note**
>
> Note that if you work in both the UNIX and MS worlds, Microsoft also refers to *paging* as *swapping*. Much confusion ensues.

Aside from process manipulation, swap space is also used to boot into miniroot and to hold memory images if the system crashes.[2] Because a memory image is literally a dump of the main memory contents, you will need at least as much swap space as RAM (plus a small margin) if you want to be able to examine the file later. In fact, there should be more swap space than RAM. The rule of thumb for sizing swap will be discussed later.

> **Note**
>
> Examining a crash dump also requires sufficient space in a filesystem (remember that swap is not formatted) to store the dump image. You should plan for this when sizing filesystems during installation—see the "Partitioning" section in this chapter.

3

FILESYSTEM ADMINISTRATION

> **So, Can You Get by Without Swap Space?**
>
> In theory, yes, you can. That being said, realize that you might have difficulty with common functions later—booting into miniroot, saving crash images, and so on.
>
> Also bear in mind that if you don't set aside swap space, your system will not be capable of paging processes properly and won't swap them at all. You will need to have a large amount of RAM available to keep even quasi-dormant processes resident.
>
> In addition, some varieties of UNIX are particularly dependant on swap space. Solaris, for example, uses swap space for its /tmp directory by default.

Referring to Partitions—Device Files

One of the two great truisms of system administration is that everything that exists in UNIX is a file.[3] This means that a UNIX system "sees" its hardware devices as files. The advantage of this management method is that it allows the Operating System to treat physical disk access like flat[4] file I/O.

At the most fundamental level, files are nothing more than strings of ones and zeros. So, file I/O is simply moving bits in and out of specific file locations. It doesn't matter to UNIX whether the file goes on to pass the bits to a disk, into memory, or off to Never Never Land; the kernel just shifts bits in and out of the file handle.

Device files are the lowest-level construct that allows the OS to interact with physical devices. Device files are required to create filesystems (see the later section "Local Filesystem Creation").

Devices can be divided into two categories: raw/character devices and block devices.

Raw/character device files are so named because no buffering is done between whatever function is generating (or retrieving) the bytes and the device that is storing them. These device files are most often used for bytewise copy procedures (like those done with dd). Most tape devices have only raw device files.

Conversely, block device files *are* buffered, meaning that data is transferred in chunks rather than 1 byte at a time. This tends to be a more efficient way to transfer data for most applications.

Note that, under Solaris, hard disks have both a character device file *and* a block device file. Each is needed at different times. Most daily disk operations will go through the block device, but filesystem creation is done via the raw/character device name.

Remember that one function of partitions is to make a disk accessible to the system as one or more devices. As you might have guessed, the naming schemes outlined in Chapter 2, "Managing Disk Hardware," identify the literal, on-disk partition and device names, not the system path to their interface files.

All standard UNIX device files were originally tidily kept in /dev. Some Red Hat implementations still maintain this system.

Under Solaris and some newer implementations of Red Hat, the contents of /dev tend to be a combination of device files and symbolic links to actual device files stored in different directories. In this sort of system, /dev acts as a sort of organizational redirector. Under Red Hat, look for a directory called /devfs; under Solaris, look for a directory called /devices.

The directories and device files in /dev vary immensely, even between versions of the same Operating System. Table 3.1 shows some of the most common and useful denizens of /dev. Although many items are in slightly different locations or have slightly different names, overall, both Operating Systems have a lot in common. We encourage you to use Table 3.1 as a starting point for your own explorations of your local system's device files.

TABLE 3.1   Items of Interest under /dev

Red Hat	Solaris	Description
No analogous directory; devices exist in the top level of /dev. Device names begin with "cu."	/dev/cua	Directory for serial line devices
No analogous directory; devices exist in the top level of /dev. Device names begin with "sd" or "hd" for SCSI and IDE disks, respectively; SCSI CD-ROMs begin with "scd."	/dev/dsk	Directory for block devices (for disk drives, CD-ROMs, and so on)
No analogous directory; devices exist in the top level of /dev. Device names begin with "fd."	/dev/fd	Directory for floppy disk devices
/dev/inet	No analogous directory in /dev.	Directory for network devices (Ethernet ports and so on)
/dev/input	No analogous directory in /dev.	Directory for mouse, keyboard, and other input devices
/dev/kmem	/dev/kmem	Kernel virtual memory device
/dev/log	/dev/log	Socket to system log
/dev/mem	/dev/mem	Physical memory device
/dev/null	/dev/null	Null device
/dev/pts	/dev/pts	Pseudoterminals
/dev/random	No analogous device, by default.	Random-number generator
/dev/rd	No analogous directory in /dev.	Directory for RAID devices
/dev/raw	/dev/rdsk	Directory for raw/character devices (for disk drives, tapes, and so on)
No analogous directory; devices exist in the top level of /dev. Device names begin with "st" or "ht" for SCSI and IDE tapes, respectively.	/dev/rmt	Directory for removable media—tapes

3

FILESYSTEM
ADMINISTRATION

TABLE 3.1 continued

Red Hat	Solaris	Description
No analogous device in /dev.	/dev/swap	Swap space device
No analogous directory; devices exist in the top level of /dev. Device names begin with "tty."	/dev/tty	Directory for line terminals
/dev/usb	No analogous directory in /dev.	Directory for USB devices
/dev/zero	/dev/zero	Null byte source

Lest you think we're done with partitions, remember that we still need to discuss sizing and actual creation mechanisms. But before we do that, we need to consider the next layer up and what goes into it.

Logical Constructs: Filesystems

As mentioned before, you can't use your system's attached disk space (except for swap) until the space is divided and filesystems[5] are created. But before you go carving up your disks, you should know what components you are arranging space for.

Note that we are not going into the kind of depth that an OS developer or low-level coder might need. This section is designed to give admins the foundational understanding they need to initially get their systems up and reliably running.

Definitions

A filesystem is a logical construct that provides a framework for storing and retrieving information from a random-access storage device.[6] In the UNIX world, all information is considered to be a file,[7] so essentially everything enduring on the system is processed, stored, and retrieved through a filesystem.

The OS is directly responsible for maintaining filesystems because they are complex, logical overlays and not simple, low-level space divisions. This also means that filesystems can be far more flexible and broad with regard to the kind of information that they manage internally. Filesystems store quite a bit of meta-information (literally, information about information) about not only their own constructs, but also the files they manage.

UNIX filesystems are generally hierarchical—that is, they consist of multiple directories organized in an inverted tree structure. Inverted tree diagrams, are depicted with the core node—or *root*—at the top. In Figure 3.1, directories are referred to as "nodes." Nodes that can contain leaf nodes or other child nodes are referred to as "child nodes"; nodes that contain no further subnodes are referred to as "leaf nodes."

FIGURE 3.1

Simple hierarchical inverted tree diagram.

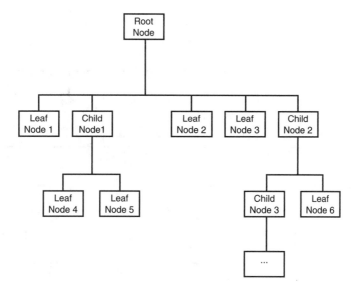

Every directory contains a reference to itself (".") and to its parent (".."). Even the initial node—or *root* of the directory structure—has the parent reference; in this special case, the parent reference simply points to itself. In Figure 3.2, you can find a node's parent by going up to the previous tier.

Pathnames specifying the location of a file from the root directory down are called "*absolute pathnames*." Pathnames that begin with "../", "./", or anything other than "/" are called *relative pathnames* because they are specified *relative* to the current directory.

What Lives Where in UNIX Filesystems

Warning: Generalizations Ahead!

In this section, we will be discussing the standard location of various files, logs, binaries, and all those other things that make UNIX what it is. Please be aware that we will be presenting generalizations and broad concepts applicable to both Red Hat and Solaris.

Figure 3.3 presents a high-level view of a "standard" UNIX filesystem. Remember that we are presenting only a generalization of what you are likely to find on your system.

FIGURE 3.2

Hierarchical inverted tree diagram with relation labels.

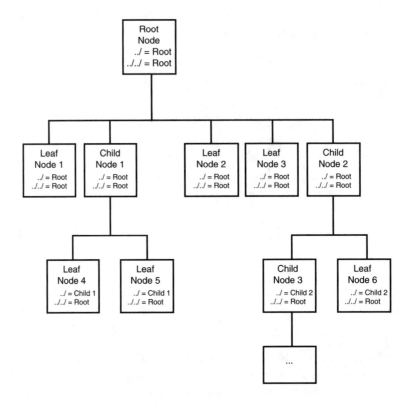

FIGURE 3.3

Hierarchical inverted tree diagram—highlights of standard UNIX filesystems.

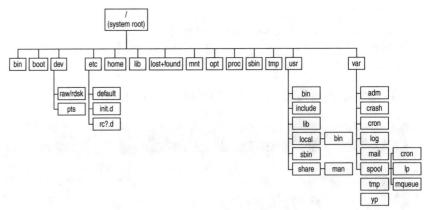

The root filesystem (/) contains a number of interesting directories:

- **/bin**—General binaries
- **/dev**—Device files

- **/etc**—System configuration files and bootup scripts
- **/sbin**—System-related binaries

Note on Interesting Directories

The existence and contents of interesting directories depend greatly on the variant of UNIX that you are using. There are no real standards for file locations, so don't be too surprised when something turns up in an unexpected location.

For instance, to track down system-related binaries, you might need to look in /bin, /usr/bin, /sbin, /usr/sbin, and even /etc. Legacy binaries might even be found in /usr/ucb or /usr/bsd. And these are only the standard system binaries; locally built software could be almost anywhere on the system.

Also be on the lookout for symbolic links between these directories; they can be helpful if you know about them and can cause confusion if you don't.

/home can either be its own filesystem or just a subdirectory of /. On Solaris NFS servers, it will often be a subdirectory of /export. /home generally holds the local system's user home directories.

Note

Beware of attempting to mount a filesystem on /home in Solaris with the automounter running (shrink-wrap default). The automounter will make /home unavailable as a mount point.

/opt can either be its own filesystem or just a subdirectory of /. It is intended to hold optional system software (for instance, compilers on Solaris systems).

Tip

We recommend sizing /opt as a separate filesystem unless there will be no additional software installed on the system. Also, /usr/local is traditionally the place for additional software installed from Open Source sources. Some sysadmins create a symlink from /usr/local to /opt, to avoid managing two "optional software" filesystems. Rather than doing this and potentially conflicting with a package install, we recommend creating an /opt/local and symlinking it to /usr/local, or vice versa, and then making that one nice-sized partition for expansion.

3

FILESYSTEM ADMINISTRATION

Temporary file storage usually is located in the /tmp directory. This directory may be accessed on most systems as /tmp, /usr/tmp, and /var/tmp. Two of the three references will be actual directories, the third will be a symlink to one of the others. The variety of UNIX determines which reference is the symlink. We recommend that you reconfigure these directories so that only one is an actual directory and the other two are symlinks to it. We further recommend that the actual directory be a distinct, mounted filesystem. Note that many applications use /tmp as temporary "scratch" space. Because this means that users can inadvertently (or deliberately) write large files to /tmp, the separate mount will protect / and /usr from filling up with temporary user files.

> **Tip**
>
> The advice given above is a special instance of a general rule: Users should not be capable of creating or deleting files in the / and /usr filesystems.

> **Tip**
>
> /tmp should always have 1777 permissions, not 777 permissions. The 777 bit setting would allow any user full rights to any file in /tmp. The 1 in 1777 sets the "sticky bit," which means that a file in that directory can be modified or deleted only by its owner.

/usr is usually in its own filesystem, although it also can be a subdirectory of /. Subdirectories of interest include these:

- **bin**—Binaries.
- **include**—Include files for programming.
- **lib**—Programming libraries.
- **local**—Locally built software packages; libraries, include files, and binaries. (/usr/local is often a mount point for a separate filesystem, to prevent software installation from filling up the /usr filesystem.)
- **sbin**—System binaries.
- **share**—Shared information, including man pages.

/var is occasionally in its own filesystem (which we recommend), although it can also be a subdirectory of / or /usr. Subdirectories of interest include these:

- **adm**—Log file storage (Solaris)
- **crash**—Crash diagnostics and memory image storage
- **log**—Log file storage (Red Hat and Solaris)
- **mail**—Mail delivery area
- **spool**—Spooling area for printing, cron, and other managed services
- **yp**—NIS configuration file storage

The /boot directory generally is found only on Red Hat machines, although there is no particular reason why it can't be used with Solaris as well. This directory, located in its own, small filesystem, has two main functions: to hold the basic files needed at boot time and to allow large disks to boot properly. Due to PC BIOS limitations, only boot sectors within the first 1024 cylinders of a disk are honored. So, a small boot partition in the very first cylinders of the disk is a wise idea.

The /proc pseudofilesystem contains system statistics and process information. /proc is considered a pseudofilesystem because the files there are not actual files on disk. Instead, each file is an interface to data about a particular running process or other system status.

Philosophy of Division

There are a number of competing philosophies about disk space divisions—the best space allocations, how many partitions to have, and so on. Like most longstanding philosophical differences, this question has blossomed into a kind of religious war. Remember that although we are going to give background information and make suggestions, we're not taking sides or saying that we have an insight on The Best™ way of doing things.

There are good reasons for each viewpoint, and the way that you finally deal with partitions must be very situation-specific. For instance, a server might not require separate home directory space, but it might need a lot of log space instead. In such a case, it might also be important to keep the logs in a separate partition from the OS so that the admins can access the machine even when the logs are brimming.

First we'll present some points to keep in mind for any kind of install and then we'll talk about specific requirements for different classes of install (server, workstation, and so on).

3

FILESYSTEM ADMINISTRATION

General Points

The most basic requirement, no matter what class of install you are doing, is that there be a minimum of two partitions: one for / and one for swap. In this most simple of systems, / holds the entire OS, logs, user home directories, and so on.

> **Note**
>
> Note that although an earlier sidebar said you can get away without swap space, we think it's a really bad idea to do so and not worth the risks. Disk space is pretty cheap these days, and your system's stability is greatly enhanced by dedicating some swap space to it.

So, then, how much swap should you allocate? (Warning: entering religious debate zone.)

Our most basic rule of thumb is to set aside somewhere between two and two and a half times as much swap space as you have system RAM. This means that when RAM increases, swap should, too (though this is only true up to a point). Remember, though, you might have applications running that require more swap space—check your documentation.

> **Tip**
>
> Allocate between two and two and a half times as much swap space as you have system RAM.

Red Hat has a good discussion of swap-related issues at `http://www.redhat.com/support/docs/gotchas/7.1/gotchas-71.html`. As they say, "It's better to have it and not need it than to need it and not have it."

The next consideration will be the number of partitions that you want on your system. Without delving into the idea of installation classes, first consider a few points:

- Are there any data areas that need to have guaranteed space allocations?

    The answer to this question is *always* "yes." If nothing else, the / and /usr filesystems must be protected. Some utilities won't operate correctly if they can't make system log entries or write scratch files to /tmp, so it's a good idea to protect the /var and /tmp filesystems, too.

- Should the machine continue running even if its logging area fills up?

  If so, then /var must have its own filesystem.

- Are there any system or data areas that will see increasing storage use?

  Again, /var is the default location for system logs and can be expected to fill up unless logs are rotated out regularly. Other examples could include a directory to which developed software is delivered for testing on a large project.

- Are there any system or data areas that will see frequent access?

  /var/mail, for instance, can be a very busy directory. Directories containing important databases also might see high access rates and should be located in their own filesystems.

- Will any directories be exported through NFS?

  Such directories should certainly have their own filesystems. *Never* export more of your system than absolutely necessary.

- Will users need especially large workspaces for large files?

  Creating data filesystems is a good way to discourage users from cluttering their home directories too much.

Data directories for a specific project accessed only by certain users might well be grouped into a single filesystem. This means that they will also require their own partition—as we mentioned earlier, there cannot be more than one filesystem on a partition.

The related question, though, is why not just keep these data areas in their own directories rather than allocating a whole filesystem? The answer is two-fold. First, you cannot *guarantee* space for a data area that is not in its own partition—there are currently no mechanisms to achieve this. Second, you cannot *limit* space consumption by a directory within a filesystem. (For those of you thinking about filesystem quotas, remember that they can only be assigned to a user, not to a directory.)

As we pointed out earlier, partitions are an ironclad way of guaranteeing space and enforcing boundaries.

So, as we go on to talk about install classes, consider which data and system areas might need room to expand and enforced limits to that expansion. Also consider whether there might be critical system areas that *must not* get crowded out (for instance, if there is no room in /tmp, users can't log into the system).

3

FILESYSTEM ADMINISTRATION

Install Classes

When considering partitioning, machines are generally classified into two types: servers and workstations.[8] There are always systems that fall into the gray areas and oddities that challenge this division, but we find that this is a good starting point.

What's a Server?

When we talk about servers, we are referring to systems that offer some kind of externally accessible service. Systems that receive and deliver email, provide DNS, offer time services, host Web sites, or furnish a remote multiuser login environment are all servers.

For reasons of security and performance, we recommend that all servers be *dedicated servers*, where possible. This means that each server offers one and only one service. Then, for example, the system hosting your site's DNS will not have to cope with the added load and major security threat of general interactive user logins.

Servers must generally dedicate a significant amount of disk space to the service that they offer.

What's a Workstation?

Broadly speaking, anything that is not a server is a workstation (of one kind or another). The key is that workstations do not offer any external services. The *only* exception could be that they allow ssh-based remote logins.

In the best of all worlds, workstations are interchangeable, cookie-cutter systems. In real life, they might not be that simple to manage, but the goal is to get as close to that as possible.

Workstation disk space should generally be dedicated to the OS itself, logs, and local user-accessible space. In some cases, local space also includes local home directories.

The first piece of information that you need to judge partition sizes is the projected amount of space that various items will need. The best way to get a feel for this sort of thing is to get a relatively large disk and simply install the OS of your choice in various ways, noting the differences in size and usability.

Most sysadmins, unfortunately, are not allowed time for this sort of constructive play, so here is a reasonable working estimate:

Red Hat

Server	650Mb
Workstation	1.2Gb
Full	2.4Gb

Solaris

Server ("Entire")	2.3Gb
Workstation ("End User")	1.6–1.9Gb
Full ("Entire + OEM")	2.4Gb

By the numbers just given, you can tell a few things about Red Hat and Sun. Although their full installs are the same size, Red Hat tends to install less by default than does Sun. Also notice that a Red Hat server install is the smallest of all the types. This is because a server is presumed to be a dedicated machine that doesn't require things like X Windows in the base install. Sun's philosophy is the opposite: Servers get all the components that a workstation gets, plus more. We tend to advocate a minimalist approach: Only install what you actually need. If it's not installed, it doesn't have to be maintained and it won't hurt you.

More About Red Hat

Red Hat officially recommends that you divide up your space into three partitions: swap, /boot, and / (root).[9] The official site recommends the following space division guidelines:

swap	32Mb minimum
/boot	32Mb maximum
/	Rest of the space

If you choose the defaults for a server-class install, your partition layout will look something like the following:

swap	256Mb
/boot	16Mb
/	256Mb
/var	256Mb
/usr	512+Mb
/home	512+Mb

A few cautions:

- If your server does not serve home directories, then the space set aside for /home should probably be reapportioned elsewhere.

- If your server's particular application generates a lot of logs or is left unattended for extended periods of time, /var should probably be larger. If you intend to keep up to *n* multiple crash images, /var should be at least *n* times the size of real memory.

- If your server is dedicated to NFS service, /usr might need to be larger (unless the applications/files being served are located elsewhere).

- If your server has large amounts of RAM or runs swap-intensive software, swap should be larger.

- All "tmp"-type directories should point into /var/tmp, to avoid filling up other key partitions, or have their own partition.

Red Hat Linux 7.1 workstation-class defaults are as follows:

swap	64Mb
/boot	16Mb
/	Rest of the space

Our concerns about these defaults:

- This is probably not enough swap space—most new machines come with more than 32Mb of RAM. Swap should be increased accordingly.

- There is no separate partition for logs. This means that if the machine is left unattended for an extended period of time, or if the logs grow very large for some other reason, the machine might not be capable of functioning properly.

- "tmp"-type directories cannot be pointed to a noncritical partition. If users or applications make heavy use of any tmp directory, it could affect system performance.

More About Solaris

Sun has a mechanism called autolayout that proposes sizes based on the amount of disk space that it detects on your system during installation.[10] Our experience suggests that a 4GB disk is a "comfortable minimum" requirement for a Solaris workstation installation.

For servers, Sun recommends the following partitions:

swap

/

/usr

/opt

/export

/export/home

/export/swap

Because a server should have space allocated for logging and for the installation of its services, it is our practice to specify an 18GB disk for Solaris server installations.

Sun's intention is that everything to be served out should be placed somewhere under /export. Note the absence of both a /boot and a /var partition. A few cautions:

- If your server does not serve home directories, then the space set aside for /export/home should probably be reapportioned elsewhere.

- If your server does not serve diskless clients, then the space set aside for /export/swap should probably be reapportioned elsewhere.

- If your server's particular application generates a lot of logs or is left unattended for extended periods of time, /var should probably be a separate partition.

- If your server is dedicated to NFS service, /opt might need to be larger (unless the applications/files being served are located elsewhere).

- If your server has large amounts of RAM or runs swap-intensive software, swap should be larger.

- All "tmp"-type directories should point into /var/tmp, to avoid filling up other key partitions, or move their own partition.

For workstations (what Sun calls "standalone" machines), the following partitions are proposed by default:

/

swap

/opt

/usr

/home

Our concerns about these defaults:

- There is no separate partition for logs. This means that if the machine is left unattended for an extended period of time, or if the logs grow very large for some other reason, the machine might not be capable of functioning properly.

- "tmp"-type directories cannot be pointed to a noncritical partition. If users or applications make heavy use of any tmp directory, it could affect system performance.

- If the workstation does not have local home directories, then the space set aside for /home should probably be reapportioned elsewhere.

- If the workstation does not have local optional software installed, then the space set aside for /opt should probably be reapportioned elsewhere.

Red Hat's Partitionless Install

There is a different kind of install supported by Red Hat that is quite outside our model. In a sort of try-before-you-buy approach, you now can install Red Hat Linux in a *partitionless* mode.[11]

The trick to this kind of install is to piggyback Linux on an existing DOS/FAT filesystem. Of course, this means that you can't boot into Linux from the local partition—you have to have a boot floppy.

See `http://www.redhat.com/support/manuals/RHL-7.1-Manual/install-guide/ch-part-less.html` for more information on partitionless installs.

Technical Details of Partitioning

Enough theory—it's finally time to make the partitions actually appear on the disk. As you have probably already guessed, Red Hat and Solaris use different means to achieve the same ends. Let's look at these tools.

Red Hat

At install time, you are presented with two front ends for disk partitioning: fdisk and diskdruid. The familiar trade-off exists between the two: diskdruid is more straightforward to use, while fdisk allows you finer control over all parameters.

If you want to partition a new disk added to an extant system, you will need to use a variant fdisk to do the job. Although plain old fdisk is the standard, we suggest that you use the curses-based front end called cfdisk. It comes standard on Red Hat 7.1 and is quite intuitive.

Invoking cfdisk with no arguments will bring up a listing of /dev/hda along with command options:

```
                        cfdisk 2.10s


                    Disk Drive: /dev/hda
                  Size: 40000000000 bytes
        Heads: 255   Sectors per Track: 63   Cylinders: 4863


       Name          Flags        Part Type    FS Type          [Label]
 Size (MB)
```

```
- - - - - - - - - - - - - - - - - - - - - - - - - - - - - - - - - - - - - - - - - - - - - - - - - -
    hda1                         Primary     Linux ext2         [/boot]
32.91
    hda2          Boot           Primary     NTFS               [^C]
26222.20
    hda3                         Primary     Linux swap
2113.90
    hda4                         Primary     Linux ext2         [/]
11630.55


    [Bootable]   [ Delete ]   [  Help  ]  [Maximize]  [ Print  ]  [  Quit  ]  [
Type  ]
    [ Units  ]   [ Write  ]

                    Toggle bootable flag of the current partition
```

This works like most curses-based[12] front ends; the keyboard arrow keys move you up
and down along the list of devices, and the Tab key moves between the command options
along the bottom. The currently selected device and command are highlighted in gray.
Also notice that there is a description of the command's purpose at the very bottom of
the output. Pressing the Return or Enter key will run the highlighted command and
refresh the display to reflect the update.

Assuming that you have a fresh disk, you will want to add a partition to it.

With the -l option, fdisk can also be used to report on current partition information:

```
[linux:6 ~]fdisk -l

Disk /dev/hda: 255 heads, 63 sectors, 4863 cylinders
Units = cylinders of 16065 * 512 bytes

   Device Boot    Start      End    Blocks   Id  System
/dev/hda1            1        4     32098+   83  Linux
/dev/hda2    *       5     3192  25607610    7  HPFS/NTFS
/dev/hda3         3193     3449   2064352+  82  Linux swap
/dev/hda4         3450     4863  11357955   83  Linux
```

Solaris

At both install-time and from within the OS, Solaris offers the format command to
partition disks. When invoked, format presents you with a list of all currently accessible
drives:

```
[sun:18: ~]format
Searching for disks...done

AVAILABLE DISK SELECTIONS:
       0. c0t0d0 <ST315320A cyl 29649 alt 2 hd 16 sec 63>
```

```
        /pci@1f,0/ide@d/dad@0,0
    1. c0t1d0 <SUN2.1G cyl 2733 alt 2 hd 19 sec 80>
        /sbus@1f,0/SUNW,fas@e,8800000/sd@1,0
    2. c1t0d0 <IBM-DNES-318350-SA30 cyl 11199 alt 2 hd 10 sec 320>
        /sbus@1f,0/QLGC,isp@0,10000/sd@0,0
    3. c1t2d0 <SEAGATE-ST118273W-6244 cyl 7499 alt 2 hd 20 sec 237>
        /sbus@1f,0/QLGC,isp@0,10000/sd@2,0
Specify disk (enter its number):
```

Simply type in the number of the disk that you are interested in. Let's select disk 0:

```
selecting c0t0d0
[disk formatted, no defect list found]
Warning: Current Disk has mounted partitions.

FORMAT MENU:
        disk       - select a disk
        type       - select (define) a disk type
        partition  - select (define) a partition table
        current    - describe the current disk
        format     - format and analyze the disk
        repair     - repair a defective sector
        show       - translate a disk address
        label      - write label to the disk
        analyze    - surface analysis
        defect     - defect list management
        backup     - search for backup labels
        verify     - read and display labels
        save       - save new disk/partition definitions
        volname    - set 8-character volume name
        !<cmd>     - execute <cmd>, then return
        quit
format>
```

To view the current partition table on the disk, enter "**verify**":

```
format>verify
Primary label contents:

Volume name = <        >
ascii name  = <ST315320A cyl 29649 alt 2 hd 16 sec 63>
pcyl        = 29651
ncyl        = 29649
acyl        =     2
nhead       =    16
nsect       =    63
Part      Tag    Flag    Cylinders        Size            Blocks
  0      root     wm    1041 - 13524     6.00GB    (12484/0/0) 12583872
  1      swap     wu       0 -  1040   512.37MB    (1041/0/0)   1049328
  2    backup     wm       0 - 29648    14.25GB    (29649/0/0) 29886192
  3      home     wm   13525 - 29646     7.75GB    (16122/0/0) 16250976
```

```
4 unassigned    wm       0               0        (0/0/0)          0
5 unassigned    wm       0               0        (0/0/0)          0
6 unassigned    wm       0               0        (0/0/0)          0
7 unassigned    wm   29647 - 29648    0.98MB      (2/0/0)       2016

format>
```

Slice 2, called backup, represents the entire disk. As a result, it is not ever a useable partition and should not be altered in any way.

Now we're done discussing partitions and can move into entirely logical constructs, such as filesystems.

More About Filesystems

If we consider filesystems as a mechanism for both storing and locating data, then the two key elements for any filesystem are the items being stored and the list of where those items are. The deeper details of *how* a given filesystem manipulates its data and meta-information go beyond the scope of this chapter but are addressed further in Appendix B, "Anatomy of a Filesystem."

Filesystem Components That the Admin Needs to Know About

As always, we need to get a handle on the vocabulary before we can understand how the elements of a filesystem work together. The next three sections describe the basic components with which you, as a sysadmin, need to be familiar.

Files

The most intuitively obvious components of a filesystem are, of course, its files. Because everything in UNIX is a file, special functions are differentiated by file *type*. There are fewer file types than you might imagine, as Table 3.2 shows.

TABLE 3.2 File Types and Purposes, with Examples

File Type	Purpose/Contents	Examples
Directory	Maintains information for directory structure	/ /usr /etc

Block special	Buffered device file	Linux:
		    /dev/hda1
		Solaris:
		    /dev/dsk/c0t0d0s0

3

FILESYSTEM
ADMINISTRATION

TABLE 3.2 continued

File Type	Purpose/Contents	Examples

Character special	Raw device file	Linux:
		    /dev/tty0
		Solaris:
		    /dev/rdsk/c0t0d0s0

UNIX domain socket	Interprocess communication (IPC)	See output of commands for files
		Linux:
		    `netstat –x`
		Solaris:
		    `netstat -f unix`

Named pipe special (FIFO device)	First-in-first-out IPC mechanism, Invoked by name	Linux:
		    /dev/initctl
		Solaris:
		    /etc/utmppipe
		    /etc/cron.d/FIFO

Symbolic link	Pointer to another file (any type)	/usr/tmp -> ../var/tmp
Regular	All other files; holds data of all other types	Text files Object files Database files Executables/binaries

Notice that directories are a type of file. The key is that they have a specific type of format and contents (see Appendix B for more details). A directory holds the filenames and index numbers (see the following section, "Inodes") of all its constituent files, including subdirectories.

Directory files are not flat (or regular) files, but are *indexed* (like a database), so that you can still locate a file quickly when you have a large number of files in the same directory.[13]

Even though file handling is generally transparent, it is important to remember that a file's data blocks[14] may not be stored sequentially (or even in the same general disk region). When data blocks are widely scattered in an uncoordinated manner, it can affect access times and increase I/O overhead.

Inodes

Meta-information about files is stored in structures called *index nodes*, or *inodes*. Their contents vary based on the particular filesystem in use, but all inodes hold the following information about the file they index:[15]

- Inode identification number
- File type
- Owners: user and group
- UNIX permissions
- File size
- Timestamps
    - •`ctime`: Last file status change time
    - •`mtime`: Last data modification time[16]
    - •`atime`: Last access time
- Reference/link count
- Physical location information for data blocks

Notice that the filename is *not* stored in the inode, but as an entry in the file's closest parent directory.

All other information about a file that `ls` displays is stored in an inode somewhere. With a few handy options, you can pull out lots of useful information. Let's say that you want to know the inode number of the Solaris kernel.[17] You just give the `-i` option, and voilá:

```
[sun:10 ~]ls -i /kernel/genunix
264206 genunix
```

Of course, `ls -l` is an old friend, telling you most everything that you want to know. Looking at the Solaris kernel again, you get the output in Figure 3.4.

FIGURE 3.4
Diagrammed Output of `ls` *on a File*

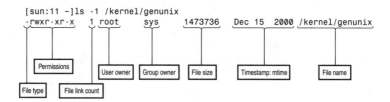

Notice that the timestamp shown by default in a long listing is mtime. You can pass various options to `ls` to view ctime and atime instead. For other nifty permutations, see the `ls` man page.

File Permissions and Ownership Refresher

Because UNIX was designed to support many users, the question naturally arises how to know who can see what files. The first and simplest answer is simply to permit users to examine only their own files. This, of course, would make it difficult, if not impossible, to share, creating great difficulties in collaborative environments and causing a string of other problems: Why can't I run `ls`? Because the system created it, not you, is only the most obvious example of such problems.

Users and Groups

UNIX uses a three-part system to determine file access: There's what you, as the file owner, are allowed to do; there's what the group is allowed to do; and there's what other people are allowed to do. Let's see what Elvis's permissions look like:

```
[ elvis@frogbog elvis ]$ ls -l

total 36
drwxr-xr-x   5 elvis     users      4096 Dec  9 21:55 Desktop
drwxr-xr-x   2 elvis     users      4096 Dec  9 22:00 Mail
-rw-r--r--   1 elvis     users        36 Dec  9 22:00 README
-rw-r--r--   1 elvis     users        22 Dec  9 21:59 ThisFile
drwxr-xr-x   2 elvis     users      4096 Dec 12 19:57 arc
drwxr-xr-x   2 elvis     users      4096 Dec 10 00:40 songs
-rw-r--r--   1 elvis     users        46 Dec 12 19:52 tao.txt
-rw-r--r--   1 elvis     users        21 Dec  9 21:59 thisfile
-rw-r--r--   1 elvis     users        45 Dec 12 19:52 west.txt
```

As long as we're here, let's break down exactly what's being displayed. First, we have a 10-character string of letters and hyphens. This is the representation of permissions, which I'll break down in a minute. The second item is a number, usually a single digit. This is the number of *hard links* to that directory. I'll discuss this later in this chapter. The third thing is the username of the file owner, and the fourth is the name of the file's group. The fifth column is a number representing the size of the file, in bytes. The sixth contains the date and time of last modification for the file, and the final column shows the filename.

Every user on the system has a username and a number that is associated with that user. This number generally is referred to as the *UID*, short for *user ID*. If a user has been deleted but, for some reason, his files remain, the username is replaced with that user's UID. Similarly, if a group is deleted but still owns files, the *GID* (group number) shows up instead of a name in the group field. There are also other circumstances in which the system can't correlate the name and the number, but these should be relatively rare occurrences.

As a user, you can't change the owner of your files: This would open up some serious security holes on the system. Only root can chown files, but if he makes a mistake, you can now ask root to chown the files to you. As a user, you can chgrp a file to a different group of which you are a member. That is, if Elvis is a member of a group named users and a group named elvis, he can chgrp elvis west.txt or chgrp users west.txt, but because he's not a member of the group beatles, he can't chgrp beatles west.txt. A user can belong to any number of groups. Generally (although this varies somewhat by flavor), files created belong to the group to which the directory belongs. On most modern UNIX variants, the group that owns files is whatever group is listed as your primary group by the system in the /etc/passwd file and can be changed via the newgrp command. On these systems, Elvis can chgrp users if he wants his files to belong to the users group, or he can chgrp elvis if he wants his files to belong to the elvis group.

Reading Permissions

So, what were those funny strings of letters and hyphens at the beginning of each long directory listing? I already said that they represented the permissions of the file, but that's not especially helpful. The 10 characters of that string represent the permission bits for each file. The first character is separate, and the last nine are three very similar groups of three characters. I'll explain each of these in turn.

If you look back to Elvis's long listing of his directory, you'll see that most of the files simply have a hyphen as the first character, whereas several possess a d in this field. The more astute reader might note that the files with a d in that first field all happen to be directories. There's a good reason for this: The first permissions character denotes whether that file is a special file of one sort or another.

What's a special file? It's either something that isn't really a file (in the sense of a sequential stream of bytes on a disk) but that UNIX treats as a file, such as a disk or a video display, or something that is really a file but that is treated differently. A directory, by necessity, is a stream of bytes on disk, but that d means that it's treated differently.

The next three characters represent what the user who owns the file can do with it. From left to right, these permissions are *read*, *write*, and *execute*. Read permission is just that—the capability to see the contents of a file. Write permission implies not only the right to change the contents of a file, but also the right to delete it. If I do not possess write permission to a file, `rm not_permitted.txt` fails.

Execute permission determines whether the file is also a command that can be run on the system. Because UNIX sees everything as a file, all commands are stored in files that can be created, modified, and deleted like any other file. The computer then needs a way to tell what can and can't be run. The execute bit does this.

Another important reason that you need to worry about whether a file is executable is that some programs are designed to be run only by the system administrator: These programs can modify the computer's configuration or can be dangerous in some other way. Because UNIX enables you to specify permissions for the owner, the group, and other users, the execute bit enables the administrator to restrict the use of dangerous programs.

Directories treat the execute permission differently. If a directory does not have execute permissions, that user (or group, or other users on the system) can't cd into that directory and can't look at information about the files in that directory. (You usually can find the names of the files, however.) Even if you have permissions for the files in that directory, you generally can't look at them. (This varies somewhat by platform.)

The second set of three characters is the group permissions (read, write, and execute, in that order), and the final set of three characters is what other users on the system are permitted to do with that file. Because of security concerns (either due to other users on your system or due to pervasive networks such as the Internet), giving write access to other users is highly discouraged.

Changing Permissions

Great, you can now read the permissions in the directory listing, but what can you do with them? Let's say that Elvis wants to make his directory readable only by himself. He can `chmod go-rwx ~/songs`: That means remove the read, write, and execute permissions for the group and others on the system. If Elvis decides to let Nashville artists take a look at his material but not change it (and if there's a group nashville on the system), he can first `chgrp nashville songs` and then `chmod g+r songs`.

If Elvis does this, however, he'll find that (at least, on some platforms) members of group nashville can't look at them. Oops! With a simple `chmod g+x songs`, the problem is solved:

```
[ elvis@frogbog elvis ]$ ls -l
total 36
drwxr-xr-x   5 elvis    users      4096 Dec  9 21:55 Desktop
drwxr-xr-x   2 elvis    users      4096 Dec  9 22:00 Mail
-rw-r--r--   1 elvis    users        36 Dec  9 22:00 README
-rw-r--r--   1 elvis    users        22 Dec  9 21:59 ThisFile
drwxr-xr-x   2 elvis    users      4096 Dec 12 19:57 arc
drwxr-x---   2 elvis    nashvill   4096 Dec 15 14:21 songs
-rw-r--r--   1 elvis    users        46 Dec 12 19:52 tao.txt
-rw-r--r--   1 elvis    users        21 Dec  9 21:59 thisfile
-rw-r--r--   1 elvis    users        45 Dec 12 19:52 west.txt
```

Special Permissions

In addition to the read, write, and execute bits, there exists special permissions used by the system to determine how and when to suspend the normal permission rules. Any thorough understanding of UNIX requires an understanding of the *setuid*, *setgid*, and *sticky* bits. For normal system users, only a general understanding of these is necessary, and this discussion is thus brief. Good documentation on this subject exists elsewhere for budding system administrators and programmers.

setuid

The setuid bit applies only to executable files and directories. In the case of executable programs, it means that the given program runs as though the file owner were running it. That is, xhextris, a variant on Tetris, has the following permissions on my system:

```
-rwsr-xr-x
1 games games 32516 May 18 1999 /usr/X11R6/bin/xhextris
```

There's a pseudouser called games on the system, which can't be logged into and has no home directory. When the xhextris program executes, it can read and write to files that only the game's pseudouser normally would be permitted. In this case, there's a high-score file stored on the system that writeable only by that user. When Elvis runs the game, the system acts as though he were the user games, and thus he is able to store the high-score file. To set the setuid bit on a file, you can tell `chmod` to give it mode `u+s`. (You can think of this as uid set, although this isn't technically accurate.)

setgid

The setgid bit, which stands for "set group id," works almost identically to setuid, except that the system acts as though the user's group is that of the given file. If xhextris had used setgid games instead of setuid games, the high score would be writeable to any directory owned by the *group* games. It is used by the system administrator in ways fundamentally similar to the setuid permission.

When applied to directories on Linux, Irix, and Solaris (and probably most other POSIX-compliant UNIX flavors as well), the setgid bit means that new files are given the parent directory's group rather than the user's primary or current group. This can be useful for, say, a directory for fonts built by (and for) a given program. Any user might generate the fonts via a setgid command that writes to a setgid directory. setgid on directories varies by platform; check your documentation. To set the setgid bit, you can tell chmod to use g+s (gid set).

sticky

Although a file in a group or world-writeable directory without the sticky bit can be deleted by anyone with write permission for that directory (user, group, or other), a file in a directory with the sticky bit set can be deleted only by either the file's owner or root. This is particularly useful for creating temporary directories or scratch space that can be used by anyone without one's files being deleted by others. You can set permission +t in chmod to give something the sticky bit.

Numeric Permissions

Like almost everything else on UNIX, permissions have a number associated with them. It's generally considered that permissions are a group of four digits, each between 0 and 7. Each of those digits represents a group of three permissions, each of which is a yes/no answer. From left to right, those digits represent special permissions, user permissions, group permissions, and other permissions.

So, About Those Permission Bits...

Most programs reading permission bits expect four digits, although often only three are given. Shorter numbers are filled in with leading zeros: 222 is treated as 0222, and 5 is treated as 0005. The three rightmost digits are, as previously mentioned, user (owner) permissions, group permissions, and other permissions, from right to left.

Each of these digits is calculated in the following manner: read permission has a value of 4, write permission has a value of 2, and execute permission has a value of 1. Simply add these values together, and you've got that permission value. Read, write, and execute would be 7, read and write without execute would be 6, and no permission to do anything would be 0. Read, write, and execute for the file owner, with read and execute for the group and nothing at all for anyone else, would be 750. Read and write for the user and group, but only read for others, would be 664.

The special permissions are 4 for setuid, 2 for setgid, and 1 for sticky. This digit is prepended to the three-digit numeric permission: A temporary directory with sticky read, write, and execute permission for everyone would be mode 1777. A setuid root directory writeable by nobody else would be 4700. You can use chmod to set numeric permissions directly, as in chmod 1777 /tmp.

umask

In addition to a more precise use of chmod, numeric permissions are used with the umask command, which sets the default permissions. More precisely, it "masks" the default permissions: The umask value is subtracted from the maximum possible settings.* umask deals only with the three-digit permission, not the full-fledged four-digit value. A umask of 002 or 022 is most commonly the default. 022, subtracted from 777, is 755: read, write, and execute for the user, and read and execute for the group and others. 002 from 777 is 775: read, write, and execute for the user and group, and read and execute for others. I tend to set my umask to 077: read, write, and execute for myself, and nothing for my group or others. (Of course, when working on a group project, I set my umask to 007: My group and I can read, write, or execute anything, but others can't do anything with our files.)

You should note that the umask assumes that the execute bit on the file will be set. All umasks are subtracted from 777 rather than 666, and those extra ones are subtracted later, if necessary. (See Appendix B for more details on permission bits and umask workings.)

Actually, the permission bits are XORed with the maximum possible settings, if you're a computer science type.

3

FILESYSTEM ADMINISTRATION

Also notice that the first bit of output prepended to the permissions string indicates the file type. This is one handy way of identifying a file's type. Another is the file command, as shown in Table 3.3.

TABLE 3.3 `ls` File Types and `file` Output Sample

File Type	`ls` File Type Character	File Display Example
Directory	d	[either:1 ~]file /usr /usr: directory
Block special device	b	[linux: 10 ~] file /dev/hda1 /dev/hda1: block special (3/1) [sun:10 root ~]file /dev/dsk/c0t0d0s0 /dev/dsk/c0t0d0s0: block special (136/0)
Character special device	c	[linux:11 ~] file /dev/tty0 /dev/tty0: character special (4/0) [ensis:11 ~]file /dev/rdsk/c0t0d0s0 /dev/rdsk/c0t0d0s0: character special (136/0)
UNIX domain socket	s	[linux:12 ~] file /dev/log /dev/log: socket [sun:12 ~]file /dev/ccv /dev/ccv: socket
Named pipe special (FIFO device)	p	[linux:13 ~] file /dev/initctl /dev/initctl: fifo (named pipe) [sun:13 ~]file /etc/utmppipe /etc/utmppipe: fifo
Symbolic link	l	[linux:14 ~] file /usr/tmp /usr/tmp: symbolic link to ../var/tmp [sun:14 ~]file -h /usr/tmp /usr/tmp: symbolic link to ➥../var/tmp
Regular	-	[linux:15 ~] file /etc/passwd /etc/passwd: ASCII text [linux:15 ~] file /boot/vmlinux-2.4.2-2 /boot/vmlinux-2.4.2-2: ELF 32-bit LSB executable,

TABLE 3.3   continued

File Type	`ls` *File Type Character*	`File` *Display Example*
		➡Intel 80386, version 1,statically linked, not stripped
		[linux:15 ~] file /etc/rc.d/init.d/sshd /etc/rc.d/init.d/sshd: Bourne-Again shell script text executable
		[sun:15 ~]file /etc/passwd /etc/passwd: ascii text
		[sun:15 ~]file /kernel/genunix /kernel/genunix: ELF 32-bit MSB relocatable ➡SPARC Version 1
		[sun:15 ~]file /etc/init.d/sshd /etc/init.d/sshd: executable ➡/sbin/sh script

Notice the in-depth information that `file` gives—in many cases, it shows details about the file that no other command will readily display (such as what *kind* of executable the file is). These low-level details are beyond the scope of our discussion, but the `man` page has more information.

Important Points about the `file` ommand

`file` tries to figure out what type a file is based on three types of test:

- The file type that the `ls -l` command returns.
- The presence of a magic number at the beginning of the file identifying the file type. These numbers are defined in the file /usr/share/magic in Red Hat Linux 7.1 and /usr/lib/locale/`locale`/LC_MESSAGES/magic (or /etc/magic) in Solaris 8. Typically, only binary files will have magic numbers.
- In the case of a regular/text file, the first few bytes are tested to determine the type of text representation and then to determine whether the file has a recognized purpose, such as C code or a Perl script.

`file` actually opens the file and changes the *atime* in the inode.

Inode lists are maintained by the filesystem itself, including which ones are free for use. Inode allocation and manipulation is all transparent to both sysadmins and users.

Inodes become significant at two times for the sysadmin: at filesystem creation time and when the filesystem runs out of free inodes. At filesystem creation time, the total number of inodes for the filesystem is allocated. Although they are not in use, space is set aside for them. You cannot add any more inodes to a filesystem after it has been created. When you run out of inodes, you must either free some up (by deleting or moving files) or migrate to another, larger filesystem.

Without inodes, files are just a random assortment of ones and zeros on the disk. There is no guarantee that the file will be stored sequentially within a sector or track, so without an inode to point the way to the data blocks, the file is lost. In fact, every file is uniquely identified by the combination of its filesystem name and inode number.

See Appendix B for more detailed information on the exact content of inodes and their structure.

Linux has a very useful command called stat that dumps the contents of an inode in a tidy format:

```
[linux:9 ~]stat .
  File: "."
  Size: 16384        Filetype: Directory
  Mode: (0755/drwxr-xr-x)        Uid: (19529/   robin)        Gid:(20/users)
  Device:  0,4   Inode: 153288707 Links: 78
  Access: Sun Jul 22 13:58:29 2001(00009.04:37:59)
  Modify: Sun Jul 22 13:58:29 2001(00009.04:37:59)
  Change: Sun Jul 22 13:58:29 2001(00009.04:37:59)
```

Boot Block and Superblock

When a filesystem is created, two structures are automatically created, whether they are immediately used or not. The first is called the *boot block*, where boot-time information is stored. Because a partition may be made bootable at will, this structure needs to be available at all times.

The other structure, of more interest here, is the superblock. Just as an inode contains meta-information about a file, a superblock contains metainformation about a filesystem. Some of the more critical contents are listed here:[18]

- Filesystem name
- Filesystem size
- Timestamp: last update

- Superblock state flag
- Filesystem state flag: clean, stable, active
- Number of free blocks
- List of free blocks
- Pointer to next free block
- Size of inode list
- Number of free inodes
- List of free inodes
- Pointer to next free inode
- Lock fields for free blocks and inodes
- Summary data block

And you thought inodes were complex.

The superblock keeps track of free file blocks and free inodes so that the filesystem can store new files. Without these lists and pointers, a long, sequential search would have to be performed to find free space *every* time a file was created.

In much the same way that files without inodes are lost, filesystems without intact superblocks are inaccessible. That's why there is a superblock state flag—to indicate whether the superblock was properly and completely updated before the disk (or system) was last taken offline. If it was not, then a consistency check must be performed for the whole filesystem and the results stored back in the superblock.

Again, more detailed information about the superblock and its role in UNIX filesystems may be found in Appendix B.

Filesystem Types

Both Red Hat and Solaris recognize a multitude of different filesystem types, although you will generally end up using and supporting just a few. There are three standard types of filesystem—local, network, and pseudo—and a fourth "super-filesystem" type that is actually losing ground, given the size of modern disks.

Local Filesystems

Local filesystems are common to every system that has its own local disk.[19] Although there are many instances of this type of filesystem, they are all designed to work *within* a system, managing the components discussed in the last section and interfacing with the physical drive(s).

Only a few local filesystems are specifically designed to be cross-platform (and sometimes even cross–OS-type). They come in handy, though, when you have a nondisk hardware failure; you can just take the disk and put it into another machine to retrieve the data.[20] The UNIX File System, or *ufs*, was designed for this; both Solaris and Red Hat Linux machines can use disks with this filesystem. Note that Solaris uses ufs filesystems by default. Red Hat's default local filesystem is ext2.

Another local, cross-platform filesystem is ISO9660, the CD-ROM standard. This is why you can read your Solaris CD in a Red Hat box's reader.

Local filesystems come in two related but distinct flavors. The original, standard model filesystem is still in broad use today. The newer *journaling* filesystem type is just beginning to really come into its own. The major difference between the two types is the way they track changes and do integrity checks.

Standard Filesystems

Standard, nonjournaling filesystems rely on flags in the superblock for consistency regulation. If the superblock flag is not set to "clean," then the filesystem knows that it was not shut down properly: not all write buffers were flushed to disk, and so on. Inconsistency in a filesystem means that allocated inodes could be overwritten; free inodes could be counted as in use—in short, rampant file corruption, mass hysteria.

But there is a filesystem integrity checker to save the day: fsck. This command is usually invoked automatically at boot-time to verify that all filesystems are clean and stable. If the / or /usr filesystems are inconsistent, the system might prompt you to start up a miniroot shell and manually run fsck. A few of the more critical items checked and corrected are listed here:

- Unclaimed blocks and inodes (not in free list or in use)
- Unreferenced but allocated blocks and inodes
- Multiply claimed blocks and inodes
- Bad inode formats
- Bad directory formats
- Bad free block or inode list formats
- Incorrect free block or inode counts
- Superblock counts and flags

Note that a filesystem should be unmounted before running fsck (see the later section "Administering Local Filesystems"). Running fsck on a mounted filesystem might cause a system panic and crash, or it might simply refuse to run at all. It's also best, though not required, that you run `fsck` on the raw device, when possible. See the `man` page for more details and options.

So where does `fsck` put *orphans*, the blocks and inodes that are clearly in use but aren't referenced anywhere? Enter the lost+found directories. There is always a /lost+found directory on every system; other directories accrue them as `fsck` finds orphans in their purview. `fsck` automatically creates the directories as needed and renames the lost blocks into there by inode number. See the `man` pages "mklost+found" on Red Hat and "fsck_ufs" on Solaris.

Journaling Filesystems

Journaling filesystems do away with `fsck` and its concomitant superblock structures. All filesystem state information is internally tracked and monitored, in much the same way that databases systems set up checkpoints and self-verifications.

With journaling filesystems, you have a better chance of full data recovery in the event of a system crash. Even unsaved data in buffers can be recovered thanks to the internal log.[21] This kind of fault tolerance makes journaling filesystems useful in high-availability environments.

The drawback, of course, is that when a filesystem like this gets corrupted somehow, it presents major difficulties for recovery. Most journaling filesystems provide their own salvaging programs for use in case of emergency. This underscores how critical backups are, no matter what kind of filesystem software you've invested in. See Chapter 16, "Backups," for more information.

One of the earliest journaling filesystems is still a commercial venture: VxFS by Veritas. Another pioneer has decided to release its software into the public domain under GPL[22] licensing: JFS[23] by IBM. SGI's xfs journaling filesystem has been freely available under GPL since about 1999, although it is only designed to work under IRIX and Linux.[24]

Maintenance of filesystem state incurs an overhead when using journaling filesystems. As a result, these filesystems perform suboptimally for small filesystem sizes. Generally, journaling filesystems are appropriate for filesystem sizes of 500Mb or more.

Network Filesystems

Network-based filesystems are really add-ons to local filesystems because the file server must have the actual data stored in one of its own local filesystems.[25] Network filesystems have both a server and client program.

The server usually runs as a daemon on the system that is sharing disk space. The server's local filesystems are unaffected by this extra process. In fact, the daemon generally only puts a few messages in the syslog and is otherwise only visible through ps.

The system that wants to access the server's disk space runs the client program to mount the shared filesystems across the network. The client program handles all the I/O so that the network filesystem behaves just a like a local filesystem toward the client machine.

The old standby for network-based filesystems is the Network File System (NFS). The NFS standard is currently up to revision 3, though there are quite a number of implementations with their own version numbers. Both Red Hat and Solaris come standard with NFS client and server packages. For more details on the inner workings and configuration of NFS, see Chapter 13, "File Sharing."

Other network-based filesystems include AFS (IBM's Andrew File System) and DFS/DCE (Distributed File System, part of the Open Group's Distributed Computing Environment). The mechanisms of these advanced filesystems go beyond the scope of this book, although their goal is still the same: to efficiently share files across the network transparently to the user.

Pseudo Filesystems

Pseudofilesystems are an interesting development in that they are not actually related to disk-based partitions. They are instead purely logical constructs that represent information and meta-information in a hierarchical structure. Because of this structure and because they can be manipulated with the mount command, they are still referred to as filesystems.

The best example of pseudofilesystems exists on both Red Hat and Solaris systems: /proc. Under Solaris, /proc is restricted to just managing process information:

```
[sun:1 ~]ls /proc
0    145  162  195  206  230  262  265  272  286  299  303  342  370  403  408
→672  752
1    155  185  198  214  243  263  266  278  292  3    318  360  371  404  52
→674
142  157  192  2    224  252  264  268  280  298  302  319  364  400  406  58
→678
```

Note that these directories are all named according to the process numbers corresponding to what you would find in the output of ps. The contents of each directory are the various meta-information that the system needs to manage the process.

Under Red Hat, /proc provides information about processes as well as about various system components and statistics:

```
[linux:1 ~] ls /proc
1       18767   23156   24484   25567   28163   4     493   674    8453       ksyms
⇒stat
13557   18933   23157   24486   25600   3       405   5     675    9833       loadavg
⇒swaps
13560   18934   23158   24487   25602   3050    418   5037  676    9834       locks
⇒sys
13561   18937   23180   24512   25603   3051    427   5038  7386   9835       mdstat
⇒tty
1647    19709   23902   24541   25771   3052    441   5054  7387   bus        meminfo
⇒uptime
1648    19730   23903   24775   25772   30709   455   5082  7388   cmdline    misc
⇒version
1649    19732   23936   25494   25773   30710   473   510   7414   cpuinfo    modules
16553   19733   24118   25503   25824   30712   485   5101  7636   devices    mounts
18658   2       24119   25504   25882   30729   486   524   7637   dma        mtrr
18660   21450   24120   25527   25920   320     487   558   7638   filesystems net
18661   21462   24144   25533   26070   335     488   6     7662   fs
⇒partitions
18684   21866   24274   25534   26071   337     489   670   8426   interrupts pci
18685   21869   24276   25541   26072   338     490   671   8427   ioports    scsi
18686   21870   24277   25542   28161   339     491   672   8428   kcore      self
18691   21954   24458   25543   28162   365     492   673   8429   kmsg       slabinfo
```

Again we see the directories named for process numbers, but we also see directories with indicative names such as cpuinfo and loadavg. Because this is a hierarchical filesystem, you can cd into these directories and read the various files for their system information.

The most interesting thing about /proc is that it allows even processes to be treated like files.[26] This means that pretty much everything in UNIX, whether it is something that just exists or something that actually happens, can now be considered a file.

For more information under Red Hat, type **man proc**. For more information under Solaris, type **man -s 4 proc**.

Logical Volumes

Finally, there are the "super-filesystems" or *logical volumes* that do what the other major types of filesystem cannot: surmount the barriers of partitions. You may well ask why anyone would want to do that. There are two reasons. First, because disks used to be a lot smaller and more costly, you used what you had at hand. If you needed a large pool of disk space, logical volumes allowed you to aggregate remnants into something useable. Second, even with larger disks, you still might not be able to achieve the kind of disk space required by a particular researcher or program. Once again, logical volumes allow you to aggregate partitions across disks to form one large filesystem.

3

FILESYSTEM
ADMINISTRATION

Crossing disk boundaries with a logical volume is referred to as *disk spanning*. Once you have logical volumes, you can also have some fairly complex data management methods and performance-enhancing techniques. *Disk striping*, for example, is a performance booster. Instead of sequentially filling one disk and then the next in series, it spreads the data in discrete chunks across disks, allowing better I/O response through parallel operations.

RAID[27] implements logical volumes at 10 distinct levels, with various features at each level. This implementation can be done either in hardware or in software, although the nomenclature for both is the same.[28]

TABLE 3.4   RAID Levels

RAID Level	Features	Implications
0	Disk striping	Fastest
		Not self-repairing
1	Disk mirroring	Fast
		Self-repairing
		Requires extra drives for data duplication
2	Disk striping	Fast
	Error correction	Self-repairing
		(Very similar to RAID-3)
3	Disk striping	Slower
	Parity disk	Self-repairing
	Error correction	Requires separate parity disk
4	Disk striping	Slower
	Parity disk	Self-repairing
		Requires separate parity disk
		(Very similar to RAID-5)

TABLE 3.4   continued

RAID Level	Features	Implications
5	Disk striping	Slowest for writes, but
	Rotating parity array	good for reads
		Self-repairing
		Requires three to five separate parity disks
		Reconstruction by parity data (not duplication)
6	RAID-5 + secondary parity scheme	Not in broad use
7	RAID-5 + real-time embedded controller	Not in broad use
0+1	Mirrored striping	RAID-0 array duplicated (mirrored)
1+0	Striped mirroring	Each stripe is RAID-1 (mirrored) array
		High cost
0+3	Array of parity stripes	Each stripe is RAID-3 array
		High cost

3

FILESYSTEM ADMINISTRATION

Clearly, the kind of complexity inherent in all logical volume systems requires some kind of back-end management system. Red Hat offers the Logical Volume Manager (LVM) as a kernel module. While the details of LVM are beyond the scope of this book, it is interesting to note that you can put any filesystem that you want on top of the logical volume. Start at `http://www.linuxdoc.org/HOWTO/LVM-HOWTO.html` for more details.

Although Sun offers logical volume management, it is through a for-pay program called "Solstice DiskSuite." The filesystem on DiskSuite logical volumes must be ufs. For more information, start at `http://docs.sun.com/ab2/coll.260.2/DISKSUITEREF`.

Another commercial logical volume manager for Solaris comes from Veritas; see: `http://www.veritas.com/us/products/volumemanager/faq.html#a24`

The beauty of all logical volumes is that they appear to be just another local filesystem and are completely transparent to the user. However, logical volumes do add some complexity for the systems administrator, and the schema should be carefully documented on paper, in case it needs to be re-created.

NAS

Normally, a file server's disks are directly attached to the file server. With *network-attached storage* (*NAS*), the file server and the disks that it serves are separate entities, communicating over the local network. The storage disks require an aggregate controller that arbitrates file I/O requests from the external server(s). The server(s) and the aggregate controller each have distinct network IP addresses. To serve the files to clients, a file (or application) server sends file I/O requests to the NAS aggregate controller and relays the results back to client systems.

NAS is touched on here for completeness—entire books can be written about NAS design and implementation. NAS does not really represent a type of filesystem, but rather it is a mechanism to relieve the file server from the details of hardware disk access by isolating them in the network-attached storage unit.

Red Hat Filesystem Reference Table

Table 3.5 lists major filesystems that currently support (or are supported by) Red Hat.[29] The filesystem types that are currently natively supported are listed in /usr/src/linux/fs/filesytems.c.

TABLE 3.5   Filesystem Types and Purposes, with Examples (Red Hat)

Filesystem Type	Specific Instances (as Used in /etc/fstab)			Purpose
Local	ext2			Red Hat default filesystem
	ufs			Solaris compatibility
	jfs			Journaling filesystem from IBM
	xfs			Journaling filesystem from SGI
	msdos			Windows compatibility: DOS
	ntfs			Windows compatibility: NT
	vfat			Windows compatibility: FAT-32
	sysv			SYS-V compatibility
	iso9660			CD-ROM
	adfs	hfs	romfs	Others
	affs	hpfs	smbfs	
	coda	mnix	udf	

TABLE 3.5   continued

Filesystem Type	Specific Instances (as Used in /etc/fstab)			Purpose
	devpts	ncpfs	umsdos	
	efs	qux4		
	coherent			Deprecated, pre-kernel 2.1.21
	ext			
	xenix			
	xiafs			
Network	afs			Network-based remote communication
	autofs			
	nfs			
Pseudo	proc			Store process (and other system) meta-information

Solaris Filesystem Reference Table

Table 3.6 lists major filesystems that currently support (or are supported by) Solaris.[30] The filesystem types that currently are natively supported are listed as directories under /usr/lib/fs.

TABLE 3.6   Filesystem Types and Purposes, with Examples (Solaris)

Filesystem Type	Specific Instances (as Used in /etc/vfstab)			Purpose
Local	ufs			Solaris default filesystem; Red Hat-compatible
	pcfs			PC filesystem
	hsfs			CD-ROM
	jfs			Journaling filesystem from IBM
Network	afs			Network-based remote communication
	nfs			
Pseudo	procfs			Store process metainformation
	fdfs	swapfs	tmpfs	Mount metainformation
	mntfs	cachefs	lofs	areas as filesystems
	fifofs	specfs	udfs	
	namefs			

Administering Local Filesystems

Now that you know what's available, it's time to decide which filesystem you want to use on your local system hard disks. (Hint: When creating a filesystem for a local hard disk, pseudo and network filesystem types are right out.)

Local Filesystem Creation

Local filesystem creation is taken care of for you at install time by the various OS install programs. To do it manually, simply invoke mkfs on the device file that you want to set up. On Solaris systems, this would be the device file in /dev/rdsk – the raw/character device file.

On both Red Hat and Solaris, mkfs is mainly a wrapper that sends arguments to a filesystem-specific filesystem-creation subprogram (such as mkfs.ext2 or mkfs_ufs). The mkfs front end for both operating systems allows you to specify things like filesystem type on the command line.

Solaris also offers a ufs-specific filesystem-creation tool called newfs. It offers more flexibility and deeper feature management than the mkfs front end. For most applications, however, the defaults for the filesystem are adequate.

The operating system will generally warn you if you try to create a new filesystem on a device that is either mounted or already has a filesystem present. Make sure that that partition is unmounted and not in use on the system before running mkfs. Also realize that if you create a new filesystem where one already exists, the original filesystem is permanently destroyed (your only hope of recovering the data is your backups). Because mkfs is a nonreversible operation, the system is generally polite enough to query before you destroy data, but don't take that for granted. Use care when (re)formatting disk space.

Note that a detailed description of logical volumes goes beyond the scope of this book, so the filesystems discussed are the usual one-to-a-partition kind.

Local Filesystem Availability Management

Of course, filesystem administration only really begins when the filesystem is created. The next task is to get the system to recognize and make available the newly formatted space, probably in a reboot-survivable way. You will also want to periodically check on space usage, both to make sure that system areas have enough free space to function well and to check that no errant processes or users are taking up inordinate amounts of space.

The mount Command

Both Red Hat and Solaris use the mount command to make filesystems available to the Operating System. When invoked from the command line, the filesystem is mounted in a temporary fashion; that is, it will disappear after a reboot. The filesystem itself, along with its data, is intact, but unless another mount command is issued, it is inaccessible.

Under both Red Hat and Solaris, mount acts as a wrapper, much in the same way that mkfs does. You can specify filesystem type via a command-line switch to mount, thereby invoking the correct routines. If no filesystem type is specified, Red Hat assumes ext2 and Solaris assumes ufs. Note that only root (or rather, only UID 0 users) has the capability to run mount.

Filesystems require somewhere to attach to the directory structure on your system, a path by which the files can be accessed. And because UNIX uses hierarchical filesystems, it shouldn't be surprising that the attachment point, or *mount point*, must be a directory. Both Red Hat and Solaris provide a mount point called /mnt, intended to be used for temporary mounts.[31] Figures 3.5 and 3.6 show part of a standard UNIX filesystem both before and after mounting a filesystem on /mnt.

FIGURE 3.5

Filesystem fragment before mount.

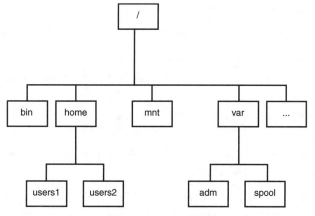

FIGURE 3.6
Filesystem fragment with /mnt mounted.

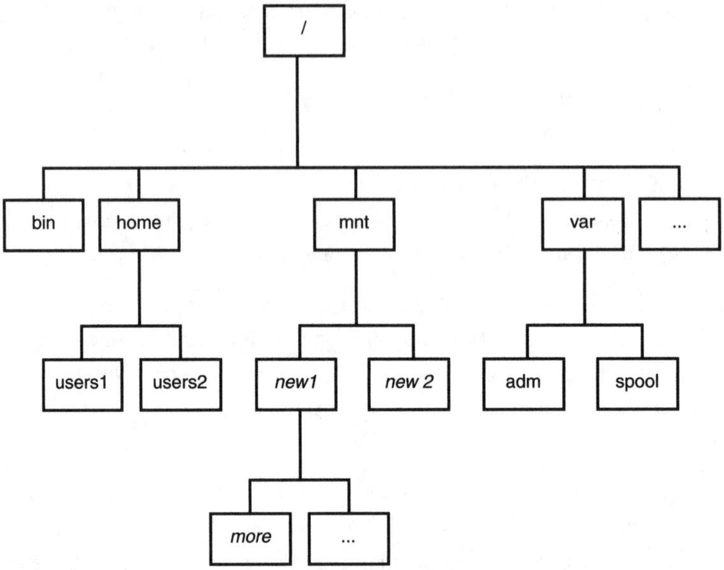

Note that `mount` is invoked on the hard disk *block* device,[32] as in the following examples:

```
[linux:16 ~]mount /dev/hda1 /mnt
```

```
[sun:16 ~]mount /dev/dsk/c0t0d0s3 /mnt
```

A successful operation produces no output.

If you want to `mount` a filesystem from a remote server, you specify both the remote server and the filesystem name as it appears on the remote server on the command line, like so:

```
[sun:17 ~]mount linuxserver:/research/data /mnt
[linux:17 ~]mount bsdserver:/accounting /accounting
```

Note that these commands assume that the NFS server is configured properly and that your system is configured for client-side NFS.

Remember that it doesn't matter what the local filesystem type is on the remote server, just that there is a network file server program that can handle passing data across the network and back into the local filesystem. This means that even though Solaris does not directly understand ext2 filesystems, it can communicate with a Linux file server via NFS. Also remember that the mount point must already exist on your local system. For more on network-based filesystems and file-sharing mechanisms, see Chapter 13.

The umount Command

Of course, what goes on must also come off (or something like that). To take a mounted filesystem offline, issue the umount command on the filesystem name (or the associated device name). As with mount, only root (or other UID 0 users) has the capability to unmount a filesystem.

Where Did the *n* Go?
or, Why Is It umount Instead of unmount?

The *n* was sacrificed on the two altars of lazy typists and limited computer memory, like the *i* and *t* in the list (1s) command or the *e* in the ch[ange]mode (chmod) command. It's yet another way you know that UNIX was written by geeks—save those keystrokes!

The umount command is polite; if the filesystem is in use, it will not be unmounted because unmounted filesystems cannot be accessed. This means that you won't be able to accidentally unmount your root filesystem (which, incidentally, holds the kernel) or interrupt a write operation.

Of course, UNIX will let you do virtually anything, no matter how foolish or detrimental, if you really want to. By passing the command-line option to *force* the operation (usually -f; see the mount man page), the filesystem will be gracelessly dropped, killing any ongoing accesses and leaving the filesystem dirty. Be prepared to fsck a forcibly unmounted local filesystem and potentially suffer file corruption. Remote filesystems gracelessly dropped create problems for the remote server to deal with.

"Filesystem Busy" Resolution

Rather than forcing your system to unmount a busy filesystem, take the time to track down the processes or users still using those resources.

Under both Red Hat and Solaris, you can invoke the fuser command on the relevant filesystem name to get a list of processes currently requiring its presence. You might be surprised to find that your own shell is the obstacle; make sure that you are not currently *in* the filesystem that you are trying to unmount!

The fstab and vfstab Files

It would be awfully tedious and time-consuming to make sysadmins manually mount all filesystems manually every time the system rebooted. From laziness (and perhaps a sense of efficiency) is born automation. Recall the rc scripts mentioned in Chapter 1, "Startup and Shutdown," that take care of mounting routine filesystems (local, pseudo, and network) at boot-time. The rc scripts must get a list of these filesystems from somewhere, though.

On Red Hat, the relevant file is /etc/fstab; on Solaris, it is /etc/vfstab. Although both have the same basic function, their formats are quite different. Note that all lines beginning with a # are comments.

What's This "tab" File Business?

As with most "<something>tab" files, the "tab" is short for *table*. fstab, therefore, is the filesystem table file—it contains information about filesystems in tabular form. vfstab is the virtual filesystem table—a mild naming-convention difference that makes cross-platform sysadmin so interesting.

Also note that, as we have mentioned before, not all the entries in the [v]fstab must be mounted at any given time. This means that you can make entries for filesystems that you might want to regularly mount but not have come up on when the system boots (it's just a matter of setting the right options in the table file).

Red Hat: /etc/fstab

Note: We added the comment lines at the beginning of this file listing for the sake of clarity.

#device #to mount #	mount point	FS type	mount options	dump frequency	fsck pass
LABEL=/	/	ext2	defaults	1	1
LABEL=/boot	/boot	ext2	defaults	1	2
/dev/fd0	/mnt/floppy	auto	noauto,owner	0	0
none	/proc	proc	defaults	0	0
none	/dev/pts	devpts	gid=5,mode=620	0	0
/dev/hda3	swap	swap	defaults	0	0
/dev/cdrom	/mnt/cdrom	iso9660	noauto,owner, kudzu,ro	0	0
bsdserver:/accounting	/accounting	nfs	rw,nosuid,nodev	0	0

The first field lists the local device name or remote filesystem to be mounted. Notice that pseudofilesystems have "none" in this field.

The second field lists the local mount point (which is also the mounted filesystem's local name). Notice that swap has "none" in this field.

The third field lists the filesystem type/instance. See the earlier table on filesystems currently supported by Red Hat.

The fourth field lists mounting options for the filesystem. These allow you to control read and write privileges, setuid bit honoring, and other performance- and security-related settings. Some recommended settings include these:

- **noauto**—Do not mount the filesystem unless specifically invoked (i.e. mount -a will not mount it).

- **nodev**—Do not honor any device files in the filesystem. This is a security precaution.

- **noexec**—Do not execute any binaries in the filesystem. This is another security precaution that should be used with care (and not on an application server's application-service filesystems).

- **nosuid**—Do not honor any setuid or setgid permission bits on any files in the filesystem. This is a security precaution that should be used with care; the filesystem containing the kernel, local password-changing binaries, and other critical programs should not have this option set.

- **usrquota**—Enable user-based quotas (for ext2 filesystems only).

- **grpquota**—Enable group-based quotas (for ext2 filesystems only).

- **ro**—Mount the filesystem read-only. This is a security precaution that is not useful on filesystems that users need to write to (including home filesystems and tmp space).

For recommended remote filesystem mount options, see Chapter 13.

The fifth field lists how often dump should back up the filesystem. A value of "0" means that the filesystem is either not dumped at all or is dumped by some other method.

The sixth field lists the order in which fsck checks and corrects filesystem inconsistencies at boot time. A value of "0" means that the filesystem is not checked at all and must

3

FILESYSTEM ADMINISTRATION

be checked manually if there is a problem. Note that network-based filesystems are never checked by `fsck`. Red Hat recommends that the root filesystem be assigned a value of "1" so that it is checked first and that all other filesystems be given a value of "2." All filesystems with the same field value are checked in parallel, if possible.

Although filesystem quotas are not indicated in the /etc/fstab file, they still need to be enabled for each filesystem that you want regulated via `quotaon`. Note that `quotaon` is called automatically at boot time via `rc` files but can be invoked manually when first setting up quotas on a filesystem.

Solaris: /etc/vfstab

```
#device                      device               mount   FS      fsck  mount    mount
#to mount                    to fsck              point   type    pass  at boot  options
#
/proc                        -                    /proc   proc    -     no       -
fd                           -                    /dev/fd fd      -     no       -
swap                         -                    /tmp    tmpfs   -     yes      -
/dev/dsk/c0t0d0s0            /dev/rdsk/c0t0d0s0   /       ufs     1     no       -
/dev/dsk/c0t0d0s3            /dev/rdsk/c0t0d0s3   /space  ufs     1     yes      -
/dev/dsk/c0t0d0s1            -                    -       swap    -     no       -
linuxserver:/research/data   -                    /mnt    nfs     -     yes      nodev,
↪noexec,nosuid
```

The first field lists the local device name or remote filesystem to be mounted.

The second field lists the raw device that is passed to `fsck`. Note that this option is not available under Red Hat and is only applicable to local filesystem instances. Entries for which this field is not applicable should contain "-".

The third field lists the local mount point (which is also the mounted filesystem's local name). Notice that swap has "-" in this field.

The fourth field lists the filesystem type/instance. See Table 3.6 for filesystems currently supported by Solaris.

The fifth field lists the order in which `fsck` checks and corrects filesystem inconsistencies at boot time. A value of "-" means that the filesystem is not checked at all and must be checked manually if there is a problem. Note that network-based filesystems are never checked by `fsck`. All filesystems with the same field value are checked in parallel, if possible.

The sixth field lists whether the filesystem should be mounted at boot time.

The seventh field lists mounting options for the filesystem. As mentioned in the last section, these options allow you to control read and write privileges, setuid bit honoring, and other performance- and security-related settings. Some recommended settings include these:

- **nosuid**—Do not honor any setuid or setgid permission bits on any files in the filesystem. This is a security precaution that should be used with care; the filesystem containing the kernel, local password-changing binaries, and other critical programs should not have this option set.
- **quota**—Turn on full quota management for the filesystem.
- **ro**—Mount the filesystem read-only. This is a security precaution that is not useful on filesystems that users need to write to (including home filesystems and tmp space).

Again, for recommended remote filesystem mount options, see Chapter 13.

So, How Do [v]fstab and mount Work Together?

1. Through the `rc` files. At boot time, the system checks the [v]fstab file for both local and remote mount specifications.

2. At manual invocation of `mount`. If you call `mount` with just a filesystem name ("`mount /space`"), the system will first check if there is a related entry in [v]fstab. If so, the appropriate device will be mounted with the options given in [v]fstab. If not, the system will complain about either a missing mount point or a missing entry in the filesystem table file. Note that `mount -a` will mount all entries in [v]fstab, if possible.

Space Management

As mentioned before, there is really only one way to enforce space usage limitations within a filesystem: set quotas. Red Hat allows you to set quotas either by user or by group. Solaris limits you to setting user quotas only.

Be aware that these settings are done on a per-filesystem basis. Although this gives you good granularity for space allocation across different storage areas, it also means that you must assign and maintain quotas across all those areas. A user with no quota assigned for a given filesystem may use as much space as is available with no limits.

> ### Tips for Handling Quotas
>
> Your user creation scripts or procedures should add a default quota for the new user.
>
> Disks with quotas should have quota checking enabled at boot time. This can be configured in [v]fstab.
>
> Your user-deletion scripts should remove quotas. Unused quota entries add overhead to each disk write operation.

Quota Guidelines

Here are a few guidelines to keep in mind when setting quotas:

- Define the goal for your use of quotas. Are you trying to prevent the disk from getting filled up by errant processes or mailer loops? Or are you trying to precisely divide out disk space, making sure that everyone gets the same-size slice of the pie?

    This is a balancing act: If you dole out disk space exactly, you are likely to leave large portions unused when users are under their usage limit. This is, of course, not a problem until you realize that there is often quite differential usage among users—some (legitimately) need a great deal of space, while others don't. Strict rationing can cause resource starvation for no reason.

- Are most of your users disk space–intensive? Will your users immediately use their entire quota or do they keep fairly minimal files on the system? General entropy (and our observations) suggests that eventually all available space will be filled, but you will need to monitor the system to find out the rate at which this occurs. This affects what kind of quotas you set and also how often you need to ask for more disk space (and how much).

- Do users have access to write to system-critical areas? The answer here should be "No," but in case it isn't (for whatever reason), consider setting a fairly stringent quota for all users with access to the area. That way they won't damage system performance by filling up a filesystem.

- Set quotas on *all* user-accessible filesystems. Though it might seem like overkill, every user should have a quota on every filesystem that they can access. This is especially important in space bill-back situations when users or departments must pay for the space they consume. If users can write to areas other than their own home filesystems, they might (intentionally or not) have files scattered and unaccounted for.

We recommend that, at the very least, you set user quotas to three-fourths of the partition size (perhaps slightly more if the partition is solely dedicated to the user in question). This will help cap runaway processes and also alert both users and admins when usage is nearing capacity.

- Use caution when assigning quotas to system accounts (such as root). In fact, system accounts should not have quotas. Should you run into some pressing need, though, remember that if root can't write any more files, the system is going nowhere after a while.

Quota Definitions

You can limit two things by filesystem quotas: block usage (file space) and inode usage (number of files). Respectively, these prevent users from filling up too much space or hoarding too many inodes when both have a finite limit.

There are also two kinds of limit: *soft* and *hard*. The soft limit is the actual quota that the user is assigned, whether of blocks or of inodes. When the user has reached or surpassed this limit, the user has a preset *grace period* in which to lower usage (or get a quota boost from the sysadmin). After the grace period expires, the user will no longer be able to create new files. This might mean that the user can no longer log in, can no longer send or receive email, or other such unfortunate consequences. In fact, if a user reports one of these dilemmas, be sure to check quota usage before panicking about a deeper systemic problem.

The hard limit represents the absolute ceiling of resources that the user may consume within the grace period allotted. If there is no grace period, the soft limit effectively becomes the hard limit. We recommend a grace period of between three and seven days and a sensible margin of space between the soft and hard limits (this will vary, depending on your specific disk space, user pool, and applications).

Red Hat

Quotas are available by default with the ext2 filesystem. To enable quotas for a filesystem (listed in /etc/fstab) called /space, do the following:

1. Become root.
2. `mount /space`.

3. Add "usrquota" and/or "grpquota" to the "mount options" column of the /etc/fstab entry for /space.

4. touch /space/aquota.user /space/aquota.group

5. chmod 600 /space/aquota.user /space/aquota.group

6. quotacheck -auvg. (Note: This will produce some "truncation" error messages. This is okay.)

7. Now you may add quotas for users on /space.

To set quotas for an individual user on a Red Hat system, you can use the command-line setquota or the interactive command edquota. Note that setquota can also be used to reset the grace period's expiration time.

When invoked, edquota reports on current usage on all filesystems that have quotas currently turned on. When edquota valjean is run, it brings up the following information with vi or your shell's current EDITOR environment variable. Simply edit the numbers to the right of the various "=" signs to set new limits:

```
Edit block and inode quota for user valjean:
Device /dev/hda1 (/space):
Used 2567KB, limits: soft=50000 hard=51000
Used 80 inodes, limits: soft=1000 hard=2000
```

Editing the informational statistics will have no effect on actual usage.

To check valjean's current space usage in all filesystems with quotas turned on, invoke quota -v valjean:

```
[linux:25 ~]quota -v valjean
Disk quotas for user valjean(24601):
    Filesystem blocks   quota   limit   grace   files   quota   limit   grace
     /dev/hda1      0   50000   51000               0    1000    2000
```

The usage numbers should only be considered fully accurate if the quotacheck command is run on the filesystem of interest first. See the man page for more details.

If valjean does not have quotas set on any filesystem, you will see a message like, "Disk quotas for user valjean(24601): None".

Solaris

Quotas are also available by default with the ufs filesystem. To enable quotas for a filesystem (listed in /etc/vfstab) called /space, do the following:

1. Become root.

2. mount /space.

3. `touch /space/quotas`

4. `chmod 600 /space/quotas`

5. Add "quota" to the "`mount options`" column of the /etc/vfstab entry for /space.

6. `/usr/sbin/quotaon /space`

7. Now you may add quotas for users.

To set quotas for an individual user on a Solaris system, you can use the interactive command `edquota`. Note that `edquota -t` can be used to reset the grace period's expiration time.

When `edquota valjean` is run, it brings up the following information with vi or your shell's current `EDITOR` environment variable. Again, all filesystems that currently have quotas turned on are displayed. Simply edit the numbers to the right of the various "=" signs to set new limits:

```
fs /space blocks (soft = 50000, hard = 51000) inodes (soft = 1000, hard = 2000)
```

Users with a UID greater than 67,108,864 cannot be assigned quotas under Solaris.

To check valjean's current space usage in all filesystems with quotas turned on, invoke `quota -v valjean`:

```
[sun:25 ~]quota -v valjean
Disk quotas for valjean (uid 24601):
Filesystem     usage  quota  limit    timeleft  files  quota  limit    timeleft
/space         2543   50000  51000              75     1000   2000
```

Again, these usage numbers should only be considered fully accurate if the `quotacheck` command is run on the filesystem of interest first. See the man page for more details.

If valjean does not have quotas set on any filesystem, you will see a message like, "no disk quota for valjean (uid 24601)".

For both Red Hat and Solaris, to make quotas take effect, `quotaon` must be run at each boot. This is done automatically via the boot-time `rc` files after the steps just outlined are completed.

Filesystem Space Monitoring

Now that you know how to invoke mounts both automatically and manually, you need to know how to query the system for its current filesystem mount status. On both Red Hat and Solaris, use the `df` command. The `-k` option makes all sizes to be reported in kilobytes (Kb):

```
[linux:17 ~]df -k
Filesystem          1k-blocks      Used       Available      Use%     Mounted
```

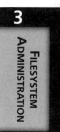

```
on
/dev/hda4          11179696   1381344   9230456      14%    /
/dev/hda1             31079      3485     25990      12%    /boot

[sun:17 ~]df -k
Filesystem           kbytes      used     avail  capacity   Mounted on
/dev/dsk/c0t0d0s0   6191949   4845981   1284049      80%    /
/proc                     0         0         0       0%    /proc
fd                        0         0         0       0%    /dev/fd
mnttab                    0         0         0       0%    /etc/mnttab
swap                 576368        16    576352       1%    /var/run
swap                 576464       112    576352       1%    /tmp
/dev/dsk/c0t0d0s3   7995933      9623   7906351       1%    /space
```

Notice that Solaris displays information about pseudofilesystems, whereas Red Hat does not.

Red Hat also supports the "-i" option for df; it reports statistics about the filesystem's inode usage:

```
[linux:18 ~]df -i
Filesystem           Inodes    IUsed     IFree    IUse%   Mounted on
/dev/hda4           1419840    79243   1340597      6%    /
/dev/hda1              8032       26      8006      1%    /boot
/dev/hda1              8032       26      8006      1%    /mnt
```

There's also a command that allows you to examine and summarize disk usage by directory rather than filesystem: du. When passed the "-k" option, du will present its usage report in kilobytes (Kb).

Normally, du will recurse and print space usage information for every subdirectory. To simply present a *summary* of all file and subdirectory space usage under the directory specified, use the "-s" option.

For example, to see the space usage of all top-level directories in /usr, the command might look like this:

```
[linux:20 ~]du -ks /usr/*
88828     /usr/bin
4         /usr/dict
4         /usr/etc
40        /usr/games
120       /usr/html
```

```
19948    /usr/include
3996     /usr/kerberos
285016   /usr/lib
2264     /usr/libexec
66344    /usr/local
48       /usr/man
5132     /usr/sbin
392388   /usr/share
102200   /usr/src
0        /usr/tmp
79568    /usr/X11R6
```

But to see the total summary usage for /usr, leave off the wildcard:

```
[linux:21 ~]du -ks /usr
1045904 /usr
```

Notice that when /usr is also its own filesystem, df -k will give you equivalent usage information.

One final tool, quot, is offered only by Solaris. This handy command summarizes filesystem usage by user, whether or not quotas have been turned on. It also allows admins to get a true picture of who is using what space, regardless of how it is scattered among directories in the filesystem. The following shows using quot to report on disk-space used, the number of files extant, and the users who own them for all mounted filesystems:

```
[sun:26 ~]quot -af
/dev/rdsk/c0t0d0s0 (/):
3380940 58973   root
1258565 63506   bin
42709    681    daemon
 8746    179    lp
  186     11    adm
    9      8    javert
    6      6    eponine
    5      5    fantine
    2      6    nobody
    1      1    valjean

/dev/rdsk/c0t0d0s3 (/space):
 7678    834    javert
 1961      4    root
```

For more on space-monitoring considerations and method, see the second half of Chapter 23, "Requirements Analysis and Performance Monitoring."

3

FILESYSTEM
ADMINISTRATION

Removable Storage Media

Just to keep things really interesting, not all devices on a system are "fixed"—that is, some support removable media. So, although the media reader may be permanently mounted in the system chassis, the presence of the media itself is not guaranteed. Some of the most common removable media types include these:

- Floppy disks
- ZIP disks
- CD-ROM, CD-R/RW
- DVD-ROM, DVD-R/RW
- Hard disks

The variable nature of the media introduces a few wrinkles to managing these devices. Removable media devices were designed with an eye to near–real-time management; in a nutshell, this means that you won't have to reboot every time you want to swap a CD or floppy. By the same token, the system configuration that you have at boot-time might not be the same one that you keep until shutdown.

In a workstation environment, this means that users must have the capability to mount new media on the system (remember that only root has had mount capability until now). Instead of having to indiscriminately hand out the root password, admins can instead run a *volume manager daemon* to handle these details.

On Red Hat, this daemon is part of the kudzu package. On Solaris, this daemon is called vold. In both operating systems, the volume manager is installed and activated by default.

Under Solaris, once vold is in command of a device, the sysadmin cannot control that device using standard UNIX commands until vold has been disabled.

Adding Swap Files

If you find that you didn't allocate enough swap space during the initial partitioning, or if you neglected the swap partition entirely, don't despair! You can always allocate more swap space in the form of *swap files*. Red Hat and Solaris handle this task in different ways, however.

Something that they have in common, though, is that swap files are intended to be temporary augmentations and, as such, can't be easily added to the system's boot-time configuration. Also note that swap files are accessed through a filesystem, thus slowing I/O times and performance.[33]

To add a swap file under Red Hat, follow these steps:[34]

1. Use dd to create a file of desired swap size.[35] The following command will create a file called swapfile in the local directory with a size of 256MB:

   ```
   dd if=/dev/zero of=swapfile bs=1024000 count=256
   ```

2. Invoke mkswap with no options to actually set up the swap file:

   ```
   mkswap swapfile
   ```

3. Call sync with no arguments to flush filesystem buffers.

4. Invoke swapon to notify the system that the new swap space is available:

   ```
   swapon swapfile
   ```

As of this writing, Red Hat supports a maximum of 2Gb in a single swap file and a total of eight swap areas. To find active swap partitions and files, examine the contents of /proc/swaps.

To add a swap file under Solaris, follow these steps:

1. Use mkfile to create a file of desired swap size.[36] The following command will create a file called swapfile in the local directory with a size of 256MB:

   ```
   mkfile -v 256m swapfile
   ```

2. Invoke swap -a with the full pathname to the swapfile you just created to actually set up the swap file. Let's assume that the swapfile was created in /space:

   ```
   swap -a /space/swapfile
   ```

To view active swap partitions and files, call swap with the "-l" option:

```
[sun:19 ~]swap -l
swapfile              dev  swaplo blocks    free
/dev/dsk/c0t0d0s1     136,1      16 1049312 1003408
/space/swapfile         -        16 524272 524272
```

Best Practices

Partitioning

- Allocate two to two and a half times the size of RAM to swap space.

Filesystems

- Assign quotas to all users on all filesystems.
- Monitor space with df, du, and quot (on Solaris).

- Include meaningful comments in your /etc/[v]fstab file that document the physical devices associated with the system's logical designation (for example, above the entry for /dev/c0t1s2, add a comment that the disk is an external Fujitsu model "foo" with SCSI ID 3).

- Document the following items in a file:
  - Physical disk arrangement, including models, disk chain type and ID, and cable arrangements
  - Logical disk arrangement, including devices and filesystem names

- When complete, print the contents of the documentation file onto actual *paper* and store it in a central location (file cabinet). Remember that you don't want to lose the text file in the same disaster that ate your filesystem in the first place!

Online References

General technology term definitions: `http://whatis.techtarget.com`

Linux Documentation Project: `http://www.linuxdoc.org`

Solaris documentation: `http://docs.sun.com`

Devices:

Red Hat:

- `http://www.kernel.org/pub/linux/docs/device-list/devices.txt`
- `http://www.linuxdoc.org/HOWTO/mini/Partition/partition-2.html`

Solaris:

- `http://docs.sun.com/ab2/coll.47.11/TRANSITION/@Ab2PageView/idmatch(DEVADM-32137)`
- `http://docs.sun.com/ab2/coll.47.11/TRANSITION/@Ab2PageView/16148`

Filesystems:

General: `http://www.angelfire.com/myband/binusoman/Unix.html`

Red Hat:

- `http://www.linuxdoc.org/LDP/gs/node6.html`
- `http://www.linuxdoc.org/LDP/tlk/fs/filesystem.html`

Logical volumes: `http://www.linuxdoc.org/HOWTO/LVM-HOWTO.html`

Partitioning:

Red Hat:

- `http://www.linuxdoc.org/HOWTO/mini/Partition/index.html`
- `http://www.redhat.com/docs/manuals/linux/RHL-7.1-Manual/ref-guide/ch-partitions.html`

Solaris: `http://docs.sun.com/ab2/coll.752.2/SPARCINSTALL/@Ab2PageView/931`

RAID: `http://www.raid-advisory.com/rabguide.html`

Swap:

General: `http://www.aplawrence.com/Boot/swap.html`

Red Hat: `http://www.redhat.com/support/docs/gotchas/7.1/gotchas-71.html`

Endnotes

[1] *Filesystems will be discussed in a later section.*

[2] *Unless you have set up a special* dump-*dedicated device ahead of time.*

[3] *The other is that everything that happens in Unix is a process.*

[4] *Flat files are just plain ASCII.*

[5] *This term is sometimes shown as two words—"file system"—and sometimes as one, as we have chosen to do here.*

[6] *This means that you would expect hard disks to have filesystems but not streaming tape media.*

[7] *Hence the name "filesystem."*

[8] *Or, if you prefer, servers and non-servers*

[9] *See* `http://www.redhat.com/support/manuals/RHL-7.1-Manual/install-guide/s1-guimode-partitioning.html#S2-GUIMODE-RECOMMENDED`

[10] *See* `http://docs.sun.com/ab2/coll.47.11/SYSADV1/@Ab2PageView/idmatch(DISKSCONCEPTS-25801)`

[11] *See* `http://www.redhat.com/support/manuals/RHL-7.1-Manual/install-guide/ch-part-less.html`

[12] *Curses uses regular ANSI text to emulate graphical interfaces, including menus, selection buttons, and so on.*

[13] *See* `http://www.cse.nau.edu/~rwood/cse178/handout.html`

[14] *Data blocks refer to the physical disk locations that store the file's contents.*

[15] *Also see* `http://www.pcwebopedia.com/TERM/i/inode.html`

[16] *Note that mtime is a subset of ctime.*

[17] *Not for any particular reason. Really.*

[18] *See* `http://www.angelfire.com/myband/binusoman/Unix.html#start`

[19] *Diskless workstations are the resurgent extremely thin clients.*

[20] *Of course, backups are intended to provide this same flexibility—see Chapter 16.*

[21] *For a full definition and more details, see* `http://whatis.techtarget.com/definition/0,289893,sid9_gci284007,00.html`

[22] *GPL = Gnu Public License = copyleft. See* `http://www.gnu.org/copyleft/`

[23] *See* `http://oss.software.ibm.com/developerworks/opensource/jfs/`

[24] *See* `http://oss.sgi.com/projects/xfs/`

[25] *Not strictly true. You can serve mounted filesystems, but it's not terribly reliable or wise.*

[26] *Æleen Frisch Essential* System Administration *(the "Armadillo book"), 2nd edition, p. 47.*

[27] *RAID stands for "Redundant Array of Independent Disks" or "Redundant Array of Inexpensive Disks," depending on whom you ask.*

[28] *A good, simple discussion of the levels can be found at* `http://whatis.techtarget.com/definition/0,289893,sid9_gci214332,00.html`

[29] *Also see* `http://www.linuxdoc.org/LDP/tlk/fs/filesystem.html`

[30] *Also see* `http://docs.sun.com/ab2/coll.47.11/TRANSITION/@Ab2PageView/6617?`

[31] *And removable media—see the later section.*

[32] *As opposed to* mkfs *under Solaris, which is called on raw devices.*

[33] *Also see* `http://www.linuxdoc.org/LDP/gs/node6.html`

[34] *Also see* `http://www.meangene.com/notes/linux_swap.html`

[35] *The swap file can't have any contents but needs to have size. Hence the use of /dev/zero as the source for the* dd *operation.*

[36] *The swap file can't have any contents, but needs to have size.*

User Administration

by Robin Anderson

CHAPTER 4

Now that you have hard disks and other local devices sorted out, it's time to populate them with users.

Broadly speaking, users are the reason for the sysadmin.[1] No one hires sysadmins for the sake of their sparkling wit alone. Organizations exist to further some specific end goal, whether to offer public services, manufacture widgets, or turn a profit. Whatever the objective of the organization is, anyone using computer systems to create, deliver or interact with it is a customer of the organization—and, by extension, of the sysadmin. So, in the most fundamental sense, users are customers and customers are users.

Naturally, sysadmins must be prepared to deal with various kinds of user-related issues. The core tasks covered in this chapter involve creating and removing users.

Definitions: Identity, Entity, Capability

Authentication and Authorization

When you log in and perhaps receive a cheery greeting addressing you by name, it is natural to feel that the Operating System has recognized you and is placing itself personally at your service. Of course, nothing of the sort has happened. Operating Systems are programs and, like all programs, operate in an internal world of symbolic constructs, which have meaning only in the context in which the program is used. You, the reader, are *not* a part of that world of symbolic constructs. In fact, even another program might not be a part of the same world of constructs, although the two programs might communicate data and instructions.

Because the Operating System can have no conception of a "user" outside its own internal universe of constructs, the only way that you (or any entity external to the program) can be identified to the system is through such an internal construct. This construct, for instance, could be a seven-field record in the /etc/passwd file or an instance in the Kerberos database. Here, constructs used for this purpose are called *identities*. The process by which the external entity is enabled to use a particular identity is called *authentication*. Authentication, then, is the means by which an entity external to the Operating System is enabled to interact with the system through an identity internal to the system. The entity still has no meaning within the system beyond its interaction through the identity.

Normally, the identity construct is standardized throughout the system. The /etc/passwd file is a list of such identities, each with the same structure of seven fields of information. One of those fields, the password hash field, is actually used in the authentication process. Each identity is an instance of that general seven-field structure.

If the system makes any pretense whatsoever of being secure, then there are limitations on what can be done within the system through a given identity. Such limitations may be defined through traditional Unix file ownership and permission settings or through some other mechanism, such as access control lists. When an instruction is given to the system through an identity, the system must determine whether the instruction is within the set of instructions permitted that identity. This process is called *authorization*.

In the standard Unix world, then, the external entity (you, the user) is authenticated as an identity recognized by the system. This process often involves the password field of one of the records in the /etc/passwd file. When the authentication has been performed, other fields in the identity instance defined by that particular record are used to determine the capabilities and limitations of that identity. In Unix, these would be the user-id and group-id fields, used in conjunction with file ownership and permission settings.

In mathematical language, authentication is the mapping of an external entity to a particular identity in a set of identities recognized by the system. Authorization is the mapping of an identity to a subset of the set of all the capabilities offered by the system.

Figure 4.1 illustrates the processes of authentication and authorization in a system.

FIGURE 4.1

Entity-identity-capability relationships.

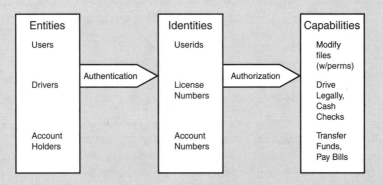

As Figure 4.1 illustrates, this model applies to many systems, even some that do not exist entirely within computers. Your driver's license number, for instance, is the key by which your state police determine whether you may legally drive. Additionally, when cashing a check, the license number is often copied onto the check. It serves as an identity with certain associated attributes (your name and home address) that are accepted as authorization to cash the check.

Another common example is the ATM card. A bank's computers have no idea who or what you are, but you can use your ATM card and PIN to authenticate yourself through an account number that the system *does* recognize. That account number (and, hence, anyone working through it) is authorized to manipulate funds in your account in various ways.

The previous model can be used to frame discussions of system security. A hacker might use a buffer overflow attack to bypass authentication completely and gain control of a process (a root shell) authorized for all the capabilities of the system. To gain access in the future, a hacker's first action upon gaining such control is to add new records to the /etc/passwd file. This creates new identities to which the hacker can authenticate. Commonly, one of the attributes of these identities is a UID of 0, authorizing the identity for the same capabilities as those held by root.

Please note also that some identities, such as bin, exist solely for use by the Operating System itself. These identities usually have locked passwords making direct authentication impossible. Access to these identities is available only from other identities authorized for full system privileges. In such cases, the system might be considered as the entity that ultimately maps to the identity.

A good high-level approach is to consider a user as an "entity," an abstract structure with specific characteristics or attributes associated with it. The most critical attributes are traditionally stored on the local machine in the /etc/passwd file (more on passwd entries in a moment).

It's important to note that these "entities" are commonly called a number of different things, including accounts, logins, and users.[2] You're also likely to find redundant combinations of these terms ("user account login" is a sententious favorite).

As an admin, you need to be aware that a user is not necessarily an individual person. Ideally, for authentication and accountability, every account would have a one-to-one mapping with an individual owner. But in some environments, shared accounts are considered the only practical way to accomplish certain tasks. This means that multiple people know the password associated with one username. We'll discuss authentication in Chapter 7, "Authentication," but for now, let's refine our definition of a user: A user is an entity that can own files and execute programs on a local system.[3]

Storing Basic User Information Locally

There are many options for maintaining user information. This section addresses common methods of storing such information directly on the local system that will use it.

/etc/passwd

As mentioned earlier, the simplest (and most critical) user information is stored in a local /etc/passwd entry. These seven fields define how the system views and interacts with the user. Here is the reference user's entry:

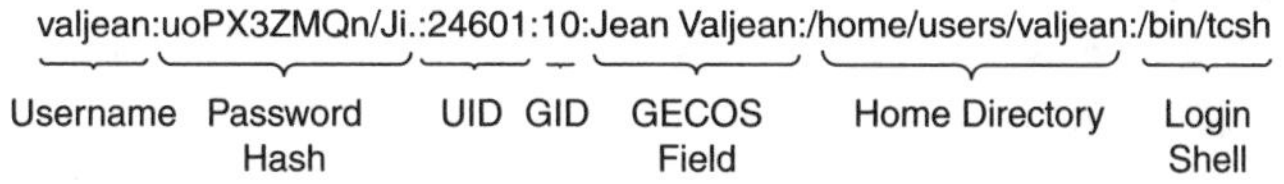

FIGURE 4.2

Diagrammed /etc/passwd entry.

valjean:uoPX3ZMQn/Ji.:24601:10:Jean Valjean:/home/users/valjean:/bin/tcsh

| Username | Password Hash | UID | GID | GECOS Field | Home Directory | Login Shell |

The format of /etc/passwd is the same under both Red Hat and Solaris. Notice that the fields are separated by a colon (:). This is very useful when writing automation scripts.

The first field contains the entry's username.[4] In the example, this is valjean. Usernames are mainly a human-friendly label for numeric UIDs (the third field), but they are directly used at login. Usernames are supposed to be unique on the local system; if there are duplicates, the first matching entry is the one used during login.

Standard Unix usernames must be a minimum of one character long and must have a maximum length of eight characters.[5] Permissible components include alphanumeric (a–z, A–Z, 0–9) characters and the period (.), hyphen (-), and underscore (_) characters. Forbidden characters include the colon (:) (because it is the field separator) and newline (\n) (because it is the entry delimiter). Remember that Unix is case-sensitive. For example, the letters *a* and *A* are distinct.

The second field contains what is often (mistakenly) referred to as the user's encrypted password. It is actually the output of a one-way hash function that takes the plain-text password as input (more on this in Chapter 7). This field is always 13 characters long and is composed of alphanumeric (a–z, A–Z, 0–9) characters, a period (.), and a forward-slash (/). In the example, the string uoPX3ZMQn/Ji. is the password hash.

Two characters have a special significance when they appear alone in this field. If a * appears, it indicates that the user is locked out or that an alternate authentication method, such as Kerberos, is being used. If an x appears, it indicates that shadow passwords are

4

USER ADMINISTRATION

being used on the system (see the later section "/etc/shadow"). If the field is empty, it means that the user has no password set.[6]

The third field contains the UID, the user's identification number for the local system. In our example, this is 24601. This is the second unique identifier for an account. UIDs are used in a file's inode (see Chapter 3, "Filesystem Administration") to indicate ownership, so if UIDs collide, *all* users with the same numeric designation can access the file. It's interesting to note that if usernames collide but have different UIDs, logins will occur under the first entry (and, thus, the first UID). But files can still be owned by the second UID. Cursory examination (with `ls -la`) would seem to show those files as being owned by the collided username.[7]

UIDs in the range 0–99 (inclusive) are typically reserved for system accounts. UID 0 is assigned to root and whatever other super-user-level accounts exist on the system. The maximum UID on a system is generally one less than the system's maximum unsigned integer value.[8]

The fourth field contains the GID, the user's default/primary group identification number for the local system. In our example, this is 10. This number is not intended as a unique identifier, but as a membership indicator. Groups are assigned names and further membership information in the /etc/group file (see the next section, "/etc/group"). As mentioned before, all files have user *and* group ownership information stored in their inodes. By default, all files created by the user will be group-owned by that user's default login group.

The fifth field has an interesting history to it. It is variously known as the GECOS or GCOS field.[9]

> **Note**
>
> GECOS is an acronym for the General Electric Comprehensive Operating System. The OS lost its first vowel to a corporate buyout and became GCOS (no "Electric"). The quirk is that Bell Labs, the birthplace of Unix, used GCOS machines for print spooling. Naturally, the company wanted some way to associate GCOS identification information with the Unix user using the service. Of course, critical attributes are stored in /etc/passwd, so a new field was born.

The field is still used to hold the user's personal information, including full name, phone numbers, and so on. In our example, only the user's full name is included in the field: Jean Valjean. A number of standard programs, such as finger, look for this information when invoked. Users can modify this field under Red Hat with `chfn` and under Solaris with `usermod -c <comment info>`. Be aware, though, that these commands are compatible only with *local* user information storage.

The sixth field contains the full path to the user's home directory. In our example, this is /home/users/valjean. This is the directory that the user automatically logs into on the system, and that contains various environment control and other user files. The base path is site-dependent, although it is common to see the terms *users* or *home* somewhere in it.

Caution

If the home directory specified in this field does not exist on your system or is unavailable at the time of the user's login, the user should receive an error message similar to the following:

```
No directory! Logging in with home=/
```

The users *will* be allowed to log in, although obviously without access to their personal files. Users are not granted any particular rights in this directory, but it is still unwise to allow this to continue. There might be broader problems on the system that need to be fixed.

The seventh and final field specifies the user's login shell. In our example, this is /bin/tcsh. Note that this is simply the program that gets executed when the user successfully logs into the system; it does not have to be a valid interactive shell.[10] A wide variety of shells are included or can be compiled for Red Hat and Solaris.

Site-approved shells should be listed with fully qualified path names in the file /etc/shells. Many applications, including standard ftp, check this file for the validity of a user's shell before granting access.

Caution

If the shell specified in this field does not exist on your system, then the user should receive an error message similar to the following:

```
No shell
```

The user then should be logged out. It's always a good idea to verify that this is actually the default behavior on your system.

Technical

Red Hat Shadow Utilities

The *shadow-utils* package is now included with Red Hat. If you have not already installed it on your system (most likely by selecting the Use Shadow Passwords option during install), you should go back to your distribution site or CD and install it now. The commands and components discussed here and in the shadow/gshadow section that follows are installed from this RPM.[11]

Caution

You should not install the *shadow-utils* RPM if your site relies on PAM or Kerberos authentication mechanisms or if your site uses NIS or LDAP for user information distribution.[12]

The `pwck` tool is very useful for checking /etc/passwd for consistent file formatting.[13] The `pwck` command checks for the following for each entry:

- Correct number of fields
- Existence, composition, and uniqueness of the username
- Existence and uniqueness of the user UID
- Existence of the default GID, and whether it appears in /etc/group
- Existence of the home directory
- Existence and executability of the login shell

Note that this tool does not *fix* the problems; it just reports the errors that it encounters.

Of course, it takes more than creating a simple /etc/passwd entry to correctly populate a system with users. The necessary steps are covered later in this chapter, in the section "Creating Accounts."

/etc/group

As mentioned before, /etc/group contains group name and membership information, providing the second half of the user/group file ownership pair. Here is a sample /etc/group entry:

```
mizusers::10:valjean,javert,bob
```

The format of /etc/group is the same under both Red Hat and Solaris. Notice that, as in /etc/passwd, these fields are separated by a colon (:).

The first field contains the group's name. In our example, this is mizusers. Group names are required to be unique, but they have more strict composition constraints than usernames: They may consist of only lowercase letters and digits.

The second field contains the (optional) group password hash. In the example, no password is set. When the field is empty, it means that nonmembers are never allowed to switch to the group. Conversely, when a password hash is specified, *any* user who knows the password can switch to the group and access files that it owns.

On a Red Hat system, if this field contains !, it indicates that shadow groups are being used on the system (see the later section "/etc/gshadow").

The third field contains the group GID, which *must* be less than 65,535. In our example, the GID is 10. For compatibility reasons, the Solaris man page encourages admins to set GIDs to 60,000 or less, where possible.

As with UIDs, it is prudent to make all GIDs unique. But in some circumstances it might be useful to have distinct group names share a GID.[14] When this happens, the file's group ownership (as shown by `ls -la`) will be listed as the first group name in /etc/group. But because file ownership is assigned and stored by number rather than name, all members of all groups with the given GID will be able to access the file.

The fourth and final field contains a comma-separated list of users who belong to the group. In our example, this is the string `valjean,javert,bob`. Note that this does not necessarily mean that this is the *default* group for the users listed; it just means that they can access group-owned files.

Be careful that no stray whitespace is inadvertently added anywhere in the entry; that kind of bad formatting causes programs that use this file to simply stop reading. This means that they keep the incomplete data that they have and simply skip over the rest— definitely not desirable behavior.

Technical

The system-wide default for the maximum number of groups to which a single user may belong[15] is 16 (this includes both local and remote groups). Users belonging to more than this number of groups will be restricted to only their default login group until the admin brings them back under the limit. We have also seen other, more ambiguous symptoms of this problem, including mysterious login denials. The system's behavior when limits are exceeded is not always well defined.

4

USER ADMINISTRATION

Some useful user-level commands for dealing with groups include:

- **groups**—Lists *all* the groups to which the specified user belongs.
- **newgrp**—Allows users to switch to the specified group. The command invokes a new shell and sets the specified group as the current file group owner default. Note that if a group has a password set, *any* user that has the password can switch to the group (not just members).
- **chgrp**—Allows a file's owner to change its group ownership, though only to a group to which the owner belongs.[16]

Some useful admin-level commands for managing groups include:

- **groupadd**—Adds a new group entry to /etc/group
- **groupmod**—Modifies the entry for a pre-existing group
- **groupdel**—Deletes a group entry from /etc/group

The key group-management tool, though, is grpck. An analog to pwck, grpck analyzes /etc/group for consistent file formatting.[17] The grpck command checks for the following for each entry:

- Correct number of fields
- Existence, composition, and uniqueness of the group name
- Existence, composition, and uniqueness of the group GID
- Whether all users appear in /etc/passwd
- Whether any users belong to more than the maximum number of groups allowed by the system
- Whether any username appears more than once in a single group entry
- Whether the entry itself exceeds 512 characters

Again, note that this tool does not *fix* the problems; it just reports on the errors that it encounters.

/etc/shadow

You might wonder why we are going to talk about yet another file in /etc when we've already covered how information is stored locally for file ownership and logins. The reason is that the contents of /etc/passwd—especially the password hashes—are stored insecurely. Any system user can read /etc/passwd, so any system user can copy out and attack the password hashes (more on this and why it's a problem in Chapter 7). Here is a standard listing of an /etc/passwd file:

```
[sun:10 ~] ls -l /etc/passwd
-r--r--r--   1 root     sys            1103 Apr 11 16:43 /etc/passwd
```

Remember that even root must have an entry in this file, so its password hash is vulnerable, too.

So why leave /etc/passwd world-readable? Because legitimate programs—including `ls`—access the file to translate common items such as UIDs to human-friendly usernames. A secret /etc/passwd file would break a lot of expected functionality.

The solution is not to cloak /etc/passwd, but to provide an alternate, secure repository for the sensitive bits of a user's information. Enter /etc/shadow, also known as "the shadow file."

The shadow file does not *replace* /etc/passwd, but supplements its functionality and security. It takes password hashes out of the public domain and stores them with other internal system information in a file that only root may access. Here is a standard listing of an /etc/shadow file:

```
[sun:11 ~] ls -l /etc/shadow
-r--------   1 root     sys             697 Apr  5 11:03 /etc/shadow
```

Note that although the default permissions are root-read-only, the admin can set them otherwise. Of course, this would defeat the major purpose of the shadow file, so keep an eye out for erroneous permissions.

Components

Shadow files have nine fields per entry and correlate to /etc/passwd solely by username. Our reference user's entry might look something like Figure 4.3.

FIGURE 4.3
Diagrammed /etc/shadow entry.

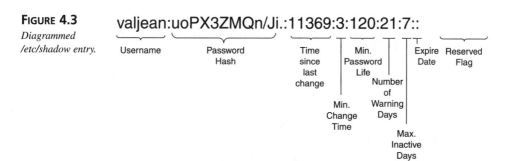

The format of /etc/shadow is the same under both Red Hat and Solaris. Notice that, as in /etc/passwd and /etc/group, the fields are separated by a colon (:).

The first field contains the entry's username. Again, this is the field that matches the shadow entry to the passwd entry. In our example, this is valjean.

The second field contains the password hash with the characteristics described in the previous section on /etc/passwd. In our example, the password hash is "uoPX3ZMQn/Ji.".

If this field is empty, it means that there is no password set for the user.[18] As in /etc/passwd, if a * appears in this field, it indicates that the user is locked out or that an alternate authentication method, such as Kerberos, is being used.

The third field contains the number of days between the epoch (January 1, 1970) and the date on which the password was last modified for this user. In our example, the number of days is 11,369, which means that valjean's password was last changed on February 16, 2001.

The fourth field contains the minimum number of days required between password changes. This is generally set so that users cannot get around certain password-changing requirements (such as having to select a different password every 120 days) by complying and then immediately reverting back.

If this value is set too high, users might be unable to legitimately change their passwords without contacting a sysadmin. Many sites choose not to use this feature; setting the value to 0 effectively disables it.

The fifth field contains the maximum number of days that the password will be valid on the system.[19] In the example, valjean's password is good for 120 days.

When there is a nonzero value in this field, the system is said to have "password aging" enabled. When a password has aged past the limit, the account is automatically locked and the user must contact a sysadmin to regain access.

The sixth field contains the number of days before password expiration that the user is warned. Just to show that Unix is not an unreasonable operating system, this field allows admins to notify users *before* their passwords expire. It's a good idea to make this a long time period if your users do not log in regularly but you enforce password aging.

Under Red Hat Linux, the seventh field is the number of days to wait before disabling an account after the password expires. Under Solaris, the seventh field contains the number of days of inactivity allowed for the user. In our example, valjean would be allowed only a seven-day hiatus under Solaris, after which his account will be automatically locked.

The eighth field contains the expiration date (expressed in days since January 1, 1970) for the *account* (not just the password). The end result is the same as if the password had aged past its limit: The account is automatically locked.

The ninth and final field contains a flag that is reserved for future use. It currently has no effect on the system, but it is recommended that the field be left blank.

Technical

We mentioned earlier that /etc/shadow is generated from /etc/passwd. The command that performs this task on both Red Hat and Solaris is pwconv. It takes no arguments and performs the following tasks:

- Checks for the existence of /etc/shadow and creates it, if necessary.

For a new /etc/shadow file:

- Creates a new entry for each user
- Adds username, password hash, and password aging information (if any) to the new entry
- Updates the Time Since Last Password Change field

For a pre-existing /etc/shadow file:

- Checks for x in the second field of each user's /etc/passwd entry. If it is found, the user's password hash in /etc/shadow will not be modified.
- Adds entries for users that appear in /etc/passwd but not /etc/shadow. Adds username, password hash, and password aging information (if any) to new entry.
- Removes entries for users that appear in /etc/shadow but not /etc/passwd.
- Updates the password hash, password aging information, and Time Since Last Password Change field for each remaining entry.

Let's look at an example conversion with our reference user to bring it all together:

Original /etc/passwd entry:

```
valjean:uoPX3ZMQn/Ji.:24601:10:Jean Valjean:/home/users/valjean:/bin/tcsh
```

After pwconv, there are two entries. Here's the modified one in /etc/passwd:

```
valjean:x:24601:10:Jean Valjean:/home/users/valjean:/bin/tcsh
```

And here's the new one in /etc/shadow:[20]

```
valjean:uoPX3ZMQn/Ji.:11369::::::
```

You might have noticed that there are a lot fewer numbers in this shadow entry than in the example shown in Figure 4.3. That is because we didn't have any password aging information stored in the /etc/passwd file.

Two steps are involved in setting all possible password aging and inactivity fields. The first step is to modify the template files used at conversion time by pwconv. The second step is to issue the usermod command to set the inactivity lockout. Of course, on either one you can always edit /etc/shadow manually after the account has already been created or converted (although this should be considered a measure of last resort).

On Red Hat systems, /etc/login.defs contains the default values to be applied to all user accounts. Three variables set the parameters for password aging on the system: PASS_MAX_DAYS, PASS_MIN_DAYS, and PASS_WARN_AGE. For valjean to have the setting shown in Figure 4.3, the settings would appear in the file as follows:

```
PASS_MAX_DAYS 120
PASS_MIN_DAYS 3
PASS_WARN_AGE 21
```

To add the further restriction of maximum inactive days, invoke the usermod command, like so:

```
usermod -f 7 valjean
```

Solaris, on the other hand, keeps password aging information in its own file: /etc/default/passwd. The pertinent parameter names are MINWEEKS, MAXWEEKS, and WARNWEEKS. For valjean to have the setting shown in Figure 4.3, the settings would appear in the file as follows:

```
MINWEEKS=1
MAXWEEKS=17
WARNWEEKS=3
```

Note

Notice that Solaris forces you to use weeks for time units. Of course, this means that you cannot set minimum aging time to anything less than seven days (unless you set it to 0). You also are constrained to make your maximum password lifetime 119 days (17 weeks) instead of 120.

Again, to add the further restriction of maximum inactive days, invoke the usermod command, like so:

```
usermod -f 7 valjean
```

Notice that this value is specified in days, even under Solaris.

Now the /etc/shadow entry for valjean looks like our earlier example:

```
valjean:uoPX3ZMQn/Ji.:11369:3:120:21:7::
```

Red Hat provides a convenient and intuitive way to back out of shadowed password architecture: pwunconv. This command is not available under Solaris. pwunconv parses through the entries in /etc/shadow and updates the password hashes for corresponding usernames in /etc/passwd. Any entries that exist in /etc/passwd but not in /etc/shadow are left unchanged by this command. After a successful run, pwunconv removes /etc/shadow. Be aware that pwunconv will lose some password aging information.

/etc/gshadow

Red Hat also offers the capability to shadow group entries in /etc/gshadow. This would be useful if you have groups on your system with non-null passwords.

Entries in the /etc/gshadow file consist of four colon-separated fields and function in much the same way as generic /etc/shadow files:

```
groupname:password_hash:<admin-list>:<user-list>
```

The first field contains the entry's group name. This is the only field that matches the shadow entry to the /etc/group entry.

The second field contains the password hash with the characteristics described in the previous section on /etc/passwd.

The third field is a new one. It contains a comma-separated list of users designated as admins for the group. Group-admins are allowed to change the group's password and membership.[21]

The fourth field is analogous to the last field in /etc/group. It contains a comma-separated list of users who belong to the group.

Red Hat offers three shadow-group management commands that, for obvious reasons, are not available under Solaris: gpasswd, grpconv, and grpunconv.

The gpasswd command gives some group control to the group-admins designated in the third field just described. It allows admins to add and delete group members and to change the group password.

The group-related analog of pwconv is grpconv. This command also requires no arguments and performs the same tasks. For each entry in /etc/group, it creates a corresponding entry in /etc/gshadow, correlated by group name. If the group-shadow file already exists, grpconv simply updates the password hashes as appropriate.

As you can probably guess from the name and its password-related analog, grpunconv acts kind of like grpconv in reverse. It parses the entries in /etc/gshadow and updates the password hashes for corresponding group names in /etc/group. Any entries that exist in /etc/group but not in /etc/gshadow are left unchanged by this command. After a successful run, grpunconv removes the source file, /etc/gshadow.

4

USER ADMINISTRATION

passwd, Revisited

The passwd command with the right switch lets you view items of interest from the local /etc/shadow file.[22] Under Red Hat, the switch is -S. Under Solaris, the switch is -s. Why they don't match is unclear; neither has a case-sensitive opposite switch in its syntax.

Be aware that if you don't have password aging information set, you will get very different output from what we are about to describe.[23] The output in those cases can be rather off-putting.[24]

Root can use this command to generate a report about any (or all) users. The output has six whitespace-separated fields:

- Username
- Password status
  - PS—Valid password is set
  - LK—Password is locked, and user cannot log in
  - NP—No password is set.[25]
- Date of last password change (in mm/dd/yy format)
- Minimum number of days required between password changes
- Maximum number of days password is valid
- Number of days relative to Maximum before the password expires and the user will be warned

When run for valjean, we get the following output:

```
valjean PS 02/16/01 3 120 21
```

This summary translates as follows:[26] The user valjean has a valid password that was last changed on February 12, 2001. This password must age at least three days before being changed again, but it is valid only for a maximum of four months (120 days). This user will get a notice 21 days before the password expires and his account is locked.

Sharing User (and Other) Information over the Network

Local user information and password storage are important, but these are really just the beginning. When your installation grows beyond 10 or 20 machines, it grows increasingly more difficult to maintain synchronization across all of them.

There are a number of network-based information sharing mechanisms that can extend the function of /etc/passwd and /etc/shadow beyond the local system. Be aware, though, that once these basic systems are in place, they are frequently used for more than just user information synchronization.

rsync, rdist, cfengine

A number of tools that admins use for file distribution also can be employed to keep password, group, and shadow files synchronized.

The `rdist` program handles remote file distribution and is something of an old standby. Admins can maintain a central control file and distribution tree. rdist performs file comparisons and full file copies when updates are required. It relies on either `rcmd` or `rsh`.

A faster and more flexible alternative to `rdist` is `rsync`. The critical difference between the two is that `rsync` uses *file deltas*—that is, it sends only the *differences* between two sets of files over the network. This results in lower bandwidth consumption and greater speed. Thus, `rsync` is ideal for synchronizing large directories of files that either change infrequently or change only in small ways. You also have the choice of using either `rsh` or `ssh` as `rsync`'s transport.

Consider a real-world application of `rsync`: keeping nameserver zone files synchronized across multiple, redundant DNS servers. With a normal, `scp`-based network copy (even over 100Mb lines), transfer time for a few thousand large files could take between 10 and 15 minutes per run. Using `rsync`, the transfer time could be reduced to something like three minutes per run. This is a major step toward keeping data up to near–real-time accuracy.

The most secure and flexible method of all broadly useful synchronization mechanisms is `cfengine` (especially when run over `ssh`). This program can compare files based on contents, ownership, timestamp, and checksum. It can also copy, link, and even directly edit files. If you are intrigued, you can read more about cfengine in Chapter 19, "Automation."

NIS (Nod to NIS+)

Covering NIS in any detail is beyond the scope of this book. As always, we are trying to prepare sysadmins for any new environments that they might encounter, but in a breadth-first manner.

Definitions

The Network Information Services (NIS) protocol is probably the most common method of sharing user information and passwords. Because it provides such a tidy infrastructure, it is also used to centralize and disseminate other information. NIS is an RPC-based protocol that was originally developed by Sun under the name Yellow Pages (YP). Because this turned out to be a trademark infringement,[27] Sun changed the package's name to NIS, but many of the commands that we will look at use the old yp prefix.

NIS+ is Sun's follow-up to NIS, offering enhanced scalability, security, and various administration functions. Although some sites use NIS+, it is not nearly as widespread as its predecessor, so we will not be detailing how to set up a NIS+ environment.

NIS Architecture

NIS is designed to use a (slightly modified) client/server model. There must be a master server for the NIS domain (more on that in a moment).[28] Now the sysadmin needs to make a design decision: Should all clients query the master server directly, or should there be more than one host available to answer queries? If you have a small number of clients or are not a network information-intensive site, you might need only one master server. Most sites, though, opt to add what are known as "slave servers" (or sometimes "secondary servers") to the environment.

Slave servers get all their information directly from the master server and store it on their own local disks. They can then share the information with clients, thus taking some of the load of the master and providing a failover in case of disaster.

Clients do not store NIS data locally, but they send out a query every time they need information. When a client selects a server to connect to for information queries, the process is called "binding."

FIGURE 4.4

NIS modified client/server model.

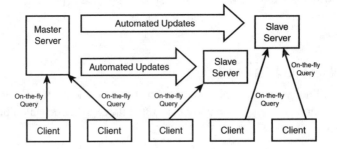

Flat Files and Maps

Sun's original intention in designing NIS was to replace *all* files in /etc with information served in a scalable network-based environment. As such, Sun also elected to replace the plain ASCII text files—or *flat files*—with ndbm-style database files—or *maps*—because database files are much easier to index and retrieve information from. Generally two database files correspond to each flat file. This is because database files must be indexed by a particular kind of value, or *key*. Each key requires that the database it indexes be organized in a particular way for optimal data retrieval, so the two database maps are each optimized for retrieval by a different key.

Table 4.1 shows the relationship between standard /etc flat files and NIS maps.

TABLE 4.1   NIS Maps and Flat Files

Local Flat File	Purpose	NIS Map Name	NIS Map Key
/etc/bootparams	Associates servers and full path to key partitions for diskless clients	bootparams	—
/etc/ethers	Associates Ethernet addresses to hostnames	ethers.byaddr	Ethernet address
		ethers.byname	Hostname
/etc/group	Associates group names and members	group.bygid	GID
		group.byname	Group name
/etc/hosts	Associates IP addresses to hostnames	hosts.byaddr	IP address
		hosts.byname	Host name
/etc/aliases or /etc/mail/aliases	Associates mail aliases to system usernames	mail.aliases	Alias
		mail.byaddr	System username/ mail address
/etc/netgroup	Associates sets of hosts or users into logical groups	netgroup.byhost	Hostname
		netgroup.byuser	Username
/etc/passwd /etc/group /etc/hosts	Associates UIDs with GIDs for particular host or associates a host with a logical group	netid.byname	Username

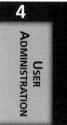

4

USER ADMINISTRATION

TABLE 4.1 continued

Local Flat File	Purpose	NIS Map Name	NIS Map Key
/etc/netmasks	Associates netmasks with local subnets	netmasks.byaddr	IP address
/etc/networks	Associates network names with network numbers/IP addresses	networks.byaddr networks.byname	Network number/IP address Network name
/etc/passwd and /etc/shadow	Provides auditing and hidden password information for C2 clients	passwd.adjunct.byname	Username
	Provides /etc/passwd entries	passwd.byname passwd.byuid	Username UID
/etc/protocols	Associates network protocol names and numbers	protocols.byname protocols.bynumber	Protocol name Protocol number
/etc/rpc	Associates RPC names and numbers	rpc.bynumber	RPC number
/etc/services	Associates network service names, ports, and transport method	services.byname services.byservice	Ports and transport methods Service name
/var/yp/binding/ <domain>/ ypservers	Provides authorized NIS server hostnames	ypservers	—

For maps that get frequent use, NIS enables you to specify a shortened "nickname" for the map. Both Red Hat and Solaris offer the same stock nicknames and store them in the same location:

```
[root@linux ~]# cat /var/yp/nicknames
passwd          passwd.byname
group           group.byname
networks        networks.byaddr
hosts           hosts.byname
protocols       protocols.bynumber
services        services.byname
aliases         mail.aliases
ethers          ethers.byname
```

Of course, you can add other map nicknames or change the ones provided.[29]

Philosophy

From a user administration perspective, the purpose of NIS is to minimize the number of iterations that must occur for any given change to take full effect across all systems. With a centralized management architecture, such as the one provided by NIS, the sysadmin only has to make the change in one location and then rebuild the maps and let them propagate across all slave and client systems. This greatly simplifies the admin's life.

Also, when there is a single authority for user and other information, all systems and users know where to get reliable information.

Almost any information can be transformed into a NIS-servable map, although the standard maps generally prove sufficient at most sites. In fact, many of the standard maps go unused and can be disabled.[30]

To set up NIS at your site, you must select a domain name. By default, on Red Hat and Solaris, the DNS domain name is assumed to be the same as the NIS domain name. This is dangerous from a security perspective because *anyone* who knows the NIS domain name can bind to it[31]—that is, anyone can request information from the server and receive responses for your site.[32] Attackers often rely on just this sort of information-gathering technique, so it's wise to block it, if possible. So, set your NIS domain name to be a short phrase with mixed-character cases (domains are case-sensitive) that does not correspond to your site's DNS domain name.

Remember that there are consequences to losing NIS service once your infrastructure is dependent on it. Users might not be able to log in or even authenticate for remote email services; host IP lookups and access rights might not be resolvable. That's why, if you decide to move to a NIS environment, it's critical to have sufficient redundancy in the way of slave servers.

The potentially ephemeral nature of NIS is one of two reasons to never have root's user information and password served over NIS: root would be unable to log in without network/NIS capability. Single-user logins would not work, either, if there were no local root entry. The other reason is security: the password hash is communicated over the network in the clear by default. It's scary enough having user password hashes on the wire; keep root's off.

The next three sections describe NIS on a master, on clients and on slaves, in that order. Configuring the master server is discussed first because, without it, you would have no NIS environment. Slave servers are addressed last because they must be configured as NIS clients before taking on service duties.

Setting Up a NIS Master Server

The first step in deploying NIS is to select a machine to be the master server. It's generally wise to use dedicated servers, but it's not always possible. In the case of NIS, it's important to keep the core flat files away from the general user population. Let your NIS master be a machine that doesn't support general user logins, although perhaps it could provide file or other non–login-related services. Also make sure that the machine can handle the overhead of updates and propagations, especially in change-rich environments.

Because NIS servers (whether masters or slaves) are likely to need access to the information they are serving out, they will have to be clients (though probably of themselves).

Also be aware that NIS relies on RPC services to function. This means that if you need to offer NIS, you cannot lock down `portmapper/rpcbind` and the RPC-based services on the master and slave servers. Clients do not need to offer RPC service; they just need to be capable of interacting with them from the other side.

The key service daemons that must run on the master server are listed in this table.

Daemon Name	*Service Provided*
portmap (Red Hat)	Routes incoming RPC requests
rpcbind (Solaris)	
Ypserv	Works as the main NIS server process
Ypbind	Serves as the client binding daemon
Ypxfrd	Works as the direct map transfer daemon
yppasswdd (Red Hat)	Facilitates password changes
rpc.yppasswdd (Solaris)	
rpc.ypupdated (Solaris only)	Facilitates changes based on other maps

First create the NIS domain; otherwise, your domain will literally be set to `"(none)"` on Red Hat and `""` on Solaris. Use `domainname` with the string that you want for your NIS domain, like so:

```
domainname WiLdRuMPus
```

Check that this worked by calling `domainname` with no arguments. You should see the string that you just entered.

Although the rest of the basic commands for this process are the same under both operating systems, we consider each separately because they respond in slightly ways.

Red Hat

The server portion of NIS is available with the Red Hat 7.1 distribution, although it might not be installed by default.[33] Check your media for the RPM ypserv-1.3.11-13.1386.rpm. Once these tools are available, you can begin configuring your NIS master server.

Verify that the domain name will survive a reboot by checking for its existence in the file /etc/sysconfig/network. Now enter the command /usr/lib/yp/ypinit -m. You will be queried for the hostnames of other NIS servers (slaves). Enter the hostnames that you plan to use for NIS slaves, even if the machines are not yet configured for it. Notice that the server being initialized is automatically included in the list.

The following is our first run at initializing the NIS master:

```
[root@linux ~]# /usr/lib/yp/ypinit -m

At this point, we have to construct a list of the hosts which will run NIS
servers. linux.my.site.com is in the list of NIS server hosts.  Please continue
to add the names for the other hosts, one per line.  When you are done with the
list, type a <control D>.
        next host to add:  linux.my.site.com
        next host to add:
The current list of NIS servers looks like this:

linux.my.site.com

Is this correct?  [y/n: y]
We need some minutes to build the databases...
Building /var/yp/ WiLdRuMPus /ypservers...
Running /var/yp/Makefile...
gmake[1]: Entering directory '/var/yp/WiLdRuMPus'
Updating passwd.byname...failed to send 'clear' to local ypserv: RPC: Program
➥not registered
Updating passwd.byuid...failed to send 'clear' to local ypserv: RPC: Program not
➥registered
Updating group.byname...failed to send 'clear' to local ypserv: RPC: Program not
➥registered
Updating group.bygid...failed to send 'clear' to local ypserv: RPC: Program not
➥registered
Updating hosts.byname...failed to send 'clear' to local ypserv: RPC: Program not
➥registered
Updating hosts.byaddr...failed to send 'clear' to local ypserv: RPC: Program not
➥registered
Updating rpc.byname...failed to send 'clear' to local ypserv: RPC: Program not
➥registered
Updating rpc.bynumber...failed to send 'clear' to local ypserv: RPC: Program not
➥registered
```

```
Updating services.byname...failed to send 'clear' to local ypserv: RPC: Program
➥not registered
Updating services.byservicename...failed to send 'clear' to local ypserv: RPC:
➥Program not registered
Updating netid.byname...failed to send 'clear' to local ypserv: RPC: Program not
➥registered
Updating protocols.bynumber...failed to send 'clear' to local ypserv: RPC:
➥Program not registered
Updating protocols.byname...failed to send 'clear' to local ypserv: RPC: Program
➥not registered
Updating mail.aliases...failed to send 'clear' to local ypserv: RPC: Program not
➥registered
gmake[1]: Leaving directory '/var/yp/WiLdRuMPus'
```

Aside from all the failures, it's important to note where some key files are assigned to
live. The directory /var/yp/WiLdRuMPus was created to hold the various database-format
maps that are associated with this NIS domain. Notice that there is a makefile in /var/yp.
This is the makefile invoked when maps are updated later.

Now why didn't the build work? Because we didn't have the requisite RPC service available to talk with the processes here. Now that you know what a typical NIS server error
looks like, let's try it again—this time, though, we'll run the ypserv process first:

```
[root@linux ~]# /usr/sbin/ypserv
[root@linux ~]# /usr/lib/yp/ypinit -m
```

```
At this point, we have to construct a list of the hosts which will run NIS
servers.  corylus.ucs.umbc.edu is in the list of NIS server hosts.  Please
continue to add the names for the other hosts, one per line.  When you are done
with the
list, type a <control D>.
        next host to add:  linux.my.site.com
        next host to add:
The current list of NIS servers looks like this:

linux.my.site

Is this correct?  [y/n: y]
We need some minutes to build the databases...
Building /var/yp/WiLdRuMPus/ypservers...
Running /var/yp/Makefile...
gmake[1]: Entering directory '/var/yp/WiLdRuMPus'
Updating passwd.byname...
Updating passwd.byuid...
Updating group.byname...
Updating group.bygid...
Updating hosts.byname...
Updating hosts.byaddr...
Updating rpc.byname...
Updating rpc.bynumber...
```

```
Updating services.byname...
Updating services.byservicename...
Updating netid.byname...
Updating protocols.bynumber...
Updating protocols.byname...
Updating mail.aliases...
gmake[1]: Leaving directory '/var/yp/WiLdRuMPus'
```

Sweet success!

Now to make the server its own client, just invoke ypbind without any options. This allows ypbind to read from the local /var/yp/ypservers file generated during the initialization with the data that you entered. If more than one hostname appears in that file, the list is processed sequentially until a server answers.

The configuration process also registered the service through Red Hat's chkconfig utility. This means that all the necessary symbolic links in the /etc/rc[0–6].d/ hierarchy pointing to /etc/init.d initialization files were correctly made. So, our configured NIS services will survive rebooting. See the man page for chkconfig for more details.

Solaris

Unsurprisingly, Solaris comes with all NIS-related commands and utilities installed by default. The creation process is also a little more verbose. We already set the domain name for the machine, but that value will disappear on reboot unless it is stored manually in /etc/defaultdomain. When this is done, we can go right into the master initialization:

```
[sun:12 root ~]/usr/sbin/ypinit -m

In order for NIS to operate successfully, we have to construct a list of the
NIS servers.  Please continue to add the names for YP servers in order of
preference, one per line.  When you are done with the list, type a <control D>
or a return on a line by itself.
        next host to add:  solaris.my.site.com
        next host to add:  ^D
The current list of yp servers looks like this:

ensis.ucs.umbc.edu

Is this correct?  [y/n: y]

Installing the YP database will require that you answer a few questions.
Questions will all be asked at the beginning of the procedure.

Do you want this procedure to quit on non-fatal errors? [y/n: n]
OK, please remember to go back and redo manually whatever fails.  If you don't,
some part of the system (perhaps the yp itself) won't work.
The yp domain directory is /var/yp/WiLdRuMPus
```

There will be no further questions. The remainder of the procedure should take 5
to 10 minutes.
Building /var/yp/WiLdRuMPus/ypservers...
Running /var/yp /Makefile...
updated passwd
updated group
updated hosts
updated ipnodes
make: Warning: Don't know how to make target `/etc/ethers'
Current working directory /var/yp
updated networks
updated rpc
updated services
updated protocols
make: Warning: Don't know how to make target `/etc/netgroup'
Current working directory /var/yp
make: Warning: Don't know how to make target `/etc/bootparams'
Current working directory /var/yp
/var/yp/WiLdRuMPus/mail.aliases: 3 aliases, longest 10 bytes, 52 bytes total
/usr/lib/netsvc/yp/mkalias /var/yp/`domainname`/mail.aliases
➥/var/yp/`domainname`/mail.byaddr;
updated aliases
updated publickey
updated netid
/usr/sbin/makedbm /etc/netmasks /var/yp/`domainname`/netmasks.byaddr;
updated netmasks
couldn't find /etc/timezone
updated auto.master
updated auto.home
couldn't find /etc/auth_attr
couldn't find /etc/exec_attr
couldn't find /etc/prof_attr
updated user_attr
couldn't find /etc/audit_user
make: Warning: Target `all' not remade because of errors
Current working directory /var/yp
*** Error code 1
make: Fatal error: Command failed for target `k'
Error running Makefile.

solaris.my.site.com has been set up as a yp master server with errors. Please
rememberto figure out what went wrong, and fix it.

If there are running slave yp servers, run yppush now for any data bases
which have been changed. If there are no running slaves, run ypinit on
those hosts which are to be slave servers.

Notice that this worked although we did not run ypserv first.

Also notice that the initialization was successful in spite of the errors. The "Warning: Don't know how to make target <filename>" and "couldn't find <filename>" errors occurred because the flat files needed to create the standard NIS maps do not exist on our reference system.

As under Red Hat, the directory /var/yp/WiLdRuMPus was created to hold the domain's maps.

Again, to make the server its own client, first run ypserv and then invoke ypbind without any options. Under Solaris, the server names for this example are stored in the file /var/yp/binding/WiLdRuMPus/ypservers.

Although Solaris does not have a chkconfig analog, all the necessary services will be started on reboot by checks performed automatically by initialization scripts.

Setting Up NIS Clients

Before setting up a client, you need to gather a bit of information from your server(s). The hostname command will tell you how the server refers to itself, both locally and over NIS. NIS requests that use anything other than the hostname as returned by hostname will fail.[34]

As before, the proper domain name must be set on the machine before proceeding.

Red Hat

Setting up a basic NIS client on a Red Hat box is very straightforward. Red Hat's "Canned Answer Number 191"[35] basically outlines the following steps:

1. Run /usr/sbin/authconfig as root. This launches a curses-based interface.
2. Enable NIS from the menu.
3. Enter the domain and server information. Remember that the domain name is case-sensitive. Remember to specify the server name as presented by the hostname command there.
4. Continue through authconfig without any further changes.

When authconfig exits, it automatically starts the appropriate services (and registers them with chkconfig as well). It also sets up appropriate entries in the /etc/nsswitch.conf file (more on that in a moment).

Solaris

You might be tempted to think that all that is required to set up a NIS client under Solaris is to invoke ypinit with a different command-line option. In fact, this is only one of two steps necessary to configure NIS to run properly on a client machine.

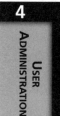

First, issue the command `ypinit -c` to set up the initial client configuration. The system will ask you to specify a list of NIS servers in order of query precedence. Note that all these hosts must have entries in your local /etc/hosts file.[36]

Second, edit /etc/nsswitch.conf, the Name Service Switch file. This file tells a system where it should look for user and various kinds of other information. Sources include local flat files (usually in /etc), local databases, network-based databases (NIS, LDAP, DNS), and potentially others. Both Solaris and Red Hat use this file.

Information types may have more than one lookup source, specified in search order. The basic format of entries in the file is as follows:

```
<information type>: <information source> [<action>] [<information source>
[<action>]]
```

You can specify what action the program executing the lookup should take after checking each information source. Here are two sample lines:

```
passwd: files nis [notfound=return] nisplus
hosts:  files nis dns
```

The first entry tells you that when you look up a user's passwd entry, you check local flat files first. This is important because local users (including root) would get overlooked otherwise. If the entry is not found in the local file, you automatically continue the search in the next information source (in this case, NIS). The `[notfound=return]` directive means that if the lookup fails because the user is not in the NIS `passwd` map, the search ends. However, if the lookup fails because NIS is unavailable at the time, the search continues in the NIS+ maps. [37] This process holds for network-based information sources other than NIS and NIS+ as well, including LDAP. In fact, you may specify any or all as successive information sources in nsswitch.conf entries.

There are three ways that evolved to ensure that both `passwd` and `group` entries are searched in the order *local, network-based-source.*

The original (now deprecated) way is to append to each local flat file a special string that tells the system to append all entries from the equivalent network-based map. This is a holdover from before the advent of nsswitch.conf, when the only network-based source for `passwd` and `group` was NIS. The special string consists of either a lone + or +:::::::.[38] With the second syntax, you can modify imported field values. For instance, if you wanted all NIS-based users to use the /usr/local/bin/zsh shell locally, you would modify the + entry like so: +:::::::/usr/local/bin/zsh.

The introduction of the nsswitch.conf file allows the admin to specify network-based sources other than NIS for passwd and group queries. Neither the new file nor its keywords obviated the need to use the original special string in the local flat files, however.

In fact, other than introducing new information source keywords, most early implementations of nsswitch.conf made little difference to existing system configurations.

The newer `compat` keyword for nsswitch.conf introduces a compatibility mode that removes the need for both the special string and the keyword pair `files nis`.[39] It specifies that lookups search local files first and, if unsuccessful, then queries NIS maps. The major benefit of `compat` mode is that it allows admins to keep all search specifications within one system file. See the man page for nsswitch.conf for more details.

The second entry in our example describes the procedure for looking up hostnames and IP addresses. You first look in the local flat file; then, if you don't find the answer, you proceed to check the NIS `hosts.byname` or `hosts.byaddr` maps (as appropriate to the request). If this, too, is fruitless, you resort to a DNS lookup. This is generally the last measure because it can have relatively high overhead and wait times.

Entries can be much more complex, specifying things such as timeouts, compatibility specifications, and so on.

Solaris provides a number of suggested templates for different primary information sources. Take a look at /etc/nsswitch.nis (NIS as the primary mechanism), /etc/nsswitch.files (local files, ignoring NIS), and /etc/nsswitch.ldap (LDAP as the primary mechanism).

The Solaris man page is especially rich with examples and detailed options. If you need to implement information lookups in a very precise manner, or if you need to juggle a lot of options, we recommend looking at them for reference.

Setting Up NIS Slave(s)

Again, although slave servers are optional, they are highly utile in large or heavy-request environments. Also, if you have multiple subnets[40] at your site, then you must have some sort of NIS server on each one. This can be done via multiple NIC cards on one server, or it can be handled by deploying multiple servers. For the purposes of illustration, we will be setting up NIS slaves on separate machines.

A system destined to be a slave server must first begin life as a client; it needs to communicate with the master server and enumerate its maps. When your client is stable and functioning normally,[41] you may issue the following command:

```
ypinit -s <master-name>
```

Again, remember to provide the proper form for the master server's hostname, both on the command line and in /etc/hosts.

Slave servers can bind either to themselves or to the master server. Just set the order that you prefer in the slave's local `ypservers` file.

Now go back to the master server and make a few modifications to ensure that the new slave server receive updates properly. The purpose of updates, of course, is to keep the maps stored locally on the slave server current. First, add the new server's hostname information to the `ypservers` file on the master server.

Next, make sure that master map updates will be propagated automatically. On Red Hat, edit /var/yp/Makefile and comment out the line containing `NOPUSH="True"`.[42] On Solaris, automatic updates are the default behavior.

Now, to manually invoke an update on Red Hat, do the following:

```
cd /var/yp
make
```

This rebuilds the map files from the flat source files and then calls `yppush` to send the new maps to the slave servers.

On Solaris, just invoke the `ypmake` command with no arguments to do the same tasks.

Caution

Do *not* manually make/update NIS maps on any machine except the master server. Doing so just asks for file corruption and mass confusion.

NIS provides a mechanism for high-speed map transfers called `ypxfr`. The master server must be running `ypxfrd` (which Red Hat and Solaris NIS masters do by default), and the slave server must be able to invoke `ypxfr`. This is the mechanism tried by default, but if it is unavailable for any reason, the older, slower method is used without any loss of data integrity.

If the slave is offline when an update happens, it will not get the new maps until the master initiates *another* update. Because you don't know how frequently maps might be updated, you don't know that the slave is keeping up-to-date. To alleviate this uncertainty, put entries in the slave server's root `crontab` to run `ypxfr` periodically. On Red Hat, that would be as follows:

```
10 *     * * *    /usr/lib/yp/ypxfr_1perhour
20 3     * * *    /usr/lib/yp/ypxfr_1perday
55 3,18 * * *    /usr/lib/yp/ypxfr_2perday
```

On Solaris, it would look like:

```
10 *     * * *     /usr/lib/netsvc/yp/ypxfr_1perhour
20 3     * * *     /usr/lib/netsvc/yp/ypxfr_1perday
55 3,18 * * *     /usr/lib/netsvc/yp/ypxfr_2perday
```

Note that the scripts are run at times a little off the hour and half-hour marks (in case other jobs are being started at those popular times).

As you can see by the script names invoked, NIS designers *planned* to have these kinds of updates run periodically. The `ypxfr_1perhour` script requests only updates of the most volatile map: `passwd`. The `ypxfr_1perday` script updates the (presumably) least volatile maps: `group`, `protocols`, `networks`, `services`, and `ypservers`. Finally, `ypxfr_2perday` handles medium-volatility maps: `hosts`, `ethers`, `netgroup`, and `mail`.

Notice that there is no overlap in the maps being updated. That's why you want to run *all three* scripts. You can also add any extra maps that your site uses, change maps to more or less frequent updates, and even delete maps that your site doesn't use.

NIS now offers a new security-related feature to help prevent unauthorized map transfers: the /var/yp/securenets file.[43] Requests for map transfers are first checked against the hosts listed in the file. Red Hat includes this file by default, but Solaris does not. In Red Hat's default configuration, all hosts are allowed to request maps, but this can be easily modified.

Entries may have one of two formats:

```
<netmask> <IP address>
```

or

```
host <IP address>
```

This allows the admin to restrict access by subnet or specific host.

Of course, if you don't remove the `0.0.0.0   0.0.0.0` entry at the end of `securenets`, the rest of the configurations will be meaningless.

When you add or delete entries from /var/yp/securenets, you must also restart both `ypserv` and `ypxfrd`.

Useful Commands

The following are useful user-level NIS commands and options not already covered:

- **ypwhich**:
  - No options—Lists the NIS server you are bound to
  - `-m`—Lists the master NIS server for all domain maps

4

USER ADMINISTRATION

- `-m <map>`—Lists the master NIS server for the specified map
- `-x`—Lists nicknames for all domain maps
- **ypmatch <key> <map>**—Displays the entry associated with the specified key in the specified map.
- **ypcat**:
- `<map>`—Displays all values in the specified map
  - `<map>| grep <item>`—Searches for the specified item entry in the specified map
  - `-k <map>`—Specifically enumerates both the keys and the values (if any) in the specified map
- **yppoll**:
  - `<map>`—Lists the domain, order number, and master server for the specified map

Now, let's take a look at the output of a few of these commands when performing common tasks. Note that the output for all these commands is very similar on both Red Hat and Solaris, so we will present output only from one box.

First, let's find out to which server we are currently bound:

```
[sun:2 root ~]ypwhich
sun.my.site.com
```

Next, let's see what map nicknames the domain offers:

```
[sun:3 root ~]ypwhich -x
Use "passwd" for map "passwd.byname"
Use "group" for map "group.byname"
Use "project" for map "project.byname"
Use "networks" for map "networks.byaddr"
Use "hosts" for map "hosts.byname"
Use "ipnodes" for map "ipnodes.byname"
Use "protocols" for map "protocols.bynumber"
Use "services" for map "services.byname"
Use "aliases" for map "mail.aliases"
Use "ethers" for map "ethers.byname"
```

Now let's see if there is a user called sendak in the `passwd` map:

```
[sun:4 root ~]ypcat passwd | grep sendak
```

Because the return answer was whitespace (or null), we know that sendak is not in the map.

Let's look for a known user; we'll try valjean:

```
[sun:7 root ~]ypcat passwd | grep valjean
valjean:uoPX3ZMQn/Ji.:24601:10:Jean Valjean:/home/users/valjean:/bin/tcsh
```

Now notice that although this is a shadowed system *locally*, valjean's password hash appeared in the lookup. This is because, by default, the /etc/passwd and /etc/shadow files are merged when building the `passwd` maps.[44] There are ways around this, but they go beyond what we cover here (see the later section "Online References" for pointers to more material).

LDAP

The Lightweight Directory Access Protocol (LDAP) is another information-sharing mechanism that is rapidly gaining popularity. LDAP is an open standard, facilitating development and acceptance. It is even more flexible than NIS and can manage a broader range of information and data types (including standard X.500).

Like NIS, LDAP employs a modified client/server architecture. Unlike NIS, which requires full file transfers for master-slave synchronization, LDAP supports incremental information updates.[45]

Setting Up an LDAP Server

Setting up and populating an LDAP server goes beyond the scope of this book, so we are going to give it very light treatment here.

Red Hat 7.1 comes with the following RPMS that support LDAP:

- auth_ldap-1.4.7-2
- nss_ldap-149-1
- openldap-2.0.7-14
- openldap12-1.2.11-4
- openldap-clients-2.0.7-14
- openldap-devel-2.0.7-14
- openldap-servers-2.0.7-14

The two RPMs from this list that *must* be installed to set up an LDAP server are openldap-2.0.7-14 and openldap-servers-2.0.7-14.[46]

Solaris supports LDAP *clients* natively, but server support is commercial (through iPlanet's Directory Server[47]). If you want a freeware LDAP server, we recommend using OpenLDAP.

> **Note**
>
> As of this writing, the most recent stable release version is openldap-2.0.11. If you connect to `ftp.openldap.org`, you can download it from `/pub/OpenLDAP/openldap-stable.tgz`.

OpenLDAP uses the GNU-style `configure` and `make` commands, so the install is fairly quick and clean.[48]

The critical daemons for LDAP servers are `slapd` (standalone LDAP directory server) and `slurpd` (standalone LDAP replication server). Thus, the critical configuration files are slapd.conf and slurpd.conf. More information about `slapd` and `slurpd` is available in their respective man pages and at `http://www.openldap.org`.

As with most information services, the really tricky bit is in populating the databases. Even more complex is migrating from one information server type to another. The folks at OpenLDAP apparently took this into consideration and included a directory full of scripts (/usr/share/openldap/migration) that facilitate migrating from flat files to LDAP.[49]

Setting Up an LDAP Client

Red Hat's "Canned Answer Number 268"[50] addresses setting up LDAP client-side support. The key is to make sure that the nss_ldap-149-1 RPM (included with the Red Hat 7.1 distribution) is installed.

As before when configuring NIS clients, you need to call authconfig to configure the LDAP client:

1. Run `/usr/sbin/authconfig` as root. This launches a curses-based interface.
2. Enable LDAP from the menu.
3. Elect whether or not to use TLS (it's off by default).
4. Enter the server's IP information.
5. Enter the base DN—for example: `dc=example,dc=com`.
6. Continue through authconfig without any further changes

When authconfig exits, it automatically updates /etc/ldap.conf with the values you entered. It also updates nsswitch.conf entries to have `ldap` as the information database type.

LDAP client support for Solaris is provided by the SUNWlldap package. Although Solaris does not have the authconfig utility, it does provide a powerful script called /var/ldap/ldapclient. This script can initialize the system as an LDAP client based on its current configuration information. It also can restore the system back to its original state, if you would just like to test LDAP but not necessarily use it as your primary information source. Simply invoke the command and point it at your LDAP server and the client profile it serves:

```
ldapclient -P <profile name> <ldap server>
```

For a deeper discussion, see the Solaris man pages and online *LDAP Setup and Configuration Guide* from docs.sun.com.

Also remember that when you actually start relying on LDAP for information or authentication, you will need to modify the nsswitch.conf files on your systems. The stock Solaris nsswitch.conf file for LDAP support looks like this:

```
#
# /etc/nsswitch.ldap:
#
# An example file that could be copied over to /etc/nsswitch.conf; it
# uses LDAP in conjunction with files.
#
# "hosts:" and "services:" in this file are used only if the
# /etc/netconfig file has a "-" for nametoaddr_libs of "inet" transports.

# the following two lines obviate the "+" entry in /etc/passwd and /etc/group.
passwd:     files ldap
group:      files ldap

# consult /etc "files" only if ldap is down.
hosts:      ldap [NOTFOUND=return] files
ipnodes:    files
# Uncomment the following line and comment out the above to resolve
# both IPv4 and IPv6 addresses from the ipnodes databases. Note that
# IPv4 addresses are searched in all of the ipnodes databases before
# searching the hosts databases. Before turning this option on, consult
# the Network Administration Guide for more details on using IPv6.
#ipnodes:    ldap [NOTFOUND=return] files

networks:   ldap [NOTFOUND=return] files
protocols:  ldap [NOTFOUND=return] files
rpc:        ldap [NOTFOUND=return] files
ethers:     ldap [NOTFOUND=return] files
netmasks:   ldap [NOTFOUND=return] files
bootparams: ldap [NOTFOUND=return] files
publickey:  ldap [NOTFOUND=return] files
```

4

USER ADMINISTRATION

```
netgroup:    ldap

automount:  files ldap
aliases:    files ldap

# for efficient getservbyname() avoid ldap
services:   files ldap
sendmailvars:   files

# role-based access control
auth_attr: files ldap
exec_attr: files ldap
prof_attr: files ldap
user_attr: files ldap

# audit
audit_user: files ldap
project:    files ldap
```

Note how similar this really is to the NIS-style nsswitch.conf file considered earlier.

Creating Accounts

Account creation is one of the most common tasks that any sysadmin must perform. It is frequently delegated to the most junior person available. Although this is not an unreasonable approach, the sysadmin should be aware of the issues that underlie this mundane procedure.

Policy

Before we discuss the technical steps of account creation, we should give a nod to policy questions. Policy of all kinds is critical for a variety of reasons. First, it protects the admins by creating a set of standards that they can refer to when questions arise. Second, it protects the organization; if policies are created and followed, then all users get treated the same way. Third, it protects the users by clearly defining what they can expect from the organization.

It's best for all concerned that policy be written down and approved by the appropriate authorities in your organization.

Here we present some critical policy questions with regard to accounts that you should get answered *before* you start creating them. These lists are by no mean exhaustive, but they provide a good starting point.

General

- After these policies are set, who can override them?

  This is a serious question—who gets to tell you to make an exception to these rules? What kind of clearance or documentation do you need to get to do it? There are *always* exceptions, so build in a mechanism to deal with them.

- Who is allowed to have an account?

  The answer to this question is *never* "anybody." "Anybody" would include your 5-year-old cousin, my cat, and your competitor's chief engineer. Although these might all be very deserving beings, you almost certainly do not want them on your systems.

  So, do all employees get accounts, or just the ones who have a business reason to use one? Can staff members sponsor accounts for friends and relatives?

  If only certain employees are allowed to have accounts, what kind of verification/paper trail is required?

- Are there special classes of machines that have extra requirements for people to get accounts?

  Some machines might be designated as holding secure information (research, accounting information, proprietary data, and so on). What extra requirements are there for people to get accounts there? What verification/paper trail is necessary in addition to what is normally required?

Usernames and UIDs

- How are usernames generated?

  It's amazing how touchy some folks can be about their usernames. Some sites address this by allowing users to choose their own.[51] Other sites present a short list of available names for the new user to choose from, generated by a predetermined algorithm. Some sites just hand out the username, end of story.

  Because standard Unix usernames can have only eight characters, make sure that whatever selection method you choose adheres to the limit. You also must be able to handle collisions when your algorithm generates the same username for more than one entity.

  One successful algorithm spotted in the wild assigns usernames based on the first letter of the first name, up to the first five letters of the last name, and up to a two-digit number (to deal with collisions). Jean Valjean would have a username of jvalje1 under this system. If Janet Valjean came along later, her username would be jvalje2, and so on. Sun Tzu would be stzu1.

Make sure that your policy is flexible enough to accommodate users whose usernames are unsatisfactory to them for some reason. Occasionally algorithms will innocently produce obscene usernames or ones that have an unfortunate meaning in another language. Users also might want their usernames changed in the event of marriage, divorce, and other such events. Even if your policy will not allow username modifications, at least decide and document this fact beforehand.

Don't forget that programs sometimes also need usernames generated on the system. Some programs are very particular about the name they require to run properly, so make allowances for them ahead of time.

- How are UIDs generated?

Usually UIDs are just created sequentially. Again, some programs will require the UID to be set a certain way, so watch out for collisions.

Also be aware that if you mount remote file systems, you also might be importing UID collisions from *there*. This is another reason why consistency across systems is so critical (see the section on NIS in this chapter).

Groups and GIDs

- How are group names generated?

If your site relies on /etc/group, then it also relies on the sysadmins to maintain it. If users can request groups, there should be a well-known process for them to do so. Also make clear to them how groups should be named, or reserve naming rights.[52]

- What are the default groups for new users?

Most sites have a number of default groups—users, research, systems, and so on. How do you determine what default group a new user should belong to? Some sites base this on departments, others use physical location, and others use clearance level.

Again, make sure that your numbering schemas match across systems. It doesn't help you if group *names* are consonant if the GID that actually owns the files is not consistent (see the section on NIS in this chapter).

- What about additional group memberships?

Will new users generally need to belong to more than one group? Although users can have only one default group, they still might need to access other group-owned files (for example, if they are working with a number of different project groups).

- What about multiuser accounts?

Will your accounting department want to have a single account called accounting for which they all share the password? Within three weeks, you will have no idea who has that password or who is using the account. It will be almost impossible to change the password as well.

If you get such a request, find out exactly why the user wants it. More often than not, all users want to get email addressed to `accounting@my.site.com`. This can be handled through a mail alias without creating an account at all. A user's request will often reflect what the user thinks is possible rather than what that user actually needs. Make sure that you understand the difference.

Passwords

- Does your site enforce strong password characteristics?

We encourage sites to require good passwords and enforce those requirements. Make sure that you get approval before rolling out this kind of policy, however, because it might upset some of your users. Informing users ahead of time and addressing their concerns can take some of the sting out of the change for them, too.

See Chapter 7 for more on strong password characteristics and how to set them.

- Does your site require password aging?

Again, if this is a new requirement at your site, get approval and give warning.

- Does your site enforce automated account lockouts?

Automated lockouts usually stem from either idle time between logins or some number of failed login attempts. Lockouts are a security precaution, but they also can impede legitimate users and cause extra work for the sysadmin. Lockouts also can be used by a malefactor to prevent legitimate users from accessing their accounts. Weigh these things carefully before deciding.

- What kind of user information management does your site support—local only, NIS, LDAP, or something else?

Make sure that you know what kind of information systems your site uses and ensure that new users are properly entered into it.

- How do you give new users their username/password pair?

This is not as simple-minded as it first sounds. You want to be sure to hand over the new account to its rightful owner, not some potentially unauthorized third party. Emailing the information offsite and giving it out over the phone are not wise distribution methods.

4

USER ADMINISTRATION

Some sites require log entries for all accounts that are distributed. Others even require that new users read and sign the site's Acceptable Use Policy before they may access their account. Sometimes this will be handled through the organization's Human Resources department.

Make sure you know what procedures already exist, and conform to them where possible. If no procedures exist, make some and get them approved.

Other Default Settings

- What is the default home directory for new users?

  This is a question of resources. Where is there enough space to put a new user? If you have a lot of disk space, you might even divide it up into logical subdirectories (based on username or department or some other schema).

- Are there disk and file quotas for new users?

  Again, this question addresses resource distribution. If you set quotas, you might protect the other users on the disk from getting squeezed out, but you also might be impeding critical work. We generally recommend setting these limits, but it might not be appropriate for your site.

  If you do set quotas, remember to consider what might happen if all users used their maximum amount. Large quotas can give users the sense that they have plenty of room to sprawl, so they don't tidy up as much as they might otherwise do. You will probably have to strike a balance between dividing up the actual disk space evenly among users and realizing that many users will not use up all the quota they are allowed.

- What is the default shell for new users?

  Although this is a relatively minor point, make sure that you know what a good site-wide default is. Some user-friendly shells include bash and tcsh, but these are not available on some older systems. Remember, if a user's shell is not available, the user might not be able to access legitimate resources. Some sites don't allow users to change their assigned shells at all.

- Are there default "dotfiles" for new users?

  Dotfiles are files that begin with a period (.) and that usually contain resource settings for shells, login behavior, and the like. System-wide defaults might live in /etc/skel, or you might have your own site-specific storage directory. Some common dotfiles include .profile, .bashrc, .cshrc, .tcshrc, .login, and .logout.

You also might want to consider making certain prudent aliases by default, such as aliasing rm to rm -i. We are not suggesting that root should have this alias, but general users should get it by default. Although it won't stop users from accidentally deleting files, it will make it a little more difficult.[53]

It is also wise to set users' default PATH variables to have the current directory (.) at the *end* of the path.[54] Otherwise, they are pretty much guaranteed to put it at the front. Of course, root should not have . in its path *at all* (for security reasons).

- Are there any policy or help documents that users should get by default?

Some sites drop key documents into new users' home directories so that they can be easily accessed. Good candidates for this include Acceptable Use Policies, HTML files pointing to online help resources, and local tips and tricks files.

- Are there default site mailing lists?

Many sites maintain mailing lists to notify users of configuration updates, security alerts, and so on. Identify whether your site has any and to which of them users should belong by default.

- Are there any other specific default access rights for new users?

This question goes hand in hand with the one about special machine access. Are there special machines, directories, or files that new users—or certain classes of new users—should be allowed (or disallowed) to access?

Technical

It's important for sysadmins to know how to manually create accounts on their systems, especially if there isn't already a script or command to do it for them.

Creating/Enabling Users—12 Steps to a Happy Account

The following 12 steps are the core of creating users—use them as the basis for your own customized checklist. We have created a sample checklist in Appendix C, "User Creation Checklist."

Step 1: Allocate a Unique UID

Check whether your site policy has anything to say about choosing UIDs. Pick the next available UID and then verify that it is not reserved, in use, or colliding with UIDs on remote servers from which you mount filesystems.

Step 2: Choose a Default GID

Check whether your site policy has anything to say about choosing GIDs, and determine what is appropriate for this user.

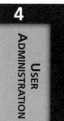

Check whether the user will need to be added to any other groups, either locally (in /etc/ groups) or remotely (as in the NIS netgroups map).

Step 3: Allocate a Unique Username

Check what your site policy has to say about generating usernames. Verify that the proposed username is not reserved or in use.

Step 4: Allocate Home Directory Space

Check what your site policy has to say about locating new user home directories. Verify that there is enough space to create the user, plus some reasonable amount of extra space for the user to create files.

Step 5: Choose a Shell

Check what your site policy has to say about selecting new user login shells. Verify that the proposed shell exists on all relevant systems and appears in /etc/shells.

Step 6: Create the /etc/passwd Entry

Use vipw to manually create an entry in /etc/passwd based on the parameters selected in the previous steps. Note that you can use any text editor for this job, but vipw performs file lock checks and prevent root's entry from being mangled.

Either keep the new account disabled or set a good password on it immediately.

Step 7: Modify /etc/group and netgroups as Necessary

Edit the /etc/group file (and netgroups, if applicable) as necessary for additional, nonde-fault group memberships for the new user. Red Hat offers the vigr command to facilitate this.

If your site uses NIS or NIS+, run ypmake to update and push out the map files. This enables you to execute chown properly later.

Step 8: Create the Home Directory

Use mkdir to create the user's selected home directory.

Step 9: Copy in Configuration Files

Check what your site policy has to say about local policy, help, and dotfiles; copy them into the user's home directory as appropriate.

Step 10: Set Quotas

Check whether your site policy has anything to say about setting quotas on home and other filesystems. Use edquota to set the values on each filesystem.

Step 11: Set Ownerships

Users need to have access to their home directory and files. Use `chown -Rh` to set user and group ownership. The switches cause `chown` to recurse down through all subdirectories but to *not* dereference any symbolic links.[55]

On Solaris, the syntax is `chown <user>:<group> <dirname>`.

Note that Red Hat supports both the previous syntax and `chown`
`<user>.<group> <dirname>`.

Step 12: Test!

Take the time to verify the new user account—it can save a lot of headaches later. Log in as the user, in the user's intended environment (where possible).

Note that you probably won't see any mail file for the user (unless you send the user email as part of your site's customizations). Nothing special is needed to enable email delivery/access for most site configurations—the file is created automagically when the user first receives mail.

Automating the Process

At this point, you must be wondering what automated tools exist to take care of such a common sysadmin task. Although there are indeed a plethora of stock automation tools, none takes care of every item outlined in the basic list of steps.

The Red Hat shadow-utils package replaces the OS-standard `adduser` command with a symbolic link to the more standard `useradd` (also supported under Solaris).

The `useradd` command is smart enough to update both /etc/shadow and /etc/passwd if you have enabled shadowing on your system.[56] It is also flexible enough to allow admins to either specify configuration parameters on the command line or accept preset defaults. Although each OS tweaks the command in extra ways, its core functions are the same:

- Selects the next unused UID greater than 100
- Sets the initial group GID, home directory, and login shell according to system default values
- Adds a new entry to /etc/passwd and /etc/shadow (if applicable)
- Creates the home directory specified in the entry
- Copies configuration files from default location into the home directory specified in the entry

4

USER ADMINISTRATION

Note that the username must be specified by the sysadmin on the command line. Except where noted here, accounts are password-locked at creation time.

Also notice that `useradd` does not set quotas or update NIS maps.

Command-line options common to both Red Hat and Solaris include these:

- `-c <comment>`—Sets the user's GECOS field to the specified string.
- `-d <home_dir>`—Sets the user's home directory field to the specified string.
- `-e <expire_date>`—Sets the account's expiration date to the specified string. Under Red Hat, the date must be specified as YYYY-MM-DD. Under Solaris, the date may be specified as MM/DD/YY or as `<monthname> <day>, <year>`.
- `-g <default_group>`—Sets the user's default login group (by group name or GID).
- `-G <group, group...>`—Grants additional group memberships to the new user.
- `-k skel_dir`—Is the system's skeleton directory. By default, /etc/skel
- `-m`—Creates the user's home directory if it doesn't already exist. Copies in dotfiles from the default skeleton directory
- `-o`—Forces the system to accept non-unique UIDs.
- `-s shell`—Sets the user's shell.
- `-u uid`—Sets the user's numeric UID.

While both Red Hat and Solaris support the `-f <inactive_time>` option, they use the value differently. Under Red Hat, this sets the number of days after a password expires until the account is permanently disabled.[57] Under Solaris, it represents the maximum number of days allowed between user logins.

By default, the version of `useradd` included with Red Hat creates a new group for every user added to the system and assigns its group name to match the username. If you pass it the `-n` option, however, this behavior is suppressed.

Red Hat also accepts the following extra switches:

- `-M`—Forces the system not to create the user's home directory.
- `-p <password hash>`—Allows the admin to specify a password hash on the command line. Without this switch, the account is locked on creation.
- `-r`—Forces the system to allow creation of an account with a UID less than 100 (that is, a system account).

Solaris offers a different set of extra command-line switches:

- `-A <authorization[,...]>`
- `-P <profile[, ...]>`
- `-R <role[,...]>`

Authorizations, profiles, and roles are special Solaris constructs that are discussed along with their defaults files in Chapter 7.

The Solaris `passmgmt -a` command performs a limited subset of user-creation tasks; it simply adds the appropriate entry to /etc/passwd (and /etc/shadow, where necessary).

System Defaults

When `useradd` is invoked with just the `-D` option, it prints out a list of current system defaults. With further command-line options, system defaults can be updated.[58]

Red Hat stores the information displayed by `useradd -D` in /etc/default/useradd.

As mentioned before, the Red Hat /etc/login.defs file tells the system where to deliver email, how to age passwords, and gives value ranges for UIDs and GIDs. The Solaris analog is /etc/default/passwd, although its purview is more strictly limited to password attributes. Either file may be updated manually, but be sure that you change values only to sensible alternatives.

The default location to store dotfiles and other configuration files on both Red Hat and Solaris systems is /etc/skel.

Solaris provides the following files by default, although we recommend modifying them before deployment:

- .profile
- local.cshrc
- local.login
- local.profile

Also note that these files are copied precisely as is; they are not renamed to more useful filenames.[59]

Red Hat provides a different set of default files, although they, too, should be modified to suit your environment:

- .bash_logout
- .bash_profile

4

USER ADMINISTRATION

- .bashrc

- .emacs

- .screenrc

As mentioned before, because these standard automation tools do not do everything on the provided checklist, many sites choose to script their own solutions. The important thing to remember when you are doing this sort of scripting is to perform sufficient error checking (something that the stock tools tend to have built in). The optimal solution is probably a combination of standard and local tools; build your own shell wrapper around stock tools, and then write additional procedures to handle the tasks that the system tools can't.[60]

Now, you should also be aware that most systems have a GUI (graphical) front end to automation tools. For example, Solaris offers `admintool` to add and manipulate users, groups, and other local files. Red Hat offers `linuxconf` to do much the same tasks. These tools are highly system-specific and are subject to a great deal of variation.

Some GUI-based tools add step-by-step information and queries to facilitate the process. This makes them very useful for busy sysadmins who need to get something done fast and don't have time to learn the standard tools thoroughly.[61] Most experienced sysadmins stay away from the GUI front ends because they are typically not as full-featured or as flexible as command line–based tools.[62]

Removing Accounts

Account creation, discussed in the previous section, leads to the subject of this section: the deletion of accounts. Account deletion and creation raise similar issues, but account deletion could be even more sensitive from a policy standpoint.

If a sysadmin is asked to create some accounts quickly, it's probably because someone is eager to get new staff to work. When the sysadmin is asked to *delete* accounts quickly, there is probably something of a sensitive nature happening.

Policy

As with so many other aspects of system administration, you need to address some policy questions before removing accounts from your systems. Here are a few suggested considerations; as always, add your own (site-specific) items.

The first, most obvious question is whether to remove accounts at all. When unused accounts[63] remain active on a system, they can present a security risk. If the account were compromised, the absent user would certainly not notice any anomaly. If the sysadmins (and their monitoring software) were unaware of the user's inactive status, they would also not flag activity on that account as being suspicious. Many system compromises rely on having local access at the outset of the attack, so it is wise to close down excess ingress paths.

Insider attacks are always a possibility, but the likelihood of occurrence increases when an account outlasts its legitimate lifetime. Any users granted extra privileges on a system are likely to retain them as long as they can access the account. A good example of such a dangerous user is an employee who was terminated but can still log into the system with full access rights and privileges.

It also takes disk space to support the contents of user accounts, whether those contents are being accessed or not. Thus, it is also prudent resource management to periodically purge old accounts.

Of course, it's not enough simply to decide to winnow accounts; you must also set the limits and process by which it will be done. To this end, you should categorize the kinds of user you can have on your systems. Some common ones include these:

- Superuser accounts (root, other UID 0)
- Stock system accounts (bin, daemon, sys)
- Application-specific system accounts (postfix, postgres)
- Full-time employee accounts
- Part-time employee accounts
- Temporary staff accounts
- Guest accounts
- Contractor/vendor-use accounts

There might be others at your site, so take the time to do a little investigation. Each category that you identify is likely to have different expiration parameters and scenarios. For example, you might want to lock down a terminated employee's account very quickly but grant a little more leeway to employees who are leaving under good terms (to retrieve personal files,[64] set mail forwarding, and so on). Employees who work for research and accounting departments might have more strict closure rules than do those in customer service. On the other hand, your site might choose to enforce the same policy across the board. If so, we advise you to err on the side of caution and close out all accounts swiftly.

It's best if you keep in close communication with local management and Human Resources for your organization so that you know when employees start and end their

4

User Administration

stints. Regardless, we recommend doing periodic usage pattern analysis to check for idle accounts, odd access vectors, and so on. It is also wise, though potentially time-consuming, to periodically verify accounts with local department heads, team leaders, and the like to make sure that the accounts on your system can *all* be linked to a verified individual who has (or can give) authorization for the account. It's amazing how many times you hear things like, "Oh, yeah, we needed that account for a contractor about three months ago, but I don't think they've been around since then." If you uncover a sufficient number of cases like that, you might want to re-evaluate your account management processes to find some way to tighten accountability and security.

Also document who has authorization to request that an account be closed or terminated. Some sites allow users who have left or taken a leave of absence to request that their account be locked, if not deleted. If this is the case, though, make sure that you sufficiently verify the requestor's identity before performing the alteration. At many sites, department heads, section managers, and other organization officials can make the request. Make sure that all site sysadmins (as well as the help desk, if any) are aware of who is on the approved list.

Now consider the *process* by which you revoke access and delete accounts. Depending on your site's particular needs, it is probably wise to employ a two-step progression: First lock the account and then delete it later.

Locking an account does not harm or alter the account's contents, but it prevents anyone from logging in or switching to the username. Be aware, though, that all the user's public- and group-accessible files will remain on the system and available. That's why it might be better to generate fresh accounts every time a vendor visits rather than retain a perpetual account that gets locked between uses.[65]

When an account is slated for deletion, consider backing up all its associated files. Remember that not all user-owned files will reside in the user's home directory. If you miss external files but delete the user from /etc/passwd or NIS, the unowned files can still happily exist on your filesystem (they just appear as being owned by a UID).

A good backup enables you to preserve files in case of any number of circumstances—files being legitimately requested by current project leads, the reinstatement of the user, or legal action being brought against the organization or user.

Technical

Due to the sensitive issues that might be involved in deleting an account, we will address technical options short of total deletion in this section. Account locking, for instance, is a common practice and is much easier to undo than account deletion.

Locking

An account can be locked in a number of ways, the best of which combine the techniques discussed here.

Locking the account's password prevents anyone from using password-based authentication to access the account or system. Note that this does *not* prevent key-based access, as implemented by `rlogin` and `ssh` (see Chapter 7 for more discussion on authentication).

Although some sites "randomize" passwords to lock accounts, this is not recommended. Randomization simply sets the password to a presumably randomly generated value unknown to either the user or admins. If the generation is done poorly, however, the password might be easily guessed or cracked.

A much better method is to add a set of one or more illegal characters to the password hash. Recall that the hash may be composed only of alphanumeric characters (a–z, A–Z, 0–9], a period (.), and a forward-slash (/). Any illegal characters added *to the hash* (not the original password) will make it impossible to successfully match. The standard password-locking characters are * and ! !.

If you prepend or append locking characters to the existing password, you can easily re-enable the account with its previous password by removing them. Some sites prefer to use a string that indicates that the account is locked in place of the password hash (such as *LK* or something similar).

The standard `passwd` command uses the `-l` switch to perform password locking. On both Red Hat and Solaris, the `passwd` command is smart enough to update the password hash in the correct location: /etc/passwd if the account is not shadowed, or /etc/shadow if it is. Their respective locking approaches differ, however: Red Hat prepends the ! character to the password hash, whereas Solaris replaces the entire string with *LK*.

Because Red Hat leaves the original hash intact, it also offers another command switch to re-enable the password: `passwd –u`.

To prevent logins of any type, you really need to change the login shell. The most straightforward method is to set the shell to a command that will execute and exit, accepting no user input or signals. Replacing the shell entry in the user's /etc/passwd entry with `/bin/true`[66] (or `/dev/null`) will do this.[67]

Some sites offer special-purpose home-brew shells that allow users to ftp into their accounts but not log in. If you intend to do this sort of thing, it is best to use compiled code.[68] If you must use a shell script, remember to trap all signals[69] and `exit` at the end. The homebrew shell must also be listed in /etc/shells for ftp to be successful.

To prevent other (nonprivileged) users from accessing files owned by the locked user, consider using `find` and `chmod`. To do this for valjean, the command would look like this:

```
find / -user 24601 -xdev -exec chmod 000 {} \;
```

Note that there is a whitespace between } and the escaped semicolon \;. The space is a necessary part of the `find` command syntax. The escape character in front of the semicolon prevents the shell from interpreting it (because `find` needs it as an argument).

We specified `-xdev` so that our `find` command would not traverse into other filesystems, whether local or remote. This means that you will have to run this command again on the remote server. Although presumably your site implements synchronized UIDs,[70] it's safer to run this sort of command locally after verifying that you really are locking down the account that you are intending to lock down. By default, `find` will not dereference symbolic links (that is, it just changes the owner of the link, not of the file to which the link is pointing). This is a useful default that you do not want to change carelessly.[71]

Deleting

The steps necessary for manual deletion of users from your system are a mirror image of the steps outlined earlier for adding them. They boil down to the following process:

Step 1: Check for User Activity

Before trying to manipulate any of the user's access rights or files, make sure that the user is not logged into the system. This becomes especially important when using the automated tool discussed in the next section.

Step 2: Make a Backup

Backup the account (including the mailspool), preferably onto removable media that can be stored offline. You can use a variety of tools for this: `cp -Rp`, `tar` (with or without `gzip` for compression), or `dd`. See Chapter 16, "Backups," for more on backups.

Verify that the backup was successful before moving on to the next step.

Step 3: Handle Mail

If your site offers email-forwarding services, add an entry to /etc/aliases on the main email server. If your site supports NIS with the `aliases` map, edit the flat file and remake the map.

Even sites that don't do forwarding sometimes provide a *redirect* service through their mail server. This service returns updated email addresses to email senders when the "To:" address is no longer valid for mail delivery.[72] This still requires an entry in /etc/aliases. See Chapter 12, "Mail," for more information on email systems.

Step 4: Check Quotas

Use `quota -v` to see which filesystems have quotas set for the user.

Step 5: Remove /etc/passwd and /etc/shadow Entries

Now it's time to remove system-use information entries. Use `vipw` to remove the user from /etc/passwd, and run `pwck` to make sure that the file is still consistent. Invoke `pwconv` to update the contents of the shadow file.

If you are using NIS, update your maps.

Remember that once the /etc/passwd entry is removed from the main email server, the user will no longer receive local mail. This is why we updated the aliases file first.

The username and UID can go back into the pool for new accounts, but they should probably not be reassigned for some appropriate length of time (in case the user should be reinstated, for example).

Step 6: Remove Username from /etc/group and netgroups

The user might have belonged to more group than just the default, so edit /etc/group and remove all references to the username. Run `grpck` to verify that the file is still consistent. If you are running NIS, do the same for /etc/netgroup and remake the maps.

Step 7: Remove Home Directory and Associated Files

The most important caution for this step is: Check where you are and what command you typed *before* you hit Return. Since you will probably be calling `rm -rf` a misplaced wildcard or bad starting directory could be disastrous to your system. Take the extra few keystrokes to run `pwd` before removing things and double-check your typing.

Step 8: Remove Mail Directory

Remove the user's mailspool from the main email server.

Step 9: Check for Stray Files

Use `find` to check for files owned either by the removed UID or, to be really thorough, by "no one"—that is, owned by a UID not listed in /etc/passwd. The format of this command is as follows:

```
find / -xdev -nouser
```

You can use the `exec` switch to get a long listing of the files.

> ### Caution
>
> Do *not* automatically remove unowned files! There might be a legitimate reason (or, more likely, an oversight) for key system files to be owned by nonexistent users. You can damage the system by passing exec an rm command without first checking what find returns.

Step 10: Remove User Quotas

Use edquota to zero out the user's space and inode quotas on all local filesystems listed in Step 4.

There are also automated ways to accomplish most of these tasks. First, verify that the user is not currently active on the system.[73] Then issue the command userdel -r to perform the following tasks:

- Remove the user's entry from /etc/passwd
- Remove the user's entry from /etc/shadow
- Remove the username from entries in /etc/group
- Remove the files in the home directory listed in the user's /etc/passwd entry
- Remove the user's home directory itself
- Remove the user's mailspool (Red Hat only)

Under Red Hat, a group with the same name as the username is created by default by useradd. The userdel command does *not* delete that group. To purge that undeleted entry in /etc/group, invoke groupdel with the username as an argument.

Note that userdel does not back up the account, perform alias updates, modify quotas, modify netgroup, check for stray files, or remove the mailspool (under Solaris). It also does not update NIS flat files (unless it is run on the NIS master), nor does it remake the maps. All these tasks must be either performed manually or scripted.

Admins also may elect to remove only the /etc/passwd and /etc/shadow entries by specifying userdel with only the username as an argument. Solaris also enables you to accomplish the same task with passmgmt -d.

Best Practices

Policy

- Have policies defined ahead of time.
- Know who can override policies and make exceptions.
- Make sure that policies are well known to all admins and, where appropriate, to users as well.
- Clearly define who may have an account.
- Clearly define how usernames are generated.
- Clearly define how accounts are assigned, distributed, and revoked.

Usernames and UIDs

- Enforce a one-to-one mapping of users to accounts.
- Reserve UIDs below 100 for system accounts.
- Enforce unique UIDs.
- Enforce unique usernames.
- Run pwck periodically.

Group Names and GIDs

- Enforce unique GIDs.
- Enforce unique group–names.
- Assign GIDs of less than 60,000, where possible.
- Don't let users exceed the local maximum number of group memberships (usually 16).
- Run grpck periodically (more frequently, if you have gpasswd available).

Passwords

More best practices can be found in Chapter 7.

- Remember length limits:

  Standard passwords: *Only* 8 characters

  MD5: Up to 256 characters

4

USER
ADMINISTRATION

- Use MD5, where possible.
- Enforce password aging. Set values in /etc/login.defs (Red Hat) and /etc/default/passwd (Solaris)

Shadowing

- Install shadow-utils RPM on Red Hat, where possible.
    - Use caution if you use Kerberos, PAM, NIS, or LDAP.
- Use shadow, files where possible:

/etc/shadow

/etc/gshadow (Red Hat only)

Account Locking

- Enforce lockouts for failed login attempts.
- Use special character in password hash field: * or !.

Better yet, use a designated special-character phrase such as *LK*.
- Do *not* just empty the password hash field, even if that would technically work.
- Lock shell access by assigning the login shell to /dev/null or bin/true.
- *At least* lock unused accounts.

Account Deletions

- Make sure that the account is not in use at the time of deletion.
- Make an archive backup first.
- Delete unused accounts and accounts of terminated or leaving employees.
- Remember to look for files outside the home directory owned by the user.

NIS

- Set up exactly one domain master. Isolate NIS master service on its own machine, if possible.
- Set up at least one domain slave.
- Set the domain name to something other than the DNS domain.
- Make the domain name hard to guess (that is, not the name of the department).
- Enable ypxfr to run via cron on slaves.
- Do not have an NIS passwd map entry for root or other UID 0 accounts.

- Make sure that nsswitch.conf reflects the order of lookups that you want and support.
- Use /var/yp/securenets to limit who can bind and request maps.

Creating Accounts

- Set disk and file quotas.
- Test new accounts before releasing them in the wild.

General

- Populate /etc/shells.
- Verify local shell existence.

Online References

Linux Documentation Project
`http://www.linuxdoc.org`

shadow password How-To:
`http://www.europe.redhat.com/documentation/HOWTO/Shadow-Password-HOWTO-7.php3`

Solaris Documentation
`http://docs.sun.com`

NIS: *Solaris 2.6 System Administrator Collection, Volume 1: Solaris Naming Setup and Configuration Guide*

NIS

Red Hat's HOW-TO Guide to Setting Up a NIS Server:
`http://www.europe.redhat.com/documentation/HOWTO/NIS-HOWTO/ypserv.php3`

Auburn University's guide to securing NIS:
`http://www.eng.auburn.edu/users/doug/nis.html`

Stern, H., M. Eisler, and R. Labiaga. *Managing NFS and NIS,* O'Reilly, 2001

4

USER ADMINISTRATION

LDAP

OpenLDAP's Quick Start Guide:

`http://www.openldap.org/doc/admin/quickstart.html`

Red Hat's Official Reference Guide on LDAP:

`http://www.redhat.com/support/manuals/RHL-7.1-Manual/ref-guide/ch-ldap.html`

Sun's Guide to LDAP:

- Server: `http://docs.sun.com/ab2/coll.736.2/LDAPCONFIG/@Ab2PageView/616?DwebQuery=ldapclient&oqt=ldapclient&Ab2Lang=C&Ab2Enc=iso-8859-1`
- Client: `http://docs.sun.com/ab2/coll.736.2/LDAPCONFIG/@Ab2TocView?Ab2Lang=C&Ab2Enc=iso-8859-1&DwebQuery=ldapclient&oqt=ldapclient`

Endnotes

[1] *Or the sysadmin's job, which is pretty much the same thing.*

[2] *We are leaving out all humorous and derogatory terms out—we encourage sysadmins and users to get along!*

[3] *And, typically, UID + GID = capability.*

[4] *As with so many other things, this field can be called many things—username, login, login name, and, confusingly, userid.*

[5] *Technically, the limit is 8 bytes.*

[6] *As you might surmise, this is a Very Bad Thing.*

[7] *Yes, this is the sort of thing that geeks find interesting.*

[8] *On a 16-bit OS, this would be ($2^{16} - 1$), or 65534.*

[9] *It is also known as the comments, full name, and user information field.*

[10] *Many sites take advantage of this to install a local "reboot" user that has shutdown or a related executable as its "shell."*

[11] *If you are using a Solaris system, you already have these tools by default.*

[12] *See* `http://www.redhat.com/support/manuals/RHL-7.1-Manual/ref-guide/ch-access-privileges.html`.

[13] *For more detailed information, see the man pages or go online through Sun's portal:* `http://docs.sun.com/ab2/coll.40.6/`

[14] *However, we can't think of any just now.*

[15] *This and other system-wide defaults are defined in /usr/include/limits.h. Also see the* man *page for* limits.

[16] *The error message* chgrp *gives when file owners try to change group-ownership to a group to which they do not belong is a bit cryptic: "chgrp:*

[17] *For more detailed information, see the man pages or go online through Sun's portal:* http://docs.sun.com/ab2/coll.40.6/

[18] *This is still a Very Bad Thing.*

[19] *This is often referred to as the time to live (TTL) or lifetime of the password.*

[20] *Again, the 11369 indicates that we ran the pwconv command on February 16, 2001.*

[21] *This is done via the* gpasswd *command. Unfortunately, there is no man page for this command.*

[22] *Notice that it does not tell you anything new; it just reports on the settings that you already gave for a particular user. The command is a succinct way of getting the information, so we cover it here.*

[23] *In fact, all you get under Solaris is <username><password status>, and under Red Hat <password status><encryption type>.*

[24] *This includes, under Red Hat, a line that reads Changing password for user <username>— even when it does no such thing!*

[25] *In some settings, this will effectively lock the account. In others, it grants access to the account for anyone who connects. In any event, it's a Very Bad Idea.*

[26] *See* http://www.computerhope.com/unix/upasswor.htm *for a redux of the Red Hat -S option's output; also see the Solaris passwd man page.*

[27] *The name Yellow Pages is a registered trademark in the United Kingdom of British Telecommunications plc, and may not be used without permission.*

[28] *Technically, you may have more than one master server (by splitting up who serves various maps), but we don't recommend this. Redundancy is provided by slave servers, and spreading out maps defeats the goal of centralization.*

[29] *This is a local file not explicitly made into a map, but it can be accessed via NIS services with ypwhich -x (more on that later).*

[30] *This is fairly easy; you edit the main* makefile *(under the /var/yp directory) and remove the unwanted map name from the* all *line. See* http://docs.sun.com/ab2/coll.47.11/NETNAME/31.

[31] *Of course, they still need to be on the same network.*

[32] *This is addressed by the more security-conscious NIS+, but most sites do not use NIS+.*

[33] *If you want the source, go to ftp.kernel.org in the directory /pub/linux/utils/net/NIS, and get ypserv-1.3.11.tar.gz.*

[34] *This is true even if the local hostname is specified in the short form (sun) and the NIS request comes in with the fully qualified form (sun.my.site).*

[35] *See* http://www.redhat.com/support/alex/191.html.

[36] *This is because you will need to reference hostname/IP information to start the NIS services (so you can't query it through NIS).*

[37] *This is not entirely intuitive, but it makes sense on about the third go-round.*

[38] *The colons delimit fields that, by default, take on the NIS map's value for each entry.*

[39] *Both are still honored, though.*

[40] *This is true for even logical, as opposed to physical, subnets.*

[41] *This includes nsswitch.conf setup.*

[42] *Just put a hash mark (#) at the beginning of the line.*

[43] *This function can also technically be handled by tcpwrappers, but because the tcpwrappers package is not built into NIS, we don't touch on it here.*

[44] *Shadowed files, by default, are local; the point of NIS is to obviate local files. If the password were stored in a local shadow file, presumably you could use the same mechanism to distribute the original passwd file, and there wouldn't be a need for a distributed passwd map.*

[45] *See* `http://www.redhat.com/support/alex/265.html`.

[46] *See* `http://www.redhat.com/support/alex/255.html`.

[47] *See* `http://www.iplanet.com/download_index/downloads_index_9_0.html` *for an evaluation copy and more information.*

[48] *Note that we used GNU utilities for the build. If you do not have gcc, gmake, and other friends, you might have a much tougher time. See Chapter 17, "Open Source Software Management."*

[49] *See* `http://www.redhat.com/support/alex/272.html`.

[50] *See* `http://www.redhat.com/support/alex/268.html`.

[51] *Be aware, though, that someone will want to be "snoogums" or "priapic" or some other horribly unprofessional name. This might not matter as much, though, if email aliases are separate from login names.*

[52] *Otherwise, you might encounter the same inappropriate name problem.*

[53] *It's an added bonus when you can save wear and tear on the admin, too!*

[54] *Many admins feel that . should not be on the PATH at all, but this would cause a lot of ease-of-use problems for users.*

[55] *No dereferencing means that if, for some reason, there were a symbolic link pointing to /, that you wouldn't accidentally transfer all system-level ownership over to the new user.*

[56] *The command checks for the x character in the password hash field of any entry in /etc/passwd.*

[57] *See the Red Hat 7.1 man page for* `useradd`.

[58] *See the* `useradd` *man pages for more specifics.*

[59] *For example, local.cshrc needs to be .cshrc if it is to be automatically sourced at login time by users whose shell is* `csh`.

[60] *Remember, there's no need to reinvent the wheel—use the tools that the system provides rather than doing it all from scratch every time.*

[61] *There are quasireligious wars about quick-and-dirty solutions vs. time-intensive "correct" solutions. The reality of the situation is that sometimes quick-and-dirty is all you are permitted.*

[62] *And sysadmins are nothing if not control freaks.*

[63] *This means unused in legitimate terms.*

[64] *This is if your site allows personal files to be stored on business machines.*

[65] *Of course, some sites do not have the infrastructure to support this kind of on-the-fly account generation and tracking.*

[66] *There is an old exploit using* /bin/false*, so it's common practice to use its counterpart now.*

[67] /bin/true *always returns 1 and then exits.*

[68] *This way, you can avoid certain security exploits that reset IFS and other nifty tricks.*

[69] *If users could interrupt the process, they may be able to gain access.*

[70] *At least after reading this chapter, it should :)*

[71] *Again, beware unexpected links to system-level directories (/, /usr, /etc).*

[72] *For Sendmail, the controlling configuration file is sendmail.cf.*

[73] *This includes interactive logins and process ownership. Also note that the specified user must have an entry in /etc/passwd.*

4

USER ADMINISTRATION

Getting on the Network

by Andy Johnston

IN THIS CHAPTER

Introduction

This chapter serves a double purpose. First and foremost, as a system administrator, you will be expected to install, configure, and maintain network services on a system. In this chapter, we describe the commands and configuration files relevant to this task on our reference systems, Solaris 8 and Red Hat Linux 7.1. In addition, we address the concepts underlying network addressing, routing, and related issues. The background provided here will help the system administrator troubleshoot problems and communicate effectively with the network support staff.

This chapter also prepares you to understand and to make use of Chapter 21 Network Intrusion Detection Systems (NIDS). Network-based attacks often make use of subtle weaknesses in the Internet protocols and poor implementation of those protocols in certain versions of Unix. We assume that you are reasonably comfortable with binary notation and arithmetic, though a brief review of this subject is provided in Appendix E "Binary/Decimal/Hexadecimal Representation."

The background concepts will be presented first to provide a context for the specific configuration procedures presented later.

TCP/IP

The TCP/IP protocol is the accepted protocol for all Internet communications. A full description of the protocol is beyond the scope of this book. This section presents the reader with an illustration of the TCP/IP fundamentals that support data communication between networked computers.

The Internet as a Network of Networks

The term "Internet" is actually a contraction of "inter-network." The name describes the communications problem that the Internet Protocol addresses. The Internet consists of countless smaller local networks, each with its own rules about data delivery, traffic management, and so forth. Transmitting data from a computer on one local network and receiving it on a computer on another network is not just a matter of running a long line connecting the two local networks. Each network might have a completely different way of representing and transmitting data.

By analogy, imagine lots of separate, local railroad lines, each with its own track gauge, rail shape, rail car capacity, and so on (see Figure 5.1).

FIGURE 5.1

Independent local railroads.

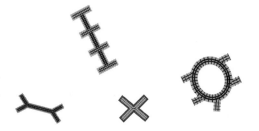

More rail lines can connect them all, but because each local railroad conforms to different specifications, the connection points will have to be a specialized type of station. At these special stations, two or more railroads will meet in such a way that cargo can be transferred from cars on one railroad to cars on another to continue the shipment (see Figure 5.2). These specialized junctions are called switchyards.

FIGURE 5.2

Interconnected local railroads.

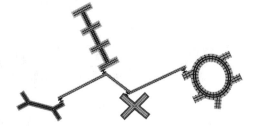

This is very much like the Internet. A local network can use any local data-transport system that seems preferable. Any data transmitted from one system to another on the same network can make use of local communications protocols. Data transmitted between systems on different networks must first be directed from the originating system to a specialized connector, a *gateway*, to leave the originating network. The data then may travel through other gateways and local networks until it reaches the network containing its destination and is finally delivered from that network's gateway to the destination system using the destination network's local delivery protocols.

> **Note**
>
> To function as a junction between networks, the gateway must be connected to more than one network. This will be an important point to keep in mind when we look at Internet Protocol (IP) addressing.

5

GETTING ON THE NETWORK

Although most networked computers are connected to only one network, it is not unusual for computers—especially those regulating network traffic—to be connected to two or more networks. Each network connection is made through a "network device" in the computer. By far the most common type of network device is the network interface card (NIC). Different types of NICs are made for different types of physical network connection. It is the job of the NIC to deal with the physical details of the connection while communicating with the computer in a standardized way. As a result, assuming that you have selected the right NIC for your network, no special configuration of the operating system is needed to accommodate different network hardware: It will all look alike to the computer. We will refer to NICs throughout this chapter as our standard network device hardware.

Note

If you aren't sure what type of NIC is appropriate, check with your network administrator. In fact, it's wise to do so anyway because there could be accepted standards for NICs and other equipment on your network.

Note on Terminology

Throughout the remainder of this chapter, we will use the term "node" to refer to any computer or other device that can transmit and receive data over a network. This means that a computer is not a node *until* it has been configured to communicate over a network, even though the physical network wiring might be in place.

Local Delivery—MAC Addresses

Internet communication depends on the successful communication of data *within* a local network. If the source and destination of a transmission are on the same network, then obviously that network supports the transmission. If the destination is on another network, the transmission must first be directed to a gateway on the local network. This first step, though, also takes place as a transmission from one local network node (the source) to another (the gateway).

As noted earlier, each node connects to the network through a NIC. The transmission through the local network is actually made from one NIC to another. If the local network contains more than two NICs (and it will), there must be some way to specify that the message is destined for one of the NICs in particular.

The most common type of local network communication uses an *Ethernet* protocol. In this protocol, all NICs receive each transmission but ignore any transmissions not addressed to them. (An increasingly common variant, *switched Ethernet*, directs each transmission *only* to its destination, but the destination must still be specified.) Each NIC on an Ethernet network has a unique address, called the *Medium Access Control (MAC)* address, used to specify both the source and the destination of local transmissions.

The MAC address consists of 6 bytes, expressed in hexadecimal notation and separated by colons. The address is actually assigned directly to the network device during manufacture and is sometimes called the "hardware" address. It is the responsibility of each manufacturer to ensure that no two devices are ever assigned the same address. To make sure that two different manufacturers don't assign the same address to different devices, each manufacturer is assigned a range of possible addresses for exclusive use. Specifically, the first 3 bytes of a NIC's MAC address must have values that have been assigned to that NIC's manufacturer. These bytes comprise the organizationally unique identifier (OUI).

> **Note**
>
> The assignment of OUIs to manufacturers of network equipment is the responsibility of the Institute of Electrical and Electronics Engineers (IEEE). Using their assignment records, it's possible to determine the manufacturer of a NIC solely from the traffic that it generates. For instance, a data transmission from Ethernet address 00:10:a4:9a:25:ac can be matched through its first 3 bytes to the IEEE OUI record:
>
> 00-10-A4   (hex)   XIRCOM
> 0010A4   (base 16)   XIRCOM
>   2300 Corporate Center Dr.
>   Thousand Oaks CA 91320

Just as a NIC takes care of the details of the physical network connection, it also handles the details of local network addressing through its built-in software and preassigned MAC address. Although the MAC address is useful in debugging network problems, the system administrator doesn't normally need to worry about it. On many systems, it is now possible for an administrator to change the address of a network device. Doing so weakens the integrity of the Ethernet protocol and should be avoided.

Commands and files involving the MAC address and its interaction with the higher-level IP address (see the next section) will be described later in this chapter.

Internetwork Delivery—IP Addresses

Now we know that the local network, using MAC addresses, manages the transmission of data between any two local network nodes. If the transmission is purely local, both nodes are computers on the local network. If the transmission is destined for a node on another network, it is first directed to a gateway node on the local network, from which it will travel (via another of the gateway's network interfaces) to another network.

There is a piece missing here, though. It is the source of the transmission that determines whether to send data to the local gateway or to a local node. That means that the source must be capable of distinguishing between addresses on its own network and those elsewhere, *and* it must be capable of distinguishing the MAC address of the local gateway(s) from the other network nodes. In turn, the local gateway (and each subsequent gateway) must be capable of determining which gateway should be the next to receive the data transmission so that it reaches its final target. If the Internet is a "network of networks," there must be a mechanism to determine *which* networks and gateways need to be traversed to get to a specific destination.

Broadly, two strategies can accomplish this. If every node on the Internet has a complete "map" of all the networks and their Internet connections, the transmission source can figure out an end-to-end "route map" for the data transmission and can include it with the transmission. As the Internet grows, however, this map becomes impossibly huge. In addition, the configurations of the local networks and connections are constantly changing, and this would also have to be reflected in constant updates of the map.

A simpler approach is to supply each node on the Internet with exactly the information needed to determine, given the final destination of a transmission, what the *next step* in the transmission should be.

Referring to the railroad analogy, if a container starting in San Francisco is destined for New York, there must be some way to determine, for any given station, which station the container should go to next to reach its final destination. For instance, destinations such as San Jose and Berkeley might well be recognized as stations on the local railroad, and cargo would be dispatched directly to them. Cargo destined for other cities not recognized as part of the local railroad would be sent to the local railroad switchyard.

The local station manager needs to know whether a destination is or isn't on the local railroad. If it is on the local railroad, cargo can go directly there. If it isn't, cargo goes to the switchyard. The switchyard manager also needs to be able to recognize whether a destination is on *any* of the local railroads that the switchyard serves. If so, cargo can be delivered directly from a local station. If the destination is *not* local, the switchyard manager must know which switchyard the cargo should go to next. Perhaps he knows that cargo destined for Seattle or Tacoma goes to the switchyard for the Northwest railroad and that cargo for Los Angeles goes to the SoCal railroad switchyard. Perhaps any destination that he can't recognize goes simply to a special switchyard in Chicago, which has no local stations but only connects switchyards to other switchyards. The key is that, at each step in the journey, the next step is determined until the final destination is reached.

Of course, while it is possible to maintain huge registers of local station names and switchyards, this system can be made far more efficient through the introduction of an addressing system with an encoding method that includes this information within the station and gateway addresses themselves.

IP Addressing

The IP address of a system is the "encoding method" referred to in the context of the Internet. While local MAC addresses serve data transfer within their local networks, the IP address is universally meaningful across the Internet. Given the IP address of the destination, a computer or gateway can determine the "next station" to travel to so that data can reach its final destination.

> **Note**
>
> Note that it is not necessary for the system that originally transmits the data packet to map out the packet's entire route to its destination. This job would become increasingly difficult to manage as the Internet grows. All that is necessary is that at any point, the next step in the journey can be determined. The design philosophy pervading the Internet is that each component knows the least it needs to know to do its job. That way, the Internet can grow without putting undue strain on any single component.

Dotted-Quad Representation

The IP address is 4 bytes long. The *dotted-quad* representation of the address is by far the most common. In this notation, each byte is represented as a decimal number, and the four numbers are separated by periods, as in 10.100.253.1. Note that a byte is 8 bits and ranges in value from 0 to 255.

> **Note**
>
> A proposal called IPv6 would make the IP address much longer. Progress toward this new standard has been glacial, at best, and IPv6 is not discussed here.

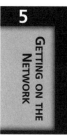

Every network device on the Internet has an IP address. In fact, being on the Internet means, as much as anything, having a unique IP address.

To ensure that IP addresses are unique, certain transnational organizations exist to assign ranges of IP addresses, called *address space*, to Internet service providers (ISPs). The ISPs assign addresses to their customers from this pool, and, finally, the system administrator is assigned an IP from a pool available to the local network administrator. The primary coordinator of IP addresses is the Internet Assigned Number Authority (IANA).

Subnets and Netmasks

Given the destination address for a data transmission, the source of the transmission needs to determine whether that destination lies on the local network or whether it can be reached only through a local gateway. The dotted-quad representation suggests a very simple approach immediately. If all systems on a given network have addresses of the form 10.100.253.*xxx*, where *xxx* ranges from 1 to 254, then any destination with the same first three numbers out of the four in its address is on the same network. Conversely, any destination differing in any of the first three numbers is on a different network and must be directed through the local gateway.

Note

The values 0 and 255 in the final octet of an IP address have a special meaning. By the accepted standard, 255 in the final octet indicates that the packet is to be broadcast to all systems on the local network (using the broadcast MAC address of ff:ff:ff:ff:ff:ff). Some early implementations of the TCP/IP protocol in Unix used a 0 in the last octet, rather than 255, to signify the broadcast address. This is nonstandard usage, but many systems honor it.

The standard defines a broadcast address literally to be one in which the host part of the binary representation of the address is all ones. As will be shown later in this chapter, the host part of the IP address consists of bits of the address not used to specify the network. If the remaining bits of the host part are all ones, then the IP address is a broadcast address. A final 255 denotes a broadcast in the common case in which the first 24 bits of the address (the first three octets) are used to specify the network.

Note

Up until now, we have been considering the Internet as a network made of smaller networks. At this point, we are considering the way that all possible IP addresses are distributed among the smaller networks to facilitate data transmission throughout the Internet. Our viewpoint has changed from the bottom-up view of the local networks that make up the Internet to the top-down view of the Internet partitioned into smaller networks. Partitioning the addresses available to a network into smaller groups of addresses is called *subnetting*. The "local networks" that we referred to previously will be considered subnets of larger networks (including the Internet) for the rest of the chapter. Anyone wanting to add a subnet to the Internet needs to be assigned an unused subnet (a range of addresses) of an existing larger network or subnet. The Internet is now a "network of subnets."

Of course, this means that every subnet gets 254 addresses. Some subnets will have far fewer nodes, leaving unassigned addresses, and some will have far more, leaving nodes with no address. To get a bigger subnet, we could fix only the first and second quads (10.100.*xxx.xxx*) or only the first quad (10.*xxx.xxx.xxx*), but these networks are very large and really huge, respectively. Fixing quads in the address doesn't give you very fine control over the address size of local networks.

New Term

The *address space* of a network is the set of addresses assigned to it.

In fact, the address space of the entire Internet was originally "carved up" using a plan based on this approach. Half of the possible addresses are assigned to subnetworks with the first quad fixed. Half of the remaining addresses are assigned to subnetworks with the first two quads fixed. Finally, half of the addresses now remaining are assigned to subnetworks with the first three quads fixed. These three types of subnet are called Class A networks, Class B networks, and Class C networks, respectively. This classification system defines two more classes, D and E, in similar fashion. These classes, however, are not available for assignment.

Note on Terminology

It will often seem that the terms "network" and "subnet" are used interchangeably. In fact, from our current point of view, the only "network" is the Internet itself. Everything else is a subnet, a subnet of a subnet, and so on. For convenience, it is common practice to refer to a large subnet of the Internet (like one assigned to an entire corporation) as "the network," and to refer to subnets in relation to that "network."

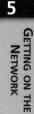

5

GETTING ON THE
NETWORK

The lack of fine control over subnet size in the ABC system has caused problems with the allocation of addresses throughout the Internet. Figure 5.3 illustrates the uneven distribution of IP address space into classes.

FIGURE 5.3

Internet address space as allocated under class-based addressing.

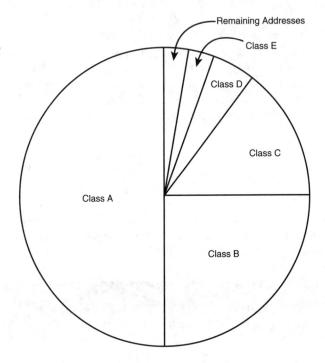

Finer control is available if, instead of looking at the IP address as four decimal numbers, we look at it as 4 bytes, or 32 bits, of addressing information.

Now, if our host has the address 10.100.253.98, we will see it as follows:

    00001010 01100100 11111101 01100010

If this host is on a Class C network, local addresses all have this form:

    00001010 01100100 11111101 *xxxxxxxx*

Here, each *x* is a 0 or a 1. The Class C network, as you see, has the first 24 bits fixed in its address space.

Suppose that you need a larger network, but not one as large as a Class B. You could fix, for example, only the first 22 bits of the address space and make all local addresses have this form:

    00001010 01100100 111111*xx xxxxxxxx*

Translated back to dotted-quad notation, this gives an address space as follows:

> 10.100.252.*xxx*
>
> 10.100.253.*xxx*
>
> 10.100.254.*xxx*
>
> 10.100.255.*xxx*

It might be a bit less obvious to you that these addresses all belong to the same network, but remember that the decision about whether a destination address is local is made by the source of the data transmission, not by you. That source is very likely a digital electronic device of some sort and represents everything internally in binary notation. This system is *very* efficient in binary.

This subnetting method described is commonly expressed using Classless InterDomain Routing (CIDR) notation. In this notation, the Class C subnet described previously as 10.100.253.*xxx* would be written as 10.100.253.0/24, indicating that the first 24 bits of the 32-bit address are fixed and that the remaining 8 are allowed to vary through the address range of the subnet. The subnet created when we fixed only 22 bits of the 32-bit address could be written as 10.100.253.0/22.

In Unix systems, a *subnet mask* is used to specify subnets. As in CIDR notation, the subnet mask describes which bits of an IP address are fixed for the subnet and which vary. Even though the subnet mask is evaluated as a 32-bit binary string, it is usually represented in Unix commands in dotted-quad notation.

For instance, the subnet mask for the Class C subnet 10.100.253.0/24 would be 255.255.255.0, and the subnet mask for the subnet 10.100.253.0/22 would be 255.255.252.0. The following table illustrates the subnets in dotted-quad and in binary notation.

TABLE 5.1   Subnet Masks

Dotted-Quad	*Binary*
255.255.255.0	11111111 11111111 11111111 00000000
255.255.252.0	11111111 11111111 11111100 00000000

The source node preparing to transmit data to a destination node determines whether the destination is on the same subnet through a simple series of computations involving the source IP, the destination IP, and the subnet mask. Suppose that the source IP is 192.168.15.5, the destination IP is 192.168.17.90, and the subnet mask is 255.255.248.0.

The first computation involves the source IP and the subnet mask:

TABLE 5.2   Subnet Mask on /24 Subnet

Source IP	192.168.15.5	11000000 10101000 00001111 00000101
AND Subnet Mask	AND 255.255.248.0	11111111 11111111 11111000 00000000
Result	192.168.8.0	11000000 10101000 00001000 00000000
Destination IP	192.168.17.90	11000000 10101000 00010001 01011010
AND Subnet Mask	AND 255.255.248.0	11111111 11111111 11111000 00000000
Result 2	192.168.16.0	11000000 10101000 00010000 00000000

If result 1 and result 2 are the same, the source and destination IP belong to the same subnet. If they differ, then the host and destination IP belong to different subnets. In this case, the results differ and the two IP addresses are on different subnets; the source of the transmission must direct it to the gateway.

Trying again with a different subnet mask, 255.255.192.0, you can repeat the computations on what is now a /18 subnet in CIDR notation.

TABLE 5.3   Subnet Mask on /18 Subnet

Source IP	192.168.15.5	11000000 10101000 00001111 00000101
AND Subnet Mask	AND 255.255.192.0	11111111 11111111 11000000 00000000
Result	192.168.0.0	11000000 10101000 00000000 00000000
Destination IP	192.168.17.90	11000000 10101000 00010001 01011010
AND Subnet Mask	AND 255.255.192.0	11111111 11111111 11000000 00000000
Result 2	192.168.0.0	11000000 10101000 00000000 00000000

Result 1 matches result 2, so the two IP addresses belong to this subnet.

The subnet masks all begin with ones and then change to zeros in their binary representation. After the first 0 appears, reading left to right, the rest of the subnet mask consists entirely of zeros. No subnet mask should contain, for instance, a byte like 00010001.

Tip

When configuring IP addressing on a computer's network device, the system administrator needs three pieces of information for successful IP communication:

- IP address associated with the network device. This will usually be assigned by the network administrator or will come from a pool of addresses that the network administrator assigns to the system administrator.

- Subnet mask associated with the local subnet. This will be provided by the network administrator.
- IP address of the gateway. This will be provided by the network administrator.

Note

Clearly, successful administration of networked computers requires a good working relationship with the person or organization responsible for maintaining the network. For some reason, systems and network people seem to be at each other's throats in many organizations. This could be because each group thinks that the other consists of arbitrary, capricious troublemakers. In many cases, this is not so. Seriously, the two groups need to work together, and each needs to have some conception of what the other is doing for either to serve the larger organization. (*Reminder: That's why they're paying you.*) Pizza with the network support staff will be a lot less unpleasant than the other system administrators might tell you it will be, and your efforts will be paid back with interest in the information that you share. In fact, when you first start on a job site, it's a good idea to find out who is in charge of networking (if the answer is "no one," consider finding a new job), introduce yourself, and ask if there is anything that you, as a system administrator, should know about the network. It helps to get off on the right foot.

It should be noted that certain ranges of IP address are not used on the Internet. That is, you can assign them, but gateways will refuse to pass traffic from them off their local network. They can be useful, in fact, if you want to configure a network device so that it can be "seen" only by other devices on the local network.

TABLE 5.4   Reserved Addresses

Reserved Address Ranges	
Range	CIDR Notation
10.0.0.0–10.255.255.255	10.0.0.0/8
172.16.0.0–172.31.255.255	172.16.0.0/12
192.168.0.0–192.168.255.255	192.168.0.0/16

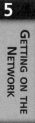

Note

The Internet Engineering Task Force (IETF) maintains standards for Internet communication, such as the reserved addresses mentioned previously. The standards, whether they are accepted or simply proposed, are called requests for comment (RFC) and are each assigned an RFC number. For instance, the reserved addresses are specified in RFC 1918. CIDR addressing is described in RFC 1519. The older system of addressing using Classes A, B, and so on is defined in RFC 0791. See the references at the end of the chapter for the IETF URL.

ARP (and RARP)

As noted previously, the system administrator must assign the IP address of a network device. The manufacturer of that device has already assigned the MAC address. Decisions about data transmission are made using the known IP addresses of the source and destination, and data transmission within a subnet depends on the MAC address. The source node knows its own IP and MAC addresses and the IP address of the destination node. If the destination lies on the same subnet, however, the source must have the destination MAC address as well to transmit the data. If the source directs the data to a local gateway, it must use the MAC address of that gateway, yet that information was not provided during configuration.

Maintaining a lookup table of MAC and IP addresses would be an impossible task for a human administrator, so there is a protocol that lets the nodes find out what they need for themselves. The Address Resolution Protocol (ARP) enables a node to broadcast a request (called an "arp" request) to all other nodes on the subnet asking the node with a given IP to respond with its MAC address. That address is then stored in an *arp cache* in the node memory and is used to transmit local data. This makes it simple to add a node to the local network, as long as it is configured with basic IP information. Any other node that needs to transmit data to it for the first time will broadcast an arp request to which the new node will respond with its MAC address. Note that arp cache entries are aged out after awhile because changes in network configuration may be quite common.

There is also a protocol named Reverse ARP (RARP), which allows a node to broadcast its MAC address and receive its assigned IP address in reply from a "RARP server." This protocol has been used with diskless workstations and "very thin" workstations that don't store an IP address when they power down. RARP is also used when a system is installed over the network from an installation server (as in Sun's Jumpstart).

> **Tip**
>
> RARP server configuration varies from one Operating System to the next. RARP servers require a method of matching a given MAC address to an IP address. This is normally done using the file /etc/ethers. In RH Linux 7.1, for example, each line of the /etc/ethers file consists of a MAC address followed by an IP address. In Solaris 8, on the other hand, a line in /etc/ethers consists of a MAC address followed by a hostname. Solaris 8 RARP service depends also on the /etc/hosts file, whose lines consist of a hostname followed by an IP address. The mapping of MAC to IP is done through an intervening hostname.
>
> If you need to deal with RARP, read your man pages carefully for ethers, rarp, and rarpd to ensure that you have a clean configuration.

DNS

Computers deal in symbol manipulation and numeric representations. People prefer names. It's much easier to remember stinky.my.com than, say, 192.168.200.76. Since there are so many nodes on the Internet, no computer can be expected to register and update a table of all the names and IP addresses. Instead, each networked installation is expected to maintain a table of *its own* names and addresses. These tables and the protocol through which they are accessed make up the Domain Name Service (DNS).

Most nodes are DNS clients. They know only the IP address(es) of themselves and the local DNS server(s). A local server has a table of local names and IPs, and will also look up the IP addresses associated with names elsewhere on the Internet. Each DNS server occupies a place in a well-defined hierarchy of servers. A server will query up its line of the hierarchy until it gets or is provided with the information that it requires. The information thus acquired is stored in a DNS cache on the local server. As with most such caches, the entries will eventually age out (see Chapter 8, "DNS," for more details about DNS behavior).

It should be noted that although DNS is most often used to look up the IP address associated with a name (known as *resolving* the name), it also can be used to find the name that is associated with an IP address. Some security tools exploit this "reverse lookup" as a way to double-check DNS entries. If a transmission is received from source IP 192. 168.200.76, reverse lookup can provide the name www.stinky.com. If subsequent resolution of www.stinky.com yields *anything* other than 192.168.200.76, there might be something severely wrong and the transmission should be either rejected or flagged as being of dubious provenance.

5

GETTING ON THE
NETWORK

> **Tip**
>
> There are three common methods for a system to get IP addresses resolved into names:
>
> - DNS—The file /etc/resolv.conf must contain the IP address(es) of the local DNS server(s). See Chapter 11, "Name Service," for a detailed discussion of DNS.
> - /etc/hosts—This is a table on the local system itself. It is often created at installation but may be updated by hand.
> - NIS. See the NIS section of Chapter 4, "User Administration."
>
> The hosts: record in the file /etc/nsswitch.conf must be configured to determine which of these three methods is used and in which order (see Chapter 4).

Figure 5.4 illustrates how the different methods of referring to a network device are mapped to one another.

FIGURE 5.4

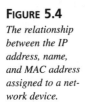

The relationship between the IP address, name, and MAC address assigned to a network device.

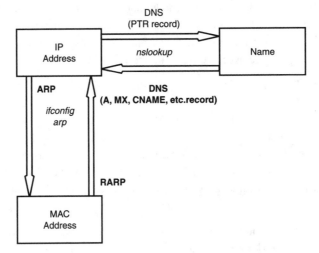

DHCP

As noted previously, a network interface must have a unique IP address assigned to it to be on the Internet. Suppose, though, that you have 30 computers with network interfaces, but you expect only about 10 of them to be in use at any given time. If you had a way to get an IP address to each computer that needed one and then "revoke" the address when it wasn't needed, you could get away with perhaps 12 IP addresses (always have a little more than you expect to need). This would be especially useful to an ISP with thousands of subscribers when no more than 200 are expected to be online simultaneously.

Dynamic Host Configuration Protocol (DHCP) supports this cooperative mechanism. As with RARP, a system requiring an IP address for its network device must request one. Unlike RARP, DHCP will not always supply the same IP address to a given requestor each time. If your site uses DHCP, it is probably maintained by or in cooperation with your network administrator.

During installation of RH Linux 7.1, there is a phase called "Network Configuration." The GUI installer with this title will appear. If you will be using DHCP, select the "Configure Using DHCP" option on that page.

Solaris 8 presents DHCP options to the user during installation in much the same way as RH Linux 7.1. If DHCP is selected at that point, the installation process takes care of the DHCP file configurations and so on.

If you want to start (or stop) using DHCP on a system that has already been configured, use the sys-unconfig utility described earlier for changing the network configuration. After running `sys-unconfig` and letting the system shut down, boot it back up and configure it for DHCP.

There are other ways to approach DHCP configuration for both of these systems, but this describes the quickest, simplest approach to day-to-day installation and maintenance tasks.

IP Configuration and Troubleshooting Commands

Now that we've covered the addressing concepts, let's look at some of the commands that we can use to examine and manage the various addressing configurations. We start by examining the configurations of a working, networked computer using our reference systems: Red Hat Linux 7.1 and Solaris 8. Then we look at the task of configuring a system from scratch and reconfiguring an existing system.

ARP and ping

Let's start with the arp cache. Remember that the arp cache associates the IP addresses of network devices that you contact with the MAC addresses that you actually use to contact them. The following arp cache listing is from our Solaris 8 reference platform:

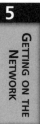

LISTING 5.1 Sample Output from the arp -a Command

```
# arp -a

Net to Media Table: IPv4
Device   IP Address              Mask          Flags   Phys Addr
------   -----------------       ------------- -----   ---------------
eri0     10.100.70.1             255.255.255.255       00:d0:d3:33:8b:58
eri0     gecko                   255.255.255.255       08:00:69:07:8b:ce
eri0     kyle                    255.255.255.255       00:10:4b:66:c5:28
eri0     ensis                   255.255.255.255  SP   00:03:ba:08:73:d3
eri0     10.100.71.1             255.255.255.255       00:d0:d3:33:8b:58
eri0     ecs020pc-14             255.255.255.255       00:b0:d0:55:a6:76
eri0     ecs020pc-15             255.255.255.255       00:b0:d0:60:98:a5
eri0     BASE-ADDRESS.           240.0.0.0        SM   01:00:5e:00:00:00
         MCAST.net
```

The command arp –a dumps the current arp cache. Notice that all the entries are associated with one network device, eri0. (There is only one on this machine, as it happens.) Among other things, those IP addresses have been replaced with DNS-defined names where available. You can see that, to transmit data to the machine named gecko, the data must be directed to the network device with MAC address 08:00:69:07:8b:ce.

The next command deletes the entry associated with kyle from the arp cache, followed by another arp cache dump to confirm that kyle is gone:

LISTING 5.2 Deletion of an arp Table Entry

```
# arp -d kyle.my.site.com
kyle.my.site.com (10.100.70.134) deleted
# arp -a

Net to Media Table: IPv4
Device   IP Address              Mask          Flags   Phys Addr
------   -----------------       ------------- -----   ---------------
eri0     10.100.70.1             255.255.255.255       00:d0:d3:33:8b:58
eri0     gecko                   255.255.255.255       08:00:69:07:8b:ce
eri0     ensis                   255.255.255.255  SP   00:03:ba:08:73:d3
eri0     10.100.71.1             255.255.255.255       00:d0:d3:33:8b:58
eri0     10.100.69.1             255.255.255.255       00:d0:d3:33:8b:58
eri0     ecs020pc-14             255.255.255.255       00:b0:d0:55:a6:76
eri0     ecs020pc-15             255.255.255.255       00:b0:d0:60:98:a5
eri0     10.100.71.86            255.255.255.255       00:a0:cc:5f:e8:17
eri0     BASE-ADDRESS.           240.0.0.0        SM   01:00:5e:00:00:00
         MCAST.net
```

Now a ping command is sent to kyle. ping sends a special type of packet, but one that still uses the IP addressing scheme. To send the packet, the node must first find out the MAC address of kyle's node, so kyle's IP-MAC association is returned to the table:

LISTING 5.3   Update of an ARP Table

```
# ping kyle.my.site.com
kyle.my.site.com is alive
# arp -a
Net to Media Table: IPv4
Device    IP Address                    Mask       Flags    Phys Addr
------    ------------------            ---------------    -----    ---------------
eri0      kyle                          255.255.255.255             00:10:4b:66:c5:28
eri0      10.100.70.1                   255.255.255.255             00:d0:d3:33:8b:58
eri0      gecko                         255.255.255.255             08:00:69:07:8b:ce
eri0      ensis                         255.255.255.255    SP       00:03:ba:08:73:d3
eri0      10.100.71.1                   255.255.255.255             00:d0:d3:33:8b:58
eri0      10.100.69.1                   255.255.255.255             00:d0:d3:33:8b:58
eri0      ecs020pc-14                   255.255.255.255             00:b0:d0:55:a6:76
eri0      ecs020pc-15                   255.255.255.255             00:b0:d0:60:98:a5
eri0      10.100.71.86                  255.255.255.255             00:a0:cc:5f:e8:17
eri0      amy                           255.255.255.255             00:10:4b:d2:91:39
eri0      BASE-ADDRESS.                 240.0.0.0          SM       01:00:5e:00:00:00
          MCAST.net
```

> **Note**
>
> ping *<system name or IP>* is a very simple command that determines whether another system is active and reachable through the network. It sends a special request (according to a specific protocol) that asks only for a reply and tells you if it got one.

netstat and ifconfig

Now we will take a look at the configuration of the network interface using the very useful commands `ifconfig` and `netstat`. Of course, you might not know what the name of that interface is, so you type `netstat -i`. The respective outputs for Red Hat Linux 7.1 and Solaris 8 are shown here:

LISTING 5.4   `netstat -i` Output

RH Linux 7.1:

```
# netstat -i
Kernel Interface table
Iface   MTU Met    RX-OK RX-ERR RX-DRP RX-OVR    TX-OK TX-ERR TX-DRP TX-OVR Flg
eth0    1500   0  1508661      0      0      0      530      0      0      0 BRU
lo      16436  0        6      0      0      0        6      0      0      0 LRU
```

LISTING 5.4 continued

Solaris 8:

```
# netstat -i
Name  Mtu   Net/Dest      Address       Ipkts    Ierrs Opkts   Oerrs Collis Queue
lo0   8232  loopback      localhost     644113  0     644113  0     0      0
eri0  1500  ensis         ensis         1651233 3     4170    0     0      0

# netstat -in
Name  Mtu   Net/Dest      Address       Ipkts    Ierrs Opkts   Oerrs Collis Queue
lo0   8232  127.0.0.0     127.0.0.1     644269  0     644269  0     0      0
eri0  1500  10.100.70.0   10.100.70.20  1651771 3     4190    0     0      0
```

Notice that the interface name appears in the first column in every case. You also might notice that both reference systems seem to have an interface named lo0 with IP 127.0.0.1. This is called the "loopback" interface, and it exists mainly for testing the NIC. A normal NIC passes data from the computer to the network and also passes data from the network back to the computer. The lo0 interface passes data from the computer through the NIC *almost* to the network and then sends it back. Most of the time, it can be ignored.

Beyond the first column, the output of netstat differs between the two reference systems. Note that Solaris includes the (Class C, in this case) subnet that the interface is attached to and the IP address of the network device. By default, Solaris will try to resolve the IP addresses into names in the output. The second invocation of netstat on Solaris uses the -n option that suppresses name resolution and just shows IP.

> **Tip**
>
> Almost all commands that try to resolve IP addresses into hostnames by default will accept the -n option to suppress that resolution. It is always advisable to use this option during network troubleshooting. *In many cases, what looks like a network failure turns out to be a problem with DNS.* A utility such as ifconfig will seem to be hanging, suggesting some horrible problem with the network interface, when, in fact, it's waiting for a slow or nonexistent DNS to finish resolving IP addresses so that it can output names. It probably has never taken us more than a day or so to figure this out.

netstat -i shows that the network interface device is named eth0 on the Linux system and eri0 on the Solaris system. Different types of interface will have different names on the same system, so always check with netstat -in.

Now we will use `ifconfig`, the command that actually configures the network devices in the first place, to examine the configuration of these devices.

LISTING 5.5 `ifconfig` Output

RH Linux 7.1

```
#  ifconfig eth0
eth0      Link encap:Ethernet  HWaddr 00:B0:D0:F0:F5:76
          inet addr:10.100.70.16  Bcast:10.100.70.255  Mask:255.255.255.0
          UP BROADCAST RUNNING MULTICAST  MTU:1500  Metric:1
          RX packets:1516313 errors:0 dropped:0 overruns:0 frame:0
          TX packets:547 errors:0 dropped:0 overruns:0 carrier:0
          collisions:22 txqueuelen:100
          Interrupt:11 Base address:0xec80
```

Solaris 8

```
#  ifconfig eri0
eri0: flags=1000843<UP,BROADCAST,RUNNING,MULTICAST,IPv4> mtu 1500 index 2
          inet 10.100.70.20 netmask ffffff00 broadcast 10.100.70.255
          ether 0:3:ba:8:73:d3
```

Beyond the obvious differences in output format, both commands produce similar information.

The Linux system has the following format:

IP:	10.100.70.16
MAC:	00:B0:D0:F0:F5:76
Netmask:	255.255.255.0

The Solaris configuration as follows:

IP:	10.100.70.20
MAC:	0:3:ba:8:73:d3
Netmask:	ffffff00

(ffffff00 is hexadecimal notation for 255.255.255.0.)

Now we turn to `netstat` again to find out where each system's gateway is and how the systems are configured to recognize local traffic versus that which goes through the gateway. By the way, the most common type of gateway system is the "router" because it obviously routes transmissions around the Internet. The tables that determine where to send traffic directed to various destinations are called routing tables.

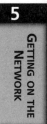

5

GETTING ON THE
NETWORK

LISTING 5.6   `netstat -rn` Output

RH Linux 7.1

```
# netstat -rn
Kernel IP routing table
Destination     Gateway         Genmask         Flags   MSS Window  irtt Iface
10.100.70.0     0.0.0.0         255.255.255.0   U       40 0          0 eth0
127.0.0.0       0.0.0.0         255.0.0.0       U       40 0          0 lo
0.0.0.0         10.100.70.1     0.0.0.0         UG      40 0          0 eth0
```

Solaris 8

```
# netstat -rn

Routing Table: IPv4
  Destination          Gateway              Flags  Ref   Use    Interface
-------------------- -------------------- ----- ----- ------ ---------
10.100.70.0          10.100.70.20           U      1     103   eri0
224.0.0.0            10.100.70.20           U      1       0   eri0
default              10.100.70.1            UG     1     208
127.0.0.1            127.0.0.1              UH     27 596678   lo0
```

Note the use of the –n option. This suppresses DNS name resolution. As noted earlier, independence from name servers is an asset when debugging network problems.

Let's take these outputs one line at a time.

The first nonheader line of the Linux output says that traffic bound for the Class C subnet 10.100.70.0/24 goes to gateway 0.0.0.0 (or rather, no gateway at all), which means that it gets transmitted to its destination on the local network through device eth0.

The second line directs traffic destined for the Class A subnet 127.0.0.0/8 to local delivery as well, but through interface device lo.

The third line seems to say that any destination at all will be sent to 10.100.70.1 through the network device eth0. The G flag on the line indicates that this is the gateway.

Why doesn't all traffic go to the gateway? Because in RH Linux 7.1, 0.0.0.0 is the address of the "default" destination. Traffic destined for specified subnets is handled by other entries in the routing table. Other traffic, by default, is handled by this table entry.

The first entry in the Solaris table is similar to the first entry in the Linux table and means pretty much the same thing.

To understand the second entry, you need to know that any address starting with the quad 224 is reserved for multicast messages. Multicast messages provide simultaneous communication among groups of systems. This line is directing all multicast messages to local delivery through device eri0.

The third entry uses the "default" entry that Linux labels 0.0.0.0. As in Linux, it specifies the handling of traffic for destinations not specified elsewhere.

The final entry in the Solaris table handles the loopback address and directs it to device lo0. The format of the entry suggests that *only* that address goes to loopback, rather than the entire subnet 127.0.0.0/8 as under RH Linux 7.1.

Most routing tables are fairly short because they deal only with whether to send a transmission through the gateway. Of course, the gateways (or *routers*) have routing tables themselves. These can get complicated. Remember that although any gateway must be connected to *at least* two networks, it is often connected to far more than two and must be capable of locating other routers on all of them.

> **Tip**
>
> A lot of software vendors really don't put a lot of effort into their `netstat` and `ifconfig` outputs, and sometimes they don't seem to make as much sense as they ought to. In Chapter 22, "Intrusion Detection," you will see how you can watch the network traffic itself to get a better idea of what is happening.

nslookup

Having avoided name resolution so far, we will check out its functionality with the `nslookup` command through direct inspection of the /etc/resolv.conf file.

LISTING 5.7   `nslookup` Output

RH Linux 7.1

```
# nslookup www.um.edu
Note: nslookup is deprecated and may be removed from future releases.
Consider using the 'dig' or 'host' programs instead.  Run nslookup with
the '-sil[ent]' option to prevent this message from appearing.
Server:         10.100.1.5
Address:        10.100.1.5#53

Name:   www.um.edu
Address: 10.100.253.114
```

LISTING 5.7   continued

Solaris 8

```
# nslookup www.um.edu
Server:   um5.um.edu
Address:   10.100.1.5

Name:    www.um.edu
Address:   10.100.253.114
```

> **Note**
>
> As you can see, nslookup has a limited future. dig and host have a lot more options and provide a lot more information. In fact, most of the time they'll tell you more than you want to know unless you use the options to quiet them down. We will describe these utilities in the Chapter 11, which will provide a more complete context for what they do.

Although the Linux implementation of nslookup is a good bit more wordy—including a warning of its own impending doom—both versions tell you that they went to the name server with IP address 10.100.1.5 and successfully resolved the name www.um.edu.

Examination of the /etc/resolv.conf file and the hosts record of the /etc/nsswitch.conf file shows this:

LISTING 5.8   Name Resolution Configuration Files—resolv.conf and nsswitch.conf

RH Linux 7.1

```
# cat /etc/resolv.conf
search ucs.um.edu
nameserver 130.85.1.5
nameserver 130.85.1.4
nameserver 130.85.1.3


# grep hosts /etc/nsswitch.conf
hosts:       files nisplus dns
```

Solaris 8

```
# cat /etc/resolv.conf
domain um.edu
nameserver 130.85.1.5
```

LISTING 5.8   continued

```
nameserver 130.85.1.3
nameserver 130.85.1.4

# grep hosts /etc/nsswitch.conf
hosts:      files dns
```

The Linux resolv.conf file specifies the correct name servers for the domain, as does the Solaris resolv.conf file. (The search and domain lines provide endings for hostnames that are not entered entirely—`telnet gleep` instead of `telnet gleep.um.edu`.)

The Linux nsswitch.conf `hosts:` record directs the Operating System to try to resolve names first from the /etc/hosts record, next from NIS, and finally from DNS. The corresponding Solaris record states that /etc/hosts be searched first, followed by DNS.

Initial Configuration

Actually, if you are installing either of the reference systems for the first time, the installation process asks you specifically for the IP address, netmask, default gateway, nameservers, and so on, and configures the system accordingly as part of the install. As long as you understand what you are being asked for (which is really what this chapter is about), you can get the information from your network administrator ahead of time and just enter it during installation.

Reconfiguration

Sometimes you need to change your networking configuration without necessarily going through a full reinstallation. On Linux, a GUI utility will help you do this. Enter the command `control-panel` to invoke it, select the Network icon, and then make whatever changes are needed. After changing network configuration, it's a good idea to reboot.

In addition, both Solaris 8 and RH Linux 7.1 provide a scary-sounding utility, `/usr/sbin/sys-unconfig` that removes all configuration data specific to the system on which it is run. It methodically reverses the configuration process that took place at installation and then shuts down the system. When the system is booted up again, it recognizes that it is not configured and goes through the same configuration process that it executed when first booted and installed. Because `sys-unconfig` confines itself to system configuration files only, it is actually fairly simple, for instance, to execute `sys-unconfig`, let the system shut down, move it to some new location with a different network, boot it up, and configure for the new network while still retaining user authentication information, home directories, and most installed software.

5

GETTING ON THE NETWORK

Services and Ports

As you probably already know, Unix is a multi-user Operating System. It runs lots of processes at the same time, some of which are started and controlled by users, and others that are started and controlled by the Operating System itself. Normally, a Unix system runs several network-based processes, both clients and servers.

We have described how a transmission gets from one node on the Internet to another. Now we need to consider what is done with it upon arrival. If the transmission payload contains email, it should go to the `sendmail` process. If the transmission is part of a telnet session, it needs to go to a telnet server. For that matter, if there are *two* telnet sessions going on, the transmission must go to the one it belongs to. Trying to sort out the nature and proper disposal of transmissions as they arrive would be a horrendous task, so the job is done by adding a bit more information to the data as it is prepared for transmission.

If a transmission is to go to the sendmail process, it is so marked. If it is to go to a telnet server, it is marked for the telnet server. If it is part of a specific telnet session, it is marked for that particular session. This is the computer world, so marking is done with numbers. Specifically, they are called *port numbers*. Just as the transmission has source and destination IP addresses, it also has source and destination port numbers.

Common Internet services are distinguished by specific "ports." Specifically, if a transmission has destination port 25, it is intended for the sendmail process running at the destination IP. A transmission with destination port 80 is intended for the Web server. In fact, port numbers below 1024 are called "well-known" ports and are reserved for specific services.

Unix systems have a file, /etc/services, in which port numbers are mapped to service names. If a port is not in /etc/services, it can still be used, but the system simply won't know what its name is and will have to refer to it by port number. In cases where an extended two-way exchange can be expected, such as a telnet or ftp session, the two communicating nodes establish a "connection." This means that both systems recognize a specific source IP/port pair and a specific destination IP/port pair allocated to support a particular communications session using a particular protocol until both sides decide to end it. A connection is often defined as consisting of five parts:

> *<source IP, source port, destination IP, destination port, protocol>*

Often, a server waiting at a well-known port will, upon receiving a transmission requesting a connection, "spawn" a copy of itself at some port above 1024 that is not currently in use. That port will then become the destination port in the five-component connection described previously.

Until now, we have considered Internet communication to take place between nodes with assigned IP addresses. That is only part of the story. Internet communication is actually between a source and destination port and is *supported* by the IP-to-IP communication between nodes. Two protocols exist "above" IP to enable port-to-port communication: Transmission Control Protocol (TCP) and User Datagram Protocol (UDP). TCP is the more robust of the two and is used when high confidence and low error tolerance are called for. In general, TCP is used for communication that often takes place between sub-nets. UDP is used more for communication that would usually take place within a subnet or when the overhead of a connection-oriented protocol would be too high to justify in terms of network bandwidth. For example, when DNS servers transfer data to one another from different parts of the Internet, they use TCP. When a local server is queried with the `nslookup` command, the query and response are usually transmitted using UDP. Streaming media applications also use UDP due to the amount of traffic they generate.

inetd/xinetd

`inetd` and `xinetd` are "super-servers," daemons that bind to multiple ports and are used to start multiple services. These services are usually lightweight, low-priority programs; the significant exceptions are `telnet` and `ftp`. More typical of services started by `inetd` or `xinetd` are `finger`, `ident`, and the AMANDA backup package, which uses several different ports. (Except when discussing configuration files, we will use "`inetd`" to refer to both `inetd` and `xinetd`.)

The advantage of using `inetd` over running lightweight services independently is that none of the programs need run until actually connected to by a user. When this occurs, `inetd` transparently spawns a server process and connects the user to the requested server.

Servers that require little or no per-user setup benefit from `inetd` primarily by reducing the amount of spawning and the number of dormant processes. Another significant advantage is that services using `inetd` may be "wrapped" with TCP Wrappers to provide additional security. (See Chapter 8 for more information about TCP Wrappers.)

Heavyweight processes, or those requiring a substantial amount of per-instance setup, are not good candidates for running via `inetd`. Examples of such services include Web servers, which must generally parse a large number of complex configuration files upon initialization, and the `ssh` server, which must generate large numbers upon starting.

Although these programs could potentially be configured to start via `inetd`, they would take an inordinate amount of time to start up, providing poor response to the user. These servers thus generally run as independent daemons.

If no services requiring `inetd` are necessary, we recommend that it be disabled completely to reduce security exposure. If `inetd` cannot be removed due to the use of programs that depend upon it, we recommend disabling all unused services. In particular, the `chargen`, `echo`, `time`, and `daytime` services are almost never used for legitimate purposes anymore; they are primarily used as part of a denial-of-service attack or to exploit a security hole in the service itself. All these services should be disabled. Similarly, `rsh`, `rcp`, `rlogin`, and `rexec` should all be disabled; they have been superseded by the `ssh` suite. (See Chapter 8 for more details on `ssh`.) If you have multiple users logged onto your system, the ident server might be useful to determine who accessed a particular remote resource, but it is unreliable and not generally necessary. `telnet` and `ftp` are both security risks and should be disabled except in situations where it is infeasible to move a particular user to `ssh`; because there are free `ssh` clients available for Unix, Windows, and Macintosh, the only reason to leave FTP enabled is if the system is running an anonymous FTP server. If the system is not running an anonymous FTP server, `inetd` can generally be disabled unless, for example, backup software such as AMANDA is running.

Although they function in a similar manner and for similar purposes, `inetd` and `xinetd` configuration files have a completely different syntax. In `inetd`'s configuration, which is located in the file /etc/inetd.conf, each service is represented by a single line of the configuration file. Lines beginning with # are comments and are ignored. Every line begins with the port number or name of the port, as found in the /etc/services file, and is followed by several other parameters, as documented on the man page. There are four such parameters, which are separated by spaces and then followed by the command to run when the port is opened. To disable services, simply add a # to the beginning of the line; to enable services that have been commented out, simply uncomment the line in question. Any services that need to run via inetd should document the configuration settings; pay attention to the installation instructions, and you should be okay.

`xinetd`'s configuration syntax bears no resemblance to that of inetd. The file is /etc/xinetd.conf, although that location might vary on systems where xinetd was built from source rather than installed with the system. Each service is represented by a group of lines that begin with the words `service` *<servicename>*, where *<servicename>* is a service listed in the file /etc/services. This is followed by an open brace ({), and then a list of attributes and values, which are essentially configuration variables. Each line provides an attribute, a space, an equals sign, and the value of that attribute. The important attribute is `disable`, which should be set to `yes` if a service is not to be run, and should be set to `no` if a service is to be run. The attributes for a particular service are followed by a line with a closed brace (}). Many additional attributes are documented on the xinetd.conf(5) man page; this makes interesting reading, and we encourage budding system administrators to learn how to take full advantage of `xinetd`.

Both `inetd` and `xinetd` reread their configurations at startup or when given a HUP signal. After editing the configuration file or files, be sure to run `kill -HUP` on the appropriate process. On some older versions of `inetd` on older platforms—notably versions of SGI's IRIX earlier than 6—the HUP signal will not cause the configuration files to be reread, and the process will need to be killed and then restarted for changes to take effect.

Solaris 8 uses a plain-vanilla `inetd` configuration, as do versions of Red Hat Linux earlier than version 7. Version 7 and up use `xinetd` with a minimal /etc/xinetd.conf that includes an /etc/xinetd.d directory. The /etc/xinetd.d directory contains several files, each of which corresponds to a single service. This makes it simple for package management to add or remove a service by adding or removing a single file; to disable a service without completely removing it from the system, just change the `disable = no` option to `disable = yes`.

netstat Revisited

You can use `netstat` without options or with the -a option to find out the status of system connections. A complete discussion of the output of `netstat`, with or without the -a option, is beyond the scope of this chapter. We'll just paste in the good bits here.

LISTING 5.9   `netstat -a` Output

RH Linux 7.1

```
# netstat
Active Internet connections (w/o servers)
Proto Recv-Q Send-Q Local Address          Foreign Address        State
tcp        0      0 corylus.ucs:ssh        umbc7.um.edu:36899     ESTABLISHED
tcp        0      0 corylus.ucs:ssh        gecko.ucs:21483        ESTABLISHED

# netstat -a
Active Internet connections (servers and established)
Proto Recv-Q Send-Q Local Address          Foreign Address        State
tcp        0      0 *:32768                *:*                    LISTEN
tcp        0      0 *:sunrpc               *:*                    LISTEN
tcp        0      0 *:x11                  *:*                    LISTEN
tcp        0      0 *:ssh                  *:*                    LISTEN
tcp        0      0 localhost.localdom:smtp *:*                   LISTEN
tcp        0      0 corylus.ucs:ssh        umbc7.um.edu:36899     ESTABLISHED
tcp        0      0 corylus.ucs:ssh        gecko.ucs:21483        ESTABLISHED
udp        0      0 *:32768                *:*
udp        0      0 *:772                  *:*
udp        0      0 *:sunrpc               *:*
```

LISTING 5.9 continued

Solaris 8

```
# netstat

TCP: IPv4
    Local Address        Remote Address       Swind Send-Q Rwind Recv-Q State
 ------------------   ------------------   ----- ------ ----- ------ -------
 ensis.22             gecko.21404          61100      0 24820      0 ESTABLISHED
 ensis.22             umbc7.um.edu.37929   49152      0 24820      0 ESTABLISHED


# netstat -a

UDP: IPv4
    Local Address        Remote Address       State
 ------------------   ------------------   -------
      *.sunrpc                              Idle
      *.*                                   Unbound
      *.32771                               Idle
      *.1023                                Idle
      *.32772                               Idle
      *.32773                               Idle
      *.32777                               Idle
      *.32779                               Idle
      *.name                                Idle

TCP: IPv4
    Local Address        Remote Address       Swind Send-Q Rwind Recv-Q State
 ------------------   ------------------   ----- ------ ----- ------ -------
      *.*                  *.*                  0      0 24576      0 IDLE
      *.sunrpc             *.*                  0      0 24576      0 LISTEN
      *.*                  *.*                  0      0 24576      0 IDLE
      *.1023               *.*                  0      0 24576      0 BOUND
      *.32771              *.*                  0      0 24576      0 LISTEN
      *.32772              *.*                  0      0 24576      0 LISTEN
      *.ftp                *.*                  0      0 24576      0 LISTEN
      *.telnet             *.*                  0      0 24576      0 LISTEN
      *.shell              *.*                  0      0 24576      0 LISTEN
      *.shell              *.*                  0      0 24576      0 LISTEN
      *.login              *.*                  0      0 24576      0 LISTEN
      *.exec               *.*                  0      0 24576      0 LISTEN
      *.exec               *.*                  0      0 24576      0 LISTEN
 ensis.22             gecko.21404          61100      0 24820      0 ESTABLISHED
 ensis.22             umbc7.um.edu.37929   49152      0 24820      0 ESTABLISHED
```

The difference in output format camouflages the similarity of content between the two reference systems. The Linux netstat command reveals that there are two ssh (port 22) connections established between the host and remote systems. netstat -a reveals that there are several TCP services in LISTEN state—that is, waiting for a connection request—and several UDP services waiting for contact as well (for technical reasons dealt with in another chapter, the term "connection" is not applied to UDP).

Notice that some of the port numbers are translated to names, such as `ssh`, and others are not. We didn't use the `-n` option with `netstat`, so it resolved anything that it could. Any port expressed as a number has no corresponding entry in the /etc/services file.

The Solaris 8 `netstat`, like its Linux counterpart, identifies the `ssh` sessions, while `netstat -a` also shows the waiting TCP and UDP servers.

Best Practices

Human Interaction

- Get to know your network administrator(s).
- Develop a good working relationship with your network administrator(s).
- Realize that there is not likely to be a lot of configuration leeway until later in the process.

Basic Network Configurations

- Get the following items from the network administrator(s) before you try to configure your system:
  - System's IP address(es) and associated hostname(s) (check whether your site is using DHCP)
  - System's local subnet mask
  - System's local gateway IP address
  - IP address(es) of local DNS servers
- Remember to populate /etc/resolv.conf.
- Remember to populate /etc/hosts; key entries include these:
  - 127.0.0.1
  - System IP address(es) and associated hostname(s)
  - Critical server IP addresses and names (especially DNS servers)
- Develop a working knowledge of the site network layout; everything is easier if you know where you fit into the grand scheme of things.

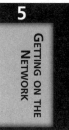

5

GETTING ON THE
NETWORK

Troubleshooting

- Use the -n switch with network troubleshooting commands (such as netstat) to suppress name resolution.

- Periodically run netstat even if you don't think there are problems, just to see what kind of activity is happening on your system.

- Use sys-unconfig when you move your machine around at a site or to wipe troublesome settings.

- When troubleshooting a network connection:

  - Use netstat to confirm that your system "sees" the network devices, and use ifconfig to check the device configurations.

  - ping the loopback address 127.0.0.1, to confirm that the network device is working (independent of the network). If this doesn't work, make sure that the NIC is firmly seated in your system. If so, try another NIC.

  - ping the IP of the system that you are troubleshooting to make sure that traffic can reach the network from your system and vice versa. If the ping fails, check the physical connection between the NIC and the network.

  - ping another system on your local network that you know to be working. This confirms that the local network connections are working. If the test fails, try another local system. If that fails, double-check your device configurations and physical network connections.

  - ping a system outside your local network. If you have the IP of a system reachable directly through your gateway without passing through any others, use that IP. If this fails, use netstat -rn to check that your routing information is correct. In particular, make sure that your local gateway is correctly defined. If the problem persists, ask the network administrator. It's possible that your IP is blocked for some reason.

Offering Services

- Minimize services being offered—don't offer *anything* unnecessary via inetd/xinetd.

Online References

Network Standards

IEEE OUI assignments: `http://standards.ieee.org/regauth/oui/index.shtml`

IETF RFCs: `http://www.ietf.org/rfc.html`

IANA home page: `http://www.iana.org`

DHCP

Red Hat's official references

Linuxconf: `http://www.europe.redhat.com/documentation/HOWTO/Net-HOWTO/x1112.php3`

Mini-How-To home:
`http://www.redhat.com/mirrors/LDP/HOWTO/mini/DHCP/x69.html`

Sun's official reference:
`http://docs.sun.com/ab2/coll.47.11/SYSADV3/@Ab2PageView/16214?Ab2Lang=C&Ab2Enc=iso-8859-1`

Logging

*by Robin Anderson and
Andy Johnston*

IN THIS CHAPTER

CHAPTER 6

Introduction

System logging is crucial for system security, monitoring, and troubleshooting. It can provide an early warning about potential or developing problems as well as forensic evidence regarding an incident.

All Unix variants are packaged with some kind of logging mechanism. The one enabled by default under both Red Hat and Solaris is based on the BSD syslog program. This service is highly configurable, and we will suggest a few sensible settings to improve on the defaults provided by the vendors.

We will also present concepts to bear in mind when designing site-wide logging systems, such as centralized collection and management. These principles are also applicable to non–syslog-based logging mechanisms, a few of which will be introduced in this chapter.

Finally, we will consider some techniques for performing routine log analysis. Remember, it's not enough to just collect the information; you need to spot anomalies and patterns to make it all worthwhile.

Standard Unix System Logging: syslog

As we mentioned before, Red Hat and Solaris both come standard with a system logger. Although the logging process is actually called different things on each system, on both it acts as a *daemon*, a process that always runs on the system in the background.

BSD System Logging

The BSD syslog program was the original system logger. It was intended to be the conduit for *all* logging on a system. Although many applications independently perform their own logging functions, syslog is still the basis for most system logging on Red Hat and Solaris systems.

Now, you might be wondering why we need to bother with an intermediary like syslog at all—why not just have processes write directly to their own log files? Syslog enables a unified, centralized control structure for logging. The exact location and style of logging is configurable by the sysadmin; the decision about how to handle logs does not require recompiling of software.

Having a centralized structure means that all log files are gathered in one place on the system, potentially even into a single file. This schema even scales over a network; syslogd can act as a conduit to pipe messages off-system to a central repository. Whichever method you use, centralized logging means that you don't have to rummage around on your system when you need to check log files or hunt down the origin of a particular error.

The syslog daemon also manages your log file(s), preventing the write-time contention that would certainly exist among numerous competing processes if they were trying to independently access the same log file. Having syslogd act as an arbiter and buffer for writes eliminates the potential for file corruption by funneling the records into the file(s) in an orderly fashion.

Finally, and most importantly, syslog prepends a standard header onto every log file record. This means that you will always have a predictable set of fields, including time-stamps. Note that the content of the message itself is unregulated—syslog just puts standardized information at the head of it. Also note that *any* system process can send messages to syslogd, which helps to explain the wide variety of messages that you'll find in the log files.

As the years have gone by, syslog's design has proven to be both flexible and scalable—so much so that its model, internal schema, and even configuration file syntax have changed very little since its creation.

Client/Server Model

Standard Unix logging operates in a client/server model, both internally on a single machine and across the network. This sort of architecture should be becoming very familiar to you; it is one of the most fundamental aspects of the Unix Operating System.

Let's look at a local system first. As we mentioned before, every Unix system runs a listening server process dedicated to logging: the syslog daemon. All processes needing to put information into the system log contact the syslogd to pass it the message. Those processes are acting as clients in our model. Figure 6.1 shows how these pieces fit together.

The syslog daemon can get its messages from the network as well as from other internal system processes. This is one of the factors that makes syslog so flexible: its capability to accept and process multiple sources of input. Since network communications are built into syslog from the ground up, it incurs very little extra overhead to send log messages off-system instead of—or in addition to—storing them on-system. Figure 6.2 shows a high-level view of a centralized log server receiving messages from remote machines.

FIGURE 6.1

Single-system syslog schematic.

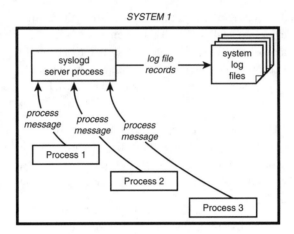

FIGURE 6.2

Centralized log server schematic (high level).

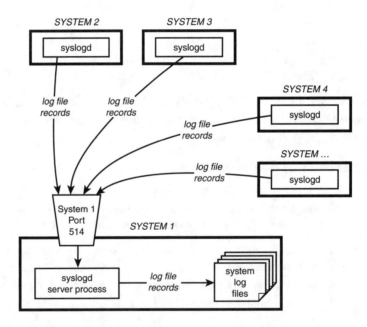

The bird's eye view of the model over-simplifies the underlying processes; there's more going on than you might first think. The processes on the remote systems are not talking directly to the central log server's daemon. They are actually passing the messages to their local syslogd, which, in turn, formats them into records. After formatting, the local syslogd forwards records to their ultimate destination.

Of course, `syslogd` can route messages to multiple locations, whether local files, remote servers, or a combination thereof. By adding the correct entries to the syslog.conf file (discussed later), you can keep both local and remote versions of all syslog entries. Figure 6.3 shows a more detailed view of what goes on inside all the machines involved.

FIGURE 6.3

Centralized log server schematic (detailed).

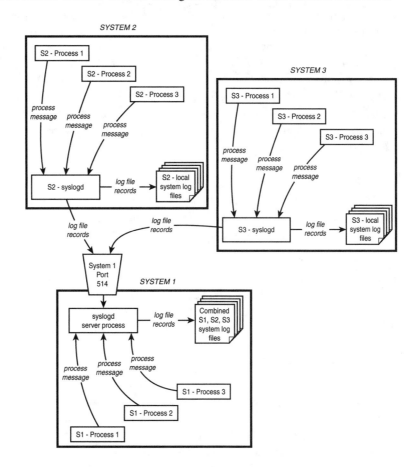

Note that there is a `syslogd` server process running on all three machines. The processes on Systems 2 and 3 are clients for their respective `syslogd` servers. These servers then act as clients to System 1's central `syslogd` server. Notice that System 1 also accepts log messages from its own local processes.

The net effect is that the same messages are logged in multiple locations. Notice that all hosts ***in our example*** store log messages in one or more local files as well as send copies out across the network. To a casual observer, this might seem like a needless waste of space. To the experienced sysadmin, multiple files provide a safety net of redundancy, protecting against loss, corruption, and intruders.

> ### Note
>
> In the preceding paragraph, we emphasized that the behavior of saving local copies of the logs before sending copies off-system was specific to our example. Syslog is highly configurable and its defaults are not consistent across Operating Systems, or even across versions.
>
> By default, Solaris will try to send copies of log file entries off-system as well as store them locally. Red Hat, on the other hand, only stores local copies in its default mode. See the later section on "syslog.conf" for more information.

Redundant log files become especially important in the event of security incidents, when local log files might be tampered with or even deleted entirely. It's much more difficult for would-be hackers to cover their tracks when they have to compromise not only the original system, but the site's central log server as well.

This is also a recurring theme that you will notice throughout this book: the importance of centralized, dedicated servers. Since dedicated servers run *only* the bare minimum of processes and services required to support their specific service, they have a lower network profile than systems that run a full panoply. Not only are dedicated servers less visible, but they also present fewer vulnerabilities to the Internet at large.

Red Hat: sysklogd

Red Hat refers to its system-logging utilities as sysklogd. Note, however, that there is no system *binary* called sysklogd; the term is a collective name for two separate processes. The first is the standard syslog daemon just discussed, if slightly modified. The second is a daemon called `klogd`, dedicated to trapping and recording kernel messages. Typically, `klogd` functions as a normal client process, sending its messages to syslog for formatting and recording in the main system log file.

But why run a separate process for kernel logging? The `klogd` man page gives us the following insight:

> In the modern Linux kernel a number of kernel messaging issues such as sourcing, prioritization, and resolution of kernel addresses must be addressed. Incorporating kernel logging into a separate process offers a cleaner separation of services.

So, if you check your Red Hat system, you will find both daemons running at any given time:

```
[linux:20 ~] ps -ef | grep logd
root      574    1   0 Sep10 ?       00:00:00 syslogd -m 0
root      579    1   0 Sep10 ?       00:00:00 klogd -2
```

By default, Red Hat stores all logs in the /var/log directory. There are a number of default log filenames, all defined in syslog.conf (discussed in the later section "syslog.conf"). The most broadly used log file is /var/log/messages.

Solaris: syslogd

Solaris runs only one logging process—`syslogd`—to handle both normal process and kernel logging needs:

```
[sun:20 ~]ps -ef | grep logd
    root   213    1   0   Sep 10 ?       0:03 /usr/sbin/syslogd
```

By default, Solaris stores local logs in /var/adm directory and logs directed off-system in the /var/log directory. Solaris also maintains a number of default log filenames, all defined in syslog.conf (discussed in the later section "syslog.conf"). The most broadly used log file is /var/adm/messages.

syslog Internal Schema

Log messages generated by local processes are tagged with two identifiers, usually referred to as *facility* and *severity*. The syslog server then processes the message based on those two labels.

The Facility Identifier

Facility indicates the type of subsystem that produced the log message. Both Red Hat and Solaris honor the keywords shown in Table 6.1.

TABLE 6.1   syslog Facility Labels

Facility Name	Intended Purpose
auth	Messages generated by the authorization subsystem
	Examples: `login`, `su`, `getty`
cron	Messages generated by periodic processes
	Examples: `cron`, `crontab`, `at`
daemon	Messages generated by system daemons
	Examples: `in.ftpd`, `inetd`

TABLE 6.1   continued

Facility Name	Intended Purpose
kern	Messages generated by the kernel
lpr	Messages generated by the printing subsystem
	Examples: `lpr`, `lpc`
mail	Messages generated by the mail subsystem
	Examples: `sendmail`, `postfix`, `procmail`
mark	Timestamp messages generated internally by syslogd; not for use by external processes (See Sidebar, "Using mark")
news	Messages generated by the Usenet network news subsystem
	Examples: `inn`
user	Messages generated by user processes. This is the default facility assigned to any logging process that does not specify another facility.
uucp	Reserved for messages generated by the UUCP subsystem; not currently used
local0 through local7	Reserved for local use

Note

Red Hat also offers three facilities not in Table 6.1: `authpriv`, `security` (a deprecated version of `auth`), and `syslog` (indicates non-timestamp information from logging processes).

Although all these facilities are fairly well delineated, remember that any process can send `syslogd` a message labeled with any facility. In the end, these identifiers are only as accurate as the programmers who implemented them; there is nothing to prevent a home-brewed program from logging under the "news" facility.

Using mark

While `mark` is defined as a facility in the man pages of both Solaris and Red Hat, it functions like a directive. While other facilities are used as labels to categorize the associated log message, the `mark` facility simply directs `syslogd` to put a timestamp in the specified log file(s).

Methodical use of the mark facility will create a clear, periodic pattern of time stamps throughout your logs. This is one of the best security measures available to highlight that log files have been tampered with; there are few script kiddies or even accomplished hackers who will go through and edit a log file to remove all the messages, but leave the mark records in place. (You should be aware however, that there are scripts designed to excise selected messages from logs without interfering with other records.)

Automated monitoring tools can easily detect interruptions in the periodic patterns of the mark records. Such interruptions can indicate that syslogd is not functioning as intended or that the log files have been tampered with.

We recommend especially that mark records be sent to at least one local file and one file on the central loghost. Both files should be routinely monitored as part of your security practices.

To help encourage coders to stick to using facilities as originally intended, syslog provides eight local-use facilities (local0-local7). These facilities can be assigned to critical subsystems or locally developed software that routinely needs to submit log entries. See the section on syslog.conf for more information on enabling these local facilities.

The Severity Identifier

Severity, also called priority, indicates the relative importance of the log message.[1] Both Red Hat and Solaris honor the keywords shown in Table 6.2, ordered from lowest to highest severity.

TABLE 6.2 syslog Priority Labels

Severity/Priority Level	Purpose
none	Indicates that no messages from the indicated facility should be logged
debug	Used for messages normally needed only when debugging
info	Used for non-emergency informational/status messages
notice	Used for non-error messages that might need special attention
warning (warn)	Used for warning messages
err (error)	Used for general errors
crit	Used for critical conditions, such as hardware errors
alert	Used for conditions that should be corrected immediately
emerg (panic)	Used for emergency conditions

Note that the severity levels listed in parentheses are deprecated keywords—still honored, but frowned on.

Facility and severity may appear as labels for a message in any combination. Of course, these identifications lose some of their impact unless the syslog daemon is prepared to handle them in differentiated ways. The syslog.conf file is where the admin can manipulate the handling of various types of log messages.

syslog.conf

The syslog.conf file can be as simple or as complex as your site requires. A one-line file can send all records to one location, whether that is a file or a remote server. Conversely, you can set up a configuration file that sends records to multiple log files by severity or by facility.

Before we take a look at some actual syslog.conf files, let's outline a few of its basic rules and behaviors. The format described below is illustrated by the example Red Hat and Solaris syslog.conf files in their respective sections below.

Grammar of syslog.conf Entries

- Line format: `<selector><TAB><destination>`
- Selector format: `<facility>.<severity>`

Note that multiple selectors are allowed, separated by semicolons. Also note that the angle brackets (< and >) are not actually part of the entry; they are just delineators.

Syntax Rules of syslog.conf Entries

- The whitespace separator *must* be `<TAB>` (not `<SPACE>`).
- Comments begin with a # mark.
- Blank lines are ignored.
- If any part of a rule is malformed, the whole thing is ignored.
- Asterisk wildcard:

  The only wildcard supported is the asterisk (*). If used as a facility, it indicates all facilities except mark. If used as a severity, it indicates all severity levels. If used as a destination, it indicates that the record should be sent via `write` to all users currently logged in .

- Semicolons:

  - Semicolons (;) may be used to specify more than one selector per destination.
  - Multiple selector format: `<selector>;<selector>;<selector>;…`

- Selectors are parsed left to right, which means that each successive selector field gets priority over the ones before it. This allows selective exclusions.

Example: `*.alert;mail.none`   `/var/adm/alerts`

Means: Append records from all facilities except `mail` to /var/adm/alerts if they have severity `alert` or `emerg`. If you have this kind of rule, you generally also have one redirecting mail log records to their own file/location.

- Severity:

By default, all messages of the specified severity *and higher* are affected by a given line. Thus, `*.crit` applies to all facilities with messages of severity `crit`, `alert`, and `emerg`.

- Red Hat uses as special syntax extension for severity:
    - To specify an exact severity level (and not include any with greater severity), prepend a = character. Thus, `*.=crit` applies to all facilities with messages of severity `crit` only.
    - To ignore messages of a given severity or higher, prepend a ! character. Thus, `*.!alert` means to ignore messages from all facilities with severity `alert` and `emerg`.
    - To ignore only one specific severity level, combine the previous two examples. Thus, `*.!=debug` means to ignore messages from all facilities with severity `debug`.

Destination Rules of syslog.conf Entries

- Legitimate destinations include files, remote servers, the console device, and lists of users (via a `write` banner).
    - To specify a file: `<full path the log file>`
      Example: `/var/log/critical`
    - To specify a remote server: `@<remote server name>`
      Example: `@loghost.my.site.com`
    - To specify the console: `<full path to console device>`
      Example: `/dev/console`
    - To specify local users: `<username>,<username>,<…>`
      Example: `root,operator,valjean`
    - To specify *all* users currently logged in: `*`

- The syslog.conf file is read and stored in memory when `syslogd` is started or receives a HUP signal. This means that changes to /etc/syslog.conf will not take effect until `syslogd` is re-initialized.

  - Individual records can have multiple destinations. A record may match more than one facility/severity pair (or none at all). Thus, one record might appear in multiple local files and also be sent off-system.

Log File Existence

There are two ways to handle the question of log file existence, and you should not be surprised to learn that Red Hat and Solaris use opposite approaches.

Under Red Hat, if the log file specified in syslog.conf does not exist, it will be created as needed. Under Solaris, if the log file specified does not exist, the rule is ignored and the log record directed to the non-existent file is silently discarded. Note that the log record *could* be processed and stored elsewhere; as mentioned before, failure on one rule in syslog.conf has no effect on evaluation of other rules.

In either case, the question of log file existence is evaluated when syslog is *started* (or re-initialized), not when it attempts to write out the record. This means that even if you create a missing log file on a Solaris system, you will need to re-initialize `syslogd` to allow records to be stored there.

Note

Red Hat offers one additional destination that Solaris does not yet support: a *named pipe* (also called a FIFO).[2] Since Red Hat's `sysklogd` only supports writing to named pipes that exist before the syslog daemon is started up, make sure you've created the pipe with the `mkfifo` command.

To specify writing to a named pipe, use the following syntax in the syslog.conf file:

```
|<full path to named pipe> <full path to executable>
```

The executable is an external program, such as a log processor, and must be capable of interacting with the named pipe.

Now let's look at these rules in action in the default system syslog.conf files.

Red Hat: Default syslog.conf File

The following listing shows the default syslog.conf file for Red Hat Linux 7.1:

```
# Log all kernel messages to the console.
# Logging much else clutters up the screen.
#kern.*                                         /dev/console

# Log anything (except mail) of level info or higher.
# Don't log private authentication messages!
*.info;mail.none;authpriv.none;cron.none        /var/log/messages

# The authpriv file has restricted access.
authpriv.*                                      /var/log/secure

# Log all the mail messages in one place.
mail.*                                          /var/log/maillog


# Log cron stuff
cron.*                                          /var/log/cron

# Everybody gets emergency messages, plus log them on another
# machine.
*.emerg                                              *

# Save mail and news errors of level err and higher in a
# special file.
uucp,news.crit                                  /var/log/spooler

# Save boot messages also to boot.log
local7.*                                        /var/log/boot.log
```

There are a few things about this file worth mentioning. First, notice that all logs are collected under /var/log. While not mandatory, this practice certainly makes it easier on the admin (you!) when looking for log files.

Second, notice the theme of collecting log records by facility. This allows you to go through far fewer records when you are searching for a particular event in a given facility. On the other hand, the split files mean that you might not be able to get a sense of all the things going on in your system at any given time. You can get the best of both worlds by creating a unifying log file where all messages are stored, regardless of facility by an entry such as this:

```
*.notice/var/adm/all_messages
```

Remember that you will have to create the file /var/adm/all_messages before you can send messages to it, however.

Also notice that this syslog.conf prevents any messages from echoing to the console. If the system console is unmonitored, then there's no reason to send messages there. If, on the other hand, you have someone monitoring the screen, then it might be wise to un-comment the third line of this file and let the messages show.

One thing that we particularly recommend adding to this file is an entry to send a copy of all messages to a remote log server. This only makes sense, of course, if you actually *have* a centralized loghost. Assuming that the machine exists and is called loghost.my.site.com, enter the following as the last line of the file:

```
*.notice@loghost.my.site.com
```

A better approach is to add an entry to your /etc/hosts file, specifying that loghost.my.site.com is also called loghost. Then the syslog.conf entry would look like this:

```
*.notice@loghost
```

This way, if the loghost changes IPs or switches hosts, you only need to update one file.

Solaris: Default syslog.conf File

The following listing shows the default syslog.conf file for Solaris 8:

```
#ident  "@(#)syslog.conf      1.5     98/12/14 SMI"    /* SunOS 5.0 */
#
# Copyright  1991-1998 by Sun Microsystems, Inc.
# All rights reserved.
#
# syslog configuration file.
#
# This file is processed by m4 so be careful to quote (`') names
# that match m4 reserved words.  Also, within ifdef's, arguments
# containing commas must be quoted.
#
*.err;kern.notice;auth.notice                   /dev/sysmsg
*.err;kern.debug;daemon.notice;mail.crit        /var/adm/messages

*.alert;kern.err;daemon.err                     operator
*.alert                                         root

*.emerg                                         *

# if a non-loghost machine chooses to have authentication messages
# sent to the loghost machine, un-comment out the following line:
#auth.notice                    ifdef(`LOGHOST', /var/log/authlog, @loghost)
```

```
mail.debug                      ifdef('LOGHOST', /var/log/syslog, @loghost)

#
# non-loghost machines will use the following lines to cause "user"
# log messages to be logged locally.
#
ifdef(`LOGHOST', ,
user.err                                /dev/sysmsg
user.err                                /var/adm/messages
user.alert                              'root, operator'
user.emerg                              *
)
```

Sun has included some fancy constructs in this file, such as the `ifdef` statements, that are useful but not actually necessary to the proper function of syslog.conf. These constructs do provide for sending copies of log records off-system, however. Note that loghost must be defined (usually in /etc/hosts) for it to have meaning here.

Caution

Solaris can be quite resourceful when trying to locate your LOGHOST system. Depending on how you have configured /etc/nsswitch.conf, your Solaris system may check any combination of your local /etc/hosts file, DNS, and NIS. Make sure that you are aware of all avenues that your system will try when looking for remote hostnames and IPs. This is critical not just for logging, but for everyday functionality as well.

All in all, we recommend that you explicitly define your loghost in /etc/syslog.conf. This also fits very well with the overall philosophy of Unix—where components can be modular and self-contained, they are made so. When syslog.conf contains the fully-qualified hostname of the remote loghost, it means that there is one less intrasystem dependency (on /etc/hosts or NIS) to worry about.

Notice that Solaris splits logs into two locations, /var/adm for local-only files and /var/log for files containing records also copied off-system. Also notice that Solaris tends to differentiate log records by severity. In the end, though, most messages will be in one file: /var/adm/messages.

Finally, note that /dev/sysmsg is a device that routes message sent by root to the appropriate system console devices (in other words, it acts as a more flexible /dev/console).

Timekeeping: ntp

Synchronized timekeeping is absolutely critical to maintaining a secure and viable logging schema at your site. If one system is recording events in Greenwich Mean Time (GMT) while another is recording events in U.S. Eastern Standard Time (EST/GMT-5), you are obviously going to have to expend some effort matching up the two sets of logs. Even worse, imagine the headache of trying to match up records from systems that are at 5 minutes' variance.

Even if you manage to deal with the correlations for internal purposes, mismatched logs are not well received by law enforcement. Remember, the more you have to massage the records, the more it looks like you are performing some sort of underhanded trick with the data.

So how can you keep consistent time across your site? System hardware clocks are known to be relatively unreliable components, prone to *drift*. What's more, they don't communicate with each other, so there is no synchronization among systems. The trick is to use your network to establish and communicate a common timeframe. The package of choice for this is ntp, which comes standard in the current Red Hat and Solaris distributions.

A Brief History of ntp

Serious work on network-based time synchronization was underway before the 1980's. The first version of the actual Network Time Protocol (NTP) was released in 1985 with RFC 958.

The third version of the ntp software was called "xntp," to differentiate it from its predecessors. If you see a package called xntp or xntpd, it is the "real" ntp (RFC 1305).

The confusion really arose, though, when ntp version 4 came under development. Its naming scheme dropped the "x" – now it is just called "ntp" again. This newest version is stable and in use.

See http://www.eecis.udel.edu/~ntp/ntpfaq/NTP-a-faq.htm for more on the history of Internet Timekeeping.

ntp Architecture

Like DNS and NIS, NTP has a hierarchical structure. Each level of hierarchy is called a *stratum* (plural: *strata*). *Stratum 1* contains *primary servers*; systems that have their own reliable timepieces. *Stratum 2* contains *secondary servers*; systems that query primary servers and replicate the information, helping to balance the query load. The higher the number of a stratum, the farther removed it is from a primary server. Note that not all strata act as replicators or servers, since the farther removed a system is from the original timepiece, the greater the potential time drift.

Since highly reliable timepieces, like cesium clocks, are very expensive and require precise maintenance, most sites defer to well-known primary servers for time generation. Note that querying one of the many secondary servers available on the Internet is considered functionally equivalent to querying one of the fewer primary servers. See the following URL for listings of publicly accessible ntp time servers (strata 1 and 2):

```
http://www.eecis.udel.edu/~mills/ntp/servers.htm
```

Note

It is considered rude to "suck clock" (i.e. query NTP) from a system that is not yours, not explicitly for public time use, or has not been offered for your use by the system's owner.

Configuring ntp at Your Site

Setting up a robust NTP server infrastructure goes beyond the scope of this book. We will tell you how to configure clients to update themselves, either from a local server/server group or from publicly accessible Internet timeservers.

There are two ways to effectively run ntp: continuous/daemon mode and intermittent update mode. Since ntp takes up relatively little network bandwidth and CPU processing time, we recommend that you run the daemon wherever possible. Systems with known hardware clock problems and high exposure should always have ntpd running. Intermittent updates are an acceptable alternative for systems that are used infrequently or are not always on the network.

Daemon mode: ntp.conf

The ntp.conf file controls the behavior of ntp under both Red Hat and Solaris. The default Red Hat /etc/ntp.conf file is well commented with explanations of some of the more subtle timekeeping settings. The default Solaris /etc/inet/ntp.conf file, on the other hand, is very sparse.

Listing 6.1 shows a simple ntp.conf file that you can drop onto a client system to get time updates from external servers.

LISTING 6.1   Sample ntp.conf file

```
# ntp.conf

# Drift file
driftfile /etc/ntp.drift

# Use three external (public) secondary timeservers.
server 128.175.1.3     # louie.udel.edu
server 128.46.128.76   # harbor.ecn.purdue.edu
server 165.91.52.110   # ntp5.tamu.edu

# Ignore ntp messages from any system; do not serve time
# or provide information, even to other systems on-site

restrict default ignore
```

Notice the entry specifying a *driftfile*; this file stores time drift information for use by ntp in the event of loss of network connectivity. We recommend that you use a driftfile on all clients.

Also notice that we specified three timeservers, all of which are publicly accessible and whose admins do not request notification prior to use. We chose these machines randomly; see the online list of secondary servers for sites better suited to your location.

We specified some fairly strict security settings on the last line of Listing 6.1. All ntp information on and about this client system is restricted by default. All requests for such information are ignored (discarded without response), even when the requestor is coming from on-site.

If you know that your site provides a cluster of ntp servers, you can substitute their IP addresses for the secondary servers we specified.

Intermittent Mode: cron

To intermittently update system time, invoke the `ntpdate` command via `cron`. We recommend that you update your system time at least twice per day. The following command line will work under both Red Hat and Solaris:

```
ntpdate -s ntp1.mysite.com ntp2.mysite.com ntp3.mysite.com
```

We specified three ntp servers, all of which happen to be run by our local site. As with the daemon mode, you can specify external primaries and/or secondaries.

The "-s" option makes ntpdate log to the system log rather than standard output. Now we've come full circle—setting system time to make logging work better and logging to the system log when we do it.

Configuring Your Site's Logging Security

We suggest taking a top-down approach when considering how to tighten your site's logging security. Your overarching goals are to protect the confidentiality and integrity of your log files, both on disk and in transit.

Your site's logging configuration can be separated into two components. The first component consists of all the systems that log messages to themselves. The second component contains the systems that send log messages to the central (remote) loghost and the central loghost itself. Of course, many systems maintain local log files and log to a remote loghost at the same time. Such systems appear in both components of the overall site configuration. Separating the components conceptually allows us to consider the local and remote logging strategies separately, and address the different security issues that each presents independently. The resolutions of the issues in the separate components can then be combined into a strategy for the entire site configuration.

Securing Your Local Logging Configuration

Let's take a look at components with local logging functions first. These systems run `syslogd` and store their own system log records locally, but are not intended to accept records from external sources.

What's Wrong with Logging External Records?

There are two major reasons why accepting external records can be dangerous: Excess logs can fill up your local filesystems and the extra network traffic can slow down your system's overall response time.

While this presents a problem even for a central loghost, a non-dedicated machine is likely to suffer more acutely since it was not designed to act as a repository.

By default, Red Hat provides logging for local system access only, refusing external network connections to `syslogd`. This kind of secure-by-default setup makes your job as an admin much easier; you actually have to provide a command-line option to get syslog to listen to the network.

The Solaris default behavior is completely opposite; `syslogd` accepts records from any external source. This model trusts every machine that can contact your system over the network. Unfortunately, relying on the goodwill of unknown admins and users is rarely a wise idea.

Fortunately, though, shutting down the syslog network listening service will stop the incoming log chatter. Solaris makes this easy: Just pass the "-t" option to syslogd at startup. The simplest way to do this is to edit syslog's init script (by default this is /etc/init.d/syslog) and add in the "-t" option to syslogd's invocation. Remember to re-initialize syslog after adding this option or it won't take effect.

So How Can I Tell if syslog is Accepting Remote Records?

Even though you've configured syslogd to ignore external log connection attempts, you will want to periodically check that the system is performing as expected.

While you could just check your various log files for external system records, this is inefficient (and depends on a fairly steady stream of input from an external source). A more reliable method is to check whether your system is listening for network connections on the syslog port.

The standard syslog implementations packaged with Red Hat and Solaris accept incoming log records on port 514, UDP (check for the syslog entry in your local /etc/services file).

Use the netstat command to see if port 514/udp is open. Note that under Red Hat, the "-p" option to netstat reveals the owning PID and the "-u" option specifies to check only UDP sockets. The following netstat listing indicates a syslogd daemon with PID 427 listening at port 514/udp.

```
[linux:24 ~]netstat -anpu | grep 514
udp        0      0 0.0.0.0:514          0.0.0.0:*           427/syslogd
```

Also note that to examine processes or sockets owned by root, you must have super-user privileges on the system.

The netstat implementation under Solaris is not nearly so forthcoming, but it still tells us that a daemon is listening at port 514/udp:

```
[sun:39 ~] netstat -an | grep 514
      *.514                            Idle
```

These ports may just be listening because syslogd has not been re-initialized since updating the configuration file. Check your invocation of syslog, re-initialize if necessary, and see if the port is still open. Once netstat does not report 514 UDP, you know that you have shut down remote logging capabilities for the machine.

Remember that you can automate this task; just use cron to invoke a simple shell script that runs the netstat command and emails you the output.

Confidentiality of Local Logs

Now that your local system is logging to itself and refusing access to external machines, there is only one other major security issue to address locally: confidentiality. You want to protect your logs using the principle of least privilege (in other words, only give out log information on a need-to-know basis).

What's So Important About Local Logs?

Many admins overlook the fact that local logs contain a great deal of critical information about the system that generated them. It may sound cliché, but information is power. If an attacker knows what hardware you have, what versions of the OS and applications you are running, and other tidbits of expected behavior about the system, that attacker has a better chance of breaking in without your detecting it.

Protecting your system logs from those without a valid need to know is another aspect of defense in depth.

The simplest way to protect your system logs is to set their file permissions and ownerships. File permissions of 640 will usually suffice, provided that the group owner has restricted membership.

Tip

Create a "loggers" group to allow specific users access to your system logs without giving away the root password or granting sudo powers.

Here's what the long listing of a protected log file should look like:

```
[sun:46 ~] ls -la /var/adm/messages
-rw-r——-   1 root     loggers     7731658 Oct 19 13:12 /var/adm/messages
```

Securing Your Remote Logging Configuration

When considering remote logging, remember that there are two kinds of system involved: the client that sends the log records and the server that acts as a central log repository.

The Client System

The client system component suffers no real security risk when sending log records to the central loghost. Your biggest concern on the client side is to ensure that the records are being sent to the correct off-system server. Check your syslog.conf file to see how the loghost is defined. Then use nslookup to verify that the loghost specified really resolves to the IP of the intended central server.

Confidentiality of Log Records in Transit

You want to protect the confidentiality of your logs whether they are resident on a system or in transit across your network. The catch is that it's more complex to set up protected network communication channels than it is to just set a few file permission bits.

The syslog implementation included on both Red Hat and Solaris transmits log records without encryption. This means that anyone sniffing network traffic on the route between the client and loghost systems will be able to see the full log records as they travel to the loghost. Some of the syslog alternatives we discuss in the later section have the capability of transmitting records over a secure, encrypted channel.

You should try to safeguard your log records in transit through appropriate network security measures. Encryption of network traffic is the most effective anti-sniffing measure that you can take. However, even if your system logger implementation encrypts communications, additional measures to secure your network are justified under the "defense-in-depth" approach to security. Two network-based security measures will help protect you log records in transit: point-to-point encrypted transfer tunnels and syslog border-blocking.

Aren't Switched Networks Enough?

It's a longstanding and beguiling myth that switched networks are the One True Solution against network sniffing. Vendors still promote this idea and even security practitioners believed it for a long time.

Switched networks were developed to route traffic point-to-point for bandwidth optimization, not to address security concerns. The switches themselves can be targeted for compromise. There are many means (for instance, ARP cache poisoning) by which an attacker can fool your switches into bypassing their normal point-to-point behavior.

Relying on switched networks to prevent network sniffing or provide data privacy is a fallacy and can foster a *false* sense of security. Also remember that the data transfer can be sniffed at the source and destination hosts more easily than on the wire.

Preventing trivial hub sniffing with switched networks is certainly part of an in-depth security posture, but should not be relied on to protect logs or other sensitive data.

Bottom line: If you don't have a switched network, you should convert, though mainly for performance reasons. Moving to switched networks can be costly and time-intensive; so don't expect this to happen overnight.

There are two types of point-to-point encrypted transfer tunnels that you might want to try at your site: ssh-style tunneling and IPSEC/VPN-style tunneling. We currently use a log transfer scheme based on OpenSSH's scp and RSA-challenge keys (see Appendix E "Cryptography in Unix"). Virtual Private Networks (VPNs) can be implemented in software or in hardware, depending on your site's needs and budget. A VPN tunnel creates an encrypted, dedicated channel between the central loghost and your client systems.

Note

We found it quite straightforward to set up scp-based log transfers. VPNs take more initial effort, but may be worth it in terms of long-term payback. Our recommendation is to secure your transfers *now* and then look into your long-term solution.

Regardless of your network infrastructure or log transfer mechanisms, you should add a syslog egress block at your border router or firewall. If you block port 514/udp traffic from leaving your site (or even a particular subnet), you will know that your system logs are not straying to the outside world.

Note that both of these measures will mean that you will need to work in concert with your site's network folks (since we presume you are not also the network admin). Remember that you are all on the same side, trying to make your site work efficiently and securely.

The Central Loghost

The first key to securing your central loghost is to make it a dedicated server. The concept of dedicated servers is one that we've been expounding throughout this book; it's one of the simplest ways to control what happens on a machine and narrow the field of security threats.

Using a Dedicated Server

As with any other dedicated server, you will need to shut down all unnecessary services and daemons. The only ports that should be accepting external connections are 514/udp (syslog) and possibly 22/tcp (ssh). For pointers on how to get rid of services maintained by `inetd` or `rpc/portmap`, see Chapter 8, "Securing Your System for Rollout."

Ingress Filtering

Consider asking your network admin to add a syslog ingress block at your border router or firewall. There's no real reason that systems external to your site should be sending their system logs to your central server. In fact, you may want to drop all connection requests to the central loghost from off-site. Note that this will require you to do your own maintenance work from an onsite IP or through some sort of VPN.

Since your central loghost must accept records from external machines, it is exposed to several security risks that can be mitigated, but not eliminated. As we mentioned before, a high volume of log traffic can fill up your local filesystems and the extra network traffic can slow down your system's overall response time. These conditions can present serious problems even if they happen unintentionally (not all bad things are the result of hackers or malicious users). You also want to consider how to block unwanted systems from logging to the central loghost.

You can avert filling up your local filesystems by keeping logs in their own partition (usually /var) and making sure that partition has "lots" of extra space. Of course "lots" is a relative term; disk allocations will depend on your budget, how many machines are logging to your central server, how long you keep the logs, etc.

> **Caution**
>
> Any syslog server is a tempting target for Denial of Service (DoS) attacks. A malicious user or hacker can flood your syslog server with thousands of requests, rendering it useless.

There is no good, reliable method for preventing DoS attacks; if someone really wants to flood your system, they will succeed. In fact, the measures we recommend that guard against network flood attacks are the same as those that guard against external systems sending unwanted log records to your central server.

Aside from DoS concerns, as more systems that log to your server, it becomes harder to spot specific problems with individual hosts. This problem is greatly compounded if not all the systems you receive logs from actually belong to your site.

Blocking unwanted systems improves your signal-to-noise ratio.

Just as we recommend egress filtering to protect your logs' confidentiality, we also recommend ingress filtering. Configure your site's border router or firewall such that incoming port 514/udp is blocked. This will prevent systems outside your domain from pretending that they are legitimate log clients.

A further measure that takes a bit more effort to both set up and maintain is a local system firewall on the central loghost. Setting up a host-based firewall goes beyond the scope of this chapter, but can be very effective in filtering message traffic by source. A local firewall can also blackhole all service requests so that machine doesn't even seem to be on the network; with this kind of configuration, the system won't even respond to ping requests. The basic principle is that hackers can't hit what they can't see.

Periodic Checks

To keep your loghost running in top condition, we recommend that you perform periodic checks on syslog's run status, log disk space usage, and other key components. Use cron to run single commands or simple scripts to keep you up to date. See Chapter 19, "Automation" for more tips on periodic process management.

There are a number of simple checks you can run to make sure syslogd is performing as expected:

- Use ps to check that the syslog daemon is running.
- Use netstat as described earlier to verify whether port 514/udp is open and accepting external log records.
- Use df once or twice a day to check on the loghost's disk space usage. If you see a sudden spike in log size, it could be an early warning sign of other problems at your site.
- Use ls -l to verify that the main log file continues growing. If the timestamp and size never change, then it's likely that the syslog process itself has died.
- Check for mark-type entries in the main log file. Missing markers may indicate that the syslog process itself has died or that the logs have been tampered with.

Log Record Validity

There is one final security issue you should be concerned about on your central loghost: Logfile content validity. Forging syslog messages is trivial, especially given that records are transmitted over UDP. Again, local firewalls will help winnow out some falsified traffic, but you could still see spoofed messages originating in-site. View all syslog records with a grain of caution and take steps to cross-reference the information you receive. The more correlations you can establish, the more likely the records you are receiving are valid and useful. Comparing local logs with those on the central loghost will catch most discrepancies.

Application Logging through syslog

Clever application programmers often code in the capacity for their applications to log through syslog. The benefits are multiple: The handling code is already written and available as a black-box, the log is probably replicated across more than one machine, and the main system logs are more likely to be perused than individual application logs.

Of course, there is nothing stopping an application from maintaining its own log files in addition to sending messages to syslog. In fact, sudo allows you to build in the kind of logging that you want: syslog only, native only, or both.

> **Note**
>
> Our advice: When you can get both kinds of logging, take both.
>
> Our reasoning: It's faster to search application-specific logs. You can also spot application event trends more easily with dedicated log files. Multispectrum system log files allow you to spot system-wide trends and problems and, as we mentioned before, are more likely to be replicated off-system.

For homegrown applications, remember that syslog has eight local logging facilities built in for your use (local0-local7). Just remember to document how you are using them with comments in both the syslog.conf file and in the application's document.

Also note that local0-local7 can be defined for use throughout a site, not just on a particular system. There is a great deal of value in coordinating the use of the "local" facilities among sysadmins throughout your enterprise, especially if you use central loghosts or shared rule-based log-monitoring tools.

To make this work, all your site's sysadmins need to thoroughly document how all third-party software is set up to log, including what syslog facility it uses. This information needs to be centrally stored and accessible by all the sysadmins in the enterprise. Enormous chaos results when badly documented systems are set to log to the same central loghost; when facilities collide, everyone loses.

Application-Specific Logging outside syslog

Many applications do not take advantage of syslog, mostly because it does not offer the kinds of features that the programmers required. System logs are not an optimal place to store current state and access records, especially if some post-filing processing must be done.

When applications start their own log files, they tend to keep most, if not all, their functional information in them. Error messages, configuration updates, and so on are usually in the same file as state and access information. Many programs also track their controlling process PID by placing it in its own file. Applications can effect graceful shutdown and restarts if they are PID-aware, and it takes less time to check a file than to `grep` through a `ps` listing.

A few examples of applications that you might expect to maintain their own logs follow:

- **httpd**—Web server daemon
- **lmgrd**—License manager daemon
- **innd**—Usenet news daemon
- **lpd, lprng**—Print spooler daemons

Note that most applications allow you to configure where their logs are stored. For the sake of convenience, you might want to keep application logs together with standard system logs in /var/log or a suitable subdirectory thereof.

Standard System Logging outside syslog

Ironically enough, some fundamental system logging is done outside the parameters of syslog. The most critical and noteworthy is the system's automatic user login tracking.

Both Red Hat and Solaris use the same basic log files to document when users log in, when users log out, and from where the activity occurred. These files are not plain text, but are rather in a database format to more efficiently store their data. The files common to both Operating Systems are listed here:

- **utmp**—Records all users currently logged into the system.
- **utmpx**—Is an extended version of utmp (more fields per record).
- **wtmp**—Records all logins and logouts. The format mirrors that of utmp, but a null username indicates a logout on the associated terminal.
- **wtmpx**—Is an extended version of wtmp (more fields per record).

These files are just so much wasted space without a command to format and display their contents. To access utmp (or utmpx, whichever is available), use the w command:

```
[linux:5 ~] w
 11:30pm  up 10 days,  8:38,  1 user,  load average: 0.00, 0.00, 0.00
USER     TTY     FROM            LOGIN@   IDLE   JCPU   PCPU  WHAT
root     pts/0   :0              11:17pm  0.00s  0.04s  0.00s  w

[sun:5 ~]w
 11:34pm  up 10 day(s),  9:15,  1 user,  load average: 0.00, 0.09, 0.11
User     tty            login@  idle   JCPU   PCPU  what
root     pts/1          10:10pm         24            w
```

Notice that although the output format differs slightly, the content is basically the same under both Red Hat and Solaris. Both show the system's uptime since the last reboot; load averages for the last 1, 5, and 15 minutes; and information on currently logged-in users.

What Red Hat provides that Solaris does not is the user's login vector. In this case, we know that root is logged in from :0, or the system console. Solaris does not provide us with that information here.

To retrieve records from wtmp (or wtmpx, whichever is available), sorted from most to least recent login time, invoke last. Note that the output of last is similar for Red Hat and Solaris. The output is separated into the following columns:

```
Username  Terminal  From  LoginTime-LogoutTime  Duration
```

The username is the one presented to the system during a successful login attempt. Terminal represents the virtual terminal assigned to that particular login session. The From field shows the name (or IP) of the host from which the user logged in. Note that this field is occasionally truncated, but can be fully displayed by passing last various command-line options. The next field shows the timestamps, in system time, of when the user logged and out. If the user has not yet logged out, the LogoutTime and Duration

fields will be marked `still logged in`. `Duration` tells how many days, hours, and minutes the login session lasted.

The following sample output from last has been trimmed due to space constraints:

```
[sun:6 ~]last
root      pts/1      remote1.my.site.com   Thu Sep 20 22:10    still logged in
root      pts/2      remote1.my.site.com   Thu Sep 20 16:01 - 21:05   (05:04)
root      pts/1      remote2.net           Thu Sep 20 12:57 - 18:33   (05:35)
root      pts/1      remote1.my.site.com   Tue Sep 18 10:30 - 15:52   (05:21)
root      pts/1      remote1.my.site.com   Mon Sep 10 20:21 - 23:55   (03:34)
root      pts/1      remote1.my.site.com   Mon Sep 10 15:42 - 17:51   (02:09)
root      pts/1      remote3.org           Mon Sep 10 14:21 - 14:53   (00:32)
reboot    system boot                      Mon Sep 10 14:19
root      pts/1      remote4.my.site.com   Mon Sep 10 14:16 - down    (00:03)
root      pts/1      remote4.my.site.com   Mon Sep 10 10:23 - 14:16   (03:52)
root      pts/1      remote1.my.site.com   Sun Sep  9 21:23 - 23:32   (02:08)
root      pts/2      remote1.my.site.com   Sat Sep  8 16:55 - 16:55   (00:00)
root      pts/1      remote1.my.site.com   Sat Sep  8 15:39 - 21:26   (05:46)
root      pts/1      remote4.my.site.com   Thu Sep  6 13:43 - 17:17   (03:34)
root      pts/1      remote5.outer.edu     Tue Sep  4 20:42 - 00:31   (03:49)
root      pts/1      remote1.my.site.com   Sun Sep  2 14:57 - 18:31   (03:34)
root      pts/1      remote1.my.site.com   Sun Sep  2 11:45 - 14:54   (03:08)
root      pts/1      remote1.my.site.com   Mon Aug 27 19:31 - 23:36   (04:04)
root      pts/1      remote1.my.site.com   Sun Aug 26 11:41 - 03:13   (15:32)
root      pts/2      remote1.my.site.com   Sat Aug 25 20:45 - 04:49   (08:03)
root      pts/1      remote1.my.site.com   Sat Aug 25 15:56 - 21:40   (05:44)
root      pts/1      remote1.my.site.com   Sat Aug 25 11:22 - 14:47   (03:24)
root      pts/1      remote1.my.site.com   Tue Aug 21 14:22 - 17:07   (02:44)
root      pts/2      remote4.my.site.com   Mon Aug 20 13:09 - 17:23   (04:13)
root      pts/1      remote4.my.site.com   Mon Aug 20 11:05 - 17:21   (06:15)
reboot    system boot                      Mon Aug 20 10:53
root      pts/1      remote1.my.site.com   Mon Aug 20 09:22 - 09:22   (00:00)
root      pts/2      remote1.my.site.com   Sun Aug 19 19:08 - 22:17   (03:09)
root      pts/1      remote1.my.site.com   Sun Aug 19 16:38 - 19:50   (03:11)
root      pts/1      remote1.my.site.com   Sun Aug 19 13:55 - 16:04   (02:09)
root      pts/1      remote1.my.site.com   Sun Aug 19 11:17 - 13:33   (02:15)
root      pts/1      remote1.my.site.com   Sat Aug 18 14:38 - 20:05   (05:27)
fantine   pts/1      jeune.femme.fr        Wed Aug 15 16:03 - 16:07   (00:03)
fantine   pts/1      jeune.femme.fr        Wed Aug 15 15:28 - 16:02   (00:34)
reboot    system boot                      Tue Aug 14 14:45
root      pts/1      remote1.my.site.com   Fri Aug  3 11:53 - 13:24   (01:31)
root      pts/1      remote1.my.site.com   Wed Aug  1 21:44 - 01:07   (03:22)
root      pts/1      remote5.outer.edu     Tue Jul 31 18:34 - 19:43   (01:09)
root      pts/1      remote1.my.site.com   Thu Jul 26 21:24 - 00:41   (03:17)
root      pts/1      remote1.my.site.com   Thu Jul 26 09:51 - 17:48   (07:57)
root      pts/2      remote5.outer.edu     Mon Jul 23 14:43 - 19:00   (04:17)
root      pts/1      remote5.outer.edu     Mon Jul 23 12:45 - 15:32   (02:47)
root      pts/1      remote5.outer.edu     Mon Jul 23 09:00 - 11:19   (02:18)
```

```
javert      pts/1      jeune.ecole.fr      Mon Jul 23 08:12 - 08:13  (00:00)
javert      pts/1      jeune.ecole.fr      Mon Jul 23 07:20 - 08:12  (00:52)
javert      pts/2      jeune.ecole.fr      Mon Jul 23 07:17 - 08:12  (00:54)
javert      pts/2      jeune.ecole.fr      Mon Jul 23 07:16 - 07:17  (00:00)
```

Use `last` with care!

If your system has been up for a long time, or if it has many users, the unabridged output from `last` will scroll for quite some time...

Try these commands to keep your output more manageable:

- `last | head -20`

Shows you the most recent 20 entries, just under a screenful.

- `last | more`   *or*   `last | less`

Lets you manage multi-screen output and search for expressions in the output

- `last | wc -l`

Gives you a metric on how many entries `last` will produce. Good indicator for when you might want to rotate the wtmp[x] file.

You can even use `last` to check on the login patterns of a particular user. It's always interesting to check on root, so here's a partial listing:

```
[linux:7 ~]last root
root      pts/1      remote1.my.site.com Thu Sep 20 22:10    still logged in
root      pts/2      remote1.my.site.com Thu Sep 20 16:01    still logged in
root      pts/1      remote2.net         Thu Sep 20 12:57 - 22:10  (09:12)
root      pts/1      remote1.my.site.com Tue Sep 18 10:30 - 12:57  (2+02:27)
root      pts/1      remote1.my.site.com Mon Sep 10 20:21 - 10:30  (7+14:09)
root      pts/1      remote1.my.site.com Mon Sep 10 15:42 - 20:21  (04:38)
root      pts/1      remote3.org         Mon Sep 10 14:21 - 15:42  (01:21)
root      :0                             Mon Sep 10 14:16 - down   (00:03)
root      pts/1      remote4.my.site.com Mon Sep 10 10:23 - 14:16  (03:53)
root      pts/1      remote1.my.site.com Sun Sep  9 21:23 - 10:23  (12:59)
root      :0                             Sat Sep  8 16:55 - down   (1+21:24)
root      pts/1      remote1.my.site.com Sat Sep  8 15:39 - 21:23  (1+05:43)
root      pts/1      remote4.my.site.com Thu Sep  6 13:43 - 15:39  (2+01:55)
root      pts/1      remote5.outer.edu   Tue Sep  4 20:42 - 13:43  (1+17:01)
root      pts/1      remote1.my.site.com Sun Sep  2 14:57 - 20:42  (2+05:45)
root      pts/1      remote1.my.site.com Sun Sep  2 11:45 - 14:57  (03:11)
root      pts/1      remote1.my.site.com Mon Aug 27 19:31 - 11:45  (5+16:14)
root      pts/1      remote1.my.site.com Sun Aug 26 11:41 - 19:31  (1+07:49)
root      pts/2      remote1.my.site.com Sat Aug 25 20:45 - 16:55  (13+20:09)
root      pts/1      remote1.my.site.com Sat Aug 25 15:56 - 11:41  (19:45)
root      pts/1      remote1.my.site.com Sat Aug 25 11:22 - 15:56  (04:33)
```

```
root        pts/1        remote1.my.site.com Tue Aug 21 14:22 - 11:22 (3+20:59)
root        pts/2        remote4.my.site.com Mon Aug 20 13:09 - 20:45 (5+07:36)
root        pts/1        remote4.my.site.com Mon Aug 20 11:05 - 14:22 (1+03:17)
root        pts/1        remote1.my.site.com Mon Aug 20 09:22 - down   (01:31)
root        pts/2        remote1.my.site.com Sun Aug 19 19:08 - down   (15:44)
root        pts/1        remote1.my.site.com Sun Aug 19 16:38 - 09:22  (16:43)
root        pts/1        remote1.my.site.com Sun Aug 19 13:55 - 16:38  (02:43)
root        pts/1        remote1.my.site.com Sun Aug 19 11:17 - 13:55  (02:37)
root        pts/1        remote1.my.site.com Sat Aug 18 14:38 - 11:17  (20:39)
root        pts/1        remote1.my.site.com Fri Aug  3 11:53 - down   (11+02:52)
root        pts/1        remote1.my.site.com Wed Aug  1 21:44 - 11:53  (1+14:08)
```

Most of the activity seems to be coming from my.site.com on hosts remote1 and remote4. This is a good time to ask who logged in as root from those machines. Are there legitimate superusers coming from those systems? Should remote root logins be permitted at all? (Hint: Probably not—have users log in as themselves and su or sudo instead.) Also look into the connection from outside your domain (remote3.org and remote5.outer.edu).

Red Hat Extras

Red Hat offers a nifty extra: It logs and can report specifically on bad logins. Note that failed logins are reported only when the login process involved uses the system's native login utility (/bin/login). This behavior is *not* enabled by default, however. The admin must create /var/log/btmp ahead of time.

The `lastlog` command processes and presents information stored in /var/log/lastlog. This is a quick way to examine the last login time for all users on the system (as listed in /etc/passwd). It also reveals whether certain accounts have never been logged into directly (although it does *not* tell you about su activity). Here's a sample from our reference system:

```
[linux:10 ~] lastlog
Username        Port     From            Latest
root            pts/0    remote1.my.site. Fri Sep 21 07:21:02 -0400 2001
bin                                       **Never logged in**
daemon                                    **Never logged in**
adm                                       **Never logged in**
lp                                        **Never logged in**
sync                                      **Never logged in**
shutdown                                  **Never logged in**
halt                                      **Never logged in**
mail                                      **Never logged in**
news                                      **Never logged in**
uucp                                      **Never logged in**
operator                                  **Never logged in**
games                                     **Never logged in**
```

```
gopher                              **Never logged in**
ftp                                 **Never logged in**
nobody                              **Never logged in**
nscd                                **Never logged in**
mailnull                            **Never logged in**
ident                               **Never logged in**
rpc                                 **Never logged in**
rpcuser                             **Never logged in**
xfs                                 **Never logged in**
gdm                                 **Never logged in**
robin          :0                   Mon Aug 27 13:33:08 -0400 2001
marius                              **Never logged in**
fantine                             **Never logged in**
```

Many accounts have never been used at all on this system. This could be an early indication that some user or system accounts are superfluous and can be removed from the system.

Cross-Platform syslog Alternatives

There are a number of syslog replacement programs freely available for both Red Hat and Solaris. This begs the question, "Why replace syslog?" There are usually two reasons: security and flexibility.

Standard syslog sends messages to the central loghost in clear text, meaning that anyone sniffing the wire can get your logs. Enough information about versions, potential problems, and general status goes into the logs that you don't want the other side getting hold of them. Some of the replacement alternatives use SSL to transfer log records or encrypt them for storage.

As for flexibility, many folks would like to be able to write a module for their logging software to directly handle local software data without resorting to the "local" labels. Some newer packages also offer filtering and expanded responses to log message content.

In-depth discussion and configuration details for these packages goes beyond the scope of this chapter, but we present some of the better known for your consideration:

- Name: syslog-ng

  Current version: 1.5.10 (September 2001)

  Benefits: TCP connections, filters

  Available from: http://www.balabit.hu/downloads/syslog-ng/1.5/ (download), http://www.balabit.hu/en/products/syslog-ng/ (information)

- Name: modular_syslog (was secure_syslog; ssyslog)

  Current version: 1.07 (July 2001)

  Benefits: Data integrity, nonrepudiation

  Available from: Core SDI, `http://www.corest.com/download/download1.html`, `http://www.core-sdi.com/english/freesoft.html`

- Name: nsyslog

  Current version: 4.00b2 (October 2000)

  Benefits: TCP connections, SSL transfer, filters

  Available from: `http://coombs.anu.edu.au/~avalon/nsyslog.html`

Log Analysis and Reporting

It is a sysadmin's job to install, maintain, and support computer systems. By extension, the sysadmin should be expected to know when a system is not behaving normally, especially when the behavior indicates a potential problem. There is little to be gained from physical examination of the system (although physical indications such as smoke, the smell of burning insulation, and so forth should be noted). Depending on the users to bring up problems is not a good strategy, either; the user often won't notice a problem until the system hangs or crashes.

The single, most general, most powerful tool at the sysadmin's disposal is the system log. The daily log entries of a configured, working system examined over a few weeks will provide the sysadmin with a baseline of normal system activity. Deviations from the baseline, whether subtle ones such as an increase in remote login activity or obvious ones such as a rapid build-up of SCSI device errors reported on a disk, tell the admin about the condition of both the system and the environment in which the system operates.

Unix is very democratic about logging. The daemon that accepts log messages for the system log will accept them from any process on the system. If the system is a loghost, the daemon will be accepting messages from processes on other systems as well. This design makes it easy for software developers to write programs that send relevant message to the system logs. It is up to the developer writing the program to decide the circumstances under which the program will send a message to the log. The developer also decides the content of the message, along with the facility and severity levels of each message.

When the syslog daemon, `syslogd`, gets this information, it uses the configuration /etc/syslog.conf file to determine what to do with the message. As described earlier, the disposition of each log message is based on its associated severity and facility level. Using these guidelines, `syslogd` writes the message to the appropriate log file (or other device such as the console). The message appears in a record with this format:

```
Timestamp               System          Originating Process[Process ID]:message
```

- The first field contains a timestamp recording the time of the message's receipt.

- The second field contains the name of the system that generated the message. This is essential when a remote loghost—a system that receives log messages from other computers and combines them into its own logs—is being used.

- The third field contains the name of the program (normally a system process or daemon that generates the message). The process ID, or PID, appears in square brackets. A colon terminates this field.

- The fourth field is simply the message itself. There is no standard format for the message.

Listing 6.2 shows a few sample log record from both of our reference systems.

LISTING 6.2   Log Records from Solaris 8 and RH Linux 7.1

```
Solaris 8 log records:
Sep 20 06:00:49 blueberry.univ.edu unix: NOTICE: realloccg /nids/special:
 file system full
Sep 20 06:00:53 blueberry.univ.edu unix: NOTICE: alloc: /usr: file system full
Sep 20 06:00:57 blueberry.univ.edu unix: NOTICE: realloccg /nids/special:
 file system full

RH Linux 7.1 log records

Sep 16 04:02:00 cobbler syslogd 1.4-0: restart.
Sep 18 10:26:47 cobbler sshd[9949]: Accepted password for ROOT from
24.180.202.116 port 3204
Sep 18 10:26:47 cobbler sshd[9949]: packet_set_maxsize: setting to 4096
```

Although this logging method makes it easy to write programs that generate log messages, the lack of standards in the messages themselves can make logs difficult to read. In addition, some programs are written to generate extensive logs, while others produce almost none at all. The inconsistencies in logging style make it very hard to automate the examination of large logs. Log analysis often appears more an art than a science.

Log Analysis

If your logs are relatively small, you might prefer to examine them directly on a daily basis. If they are too large to examine completely, you might want to use tools ranging from simple scripts to relational databases to extract information from them.

> **Tip**
>
> As of this writing (September 2001) there is an extraordinarily complete reference site for all aspects of log analysis at `http://kubarb.phsx.ukans.edu/~tbird/log-analysis.html`. We recommend it to all readers interested in this topic.

Whether you examine the logs directly or use tools to generate summary reports, a good sysadmin examines system activity daily. If you work five days a week, spend extra time on Monday looking at the weekend's logs. There could be specific events that interest you. These are excellent candidates for automated reports generated daily. We have such reports e-mailed to us each night to provide summary information the following morning.

Daily examination of such events keeps the sysadmin abreast of specific activities on the system, but, more importantly, it provides the sysadmin over time with a profile of the activity normal to that system. The sysadmin should be alert for deviations from that normal profile—for example:

A filesystem containing user data from an astrophysical simulation might fill up one or two times a year on average because of errors in the simulation code. If the logs show that it is filling up daily, it could be time to buy a new disk.

Perhaps a user who never works from home appears to be logging in remotely. If the user denies logging into the system at that time, the user's password has probably been compromised and the source IP of the session should be investigated.

> **Note**
>
> In one instance, our logs indicated that a user account had been accessed from three different countries over two separate continents in one day. In such a case, it is usually not necessary to question the user before disabling the account.

snarfstring

Our daily logs, directed to a loghost, are too large for direct inspection. When investigating a specific activity, system, user ID, or other item, we often use the simple script shown in Listing 6.3, called snarfstring.

LISTING 6.3   snarfstring

```perl
#!/usr/local/bin/perl

if ($#ARGV >= 0)
{
        $log = shift @ARGV;
        open (LOG,$log) || die "Cannot open $log";
}
else
{
        $log = "-";
}


print "Extract from log $log";

if ($#ARGV == 0)
{
        $searchstring = shift @ARGV;
        print "\tSearch string: $searchstring";
}

print "\n\n";

if ($log eq "-")
{
        while (<STDIN>)
        {
                if ($searchstring)
                {
                        /$searchstring/i || next;
                }

                ($mon, $day, $time, $host, $process, @therest) = split (/\s+/);

                if ($process !~ /sendmail/)
                {
                        print ("$mon-$day $time          $host/$process\n",
                                join (" ", @therest),"\n",
                        "----------------------------------------------\n");
                }

        }
}
```

LISTING 6.3 continued

```
else
{
        while (<LOG>)
        {
                if ($searchstring)
                {
                        /$searchstring/i || next;
                }

                ($mon, $day, $time, $host, $process, @therest) = split (/\s+/);

                if ($process !~ /sendmail/)
                {
                        print ("$mon-$day $time          $host/$process\n",
                                join (" ", @therest),"\n",
                                "-------------------------------------------------\n");
                }
        }
}
```

A good Perl scripter could create a more compact version of this script, but its current form makes it easy to follow.

snarfstring takes one or two arguments. The first argument is either the name of a log file or a −, indicating standard input. The second (optional) argument is a string to search for in the log records. If no string is specified, all records other than those produced by sendmail are reported. If a string is specified, records (other than those from sendmail) containing a matching string are reported.

Records are reported in a format that parses the fields before the message and prints them in a way that makes it easier to examine the message itself. We have found this format easier to follow than that of the log files.

Sendmail Records versus Other Records

Generalizations are dangerous, and you will have to let your own experiences develop and guide you over time. Our experience is that sendmail records dominate our log files and tend to obfuscate patterns in other system activities. snarfstring is written as a "first-cut" analysis tool to report records of interest other than sendmail log messages. As a rule, either we are interested in the activities other than sendmail or we are interested in sendmail activities alone. In the latter case, we have found that different tools, particularly those that match the "from" and "to" records of a single sendmail transaction, are more useful than snarfstring.

If you use your own tools to examine logs, take advantage of the regularity of the fields at the beginning of the message. These fields allow you to specify time intervals, the name of the system producing the messages, the process that produced the messages, and the specific process ID of that process. Selecting different fields provides different viewpoints of activity. For instance, selecting only a specific system will produce the equivalent of that system's local logs. Selecting only the process imapd will provide a picture of imap activity across all systems reporting to that loghost.

The log records in Listing 6.4 were extracted by filtering first for records produced by the process ftpd and then for those referencing username harvey. As with a similar incident mentioned previous, it was not impossible that harvey was logging into systems around the country and creating ftp session back to the system harlech. In fact, harvey might even have had good and honest reasons for doing so. After a brief inquiry, however, it was clear that the account had been compromised.

LISTING 6.4   Logs Showing Suspicious Account Activity

```
/var/adm/SYSLOG.5:Jan 31 10:02:31 6E:harlech ftpd[347892]: login from
numen.elon.edu as harvey
/var/adm/SYSLOG.5:Jan 31 10:13:29 6E:harlech ftpd[947816]: login from
flatland.dimensional.com as harvey
/var/adm/SYSLOG.5:Jan 31 10:23:38 6E:harlech ftpd[1030918]: login from
statepi.epi.jhsph.edu as harvey
/var/adm/SYSLOG.5:Jan 31 10:29:51 6E:harlech ftpd[933442]: login from
hershey.eas.harvard.edu as harvey
/var/adm/SYSLOG.5:Jan 31 10:32:27 6E:harlech ftpd[1024839]: login from
hershey.eas.harvard.edu as harvey
```

Central Loghost vs. Local Logs

A central loghost can provide information about patterns of activity across all the systems that you support. If you want information about a single system, it is easy to extract. By contrast, merging the logs from several different systems to provide the "big picture" is considerably more difficult.

Real-Time/Near–Real-Time Alerting and Notifications

Although we emphasize the importance of "profiling" the normal activity of your systems, some events really should be brought to your attention as quickly as possible. If a system partition fills up on an important server, or if a SCSI device is generating errors with every access, the sysadmin will want to know about the problem before the next day's log reports.

A number of utilities monitor system logs as they are written and report specific events in several useful ways. Many such utilities are available for free and run on both of our reference systems and most other Unix varieties as well. We will look at one of the oldest and simplest in some detail here. Others will be described briefly, along with the URLs where they can be found.

Swatch: The Simple WATCHdog

Swatch is the old workhorse of log monitoring packages. It is written in Perl and is available in its third major release, maintained by Todd Atkins. Its current (September 2001) version is 3.0.2.

The principle behind Swatch is simple. It is an extension of the Unix utilities `tail -f` and `grep`. For instance, if you wanted to see any record in your system log, /var/adm/messages, containing the string `Fred`, you could enter this command:

```
tail -f /var/adm/messages | grep Fred
```

`tail` with the `-f` option reads the end of the file and continues to read records as they are appended to the file. `grep` echoes any record containing the specified string. This command echoes any record containing the string `Fred` that is added to the log.

Swatch improves on this basic concept by providing more sophisticated pattern matching, by allowing for multiple patterns to be matched and by providing far more response options to a match than simple echoing to a terminal (though that option is provided as well.)

Installation of Swatch is straightforward. The package can be downloaded from `ftp://ftp.stanford.edu/general/security-tools/swatch/swatch-3.0.2.tar.gz` or `http://www.oit.ucsb.edu/~eta/swatch/swatch-3.0.2.tar.gz`.

After the distribution is unpacked, this command gets the build started:

```
Perl Makefile.PL
```

This Perl script will examine your system and, if necessary, attempt to download and install other Perl modules required by Swatch. When you are asked if you are ready for "manual configuration," we recommend saying "no" and taking the defaults. For some reason, the script often stops after downloading and installing a needed module, so you might need to invoke the script several (up to four) times before you get a clean configuration.

When that is done, type this to complete the build:

```
make
make install
make test
make realclean
```

The Swatch program will be in the /usr/local/bin directory.

Swatch requires a configuration file. By default, the file is .swatchrc in the invoking user's home directory. The simple examples in Listing 6.5 are from examples distributed with the Swatch package.

LISTING 6.5   Swatch Configuration Examples

```
# System crashes and halts
watchfor    /(panic|halt)/
        echo
        bell
        mail
        exec "call_pager 3667615 0911"

# System reboots
watchfor    /SunOS Release/
        echo
        bell
        mail
        exec "call_pager 3667615 0411"
```

The watchfor command tells Swatch to look for matches to the specified string. The syntax (string1|string2) displayed in the first example specifies a match to either string1 *or* string2. (Another command, ignore, tells Swatch to *ignore* matches to the specified string.)

Beneath the watchfor command, several other commands tell Swatch what to do in the case of a match. echo causes the record to echo to the terminal. Bell echoes the record and rings the bell. mail mails the record to the user ID executing Swatch. exec executes a specified system command.

These commands support a wide array of options, and there are more commands as well. A very good guide to the installation and configuration of an older version (2.2) on Solaris 2.*x* systems can be found at http://www.cert.org/security-improvement/implementations.

Using command-line options, Swatch can be run to examine a single file and then quit, or it can be run, like the tail -f command, to monitor endlessly any records that are appended to the growing log file.

Other Log Monitors

Swatch is a very useful package, but it has several limitations. Perhaps the most serious is that it can evaluate only one record at a time. Logsurfer provides, among other things, the capability to monitor logs for patterns involving more than one record. On the downside, it requires more effort to install and configure than the Swatch package. In fact, it could be more profitable to install and configure a Swatch package to your preferences and then use that as a starting point for a logsurfer configuration.

An excellent reference to other log-monitoring packages can be found at
`http://kubarb.phsx.ukans.edu/~tbird/log-analysis.html`.

Log Rotation and Retention

`syslogd` is designed to deliver messages to the log files, appending each to the end of the file. Obviously, these files will keep growing—eventually reaching the limits of disk storage—unless something is done to keep their growth under control. Most Unix systems do this through log rotation. At intervals, log files are renamed in a way that represents their archival status, and new log files are begun. The actual mechanism through which this takes place differs from one operating system to another. Here we examine log rotation in our reference systems, Solaris 8 and RH Linux 7.1. Log rotation on both systems is configurable, although the default values are generally reasonable for local logging.

If you want to configure your own log rotation, there are two factors in particular to take into account:

- **Rotation period**—This is the time between rotations. In some cases, this will not be a fixed period of time. For instance, the logs could be rotated when they have reached a particular size.

- **Log retention**—This is the rule for deleting old logs. Usually, log files are deleted after a certain number of rotation periods, with each period "aging" the files until they are eligible for deletion. Other factors, such as calendar age of the files, also can be used.

The longer the rotation period is, the longer the logs will be in rotation. An overly short rotation period, however, makes it difficult to spot longer-term system behavior that might be of interest. For instance, if there is a suspicious login, it is helpful to find the logout in the same file so that any activity that took place during that session can be bounded in time. For busy systems or loghosts, we find that daily log rotation is reasonable. For systems that don't generate large logs, such as small workstations, weekly rotations may be preferable.

Log Rotation in RH Linux 7.1

Log rotation in RH Linux 7.1 is supported by a more complex mechanism than that in Solaris. The actual rotation is performed by the executable /usr/sbin/logrotate. logrotate is invoked by cron through the script /etc/cron.daily/logrotate, which, in turn, is invoked by the script /etc/crontab. This latter script defines the system cron jobs.

logrotate takes the name of a configuration file as an argument—by default, /etc/ logrotate.conf. This file defines the various parameters of log rotation. (See Listing 6.6.)

LISTING 6.6 Default logrotate.conf File

```
# see "man logrotate" for details
# rotate log files weekly
weekly

# keep 4 weeks worth of backlogs
rotate 4

# send errors to root
errors root

# create new (empty) log files after rotating old ones
create

# uncomment this if you want your log files compressed
#compress

# RPM packages drop log rotation information into this directory
include /etc/logrotate.d

# no packages own lastlog or wtmp -- we'll rotate them here
/var/log/wtmp {
    monthly
    create 0664 root utmp
    rotate 1
}

# system-specific logs may be configured here
```

As Listing 6.5 indicates, configuration details can be found on the logrotate man page. The logrotate.conf file provides considerable control over log rotation.

The term weekly, at the beginning of the configuration file, essentially means that logs will be rotated each Sunday.

Log Rotation in Solaris 8

Log rotation in Solaris is performed by the script /usr/lib/newsyslog. By default, cron executes this script at 03:10 on the first day of the week (Sunday).

Current logs in the /var/adm directory are renamed by appending a .0 to the log name and are replaced by empty files, waiting to receive messages. Logs already ending in .0 are renamed to end in .1, and so forth. The oldest logs, by default, end in .3, so they survive four "generations" after they are no longer current.

Current logs in the /var/log directory are renamed as indicated previously, unless they have no entries. The oldest log files in this directory are seven generations old, ending in .7.

The newsyslog script also restarts syslogd using a kill –HUP command. This is essential. syslogd opens the files by name but then keeps them open and writes to them through the file inodes. When the current log files are renamed, their inodes stay the same and syslogd keeps writing to them. When syslogd is restarted, it locates and opens the log files by name, selecting the new, empty files created by newsyslog.

If you want to change the log-rotation schedule, the tidiest way is to create a new newsyslog script, taking advantage of the existing mechanisms.

Log Retention Policy

As repeatedly emphasized in this book, written policies make a sysadmin's job much easier in the long run, if only by clarifying responsibilities and expectations of the job. Specific policies for log retention also help the sysadmin avoid legal entanglements.

A sysadmin may, at any time, be presented with a subpoena for stored electronic information. In many cases, this subpoena will be fairly broad, specifying that all backup data stored on tape be delivered to law enforcement. A written policy defining the length of time that backups are kept and where they are stored will make it much easier to respond to the subpoena. Written policy also relieves the sysadmin from defending "judgment calls" about log retention made in the absence of other guidance.

In fact, the sysadmin may assist in wording the subpoena in conformance with the policy, specifying a range of time and location from which data should be retrieved. In the absence of established guidelines, the subpoena would need to specify "all written or electronic records in reference to X" and then you end up trying to sift *everything* to make sure that all such records are found.

Your log retention policy should also define who has the authority to retrieve or to request the retrieval of the information you store. Such a policy will go a long way towards shielding the sysadmin and the organization from problems with privacy issues. In particular, your policy should define what sorts of request require a subpoena.

Badly written subpoenas can cause hassles for everyone. Your written log policies can help simplify these routine legal demands for information by defining your "standard practice" and by providing a framework in which the demands can be clearly phrased.

Best Practices

General

- Enable detailed logging.
- Baseline expected system behavior.
- Make sure you have consistent timekeeping across your site. Use ntp to synchronize system times across your network.
- Use a central loghost in addition to maintaining local logs; *all* messages should be mirrored centrally.
- Keep application-specific logs and combined system logs.
- Rotate your logs regularly, according to your site's log retention policy.
- Examine logs (or summary reports) daily.
- Use log-monitoring packages for more urgent events.

syslog.conf

- Make sure 'syslog 514/udp' is in the /etc/services file.
  If this entry is missing, syslog can't send records off-system (or receive records, if the system is a central loghost).
- Make sure `nslookup` reports the same IP address that you are expecting for servers specified in syslog.conf.

Hardening the Central Loghost

- Make the central loghost a dedicated server.
- Turn off all ports except 5124/udp (syslog) and 22/tcp (ssh).

- Set up and configure a local firewall to filter incoming connections. Blackhole all connection attempts to other than 514/udp and 22/tcp.

- Use an automated script to compare records from local hosts with corresponding records from the central loghost to detect discrepancies.

Periodic Checks

- Use `ps` to check that the syslog daemon is running.

- Use `netstat` as described earlier to verify whether port 514/udp is open and accepting external log records.

- Use `df` once or twice a day to check on the loghost's disk space usage. If you see a sudden spike in log size, it could be an early warning sign of other problems at your site.

- Use `ls -l` to verify that the main log file continues growing. If the timestamp and size never change, then it's likely that the syslog process itself has died.

- Check for mark-type entries in the main log file. Missing markers may indicate that the syslog process itself has died or that the logs have been tampered with.

Online References

Red Hat Logging

- Official Log File Information

  http://www.redhat.com/mirrors/LDP/LDP/lasg/logging/index.html

- Creating and Securing a Remote Log Server

  http://linuxsecurity.com/feature_stories/feature_story-64.html

Computer Emergency Response Team (CERT)

- Log management practices

  http://www.cert.org/security-improvement/practices/p092.html

- Understanding Solaris logging

  http://www.cert.org/security-improvement/implementations/i041.12.html

- Setting up Solaris logging

  http://www.cert.org/security-improvement/implementations/i041.08.html

ntp

- ntp Home

  `http://www.ntp.org`

- List of Public Timeservers

  `http://www.eecis.udel.edu/~mills/ntp/servers.htm`

- ntp FAQ

  `http://www.eecis.udel.edu/~ntp/ntpfaq/NTP-a-faq.htm`

- Setting Up ntp on Solaris

  `http://docs.sun.com/ab2/coll.47.11/SYSADV2/@Ab2PageView/`
  `34355?DwebQuery=ntp&Ab2Lang=C&Ab2Enc=iso-8859-1`

- Network Time Protocol presentation by Hal Pomeranz

  `http://bullwinkle.deer-run.com/~hal/ns2000/ntp2.pdf`

syslog Replacement Packages

- syslog-ng

  - Download

    `http://www.balabit.hu/downloads/syslog-ng/1.5/`

- Information

  `http://www.balabit.hu/en/products/syslog-ng/`

- modular_syslog (was secure_syslog; ssyslog)

  - Download

    `http://www.corest.com/download/download1.html`

  - Information

    `http://www.core-sdi.com/english/freesoft.html`

- nsyslog

  `http://coombs.anu.edu.au/~avalon/nsyslog.html`

Log Analysis

- General

  `http://kubarb.phsx.ukans.edu/~tbird/log-analysis.html`

- Packages
    - Swatch

        `http://www.stanford.edu/~atkins/swatch/`
    - LogCheck

        `http://www.psionic.com/abacus/logcheck/`

Endnotes

[1] *Or at least its importance to the programmer....*

[2] *See Chapter 3, "Filesystem Administration" for more on file types, including pipes.*

Authentication

by Matt Bishop

In This Chapter

Introduction

This chapter presents the basic ideas behind authentication. It then shows you how to configure and use the various mechanisms for authentication in a UNIX environment. We'll discuss several different tools and techniques, and we'll give you a rough idea of the underlying protocols.

What Is Authentication?

Authentication is the binding of an entity to an identity (see Chapter 4 "User Administration"). For example, when Matt Bishop logs into a UNIX system, the system must associate (bind) him to the identity to any processes that he runs. The mechanism that identifies the user as Matt Bishop to the computer is an authentication tool.

Authentication occurs for two aspects of identity. When people authenticate themselves, they typically are placed into a *user identity* (represented by the UID) and a *primary group identity* (the GID). Many UNIX systems also add a list of *supplementary* groups to which the user belongs, so a user can be in multiple groups at the same time.

Authentication mechanisms fall into one of five categories:

1. What the entity knows, such as a password
2. What the entity possesses, such as a dongle (a mechanism whose presence is required for something to function) or a smart card (a card containing an embedded mechanism used for authentication, such as a cryptographic chip or a precise time-keeper)
3. What the entity is, such as a retinal scan or a fingerprint
4. Where the entity is, as determined to some acceptable precision
5. Some combination of these

Traditionally, UNIX systems heavily favor the first category. Some vendors support tokens for UNIX systems with additional hardware and software. We will discuss one such system and provide references to vendors in the "References" section.

Overview of UNIX Password Authentication

Storing the user's password in a file invites compromise of the password. Even if the file were read-protected, the superuser could read it and determine the users' passwords. The problem is that many people use the same password on multiple systems. Those systems would therefore be compromised. Finally, UNIX access controls do not protect against carelessness or an unintentional missetting of read permissions, so the passwords might be exposed accidentally. For this reason, the UNIX system does not store the user passwords online.

When users select passwords, the passwd program may run simple checks to ensure that the password is not too easy to guess. It then applies a mathematical transformation called a cryptographic hash (see Appendix E, "Background for Authentication: Outline of Some Cryptographic Methods") to the password, and generates a printable representation of the output. This is stored in the password file /etc/passwd. Therefore, the user's password is not stored in a readable form by the system.

To authenticate a user, the system asks the user to enter a name and a password. The system retrieves the user's stored data. It then computes the cryptographic hash of the supplied password and compares that to the stored hash. If the two match, the user is authenticated. Otherwise, either the name or the password is incorrect.

One problem with this scheme is that the cryptographic hashes are visible. An attacker can guess a potential password, compute its cryptographic hash, and compare the result to the stored hash. If the two match, the attacker has guessed the user's password. This is called a *dictionary attack*. To keep hashes hidden, systems can be configured to use a *shadow password file*. The shadow file, which only root can read, contains the username and associated hash as its first two fields. Authentication programs run with root privileges and thus can access the hashes. The original password file is still present and still world-readable, although the password hashes are not present.

Good Passwords and Bad Passwords

Passwords provide the basis for authentication on most UNIX systems. If attackers can guess a user's password, that account—and the system itself—is compromised. The attackers can impersonate (or *spoof*) the legitimate user. Hence, good passwords must be difficult for attackers to guess. "Password-guessing attacks," "dictionary attacks," and "brute-force attacks" refer to attacks in which an attacker tries to guess a user's password.

Selecting good passwords is a widely discussed topic. Unfortunately, innumerable security breaches make clear that good password selection is still a problem. Even when sophisticated methods based on (for example) public-key cryptography become widespread, users still have to protect their private keys and other cryptographic data. The protection mechanism invariably requires a password, passphrase, or other cryptographic key to encode the data. so this topic will continue to be critically important in the protection of computer systems. It is vital that sysadmins know, understand, and preach the need for good password security.

Passwords are selected from a set of potential passwords (sometimes called a password space). Given such a set of passwords, the probability that each will be selected makes up the *password distribution*. Two properties must hold to make passwords hard to guess:

1. The set of potential passwords must be too large for an attacker to try each possible password.

2. Each password must be as likely to be selected as any other potential password.

Unfortunately, people do not choose random passwords. They select passwords that are easy to remember—usually words, names, meaningful sequences of numbers (such as Social Security or identity numbers), or some simple transformation of these. Because the UNIX password-hashing algorithm allows only eight characters, a relatively small number of passwords fall into these categories. If attackers begin guessing passwords by using words from the previously mentioned set, they are more likely to find at least one user's password.

Passwords that are easy to guess fall into several categories. Here is a list of types of passwords to avoid (in this list, "dictionary" includes both English language and non-English language dictionaries):

*   An account name or variations of it, such as the account name followed by a number or punctuation mark

*   A user's real name or initials, or some variations of them, such as the initial of the first name followed by the last name

*   Dictionary words or some variation of them, such as a word with some letters capitalized or reversed, or a plural or participle

*   Dictionary words with some letters replaced by control characters or "elite-speak" characters (such as replacing *a* with 2 or 4, *e* with 3, *s* with 5 or $, l and *i* with 1, and so forth)

*   Dictionary words with vowels, consonants, or whitespace deleted, such as sbbkkpper (subbookkeepper)

*   Concatenations of dictionary words, such as catdog

*   Keyboard patterns, such as qwerty for an American keyboard

- Too-short passwords (less than six characters) or those that contain only digits or letters and numbers

- License plate numbers, driver's license numbers, or other administrative data

- Acronyms, such as ACM or USAEUR

- Passwords that have been used in the past

- Passwords that have a significant number of characters in common with the previous password (for example, changing your password from hi!there to bi!there).

7

AUTHENTICATION

Consistent Passwords: A Lesson

One system administrator was given an old UNIX system and was told, "We have lost the root password. If you can figure it out, the machine is yours." The sysadmin used crack to guess the passwords (discussed later). crack guessed all the administrative account passwords except root's. Upon scanning the list of guessed passwords, the sysadmin noticed that they were all names of Greek gods and goddesses. A trip to Bulfinch's Mythology gave him several additional names not in the crack word lists. One of those new names was, in fact, root's password.

Moral of the story: Do not pick passwords according to a predictable pattern!

Examples of easy-to-guess passwords are stupendous (dictionary word), d00dz (too short), MattB (based on a username, 1plk107 (a California license plate), and 311t3$p32k (the word *elitespeak*, with obvious character substitutions).

An effective method of creating passwords that are easy to remember but difficult to guess is to base the password on an obscure poem, song, piece of prose, or something involving mathematics. For example, the value of π is 3.1415927..., and the value of e (the base of the natural logarithms) is 2.718281828.... So, one password might be 3.748pei. The third line of the poem "Tyger! Tyger" ("What immortal hand or eye") when combined with the author's initials, might give WB/amn e as a password.

Linux Red Hat 7.1: Password-Checking Rules

When users change passwords, Red Hat 7.1 first checks the proposed password to see if crack could guess it. If so, the password is rejected. If not, crack then compares the proposed password to the user's current password (if that exists). The proposed password is rejected under the following circumstances:

- The proposed password is a palindrome or a rotation of the current one.

- The proposed password and the current password differ only by changes of case.

- The proposed password is less than five characters long (to change this, change the value of PASS_MIN_LEN in /etc/login.defs) or does not contain a sufficiently rich mixture of uppercase and lowercase characters, digits, and other characters.

- The new password has too many characters in common than the old one (by default, it is the minimum of 10, or half the length of the new password).

If root chooses a password that violates these rules, a warning is given but the proposed password is accepted.

Solaris 2.8: Password-Checking Rules

The default requirements for passwd to accept a proposed password are listed here:

- The proposed password must be at least six characters long. (To change this, change the value of PASSLENGTH in /etc/defaults/passwd.)

- It must contain two alphabetic (uppercase or lowercase) letters and at least one nonalphabetic character.

- It cannot be the login name, any circular shift of the login name, or any reverse shift of the login name (the comparison ignores case).

- It must differ from the current password by at least three characters (again, ignoring case).

Again, these requirements are *not* applied to passwords set by root.

Proactive Password Changers

Several programs let sysadmins force users to pick good passwords. The better-known ones are anlpasswd, at `ftp://info.mcs.anl.gov/pub/systems`, and npasswd, at `http://www.utexas.edu/cc/unix/software/npasswd`.

Both support shadow files and NIS. It is also easy to write a simple password checker using shell or Perl scripts.

Tip

Tell your users that lists of "good" or "hard-to-guess" passwords are examples; do not use them. If attackers see the password listed as a good one, they will immediately try it. This attack is extremely effective!

Some UNIX sysadmins want users to be assigned passwords. This eliminates the problem of users selecting poor passwords. Experience suggests that this approach is productive only in certain cases:

- The passwords are computer-generated.
- They are easy to remember.
- They are generated randomly.

Generating pseudo-random data can be difficult (see the accompanying sidebar "Pseudo–Random Password Generation"). In particular, the starting point of the pseudo–random number generator must not be predictable! There is considerable tension between the second and third requirements, and, in practice, people will write down random passwords.

Pseudo–Random Password Generation

When you need to generate random data, use a good pseudo–random-number generator (see Appendix E). You'll also need to pick a starting point (called the seed). Do not use a predictable seed, such as the time of day or a PID, or any combination of the two. Once someone wrote a random password-generation program that used the time of day for the seed. An attacker used the times within 1 minute of the time that the password file was last changed.

To get a good seed, run transient data through a cryptographic hash function. For example, if md5 is a program that computes the MD5 hash of its input, a command to generate a good seed would be this on Linux

```
ps gaux | md5
```
or this on Solaris:
```
ps -ef | md5
```

Here are some tips on protecting your passwords:

Tip

- Protect backups that contain the password or shadow files.
- Use different passwords for different systems.
- Never store passwords in clear text.
- Change passwords at secure locations (where you are certain that you are not being spoofed).

> - Beware of social engineering: Never change a password for a user without being convinced of that user's identity.
> - Do not share passwords, even with family.
> - Beware of shoulder surfers (people who look over your shoulder to read your keystrokes as you enter your password).
> - Pass on these tips (except possibly for the first) to your users.

People should not write down passwords. If an attacker finds the passwords, the user can be successfully impersonated. People sometimes write down passwords in obvious places, such as on paper taped to the console or under the keyboard. In one case, a password taped to a terminal in a bank led to the theft of several million dollars!

At some installations, sysadmins are responsible for many different systems. Because they share responsibilities for each system with other sysadmins, the passwords also must be shared. Remembering a large number of passwords is infeasible. In this case, writing down passwords becomes a necessity.

One way to write down passwords safely uses a pass-algorithm that is changed frequently, at least as often as the passwords are distributed. Suppose that the root password for the system hecuba is Th3%B1g@. Each sysadmin is given a slip of paper with this line:

```
hecuba   Th3B1G
```

Each sysadmin also is told (verbally) the pass-algorithm: "Insert % after the third character, make the last character lowercase, and append @." An attacker who acquires the slip of paper still must guess the pass-algorithm.

One way to counter password guessing is "password aging." Password aging forces the user to change a password after some period of time has passed (the password is said to "expire"). However, the choice of password must be restricted, lest the user simply set the new password to the current password. There are two common ways to do this.

The first method keeps track of the last n passwords and prevents the user from reusing them. For example, if a user picks 34gtre% and the system tracked the last 10 passwords for each user, then the user could not reuse that password until after the 10th password change. This method is poor for two reasons. First, the user can simply cycle through 10 passwords to reinstall the current password. Second, the system must keep a list of previously chosen passwords. Even if the hashes of these passwords are kept, an attacker might be able to obtain the file, guess some passwords in it, and deduce from those passwords a pattern enabling the attacker to guess the current password.

The second method sets a minimum and maximum time between which a password can be changed. When users change passwords, they may not change the passwords again until the minimum time has passed. When the maximum time passes, then the users must change the passwords. This prevents users from cycling through passwords. Normal password checking ensures that the current and new passwords differ.

Password aging should be used with caution. Users should be given warnings to change their passwords as the expiration time draws near. When a password expires, the user should not be permitted to log in except to change the password. However, the user should be able to terminate the procedure at any time during the login without having to pick a new password, and any proposed password should be tested to ensure that it is hard to guess. Otherwise, the user might choose a bad password simply to complete the login.

Linux Red Hat 7.1: Password Aging

By default, password aging is not enabled. To turn it on, use the program chage(1). For example, to force user marge to change her password every 90 days, the sysadmin could use this command:

```
chage -m 7 -M 90 -W 7 marge
```

This says that marge must change her password after 90 days (-M 90) and will be warned to change it 7 days before that (-W 7). When marge changes her password, she cannot change it until seven days (-m 7) have passed. If the minimum number is *greater* than the maximum number, marge cannot change her password. To turn off password aging, set the maximum time to -1. If both the maximum time and the minimum time are set to 0, the user will be asked for a new password at the next login. Default values are given in /etc/login.defs.

Solaris 2.8: Password Aging

By default, password aging is not enabled. To turn it on, use the program passwd(1). This command has the same effect as the Linux chage command:

```
passwd -n 7 -x 90 -w 7 marge
```

If the maximum value is -1, aging is turned off; if both the maximum and minimum times are set to 0, the password must be changed when the user next logs in. Default values are given in /etc/defaults/passwd.

Basic UNIX Password Implementations

The original UNIX password-hashing algorithm uses the Data Encryption Standard. This cipher takes 64-bit input and a 56-bit key, and generates 64 bit outputs. The password hash function uses the password as the cryptographic key and sets the input message to all 0 bits. The DES then is iterated 25 times. The 64-bit output is the hash. Because the DES has a 56-bit key, passwords are restricted to, at most, eight characters.

Were this all there is to the hash, it would be easy to use standard DES hardware to hash possible passwords quickly. To prevent this, the designers added a perturbation to the standard algorithm. The "salt" is a 12-bit number. It is applied to the DES algorithm in such a way that each different salt modifies the algorithm differently. Hence, there are $2^{12} = 4096$ different password-hashing algorithms, each identified by a unique salt. The 12-bit salt is prepended to the 64-bit output, and the resulting 76 bits are converted to printable form (see the accompanying sidebar, "Salts and UNIX Password Hashes"). This 13-character representation is stored in the password file.

Salts and UNIX Password Hashes

First, two 0 bits are appended to the 76 bits (12-bit salt, 64-bit DES output) of the hash. The resulting 78 bits are broken into 13 sets of 6 bits. Each set is mapped into the alphabet in the table that follows. The result is a 13-character string.

This table is a mapping of bits to printable characters. The rows represent the most significant bits, and the columns represent the least significant bits. For example, 001100 maps to *A*, and 110101 maps to *p*.

	000	001	010	011	100	101	110	111
000	.	/	0	1	2	3	4	5
001	6	7	8	9	A	B	C	D
010	E	F	G	H	I	J	K	L
011	M	N	O	P	Q	R	S	T
100	U	V	W	X	Y	Z	a	b
101	c	D	e	f	G	h	i	j
110	k	L	m	n	O	p	q	r
111	s	T	u	v	W	x	y	z

The salt is the bit pattern corresponding to the first two characters of the password hash. The salt performs three functions:

1. It eliminates the capability of the attacker to use chips designed to compute the DES quickly, unless the salt is ".." (because the hashing algorithm with that salt is equivalent to the DES).

2. If a system has users whose password hashes have more than one salt, an attacker launching a password-guessing attack must generate one password hash per salt per guess, rather than just one password hash per guess. This takes considerably more computation.

3. If users use the same password but have different salts, the resulting password hashes will be different.

The password hashes are stored in the user database file /etc/passwd, which has the following format:

```
bishop:xyAz1/rxpqrzt:1318:53:Matt Bishop:/home/bishop:/bin/csh
```

The fields are listed here:

- User login name
- Password hash
- UID
- GID
- User information (GECOS) field
- Home directory
- User's login shell

The password hash field indicates how the system handles password authentication for that user. It contains the password hash. In some cases, it may be set to an illegal hash. A common example is setting it to *. This indicates that the user is not allowed to authenticate using a password. Either the user is not to be given access to the system or some other method is used to authenticate the user.

Linux Red Hat 7.1: Password Hashes

Special values for the password hash field are listed here:

- x for shadow password files (in /etc/passwd only).
- !hash (where *hash* is a legal password hash) for locking the account. This prevents authentication *only* via the password file. If the user can use another method of authentication (such as .rhosts, discussed later), that user still can log in. Use the -l option to passwd(1) to lock an account; use the -u option to unlock it.
- * (or any nonhash value) for locking the account. To unlock it, use passwd to assign a password.

Solaris 2.8: Password Hashes

Special values for the password hash field are as follows:

- x for shadow password files.
- *LK" for locking the account. This prevents authentication *only* via the password file. If the user can use another method of authentication (such as .rhosts, discussed later), that user still can log in. Use the -l option to passwd(1) to lock an account. To unlock it, assign a password using passwd(1).
- * (or any nonhash value) for locking the account also (same effect as *LK*).

Many UNIX systems do not use the /etc/passwd file directly. Instead, they use it to generate a database file that requires fewer reads to obtain the desired user information. (The exact database format varies from system to system.) Systems may automatically regenerate the database files whenever /etc/password is changed, or the sysadmin might need to do so manually.

Linux Red Hat 7.1 and Solaris 2.8: Local Password File Format

Both Linux Red Hat 7.2 and Solaris 2.8 use ASCII text for the password and shadow files. They do not use a binary database format for this information.

If attackers can see the password hashes and salts, then they can launch password guessing attacks. As discussed earlier, *shadow password files* hide this information. An example line from a shadow password file follows:

```
bishop:xyAz1/rxpqrzt:::::::
```

The first field is the username; the second field is the hash. The contents of the remaining fields vary among systems but usually include password-aging information (omitted here). When shadow password files are used, the password hash field of /etc/passwd is set to x to indicate that the password is stored elsewhere.

Linux Red Hat 7.1: Shadow Password Entry Fields

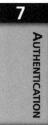

The fields of the Red Hat shadow password file are as follows:

- Username
- Hashed password
- Date that the password was last changed (in number of days since January 1, 1970)
- When the password can next be changed (in number of days)
- When the password must be changed (in number of days)
- When to warn the user that the password will expire (in number of days before expiration)
- When to disable the account (in number of days after password expires)
- When the account was disabled (number of days since January 1, 1970)
- A field reserved for future use, empty by default

To create shadow password files, use the command pwconv. To revert to the standard (nonshadow) scheme, use pwunconv (beware: this will delete the shadow files).

Solaris 2.8: Shadow Password Entry Fields

The fields of the Solaris shadow file are the same as for Red Hat, with two exceptions:

- The seventh field is the number of days of inactivity allowed for the account (in number of days).
- The last field is reserved for future use and is set to 0 by default.

To create or update shadow password files, use the command pwconv.

> **Tip**
>
> Use shadow files if your system supports them. They force attackers to gain *root* access before using hashes to guess passwords (unless the attackers find some security holes that give them access to the data).

A number of programs allow sysadmins to manipulate /etc/passwd and /etc/shadow. When these files are edited, a specific locking protocol must be observed to avoid multiple entities simultaneously writing to the file. Hence, direct editing should be avoided. When it cannot be avoided, the program vipw honors the locking protocol and should be used. On some systems, vipw will merge /etc/passwd and /etc/shadow for the edit session and will save them correctly. On other systems, vipw ignores /etc/shadow.

Linux Red Hat 7.1: Editing the Password File

To edit the password file directly, invoke vipw, edit the file as though you were using vi, and save it. You can change the editor by setting the shell variable EDITOR to the full pathname of your favorite editor. Be careful—vipw does not check the file, so you can accidentally lock yourself or other users out of the system!

Solaris 2.8: Editing the Password File

To edit the password file directly, invoke vipw, edit the file as though you were using vi, and save it. You can change the editor by setting the shell variables EDITOR and VISUAL to the full pathname of your favorite editor. vipw sanity-checks the root entry in the password file, including checking that the named login shell is legal.

If you edit the password file directly, you should follow the following tips:

> **Tip**
>
> - If you have to edit the password file, use vipw. That not only locks the password file (preventing anyone else using passwd(1) from changing it), but it also rebuilds any password database and shadow files that your system uses.
> - Do *not* use vipw to change password hashes (unless you are disabling password authentication for that account). Use the passwd program. It's just too easy to mistype a hash and accidentally lock out the user.

Linux Red Hat 7.1: The newusers Program

Sometimes hundreds of accounts need to be created and assigned passwords (for example, at the beginning of a term at a college or university). The program newusers does this. Create a file with the same format as the standard UNIX password file. One such line might be this:

```
marge:orig_pwd:2222:36:Marge Casey:/home/marge:/bin/csh
```

Then run newusers with the name of the file as an argument. The entry in the password file for marge will be updated (if it exists) or added (if it does not exist). The password orig_pwd will be hashed, and the hash will be put in the second field of /etc/passwd or /etc/shadow (whichever is appropriate).

No equivalent program is installed on Solaris 2.8.

Password Cracking

If attackers can guess passwords, why can't the sysadmins do the same thing? To use this approach, called *reactive cracking*, a sysadmin acquires a password-guessing program and tries to find local users' passwords. The sysadmin then notifies the local users that their passwords have been guessed and that they must be changed. This method effectively turns the sysadmin into a benign attacker.

Two words of caution apply: First, before you do this, *get management's approval in writing*. Otherwise, when people discover your password guessing, they will assume that you are attacking their system. This can lead to disciplinary action (at best) or you being fired, charged, and convicted in court. Even if matters do not proceed to trial, you don't need this extra hassle. Get permission before you start guessing passwords!

Second, use discretion in the guesses that you make. *Any* password can be guessed; just try each set of possible passwords. The object of guessing passwords is for the sysadmin to discover the passwords that can be guessed in too short a time. The exact definition of "too short" varies from site to site (and sometimes from sysadmin to sysadmin), but a good rule of thumb is "less than the time between password changes." In other words, if your password-guessing program takes 2 days to guess a password and your users are required to change passwords every 90 days, the password is too weak. If it takes 91 days to guess the password, the password is satisfactory.

When you guess passwords, try the ones that seem most likely first. These possible passwords include login and usernames (and their transformations). Then go to site-specific words and acronyms. Then move on to dictionary words, then patterns, and so forth. This approach maximizes the probability of finding passwords quickly. Also, gather dictionaries of words from different sources.

You can guess passwords in two ways. The first is to try them. This requires time to type the login names and passwords. Also, some systems allow the administrator to disable accounts if there are too many failed logins. Neither Linux Red Hat 7.1 nor Solaris 2.8 offers this feature.

Tip

If you set your system to disable an account after *n* failed login attempts, *always* exempt the superuser account. On one system, this lockout applied to *root*. An attacker broke in and then tried to log in as root three times. That locked the root account, and the sysadmins could not analyze and fix the hole, or track the attacker. They had to reboot the system to get access to the root account again!

You can use a program to guess passwords. Several good ones exist for UNIX password schemes. crack, by Alec Muffett, is a good example of this type of program. (See the accompanying sidebar "Installing crack.")

Installing crack

To install crack, go to the main directory c50a after downloading it. The steps now differ slightly between Red Hat 7.1 and Solaris 2.8.

Linux Red Hat 7.1: If you have configured your system to use the MD5 hashes, you cannot use the standard password-hashing routines. Instead, replace that with an interface to the MD5 routine, as follows:

1. Move the libdes source out of the way:

   ```
   mv src/libdes src/libdes.orig
   ```

2. Put the interface in place:

   ```
   cp src/util/elcid.c,bsd src/util/elcid.c
   ```

3. Now edit crack. Uncomment the LIBS line for the cc compiler by deleting the # at the beginning of Line 47:

   ```
   #LIBS=-lcrypt # uncomment only if necessary to use...
   ```

Authentication

CHAPTER 7

317

4. You also will need to change the location of the system dictionary. Edit the file conf/dictgrps.conf. Change Line 23 to read this:

```
1:/usr/share/dict/*words* dict/1/*
```

Solaris 2.8: Change into the src/libdes directory and build libdes. You might have to change the compiler from cc to gcc.

For both systems, merge the shadow and password files using scripts/shadmrg.sv (if using shadow files) or get a local copy of the NIS map (if using NIS). Save this in the file crack-passwd. Then build the binaries:

```
./Crack -makeonly
```

Also build the dictionaries:

```
./Crack -makedict
```

If you get an error message saying that crack could not find /usr/dict/*words*, your system dictionary is in a nonstandard place. Locate it, change the line in conf/dictgrps.conf, as described previously for Red Hat 7.1; then delete the file run/dict/.dictmade and run ./Crack -makedict again.

To run crack, simply use this line:

```
./Crack crack-passwd
```

(You should consider using the -nice option if people are using the system.) The program will check the binaries and dictionaries and go into the background. To see the results, run this line:

```
./Reporter
```

(This may be run at any time, and it will show incremental results).

Finally, remember that users might expose their passwords. This occurs when users log in through unencrypted links such as telnet or rlogin. Attackers monitoring the network can sniff the password and reuse it later. Users also might put passwords in their files. For example, the file .netrc allows users to store ftp logins and passwords. Such files should be readable only by their owners—even then, putting clear-text passwords in files is poor practice.

Network Information System (NIS)

The Network Information System (NIS) is a tool that supports a number of databases. It is used to create a central repository for system-related information such as trusted hosts, mail alias files, and password files. We will focus on the authentication-related parts only.

A set of workstations (the *NIS clients*) communicates with a central server (the *NIS master*). The main reason to use NIS is to ensure that login names, UIDs, and passwords are consistent among the clients and server. Users can log in at any NIS client using the same password. Their UIDs also will be the same on any client; if they change a password at any client, the new password will work on any client.

NIS uses a password map identical to the format of the /etc/passwd file. The password is hashed and stored as described previously. The difference between using NIS and not using NIS lies in how the clients locate the password hash (and other information).

Some systems use a character-based mechanism to determine whether to use the local password information or the information from the NIS password map (called "compatibility mode"). If the first character of a line in /etc/passwd is +, the NIS map is consulted. The line is interpreted as follows:

- If the first field is +, the contents of the NIS map are interpolated at that point.
- If the first character of the first field is + (for example, +mab:...), then the contents of the line in the NIS map for that user are interpolated at this point (in the example, the line for user mab would be brought over). If the first two characters are +@, the name following the @ refers to a netgroup. If the GECOS, shell, or home directory fields in the local password file are not empty, the contents of the field override the contents of the corresponding fields in the NIS map entries. The NIS map *always* supplies the password hash.
- If the first character of the first field is -, the contents of the line in the NIS map for that user are ignored when the contents of the NIS map are interpolated. As with +, if the first two characters of the line are -@, the name following the @ is a netgroup, and the effect is to ignore the NIS map lines for all users in the netgroup.

Password lookups are sensitive to order. The *first* match of a username terminates the lookup. For example, if user mutt has an entry in the local password file and a different entry in the NIS password map, then the entry that is found first is used. If using compatibility mode, this sequence would require mutt to use the password in the NIS map (and his `finger` information would identify him as Mutt Henderson):

```
+mutt:*:100:100:Mutt Henderson:/home/mutt:/bin/csh
mutt:abQr43891OpwD:1359:1359:LTC Henderson:/home/mutt:/bin/csh
```

If the lines were reversed, mutt would use the password hashed in the local password file (and his `finger` information would identify him as LTC Henderson).

> **Tip**
>
> *Always* make sure that you have a line for root in /etc/passwd on the NIS client. If the client cannot reach the NIS server, sysadmins still can log into the NIS client to diagnose the problem.

One drawback with this scheme arises when the NIS server is unavailable. In this case, some implementations ignore the special meaning of + and –. This might enable accounts that have no passwords. For example, under normal circumstances, this line would allow the user to log in as user +mab without a password:

```
+mab::312:23:Matt Bishop::
```

To avoid this, put * in the second field.

Newer systems use a mechanism called nsswitch.conf. This scheme uses the standard password file; no + characters are needed. The file /etc/nsswitch.conf controls the order in which the local password file and the NIS map are checked. The format of the relevant line is as follows:

```
passwd  options
```

Valid options vary among systems. The options in Table 7.1 are usually available.

TABLE 7.1 Options for nsswitch.conf

Option	Meaning
files	Use the local password files.
nis	Use the NIS password map.
compat	Use the local password files, but honor the + convention for referencing NIS map entries.

In addition, specific actions can be taken during the search. These are options of the form [*status=action*], where *status* is given in Table 7.2. *action* is either return (end the search) or continue (don't end the search). If *action* is omitted, the stated default is used.

TABLE 7.2   Status and Actions for nsswitch.conf

Status	*Meaning*	*Default Action*
success	Desired entry found	return
notfound	Desired entry not found	continue
unavail	Database access failed (nontransient—for example, server down, query disallowed)	continue
tryagain	Database access failed (transient—for example, file locked, too many connections)	continue

The *status* and *action* keywords are not case-sensitive; the option keywords are case-sensitive.

Linux Red Hat 7.1: The nsswitch.conf File

Here is a portion of an /etc/nsswitch.conf file:

```
passwd: db files nis
shadow: db files nis
group: db files nis
hosts:  dns [!UNAVAIL=return] files nis
```

The first three lines check for the password, shadow, and group information in database format files first; then in the flat files /etc/passwd, /etc/shadow, and /etc/group; and finally in the NIS server. The last line instructs host lookups to go to the DNS first. If the DNS is available, the result is returned even if the lookup fails (the leading ! reverses the sense of the status). If the DNS is unavailable due to a nontransient failure, the lookup proceeds to the file /etc/hosts; if that fails the lookup continues to the NIS server. To have the password lookups honor the + field, the first two lines would be changed to this:

```
passwd: compat
shadow: compat
```

If you turn on NIS and the /etc/nsswitch.conf file seems not to work, check the libraries that begin with /lib/libnss_*xxx*.so.*n*. There should be a library named like that for each of the options (for example, /lib/libnss_db.so.1, /lib/libnss_files.so.1, and /lib/libnss_compat.so.2). If those do not exist, then /etc/nsswitch.conf will not work. Try reinstalling NIS to fix this problem.

Solaris 2.8: The nsswitch.conf File

Here is a portion of an /etc/nsswitch.conf file:

```
passwd: files nis
shadow: files nis
group:  files nis
hosts:  dns [TRYAGAIN=forever] files nis
```

Here, the first three lines are like those in the Red Hat example. Solaris defines an additional action keyword `forever`. It can be used only with the status `tryagain`, and it means to continue trying until the status changes or the request succeeds. The action for `tryagain` also can be a non-negative number indicating how many retries to make. The last line in the previous file says that if the attempt to reach the DNS fails for a transient reason, continue trying. If the failure is nontransient, go on to the file /etc/hosts and then to the NIS database. As in Red Hat, option *xxx* is implemented using the libraries /usr/lib/nss_*xxx*.so.1 (for example, /usr/lib/nss_compat.so.1, /usr/lib/nss_files.so.1, and /usr/lib/nss_dns.so.1 implement the `compat`, `files`, and `dns` options, respectively).

Although shadow password files will work with NIS, the hashes are sent from the server to the client over the network in the clear. Furthermore, anyone who can build a request to the NIS server program can request that the contents of the shadow file be sent. So, there seems little point in using shadow password files over NIS, unless the network and network servers are strengthened to provide strong authentication and encryption.

Alternate UNIX Password Algorithms

Each password can be composed of characters drawn from a set of about 100 characters (the exact number varies among systems), for a total of roughly 10^{16} possible passwords. When the UNIX algorithm was devised, this was sufficiently large to prevent an exhaustive search. However, as computers have become more powerful and distributed computations have become more common, password guessing attacks have become correspondingly more successful. The capability to use longer passwords is essential.

Some UNIX systems use a hash function called crypt16 or bigcrypt that allows passwords of 16 or fewer characters. This function splits the password into two sets of 8 characters (passing with 0 bytes, if needed). Each is run through the standard UNIX crypt function (using the same salt), and the resulting printable hashes are concatenated. This scheme allows some optimizations to password-guessing attacks and is not used much.

The more common approach is to replace the UNIX crypt function with a standard cryptographic hash function, such as SHA-1 or MD5. These take strings of arbitrary length. The UNIX scheme combines them with a salt, computes the hash of the salt and the password, and converts the result to a printable string using the same method as for the traditional password scheme. Because passwords can be any length using these schemes, users have the capability to use passwords selected from a much larger set of possible passwords.

Linux Red Hat 7.1: Hashing Algorithms

Red Hat can use either the standard UNIX password hashing scheme or one based on MD5. You can choose the version at installation time, or by changing the appropriate PAM module (see the section "Integrating with PAM," later in this chapter). You can tell which scheme is in use by looking at the hashed password. If the hash begins with "1", the hash is generated using MD5. The characters between the second and third $ represent the salt. Other hashes may be added. When they are, they will be numbered, and the number between the first two $ signs indicates the specific hash (here, of course, 1 means MD5).

Solaris 2.8: Hashing Algorithms

Solaris 2.8 uses the standard UNIX password-hashing algorithm.

The main problem with alternate password algorithms is that they are incompatible with many systems and software. For example, NIS does not support the MD5 and SHA-1 styles of passwords.

Tip

If your system supports a password mechanism that allows more than eight-character passwords, use it unless you have a good, specific reason not to.

Alternate Authentication Schemes

One objection to the standard UNIX schemes and the variants described previous is that the passwords are reusable: Users use the same password to log in every time. If the password is monitored or guessed, the attacker immediately can use it to gain access to the compromised user's account.

The first solution, called *trusted hosts*, eliminates the sending of the password. Users create a file called .rhosts in their home directories. Each line of that file contains a hostname and a username:

```
ee.com.com      scott
home.univ.edu   matoon
```

This file instructs the *r-protocols* (rlogin, rsh, rcp programs) *not* to ask for a password when the user scott from the host ee.com.com tries to log into this account. Similarly, the user matoon from the host home.univ.edu need not supply a password to log into this account. The hostname + and the username + match *any* host or username throughout the

Internet, so these files should *never* contain those characters! The theory underlying the use of this mechanism is that the remote host adequately authenticated the user, so the local system need not repeat the authentication.

The .rhosts file applies to the user whose home directory the file lies in. The sysadmin may create a file called /etc/hosts.equiv. This file has the same format as a user's .rhosts file. The difference is that the trust is extended for *all* users. For example, suppose that host ee.com.com has a user named casey, and the local host does, too. If the hosts.equiv file on the local system contains the following, then casey on ee.com.com need not supply a password to access the account casey on the local system:

```
ee.com.com
home.univ.edu
```

As with .rhosts, + matches any host on the Internet and should not be in this file.

Tip

Here are some suggestions for using host-based authentication:

- Because IP spoofing programs are widely available, and because the name of the remote host is determined by converting the IP address to a hostname, the use of .rhosts and hosts.equiv is easy to subvert. Disable this method unless your site cannot function without it. To do so, comment the `rlogind`, `rexecd`, and `rshd` lines out of your /etc/inetd.conf file, and restart inetd.

- The rexd daemon deserves special mention. Under no circumstances should you run this daemon. It does no authentication, yet it will execute commands on your system. If you are running it, disable it immediately.

- Do not use hosts.equiv to extend trust to a remote host unless you have complete control over that host. In particular, if the remote host and the local host have accounts with the same name, the same entity must be associated with each account.

Consistency in Usernames Across Hosts

Sometimes account ownership is not consistent across workstations in the same installation. For instance, imagine that a user has an account casey on the central system and, for some reason, is assigned the account jiggs on a workstation. One day he types `rlogin mainserver`, forgetting to add the `-l casey` that would get him to his account on the server. Figuring that the connection would be rejected, he just waits—and is promptly put into the jiggs account on the server, which belongs to a different user! (He should report this to the site administrator, who promptly should change the workstation account name to casey.)

An alternative to the trusted host approach is to take password aging to its logical conclusion: A password may be used once before being changed. This is called a *one-time password*, and it uses a type of protocol called *challenge-response*. When users initiate the login sequence, the computer sends or displays some information (the *challenge*). The user enters the appropriate password (the *response*). The computer validates the response and, if correct, completes the login. At the next login, a different challenge is presented, leading to a different response (password). Hence, even if attackers record the previous password, they cannot replay it to gain access to the system. The recorded password is no longer valid; it is used only once.

This method has several advantages over reusable passwords, including these:

- The hash of the next password is not kept online, so an attacker cannot guess the next password and compare it to an existing hash. However, some implementations of one-time passwords are vulnerable to similar attacks.
- Users can either work from a printed list of passwords or use a password-generation program (the latter is convenient if the login originates at a laptop or other computer). Most systems also require the user to supply a fixed, reusable password to help generate the response.
- If the algorithm that generates responses from the challenges is well chosen, deriving the algorithm from a list of challenges and corresponding responses is computationally infeasible.

However, this method also poses some problems:

- Software that handles passwords must be modified to handle the challenge-response scheme.
- Challenge-response methods must be used everywhere throughout an infrastructure.
- Challenge-response methods authenticate the user. They may, but usually do not, authenticate the server. Also, they do not protect the following session.

The second and third points are important and subtle enough to warrant a more detailed explanation.

The second point raises the issue of incomplete integration. Suppose that a company uses a challenge-response scheme internally but does not support it at the boundaries, for compatibility reasons (it is not integrated into external server software, for example). Then users must use reusable passwords to connect to the company systems, after which they can use the challenge-response scheme. This means that the reusable passwords are exposed to the external network, but not to the internal network (where the company might be able to control sniffing by using encrypted connections). *The moral:* If you use one-time passwords, use them everywhere and not just internally!

The third point states the limits of challenge-response protocols. They establish identity. If a connection then is hijacked, the server will *not* realize that the entity that it authenticated is no longer at the other end. Furthermore, unless the connection is encrypted, any eavesdropper can read all messages. Finally, in most implementations, although the users authenticate themselves to the server, the server does not authenticate itself to the user. Hence an attacker might be able to impersonate a server and trick users into revealing information.

To demonstrate how challenge-response systems work, we discuss the S/Key system as an example. This is the basis for several other schemes, including OPIE. The references listed at the end of this chapter include information on how to get OPIE and OTPW.

To initialize S/Key, the user supplies a reusable password (the *S/Key password*) and the computer generates a random *seed*. Suppose that the user wants to generate 100 passwords. The S/Key password and the seed are combined, and a hash function (usually MD5, but sometimes MD4) is applied 100 times. The system stores in the skeykeys file the username, the seed, the 100th hash, and some other information not relevant to the hashing.

To log in, the user supplies the 99th hash, which is the next password (this can be obtained from a list or from special-purpose software that takes the user's S/Key password and the seed). When the system gets the user-supplied hash, it hashes that password. Because the supplied password is (supposedly) the 99th hash, hashing it again will produce the 100th hash, which the computer has stored in the file. So, the results of hashing the password should produce the hash stored in the file.

If not, the login is rejected. If so, the hash in the skeykeys file is replaced with the password (99th hash), and the user is logged in.

Hardware-based challenge-response mechanisms work similarly. They send a cryptographic challenge to the user. The user has special-purpose hardware (a calculator or program on another computer) that computes the appropriate response. The user might have to supply a fixed password, in addition to entering the challenge. The user sends the response back to the computer, and, if the response is correct, the login completes. Other hardware systems use a reusable password and a random number based upon time. Every minute, the "smart card" generates a new random number. The user logs in by supplying the reusable password and the number currently displayed. The server knows the number that should be displayed, and if the reusable password and the number are correct, the login completes. The number is invalidated so that another user cannot log in during the remainder of the interval when that number is valid.

ssh and Authentication

Secure Shell (or SSH) is a program and a protocol to provide authenticated, enciphered connections. Appendix E discusses the protocols in detail. Basically, SSH uses a public key cryptosystem to authenticate the server to the client. It can authenticate the user in a variety of ways:

- The user can send a reusable password. In this case, the password is sent over an encrypted connection. It is *not* visible to attackers (unless the encryption is turned off).

- The SSH system can be configured to use the trusted host mechanism using .rhosts and hosts.equiv. Here, the host is identified by the public key authentication mechanism in the protocol, not by the IP address.

- The SSH mechanism can be configured to use the trusted host mechanism using .shosts. This works the same way as the .rhosts file, but if the server is running the r-protocols, those programs will ignore the .shosts file.

- The SSH mechanism can be configured to use public key authentication for the user as well as for the host.

We will discuss how to set the authentication method when we discuss the configuration files.

Chapter 8, "Securing a System for Rollout," describes how to install the SSH program. In what follows, we assume that the program is installed correctly, and we review a subset of the authentication-relevant options. There are three different servers, OpenSSH, SSH2, and SSH1. The options are largely consistent for all versions; we note differences where they occur.

Linux Red Hat 7.1: OpenSSH

Red Hat 7.1 comes with OpenSSH. You can have it installed at installation time. When it asks for the daemons that you want to enable, indicate SSH. Otherwise, you can install it later.

Solaris 2.8: ssh Options

Solaris 2.8 does not come with a version of SSH. You will need to obtain and install one. OpenSSH is free; other versions might cost money.

SSH consists of two components, a server and a client. Options for both are set in configuration files specified at compile time or runtime (with the −f option). Table 7.3 summarizes some options relevant to authentication in the SSH server configuration files.

TABLE 7.3 SSH Server Configuration Keywords

Keyword	Meaning
AllowGroups group,group,... DenyGroups group,group,...	Allows (denies) logins only if the user's primary GID matches a group. The group cannot be numeric but may be a pattern, with ? matching exactly one character and * matching zero or more characters. Default: Allows login.
AllowHosts host,host,... DenyHosts host,host,...	Allows (denies) logins only from the named hosts. The host may be a pattern, with ? matching exactly one character and * matching zero or more characters. (The OpenSSH server does not support this option.) Default: Allows login.
AllowUsers user, user,... DenyUsers user,user,...	Allows (denies) logins only if the user's login name matches a *user*. The *user* cannot be numeric but may be a pattern, with ? matching exactly one character and * matching zero or more characters. Default: Allows login.
ChallengeResponseAuthentication *yesno*	If *yesno* is yes, allows challenge-response authentication for SSHv2 protocol. Currently OpenSSH supports only S/Key and PAM authentication. If *yesno* is no, does not allow it. Default: yes
IgnoreRhosts *yesno*	If *yesno* is yes, does not use the user's .rhosts file or .shosts file. If *yesno* is no, honors them. Default: yes
PasswordAuthentication *yesno*	If *yesno* is no, authentication using passwords is disallowed. If *yesno* is yes, authentication using passwords is permitted. Even if this is no, when ChallengeResponseAuthentication is yes, users can use those mechanisms. Default: yes
PermitEmptyPasswords *yesno*	If *yesno* is set to yes, the server will accept connections to accounts with empty passwords. Otherwise, those connections are rejected. Default: no

TABLE 7.3 continued

Keyword	Meaning
PermitRootLogin *value*	This controls root logins. If *value* is no or yes, access is denied or granted always. If it is without-password (OpenSSH) or nopwd (SSH2), password authentication is not allowed for root (but other forms of authentication, such as public key, are allowed). If it is forced-commands-only (OpenSSH), root can use public key authentication only when a command is defined; see Chapter 8, "Securing a System for Rollout," for more details. Default: yes
PubkeyAuthentication *yesno*	If *yesno* is yes, allows public key authentication. If *yesno* is no, disallows it (SSHv2 protocol only). Default: yes
ReverseMappingCheck *yesno*	If *yesno* is yes, maps the IP address to a hostname and maps the name to an IP address, and compares. Disallows the connection if the two differ. If *yesno* is no, does not check the IP address this way. Default: no
RhostsAuthentication *yesno*	If *yesno* is yes, allows .rhosts authentication. Otherwise, disallows such authentication. (If you want .rhosts authentication, use RhostsRSAAuthentication because that uses cryptography to establish the remote host identity.) Default: no
RhostsRSAAuthentication *yesno*	If *yesno* is yes, allows .rhosts authentication, basing host identification on public keys. Otherwise, disallows such authentication. Default: no
RSAAuthentication *yesno*	If *yesno* is yes, allows authentication using the RSA public key system. Otherwise, disallows such authentication. Default: yes

The SSH clients have several authentication options.

PasswordAuthentication, PubkeyAuthentication, RhostsAuthentication, RhostsRSAAuthentication, RSAAuthentication, and

ChallengeResponseAuthentication dictate what authentication methods are to be used and can take the values yes and no only. They apply to the versions of the protocol as indicated in Table 7.3.

If FallBackToRsh is yes, then if the client is told that there is no ssh daemon on the server system, it will use rsh(1). Needless to say, this should always be set to no to force ssh to quit if there is no daemon on the server system.

The final option requires some background. When the client contacts an SSH server, it receives the host key from that server. The client then checks its host key database. If that host is named in the database, the client compares the stored key with the one that it just received. If the two match, the server is authenticated. If not, or if the host is not named in the database, the option StrictHostKeyChecking controls what happens.

If StrictHostKeyChecking is no, the new key and host are inserted into the database (possibly overwriting the existing key). If the option is yes, the key is rejected. If the option is ask, the user is asked if the key and host should be added. This option always should be set to ask or yes. Otherwise, a spoofed key might be silently accepted and inserted into the database.

The advantage of SSH is that passwords are never sent in clear text over the network. In fact, by setting PasswordAuthentication and IgnoreRhosts to no, all logins must use public key authentication. Furthermore, when the connection is established, all messages sent over it are encrypted. Other protocols can be tunneled through that connection, too.

As an example, suppose that you want to access a POP server on a host. However, you do not want the POP password to be sent in clear text over the network. If the host runs an SSH server, you can arrange to POP mail to your local system as follows. First, establish an encrypted tunnel from your system to the host:

```
ssh -L 110:host:110 host
```

This says to forward all connections to port 110 (the POP port) on the local host to port 110 on the host. The forwarding is through SSH's tunnel, which is encrypted. Then, to pop your mail, have your POP client access port 110 on the local host. The request and the password will be forwarded to the host, where the POP server will process it and return the results through the SSH connection.

Tip

Install a version of SSH. Disable daemons that accept clear-text passwords (the main ones are telnet, ftp, POP and IMAP daemons, and rlogin), or allow them to accept connections from the local host. Teach your users to use SSH and its tunneling capabilities to reach the other daemons.

Kerberos

Kerberos is an authentication mechanism offering centralized password management. It is a challenge-response system and uses classical cryptography. At no time is the cleartext password placed on the network.

With Kerberos, users authenticate themselves to the authentication server. The authentication server issues a sealed credential (called a ticket) that identifies the user to a server. The user cannot alter the ticket. The user transmits the ticket and a second token, called an authenticator, to the server. The server unseals the ticket, checks that it was issued to the sender, and checks that the authenticator originated from the sender. If so, the server knows who the sender is and can determine whether to allow the sender to use the service. Kerberos also allows encrypted communications between the user and the server.

Kerberos is not as widely used as the other methods discussed here.

Integrating with PAM

Pluggable Authentication Modules (PAM) is a framework for a collection of authentication modules that provides different authentication methods. There is a common interface to programs using PAM. Programmers can treat the notion of authentication as an abstraction. The modules can be "stacked," meaning that multiple methods of authentication can be used by the same program. Changing authentication mechanisms for a particular program requires changing a configuration file rather than changing, recompiling, and relinking the program.

PAM provides four different types of modules, as shown in Table 7.4.

TABLE 7.4 PAM Module Types

Module	Type Function
account	Account management not involving authentication
auth	Authentication of the user, and (possibly) granting of additional privileges
password	Updated authentication information
session	Actions needed to begin or end a session not involving authentication

Modules can be "stacked" or invoked in succession as part of the authentication process. If a module fails, the authentication might or might not fail. The PAM configuration file uses control flags to describe how the failure is handled, as shown in Table 7.5.

TABLE 7.5 PAM Control Flags

Control Flag	Effect
optional	If no other module returns success or failure, returns the success or failure of this module
required	If this module fails, executes the other modules and reports failure, regardless of the results from the other modules
requisite	If this module fails, does *not* execute any other modules and reports failure immediately
sufficient	If this module succeeds and no previous required modules have failed, returns success. No other modules of this type are executed.

The module is named in the configuration file, along with a set of module-specific arguments that are passed to the module. If an erroneous argument is given, that argument is ignored and an error is written to syslog. Some arguments are common to a large number of modules, as shown in Table 7.6.

TABLE 7.6 PAM Module Arguments

Argument	Effect
debug	Writes debugging information to syslog.
expose_account	Does not conceal information about user accounts that attackers might find useful (such as username or home directory). This is mainly useful in facilities that are willing to expose this information during the authentication process.
no_warn	Does not give warning messages to the caller (application).
try_first_pass	Uses the password supplied to the preceding auth module. If that cannot be obtained, prompts for a password.
use_mapped_pass	Uses a clear-text password obtained by a previous module to generate a cryptographic key that can be used to store or retrieve the authentication token for this module. This is intended for single sign-on, but it requires strong encryption and thus is not widely supported yet.
use_first_pass	Does not ask for a password; uses the one supplied to the preceding auth module. If that cannot be obtained, fails.

7

AUTHENTICATION

PAM control files have two formats. In one form, the lines are placed in the file /etc/pam.conf and have this form:

```
program module-type     control-flag     module   arguments
```

For example, when the program login runs, the lines that control authentication all begin with `login`. The second form uses a directory called /etc/pam.d. That directory contains files with the same names as programs. Each file contains lines of this form:

```
module-type     control-flag     module   arguments
```

With this arrangement, when the program login runs, the lines that control authentication are in the file etc/pam.d/login. In both cases, the program other refers to any program not listed in the configuration file or directory.

Let's consider the login program as an example. We'll walk through the login procedure and build the appropriate PAM configuration lines for authentication (the actual entries would include account and session modules, and, if password aging were in force, password modules). We'll assume that the PAM modules are in the pamdir directory and that all are dynamically loaded (and so end in ".so"). The following steps take place:

1. When root logs in on a tty, that tty must be listed in the set of secure ttys. The module pam_securetty succeeds if the user is not root or if the tty is listed as a secure tty (in the /etc/securetty file). The line would be as follows:

   ```
   auth required     pamdir/pam_securetty.so
   ```

2. User authentication comes next. Here we use the idea of stacking because we want to have user authentication listed in one file rather than once in all configuration files (that way, if we change the authentication procedure for one program, we change it for all). So, we refer the authentication to the system-auth module using the stacking PAM module:

   ```
   auth required     pamdir/pam_stack.so service=system-auth
   ```

   (If your system does not have this module available, simply list the next two lines directly.)

3. Now, let's set up a typical system_auth configuration file. The goal here is to authenticate the user using a password and to deny access if the user fails to authenticate.

   a. We need to have the password checked. The module pam_unix obtains the password from the appropriate source (with the password file, or using /etc/nsswitch to locate the appropriate source). If the user has a blank password, this module will deny access. We want access to be allowed, so we give the option `nullok`. The line looks like this:

      ```
      auth sufficient     pamdir/pam_unix.so nullok
      ```

   b. If that module fails, we want to deny access. The PAM module pam_deny always fails, so we add another line:

```
auth required          pamdir/pam_deny.so
```

To summarize, using the /etc/pam.d method, the appropriate lines for login authentication would be in a file called login:

```
auth    required       pamdir/pam_securetty.so
auth    required       pamdir/pam_stack.so service=system-auth
```

The file system-auth in that same directory would contain the following:

```
auth    sufficient     pamdir/pam_unix.so nullok
auth    required       pamdir/pam_deny.so
```

An equivalent setup would be to put everything into the login file:

```
auth    required       pamdir/pam_securetty.so
auth    sufficient     pamdir/pam_unix.so nullok
auth    required       pamdir/pam_deny.so
```

If you are using the /etc/pam.conf method, the following lines would be put into /etc/pam.conf:

```
login   auth   required       pamdir/pam_securetty.so
login   auth   sufficient     pamdir/pam_unix.so nullok
login   auth   required       pamdir/pam_deny.so
```

As a second example, let's look at the PAM modules for the password-changing program, passwd. This program uses three types of modules: auth, to authenticate the user; account, to check account parameters such as password age; and password, to change and check the proposed password. We walk through the steps to check that the user is allowed to change the password and to verify that the password is acceptable.

1. Users must authenticate themselves before changing passwords. Hence, we invoke the system-auth module described previously:

```
auth required      pamdir/pam_stack.so service=system-auth
```

2. Next comes the account information module. This checks that the user can change the password. The pam_unix module performs these functions:

```
account    required       pamdir/pam_unix.so
```

3. The proposed password is to be vetted by the password-checking module. Here, we use a version of crack that checks whether crack would be capable of guessing a password and then tries some other tests comparing the proposed password with the current one. The module is pam_cracklib. We allow the user to try three different passwords before giving up. The line is as follows:

```
password   required       pamdir/pam_cracklib.so retry=3
```

4. The password now is updated using the ubiquitous pam_unix module. We allow empty passwords. On this system, we are using the MD5 alternate password scheme with shadow files. We also want to force this module to set the password to the one entered to the previous module. The appropriate line is as follows:

```
password   sufficient      pamdir/pam_unix.so nullok use_authtok \
        md5 shadow
```

5. Finally, if the password could not be set, we want to force failure:

```
password   required      pamdir/pam_deny.so
```

These examples give a flavor of how PAM works.

Locking Yourself Out

If you misconfigure PAM, you might accidentally lock yourself out of your system! If that happens, *don't panic*. You can regain access easily, provided that you can get access to root or boot your machine into single-user mode. When you're in that mode, you'll get the *root* prompt. Save all your PAM files somewhere (so that you can figure out what you did wrong):

```
cd /etc
mv pam.d pam.d.old
mv pam.conf pam.conf.old
```

Next, create a new PAM configuration file that does basic authentication and management. On Linux, the file contains the following:

```
other auth       required      pam_unix_auth.so
other account    required      pam_unix_acct.so
other password   required      pam_unix_passwd.so
other session    required      pam_unix_session.so
```

On Solaris, the file contains this:

```
other auth       required      pam_unix.so
other account    required      pam_unix.so
other password   required      pam_unix.so
other session    required      pam_unix.so
```

Then log in normally. If that fails, something else is wrong. (Check the syslog messages for an indication.)

Linux Red Hat 7.1: PAM

The default distribution uses the directory /etc/pam.d to store files named by the programs that use PAM. Furthermore, the system authentication components, which most programs use, are in the file system-auth. This includes all the module types.

```
auth          required        /lib/security/pam_env.o
auth          sufficient      /lib/security/pam_unix.so nullok
auth          required        /lib/security/pam_deny.so
account       required        /lib/security/pam_unix.so
password      required        /lib/security/pam_cracklib.so retry=3
password      sufficient      /lib/security/pam_unix.so nullok \
use_authtok md5 shadow
password      required        /lib/security/pam_deny.so
session       required        /lib/security/pam_limits.so
session       required        lib/security/pam_unix.so
```

The first three lines were discussed in the previous login example. The account line invokes the module pam_unix.so, which, in that guise, checks any password aging and acts accordingly. The next three lines are invoked when a password is being changed; these were discussed in the previous passwd example. Finally, the first session line instantiates any limits, and the second logs the username and type of service to syslog(3).

Solaris 2.8: PAM

By default, Solaris 2.8 uses the configuration file /etc/pam.conf to control the use of PAM. As an example, the rlogin program's auth modules are listed as follows:

```
rlogin auth sufficient /usr/lib/security/$ISA/pam_rhosts_auth.so.1
rlogin auth required   /usr/lib/security/$ISA/pam_unix.so.1
```

The first line checks to see if the .rhosts or /etc/hosts.equiv files allow the user access without supplying a password. If not, the second line forces the user to supply a password.

The ident Server and Authentication

Although it is not an authentication mechanism, the ident protocol often is misused as one and so deserves mention. The ident protocol identifies the user running the program at the remote end of a connection. The host sends an ident request to the remote host identifying the local port number and the remote port number (which can be obtained from the connection). The remote host returns the username corresponding to the real UID of the process at the other end of the connection.

To use this as an authenticator, the local host queries the remote host when the connection is initiated. Access rights are based upon the username returned.

The problem with using ident to authenticate the remote user is the same as for the trusted host mechanism. Like .rhosts files, the authentication trusts properties of the connection (such as the remote IP address and the assignment of usernames remotely to the same entities as the local name), these can be spoofed or simply might be false. Unless the remote host is under the physical control of the local sysadmin, the information that the ident protocol returns should be treated with extreme skepticism. It may be logged for any future investigations, but it should be seen as a starting point and not as correctly identifying the user.

The situation is worse than the one discussed previously. Suppose that an attacker breaks into a computer system. The attacker wants to attack other targets. By sending ident queries to all remote hosts that have connections to the local host, the attacker can get a set of login names and hosts to probe. For this reason, ident never should return a legitimate username. Instead, it should return a randomly generated string. The host also should log the string and the correct username in a log file (such as syslog). If sysadmins of the querying host need the correct name, they then can call the sysadmins of the responding host and, after demonstrating the need, can supply the random string. The sysadmins of the responding host can supply the corresponding username.

> ### Tip
>
> Here are some tips about ident and other servers (such as the finger server) that return usernames:
>
> - Unless absolutely necessary, do not run the ident service.
> - If this service must be run, have it return a random string rather than an actual username, and log the random string and corresponding username. The remote sysadmin can contact you to get the real username later, if necessary.

Linux Red Hat 7.1: The identd Daemon

By default, the ident daemon is disabled. To run it in multiuser mode, go to /etc/rc5.d (or the directory for the runlevel that you want identd to run at) and execute this:

```
./K65identd start
```

To have it execute when booting into runlevel 5, link the file to the name S35identd. *Do not delete the original file or change its name: You need it at shutdown.*

By default, the daemon will return the name of the user (such as root or marge). As discussed previously, this is strongly discouraged. The Red Hat version of identd allows you to return an enciphered token that then can be deciphered. To do this, edit the file /etc/inetd.conf. Change this line

```
# result:encrypt = no
```

to this:

```
result:encrypt = yes.
```

Then the username to an identd query will be returned like this (for example):

```
[AX8LoV0wiQt3tf6jbCMjqapwh3KNLJks]
```

This is of no use to a remote attacker. If the query is legitimate, the requester can contact you and convince you of the necessity for revealing the username. If you decide to do so, run the program idecrypt(8) and give the token on the standard input. The standard output will contain the time at which the token was generated and the UID of the corresponding user. Here, you type the **bold** part, and the rest comes from the computer:

```
# idecrypt
[AX8LoV0wiQt3tf6jbCMjqapwh3KNLJks]
Sun Sep 30 12:12:12 2001 0
```

If you use identd, this mode is *strongly* recommended.

Solaris 2.8: The identd Daemon

Solaris 2.8 does not come with an ident daemon. The one that Linux has will work with Solaris 2.8. Download it (see the "References" section in this chapter), and follow the directions in the INSTALL file. As with the Linux version, if you decide to run identd, you should install the cryptographic support (described in the instructions) and set identd to return the encrypted token. (After installation, change the line indicated in the configuration file to say `result:encrypt = yes`, just as for Linux.)

Best Practices

- Tell your users that lists of "good" or "hard-to-guess" passwords are examples; do not use them.
- Protect backups that contain the password or shadow files.
- Use different passwords for different systems.
- Never store passwords in clear text.
- Change passwords at secure locations (where you are certain that you are not being spoofed).

- Beware of social engineering: Never change a password for a user without being convinced of that user's identity.

- Do not share passwords, even with family.

- Beware of shoulder surfers (people who look over your shoulder to read your keystrokes as you enter your password).

- If you use password aging, force users to change passwords as infrequently as you consider wise, and give them plenty of notice before their password expires.

- Use shadow password files if your system supports them.

- If you have to edit the password file, use vipw.

- Do *not* use vipw to change password hashes (unless you are disabling password authentication for that account).

- If you set your system to disable an account after *n* failed login attempts, *always* exempt the superuser account.

- If you are using NIS, *always* make sure that you have a line for root in /etc/passwd on the NIS client.

- If your system supports a password mechanism that allows more than eight-character passwords, use it unless you have a good, specific reason not to.

- Disable the r-protocol daemons, *especially* rexd.

- Do not use .rhosts or /etc/hosts.equiv to turn off password authentication unless you have both physical and administrative control over the systems named in those files *and* have secured them as well as the local host.

- Install, use, and have your users use some implementation of SSH.

- Unless absolutely necessary, do not run the ident service. If this service must be run, have it return a random string rather than an actual username, and log the random string and corresponding username for later reference.

References

Authentication in general:

Bill von Hagen. "Logging in from Anywhere: Distributed Authentication for Linux." *Linux Magazine.* January 2001. http://www.linux-mag.com/2001-01/authentication_01.html.

Passwords and password files:

Morris, Robert, and Ken Thompson. "Password Security: A Case History."

Communications of the ACM. Vol. 22, no. 11 (November 1979). p. 594–597. (This discusses the original UNIX password-hashing algorithm.)

Holbrook, Paul, and Joyce Reynolds. RFC 1244, "Site Security Handbook." July 1991. (The recommendations are in Section 4.3.1.)

Eastlake, Donald III, Stephen Crocker, and Jeffrey Schiller. RFC 1750, "Randomness Recommendations for Security." December 1994. (This discusses random number generation and seeding.)

http://www.cert.org/tech_tips/passwd_file_protection.html.

Russell, Paul. "Passwords That Don't Suck." *Linux Magazine*. December 1999. http://www.linux-mag.com/1999-12/bestdefense_01.html.

NIS:

Stern, Hal, Mike Eisler, and Ricardo Labiaga. *Managing NFS and NIS, 2nd Edition*. O'Reilly and Associates: Sebastopol, California, July 2001.

Password-guessing programs:

crack: http://ftp.cerias.purdue.edu/pub/tools/unix/pwdutils/crack

John the Ripper: http://ftp.cerias.purdue.edu/pub/tools/unix/pwdutils/john

Commercial token-based challenge-response implementations:

Axent Defender: http://www.c2000.com/products/sec_dfdr.htm

FiPass: http://www.fipass.com/corporate/authentication.asp

RSA SecurID:
http://www.rsasecurity.com/products/securid/authenticators.html

One-Time password programs:

S/Key: ftp://ftp.cert.dfn.de/pub/tools/password/SKey/;
(http://lheawww.gsfc.nasa.gov/~srr/skey_info.html has some helpful hints.)

OPIE: http://www.inner.net/pub/opie/

OTPW: http://www.cl.cam.ac.uk/~mgk25/otpw.html

Kerberos: http://web.mit.edu/kerberos/www/

PAM:

Morgan, Andrew. *The Linux-PAM System Administrators' Guide*. Version 0.74, /usr/share/doc/pam-0.74 (January 2001).

`http://www.sun.com/solaris/pam` (contains whitepapers and documentation)

ident daemon:

St. Johns, Mike. RFC 1413, "Identification Protocol." February 1993.

`http://sf.www.lysator.liu.se/~pen/pidentd`

Securing a System for Rollout

by Jay Beale

IN THIS CHAPTER

You Must Harden the System

A system really can't be considered to be fully set up until you've performed some basic security steps. This isn't simply dogma—there's a real practical reason for this: Almost every freshly installed system can be broken into.

Actually, the HoneyNet project estimated that the average life expectancy of a default install of a Red Hat 6.2 server is 72 hours. Many people initially are shocked by this estimate. Honestly, it gets worse. One interviewed student installed her operating system, went to bed, and got a call from campus authorities the next day—her system had been hacked and was being used to attack other students. A man at another college reported that he installed his operating system, went to dinner, and came back to find that his system had been hacked while he was eating. Really, you just can't trust the default install. Let's consider why.

Well, during the time between the packaging of your operating system and the time of your install, creative analysts will find a number of security vulnerabilities in *any* operating system. The older your operating system is, the more time that analysts have had to discover vulnerabilities. Now, most of these vulnerabilities will be *exploitable*. A vulnerability is exploitable if some knowledgeable person, armed with a little ingenuity, could use it to gain any level of unauthorized access to your system. If someone automates the exploitation process, the resulting program/script is called an *exploit*. These exploits are easy to find on the Internet, widely circulated via hacker and security sites alike.

As we said, vulnerabilities are discovered in every operating system. You're probably thinking right now, "Yeah, but I won't get hacked. My site's not very interesting. I'm just running the computers at a five-person company." Well, remember the statistics? Most computers plugged into the Internet get scanned over the Internet within a few days of coming online. Many universities see a new machine get scanned within 5 minutes of being plugged into the Internet. There's a value to any system on the Internet, even if it's not obvious. Computers with an even slightly fast Internet connection make a wonderful depot/trading point for warez (illegally copied software), porn, music and movie files. Without a fast Internet connection, the system can still be used with an IRC "bot" to control IRC channels. Further, an attacker will often use each computer he cracks as a jumping-off point for future attacks — this makes it much harder to trace the attacks back to him. I have seen a number of times where an attacker cracks one system in the US, uses it to crack a system in Russia, then cracks another system in the US from the one in Russia. Anyone trying to track the cracker often has to coordinate across oceans, timezones and language barriers, not to mention differing legal systems. There is extreme value here to each and every system the cracker can nail, whether or not it is "interesting" in its own right.

So, how do you avoid being hacked? We'll cover that in this section, to the extent that we can cover it in a single chapter[1] of a comprehensive book like this one. Ideally, you should spend some time over the course of the next year of your career learning about security. In considering what you as a new administrator could accomplish in the meantime, we settled on the following: patch, do a password audit, do a network daemon audit, and use an automated solution like Bastille Linux or Titan to perform much more comprehensive steps.

Before we get to that, though, let's take a look at physical security.

Physical Security

In the whirlwind of technical details surrounding system and network security, it is easy to forget one of the most basic issues: physical security. As described in the Beale article "Anyone With a Screwdriver Can Break In," a capable attacker with physical access to the machine is nearly guaranteed illicit root privilege, so long as he has time, tools and a strong understanding of the target operating system's boot process. To paraphrase the article, we simply note that most systems can be easily hacked by simply interrupting or replacing the normal boot process. On top of this, an attacker who can mount your hard drive on a system that he controls generally wins by default.

On top of this, there's the simple matter of physical reliability. No matter how well audited and patched the software is, if the power is lost or the sprinklers go on, it's all over.

Before the system is even taken out of the box, the sysadmin should take a moment to inspect the intended site of the hardware. If the system is physically large, expensive, and important, it would be wise to write up a brief one-page report on physical site requirements. We have seen systems ordered, delivered, uncrated, assembled, installed, and configured in a staging area before anyone realizes that there is no place to put them.

Is there actually room for the system at the site? Remember that many systems come with physical specifications that include the amount of free space required for proper ventilation. Include this "breathing room" in your measurements.

Is there sufficient, reliable electric power at the site? If it's a desktop system, make sure that a power supply is available. If backup power, such as a UPS, will be required, it should be specified, ordered, and in place before the system is installed.

What happens if there is a fire at the site? Will the power be cut? Will the sprinklers go off? Is the system on a UPS that will keep it running while the sprinklers go off? You might not be able to do anything about any of this, but if you think ahead, you might get a more appropriate backup strategy.

We have seen problems arise when these questions weren't asked ahead of time. In the case of large system, questions such as "Will it fit through the door?" and "Will the floor hold it?" have arisen as well. Most computers are simple desktop models, of course, but a few seconds of consideration about appropriate physical site could save you hours of headache later.

From here, let's examine patching.

Patching: Process and Policy

You had better patch that system immediately! Remember, the attackers have the exploits, and they start scanning your system immediately. This means that the only safe move is to patch as soon you finish your installation procedure. If you can, try to install the patches before plugging the system into the network. In this vulnerable state, an attacker can compromise the system while you're downloading or installing patches! Even if you need to keep the system plugged into the network, say, to download patches, you should still do this in *single-user mode*. In single-user mode, your computer has minimal programs and services running, no one else can log in, and the network usually is disconnected. While logged in as root, you can switch your computer to single-user mode with this command:

```
# telinit 1                    OR        # telinit s
```

To bring the network back up, type the following:

```
# /etc/rc.d/init.d/network start     (Red Hat Linux or Mandrake Linux)
# /etc/init.d/network start          (other Linux distributions)
# /etc/rc2.d/S69inet                 (Solaris)
```

To get back into a multiuser runlevel, you can run "telinit <runlevel>", where <runlevel> is the appropriate runlevel. If you're not sure which one that is, either get it from the :initdefault: line in the /etc/inittab file, like this:

```
# grep :initdefault: /etc/inittab
```

or just reboot the system. As a patch might involve kernel changes, it's safer to simply reboot the system until you're more familiar with your vendors' patches and patch process.

Now, where do you get patches? Well, that depends on which UNIX you're running.

Solaris: At Install Time

Solaris system administrators should explore `http://sunsolve.sun.com` to find out about patching and the most recent security bulletins. After installing a new system, you should pull down the most recent "recommended patch cluster" from Sun. This is the set of all patches, updated each week, for each version of Solaris. You can download the cluster via the ftp link `ftp://sunsolve.sun.com/pub/patches/X.Y_Recommended.tar.Z`, where X.Y is the Solaris release version. For example, for Solaris 2.8, the link is `ftp://sunsolve.sun.com/pub/patches/2.8_Recommended.tar.Z`. Download the most recent patch cluster to /tmp, and install like this:

```
# cd /tmp
# compress 2.8_Recommended.tar.Z | tar -xvf -
# cd 2.8_Recommended
```

Read through the file CLUSTER_README, and remove any patches from the cluster, if you've made special modifications to your Solaris install. For example, many sites replace Sun's build of sendmail with their own build, compiled from source. To not inter-fere with this build, they have to remove any Sun sendmail patches before running the next command.

```
# ./install_cluster
```

This begins the Sun patch cluster process, which can take a while. Although it's intended to be interactive, the installation program always assumes that you want to proceed if you don't answer a question within some length of time. This allows you to automate the installation process, which makes running a large server farm much easier.

Often a reboot is necessary, especially if you've applied a kernel patch. You can find out what patches were included in the cluster by looking at the file CLUSTER_README in the patch cluster's main directory. This same file can be downloaded independently as X.Y_Recommended.README, which would be 2.8_Recommended.README in the case of our previous example.

Solaris: Maintenance

After install time, it's generally safest to continue downloading and installing the cluster patch. Some sites choose to fine-tune this process. All of Sun's available patches, in their

latest versions, are available in the same download location as the cluster patch. If you download a given patch—say, patch number 107758-01—into /tmp, here's how you would install it:

```
# cd /tmp
# compress 107758-01.tar.Z | tar -xvf -
# cd 107758-01
# ./installpatch
```

If you had to back out this patch, you could run the program backoutpatch out of the same directory. This is seldom, if ever, necessary, but it is good to know that Sun makes this option available.

A Security Note on Reversible Patches
by Rob Jenson

The problem with installing patches in a reversible fashion is that they end up storing all the offending code on the same system, somewhere in /var/adm/patch/patch#/?. The files are stored there with the same permissions as in their original locations. So, if there is a buffer overflow that can be exploited in a broken setuid root version of /usr/sbin/lpd, for example, that is fixed by a patch, and the patch is installed reversibly, it's easy enough for a script kiddie to look for /var/adm/patch/patch#/usr/sbin/lpd, and execute it (it's still setuid root). The later application of Titan or Bastille to remove the setuid bits will clear this risk somewhat, but then the patch is no longer reversible. My recommendation is: thoroughly test the effects of patches on an expendable system first (i.e., a test box). When confident that the patch does no harm to functionality, install it (non-reversibly) on the rest of your systems. An alternative (because this chapter is about patching as soon as is feasible) is to back up the patch "back-out" directories BEFORE installing the patch sets. After the patches are applied and the system seems to be good, back up the patch "backout" directories AFTER installing the patch sets, then delete them (the backout files, not the actually patch database). The backups should be stored on an external media that is easily retrievable, but not on the system itself. This ensures that (a) the system is patched expeditiously, (b) the broken binaries that are the risk are removed from the system, and patches can be reversed if necessary.

Patching Red Hat Linux

Red Hat system administrators should take a look at Red Hat's Errata page. Unlike Sun, most of the Linux vendors, including Red Hat, do not keep their sites constant enough for you to expect these links to remain usable. If these don't work, search around Red

Hat's Web site at `http://www.redhat.com`. With that said, Red Hat's errata page is currently at `http://www.redhat.com/apps/support/errata/`.

If this stays constant, you can download each of the patches for your version of Red Hat via `http://www.redhat.com/support/errata/rhXY-errata-security.html`, where X and Y are the first two digits of the distribution version. For example, for Red Hat 7.1, this link is `http://www.redhat.com/support/errata/rh71-errata-security.html`.

If you download the patches into /tmp/patches, you can install them like this:

```
# cd /tmp/patches
# rpm -Uvh *.rpm
```

Although patching on Red Hat isn't as easy as just pulling down a nice big patch cluster, it actually can be made much easier. Red Hat's Update Agent, up2date, automatically can pull down and install patches. It appears to be very robust and might make patching a variety of systems much easier. On the other hand, it's also part of a for-pay service called Red Hat Network, so that complicates the decision to start using it.

Mandrake Linux

Mandrake Linux system administrators should take a look at MandrakeSoft's "Update and Security Advisory" page. Unlike Sun, most of the Linux vendors, including MandrakeSoft, do not keep their sites constant enough for you to expect these links to remain usable—if these don't work, search MandrakeSoft's Web site, at `http://www.mandrakesoft.com`. With that said, MandrakeSoft's errata page is currently at `http://www.linux-mandrake.com/en/security/`.

If this stays constant, you can download each of the patches for your version of Mandrake Linux via `http://www.linux-mandrake.com/en/security/mdk-updates.php3?dis=X.Y`, where X.Y is the distribution version. For example, the page for Mandrake Linux 8.0 is `http://www.linux-mandrake.com/en/security/mdk-updates.php3?dis=8.0`.

If you download the patches into /tmp/patches, you can install them like this:

```
# cd /tmp/patches
# rpm -Uvh *.rpm
```

MandrakeSoft also offers an easier patching mechanism, although it doesn't have any cost associated with it at the time of this book's printing. This mechanism is embodied in the program MandrakeUpdate, which can be launched from the shell via this command:

```
# MandrakeUpdate
```

After you configure with a Mandrake mirror server, this tool can detect which patches you need and then automatically download and install them. Although this is a relatively new feature in Linux distributions, it can really help ease the process of patching.

General Considerations for Patching

Whichever way you patch, you should consider some standard precautions. First, always try out a patch on a system that does not have to maintain high availability first. Although the chances of a patch causing a disruption are very slim, you cannot always count on your vendor to never make mistakes and also have an identical system to the one that you're patching.

Second, it's a very good idea to have a second copy of your kernel stored somewhere else on your system, in case a patch replaces your main kernel with one that won't boot. You might even want to go further than this by making sure that every system administrator at your site has a "rescue disk," a piece of boot media with a working kernel and enough tools to diagnose and correct any problems.

Third, try to patch each system as soon as possible. As we'll consider in the next section, there are enough delays in getting each security/functionality problem patched. You don't want to add to these, if you want to keep your site running properly.

Why You Must Do More Than Patch

The thing is, patching won't keep you completely safe. The problem comes down to what some call *temporal windows of vulnerability*. Let's examine these in depth by considering the life cycle of the modern security exploit.

Step 1: Someone Discovers a Bug in a Program

As we pointed out before, every operating system ships with a number of bugs. These bugs can take the form of implementation errors and design oversights. In the case of the implementation error, the coding programmer makes a mistake in translating design into execution. One very common example of this type of bug is the *buffer overflow*.[2] A programmer copies user input into a memory buffer without limiting the amount of that input to the size of the buffer. This might sound trivial, but a competent programmer often can exploit this vulnerability to make the buggy program do all kinds of things that the designer never intended.

Design problems work the same way, although they cut more deeply to the heart of the program itself. Here, the designer makes a mistake that might or might not be correctable. For instance, he designs a method of administering systems remotely, such as telnet, that does not properly protect the authentication secret, such as a password, used to establish privilege. In the example of telnet, the password used to connect to the remote machine is sent "in the clear" over the network. Any computer on the network can run a network analyzer, or *sniffer*, to capture a copy of all traffic on the network.[3] Unfortunately, this design problem in telnet can't be as easily fixed as a normal buffer overflow. Although the buffer overflow usually can be corrected with a few lines of code, the entire telnet authentication mechanism is faulty!

Not every bug will be a security vulnerability; many bugs are simply bugs. For example, if the program crashes every time you select menu option 1, the problem is probably fairly benign. So, this bug might or might not make it to Step 2.

Step 2: Someone Realizes That This Bug Is a Security Vulnerability

To be a security vulnerability, the bug in your program must be exploitable to make the program do something relatively dangerous that the designer never intended it to do. For example, let's look at the buffer overflow. In most buffer overflows, the attacker can make the program execute arbitrary system commands, usually by forcing the program to execute an interactive shell.[4] It's not always this clear cut, so this step sometimes can happen some time after the initial bug discovery.

Additionally, to be a dangerous security vulnerability, the bug usually must be in a program that has some level of *privilege*. Remember, each program runs "as a user," where it has the exact same privileges as that user and no more. The two most common types of programs that have elevated privilege are Set-UID programs and system daemons. Let's consider Set-UID programs first.

Most of the time, a program starts with[5] the privilege level of the user who ran the program. In the case of a Set-UID program, the program starts with the privilege level of the actual owner of the program file. This makes Set-UID root programs especially juicy targets because they are often executable by any user on the system and because they give that user root privileges, subject to the confines of the program. If one of these is exploitable, it often gives the attacker a *root shell*, which is an interactive shell running as the root user. Now, what about those system daemons that we mentioned?

System daemons are programs that help provide vital functions to the operating system or users. One example is syslogd, which receives, stores, and handles all system logging on UNIX systems. Another example is the Web server, responsible for serving up access to resources over the Web. To perform some or all of their functions, these programs need an enhanced level of privilege above that of a normal user. To understand why, think of the example of syslogd—you don't want any old user on the system to be capable of modifying or deleting the system log files. So, syslogd runs with privilege. Now, what if syslogd has a security vulnerability through which an attacker could send a specially crafted log message that could make the syslogd program execute arbitrary commands of the attacker's choosing? Well, an attacker with normal privileges on the system could run programs as the syslogd user, which is usually root! In some configurations, syslogd listens on the network, so the attacker wouldn't even need an account on the system to be capable of doing this. Security bugs in the little subsystems that we rarely think about can turn out to be quite dangerous.

Now, take heart. At this point, the person who found the vulnerability often will communicate with the vendor and the public so that others know about it and can address it. Unfortunately, upon public release, this can give many others the opportunity to think up an exploit. Fortunately, it also gives the good guys a chance to do something about it.

Now, just because the security vulnerability has been discovered doesn't mean that someone will discover an easily reproducible exploit. Even if someone does, it might take some time, which gives the good guys more opportunity to fix the problem before it becomes more dangerous.

Step 3: Someone Figures Out How to Exploit This Vulnerability

This is where the vulnerability becomes truly dangerous. Now someone has a fully functional method of getting unauthorized access to your system. In essence, the attacker is escalating his level of privilege, possibly from no privilege at all.[6]

This is where you should take note. You're at a high level of danger, and there's probably no patch available yet. There's even some chance that no one knows about the problem. This is the opening of the temporal window of vulnerability, the time during which the system can be compromised by an attacker.

Now, there are some other things to think about. The discoverer might share his exploit with other people. He doesn't have to, though. Things are especially dangerous if neither he, nor anyone else, ever shares the vulnerability with the public. See, you'll never know that you're vulnerable, even though there is at least one person out there with the capability to crack your systems. It's even worse if he's able to quietly circulate his exploit among a closed group of people, as can often happen in the Cracker Underground, because it increases the number of people who can break in without increasing your chances of knowing about the hole!

So, the exploit exists and is held by some limited group of people. At this point, the following might or might not happen.

Step 4: Someone Might Share the Vulnerability and Exploit with the Public

The exploit can be shared through a Web or FTP server, or possibly can just be announced on a security mailing list. Hopefully, the vulnerability, if not the exploit, makes it to the full-disclosure mailing list BugTraq. Once publicly released, you're in both worse and much better shape.

You're in worse shape because now a huge group of would-be attackers has a tool that can penetrate your systems. These attackers, known as script kiddies, are not very knowledgeable, but they are empowered by the release of these exploits, whether the release is public or only in the underground community.

You're also in better shape because you now understand the exact threat! This knowledge is invaluable to you as a defender because you can take immediate action. You can decide what to do about the threat, from temporarily deactivating a given service to moving vital information or assets off the vulnerable server. You even can replace the affected program with a nonvulnerable substitute. If you've got someone on staff with the needed competence, you might even be capable of devising a source-level workaround to the vulnerability itself, if you have the source code for the program. If you have the exploit itself, you can test your modified version of the program for vulnerability using the exploit itself.

Finally, you're in better shape now because the program's vendor definitely knows about the problem. In fact, many vendors will put off fixing a problem either indefinitely or until the next version, ignoring the security needs of the customers affected by this delay. Public release of the problem tends to bring public pressure to bear on these vendors, who now have the demands of a large portion of their customer base to get them to take the problem seriously. Take note: Most security professionals are rather careful to give the vendor sufficient time to respond before taking a vulnerability public. When all goes well, the discoverer and the vendor make a joint public announcement, hopefully with a workaround attached.

As you can see, you've gained a great deal if you're following the vulnerability/exploit announcements. How do you do this? Well, a number of resources for this are cited at the end of this chapter, but the foremost has to be BugTraq. BugTraq is an amazing community resource that every organization should have at least one person following. It's an online forum where the community itself can announce vulnerabilities, which allows the entire Internet community to be on equal footing in getting the news and moving to address the problem. BugTraq can be found via the SecurityFocus Web site, at `http://www.securityfocus.com`.

Now, possibly some time after public announcement, the next positive event occurs.

Step 5: A Source-Code Patch Is Released

Finally, someone releases a fix to the problem. Many security problems can be fixed in one to three lines of code, so this can happen very fast. Often, the patch is made available via the same resource that announced the problem, hopefully at the same time. Unfortunately, this does not always happen. Usually, the process takes a few days[7] when the source code is freely available—or much longer when it isn't.

At this point, people who compile their programs from source are out of the water. You don't have to be on a source-available operating system for this to be the case; you simply need the source code for the affected program. On the other hand, people who don't compile their programs from source code or who don't have the source code to the affected program are still in hot water. Unfortunately, this group includes the majority of users out there.

So, what do they wait for?

Step 6: A Binary (Vendor) Patch Is Released

After some time, a binary patch is released by the operating system or program vendor. This is where the entire world actually has the chance to fix the problem. Although far from ideal, there's definitely some real waiting for this step. According to the January 17, 2000, cover story on SecurityPortal.com by Kurt Seifried, the times between Step 4 (worldwide announcement of the vulnerability/exploit) and Step 6 (binary patch released by the vendor) averaged like this:

Red Hat	11 days
Microsoft	16 days
Sun	89 days

To be fair, please note that this time includes all the time that it takes these vendors to test their patches before they feel comfortable releasing them to the public. When asked for an update on these figures, Kurt had this to say:

> Average times for vendor patch releases continue to fluctuate. A small group of vendors maintains relatively quick rates; however, extended testing of updates can significantly reduce turnaround time on some patches (from days to months). Generally, the larger vendors move slower because they must do extensive testing to ensure that mission-critical systems will not misbehave if the patch is applied. This is even more true for closed source vendors that tend to service larger clients with extremely stringent needs for stability.
>
> Basically you can have it quick, or you can have it working.

Even if the vendors had magically gotten twice as fast, you're still left with a great deal of time to be vulnerable. The scary thing is this: Even though the patch is now available, there's often substantial delay[8] until most people apply it.

Step 7: People Apply the Patch

For a variety of reasons, it's not amazingly practical to patch every system every day. Although some sites can patch every workstation or development system on a daily basis by using automated tools, many sites can't patch every production system every day. It's not even considered prudent to apply patches to high-availability production systems before first testing them on less vital machines. On the other hand, you should definitely patch your system as often as you can manage. In any case, your patch interval adds to the window of vulnerability.

With that said, consider all the delays between when an exploit is created and when the vulnerability actually is corrected. These all add up to form a nontrivial window of vulnerability during which your system can be successfully cracked. Because you can't avoid the window itself when you have a vulnerability in your system, your best bet is to try to contain the vulnerability itself. You do this by *hardening* your system.

The act of hardening, or tightening, your system involves creating an overall improved configuration that is harder to exploit. We'll spend the remainder of this chapter explaining how to harden your system. In short, the primary ways to accomplish this are as follows:

- Contain the attacker's access to any program that might develop a security problem.
- Avoid having a program with a security problem running on your system.
- Minimize the privilege that any vulnerable program can grant a successful attacker.

Let's first look at auditing network services, which falls under the first bullet point.

Auditing Services

The first step of hardening your system has to be auditing the network services on your system. Network "services" hereby are defined as every program that listens on the network for connections. Because each provides a method of remotely interacting with your system, you have to protect each one. The first, and easier, method of protection is to simply remove the service. For those that you absolutely cannot remove, your only option is to go through the more difficult[9] process of hardening their configuration. Let's look at the easier method first.

To do a real network service audit, you basically need to sit down and take a look at each program listening to the network, learn its function, and decide whether it's necessary on this particular machine. With the help of this book, UNIX man pages, and the World Wide Web, Step 2 is fairly easy. By way of example, we'll follow the process on Red Hat 7.1, the current version of Red Hat at the time of this printing. This will be a two-part process. In the first part, we'll audit inetd/xinetd, which handles the initial network connection for many of the smaller daemons. In second part, we'll track down each of the other programs listening on the network, research them, and decide which ones to keep.

Part I: The inetd/xinetd Audit

In UNIX, each network daemon's designer had the choice of either running the daemon standalone or having it launched by inetd. In standalone mode, the program simply is started during the boot process and is left to listen on the network for connections. It is responsible for figuring out how to handle multiple connections, if it will at all. On the other hand, for inetd-managed services, the situation is different. Upon startup, these programs don't need to be started at all—inetd simply starts listening on the appropriate ports. When a connection comes in on, say, the ftp port (21), inetd starts up a single instance of the ftp daemon and passes off the connection to it. When that network session is done, the ftp daemon dies off again. The advantage of this approach is that it usually saves memory and conserves system resources.

To see this, think about the situation with 10 network daemons replaced by a single inetd process listening on 10 ports. The disadvantage of this approach is that each connection is delayed a little by the time that inetd requires to fork off a process and start a new instance of the responsible program. This becomes very pronounced with a program such as sshd, which does some hard-core computation every time that it starts. For this reason, most people recommend running sshd as a standalone program.

Most systems run inetd or xinetd, listening on the assigned ports for some number of network daemons, as instructed in their configuration files. Although it's rarely done, it's even possible to run both inetd and the less-ported[10] xinetd on the same system—you simply have make sure that they're listening to two completely disjointed sets of ports. Now, although they still need to be audited, most distributions have developed more minimal default configurations for inetd/xinetd with fewer ports open. They're both relatively easy to audit. We'll start by looking at inetd, and then move on to a consideration of xinetd.

Let's audit a sample inetd configuration from a Red Hat Linux 6.0 system. inetd's configuration is stored in a single file, which is /etc/inetd.conf on most[11] systems. Let's look at that file:

```
#
# inetd.conf    This file describes the services that will be available
#               through the INETD TCP/IP super server.  To re-configure
#               the running INETD process, edit this file, then send the
#               INETD process a SIGHUP signal.
#
# Version:      @(#)/etc/inetd.conf    3.10    05/27/93
#
# Authors:      Original taken from BSD UNIX 4.3/TAHOE.
#               Fred N. van Kempen, <waltje@uwalt.nl.mugnet.org>
#
# Modified for Debian Linux by Ian A. Murdock <imurdock@shell.portal.com>
#
# Modified for RHS Linux by Marc Ewing <marc@redhat.com>
#
# <service_name> <sock_type> <proto> <flags> <user> <server_path> <args>
#
# Echo, discard, daytime, and chargen are used primarily for testing.
#
# To re-read this file after changes, just do a 'killall -HUP inetd'
#
#echo           stream  tcp     nowait  root    internal
#echo           dgram   udp     wait    root    internal
#discard        stream  tcp     nowait  root    internal
#discard        dgram   udp     wait    root    internal
#daytime        stream  tcp     nowait  root    internal
#daytime        dgram   udp     wait    root    internal
#chargen        stream  tcp     nowait  root    internal
#chargen        dgram   udp     wait    root    internal
#time           stream  tcp     nowait  root    internal
#time           dgram   udp     wait    root    internal
#
# These are standard services.
#
ftp     stream  tcp     nowait  root    /usr/sbin/tcpd  in.ftpd -l -a
telnet  stream  tcp     nowait  root    /usr/sbin/tcpd  in.telnetd
#
# Shell, login, exec, comsat and talk are BSD protocols.
```

8

SECURING A
SYSTEM FOR
ROLLOUT

```
#
shell    stream  tcp     nowait  root     /usr/sbin/tcpd  in.rshd
login    stream  tcp     nowait  root     /usr/sbin/tcpd  in.rlogind
#exec    stream  tcp     nowait  root     /usr/sbin/tcpd  in.rexecd
#comsat  dgram   udp     wait    root     /usr/sbin/tcpd  in.comsat
talk     dgram   udp     wait    root     /usr/sbin/tcpd  in.talkd
ntalk    dgram   udp     wait    root     /usr/sbin/tcpd  in.ntalkd
#dtalk   stream  tcp     waut    nobody   /usr/sbin/tcpd  in.dtalkd
#
# Pop and imap mail services et al
#
#pop-2   stream  tcp     nowait  root     /usr/sbin/tcpd ipop2d
#pop-3   stream  tcp     nowait  root     /usr/sbin/tcpd ipop3d
#imap    stream  tcp     nowait  root     /usr/sbin/tcpd imapd
#
# The Internet UUCP service.
#
#uucp    stream  tcp     nowait  uucp     /usr/sbin/tcpd /usr/lib/uucp/uucico
-l
#
# Tftp service is provided primarily for booting.  Most sites
# run this only on machines acting as "boot servers." Do not uncomment
# this unless you *need* it.
#
#tftp    dgram   udp     wait    root     /usr/sbin/tcpd  in.tftpd
#bootps  dgram   udp     wait    root     /usr/sbin/tcpd  bootpd
#
# Finger, systat and netstat give out user information which may be
# valuable to potential "system crackers."  Many sites choose to disable
# some or all of these services to improve security.
#
finger    stream  tcp    nowait  root     /usr/sbin/tcpd  in.fingerd
#cfinger  stream  tcp    nowait  root     /usr/sbin/tcpd  in.cfingerd
#systat   stream  tcp    nowait  guest    /usr/sbin/tcpd  /bin/ps  -auwwx
#netstat  stream  tcp    nowait  guest    /usr/sbin/tcpd  /bin/netstat    -f inet
#
# Authentication
#
auth    stream  tcp     nowait   nobody   /usr/sbin/in.identd in.identd -l -e -
o
#
# End of inetd.conf

linuxconf stream tcp wait root /bin/linuxconf linuxconf —http
#swat       stream  tcp     nowait.400      root /usr/sbin/swat swat
```

Each line of this file is for a different daemon. We really need to consider only the first, sixth, and seventh columns, although though you can refer to the discussion of inetd in Chapter 5, "Getting on the Network," or the appropriate man page to remember what the other columns do. The first column tells which port[12] the inetd program should listen to, while the sixth column tells inetd what network daemon to launch in response to any new connections on that port. Column 7 doesn't really exist as far as inetd is concerned; it's just an extension of column 6. For example, in the case of the finger port, when inetd receives a new connection on the finger port, TCP port 79, it runs this:

```
/usr/sbin/tcpd in.fingerd
```

Originally, inetd would have just run /usr/sbin/in.fingerd. The problem was that inetd didn't offer any access control or sanity checking. Wietese Venema wrote TCP Wrappers, or tcpd, to cure these problems. When tcpd is run, it checks the source hostname or IP address against access control lists, if present, and also makes some effort to make sure that the source IP address doesn't have a spoofed[13] domain name. If these check out, it runs in.fingerd. In any case, let's start auditing.

To run the audit, just look at each line that isn't commented out (with a # mark), and decide whether you want to run that service. If necessary, you can look up each of these services in man pages, Web pages, or any book on firewalling.

Before we start our audit, let's save a copy of this configuration file. This way, we can restore our old configuration file if we make a simple mistake. To save the file:

```
# cp /etc/inetd.conf /etc/inetd.conf.orig
```

Let's start with the first noncommented line:

```
ftp     stream  tcp     nowait  root    /usr/sbin/tcpd  in.ftpd -l -a
```

This line starts an FTP daemon listening on port 21. This is a great first example for us to rant on bad protocols. FTP really stinks because it's full of weaknesses. First, the protocol is completely unencrypted, so an eavesdropper can steal any passwords that your users use to authenticate. If an attacker owns,[14] legitimately or illegitimately, a computer on the same network as either the FTP client or the server's machine, he can overhear the entire communication and steal the password used. This represents one of the major ways that accounts are stolen. There several other problems with FTP, though.

Tip

The term "owned" in hacker slang has nothing to do with legal ownership. A person who has full control (root) of a system is said to "own" it.

FTP is just a mess. It uses two ports, to transfer files on a separate connection. The default "active" mode actually breaks the normal client-connects-to-server custom by making the second port's connection go from server to client, making FTP much more difficult[15] to firewall. Because the protocol is completely clear-text, it's possible to take over the connection by inserting packets into the data stream. Even when you can't do this, you can steal people's files by either eavesdropping or, when the connection is in passive mode, simply grabbing the file before the client can. Finally, to make things much worse, most FTP servers have had at least one remote root hole in the last three years. It's not clear whether this is caused by complexity in the design aiding in implementation problems or the inbreeding[16] in FTP daemon development. The only thing that has made this last point more bearable is that the attacker generally needs upload privileges to crack the daemon; he gets this only if he can use a stolen account or if you have anonymous upload available.

FTP daemons are fairly unsafe. If you must run one, we recommend that you use it only for anonymous downloads. In our example, we'll turn this off by placing a # mark at the beginning of the line, like this:

```
#ftp    stream  tcp     nowait  root    /usr/sbin/tcpd  in.ftpd -l -a
```

Let's move onto the next line, referencing telnet:

```
telnet  stream  tcp     nowait  root    /usr/sbin/tcpd  in.telnetd
```

telnet shares two of FTP's major problems because it's unencrypted. An observer can steal your password as you're logging in and can eavesdrop—and possibly take over—your session. Honestly, this is where most accounts are stolen. An attacker breaks into one machine and runs a network sniffer to capture name and password pairs out of telnet, FTP, POP, and IMAP. He then uses these to gain access on other machines, one or more of which he'll grab root on. He then sets up another[17] sniffer....

There are even reports of past root holes in telnet as well, which only add to the significant danger inherent in its design. You should disable telnet as soon as possible. It can be easily replaced with the encrypted-channel Secure Shell (ssh) without much user training.

I only give this warning: before you deactivate telnet at your site, make sure to obtain agreement and consensus within your organization. While clients exist for Windows, they don't ship by default with the operating system. Dial-up Windows users will need some time to obtain, install and configure a solution. Exercise patience, but not to the point of futility.

Just comment out that telnet line, like so:

```
#telnet stream  tcp     nowait  root    /usr/sbin/tcpd  in.telnetd
```

Let's look at the next port:

```
shell   stream  tcp     nowait  root    /usr/sbin/tcpd  in.rshd
```

This line listens on TCP port 514 (shell) and accepts rsh connections via in.rshd. rsh is problematic, too, unfortunately. It uses IP addresses as authentication, which, unfortunately, can be faked, or *spoofed*. Furthermore, because it uses a clear-text protocol, it can be taken over. At this point, most security-conscious sites take pains to replace this with ssh whenever possible. Let's turn this off in our example:

```
#shell  stream  tcp     nowait  root    /usr/sbin/tcpd  in.rshd
```

It might seem like we're being completely negative here, but there's a good reason that inetd/xinetd configurations are starting to get emptier in Linux distributions: Most of the network daemons originally run out of them are flawed in some way. The interactive login and file-copy daemons have been replaced by Secure Shell (ssh), while the mail-retrieval programs now have replacements and add-ons that do not use clear-text passwords as authentication tokens. Most Linux machines are capable of deactivating inetd entirely. On Solaris and other UNIX types, more daemons run out of inetd than just these simple bad ones, which means that inetd rarely is deactivated.

Let's consider the next port, login, or TCP port 513:

```
login   stream  tcp     nowait  root    /usr/sbin/tcpd  in.rlogind
```

This launches in.rlogind in response to connections on port 513. rlogin can authenticate in one of two modes. It either uses IP addresses, like rsh, or passwords, like telnet. The issues are thus the same as in our examination of telnet and rsh. Running rlogin is very inadvisable.

```
#login  stream  tcp     nowait  root    /usr/sbin/tcpd  in.rlogind
```

What about talk and ntalk? These are relatively safe chatting protocols, although you should never assume that no one is eavesdropping or inserting text. When used across a network, someone can eavesdrop and possibly insert text into the conversation. As long as you don't use these in a critical capacity, there isn't much risk of this. If you use these in such a capacity, consider tunneling through an encrypted channel.

Next we examine the finger service:

```
finger  stream  tcp     nowait  root    /usr/sbin/tcpd  in.fingerd
```

finger is a information-gathering and broadcast service. You can use it to find out which users are logged into a system, how long they've been logged on, and even how long they've been idle. Although this is very friendly, it's also very useful information to an attacker who takes his time to find out when the system administrator goes on lunch break or leaves for the night. You probably should deactivate this service or at least use TCP Wrappers to restrict which IP addresses have this capability.

Let's look at in.identd now:

```
auth    stream  tcp     nowait   nobody    /usr/sbin/in.identd in.identd -l -e -
o
```

identd is actually a very useful tool. For any TCP connection originating from its machine, identd can tell you what user has created the connection. This can be very useful in a security incident, although it's mostly useful to the sysadmin of the machine running the identd daemon. If someone has rooted this machine, the other machine can't trust that this person will continue using the same account; he can switch among all the accounts. As the sysadmin of the rooted machine, though, logs from the other sysadmin can help you see which of your accounts were compromised. Then again, you can't trust anything that your system says when it has been rooted. Although the decision is never obvious, this seems safe enough to keep on at most sites.

The last port is odd and Linux-specific. This is the linuxconf port, defined in /etc/ services as TCP port 98:

```
linuxconf stream tcp wait root /bin/linuxconf linuxconf --http
```

Here we've got linuxconf listening on port 98, awaiting remote administration through a Web browser. In our opinion, this is just not good news. If you were going to use it, do you really want to trust the administration of your system to a clear-text Web browser-based tool? If you're saying yes, it's time to read BugTraq and look into Web attacks, including the cross-site scripting problems. Among other things, perhaps an attacker could include a page/image link that tricks you or your browser into following an illegitimately inserted hyperlink—say, to http://your_net:98/change_root_password_ to_foo. An attacker with some knowledge of your network could leave you hurting from the actions of your own browser.

In any case, Web-based administration might have sounded cool, but you definitely should put this idea away immediately. Let's further note that this program runs as root, listens to the network, and, in this case, isn't wrapped with TCP Wrappers. None of these things raises confidence. As a rule[18], if you're feeling uncomfortable, turn off a program until you can do proper research into why it should be on.

```
#linuxconf stream tcp wait root /bin/linuxconf linuxconf --http
```

So, now that we've gone through the entirety of the inetd.conf file, we want the changes to take effect. You can either stop and restart the inetd daemon or simply pass it a HUP signal, like this:

```
# kill -HUP <PID of inetd>
```

After auditing this file, it's important to store a printed copy of it somewhere and to revisit this audit in the future. You need to make sure that no new network daemons appear that you don't know about. Mysteriously appearing new lines in inetd.conf are often signs of a compromised system.

Finally, before we get into the xinetd audit, let's revisit this clear-text password issue. Many people consider Kerberos a safe exception to the "don't use clear-text protocols" rule. Many of the programs can be configured to use Kerberos authentication, which appears safe, since people can't steal your authentication information as easily. Then again, take note of the remaining problems inherent in clear-text protocols. If an attacker can sniff or take over your connection, you might have just as many problems as if he could steal your password.

Now, what if you're running a recent Linux distribution and thus might be running xinetd? Well, the principles are the same, so we won't spend much time discussing xinetd. First, let's get some background on xinetd; then we'll take a look at how to configure it.

xinetd was designed as a more security-conscious inetd replacement. Among other things, it includes TCP Wrappers–like IP-based access control as a core function. It goes even further than this, allowing you to specify what time of day connections to a given service will be allowed. There are a wealth of other functions, as you can learn from the xinetd.conf man page. For now, let's focus on what you need to know to audit the services launched by this daemon.

xinetd uses a more involved configuration system, at least on the current default setups on Red Hat and Mandrake Linux. The file /etc/xinetd.conf is technically the configuration file, although it includes a line that reads as follows:

```
includedir /etc/xinetd.d
```

This means that all the files in /etc/xinetd.d become configuration files for the program, too. Looking at this directory on a stock Red Hat 7.1 system, you can see that each file is named for a particular program or service:

```
# ls /etc/xinetd.d/
chargen       daytime-udp  finger  rlogin  talk    time-udp
chargen-udp   echo         ntalk   rsh     telnet  wu-ftpd
daytime       echo-udp     rexec   rsync   time
```

If you look at one of these files—say, the telnet file—you find this:

```
# default: on
# description: The telnet server serves telnet sessions; it uses \
#        unencrypted username/password pairs for authentication.
service telnet
{
        flags              = REUSE
        socket_type        = stream
        wait               = no
        user               = root
        server             = /usr/sbin/in.telnetd
        log_on_failure     += USERID
        disable            = yes

}
```

The lines in this file that are important are the `service` line, which names which port we're listening to; the `server` line, which lists which program xinetd is to run after connecting to that port; and the `disable` line, which tells whether this service currently is disabled. As you can see here, there is a file for telnet, which does, in fact, point the standard telnet port, TCP 23, to the standard in.telnetd. You also can see that telnet is disabled on this machine.

Although it's not as simple as auditing inetd, auditing xinetd is not too difficult. You can just look through each file and check the `disable` line, if present. If it's present and set to `yes`, then you don't need to worry about this service. If it's either not present or set to `no`, then examine the service and decide whether you want it running. If you want to deactivate it, you can either set `disable = yes` in its file or just delete the file itself. When you're done, you can tell the xinetd program to reread its configuration file in one of the following three ways:

- **kill -USR1 <PID of xinetd>**—This tells xinetd to stop listening to any ports that it is no longer responsible for and to start listening on any ports that you've newly added to its configuration. The xinetd man page calls this a "soft reconfiguration."

- **kill -USR2 <PID of xinetd>**—This tells xinetd to stop listening to any ports that it is no longer responsible for and to start listening on any ports that you've newly added to its configuration. Additionally, xinetd will enforce any new access restrictions on existing connections. This means that it will shut down any network daemon instances that it might have started before the reconfiguration if they don't comply with the new configuration. The xinetd man page calls this a "hard reconfiguration."

- **`/etc/rc.d/init.d/xinetd restart`**—Although it's the least elegant option, you can simply stop and restart the xinetd daemon. Aside from causing a delay during which no new connections to xinetd-monitored ports can be made, this has much the same effect as a soft reconfiguration.

Each system administrator can decide which of these is appropriate, although we recommend the second choice for any vital changes to the security configuration.

Our installation of Red Hat 7.1 had `disable = yes` in every service, so no additional hardening was necessary. If there had been any additional hardening required, the ideas, of course, are the same as those in the inetd audit—only the implementation differs. Now that we're done with that stage of our network daemon audit, let's move on to the other part. Let's track down all the network daemons that don't use inetd/xinetd.

Part II: Tracking Down the Rest with `netstat`, `lsof`, and a Few Detective Tools

We first need to find out what programs are listening on the network for new connections. We can do this with the netstat utility in UNIX. Although the command-line options differ from version to version, you can always learn them from the man pages. You can use the following commands to get a list of all listening TCP-based services on either Linux or Solaris:

Linux: `netstat -vat`

Solaris: `netstat -aP tcp`

You can use these commands to get a list of all listening UDP-based services on the same operating systems:

Linux: `netstat -vau`

Solaris: `netstat -aP udp`

The Miscellaneous TCP Audit

Let's follow the exercise on a sample, deliberately wide-open Red Hat 7.1 system. Let's start by looking at the TCP ports that are listening:

```
# netstat -vat
Active Internet connections (servers and established)
Proto Recv-Q Send-Q LocalyAddress         Foreign Address        State
tcp       0      0 *:1026                 *:*                    LISTEN
tcp       0      0 *:acap                 *:*                    LISTEN
tcp       0      0 *:netbios-ssn          *:*                    LISTEN
tcp       0      0 *:sunrpc               *:*                    LISTEN
```

```
tcp       0      0 *:http                 *:*                    LISTEN
tcp       0      0 *:auth                 *:*                    LISTEN
tcp       0      0 192.168.71.128:domain  *:*                    LISTEN
tcp       0      0 localhost.locald:domain *:*                   LISTEN
tcp       0      0 *:ssh                  *:*                    LISTEN
tcp       0      0 *:postgres             *:*                    LISTEN
tcp       0      0 localhost.localdom:smtp *:*                   LISTEN
```

Looking in the fourth column, we find our list of listening ports. Some ports are spelled out, whereas others are only listed numerically. The operating system has found the port numbers and names in the /etc/services file for these. If the port is listed numerically, it wasn't found[19] in this file.

Let's go through our netstat output line by line. The first line notes that TCP port 1026 is open. We can find out what program is listening on this port using the lsof command, downloadable from http://freshmeat.net/projects/lsof/. This command is standard on most operating systems, although you might have to download it separately from your vendor. Let's look at our lsof output:

```
# lsof -i tcp:1026
COMMAND      PID USER    FD    TYPE DEVICE SIZE NODE NAME
rpc.statd 11009 root     6u    IPv4 110288      TCP *:1026 (LISTEN)
```

The first column shows which program has bound to the port. What if you don't know what rpc.statd does? Luckily, Linux tends to have fairly comprehensive man pages. The man page says that rpc.statd implements the Network Status Monitor protocol for NFS. It is necessary only for machines that are using NFS, either as clients or server. Now, this is where we decide whether we want this machine to use this service. If we're not using NFS here, we can definitely deactivate this.

Deactivating a network program is mostly easy. Just figure out where it starts in the UNIX boot process and deactivate it. If you're weak on the boot process, a quick browse of Chapter 1, "Startup and Shutdown," should help. At some point, a valuable exercise is to follow the UNIX boot process from the very beginning, from boot loader to kernel to init to each of the scripts run by init. A thorough understanding of this process is part of what graduates a junior-level system administrator to an intermediate-level one. With that said, let's track down the script that starts rpc.statd.Because we're on Red Hat Linux, with SysV init scripts, we start by looking at the active rc-scripts (the main startup scripts) for our current runlevel. We know that, upon booting, the kernel runs init, the direct or indirect parent of all processes on the system. init then runs the main rc-script—in this case, /etc/rc.d/init.d/rc—with the parameter of the current runlevel. In this case, the runlevel is 3, as we can learn if we look at the :initdefault: line in /etc/inittab. So, the main rc-script gets run with the parameter 3.

The main rc-script starts every script[20] in /etc/rc.d/rc3.d/ that begins with S (for "start"), so these are the ones that we need to look at. Let's look at a listing of the scripts here:

```
# ls -l /etc/rc.d/rc3.d/
S08iptables  S25netfs    S50snmpd       S60mars-nwe    S80isdn      S95innd
S10network   S26apmd     S50tux         S60nfs         S80sendmail  S97rhnsd
S12syslog    S26ypserv   S55arpwatch    S60rstatd      S85gpm       S99kdcrotate
S13portmap   S27ypbind   S55named       S60rusersd     S85httpd     S99local
S14nfslock   S28autofs   S55sshd        S60rwalld      S90crond
S17keytable  S30nscd     S56rawdevices  S60rwhod       S90xfs
S20pcmcia    S35identd   S56xinetd      S66yppasswdd   S91smb
S20random    S40atd      S60lpd         S78postgresql  S95anacron
```

Because none of these obviously starts rpc.statd, we can either read each one or employ a little ingenuity. As career UNIX sysadmins, we prefer[21] ingenuity. Let's grep all the start scripts for rpc.statd:

```
# grep rpc.statd /etc/rc.d/rc3.d/S*
S14nfslock:[ -x /sbin/rpc.statd ] || exit 0
S14nfslock:     daemon rpc.statd
S14nfslock:     killproc rpc.statd
S14nfslock:     status rpc.statd
S14nfslock:     /sbin/pidof rpc.statd >/dev/null 2>&1; STATD="$?"
```

Okay, it looks like the nfslock script is our culprit. We could just comment out the lines that start with "rpc.statd," but it's usually cleaner to deactivate the entire script, if possible. If you read through the script, you quickly learn that it starts both the rpc.statd program and the rpc.lockd program, which are necessary if this machine is an NFS client or server. Because this machine is not, we can safely deactivate this script.

The canonical way to do this is to remove or rename the S14nfslock link. On most systems, the common practice is to rename the file to a lowercase *s* version, as in s14nfslock. This keeps the link around so that it's easy to restore when you need to turn the service back on, but it removes the script from the list started by rc because rc starts only scripts that begin with a capital *S*.

On Red Hat Linux systems, along with a few others, there's an even easier way to manage this. The chkconfig tool actually adds and removes symbolic links automatically when you ask it to activate or deactivate an rc-script. It doesn't use anything as breakable as a master database, but instead it uses a simple commented header in the file, like this one:

```
# chkconfig: 345 14 86
# description: NFS is a popular protocol for file sharing across \
#              TCP/IP networks. This service provides NFS file \
#              locking functionality.
```

8

The first line here tells chkconfig about the runlevels that the script gets activated in and what numbers should go in the S and K symbolic links. Actually using chkconfig to deactivate scripts is very easy—this is all that's needed:

```
# chkconfig nfslock off
```

With that done, we've deactivated nfslock for the next boot. If we want to actually turn it off now, we can stop it with this command:

```
# /etc/rc.d/init.d/nfslock off
```

At this point, we're done and we can move on to the next port/program listed in the netstat output. Although this might seem complicated, it gets easier as you get to know your system. Especially if you're new to system administration, the remainder of this example should be very instructional.

Let's look at the netstat output from earlier again:

```
# netstat -vat
Active Internet connections (servers and established)
Proto Recv-Q Send-Q Local Address          Foreign Address    State
tcp        0      0 *:1026                  *:*                LISTEN
tcp        0      0 *:acap                  *:*                LISTEN
tcp        0      0 *:netbios-ssn           *:*                LISTEN
tcp        0      0 *:sunrpc                *:*                LISTEN
tcp        0      0 *:http                  *:*                LISTEN
tcp        0      0 *:auth                  *:*                LISTEN
tcp        0      0 192.168.71.128:domain   *:*                LISTEN
tcp        0      0 localhost.locald:domain *:*                LISTEN
tcp        0      0 *:ssh                   *:*                LISTEN
tcp        0      0 *:postgres              *:*                LISTEN
tcp        0      0 localhost.localdom:smtp *:*                LISTEN
```

Now look at the second port, acap, TCP port 674. Using our handy lsof, we see this:

```
# lsof -i tcp:acap
COMMAND   PID USER   FD   TYPE DEVICE SIZE NODE NAME
ypserv 11093 root    5u   IPv4 110371      TCP *:acap (LISTEN)
```

ypserv, as we learn through the man page, is run on a machine if it is being used as a Network Information System (NIS) server. This facility usually is used to allow people to log into a number of workstations with the same name and password. Most sites have moved away from this service because of the security problems inherent in the design. Even if your site uses it, only one to three systems needs to function as an NIS server. For the rest of the machines out there, this can be very safely deactivated.

Now, how do we deactivate ypserv? Well, this one's easy. If we look at the list of *S* scripts in /etc/rc.d/rc3.d/ from earlier, we find one called S26ypserv. Deactivating the

NIS service is as easy as renaming/deleting this script. Use chkconfig to deactivate it upon boot, and use the script itself to stop the current instance of the program:

```
# chkconfig ypserv off
# /etc/rc.d/init.d/ypserv stop
```

We can keep moving through this process. The next port on the list is netbios-ssn. Although this port is quoted non-numerically,[22] we can still look it up with lsof:

```
# lsof -i tcp:netbios-ssn
COMMAND  PID USER   FD   TYPE DEVICE SIZE NODE NAME
smbd    7706 root    5u   IPv4 12083       TCP *:netbios-ssn (LISTEN)
```

We see that this port is used by the smbd program. smbd is the main Samba daemon. Samba is a program that permits UNIX computers to participate in standard Windows network file sharing. We can learn this from the man page or even from a good Web search. Now, suppose that we decide that this machine won't be using Windows file-sharing protocols—for example, there isn't any Windows file sharing going on or this machine is a dedicated Web server. Looking in the /etc/rc.d/rc3.d/ directory listing from before, we find that smbd is started in the smb script. We can figure this out either via visual inspection or through our grep trick from before. In any case, we know how to deactivate scripts on this system:

```
# chkconfig smb off
# /etc/rc.d/init.d/smb stop
```

Moving on, our next port to investigate is sunrpc. Using lsof, we note that sunrpc is being listened to by the portmap program. portmap, also known as rpcbind on many other systems (including Solaris), is a rather important program. It serves as the backbone of several other systems, including NFS and NIS. For now, we're going to hold off on making a decision on this program. There's a very good reason for this: All of the *remote procedure call* (RPC) programs on the system tend to depend on this a bit.

The RPC interface was created by Sun as a new system for networking applications. As the name implies, the idea is to allow a program on one computer to ask a program on another to run a given procedure/function/subroutine. For the purposes of our audit, you should know that although most servers always listen to a predefined static port, RPC-based programs choose a port dynamically and then register that port with the portmapper, also known as rpcbind or portmap. When an RPC-based client program wants to contact an RPC-based server, it uses portmapper to discover which port it should contact. We can query this systems portmapper for a list of checked-out ports, like this:

```
# rpcinfo -p
   program vers proto   port
    100000    2   tcp    111  portmapper
    100000    2   udp    111  portmapper
```

```
100004   2   udp   671   ypserv
100004   1   udp   671   ypserv
100004   2   tcp   674   ypserv
100004   1   tcp   674   ypserv
100002   3   udp  1035   rusersd
100002   2   udp  1035   rusersd
100009   1   udp   976   yppasswdd
100008   1   udp  1039   walld
```

Because we don't know which RPC services we'll be turning off, we'll have to withhold judgment on portmap until we've investigated each of these ports. For now, let's move on with the audit.

The next port to investigate is http, or port 80. lsof reports nine separate httpd processes:

```
COMMAND   PID USER   FD    TYPE DEVICE SIZE NODE NAME
httpd    1162 root   17u   IPv4 160916      TCP *:http (LISTEN)
httpd    1163 root   17u   IPv4 160916      TCP *:http (LISTEN)
httpd    1164 root   17u   IPv4 160916      TCP *:http (LISTEN)
httpd    1165 root   17u   IPv4 160916      TCP *:http (LISTEN)
httpd    1166 root   17u   IPv4 160916      TCP *:http (LISTEN)
httpd    1167 root   17u   IPv4 160916      TCP *:http (LISTEN)
httpd    1168 root   17u   IPv4 160916      TCP *:http (LISTEN)
httpd    1169 root   17u   IPv4 160916      TCP *:http (LISTEN)
httpd    1170 root   17u   IPv4 160916      TCP *:http (LISTEN)
```

Don't be alarmed. As a ps process listing shows, this is just a single instance of Apache that is started by init, process 1, that is then the parent of all the others:

```
UID        PID  PPID  C STIME TTY       TIME CMD
root      1161     1  0 14:42 ?      00:00:00 httpd start
apache    1162  1161  0 14:42 ?      00:00:00 httpd start
                          ...
apache    1170  1161  0 14:42 ?      00:00:00 httpd start
```

This just allows Apache to handle more connections while divvying up the work among multiple instances, which can even be run on different processors on a multiprocessor system. The audit continues as normal.

Now you get into the question of whether this system needs a Web server. If this machine won't be serving Web pages for consumption, we can safely turn off our Web server. A simple look through /etc/rc.d/rc3.d/ once again shows an obvious script to deactivate, httpd. After reading through the script to make sure that it's safe, we deactivate it with the chkconfig command:

```
# chkconfig httpd off
# /etc/rc.d/init.d/httpd stop
```

The next port on our list is called, rather nondescriptively, auth. Running `lsof`, we find that the identd program is listening on that port.

```
# lsof -i tcp:auth
COMMAND  PID USER   FD    TYPE DEVICE SIZE NODE NAME
identd  7387 root   4u    IPv4 10620       TCP *:auth (LISTEN)
identd  7390 root   4u    IPv4 10620       TCP *:auth (LISTEN)
identd  7391 root   4u    IPv4 10620       TCP *:auth (LISTEN)
identd  7392 root   4u    IPv4 10620       TCP *:auth (LISTEN)
```

Checking the man page reveals that this is the TCP/IP IDENT protocol server. This program tells remote machines which user is responsible for a given TCP/IP connection. Because the queried machine could spoof the response, this is not generally used for authentication[23] or auditing by the computer that asks. Instead, when it does find use, it is generally the queried machine's system administrator, who, upon finding that his machine was used in a cracking attack or other nefarious purpose, wants to know which user was running the offending/attacking program. Because it serves so little purpose, many sysadmins deactivate it. In this example, we'll leave it on because it might prove useful for security.

Moving on, the next two netstat lines reference the domain port, port 53. As shown by the `lsof` output, this is used by the DNS server process called named. Most sites need only one or two, if any, DNS servers. If this machine will not be one of them, we can deactivate this program. Again, because there's a script called S55named in /etc/rc.d/init.d/, it appears that we can deactivate this program simply by running the following:

```
# chkconfig named off
# /etc/rc.d/init.d/named stop
```

Let's look at the next port on our list, ssh, or port 22. As `lsof` can show, this port is checked out by sshd, the Secure Shell Daemon. Secure shell allows interactive remote login[24] to this machine. It was designed as a secure replacement for the rlogin, rsh, rcp, telnet, and, to some extent, ftp programs, each of which uses an insecure method of authentication. Most system administrators leave sshd running on each machine that they might need to remotely administer. For our example, let's leave this running.

The next port on our list is postgres, which /etc/services shows is port 5342. This one might be a mystery at first because it's a fairly uncommon port. If we use our `lsof` to track the program down, we get this:

```
COMMAND     PID    USER   FD   TYPE DEVICE SIZE NODE NAME
postmaste 11456 postgres   3u  IPv4 111664      TCP *:postgres (LISTEN)
```

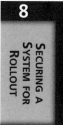
8
SECURING A
SYSTEM FOR
ROLLOUT

Because the command is cut off, we use ps to get the full command line:

```
postgres 11456 11453  0 Sep25 ?         00:00:00 /usr/bin/postmaster -i
```

From here, we try our standard method. We read the man page for postmaster. This reveals that postmaster runs the Postgres multiuser back end. Unfortunately, this still doesn't tell what Postgres actually does. At this point, we move to the Web search, using Google or another search engine. Google brings us right to the Web page for PostgreSQL, which describes itself as an "Object-Relational DBMS... supporting almost all SQL constructs." So, we've got an SQL database on our hands.

Are we trying to run a database server here? If yes, leave this turned on. In this example, in which we didn't know what Postgres was, we probably aren't running it!

Let's turn it off. Looking in /etc/rc.d/rc3.d/, we find S78postgresql, which starts up the *PostgreSQL* system. We can deactivate it easily:

```
# chkconfig postgresql off
# /etc/rc.d/init.d/postgresql stop
```

This brings us to our last port, smtp, or port 25. This is the Simple Mail Transfer Protocol port, which generally is checked out by your mail transfer agent (MTA) of choice. In this case, lsof tells us that our MTA is the program sendmail. This is where we must decide carefully whether sendmail should be running on this host and whether it should be listening to the network. This is actually not as easy than you might think.

Let's briefly take a look at how email works. Email is moved between systems over the network primarily via SMTP by mail-transfer agents. To send out an email, your mail user agent (MUA), such as mutt, pine, or Netscape Messenger, talks to an SMTP server, which actually goes through the effort to deliver the mail. Now, the situation differs next in how your mail user agent actually receives mail. In the classic model, it reads your mail out of a mailspool file on your system, usually called something like /var/mail/username. The mail is placed there by the SMTP server running on the same machine, which originally received the mail from the sender's SMTP server. For some users, especially at universities where everyone is logging in interactively to a shell server, this is still the model. For most users now, the mail is received by an SMTP server on another machine; they download their mail periodically from that server via the POP or IMAP mail protocols. If you're using mutt, pine, or elm, chances are very good[25] that you're using the classical model. If you're using Netscape Messenger, you're using the POP/IMAP method.

What does all this mean in our network services audit? Well, in the classical model, you need an SMTP server listening on the network on each machine that you read mail from.

This means that if we're using this machine to read mail and we're using one of the classical mail user agents, we need to leave sendmail running. On the other hand, if we're using one of the POP/IMAP–based clients, such as Netscape Messenger, and this machine is not the central mail server, we can feel totally free to deactivate sendmail.

Now, does this stop the machine itself from sending out automated emails? Well, no, not really. When a program on the machine itself (including mutt/pine/elm) wants to send mail, it just runs a new sendmail process in `-bs` mode, in which the program talks to sendmail using normal SMTP but does so over STDIN/STDOUT rather than over the network. For its part, sendmail then can talk to the network, if necessary. If the mail is destined for a user on the current machine, sendmail just hands over the mail to the local delivery[26] agent. If the mail is destined for another machine, sendmail, acting as a network client rather than the server that we normally expect, contacts the remote machine's mail server. It attempts to deliver the mail and then terminates. If it isn't successful, the mail is placed in a *queue* for later delivery. If we deactivate sendmail's normal "daemon[27] mode," we generally need to compensate by having cron occasionally rerun sendmail in queue cleanup mode, in which it tries to resend each failed email. To do this, just add a line to root's crontab that occasionally runs `sendmail -q`. Here's a sample line that would run sendmail at the top of every hour on a Linux system:

```
0 * * * *   /usr/sbin/sendmail -q
```

After this thorough a discussion, we should be ready to make this decision. In the case of this machine, no one is using it to send email, so we can safely deactivate sendmail's daemon mode. On our Linux system, this is as easy as using the following lines:

```
# chkconfig sendmail off
# /etc/rc.d/init.d/sendmail stop
```

Now we've finished the TCP port audit. Hopefully it has been very instructional, not only in the background that you've gained about parts of your system, but also in the skills necessary to do this audit yourself. Let's finish up with an audit of the services listening on UDP ports.

The Miscellaneous UDP Audit

To get a list of all listening UDP-based services on our sample Linux system, we just run our `netstat` command, slightly modified:

```
# netstat -vau
Active Internet connections (servers and established)
Proto Recv-Q Send-Q Local Address           Foreign Address         State
udp        0      0 *:who                   *:*
udp        0      0 *:1035                  *:*
udp        0      0 *:1038                  *:*
```

```
udp      0      0 *:1039              *:*
udp      0      0 *:671               *:*
udp      0      0 *:976               *:*
udp      0      0 *:sunrpc            *:*
```

Just as before, we can use the lsof command to figure out what program started each of these. Let's start with the who port, UDP port 513:

```
# lsof -i udp:who
COMMAND    PID USER    FD   TYPE DEVICE SIZE NODE NAME
rwhod    11385 root    3u   IPv4 111150      UDP *:who
rwhod    11386 root    3u   IPv4 111150      UDP *:who
```

We see that we need to track down the rwhod program. Calling up its man page, we read that rwhod basically has two primary purposes, which is to give out the following types of information:

```
# ruptime localhost
localhost      up      5:18,    2 users,  load 0.01, 0.02, 0.00
```

```
# rwho localhost
root      localhost:tty1 Sep 25 14:47
root      localhost:tty2 Sep 25 19:49
```

It gives anyone querying over the network access to either uptime information or a list of locally logged-in users, along with what time they logged in. From a security perspective, this shouldn't necessarily give us the warmest feelings. This information might give an attacker too much information about the system, in the same way that finger does. From a purely technical perspective, this service also represents yet another network-available entry point, which could be dangerous if a security vulnerability is discovered in it. Again, you must exercise your own judgment. For this example, we'll turn it off.

Looking in the /etc/rc.d/rc3.d/ directory, we find the start script /etc/rc.d/rc3.d/S60rwhod. After reading the script, we realize that it only starts rwhod, so it's an easy call to deactivate the entire script:

```
# chkconfig rwhod off
# /etc/rc.d/init.d/rwhod stop
```

Let's move on to the next port, 1035:

```
# lsof -i udp:1035
COMMAND      PID USER   FD   TYPE DEVICE SIZE NODE NAME
rpc.ruser 11361 root    3u   IPv4 111117      UDP *:1035
```

Looking at the ps listing for process 11361, we find the full command to be rpc.rusersd:

```
nobody    11361     1  0 Sep25 ?        00:00:00 rpc.rusersd
```

Well, there's no man page for that on this system, so we find ourselves running another Web search. This search turns up what we might expect, based on our experiences with rwhod earlier in this section. rpc.rusersd is a daemon that gives a list of all users logged in to anyone who queries it, as we show here:

```
# rusers -l localhost
root     localhost.localdomain:tty1    Sep 25 14:47    1:06
root     localhost.localdomain:tty2    Sep 25 19:49    1:15
root     localhost.localdomain:pts/0   Sep 25 20:53         (192.168.70.1)
```

Again, this really does give an attacker way too much information, especially because this lists where everyone is logged in from and how long they've been idle. An attacker who is profiling this network as a target learns a great deal, including the following:

- When the system administrator and other users are online and active

- Where the system administrators log in from

- A list of other target machines that might even have trust relationships with this one

We choose to deactivate this one straight out. Investigating /etc/rc.d/rc3.d/, we find S60rusersd. Because this one only starts rpc.rusersd, we can safely shut it off.

```
# chkconfig rusersd off
# /etc/rc.d/init.d/ruserd stop
```

The next port to investigate is UDP port 1038. Firing off `lsof` and `ps` at this gives us the responsible program rpc.rwalld. From the man page, we learn that this program allows users on other systems to send broadcast messages to everyone on our system. This, like rpc.rusersd and rwhod, appears to be a holdover from more trusting times on the Internet. The days of dynamically assigned IPs and low traceability were not here just yet, and they seemed to mostly trust most of the traffic on the Net. These days, we would rarely leave such a service running, unless we have a large number of users at a site with many, many machines. Even in this case, we'd probably try to use the routers and firewalls to disallow access to this service by all but a few machines. Let's turn this off in this example because we don't need this functionality enough to want to worry about it.

Looking in /etc/rc.d/rc3.d/, we find the script S60rwalld, which solely starts the rpc.rwalld program. We can safely shut this off:

```
# chkconfig rwalld off
# /etc/rc.d/init.d/rwalld stop
```

Moving on, our next port is UDP 1039. Firing up `lsof`, we find that the responsible program is missing. Well, remember our `rpcinfo` output from before, back when we first looked at portmap? Here it is again, filtered so that only the UDP ports remain:

```
# rpcinfo -p | grep udp
   program vers proto    port
    100000    2   tcp     111   portmapper
    100000    2   udp     111   portmapper
    100004    2   udp     671   ypserv
    100004    1   udp     671   ypserv
    100004    2   tcp     674   ypserv
    100004    1   tcp     674   ypserv
    100002    3   udp    1035   rusersd
    100002    2   udp    1035   rusersd
    100009    1   udp     976   yppasswdd
    100008    1   udp    1039   walld
```

It turns out that UDP port 1039 was reserved by rpc.rwalld as well. With that mystery cleared up, let's look at the next port, UDP port 671. lsof shows that this port is checked out by the program ypserv. As you can learn from the ypserv man page, this is the main NIS daemon. NIS, or the Network Information System, is an old system dreamed up by Sun to go with its Network File System (NFS). Among other things, it allows all UNIX computers on a network to look up user entries in a global /etc/passwd without having to actually send the passwd file over NFS. Instead, a set of NIS servers serve user information to each machine on the network. Sites often pair NIS with NFS to allow a user to sit down at one of many different machines at a campus, log in with a single common password, and have equal access to centrally stored files.

In our example, this machine won't be an NIS server, so let's shut this down. We look in /etc/rc.d/rc3.d/ and quickly find S26ypserv. Because this only starts the ypserv program, we can simply deactivate the script:

```
# chkconfig ypserv off
# /etc/rc.d/init.d/ypserv stop
```

Let's move on to UDP port 976. lsof and ps show that this port is reserved by rpc.yppasswdd. As the man page for yppasswdd describes, this provides a facility for users to change their passwords in an NIS domain. Because we're not running one, we can simply deactivate this.

We find a script in /etc/rc.d/rc3.d/ called S66yppasswdd, which is responsible only for starting rpc.yppasswdd, so it's safe to simply chkconfig this off:

```
# chkconfig yppasswdd off
# /etc/rc.d/init.d/yppasswdd stop
```

Finally, we're at our last port, sunrpc, or UDP port 111. This just so happens to belong to portmap, the program that we delayed judgment on earlier. We had to wait until we had visited all the RPC-based servers. Well, because we're not running any RPC programs, we don't need to tell other computers what ports they're running on. This means that we can deactivate the portmap program safely.

```
# chkconfig portmap off
# service portmap stop
```

This concludes our post-install network daemon audit. At this point, we need to see what remains using netstat. We should definitely log this, hopefully on hard copy. We can email the output to a central system administration account to start:

```
# netstat -vatu | mail sysadmin@some.other.machine
```

From here, you should check your results externally from another machine.

Best Practice: Checking the Audit with nmap

At this point, we should make sure that the netstat readout was accurate. Although this may sound paranoid, you might be surprised to know that there are tools called *rootkits* in common use that can hide a port or two from netstat output. Then again, if a port is open and listening, it can't be hidden from an external network scanner. Let's try out nmap, an excellent scanner by Fyodor from `http://www.insecure.org/nmap/`:

```
$ nmap -sT -sU -sR 192.168.71.128

Starting nmap V. 2.53 by fyodor@insecure.org ( www.insecure.org/nmap/ )
Interesting ports on  (192.168.71.128):
(The 1513 ports scanned but not shown below are in state: closed)
Port       State       Service
22/tcp     open        ssh
5432/tcp   open        postgres
Nmap run completed — 1 IP address (1 host up) scanned in 3 seconds
```

Note that our nmap command tells nmap to scan TCP and UDP ports, but also to do an RPC scan. We can check this against the open ports list that we just generated with netstat so that we can make sure that they match up.

Periodic Checks for Integrity

Finally, you should periodically run these checks to verify integrity. If a new network port starts listening, then you've possibly added a program that you need to check into. If you don't recognize whatever program netstat and lsof show up, you might have direct evidence of an intrusion. If a port appears in your periodic nmap[28] scans but doesn't appear in either past or current netstat listings, you almost certainly have evidence of an intrusion.

We've mentioned and used a number of security audit tools. Let's take a look at how we can replace a number of network daemons with more secure replacements.

Secure Network Daemon Replacements

There are three common security-focused replacement network daemons, each of which have become standard parts of major Linux distributions. These include TCP Wrappers, Secure Shell (ssh), and Wietese Venema's secure portmapper.

TCP Wrappers (tcpd)

TCP Wrappers adds access control to inetd and other network daemons that don't include it natively. We mentioned this earlier when we were examining the inetd.conf file. In essence, inetd runs tcpd instead of the actual daemon that is responsible for the protocol supported. inetd runs *tcpd <daemon>*, passing the daemon name as a parameter to tcpd. tcpd checks its access control lists in /etc/hosts.allow and /etc/hosts.deny, does a consistency check on the IP address,[29] and, should these check out, starts the daemon.

You can learn exactly how to configure this functionality by reading the man pages hosts_access(5) and hosts_options(5):

```
man 5 hosts_access
```

```
man 5 hosts_options
```

We present the short version here, but urge you to read the documentation on TCP Wrappers. The first thing to understand is that TCP Wrappers can be configured via one of two methods.

First, the simpler and much more common implementations is the two-file method. Here, you create a hosts.allow file, listing which machines are allowed access to which servers, and a hosts.deny file, listing which servers are off limits to which machines. While this may sound complicated, most people opt for the following configuration:

```
hosts.allow:
        daemon1: machineA, machineB
        daemon2: machineA, machineB
hosts.deny:
        ALL: ALL : (safe_finger -l @%h | mail -s %d-%h root) &
```

This has the effect of allowing access to daemon1 and daemon2 from machineA and machineB, but setting a default-deny policy on everything else. While other combinations are possible, this is both the safest and the most common. By the way, note the last column in the hosts.deny line — this runs a finger lookup against the offending client and mails the result to the sysadmin. Many sysadmins use this to track probes in general— this information can even be very helpful in predicting when a new vulnerability or exploit has been released.

The second method of configuring TCP wrappers uses only a single file, specifically, the hosts.allow file. Here's the example above, translated into this format:

```
hosts.allow
        daemon1: machineA, machineB : allow
        daemon2: machineA, machineB : allow
        ALL:ALL:spawn (safe_finger -l @%h | mail root) &: deny
```

The primary difference here appears to be that we've added a final column, which simply says "allow" or "deny." This difference is important, in that the configuration becomes easier to read and thus to audit. On the other hand, this is not the only difference. As you'll discover if you read the man pages referenced above, many options are only available under the single-file configuration method.

A full discussion of TCP wrappers is beyond the scope of this chapter. For now, let's move on to the Secure Shell, or ssh.

Secure Shell (ssh)

ssh was created, as we mentioned in the Network Daemons Audit, to address the extreme weaknesses in the telnet, rsh, rlogin and ftp protocols. For the most part, this protocol just adds encryption to existing applications. This stops attackers from stealing your passwords or using IP spoofing to access machines illicitly, but it also has a more subtle effect: it prevents an attacker from watching and taking over your session. This is all quite valuable. You should definitely work hard to replace each of these protocols with an ssh-equivalent. The dangers of not doing so are detailed in the Beale article[30] "Stupid, Stupid Protocols: Telnet, FTP, rsh/rcp/rlogin."

ssh is used very simply, designed to be easily learned by Unix users. While it has many advanced features and purposes, the primary purpose of remote login can be accessed via a command like so:

```
ssh account@server
```

The other two main purposes, running commands on remote systems and copying files to/from remote systems, are illustrated here:

```
ssh account@server "run some command"

scp file_here account@server:target_directory/
```

Finally, let's take a look at Wietese Venema's portmapper.

Secure Portmapper (portmap/rpcbind)

Wietese Venema basically wrote a more secure portmapper along the same lines as his popular TCP Wrappers suite. In essence, it replaces the standard portmapper[31] with one that allows for access control. Now, why don't we use TCP Wrappers to do this?

The answer to this question has a great deal to do with how RPC-based programs work. While most network daemons have established static port numbers, usually listed in /etc/services, RPC-based daemons work differently. When an RPC daemon starts, it checks out a port number and registers it with the portmapper program, called either portmap, portmapper or rpcbind. When another program wants to contact that daemon, it contacts the portmapper and requests the port number.

Since most RPC-based services don't run out of inetd, they can't be wrapped in quite the same way that normal services are. Further, the portmapper itself isn't run by inetd, so it can't be wrapped. Venema hacked on the portmapper program itself to add access control, which is controlled through the TCP Wrappers configuration files /etc/hosts.allow and /etc/hosts.deny.

This access control stops machines using unauthorized IP addresses from using the portmapper to discover and access RPC services on the machine. This is amazingly helpful, though it can still be bypassed by a clever attacker. While the attacker can't make the relatively quiet normal queries of the portmapper, he can still use nmap to scan each port directly. This will be very noisy and noticable, but it will reveal the port numbers of each of the running RPC programs.

This kind of feature is still very important, so we should take the time to configure it. Simply add a line to the /etc/hosts.allow file like this:

```
portmapper : 192.168.1.0 192.168.2.0
```

if you use the two-file method, or like this

```
portmapper : 192.168.1.0 192.168.2.0 : allow
```

if you use the single-file method. Still, though, the portmapper replacement was also written to fix a number of old security vulnerabilities. While these are usually not a concern on newer operating systems, it's generally a good idea to use a secure replacement for any system that has had bugs. Luckily, most Linux distributions have included this for a long time. You may have to download it seperately for Solaris or for older distributions.

So, we've discussed a number of security enhancement tools. Now, let's take a look at auditing your passwords.

Auditing Passwords

Another critical step, especially on older UNIXes, is auditing all accounts and passwords. The first thing that you should do here is make sure that every account on the system actually has a password or has been set to not allow direct login. Exactly how the latter is done varies with UNIX type and version, so you should read both the passwd and shadow man pages to learn. Remember, you must check to make sure that each entry in /etc/passwd has a * in the password field, signifying that the password is stored in /etc/shadow. Each line in /etc/shadow should have either a password or some symbol that indicates that no password, empty or otherwise, will be accepted. In Linux, this symbol is either ! ! or *.

Over time, you definitely should test the strength of your passwords with a tool such as Crack or John the Ripper. It is necessary to get permission before doing anything like this, of course, but it is a standard step at most security-conscious UNIX sites. In essence, you use a tool such as Crack to see if an attacker could crack any of the passwords at your site in reasonable time. You should expect at least one or two—or perhaps as many as 50%—of your passwords to be cracked the first time that you audit a site, especially if the operating system allows fairly weak passwords. As Chapter 7, "Authentication," pointed out, weak passwords often can be guessed or cracked with proper tools. After you educate your staff on the dangers (and show them their cracked passwords), their passwords probably will improve significantly.

From there, you can try to enforce stronger passwords using tools such as npasswd or Matt Bishop's passwd+, if your operating system doesn't already do this for you. These types of tools can allow you to configure mild to very strict standards on your user passwords. Be careful, though, that you don't set the standards so high, either in password difficulty/randomness or password lifetime, that your users begin to resent it. When this happens, such as when you configure a firewall so tightly that people can't get their jobs done, you'll find that the users begin to work around you. They'll pick difficult passwords and change them every four days, but then you'll find that those passwords are taped to everyone's monitors or keyboards. Enforcing good passwords is definitely a game of balance. This practice represents a much more proactive solution, although you still should audit your password security on a regular basis.

We've just touched the surface here of a full system audit. Programs such as Bastille Linux, which works on Linux, HP-UX, and is being ported to a number of other operating systems (including Solaris), and Titan, which works on Linux and Solaris, can automate much of this process. In the next two sections, we'll take a general look at what each of these programs can do.

The question of whether or not to use automation is a common one. Experienced sysadmins know that any task that you can reliably automate is another task that:

- Will not take up much time on a regular basis.
- Will be performed consistently, the exact same way every time.

The latter is very important for avoiding problems. The former is probably the most important, since it frees you up to work on architectural decisions and attack future problems proactively. I know more than one system administrator who fervently believes that if his job is not easier to do by the time he leaves than when he first arrived, he has not done it very well. I wholeheartedly agree—automation is the Way.

There are other reasons to use automated solutions. One of the most basic here is that you benefit from the experience of the people who wrote the automation solution. Well, even if you choose not to employ automation, please do read on anyway — you'll learn a great deal by examining these solutons up close. For example, Bastille Linux is widely regarded as an educational security checklist that many experienced sysadmins use even when they do all the work manually.

Automating Linux/UNIX Lockdown with Bastille Linux

Bastille Linux locks down a Linux/UNIX machine by making intelligent configuration changes and educating the end user or system administrator about operating system security. The central idea is to proactively change the configuration to one that is more resistant to attack. It initially was dreamed up at a SANS conference by Jon Lasser (the project's lead coordinator), Ben Woodard, and a team of other sysadmins who all were annoyed with the current state of operating system security. This chapter's author, Jay Beale, joined later as the author of the Bastille program itself and now serves as the lead developer. Jay's efforts, to this end, are even sponsored by MandrakeSoft, which includes Bastille in its Mandrake Linux distribution.

At this point, Bastille has become a collaborative effort, with people developing modules and helping to port Bastille to other operating systems. Peter Watkins wrote the firewalling module and has since taken a role as a core developer. Michael Rash created a port scan–detection utility called psad, which has since been integrated into Bastille. Hewlett-Packard has graciously donated the time of several of its employees to make the port to HP-UX, including Keith Buck, John Diamant, Robert Fritz, and Tyler Easterling.

Bastille differs from most hardening scripts in that it has an educational component. When we designed the original program, we had to decide what hardening steps to take. In any system-hardening process, some steps could "break" functionality for a user. Remember, the audit in the section "Auditing Services" deactivated NFS services. If our machine had needed those services, we would have upset someone. The best way to avoid this problem, while still doing as much good as possible, is to ask the user which actions could be taken. Unfortunately, most users (and many system administrators) haven't had time for much training in computer security. This means that the program would ask them questions that they didn't have the background to carefully consider.

For example, most people who have used telnet think that it's a very useful tool and that it should not be disabled on a system that you want to connect to remotely. Unfortunately, telnet is absolutely horrible from a security standpoint. Because it's a clear-text protocol, someone can eavesdrop, steal the password used for authentication, and even take over the session. For Bastille to function optimally, we felt that it would need to teach the user this. As a result, Bastille gained what has turned out to be a very valuable educational component. We like to believe that Bastille not only secures the machine, but also secures the administrator by giving him a stronger background in security. That's enough history and introduction. Let's get into what Bastille actually *does*.

Bastille applies some basic security concepts to a Linux/UNIX installation. The primary one, and the one that is at the core of most proactive security solutions, is the principle of minimalism applied to computer security.

Principle of Applied Minimalism

If we give each account or program only the access or privilege that it actually needs, then an attacker both has a smaller chance of compromising our system and less access if he is successful.

Let's see this in action as we look at each of Bastille's modules. Remember, every action that Bastille takes is *optional*.

8

SECURING A
SYSTEM FOR
ROLLOUT

Account Security (AccountSecurity.pm)

This module takes a number of actions to protect user accounts and minimize the effect of a compromise of one of these. It prevents the flawed IP-based rhosts authentication that we discussed in the section "Auditing Services," and it disables the clients and daemons that use these. It implements password aging to disable old, unused accounts. It restricts cron usage to a more minimal set of users, and, finally, it prevents direct root login so that a user logging in as root first must log in as a regular user. This last step has the effect of forcing someone who steals root's password to steal a second user's password as well before being able to log in as root, at least on the ttys.

File Permissions (FilePermissions.pm)

This module sets some general file permissions and then does a Set-UID audit. This kind of audit, while often ignored, is one of the most effective measures that you can take to prevent *privilege escalation*. In this instance, an attacker who has compromised one program—say, Apache—and thus has the privileges of user nobody exploits another vulnerable program on the system that has greater privileges. Privilege escalation usually involves a vulnerable Set-UID root program. If we can trim the number of Set-UID root programs that the attacker can run, there's a better chance that there won't be any vulnerable ones for him to use to escalate.

The purpose of the audit is either to remove the Set-UID quality from the programs found or to limit the group of people who can run each program. The optimal way to do the latter is to create a new group owner for each program and then make the program mode 750, so that only members of the group can run the program. Because this involves much user education, Bastille chooses instead to simply deactivate or leave active each Set-UID root program.

Here are some of the programs that Bastille can limit—these are all Set-UID root and can be run by any user:

```
mount     dump      ping          lpr     rsh       inndstart
umount    restore   traceroute    lpq     rcp       startinnfeed
dos 32    at        usernetctl    lprm    rlogin
```

Deactivate Miscellaneous Daemons (MiscellaneousDaemons.pm)

This module deactivates many of the standalone daemons on the system, both network and otherwise. This reduces both the number of privileged programs on the system and the number of avenues for attack. The informational component alone in this step and the previous one can be one of the better reasons to download Bastille. Here are some of the daemons that Bastille deactivates:

```
rpc.mountd    apmd    dhcpd    routed     atd        ypbind
rpc.statd     smbd    gpm      gated      amd        ypserv
rpc.lockd     nmbd    innd     snmpd      rpc.nfsd   portmap
```

Boot Security (BootSecurity.pm)

This module takes actions to protect the boot process, preventing an attacker from subverting the boot process to get root. It password-protects the LILO prompt so that an attacker can't reconfigure the boot loader, which he might do to boot from an alternate medium or to replace the normal init program with an interactive shell. It also password-protects single-user mode, to stop an attacker from booting to single-user mode to get root.

Add Enhanced Logging (logging.pm)

This module configures additional logging for the system, to better warn the system administrator of an attack. This includes logging all kernel messages, all high-severity messages, and all logins to their own log files. This last step (creating loginlog) is a vital one on all operating systems because it helps create a good audit trail of which users were logged in when a security incident occurs.

This module also helps you configure logging to a remote system, which can both make centralized log analysis possible and protect the system logs from deletion.[33] Finally, it can activate process accounting, which can log every program started on the system.

Configure Miscellaneous PAM Settings (ConfigureMiscPAM.pm)

This module sets PAM resource limits to help protect against resource-starvation attacks. This can be controversial because these settings really should be tuned for each site. Bastille sets core dump maximum sizes to 0, limits the number of processes per user (to stymie fork bombs and such), and sets a user file size maximum.

Disable User Tools (DisableUserTools.pm)

This module disables the compiler, slowing down or halting an attacker who needs to compile his exploits on the system. Although this is less common on Intel x86 Linux systems, here's a very common scenario: An attacker steals a telnet user's password as he telnets from some other system to ours, and then logs into our system. Once on our system, he downloads exploit code from an FTP archive, which he then compiles and runs against our system to gain root access. He also might compile a sniffer or other attack tools on our system, to gain access to others. Removing the compiler can break this cycle early, especially on less common architectures.

Printing (printing.pm)

This module deactivates the printer daemons and binaries, if they aren't necessary. This just follows from our principle of minimalism from before because we're trying to reduce the number of accessible privileged programs.

Apache (Apache.pm)

This module fine-tunes Apache's configuration to make it harder to compromise. This includes deactivating Apache, turning it into a personal Web server (by forcing it to listen only to the loopback interface), or binding it to only one interface. Bastille also can turn off CGI script execution, server-side include parsing, index generation, and symbolic-link follow—each of these can potentially be dangerous, based on the server's content.

DNS (DNS.pm)

This module runs the BIND named program more safely, to stop an attacker who can successfully compromise it from having full privileges on the system. BIND has had a number of bad security vulnerabilities in recent years, several of which granted an attacker a remote rootshell. Bastille configures named to run in a chroot-prison as a non-root user. Instead of a completely unrestrained root shell, the attacker find himself with a highly boxed-in shell, running as a user who owns only one file. This is the essence of containment and has been highly effective.

This seems like a good place to take a break and introduce another critical concept in hardening operating systems.

Defense in Depth

For each potential avenue of attack, protect it in as many ways as possible so that if one method of defense is breached, your system isn't compromised.

Bastille applies this in multiple ways. For instance, it tightens configurations of programs such as named, even when you've also chosen to turn these off. The idea is that if named gets reactivated, either by you or by the system administrator who replaces you when you get that promotion, it's at least a much safer program. With network daemons, we go even further. We harden, deactivate, and then even firewall them off, if possible. In this case, if two layers of security fail, you've still got the third protecting you from remote root compromise.

FTP (FTP.pm)

This module fine-tunes WU-FTPd's configuration to reduce an attacker's avenues for attack. As we discussed in the inetd audit in the section "Auditing Services," FTP is highly dangerous. Bastille can help you remove whichever of the two modes (user/password mode or anonymous mode) you aren't using. It also takes some great pains to explain the problems inherent in FTP.

sendmail (sendmail.pm)

This module shuts down sendmail's profiling/spam-friendly features and allows you to deactivate daemon mode. In daemon mode, sendmail listens to the network for incoming email. As we saw in our daemon audit in the section "Auditing Services," it doesn't need to do this if the machine that it's running on doesn't need to receive email from outside the system. Bastille can either deactivate sendmail or simply replace daemon mode with queue-cleanup mode. In this mode, sendmail still can send email off the machine from classical model mail clients, such as pine, mutt, and elm.

As we noted before, Bastille also shuts down the profiling/spam-friendly VRFY (verify account) and EXPN (expand alias) SMTP commands. These commands allow an attacker to discover which accounts exist on the system and what relationships might exist between them. For instance, you might expand the sysadmins alias or verify that the sysadmin account exists on a system.

Secure inetd Configuration (SecureInetd.pm)

This module fine-tunes inetd's configuration to reduce an attacker's avenues for attack. It deactivates the telnet and ftp daemons and gives you the opportunity to use TCP Wrappers to set a default-deny policy on all inetd/xinetd–supported programs. These are the same themes as in our inetd/xinetd audit. Luckily, as we showed in our Red Hat 7.1 xinetd audit, this part has become easier and less necessary because vendor defaults have gotten much better.

tmp Directory Defense (TMPDIR.pm)

This module, by Pete Watkins, defends users against /tmp directory exploits, a special class of exploit that works against programs that make bad assumptions about temporary files. Basically, it gives each user a randomly named subdirectory[34] of /tmp, to prevent race condition attacks and general spying. This pushes each user's temporary files into a directory that other users don't have access to, so other users cannot subvert the temporary files or read them.

Firewall (firewall.pm)

This module, by Pete Watkins, configures stateful or nonstateful firewalling in the kernel. It creates a firewall either for a single system or for a small number of networks. The Bastille firewall is very flexible and expandable, allowing it to work in a variety of network designs. At the same time, you always should take note that configuring and maintaining a firewall involves study and maintenance. This is definitely the step that gives new users the most trouble.

Port Scan Attack Detector (psad.pm)

This module implements Mike Rash's psad tool, written to compete with PortSentry as an active port scan–detection tool. Whereas PortSentry can detect only scans that get through to the system itself, psad can work with the Linux kernel to detect scans that are blocked by the firewall, even when there are no special firewalling rules to log the offending packets. psad also incorporates several IDS signatures from Snort to detect other types of attacks and is easily extendable. Although it is still in development, psad is ready for use.

This wraps up our coverage of Bastille's automated hardening. Now that you know what an automated solution can do, you might be wondering, "So, should I do this myself or automate the task?" The answer to this, as you should be getting used to in UNIX, is multifaceted. If you've got the time, education[35] and inclination, you can always do a better job than any automated solution. You're smarter than a computer! On the other hand, if you don't have the time, education, or inclination, an automated solution can really help. Heck, Bastille can help you with the education part even if you don't want to use it to do the work itself. The other main reasons that people like automated solutions are that the solutions do the following:

- Leverage someone else's experience, removing the need to figure out the implementation of each change
- Give consistent results every time, with little chance for error
- Can duplicate configuration choices/policy across a large number of machines

Automating Solaris/UNIX Lockdown with Other Tools

Although Bastille is being hastily ported to many other UNIXes, you might be looking for a tool to harden Solaris now.[36] There are several competing solutions, which we cover here in brief.

Titan

Titan was one of the first hardening programs for UNIX, written by Brad Powell, Matthew Archibald, and Dan Farmer. It is made up of a host of small shell scripts that each takes a specific small set of actions on a host. Titan originally was written for Solaris, although it appears to be minimally ported to Linux and FreeBSD.

Titan was originally written to automate security steps that the authors had to make over and over during the course of their careers. Sooner or later, they were continually asked by colleagues for copies of "those scripts to tighten down the OS." In response to those requests, they began to formally work on the project — at this point, the name "Titan" was attached to the as-yet-unnamed scripts.

Titan performs a variety of security steps and is quite thorough on Solaris systems. It also works on FreeBSD and Linux, though the modules are admittedly more minimal. Titan religiously follows the "Keep It Simple Stupid (KISS)" Principle. Instead of a single script which does everything, the functionality is broken out into a large number of small scripts, each of which has a single purpose. To configure Titan, you simply choose which scripts to run on your system.

Keep It Simple Stupid (KISS)

Simplicity is highly underrated in most aspects of our society. In computer security, it is totally prized. A simpler program has a much lower chance of bugs. With a simpler configuration process, a user is less likely to create a harmful configuration mistake.

Titan's modules take much the same steps as every other Solaris hardening script. Since it was the first, this says a great deal for its strength — it is often said that imitation is the highest compliment! Let's take a look at a number of Titan modules for Solaris.

`addumask.sh`: Adds a system-wide umask so that the rc-scripts all run with a strong umask. This prevents the files they create from having weak permissions.

`adjust-arp-timers.sh`: Shortens the ARP expiration timers from 20 minutes to 1 minute. This prevents specific types of spoofing or DoS attacks.

`aset.sh`: Wraps the Automated Security Enhancement Tool which can, among other things, do Tripwire-like file integrity checking.

`automount/automount.sh`: Prevents the automounter program from starting at boot time. The automounter has had a number of security problems in its history.

`bsm.sh`: Configures auditing on the system.

`cde.sh`: Configures CDE to not allow remote X logins through XDMCP.

`create-issue.sh`: Creates an /etc/issue file that is displayed at login time.

`cronset.sh`: Tightens the cron configuration and activates logging of all cron-run programs.

`decode.sh`: Looks for any "|" statements in /etc/aliases and replaces them if necessary. This was an old vulnerability/feature in sendmail—since sendmail ran as root, a "account: | foo" into /etc/aliases would run the command *foo* as root whenever a mail came for *account*. This command would get whatever input was contained in the incoming email.

`defloginparams`: Sets better parameters in /etc/default/login—these should be tuned to your site to prevent disruptions in service.

`defpwparams.sh`: Sets better parameters in /etc/default/password to improve password aging.

`disable-L1-A.sh`: Deactivates the Stop-A/L1-A key sequence, making it much harder to employ physical attacks against the machine.

`disable-NFS-2.6.sh`: Sets the NFS ports as additional privileged ports, blocking some early NFS-based attacks.

`disable-accounts.sh`: Disables "system accounts" like *bin, daemon* and *nobody* so no one can use them to login.

`diable-core.sh`: Sets the system-wide core dump filesize limit to zero, preventing many attacks against applications that dump sensitive data into a core file when they crash.

`disable-ping-echo.sh`: Disables replying to icmp-echo packets, or "pings." This has the effect of both hiding the host from simple network scans and of blocking ICMP-echo-based DoS attacks.

`disable-ip-holes.sh`: Sets better parameters on the IP stack, including forbidding source-routed packets and forwarding directed broadcasts. The former is almost always used for IP spoofing, while the latter is often used in Distributed Denial of Service (DDoS) attacks.

`dmi-2.6.sh`: Disables the relatively unncessary and undocumented dmi daemons.

`eeprom.sh`: Checks to see if an eeprom password has been set. This prevents many physical attacks, most of which involve booting from alternate media. It also stops one Denial of Service (DoS) attack where an attacker sets an eeprom password himself and then halts your system, leaving you unable to boot your own system back up.

`file-own.sh`: Sets many system files to be owned by root, which is generally much smarter and safer.

`fix-cronpath.sh`: Sets ownership and permissions on programs run out of cron to prevent a specific trojan horse technique.

`fix-modes.sh`: Runs Casper Dik's fixmodes program, which makes a number of file permissions on the system much safer. This is very standard and safe in virtually every environment. It appears that each release of Solaris actually gets closer to the standard set by fixmodes.

`fix-stack-sol2.6.sh`: Configures a non-executable stack, preventing most stack-smashing attacks from working. Though many are squeamish about this, there are very, very few applications that are negatively affected by this. The only well-known one is a specific functionality in the GNU debugger.

`ftp-2.6_secure.sh`: Sets a tighter umask for ftpd and creates a banner to be displayed for each user. Be careful to audit the umask set by this script.

`ftpusers.sh`: Creates a strong ftpusers file which prevents root and system accounts from using FTP.

`hosts.equiv.sh`: Checks for the presence of a hosts.equiv file. This practice of using rhosts IP-address authentication is quite flawed, as IP addresses can be easily spoofed, especially in the LAN setting where rhosts files are normally used.

`inetd.sh/inetd2.sh`: Creates a much stricter inetd configuration. Make sure to examine this one carefully, as it may deactivate services that you need.

`inetsvc.sh`: Deactivates the system's DNS server, DHCP client and ability to respond to multicast packets.

`keyserv2.8.sh`: Disable the "nobody" key. Default accounts like these should very often be disabled.

`log-tcp.sh`: Alters inetd's configuration to log all connections.

`loginlog.sh`: Sets the system to log all failed login attempts.

`lpsched.sh`: Deactivates the print server. This is not a good idea for print servers or any machine that needs to print to those servers. It is, on the other hand, a wonderful idea for firewalls and bastion hosts (dedicated Web servers and the like).

`nddconfig.2.8.sh`: Creates an nddconfig script with a basic ndd configuration. ndd controls a number of kernel paramaters related to the network stack.

`nfs-portmon.sh`: Activates NFS port monitoring for Solaris.

`nsswitch.sh`: Sets nsswitch.conf to not use NIS, NIS+ or DNS. This can be perfect for firewalls, but will break things on just about any other type of host. Still, try to do some of this manually, as disabling NIS at least is a very good idea.

`nuke-nscd.sh`: Deactivates the name service cache daemon. This is more useful on firewalls.

`nuke-sendmail.sh`: Deactivates sendmail. Look at our description of Bastille's sendmail.pm to decide whether or not this is a wise move on the target machine.

`pam-rhosts-2.6.sh`: Configures PAM to totally disallow all types of rhost-booting.

`passwd.sh`: Checks for accounts with no password, disabling those that don't have one.

`powerd.sh`: Checks that the power suspend program can only be run by root.

`psfix.sh`: Makes sure that the /tmp directory will always have the sticky bit set on boot.

`rhosts.sh`: Checks for and possibly removes .rhosts files in local directories and in NIS. Again, rhosts is severely broken and should not be used. With today's hardware speeds, there is virtually no excuse to continue to use rsh/rlogin when ssh can replace them easily.

`rmmount.sh`: Makes sure that CD-ROMs and floppies are always mounted with the nosuid option. This makes sure that a user cannot create a special CD-ROM/floppy that would let them easily escalate privilege.

`rootchk.sh`: Runs through root's path and makes sure that root owns each and every directory listed in the path. This prevents an attacker from writing a trojan binary into one of the directories is root's path.

`routed.sh`: Make sure that in.routed starts in quiet mode, whereby it doesn't advertise routes.

`sendmail-forward.sh`: Disables forwarding of mail, deterring spammers.

`sendmail.sh`: Disables the EXPN (expand alias) and VRFY (verify) SMTP commands so that a curious user can't use sendmail to learn about the accounts and aliases/lists that sendmail knows about.

`smtpbanner-8.8.sh`: Configures sendmail to give out less information to clients connecting to it.

`syslog-block-remote.sh`: Configures syslog to not accept remote logging attempts. This should run on every system that is not your site's central logging host. If you don't have a logging host, it is highly recommended that you create one. This machine doesn't need to be powerful, but should be highly hardened. It keeps a second copy of all of your machines' logs, so that an attacker who compromises a specific machine on your network can only delete the local copy of the logs.

`snmpdx-2.6.sh`: Deactivates the SNMPd daemon. This is **highly** recommended. SNMP is a nightmare, as it advertises a huge amount of information publically and has even been known to allow an attacker to remotely reconfigure or shut down machines.

`syslog.sh`: Sets syslog to log all console messages to log files.

`syslog_failed_logins.sh`: Sets syslog to log all failed login attempts.

`tcp-sequence.sh`: Sets more random TCP initial sequence number generation, which can strengthen the system against TCP/IP spoofing attacks.

`telnet-banner.sh`: Prevents telnet from giving out the Solaris version number to every remote telnet user.

`tmpfs-fixsize.sh`: Sets up a size limit on any tmpfs volumes. This prevents some DoS attacks.

`userumask.sh`: Sets a minimal umask of 022 in /etc/skel/ files.

`useraddset.sh`: Modifies the useradd program for better security.

`utmp2.7.sh`: Makes sure utmpx isn't world-writable.

`vold.sh`: Deactivates the volume management daemon which is responsible for mounting removable media. This is a good idea on any system where non-root users don't need to mount floppies or CD-ROMs. It is a necessity on firewalls and bastion hosts.

`ziplock.sh`: Sets very, very tight file permissions on the system. Please carefully research this script before running it.

Well, as you saw, Titan is quite comprehensive. It also, like any other solution, must be very carefully configured. A wrong choice can better your security, but leave you with an angry manager. Make sure to educate yourself on each script before putting it into play. This is one place where the Bastille Linux approach to ask the user about each step, while educating said user about said step, can be very safe and useful. On the other hand, Titan is faster to run when you're more experienced and don't need the education.

From here, let's take a quick look at the other hardening programs available for Solaris.

Solaris-Specific Hardening Tools: YASSP and jass

YASSP was written by Jean Chouanard, sponsored by Xerox PARC at the time. It takes many of the same hardening steps as Titan and jass, but it also changes the way that the core system is administered. YASSP centralizes much of the security configuration options into one central file, which makes administration of these easier but adds a significant learning curve to its use. At the time of this chapter's composition, YASSP also has remained inactive for some time, having published a "Release Candidate" in November 2000.

`jass` appears to represent the most recent foray by Sun into the system-hardening space. It has much stronger integration with system installation, although it apparently takes much of the same actions as Titan and YASSP.

All three of these solutions implement Sun and the general community's recommendations for hardening the Solaris operating system. This process is remarkably similar to Bastille's, although it doesn't include a Set-UID audit, a kernel-based firewall, or a port-scan detector. On the other hand, Solaris hardening does kernel options such as setting a nonexecutable stack and tweaking the networking subsystem for better security.

This wraps up our chapter on securing a system for rollout. This is an introduction and by no means a complete process—such a process would take a complete book in and of itself. Watch this author's Web site, listed under the references here, for articles and a future book on the topic.

Best Practices

- Never assume that a system is not worth someone's trouble to hack.

- Never assume that one of your systems can be hacked without consequences.

- If a service is not required, it should not be enabled.

- Encrypted channels are preferable to clear channels.

- More than one method should be used to audit a system.

- Never rely on a single method of securing your system.

- Always check out a system's physical site *before* putting the system in it.

- Learn everything you can, especially about security. This will make your job much, much easier and will even earn you raises.

Resources

`http://www.securityfocus.com`: If you read no other mailing list, begin reading BugTraq now. This full-disclosure mailing list that we introduced in the section "Why You Must Do More Than Patch" generally represents the very first public release of vital information about vulnerabilities in your operating system and software.

`http://www.vulnwatch.org`: Vulnwatch, a new mailing list begun this year, has a similar purpose to BugTraq, but it was begun as a completely noncommercial community resource. This bears watching.

`http://www.bastille-linux.org`: Bastille Linux, perhaps more appropriately called "Bastille," tightens the configuration of a system to reduce the possibility and impact of a compromise.

The Solaris hardening programs discussed here are available via:

- Titan: `http://www.fish.com/titan`
- YASSP: `http://www.yassp.org`
- jass: `http://www.sun.com/blueprints/tools/`

`http://www.bastille-linux.org/jay/`: The author of this chapter, Jay Beale, publishes a Web site on Linux/UNIX security, complete with articles and references on system hardening and security.

8

SECURING A
SYSTEM FOR
ROLLOUT

Endnotes

[1] *We can write an entire book on the topic of this chapter.*

[2] *The buffer overflow vulnerability is one of the chief security holes that crackers use to penetrate systems. To learn more about how attackers use this, and how to avoid the programming mistakes that are responsible, see Aleph1's seminal paper, "Smashing the Stack for Fun and Profit."*

[3] *By the way, we used to think that this was possible only on a hub-based network. Switch-based networks also can be sniffed, although the process involves one or more active components. Don't assume that network switches protect you from sniffing.*

[4] *In cases when he can't execute an arbitrary shell, he'll often force the program to do something else that can be used to eventually get a shell on the system. For example, he might get a program that runs with root privilege to add another account to the system, by modifying /etc/passwd.*

[5] *A root-level program (one that runs with UID 0) can drop privilege down to any arbitrary user. This is a safer coding practice that has become more common in system daemons, to make root access harder to obtain. Unfortunately, programs that do this can still sometimes be compromised before they drop privilege—even if this isn't possible, whatever user they drop down to might still have a level of privilege that an attacker desires.*

[6] *If the attacker can communicate with the system only over the network but doesn't yet have an account, we say that he has "no access."*

[7] *The Linux community, in particular, is very fast at this. When the "ping of death" vulnerability was announced years ago, in which most any computer on the Internet could be crashed by sending a single overly long ping packet, the Linux community developed a source-code patch faster than any other operating system. According to the "Ping O' Death" page at http://www.dfm.dtu.dk/netware/pingod/ping.html, the Linux community developed a patch in 2 hours, 35 minutes, and 10 seconds.*

[8] *In 2001, there were substantial Internet slowdowns and outages due to a worm called Code Red. What the news media failed to cover in this incident was that Microsoft had released a patch to fix the vulnerability that Code Red exploited months before Code Red was developed. Each machine that was taken over and that became an unwilling attacker was another machine that had not been patched promptly, if ever.*

[9] *Don't worry too much about this—we'll talk in a later section about some tools and books that will help you substantially with this process.*

[10] *xinetd has been ported to a very small number of UNIX types. At the time of this printing, it does not support Solaris, HP-UX, or Irix.*

[11] *Solaris uses /etc/inet/inetd.conf but makes a symbolic link to it from /etc/inetd.conf.*

[12] *By the way, the port usually is listed symbolically. UNIX automatically remaps this symbol to the port number listed in /etc/services. UNIX commands even will output ports by their symbolic names, unless instructed to use the numeric equivalents, as long as the name/number pair is in /etc/services.*

[13]*TCP Wrappers does a reverse DNS lookup on the source IP address and then does a forward DNS lookup on the response. If the IP address that it receives as an answer does not match the source IP address of the connection, Wrappers suspects that there might be some DNS spoofing going on. Here's where that becomes important: Suppose you've configured Wrappers to allow FTP connections only from machines in the .bastille-linux.org domain. You want some assurance that there's no DNS spoofing involved.*

[14]*Whether this ownership is legitimate, such as when he's in the cubicle next to the user, or illegitimate, when he has cracked (owned) the machine, is something to consider.*

[15]*Stateless firewalls, such as most filtering routers, many embedded firewalls, and the Linux kernel before 2.3 aren't designed to easily firewall FTP. This has led to a number of attacks, including the FTP bounce attack, that could pass through many of these types of firewalls.*

[16]*Many of the FTP daemons available are based on an initial implementation of ftpd.*

[17]*Interestingly, "steal, sniff, repeat" sounds a lot like "rinse, wash, repeat."*

[18]*As an exception, if you're not the only one responsible for this machine/network, you might want to check with the others who are responsible for it before making these changes.*

[19]*You can add any service to this easily. Some people actually have spent some time compiling a more comprehensive /etc/services file.*

[20]*Note that these scripts are actually links to the real scripts in /etc/rc.d/init.d/. The links are symbolic links under Linux and hard links under Solaris. It doesn't really matter—most Solaris sysadmins use symbolic links when they add scripts to the boot process.*

[21]*Many of us in the profession actually use the term "enlightened laziness." This describes the use of a little cleverness, a bit more creativity, and a whole lot of tools and automation to make our jobs easier.*

[22]*Remember, if we want to number the number of the port, we can look it up the same way that the system does. We simply find it listed in /etc/services.*

[23]*The port name auth is either a misnomer or a product of history; this is not used for authentication, especially because this would require the system asking for authentication to "take the client system's word for good" that the user was who he said he was. When the queried system is owned by the attacker, either for real or simply in the cracked sense, the answer cannot be trusted.*

[24]*It also allows interactive and automated file transfer, as well as automated command execution.*

[25]*Many of these clients can be configured to use POP or IMAP, although it is not their native behavior. It is also fairly uncommon because it is usually a user choice. Still, check with your site's email administrator to learn about how users are reading their mail.*

[26]*Most people don't realize this until their local delivery agent breaks, but sendmail does not actually deliver local mail itself on most systems. For instance, on Solaris systems, the local mail delivery agent is /bin/mail. Oddly enough, on most Linux systems, procmail does this job.*

[27]*In daemon mode, sendmail runs constantly, listening to port 25 for incoming messages from remote machines.*

8

SECURING A
SYSTEM FOR
ROLLOUT

[28]*One warning about nmap: It's generally better to nmap a single computer at a time, to avoid saturating your network or network interface. Furthermore, you need to be careful when scanning routers and such. Although nmap has no trouble scanning UNIX machines, we have caused our network routers to crash and reboot; this is a documented issue with a number of old routers.*

[29]*tcpd checks the client IP address's reverse map, that is, the name associated with that IP address. It then resolves this name into an IP address. If this IP address doesn't match the first IP address, tcpd suspects that there is some spoofing going on and it denies the connection.*

[30]`http://www.bastille-linux.org/jay/stupid-protocols.html`

[31]*The portmapper is also called "rpcbind" on Solaris and other Unix systems.*

[32]*dos is the default SUID program for dosemu, whose man page, ironically, states that it should not be SUID.*

[33]*A smart attacker often will delete the logs on a system that he compromises. If the system is also logging to a highly tightened dedicated log host, you have a second copy of the logs.*

[34]*Originally, this was done in the user's home directory, but this is problematic in situations in which the home directories are NFS-mounted.*

[35]*Actually, given more time, you can educate yourself, so this really reduces to "time and inclination."*

[36]*Bastille's Solaris version might be done now—go check* `http://www.bastille-linux.org`*!*

Day-to-Day System Management

by David Ennis

IN THIS CHAPTER

Overview

As the name of this chapter implies, we deal here with the day-to-day details of system administration. These details are divided into two broad groups: proactive, those things that an administrator can do in advance to help a system run smoothly and avoid problems, and reactive, things to do if the proactive steps don't avoid a problem.

The goal of this chapter is not to present detailed implementation, but rather to discuss concepts and general commands used to achieve the goal. The nitty gritty details of "how to" are left for the other chapters in this book.

System administration is all about control. It is just a matter of whether you, the admin, control your systems or whether they control you. Hopefully, the material in this chapter, along with the rest of the book, will put you in control of your systems.

Probably every book on UNIX and system administration has dire warnings about being root and doing things such as `rm -rf *`. These are catastrophes in the making. And you say to yourself, "I would never do that!" Well, there may well come a time when you are tired or under pressure of a deadline or some other serious problem. You will be rushing to get things fixed and the system back online, the phone will be ringing, your pager will be beeping, and you know that any minute your boss will call for an ETA or a status report. It is the voice of experience talking to you here—be careful! And, with that, enough said on the topic....

The Proactive Administrator

A proactive administrator, as the name implies, needs to look ahead and anticipate problems before they occur. The idea is to close the loopholes, so to speak, so that the problems don't occur.

The first part of this chapter makes some suggestions of areas where proactive opportunities exist. Some of the topic areas covered are security, performance monitoring, log management, resource management, and, last but by no means least, backups.

Hopefully, the material presented here will be food for thought and will aid you as an administrator.

The Importance of Being Root

As an admin, you should be familiar by now with the concept of being root. You know the significance of the root, or superuser, account on your systems. You surely have read repeatedly about the many things that you can do wrong while logged in as root. This chapter focuses on how to do things right to avoid problems or catastrophes. Many tasks that you perform require that you log in as root for them to succeed. Just keep in mind that a crucial part of systems administration is proper management of the root account.

Precisely because of the importance of the root account, you should limit and control access to the root account. The methods used to do this are varied, and which one you select depends on security issues, policy, and procedures at your installation.

Keeping Control Within Limits

In a medium to large-scale systems environment, there is usually more than one administrator. Each requires access to the root account to do his job—this is unavoidable but somehow still needs to be managed.

It is a good idea to give each root user his own personal account, separate from the root account. These personal accounts can be given a substantial amount of root authority without actually being *the* superuser account. You can make the personal account a member of the same groups that root is a member of. Some versions of UNIX will even allow root alias accounts that have the same UID as root (0) and the same primary group ID (0), therefore being identical to root except for the account name. Creating these alias accounts has pros and cons that we will discuss in more detail throughout this chapter.

From a general security standpoint, the password to the root account should have as limited a distribution as possible and should be changed on a regular basis (a good general policy for *all* accounts). Logging access to root is also a good policy to provide accountability and audit of root activity.

Putting on Your Superuser Cape

The "switch user" command, su, is used to switch from one account to another. The account that you are switching to is the only argument on the command line, along with optionally the - switch. The su command prompts for the password of the destination account identical to a login. When the correct password is entered, a new shell is started as the selected account. If no account argument is provided, the command defaults to the root account.

The most useful feature of the su command is that it logs each use, noting the issuing and destination account and the success or failure of the command. A policy or guideline for using the su command when accessing the root account provides control and audit of the superuser admin(s) on your systems.

System Administration in Shades of Gray: The sudo Command

Administering a system is not always just black or white, yes or no. Often you will find that you need to grant limited root access to selected users. It might be limited by function or period of time, or both. The native UNIX account structure is not well equipped to allow shades of gray for root access.

Enter the sudo command, which allows you, the admin, to create a configuration in which specified users are permitted the use of selected commands as the root user. This configuration is kept in the sudoers file.

The sudo command has a number of advantages even for admins that possess the root password and full access to the root account:

- Logging all sudo activated commands through the syslogd facility
- Additional authentication via password input prompt for selected users
- Assignment of permissions by purpose to users or groups to selected commands
- "Quick root login" for admin users in lieu of using su

A typical scenario for using sudo is to permit operations staff to run selected backup system commands. This allows them to perform their job functions without having to know the root password and have access to the superuser account.

The configuration options for sudo are varied and can be used in combination to create as loose or as structured an access plan as needed, depending on your needs or company policy.

Your sudo user includes the entire command to be executed as root on the command line. The sudo command validates that the user is in the sudoers file and is authorized to use the requested command. It is even possible to require the user to enter a personal password to validate that this is the valid user.

There is not enough space in this chapter to give every command a complete explanation. The sudo command is one that is well worth further exploration to understand its capabilities.

Process Management

Process management is one of the ongoing tasks that you, as an admin, will do regularly. The task of process management takes many forms. You will be monitoring them, scheduling them, and overall controlling them to keep your system(s) running effectively and efficiently. As usual, UNIX has a number of commands that enable you to manage the processes running on your system.

Each process has attributes associated with it, information that is essential when managing the activity on your system:

- Process ID (PID), the unique number assigned to each process
- User ID (UID), the number associated with the account of the user who owns the process
- Current working directory (CWD), the default directory used by the process for file references
- File descriptors, a list of the files opened by the process

In the following sections, you will find that all of these process details are important to their management.

Process Status Using the ps command

The ps command is one of the basic tools of process management. This command, with its numerous options, gives you information on the processes that are running on your system. You can find their status and the resources that they are using, as well as who they belong to and other processes to which they are related. The following is some of the information that can be displayed for each process with selected options:

- Process ID
- Parent process ID
- User ID
- Current status of the process
- Priority
- nice number
- CPU time used
- Memory used

Every UNIX process can be identified by a unique process ID or PID. With the exception of init, PID 1, every process is a child of another process known as its parent process. When first started, a process inherits its environment from this parent process. Part of this environment is the ID of the user (UID) initiating the process.

At any moment, a process has a status, such as running, swapped, sleeping blocked, or stopped, to name a few common states. When running, a process has a priority that is used by UNIX to decide when it actually gets CPU time. The lower the number is, the higher a process's priority is.

UNIX dynamically changes process priority to ensure that every process gets some CPU time. The owner of a process can decide to lower the priority (raise the number) using the nice command. The priority of a process combined with its nice number gives the true priority ranking at any moment. Only the root user can increase a process priority (lower the nice number) using nice.

With the ps command, you also can monitor how much memory (real and virtual) and CPU time is used by a specific process. Refer to the ps man page to find out more about the CPU, memory, and other resources reported by the command on your version of UNIX.

In a script, the ps command can be combined with grep, sed, or awk to filter the output. You then can gather selected information about processes running on your system to suit the purpose of your script.

By analyzing the output of ps, you can look for processes using a significant amount of memory or CPU resources. For example, you might find that a process or group of processes is using significant amounts of CPU. By reducing the priority of the process(es) using nice, it might be possible to better balance CPU utilization.

Who's on top?

Although the ps command is sufficient to provide a quick snapshot of processes on your system, sometimes you need to see a trend of the activity. The top command is better suited to this task.

The first few lines of the information that top displays shows a summary of uptime and load average. The status of the CPU(s) and memory also is given, including swap as well as physical and virtual memory. This information can be a very valuable tool in evaluating a current problem on your system. For example, if you are experiencing system slowdowns, it could be due to excessive memory utilization or process swapping, which would be indicated by top.

The top command, unlike ps, runs continuously until it is stopped. While top is running, it displays a real-time table of the current processes on the system. The table is ordered from highest to lowest by CPU usage. By default, top updates the display every 5 seconds, but this can be changed to suit your needs.

Looking at the output of top as it updates gives you a quick view of the state of your system. You can readily see the process(es) that are using the most significant amount of system resources.

By looking at the percentage utilization of CPU and memory for top processes, you can easily determine whether a few processes are the source of your slowdown. A quick fix might be to look at the process priority and nice value of selected processes to see if they might be "throttled back" to allow other processes a fairer share of the system resources.

The top command has a built-in help facility that displays all its commands. Typing **h** while top is running displays the help information.

Killing Process with Signals

Identifying performance issues or problem processes with ps or top is the first step to getting your system back in good running order. Occasionally the only solution is to stop a problem process. The process might be consuming a large percentage of CPU time, memory, or other system resource.

The kill command is the typical tool used to stop processes, but, for us, it is the last resort as well. If the process in question is part of an application that has tools for managing or monitoring its own processes, we suggest using these tools on your first attempt to stop the process(es). Sometimes these tools will fail to remedy the problem, either restarting or stopping a problem process. In that event, then kill is the answer.

Communication between UNIX processes is done with signals, predefined messages each with its own meaning. The kill command sends a specified signal to one or more processes identified by their ID numbers (PIDs). The typical end result of a process receiving a signal is the demise of the process.

A well-written UNIX application traps signals sent to it and responds accordingly. Usually, this means closing files, releasing memory pages, and so on before stopping. At a minimum, you hope that a process will at least stop on receipt of a signal issued from kill.

Table 9.1 lists the common signal names and numbers.

TABLE 9.1 Common Signals

Signal Name	Signal Number	Signal Meaning
HUP	1	Hang up; stop running. (logoff)
INT	2	Interrupt; stop running. (Ctrl+C)
QUIT	3	Quit; stop running, dump core. (Ctrl+\)

TABLE 9.1 continued

Signal Name	Signal Number	Signal Meaning
KILL	9	Kill; unconditionally stops immediately, as an emergency kill. (Cannot be ignored.)
SEGV	11	Segmentation violation; process attempted illegal memory access.
TERM	15	Terminate; stop running nicely, if possible.
STOP	17	Stop unconditionally and immediately. Continue with CONT.
TSTP	18	Stop/pause; continue in foreground or background. (Ctrl+Z)
CONT	19	Continue; resume execution after STOP or TSTP.

The `kill` command can be used with or without a signal name or number, but it must include one or more PIDs to receive the signal. The TERM signal (15) is sent by default if no value is given on the command line.

Application software (homegrown or commercial) often is designed to trap specific signals. A number of UNIX system commands trap signals for special purposes as well. For example, sending HUP to init (PID 1) causes it to reread configuration files. It is a good idea to familiarize yourself with the specific behavior of the software running on your system by consulting available documentation. You might find specific suggestions regarding signals and the actions that they initiate when issued via `kill`. Some signals that might otherwise stop a process instead could be used for other purposes.

A good general rule is to try TERM, INT, or HUP signals first to stop a process. If they fail, then use the KILL signal. The reason for this is that the KILL signal cannot be trapped by a process. If a signal cannot be trapped, the process cannot stop nicely. The KILL signal should be your last resort.

Processes that are waiting for unavailable NFS resources (an NFS server is down, for instance) actually respond better to a QUIT or INT signal, not the KILL signal. Processes that do not respond to any signal are known as zombies. On the output displayed by the `ps` command, `zombie` processes are shown as `<defunct>`. Zombie processes are not usually a problem and are cleared with the next reboot of the system.

A zombie exists because of a lost signal that leaves the residual information in the process table.

Who's Using My Files?

You might have encountered a situation in which you find that a device, file, or even filesystem that you need is tied up or busy. You now have a riddle to solve! Which user has the resource busy, and which of the user processes is the culprit?

The `fuser` and `lsof` commands often can provide the answer to these questions. `fuser` is available on most every UNIX system, while `lsof` is a part of the Linux command set.

To find out who has a file open, use `fuser -u filename`. The output from `fuser` is a list of PIDs that have the specified file in use. Each PID displayed can have a letter qualifier appended to it, to indicate attribute(s) of how the process has the file opened.

Using the list of PIDs supplied by `fuser`, you can find out the user(s) and what command(s) have them open. This is often the best and most cautious approach. The user(s) can be notified to stop what they are running and free the file.

In an emergency situation, the `-k` option can be used on `fuser`. With this option, `fuser` automatically issues a `kill` against each process that has the selected file open. Of course, you must be the owner of the process or be the root user for this to have any effect.

As mentioned earlier, a simple `kill` sent to a process might not cause it to stop executing. You might need to run `fuser` again or run a `ps` to see if the process has, in fact, been stopped. If not, you will need to manually attempt to stop it with a more potent signal than the default `kill`.

`lsof` gives you a very verbose output report showing every file opened by every process running on your system. On a large system, needless to say, this volume of output can be hard to work with. The obvious solution is to use something like `grep` to select the needle that you are looking for from within this large haystack.

After you have culled the desired output from `lsof`, you will have still quite a bit of information at your disposal. Each line of `lsof` output gives you the command, its PID, the user executing it, a file descriptor/attribute, the type of the file, the device that it resides on (major and minor number usually), the size of the file, its inode number, and the name of the file itself.

Whew! That is a lot of information. But if you are looking for a specific file, for example, it can easily be `grep`ed from this output. Likewise, it is helpful if you want to find all files in use by a particular user, or on a specific device.

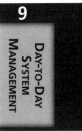

When you have selected the criteria for your file search and have selected your records from the output, you then have a list of PIDs of processes to investigate, as before. Then, by either notifying the user(s) or killing the processes yourself, you can free up the file or device.

Looking at System Logs

One of the main resources of the admin in maintaining a system is the various logs generated by your system. Solaris and Linux each have a main or primary log file, syslog for Solaris and messages for Linux. These are by no means the only logs available, though. Many applications, such as mail, ftp, the Apache Web server and numerous others generate their own log files.

Writing to the syslog or messages file is an option on any system. By configuring syslogd to run (or not) as desired, you turn system logging on or off. The volume of logging and what gets logged can be configured with a variety of options and a great degree of control. The /etc/syslog.conf file controls the operation of syslogd and contains all the options for what gets logged, when it gets logged, and where the logs are written. Each system has a default version of syslog.conf. You can modify this file and exercise a surprising degree of control over the logging on your system. You might need to make changes to the syslog.conf file, depending on the level of activity on your system and your need to capture logging information.

The output from `syslogd` can be substantial, depending on the activity on you system. The syslog.conf file gives you a way to control and better manage this important information source. The goal is to get the information that you want without having to wade through a large volume of less important messages. By modifying the syslog.conf file, you can quickly make two important changes in your log output.

1. Suppress warning, notice, and information messages that will leave only the more important or critical messages to be viewed.

2. Set up different file destinations for different importance levels or messages origins.

These two steps will make log processing and maintenance easier. Also, by separating the messages by importance or origin, you can visually see problems quickly by looking in the file that is of interest.

It is a good idea to become familiar with the logging done by critical applications on your system. Occasionally logs written by some applications are in addition to messages posted to the system log, or they might duplicate some or all of the syslog messages. It is a good idea to create checklists by application, showing where message files reside. Also, a quick summary of the most important messages or general message characteristics can be a big aid in troubleshooting application problems. For critical applications with recurring problems, these checklists can be invaluable guides when constructing scripts for monitoring error logs.

The variety of logs is not your only problem. Keeping track of where they reside and ensuring that they don't fill up your disk is a never-ending task of the admin. Again, understanding where logs are and what is being logged is important.

You might need to create scripts to monitor log sizes on a regular basis. Also, log backup, rollover, and pruning can be important steps to help avoid space problems. Refer to Chapter 6, "Logging," for an in-depth discussion of logging and log management. There you will find more detailed suggestions to help you with this task.

Check Partition Usage

Checking up on your disk space utilization is a never-ending task, as you probably well know. You hopefully are also aware that you need to respond to the problem before a partition gets totally filled, preferably before usage exceeds 90%.

Even though as root you still can write to a partition when it is at 100%, it can make some actions that you need to perform near to impossible, if not actually impossible, for lack of space. Also, when a partition reaches 100% usage, your users cannot write to it. In all likelihood, they will be experiencing problems well before that, due to some characteristics of how UNIX filesystems work. So, get to it before it is a problem.

Using `df` for Partition Management

Using the `df -kl` command, you can see all your partitions and their current state. The default output of `df` reports space in 512-byte blocks, often hard to relate to in terms of common storage sizes. Adding the `-k`, option your space will be reported in 1KB blocks (1024 bytes). The 1KB blocks map better to the megabyte (MB) and gigabyte (GB) storage capacities of today's drives. The `-l` option expands the output to report more information such as inode statistics.

You also can specify a file argument on the command line. It can be either a filesystem or an individual file in which the single filesystem will be reported. This can be handy for determining the actual filesystem where a file resides.

If you decide to write a script using `df -kl` to monitor partitions, don't forget to also watch out for inode usage approaching some percentage over 90%. You can have plenty of physical space left in a partition and have it be unusable because not enough inodes are left to create a new file. On most UNIX systems, increasing the number of inodes in a partition is a nontrivial process involving downtime for the partition.

Who (or What) Is Using Up All the Disk?

Using df will show you the status of a disk partition on your system. To find out in more detail where space is being taken up, you need to use the du command.

The du command with no options shows the total space used by the current directory and each of its subdirectories. By default, it reports the space in 512-byte blocks, but with the -k option that changes to 1KB (1024 bytes) blocks.

In a directory that has a number of subdirectories, the du output can get lengthy. The results are in order by directory name, which is not as useful when hunting for large usage. When you are looking to find where the high usage is, pipe the du output through sort and then perhaps even head to get the top 10 or top 20 directories.

```
% du -sk | sort -rn | head
```

Using the same technique, you can do a quick analysis on a single directory to find the large files. If you want to report the space used by individual files, use the -a option with du, which otherwise just reports usage by directory.

Quota Pros and Cons

One way to manage some of your disk space is by using the UNIX quota facility. Enabling quotas has both plusses and minuses associated with it, but it is a viable way to manage filesystems that are used for user space, home directories, and the like. Refer to Chapter 3, "Filesystem Administration," for more details on implementing quotas.

The obvious pro to using quotas is that this is a way for the system to help you manage user space. One of the main cons to quotas is that they can be a clerical burden, if not a nightmare. A quota needs to be set for each user who will be using space on a filesystem. With our opinions about quotas out of the way, here's the way to do quotas.

Enabling Quotas

To enable quotas on a specific filesystem, use quotaon <filesystem_name>. This sets quotas for the selected filesystem. Next, you should set the limits for each user using edquota. Typically, quotaon is started when your system is booted. The command should be included in an rc file in /etc. Often it is included in the appropriate file by your UNIX vendor but is commented out. A search of files in /etc will find it if it exists.

With `edquota`, you set a soft limit, a hard limit, and a time limit. As a user creates files, he approaches the soft limit. When a user exceeds the soft limit, a timer starts. If the time goes over the limit set, it is treated the same as exceeding the hard limit.

If the user is over the soft limit for more than the time allotted, or if the user exceeds the hard limit, no more space can be used on that filesystem to create new files or expand existing files. If the soft limit is exceeded for only a short period less than the time limit, it is ignored without consequence.

To get a quota status list of all users on a filesystem, use the `repquota` command. For each user on the filesystem, the output will show block and file usage and indicate whether the user has exceeded the limits.

Used judiciously, quotas can be an effective tool for space management. The goal is to set reasonable limits to allow users to do their work without impact, while at the same time keeping storage usage at an efficient level. This often can be a hard balance to achieve.

When Was the System Booted?

It has been our experience that the UNIX operating system is pretty resilient. We have seen some servers stay up and operating for hundreds of days at a time. But, like all computer software, UNIX can have its problems and crash on you unexpectedly. When this happens, the system often will reboot and recover without further problems.

It is fairly easy to set up scripts to monitor the systems in your environment, to check that they are up and responding. A script that periodically `pings` all critical servers, for example, is a good first step in this direction. But, depending on the time period between these checks, it is possible that a system has crashed and recovered without being noticed.

We have always liked to use `uptime` periodically as well. In a single line of output, you get a lot of information about the system. You can see how long it has been up since the last reboot, how many users are logged on, and the current load average. A short script to run `uptime` on a group of servers tells you that they are up and running. If you expect to see users logged on and you do, then you know that there is a good chance that the systems are functioning normally. This is even more true if the load averages shown are reasonable levels as well.

Not every company has the resources to purchase an expensive commercial system-monitoring software package. With a little bit of ingenuity, though, you can assemble a set of scripts that can provide the essential tools for monitoring your systems. By using ping to test connectivity, uptime to indicate responsiveness and load levels, and df to check on filesystems, you have a good start.

Is Everything Running?

You know that a system is up when it responds to a ping. With uptime, you see it has been up all month and that there are users using it, or so it seems. But are they really using it, or are they just sitting there at their computers frustrated? Is everything running on the system that should be?

Here are a couple of scenarios to illustrate what we mean. You have a server that is running your financial applications, and they depend on some database software that might not run on the same system. What happens if the database software stops because of an error?

Your users are sitting there with their screens containing data, waiting for a response, but their application is waiting for a reply from a database program that no longer is running! A simple script that runs continuously, sleeping for a few minutes between each check or perhaps cron initiated, can check for the critical processes. If a specific process is missing, it means that the database is not running. If the database is not running, steps need to be taken immediately.

Perhaps you need to be notified by something like a 911 page. Another solution instead of, or in addition to, the page is to attempt a restart. Investigate the software in question to see if there is a method for doing this. Restart the Web server, or stop and then start the database server. For some simple processes, starting them from a loop in a script, where they are restarted if they terminate, can be very effective.

Doing this kind of automated resuscitation can be very effective and can save you from a late-night page or wakeup call to drive into work. Using the commands and tools at hand such as ping and uptime, and checking for critical processes is a quick and easy way to monitor the health of your systems.

For some typical critical process checks, you can use telnet as a simple diagnostic tool. A number of critical processes will give some predictable response when they receive a connection on a specific TCP port. Some examples are lpd on port 15, sendmail on port 25, and Web servers (httpd) on port 80. You can create fairly simple scripts to test for signs of intelligent life using this technique. If you can ping a server but you don't get a response from a specific process on a known port, then it is a good bet that the process is not running or that it otherwise has ceased to function normally. Your script then can issue a page or some other form of alert to bring attention to the problem.

Are the Backups Getting Done?

We probably do not have to tell you about the importance of doing backups on your system. In any event, that is not the topic of this chapter. Checking that the backups are running successfully and doing what they are supposed to be doing is another story. Look in Chapter 16, "Backups," for further discussion on backup administration.

Any number of things can happen to cause a backup to fail partially or totally. A tape drive could need maintenance (cleaning), and you are getting errors writing to tape. The tape drive could be dead, and your backup may have failed because it could not write to the tape. There might be nothing wrong with the drive at all, but the tape in it could be write-protected. The backup software that you use might require some initial formatting of some sort on the tape, and that might not have been done, so the tape was not recognized.

We could go on and on about reasons that a backup could fail. Murphy lives! Backups fail occasionally. You need to be diligent about checking the status of the backups on your system. It is not enough to check the schedule and visually see that a tape is in the drive.

The task of checking on backups can be significant. Depending on the size of your environment and the number of backups that you do, the number of tapes that are written, and so on, it can be a full-time job for one person. You might be doing backups with a well-known commercial software package, or you might just be using `tar` or `cpio` or a backup command available on your version of UNIX. You can use more than a few different commands to get the job done.

The important point here is that you need to keep tabs on the process regularly. Monitor the status of your devices, and keep up on their maintenance. Make sure that your media is in good shape, too, because writing to an old tape can be as bad as writing a new tape on a dirty drive.

A set of scripts to scan backup logs and report status, success as well as failure, is well worth the peace of mind that it will bring.

Monitoring the success or failure of backups is a highly critical task for an administrator. If backups are failing or are not running with total success, steps should be taken to quickly correct any problems. It is too late, once you need a backup, to discover that a backup is bad.

Typical backup problems include bad media, faulty tape device(s), or out-of-date backup configuration. I often found that backups failed because a partition was moved and the configuration was not changed. Also, don't forget to update the configuration if you have

added new partitions that need to be backed up. Communication between admins at a large site is a critical issue.

Be a System Environmentalist

The environment that your system runs in is often overlooked. For large installations, the big servers are housed in a nice room with raised flooring and air-conditioning and all the comforts of the data center. This is not always the case, of course—and even if it is, some things often are overlooked.

For starters, check the specifications from your vendor(s) for power, temperature, humidity, and air flow. For medium to large-scale installations, usually a preinstallation site check is done to make sure that all the requirements are met. For smaller sites, this might be overlooked.

Air flow? What's that? The air-conditioning is running—what more do you need? We have seen sites that are nice and cool—if not cold—in the computer room. But then all the systems are jammed close together, perhaps even more than one in a cabinet, with several cabinets side by side. When we open the back door of a cabinet, it's like a sauna inside.

There might be a raised floor in the room, but there could be few vent panels in the floor; the systems might not be getting sufficient cool air through the cabinets. You might find that you meet the specifications when the systems are first installed, but you later add more memory or disks or another CPU chassis in the cabinet. If you don't check to see that a proper environment is still being maintained, you are just asking for trouble.

Unfortunately, unlike the software side of your system, checking the environment cannot usually be scripted. You might not have the expensive equipment to monitor and report on power, temperature, humidity, and air flow for your systems. Getting in the habit of a regular walkthrough to inspect the systems is a good idea. The frequency and degree of thoroughness of these checks will depend on your particular needs.

Often overlooked is the cabling between and even within system cabinets. You want to ensure that they will not be stepped on or pinched or worn by cabinet doors or rollers. Check to be sure that cables have sufficient slack so that they won't be disconnected and also so that they are not blocking airflow within the cabinet.

Reactive Administration

Reactive administration is the stuff that you do day-to-day that you cannot predict having to do from one day to the next. Some of it is trivial and not what you would class as problems: setting up users or new printer queues or the like. Some of it is not as trivial, and the rest of it is down right critical! When these requests, problems, and crises occur, all you can do is react and handle them, hopefully in a calm and collected manner.

Lowering the Defenses

In an ideal world, you would be able to put up a nice strong wall around your systems and have total control over who accesses it and when. But then there is reality—multiple systems communicating with each other, multiple admins, third-party packages, automated tools, outside vendors, remote sites, and the Web. What is an admin to do?

On a day-to-day basis, you need to decide where, when, and how to permit access to your system and its processes, when necessary. This often is part of the larger issue of system security, about which whole books have been written. Some, such as user access and other admins, are easy to handle. Others, such as access by external sites or vendors, get more difficult and also often have to consider company policy as part of the decision process.

Firefighting

Your pager goes off or your phone starts ringing, the end result of a crisis or catastrophe in the making. Something is broken or has stopped working, and you are now the focus of attention. It might be something fairly simple, or it could be a major nightmare, but you're the admin and it is your job to fix it and make things right.

The problem, though, is that very often you are dealing with a complex environment of network, computer hardware, software, and data. Where in all of this is the source of the problem, who has the solution, and what will it take to get it fixed?

Get to Know Your Environment

As an admin, you should know as much as you can about your hardware and its configuration. The same goes for the software running on the system: OS, applications, tools, and databases. When an application is installed on your system, you should know a few things about it:

- Where do the executables, configuration files, and data files reside?
- How is the application started and stopped, and is it dependent on other processes or services?
- What required processes should be running on the server? On the client?
- What are their ownership and permissions for proper operation?
- If a database is involved, where are the instance datasets located?

- Do the users log into the server, or is it a client/server type of application?
- Maintain a contact database with vendor numbers, license information, and handles, as applicable.
- For locally developed applications, include contact information for developers and DBAs, where applicable with escalation procedures.

Armed with this kind of information about each of the applications running on your system, you stand a better chance of quickly resolving problems. You don't need to have in-depth information about what is in the database or the details of how the application works. Basically, the more, you know the better chance you have of figuring out the nature and source of a problem.

Document, Document, Document

As you learn more about each application system, you can compile a folder or notebook for reference. This will help you as a refresher and also will help you communicate with other admins working on the systems.

Several companies have instituted a very helpful procedure. One or more spreadsheet or text files are created to log various events. These usually are kept separate by category such as hardware trouble calls, software trouble calls (OS and third-party applications), and in-house application problems.

Each time a call is opened with a vendor for a hardware or software problem, it is entered in the appropriate file. This then can be used to follow up on open problems and document repeat problems with the vendor, and it is invaluable in researching repeat or similar problems with software.

This turns out to be very helpful when more than a couple of admins are responsible for a medium to large-scale installation. It is time-consuming to keep everyone informed about each and every problem that they are all handling on these systems.

Although online files are great because they can be searched for keywords, they are not much help when the system is down. Generating regular hard-copy sets of critical documentation files is a good idea. Additionally, you can push a set of the files to an alternate system to provide for emergency access online if this is needed as well.

Software Versions and Patches

If you have a large mountain of details, it is hard sometimes to keep it all sorted out. This can be particularly true with multiple systems, various versions of software, and the variety of patches required to keep it current and working properly.

Our solution for this is some quick scripting to generate a text file, or perhaps several, with the list of installed software, their versions, and their installed patches. A quick cronjob to run this on a regular basis and perhaps even print it for yet another notebook keeps things current. Then, when on a call with a vendor, you can grab the hard copy or call up the file for a quick answer.

Plan for a Brighter Future

Armed with a lot of accumulated documentation on hardware and software, you should be better able to solve problems as they occur. But the best way to solve problems is to learn from experience and cut them off at the pass.

A periodic analysis of the trouble logs can help you spot recurring problems or trouble areas. Where possible, make a proactive investment and write some scripts as tools to help you in the future—perhaps to sense that a critical process is not running and send a notice. Check that critical resources are available, such as a remote database server or sufficient scratch disk space for work files. Basically, learn from the past and think ahead.

Deciphering User Requests

If we had a nickel for each time we got a call saying, "It's broken! Fix it!", we'd be rich. Very often you are given the barest description of the symptoms, and you need to figure out the true nature of the problem.

Here are some typical complaints and some insights into the cause and possible solutions. No doubt your own experiences will help you as well in the process of getting to the bottom of these and other mysteries that you will encounter.

"I Can't Log In"

One of the most common day-to-day problems is a user having access problems. The typical reasons include the following:

- A forgotten, lost, or compromised password
- A mangled shell
- A mangled .rc file
- Quota exceeded
- An attempt to log in on a system where no account exists
- Unavailability of the home directory due to NFS or network problems

Password Problems

Password problems are regular occurrences, especially in medium to large user environments. If you expire user passwords (a good security practice), a few of your users will forget their new passwords. The solution is to reset the password and then have them change it again.

User education on proper password safeguards is another good practice. Expiring passwords on a regular basis and using a tool such as Crack to monitor user password choices will help reduce password and security issues.

Mangled Shell or .rc Files

Mangled shells and .rc files are rare occurrences in our experience, but they do happen occasionally. Again, it is just a matter of correcting the problem by replacing the bent file. This might require a restore from backup of the .rc file, but it is still usually a quick fix.

To simplify both user setup and troubleshooting, give your users a standard .profile—for example, one that is write-protected (owned by root with permissions 755). At the end of that file, invoke something like $HOME/.userenv. Creating an empty .userenv in their home directory allows the user to customize the environment but doesn't allow changes to critical settings. This also reduces the number of places where problems can exist. The assumption is that things should work with just the standard file (.profile, for example), so you can test by commenting out the .userenv line and see if the problem continues. If so, your user needs to figure out what was changed to cause the problem.

The Dreaded Quota

When a user exceeds the quota set on his home directory, it needs to be corrected. If it is not remedied within the allowed time period, your problem user can experience login problems. Then you need to step in to assist in cleanup or to suspend or modify the quota until the user can reduce his space usage. We don't care for quotas, and we use them only when all else fails.

No Account

In a medium or large environment, not all users will have accounts on all systems. We have seen this handled in a variety of ways, for a variety of reasons.

In an effort to keep UID assignments consistent across systems, some create an account on each one for every user. The account is disabled on the systems that the user will not access.

Another approach is to use some form of menu to provide each user easy access to only the systems where they have authorized accounts. The menu approach also helps with security because users easily can be blocked from access to shells and applications that they are not permitted to use.

NFS or Network Problems

We try to avoid using NFS mounts as a general rule. Sometimes, however, it is unavoidable to provide a consistent set of files across multiple systems or to reduce the duplication of file space.

Improvements in systems performance and even the NFS software performance have made NFS more viable for use in production environments. Every effort should be made to ensure that the NFS server performs well and stays up and online if it is a component of production systems.

"I Can't Read My Email"

Electronic mail (email) is now the backbone of most companies, who use it to communicate internally for corporate communications. Email also is used to communicate with vendors as well as with customers on a frequent basis.

Many companies encourage their customers to communicate with them via email instead of tying up expensive phone and personnel resources to handle questions or complaints. With the growth of the Web, this is even more true with the availability of Web-based response forms used to communicate with the customer.

If email stops working, even for a single person or a small group, it can be critical to get the problem resolved quickly.

Typical problems affecting email are as follows:

- Login problems
- Quota problems
- Deleted mailspool
- Efforts to read on the wrong system
- Misconfiguration of IMAP/POP server pointer
- Hanging mail processes caused by excessive mail
- Lock contention problems when user starts more than one session reading mail

9

DAY-TO-DAY
SYSTEM
MANAGEMENT

Login Problems

Login problems were covered earlier in this chapter in a bit more detail. To read mail, the user first needs to be logged in for proper authentication by the email server. Typically, resolving the login issues will solve the email problem as well.

Quota Problems (Read or Receive)

We discussed quotas in the first part of this chapter and said that there are pros and cons to using quotas. Here is one of the negative aspects. If a user has exceeded the quota set on his home directory, it can affect his capability to read email.

The typical user email configuration creates an "inbox" as a file somewhere in the user's home directory or a subdirectory of the home directory. When quotas are exceeded, it is possible that new mail will not be written to the user's inbox. Then you will get a complaint call that mail cannot be read.

The solution is to have the user resolve the quota issue by doing some cleanup in his home directory. Barring that, you will need to suspend quotas for the user using `edquota` or, for the entire filesystem, using `quotaoff`.

You might have figured out by now that we are not big fans of quotas, and this is just one example of why that is the case. There are enough unexpected sources of problems on a computer system without artificially creating more.

Deleted Mailspool

At one time or another, every novice admin creates a problem by inadvertently deleting a file that is critically important. One of these files is the mailspool or mailqueue file (actually, a directory in most cases).

The mail daemon, sendmail, places both incoming and outgoing mail in the mail queue when it gets busy. When sendmail gets caught up, it then processes the mail queue, placing incoming mail in the users' individual mailbox files and sending the outgoing mail from the queue.

Deleting the mail queue directory and the files contained in the directory will affect mail operation. Unfortunately, if mail files are deleted, the incoming or outgoing mail that they contained will be lost. It is a good idea to get familiar with the version of sendmail on your system as well as its auxiliary problems and files

Trying to Read Mail on the Wrong System

Users often have accounts on more than one system or server in a company. Each system is accessed to use a specific application typically. One of the systems is designated as the "home system" for the user, where his home directory resides and where he can read his email.

If your users have regular logon accounts on several systems where they can then run different applications, they might forget which system they are on when checking mail. Your user might try to start up his favorite mail reader, but there is no configuration on the system to point to the mail server. Oops! He can't read mail.

One solution to this problem is to provide the user's home directory to all systems using NFS. This will work, but it is not a solution that I personally like very much. I am more in favor of the user "home system," which enables the user to read mail and create his own files. This avoids the situations created when NFS problems arise.

IMAP/POP Server Pointer Misconfigured

Two popular email protocols are the Internet Message Access Protocol (IMAP) and the Post Office Protocol (POP). Both are used by email servers running on non-UNIX servers typically. To read and write email, users employ various email clients, including elm and pine.

The email client needs to be configured with the correct address (pointer) and protocol settings to work properly. If the client configuration is changed, corrupted, or deleted, then the user will not be capable of reading or writing email.

In most cases, the client and its configuration will be standardized among your users. But different clients might be available as choices to your users. At a minimum, each user should know the name of the server being used to send and receive mail.

A quick fix to this problem, if you use standardized client configuration, is to push a good copy of the configuration file to the user's home directory. If this is not the case, then you will most likely have to check the settings of the user's email client and correct them as needed.

sendmail Hangs or There Is a Locking Problem

These two issues often are related to each other. If the user has a lot of backed-up email due to inactivity, sendmail might hang trying to process the backlog. The same thing might occur due to just a single very large email.

Sometimes due to general system loads or the problem just described, the user loses patience. One typical response is to try to start another session or window to read mail. The result, rather than enhancing the process of reading mail, is to create a nasty lock contention problem. Sometimes the only solution is to get the user to log off, kill off hung mail processes, clear the lock file, and start again. If the problem is excess mail or a single large email remedial, cleanup by the root user could be the only solution.

9

DAY-TO-DAY SYSTEM MANAGEMENT

"I Can't Send My Email"

This problem is one that often goes hand in hand with not being able to read email. Similar reasons are the cause of this general problem:

- Quota problems (again!)
- Misconfiguration of SMTP server pointer
- Off-site connectivity problem

Quota Problems

Quotas are less often a problem with sending mail than they are with reading mail. But the nature of quotas and their penalty can be a source of a variety of problems when they are exceeded. See the other topics in this chapter related to quotas to get a better picture of what they are and what their effects can be. You will get a sense of our opinions regarding quotas.

SMTP Server Pointer Misconfiguration

Simple Mail Transfer Protocol (SMTP) is the standard email protocol found on most every UNIX system. It is used very frequently by Internet mail servers because of its ease of implementation. Like IMAP and POP, if the user's client is not properly configured, email fails.

The solution options for the problem are the same as well. Either replace the configuration file for the client with a known good copy or manually fix the user's configuration to correct errors.

Off-Site Connectivity Problem

This is a fancy way to say that the network is down in some way. If the user's home server is not also the user's email server, then they are dependent on a good network connection to send and receive email.

Network issues could affect NFS as well. If the user home directories are NFS-mounted and NFS is not functioning well, the result could be email problems.

General network issues also can affect email if, for example, a local email server (such as one for a department or business unit) must communicate with the outside world through a central corporate mail server. If connectivity between the two is marginal or down, mail will pile up in the local queue until a proper connection is re-established.

Often in larger company environments, a group or department other than the systems administrators handles the network infrastructure—and, therefore, problems. You might find that you have to coordinate your efforts with this group to get complete problem resolution. The more you know about network issues and your local infrastructure, the better you will be at working with the outside group.

"These New Guys Need Accounts"

One of the most frequent tasks of an admin is adding users. Depending on the size of your site, it can be a cumbersome task. Often complicating things is the issue of where to create accounts for each user. On which systems should this be done?

When working at a site with numerous applications and a large user base, scripting often is the answer. Look at whether users can be classified by work area or job classification. Then the script can be a matter of selecting the proper class or category of the user after entering name and department descriptive information. Then the script hopefully can be made smart enough to figure out on which systems accounts should be created.

An additional task related to new users that can be scripted is environment setup. The same script also can be responsible for pushing appropriate user startup and environment scripts, again based on the system and applications that the user will have access to.

It is not that the task of setting up an account and moving scripts is difficult. When it occurs often and is not simple or the same for each user, it is good to figure out the rules and let the script handle the task and get it right.

"We Need a Group Account for Our Group Web Page and Mail"

A group account means different things to different people. It can be implemented in more than one way as well. There are two parts to this request in reality. One is a group account or space for the "group Web page" content; the other is the mail account.

To set up a group account, create a new group ID (GID) entry in /etc/group. Then add a user account with the group name and assign it the new GID. The common area containing the Web page content and associated files can be owned by this "master group" account.

When there is a need for multiple users to have access to a group account or files owned by a group account, security and accountability need to be considered. We do not like having a single account on which everyone knows the password. Instead, we like to use one of two methods, depending on company policy. You can add each user who needs access to the group in /etc/group, thereby granting them access to all files in the same group. You do need to make sure that all files associated with this group or project are owned by the group account or, at the very least, are assigned the GID of the group with permissions to allow all members required access privileges.

The other method involves creating a number of alias accounts, user accounts with the same UID and GID of the "master group" account. Each alias account then is assigned to a different user, who can set his own password. Then the knowledge of the password to the master account can be limited and controlled, and there is more accountability as well.

"<Insert Application Name Here> Is Broken"

There is no substitute for experience when troubleshooting application problems. That's the bad news. The good news is that a good set of documentation speeds the process of gaining that experience. As mentioned earlier in this chapter, documentation is a good investment for an admin.

If a documentation standard is available, use it. Otherwise, create your own, perhaps using some of the suggestions made earlier. Having a source of information available when troubleshooting problems refreshes your memory or saves you from having to chase down the local guru for the application.

It will help you to know where the application lives—what server, what filesystem, what directory? Where are the configuration files? Is a program included with the application for configuration maintenance? Are tools included to help you get status on the application?

Putting together this kind of information serves as a good learning exercise for you while you are compiling it, and it will help the others in your group when they need to solve problems.

When problems with an application arise, log them; when solved, note what was done to fix the problem. If you have support with the vendor, document all the contact information, phone numbers, contract numbers or support handles, and the like. Log each call instance to the tech support. If you have to hand off the problem to another admin, it will help that admin to pick up where you left off.

Obviously, we can't address specific problems and their solutions in the space in this book. We can tell you that keeping notes and logs in a consistent and diligent manner goes a long way toward filling the gaps in experience when troubleshooting. It also helps to spread the knowledge around a group when you have documentation that can be shared and learned from.

Request for New Hardware

A new hardware request in most organizations has two parts to it: technical and budget. The budget part is not something that we can help you with or that you, as an admin, usually should have to deal with (hopefully your manager has taken care of that for you). The technical portion is typically something that you will have to contend with.

New hardware requests start out primarily as a planning exercise. There are usually a few questions to be answered and possibly some issues to be resolved before receiving and installing new hardware.

With a new hardware request, the first issue is whether the new hardware is supported by your version of UNIX. Most often this is a question of whether a driver is available for the hardware that is compatible with your UNIX. Between the vendor for the new hardware and the vendor for your system, you should be able to get an answer.

Another question that you need to answer is whether you have the capacity and resources to support the new hardware. By this, we mean issues such as available slots for new cards or physical space for new drives, for example. Also, do you have available SCSI address space, if needed, on the bus where the device will be attached?

Again, keeping accurate and fairly detailed documentation on your hardware can be beneficial and important:

- It helps to communicate with management regarding hardware issues.
- Share information with other admins at your site about systems that might not be their primary responsibility.
- Provide configuration information to vendors in support of new hardware or software requests.

Request for New Software/License

New software is similar to new hardware. You need to verify that the software being requested is compatible with your current version of the OS. Often requirements for specific additional patches also must be applied to your system. In addition, hardware requirements need to be verified to meet vendor requirements before installation.

If you are going to install the new software along with other applications on a server, you should ensure that all are compatible with the others—not only the individual applications, but their specific patch requirements as well.

Check to see what your typical available resources are, including memory, disk space, and any other system resource requirements cited by the vendor. Installation of the package will be much easier if you identify all the requirements in advance and verify that they are met. You might still miss one or two, but that is better than having to resolve these critical issues at the last minute. It can be a real problem to find out that you need to get more memory or disk and have to wait for budget, then ordering delays, and installation with possible downtime. You want to plan the time to get everything in place before it is time to do the installation.

We have found that most vendors are very helpful in supplying installation manuals and materials in advance to help you in your planning. Often they provide useful worksheets to help in the preparations necessary before actually starting the install.

This can be exceedingly useful to have in advance. Often some of the requirements entail changes to kernel parameters or other configuration files that require a reboot to take effect. We have worked at many sites where this kind of activity (reboots) has to be planned in advance and scheduled for off-hours or maintenance windows.

When a new software package is installed, you should include information such as kernel parameters, special services, and special user accounts in your system and application documentation. It can be very helpful to know which applications required specific kernel parameter values or services. Otherwise, another admin might inadvertently break an application when making a change that seems to be harmless.

If the software is licensed, you will need to be familiar with the method or mechanism used to enforce the license. Licenses come in various types. Typically a software package will be licensed to run on a specific server. You usually need to provide the vendor with the hardware ID of your server so that a proper license key can be constructed. Most vendors will want the ID number reported by the `hostid` command.

If you have other applications running on a server, they might share the same license server software and key file. Be sure that you keep backup copies of the license key file before adding new software license keys. It is a good idea to do the license maintenance during a quiet time on the system and test all applications sharing the same license server. You will be a happy hero after you have installed the new software if you don't break the other applications due to license key issues.

License keys are yet another piece of important information that should be kept with system documentation. We strongly suggest keeping a hard-copy record of each key supplied by your software vendors in a file or notebook. Also, it is a good idea to print the license key file(s) after each change, date them, and keep them to record what changes were made when and for what reason. You will thank yourself for it someday.

Best Practices

Proactive Administration

- The root account is very important. Limit and control access to this critical account.

- Change the root password on a regular basis.

- Give each root user his own personal account. Each root user should use su to access the root account from there.

- Provide root access to nonadmin users via sudo to provide control and accountability.

- Document system configuration, hardware and software, as completely as possible.

- Document application software, including vendor contact information, file locations, license keys, and message file locations.

- Keep OS and application software patched according to vendor recommendations two to four times per year.

- Log hardware and software trouble calls, with detailed description of problem and solution. Include vendor reference numbers and contacts.

- Log internal (in-house) application problems the same way that you log OS and third-party software problems.

- Analyze system and application logs to spot trends or recurring problems.

Reactive Administration

- Log hardware and software trouble calls, with detailed description of problem and solution. Include vendor reference numbers and contacts.

- Log internal (in-house) application problems the same way that you log OS and third-party software problems.

- Analyze system and application logs to spot trends or recurring problems.

Online References

Software Web resources:

lsof software:

ftp server: ftp://vic.cc.purdue.edu/pub/tools/unix/lsof

sudo software: http://courtesan.com/sudo

9

DAY-TO-DAY
SYSTEM
MANAGEMENT

ftp server: `ftp://ftp.cs.colorado.edu/pub/sudo`

top software:

ftp server: `ftp://ftp.groupsys.com:/pub/top`

Linux resources on the Web:

Linux World: `http://www.linuxworld.com`

Linux Journal (magazine): `http://www.linuxjournal.com`

Linux News: `http://www.linux.com`

Linux Online: `http://www.linux.org`

General system admin Web resources:

UNIX Guru Universe (UGU): `http://www.ugu.com`

BigAdmin: `http://www.sun.com/bigadmin`

Sys Admin Magazine: `http://www.samag.com`

UNIX system administrator's resources:
`http://www.stokely.com/unix.sysadm.resources`

UNIX resources on the Internet: `http://herbie.ucs.indiana.edu/internet.html`

Solaris sysadmin tools: `http://darkwing.uoregon.edu/~hak/unix.html`

Critical Subsystems

PART

II

The X Window
System

by Robert Banz

In This Chapter

Introduction

This chapter is an overview to certain X Window System administrative and advanced user tasks. It is not a basic introduction to X, and it is assumed that the reader has a basic knowledge of using the X Window System. Many books accomplish this basic introduction, including Jon Lasser's *Think Unix*, published by Que. Before you read on, you should know how to use a mouse, you should know what an X server is, and you should have spent some time using it. We'll start by taking a look at the installation layout of the X Window System installation. Then you'll discover how to customize the behavior of some of the more important elements of the system, such as its security features, as well as fonts and keyboard layout.

The X Directory Structure

As anyone familiar with Unix and Unix-like operating systems knows, things are "just a bit different" from one implementation to another. The X Window System is no exception. Vendors probably do this to make more money off certifications…. Conspiracies aside, that's the way it is, so we'll have to deal with it. Some vendors have taken the time to integrate the X directory structure tightly with their operating system's tree, while most tend to keep the X software and configuration files isolated in a single section of the tree. There are benefits to both methods, and it's all generally a matter of personal preference as to which is better. Because the focus of this book is Red Hat Linux and Solaris, we can look at two quite differing styles of X installation.

XFree86 Style

Most readers have been exposed to the preferred directory layout of XFree86, a distribution of the X Window System targeted at Intel-based operating systems, which include Linux, FreeBSD, and OpenBSD, as well as some commercial Intel Unix variants. Although these operating systems vary widely when it comes to their directory layout, XFree86 is generally found in the same places—neatly under the /usr/X11R6 (or sometimes /usr/X11R6.4) directory tree.

Solaris Style

The distribution of the X Window System that is provided with Sun Microsystems' Solaris operating system is very common, but it has a strange directory layout rooted deeply in its history. You can find most of the X Windows files under /usr/openwin, named for Open Windows—Sun bestowed that name upon its windowed operating environment from the time before it was X-based (ever heard of NeWS?). Since then, the preferred Solaris environment had switched to the Common Desktop Environment (CDE), which is housed in the /usr/dt directory tree. The "greeter" program, dtlogin, is located in /usr/dt, and the X server that it runs is in /usr/openwin. Most of the shared libraries are in /usr/openwin/lib, and, er, it's kind of confusing.

Navigating the X Distribution

As hinted in the two previous examples, the biggest obstacle to fully grasping all there is to know about X is knowing where everything is. So, to show you the how and why of where things are—and to avoid having to show 12 locations for each configuration file— we'll use symbolic names such as $LibDir to refer to portions of paths that vary from system to system. These same symbolic names are used as part of the X Window build system (xmkmf and imake) when creating makefiles for building X applications and the X Window System itself. If you can find a directory full of files ending in .def and .tmpl on your system, you could very well figure out these paths for other operating systems on your own.

In this chart, we'll provide you with the symbolic name of the path, a short description of it, and what this path is in an out-of-the box build of X11 Release 6.4, Red Hat Linux, Solaris, and IRIX. IRIX is given as an example of a more "integrated" configuration of the X Window System, where bits are scattered to different places in the host operating system's directory tree.

Symbolic Name	Description/Contents	Values
ProjectRoot	"Top" of the X Window System installation	X11R6.4: /usr/X11R6.4 Red Hat: /usr/X11R6/lib Solaris: /usr/openwin IRIX: —
ShLibDir	X Window shared libraries	X11R6.4: /usr/X11R6.4/lib Red Hat: /usr/X11R6/lib Solaris: /usr/openwin/lib IRIX: /usr/lib
UsrLibDir	Nonshared X libraries	X11R6.4: /usr/X11R6.4/lib Red Hat: /usr/X11R6/lib Solaris: /usr/openwin/lib IRIX: /usr/lib
AdmDir	System log files	X11R6.4: /usr/adm Red Hat: /usr/adm Solaris: /usr/adm IRIX: /usr/adm

Symbolic Name	Description/Contents	Values
BinDir	Binaries/program files	X11R6.4: /usr/X11R6.4/bin Red Hat: /usr/X11R6/bin Solaris: /usr/openwin/bin IRIX: /usr/bin/X11
ConfigDir	Build system configuration files	X11R6.4: /usr/X11R6.4/lib/X11/config Red Hat: /usr/X11R6/lib/X11/config Solaris: /usr/openwin/lib/config IRIX: /usr/lib/X11/config
FontDir	Font directories	X11R6.4: /usr/X11R6.4/lib/X11/fonts Red Hat: /usr/X11R6/lib/X11/fonts Solaris: /usr/openwin/lib/X11/fonts IRIX: /usr/lib/X11/fonts
LibDir	Support files	X11R6.4: /usr/X11R6.4/lib/X11 Red Hat: /usr/X11R6/lib/X11 Solaris: /usr/openwin/lib/X11 IRIX: /usr/lib/X11
ServerConfigDir	X server configuration files	X11R6.4: /usr/X11R6.4/lib/X11/xserver Red Hat: /usr/X11R6/lib/X11/xserver Solaris: — IRIX: —
VarDirectory	X logs and system-specific configuration files	X11R6.4: /var/X11 Red Hat: /var/X11 Solaris: — IRIX: /var/X11
XAppLoadDir	Application defaults	X11R6.4: /usr/X11R6.4/lib/X11/app-defaults Red Hat: /usr/X11R6/lib/X11/app-defaults Solaris: /usr/openwin/lib/app-defaults IRIX: /usr/lib/X11/app-defaults

Symbolic Name	Description/Contents	Values
XdmDir	Configuration files and scripts for xdm	X11R6.4: /usr/X11R6.4/lib/X11/xdm Red Hat: /etc/X11/xdm Solaris: /usr/openwin/lib/X11/xdm IRIX: /var/X11/xdm
XinitDir	Configuration files and scripts for xinit	X11R6.4: /usr/X11R6.4/lib/X11/xinit Red Hat: /usr/X11R6/lib/X11/xinit Solaris: /usr/openwin/lib/X11/xinit IRIX: /usr/lib/X11/xinit

Not-So-Basic Basics

The X Window System is network-based. In fact, while other operating systems have needed to look to external applications such as PC Anywhere or Citrix to enable remote access to graphical applications, Unix has had this capability since the mid-1980s, thanks to X. It is also important to note that Unix was not the only operating system to integrate X in a major way. Digital Equipment Corporation's VMS operating system used a port of the X Window System, called DECWindows, as its graphical interface. The DECWindows environment was also available in Ultrix, DEC's BSD Unix port. Other major operating systems, such as Microsoft Windows and MacOS, have ports of X available to them—some provide only X server functionality, and some provide the libraries to build and run X applications locally, making X a viable platform for highly portable development.

X applications require a bidirectional data stream to communicate between themselves and the X server, where their user input and output is handled. On Unix-like operating systems, a string identifying the display that the application is destined for is most commonly found in the environment variable DISPLAY. A display setting typically looks like this:

```
holly.membrain.com:0.0
```

The first portion describes the host on which you are attempting to display the application. It can be a valid hostname (something that your operating system's gethostbyname() function will think is sane) or an IP address in numeric format, such as 192.168.3.1. The second section, after the colon, describes the display number before the period and then screen number. A host can—but typically does not—house multiple displays (a display is a collection of input and output devices that are tied together). When using IP, the first display (0) is accessed on port 6000, and each successive display is allocated port 6000 + *n*, where *n* is the display number. The screen number refers to the video screens allocated to a specific display. Usually there's only one (referred to as 0), but multihead displays are becoming more common.

Setting the DISPLAY in an environment variable is not the only option for telling an application where to go. Most X applications also accept a command-line argument of -display, followed by a display string:

gate% xterm -display fritz.membrain.com:0.0

This works for 99% of the X applications that you will encounter, but keep these pointers in mind:

- Not all applications support this.
- Some that don't might support it under a different argument name, such as -d.
- Those that don't support it might listen to DISPLAY, or they might not. As with anything, your mileage might vary.

If our machine name happens to be holly.membrain.com, you could use either of these settings as your display, and it would get to the right place:

holly.membrain.com:0.0

Or, the shorter version:

localhost:0.0

However, neither of these is recommended for local display access. Instead, this much shorter and simpler code is recommended:

:0.0

If just being shorter isn't reason enough for you to choose it (that should be enough—all system administrators should be lazy by nature), increased performance should be. When set using a hostname or IP address, the X traffic is chopped up into TCP packets and forced through your host's network stack, causing a lot of unnecessary work for information to end up not going very far. Using the "short" version described causes the connection to be made through a *Unix domain socket*, which, at its most basic, provides a bidirectional pipe between your application and X server. This means no little packets, no network stack, and better interactive performance.

A third method of transport is available on some systems that have System V (SYSV)–style shared memory (most modern systems do.) Like the Unix domain socket, it is a local-only transport, meaning that you can't use it from another machine. Called *shared memory transport,* it works by allocating a chunk of memory that both the server and the client can quickly access using standard memory operations. For common purposes, both it and the Unix domain socket will give about the same performance. Where the shared memory transport really shines, though, is when manipulating and displaying large images.

Shared memory transport has its limitations, however. Most systems place a restriction on the number and size of shared memory resources available to applications, and, as a result, restrictions are placed on how many shared memory connections can be open by the X server to prevent system-wide resource exhaustion. There have also been problems regarding security tied to the shared memory transport. Although many have been resolved, you might find that the risk is unacceptable on some systems. Most applications that use shared memory transport negotiate for it with the server on their own. Some X Window implementations, such as that on SGI's IRIX operating system, allow you to ask for shared memory transport directly by setting your display to `shm:0`. (What happens if you have a machine on your network called shm, though?)

Security

An X server is a network service, and, as with any network service, security must be an issue. As you might expect, a remote X application is expected to be capable of doing almost anything to a display. *Almost anything* means just that. A remote X connection can open and modify windows, respond to input events, and grab the contents of portions of the screen. There are even X extensions to provide access to a workstation's audio devices. These features, of course, can be used for evil purposes as well, including these:

- **Nuisance attacks**—A favorite among novice X Window System users once they've found out about the `-display` option is popping up the popular xeyes application on their friends' displays. (Incidentally, some other applications that are good for this are xroach, in which roaches hide under the windows and scurry when exposed, and xcrabs, in which little mites eat the screen's background image. You can find these applications at your favorite FTP site.)

- **"Real" attacks**—Any application can intercept and interject input or grab the contents of an area of the screen or window, making possible much less humorous exploits of the X architecture. The most basic and perhaps most potentially dangerous of these is password sniffing.

Host-Based Authorization

A "first response" to the keyboard-sniffing problem is to use a function of the X protocol that allows an application to *grab*, or get exclusive access to, the input device. The secure keyboard option of xterm uses this function (it is typically the first option of the Ctrl+left mouse button menu, and it also can be bound to a key sequence—more on that later). Many users have found it good practice to enable this typing information, such as a password or a PIN, that could cause them trouble when compromised.

The second step is to keep applications from remote hosts—or, at least, remote hosts that you don't want to have access to your X server. To this end, the X server has a host-based access control list, manipulated by the xhost command. To see the current status of the X access list, just type xhost with no arguments:

```
gate%  xhost
access control enabled, only authorized clients can connect
INET:gate.membrain.com
INET:localhost
```

This means that xhost-based authentication is enabled. Specific hosts that have been granted access to this server are listed next. On systems that are using host-based access control, it is typically initially set to *localhost* and the hostname of the machine. To completely disable access control, use the command xhost +. This is dangerous because anyone who has TCP access to your machine (potentially the entire Internet) can access your display.

```
gate%  xhost +
access control disabled, clients can connect from any host
INET:gate.membrain.com
INET:localhost
```

As said, this is probably a bad idea, and you might want to turn the restrictions back on with xhost -:

```
gate%  xhost -
access control enabled, only authorized clients can connect
INET:gate.membrain.com
INET:localhost
```

To be slightly more picky about whom you allow access to, you can manipulate the access control list by adding to the xhost + statement above a hostname or IP address of the host that you want to allow access from:

```
gate%  xhost +fritz.membrain.com
fritz.membrain.com being added to access control list
```

A concern with host-based access control is that it's just that—everyone on fritz. membrain.com is allowed to access the display. Depending on the environment, this might be sufficient. However, allowing access by any user from a machine that might be accessed by a number of people outside your administrative control might not be advisable. For that, you need the xauth command, and you'll want to read on.

> **Note**
>
> For further information on the xhost command, see the manual page provided with your X distribution.

xauth: Stronger Authorization Methods

The next step in access control is user-based, relying on some individualized piece of information to allow an application access to the server. To that end, the first of these methods devised was called MIT-MAGIC-COOKIE-1. Developed at MIT, it works with xdm (more on this later) generating a random string (the "magic cookie") at the time of user login and storing it in a file that the user has access to—typically a file named .Xauthority in the user's home directory. A client X application then reads this file, finds the cookie that corresponds to the host it is trying to connect to, and presents it to the target server when establishing the connection. If you are in an environment where home directories are shared across machines that you will be running applications from, X applications should be capable of displaying back to the workstation that you logged into without adding them with xhost.

This is convenient for the "shared file space" environment, but it is not out of the question to use MIT-MAGIC-COOKIE-1 without it. To do so requires the manipulation of the data within the .Xauthority file, which is done with the command xauth. The basics of what needs to happen are listed here:

1. Extract the magic cookie for the particular display that you want to connect to.
2. Copy the extracted information to the remote system.
3. Import the magic cookie into the remote system or account's .Xauthority file.

There are a few ways to do this. The first is to extract the contents, save them to a file, copy the file to the remote machine, and then import them from that file. Sounds like a few steps, and it is—there's an easier way to do it using rsh and a pipe. (If you're wondering, "Why don't you use ssh?" you should be—just assume that you don't have ssh for now because, if you did, you probably wouldn't need to be doing this.)

```
xauth extract - $DISPLAY | rsh <remotehost> xauth merge -
```

Of course, to do this, you'll need to run this command before logging into any remote server and expecting to run an X application. Here is a script, called xrlogin, that does this and makes sure that your DISPLAY variable gets set correctly on the remote machine. Because this uses the rlogin command, it does not propagate the DISPLAY setting. However, it does propagate the TERM setting, so the appropriate DISPLAY setting is piggy-backed on the TERM setting, requiring the target system to unsplit this variable during login. The appropriate code snippet for this is listed afterward.

```sh
#!/bin/sh
#
# at the very least we need a hostname
#

if [ $# -lt 1 ]; then
    echo "usage: xrlogin hostname [ username ]"
    exit
fi

#
# set the host and username
#

r_host=${1}
r_user=${2:-`whoami`}

#
# display name must be fully qualified
#

if [ "$DISPLAY" = ":0" -o "$DISPLAY" = ":0.0" ]; then
    if [ "$REM_DISPLAY" != "" ]; then
        disp=$REM_DISPLAY
    else
        disp=`hostname`$DISPLAY
    fi
fi

#
# if we have a display and a magic cookie, propagate the cookie
#

if [ -n ${disp} ]; then
    foo=`xauth extract - ${disp} 2> /dev/null`
    if [ "$foo" = "" ]; then
```

```
        echo "No authority propagated"
    else
        xauth extract - ${disp} | rsh ${r_host} -l ${r_user} xauth merge -
        echo "Auth OK to ${disp} from ${r_user}@${r_host}"
    fi
    # munge the TERM variable
    TERM=$disp.$TERM
    export TERM
fi

#
# exec the connection
#

exec rlogin ${r_host} -l ${r_user} -e -8
```

The appropriate magic for the target system's shell—this is in csh/tcsh format for a
.cshrc—should be modified appropriately for other shell types:

```
if ($TERM =~ *.*) then
set foo=$TERM
setenv TERM $foo:e
setenv DISPLAY $foo:r
unset foo
endif
```

At this point, it is appropriate to mention that if you are using ssh or any of its functional
equivalents, such as OpenSSH, none of this should be necessary. Why should you be
using ssh? One of its features, called X Forwarding, sets up a channel for your X
Window applications to communicate with your local X server through the encrypted
SSH channel. It does this by listening on a TCP port on the remote machine that would
typically be allocated to an X server—usually the first unused port after the one that
would have been allocated for display number 10. It then sets the DISPLAY variable in the
remote environment to the appropriate setting, and it also takes care of setting up an
appropriate .Xauthority entry for that display so that unauthorized users cannot take
advantage of it. Some ssh clients for other operating systems, such as TeraTerm for
Windows, also support X forwarding.

Other Authentication Schemes

The MIT-MAGIC-COOKIE-1 authorization scheme is not the only scheme supported,
but it is the one most commonly used. Other authorization schemes include XDM-
AUTHORIZATION-1, which works by encrypting the authorization cookie, making it
more resistant to network sniffing attacks. SUN-DES-1 is a scheme that relies on Sun's
Secure RPC mechanism.

Turning On Security

Not all X11 distributions come configured by default to use X authorization, and they rely totally on xhost-style authorization. In fact, some operating system vendors, such as SGI in earlier releases of the IRIX operating system, turned off even that by placing xhost + in their X startup scripts. Steps to take to turn on X authorization will be covered later when we look at configuring xdm.

Customizing the Environment (as a User)

For the most part, almost every aspect of the X Window System can be customized on a per-user basis. We'll take a look at some of the customizations that can be done, and, later, we'll look at how integrate the changes and make some others to the system's default environment.

.xsession

In most environments, a user can customize the entire environment from the command .xsession (usually a shell script), located in the user's home directory. When the user is logged in and this script exists, it is executed in lieu of the system's standard session. For example, a simple, correct, and completely useless .xsession could consist of the following:

```
#/bin/sh
exit
```

When the unlucky possessor of such an X session tries to log in (via X), the session would immediately end, and the user would be presented again with the login screen. To make the session slightly more useful, we can add the xterm application to the script. We'll make an assumption that the OS or clueful system administrator has been thoughtful enough to include $BinDir in the default execution path for the shell.

```
#/bin/sh
xterm
```

That doesn't do much, but we're getting somewhere. The user is presented with a single xterm window (but no window management functionality), usually in the upper-left corner of the screen as shown in Figure 10.1. When this window is terminated (by the user exiting the shell that is in it), the session will close.

FIGURE 10.1

A display running just an xterm.

To add a bit more functionality, you should add a window manager to the mix. For the sake of example, we're going to use the only window manager that comes with X: twm. (Yes, twm is probably not the window manager of choice nowadays, but it's the only one we're "sure" to have, and some people still like it.) When it's executed, the window manager will not exit until it is killed in some way, so it will have to run in the background.

```
#/bin/sh
twm &
xterm
```

Now you can at least drag your window around—you're well on your way to a usable X environment. To add other applications to your environment, just add them (backgrounded) to your session—of course, before the "terminal" program (the one that isn't in the background).

FIGURE 10.2

A display running an xterm, *and the twm window manager.*

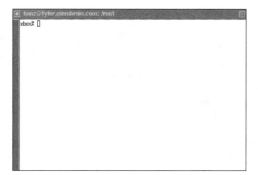

Many more modern window managers (some of which have become more than window managers, almost entire environments) have facilities to manage the launching and running of other applications integrated into them, and they can be placed by themselves (and not run in the background) in a user .xsession file. Examples of these window managers include fvwm, enlightenment, and AfterStep.

SGI's IRIX takes a different tack for X session termination. It uses a small program called reaper, which is placed as the terminal program in the session. Reaper terminates when a property called _SGI_SESSION_PROPERTY is removed from the display. (This is done using a utility called xprop—see the script /usr/bin/X11/endsession on an SGI; the way it handles the X session is pretty nifty.)

Resources

Who decided that the sky would be blue? Or that the grass would be green? Or that the length of that hill would be 100 feet tall instead of 200 feet? And, when they did, where did they record all this information so that the sky could see what color it was supposed to be and the hill could tell how tall it should be? And then, wouldn't it be neat if when you got bored of the green grass, you could simply tell it (and any new grass) to be "lemon chiffon" by putting its new color in some "well known place"? The designers of the X Window System thought this would be a good idea. (Maybe not some of the specifics, though—I don't think I could deal with lemon chiffon–colored grass.)

For X applications that choose to "follow the rules" and use the toolkits, almost every bit of every widget is identified by a resource name. Here's an example: Run the application editres (it's included in most X distributions). From the Commands pull-down menu, choose Get Tree. Then click on your favorite xterm window. The editres window should now look something like Figure 10.3.

FIGURE 10.3

editres displaying the resource tree for an xterm.

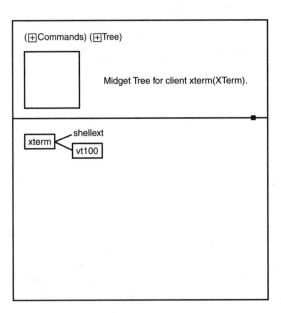

Now click on the box labeled vt100. This refers to the vt100 terminal emulation window that is part of the `xterm` application. From the Commands menu, select Show Resource Box. A window similar to Figure 10.4 should appear.

FIGURE 10.4

editres displaying the resources for the vt100 widget.

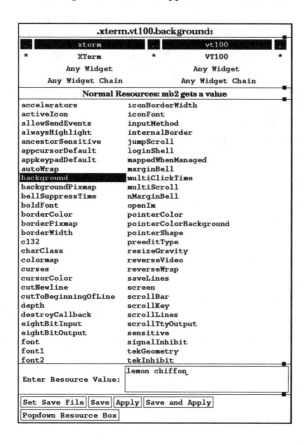

Choose Background from the list of available resources for this widget, and type in **lemon chiffon** in the box labeled Edit Resource Value at the bottom. Then choose Apply. Your terminal window should turn a beautiful shade of yellow. We'll leave it as an exercise to the reader to undo this....

Although there might not be much of a need to change the background color of your terminal windows interactively—and, in most cases, you'll find that not all applications or window elements respond to interactive changes quite as easily as `xterm` does in this example. However, using editres to examine the resource tree of some random application (say, Netscape Communicator) and identifying specific buttons and disabling them through their resources can be of great utility (for, say, limiting the capabilities of an application so that it can be placed in a public kiosk.)

Resources in text form are a set of ordered path elements, separated by periods. The head of the path is specified by the application. First, the window's *name* is checked, followed by the application's *class name*. The window's name is usually what you see in the title bar (for example, xterm), and it can be customized by specifying a -name argument to most X applications (for example, running xterm -name Bob). The class name is defined by the application; in the instance of xterm, it is XTerm (take note of the capitalization). So, XTerm.vt100.background means "the background of the vt100 widget of applications with the class Xterm." Likewise, Bob.vt100.background means "the background of the vt100 widget of applications with name Bob." This overrides the resource that was set by the class name (XTerm) method.

The other part of the X resource is the actual *value*. The values are given as strings separated by a colon from the resource name:

```
XTerm.vt100.background: black
BigYellow.vt100.background: yellow
```

In this example, if you fire up an xterm as xterm -name BigYellow, you'll get one with a yellow background, but any other xterm will be black.

So far, we have discussed the use of only the "tight" resource bindings—fully qualified resource names. Another way of setting resource values is via *loose* bindings, which use an asterisk (*) as the separator. A loose binding is similar to using a wildcard in a shell, with the exception of being name-based, not character-based. So, this next line will set an xterm's background to black:

```
XTerm*background: black
```

On the other hand, this next line won't:

```
XT*background: black
```

"Tight" resource bindings are preferred over "loose" bindings, making the following possible:

```
BigYellow.vt100.background: yellow
BigYellow*background: green
```

This kind of setting will cause the background of the emulation window to be yellow, but the background of everything else (scroll bars, menus, and so on) will be green.

Resources not only control colors, but they also can control fonts, geometry, application-specific key bindings, or text labels. They also can control whether a specific widget actually appears at all, making them very powerful. However, some of the newer GUI toolkits, such as GNOME, have chosen not to go the route of using the existing resource structure to control their functionality. This decision has befuddled many X users.

xrdb and .Xresources

The X resource database is stored by the X server, and manipulated with the command `xrdb`. Typical operations with `xrdb` are listed here:

- **-query**—Lists the contents of the X resource database
- **-load**—Clears out the current contents of the database and reloads it from scratch
- **-override**—Adds the current contents to the resource database
- **-merge**—Merges with and lexigraphically sorts the current contents of the database

`xrdb` takes input from standard input or from a filename that you specify on the command line. Most people tend to store their resources in a file called .Xresources in their home directory, which is typically loaded with the command `xrdb -merge` `$HOME/.Xresources` from the X session script. Because .Xresources is the common filename for this purpose, most systems' X sessions will load this for you automatically.

`xrdb` doesn't just load in your resource settings from a file; it also runs that file against the C preprocessor, with certain symbols predefined. These symbols can help you tailor your resources to the machine or display that you are using. Some of the more useful of these include the following:

- **SERVERHOST**—The hostname portion of the display you are using
- **COLOR**—Defined if your display is color-capable
- **HEIGHT**—The height of your display, in pixels
- **WIDTH**—The width of your display, in pixels
- **X_RESOLUTION**—The horizontal resolution in "pixels per meter" of your display, as reported by the server
- **Y_RESOLUTION**—The vertical resolution in "pixels per meter" of your display, as reported by the server

For an exhaustive list of the symbols defined, see the manual page for `xrdb`. You can also query `xrdb` for what symbols are defined when running on a particular server with `xrdb -symbols`.

Application Defaults

Application defaults are the default resource settings for specific programs, such as `xterm`. They are stored in plain-text files, named by application *class name*, typically in

$XAppLoadDir. Applications "know" where these files are, either from compiled-in defaults or from the settings of XUSERFILESEARCHPATH and XFILESEARCHPATH. The contents of these strings are governed by the same rules and semantics; the only difference is that XUSERFILESEARCHPATH is searched before XFILESEARCHPATH.

These paths aren't typical in the way you would think of the PATH shell variable. They contain what amounts a colon-separated list of filenames for the application to check the existence of. Luckily, you don't have to list the *name* of every resource file that you have because the application will do some variable expansion for these popular values:

- %L is replaced with the language string (value of the xnlLanguage resource).
- %C is replaced with the customization string (value of the customization resource).
- %N is replaced with the class name of the application.

A sane value for the XUSERFILESEARCHPATH variable, assuming that your $XAppLoadDir is /usr/lib/X11/app-defaults, could be as follows:

```
/usr/lib/X11/app-defaults/%N-%C:/usr/lib/X11/app-defaults/%N
```

If your application's class is XTerm and your *customization: resource is set to color, you could expect that the application would try to read /usr/lib/X11/app-defaults/XTerm-color and, if that failed, /usr/lib/X11/app-defaults/XTerm.

This has been a very cursory discussion of how X handles resources and application defaults, but it should have cleared up some of the mystery. For more information, we recommend reading Chapter 10 of the *X Toolkit Intrinsics Programming Manual* (O'Reilly & Associates), which completely covers the ins and outs of this system (in about 40 pages.)

Key Mapping

As in any reasonable GUI, an interface is provided to remap the keyboard to meet your needs, ranging from swapping the Caps Lock and Ctrl keys, to changing the entire keyboard mapping to the Dvorak style, X has got you covered. It can modify not only how keyboard events are translated, but also how mouse buttons are mapped.

Mouse buttons are simply referred to numerically (usually numbered 1 through 3) and can be easily swapped around. Keyboard mappings are a bit more confusing. Not only are there more keys than on a mouse, but the keys can be *modified* with other key presses, such as Shift, Ctrl, and Alt. When discussing keyboard mappings on X, the following terms are used:

- **Keycode**—The numeric value of the key that generated the event.

- **Keysym**—The symbolic name for the event that a key will generate. In most cases, it's directly related to the label on the physical keyboard.

- **Modifier**—A special type of key, usually held down while another key is pressed. (Shift, Alt, Ctrl, and Caps Lock are all modifiers.)

`xmodmap` and `.xmodmaprc`

The command `xmodmap` is used to query and modify key mappings. The manual page is very useful in this case because it gives solid and understandable explanations of the different options. However, we'll touch on a few of them here. First, to get the current keyboard mapping, use `xmodmap -pke`. This will display output similar to the following:

```
keycode    8 = Escape
keycode    9 = 1 exclam
keycode   10 = 2 at
keycode   11 = 3 numbersign
keycode   12 = 4 dollar
keycode   13 = 5 percent
keycode   14 = 6 asciicircum
keycode   15 = 7 ampersand
keycode   16 = 8 asterisk
keycode   17 = 9 parenleft
keycode   18 = 0 parenright
keycode   19 = minus underscore
keycode   20 = equal plus
keycode   21 = BackSpace Delete
keycode   22 = Tab KP_Tab
keycode   23 = Q
keycode   24 = W
keycode   25 = E
keycode   26 = R
keycode   27 = T
...
```

The keys with multiple symbols listed refer to what the key returns when the key is pressed in association with the key bound to the Shift modifier. Keys associated with the modifiers can be viewed with `xmodmap -pm`:

```
xmodmap:  up to 2 keys per modifier, (keycodes in parentheses):

shift       Shift_L (0x31),  Shift_R (0x3d)
lock        Caps_Lock (0x41)
control     Control_L (0x24),  Control_R (0x5e)
mod1        Alt_L (0x3f),  Alt_R (0x61)
mod2
mod3        Num_Lock (0x62)
mod4
mod5
```

There are a few other parameters to xmodmap for querying the configuration, and they're well explained in the manual page. It's one of those applications with a really good one.

Modifications are made with text expressions similar to the previous two examples. For example, to have key 23 send a *Z* instead of a *Q*, you would need a statement like this:

```
keycode 23 = Z
```

To make it easier to reassign keys, you can use the current defined value for the key in the left side of the expression, like this one to change the Backspace key to send Delete:

```
keycode Backspace = Delete
```

These expressions can be loaded in on the command line of xmodmap with the -e argument or from a file named in the command line. Many default X environments call xmodmap at startup to load a file called .xmodmaprc from the user's home directory.

Useful Application: xkeycaps

Configuring key mappings can be a bear. We highly recommend an application called xkeycaps, available from many FTP sites (`ftp://ftp.x.org/pub/contrib/applications` is one) and included in most Linux distributions. It enables you to graphically examine and set the key mappings, and it can generate a text file for xmodmap to take as input. (See Figure 10.5.)

FIGURE 10.5

xkeycaps.

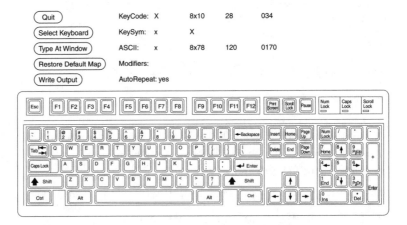

Window Managers and Environments

A window manager is an application that provides the user's interface for moving, resizing, iconifying—generally doing any to a window that the stuff inside the window doesn't handle. Many window managers provide pop-up menus that house common operations. Some are not just window managers but are part of full-fledged desktop environments, such as KDE (`http://www.kde.org`), GNOME (`http://www.gnome.org`), and CDE (`http://www.opengroup.org/tech/desktop/cde`). CDE is popular for many commercial Unix environments, including Solaris and AIX. Silicon Graphics IRIX has its own desktop (IRIX Interactive Desktop, previously called Indigo Magic). CDE was in the running to be "the" desktop environment and at one time was adopted by most commercial Unix vendors. However, as Open Source solutions such as GNOME have matured, many commercial vendors have changed their tune and have been migrating or planning to migrate to GNOME as their default desktop environment.

A good overview and comparison of most window managers is available at `http://www.xwinman.org`, including screenshots and download information.

twm: As Basic as They Come

twm, the Tab Window Manager, comes as part of the X distribution. It provides very basic window management functions, so it's also pretty lightweight. It's configured by the file $LibDir/twm/system.twmrc at the system level and by .twmrc at the user level; read the manual page if you're really interested in customizing twm. If you're like most users, you'll just be using twm until you get something more substantial configured on your workstation.

twm has also been spun off to create tvtwm, Tom's Virtual Tab Window Manager, which at first added "virtual desktops" and has been expanded since. There are also a few other derivatives of twm, such as ctwm.

mwm: The Motif Window Manager

mwm is part of the Open Group's Motif toolkit. Like twm, it provides basic window-management functions and is a little "prettier." Of course, you pay for the prettiness: mwm can be quite a beast as far as resources go, in comparison to twm. The Motif toolkit was never known for efficiency. It is configured at the system level with $LibDir/ system.mwmrc (this varies a lot, depending on where your Motif libraries come from) and with .mwmrc at the user level.

CDE

CDE was obviously designed by committee. Well, that's our opinion, and we're sticking with it. Actually, the only part of CDE that we like is dtlogin, CDE's replacement for xdm. It allows the user to choose what environment they want to be logged into (in the case of Solaris, that's OpenWindows or CDE), but this is fully configurable. This means that an administrator can have lots of fun defining default user environments. The window manager is dtwm—basically mwm with some more bloat, er, features. Actually, it's not as bad as we make it out to be—lots of people really like it.

Most of the CDE software, libraries, and so on live in the tree /usr/dt (at least under Solaris) and the configuration files under /usr/dt/config. Explore at your own risk—on the outset, they seem overly complicated but are actually pretty powerful. To make it easier for system administrators to customize their environment, CDE checks the directory /etc/dt/config before using files in /usr/dt/config. You *should* put your customized versions of scripts and such there, but people have been known not to.

Other Window Managers

Window managers and environments are popping up (and dying) like mosquitoes in midsummer. The rest of this book could probably be filled with in-depth discussions of all the current ones. However, some resources on the Net will be more complete and more up-to-date than this chapter ever could be. Here are some pointers to some of the popular window managers. If you don't find what you're looking for here, `http://www.xwinman. org` is a good starting point.

- **Fvwm, Feeble Virtual Window Manager**—(`http://www.fvwm.org`) This is a lightweight, quite customizable window manager and our personal preference. It does its job and stays out of your way. It's actually based on the twm code.

- **Enlightenment**—(`http://www.enlightenment.org`) This window manager started out as a very artistic approach to window management. But as it has matured, it has become a keystone of the GNOME desktop environment and has become much more efficient as well. It's still pretty darned big, though.

- **Sawfish (nee SawMill)**—(`http://www.sawfish.org`) This is a pretty lightweight and highly configurable window manager (via Lisp).

- **Fvwm95**—(`ftp://mitac11.uia.ac.be/html-test/fvwm95.html`) Here's a window manager based on the fvwm codebase. As its name suggests, it strives to look like Windows 95. Weren't you using Unix to get away from this?

- **AfterStep**—(`http://www.afterstep.org`) This looks like the 'ole OpenStep/NextStep environment. Based on the fvwm code, its configuration files are similar.

- **WindowMaker**—(`http://www.windowmaker.org`) Like AfterStep, WindowMaker strives for the NeXT look, but it's not based on the fvwm code.

The System-wide X Environment

Some system administrators are satisfied with the environment that their vendor provides—and that's okay. Some aren't. That's what this section is for.

xdm

xdm, the X Display Manager, provides two functions. The first is to execute X servers that provide displays for the local machine. These are usually listed in the file $LibDir/xdm/Xservers, one per line. Each line is formatted as follows:

```
<display name> [<display class>] <type> [<server to execute>]
```

Here, the following is true:

- <display name> is the name of the display that XDM is controlling (what would be set for $DISPLAY for xdm to find out where it is)

- <display class> is optional and defines a class name defined for this display. It is not frequently used.

- <type> is either local or foreign. If it's local, the next argument is what XDM needs to execute. If it's foreign, xdm simply tries to contact the display name listed previously to display the login window. This is also used infrequently because XDMCP should be used to better manage foreign displays.

- <server to execute> is the pathname and arguments of the X Server executable.

For example, for a single display under Xfree86, the line would consist of this:

```
:0 local /usr/X11R6/bin/X
```

When xdm controls a display, it pops up a *greeter* window, usually asking for a username and password. It will verify the information and execute the scripts that produce the machine's configured X Window environment.

xdm can control a display in two ways. The first is to have it explicitly listed in its configuration, as described previously. The second is to have a remote display "ask" to have it managed, using the X Display Manager Control Protocol (XDMCP). XDMCP has multiple modes of operation:

- **Direct**—A client X server asks an individual machine (via IP/hostname) to manage a display.

- **Indirect**—A client X server asks an individual machine (via IP/hostname) to provide a *chooser* process, showing hosts that are available to provide display

10

management. The host list is either preconfigured or generated via an XDMCP broadcast message.

- **Broadcast**—A client X server broadcasts on a LAN to all hosts that can provide display management, and it enables the user to choose which one will manage the display.

An xdm instance will manage a host's display or determine what hosts are displayed in a chooser window configured in the Xaccess configuration file (usually $LibDir/xdm/Xaccess). As with any network service, providing display management to other hosts, whether on your network or not, is a potential security risk. It is recommended that it be disabled if not used, by removing or commenting out the appropriate lines in the Xaccess configuration file. In most X distributions, the lines that you'll want to comment out are listed in bold. Placing a hash mark in front of these lines should do the trick.

```
# match, for Direct and Broadcast Query messages, only entries without
# right hand sides can match.
#

*                                 #any host can get a login window

#
# To hardwire a specific terminal to a specific host, you can
# leave the terminal sending indirect queries to this host, and
...
#
# The nicest way to run the chooser is to just ask it to broadcast
# requests to the network - that way new hosts show up automatically.
# Sometimes, however, the chooser can't figure out how to broadcast,
# so this may not work in all environments.
#

*           CHOOSER BROADCAST        #any indirect host can get a chooser

#
# If you'd prefer to configure the set of hosts each terminal sees,
# then just uncomment these lines (and comment the CHOOSER line above)
```

Most of xdm's configuration can be found in $LibDir/xdm/xdm-config. This file's format will look familiar because it uses X resources for configuration settings. All xdm resources begin with the class DisplayManager. Configuration options that are not made on a display-by-display basis are directly off the DisplayManager class (such as the resource that defines where the Xservers file is, DisplayManager.servers). For configuration options that can be specified on a per-server or per-server-class basis, the second

portion of the resource string is the display number (with the : and . replaced with a _—
for example, :0 becomes _0) or the class name that is specified in the Xservers file or
provided by the display itself.

The resources are listed and well described in the manual page for xdm. Some of the
more interesting ones are these:

- **DisplayManager.*DISPLAY*.resources**—Specifies the file that contains resource
  settings that will be loaded for this display. The Greeter/Login or Chooser applications will use these resource settings for their fonts. These resources are explained
  in the xdm manual page.

- **DisplayManager.*DISPLAY*.setup**—Pathname of an executable/script that is run by
  root before offering the login window (usually $LibDir/xdm/Xsetup).

- **DisplayManager.*DISPLAY*.startup**—Pathname of an executable/script that is run
  by root after a user is authenticated (usually $LibDir/xdm/Xstartup).

- **DisplayManager.*DISPLAY*.session**—Pathname of an executable/script that is run
  by the user after the user is authenticated. This is the system's Xsession file
  (usually $LibDir/xdm/Xsession).

- **DisplayManager.*DISPLAY*.reset**—Pathname of an executable/script that is run by
  root after the user's session has terminated (usually $LibDir/xdm/Xreset).

- **DisplayManager.*DISPLAY*.authorize**—Boolean (true/false) of whether to use X
  authorization with this display. (See the previous section on X security.)

Remember, to set one of these configuration resources for "all" displays, use the loose
binding operator *.

Some xdm implementations contain modifications made by the operating system vendor.
For example, SGI has created another script called Xlogin, which, like Xsetup, is run as
root before the user logs in. However, it has some other properties.

The most commonly modified file is the system X session script. Here is an example X
session script, taken from the X11R6 distribution:

```sh
#!/bin/sh
# $Xorg: Xsession,v 1.4 2000/08/17 19:54:17 cpqbld Exp $

# redirect errors to a file in user's home directory if we can
for errfile in "$HOME/.xsession-errors" "${TMPDIR-/tmp}/xses-$USER" "/tmp/xses-$USER"
do
        if ( cp /dev/null "$errfile" 2> /dev/null )
        then
                chmod 600 "$errfile"
                exec > "$errfile" 2>&1
```

```
                  break
         fi
done

case $# in
1)
         case $1 in
         failsafe)
                  exec xterm -geometry 80x24-0-0
                  ;;
         esac
esac

#  The startup script is not intended to have arguments.

startup=$HOME/.xsession
resources=$HOME/.Xresources

if [ -s "$startup" ]; then
         if [ -x "$startup" ]; then
                  exec "$startup"
         else
                  exec /bin/sh "$startup"
         fi
else
         if [ -f "$resources" ]; then
                  xrdb -load "$resources"
         fi
         exec xsm
fi
```

The first portion of the file attempts to redirect any error output from the session to, in order of preference, a file in the user's home directory called .xsession-errors or to a file in TMPDIR called xses-$USER or /tmp/xses-$USER. The next section checks to see if a user provided the keyword failsafe after the login name while signing in. If the user did, it executes a simple terminal window, bypassing all user and system customizations. The final section of the script checks to see if the user has an .xsession script in the home directory, and it executes it if the user does. If the user doesn't have this script, the script attempts to load the user's .Xresources file (if one is present) and then executes the X Session Manager, which then runs the default applications, such as the window manager and an xterm. xsm is new in X11R6 and isn't taken advantage of by many users. For more information, check out the documentation and manual page.

Other Display Managers

It seems that every new desktop environment has had to create its own replacement for xdm. We touched on CDE and its display manager, dtlogin, earlier. After a bit of checking, you'll see that many similarities exist between it and xdm. (We suspect that they share a large bit of code.) The creators of the GNOME environment seemingly started from scratch with their display manager, gdm. If you look around, you'll find very little in common between gdm and xdm.

X Fonts

No discussion of the X Window System would be complete without an overview of its font-handling system. Fonts are identified by a set of terms separated by -, as in this example:

```
-adobe-helvetica-bold-o-normal—*-100-100-*-p—iso8859-1
```

In order of appearance in the font string, the parameters are as follows:

1. Foundry
2. Font Family
3. Weight
4. Slant
5. Set Width
6. Additional Style
7. Pixels
8. Points
9. Horizontal Resolution
10. Vertical Resolution
11. Spacing
12. Average Width
13. Registry
14. Encoding

The Foundry is the company that produced the font. The Font Family is the name of the font. Weight refers to the "blackness" of the font—medium, strong, bold, and so on. Slant describes the angle of the typeface—oblique, italic, roman (upright). Set Width refers to the horizontal width of the font, such as normal or semicondensed. Additional Style is a string that contains other style information that may identify the font. Pixel Size and Point Size refer to the height of the font, in pixels, and tenths of a point, respectively. Horizontal Resolution and Vertical Resolution are the parameters, in dpi, of the font; when referring to fonts by pixel size, this information isn't typically important. Spacing is either c for character box, p for proportional, or m for monospaced.

10

THE X WINDOW SYSTEM

`Average Width` is the width of the average character in the font, in tenths of a pixel. `Registry` and `Encoding` refer to the character encoding that characters in the font are referred to by, such as ISO8859-1.

Fonts also can be referred to by *aliases*. For example, all X servers have a font called fixed that is used as a fallback if a font requested is not available. Font aliases are defined by a file fonts.alias located in each directory of the font path (more on this later).

As with resources, font names have weak and strong bindings. A *strong* binding, as with resources, has all the components of the font's name filled out. A *weak* binding may contain a * as a font-naming component. You hardly ever will see a fully qualified path in use because some elements of the name (such as pixels and points) are different and potentially contradictory ways of describing the size of the font. The two resolution portions probably should not be used in conjunction with choosing a font by pixel size because resolution wouldn't play into that setting. When using a weak binding, if multiple fonts match, the first one matching (the first one in the X server's font path) will be used.

A few fonts are typically available on all X distributions, and these include representatives of the Courier, Helvetica, and Times Roman font families.

To play around with choosing and viewing fonts, use the xfontsel application that comes standard with X11 distributions (see Figure 10.6).

FIGURE **10.6**

xfontsel.

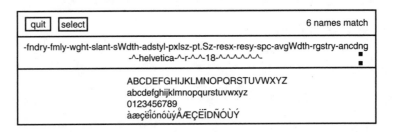

xlsfonts is also a useful application. As the name implies, it shows a list of fonts available to an X server. With no arguments, it prints a list of *all* the fonts available. Or, optionally, the `-fn` argument enables you to specify a font name and list the matching fonts. For example, for a list of all Courier fonts of medium weight, monospaced, and 14 pixels high, you would do this:

```
gate% xlsfonts -fn '-*-courier-medium-r-*-*-14-*-*-*-m-*-*-*'
-adobe-courier-medium-r-normal—14-100-100-100-m-90-iso8859-1
-adobe-courier-medium-r-normal—14-101-100-100-m-0-iso8859-1
```

```
-adobe-courier-medium-r-normal—14-101-100-100-m-0-iso8859-1
-adobe-courier-medium-r-normal—14-140-75-75-m-90-hp-roman8
-adobe-courier-medium-r-normal—14-140-75-75-m-90-iso8859-1
```

If you were using the font string listed as an argument to xlsfonts while connected to a particular X server as, say, the setting for the XTerm*vt100.font resource, the font -adobe-courier-medium-r-normal—14-100-100-100-m-90-iso8859-1 would be the one chosen by the server. When specifying font resources, you should use the least-specific name to get you what you are expecting most of the time. Using fully qualified names all the time can get you into trouble because different X servers might not have the exact font that you were looking for—but they might have something pretty close.

How Fonts Are Stored

Fonts come in may different packages. Most typically used fonts come in a bitmap form. These come in prerendered, typically from vector-based sources, in a variety of popular sizes, styles, and resolutions. Because they are already in bitmap form, they are the most efficient kind of font for an X server to use. Some X servers allow *scaling* of bitmap fonts, giving the server the capability to match more font requests. However, scaled bitmap fonts also can look pretty ugly.

Vector-based fonts, on the other hand, scale very well. The files that store vector-based fonts "describe" the look of the font instead of actually saying which pixel should be what, as in the case of bitmap fonts. Some of these fonts also can rely on various parameters, not just limited to the size of the font, to affect appearance. However, this flexibility comes with a cost: The server must calculate the "bitmaps" of the font on the fly, potentially driving down performance. There are also multiple types of vector-based fonts. The ones most supported by X servers are as follows:

- **Speedo**—This vector-based format is part of the core X11 distribution and is supported by most, if not all, X server software.

- **Type1**—This font format is based on the PostScript language. It is supported only by X servers that supported Display PostScript, which is an X extension that enabled the interpretation of the PostScript language directly by the X server.

- **TrueType**—TrueType is a font format originally designed by Apple. It is supported on some X servers.

These are just the most popular ones. Just like anything, there's more out there than the world probably needs.

Broad support for vector-based fonts has been something that X has needed for quite some time. Many vendors have included varying kinds of vector-based support in their proprietary servers for quite some time, but now, FreeType (`http://www.freetype.org`) has made it much easier to provide vector-based support in the Open Source community. It is included by default in XFree86.

Where Fonts Are Stored

Because providing fonts is a "server" function, the fonts must be available to the X server process and typically are stored locally on the machine that it is running on—or at least somewhere where the server knows how to find it. Fonts also can be housed on a remote machine and retrieved through an X Font Server; this method typically is used for standalone X Terminals that have no local storage for such things. Some vendors, such as Red Hat, ship with an X Font Server configured, used by the server running on the local machine. You'd have to wonder, though, why you'd add another network service and level of complication if you really don't need it.

The Font Path

The font path contains a list of resources where the server can find fonts. These can be paths to directories where fonts are stored on the X Server's machine or references to an X Font Server running locally or remotely. A font server can be referred to as `unix/:-1` if referring to a local font server through a socket, or as `tcp/hostname:port` when referring to a font server running on a specific host or port. The port is usually 7100.

When the X server is started, font paths can be read and changed with the `xset` command. (`xset` does a whole lot of things other than play with fonts, but that's all you'll be using it for here). The q argument to `xset` dumps some configuration flags about the server—we're interested in the Font Path section here:

```
Font Path:
/usr/lib/X11/fonts/100dpi/,/usr/lib/X11/fonts/75dpi/,/usr/lib/X11/fonts/misc/,/u
sr/lib/X11/fonts/Type1/,/usr/lib/X11/fonts/Speedo/,/usr/lib/X11/fonts/CID/
```

The font path is searched in order—you want to have your pre-rendered (bitmap) fonts first in the path because they are the most efficient to use, and then list all the vector fonts. Some X servers, such as the Xfree86 server, support the scaling of bitmap fonts. In this case, you can put items in your font path like this:

```
/usr/lib/X11/fonts/100dpi/:unscaled
```

If you know that your server supports scaling of bitmap fonts, you probably should put the `:unscaled` identifier on all the bitmap font directories (usually 100dpi, 75dpi, and misc) in the beginning of the list and then list the vector fonts, followed by the bitmap font directories again, without the `:unscaled` appended to them. (To our dismay, many vendors ship without their fonts configured like this, and those scaled bitmap fonts are quite unsightly.) This can be configured as default on XFree86 through the XF86Config file (usually found in /etc/XF86Config, although this widely varies by vendor); the Fonts section should be pretty obvious. On most other X servers, it is easiest to redefine the default font path in the command line used to execute the server by placing the information in the .Xservers file.

References

You can find information on the X Window System in many good places; this has been just a primer to get you over some of the most common hurdles. The most detailed reference to date is the series *The Definitive Guides to the X Window System*, from O'Reilly and Associates. This multivolume series is *the* reference to the X Window libraries, toolkits, protocols, and bundled applications. Many other fine publishers and authors have written on the subject, of course, and we suggest that you peruse the aisle of your favorite bookstore and find the one you like. Random places on the Internet are also good to look at, especially because new features are being added to operating systems and the X Window System constantly. Keep a really close eye on the "What's New" sections at `http://www.x.org` (*the* Web site for all that is X) and `http://www.xfree86.org` (the home page of XFree86) for new developments and features. These sites also contain pointers to other sites and documentation on X—it might take a little digging, but the answer is out there.

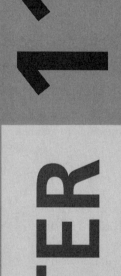

Name Service (DNS)

by Carolyn Sienkiewicz

In This Chapter

Introduction

Each system that is attached to a network has its own name and IP number. UNIX servers typically have IP numbers that are permanently assigned to them. When a user on one system wants to access an application or service that resides on some remote server, the user must connect to that remote server in some manner to access the application or service. Typically people use names to refer to computers. Because computers address their packets to one another by IP numbers, and because people couldn't possibly begin to remember the IP numbers of systems or sites that they need to access, a mechanism was needed to provide a translation from hostnames to IP numbers. The Domain Name Service (DNS) is the network-based service that provides a system-name–to–IP-number mapping and an IP-number–to–system-name mapping. The default port number used for this communication is port number 53. This network service is used in networks all over the world as an important part of what enables users to get from one machine to another.

In the 1970s, the systems on the ARPAnet all had a HOSTS.TXT file with roughly the same kind of information that you will find in an /etc/hosts file today. This information was the address book of how the various systems could reach each other. Going from a few hundred machine names in the 1970s to anything much larger just was not going to scale. This was especially true if you had to run around updating a HOSTS.TXT file and then distributing it to every computer on the network. Plus, once a name was used for a host, that was it—no one else could use it, or there would be a name collision (or conflict).

The DNS doesn't just provide a universal translation mechanism, though. It also provides the structure for having different domain names. Having numerous different domain names is the thing that keeps us from running out of hostnames (at least, within any one human language).

DNS was created for these reasons:

- To be an easily accessible service to provide the hostname–to–IP-number translations
- To provide a means of parceling out different subsets of names (also called sub-domains) and addresses to be independently administered by organizations
- To provide the means for a relatively simple method of updating the world's address book of systems

In this chapter, we'll explore the concepts and the basic constructs that go into making DNS work. The overall topic of DNS is enormous and cannot possibly be covered in full detail in a single chapter. The information presented here will provide you with a

reasonable understanding of how to run an existing name server for which you might suddenly be given administrative responsibility.

Domains and Subdomains

Different subsets of names can be parceled out to be independently administered because DNS is essentially a distributed database. The hierarchical structure of the DNS can be represented in the same inverted tree-like structure that might be used to show a UNIX filesystem. But whereas in building up a filesystem path, names are appended and separated by "/" (forward slash), in domain names, as you traverse the tree, the names are prepended and separated by a "." (dot).

FIGURE 11.1

Domain and sub-domain structure.

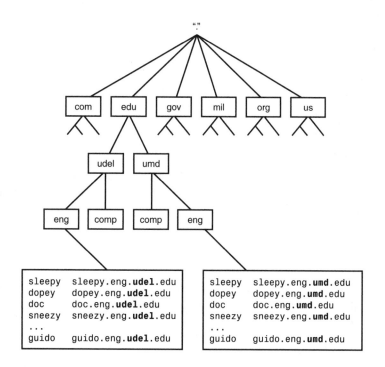

Every domain has its own unique name, and each domain can be further subdivided to provide as many names as any one organization needs. This creates a large naming space and also a way to delegate the responsibility for a naming space or domain. Upon delegating the domain .umd.edu to the University of Maryland, the responsibility and control of this namespace lies with the university. It is the university's to subdivide as it sees fit, and it is the university's responsibility to run its own *name servers*. These name servers are the server half of the client/server equation. They contain the portion of the distributed database of names and addresses for their domain, and they exist to answer the query of any other name server that asks for an address in their domain. More often than not, a domain is divided into enough subdomains that some of the subdomains also will be delegated yet again, and another level of name servers then is required.

For example, the University of Maryland might delegate a subdomain to the engineering department and another to the computer science department. Each of these departments then would have its own separate subdomain name (.comp.umd.edu and .eng.umd.edu) and could have its own name servers. The server providing name service for eng.umd.edu would house the database of addresses and, therefore, would be the final authority on what the hostnames and IP addresses are for that subdomain. That server would be considered *authoritative* for that subdomain.

BIND

On the server side of the DNS equation, BIND is the name of the software package that name servers run to serve the name and address information kept in their databases. BIND originally was developed at the University of California, Berkeley, and the name is an acronym for Berkeley Internet Name Domain. Most vendors ship this code as a regular part of their operating systems. We'll examine setting up and configuring BIND in a later portion of this chapter.

The client machines (the machines that are not running the name server) are utilizing something called a *resolver*. The resolver is used to formulate a query to send to the name server when the client machine needs a hostname *resolved* (or translated) to an IP number.

The Basics of How Name Service Works

It's important to understand the basic mechanics of how a name resolution (or translation) works under the covers. Imagine that you are logged onto a UNIX workstation named snorkel.eng.umd.edu. From there, perhaps you want to `ping` guido.eng.umd.edu. When you do this, a name resolution is set into motion:

```
$ ping guido.eng.umd.edu
```

Let's assume that your workstation is a client here, not a name server. Your system is configured to use ns1.eng.umd.edu as its name server. snorkel's resolver forms a query to request the address of guido so that it can be `ping`ed. The resolver contacts the name server—in this case, ns1—and hands it the query. If the name server, ns1, is authoritative for the subdomain (eng.umd.edu), or if the name server has the answer in it cache and the query did not require an authoritative response, it returns the answer to the resolver.

Let's say that you want to `ping` some machine outside your own subdomain. Let's use the name rex.cs.purdue.edu. snorkel's resolver will form the query and send it to its name server, ns1. ns1 might not be authoritative for anything other than eng.umd.edu. For the sake of this example, we'll say that that is the case. ns1 does not keep any other domain's database. Therefore, ns1 needs to hand off the query to some other name server to get an answer. If ns1 knows which name server is authoritative for the queried name, it sends the query directly there. If not, ns1 strips off the hostname and sees if it knows who is authoritative for the domain—in this case:

```
cs.purdue.edu
```

If it knows who is authoritative, it sends the query there. If it doesn't know that, it strips off the first layer of the domain name and sees if it knows who is authoritative for that:

```
purdue.edu
```

If it doesn't know that, it strips off the next layer and sees if it knows who is authoritative for that:

```
edu
```

If it doesn't know that, it strips off another layer. Because there is no additional layer (technically, there is an implied . at the end of each of the names), the name server defaults to sending its query to one of the root name servers (more about root name servers in a moment). All name servers know the names and addresses of the root name servers.

Going back a little bit, let's say that ns1 believes that names.purdue.edu is authoritative for purdue.edu. The query is sent to names.purdue.edu. Now maybe names is not authoritative but it knows who is. It sends back a referral answer to ns1, telling ns1 that it should ask ns2.cs.purdue.edu. Now ns1 follows through on this referral and asks ns2.cs.purdue.edu, who has an answer. ns2 sends the answer back to ns1, who then sends the answer back to you.

Queries are processed in this way to always guarantee the shortest lookup path available from the name server.

Whether the second name server does subsequent lookups instead of returning a pointer record depends on the configuration parameters of the client and the server involved in the query. Name servers act as both DNS servers and DNS clients, depending on the query, their data, and the state of their cache.

Zones

There is a subtle difference in concept between a domain (or subdomain) and what is called a *zone*. Whereas a domain or subdomain refers to a distinct set of names, the concept of a zone speaks more specifically to responsibility for a domain or subdomain. A domain or subdomain is a syntactic construct, based on the domain name. A zone or subzone is a chunk of data that includes the IP numbers and other data for some part of the DNS. When a nameserver is authoritative for a zone, it is expected that the responses from that nameserver for queries from that zone are the truth—regardless of whether the nameserver has the data.

The domain named umd.edu names the set of all devices having a name that ends in umd.edu. The domain (or subdomain) named eng.umd.edu, while a subset of umd.edu, names the entire set of all devices having a name that ends in "eng.umd.edu." Likewise, the domain (or subdomain) named comp.umd.edu, while a subset of umd.edu, names the entire set of all devices having a name that ends in "comp.umd.edu."

It is possible that a single name server—let's say, nameserver5.umd.edu—could be authoritative, or responsible for the name database that covers both eng.umd.edu and comp.umd.edu. In this case, the zones that the name server is responsible for would be both eng.umd.edu and comp.umd.edu. The name server responsible for umd.edu—let's call it nameserver1.umd.edu—would know this and have records in its database indicating that both the comp and eng subdomains are delegated to nameserver5. nameserver1's database would not contain any systems from those subdomains because responsibility for that zone has been delegated to nameserver5.

Root Name Servers

The *root name servers* that were referenced a moment ago are the root-level name servers for the entire Internet. There are more than a dozen of them spread around the world. Their job is to know who is authoritative for the top-level domains (.edu, .com, and so on) and to provide those names and addresses when a query is received. The requesting name server then can use that information to contact the top-level domain name server, which then can refer it to who is authoritative for the next level down. This continues until eventually the name server is reached that is authoritative for the precise zone for which an address originally was requested.

Caching

It might appear at first blush that this entire mechanism is terribly complicated and that it could take a long time to get the answer to the query. You'd be surprised how fast these query responses come, even when multiple name servers must be consulted to get the answer. A method that is in place to assist in cutting down on the potential time, and also cutting down on the number of name server queries going out to additional name servers, is *caching*.

Let's say that you want to `ping` raffles.cs.purdue.edu. When the name server has just answered your system's query, the answer is stored, or cached, so that the next machine that comes along and wants to reach raffles.cs.purdue.edu can be given the answer without again performing several external queries. At the same time the name server also caches the names and addresses of the purdue.edu name server and the cs.purdue.edu name server. If the answer that your name server received about raffles was that no such host exists, that information would be cached as well. The bottom line is that whatever information a name server learns about other hosts and name servers, whether positive or negative, gets stored in a cache to speed up the response time of subsequent lookups and to cut down on the amount of work that the name server has to do to provide answers. The name server always consults its own database and then its own cache before it sends queries to external sources.

Each administrator of a zone must decide how long other name servers can be allowed to cache data from the zone. As an administrator, if you are running the zone for cs. purdue.edu, you might configure the zone for expiration (often referred to as the TTL, or time-to-live) in one week. Then any other name server coming to your name server and getting answers will cache those answers for a week before timing out the data in their cache. This means that if a name server ask you for a name resolution on raffles. cs.purdue.edu on Monday and there is no entry in your DNS, then it will cache the information that no such address exists. If you install raffles the next day, on Tuesday and add the entry for it to your DNS, the people who tried to reach it on Monday can't reach it until the following Monday, after their DNS cache has timed out. At that time, that name server will query your name server and get the answer. But, until the cache expires, whatever is in the cache is believed to be the answer.

The administrator of each zone determines how long other name servers should cache information about that zone. Consequently, as a zone administrator, you need to be aware of the need to balance consistency and name server work load. You don't want to have such a short TTL that no one caches your information. You also don't want the TTL to be so long that caches of your zone's information are regularly outdated. A good rule of thumb is to limit the caching to 24 hours.

The Difference Between Server and Client

We'll briefly summarize the difference between how the server and client operate for DNS. The name server runs BIND and provides responses to queries. The client function occurs on systems that do not run BIND but that instead have just the subset of BIND, called the *resolver*. These resolver libraries are linked to other programs that need name-to-address mappings, such as telnet or `ping`. When a program such as telnet needs to resolve a hostname to an IP number these libraries are responsible for formulating the query. Upon receipt of the answer from the name server, they interpret the answer and return that to the calling program. The resolver software piece is what generates the query, both for a client and for a name server when it needs to ask another name server for more information. The BIND server also plays the additional role of looking up the information that it does have and providing the answers to queries that it receives.

FQDN

Before going any further, we want to take this opportunity to define a term that you'll often hear in conversations revolving around DNS. Let's say that you are sitting at a machine named guido.eng.umd.edu. When you want to `ping` raffles.cs.purdue.edu, you, as a user on the eng.umd.edu network, need to explicitly state raffles's entire name. This is also what is called its fully qualified domain name, which is usually referred to as FQDN for short. If you say this without qualifying what domain raffles is in, the default action is that raffles is assumed to be in the same domain as the machine you are on:

```
$ ping raffles
```

Therefore, raffles would be looked for in the eng.umd.edu domain. If such a hostname coincidentally exists in eng.umd.edu, the IP number will be returned by the name server to your resolver, which will return it to the `ping` program, and `ping` will send ICMP packets to that address. However, raffles.eng.umd.edu and raffles.cs.purdue.edu are different machines (at least, for argument's sake). You'll see that you are `pinging` raffles.eng.umd.edu, and that's when you'll realize (hopefully) that you forgot to specify the machine accurately enough. In summary, when you want to reach some system that is not in the exact same domain as the system that you are typing at, you must use a fully qualified domain name to get the result you are seeking.

The Client (a.k.a. the Resolver)

Typically all UNIX systems need to be capable of resolving names. Adding entries to an /etc/hosts file and distributing it to every device on your network can get very unwieldy very fast.

The resolver libraries for BIND come as a common subsystem in all UNIX operating systems. To make use of DNS to resolve names, you'll need the address of a name server that will answer your queries. You'll want to use the nearest name server (in terms of numbers of network hops) as your first choice of name servers. This will theoretically be a name server run by the organization that you work for (or are a part of). If you want to use another company or organization's name server, you should ask permission first before configuring your resolver to point to it.

Resolver Configuration

Two files should be configured (or reconfigured) when adding DNS name lookups to a system. For Red Hat Linux 7.1 and Solaris 8, these are as follows:

/etc/resolv.conf

/etc/nsswitch.conf

resolv.conf

The /etc/resolv.conf file can contain five different types of directives:

```
domain
search
nameserver
sortlist
options
```

Each of these keywords must always begin in column 1. The `domain` directive is used to set the local or default domain name for a machine. Placing a `domain` directive in /etc/resolv.conf will override the domain that you might have set in `hostname`. This directive is formed with the keyword beginning in column 1, constructed like so:

```
domain  eng.umd.edu
```

The `search` directive is used to specify a list and order of domains to be searched. The list can contain one to six domains. The first domain in the search list becomes the default domain and overrides the `domain` directive if it comes after the `domain` directive. Whichever of these two directives appears latest in the file will override the other. Consequently, the `search` and `domain` directives are mutually exclusive. Here's an example of a `search` directive:

```
search  eng.umd.edu comp.umd.edu umd.edu
```

With this statement, the resolver is being directed to first search eng.umd.edu for the hostname in question. If no entry is found, then comp.umd.edu and then umd.edu will be searched.

The `nameserver` directive specifies to the resolver the IP address of a name server to send all queries to. Again, this is typically a name server within your own network, company, or organization. If resolv.conf has no `nameserver` directive in it, then the resolver will attempt to connect to a name server running locally. You can specify zero to three *nameserver* directives. Here is an example of three:

```
nameserver    10.10.13.100
nameserver    10.10.12.100
nameserver    10.10.11.100
```

Additional name servers are consulted only in the event of a total failure to receive a valid response from the first name server. The default time to wait for a response is five seconds. After five seconds, the query times out. The second name server is queried only if the query to the first one times out or if the resolver receives a network error back from the query. The same goes for the third name server after a query timeout of another five seconds with the second name server. If the third name server times out as well, the resolver goes back to the first name server and attempts another round. Solaris 8 makes as many as four rounds before giving up. Red Hat 7.1 gives up after two rounds.

If an answer is received from the first name server to the effect that there is no such host, additional name servers are not consulted. It is assumed that the same answer would be received from any other name server. Specifying multiple name servers is done strictly to provide backup name servers to connect to, in the event of an outage of your principal nameserver.

The `sortlist` directive is a way to prefer some networks over others. This can be used in cases when systems have multiple network interfaces—say, one that is Gigabit Ethernet and one that is on a FDDI ring. The DNS entries for a system with multiple interfaces can be defined so that all interface addresses are returned when a resolver queries. If you want to be sure to use the Gigabit Ethernet, then you could specify it on the `sortlist`. This directive can take up to 10 different networks or subnets. Here is an example indicating to prefer the 10.10.12.0 network whenever multiple addresses are returned to the resolver by a name lookup:

```
sortlist10.10.12.0
```

The last directive that we'll talk about is the `options` directive. This directive takes an argument of any of the following:

```
debug

attempts

timeout
```

There are a couple others, but these are the ones that you're most likely to want to use. `debug` is turned on with this line:

```
options debug
```

However, this works only if the resolver libraries on your system have been compiled with debugging turned on. This option can be helpful if you're trying to resolve problems with your resolver or DNS.

`attempts` refers to the number of times to try each name server before giving up. The maximum value is 5. Here is an example with a value of 3:

```
options attempts:3
```

`timeout` refers to the number of seconds to wait for a response from a name server before sending a retry. This number can change the timeout period only for the first round through the name server list. Subsequent rounds will be per each vendor's resolver's typical round and beyond. Here is an example:

```
options timeout:2
```

Finally, here is an example of the typical contents of a sample /etc/resolv.conf:

```
search          eng.umd.edu comp.umd.edu umd.edu
nameserver 10.10.12.100
nameserver          10.10.11.100
```

nsswitch.conf

The /etc/nsswitch.conf file can determine the ordering of hostname lookup methods. This ordering can be specified by the use of the keyword `hosts`. The sources (and, in this case, the additional keywords) that might be consulted for host information include `dns`, `files`, `nis`, and `nisplus`. An entry of *files* refers to the file /etc/hosts. If you want name-resolution ordering of DNS first and then /etc/hosts, you would place a line like this in the nsswitch.conf:

```
hosts:  dns files
```

For more information on this configuration file, consult the man page.

The Name Server

The server side of the DNS equation involves running BIND on a machine to provide answers to name lookups.

It really is best to have dedicated machines for serving DNS to a site. There are a few reasons for this. One of the most important is that name servers need to be capable of responding to many requests very quickly. Another is that a name server needs to be up and available all the time. If other applications or services are being provided by a DNS server, there is a much greater chance that there will be a conflict of interest between the application users and the admin (who knows that the machine can't just be rebooted any time). For any essential services such as DNS, it is always best to run it on a box that has no other purpose than providing that service. This philosophy also makes for cleaner troubleshooting because the scope of what is running on the box is clearly defined.

Primary or Master Name Server and Slave Name Server

To assist with issues of availability and redundancy, it is required that a minimum of two name servers be available. This is especially important for system-maintenance purposes. Hardware failures do occur, and systems need to be patched and upgraded. Having multiple name servers running can prevent a site from being completely without name service during these normally occurring system-maintenance events.

A Word on Terminology

The older term for *master* is *primary*. The older term for *slave* is *secondary*. You'll need to realize that those terms are interchangeable. Although we have consistently used the newer terms *master* and *slave* in this chapter, you'll want to be able to converse with other sysadmins who might use only the older terminology of *primary* and *secondary*.

It is recommended that one name server be set up as the *primary* or *master name server* and the others be set up as *secondary* or *slave name servers*. The master for a zone is whichever server contains the actual data records for that zone. A slave name server for a zone receives the data for that zone from the master in a transaction called a *zone transfer*. Both master and slave can give authoritative responses for the zone.

A zone can have multiple master name servers. In this case, each name server must individually have records added for any new hosts. Because there is more room for error, this is not recommended (but it can be done).

A zone can have multiple slave name servers. A slave name server can receive its zone transfer from the primary master or from another slave.

We'll cover the configuration differences between these two types a little later.

Configuring the BIND Startup

BIND is the name of the package of code that we run for a name service. The actual *process* that is run when we start name service, and the process name that you'll look for to see if it's running, is called named (the name server daemon). The configuration file that is first examined as part of the initialization of named is called /etc/named.conf.

For the purposes of example, we'll be building named.conf and the zone files for a make-believe zone named eng.umd.edu. For our example, eng.umd.edu consists of the networks and hosts shown in Figure 11.2.

FIGURE 11.2

Example zone eng.umd.edu.

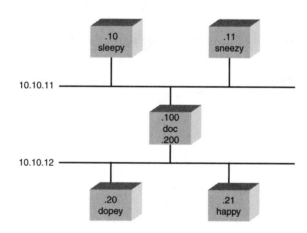

The /etc/named.conf for our example would look like this:

```
# named configuration file

options {
        directory "/var/named";
};

zone "eng.umd.edu" in {
        type master;
        file "forward.eng.umd.edu";
};
```

```
zone "11.10.10.in-addr.arpa" in {
        type master;
        file "reverse.10.10.11";
};

zone "12.10.10.in-addr.arpa" in {
        type master;
        file "reverse.10.10.12";
};

zone "0.0.127.in-addr.arpa" in {
        type master;
        file "reverse.127.0.0";
};

zone "." in {
        type hint;
        file "cache.root";
};
```

This tells us that there will be five additional configuration files in the /var/named directory:

> forward.eng.umd.edu
>
> reverse.10.10.11
>
> reverse.10.10.12
>
> reverse.127.0.0
>
> cache.root

When the named process is started, it will read this configuration file and load all of its zone data by reading each of the specified files.

Configuring a Zone

It's time now to cover the information needed by a name server so that it can serve up information about a zone. To review, the word *zone* denotes the authoritative information for a domain or subdomain. A name server can provide service for multiple domains. It also can be the primary master for some zones and, at the same time, be a slave name server for other zones.

Zone Files

The minimum set of zone files that must exist on a primary master name server consists of the following:

- A forward-mapping file
- A reverse-mapping file (a separate one for each subnet—but only when you have the full subnet)
- A cache file
- A loopback file

The forward-mapping file is used for translating from a name to an address, and the reverse-mapping file is used for translating from an address to a name. The cache and loopback files are required for any system running a name server, but the contents are virtually identical for all name servers.

There is no requirement for what you name any of these files. For purposes of example in this chapter, we'll refer to forward-mapping files with names such as forward.*domainname*, and we'll refer to reverse-mapping files as reverse.*networknumber*.

Forward Lookup or Mapping

The entries in zone files are referred to as *DNS resource records*. We'll be reviewing the use of the following list of resource record types as each one comes up in the discussion of zone files:

- **SOA**—Start of authority record
- **NS**—Name server record
- **A**—Name-to-address record
- **PTR**—Address-to-name record
- **CNAME**—Alias to canonical (official) name record

Other resource record types exist, but these are the most important.

For our example, we will name the forward lookup file forward.eng.umd.edu. If the same system was going to be serving up both the eng.umd.edu and comp.umd.edu zones (or subdomains), there would be a separate forward lookup file for each zone.

The first thing in every zone file will be the TTL value. This value says how long anyone else who is caching this data may answer with the value held in that person's own cache. If the cache entry is older than this value, the cache entry must be removed and a new query must be sent out. Note that this value that appears at the beginning of each zone file is specifically for positive answers received from the name server, or, in other words a response where the requested entry was found. There is a separate TTL for negative responses, or "no such host" responses. We'll see this negative TTL in a little bit.

We'll use a value of 6 hours for all of our zone records.

```
$TTL 6h
```

The value that you use for this and other time values in zone files will vary depending on how static your zone data is and how much load your name servers can handle. If your data is never changing, it makes more sense to let other servers cache your data for longer periods. If your name servers are having difficulty responding to requests quickly enough, you might have your time values set too low.

The first resource record statement in the forward lookup file is the SOA record. There is exactly one SOA record in each zone file. For our eng.umd.edu example, this statement would look like the following:

```
eng.umd.edu. IN SOA doc2.eng.umd.edu. root.sleepy.eng.umd.edu. (
1;              serial number
4h              ;refresh after 4 hours
1h              ;retry after 1 hour
1w              ;expire after 1 week
8h )     ;expire negative cache ;after 8 hours
```

The first interesting thing to note is that you must make sure that each name in the first line ends with a trailing dot. This is critical.

Also note that comments can be added to the file by placing a semicolon before the comment text. The comment begins at the semicolon and ends at the end of the line.

Let's examine each of the components of the SOA record in turn from our example:

- **eng.umd.edu**—This is the zone for which we are claiming authority. Note the trailing dot.
- **IN**—This indicates that the data contained in this file is of the class of data called Internet. There are other classes, but none currently is in widespread use.
- **SOA**—This indicates a "start of authority" resource record type.
- **doc2.eng.umd.edu**—This indicates the name of the master name server for the zone named at the beginning of the resource record. Note the trailing dot.
- **root.sleepy.eng.umd.edu**—This indicates the mail address where you can reach the administrator(s) for this zone. Note the @ symbol has been replaced with a dot. Also note the trailing dot.
- **(**—The opening parenthesis indicates the beginning of settings that direct the behavior of any slave name server(s) for this zone.
- **1 ;serial number**—The first entry inside the parenthesis is the serial number. Whenever you finish making a set of changes to the zone files, you must increment

this number. When a slave name server contacts a master server for data, it first checks the serial number in the master's SOA record. If the serial number is greater in the master's SOA record, the slave reloads the zone data over the network from the master. If you've updated zone files with new host information and are wondering why other people aren't seeing the updates, check your serial number. Forgetting to increment it is a classic mistake.

- **4h ;refresh after 4 hours**—This indicates to a slave how often to check with the master to see if the slave's information is up-to-date.

- **1h ;retry after 1 hour**—This indicates to a slave how long to wait before retrying to contact the master (it might have been down for maintenance).

- **1w ;expire after 1 week**—This indicates the maximum length of time that a slave will continue to wait to reach the primary master before expiring the zone data. In our example, if the slave hasn't been capable of reaching the master for a week, it expires the zone information and stops providing answers to queries for the zone.

- **8h) ;expire negative cache ;after 8 hours**—This indicates the length of time that a slave will retain a negative cache result. This is when a slave has received a "no such entry" response to a query. Also note the closing parenthesis.

The data in the SOA record is used by the named process to set defaults on responses that a nameserver gives. It also is forwarded to slave nameservers of this zone to set defaults on responses that they give about this domain, and it contains parameters that tell the slave nameservers how often to synchronize with the master. Data in the SOA record can be queried by any host on the Internet that can directly reach the name server (in other words, not an intranet name server behind a firewall).

The next resource record to appear in this file is the NS record(s), or name server record(s). Place a single line for each name server that is authoritative for this zone. For our example, we'll say that doc2 and sleepy are both authoritative for eng.umd.edu. doc2 is the master name server, and sleepy is a slave name server.

The NS entries would be these:

```
eng.umd.edu. IN NS doc2.eng.umd.edu.
eng.umd.edu. IN NS sleepy.eng.umd.edu.
```

This is pretty simple after the SOA record:

- **eng.umd.edu**—Again, this indicates the zone. (Note the trailing dot.)

- **IN**—Again, the class of data is Internet.

- **NS**—This tells us that this record specifies who is an authoritative name server for this zone.
- **doc2.eng.umd.edu**—The name that appears here is designated an authoritative name server for this zone. Note the trailing dot.

The next record type that we'll cover is the A record, or address record. This record type provides a name-to-address translation. We'll put in an address record for every network interface that is used. For our example network in Figure 11.2, the A record entries might read as follows:

```
localhost.eng.umd.edu.   IN A   127.0.0.1
sleepy.eng.umd.edu.            IN A   10.10.11.10
sneezy.eng.umd.edu.            IN A   10.10.11.11
doc1.eng.umd.edu.              IN A   10.10.11.100
doc2.eng.umd.edu.              IN A 10.10.12.200
dopey.eng.umd.edu.             IN A   10.10.12.20
happy.eng.umd.edu.             IN A   10.10.12.21
```

The record syntax is straightforward. When a hostname is requested, the name is searched in these A records. If a match is made, the right, or data, portion of the record is returned, which contains the address. Note that hostnames still end with a trailing dot.

In the case of a multihomed host such as doc, note that there are multiple network addresses.

The next record type is the CNAME record. A CNAME record provides an alias name to canonical (or official) name lookup. Let's say that people using our sample network need to access the accounts payable application that runs on happy. We might not want these users to have to know which server their application runs on, so we might choose to provide an alias that describes the function or uses the application's name:

```
acctpay.eng.umd.edu.    IN CNAME  happy.eng.umd.edu.
```

There are many different reasons to use CNAME records. They often are used to pre-serve an old existing name that users have used to connect to a service that might have moved from machine to machine.

Our completed forward lookup, forward.eng.umd.edu, would look like this:

```
$TTL 6h
eng.umd.edu. IN SOA doc2.eng.umd.edu. root.sleepy.eng.umd.edu. (
1                ;serial number
4h               ;refresh after 4 hours
1h               ;retry after 1 hour
1w               ;expire after 1 week
8h )    ;expire negative cache ;after 8 hours
```

```
; NAME SERVERS FOR eng.umd.edu.
;
eng.umd.edu.                         IN NS doc2.eng.umd.edu.
eng.umd.edu.                         IN NS sleepy.eng.umd.edu.

; ADDRESSES
;
localhost.eng.umd.edu.       IN A    127.0.0.1
sleepy.eng.umd.edu.          IN A    10.10.11.10
sneezy.eng.umd.edu.          IN A    10.10.11.11
doc1.eng.umd.edu.            IN A    10.10.11.100
doc2.eng.umd.edu.            IN A    10.10.12.200
dopey.eng.umd.edu.           IN A    10.10.12.20
happy.eng.umd.edu.           IN A    10.10.12.21

; ALIASES
;
acctpay.eng.umd.edu.         IN CNAME  happy.eng.umd.edu.
```

Now that we've covered the full or verbose version of the forward lookup zone file, we need to show the same data in a shortened format. This format is the one that you are most likely to encounter. But having seen the fully fleshed-out version, you will be able to compare it with the abbreviated version that follows and have a better understanding of what is really being implied.

```
$TTL 6h
@ IN SOA doc2.eng.umd.edu. root.sleepy.eng.umd.edu. (
1               ;serial number
4h              ;refresh after 4 hours
1h              ;retry after 1 hour
1w              ;expire after 1 week
8h )    ;expire negative cache ;after 8 hours

; NAME SERVERS FOR eng.umd.edu.
;
                        IN NS doc2.eng.umd.edu.
                        IN NS sleepy.eng.umd.edu.

; ADDRESSES
;
localhost                   IN A    127.0.0.1
sleepy           IN A    10.10.11.10
sneezy           IN A    10.10.11.11
doc1                        IN A    10.10.11.100
doc2                        IN A 10.10.12.200
dopey                       IN A    10.10.12.20
happy            IN A    10.10.12.21

; ALIASES
;
acctpay                     IN CNAME  happy
```

Reverse Lookup or Mapping

A new record that you'll encounter in the reverse lookup file is the PTR (or pointer) record. This record provides a network-address–to–name mapping. There will be a separate reverse lookup file for each network. For the 10.10.11 network, there will be an entry for sneezy, like so:

```
11.11.10.10.in-addr.arpa.        IN PTR sneezy.eng.umd.edu.
```

Its shortcut version would look like this:

```
11 IN PTR sneezy.eng.umd.edu.
```

Here, then, are the complete reverse lookup files for both of the networks that are part of our sample network:

reverse.10.10.11:

```
$TTL 6h
@ IN SOA doc2.eng.umd.edu. root.sleepy.eng.umd.edu. (
                                1                       ;serial number
4h              ;refresh after 4 hours
1h              ;retry after 1 hour
1w              ;expire after 1 week
8h )     ;expire negative cache ;after 8 hours


; NAME SERVERS FOR eng.umd.edu.
;
                        IN NS doc2.eng.umd.edu.
                        IN NS sleepy.eng.umd.edu.


; ADDRESS TO NAME
;
10                              IN PTR sleepy.eng.umd.edu.
11                              IN PTR sneezy.eng.umd.edu.
100                             IN PTR doc1.eng.umd.edu.
```

reverse.10.10.12:

```
$TTL 6h
@ IN SOA doc2.eng.umd.edu. root.sleepy.eng.umd.edu. (
1               ;serial number
4h              ;refresh after 4 hours
1h              ;retry after 1 hour
1w              ;expire after 1 week
8h )     ;expire negative cache ;after 8 hours


; NAME SERVERS FOR eng.umd.edu.
;
                        IN NS doc2.eng.umd.edu.
                        IN NS sleepy.eng.umd.edu.
```

```
; ADDRESS TO NAME
;
20                                 IN PTR dopey.eng.umd.edu.
21                                 IN PTR happy.eng.umd.edu.
200                             IN PTR doc2.eng.umd.edu.
```

From these two files, you can see that the SOA and NS records appear exactly the same. The only other records that occur in these reverse lookup files are the records for each specific network.

Also note these files named as per the *zone* statements that we specified earlier in the /etc/named.conf configuration file.

Loopback File

One more reverse lookup file is needed, and that is for the loopback interface. In our case, it is named reverse.127.0.0 and contains the following:

```
$TTL 6h
@ IN SOA doc2.eng.umd.edu. root.sleepy.eng.umd.edu. (
1               ;serial number
4h              ;refresh after 4 hours
1h              ;retry after 1 hour
1w              ;expire after 1 week
8h )    ;expire negative cache ;after 8 hours

; NAME SERVERS FOR eng.umd.edu.
;
                    IN NS doc2.eng.umd.edu.
                    IN NS sleepy.eng.umd.edu.

1                                 IN PTR localhost.
```

Root Hints Cache File

Our name server also needs to know where to find the root name servers. For this information, the named.conf references the zone ., which indicates the root of all domains. You can find the current list of root servers at ftp.rs.internic.net (198.41.0.6). Use anonymous ftp to retrieve the file named.root from the subdirectory domain and then rename it to the filename that we've used in our named.conf (in our case, cache.root). You should retrieve a new copy every two or three months because the root name servers do change.

Serial Numbers

It's time now for a word about the serial numbers that appear in each file's SOA record. Each time you make a change to a zone file, you must increment the serial number so that slave servers will know that they must reload the file that you have changed. Failing to increment the serial number is the most common mistake that administrators make when working with DNS.

Use only integers for serial numbers. A common numbering scheme that many people like to use is the date plus a two-digit number:

```
YYYYMMDDNN      or for today:    2001091801
```

This provides an indication of when a file was last changed. The last two digits can help to show how many changes were made on a given day. There's nothing wrong, though, with using simple consecutive numbers. It is important that your numbering sequence is always numerically increasing; if you use a date scheme, it's important that the numerical value of tomorrow is greater than the numerical value for today, even across month/year boundaries. A bad numbering system would be DDMMYYYYNN because 0110200101 would be numerically smaller than 2609200101.

Starting Name Service

Now that the named.conf file has been completed, along with all of the supporting zone files, we're ready to actually start the name server process, which is called named. Start it by running the program (as root) /usr/sbin/in.named. You'll want to be sure to check the syslog file for any indication of errors.

To complete things, alter your system's startup files to set hostname(1) to the appropriate domain name and configure name service to start automatically. These startups already are available in the /etc/rc files area as commented-out code, so just grep for hostname and named to find them and uncomment the code so that it will run when the system is next booted. It's best, of course, if you can test this startup change right away. This can help to avoid a potential unpleasant surprise later if the system reboots and does not starting up in precisely the way you expect.

Adding a Slave Name Server

It is necessary to have more than a single master name server. You must have at least one other machine that can provide name service for your domain. Typically, a slave name server will provide this service for your domain.

A slave name server loads the zone data from the master name server (or from another slave server) over the network in what is called a *zone transfer*. Let's implement a slave name server on sleepy (which we already mentioned is listed as a name server in the files that we examined previously). sleepy will act as a slave to doc2, which is our master name server.

On sleepy, we would copy over the following three files from doc2:

> named.conf
>
> reverse.127.0.0
>
> cache.root

Both reverse.127.0.0 and cache.root can be used as is. Here is sleepy's version of named.conf after altering it to have sleepy act as a slave server:

```
# named configuration file

options {
        directory "/var/named";
};

zone "eng.umd.edu" in {
        type slave;
        file "slave.eng.umd.edu";
        masters { 10.10.12.200; };
};

zone "11.10.10.in-addr.arpa" in {
        type slave;
        file "slave.10.10.11";
        masters { 10.10.12.200; };
};

zone "12.10.10.in-addr.arpa" in {
        type slave;
        file "slave.10.10.12";
masters { 10.10.12.200; };
};

zone "0.0.127.in-addr.arpa" in {
        type master;
        file "reverse.127.0.0";
};

zone "." in {
        type hint;
        file "cache.root";
};
```

The first change is that sleepy is type slave, whereas doc2 was type master. This applies to all the zones except the loopback and the root hint cache. For the latter two, we've already copied over the files from doc2 and will leave them as is.

The zone statement for eng.umd.edu indicates that sleepy is acting as a slave, that the zone transfer data should be stored in a file named slave.eng.umd.edu, and that the master to get the zone transfer from is at address 10.10.12.200. You'll notice that this pattern holds true for the other zone files as well. Now when a new machine gets added to this domain, you just update the appropriate files on the master name server, and the information is transferred to the slave server via a zone transfer.

As with the master server, after completing the configuration files, you should do the following:

- Start the named process.
- Check syslog for errors.
- Configure in the rc file for auto startup.
- Set the hostname(1) to the domain.

Maintaining DNS

The main task of maintaining the DNS is updating the zone files with changed host information when systems are being added, removed, or modified. After editing the affected zone files (and remembering to increment the serial numbers in each zone file that has been edited), the named process must be told to reload zone data. This can be done by using a program named ndc. Use ndc reload to reload zone data after an update on a master server or to force a zone transfer on a slave server (rather than letting the slave wait until its time has expired). The named process also can be stopped and started with the commands ndc stop and ndc start. Check the ndc man page for more information on its other capabilities.

To verify that your changes are being served, use nslookup to query the server for the changed entries. If you don't see any evidence of the change you made, check to be sure that you increased the serial number and reloaded the zone.

Another maintenance task is to keep the root hints file current. Again, we recommend checking this every two or three months. Download the latest from ftp.rs.internic.net.

Finally, be sure to review the syslog file on a regular basis, checking for any indications of problems with the DNS so that they can be caught early.

Management with Front Ends

Some freely available tools can be used to make the upkeep of the zone files simpler. Here are a few and where to find them:

webmin	`http://www.webmin.com`
h2n	`ftp.uu.net/published/oreilly/nutshell/dnsbind/dns.tar.Z`
webdns	`ftp.lcs.mit.edu/pub/webdns`

Caching-Only Name Servers

If your name servers get too busy, you might add additional master servers or additional slave servers. Adding another master server could be the answer, but remember that you will have to make all the same configuration changes to each master server. Adding another slave server also might be the answer—the only downside is the potential added overhead burden on the master server(s) for more zone-transfer traffic. A caching-only name server provides another option to add to your arsenal when you find that your name servers are getting too much traffic.

This type of name server isn't authoritative for anything but can serve as a big cache repository for things that it has looked up. Over a period of time, it can build up a quite comprehensive cache, at which point it becomes quite valuable in terms of what traffic it can provide relief from for the other name servers. It doesn't pose the issue of an additional copy of files to be maintained like another master would, and it doesn't have the issue of burdening the master with polls for zone transfers. Instead, a caching-only name server applies its own special set of overhead burden by having to get the initial data that it then caches.

Everything is a trade-off, but a caching-only name server provides another option.

Tools and Troubleshooting

Sometimes you need something that you can use to test or verify DNS changes. Sometimes things also don't seem to be working as expected with the DNS, and you need a view into its behavior (or, rather, misbehavior). For just such times, there are a few good tools to know about. The most commonly used tools for troubleshooting purposes are nslookup and dig. These two tools have much more capability than we will go into detail about here, but we will cover their basic uses. This introduction will provide an introduction to these tools that you will want to supplement with further examination of each tool's man pages. For additional tools, check out `http://www.dns.net/dnsrd/tools.html`.

nslookup

The first tool that we'll discuss, nslookup, is considered by many to be history. However, it is available just *everywhere*, so, purely by its pervasiveness alone, it is a tool that you should know how to use and one that you should take advantage of. In general, nslookup is a useful tool because it is capable of the following:

- Emulating the query that a resolver would generate
- Emulating the query that a name server would generate
- Emulating a zone transfer
- Providing detailed debugging information

A single lookup can be performed by including all requested information directly on the command line.

```
# nslookup sneezy
Server: doc2.eng.umd.edu
Address: 10.10.12.200

Name:    sneezy.eng.umd.edu
Address:10.10.11.11
```

An interactive mode also can be entered by using the `nslookup` command only. With the interactive mode, at each succeeding > prompt, you can give a different name or address or other record to look up, or you can enter options to affect how nslookup will function.

Use `set debug` to have nslookup show detailed debugging information for the responses that it gets from name servers. Use `set debug2` to have it also show detailed debugging information about the query that it sent out. Debugging can be turned off with `set node-bug`. By the way, you'll want to do this in a window that you can scroll backward to look at all the debugging text that has drifted past.

If you want to query another name server (other than the one that your system is configured to talk to) you can specify `server otherservername`, and all subsequent interactive queries will go to that name server.

To exit the interactive mode of nslookup, type `^d` or `quit`.

You can do lots more with nslookup. These are really just the barest basics. Read the man page and play with it. You will find that even playing with it is instructional.

dig

The next tool to examine is dig, which, believe it or not, stands for Domain Information Groper. dig does not have an interactive mode. To do a simple lookup of sneezy again, just do this:

```
# dig sneezy
```

To specify that a different name server (other than the one in your resolv.conf) be queried, include it after an @:

```
# dig raffles @ns.comp.purdue.edu
```

As with nslookup, the things that you can do with dig are too numerous to mention here. Again, you'll want to read the man page and play and experiment with it to find out what you can do with it.

Best Practices

Maintaining DNS

- Use revision control (RCS/CVS/SCCS) to maintain previous revisions so that you can "back out" erroneous changes and keep track of how and when changes happened.
- Edit both the forward and reverse file for each entry being added, deleted, or modified.
- Verify the syntax and the correctness of changes made to the zone files before reloading them.
- Increment the serial number in any file that is changed.
- Reload the zone (`ndc reload`).

Online Resources

Obtaining BIND:

- `ftp.isc.org`
- `http://www.dns.net/dnsrd/bind.html`

BIND Users Mailing List: `http://www.isc.org/ml-archives/bind-users`

The future of DNS: `http://www.ietf.org/html.charters/dnsext-charter.html`

Current root name servers: `ftp.rs.internic.net (198.41.0.6)`

Other Information on DNS: `http://www.dns.net/dnsrd`

CHAPTER 12

Mail

by Rich Blum

In This Chapter

Internet email has become a vital resource for businesses and home users alike. Many corporations use email for official communications both internally and with external customers. Email server downtime can severely affect communications in many corporations.

As the Unix administrator, it most likely will be your job to run some kind of email process on your Unix system. Many organizations use a corporate-wide Unix email server that accepts mail messages for the entire domain. Alternatively, many organizations use individual Unix client workstations that must connect to a central mail hub to send and receive mail messages. In either situation, it is imperative that you know how Internet email works and how to configure the Unix email system properly.

This chapter describes some of the basics of Unix email, as well as how email is transferred across the Internet. After that, it describes how to install and manage email software on your Unix system for both mail clients and mail servers.

The Unix Mail Process

The Unix operating system breaks the different functions of Internet email into separate processes, each handled by separate programs. Figure 12.1 shows how most Unix email software modularizes email functions.

FIGURE 12.1

Unix modular email environment.

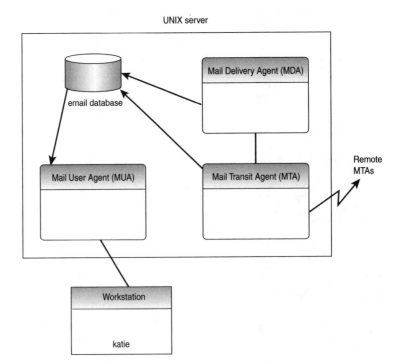

As can be seen in Figure 12.1, the Unix email function normally is broken into three separate processes:

- The Mail Delivery Agent (MDA)
- The Mail Transfer Agent (MTA)
- The Mail User Agent (MUA)

The MTA process is the core of the system. It is used to control how messages are received from both local and remote users, and how messages are delivered to remote users. It is often the most difficult of the processes to configure. The MDA process is responsible for ensuring that messages are delivered to the local users on the Unix system. It usually receives messages identified as local from the MTA process. The MUA process is often separated out from the MTA and MDA processes, in that it doesn't deliver messages. It is used to allow remote users to read messages already stored in the users' mailboxes.

The lines between these three functions sometimes can be fuzzy. Some email packages combine functionality for the MDA and MTA functions, while others combine the MDA and MUA functions. The following sections describe these basic email agents and how they are implemented in Unix systems in more detail.

Unix Mail Delivery Agent

The most basic mail delivery function is the capability to send messages to users on the local host. Often Unix email implementations rely on separate standalone MDA programs to deliver messages to local users. Because these MDA programs concentrate only on delivering mail to local users, they can add additional bells and whistles that aren't available on MTA programs that include MDA functionality. This enables the mail administrator to offer additional mail features to mail users.

When the MTA program determines that a message is destined for a local user, it passes the message to the MDA program. At this point, the MDA program must ensure that the message gets delivered to the proper location, either to the local user's mailbox or to an alternate location defined by the local user.

MDA Functions

As mentioned, the main function of the MDA program is to deliver mail to users on the local mail server. To do this, the MDA program must know the location and type of mailboxes that are used by the email system. Three different types of user mailbox systems commonly are used on Unix servers:

- /var/spool/mail files
- $HOME/mail files
- Maildir-style mailbox directories

Each mailbox type has its own features that make it attractive to use. The /var/spool/mail file method creates a separate file for each user. Each message stored for a particular user is appended to the user's file. For systems with lots of users, this can create a directory with lots of files. The $HOME/mail method uses the same system of appending messages to a single file but moves the files to each users' $HOME directory. This can greatly increase access times for systems with lots of users. Another benefit of the $HOME/mail method is that, by moving the users' mailboxes to their $HOME directories, they can be controlled by system quota systems, allowing you to control how large the mailboxes can get.

The Maildir method takes the $HOME/mail method one step further. Not only does it place each user's messages in the correct $HOME directory, but it also creates a separate mail directory in $HOME where each message is stored as an individual file. Not only does this increase performance, but it also helps prevent corruption of the entire mailbox when one bad message is received. Although Maildir-style mailbox directories offer increased performance, security, and fault tolerance, many popular MDA and MUA programs are not capable of using them. Just about all MDA and MUA programs can use the /var/spool/mail mailbox files.

Several other features may be added to the basic MDA program. Different MDA programs offer different features that make them attractive to the mail administrator. Some of the more popular features are listed here:

- Automatic mail filtering
- Automatic mail replying
- Automatic program initialization by mail

The following sections describe these features and how they are implemented.

Automatic Mail Filtering

Possibly the nicest and most used feature of MDA programs is the capability to filter incoming mail messages. For users who get lots of email, this can be a lifesaver. Messages can be automatically sorted into separate folders based on a subject header value or even just one word within a subject header. Figure 12.2 demonstrates this process.

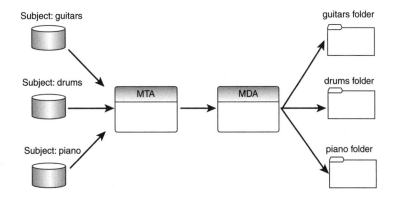

FIGURE 12.2
Sorting incoming mail messages to separate folders.

The MDA program must utilize a configuration file that allows the user to specify regular expressions to search fields in the incoming message header or body. As expressions are matched, the message will be saved in a predetermined folder in the user's mail area.

A similar feature is the capability to filter messages and throw away undesirable ones. This feature can help reduce unwanted unsolicited commercial email (UCE), also known as spam.

Automatic Mail Replying

Another feature of MDA programs is the capability for the mail user to configure an autoreply for email messages. As with message filtering, many MDA programs allow the mail user to send replies to mail senders based on values in the subject header field. Mail users can customize the autoreply function to support many different types of responses to received messages.

The mail user also can configure the MDA program to send mail responses to the original message sender based on predetermined values in the configuration file. Different values can elicit different messages in the reply. The mail user also can determine whether the original message will be stored in a mail folder or discarded after a response has been sent.

Automatic Program Initialization by Mail

Still another common feature with MDA programs is the option to run a program based on the contents of a message. The MDA program also can start different programs based on different text in messages.

Many MDA programs allow the mail user to create a configuration in which other programs are started based on values within the mail message, such as subject header values. This can provide such exotic functions as the production of different workstation sounds based on the particular subject heading of a new message or the execution of different monitoring programs based on a subject header field value.

Unix MDA Programs

Several Open Source MDA programs are available for the mail administrator to incorporate into the email system. Three of the most popular programs are binmail, mail.local, and procmail. This section describes these programs.

binmail

The binmail program is the most popular MDA program used on Unix systems. You might not recognize it by its official name, but you most likely have used it by its system name, mail.

The name "binmail" comes from its normal location on the system, /bin/mail. Really two separate versions of the binmail program exist: one for SRV4 versions of Unix and one for V7 versions. You must be careful to use the version that is applicable to your version of Unix. Most Linux distributions use the V7 version of binmail. This is the version that is used in Red Hat 7.1.

Messages are passed from the MTA program to the binmail program, which delivers the messages to the standard /var/spool/mail directory.

mail.local

Unix systems based on the BSD model use the mail.local program for local mail delivery (on Solaris systems, it is located in the /usr/lib directory). Similar to the binmail program, the mail.local program receives messages from the MTA program and then determines how to deliver them. The mail.local program is also similar to the binmail program, in that it uses the standard /var/spool/mail format of mailboxes (although most BSD systems use /var/mail as the mailbox directory). The mail.local executable is found in the /bin directory.

procmail

One of the more popular MDA programs in use is the procmail program, written by Stephen R. van den Berg. It has become so popular that many Unix implementations now install it by default, and many MTA programs utilize it in default configurations. Both Red Hat 7.1 and Solaris 8 use the procmail program for local mail delivery.

The popularity of the procmail program comes from its versatility in accepting user-configured "recipes" that allow a user to specify the processing of received mail. The user can create his own .procmailrc file to direct messages based on regular expressions to separate mailbox files, alternative email addresses, or even the /dev/null file, to automatically trash unwanted mail.

Unix Mail Transfer Agent

The MTA software is responsible for handling both incoming and outgoing mail messages. For each outgoing mail message, the MTA determines the destination of the recipient addresses. If the destination host is the local machine, the MTA can either deliver it to the local mailbox directly or pass the message off to the local MDA for delivery.

However, if the destination host is a remote mail server, the MTA must establish a communication link with the remote host to transfer the message. For incoming messages, the MTA must be capable of accepting connection requests from remote mail servers and receiving messages for local users. Many different types of protocols can be used to transfer messages between two remote hosts. The most common protocol used for Internet mail transfer is the Simple Mail Transfer Protocol (SMTP).

The Unix environment has many different types of Open Source MTA programs. Each program offers different features that distinguish it from the others. The following section describes some of the various features that can be found in MTA programs.

MTA Features

Much like the MDA programs, different MTA programs have been created to offer different features for the mail administrator. You should choose the MTA program that best meets the requirements of your particular email environment. Some of the most common features MTA programs offer are these:

- Security
- Ease of configuration
- Processing speed

The following sections describe these features in more detail.

MTA Security

In these days of increasing security awareness, any software that interacts with remote hosts is scrutinized for weaknesses that can be exploited by hackers. MTA software is no different.

Various safeguards are used to protect the MTA software from attacks from remote hosts. Many MTA programs run under separate usernames rather than as the root user, to help protect the mail server. Many MTA programs use special user accounts on the server to prevent a hacker from taking over the server if the software is compromised. Even tighter security is available in some packages that create a `chroot` environment, limiting the MTA package to a specific area on the filesystem. Extensive logging of each connection attempt is also a valuable feature found in most MTA packages.

Ease of Configuration

Although the advent of security features has made MTA software more complex, it is still nice to see software that can be fine-tuned for a particular email environment. Most MTA software packages allow the administrator to make configuration changes to control the behavior of the MTA software and how it reacts to particular email situations.

Different MTA software packages handle configuration options differently. Some software packages create one or two monolithic configuration files that contain all of the parameters used by the MTA software. A current trend in MTA software is the division of configuration parameters into separate configuration files, with each file containing parameters controlling a particular aspect of the software behavior.

Processing Speed

With many companies and ISPs implementing large email systems, performance is crucial. Most customers expect email recipients to receive the messages instantly. Having servers hold messages in message queues for a few hours is not often tolerated in today's email environment.

Most MTA packages implement some form of queuing strategy to handle email traffic as efficiently as possible. Some newer features include creating separate message queues to handle different classes of messages (such as new messages, bounced messages, mail list messages, and so on). By prioritizing messages, the MTA program can efficiently transfer messages even in high-volume situations. It is extremely frustrating to have your email held up while the mail server is processing the company's 10,000-member mailing list.

Unix MTA Programs

Many Open Source MTA programs are available for the Unix environment. Again, it is the job of the mail administrator to determine which MTA program meets most of the email requirements of his particular environment. This book covers three popular MTA packages that are in wide use on the Internet:

- sendmail
- qmail
- Postfix

The following sections describe these three MTA programs.

sendmail

The sendmail MTA program, originally written by Eric Allman, is one of the most popular Unix MTA programs available. The Sendmail Consortium (`http://www.sendmail.org`) currently maintains the source code for it. Eric has moved on to Sendmail, Inc., which provides commercial versions of the sendmail program and also provides support to the Sendmail Consortium.

The sendmail program has gained popularity mainly because of its great versatility. Many of the standard features of sendmail have become synonymous with email systems—virtual domains, message forwarding, user aliases, mail lists, and masquerading.

The sendmail program can be used for many different types of email configurations—large corporate Internet email servers, small corporate servers that dial into ISPs, and even standalone workstations that forward mail through a mail hub. Simply changing a few lines in sendmail's configuration file can change its characteristics and behavior.

Besides having the capability to change its server characteristics, sendmail also can parse and handle mail messages according to predefined rule sets. As the mail administrator, it is often desirable to filter messages depending on particular mail requirements. All that is needed to do this are new rules added to the sendmail configuration file.

Unfortunately, with versatility comes complexity. Handling the sendmail program's large configuration file often becomes overwhelming for novice mail administrators. Many books have been written to assist the mail administrator in determining the proper configuration file settings for a particular email server application.

qmail

The qmail program is a complete MTA program written and maintained by Dan Bernstein (`http://www.qmail.org`). It supports all the MTA functionality of the sendmail program.

The qmail program takes the idea of modular email software one more step. It breaks the MTA functions into several modules and uses separate programs to implement each function.

The qmail program requires several different user IDs to be added to the mail server. Each program module runs under a different user ID. If an intruder compromises one module, it most likely will not affect the other modules. The security features of qmail are often touted as the program's best feature.

Still another feature of qmail is its reliability. As each message enters the qmail system, it is placed in a mail queue. Then qmail uses a system of mail subdirectories and message states to ensure that each message stored in the message queue is not lost. As an added feature, qmail also can use Maildir-style mailboxes, decreasing the chance of corruption or lost messages in the message mailbox.

In addition, qmail uses multiple configuration files, one for each of its features. This can be a drawback of the program because, although it avoids the problem of managing one large configuration file, novice administrators often get confused over which feature is configured in which file.

Postfix

Wietse Venema wrote the Postfix program to be a complete MTA package. Similar to qmail, Postfix is written as a modular program. Postfix uses several different programs to implement the MTA functionality; it can be downloaded from the Postfix Web site (`http://www.postfix.org`).

Postfix requires a separate user ID to be added to the mail server. Unlike qmail, which uses a separate user ID for each module, Postfix runs each module under one user ID. Although it uses only one user ID, if an intruder compromises a Postfix module, he most likely will still not be able to control the mail server.

One of the nicest features of Postfix is its simplicity. Instead of using one large complex configuration file or multiple small configuration files, Postfix uses two files that use plain-text parameters and value names to define functionality. Most of the parameters default to standard values that allow the mail administrator to configure a complete mail server with a minimum amount of effort.

Unix Mail User Agent

The Unix email model uses a local mailbox for each user to hold messages for that user. MUA programs became available to provide a method for users to interface with the mailbox to read messages stored there.

MUAs do not receive messages; they only display messages that are already in the user's mailbox. Many MUA programs also offer the capability to create separate mail folders so that the user can store mail in separate locations.

Throughout the years, many different Open Source MUA programs have been available for the Unix platform. The following section describes some of the more popular features that MUA programs try to implement.

MUA Features

MUA programs use different features to distinguish themselves from other MUA programs. Two of the most significant features of an MUA program are the location in which it stores mail that has been read and the method by which it displays messages. The following sections describe these features in detail.

Mail Location

Over the brief history of Internet mail, two different philosophies regarding the storage location of user mail messages have developed. Both philosophies have proponents and opponents. In reality, both philosophies have advantages in their own right, given a particular email environment.

One philosophy supports the download of messages directly to the user's workstation, thus freeing up disk space on the mail server. Although this makes the job of the mail administrator easier, it often leads to confusion for users who check their mail from multiple workstations.

Users often check mail messages from home (thus downloading them to their home workstation) and then go into work and check mail messages from their office workstations. Unfortunately, the earlier messages are on the home workstation and have been deleted from the mailbox account. When the users get to work, they find that the messages are not retrievable from their offices. This can create considerable confusion.

The second philosophy solves the problem of multiple workstations by keeping all the messages on the mail server. As users read their mailboxes, only a copy of the message is sent to the workstation for display purposes. The actual messages still are stored in a file or directory on the mail server. No matter which workstation the users check their mail from, the same messages will be available for viewing. Although this makes life much simpler for users, the mail administrator's life is more complicated. With all messages stored on the mail server, disk space becomes a crucial factor.

Displaying Messages

With the advent of fancy GUI devices, MUA programs have become more sophisticated in their message display. Many Unix MUA programs still use text-mode graphics to display text messages. However, many Windows-based programs now have the capability to display rich-text and HTML-formatted documents.

To accommodate this, many email messages use the Multipurpose Internet Mail Extensions (MIME) format. MIME allows the message to contain multiple versions of the same information, each formatted using a different display method. It is the job of the MUA to determine the best method for message display. Thus, text-based terminals can display the message in text mode, while GUI terminals can display the same message as an HTML-generated page.

Although HTML-formatted messages are nice for users, they quickly become trouble-some for mail administrators. Often a simple three-sentence message turns into a large mail message due to added HTML formatting, complete with fancy background graphics and signature blocks that include pictures. It doesn't take long for these messages to clog a mail system.

Unix MUA Programs

Again, several very good Open Source MUA programs are available for the mail administrator to choose from. When choosing an MUA program, the administrator must find one that works on the operating system that the client workstations will be using.

The Open Source movement has created several very good MUA programs for Unix operating systems. This section describes three popular Unix MUA packages:

- binmail for text terminals
- PINE for graphical text terminals
- kmail for X Window terminals

binmail

Although binmail was discussed earlier as an MDA program, it does double duty as an MUA program. It allows users to access their mailboxes to read stored messages, and it allows them to send messages to other mail users as well. Listing 12.1 shows a sample mail session.

LISTING 12.1 Sample Mail Program Session

```
$ mail
Mail version 8.1 6/6/93.  Type ? for help.
"/var/spool/mail/rich": 4 messages 4 new
>N  1 barbara@shadrach.isp   Tue Apr 10 18:47 12/417 "This is the first tes"
 N  2 katie@shadrach.isp1.   Tue Apr 10 18:57 12/415 "Second test message"
 N  3 jessica@shadrach.isp   Tue Apr 10 19:23 12/413 "Third test message"
 N  4 mike@shadrach.ispnet   Tue Apr 10 19:42 12/423 "Fourth and final test"
& 1
Message 1:
From barbara@shadrach.isp1.net Tue Apr 10 18:47:05 2001
Date: 10 Apr 2001 23:47:05 -0000
From: barbara@shadrach.isp1.net
To: rich@shadrach.isp1.net
Subject: This is the first test message

Hi, This is a test message

& d
```

LISTING 12.1   continued

```
& 2
Message 2:
From katie@shadrach.isp1.net Tue Apr 10 18:57:32 2001
Date: 10 Apr 2001 23:57:32 -0000
From: katie@shadrach.isp1.net
To: rich@shadrach.isp1.net
Subject: Second test message

Hi, this is the second test message

& q
Saved 3 messages in mbox
$
```

The first line shows the mail program being executed with no command-line options. By default, this allows users to check the messages in their mailboxes. After entering the `mail` command, a summary of all the messages in the user's mailbox is displayed. The mail program reads messages only from either /var/spool/mail–style mailboxes or $HOME/mail–style mailboxes.

Each user has a separate file that contains all of that user's messages. The filename is usually the system username of the user, and the file is located in the system mailbox directory. Thus, all messages for username rich are stored in the file /var/spool/mail/rich. As new messages are received for the user, they are appended to the end of the file.

PINE

As advancements were made to the Unix environment, MUA programs became fancier. One of the first attempts at implementing graphics on Unix systems was the ncurses graphics library. Using ncurses, a program could manipulate the location of a cursor on the terminal screen and place characters almost anywhere on the terminal.

One MUA program that takes advantage of the ncurses library is the Program for Internet News and Email (PINE) program, developed at the University of Washington. Both Red Hat 7.1 and Solaris 8 include the PINE package, although it is included as an optional package in Solaris. When PINE is started, it paints a user-friendly menu on the user's terminal screen, as shown in Figure 12.3.

The PINE program assigns any messages in the user's mailbox to a special folder labeled INBOX. All new messages appear in the INBOX. The user can create separate folders to hold mail that already has been read, thus making message storage and retrieval easier. As can be seen from Figure 12.3, PINE also includes an address book feature, allowing the user to save important email addresses in a single location.

FIGURE **12.3**

The PINE program main menu screen.

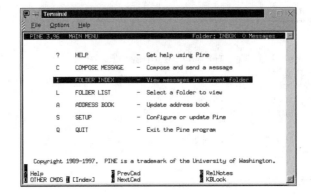

kmail

Almost all Unix systems support the graphical X Window environment. Red Hat Linux uses the Xfree86 software, and Solaris uses the openwindow software to run X Window programs on either the system console or a remote X terminal on the network. Many email MUA programs utilize the X Window System to display message information. The Open Source kmail MUA program can be used to read and send messages using the X Window System. Figure 12.4 shows a sample kmail session screen.

FIGURE **12.4**

The kmail MUA program main screen.

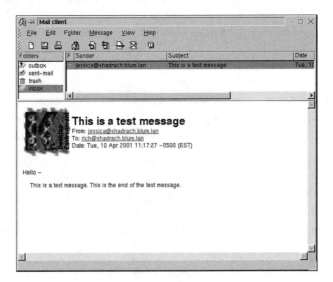

The SMTP Protocol

MTA programs must be capable of forwarding mail messages for remote users to the mail host that is responsible for that user. This requires some method of communication between the two mail servers. The Simple Mail Transfer Protocol (SMTP) was developed to allow two mail servers to transfer messages between themselves. Today, the most common medium for the SMTP protocol is the Internet, which uses the TCP/IP protocol to transfer data between hosts.

When a TCP session has been established and the SMTP server acknowledges the client by sending a welcome banner, it is the client's responsibility to control the connection between the two computers. The client accomplishes this by sending special commands to the server. The server should respond accordingly to each command sent.

RFC 821 defines the basic client commands that an SMTP server should recognize and respond to. There have been several extensions to the SMTP protocol since RFC 821 that not all servers have implemented. This section documents the basic SMTP keywords that are defined in RFC 821.

The basic format of an SMTP command is as follows:

`command [parameter]`

Here, `command` is a four-character SMTP command and `parameters` are optional qualifying data for the command. Table 12.1 shows the basic SMTP commands that are available. The following sections describe the commands in more detail.

Table 12.1 SMTP Basic Commands

Command	Description
HELO	Gives opening greeting from client
MAIL	Identifies sender of message
RCPT	Identifies recipients
DATA	Identifies start of message
SEND	Sends message to terminal
SOML	Stands for SEND or MAIL
SAML	Stands for SEND and MAIL
RSET	Resets SMTP connection
VRFY	Verifies username on system
EXPN	Queries for lists and aliases
HELP	Requests list of commands

TABLE 12.1   continued

Command	Description
NOOP	Stands for "no operation"; does nothing
QUIT	Stops the SMTP session
TURN	Reverses the SMTP roles

It is important for the mail administrator to understand the SMTP protocol and how messages are transferred between mail hosts. Mail problems often can be solved by understanding the SMTP errors returned by the mail server. The following sections describe the SMTP commands in more detail.

HELO Command

This is not a typo. By definition, SMTP commands are four characters long—thus, the opening greeting by the client to the server is the HELO command. The format for this command is shown here:

HELO *hostname*

The purpose of the HELO command is for the client to identify itself to the SMTP server. Unfortunately, this method was devised in the early days of the Internet before mass hacker break-in attempts. As you can see, the client can be identified as whatever it wants to use in the text string. That being the case, most SMTP servers use this command just as a formality. If they really need to know the identity of the client, they try to use a reverse DNS lookup of the client's IP address to determine the client's DNS name. For security reasons, many MTA packages can be configured to refuse to talk to hosts whose IP address does not resolve to a proper DNS hostname.

By sending this command, the client indicates that it wants to initialize a new SMTP session with the server. By responding to this command, the server acknowledges the new connection and should be ready to receive further commands from the client.

MAIL Command

The MAIL command is used to initiate a mail session with the server after the initial HELO command is sent. It identifies from whom the message is being sent. The format of the MAIL command is shown here:

MAIL *reverse-path*

The *reverse-path* argument not only identifies the sender, but it also identifies how to reach the sender with a return message. It always starts with the keyword FROM:. If the sender is a user on the client computer that initiated the SMTP session, the format for the MAIL command would look something like this:

```
MAIL FROM:rich@shadrach.ispnet1.net
```

Notice how the FROM section denotes the proper email address for the sender of the message, including the full hostname of the client computer. This information should appear in the text of the email message in the FROM section (more on that later). If the email message has been routed through several different systems between the original sender and the desired recipient, each system will add its routing information to the *reverse-path* section. This documents the path that the email message traversed to get to the server.

Often, mail from clients on private networks must traverse several mail-relay points before getting to the Internet. The *reverse-path* information is often useful in troubleshooting email problems or in tracking down senders who are purposely trying to hide their identity by bouncing their email messages off several unknowing SMTP servers.

RCPT Command

The RCPT command defines who the recipients of the message are. There can be multiple recipients for the same message. Each recipient normally is listed in a separate RCPT command line. The format of the RCPT command is shown here:

```
RCPT forward-path
```

The *forward-path* argument defines where the email is ultimately destined. This is usually a fully qualified email address, but it could be just a username that is local to the SMTP server. The forward path always starts with the keyword TO:. For example, the following RCPT command would send the message to user haley on the SMTP server that is processing the message:

```
RCPT TO: haley
```

Messages also can be sent to users on other computer systems that are remote from the SMTP server to which the message is sent.

For example, sending the following RCPT command to the SMTP server on computer shadrach.ispnet1.net would require shadrach.ispnet1.net to make a decision:

```
RCPT TO: riley@meshach.ispnet1.net
```

Because the user is not local to shadrach, shadrach must decide what to do with the message. There are three possible actions that shadrach could take with the message:

- shadrach could forward the message to the destination computer and return an OK response to the client. In this scenario, shadrach would add its hostname to the *reverse-path* of the MAIL command line to indicate that it is part of the return path to route a message back to the original sender.

- shadrach could refuse to forward the message but would send a reply to the client warning that it was not capable of delivering the message. The response also could verify that the address of meshach.ispnet1.net was a correct address for another server. Thus, the client then could try to resend the message directly to meshach.ispnet1.net.

- Finally, shadrach could refuse to forward the message but would send a warning to the client specifying that this operation is not permitted from this server. It would be up to the system administrator at shadrach to figure out what happened and why.

In the early days of the Internet, computers commonly used the first scenario and blindly forwarded email messages across the world. Unfortunately, that technique became popular with email spammers. Many ISPs allow their customers to relay email from their mail server but restrict outside computers from that privilege.

In the case of multiple recipients, it is up to the client to handle situations in which some of the recipients are not acknowledged. Some clients will abort the entire message and return an error to the sending user. Some will continue sending the message to the recipients that are acknowledged and will list the recipients that aren't acknowledged in a return message.

DATA Command

The DATA command is the meat and potatoes of the SMTP operation. After the MAIL and RCPT commands are hashed out, the DATA command is used to transfer the actual message. The format of the DATA command is shown here:

```
DATA
```

Anything after that command is treated as the message to transfer. Usually the SMTP server will add a timestamp and the return-path information to the head of the message. The client indicates the end of the message by sending a line with just a single period. The format for that line is shown here:

```
<CR><LF>.<CR><LF>
```

When the SMTP server receives this sequence, it knows that the message transmission is finished and that it should return a response code to the client indicating whether the message has been accepted.

Much work has been done on the format of the actual DATA messages. Technically, there is no wrong way to send a message, although work has been done to standardize a method. Any combination of valid ASCII characters will be transferred to the recipients. Listing 12.2 shows a sample session sending a short mail message to a local user on an SMTP server.

LISTING 12.2   Sample SMTP Session

```
$ telnet localhost 25
Trying 127.0.0.1...
Connected to localhost.ispnet1.net.
Escape character is '^]'.
220 shadrach.ispnet1.net ESMTP
HELO localhost
250 shadrach.ispnet1.net
MAIL FROM: rich@localhost
250 ok
RCPT TO:rich
250 ok
DATA
354 go ahead
This is a short test of the SMTP email system.
.
250 ok 959876575 qp 40419
QUIT
221 shadrach.ispnet1.net
Connection closed by foreign host.
you have mail
$ mail
Mail version 8.1 6/6/93.  Type ? for help.
"/var/mail/rich": 1 message 1 new
>N  1 rich@localhost        Thu Jun  1 12:22    8/339
& 1
Message 1:
From rich@localhost Thu Jun  1 12:22:55 2000

This is a short test of the SMTP email system.

& x
$
```

Listing 12.2 shows a typical SMTP exchange between two hosts. After entering the message header information, the client enters the DATA command, and the server responses.

Next the client sends the text message. Following the completed message is the terminating period, indicating the end of the message to the server. As you can see, the SMTP server transferred the message to the local user's mailbox account exactly as the server received it. Also note how the SMTP server included a timestamp and the return path information in the text of the email message.

Much work has been done in an attempt to standardize the format of Internet mail messages. RFC 822 specifies a standard format for sending text mail messages between hosts.

SEND Command

The SEND command is used to send a mail message directly to the terminal of a logged-in user. This command works only when the user is logged in, and it usually pops up as a message much like the Unix write command. This command does have a serious drawback: It is an easy way for an external user to determine who is logged into a computer system at any given time without having to authenticate to the system. Hackers have exploited this "feature" by searching the Internet for unsuspecting victims' user IDs and the times that the victims are logged in. Because it is such a security threat, most SMTP software packages do not implement this command anymore.

SOML Command

The SOML command stands for "SEND or MAIL." If the recipients are logged onto the computer system, the command behaves like the preceding SEND command. If not, it behaves like the MAIL command and sends the message to the recipients' mailbox. The "exploitability" of this command has made it another hacker tool, and it often is not implemented on newer SMTP server packages.

SAML Command

The SAML command stands for "SEND and MAIL." This command tries to cover both bases by both sending a message to the terminal of a logged-in user as well as placing the message in the user's mailbox. Again, the "exploitability" of this command has rendered it unsafe to implement.

RSET Command

The RSET command is short for "reset." If the client somehow gets confused by the responses from the server and thinks that the SMTP connection has gotten out of sync, it can issue the RSET command to return the connection back to the HELO command state. Thus, any MAIL, RCPT, or DATA information entered will be lost. Often this is used as a "last-ditch effort" when the client either has lost track of where it was in the command series or did not expect a particular response from the server.

VRFY Command

The VRFY command is short for "verify." You can use the VRFY command to determine whether an SMTP server can deliver mail to a particular recipient before entering the RCPT command mode. The format of this command is shown here:

VRFY *username*

When received, the SMTP server will determine whether the user is on the local server. If the user is local to the server, it returns the full email address of the user. If the user is not local, the SMTP server can either return a negative response to the client or indicate that it is willing to forward any mail messages to the remote user—depending on whether the SMTP server will forward messages for the particular client.

The VRFY command can be a very valuable troubleshooting tool. Often users incorrectly type a username or hostname in an email message and don't know why their mail message did not get to where they wanted it to go. Of course, the first thing they will do is complain about the lousy mail system and then contact you—the mail administrator. As the mail administrator, you can attempt to verify the email address in two ways. First, use the DNS host command to determine whether the domain name is correct and has a mail server associated with it. Then you can telnet to port 25 of the mail server and use the VRFY command to determine whether the username is correct. Listing 12.3 shows an example of using the VRFY command to check the validity of usernames.

LISTING 12.3 Example of the VRFY Command

```
[riley@shadrach riley]$ telnet localhost 25
Trying 127.0.0.1...
Connected to localhost.
Escape character is '^]'.
220 shadrach.ispnet1.net ESMTP Sendmail 8.9.3/8.9.3;
[ic:ccc] Thu, 26 Aug 1999 19:20:16 -050
HELO localhost
250 shadrach.ispnet1.net Hello localhost [127.0.0.1], pleased to meet you
VRFY rich
250 <rich@shadrach.ispnet1.net>
VRFY prez@mechach.ispnet1.net
252 <prez@mechach.ispnet1.net>
VRFY jessica
550 jessica... User unknown
QUIT
221 shadrach.ispnet1.net closing connection
Connection closed by foreign host.
[riley@shadrach riley]$
```

12

MAIL

Note the difference between the return codes for the usernames rich and prez. The VRFY command for rich returns a 250 code, which indicates that the server will accept messages for rich, who is a local user. The result from the prez VRFY command is 252, which indicates that the user is not local but that the mail server is willing to forward the message for him. The result codes will be explained in more detail later.

Much like some of the other useful commands, the VRFY command can be exploited by hackers and spammers. Because of this, many sites do not implement the VRFY command.

EXPN Command

The EXPN command is short for "expand." This command queries the SMTP server for mail lists and aliases. Mail lists are handy ways of sending mass mailings to groups of people with just one address. The format of the EXPN command is shown here:

```
EXPN mail-list
```

Here, mail-list is the name of the mail list or alias. The SMTP server returns either an error code, if the client does not have privileges to see the list, or the complete mailing list, one email address per line. Hackers and spammers have abused EXPN to obtain lists of valid user accounts on the mail server. Thus, many MTA packages offer configuration options to disable this command.

HELP Command

The HELP command is used to return a list of SMTP commands that the SMTP server will understand. Almost all SMTP software packages understand and process the basic RFC 821 commands listed here (except, of course, those disabled due to security issues). Extended SMTP commands (those added after RFC 821) supported by the mail server often are listed in the HELP command output, allowing remote servers to determine which extended SMTP commands are supported by the server.

Listing 12.4 shows the output from a HELP command issued to a Linux server running the sendmail SMTP package version 8.11.3.

LISTING 12.4 SMTP HELP Command Output

```
$ telnet localhost 25
Trying 127.0.0.1...
Connected to localhost.
Escape character is '^]'.
220 test.ispnet.net ESMTP Sendmail 8.11.3/8.11.3; Fri, 6 Apr 2001 07:25:37
HELO localhost
250 test.ispnet.net Hello IDENT:rich@localhost [127.0.0.1], pleased to meet you
HELP
214-2.0.0 This is sendmail version 8.11.3
```

LISTING 12.4 continued

```
214-2.0.0 Topics:
214-2.0.0      HELO    EHLO    MAIL    RCPT    DATA
214-2.0.0      RSET    NOOP    QUIT    HELP    VRFY
214-2.0.0      EXPN    VERB    ETRN    DSN     AUTH
214-2.0.0      STARTTLS
214-2.0.0 For more info use "HELP <topic>".
214-2.0.0 To report bugs in the implementation send email to
214-2.0.0      sendmail-bugs@sendmail.org.
214-2.0.0 For local information send email to Postmaster at your site.
214 2.0.0 End of HELP info
HELP RCPT
214-2.0.0 RCPT TO: <recipient> [ <parameters> ]
214-2.0.0      Specifies the recipient.  Can be used any number of times.
214-2.0.0      Parameters are ESMTP extensions.  See "HELP DSN" for details.
214 2.0.0 End of HELP info
QUIT
221 2.0.0 test.ispnet.net closing connection
Connection closed by foreign host.
$
```

12

MAIL

Two levels of help are available. By sending the HELP command alone, the SMTP server will give a brief overview of all of the available commands. By sending the HELP command with an argument that is another SMTP command, the server will return a more detailed description of the command, including any parameters that are required.

NOOP Command

The NOOP command is short for "no operation." This command has no effect on the SMTP server other than to elicit a positive response code. It is often a useful command to test connectivity without actually starting the message transfer process.

QUIT Command

The QUIT command does what it says. It indicates that the client computer is finished with the current SMTP session and wants to close the connection. It is the responsibility of the SMTP server to respond to this command and to initiate the closing of the TCP connection. If the server receives a QUIT command in the middle of an email transaction, any data previously transferred is deleted and not sent to any recipients.

TURN Command

The TURN command is not implemented on SMTP servers today, for security reasons. It is part of the RFC 821 standard because it was a great idea that, unfortunately, was exploited by hackers. The TURN command idea was modified in the extended SMTP RFCs to the ETRN command.

The TURN command allows two-way mail transfer between two computers using one TCP connection. Normally, the SMTP protocol sends mail in only one direction for each connection. The client host is in control of the transmission medium, and it directs the actions of the server through the SMTP commands that it sends. Mail can be sent only from the client to the server. It might be desirable, though, for a computer to make contact with an SMTP server and not only send mail to the server, but also receive any mail that the server had waiting to send back to the client.

As discussed previously, the server uses the domain name indicated by the HELO command text string to identify the client it is talking to. The TURN command allows the SMTP server to switch roles with the client and send any mail destined for the client's domain name to the client. The problem with TURN is the SMTP server's reliance on the client's identification of itself. If a hacker connects to the SMTP server and identifies himself as another computer's domain name, the server trustingly would send all the mail messages destined for that domain name to the hacker.

The sendmail MTA Package

Before you start configuring the sendmail MTA package for your email server, it is a good idea to understand all the parts that make up the package. Each part of the sendmail package performs a separate function of the MTA process, each working together to route mail messages to the proper destination. Figure 12.5 shows a block diagram of how these parts interact with one another.

FIGURE 12.5

Block diagram of the sendmail package.

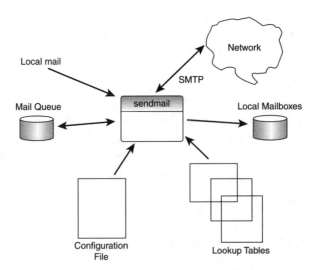

Besides the main sendmail program, there is a configuration file and several tables that can be created to contain information used by sendmail while processing incoming and outgoing mail messages. Table 12.2 lists the parts used in a normal sendmail installation.

TABLE 12.2 sendmail Parts

Part	Description
sendmail	Receives messages from local and remote users, and determines how to deliver them
sendmail.cf	Is a configuration file that controls the behavior of the sendmail program
sendmail.cw	Contains a list of domain names that the sendmail program will receive messages for
sendmail.ct	Contains a list of trusted users that can control the sendmail operations
aliases	Contains a list of valid local mail addresses that can redirect mail to another user, a file, or a program
newaliases	Creates a new aliases database file from a text file
mailq	Checks the mail queue and prints any messages
mqueue	Is the directory used to store messages waiting to be delivered
mailertable	Used to override routing for specific domains
domaintable	Used to map old domain names to new ones
virtusertable	Used to map users and domains to alternate addresses
relay-domains	Used to allow specific hosts to relay messages though the sendmail program
access	Used to allow or refuse messages from specific domains

Configuring sendmail

The sendmail program needs to be told how to handle messages as the server receives them. As an MTA, sendmail processes incoming mail and redirects it to another mail package, either on a remote system or on the local system. The configuration file directs sendmail in determining where and how to forward the message based on the destination mail address. The default location for the configuration file is /etc/mail/sendmail.cf.

The sendmail.cf file consists of rule sets that parse the incoming mail message and determine what actions to take. Each rule set is used to identify certain mail formats and instruct sendmail on the method of handling that message. As a message is received, its header is parsed and passed through the various rule sets to determine an action to take. Rules are available allowing sendmail to handle mail in many different formats. Mail received from an SMTP host has different header fields than mail received from a UUCP host. Sendmail must know how to handle any mail situation.

Rules also have helper functions defined in the configuration file. Three different types of helper functions can be defined:

- Classes define common phrases that are used to help the rule sets identify certain types of messages.
- Macros are values that are set to simplify the typing of long strings in the configuration file.
- Options are defined to set parameters for the sendmail program's operation.

The configuration file is made up of a series of classes, macros, options, and rule sets. Each function is defined as a single text line in the configuration file. Each line begins with a single character that defines the action for that line. Lines that begin with a space or a tab are continuation lines from a previous action line. Lines that begin with a pound sign (#) indicate comments and are not processed by sendmail.

The action at the beginning of the text line defines what the line is used for. Table 12.3 shows the standard sendmail actions and what they represent.

TABLE 12.3 sendmail Configuration File Lines

Configuration Line	Description
C	Defines classes of text
D	Defines a macro
F	Defines files containing classes of text
H	Defines header fields and actions
K	Defines databases that contain text to search
M	Defines mailers
O	Defines sendmail options
P	Defines sendmail precedence values
R	Defines rule sets to parse addresses
S	Defines rule set groups

If creating a configuration file using cryptic codes doesn't sound like fun to you, don't worry. Fortunately, there is a much easier way to create sendmail configuration files. The next section describes how to use the m4 macro preprocessor to create sendmail.cf files.

Using the m4 Macro Preprocessor

The GNU m4 macro processor is used to create the sendmail configuration file from a set of macro files. Each macro file uses keywords that represent the various functions that are used in the sendmail configuration file. As a macro file is read into the input, macros are expanded to their actual sendmail codes before being written to an output file. Some macro definitions are built into the m4 processor program, while other macro definitions are defined in the sendmail configuration distribution. Besides expanding macros, the m4 macro processor also can contain built-in functions such as running shell commands, manipulating text, and performing integer arithmetic.

Table 12.4 lists some of the m4 macros that are available to use in the sendmail configuration file.

TABLE 12.4 sendmail Macro Definitions

Macro	*Description*
divert(n)	Defines a buffer action for m4. When $n = -1$, the buffer is deleted; 0 starts a new buffer.
OSTYPE	Defines the operating system the macro is used on. This allows the m4 program to add operating system–specific macro files.
Domain	Defines what domain(s) the MTA will be using to transfer messages.
Feature	Defines a special feature set that will be used in the configuration file.
Define	Defines specific option values in the configuration file.
MASQUERADE_AS	Defines an alternative hostname that sendmail will answer messages as.
MAILER	Defines a method of mail transport for sendmail.

The entries in the macro definition file are expanded by the m4 preprocessor to create the complete configuration file. Listing 12.5 shows a sample macro file that can be used to create a standard sendmail configuration file.

LISTING 12.5   Sample sendmail Macro File

```
divert(-1)
divert(0)dnl
include(`/usr/lib/sendmail-cf/m4/cf.m4')dnl
OSTYPE(`linux')dnl

FEATURE(`allmasquerade')dnl
FEATURE(`masquerade_envelope')dnl
FEATURE(`always_add_domain')dnl
FEATURE(`virtusertable')dnl
FEATURE(`local_procmail')dnl
FEATURE(`access_db')dnl
FEATURE(`blacklist_recipients')dnl

MASQUERADE_AS(`ispnet1.net')dnl

MAILER(`smtp')dnl
MAILER(`procmail')dnl
```

As seen in this example, many different features can be defined with the Feature macro command. Each feature represents a separate set of action lines in the final configuration file. Note how each line ends with the text dnl. This represents the end of a line entry in the macro file.

Caution

You might have noticed the odd way of quoting text strings in the m4 macro file. The m4 preprocessor uses the backtick (`) and the single tick (') to represent quote marks. If you do not use these characters properly, the m4 program will not create the final configuration file properly.

After the .mc file is created, you must use the m4 preprocessor program to create the text configuration file. The output of the m4 preprocessor is the complete sendmail.cf configuration file, but it is sent to the standard output. You can redirect the output to a file this way:

```
m4 test.mc > sendmail.cf
```

After creating the sendmail.cf configuration file, you must copy it to the standard sendmail location, /etc/mail/sendmail.cf (you might want to copy the old sendmail.cf file to an alternate location, just in case). The new sendmail configuration will take effect the next time the sendmail program is started.

Unix Mail Clients

Many organizations such as programming and engineering shops contain Unix workstations. Although having lots of high-powered Unix workstations on the network is great for some applications, mail is not necessarily one of them.

If each Unix workstation were configured to act as an individual mail server, sending mail messages on the network could become complex and confusing. Each workstation would need to be uniquely identified on the network, and all users would have their own email address on their workstations. Figure 12.6 shows an example of what this would look like.

FIGURE 12.6

A fully routed workstation mail network.

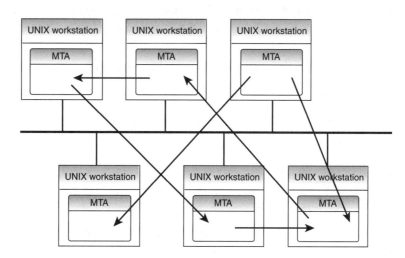

Each workstation MTA program would have to route each message to the appropriate workstation on the network. Each time a workstation was removed from the network (or a new one was added) the mail routes would change. Of course, this environment also would not be good for sharing or changing workstations. Each time users switched workstations, their email addresses would change! This would get very confusing, very fast.

To compensate for this environment, a Unix server dedicated as a central mail hub should be established. This server maintains a user account for everyone in the organization. The individual Unix workstations then can be configured as email clients, retrieving messages from the central mail hub.

This section describes the MTA configuration necessary to configure a Unix mail client in this environment, as well as the PINE software package used by the workstation user to read messages from the central mail hub and send messages through the central mail hub to remote mail hosts.

Unix Workstation Mail Configuration

When a Unix workstation is connected to an office network, instead of configuring the MTA package to send messages directly to each remote host as an email server would do, you can configure it to send all messages to the central mail hub. The central mail hub then can be configured to determine where the message should be transferred.

This also has the added benefit of simplifying the software requirements on the workstation. Although an MTA package must still be installed, no local mail delivery is required, so there is no need for a separate MDA package. Similarly, there is no requirement for remote users to access mail on the workstation, so there is no need for an MUA package as well.

Listing 12.6 shows a sample sendmail macro file that can be used to generate a configuration file for this purpose.

LISTING 12.6   Sample Unix Workstation Macro File

```
divert(-1)
divert(0)
include(`/usr/lib/sendmail-cf/m4/cf.m4')dnl
OSTYPE(`linux')dnl
FEATURE(`nullclient', `[192.168.1.1]')dnl
```

As you can tell, this configuration file is not too difficult. It defines the standard operating system sendmail files (Linux, in this example) and one sendmail FEATURE line, which defines the nullclient feature. This feature configures sendmail to forward all mail messages to the mail server specified in the FEATURE line. In this example, it is the IP address 192.168.1.1. This even includes messages for other usernames configured on the same local host. No messages will be stored in the local host mail queue.

You can create the sendmail.cf file by using the m4 macro preprocessor and copying the newly created file to the appropriate directory:

```
m4 test.mc > sendmail.cf
cp sendmail.cf /etc/mail/sendmail.cf
```

Normally this configuration would result in sendmail forwarding each message individually to the central mail hub. Occasionally, a message destined for the mail hub might get "stuck" in the mail queue on the local host. It is a good idea to run the sendmail program as a background cron process once in a while to flush out any stuck messages.

The format to use for sendmail to run once, process messages in the queue, and exit is this:

`/usr/bin/sendmail -q`

The `-q` option is used to instruct sendmail to process any messages in the mail queue immediately. Thus, any stuck messages can be processed manually by sendmail each time the cron job executes.

Using PINE to Read and Send Mail Messages

Because all the mailboxes for the organization are located on a separate central mail hub, users must be able to connect to the mail server using an MUA program to read their messages. The most popular MUA program for the Unix environment is the PINE package, described earlier in our discussion of PINE.

You must configure the PINE program to access the proper remote mailbox on the central mail hub for the workstation. Each of the users on the workstation should have a PINE configuration file, .pinerc, which is located in the users' $HOME directory.

You can change the value for the remote mailbox using the PINE Setup option in the main menu. Pressing the C key brings up the Config option, displaying the PINE SETUP CONFIGURATION screen. This enables you to change values for the PINE configuration settings. To set the location of the central mail hub mailbox, you must change the value for the inbox-path parameter. Of course if all of your users connect to the same central mail server, you can create a standard .pinerc file that can be used on all of the users' home directories.

The inbox-path parameter points to the location of the default mailbox where all incoming messages are stored. By default, it is set to the /var/spool/mail mailbox for the user on the local host. Because the workstation does not receive any messages, you must change this default value to point to the mailbox on the central mail hub. This can be done using the following format:

`{mailhost}inbox`

Here, `mailhost` is the name or IP address of the central mail hub. The completed entry should look similar to the value shown in Figure 12.7.

After entering the new value, you must exit the setup screen and save the settings. The PINE program then attempts to log into the central mail hub using the IMAP protocol to read the mailbox for the username supplied.

FIGURE **12.7**

*PINE setup con-
figuration screen.*

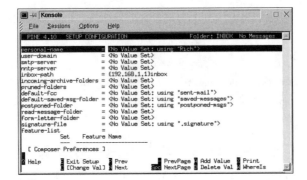

Server Topics

As mentioned in the "Unix Mail Clients" section, you can create a mail server that acts as the central mail hub for your organization. A central mail hub often is configured to accept messages addressed to the specific domain name of the organization as the mail host address.

This section describes the parts of a central mail hub and tells how to configure them.

Dedicated Domain Mail Hub

The sendmail configuration file used for the central mail hub is more complicated than the client configuration file shown in the previous section. Some common features used for central mail hubs are listed here:

- Allowing internal users to forward messages through the mail hub to external email addresses
- Using the organization domain name as the mail host address (such as prez@company.com instead of prez@mailhost.company.com)
- Using sophisticated MDA programs (such as procmail) to allow mail filtering to block spam

For the mail hub to be capable of processing messages for remote hosts, it must be on a dedicated Internet connection (one that is active 24 hours a day, 7 days a week). If the server is on a dial-up connection, any mail sent to the server while it is disconnected will be lost. When the mail hub is on a dedicated Internet connection, precautions must be taken to ensure that spammers can't use the mail hub to forward their own email messages sent from other sites. However, because this is the mail gateway for internal users to send mail out to the Internet, it should allow your domain clients access to relay messages. The sendmail access table is used to create a table of addresses that are allowed to forward messages through the mail hub. Messages received from addresses not in the table are blocked.

> **Note**
>
> When operating a mail gateway, care should be taken to ensure that it doesn't forward messages for all remote hosts. This feature (called an *open relay*) can be exploited by spammers to help hide their identity. Spammers can bounce their messages off your mail server to their destinations. When the spam message is forwarded by your mail server to an unsuspecting recipient, your mail server address will be on the Received By header field, and you might get blamed for the spam message. Many organizations track open relay servers and black list their addresses, refusing to accept any messages from them (even legitimate ones). When creating the sendmail access table, take care that you are not overly general in the address definitions.

The sendmail masquerade feature allows the mail server to accept messages destined for an address other than the standard hostname. This feature can be used to accept messages addressed to the domain. Along with this feature, most administrators also add the masquerade_envelope feature that changes the address of all outbound messages to the domain name, which eliminates confusion in reply addresses.

Finally, the sendmail mailer feature can be used to define the procmail mailer for local messages. Listing 12.7 shows a sample macro file that will produce the necessary sendmail configuration file.

LISTING 12.7 Sample Dedicated Linux Mail Server Macro File

```
divert(-1)
divert(0)dnl
include(`/usr/lib/sendmail-cf/m4/cf.m4')dnl
OSTYPE(`linux')dnl

FEATURE(`allmasquerade')dnl
FEATURE(`masquerade_envelope')dnl
FEATURE(`always_add_domain')dnl
FEATURE(`local_procmail')dnl
FEATURE(`access_db')dnl

MASQUERADE_AS(`smallorg.org')dnl

MAILER(`smtp')dnl
MAILER(`procmail')dnl
```

The macro file defines FEATURE commands that the mail hub needs for this environment. Each FEATURE line generates the necessary sendmail.cf configuration lines to perform the function. The access_db feature uses the sendmail access database that contains the domain name or the subnet IP address of the local network. This will allow local users to relay messages intended for external users through the mail gateway. The allmasquerade and masquerade_envelope features allow the mail hub to send messages using the domain name (smallorg.org, in this example) instead of the local hostname. The MASQUERADE_AS function defines the masquerade name to be used.

Finally, the types of mailers that will be used by sendmail are defined. The smtp mailer is used to route messages for users on remote SMTP hosts using the SMTP protocol, while the procmail mailer is used to forward messages for local users using the procmail program.

After the configuration macro file is created, you must create the sendmail.cf file and copy it to the proper directory:

```
m4 test.mc > sendmail.cf
cp sendmail.cf /etc/mail/sendmail.cf
```

Next, you must create the access table, listing the addresses of the local workstations that are allowed to forward mail through the central mail hub. The access table is created as an ASCII text file and is converted into the binary database file using the makemap command.

Each entry in the access table represents an address or address range that should be either specifically blocked or allowed to forward messages. The format of the entry is as follows:

```
address    value
```

The *value* parameter may be one of the following:

- OK—Accepts mail for the mail server from the address specified
- RELAY—Accepts all mail from the address specified
- REJECT—Refuses all mail from the address specified and returns an error message
- DISCARD—Refuses all mail from the address specified and does not return an error message

A simple access table for a small network would have a single entry and would look like this:

```
192.168.    RELAY
```

This entry allows all workstations on the local 192.168.0.0 network to forward messages through the mail server, and it prevents all other servers from using the mail server as an open relay. To convert this file into the binary database file used by sendmail, the `makemap` command is used:

```
makemap hash /etc/mail/access < /etc/mail/access
```

After restarting sendmail, the new configuration and access table would take effect.

Using procmail for the Local Mail Delivery Agent

MTA packages often use an external MDA program to deliver messages to local users. This allows the MDA package to include fancy features lacking in the MTA package. The procmail package is a popular MDA package that includes its filtering capability to help block spam and virus-infected messages.

The .procmailrc file located in each user's $HOME directory controls the delivery of mail messages from the procmail program. Individual users can create their own .procmailrc file to specify how their messages are handled.

Mail delivery is controlled by recipes defined in the .procmailrc file. Each recipe defines a matching expression value and an action for procmail to take when a message matches the expression. The format of a procmail recipe is shown here:

```
recipe header line
condition line(s)
action line
```

The recipe header line defines the basic action of the recipe. All recipe lines start with this heading:

```
:0 [flags] [: locallockfile]
```

The flags identify the basic function that the recipe will perform. Table 12.5 lists the flags that are available.

TABLE 12.5 Recipe Flags

Flag	*Description*
A	Is not executed unless the conditions of the last preceding recipe are met.
a	Is not executed unless the conditions of the immediately preceding recipe are met.

TABLE 12.5   continued

Flag	Description
B	egreps the body of the message.
b	Feeds the body of the message to the destination (default).
c	Generates a carbon copy of this message.
D	Distinguishes between upper and lower case (default is to ignore case).
E	Is not executed unless the conditions of the last preceding recipe were not met.
e	Is not executed unless the immediately preceding recipe failed.
f	Considers the pipe as a filter.
H	egreps the message header (default).
h	Feeds the header of the message to the destination (default).
i	Ignores any write errors on the recipe.
r	Does not ensure that messages end with an empty line (raw mode).
W	Waits for the filter or program to finish and checks the exit code. Suppresses any "Program failure" messages.
w	Waits for the filter or program to finish and checks the exit code. Does not suppress any error messages.

The flags are listed in the recipe header line after the :0 header. More than one flag can be entered on the recipe header line.

After the flags, if a lock file is required, the mail administrator either can specify a specific lock file by name or can omit the lock filename to allow procmail to use a default lock file. For example, this recipe header line directs procmail to use the default flags (Hhb) and to utilize the default lock file when processing the message:

```
:0:
```

Alternatively, the mail administrator can stipulate a specific lock file to use:

```
:0 Whc: msgid.lock
```

After the header line, one or more recipe condition lines must be defined. Each condition line must start with an asterisk (*). After the asterisk, a normal regular expression is used as the matching condition. Besides normal regular expressions, procmail defines seven special conditions. Table 12.6 lists the special conditions.

TABLE 12.6   procmail Special Conditions

Condition	Description
!	Inverts the condition
$	Evaluates the condition according to shell substitution rules inside double quotes
?	Uses the exit code of the specified program
<	Checks whether the total message length is less than the specified number of bytes (in decimal)
>	Checks whether the total message length is greater than the specified number of bytes (in decimal)
variable ??	Matches the remainder of the condition against the environment variable specified
\	Quotes any of the special characters to use as normal characters

The easiest way to learn how to write condition lines is to see a few examples. This condition line checks whether the message subject header field contains the word *guitars*:

```
^Subject:.*guitars
```

Any received messages with the word *guitars* in the message subject header field would match this condition. This condition line checks whether the message subject header field contains the words *guitars* and *bass*:

```
^Subject:.*guitars.*bass
```

Received messages with both of the words *guitars* and *bass* in the message subject header field would match this condition line. Finally, this condition line checks the entire message for the word *meeting*:

```
* meeting
```

Any received message with the word *meeting* anywhere in the message would match this condition line.

After defining the condition lines, the procmail action line must be defined. The action line defines the action that procmail will take if the condition line is matched with a message.

Much like the condition line, the action line can start with a special character that describes the basic action that will be taken. Table 12.7 describes the action line special characters.

TABLE 12.7   procmail Action Line Special Characters

Character	Description
!	Forwards the message to the specified addresses
|	Starts the specified program
{	Starts a block of recipes checked if the condition is matched
}	Ends a block of recipes checked if the condition is matched
text	Forwards the message to the mailbox defined by text

Each recipe has only one action line. The action line defines what procmail will do with any messages that match the condition lines. Again, the easiest way to explain this is to show some examples.

Listing 12.8 is an example of a simple .procmailrc file for a sample user on the mail server.

LISTING 12.8   Sample .procmail File

```
:0 c
messages

:0
* ^From.*guitar-list
{
    :0 c
    ! rich@ispnet3.net

    :0
    guitars
}

:0 hc
* !^FROM_DAEMON
* !^X-Loop: rich@ispnet1.net
| (formail -r -I"Precedence: junk" \
-A"X-Loop: rich@ispnet1.net" ; \
echo "Thanks for your message, but I will be out of the office until 1/4") \
| $SENDMAIL -t
```

LISTING 12.8 continued

```
:0
* ^Subject.*spammer
/dev/null
```

The .procmailrc file shown in Listing 12.8 contains four separate recipes that are processed by procmail:

1. The first recipe places a copy of all received messages in the mail folder named messages.

2. The second recipe demonstrates the use of recipes within a recipe. The main recipe first checks whether the received message is from the guitar-list user. If it is, both of the internal recipes are checked. First, a copy of all the messages is forwarded to the email address rich@ispnet3.net. Next, a copy of all the messages is placed in the mail folder named guitar.

3. The third recipe demonstrates both invoking an external program and creating an autoreply. The recipe states that all messages that are not sent from either a daemon process or the original user are forwarded to the formail program. This program is included with the procmail distribution. It is used to help filter header information from messages. Two header fields are added, a `Precedence:` line and an `X-Loop` line to help prevent message loops. After that, a message is generated and sent to the local MTA process.

4. The last recipe demonstrates filtering messages based on a `Subject` header line. Any message with a subject containing the word *spammer* is placed in the mail folder /dev/null. System administrators will notice that this is a special file—it maintains a 0-byte file size. Any information copied there is lost forever. Thus, this recipe deleted any messages with the subject "spammer." This technique often is used for blocking known spam messages from your email server.

Each message is processed against each recipe. Any recipes whose condition line matches the message are processed. However, recipes that match a message but that are not specifically set to copy the message will redirect the message from the normal inbox. For example, the second example in Listing 12.8 redirects messages from the guitar-list to the guitar folder. These messages will not appear in the normal inbox mail folder.

The third example shown previously—creating autoreply messages—is a great feature to use when you know that you will be away from your mail server for an extended period of time. Any message sent to your email account will generate an automatic reply message to the sender with any text that you need. Listing 12.9 shows an example of this feature.

LISTING **12.9**   Sample Autoreply Session

```
$ mail rich
Subject: Test message
Hi -

     This is a test message sent while you were out.
.
Cc:
$ mail
Mail version 8.1 6/6/93.  Type ? for help.
"/var/spool/mail/jessica": 1 message 1 new
>N  1 rich@shadrach.ispnet1.n  Tue Dec  5 18:01  17/673   "Re: Test message"
&1
Message 1:
From rich@shadrach.ispnet1.net  Tue Dec  5 18:01:22 2000
Delivered-To: jessica@shadrach.ispnet1.net
To: jessica@shadrach.ispnet1.net
Subject: Re: Test message
References: <20001205160122.10428C352@shadrach.ispnet1.net>
In-Reply-To: <20001205160122.10428C352@shadrach.ispnet1.net>
X-Loop: rich@shadrach.ispnet1.net
Precedence: junk
Date: Tue,  5 Dec 2000 18:01:22 -0500 (EST)
From: rich@shadrach.ispnet1.net (Rich Blum)

Thanks for your message, but I will be out of the office until 1/4

&
```

Note that the recipe created for the autoreply function uses the c flag. Thus, only a copy of the message is used for the autoreply. The original message should be safely stored in the normal mailbox for when the user returns to read his mail.

Many other recipes are useful for local mail users. There are links on the procmail Web site (http://www.procmail.org) to posted recipe examples. These examples can help users create their own procmail delivery masterpieces.

Care should be taken when allowing individual users to create their own .procmailrc files. It is possible for a wayward user to create a recipe that does not do what you would want, such as create endless mail loops, overwrite personal mail files, or allow hackers to run programs on the server illegally. The procmail program is a complicated application that should not be taken lightly.

SMTP Authentication

A popular method of allowing remote hosts to relay messages through email servers is to use an SMTP authentication method. The SMTP authentication method can uniquely identify the remote mail server so that your mail server can determine whether it is allowed to relay messages.

One of the most popular methods of authenticating network connections is the Simple Authentication and Security Layer (SASL). This protocol defines a set of authentication mechanisms that can be used by any network application to authenticate remote users. Many Open Source MTA packages use SASL to implement the ESMTP AUTH command, which allows ESMTP hosts to use client authentication within a standard ESMTP session.

RFC 2222 describes how SASL can be used to provide an authentication mechanism for network applications that use client/server commands, such as POP3, IMAP, and SMTP. SASL itself is not a complete application; it just provides authentication support for existing applications. It should be used as a plug-in for network applications, such as the sendmail program used to receive mail from remote network hosts.

This section describes SASL and tells how it is used to authenticate SMTP users with the SMTP AUTH command.

How SASL Operates

SASL support must be compiled into the network application program. It operates within the network application, providing an application program interface (API) that can be called on to validate authentication attempts by remote users.

The network application must provide a method to accept an authentication token from the remote network client. This usually is done in the form of a text command, such as the SMTP AUTH command described later. The authentication token is passed to the SASL layer for verification.

If the authentication token is verified, SASL returns a positive response to the application, and the remote network client is allowed to continue using the network application as normal. If the authentication token is rejected, SASL returns a negative response and the remote client is not allowed access to the application.

It should be noted that SASL does not provide for encrypting the network session. All SASL provides is a means to authenticate the remote user. In fact, it is possible to choose an SASL authentication method that sends the authentication data in clear text, providing no confidentiality.

SASL Authentication Mechanisms

Each authentication session must use a specific authentication mechanism. The authentication mechanism is an underlying protocol that is used to send the authentication tokens to the server. Many different mechanisms can be used to authenticate the user within the SASL framework. RFC 2222 defines three specific mechanisms:

- **KERBEROS_V4**—The Kerberos encryption algorithm
- **GSSAPI**—The Generic Security Service authentication key
- **SKEY**—The MD4 digest algorithm

A username and password pair is encoded using the encryption technique. Obviously, both the client and the server must use the same encryption technique for the SASL session.

Since the publication of RFC 2222, several other mechanisms have been defined for SASL. The CRAM-MD5 and DIGEST-MD5 mechanisms provide another common encryption technique that uses Message Digest 5 challenge/response model similar to the KERBEROS and SKEY methods. These have become common mechanisms for secure mail clients.

The PLAIN mechanism allows the client to send clear-text ASCII user IDs and passwords to the server. This method by itself provides no security because the tokens easily can be intercepted on the network and can be compromised. It is assumed that the PLAIN mechanism should be used only in secure (encrypted) network connections.

Possibly the most popular mechanism is LOGIN. This mechanism uses Base64 encoding of the user ID and the password. Although the user ID and password are encoded, encoding itself does not mean secure communication. If the encoded user ID and password are captured, it is a trivial exercise to decode them to their text equivalents.

Note

Although the LOGIN mechanism is not recommended by most SASL software packages, if you need to support Microsoft Outlook and Netscape Messenger clients, you must include support for the LOGIN mechanism in your SASL environment because both of these packages use the LOGIN mechanism to encode user IDs and passwords.

Using SASL in SMTP

RFC 2554 provides an additional command for SMTP servers to support SASL authentication. A remote client can send an authentication token using the SMTP AUTH command. The AUTH command can be used as a standalone command or as an option to the MAIL FROM: command to identify that a trusted host already has authenticated the message.

As a standalone command, the format of the AUTH command is as follows:

AUTH *mechanism*

The *mechanism* parameter defines what authentication mechanism the remote client wants to use for the SASL session. The local server and the remote client must be capable of agreeing on a common mechanism for the authentication to work. To help this process, the ESMTP command allows the server to advertise what authentication mechanisms it supports within the EHLO greeting banner. Listing 12.10 shows the start of a sample ESMTP session.

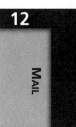

LISTING 12.10   Sample ESMTP Session

```
$ telnet localhost 25
Trying 127.0.0.1...
Connected to localhost.
Escape character is '^]'.
220 shadrach.ispnet1.net ESMTP Sendmail 8.12.3/8.12.3; Thu, 5 Apr 2001
[ic:ccc] 09:12:36 -00
EHLO shadrach.ispnet1.net
250-shadrach.ispnet1.net Hello IDENT:rich@localhost [127.0.0.1], pleased
[ic:ccc] to meet you
250-ENHANCEDSTATUSCODES
250-EXPN
250-VERB
250-8BITMIME
250-SIZE
250-DSN
250-ONEX
250-ETRN
250-XUSR
250-AUTH LOGIN DIGEST-MD5
250 HELP
```

The EHLO greeting banner lists the ESMTP commands that the mail server accepts. The AUTH command is listed, along with the authentication mechanisms that it supports. The remote client must determine which common authentication mechanism is appropriate for the network environment. Obviously in this example, if the remote client also supports both the LOGIN and DIGEST-MD5 mechanisms, it would be better to select the DIGEST-MD5 mechanism because it is more secure.

When the client sends the AUTH command, the server must respond with an authentication challenge phrase. The phrase will differ, depending on the authentication mechanism used. Listing 12.12 shows a sample SMTP session using the LOGIN mechanism.

LISTING 12.12   Sample SMTP Authentication Session

```
$ telnet localhost 25
Trying 127.0.0.1...
Connected to localhost.
Escape character is '^]'.
220 shadrach.ispnet1.net ESMTP Sendmail 8.12.3/8.12.3; Thu, 5 Apr 2001
[ic:ccc] 09:12:36 -00
EHLO shadrach.ispnet1.net
250-shadrach.ispnet1.net Hello IDENT:rich@localhost [127.0.0.1],
[ic:ccc] pleased to meet you
250-ENHANCEDSTATUSCODES
250-EXPN
250-VERB
250-8BITMIME
250-SIZE
250-DSN
250-ONEX
250-ETRN
250-XUSR
250-AUTH LOGIN DIGEST-MD5
250 HELP
AUTH LOGIN
334 VXNlcm5hbWU6
cmljaA==
334 UGFzc3dvcmQ6
cHJsbmpn
235 2.0.0 OK Authenticated
MAIL FROM: rich@shadrach.ispnet1.net
250 2.1.0 rich@[158.18.1.153]... Sender ok
RCPT TO: richard.blum@meshach.ispnet2.net
250 2.1.5 richard.blum@meshach.ispnet2.net... Recipient ok
DATA
354 Enter mail, end with "." on a line by itself
Subject: test
From: rich@shadrach.ispnet1.net
To: richard.blum@meshach.ispnet2.net

This is a test message.
.
250 2.0.0 f35EDFB04406 Message accepted for delivery
QUIT
221 2.0.0 shadrach.ispnet1.net closing connection
Connection closed by foreign host.
$
```

The server accepts the AUTH LOGIN command sent by the client, and a challenge phrase is returned. The client then responds to the challenge phrase using the negotiated mechanism (LOGIN, in this example). At the end of the challenge/response, the server indicates whether the authentication attempt has been successful. If it has, the SMTP session can continue as normal.

RFC 2554 also provides a method of identifying authenticated messages relayed through mail servers. If a mail server receives a message using the SMTP AUTH command but must relay it on to another mail server, it should indicate to the receiving host that the message already has been authenticated.

RFC 2554 provides an extension to the standard MAIL FROM: SMTP command to add authentication notification. The command format is shown here:

```
MAIL FROM: reverse-path AUTH=address
```

The AUTH parameter identifies the address of the host that has previously authenticated the messages and vouches for its authenticity. If *address* is set, the listed host already has authenticated the message using the AUTH command, and no further authentication is required (assuming that the receiving host trusts the sending host listed in the AUTH parameter). If *address* is set to an empty set (<>), the sending host has not authenticated the message.

IMAP and POP Servers

Users who have physical access to the mail host can log into an interactive session such as a console screen or an X Window session. After logging into the mail server, a user can use a Mail User Agent (MUA) program such as PINE, elm, or kmail to access the local mailbox and manage messages. These types of programs allow users to view and delete mail messages from an interactive session on the local mail server.

Unfortunately, many users do not have physical access to the mail server host. In fact, in most cases it is impossible for all users on the network to have physical access to read email messages on the same mail server. The next approach for remote clients is to utilize programs such as telnet or X terminal to establish a connection with the remote mail server. Although this works, it is extremely inefficient for reading mail messages. Both telnet and X terminal sessions create a large network overhead for reading just a few lines of text messages.

The best solution that mail administrators have available is to use remote MUAs. Remote MUAs offer a method for remote users to access their mailboxes on the local mail server without a large network overhead. The MUA can access the remote mailbox and download just the information necessary for the client computer to present the message to the user.

Two protocols that allow remote access of mailboxes are the Post Office Protocol (POP3) and the Interactive Mail Access Protocol (IMAP). The POP3 and IMAP protocols allow remote users to view and delete mail messages on the local mail server from a remote workstation using an email client program. The Unix mail server must run server software that supports either the POP3 or the IMAP protocols to allow remote users access to their mailboxes.

The POP Protocol

The Post Office Protocol (POP) has been an extremely popular protocol. Currently it is on its third official release version (thus, the name POP3). Figure 12.8 demonstrates how the POP3 protocol can be used to retrieve mail from a mail server.

FIGURE 12.8
Overview of the POP3 protocol.

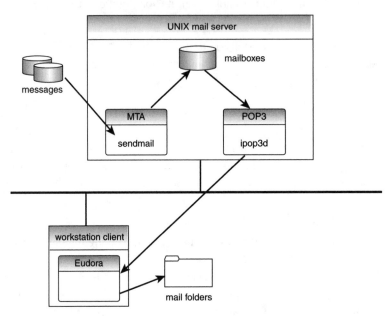

The user's client computer can use the POP3 protocol to download messages from the user's mailbox on the mail server. After it's downloaded, the message can be deleted from the mail server or the user can elect to keep the mail message on the server. Either way, the message is downloaded in its entirety for the user to be able to view on the remote client computer using email client software.

The IMAP Protocol

The Interactive Mail Access Protocol (IMAP) has been a lesser-known protocol in the email world, but it is quickly gaining popularity. Currently, it is at release version 4, revision 1 (commonly called IMAP4rev1). Figure 12.9 demonstrates how the IMAP protocol works.

The IMAP protocol uses a series of text commands that can be sent from the network client to the mail server. Each command instructs the mail server to perform a particular function. Table 20.2 shows the IMAP commands that can be used by the network client.

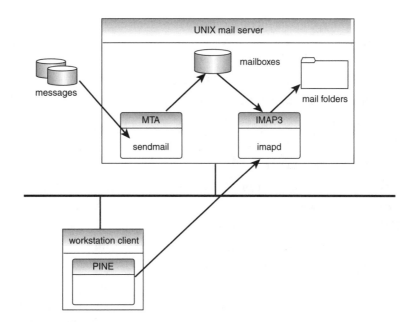

FIGURE **12.9**
Overview of the
IMAP protocol.

The UW IMAP Server

One of the most popular POP and IMAP server packages was developed at the University of Washington. The UW IMAP package includes the ipop3d and imapd programs to provide both POP3 and IMAP servers for the Unix host. Both Red Hat 7.1 and Solaris 8 include the ipop3d and imapd programs in their installations.

If you want to download the latest version of the ipop3d and imapd programs, they are available from the UW IMAP Web site at http://www.washington.edu/imap/. This site contains information about the UW IMAP project at the university, as well as links to the current release of UW IMAP. The current release at the time of this writing is version 2001.

Note

Note that prior to the imap-2000 release, the version name for UW IMAP was different. The previous version to the 2000 release was version 4.0.7.

You also can download many development versions as new features and patches are developed. The development versions are marked with the phrase BETA.SNAP-*yymmddhhmm*, where *yymmddhhmm* is a number that represents the year, date, and time of the development release.

You can download the source code distribution by the link provided at the Web site. Alternatively, you can connect directly to the FTP site at ftp.cac.washington.edu and check the /imap directory for the current release version. A link named `imap.tar.Z` is always set to the current release version. At the time of this writing, it is imap-2001.BETA. SNAP-01008162300. Remember to use BINARY mode when retrieving the file.

After you have downloaded the source code distribution file, you can unpack it into a working directory using this command:

```
tar -zxvf imap.tar.Z -C /usr/local/src
```

This produces a subdirectory named after the release version and places the source code in subdirectories underneath it.

The UW IMAP program does not use a config script in its installation because it does not have any feature options that are necessary to add at compile time. Instead, features are defined as `make` command-line options.

One feature that must be included is the type of password method that you are using on your Unix system. The UW IMAP makefile uses a three-character code to define different types of Unix systems and password methods.

Many Unix distributions offer only one password method. If your system is one of these, all you must do is find the three-character code for your Unix system to use on the `make` command line. For Unix distributions that offer multiple password-authentication methods (such as Linux), you must determine the password method that your system uses and include the three-character code appropriate for it. All the codes can be found in the comments in the makefile. Table 12.8 shows a few common system codes for various Unix systems.

TABLE 12.8   UW IMAP make Options

Option	Description
bsd	Generic BSD-based systems
bsf	FreeBSD systems
gso	GCC Solaris
gsu	GCC Sun-OS
hpx	HP-UX 10.*x* systems
lnx	Traditional Linux systems
lnp	Linux with Pluggable Authentication Modules (PAM)
neb	NetBSD systems
s40	Sun-OS 4.0
sl4	Linux using –lshadow for passwords
sl5	Linux using shadow passwords
slx	Linux using –lcrypt for passwords

Each code represents a different makefile section used to compile IMAP for your system. For Linux systems that use shadow passwords, you can use the slx option.

After you have determined the options required to compile UW IMAP in your environment, you can run the make program:

```
make slx
```

This compiles the source code and produces the IMAP executables located in the subdirectories in the distribution. The next step is to install and configure the individual pieces of IMAP.

Three executable programs are produced by UW IMAP:

- **ipop2d**—A POP2 server
- **ipop3d**—A POP3 server
- **imapd**—An IMAP server

The two POP servers are located in the ipopd directory, while the imapd server is located in the imapd directory. You must copy these files to a common location on the mail server so that the inetd program can access them:

```
cp ipopd/ipop2d /usr/sbin
cp ipopd/ipop3d /usr/sbin
cp imapd/imapd /usr/sbin
```

Both the ipop3d and imapd programs use either the inetd or the xinetd programs to monitor the network for incoming connections. You must add the ipop3d and imapd entries to the appropriate configuration file for your Unix system.

On Red Hat 7.1 systems, you must create two separate configuration files in the /etc/xinetd.d directory. The first one should be ipop3, which contains the ipop3d server definitions:

```
service pop3
{
        socket_type         = stream
        wait                = no
        user                = root
        server              = /usr/sbin/ipop3d
        log_on_failure      += USERID
        log_on_success      += USERID
}
```

12

MAIL

The second configuration file should be the imap file, which contains the imapd server definitions:

```
service imap
{
        socket_type       = stream
        wait              = no
        user              = root
        server            = /usr/sbin/imapd
        log_on_failure    += USERID
        log_on_success    += USERID
}
```

On Solaris 8 systems, you must add two entries to the standard /etc/inetd.conf file, which defines all network services:

```
ipop3d stream tcp nowait root /usr/sbin/ipop3d ipop3d
imapd stream tcp nowait root /usr/sbin/imapd imapd
```

After adding the new entries to the proper configuration files, you should send the running inetd or xinetd program a SIGHUP signal to reread the configuration using the `kill -HUP` command.

You can telnet to the POP and IMAP TCP ports to test the new installation. Listing 12.12 shows an example of this.

LISTING 12.12 Sample POP and IMAP Sessions

```
$ telnet localhost 120
Trying 127.0.0.1...
Connected to localhost.
Escape character is '^]'.
+OK POP3 localhost v7.63 server ready
USER katie
+OK User name accepted, password please
PASS signing
+OK Mailbox open, 5 messages
QUIT
+OK Sayonara
Connection closed by foreign host.

$ telnet localhost 143
Trying 127.0.0.1...
Connected to localhost.
Escape character is '^]'.
* OK localhost IMAP4rev1 v12.261 server ready
a1 LOGIN jessica sharks
a1 OK LOGIN completed
a2 SELECT INBOX
* 0 EXISTS
```

LISTING 12.12 continued

```
* 0 RECENT
* OK [UIDVALIDITY 940284862] UID validity status
* OK [UIDNEXT 2] Predicted next UID
* FLAGS (\Answered \Flagged \Deleted \Draft \Seen)
* OK [PERMANENTFLAGS (\* \Answered \Flagged \Deleted \Draft \Seen)]
[ic:ccc] Permanent flags
a2 OK [READ-WRITE] SELECT completed
a3 LOGOUT
* BYE shadrach.smallorg.org IMAP4rev1 server terminating connection
a3 OK LOGOUT completed
Connection closed by foreign host.
$
```

Both the POP3 and IMAP servers worked fine, allowing the users to connect, log in, and query their prospective mailboxes.

Secure IMAP and POP

Most email environments require users to communicate across a network with the email server to send and receive messages. As seen in the previous section, this usually is done with either POP3 or IMAP. The problem with these protocols is that they transfer messages across the network using plain ASCII text. This could leave your users vulnerable to network snooping by others.

To address the problem of sending ASCII text across the network, the Secure Socket Layer (SSL) family of protocols has been developed. SSL allows network hosts to encrypt data before sending it across the network, and it allows the receiving host to decrypt the data back into its normal form. By using SSL, you can create a more secure environment for your users to read their mail messages.

The OpenSSL package has become the most popular method used by Open Source programs to supply SSL functionality. OpenSSL provides an Open Source set of libraries and utilities that enable a network application to incorporate SSL versions 1.0, 2.0, and 3.0 as well as TLS.

The UW IMAP package can use the OpenSSL libraries to provide a secure POP3 or IMAP server connection with remote clients. The OpenSSL package can be downloaded from the OpenSSL Web site, `http://www.openssl.org`. After it is installed, the UW IMAP package can be recompiled using this command:

```
make option SSLTYPE=unix
```

Here, *option* is the password-authentication method used for the POP3 or IMAP server. The new ipop3d and imapd executables will now support SSL connections on TCP port 995 (for POP3) and 993 (for IMAP).

Best Practices

The Unix Mail Process

- Unix MTA packages should separate MDA packages to provide advanced filtering in local mail delivery. This helps reduce spam and viruses in the mail.
- Unix MUA packages should be installed to allow remote users to read messages from the mail server. If server disk space is critical, a POP3 server should be used to force users to download their mail messages to their workstations.
- Unix mail servers should be configured to use the SMTP protocol to transfer data between hosts via the Internet. Servers receiving mail from Internet hosts should have a dedicated Internet connection available.

The sendmail MTA Package

- The sendmail program uses a single configuration file, sendmail.cf, to hold all the parameters used to control its behavior. Care should be taken that this file is not accessible by normal system users.
- Instead of manually coding the sendmail.cf configuration file, you should use pre-configured macros and the m4 macro preprocessor to produce the file.

Unix Mail Clients

- Organizations in which lots of users have Unix workstations should maintain a central mail hub instead of using each workstation as a mail server.
- You should configure the sendmail MTA package on each workstation to auto-matically route all mail messages to the central mail hub.
- The users should use MUA programs such as PINE to access mail messages from the central mail hub.

Server Topics

- You should create a dedicated domain mail server to accept messages sent to any user in the domain.
- Each user should use the procmail MDA package to set filters on their incoming messages to help limit spam and viruses received via email.

- The mail server should be configured to support SMTP authentication (SASL) to allow for authenticating local users and to allow them to relay messages through the central mail hub.

- The mail server also should be configured to support POP3 and IMAP servers to allow remote users to read messages in their inbox.

- The mail server POP3 and IMAP servers also should incorporate the SSL protocol to encrypt messages retrieved from the mail server.

Online Resources

The Unix mail process

- `http://www.cis.ohio-state.edu/cgi-bin/rfc/rfc0821.html`
- `http://www.cis.ohio-state.edu/cgi-bin/rfc/rfc0822.html`

The sendmail MTA package

- `http://www.sendmail.org`
- `http://www.sendmail.net`
- `http://www.sendmail.com`

Unix mail clients

- `http://www.washington.edu/pine/`

Server topics

- `http://www.procmail.org`
- `ftp://ftp.andrew.cmu.edu/pub/cyrus-mail` (Cyrus-SASL)
- `http://www.washington.edu/imap/`
- `http://www.openssl.org`

File Sharing

by Todd Herr

IN THIS CHAPTER

CHAPTER 13

Overview of File Sharing

Since the beginning of modern computing, any site with more than one computer connected to its local network has wrestled with the problem of allowing those computers to share data in the most secure and efficient means possible. In this chapter, we will discuss this problem and try to provide solutions that strike the best balance between the two goals of security and efficiency. Our primary focus in this chapter will be on the Network File System (NFS) and Samba, but we will touch on other methods and try to provide some history of the problem as well.

As you read, you will discover (if you didn't know already) that when it comes to file sharing, security and efficiency can and usually do conflict with each other. As a sysadmin, part of your job is to work with your organization's security folks to define system usage policies, ones that allow the hosts that you manage or the users that you support to do their jobs without undue burden. At the same time, you want to protect your organization's sensitive data from access by outsiders.

File-Sharing Concepts

To fully understand any new topic, you must develop an understanding of the underlying concepts of that topic. When we discuss file sharing, there are really only three concepts to master:

- The definition of the term *file sharing*
- The server and its role in file sharing
- The client and its role in file sharing

The rest is just details on how to set things up, what's going on when files are being shared, and how to make sure that files are shared with only the hosts that you want them shared with. We'll discuss all of that in this chapter because those details are important, but first let's talk about the basic concepts.

File Sharing Defined

We define file sharing to be the capability of a group of hosts to access one or more files that reside on only one host in the group. In practice, this access is usually simultaneous access (with all hosts having the capability to access the same file at the same time), but in some cases it is not. We'll discuss both kinds of access in this chapter, although we'll talk much more about simultaneous access.

The Server

A server is a provider of resources; that's the purest definition. In the context of file sharing, the server is the host that is providing the other hosts in the group access to its files.

In a typical computing environment, the largest, most powerful hosts are configured as servers, but there is no requirement that a server be the most powerful machine on your network; any UNIX host can be a server, as long as the required pieces of the operating system are installed and configured on that host. As a practical matter, however, it is better to configure those hosts with the most memory, CPU, and disk space as your servers because they are better equipped to provide resources.

The Client

A client is a consumer of resources. When we speak of a client in this context, we are speaking of a host that is accessing one or more files that physically reside on a different host.

Why Bother with File Sharing?

At one time, disk space was at a premium, at least compared to today. Disk sizes were measured in tens, or perhaps hundreds, of megabytes. In those days, any sysadmin lucky enough to have a host with a gigabyte or more of disk space would cram as much data as possible onto that host; all the other hosts on the network would access many, most, or sometimes all of their files from this central server. Now that disk prices are a few dollars or less per gigabyte, some might wonder why to even bother with file sharing. If a workstation has tens of gigabytes of storage capacity, can't it hold all the data that it needs?

Although today's larger disks have eliminated one need for file sharing, there are still other reasons to do it. In an environment that relies on third-party applications, file sharing makes the sysadmin's job easier because it means that there are fewer copies of an application's configuration files to maintain. This will keep you happy, which is always something that you strive for in your job. In an environment with multiple users who don't have their own dedicated workstations or who might use multiple hosts, file sharing allows the users easier access to their environment settings and personal files if all home directories are shared to all workstations from one central server. This keeps the users happy, and happy users are more likely to appreciate your efforts, or at least leave you alone so that you can concentrate on that big project you've got to finish.

Finally, file sharing in any environment means that there are fewer files to back up, meaning that your backup times should be shorter and your costs for media should be lower. Shorter backup times can mean less network congestion, and that, coupled with the lower costs associated with your need to buy comparably fewer tapes for your backup jobs, will keep your users, your boss, and yourself happy.

History of File Sharing

If you've got an immediate need to setup either NFS or Samba in your environment, you may want to skip the next few pages. They're here to provide you with background information on different methods of file sharing that have been employed throughout the history of computing, and you can read them at your leisure. Regardless of whether you read them now or later, we at least want you to be aware of them.

Sneakernet

Before computer networks came into existence, *sneakernet* was the only method of file sharing available. Sneakernet is the generally accepted term for the act of loading files that you want to share on removable media (tape, CD, or floppy disk) at one computer, carrying the media to a second computer, and reading the files from the media onto that second computer. (Among other terms that you might hear used for this technique are *shoenet* and *walknet*). Sneakernet is the lowest-tech form of file sharing that has ever been available, and it is still practiced at some sites today. Any time that you find yourself in a situation in which you need to share files between hosts, and the hosts cannot communicate over a network, sneakernet will be the solution to your problem.

UUCP

UUCP is an acronym for UNIX to UNIX Copy, and it represents a batch method of transferring files from one host to another, using a small set of commands. Originally developed at AT&T, UUCP is recognizable for its use of "bang-style" addressing, in which you must specify not only the source host, source file(s), and destination host, but also any hosts in between, such as in this example:

```
uucp bassoon!/usr/local/lica/newlibrary.soguitar!violin!cello!/usr/
local/lib/newlibrary.so
```

In this example, the command is being issued to copy a file named /usr/local/lib/ newlibrary.so from a host named bassoon to a host named cello, passing it through hosts named guitar and violin, which must allow such a transfer. UUCP does not understand

DNS-style addressing, so each host must be known to the system issuing the command; this typically is done by listing all known hosts in a text file, usually called Systems, in the UUCP configuration directory.

UUCP provides not only a facility to transfer files from one host to another, but also the capability to execute commands on the remote host after the transfer is complete. Its design lends itself well to use in isolated sites that connect to the Internet only when necessary, usually through long-distance dialups and other costly methods. Because of its design for use in batch mode, UUCP was quite popular at one time for both email and Usenet news. Both required transferring large files whose contents were not time-sensitive enough to warrant immediate attention; the transfers could be scheduled at hours when it was cheapest to establish the connection. The Simple Mail Transport Protocol (SMTP) and the Network News Transfer Protocol (NNTP) have replaced UUCP, for the most part, because today's world allows for relatively cheap network access and demands immediate transfer of these types of files, especially email.

Vestiges of UUCP still remain in use today. You occasionally might receive an email message or see a Usenet posting that contains binary data that has been uuencoded as text for transfer between hosts; you'll have to uudecode it to make the contents useable. Fortunately, some mail clients and news readers have hooks built into them to provide you with capabilities to uudecode files without exiting the program to get to a command line.

DECnet

Developed by Digital Equipment Corporation (DEC), the Digital Network Architecture (DNA, more commonly called DECnet) is an implementation of file sharing originally designed to support nearly every operating system that DEC shipped, including, but not limited to, VMS, Ultrix, VAXeln, and OpenVMS. The DECnet specification defines not only file-transfer methods, but also the lower-level communications protocols that two hosts use to communicate with one another when sharing files using an implementation of DECnet. Later implementations of DECnet have been designed with built-in support for TCP/IP transports and use of DNS naming conventions.

Although an in-depth discussion of DECnet is beyond the scope of this book, it is worth noting that work has been done to implement DECnet in several distributions of UNIX, including Compaq's Tru64 UNIX, and Linux.

File Sharing Today

It's now time to move on to a discussion of today's more popular implementations of file sharing. Although the techniques mentioned previously certainly have their supporters and no doubt are in use today, you're much more likely to run across sites that employ the methods that we're going to discuss next.

"Free" or Non-Commercial File Sharing Products

We'll use the term "free" loosely here to describe methods of file sharing that are available either as part of an operating system distribution or free for download.

NFS

The Network File System, originally developed at Sun Microsystems, is generally available with any UNIX distribution on the market today. NFS allows a UNIX host on a network (the server) to provide simultaneous access to its directories and filesystems to any number of other hosts (the clients) on that network; on the client systems, the server's files appear to be local files. Given proper file permissions and access, clients can read, modify, create, and destroy files on the server's shared directories.

Samba

Samba, available as part of some UNIX distributions, including Red Hat Linux, and available for download by anyone, is a UNIX-based implementation of the Microsoft Windows Server Message Block (SMB) protocol. (Samba derives its name from the SMB acronym.) UNIX hosts that implement Samba then can share their files with other SMB clients and access files shared by any other server that implements the SMB protocol.

HTTP

Although it's perhaps not thought of in the traditional sense as a pure file-sharing protocol, the Hypertext Transfer Protocol can be useful for file sharing under certain conditions. Because free implementations of HTTP servers (such as Apache) are available for UNIX, HTTP qualifies as a free method of sharing files.

One common place for using HTTP for file sharing is a document repository, either for a work team, a department, or even an entire organization. A Web server can provide paperless access to a group's "How To" documents, contact lists, and any other document that needs to be available to more than one person. Proper configuration of a Web server can make all of these documents, regardless of their format, just a click away for any user in that organization. More robust implementations even allow sharing of a document by its authors during the creation of the document.

Commercial Methods–File Sharing Products

Methods of file sharing also are available today as products sold by corporate entities. These implementations provide features that are not available in the "free" methods mentioned previously. We'll briefly discuss two commercial methods here.

AFS

AFS is a distributed filesystem provided by the Transarc Corporation of Pittsburgh, Pennsylvania. AFS is based on the Andrew File System developed at Carnegie-Mellon University, also in Pittsburgh. When AFS became a product of Transarc, (Transarc is now owned by IBM, and is known as IBM Pittsburgh Lab) the name Andrew was dropped, but it is still called AFS.

AFS is built around the concept of the cell. Rather than using independent servers sharing distinct resources, with AFS, servers can be grouped into a cell that provides a single addressable point for clients to access. Taken together, the servers that make up the cell then share all their resources as a single filesystem, which clients access by addressing the cell, not each server that makes up the cell, to map remote resources to local access points. This is a marked difference from both NFS and Samba because it provides for what is known as location independence: The server, rather than the client, keeps track of which host contains each shared resource. This frees administrators to move shared resources from one host to another within the cell, with no changes required on the clients, as long as the filesystem path names are not altered by the move.

Some other features of AFS include a caching facility (clients cache chunks of recently accessed files locally, thereby speeding up the next access); Kerberos-based user authentication, providing a higher level of security than NFS or Samba because passwords travel across the wire in encrypted form; and better scalability because AFS is designed to support a larger number of clients per cell than is practical with NFS or Samba.

DFS

DFS is another distributed filesystem implementation that shares some similarities with AFS, but it is different in its own right.

Unlike AFS, DFS is not a standalone product; it is designed to sit on top of a larger product called the Distributed Computing Environment (DCE), or other DCE-based applications. The DCE architecture integrates multiple host computers, independent of platform, into a collection called a cell, with the goal of allowing applications to use the resources available on all host computers in the cell. For instance, a CPU-intensive application could make use not only of the CPU on the host on which the application is launched, but also of the CPUs of other hosts in the cell during periods of idle time for those

CPUs. DFS, then, is layered on top of the underlying core of the DCE-based application and is an implementation of file sharing within the DCE-based application.

In keeping with the DCE's cross-platform design, DFS is available as a server product for not only UNIX platforms, but also other operating systems, including Windows and the OS/390. AFS offers both UNIX and Windows client capabilities, but its server implementations are UNIX-based.

DFS offers many of the same features available in AFS, including the concept of the cell and the location independence that it brings. Like AFS, DFS is also available from the Transarc Corporation.

Alternatives (When Your Network Policies Don't Allow Simultaneous File Sharing)

If you find yourself working in or supporting an environment that forbids NFS, Samba, HTTP, or any other kind of simultaneous file sharing, you are going to have some work to do. You likely will still need to share files between hosts on your network. We'll briefly discuss some alternatives that you can use in this situation.

Sneakernet

Sneakernet, which we discussed earlier in this chapter, is one possibility. Environments with tight controls on file sharing also might have security policies in place that forbid the use of removable media, so burning CDs or writing files to tape would not even be possible in those organizations. In that situation, if the files to be shared are text and are small enough, you could still go from host to host and actually type in the files, although that way lends itself to human error, so it is not the most elegant solution to this problem.

Email

If the network forbids simultaneous file sharing but still has an email system in place, you conceivably can use email to share files between hosts. This method requires that there be a running SMTP process on each host that requires the file, and that there be a local user on that host to receive the email. This method can work for text and binary files, provided that neither type is so large that it chokes your network or is rejected by the SMTP process on the receiving host.

scp

Secure Copy (scp) usually is found as part of any installation of the Secure Shell (ssh) package. scp uses the same authentication and encryption methods as ssh, and it is probably the best choice for sharing files when simultaneous access is forbidden.

scp provides the capability to copy multiple files at once, and both the passwords used to authenticate and the data itself are encrypted as they traverse the network. scp also can be used to share files between remote sites, where NFS would not be practical.

ftp

File Transfer Protocol (ftp) commonly is used to provide access to files at remote sites; in fact, many sites set up anonymous ftp servers to provide access to the Internet community. Although ftp can be useful to you for file sharing, it is a service that commonly is targeted for exploit by hackers, and it often is turned off at many sites. The use of ftp also can be dangerous because passwords travel the network in unencrypted form, so bad guys sniffing your network can gather data that would allow them to exploit your site. Use ftp only in situations when scp or http are not available, and then use it only behind firewalls, if at all possible.

rdist and rcp

rdist(1), the remote file distribution program, and rcp(1), the remote copy program, are two other alternatives available for sharing files. Both require that the destination host trust the sending host, through the use of either the .rhosts file or the hosts.equiv file. The presence of this trust relationship allows the sending host to not only transfer files to the destination host, but also to execute commands on the destination host using rsh(1), or to log into the destination host, unchallenged, using rlogin(1). Sites with enough concern about security to forbid NFS and Samba are also likely to have policies in place to forbid rdist, rcp, rsh, and rlogin; if yours forbids traditional file sharing but not these commands, then your organization might need to rethink its policies.

Setting Up NFS

Now that we've got all the background information out of the way, we can discuss the topics that led you to turn to this chapter in the first place. For the rest of this chapter, we'll talk about how to configure NFS and Samba servers on Red Hat Linux 7.1 and Solaris 8, how to configure NFS clients, and how to configure Samba clients. We'll present not only step-by-step task lists, but also information about what's going on behind the scenes, how to configure things so that your data is protected from outsiders, and the causes of common problems and how to fix them.

NFS Overview

The Network File System (NFS) is probably the most prevalent form of file sharing used by UNIX-based computers. Originally developed at Sun Microsyuters, NFS

13

FILE SHARING

implementations exist today for nearly all distributions of UNIX, as well as Windows and other non-UNIX operating systems.

NFS defines a method of sharing files in which files residing on one or more remote servers can be accessed on a local client system in a manner that makes them appear as local files and directories. Although the client system must "know" which remote servers are providing the files, users of the system do not have to know these details and might not even be aware that they are accessing remote files. To them, the /usr/local filesystem that physically resides on another host will appear no differently than the /, /var, or /tmp filesystems that are local to the host that they're using at that time. Users will be able to cd into any location of the /usr/local filesystem to which they have permission, run commands that reside in /usr/local/bin, or build their own programs using libraries in /usr/local/lib. They can do any of these activities just like they would if /usr/local physically resided on the local host.

Implementation Details

Sun Microsystems first released Version 2 of the NFS protocol (more commonly called NFSv2; Version 1 never was released outside Sun) in 1985, and it has licensed NFS to other vendors ever since. RFC 1094, published in March 1989, defines the NFSv2 proto-col. (The online references section at the end of this chapter has pointers to all relevant RFCs mentioned here.) Vendors who want to include NFS as part of their UNIX distribu-tions can either license NFS from Sun or write their own implementation based on the published protocol. Because the licensing fees historically have been at levels that make it cheaper for a vendor to license NFS rather than create its own implementation, most UNIX distributions include NFS that has been licensed from Sun.

NFS is built on the Remote Procedure Call (RPC) protocol, (defined in RFCs 1057 and 1831) and makes use of the eXternal Data Representation (XDR) standard (RFCs 1014 and 1832) to define the objects that contain the data being passed between hosts. The idea at the core of the RPC protocol is that services on remote hosts can be accessed through a procedure-oriented interface. Server hosts would provide these services in the form of programs, which are just collections of procedures. Each remote procedure or service is uniquely defined by three numbers: the remote program number, the remote program version number, and the remote procedure number. These numbers are the same for a given service across all platforms that implement RPC.

In Red Hat Linux 7.1, the file /etc/rpc, described in rpc(5), is a database of RPC program numbers; the rpcinfo(8) command will tell you which RPC programs are currently avail-able on a given host.

In Solaris 8, the file /etc/rpc is also there, although it's discussed in Section 4, not 5, of the online manual; the rpcinfo(1M) command is also present, although with some different options.

The following example shows output from the rpcinfo -s command on a Solaris 8 host, showing the concise listing of all RPC programs on that host:

```
program version(s) netid(s)                              service     owner
100000  2,3,4     udp6,tcp6,udp,tcp,ticlts,ticotsord,ticots rpcbind
superuser
100029  3,2,1     ticots,ticotsord,ticlts              keyserv     superuser
100024  1         ticots,ticotsord,ticlts,tcp,udp,tcp6,udp6 status
superuser
100133  1         ticots,ticotsord,ticlts,tcp,udp,tcp6,udp6 -
superuser
100021  4,3,2,1   tcp,udp,tcp6,udp6                    nlockmgr    superuser
100099  3         ticotsord                            -           superuser
100231  1         ticots,ticotsord,ticlts              -           superuser
100005  3,2,1     ticots,ticotsord,tcp,tcp6,ticlts,udp,udp6 mountd
superuser
100003  3,2       tcp,udp,tcp6,udp6                    nfs         superuser
100227  3,2       tcp,udp,tcp6,udp6                    nfs_acl     superuser
```

As you can see from the listing, this particular host has 10 different server processes available through RPC; NFS is RPC program number 100,003, found on the next-to-last line of the output. As stated earlier, this program number is the same regardless of the operating system that the host is running. This host provides NFS Version 3 and Version 2. Individual procedures are not part of the rpcinfo listing.

An NFS server is stateless; this means that the server does not keep track of which clients are accessing which shared filesystems at a given time. Because NFS is all about providing access to files and directories, objects that themselves have state, the protocol designers chose not to introduce additional state into the protocol itself. Instead, they left the details of file mounting and file and record locking outside the scope of the protocol, although both are discussed in appendixes to the RFCs defining NFSv2 and NFSv3. Because mounting and locking are not part of the NFS protocol, separate processes are run to perform their functions. Typically, a server will run an NFS daemon to handle client requests (this daemon usually will be bound to port 2049 on the server) and a mount daemon to actually satisfy the mount requests, while an NFS client will run a lock daemon to implement file and record locking.

The stateless server design also has effects on a client. The main consequence of this design is that if a server becomes unavailable for a period of time, the client will just keep retrying commands until the server becomes available again. This design can cause some performance issues on the client, especially if a user's current working directory is an NFS-mounted directory when a server becomes unavailable. Users in this situation will be left with an unresponsive workstation, and you're sure to hear about it immediately if you weren't already aware of it. However, when the server does become available again, no time is spent on either the client or the server rebuilding any state tables, so the implementation is simpler than it otherwise would be.

Note that, in the previous paragraph, we used the phrase "server becomes unavailable" instead of "server crashes." This is because any hiccup in the network, such as problems with switches, routers, hubs, and other devices along the path between server and client, as well as an actual failure of the server itself, can cause NFS problems. All will manifest themselves as what appears to be a down server, so you'll have to be aware of your local network topology in case you start having problems that can't be explained by a dead server.

Although Version 2 of the NFS protocol was sufficient for its purposes when it was designed, as technology evolved, changes to NFS became necessary. Some of these changes were just improvements that were put into implementations and did not require updating the protocol itself; others, however, did. In 1995, RFC 1813 was released. This document contained the specification for NFSv3, which did not supersede NFSv2 as much as extend it. In fact, because RPC is designed to support multiple versions of a given protocol, and NFS is built on RPC, NFSv3 servers typically are backward-compatible with NFSv2 clients.

NFSv3 extensions or changes to the Version 2 protocol were designed to either improve performance or take advantage of new technology. By 1995, some CPUs had evolved to the point that they were capable of supporting 64-bit integers, and this lead to systems being capable of supporting file sizes greater than 2GB. (The largest 32-bit signed integer is 2,147,483,647, so systems could not specify file sizes, as measured in bytes, larger than that number using 32-bit integers.) The NFSv3 protocol changed its specification of file size from a 32-bit integer to a 64-bit one to include support for these larger files. NFSv3 removed the NFSv2 requirement for synchronous writes; in NFSv2, servers were required to finish writing data to disk before returning results to the client, and this was seen as a performance bottleneck. NFSv3 specified methods to improve speed here by allowing the server in some cases to return results to the client before it had written all data to storage.

In another step toward taking advantage of newer technology to improve performance, NFSv3 changed the specification for the size of data blocks that were being passed back and forth between the client and the server. NFSv2 limited these blocks to 8KB in size, but NFSv3, with an eye toward faster networks than might have existed in the late 1980s, changed this limit to one that could be negotiated between client and server at transmission time. One last change worth mentioning that was done for performance was a change in which file attributes were passed from the server to the client. In NFSv2, the server would not pass the attributes of the file back to the client when returning results from some operations, forcing the client to immediately look them up before doing anything else; with NFSv3, the server was required to pass file attribute information back to the client with every operation, which cut down a bit on network traffic.

RFCs 2054 and 2055 defined the client and server protocol, respectively, for WebNFS. Although it was not widely adopted, the idea behind WebNFS is to allow Web browsers to access files on NFS servers through a URL (such as `nfs://server.doma.in:2049/path/to/shared/directory`). The goal of WebNFS is to eliminate the overhead of the RPC and mount protocols inherent in traditional NFS, and perhaps to replace FTP. It is likely that WebNFS has not been widely adopted because organizations typically put in place security policies that don't allow NFS traffic through their firewalls and that restrict available services on hosts outside their firewalls. Because WebNFS is an extension of NFS, it relies on the RPC protocol just like NFS does; RPC is a common target of system crackers, and most organizations turn it off on hosts outside their firewalls.

December 2000 saw the release of RFC 3010, which defined NFSv4. Among the goals of NFSv4 are to extend the NFS protocol even further to allow for better use in WANs and on the Internet, and to provide much stronger security than that found in earlier implementations of the NFS protocol.

NFS Operating System Compatibility

NFS is available with all major distributions of UNIX, and server and client implementations are also available for Windows and other non-UNIX operating systems. Because of the nature of its design, NFS is operating system-independent. A server running one operating system can share files with clients running any other operating system, as long as the NFS implementation adheres to the specification laid out in the RFCs. The only caveat here is that the version of NFS running on the server must be at least as new as the version of NFS running on the client.

Security Issues

There is a time-worn adage in the computer industry that the only way to truly secure a given computer is to disconnect it from any network; place it in a locked room with lead lining the walls, floor, and ceiling; and station several heavily armed soldiers outside the door 24 hours a day, 7 days a week. Although this is a true statement in the abstract, a computer secured this way is likely to be underutilized because it won't have access to all of the resources that networking can provide. In today's world, computers usually need access to networks and to the Internet at large to best perform their functions. Although networked computers do make easier targets for system crackers, you, as a sysadmin, can lock down your hosts well enough to keep intruders out by putting up barriers that will make their attempts difficult, if not impossible.

Although the combination of Open Source software and publicly defined protocols, the latter in the form of RFCs, has brought innumerable benefits to the world of computing, an unintended consequence also has emerged. Both have allowed millions of computer users the world over to download, inspect, augment, and build software that is some of the best in the world at what it does and that can function independently of the platform because of its compliance with protocols. Unfortunately, among those millions of users are system crackers, and they have been able to inspect, ingest, and exploit any security vulnerabilities that might exist in this software.

This statement is not to be construed in any way, shape, or form as an indictment of the Open Source community, or the software that it has produced. Open Source, protocol-compliant software is often the best tool for the job, and the Open Source movement has allowed software to be built by teams that never would have been created in any organization. Furthermore, Open Source software does not have a monopoly on vulnerabilities by any stretch of the imagination; all software produced by humans is likely to have code in it that can be exploited because humans are not infallible. Moreover, history has shown that proprietary software is just as vulnerable to attack and exploit as Open Source software is. Sometimes, however, vulnerabilities in Open Source software might be easier to find than those in proprietary software, because it's all laid out for anyone to see. In fact, allowing system crackers access to the source code for a given piece of software is not unlike what you might see in a movie when the bad guys get the blueprints to the installation that they want to attack. It makes their task easier because they can find any weaknesses that might exist just by poring over the code, and it makes your job as a sysadmin that much tougher. You need to stay aware of vulnerabilities that might exist and take steps to close them up as soon as possible. If you make your systems invulnerable to as many known exploits as you can, you'll be ahead of the game. Fortunately, the Open Source community is quick to respond to any security issues that do arise, and patches and new versions of software are made available very quickly.

The first rule of security when it comes to NFS is simple: You should run NFS servers only where it is absolutely necessary. The corollary to this rule is that you should never run NFS servers on hosts outside your organization's firewall. NFS servers require that RPC be running, and RPC is a favorite target for crackers trying to exploit system vulnerabilities. Many security professionals recommend disabling RPC entirely on any host that is not functioning as a server, and this is good advice to heed (NFS clients do not require that RPC be running). So, if a particular host isn't designed to share files, don't run any NFS server processes, and turn off RPC if you can.

Another rule to heed is to not even put NFS clients outside your organization's firewall; doing so requires that you have another port open on your firewall to allow NFS traffic to pass through, and it's good practice to minimize the number of open ports in your firewall. Building on this rule is also the idea that NFS services should never cross networks of different trust levels. A network is only as secure as the most permissive host that has access to it. Put another way, if your NFS server is on a network that permits a limited set of hosts to access it, but one of those hosts is connected to a different network with few or any limits, then anyone with access to that host has access to your server, thus defeating your network's security policies.

Next, share files only with those clients to which you want to permit access. The majority of computer crimes perpetrated against organizations are "inside jobs," so make sure that you limit the hosts that can access your server's shared file to only those that require it. Without any security or network restrictions, any NFS client can access all the shared files of any NFS server, so make sure that you limit this access as much as possible.

Another good rule to live by is to share files with the most restrictive permissions possible. By default, Solaris 8 NFS servers share filesystems to all clients in read-write mode, which means that every shared file and directory will be bound by only the individual permissions (owner, group, and world) on each. Although this access is necessary in many situations, there are options available on the server to make access even more restrictive; you should take advantage of these options whenever possible.

13

FILE SHARING

Server Setup

Now we turn our attention to setting up servers to allow other hosts to access their files. We'll show you how to setup NFS servers first on Red Hat 7.1 systems, and then on Solaris 8 servers. We'll discuss in detail the files and processes involved, and show you in-depth examples that take you "behind the scenes" so that you get a good understanding of what's going on.

Sharing Filesystems

Sharing filesystems is all about determining which filesystems you want to share and then making sure that the required processes are running on the server. You can make either permanent or temporary configuration changes to a host to make it an NFS server; we'll show you how to do both. The good news is that in both Red Hat 7.1 and Solaris 8, configuring an NFS server can be as simple as editing one file and running one command.

Setting Up a Red Hat 7.1 System as an NFS Server

If you want to set up a Red Hat 7.1 host as an NFS server, you must take one very important preliminary step. Red Hat 7.1 distributions give you an option to configure a firewall during your system installation. If this firewall is set to the high or medium level of protection, RPC-based services such as NFS will not function properly (see `http://www.redhat.com/support/docs/gotchas/7.1/gotchas-71.html`). To verify your firewall settings—and turn off your firewall, if necessary—on the command line, as root, type **setup** and then choose Firewall Configuration and No Firewall.

Now that you've got your system ready to be an NFS server, it's time to make it happen. We'll first discuss "permanent" configuration (setting its configuration as an NFS server so that it survives system boots), and then we'll talk a bit about "temporary" configuration.

The /etc/exports file lists which filesystems are to be shared by an NFS server, along with the options for sharing them. The format for this file is discussed in detail in the exports(5) man page, but we'll talk about some of the more interesting options here. The first time you configure an NFS server, this file will exist and will be empty. You will need to add lines to it to specify the filesystem(s) that you want to share. The following example /etc/exports file demonstrates the format and use of some of the options available:

```
# Filesystem to share      Allowed client hosts(optional list of options)
/usr/local                 *.angrysunguy.com(ro,async,root_squash)
/var/mail                  @dept_hosts(rw,sync)
/var/spool/news            192.168.192.0/19(all_squash)
/opt                       ws1.angrysunguy.com(rw)
```

The first line in the example is a comment line; comments may occur anywhere in the file, either at the beginning or end of a line. The # character delimits comments, and everything after it until the end of the line is considered to be a comment. This particular comment line is just there to remind the sysadmin of the format of each line in the /etc/exports file.

The next four lines each demonstrate different ways to specify options for sharing filesystems. As you'll note from the comment line, each line in the file lists the filesystem being shared, the hosts that are allowed to access it, and an optional parenthetical list of other options. On each line, we've tried to show you all the possible ways to specify which hosts are allowed to access the shared filesystems. In the order shown here, they are:

- By using wildcard characters (`*.angrysunguy.com` means that any host in the angrysunguy.com domain can access the /usr/local filesystem; the ? character, which will match exactly one character, is also valid).

- By NIS netgroup (all hosts in the NIS netgroup dept_hosts are allowed to mount /var/mail). Note that this example only works when NIS is running.
- By IP network (all hosts with an IP address in the 192.168.192.0/19 network can mount /var/spool/news)
- By specific host (only the host ws1.angrysunguy.com can mount the /misc file-system)

Each line also shows some different options that you can use to share files. Although the list shown here is not all-encompassing, we think that these are the most interesting options.

The options `ro`, `async`, and `root_squash` on the /usr/local line are actually the default options for any shared filesystem in Red Hat 7.1. Although it is not incorrect to explicitly list them in /etc/exports, it is not necessary to do so. We have chosen to do so here for illustrative purposes. The `ro` option means that the filesystem should be shared read-only so that no client will be capable of modifying any files on that filesystem, regardless of file permissions. The `async` option controls how writes are done to disk by the file server. Recalling our earlier discussion about NFSv3 and its method of allowing the server to return results to the client before the server had finished its writing to disk, the async option specifies the NFSv3 method. Finally, the `root_squash` option means that the root user on the client should be mapped to the UID of the nobody user on the server. This is usually the desired behavior in any NFS setup because to do otherwise would mean allowing the client root user to have root-level privileges on your server's exported filesystems—and that's almost never a good thing.

The /var/mail line shows the opposite of the default for two of the options discussed previously. The `rw` option means that the filesystem should be shared read-write so that only the permissions on each individual file would control the level of access granted to the client. The `sync` option specifies that the server should follow the NFSv2 method of writing data to disk, whereby it should write all data to disk before returning control to the client.

In the /var/spool/news line, we see the option `all_squash`; this option extends the idea of the `root_squash` option to all users so that all UIDs on the client will be mapped to the UID of the nobody user on the server. This is the opposite of the default behavior, which can be explicitly specified with the `no_all_squash` option. The default behavior usually is desired for most shared filesystems because users will want to have their expected levels of privilege to any shared files that they own.

The /opt line introduces no new options to the discussion; it's there more to show how to limit the clients that can mount a given filesystem to a specific host.

13

FILE SHARING

With the files ready to export, it's time to start up the programs and daemons that will share the files and deals with client requests: exportfs(8), rpc.rquotad(8C), rpc.mountd(8), and rpc.nfsd(8). The easiest way to do this is by running (as root) the command /etc/init.d/nfs start. This will start up each of the four programs listed, and you've now got an NFS server on your hands. We'll now turn our attention to what each of the four does; refer to the manual pages for more information.

The exportfs(8) command maintains the table of filesystems that the server currently is sharing. This table is the file /var/lib/nfs/xtab. For a typical NFS server, exportfs gets run at boot time with the -r option, which causes it to synch /var/lib/nfs/xtab with the /etc/exports file, and it never is run again except to check which filesystems are currently exported; this is done by running exportfs(8) with no options on the command line. However, sometimes you'll want to run exportfs by hand, either when you've made a change to /etc/exports or when you just need to share a filesystem for a time without making the change permanent. We'll get to those in a moment. Note that you should never edit /var/lib/nfs/xtab by hand; use the exportfs(8) command.

rpc.rquotad(8C) provides an interface for the client machine to obtain user quota information about filesystems on the server.

rpc.mountd(8) implements the mount protocol; it receives client requests to mount filesystems and, if the filesystem is exported and the client is permitted to access it, provides a file handle to the client to use to access the filesystem.

rpc.nfsd(8) implements the NFS protocol on the server; all procedures that are defined as part of the protocol (NFSPROC_READ, NFSPROC_WRITE, and all the rest) and all other details of the protocol are implemented by rpc.nfsd.

To make your host start NFS server services at boot time, as root, run the setup command, choose System Services, and make sure that nfs is selected to start at boot time. Doing this will cause the system to effectively run this command:

```
chkconfig -level 5 nfs on
```

This moves the script /etc/rc5.d/K20nfs to /etc/rc5.d/S60nfs, ensuring that NFS services start at boot time in init state 5, the default init state. If your system's default init state is something else, you also can manually run this command:

```
chkconfig -level $LEVEL nfs on
```

Here, $LEVEL is the number representing your system's default init state. (Init states and their scripts are covered in detail in Chapter 1, "Startup and Shutdown;" review that chapter if the above is not clear.)

You might find yourself in a situation in which you've got a running server and you need to change which filesystems are being shared. If the change is a temporary one, your best bet is to just export the filesystem at the command line, using the `exportfs(8)` command in the manner shown in this example:

```
exportfs -o ro client.angrysunguy.com:/mnt/cdrom
```

This particular example demonstrates how to share the /mnt/cdrom filesystem to the client host named client.angrysunguy.com, and to share it as a read-only filesystem. Although CD-ROM drives are nearly ubiquitous on PCs today, you still might find yourself in a situation in which a client has a CD-ROM drive that is busy or broken, and you need to access data on a CD. Putting the CD in an NFS server and using this example command (substituting your client's hostname, of course) will solve your problem in that situation. The export of the /mnt/cdrom filesystem will be temporary, in that a reboot of the system will cause it to no longer be exported. That is not to say that you have to reboot to stop exporting /mnt/cdrom; you can stop the export by running this command:

```
exportfs -u client.angrysunguy.com:/mnt/cdrom
```

You also might find yourself in a situation in which you need to share a filesystem that is not currently shared, and you want to share it permanently. In this case, you would edit the /etc/exports file and then run `exportfs(8)`, either with the –a or the –r option, but you need to choose carefully which option you use. Remember that `exportfs(8)` with the –r option synchs up /var/lib/nfs/xtab with the contents of /etc/exports, so any temporary exports that you've put in place will disappear from the system if you run `exportfs(8)` using this option. If you haven't shared any filesystems in this manner, then use –r; on the other hand, if you have shared filesystems temporarily, use –a, which maintains all current shared filesystems and also adds any that are listed in /etc/exports. The following example should illustrate the difference.

An /etc/exports file:

```
# Filesystem to share      Allowed client hosts(optional list of options)
/usr/local                 *.angrysunguy.com(async,ro,root_squash)
/var/mail                  @dept_hosts(rw,sync)
/var/spool/news            192.168.192.0/19(all_squash)
/opt                       ws1.angrysunguy.com(rw)
```

Output from the `exportfs -v` (verbose mode) command, showing what's currently being shared:

```
/opt            ws1.angrysunguy.com(rw,async,wdelay,root_squash)
/var/spool/news
                192.168.192.0/19(ro,async,wdelay,root_squash,all_squash)
```

```
/usr/local        *.angrysunguy.com(ro,async,wdelay,root_squash)
/var/spool/mail
@dept_hosts(rw,wdelay,root_squash)
```

Temporarily exporting a file from the command line:

```
exportfs -o ro ws1.angrysunguy.com:/mnt/cdrom
```

New output from the `exportfs -v` command:

```
/mnt/cdrom        ws1.angrysunguy.com(ro,async,wdelay,root_squash)
/opt              ws1.angrysunguy.com(rw,async,wdelay,root_squash)
/var/spool/news
                  192.168.192.0/19(ro,async,wdelay,root_squash,all_squash)
/usr/local        *.angrysunguy.com(ro,async,wdelay,root_squash)
/var/spool/mail
                  @dept_hosts(rw,wdelay,root_squash)
```

Adding a line to /etc/exports to permanently share a filesystem:

```
# Filesystem to share      Allowed client hosts(optional list of options)
/usr/local                 *.angrysunguy.com(async,ro,root_squash)
/var/mail                  @dept_hosts(rw,sync)
/var/spool/news            192.168.192.0/19(all_squash)
/opt                       ws1.angrysunguy.com(rw)
/home                      *.angrysunguy.com(rw)
```

Output of `exportfs -v`, after running `exportfs -a` to share the new filesystem:

```
/mnt/cdrom        ws1.angrysunguy.com(ro,async,wdelay,root_squash)
/home             ws1.angrysunguy.com(rw,async,wdelay,root_squash)
/opt              ws1.angrysunguy.com(rw,async,wdelay,root_squash)
/var/spool/news
                  192.168.192.0/19(ro,async,wdelay,root_squash,all_squash)
/usr/local        *.angrysunguy.com(ro,async,wdelay,root_squash)
/var/spool/mail
                  @dept_hosts(rw,wdelay,root_squash)
```

Output of `exportfs -v`, after running `exportfs -r` to share the new filesystem:

```
/home             ws1.angrysunguy.com(rw,async,wdelay,root_squash)
/opt              ws1.angrysunguy.com(rw,async,wdelay,root_squash)
/var/spool/news
                  192.168.192.0/19(ro,async,wdelay,root_squash,all_squash)
/usr/local        *.angrysunguy.com(ro,async,wdelay,root_squash)
/var/spool/mail
                  @dept_hosts(rw,wdelay,root_squash)
```

You'll notice that after running `exportfs(8)` with the `-r` option, /mnt/cdrom no longer is shared. The lesson here is to be careful when sharing filesystems so that you don't needlessly undo work that you've already done.

Setting Up A Solaris 8 System As An NFS Server

We'll begin the discussion of Solaris 8 NFS servers by showing you how to do initial setup of a server, and then we'll follow up with how to make changes on the fly.

To set up a Solaris 8 NFS server, you first must list the files that you want to share in the file /etc/dfs/dfstab. This file is not just a list of filesystems to be shared, however; it is actually a list of share(1M) commands to run when NFS services are started. The share(1M) command does just what its name implies; it makes local filesystems available to be accessed by remote client machines. Let's now look at a sample /etc/dfs/dfstab file, and then we'll discuss it and give you some background on the share(1M) command.

```
#  A sample /etc/dfs/dfstab file
#  Format: share [-F fstype] [ -o options] [-d "<text>"] <pathname>
share -F nfs -o rw=.angrysunguy.com -d "Home directories" /export/home
share -F nfs -o ro /cdrom
share -F nfs -d "Mail files" /var/spool/mail
```

The share(1M) command has only a few parameters, and they are all optional parameters (run with no options, the share(1M) command just reports which filesystems currently are shared by the given host). The -F parameter specifies the type of the filesystem to share; we'll limit our discussion here to the use of the nfs type, although other types specified here might be cachefs or autofs, among others. The /etc/dfs/fstypes file lists which filesystem types are available to share. Note that the actual filesystem type on the server is not nfs; nfs specifies the filesystem type as it will appear to any clients that access it. The -d parameter is a text description of the filesystem being shared; you can think of its function as a comment, almost—one that will give you some detail in the output of the share(1M) command when it's run with no parameters.

The -o parameter is where you specify the options for sharing the filesystem. These options will be both generic to the share(1M) command and specific to sharing of nfs filesystem types. In fact, when you specify a value of nfs to the -F parameter, you're actually running the share_nfs(1M) command, not just share(1M). All of the nfs type-specific option are discussed in the manual page for the share_nfs(1M) command, but we'll talk about some of the more interesting ones here.

First, though, we want to discuss the generic options, rw (read-write) and ro (read-only). By default, Solaris 8 shares filesystems read-write, so only each file's individual permissions govern its access control. When sharing a filesystem, you can specify a blanket rw or ro directive for all clients, or you can further limit which clients may have rw permission and ro permissions by specifying them as part of the ro or rw options. The ro and rw options can be combined so that you can limit one group of clients to just read-only access while permitting read-write access to another group of clients or all other clients. Sample uses of ro and rw include these:

- **-o ro**—All clients will have read-only access.
- **-o ro=*access_list***—Only the clients specified in *access_list* will be allowed read-only access. (We'll discuss the syntax of *access_list* in a moment.) No other clients will be permitted any access.
- **-o rw**—All clients will have read-write access (this is the default behavior).
- **-o rw=*access_list***—Only the clients specified in *access_list* will be allowed read-write access to the filesystem. No other clients will be permitted any access.
- **-o ro=*access_list*,rw**—Clients in *access_list* will be granted read-only access, while all other clients get read-write access.
- **-o ro=*acl1*,rw=*acl2***—Clients in *acl1* will be granted read-only access to the filesystem, while clients in *acl2* will be granted read-write access to the filesystem. No other clients will be permitted any access to the filesystem.

Client access lists are colon-separated lists containing any combination of hostnames, netgroups, domain name suffixes (such as .angrysunguy.com), or networks. The use of the minus sign in the access list gives you the option of exercising access control over individual members of a group, such as a netgroup or a domain, by excluding those members from permissions granted to the rest of the group. For instance, this share(1M) statement would grant read-write access to all hosts in the domain foo.com, with the exception of ws1.foo.com:

```
share -F nfs -o rw=-ws1.foo.com:.foo.com /export/home
```

Among the more interesting of the options specific to the share_nfs(1M) command are the options root=*access_list*, anon=*uid*, sec=*mode*, and window=*value*.

The default configuration for a Solaris 8 NFS server is to set the effective UID of the root user on all clients to the UID of the nobody user. The root=*access_list* option gives you the capability to permit root users on the clients specified in *access_list* (same format as described previously) to have root-level access to the shared filesystems.

The anon=*uid* option gives you the option of changing the UID that root client users and nonauthenticated users from the nobody UID to another of your choice. Setting this value to –1 denies access to nonauthenticated users and root users on clients not in the access list of the root= option.

The sec=*mode* option allows you to specify one or more security modes for sharing files. These modes are actually representations of different types of the RPC auth_flavor enumerated type first defined in RFC 1057, and they are discussed in the nfssec(5) manual page. You may specify one or more modes in a colon-separated list, with these possible values:

- **sys**—The default setting for Solaris servers and NFS version 2 clients, it means that UIDs and GIDs are passed in the clear and are not authenticated by the NFS server.
- **dh**—Use a Diffie-Hellman public key system.
- **krb4**—Use the Kerberos Version 4 authentication system.
- *none*—Use null authentication, mapping clients that cannot authenticate using the other mode(s) by which the filesystem is shared to the UID specified by the anon=*uid* option.

For Solaris 8, then, we can see that the following example statement would share the /export/tools filesystem only to clients that could properly authenticate themselves using either Diffie-Hellman or Kerberos Version 4:

```
share -F nfs -o anon=-1,sec=dh:krb4 /export/tools
```

It can be argued that this combination makes for more secure, if not the most secure, sharing of files.

The window=*value* option is meaningful only when used in conjunction with sec=dh or sec=krb4. You can use this option to specify the number of seconds for which a client's authentication using either system is valid; the default is 30,000 seconds, or 8 hours and 20 minutes.

Having any lines in the /etc/dfs/dfstab file that are not blank and that do not begin with the # character is enough criteria for a Solaris 8 host to act as an NFS server at boot time. The startup script /etc/rc3.d/S15nfs.server, which is a hard link to /etc/init.d/nfs.server, is installed by default and will start up the processes necessary to be an NFS server. You don't have to reboot, however, to start them; once you've configured your /etc/dfs/dfstab file, just run (as root) /etc/init.d/nfs.server start.

If the startup script finds appropriate lines in /etc/dfs/dfstab, will first run the shareall(1M) command to export the filesystems that are supposed to be shared; then it will run the mountd(1M) daemon, which implements the mount protocol, and the nfsd(1M) daemon, which implements the NFS protocol on the server. As a side note, the script also starts up mountd(1M) and nfsd(1M) if the file /etc/rmmount.conf contains any share entries, starts up NFS logging on the server if it's configured, and configures the server as a boot server for SPARC or x86 clients, if appropriate. Some security organizations recommend removing /etc/rc3.d/S15nfs.server from Solaris 8 hosts if not running

NFS; that might not be necessary because the script does work only if other files are in place and contain specific instructions. You can use your best judgment here.

The shareall(1M) command exports all filesystems that it finds in /etc/dfs/dfstab. Although it usually is run just at boot time, you also can run it after adding entries to the /etc/dfs/dfstab file.

The mountd(1M) daemon answers client requests for mounting shared filesystems and provides file handles to clients if they are properly authenticated and the filesystem is shared. It uses the file /etc/dfs/sharetab (which is built by the shareall(1M) and share(1M) commands) as its reference point for which filesystems actually are shared.

The nfsd(1M) daemon implements all the procedures and other objects defined in the NFS protocol. By default, it is started with two options, as follows:

```
nfsd -a 16
```

The -a option tells the daemon to listen for connections on all transport protocols, including UDP and TCP. Recall that NFSv2 uses UDP to communicate, while NFSv3 uses TCP. If you want your server to be solely NFSv2 or NFSv3, then you could run it using either of these commands, as appropriate:

```
nfsd -p udp 16
nfsd -p tcp 16
```

The number 16 specifies the maximum number of NFS threads that can be created in the kernel and corresponds to the number of concurrent NFS requests that the server can handle. This does not limit the server necessarily to just 16 clients; it merely limits it to 16 concurrent requests. NFS client requests are not persistent connections, in that clients receive data from the server, cache the data locally and operate on it, and then send further requests back to the server, which might include both reads and writes. Each request can be satisfied in fractions of seconds, given appropriate network speeds, so a server thus configured likely can support many more than 16 clients. If you are in a situation in which your clients are doing intensive NFS file access, with lots of reads and writes per second, you can adjust this number upward. However, but you might want to reconsider the feasibility of NFS as a solution to your particular problem. Local disk reads and writes always will be faster than NFS, and some applications just function better using local disk storage.

When you've got your server up and running, you might find that you want to share additional filesystems or stop sharing some filesystems that you're sharing. We'll spend a few moments now talking about both situations.

If you want to share additional filesystems, you can do so either permanently (the sharing will still be in place after you reboot your server) or temporarily. To do so permanently, simply edit the /etc/dfs/dfstab file, adding the appropriate line(s), and run the shareall(1M) command. For temporary sharing of filesystems, you can run the share(1M) command on the command line as root, as shown in the following example:

```
share -F nfs -o ro /cdrom
```

This command will make the contents of the /cdrom filesystem available to every host on the same network as the server until sharing is stopped, either by reboot or until the system is told to no longer share the filesystem, by using the unshare(1M) command:

```
unshare /cdrom
```

Although the unshare(1M) command can be easily used to stop temporary sharing of filesystems, stopping permanent sharing is a two-step process. You must not only unshare(1M) the filesystem at the command line, but you also must remove the line that shared the filesystem from the /etc/dfs/dfstab file so that it is not shared again the next time the system boots.

The unshare(1M) command can cause some difficulty for clients that currently are mounting a shared filesystem. Because the NFS protocol defines a stateless server, servers will just stop providing access to clients regardless of which clients might be using the filesystem. You will need to exercise care here, then, to make sure that all clients that are mounting the filesystem umount(1M) it before you stop sharing it. The showmount(1M) command, run with the - option, will give you a list of which clients currently are mounting which filesystems from the server.

Client Setup

NFS servers aren't really worth anything unless there are NFS clients to make use of the resources that they're providing. In this section, we'll look at how to set up NFS clients using standard methods and using automount. For purposes of our discussion, we'll distinguish between the two methods by referring to "standard" clients and "automount" clients. Although the specification of remote filesystems to mount does differ between the two, both methods are used to configure NFS clients.

Standard Client Setup

Setting Up a Red Hat 7.1 System As An NFS Client

A Red Hat 7.1 standard NFS client can access shared filesystems either at boot time or on demand.

To mount a shared filesystem at boot time, you must declare the filesystem in the /etc/fstab file. A sample /etc/fstab file, with a line for mounting a filesystem from a server, is shown here:

```
LABEL=/                    /                       ext2     defaults            1 1
/dev/fd0                   /mnt/floppy             auto     noauto,owner        0 0
none                       /proc                   proc     defaults            0 0
none                       /dev/pts                devpts   gid=5,mode=620      0 0
/dev/hda2                  swap                    swap     defaults            0 0
/dev/cdrom                 /mnt/cdrom              iso9660  noauto,owner,kudzu,ro 0 0
deptfs:/usr/local          /usr/local             nfs      defaults
```

The last line of the file in the previous example is the line for mounting a remote shared filesystem on this client. It tells the client to mount the filesystem /usr/local, shared by the server named deptfs on the local mount point /usr/local. The third column of each line specifies the filesystem type, so it becomes obvious that this is an NFS filesystem. The fifth and sixth columns are optional and either should not be used for nfs filesystems or should both be zero. The fifth column instructs the dump(8) command whether to dump the filesystem, while the sixth column is the pass number for the fsck(8) run at boot time. Neither is appropriate on the client for a filesystem shared from another server. A full discussion of the /etc/fstab file can be found in Chapter 1.

In the fourth column of the last line, you see the word defaults. The fourth column is where options get specified, and lots of them are detailed in the nfs(5) manual page. Some of the possible options that can be configured here include rsize=*bytes* and wsize=*bytes*. The rsize and wsize options specify the size in bytes of the objects being passed from the client to the server and back during reads (rsize) and writes (wsize). Recall from our earlier discussion that the NFSv2 specification limited these sizes to a maximum of 8K (8,192) bytes, while NFSv3 changed the limit to allow for negotiation between the server and the client. The nfs(5) manual page from the Red Hat 7.1 distribution that was used as a reference source while writing this chapter in summer 2001 is dated 20 November 1993, and it indicates that the default for rsize and wsize is 1,024 bytes, with recommendations to set them to 8,192 for better performance. Your best bet is to set these values explicitly to best take advantage of network capabilities at your site.

A default Red Hat 7.1 configuration starts up the NFS client daemons in init states 3, 4, and 5. It does this by running the script S14nfslock at boot time out of the appropriate /etc/rc?.d directory. Because of this, when you've changed your /etc/fstab file, you just need to run the mount(8) command to get your host functioning as an NFS client.

The S14nfslock script, which is a symbolic link to /etc/init.d/nfslock, starts up the rpc.lockd(8) and rpc.statd(8) daemons. The rpc.lockd(8) daemon implements the NFS lock manager on systems whose kernels don't automatically start the lock manager.

Because most kernels do start the lock manager automatically, rpc.lockd usually is not required. rpc.statd(8) on the server performs a reboot notification function by tracking which clients are mounting filesystems and notifying the rpc.statd(8) daemon on each client after a server reboot. The clients are tracked in the /var/lib/nfs/statd/sm directory on the server.

Mounting a shared filesystem on demand requires no changes to any files; assuming that the S14nfslock script ran at boot time, simply typing the `mount(8)` command with the appropriate options on the command line will mount your filesystem. For instance, this next line will mount the /usr/local filesystem shared by the host deptfs on the local filesystem /usr/local:

```
mount deptfs:/usr/local /usr/local
```

You can also use mount(8) with the –a option to mount all filesystems mentioned in the /etc/fstab file.

Although the system will attempt to mount every filesystem specified in /etc/fstab at boot time, problems can occur if servers are unreachable when a client boots. Red Hat 7.1 is designed to note a failure to mount an NFS filesystem during boot, but to continue with other startup operations without incident.

Hard vs. Soft Mounts

NFS clients have the option of mounting shared file systems either "hard" or "soft." There is a key difference to the two choices. A hard mount attempt will return an error if a server doesn't respond to its request, while a soft mount will keep trying until the server responds. We recommend hard mounts for clients mounting filesystems read-write (since any application needing to write to a resource needs to know whether or not the resource is available) and soft mounts for read-only filesystems. Also, since hard mounts can cause a client system to hang if a server becomes unavailable, we recommend that hard mounts also employ the "intr" option. This option allows for keyboard interrupt (i.e., Ctrl-C) of operations that are hanging while trying to access an unavailable server.

Setting Up A Solaris 8 System As An NFS Client

In Solaris 8, a standard NFS client also can mount a shared filesystem either at boot time or on demand.

Mounting a shared filesystem at boot time requires you to edit /etc/vfstab on the client to specify the filesystem to mount. A sample /etc/vfstab, with a line for an NFS filesystem is shown here:

```
#device             device             mount     FS      fsck    mount    mount
#to mount           to fsck            point     type    pass    at boot  options
#
#/dev/dsk/c1d0s2    /dev/rdsk/c1d0s2   /usr      ufs     1       yes      -
fd                  -                  /dev/fd   fd      -       no       -
/proc               -                  /proc     proc    -       no       -
/dev/dsk/c0t0d0s1   -                  -         swap    -       no       -
/dev/dsk/c0t0d0s0   /dev/rdsk/c0t0d0s0 /         ufs     1       no       -
/dev/dsk/c0t0d0s6   /dev/rdsk/c0t0d0s6 /usr      ufs     1       no       -
/dev/dsk/c0t0d0s3   /dev/rdsk/c0t0d0s3 /var      ufs     1       no       -
/dev/dsk/c0t0d0s7   /dev/rdsk/c0t0d0s7 /stuff    ufs     2       yes      -
/dev/dsk/c0t0d0s5   /dev/rdsk/c0t0d0s5 /opt      ufs     2       yes      -
swap                -                  /tmp      tmpfs   -       yes      -
deptfs:/usr/local   -                  /usr/local nfs    -       yes      -
```

The last line, beginning with deptfs:/usr/local, is the line that defines this host as an NFS client. It instructs the client to mount the filesystem /usr/local shared by the server named deptfs on the local mount point /usr/local. This line has three key differences from the lines for local filesystems:

- There is no device to fsck(1M) specified in column 2 because it is not the client's job to do filesystem checking of remote filesystems, nor is it possible for it to do so.
- The filesystem type for this filesystem is nfs, not ufs, as it would be for local filesystems.
- There is no fsck(1M) pass specified because fsck(1M) is not being run on this filesystem on the client.

Although this particular example shows the NFS filesystem configured to mount at boot time, with no mount options specified, this is not necessarily the best way to configure things. A failed network connection at boot time or an uncooperative server can cause the client to fail to boot in this case, and that might not be acceptable for your situation. You can take steps to guard against this either by not mounting the filesystem at boot time or by mounting in the background, using the bg option. The background option will cause a client whose first request to mount a filesystem fails to retry in the background, while letting other work proceed. The mount_nfs(1M) manual page contains lots of information on this option and many others.

With a default system configuration, the only thing left to do to make your system an NFS client after altering the /etc/dfs/dfstab file is to mount the filesystems by using the mount(1M) command. The default Solaris 8 configuration runs the startup script /etc/rc2.d/S73nfs.client (a hard link to /etc/init.d/nfs.client) at boot time. This script starts up the statd(1M) and lockd(1M) daemons for client-side NFS activities.

The function of the statd(1M) daemon is to assist the client in recovering from an NFS server crash. Although NFS servers are stateless, the Solaris implementation of NFS provides for a daemon process that monitors which clients have locks on a server. If a server crashes, during reboot the statd(1M) daemon on the server will contact the statd(1M) daemon on each host that held a lock on the server when it crashed. The list of hosts is kept in the /var/statmon/sm directory.

The lockd(1M) daemon is responsible for handling file and record locking requests on the client and passing them along to the lockd(1M) daemon on the server, when appropriate.

To mount a shared filesystem on demand, use the mount(1M) command on the command line, as in the following example:

```
mount -F nfs deptfs:/cdrom /mnt/tmp
```

This command will mount the shared /cdrom directory on the server deptfs at the /mnt/tmp mount point on the client.

Automount Client Setup

Another option available to you for managing NFS clients is to use the automounter, especially in an environment in which you've got NIS or NIS+ running. Although you don't have to be running NIS or NIS+ to use the automounter, implementing automount clients in an environment that doesn't use NIS or NIS+ adds some administrative overhead to your work, for reasons that we'll see below.

The automounter provides an on-demand method of mounting NFS filesystems and automatically unmounts them after a designated time period of inactivity. It is designed around the concept of a series of maps that will direct clients to the location of needed resources. A central master map contains a list of other maps to be referenced by clients. These other maps then point the clients to the servers containing shared filesystems. Each entry in these maps will contain a key field and a value field. The key field is the entry point into the map; the client specifies the key when searching for resources. The value field is a series of one or more server:directory pairs that will tell the client which server(s) have the shared filesystems containing the requested data.

13

FILE SHARING

A master map might look something like this:

```
/home           auto.home
/software       auto.software
/usr/local      auto.local
```

This master map contains three entries, each referencing a directory as the key and another map as the value. A client request to access a directory in a tree whose root is listed in the master map (such as `cd /home/joe` or `cd /usr/local/bin`) will cause the automounter to search the specified map for a server to satisfy the request.

Each of the maps specified in the master can be one of two types: indirect maps or direct maps. Indirect maps allow you to logically create entire new filesystems on a client, all grouped under a given mount point; direct maps are used to augment already existing filesystems with specific mount points. In the previous example, the /home and /software entries reference indirect maps; these maps will contain all of the possible directories that exist on a client under the /home and /software directories. The /usr/local entry, on the other hand, references a direct map that would give each client access to /usr/local as shared by a remote fileserver.

To better illustrate this point, let's look first at an indirect map, in this case, the auto.home map mentioned in the auto.master file above:

```
joe         joesws:/export/home/joe
docs        server1:/export/docs server2:/export/docs
*           deptfs:/export/home/&
```

This map has three entries. If any client attempted to access the directory /home/joe, the first entry would cause the client to mount /export/home/joe from joesws at the local mount point /home/joe. The next entry is an example of a simple way to try to load-balance servers that have identical data to share. Built into the automounter is the capability to have clients choose their closest server from a list as the server from which they will mount filesystems. "Closest" here is defined in terms of network location and is decided based upon which server responds first to an NFS `ping`. (The `ping` is a request sent to the null procedure of the NFS servers.) The theory behind this is that servers on distant networks (those that can be reached only by traversing routers, bridges, or switches) will respond more slowly to these `ping`s than those on the client's local subnet. Any client that tries to mount /home/docs will mount the appropriate shared resource from either server1 or server2, whichever is closest.

The last line shows an example of wildcard matching. Because maps are checked sequentially for matches, the wildcard always should go last. This line is illustrating a situation in which almost all users have their home directory located in the same file-system on the same server; rather than listing each and every user on the network, and worrying about maintaining this map each time a user is added or deleted, you can use an entry like this. The effect of this line is that any request by a client to mount any directory /home/$key, where $key is not joe and not docs, will be passed on to the server deptfs as a request to mount /export/home/$key. That is to say, an attempt to mount /home/sally will be passed along to deptfs as a request for /export/home/sally, an attempt to mount /home/pete as a request for /export/home/pete, and so forth.

Direct maps have a slightly different syntax to the key fields; rather than just listing the basename of each directory to be mounted, they list the full path of the mount point, like this:

```
/usr/local          server1:/usr/local
```

This map has only one entry, pointing clients trying to access /usr/local to the shared /usr/local filesystem on server1. This map allows the client to have local data in most directories under /usr but still access /usr/local as an NFS directory shared by the server server1.

As we mentioned earlier, it's possible to use the automounter in environments that don't run NIS or NIS+; if you do so, you'll still enjoy many of the benefits that it provides. However, one benefit that will be missing will be the ability to manage all maps in one central point and have them updated automatically on all clients. Instead, you'll have to manage the maps on each automount client on your network. Depending on the number of hosts on your network, this can increase your workload a bit; however, an inability or unwillingness to run NIS or NIS+ should not preclude you from using the automounter if it's appropriate to your situation.

One benefit of the automounter comes from the fact that the it does its mounting of filesystems when they're needed and unmounts them when they're not; this provides some protection to clients against NFS server outages. If the client isn't accessing a given NFS filesystem when a server goes down, it won't suffer any ill effects because it won't have had the filesystem mounted.

The load-balancing capability described is another advantage that the automounter has over a standard NFS client setup. You cannot specify more than one server as the location of any given mount point in a traditional setup, but, as seen with the automounter, you can. Doing so allows you to have multiple copies of the same data in multiple locations and to have those locations share the load of providing it to your network.

One final advantage that the automounter provides is that it gives nonprivileged users (those without root access) the capability to mount specific filesystems without becoming privileged users or requesting the services of a privileged user (you) every time they want to access an NFS filesystem. The simple act of cding into an automounted filesystem

will mount it for them, without their having to update the (v)fstab file and run the
mount command.

Let's turn our attention now to setting up the automounter.

Setting Up Automount On A Red Hat 7.1 System

A default Red Hat 7.1 installation contains the master map file /etc/auto.master, which
includes one direct map, but it's not an NFS map. As discussed in the auto.master(5)
manual page, an automount map does not have to be a map for mounting NFS filesystems, but that is the default filesystem type for any entry in any automount map. You can
create your own maps for NFS mounting filesystems and list them in /etc/auto.master.
These maps define what are known as autofs filesystems.

The /etc/init.d/autofs(8) script, which has symbolic links at /etc/rc3.d/S28autofs,
/etc/rc4.d/S28autofs, and /etc/rc5.d/S28autofs, starts up the automount program at boot
time. The automount program reads the /etc/auto.master file, configures automount
mount points, and then answers mount and unmount requests for autofs filesystems.
Requests to mount autofs filesystems are any attempt to access that filesystem, usually in
the form of the cd(1) or ls(1) commands. Filesystems automatically are unmounted
after a period of inactivity; the default is 5 minutes, but this can be changed through the
-t or -timeout option, as specified in the auto.master file.

If you want to add any automount maps to your system, you first should read the
auto.master(5) and autofs(5) manual pages for information on the proper format for your
map. After you've built it, or whenever you make any changes to the auto.master file or
any map, you must run this to make your changes take effect:

```
/etc/init.d/autofs reload
```

Setting Up Automount On A Solaris 8 System

A default Solaris 8 installation includes a master map file (/etc/auto_master), which will
contain both direct and indirect map entries. If you create any new maps, you should list
them in this file. Any entry starting with a plus sign in the auto_master map or any other
map indicates that the NIS or NIS+ map of the same name should be read into the map
at that point, augmenting the file just as if it were part of the map.

By default, a Solaris 8 system runs as an automount client. The script /etc/rc2.d/
S74autofs, which is a hard link to /etc/init.d/autofs, starts up two programs at boot time:
automountd and automount. The automountd program runs as a daemon to answer
requests to mount and unmount automounted (or, more appropriately, autofs) filesystems.
Requests to mount an autofs filesystem come in the form of any attempt to access
that filesystem, usually by the cd(1) or ls(1) commands. Filesystems of this type

automatically are unmounted after a designated period of inactivity; the default is 10 minutes, but that can be changed with the -t option to the automount command. The automount program creates the mount points for the autofs filesystems by parsing the auto_master file at boot time and creating what it finds there. The automount program then exits, leaving the autofs filesystem to monitor activity and pass requests along to the automountd daemon.

One of the default maps included in Solaris 8 distributions is the special map –hosts, used with the /net mount point. This map allows clients to mount any and all filesystems exported by a given server simply through accessing the autofs filesystem /net/ <hostname>, where <hostname> can be either the simple hostname or the fully qualified domain name of an NFS server. If you have Solaris hosts on your network, especially hosts that you do not control, you should be cognizant of this feature. Because any Solaris client has a default map to mount all shared filesystems from any server on its network, it's important that you share your filesystems only with those clients to which you want to allow access.

Performance-Tuning and Troubleshooting NFS

In any NFS environment, you're likely to experience times when performance is perceived to be an issue, either by your users or by yourself. Sometimes the problem will manifest itself subtly, with reads and writes seemingly taking longer than they should; other times, things are more overt, with messages showing up on all of your consoles that your NFS server is not responding or is unavailable. You can employ some strategies to improve performance, but you'll have to do some work up front to see where you might have problems first. You also need to enter any performance-tuning exercise with the notion that sometimes you might not be able to do anything. There simply will be times when your servers and your network are performing at their peak levels, given the constraints imposed on them by the applications that are using them.

There can be no question that the speed of any I/O operation degrades the farther down the chain it must go. Read and write operations to memory are faster than to local disks, and those local disk operations, in turn, are faster than any that must travel over a network. It is simply a fact of life that NFS performance will always be slower than anything done locally, so your thinking with regard to NFS performance always must focus on whether NFS is the right solution to the problem of providing file access. Many times NFS is the right solution, but the performance trade-offs must be taken into consideration.

Although there is no magic bullet that you can use to fix all NFS problems, some tools available to you as a sysadmin can help you pinpoint what problems you might be having and devise solutions to them. These solutions might not involve NFS at all, so be prepared to look at problems from many different angles.

If you have the opportunity to do so, you can do a lot of your work in this area when you're first setting up a network. NFS performance will be best in environments that have reliable network connections whose speed is measured in hundreds of megabits per second. Moreover, the servers on that network will have been designed to have enough memory, CPU, and disk to deal with at least twice the peak expected loads and will be configured to take full advantage of the fast networks that they're attached to. Beyond that, lots of thought will need to be given to filesystem planning and layout, and filesystems on the server will be spread across multiple controllers to allow for fast reads and writes. Of course, if you were lucky enough to be in an environment like that, you probably wouldn't have purchased this book in the first place. Because you did buy this book, we'll assume that you're not working in this Utopian ideal.

Any time you're faced with perceived or actual NFS performance problems, your best course of action will be to look first at NFS, then at the network, next at the server, and finally at the application. The nfsstat command is available in both Red Hat 7.1 and Solaris 8 (in slightly different forms), and it can give you a quick idea of whether you're actually experiencing NFS problems. If you are, there could be some tuning that you can do on the server or the network to fix your problems. If nfsstat doesn't show you any indications of problems, however, you'll have to look at the other factors that might impact performance.

We'll talk about the specifics of nfsstat later because there are some differences between the command options and system tuning steps for Red Hat and Solaris. The other issues are platform-independent, so we can look at them here.

If you don't see any problems indicated by nfsstat, but you still see evidence that reads or writes are slower than they could be, your network might be the issue. Too much data in general moving across you wires will slow down everything on those wires, including NFS traffic. How much data is too much is a subjective thing and depends on your site's network infrastructure. You'll have to look at the output of commands such as netstat and sar, or use a network sniffer tool to see if there is too much traffic and then takes steps to alleviate it. You also can use ping and traceroute to get a feel for the general speed of traffic between your clients and your servers.

If the network doesn't appear to be a problem, your next step is to look at the configuration of the server. NFS performance issues might be symptoms of issues with the server itself. You can look at several things on the server, including memory utilization, CPU utilization, network statistics, and disk utilization. A heavily loaded server could be exhausting its available memory or might have CPUs that are at or near 100% utilization, and it could benefit from more memory or more CPUs. If your network traffic and infrastructure allow, your server might benefit from additional network interfaces, especially if they can be trunked together to effectively create one virtual interface whose capacity is the sum of the physical interfaces that make it up. Sun Microsystems produces a Quad Fast Ethernet (QFE) with four 100Mb interfaces that can be trunked in this manner to produce a 400Mb interface, for instance.

Finally, you can look at the disk utilization using programs such as iostat and sar. You might find situations in which a relatively small number of disks on your server are handling the bulk of the I/O requests, and you might be able to spread your data around to better balance things. In some cases, when you have a large number of clients using one server, a second, replicated server could be the answer to splitting up the load among your clients, especially if you're using the automounter. Standing up a second server can be a costly solution, but it might be the best approach sometimes.

If it's not NFS, it's not the network, and it's not the server, then chances are good that any problem is with your application. There are just some applications that are better off using local disk storage than NFS storage. Your job, in this case, is to find a way to accommodate those applications.

Let's turn our attention now to the nfsstat command.

nfsstat on Red Hat 7.1

In Red Hat 7.1, the nfsstat(8) command can gather statistics on both servers (when run with the -s option) and clients (when run with the -c option). In either case, the first three lines, listing the RPC statistics, are the ones to look at when trying to diagnose problems; the rest are basically counters showing you how many times each kind of NFS procedure was requested. The statistics shown are cumulative since the server was booted.

Let's examine each of the headings on the RPC statistics on an NFS server. The first, calls, is the total number of RPC calls received by the server. This number always should be greater than 0 and will continually trend upward over time.

The next one, badcalls, shows the number of RPC calls rejected by the RPC service before passing them to the NFS service. RPC calls will be rejected if a client doesn't authenticate itself properly or if a client attempts to modify, as root, a filesystem that doesn't allow it. A badcalls number greater than 0 might indicate a problem with NFS clients if badcalls is also greater than badauth.

13

FILE SHARING

The badauth counter will increment each time that a client makes a root attempt to modify an exported filesystem that doesn't allow this kind of modification. A number greater than 0 here does not necessarily indicate an NFS performance problem. However, if the number steadily is increasing over time, it might indicate either a poorly configured client application or nefarious attempts by those on your network to corrupt your data.

The last two, badclnt and xdrcall, can indicate network problems because both are counters of badly formed RPC packets that have been received from clients. Packets can become corrupted due to intermittent network problems, so these problems are more likely to occur when there are several hops between the client and the server. If your clients and your server are on the same subnet and either of these numbers is increasing, then you must suspect a network problem. In this case, you should investigate the physical components of the network, including networking equipment, interface cards on your clients and server, and even the networking cables.

If you run nfsstat(8) on your server and see no indication of any problems there, your next place to look should be the client. It's almost paradoxical to say, but nfsstat(8) results on the client might be the better way to get a picture of performance issues on the server.

Running nfsstat -c yields three RPC statistics, and only one is meaningful in most situations. The first, calls, is again the total number of RPC calls, but this time it's a tally of all RPC calls that this client has transmitted to all NFS servers.

The retrans number is most meaningful here because it shows the number of calls that had to be retransmitted to a server due to a lack of timely server response. Although ideally this number will be 0, a good rule of thumb to follow is that if this number is 5% or more of the number in the calls column, it could indicate a server that is overloaded to the point that it can't keep up with client requests.

Finally, the authrefrsh column shows the number of times that the client had to refresh its authentication credentials. This counter is useful only if you're running NFS with any kind of authentication option. If you are, and it's increasing, this number might indicate that a server sharing files under an enhanced security mode (as defined in RFC 1057) might have the credential's lifetimes set too low.

Among the NFS statistics, the ones that could indicate performance bottlenecks include read and write, readlink, and getattr.

If you see one client on your network that's making the vast majority of NFS read and write requests (e.g., more than all other clients combined) that client might be a candidate for getting some of this data moved to its local storage. Remember, local disk access always will be faster than NFS, so if you have a client accessing a lot of data over the network, consider moving that data to the client permanently.

The `readlink` column tells you how many times a client had to follow a symbolic link on a server to access a file. If a client is spending much of its time executing readlink operations, this might indicate that a filesystem (the one being linked to) on the server should be its own exported filesystem to be mounted directly onto clients.

The `getattr` column is a count of the number of times that a client had to request the attributes of any file from the server. If you recall our earlier discussion of the evolution of the NFS protocol, one of the changes in NFSv3 was that the server passed a file's attributes back to the client with every operation. This was done to improve performance so that the client didn't have to request the file's attributes again. Clients then can cache a file's attributes for a period of time, again to help ease network load. If you see this number steadily increasing on a client, you might want to investigate setting the `actimeo` option to the `mount` command higher on the client. See the nfs(5) manual page for more details.

So, what do you do if the `retrans` number indicates that you've possibly got an overloaded Red Hat NFS server? Well, if you're lucky enough to have only one NFS server on your network, or if the client with the high `retrans` number is mounting files from only one server, you can breathe a little easier because you at least know which server is having the problem. If you've got more than one server, you'll have to do a little work to track it down first. When you find it, you'll have to go through the steps outlined previously to figure out why it's having performance problems; it can be either disk, memory, or CPU, or it could be that there just aren't enough rpc.nfsd threads running.

NFS isn't terribly intensive with regard to memory or CPU, so a server doing nothing but NFS should not have any problems with running out of memory or CPU. If your server is running out of CPU or memory, chances are good that it's doing lots more than just serving NFS, so you should try to offload some of that work to other hosts, if possible. Servers running nothing but NFS can experience disk I/O problems, if the data on the server isn't properly balanced across all available disks and I/O controllers, whether they are SCSI, FC-AL, IDE, or something else. If you see signs of unbalanced disk utilization, do what you can to spread the load across your available, underutilized disks. If it's not disk, CPU, or memory, then try increasing the number of rpc.nfsd threads by changing the variable `RPCNFSDCOUNT` in /etc/init.d/nfs. The default is 8, and you should increase it a little at a time, gathering statistics for a while at each iteration before increasing it again. When you do increase it, use factors of 2 (as in, 16, then 32, and so on).

13

FILE SHARING

nfsstat on Solaris 8

In Solaris 8, the `nfsstat(1M)` command also has options to display both server statistics (the `-s` option) and client statistics (the `-c` option). The RPC statistics at the top of the output are meaningful for diagnosing problems; the NFS statistics just show the breakdown of NFS procedure calls as both counts and percentages. On a particular client, relatively high numbers of reads and writes in the NFS statistics (relative to other clients on your network) could indicate that a particular client is a candidate for having this data moved to local storage. In general, however, the RPC statistics are the real windows to any NFS problems on your network. The statistics shown are cumulative since the server last was booted or since the statistics were zeroed out, using the `-z` option, whichever is later.

Running `nfsstat -s` on an NFS server will yield two sections of RPC statistics, one for connection-oriented (TCP/IP protocol) RPC calls and one for connectionless (UDP) RPC calls. The headings in both sections are the same.

The first column, `calls`, is the total number of RPC calls made on that communication protocol. The next, `badcalls`, shows the total number of calls rejected by the RPC service without being passed to the NFS service. This will be a sum of `badlen` and `xdrcall`.

The `nullrecv` column might show a number greater than 0 on servers running more nfsd daemons than their client load requires. It is incremented when an nfsd process is awakened by the scheduler and finds no requests to service.

The last two, `badlen` and `xdrcall`, can indicate network problems because both are counters of badly formed RPC packets that have been received from clients. Packets can become corrupted due to intermittent network problems, so these problems are more likely to occur when there are several hops between the client and the server. If your clients and your server are on the same subnet and either of these numbers is increasing, you must suspect a network problem. In this case, you should investigate the physical components of the network, including networking equipment, interface cards on your clients and server, and even the networking cables.

When running `nfsstat -c` on a client, you will see some different RPC statistics than those displayed with the `-s` option. The `calls` column again shows the total number of RPC calls made on that communication protocol, and the `badcalls` column shows the total number of calls rejected by the RPC service; ideally, this latter number will be 0.

Any nonzero number in any of the other RPC columns (`badxids`, `timeouts`, `newcreds`, `badverfs`, `timers`, `cantconn`, `nomem`, `interrupts`, `retrans`, and `cantsend`) can indicate network problems, server resource issues, or server configuration problems either alone or in some combination. These metrics count occurrences of bad or unexpected packets traversing the network or occurrences of network unavailability. Consult your Solaris documentation and the `nfsstat(5)` man page for specific information on these columns and recommended solutions to problems that they might indicate.

Among the NFS statistics, the ones that could indicate performance bottlenecks include `read` and `write`, `readlink`, and `getattr`.

Any given client on a network that is requesting an inordinate number of NFS reads and writes in comparison to other clients on your network might be a candidate for getting some of this data moved to its local storage. Remember, local disk access always will be faster than NFS, so if you have a client using accessing a lot of data over the network, consider moving that data to the client permanently.

The `readlink` column tells you how many times a client had to follow a symbolic link on a server to access a file. If a client is spending much of its time executing readlink operations, this might indicate that there is a filesystem (the one being linked to) on the server that should be its own exported filesystem to be mounted directly onto clients.

The `getattr` column is a count of the number of times that a client had to request the attributes of any file from the server. If you recall our earlier discussion of the evolution of the NFS protocol, one of the changes in NFSv3 was that the server passed a file's attributes back to the client with every operation. This was done to improve performance so that the client didn't have to request the file's attributes again. Clients then can cache a file's attributes for a period of time, again to help ease network load. If you see this number steadily increasing on a client, you might want to investigate setting the `actimeo` option to the `mount` command higher on the client. See the `mount_nfs(1M)` manual page for more details.

The `nfsstat(1M)` command has another option, `-m`, that can be used on clients to determine whether a particular server might be having resource issues. Running `nfsstat -m` will show information for all currently mounted NFS filesystems, including dynamic retransmission rates; again, consult your Solaris documentation for details on their meanings and guidelines for tuning.

If you arrive at the conclusion based on the available data that you've got NFS performance problems and that they're due to a server on your network, you've got to figure out why the server isn't performing to your satisfaction. You can immediately isolate the problem to either disk, memory, or CPU, or the need for actual NFS-related system tuning. NFS isn't terribly intensive with regard to memory or CPU, so a server doing nothing but NFS should not have any problems with running out of memory or CPU. If your server is running out of CPU or memory, chances are good that it's doing lots more than just serving NFS, so you should try to offload some of that work to other hosts, if

13

FILE SHARING

possible. Servers running nothing but NFS can experience disk I/O problems if the data on the server isn't properly balanced across all available disks and I/O controllers, whether they are SCSI, FC-AL, IDE, or something else. If you see signs of unbalanced disk utilization, do what you can to spread the load across your available, underutilized disks.

If it's not disk, CPU, or memory, you might try increasing the number of nfsd threads by changing the default of 16 in /etc/init.d/nfs.server. If you decide to go this route, you should increase it a little at a time, gathering statistics for a while at each iteration before increasing it again. When you do increase it, use factors or 2 (such as 32, then 64, and so on). Alternatively, lots of kernel parameters related to NFS and networking can be tuned; a discussion of them is outside the scope of this book, so consult your Solaris documentation.

Setting Up Samba

If you're working in an organization that requires interoperability between UNIX and Windows hosts, Samba may be the right tool for the job. Samba allows hosts running these diverse operating systems to share files and print resources. With Samba, a UNIX host can be configured to be either a client, a server, or both, depending on the needs of the network.

Samba Overview

Samba is a UNIX-based implementation of the Server Message Block (SMB) protocol (its name is actually a play on the acronym SMB). The SMB protocol defines a method for sharing not only files, but also printers, serial ports, and other objects between computers. The SMB protocol first was developed by IBM, and it has been greatly expanded upon by Microsoft and others. The SMB protocol supports resource sharing over multiple networking protocols, including NetBIOS over TCP/IP (defined in RFCs 1001 and 1002), NetBEUI, and IPX/SPX. The SMB protocol sometimes is called the NetBIOS protocol or the LanManager protocol. We'll focus just on the TCP/IP implementation in this chapter.

Given its history, it should come as no surprise to you that the SMB protocol has enjoyed its widest deployment in the PC- and Intel-based server arena. Windows-based computers have used SMB for years as a means to share files and other resources, and it has met the needs of many homogenous computing environments. However, as interoperability has become more of an issue in today's computing world, the need for clients to access files on different types of servers running different operating systems has increased.

Samba provides one way for Windows clients to access files on UNIX servers and also a way for UNIX clients to access files on Windows servers because there is both a server component and a client component to Samba. This provides a nice flexibility for an organization because users can use the tools that they're most familiar with to access the resources that they need, without a lot of retraining. For instance, years ago, UNIX users had limited, if any, means of accessing files built by Windows word-processing or spreadsheet application; today, however, software applications are available that make this kind of access possible, and Samba can be the conduit to provide that access. Similarly, organizations now can deploy UNIX servers in their data centers to house user data and application files, and PC users can access this data in a manner that's transparent to them by using Samba. This can represent a big win for the IT department and its budget because they will have to outfit users in mixed environments with only one desktop computer, not two.

Samba Servers and Clients—Programs and Configuration Files

A Samba server installation consists of two programs (smbd and nmbd, typically but not necessarily run as daemons) and a configuration file, smb.conf. A UNIX Samba client is implemented through a program called smbclient.

The smbd program implements the SMB protocol by providing file and print services to SMB clients, which are typically computers running Windows 95, 98, or NT. Its configuration, as far as which resources to share and how to share them, is spelled out in the smb.conf file. By default, smbd binds port 139, which is the commonly defined NetBIOS port. It typically is run as a daemon at boot time, but it alternatively can be run on demand under the control of the inetd daemon. You must choose one of the two methods; you cannot do both. Running smbd as a daemon yields a small performance win because it will respond slightly quicker to requests, but this gain will be noticeable only on more heavily loaded servers.

The nmbd daemon provides support for browsing and name services to clients running the NetBIOS protocol. Its configuration also is defined in smb.conf. Like smbd, nmbd can be run as either a daemon or on demand under the control of inetd, with a slight performance gain when run as a daemon. nmbd participates in browsing by advertising the services provided by the Samba server on which it is running; this is effectively what browsing is. Clients send out requests to the network, asking which services are available and which servers are providing the services. The nmbd daemon answers these requests on a Samba server. The nmbd daemon also can act as a Windows Internet Name Service (WINS) server, providing name-to-address resolution to hosts on the network.

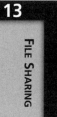

The smb.conf file is the configuration file for Samba programs. It contains a collection of rules defining which resources are to be shared and the methods by which they should be shared. Although it is possible to edit this file by hand, the recommended way to do so is to use the swat(8) program.

The swat(8) program (it's an acronym for Samba Web Administration Tool) is a tool that provides a Web browser interface to the configuration of an smb.conf file. swat(8), runs under the control of inetd and listens for connections on port 901. This makes it accessible on a given Samba server using the URL `http://<servername>:901/`. It is recommended that you access this URL only while logged into the server itself; that is, you should access it only by `http://localhost:901/`. To do otherwise would cause passwords to go over the network in clear text, which can be a security vulnerability. The swat(8) configuration page also has links to all kinds of help, which allow you to better understand what changes you might be making. When we discuss Samba configuration in this chapter, we'll focus on using swat, but we'll discuss the resulting smb.conf file so that you get a better understanding of what's going on. Although GUI-based configuration tools can be quite helpful to you as a sysadmin, you must understand which files they modify and know the proper format of those files. You never know when you'll be in a situation when you've got to fix an ailing server, and all you've got is a VT100 terminal attached to a serial port.

The smbclient program provides a method for UNIX clients to access SMB shares from non-UNIX servers (usually Windows NT servers) that have implemented the SMB protocol. The smbclient program can be used by clients to gain access to files and print services on these servers.

Although Samba can provide you many benefits, it also can provide you with a challenge to set it up properly and securely. As you are probably aware, several entire books have been written on the subject of Samba, and this section of this book cannot go into the detail that they do. This book can provide you with the basics of how to set things up and get things running, but it is outside the scope of this book to try to match those other books for depth of coverage.

You also should be aware going in that there are alternatives to Samba, including NFS server and client implementations for Windows. These implementations usually are commercial products (unlike Samba, which is free) and can present user training issues because getting access to shared filesystems under a Windows-based NFS implementation might involve different methods than the mapping of drives that users are used to. You should choose the best method for your environment to allow file sharing in a mixed environment.

Samba Operating System Compatibility

Samba is available for download in source form and can be successfully compiled and configured as a server on practically all popular flavors of UNIX. Over time, the SMB protocol has evolved, with each new evolution being referred to as a dialect. (Dialects can be thought of as versions.) As of this writing, Samba can support five SMB protocol dialects: CORE, COREPLUS, LANMAN1, LANMAN2, and NT1. Of those five, NT1 is the most "modern" and is the appropriate choice for most sites.

Authentication and Security Issues

Samba can be configured to require that clients authenticate themselves when requesting access to shares by providing passwords. Unfortunately, password management presents probably the biggest challenge to a Samba administrator, and it is certainly one of the more frequently discussed topics on Samba-focused mailing lists.

Modern Windows-based clients use encrypted passwords by default. This is a good thing because sending passwords across the wire in clear text is just asking for trouble. However, the encryption scheme used by Windows is different from that used by UNIX. Thus, Samba presents a password-management challenge because there are two password files to maintain, the UNIX password file (/etc/passwd) and the Samba password file (/usr/local/samba/private/smbpasswd). To use encrypted passwords on the server, you must create and seed the smbpasswd file with any users who may connect, and those users also must exist in the /etc/passwd file. The problem comes in because there's just no good way to add your current UNIX users to the smbpasswd file automatically; each must be added by hand, using the smbpasswd(8) program with the -a option. Because this program prompts you for the SMB password, unless you know your users' UNIX passwords or you don't care about keeping them the same as their SMB passwords, you'll need to get each of them sit with you for a moment to get them added. Alternatively, you can just give them a default SMB password; if they have login access to the Samba server, they can run the smbpasswd program themselves to change their passwords. (Remember, their presence in the /etc/passwd file doesn't necessarily imply login access because their shell could be set to /bin/false or some other nonshell.)

When you've got the password files setup, the next step is keeping them synched up, if you choose. Configuration options are available to you in the [global] section of the smb.conf file to make this happen, but they can be a little tricky to get right. The net effect of this configuration is that, when users run the `smbpasswd` command to change their Samba password, their UNIX passwords get changed at the same time without them doing anything extra. The parameters that you'll need to look at closely are unix password sync, passwd program, and passwd chat. These should be set to `Yes`, the location of the program users run to change their UNIX passwords, and a chat script, respectively. The last of these is not unlike an expect script; you list text prompts that will be displayed in an interactive session along with the answers to these prompts. The configuration is operating system-dependent, obviously, because different ones have their programs in different locations. You also can use the passwd chat debug option to enable logging of smbpasswd runs to see what's going on and to help you debug things if you're having problems.

Of course, you may choose to set up a Samba server that does nothing but serve file and print shares to the network, with direct logins to the server forbidden. In this case, your password maintenance chore is greatly reduced because you can have the users set their UNIX and Samba passwords at the time that you create their accounts (with the shell set to /bin/false) and then be done with it. The choice here is yours, and it depends on the needs of your organization and its user community.

As far as security goes, a good rule to follow is that any server configured to share resources across a network is more vulnerable to exploit than a comparable host that is sharing nothing. Resource sharing works because programs listen for requests on well-known ports, and everyone involved (the servers and the clients) understands the rules and knows which ports should be contacted to request a given service. In some cases, due to the nature of the service being provided, the server not only listens for incoming requests, but it also advertises its willingness to provide the service to anyone who will listen. Regardless of whether a service is passively listening or actively advertising, others outside your network frequently will scan all known ports to see what services are being provided and, by extension, what vulnerabilities might exist. These people might be looking to do harm to your server, your data, or your network.

As we recommend with NFS, rule 1 is that you should not run a Samba server if you don't need it. If you do need it, it is imperative that you run it only behind your organization's firewall, one that prohibits inbound traffic to ports 137, 138, and 139. NetBIOS is a favored target of hackers, crackers, and script kiddies; indeed, an Internet search for the phrase "NetBIOS hack" will yield lots of hits. Many of these sites are redundant in their content, but the point is that they're out there in large numbers. Those sites contain links to precompiled tools for crackers to use to attempt to gain access to your servers. There is no need for you to make your servers a target; put them behind a firewall.

If you do make the choice to run a Samba server, after you place it behind your firewall, configure it to share resources with the most restrictive permissions possible. Although it is possible to provide shares that can be accessed by guest users (that is, no password is required to access those shares) you should require passwords on as many shares as you can. While you're at it, consider whether to allow browsing (the capability of clients to see what resources your server is sharing before requesting a connection to them) of some or all of your shares. Although no doubt in some instances you'll want to advertise the availability of some shares, you might want to make others hidden.

Server Setup

The tasks involved in setting up a Samba server are basically the same, regardless of the operating system. The only substantial difference between setting up Samba on a Red Hat 7.1 server and setting up Samba on a Solaris 8 server is in how you get Samba onto the computer. Samba is part of the Red Hat 7.1 distribution; for Solaris, you must either install it from the Software Companion CD or download and compile it. We'll talk a little bit about how to start up the necessary daemons on both platforms, but we'll spend the majority of the time discussing the smb.conf file. The format of this file does not change from platform to platform, so there will be a combined section discussing it, rather than two sections.

Setting Up A Red Hat 7.1 System As A Samba Server

To configure Samba services to run at boot time, on the command line, run setup as root, choose System Services, and then select both smb and swat. Activating smb in this manner has the effect of running this command, although it doesn't start the services for you at that time:

```
chkconfig -level 5 smb
```

You'll still need to run this to start up smbd and nmbd in daemon mode:

```
/etc/rc5.d/S91smb start
```

However, because you don't yet have an smb.conf file in place, let's not start the daemons just yet.

Activating swat through this menu has the effect of changing the value of the `disable` line in /etc/xinetd.d/swat from `yes` to `no`; to make this change take effect, you'll have to run this command to signal your xinetd process to reread its configuration file and allow connections to swat:

```
kill -SIGUSR1 `cat /var/run/xinetd.pid`
```

If you'd rather run Samba daemons on demand instead of at boot time, you'll need to create two files in /etc/xinetd.d and put appropriate entries in /etc/services. Port 139 is the default. If they're not already there, add the following lines to your /etc/services file:

```
netbios-ns      137/tcp             # NETBIOS Name Service
netbios-ns      137/udp             # NETBIOS Name Service
netbios-dgm     138/tcp             # NETBIOS Datagram Service
```

13

FILE SHARING

```
netbios-dgm      138/udp                 # NETBIOS Datagram Service
netbios-ssn      139/tcp                 # NETBIOS Session Service
netbios-ssn      139/udp                 # NETBIOS Session Service
```

Next, you'll need to create two files in /etc/xinetd.d; we'll call them netbios-ns and netbios-ssn, to match the /etc/services entries:

```
service netbios-ns
{
        disable = no
        port    = 137
        socket_type    = dgram
        wait    = no
        user    = root
        server  = /usr/sbin/nmbd
        log_on_failure  += USERID
}

service netbios-ssn
{
        disable = no
        port    = 139
        socket_type    = stream
        wait    = no
        user    = root
        server  = /usr/sbin/smbd
        log_on_failure  += USERID
}
```

Last, you'll have to signal the xinetd process to reread its configuration file:

```
kill -SIGUSR1 `cat /var/run/xinetd.pid`
```

Now that you've got your system properly configured to provide Samba services, it's time to move on to discussing the smb.conf file. You must read and understand this section before you allow clients to connect to your server, so skip to that section now.

Setting Up A Solaris 8 System As A Samba Server

Because Samba is not part of the Solaris 8 Operating Environment distribution, you have the choice of either installing it from the software companion CD or downloading it from the Samba project Web site at http://www.samba.org/. The latter approach likely will yield a more current version of Samba, depending upon which hardware release of Solaris you have, and this is often the better approach.

Assuming that you're going to download and compile it, your first step is to make sure that you have a proper C compiler. The GNU Project's gcc compiler is on the software companion CD, so, if necessary, take a moment and install it.

After downloading and unpacking the distribution into a directory (we use /usr/local/ staging as a matter of preference), your next step is to change directories to the source directory underneath the samba directory (`cd /usr/local/staging/samba-2.2.1a/ source`). From there, installation can be as easy as just typing this (although that might or might not be appropriate for your setup):

```
./configure ; make install
```

In particular, the `configure` command has a host of options available to allow you to change the default settings. Among these options are the directory locations for the software and support for various filetypes an security options. Running the following will show you a list of all options available, and you should choose those which are best for your site:

```
./configure -help
```

Review the Samba software documentation for explanations of the options. We will confine our discussion at this point to an installation in the default location (/usr/local/ samba) using standard options.

Successful compilation and installation will leave you with all the pertinent files in subdirectories of /usr/local/samba, including /usr/local/samba/bin/smbd, /usr/local/samba/ bin/nmbd, and /usr/local/samba/bin/swat. Your next step is to decide whether you want to run Samba services as daemons that start at system boot time or on demand.

To run smbd and nmbd at boot time, first create a script called /etc/init.d/samba, owned by root, with permissions rwxr–r– that looks something like this:

```sh
#!/bin/sh

case $1 in
        'start')
                echo "Starting smbd..."
                /usr/local/samba/bin/smbd -D
                echo "Starting nmbd..."
                /usr/local/samba/bin/nmbd -D
                ;;
        'stop')
                echo "Stopping smbd and nmbd..."
                pkill smbd
                pkill nmbd
                rm -f /usr/local/samba/var/locks/smbd.pid
                rm -f /usr/local/samba/var/locks/nmbd.pid
                ;;
        *)
                echo "usage: samba {start|stop}"
                ;;
esac
```

13

FILE SHARING

Next, create links to this file, one to start Samba services at boot time, and several to stop them at system shutdown time or when the system changes to an init state where file sharing is not appropriate. You can use the location of the /etc/rc.d/*nfs.server links for guidance here; just start or stop Samba at the same time that the system would start or stop NFS services. This is a good idea because the networking services that must be in place to allow either Samba or NFS services to be provided are approximately the same for both. The commands to do this are shown here:

```
ln /etc/init.d/samba /etc/rc3.d/S16samba
ln /etc/init.d/samba /etc/rc0.d/K27samba
ln /etc/init.d/samba /etc/rc1.d/K27samba
ln /etc/init.d/samba /etc/rc2.d/K27samba
ln /etc/init.d/samba /etc/rcS.d/K27samba
```

Without rebooting your system, you'll still need to run this to start up smbd and nmbd at this time:

```
/etc/init.d/samba start
```

However, because you don't yet have an smb.conf file in place, let's hold off on that step for now.

If you'd rather configure your system to start smbd and nmbd only on demand, then, rather than creating a system startup script, you'll need to edit the /etc/services and /etc/inetd.conf files. In the /etc/services file, assuming that you'll be using the standard ports, add the following lines, if they're not already there:

```
netbios-ns      137/tcp             # NETBIOS Name Service
netbios-ns      137/udp             # NETBIOS Name Service
netbios-dgm     138/tcp             # NETBIOS Datagram Service
netbios-dgm     138/udp             # NETBIOS Datagram Service
netbios-ssn     139/tcp             # NETBIOS Session Service
netbios-ssn     139/udp             # NETBIOS Session Service
```

Next, you'll have to add the following lines to /etc/inetd.conf:

```
netbios-ssn stream tcp nowait root /usr/local/samba/bin/smbd smbd
netbios-ssn dgram  udp nowait root /usr/local/samba/bin/smbd smbd
netbios-ns  stream tcp wait   root /usr/local/samba/bin/nmbd nmbd
netbios-ns  dgram  udp wait   root /usr/local/samba/bin/nmbd nmbd
```

Finally, you'll need to signal inetd to reread its configuration file as follows:

```
pkill -HUP inetd
```

To set up your server to run swat, you'll need to edit /etc/services and /etc/inetd.conf, regardless of whether you're running Samba services at boot or on demand. The standard port for swat is 901, although you can choose any unused port; it really doesn't matter because you're going to be connecting to swat only while on the local host, not over the network. Assuming that you want to use port 901, add the following line to /etc/services:

```
swat        901/tcp
```

No matter what port you choose, you'll have to also add this line to /etc/inetd.conf:

```
swat stream tcp nowait root /usr/local/samba/bin/swat swat
```

Signal inetd to reread its configuration file by sending it a HUP signal:

```
pkill -HUP inetd
```

Now you're ready to configure the smb.conf file.

The smb.conf File

The smb.conf file is what makes Samba go. It defines the resources that you're going to share and the methods and policies by which these resources will be shared.

The basic format of the smb.conf file is as follows:

```
[sectionName]
        parameter = value
        parameter = value
        ...
        parameter = value
```

Lines that start with a semicolon or the hash character (#) are ignored, so you can use either character to begin any comment lines that you want to put into your smb.conf file.

The [sectionName] line represents the start of the policies and methods for a shared resource, and all *parameter = value* lines underneath it apply to that particular resource until the next [sectionName] line is encountered. Sections define either file shares (that is, filesystems or directories that you want to make available to clients) or printer shares (making print services on a UNIX server available to non-UNIX clients on your network). The [sectionName] line not only defines the start of a particular shared resource definition, but it also defines the name by which this share will be accessed by clients. For instance, given a Samba server with a hostname of fs.angrysunguy.com, which has an smb.conf file with a section name of [tools], Windows-based clients would access this shared resource as follows:

```
\\fs.angrysunguy.com\tools
```

There are three special sections: [global], [homes], and [printers]. The [global] section is just what its name suggests; it defines parameters that apply to all other shared resources described in the smb.conf file, although any given section can override any parameter specified in the [global] section. Think of this section as a combination of global and default settings.

The [homes] section represents an easy way to configure a server to provide access to many users' home directories. If a client requests a resource from a Samba server, the server first looks through the smb.conf for a matching section name. If no match is found but a [homes] section exists, then the server assumes that the requested name is a user-name and looks up that name in the passwd file. If there's a match there and the client has provided a correct password, that user's home directory is shared to the client. When we discuss some different parameters a little later, we'll show you how this can be easy to set up.

The [printers] section defines the methods for providing access to any print servers running on the server. As described in the previous paragraph, if a client requests a resource from a server, the server first checks for a match in the smb.conf's section names. If no match is found but a [printers] section exists, it attempts to match the request against the printer names as defined by the system's printcap file. If both a [homes] and a [printers] section exist, the [homes] section match attempt is done first; if there is no username to match the requested name, the server will attempt to match the request against known printers.

Literally hundreds of possible parameters can be set for a given resource; describing them all here is outside the scope of this book. The smb.conf(5) manual page, which runs to 127 printed pages itself, should be your definitive source for all the options. We'll talk about a few of the more common ones here, but we can't cover all of them.

A default smb.conf file is included with all Samba distributions; it's a good starting place if you want to see practical applications of what you read about here, in the smb.conf(5) manual page, or in other documentation sources. The example file is heavily commented, so you won't necessarily need the manual page next to you while you're looking at it; still, it's never a bad idea.

Although the format of the smb.conf file is straightforward, like any configuration file, a typographical error or two can really gum up the works and leave you with a nonfunc-tioning system. To that end, the swat(8) program is the recommended way of making updates to your smb.conf file. However, you must note that if you use swat(8), it will rewrite your smb.conf file, and any comments that you might have had in your file will be lost. If you choose to use swat, make sure that you back up your smb.conf file first.

Let's now set up a basic smb.conf file using swat; we'll define a [global] section, a [homes] section, a [printers] section, and a section named [docs] that will mimic a department-level document repository.

To run swat(8), you'll have to have set up your system as described in the appropriate section earlier in this chapter. When you've done that, start up a Web browser and enter the URL `http://localhost:901/` into the location bar. After entering the username root and the root password, the first screen that you'll see will look like Figure 13.1.

FIGURE 13.1

swat startup screen.

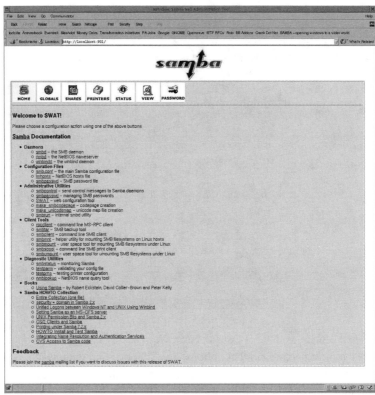

The buttons at the top of the screen give you access to various swat configuration screens and functions, while the links provide you access to all kinds of Samba documentation. Although we can't recommend that you make this your home page in your browser, it's probably not a bad idea to bookmark it.

Begin building your smb.conf by setting values for the [global] section. Figure 13.2 shows our GLOBALS screen with our values filled in.

13

FILE SHARING

FIGURE 13.2

swat GLOBALS screen.

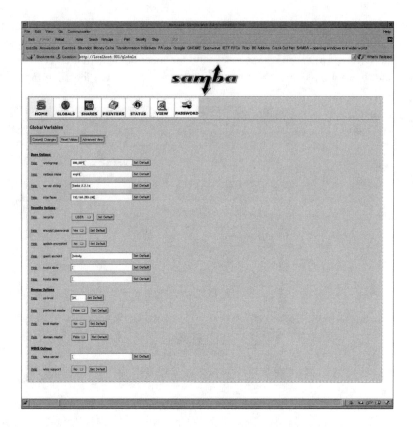

The screen shown here is just the basic view, which gives you the opportunity to configure the most common global options. You'll notice that there is a hyperlink to Help for
each of the options; we recommend that you take full advantage of this feature. If you
click on the Advanced View button, you'll be presented with a screen that allows you to
change all global-specific options. We've changed a few values from their defaults,
including workgroup, NetBIOS name, interfaces, encrypt passwords, preferred master,
local master, and domain master. Clicking on the VIEW button (see Figure 13.3) shows
what the configuration file currently looks like, with only the values that we've changed
from the default shown.

FIGURE 13.3

swat VIEW screen.

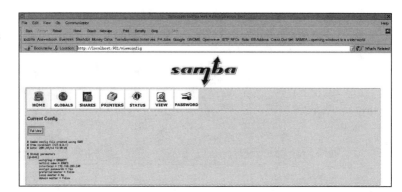

The Full View button on this screen shows you every parameter available to be set in the
[global] section.

As you can see, we set seven parameters different from their defaults:

- We changed workgroup to ENGDEPT from WORKGROUP.
- We set our NetBIOS name to ENGFS from its default of the DNS hostname of the
  server.
- We limited the interface that the nmbd process will service requests on to just
  192.168.203.240, as opposed to the default of all active interfaces on the server.
- We set encrypt passwords to YES because we want to support Windows NT and 98
  clients and because they send encrypted passwords by default.
- We set preferred master, local master, and domain master to False, No, and False,
  respectively, because we do not want our nmbd process acting as any kind of
  browser master on this server. This is not because Samba is incapable of being a
  browse master; on the contrary, Samba is a fine choice for this role in circumstances when you need to provide NT services but don't have the resources to buy
  an NT server. However, we did our configuration on a network that already had NT
  servers and services in place, and we didn't want to disrupt anyone.

Now that the global section is finished, it's time to set up some file shares.

The first task is to set up a [homes] section. After you click on SHARES, type the word
homes into the text box next to the Create Share button, as shown in Figure 13.4.

13

FILE SHARING

FIGURE 13.4

*Preparing to cre-
ate a homes share.*

After clicking on Create Share, you get the screen shown in Figure 13.5.

FIGURE 13.5

*The Create Share
screen, to set the
parameters for the
share.*

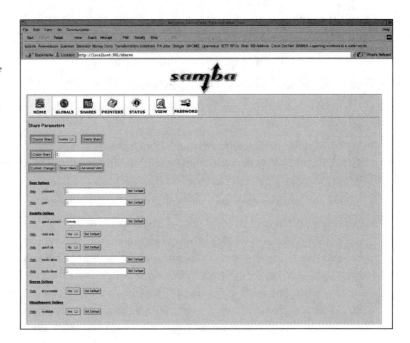

Finally, set some parameters for this share (see Figure 13.6).

We've used these nondefault settings:

- We added the comment Home Directories; the comment line is displayed when
  the share is shown to clients that use their browse capabilities to view which
  shares are available.

- The path of the share is set to /export/home/%u, taking advantage of Samba's variable substitution capability. If the server maps the requested share to the [homes] section, following the rules we outlined earlier, and there is a match in the passwd file, the %u variable will be replaced by the share name. Thus, a request for \\ENGFS\therr will be mapped to the server directory /export/home/therr, for instance. This provides a convenient way to specify home directory shares for multiple users on your network. The smb.conf file provides many variable substitution possibilities, which can be quite powerful in helping you with your configuration.

- Read Only is set to No because we want our users to be capable of creating and deleting files in their home directories. We also left Guest OK as No, because we don't want anyone accessing these shares without a password.

- Finally, Hosts Allow has the value 192.168.203.0/255.255.255.0, to illustrate one method of specifying which hosts may use this share.

FIGURE 13.6

Setting parameters for the homes share.

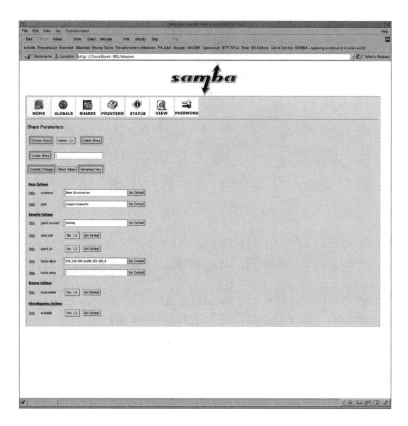

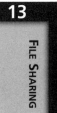

13

FILE SHARING

We also used the SHARES screen to setup a second share, called [docs]. This one is read-only, and serves as a repository for department reference documentation.

Last, you set up print services. First select the PRINTERS button, enter the name of the printer share that you want to create (here we'll use ENGPRINTER), and click on Create Printer. This brings up the screen shown in Figure 13.7.

FIGURE 13.7

Printer setup screen.

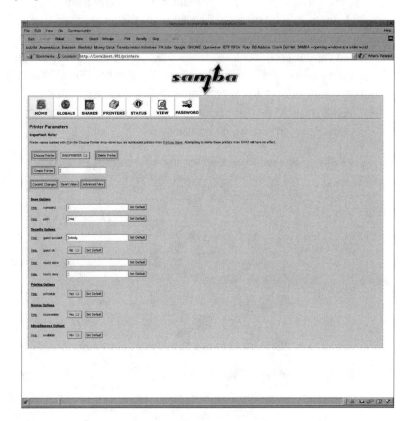

Accept the defaults here; after clicking on Commit Changes, you can view our new smb.conf file by clicking on the VIEW button (see Figure 13.8).

Remember that the view shown here is just of the nondefault parameter settings for each section; you can see the values of all parameters by clicking on the Full View button.

FIGURE **13.8**

A view of the new smb.conf file.

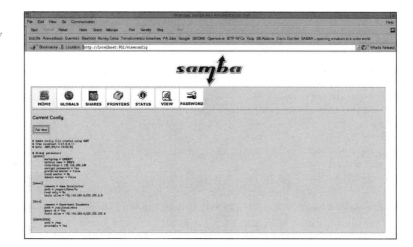

Recall from our previous discussion about authentication that a few parameters need to be set in concert with encrypt passwords to support modern Windows clients. Because the Full View look at the GLOBALS screen would cover too much real estate in this book, we'll just go ahead and add them by hand. We're adding parameters to set the location of the smbpasswd file, as well as the parameters necessary to synch up the Sambaand UNIX passwords, with debugging enabled. This leaves the smb.conf file looking like this:

```
# Global parameters
[global]
    workgroup = ENGDEPT
    netbios name = ENGFS
    interfaces = 192.168.203.240
    encrypt passwords = Yes
#   Added by hand
    smb passwd file = /usr/local/samba/private/smbpasswd
    unix password sync = yes
    passwd program = /bin/passwd %u
    passwd chat = *new*password* %n\n new*password* %n\n *changed*
    passwd chat debug = Yes
;   log level must be set to 100 to enable passwd chat debug logging
    log level = 100
#   End Added by hand
    preferred master = False
    local master = No
    domain master = False

[homes]
    comment = Home Directories
    path = /export/home/%u
```

13

FILE SHARING

```
    read only = No
    hosts allow = 192.168.203.0/255.255.255.0

[docs]
    comment = Department Documents
    path = /usr/local/docs
    guest ok = Yes
    hosts allow = 192.168.203.0/255.255.255.0

[ENGPRINTER]
    path = /tmp
    printable = Yes
```

Now that we've got an smb.conf file that we're happy with, we're ready to turn on the smbd and nmbd daemons. You can do this by clicking on the STATUS button, which brings up the screen in Figure 13.9.

FIGURE 13.9

The STATUS screen.

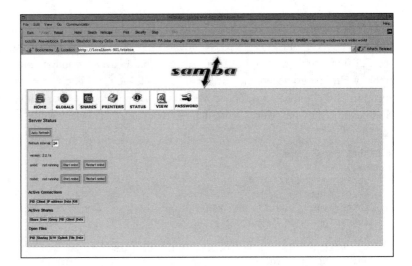

Click on Start smbd and Start nmbd, and you've got yourself a Samba server!

You can further use swat to maintain your Samba installation, by adding or deleting shares or tweaking the ones that you have. Just remember that swat will overwrite your existing smb.conf file, so you'll lose any comments that you might have added. On the other hand, as you get more comfortable, you can choose to maintain your smb.conf file by hand. Regardless of how you do it, it is important that you first test the changes using the testparm(1) program that's distributed with Samba. If testparm(1) reports no errors, then you know that your smb.conf file is acceptable. The smbd daemon automatically reloads its configuration file every minute, but you can speed up the process if you're impatient by sending it a SIGHUP signal. Configuration changes loaded by a running smbd daemon do not have an effect on existing connections; users must either disconnect and reconnect, or you'll have to stop and restart the smbd process for them to benefit from your changes.

Samba Client Setup

In the context of this book, where we're discussing UNIX systems administration, and in a narrower focus, where we're discussing UNIX-based Samba servers, when we speak of clients of those servers, we usually think of Windows-based computers. A discussion of setting up those clients is outside the scope of this book, although we can say that a properly configured Samba server can be accessed by Windows clients just as a Windows NT server would be. Those clients map network drives and access printers the same way they would if it were an NT server. We would be remiss, however, if we didn't mention UNIX-based Samba clients because it is possible to use Samba to access shares on either an NT server or a UNIX-based Samba server.

The Samba software distribution includes a program called smbclient(1), which provides access to SMB shares through an ftp-like interface. The basic method for starting up the program is simply this:

```
smbclient //servername/sharename
```

Here, `servername` is the NetBIOS name of the Samba server, not necessarily the DNS name. To illustrate its usage, let's look at a snippet of a session accessing the [homes] share set up earlier:

```
$ smbclient //ENGFS/therr
added interface ip=192.168.203.186 bcast=192.168.255.255 nmask=255.255.0.0
Got a positive name query response from 192.168.203.240 ( 192.168.203.240 )
Password:
Domain=[ENGDEPT] OS=[Unix] Server=[Samba 2.2.1a]
smb: \> ls
  .                                   D        0  Fri Sep 14 21:57:47 2001
  ..                                  D        0  Tue Apr 24 13:26:00 2001
  .dt                                 DH       0  Fri Aug 17 10:33:20 2001
  .dtprofile                          AH    5193  Fri Aug 17 13:39:52 2001
  .solregis                           DH       0  Fri Aug 17 10:33:24 2001
  .hotjava                            DH       0  Mon Mar 27 15:27:50 2000
  .Xauthority                         H     3847  Fri Sep  7 11:54:32 2001
  .mime.types                         H     1149  Tue May  1 11:27:48 2001
  .netscape                           DH       0  Fri Sep 14 19:14:33 2001
```

Many more commands than just `ls` are available; consult the manual page and the Samba documentation for further information.

Troubleshooting and Performance-Tuning Samba

Like any stable, robust software package operating under ordinary conditions, Samba problems usually occur during the setup and "break-in" period. New administrators might be overzealous when confronted with Samba's myriad options and might overconfigure things, or they might just misconfigure something when setting it up, causing problems that need to be ironed out. When you've got Samba set up, it usually just runs and runs and runs, with little or no involvement on your part. If problems do arise, however, you'll need to know where to look.

Samba Troubleshooting Strategies

In any situation when you've got problems reported, your first goal should be to gather as much information about the problem as possible. With Samba, you'll want not only information on the client and the resources that it's trying to access, but also as much information as possible on what's happening during the faulty transactions.

Assuming that network connectivity is normal between the client and server, a good checklist to follow is this one:

- Are the smbd and nmbd daemons running, if appropriate? It's possible to configure smbd and nmbd to run on demand, so the fact that they're not running might or might not be a sign of trouble.

- Are the daemons listening on the ports that they're supposed to be listening on? Can you connect to ports 137, 138, and 139?

- Is your smb.conf file okay? Run testparm(1) to verify that all is well with it.

- Can you use a network traffic-sniffer program such as tcpdump or snoop to see what kind of traffic is passing between the client and the server?

- What's happening when clients try to access shares on the server? Are they connecting? Is it a problem with passwords? Are they not capable of accessing shares that they want to access? If not, are there problems with the permissions on the shares, or is a share name spelled wrong either on the client or the server? Tools that you can use here would include smbclient and nmblookup on the server, as well as NET USE (at a DOS prompt) and Windows Explorer on clients.

- What's in the Samba log files? By default these are in the /usr/local/samba/var directory, and they are named log.smbd and log.nmbd. Run tail -f against either or both of these files to see what's going on. If you don't see anything particularly interesting going on, increase the logging level by incrementing the log level parameter in the globals section of the smb.conf file, and send a HUP signal to the smbd daemon process. (When you find and fix your problem, set this back down to a less noisy level.)

- Still stumped? Check out the public resources, such as Usenet, Samba mailing lists, books and documentation on the Web, or professional colleagues to see if your problem has a solution.

Samba Performance Tuning

As we discussed with NFS, file access across a network always will be slower than file access locally. Because of this fact of life, you invariably will run into times when your users perceive a problem with the performance of your Samba server. When this happens, you'll have a little bit of work to do.

Your first step is to decide whether you really do have a problem. Although its function might seem analogous to NFS, especially where Windows clients are concerned, FTP is the performance benchmark that you should use to decide whether you have a problem. Use smbclient and ftp on the same host to get and put files to your Samba server, and compare the times of the file transfers. Samba should run at a speed around 75% of ftp (for example, if ftp takes 3 seconds, Samba should take roughly 4 seconds). If it's slower than that, it's time to do some tuning.

First things first: Look at the overall server; make sure that it hasn't exhausted its memory and that its CPU isn't being overtaxed. Check on how many processes are running on the box, and make sure that you don't have any disk "hotspots," where one disk is getting a disproportionate number of reads and writes directed to it. If all looks well there, then it's time to look at Samba itself.

One of the first things that can have an impact on Samba performance is its logging. If you've got the log level parameter set higher than 1 and you're not in a troubleshooting situation, set it lower and see if that helps.

Beyond that, network-specific Samba parameters might yield some performance gains. Chief among these is the socket options parameter, which could yield some gains by setting the value of SO_SNDBUF and SO_RCVBUF to higher values, thereby increasing the size of the data packets traversing the network. This can produce small performance increases, up to a point.

A few other parameters are available that might yield gains, but you should consider very carefully their intended effects before changing them from their default values. Consult the smb.conf manual page and other Samba documentation for further discussion of these options.

13

FILE SHARING

Best Practices

In this section, we reiterate some of the ideas that we discussed in this chapter; the best practices for file sharing are tool-independent, so we don't have to split things up between NFS best practices and Samba best practices.

The best practices in file sharing can be summarized in this short list:

- Share files only when you have to; local file access is always faster than network access, but in many situations you'll want one central location to store and share files.

- Configure your servers to share files only to a limited group of clients and to share them at the most restrictive permissions possible.

- Keep your servers and clients behind firewalls that limit inbound traffic.

- When not required for other reasons, turn off RPC services on client systems.

- Stay current on security patches for your operating system, to make sure that you aren't vulnerable to any new exploits.

- Pay attention to security-focused mailing lists and Web sites to stay abreast of any new trends in intrusion activities.

- When faced with server performance issues, first confirm that you have a problem. Then look at the network and the overall server before focusing on the program that's actually sharing resources.

Online References

RFC 1001, "Protocol Standard for a NetBIOS Service on a TCP/UDP Transport: Concepts and Methods." http://www.faqs.org/rfcs/rfc1001.html

RFC 1002, "Protocol Standard for a NetBIOS Service on a TCP/UDP Transport: Detailed Specifications." http://www.faqs.org/rfcs/rfc1002.html

RFC 1014, "XDR: External Data Representation Standard." http://www.faqs.org/rfcs/rfc1014.html

RFC 1057, "RPC: Remote Procedure Call Specification, Version 2." http://www.faqs.org/rfcs/rfc1057.html

RFC 1094, "NFS: Network File System Protocol Specification (Version 2)." http://www.faqs.org/rfcs/rfc1094.html

RFC 1813, "NFS Version 3 Protocol Specification."
`http://www.faqs.org/rfcs/rfc1813.html`

RFC 1831, "RPC: Remote Procedure Call Specification, Version 2."
`http://www.faqs.org/rfcs/rfc1813.html`

RFC 1832, "XDR: External Data Representation Standard."
`http://www.faqs.org/rfcs/rfc1813.html`

RFC 2054, "WebNFS Client Specification." `http://www.faqs.org/rfcs/rfc2054.html`

RFC 2055, "WebNFS Server Specification." `http://www.faqs.org/rfcs/rfc2055.html`

RFC 3010, "NFS Version 4 Protocol." `http://www.faqs.org/rfcs/rfc3010.html`

Red Hat Support Web site: `http://www.redhat.com/apps/support/`

Sun Microsystems Product Documentation Web site: `http://docs.sun.com/`

The Samba project: `http://www.samba.org/`

13

FILE SHARING

CHAPTER 14

Printing

by Andrew R. Senft

IN THIS CHAPTER

Introduction

Printing within Unix has historically been accomplished by using one of two printing spooling systems—the AT&T Line Printer system and the Berkeley Line Printer Daemon (LPD). These printing systems were designed back in the 1970s for the sole purpose of printing text to line printers. Since then, Unix vendors have been adding varying levels of support for other types of printers. Most people refer to the AT&T Line Printer system as the System V printing system, named after its last major release version. The Berkeley LPD system is usually referred to as the Berkeley Software Distribution (BSD) printing system.

Today, most Unix operating systems offer both System V and BSD user commands, regardless of the underlying spooler. Few have even added a newer type of print spooler as their primary or alternative printing system. Two that will be described in this chapter are the systems LPRng and the Common Unix Printing System (CUPS). LPRng is an enhanced implementation of the BSD printing system. CUPS is a newer printing system based on the Internet Printing Protocol (IPP) that replaces the native print spooler completely.

In this chapter, we will discuss these four printing spooling systems, System V, BSD, LPRng, and CUPS. We'll also give you a general view of the Unix printing system, plus a detailed tutorial of each printing system. Table 14.1 lists these four printing systems.

TABLE 14.1 Unix Printing Spooling Systems

Printing System	*Stands For*	*Created By*	*Created*
System V	n/a	AT&T	1970s
BSD	Berkeley Software Distribution	Berkeley University	1970s
LPRng	Line Printing	Patrick A. Powell	1992
CUPS	Common UNIX Printing System	Easy Software Products	1999

Table 14.2 is a comparison of functionality among the four printing systems. Please note that even if a feature doesn't exist for a printing system, it still might exist for a particular operating system. Operating system vendors' implementations of the printing system are different. A good example of this is the GUI interface. Although there might be a GUI interface for Solaris and one for HP-UX, they are completely different programs and are not part of the native printing system.

TABLE 14.2 Comparison of Native Features

Description	System V	BSD	LPRng	CUPS
Automatic UNIX Client Configuration	no	no	no	yes
Backend Support (Modular Device Interfaces)	no	no	no	yes
Client printing from MacOS	no	no	yes	yes
Client printing from UNIX's	yes	yes	yes	yes
Client printing from Windows	no	no	yes	yes
Dynamic Redirection of Jobs	yes	no	yes	yes
Filtering for ASCII Text	yes	yes	yes	yes
Filtering for Image and PostScript	no	no	yes	yes
IPP Support	no	no	no	yes
PPD Support	no	no	no	yes
Support Classes	yes	no	yes	yes
Unified Printer Driver Architecture	no	no	no	yes
Web Interface	no	no	no	yes

Printing Spooling System

Under Unix, you can print directly to a printer's device (example /dev/lp0) even without a print spooler. The output will almost certainly not be of your liking, even for ASCII text output. Another caveat is that no other print jobs can be issued to that printer device until your first print job is completed. This is the reason why you need to use a printing spooling system. Basically, the printing spooling mechanism facilitates scheduling of print jobs into a queue (scheduler), filtering the print jobs so that your printer can recognize the input and finally sending the job output to the printer device:

Queue the print job → Filter the print job → Output the print job

All four printing spooling systems that are discussed in this chapter use this basic principle, although some are more glorified than others.

Queuing Jobs

The purpose of queuing Unix printing jobs is to schedule print jobs so that they don't clobber one another. This implies that multiple jobs can be initiated from multiple users at the same time. Figure 14.1 demonstrates this.

14

PRINTING

FIGURE 14.1

Multiple jobs to the queue

Queuing jobs in a network environment usually involves one computer (server) designated to "serve" its networked computers (clients) for their printing needs. Printing systems must be loaded on both the server and the clients. Servers are said to print "remotely" for their clients. This results in the server's print spooler listening to other client's print spoolers. For full capability, clients must run the same print spooler. In some cases, though, you might be able to send jobs from a client that is running an entirely different print spooler. In this situation, don't expect full functionality between the two spoolers. Your jobs might print properly, but you might lose some capabilities, such as accounting and status feedback. There is no hard-and-fast rule of which print spoolers will accept jobs from other print spoolers, mainly because of each Unix vendor's implementation of them. Figure 14.2 demonstrates this.

FIGURE 14.2

Multiple clients and single server queues.

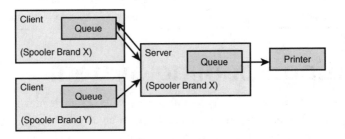

There are different variations of how to configure your queues. The simplest and most used is a single queue for a single printer. In this one-to-one relationship, your print jobs will always go to one printer. Figure 14.3 demonstrates this.

FIGURE 14.3

Single queue with single printer.

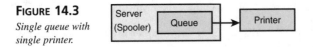

Multiple queues can also be configured. A common configuration is when multiple printers have their own queue. Because the printer relationship is still one-to-one, print jobs have a distinct destination. Figure 14.4 demonstrates this.

You also can configure multiple queues for a single printer. This many-to-one relationship is used when you have more than one common printing configuration for a printer. For example, let's say that you have a printer with two trays: one an envelope feeder and the other a letter-size paper tray. You can set up two queues, such as Envelope_Feeder and Letter_Paper. This predefined configuration eliminates the need to modify the printer setup each time you are about to print, not to mention helping you remember what you are really printing to with the meaningful alias names in place. Figure 14.5 demonstrates this.

FIGURE 14.4

Multiple queues with multiple printers.

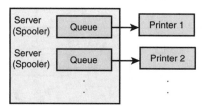

FIGURE 14.5

Multiple clients and single server queues.

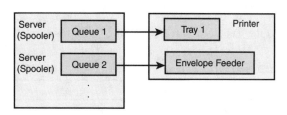

Queues can be configured as classes. Classes are simply a group of printers or instances of printers. One scenario of a class might be a computer lab environment in which you have multiple users printing at the same time and you want to balance the workload on several printers. A second scenario might be a fail-safe environment in which you don't want to lose any of your print jobs, so you have a backup printer just in case the first one breaks down or goes offline. Whatever the case, the scheduler will manage each print job, sending them to the next available printer. Figure 14.6 demonstrates this.

FIGURE 14.6

Single class to multiple printers.

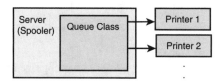

With some printing spooling systems, you can even configure multiple servers and printers as classes. Instead of grouping the printers to a class, you can group the servers and printers as a class. Print jobs still will be printed even if one server or one printer breaks down or goes offline. Again, what you achieve is a fail-safe and load-balancing printing environment. Figure 14.7 demonstrates this.

14

PRINTING

FIGURE 14.7

Single class to multiple servers with multiple printers.

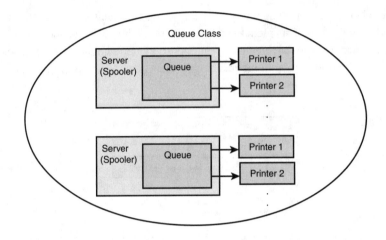

Table 14.3 summarizes the basic types of the queuing scenarios mentioned to this point.

TABLE 14.3 Queuing Scenarios

Type of Queuing	Description
Single queue to a single printer	One-to-one relationship
Multiple queues to multiple printers	One-to-one relationships
Multiple queues to a single printer	Used to print in different printer configurations
Single class to one group of printers	Used for failsafe and load balancing
Single class to one group of servers	Used for failsafe and load balancing

Filtering Jobs

Filtering Unix print jobs is required so that your printer can recognize the format of its input. It is the filter's job to translate the format of the language that the printer knows and accepts. Most printers accept ASCII text, while only some accept languages such as Adobe PostScript or HP-PCL. Many have a bitmap mode or a raster mode. Possible formats of input can include Adobe PDF, Adobe PostScript, ASCII text, GIF, HP-GL, HP-GL/2, international text, JPEG/JFIF, PNM, PBM, PGM, PNG, PPM, TIFF, and so on. Note that the System V and BSD printing native systems only translate ASCII text to the printer. Several third-party software solutions add image Raster Image Processors (RIP) and PostScript RIPs to these systems to complete the filter. Unfortunately, there is no standard solution, and they seem to work only for a unique set of Unix operating systems. With LPRng, we recommend installing its filter companion module, IFHP. CUPS already includes the image and PostScript RIPs, and needs no other add-on modules for this functionality. Figure 14.4 lists the input and printer formats.

TABLE 14.4   Possible Job and Printer Formats

Possible Job Input Formats	Possible Printer Formats
Adobe® PDF	Adobe® PostScript®
Adobe® PostScript®	ASCII Text
ASCII Text	Bitmap Mode
GIF	ESC/P
HP-GL	HP-PCL
HP-GL/2	Raster Mode
International Text	
JPEG/JFIF	
PNM, PBM	
PGM	
PNG	
PPM	
TIFF	

Commands

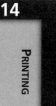

Three types of commands comprise a Unix printing spooling system: administrator, daemon, and user types. The administrator commands, issued by user root, are used to install and configure the printing spooling system. The daemon commands are responsible for spooling, filtering, and outputting print jobs. They run constantly in the background and are usually started automatically at bootup. Basic user commands start, move, list, and cancel print jobs.

Table 14.5 is a comparison of the basic commands of each printing spooling system. Notice the similarity in functionality among them.

TABLE 14.5   Comparison of Printing System Commands

Description	System V	BSD and LPRng	CUPS
Printer daemon	lpsched	lpd	cupsd
Submit a print job request	lp	lpr	lp, lpr
Lists pending print job requests	lpstat	lpq	lpstat, lpq
Removes a print job request	cancel	lprm	cancel, lprm
Administrator's interface	lpadmin	lpc	lpadmin, lpc
Enables a queue	enable	lpc	start enable
Disables a queue	disable	lpc	stop disable
Accepts printing queue requests	accept	lpc enable	accept
Rejects printing queue requests	reject	lpc disable	reject

Printing Under System V

The System V printing system is more flexible than the BSD system, solely because it supports classes. One note to remember is that, when submitting a print job, the print file is normally symlinked but can be copied with a command-line option.

Configuration Files

The configuration files for the System V printing system are shown in Table 14.6.

TABLE 14.6   System V Configuration Files

Pathname	Description
/usr/spool/lp/model/	Location of printer model configurations
/usr/spool/lp/interface/ or /etc/lp/interfaces/	Location of printer interface configurations
/var/lp/logs/ or /var/spool/lp/log/	Location of accounting file
/var/spool/lp/request/ or /var/spool/lp/requests/	Location of spooled jobs

Commands

Commands under System V are pretty straightforward. They permit you to make the fundamental printing configurations and allow basic printing control. Table 14.7 lists these commands.

TABLE 14.7   System V Printing Commands

Command	Description
lpsched	Printer daemon
lp	Submit a print job request
lpstat	Lists pending print job requests
cancel	Removes a queued job request
lpadmin	Administrator's interface
lpmove	Moves a job requests from one queue to another
enable	Enables a queue
disable	Disables a queue
accept	Accepts printing queue requests
reject	Rejects printing queue requests
lpshut	Stops the daemon (not implemented on all OSs)

Adding a Local Printer Configuration

Configuring a local printer on the System V Unix printing system is accomplished solely on the command line, although some Unix vendor's implementations do have a supplementary GUI. The following sequence of commands is used to configure a single printer connected to a parallel port.

1. Issue the su command to log in as root:

   # su

2. Locate the model and interface files. It's usually located under the directory /usr/spool/lp but issue a man command to make sure. There you will find which model files and interface files to use in Step 3.

   # man lpadmin

3. Use the lpadmin command to add a printer configuration. Its -p argument is an alias name that you give your destination printer or class. The destination alias

name will be used in the rest of this example for adding a local printer configuration. The -h argument is used only if the device is hardwired to the server's port. The -m argument specifies the name of the existing model interface program. The -i argument identifies the complete pathname of the interface program. The -v argument identifies the device file located under the /dev/ directory. Following are two examples of configuring for a parallel port. Device /dev/lp0 represents the first parallel port, although it might be specified differently on your operating system. This example uses the model argument:

```
# lpadmin -p destination -h -m model -v /dev/lp0
```

This example uses the interface argument:

```
# lpadmin -p destination -h -i interface_pathname -v /dev/lp0
```

You might want to use the -i argument when your script is not located under the model directory.

4. Issue the accept command. This enables the line-printer daemon to accept requests to queue print jobs for the destination, where destination is the value that you specified in the -p option of the lpadmin command previously.

```
# accept destination
```

5. Issue the enable command. This allows the line-printer daemon to send queued print jobs to the new destination, where destination is the value that you specified in the -p option of the lpadmin command previously.

```
# enable destination
```

6. Test the printer by piping the current directory listing to it.

```
# ls | lp -d destination
```

Adding a Remote Printer Configuration on Your Client

Adding a remote printer queue is similar to the local printer configuration for System V, just discussed. The only exception is the use of the lpadmin command in Step 3. You will use the server's IP address or hostname, plus its queues destination alias. The following is an example of configuring a client system with the alias name destination to a server with the alias name remote_destination:

```
# lpadmin -p destination -m netstandard -v /dev/null -o \
dest=remote_destination_ip_address_or_hostname:remote_destination
```

Deleting a Printer Configuration

To delete a printer configuration, you don't need to shut down the line-printer daemon. The -x flag of the lpadmin command removes the destination (a printer or a class) from the printing system. If the destination is a printer and is the only member of a class, the class is deleted. If the destination is all, all printers and classes are removed. Issue the following command to delete a destination:

```
# su
# lpadmin -x destination
```

Changing the Default Destination

The default destination can be specified in two ways. The first is the system default, which affects all users on a machine:

```
# su
# lpadmin -d destination
```

The second way is the users default, which does not affect other users on a machine. Users can define their personal default destination by setting the environment variable $LPDEST:

```
# setenv LPDEST destination; export LPDEST=destination
```

Submit a Print Job Request

lp adds a print job to a specified or default destination. By default, the file to be printed is symbolically linked in the spool area. Unless you specify the -c argument, you should not delete or modify the print file before it has completely printed. If you're printing from the command line, a job ID is displayed after issuing the lp command:

```
# lp -d destination -c file_to_print
```

Status Information

The lpstat command lists the status of one or more queues. This is an example of a long, verbose status listing of all queues:

```
# lpstat -ta
```

Canceling a Print Job Request

cancel removes previously requested jobs from the print queue. It uses a job ID argument or a destination argument specifying a printer or class. Any user can cancel any job,

14

regardless of ownership. Email is sent to the user of the cancelled job if someone else cancelled it. Here is an example of how to cancel a print job:

```
# cancel job_ID
```

If you want to cancel all your print jobs from a destination, issue this command:

```
# cancel destination
```

Stopping/Starting the Spool Queue

accept and reject starts and stops the queuing on a specific queue destination. The reject command instructs the line-printer daemon to stop queuing new job requests but allows printing of jobs already in the queue. The next example demonstrates how a job gets lost after stopping the queue.

```
# su
# ls | lp; reject destination
# ls | lp
# accept destination
```

Notice that printing starts only after the accept command is issued.

Stopping/Starting Printing

enable and disable start and stop sending jobs to a specific destination. The disable command instructs the line-printer daemon to stop sending jobs but allows it to keep queuing current and new job requests. If queued jobs are pending, the enable command flushes them out, printing every job. The following is an example of this, printing the directory listing after the enable command is issued:

```
# disable destination
# ls | lp
# enable destination
```

If you issue a ls | lpr command again, it should print.

Moving a Job to Another Destination

The lpmove command redirects the specified job ID on a queue from destination 1 to the queue of destination 2. lpmove also can move all jobs queued from destination 1 to destination 2 just by specifying the printer names. In this instance, a reject command is executed for destination 1. Here's an example of rerouting jobs from one destination to another:

```
# su
# lpmove destination_1 destination_2
```

Accounting

System V accounting is basic, but it does log some feedback on each print job. You should find some log files under the /var/lp/logs/ or /var/spool/lp/log/ directory, depending on your operating system.

Printing Under BSD

The BSD printing system is similar to the System V printing system, except that it doesn't support classes and dynamic job redirection. Unlike the System V printing system, print jobs are copied to the spool directory and are not symlinked, unless specified otherwise. This implies that print jobs will always print even if users modify or delete the file before it has completed printing.

Configuration Files

The configuration files for the BSD printing system are shown in Table 14.8.

TABLE 14.8 BSD Configuration Files

Pathname	Description
/etc/printcap	Printer database file
/etc/hosts.lpd	Lists client names allowed for printer access
/var/log/lpr/	Location of accounting files specified from printcap
/var/spool/lpd/	Location of spooled jobs

Commands

The command set of the System V printing system is similar to that of the BSD printing system. Notice the use of the lpc command instead of individual commands used by the System V printing system. With no arguments, lpc runs interactively, so you can issue multiple lpc commands in a session. Table 14.9 lists these commands.

TABLE 14.9 BSD Printing Commands

Command	Description
lpd	Printer daemon
lpr	Submits a print job request
lpq	Lists pending print job requests

14

PRINTING

TABLE 14.9 continued

Command	Description
lprm	Removes a queued job request
lpc	Line printer control program
lpc abort	Like lpc stop but aborts printing the current job
lpc clean	Cleans the spool directory: /var/spool/lpd
lpc disable	Rejects printing queue requests
lpc down	Simulates lpc stop and lpc disable
lpc enable	Accepts printing queue requests
lpc restart	Restarts a queue
lpc start	Enables a queue
lpc status	Displays the status of a printer or queue
lpc stop	Disables a queue
lpc topq	Changes the order of print jobs
lpc up	Simulates lpc start and lpc enable

Adding a Local Printer Configuration

Configuring a local printer on the BSD Unix printing system is not for the faint of heart, although some Unix vendors' implementations do have a supplementary GUI. The following sequence of commands is used to configure a single printer connected to a parallel port.

1. Issue the su command to log in as root:

   ```
   # su
   ```

2. Create the spool directory for your print queue. Notice that the alias name that you give the spool directory will be used in the rest of this example.

   ```
   # cd /var/spool/lpd
   # mkdir destination
   ```

3. Alter the ownership and group settings of the directory to daemon. Assign it readable, writeable, and executable for all, but only readable and executable for regular users.

   ```
   # chown daemon /var/spool/lpd/destination
   # chgrp daemon destination
   # chmod 775 destination
   ```

4. Write a very simple text filter script and save it as printfilter under the /usr/local/ bin/ directory. Alter the permissions of the file printfilter so that everyone can execute it. This is an example of creating a very simple filter:

```
# cd /usr/local/bin
# vi printfilter

#!/usr/bin/perl
while (<STDIN>)
{
chop $_;
print "$_\r\n";
}
print "\f";          # Delete this line if double form feeds

# chmod 755 /usr/local/bin/printfilter
```

5. Add a description entry to the /etc/printcap file. The first line signifies the alias names, destination, and lp. lp represents the default system printer. Please note that "destination" will be used in the rest of this example for adding a local printer configuration. Device /dev/lp0 identifies the first parallel port, although it might be different on your operating system. The mx#0 directive does away with file size limits. The lf and af directives are for accounting purposes and will be discussed later in this chapter. The sh directive suppresses banner pages.

```
# cd /etc
# vi printcap

    destination|lp:\
     :sd=/var/spool/lpd/destination\
     :if=/usr/local/bin/printfilter\
     :lp=/dev/lp0:\
     :mx#0:\
     :lf=/var/log/lpr/destination.log:\
     :af=/var/log/lpr/destination.acct:\
:sh:\
```

6. Alter the permissions on the printcap file so that everyone can read it.

```
# chmod 644 printcap
```

7. Create the necessary files and directories needed for a printing log and accounting purposes.

```
# mkdir /var/log/lpr
# cd /var/log/lpr
# touch destination.log
# touch destination.acct
```

14

PRINTING

8. Start the daemon.

   ```
   # lpd
   ```

9. Test the printer by piping the current directory listing to the printer.

   ```
   # ls | lpr -P destination
   ```

Adding a Remote Printer Configuration on Your Client

Adding a remote printer queue is similar to adding a local printer configuration for BSD, as just discussed. The only exception is the /etc/printcap file. In place of the lp directive are two new directives: rp and rm. The new rp parameter specifies the remote host's (server) queue name. Also, the new rm parameter identifies the remote host's (server) IP address or hostname. There is no need to specify filtering and accounting files because these functions will be performed on the server. Here is an example of configuring a client system with the alias named destination to a server with the alias name remote_destination:

```
destination|lp:\
:rp=/remote_destination:\
:rm=/remote_destination_ip_address_or_hostname:\
:sd=/var/spool/lpd/destination:\
:mx#0:\
:lf=/var/log/lpr/destination.log:\
:sh:\
```

Verify that the client's hostname or IP address is entered in the /etc/hosts.equiv file or, better yet, the /etc/hosts.lpd file. /etc/hosts.lpd restricts you only to clients that need to print.

Deleting a Printer Configuration

To delete a printer configuration, you need to disable and stop its print queue:

```
# lpc down destination
# vi /etc/printcap
```

Take away the printer configuration entry. For example, to delete the above "printcap" entry, you would delete all nine lines of the destination entry.

```
# lpd
```

Changing the Default Destination

The default destination can be specified in two ways. The first is the system default, which affects all users on a machine. To accomplish this, edit the /etc/printcap file. Then move the lp alias from the old entry to the new default printer. In the previous example of adding a local printer configuration for System V, the lp portion signifies that this queue is the default printer.

```
destination|lp:\
```

The second way is the users default, which does not affect other users on a machine. Users can define their personal default destination by setting the environment variable $PRINTER:

```
# setenv PRINTER destination; export PRINTER=destination
```

Submit a Print Job Request

lpr adds a print job to a specified or default destination. Unlike the lp command from the System V printing system, the file to be printed is copied to the spool area. This means that you can delete or modify the file before it has completed printing:

```
# lpr -P destination file_to_print
```

Status Information

The lpq command lists the status of one or more queues. The following is an example of a long verbose status listing of all queues:

```
# lpq -al
```

Also, the lpc command includes a status argument that is useful in listing the status of all queues:

```
# lpc status
```

Canceling a Print Job Request

lprm removes previously requested jobs from the print queue. It uses a job ID argument or a destination argument specifying a print queue. Unlike the System V printing system, users may remove only their own jobs, except for user root, who can remove any job. Here is an example of removing a print job:

```
# lprm job_ID
```

14

PRINTING

If you want to remove the current print job from a destination, issue this command:

```
# lprm -P destination
```

Stopping/Starting the Spool Queue

`lpc enable` and `lpc disable` start and stop the queuing on a specific queue destination. The `lpc disable` command instructs the line-printer daemon to stop queuing new job requests, but it allows printing of jobs already in the queue. The next example demonstrates how a job gets lost after stopping the queue:

```
# lpc disable destination
# ls | lpr
# lpc enable destination
```

If you issue a `ls | lpr` command again, it should print.

Stopping/Starting Printing

`lpc start` and `lpc stop` start and stop sending jobs to a specific destination. The `lpc stop` command instructs the line-printer daemon to stop sending jobs, but it allows the line-printer daemon to keep queuing current and new job requests. If queued jobs are pending, the `lpc start` command flushes them out, printing every job. The following is an example of this:

```
# lpc stop destination
# ls | lpr
# lpc start destination
```

Notice that printing starts only after the `lpc start` command is issued.

Accounting

Simple accounting files are identified in the /etc/printcap file. From the previous example, the *destination*.log and the *destination*.acct files should be located under the directory /var/log/lpr/. Print job logs and accounting logs can be viewed in their respective files.

Printing Under LPRng

The LPRng printing system is an enhanced and portable implementation of the BSD print spooler system. It was created by Patrick A. Powell and is offered to the public under the GNU GPL and Artistic licenses. The IFHP module of LPRng filters to PostScript, PCL, and text, and provides diagnostic, error, and accounting information.

Configuration Files

The configuration files under LPRng are shown in Table 14.10.

TABLE 14.10 LPRng Configuration Files

Pathname	Description
/etc/printcap	Print queue database
/etc/lpd.conf	Configuration options for the printer daemon
/etc/lpd.perms	Permission information for the printer daemon
/var/log/lpr/	Location of accounting files specified from printcap
/var/spool/lpd/	Location of spooled jobs

Commands

As you can guess, LPRng commands are similar to the commands used in the BSD printing system, but they encompass a lot more. Automatic job holding, dynamic redirection of jobs, load-balancing class queues, and enhanced security are just some of the features that it has over the BSD printing system. Also, LPRng simulates the System V command lpstat. Table 14.11 shows all LPRng commands, with the BSD subset of commands grayed out.

TABLE 14.11 LPRng Printing Commands

Command	Description
/usr/bin/lpr	Submits a print job request
/usr/bin/lpq	Lists pending print job requests
/usr/bin/lprm	Removes a queued job request
/usr/sbin/lpd	Printer daemon
/usr/sbin/lpc	Line printer control program
/usr/sbin/lpc abort	Like lpc stop but aborts printing the current job
/usr/sbin/lpc clean	Cleans the spool directory: /var/spool/lpd
/usr/sbin/lpc disable	Rejects printing queue requests
/usr/sbin/lpc down	Simulates lpc stop and lpc disable
/usr/sbin/lpc enable	Accepts printing queue requests
/usr/sbin/lpc restart	Restarts a queue
/usr/sbin/lpc start	Enables a queue

14

PRINTING

TABLE 14.11 continued

Command	Description
/usr/sbin/lpc status	Displays the status of a printer or queue
/usr/sbin/lpc stop	Disables a queue
/usr/sbin/lpc topq	Changes the order of print jobs
/usr/sbin/lpc up	Simulates lpc start and lpc enable
/usr/bin/lpstat	Lists pending print job requests
/usr/sbin/lpc active	Checks to see if server is accepting connections
/usr/sbin/lpc class	Displays and sets class printing
/usr/sbin/lpc debug	Sets debug level
/usr/sbin/lpc move	Redirects current jobs to another queue
/usr/sbin/lpc redirect	Redirects current and future jobs to another queue
/usr/sbin/lpc kill	Simulates lpc abort and lpc redo
/usr/sbin/lpc hold	Holds one job until lpc release is issued
/usr/sbin/lpc holdall	Holds all jobs until lpc release is issued
/usr/sbin/lpc local	Displays client printcap and configuration info
/usr/sbin/lpc lpd	Displays the line printer daemon's PID
/usr/sbin/lpc lpq	Invokes lpq
/usr/sbin/lpc lprm	Invokes lprm
/usr/sbin/lpc msg	Sets status message
/usr/sbin/lpc noholdall	Disables the holdall operation
/usr/sbin/lpc printcap	Reports printcap values
/usr/sbin/lpc redirect	Redirects current and future jobs to another queue
/usr/sbin/lpc redo	Releases job by reprinting it
/usr/sbin/lpc release	Releases job
/usr/sbin/lpc reread	LPD reread database information
/usr/sbin/lpc server	Displays server printcap and configuration info
/usr/sbin/checkpc	Checks the validity of the configuration files
/usr/libexec/filters/lpf	Simple text filter
/usr/libexec/filters/ifhp	Postscript, HP PCL, text and raster filter
/usr/libexec/filters/pclbanner	HP PCL banner filter
/usr/libexec/filters/psbanner	PostScript banner filter
/usr/libexec/filters/lpbanner	ASCII text filter
/usr/libexec/filters/accounting.pl	Accounting filter

TABLE **14.11**   continued

Command	Description
/usr/libexec/filters/getpc	Filter that works with Samba
/usr/libexec/filters/update_z	Filter that deals with control options
/usr/libexec/filters/smbprint	Filter that works with SMB

Adding a Local Printer Configuration

You can add a local printer configuration in LPRng the same way that you might in the BSD printing system. LPRng recognizes the same BSD syntax, excluding configurations of printers connected to the serial ports. LPRng does have its own syntax layer that offers advanced features, and it does permit configuring a printer connected to the serial port. You will see LPRng's printcap syntax in the example that follows. This sequence of commands is used to configure a single printer connected to a parallel port:

1. Issue the su command to login as root:

   ```
   # su
   ```

2. Add a description entry to the /etc/printcap file. The first line signifies the alias names, destination, and lp. lp represents the default system printer. Note that "destination" will be used in the rest of this example for adding a local printer configuration. Device /dev/lp0 identifies the first parallel port, although it might be different on your operating system. Instead of creating your own filter like you might under BSD, use the IFHP filter that comes packaged with LPRng. The lf, af, as, and ae directives are for accounting purposes and will be discussed later in this chapter.

   ```
   # cd /etc
   # vi printcap

       destination|lp
               :sd=/var/spool/lpd/%P
               :lp=/dev/lp0
               :filter=/usr/local/libexec/filters/ifhp
               :lf=/var/log/lpr/destination.log
               :af=acct
               :as=|/usr/local/libexec/filters/accounting.pl start
   :ae=|/usr/local/libexec/filters/accounting.pl end
   ```

3. Create the necessary files and directories needed for printing log and accounting purposes.

   ```
   # mkdir /var/log/lpr
   # cd /var/log/lpr
   # touch destination.log
   # touch destination.acct
   ```

14

PRINTING

4. Execute the `checkpc` command to verify that the printcap file is accurate and to create the necessary spool directories.

   ```
   # checkpc -f -V
   ```

5. Tell the line printer daemon to reread the printcap file by issuing the following command:

   ```
   # lpc reread
   ```

6. Start the daemon, if it hasn't already been started.

   ```
   # lpd
   ```

7. Test the printer by piping the current directory listing to it.

   ```
   # ls | lpr -P destination
   ```

Adding a Remote Printer Configuration on Your Client

Adding a remote printer queue is similar to adding a local printer configuration for LPRng, just discussed. The only exception is the /etc/printcap file. In place of the `lp` directive are two new directives: `rp` and `rm`. The new `rp` parameter specifies the remote host's (server) queue name. Also, the new `rm` parameter identifies the remote host's (server) IP address or hostname. There is no need to specify filtering and accounting files because these functions will be performed on the server. The following is an example of configuring a client system with the alias named destination to a server with the alias name remote_destination:

```
destination|lp:\
:rp=remote_destination
:rm=/remote_destination_ip_address_or_hostname
:sd=/var/spool/lpd/%P
:lf=/var/log/lpr/destination.log
```

Verify that the client's hostname or IP address is entered in the /etc/hosts.equiv file or, better yet, the /etc/hosts.lpd file.

Deleting a Printer Configuration

To delete a printer configuration, you need to disable and stop its print queue, but you do not need to invoke `lpd` like you would under the BSD printing system. Instead, the `lpc` command tells `lpd` to reread the printcap file.

```
# lpc down destination
# vi /etc/printcap
```

Take away the printer configuration entry. For example, to delete the previous printcap entry, you would delete all eight lines of the destination entry.

```
# lpc reread
```

Changing the Default Destination

The default destination is specified the same way as in the BSD printing system. In addition to the user's PRINTER environment variable, LPRng recognizes three other environment variables: LPDEST, NPRINTER, and NGPRINTER. The order in which LPRng recognizes the environment variables is PRINTER, LPDEST, NPRINTER, and NGPRINTER.

Submit a Print Job Request

LPRng uses the BSD command lpr and the System V simulated command lp to submit a print job request.

Status Information

LPRng uses the BSD commands lpq and lpc status to lists the status of one or more queues.

Canceling a Print Job Request

LPRng uses the BSD command lprm to remove previously requested jobs from the print queue.

Stopping/Starting the Spool Queue

LPRng uses the BSD commands lpc enable and lpc disable to enable and disable queuing on a specific queue destination.

Stopping/Starting Printing

LPRng uses the BSD commands lpc start and lpc stop to start and stop sending jobs to a specific destination.

Moving a Job to Another Destination

The lpc move command redirects current queued jobs or a specific queued job to a new destination. Note that it does not continuously move jobs from one queue to another. Here is an example of redirecting current queued jobs to a new destination:

```
# lpc move destination_1 destination_2
```

14

PRINTING

Here is an example of rerouting a single job from a queue to another:

```
# lpc move destination_1 job_ID destination_2
```

The `lpc redirect` command continuously redirects all jobs queued from destination 1 to destination 2. You can expect current and future jobs to be redirected. Here is an example of this:

```
# lpc redirect destination_1 destination_2
```

Accounting

Similar to the BSD printing system, accounting files are specified in the /etc/printcap file. From the previous example, the destination.log file should be located under the /var/log/lpr directory. With the new Perl accounting program identified in the printcap file, page log information can now be viewed.

Printing Under CUPS

In its true sense, CUPS has replaced the native printing system by using the next generation of network printing, Internet Printing Protocol (IPP), as its foundation. This modern printing system has been developed by Easy Software Products, promoting it as a standard cross-platform printing solution for all Unix vendors and users. CUPS adds network printer browsing and PostScript Printer Description (PPD)–based printing options to support today's demands for printing under Unix. CUPS also includes a customized version of GNU Ghostscript and an image file RIP that are used to support non-PostScript printers.

Configuration Files

The configuration files for CUPS are shown in Table 14.12.

TABLE 14.12   CUPS Configuration Files

Pathname	Description
/etc/cups/classes.conf	Printer classes configuration file
/etc/cups/client.conf	Default server name for client machines
/etc/cups/cupsd.conf	The daemon's configuration file
/etc/cups/printers.conf	The printer configuration file
/etc/cups/passwd.md5	Digest authentication passwords
/etc/cups/ssl/server.crt	SSL certificate key
/etc/cups/ppd/	Location of PPD files

TABLE 14.12   continued

Pathname	Description
/etc/cups/certs/	Location of authentication certificate files
/etc/cups/interfaces/	Location of System V interface printer scripts
/var/log/cups/access_log	Lists each HTTP resource that is accessed by a Web browser or CUPS/IPP client
/var/log/cups/error_log	Lists error and debug messages from the daemon
/var/log/cups/page_log	Lists each page that is sent to a printer
/var/spool/cups/	Location of spooled print jobs

Commands

CUPS's commands comprise the same basic commands from both the System V and the BSD printing systems, for compatibility incentives. The only exception is the use of the printcap file, which is used only for display purposes and is not used for printer configurations. Also, instead of the lpd or lpsched daemons, a cupsd daemon is spawned at bootup. In addition, a lpinfo command displays the printer devices with its PostScript Printer Description (PPD) details. Table 14.13 lists these commands.

TABLE 14.13   CUPS Printing Commands

Command	Description
/usr/bin/lp, /usr/bin/lpr	Submits a print job request
/usr/bin/lpstat	Lists pending print job requests
/usr/bin/disable	Stops a queued job request
/usr/bin/enable	Starts a queued job request
/usr/bin/cancel, /usr/bin/lprm	Removes a queued job request
/usr/bin/lpoptions	Sets user-defined printing options and defaults
/usr/bin/lppasswd	Adds, changes, or removes Digest password accounts
/usr/sbin/cupsd	Printer daemon
/usr/sbin/lpadmin,/usr/sbin/lpc	Administrator's interface
/usr/sbin/accept	Starts a print queue
/usr/sbin/reject	Stops a print queue
/usr/sbin/lpmove	Moves job requests from one print queue to another
/usr/sbin/lpinfo	Lists printer devices and PPDs

14

PRINTING

Many of these administration commands can be performed locally or remotely by using a Web browser (for example, Netscape). To accomplish this, bring up a Web browser and enter the URL: `http://localhost:631` or `http://hostname:631`. `localhost` represents the local server that you are currently on. `hostname` can represent either a local or a remote server. Port 631 denotes the port for IPP. Figure 14.8 shows an example of entering the hostname notation.

FIGURE 14.8

Main page of CUPS's Web interface.

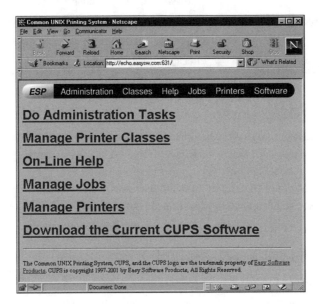

Adding a Local Printer Configuration

Adding a local printer configuration can be accomplished on the command line or a Web browser. To add a printer from the command line, follow the instructions under the System V printing system. We recommended using a Web browser because it's more intuitive and a great time saver. The following sequence of commands is used to configure a single printer connected to a parallel port:

1. Go to the main Web page of the CUPS interface by entering either URL `http://localhost:631` or `http://hostname:631`. In this example, we are specifying a hostname (see Table 14.21).

2. Click on the Do Administration Tasks link. Unless you already are logged in as user root, it will prompt you for the root login. Go ahead and input root and its password. This should take you to the next Web page.

3. Click on the Add Printer image button to proceed to the next Web page.

4. On the next page, enter an alias name, a location, and a brief description of the printer that you are configuring. In Figure 14.9, we are naming the alias Unleashed_Printer. Click on the Continue image button to proceed.

FIGURE 14.9

Adding a new printer in CUPS.

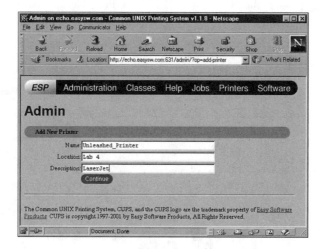

5. A selection of devices that your server is configured for should be displayed on the next page. In Figure 14.10, we are choosing the selection Parallel Port #1. After you have made your choice, click on the Continue image button to proceed.

FIGURE 14.10

Specifying the printer device in CUPS.

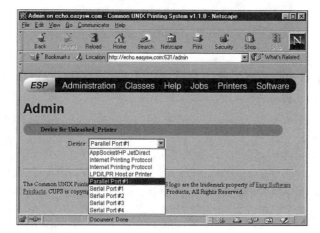

14

PRINTING

6. Select the model of your printer on the next page. Click on the Continue image button to proceed.

7. Select the make of your printer on the next page. Click on the Continue image button to proceed.

8. You should see a success page next. Click on the alias name Unleashed_Printer to bring you to its administrative tools.

9. To test the printer, click on the Print Test Page image button that is shown in Figure 14.11.

FIGURE 14.11

Specific printer admin in CUPS.

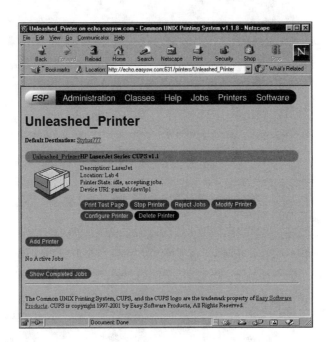

Adding a Remote Printer Configuration on Your Client

Adding a remote print queue configuration is very straightforward in CUPS. Follow the instructions under "Adding a Local Printer Configuration" for CUPS, earlier in this chapter, until you reach Step 5. On the client system, instead of selecting a parallel port for the device in Figure 14.10, you select either AppSocket/HP JetDirect, Internet Printing Protocol, or LPD/LPR, depending on your print server's interface. After you choose your selection, enter the device URL on the next page. In Figure 14.12, we chose LPD/LPR as a device and named it Unleashed_Client_Printer. We then entered the URL `lpd://lab3.easysw.com/inkjet`. The rest of the setup is what you would expect for adding a local printer configuration.

FIGURE 14.12

Identifying the network device in CUPS.

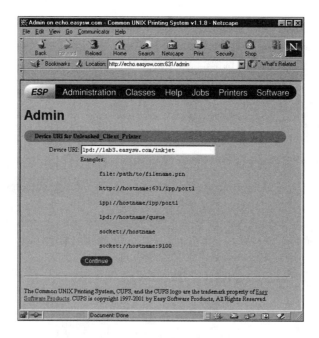

Deleting a Printer Configuration

The System V command `lpadmin -x` is used to delete a printer configuration. To delete a printer configuration from the Web interface, click on the Delete Printer image button from the printers Web page (see Figure 14.11).

Changing the Default Destination

CUPS uses the System V command `lpadmin -d` to change the default system destination. Users can define their personal default destination by setting either the `$PRINTER` or `$LPDEST` environment variables. Another alternative for users is to use the `lpoptions` command:

```
# lpoptions -d destination
```

Submit a Print Job Request

CUPS uses both the System V command `lp` and the BSD command `lpr` to submit job requests. The only exception is that it defaults with the `-c` option, so the print file is never symlinked to the spool directory.

14

PRINTING

Status Information

CUPS uses the System V command lpstat and the BSD commands lpq and lpc status to list job requests and queue statuses.

Canceling a Print Job Request

CUPS uses the System V command cancel and the BSD command lprm to cancel jobs.

Stopping/Starting the Spool Queue

CUPS uses the System V commands accept and reject to start and stop the print queue mechanism on a specific queue destination. To accomplish this through the Web interface, click on the Accept Printer or Reject Printer image buttons, respectively. These image buttons are located when you display the printers Web page (see Figure 14.11).

Stopping/Starting Printing

CUPS uses the System V commands enable and disable to start and stop jobs being sent to a specific destination. To accomplish this through the Web interface, click on the Stop Printer or Start Printer image buttons, respectively. These image buttons are located when you display the printers Web page (see Figure 14.11).

Moving a Job to Another Destination

CUPS uses the System V command lpmove to relocate print jobs to another queue.

Accounting

CUPS maintains a log of all accesses, errors, and pages that are printed. The log files are normally stored in the /var/log/cups directory. You can change this by editing the etc/cups/cupsd.conf configuration file. The access_log file lists each HTTP resource that is accessed by a Web browser or CUPS/IPP client. The error_log file lists messages from the scheduler such as errors and warnings. The page_log file lists each page that is sent to a printer.

Printer Configuration

If you select the Printer Configuration image button from the printers Web page (see Figure 14.11), you will be able to change the basic configurations. From the Unleashed_Printer example in Figure 14.13, you can modify the resolution, duplex mode, media size, media source, duplexer availability, and banner configurations.

FIGURE 14.13

Printer configuration in CUPS.

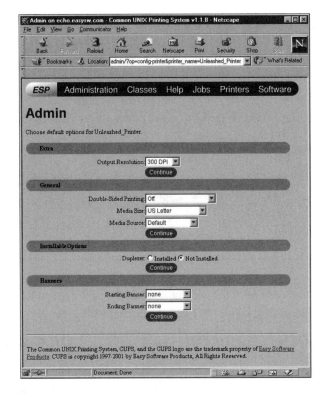

Best Practices

We recommend using the CUPS printing system because it's clearly the most full-featured printing system available. Even though it's a relatively new system (1999), many Linux vendors are already bundling it as their primary or secondary printing system.

BSD and System V users should investigate using a decent filter program rather than a simple text filter. Most operating systems have some kind of solution, so search for this in their manuals. Some operating systems have their own printer administrative GUI, so look out for that, too.

We also advise using multiple queues for one printer if you have an array of reoccurring configurations. It's not uncommon to set up predefined configurations for your printer by use of multiple queues. It's a time saver when it comes time to print.

Online Resources

The LPRng home page contains documentation and software in source code form. Unfortunately, there are no binaries available, so you need to compile the source code using the ANSI-compliant C and C++ compilers if you want to install it on your system.

The CUPS home page contains documentation and software in both source code and binary form. Included binaries are for AIX, Compaq Tru64, HP-UX, IRIX, Linux, Solaris for Intel, and Solaris for SPARC operating systems.

Information on IPP can be found at the Printing Working Group (PWG) organization's home page, `http://www.pwg.org`. There you will find information on the latest technologies and standards for printing.

TABLE 14.14 Web Site References

URL	Description
`http://www.lprng.com/`	LPRng's home page
`http://www.cups.org/`	CUPS's home page
`http://www.easysw.com/`	Easy Software Product's home page
`http://gimp-print.sourcefourge.net`	Free printer drivers for CUPS
`http://pwg.org/`	Printing Working Group with info on IPP

Basic Web Services

by Kurt Wall

Introduction

Unix servers dominate the Internet, despite claims by other OS vendors to the contrary. In July 2001, the Code Red Internet worm crippled Internet servers running Microsoft's Internet Information Server (IIS), but Unix- and Linux-based servers were largely unaffected, even in the face of a sharp upward spike in network traffic generated by Code Red worms. This chapter walks you through the process of setting up a stable, sane, no-frills Web server using Apache, the most popular Unix-based/free Web server in the world. You will learn how to build, install, configure, and maintain a common, albeit unexciting, Apache Web server. In addition, you will learn some measures that you can take to strengthen Apache's security:

- Providing basic Web services
- Obtaining and installing Apache
- Configuring Apache
- Using server-side includes
- Configuring MIME
- Using CGI scripts
- Adding features with Apache modules
- Running a chrooted Web server
- Using Apache and SSL

Providing Basic Web Services

At its simplest, the phrase *basic Web services* means running a Web server that sends out HTML-formatted documents on request. Setting up Apache and opening its default port, 80, is easy enough to do, as you will see shortly. Only slightly less simple are the administrative duties necessary to ensure that Apache *does* serve the desired content, that it runs efficiently, that it is properly maintained and monitored, and that it behaves as expected. You can thank the Apache team for this because its out-of-the-box configuration meets all the requirements for providing basic Web services.

For better or worse, few environments seem to be so simple anymore. The Apache team, including a crew of exceptionally dedicated documentation writers, helps you in this respect, too. With more than 200 configuration statements (don't scream—you might use 25 of them frequently and perhaps another 50 less frequently), you can persuade Apache to do almost anything demanded of a Web server. So, this chapter extends the definition of *basic* to include using a limited amount of server-generated content (with server-side includes), setting up virtual hosts (covered in depth in Chapter 20, "Advanced Web

Services"), extending the default MIME configuration, supporting CGI scripts, and setting up a secure server using SSL (also covered in greater detail in Chapter 20).

Before you get to any of that, though, you have to obtain and install Apache.

Obtaining and Installing Apache

Although binary versions of Apache might be available, we recommend downloading and installing from source. Not only can you customize Apache to your own needs, but you also can apply critical bug fixes and patches for security exploits more quickly if you already have the source code tree on hand and are familiar with the configure/build/install process, which is this section's purpose. After a short introduction to Apache's history, which also explains (with apologies to Kipling) how the Apache Web server got its name, this section discusses downloading, configuring, and building Apache from source code. Next, it shows you how to install the newly built server, as either a test or a primary server. Finally, it points you to a few key sources of additional information about running and maintaining Apache.

> **Note**
>
> Chapter 17, "Open Source Software Management," discusses obtaining and installing the necessary open source development tools to build other open source packages, such as Apache.

Obligatory Introduction to Apache

The Apache Web server is based on the HTTP server that the National Center for Supercomputing Applications (NCSA) originally wrote in the early 1990s. In late 1994 and early 1995, the NCSA stopped actively developing its httpd (HTTP daemon), so a small group of Web administrators who had modified the source code in various ways began to coordinate their activities and eventually merged them into a single code tree. In April 1995, this proto–Apache Group released the first public version of Apache version 0.6.2.

> **Note**
>
> The "About Apache" article on the Apache Web site (`http://httpd.apache.org/ABOUT_APACHE.html`) provides more information about the history of Apache and the Apache Group.

Even as the development team continued to stabilize the existing code base, add new features, and generate documentation, other development members completed a fundamental redesign that resulted in Apache 1.0, released on December 1, 1995. Version 1.0 cemented Apache's status as the Internet's no. 1 HTTP server. Seven years later, Internet-wide surveys conducted by Netcraft(`http://www.netcraft.com/survey/`) continually demonstrate that Apache is the most widely used Web server, surpassing all other Web servers.

Okay, So What's with the Name "Apache"?

The answer to what might be the most frequently asked question about Apache is best answered by, you guessed it, the Apache FAQ (`http://httpd.apache.org/docs/misc/FAQ.html#name`):

3. Why the name "Apache"?

A cute name which stuck. Apache is "A PAtCHy server." It was based on some existing code and a series of "patch files".

For many developers, it is also a reverent connotation to the Native American Indian tribe of Apache, well-known for their superior skills in warfare strategy and inexhaustible endurance. For more information on the Apache Nation, we suggest searching Google, Northernlight, Infoseek, or AllTheWeb.

Getting the Source Code

The source code for the latest version of Apache available as of this writing, Apache 1.3.20, can be downloaded from `http://httpd.apache.org/dist/httpd`. However, check the Apache server home page, `http://httpd.apache.org/`, to see if a newer version is available and also to check for any patches that may have been released, particularly patches that address security issues. We recommend using the latest and greatest version in the 1.*x* series. Fortunately, the build process described here will remain substantially unchanged:

1. Download apache_1.3.20.tar.gz (or the latest version) from the Apache Web site (`http://httpd.apache.org/dist/httpd`) or one of its mirrors. We downloaded it to /tmp, but you can use any directory to which you have write access.

2. Become root using su, and then cd to /usr/local/src (or another directory, if /usr/local/src is not available):

```
# cd /usr/local/src
```

3. Unpack the archive:

   ```
   # gzip -cd < /tmp/apache_1.3.20.tar.gz | tar xf -
   ```

4. `cd` into the base directory of the source code tree:

   ```
   # cd apache_1.3.20
   ```

5. Read the release documentation to familiarize yourself with changes, updates, new features, and known problems. At a bare minimum, read the files INSTALL, README, and README.configure.

If you have trouble with the build process or need more information about building applications, see Chapter 17.

Configuring the Source Code

If you are feeling impatient, just execute the command `./configure` in the Apache directory to create a configuration that will build and install. This is the no-fuss approach that works on most versions of Unix but creates a very basic installation that has no features, frills, bells, or whistles.

For those of you blessed with slightly more patience, you can customize the build configuration using the `./configure` command, shown next:

```
# OPTIM="-O2" CFLAGS="-march=CPU -mcpu=CPU" \
./configure \
--prefix=/usr/local/apache \
--enable-module=all \
--enable-shared=max
```

The syntax shown works for Bourne and similar shells (notably Bash and Korn shell). C shell–friendly syntax should resemble this:

```
# setenv OPTIM -O2; setenv CFLAGS "-march=CPU -mcpu=CPU"; \
./configure \
--prefix=/usr/local/apache \
--enable-module=all \
--enable-shared=max
```

What does this do? `OPTIM="-O2"` defines the optimization level passed to GCC. The `CFLAGS` option uses *CPU* to generate code in the Apache binaries that takes advantage of your CPU's features. If you are using Sun hardware, *CPU* can be one of v7, cypress, v8, supersparc, sparclite, hypersparc, sparclite86x, f930, f934, sparclet, tsc701, v9, or ultrasparc. For Intel x86 and compatible CPUs, *CPU* can be one of i386, i486, i586, i686, pentium, pentiumpro, or k6. `--prefix=/usr/local/apache` sets /usr/local/apache as the server's base installation directory. `--enable-module=all`

15

compiles and activates all the modules shipped in the standard Apache distribution (you can selectively disable modules later, as explained in the upcoming section "Configuring Apache"). *Modules* are pieces of code that provide both basic server functionality and extensions to core functionality. Using `--enable-shared=max` allows the modules built with `--enable-module=all` to be built as shared objects. *Shared objects*, which are similar to dynamically linked libraries, are modules that Apache can load and unload at runtime as needed.

Building Apache

Regardless of how you configured Apache—that is, whether you used the fast or slightly less fast method—building it is simple. Type **make** in the top level of the source-code tree:

```
# make
```

Even on a slow machine, it should not take more than 10 minutes to complete the process.

On some architectures and operating systems, especially if you use the GNU development tools described in Chapter 17 (primarily GCC and its linker), you might see one or both of the following error messages:

```
htpasswd.o: In function `main':
htpasswd.o(.text+0xa9a): the use of `tmpnam' is dangerous, [ic:ccc]
better use `mkstemp'
htdigest.o: In function `main':
htdigest.o(.text+0x462): the use of `tmpnam' is dangerous, [ic:ccc]
better use `mkstemp'
```

The linker generates these messages during the final link stage to remind programmers that the tmpnam call, part of the standard C I/O library, has known security problems and should be replaced with the safer mkstemp call.

Installing the New Server

When the build is complete, install the server with another simple command:

```
# make install
```

This command copies all the necessary binaries and configuration files into their appropriate locations in the filesystem, the one specified using `--prefix` (`--prefix=/usr/local/apache` in the example).

Next, decide whether you want to put the server directly into production or whether you want to test it. If you put it into production, it will be your primary server. Otherwise, it will be a test server. In this context, a *primary server* is a Web server running on the default HTTP port, 80. A *test server*, for purposes of this discussion, is a Web server running on a nonstandard port and, optionally, with restricted access. We recommend configuring a test server first to avoid adversely impacting a production environment and because it is very easy to convert a test server to a production server, as you will see shortly.

Setting Up a Test Server

To set up a test server, especially if you are already running a primary server on port 80, edit /usr/local/apache/conf/httpd.conf and change the line that reads `Port 80` to `Port 8080` (or any other port that is not currently being used). Using port 8080 or another unused port keeps the test server from interfering with the primary and also allows you to easily restrict access to the test server using a firewall or other means without affecting access to your primary server. Next, start the server using the following command:

```
# /usr/local/apache/bin/apachectl start
/usr/local/apache/bin/apachectl start: httpd started
```

Then, from any system that can access the server, try the URL `http://server.host. name:8080/` or `http://web.server.ip.addr:8080/`, replacing `server.host.name` with your system's hostname, or replacing `web.server.ip.addr` with your system's IP address. If these options do not work, there is most likely some sort of network configuration problem. From the server system itself, try `http://localhost:8080/` or `http://127.0.0.1:8080/`. If the server is working, you'll see the page shown in Figure 15.1.

FIGURE 15.1

The Apache Web server test page, delivered via port 8080.

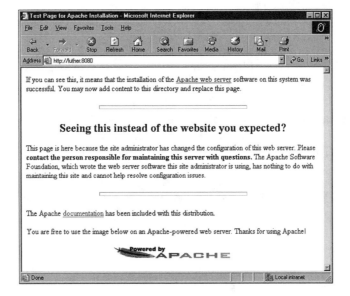

The test page shown in Figure 15.1 indicates that the server is up and running. If you want, stop the server with the following command:

```
# /usr/local/apache/bin/apachectl stop
/usr/local/apache/bin/apachectl stop: httpd stopped
```

Setting Up a Primary Server

To set up a primary server, you really have very little to do. If you configured the server as described in the previous section, edit httpd.conf and reset the `Port` directive to `Port 80`. Then start the server using the command shown previously—or, if the server is still running, restart it using the following command:

```
# /usr/local/apache/bin/apachectl restart
/usr/local/apache/bin/apachectl restart: httpd restarted
```

`apachectl` is a script provided with Apache that provides easy command-line access to working with the server. The `start` argument starts the server. Now try to access the Web server using a browser. Use the same URLs as before, but omit the `8080` from the end—that is, try one of these:

```
http://server.host.name/
http://web.server.ip.addr/
http://localhost/
http://127.0.0.1/
```

Again, if the server is working properly, you should see the Apache Web server test page shown in Figure 15.1.

If you want the Web server to continue running after a system reboot, add a call to apachectl to your system startup files, usually rc.local (if you do not want to do full SystemV initialization), a file in an init.d directory with symbolic links in various run-level directories, or a file in the rc.*N* directory. Because starting Apache at boot time will run the master server as root, make sure that your server is properly configured for security and access restrictions, as explained in the sections "Configuring Apache" and "Running a chrooted Web Server." In fact, the apachectl script is written in such a way that it can be used directly as an init script, but be sure to check the exact requirements of your system.

To stop the Web server, use the command `/usr/local/apache/bin/apachectl stop`, or let it keep running while you read the next section, "Configuring Apache."

Configuring Apache

Apache is highly configurable. Its configuration language consists of more than 200 separate *directives*, keywords that configure a particular feature. They are divided into several groups:

- General-purpose directives
- Operating system–specific directives
- Directives for backward compatibility with the NCSA httpd
- Special-purpose directives applicable to very specific situations

Because the next chapter discusses advanced Web server configuration issues, the directives discussed in this chapter affect basic server configuration; those that support SSI, modules, CGI; and those that enable support for virtual hosts.

Configuration Files

When Apache starts, it reads and processes three files, in the following order:

1. *server-root*/conf/httpd.conf
2. *server-root*/conf/srm.conf
3. *server-root*/conf/access.conf

server-root is the root of the Apache server—/usr/local/apache, in this chapter. The default location for each of these files is compiled into Apache but can be overridden using the -f option discussed later in the chapter. Apache also reads *server-root*/conf/ mime.types, which configures the MIME subsystem by mapping filename extensions to content types (see the section "Configuring MIME" for detailed discussion of Apache's MIME support).

httpd.conf is the primary configuration file, and, in fact, the srm.conf and access.conf files are empty in the standard Apache distribution. Why support three files when only one really counts? Using a single file simplifies maintaining the configuration file. However, for backward compatibility with the original NCSA server configuration and with early versions of Apache (neither of which anyone *ought* to be using at this point), srm.conf and access.conf are also supported. Do not use these files, but remember that they exist. All configuration directives can and should be placed in httpd.conf or included from other files specified using the Include directive discussed shortly.

> **Note**
>
> If you need a good belly laugh, read the alternative approach to explaining why Apache has three configuration files, two of which are redundant. It is explained in the article "Why are there three config files? Is this a throwback to NCSA?" available on the Apache Project's home page at `http://www.apache.org/info/three-config-files.html`.

httpd.conf is organized into three sections. The first section controls Apache's global characteristics. The second controls the *primary* or *default* server, the Web server that responds to all requests not handled by virtual hosts and default values for virtual servers. The third section configures any virtual hosts.

Global Configuration Directives

Table 15.1 lists the most commonly used global configuration directives.

TABLE 15.1 Global Configuration Directives

Directive	*Description*
ServerType	Controls whether Apache runs as a standalone process or runs from inetd
ServerRoot	Defines the top-level directory for Apache's configuration files and log files
PidFile	Defines the file containing the process ID (PID) of the master server process
Timeout	Defines the maximum time in seconds that Apache waits for packet send and receive operations to complete
KeepAlive	Permits multiple requests on the same connection, speeding up delivery of HTML documents
MaxKeepAliveRequests	Sets the number of requests permitted per connection
KeepAliveTimeout	Sets the number of seconds permitted to elapse between requests from the same client on the same connection when KeepAlive is On
MinSpareServers	Defines the minimum number of spare (idle) child servers permitted
MaxSpareServers	Defines the maximum number of spare (idle) child servers that the master server spawns

TABLE 15.1 continued

Directive	Description
StartServers	Defines the number of child servers created when Apache starts
MaxClients	Sets the maximum number of simultaneous connections (child servers) supported
MaxRequestsPerChild	Sets the maximum number of requests that each child server fills before terminating
Listen	Determines the combination of IP address and port on which Apache listens for connections; multiple Listen directives may be used
LoadModule	Links a module or library file into the server and adds it to the list of active modules
ClearModuleList	Clears Apache's built-in list of active modules, which must then be rebuilt using the AddModule directive
AddModule	Activates a built-in but inactive module

When specifying the names of log files or additional configuration files, these names are appended to ServerRoot unless they begin with /. That is, if ServerRoot is /usr/local/apache and you specify a log file logs/mylog.log, the complete pathname is /usr/local/apache/logs/mylog.log, whereas /logs/mylog.log is interpreted as an absolute pathname.

Specifying KeepAlive On results in significant performance improvements because it eliminates the overhead involved in initiating new HTTP connections between clients and the Web server. Rather than initiating a new connection for each request from the same client, KeepAlive On keeps the initial connection open.

When Apache starts, the master server starts a number of idle child processes, up to the number specified by MinSpareServers. If the number of *spare servers* (idle child processes) falls below MinSpareServers, the master server spawns additional spares. If the number of spares exceeds MaxSpareServers, the master server kills the excess servers. Thus, Apache self-regulates, adding and deleting child processes as Web server usage fluctuates.

When more than MaxClients attempt to connect to the server, each excess connection request enters a queue (in particular, a first-in, first-out [FIFO] queue) and is serviced in the order received as current connections close. Too long of a wait, however, will cause users either to think that they need to send another request or to disconnect. Busy Web sites might need to adjust this value to accommodate heavy traffic.

15

BASIC WEB
SERVICES

Listing 15.1 shows the default values for the directives listed in Table 15.1 (taken from /usr/local/apache/conf/httpd.conf).

LISTING 15.1 Default Apache Global Configuration Values

```
ServerType standalone
ServerRoot "/usr/local/apache"
PidFile /usr/local/apache/logs/httpd.pid
Timeout 300
KeepAlive On
MaxKeepAliveRequests 100
KeepAliveTimeout 15
MinSpareServers 5
MaxSpareServers 10
StartServers 5
MaxClients 150
MaxRequestsPerChild 0
LoadModule mmap_static_module libexec/mod_mmap_static.so
LoadModule vhost_alias_module libexec/mod_vhost_alias.so
LoadModule env_module          libexec/mod_env.so
...
ClearModuleList
AddModule mod_mmap_static.c
AddModule mod_vhost_alias.c
AddModule mod_env.c
...
```

The ellipses indicate `LoadModule` and `AddModule` directives deleted from the listing to conserve space. The section titled "Adding Features with Apache Modules" discusses modules in greater detail.

For most sites, many of the default values for the global directives in Table 15.1 should be sufficient. In particular, do not modify the order in which modules are loaded and activated using the `LoadModule` and `AddModule` directives unless you know what you are doing. Some modules depend on other modules to function properly. Apache will not start if problems occur during the module-loading procedure.

Values that you might consider changing include `MaxClients` and `MaxRequestsPerChild` and the file locations. File locations (`ServerRoot` and `PidFile`) should reflect your server's needs. For example, `PidFile` might be changed to point to /var/run/httpd.pid or any directory in which PID files are normally stored. You might need to change `MaxClients` to a smaller value if your server has limited bandwidth or limited hardware capacity. If traffic is heavy and the server logs indicate dropped connections, on the other hand, and *if* your server can handle the load, you can increase `MaxClients`.

You will almost certainly want to change `MaxRequestsPerChild` to a large value (say, 300). A value of 0 means that a child server never dies. The problem with immortal child servers is that a memory leak or other abnormal resource consumption problem either in Apache itself or in the underlying system libraries will continue to grow. Forcing the child servers to die after a specific number of requests returns consumed resources to the operating system's resource. Using a large value simply makes sure that child servers don't continually die in the middle of a session, especially if `KeepAlive On` is also set.

Configuring the Default Server

As just noted, the *default server* is the Web server that responds to all HTTP requests not handled by virtual hosts, also known as virtual servers. Without going into detail yet, a virtual server or virtual host is a Web server that runs on the same machine as the default server but that is distinguished from the main server by a different hostname or IP address. Nonetheless, configuration directives defined for the primary server also apply to virtual servers unless specifically overridden. Conversely, directives used to configure the default server can be used to configure virtual servers. Table 15.2 lists the most common directives for configuring the default server.

TABLE 15.2 Default Server Configuration Directives

Directive	Description
Port 80	Defines the port on which the primary server listens for connections if no `BindAddress` or `Listen` directive specifies a port number; has no effect otherwise.
User	Specifies the username or, if prefixed with #, the UID under which the child servers execute.
Group	Specifies the group name or, if prefixed with #, the GID under which the child servers execute.
ServerAdmin	Defines the email address included in error messages displayed to client connections.
DocumentRoot	Sets the base directory from which all requested documents will be served. Document URLs (filenames) are interpreted relative to `DocumentRoot`. See also `UserDir`.
UserDir	Defines the subdirectory in a user's home directory that is used when clients request documents belonging to a specific user.
DirectoryIndex	Specifies one or more filenames that serve as a directory index when a request does not request a specific file or document.

15

BASIC WEB SERVICES

TABLE 15.2 continued

Directive	Description
AccessFileName	Lists one or more filenames in the complete path to the requested document that define and control access to documents in each directory or subdirectory at the same level as or below the topmost directory where the file(s) specified by AccessFileName (if any) is found.
UseCanonicalName	Controls how Apache constructs a self-referential URL. If set to On, use ServerName and Port; if set to Off, use the hostname and port supplied by the client (if any) or the canonical name.
ServerName	Defines the server's fully qualified domain name (FQDN); if not specified, Apache uses its IP address to determine ServerName.
TypesConfig	Sets the filename of the MIME types configuration file (relative to ServerRoot if the filename does not begin with /), which maps file name extensions to content types. (See also AddType.)
DefaultType	Defines the default MIME type when a requested document's MIME type cannot be determined using the TypesConfig or AddType directives
HostnameLookups	Controls whether Apache performs DNS lookups on connecting hosts to log hostnames.
ErrorLog	Defines the name of Apache's error log, relative to ServerRoot if the filename does not begin with /.
LogLevel	Sets the amount and detail of information Apache records in its error log.
LogFormat	Defines the format that Apache uses for messages that it logs in the access log. (See also TransferLog and CustomLog.)
CustomLog	Defines the name of Apache's access log and the log format used when logging requests to the server.
ServerSignature	Directs Apache to append the ServerName and version number to generated documents, such as error messages, FTP file listings, and so forth
Alias	Links a directory specified relative to DocumentRoot to a filesystem directory outside ServerRoot.

TABLE 15.2 continued

Directive	Description
ScriptAlias	Functions exactly like the Alias directive and also indicates that the target directory contains executable CGI scripts.
IndexOptions	Specifies the behavior of Apache's directory indexing feature.
AddIconByEncoding	Sets the icon to display next to files with a given MIME encoding; used with the FancyIndexing directive.
AddIconByType	Sets the icon to display next to files with a given MIME type; used with the FancyIndexing directive.
AddIcon	Sets the icon to display next to files ending with a given extension; used with the FancyIndexing directive.
DefaultIcon	Sets the default icon displayed next to files whose MIME or content type cannot be determined; used with the FancyIndexing directive.
AddDescription	Adds a string used to describe files with a given a name (extension); used with the FancyIndexing directive.
ReadmeName	Defines the name of the file whose contents will be appended to the end of a directory listing.
HeaderName	Defines the name of the file whose contents will be inserted at the top of a directory listing.
AddEncoding	Adds a MIME encoding for files ending with a specific extension, overriding previous encodings for the name.
AddLanguage	Maps a filename extension to a specific language, overriding existing mappings for that filename extension.
AddType	Adds a MIME type for files ending with a given extension to the list of MIME types read from the TypesConfig file.
<Directory> </Directory>	Encloses a set of configuration directives that apply only to the named directory and its subdirectories.
<IfModule> </IfModule>	Encloses a set of configuration directives that apply only if the named module is loaded (or not loaded).

Admittedly, Table 15.2 contains a lot of information, but many of these directives are set-and-forget, meaning that you set them once and do not need to change them again. The ones that you actively use are few in number. To be frank, once you have an Apache server initially configured and, if necessary, tuned for your environment and usage patterns, you should not need to constantly tweak it.

15

BASIC WEB SERVICES

The User and Group directives allow you to run the child servers under less privileged user and group IDs. The key caveat is that the specified user and group should not have access to files that you do not want the world to see. Many administrators use the nobody user and group, but Apache's documentation recommends creating a new user and group. Regardless, no one should ever need to log in as this user, so set the login shell to something like /bin/false or /sbin/nologin to prevent user logins. For example, Red Hat Linux currently uses the user and group apache, with the following entries in /etc/passwd and /etc/group, respectively:

```
apache:x:48:48:Apache:/var/www:/bin/false
apache:X:48
```

The stock Apache installation on Solaris 8 uses the nobody user and group, which has these entries in /etc/passwd and /etc/group, respectively:

```
nobody:x:60001:60001:Nobody:/:
nobody::60001:
```

Use the UserDir directive if you want user's Web pages to be served. A common UserDir setting is:

```
UserDir public_html
```

This directive means that users must place their Web pages in $HOME/public_html and that they must be world-readable for clients to request them.

If you do not use the ServerName directive, Apache will use the host IP address to determine its name. For example, if the hostname is webbeast.my.domain and ServerName is blank, Apache will use webbeast.my.domain. However, if you specify, for example, ServerName www.my.domain, that will be the official server name (and the one used if ServerSignature On is set). If possible, use the ServerName directive because hostname lookups might not be reliable.

With UseCanonicalName On (discussed shortly), Apache uses the ServerName and Port directives to construct the server's canonical name. This name is used in all self-referential URLs—that is, URLs that refer back to the same server. With UseCanonicalName Off, Apache builds self-referential URLs using the hostname and port supplied by the client, if any are supplied; otherwise, it uses the canonical name defined by ServerName, if set, or the server system's hostname. Apache will perform a reverse DNS lookup on the server machine's IP address to which clients are connected to build self-referential URLs if UseCanonicalName DNS is specified. This feature supports IP-based virtual hosting (see the upcoming section titled "Configuring Virtual Servers" for more information about virtual hosts) and old Web clients that do not provide a Host: header in the HTTP request.

The `Alias` and `ScriptAlias` directives permit documents and other resources to be stored in the `DocumentRoot` directory. For example, consider these directives:

```
DocumentRoot /usr/local/apache/htdocs
Alias /ftp /var/ftp/pub
```

The `Alias` statement essentially creates a link from the target directory, /usr/local/apache/htdocs/ftp, to the destination directory /var/ftp/pub. So, a URL of `http://webbeast.my.domain/ftp/bigfile.tar.gz` would return the file /var/ftp/pub/bigfile.tar.gz. `ScriptAlias` has precisely the same effect, except that it *also* indicates that the destination directory, /var/ftp/pub, contains executable CGI scripts.

The `<Directory> </Directory>` directive is used to apply configuration directives and configuration options to a named directory and its subdirectories. For example, the following block indicates that the `FollowSymlinks` option and `AllowOverride None` directive apply specifically to the server root (/) and its subdirectories:

```
<Directory />
    Options FollowSymlinks
    AllowOverride None
</Directory>
```

The `AllowOverride` directive disables the use of directory access files (.htaccess, for example). The `FollowSymlinks` option means that the server will follow symbolic links in this directory tree.

Listing 15.2 contains the default values for the primary server configuration directives listed in Table 15.2.

LISTING 15.2   Default Apache Main Server Configuration Values

```
Port 80
User nobody
Group nobody
ServerAdmin root@luther.kurtwerks.com
DocumentRoot "/usr/local/apache/htdocs"
<Directory />
    Options FollowSymLinks
    AllowOverride None
</Directory>
<Directory "/usr/local/apache/htdocs">
    Options Indexes FollowSymLinks MultiViews
    AllowOverride None
    Order allow,deny
    Allow from all
</Directory>
```

15

BASIC WEB
SERVICES

This first section sets some standard defaults. A `User` and `Group` of nobody (which might not be supported on all systems) severely restricts system access, an important security measure if a malformed URL, especially in a CGI script, is used in an attempt to *root*, or compromise, the system.

```
<IfModule mod_userdir.c>
    UserDir public_html
</IfModule>
<IfModule mod_dir.c>
    DirectoryIndex index.html
</IfModule>
AccessFileName .htaccess
<Files ~ "^\.ht">
    Order allow,deny
    Deny from all
</Files>
UseCanonicalName On
<IfModule mod_mime.c>
    TypesConfig /usr/local/apache/conf/mime.types
</IfModule>
```

This `IfModule` block tells Apache which file contains the standard MIME type definitions and MIME encodings.

```
ErrorLog /usr/local/apache/logs/error_log
LogLevel warn
LogFormat "%h %l %u %t \"%r\" %>s %b \"%{Referer}i\" [ic;ccc]
\"%{User-Agent}i\"" combined
LogFormat "%h %l %u %t \"%r\" %>s %b" common
LogFormat "%{Referer}i -> %U" referer
LogFormat "%{User-agent}i" agent
CustomLog /usr/local/apache/logs/access_log common
```

These directives configure Apache's logging characteristics, including the location, the verbosity level, or the amount of information that Apache streams into the logs, and also the format of the log entries. Each `LogFormat` line uses a series of tokens to define the format of the log entry, ending with a single word used that serves as the name or alias for that format (in particular, combined, common, referrer, and agent). The last directive, `CustomLog`, uses the format named common to store information about client connections and requests in the access log, /usr/local/apache/logs/access.log.

```
ServerSignature On
<IfModule mod_alias.c>
    Alias /icons/ "/usr/local/apache/icons/"
    <Directory "/usr/local/apache/icons">
        Options Indexes MultiViews
        AllowOverride None
        Order allow,deny
        Allow from all
```

```
        </Directory>
        ScriptAlias /cgi-bin/ "/usr/local/apache/cgi-bin/"
        <Directory "/usr/local/apache/cgi-bin">
            AllowOverride None
            Options None
            Order allow,deny
            Allow from all
        </Directory>
</IfModule>
<IfModule mod_autoindex.c>
    IndexOptions FancyIndexing
    AddIconByEncoding (CMP,/icons/compressed.gif) x-compress x-gzip
    AddIconByType (TXT,/icons/text.gif) text/*
    AddIconByType (IMG,/icons/image2.gif) image/*
...
<IfModule mod_mime.c>
    AddEncoding x-compress Z
    AddEncoding x-gzip gz tgz
    AddLanguage da .dk
    AddLanguage nl .nl
...
```

Configuring Virtual Servers

This section explains how to configure Apache to support virtual servers. Primarily used to support multiple domains on a single system, virtual servers can also be used to allow multiple workgroups or departments on the same network to maintain independent Web sites without requiring additional expenditures on hardware or excessive administrative attention on your part. Table 15.3 shows directives used to configure virtual servers.

TABLE 15.3 Virtual Server Configuration Directives

Directive	*Description*
<VirtualHost> </VirtualHost>	Encloses a set of directives that define and configure a virtual host with a specific IP address (listening on a specific port, if specified). Configuration directives in the block override the directives defined for the default server.
NameVirtualHost	Defines the server IP address (listening on a specific port, if specified) for a name-based virtual host.
ServerName	Sets the fully qualified domain name of the virtual server when used with name-based virtual hosts.
ServerAlias	Allows the virtual server to respond to one or more alternate hostnames when used with name-based virtual hosts.

A typical virtual server block might look like the following:

```
...
Port 80
ServerName serverbeast.domain.com
NameVirtualHost 192.168.0.1

<VirtualHost 192.168.0.1>
    DocumentRoot /www/hers
    ServerName www.domain.com
</VirtualHost>
<VirtualHOst 192.168.0.1>
    DocumentRoot /www/his
    ServerName www.his.domain.com
</VirtualHost>
```

The `NameVirtualHost` directive defines the server's IP address, 192.168.0.1, and `ServerName` names the machine (serverbeast.domain.com). In addition, DNS must be configured with www.domain.com and www.his.domain.com as aliases (strictly speaking, CNAME resource records) for the IP address 192.168.0.1 so that lookups for any of the three names resolve to 192.168.0.1. A request to www.his.domain.com will be served out of the /www/his tree, but requests to www.domain.com will be served out of /www/hers. The main server will serve only requests to `localhost` because all other IP addresses that Apache knows about are served by the www.domain.com except those specifically sent to www.his.domain.com.

Server-Side Includes

Server-side includes, commonly referred to as SSI, are specially formatted statements placed in HTML pages and executed on the server when a document is served. SSI lets you add dynamically generated content to an existing HTML page without needing to generate the entire page using CGI or another dynamic page generation technique.

Why Use SSI?

SSI makes Web pages more active because they change, or can change, between views. SSI is best used to add small amounts of dynamically generated content to otherwise static documents. If most of a document must be generated dynamically, look for some other solution, such as PHP. SSI is a great way to add small pieces of information, such as the current time or the most recent modification date of the page. That said, the concern here is simply to enable Apache to use SSI and confirm that it works. Let the Web designers struggle with using SSI in their Web pages.

Configuring Apache for SSI

To enable SSI, add the following directive to your httpd.conf file in a `Directory` block:

```
Options +Includes
```

So, for example, a `Directory` statement that configures `DocumentRoot` might resemble the following after adding the `+Includes` option:

```
<Directory "/usr/local/apache/htdocs">
    Options Indexes FollowSymLinks MultiViews +Includes
    AllowOverride None
    Order allow,deny
    Allow from all
</Directory>
```

This directive enables Apache to process files that it serves for SSI directives. You also have to tell Apache *which* files to parse. You can use two approaches. One is to use the `AddType` and `AddHandler` directives to identify SSI files:

```
AddType text/html .shtml
AddHandler server-parsed .shtml
```

The first line adds the file extension .shtml to the text/html MIME type. The next statement instructs Apache that the .shtml extension should be evaluated using `mod_include`, which provides Apache's SSI support. The next section, "Configuring MIME," discusses Apache's MIME support and configuration minutiae.

The shortcoming of this approach is that pages using SSI would have to be renamed, and any pages that refer to them would have to be edited to reflect the name change. On the other hand, using a specific file extension makes it easy to scan directories looking for SSI-enabled pages, and it lets you avoid the rather ugly hack of the other approach, which uses the appropriately named `XBitHack` directive.

The `XBitHack` directive tells Apache to evaluate SSI directives in a document file if the file's execute bit is set. The syntax for this directive is shown in the following line:

```
XBitHack o
```

So, after adding SSI directives to a page, make it executable using `chmod`:

```
chmod +x ssi-page.html
```

After making these changes to httpd.conf, restart the server (using `apachectl restart`) to make all the changes take effect.

Do not tell Apache to parse all HTML files for SSI, however. That is, to enable SSI, *do not* do something like this:

```
AddType text/html .html
AddHandler server-parsed .html
```

Why? This approach requires Apache to read and parse *every file that it delivers to clients.* As a result, the server will incur a significant performance penalty, especially if it is busy.

Testing an SSI Example

SSI directives look like HTML comments. Their general form is as follows:

```
<!--#element attribute=value ... -->
```

If SSI is improperly configured, the browser will ignore the directive. Listing 15.3 shows a short HTML document that tests the server's SSI configuration.

LISTING 15.3   Sample SSI Document

```
<html>

<head>
 SSI Test Page
</head>

<body>
<center>
 SSI Test Page Output
 <hr>
 <p>
  This file last modified:
 <p>
  <!--#echo var="LAST_MODIFIED" -->
 <p>
 <hr>
</center>
</body>
</html>
```

The SSI directive is `<!--#echo var="LAST_MODIFIED" -->`, which uses a built-in variable, `LAST_MODIFIED`, which contains the date that the current file was last modified. Figure 15.2 shows how it appears in the Mozilla Web browser.

FIGURE 15.2

The sample SSI test page in the Mozilla graphical browser.

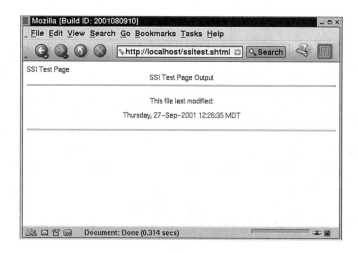

As you can see in Figure 15.2 the directive's output states that the file in question (ssitest.shtml) was last modified on September 27 at 12:26 P.M. The output of `ls -l` confirms this:

```
-rw-r--r--   1 root     root           203 Sep 27 12:26 ssitest.shtml
```

After confirming that SSI is properly configured using the test page, your configuration is complete. For more information, review the following directives in the Apache documentation

- `Options Includes`
- `Options IncludesNOEXEC`
- `AddHandler`
- `AddType`
- `XBitHack`

Also review the documentation on `mod_include`, the Apache module that handles SSI. Finally, if you want to learn how to use SSI in your Web pages, the Apache documentation includes a short SSI tutorial.

Configuring MIME

MIME is an acronym for *Multipurpose Internet Mail Extensions* that specifies how messages must be formatted so that they can be exchanged between different email systems. Although originally intended for exchanging email, the MIME standard has proven to be a very flexible format that can apply to transmission of virtually any type of data between a server and a client. Specifically, MIME messages can contain text, images, audio, video, or other application-specific data. MIME is essential, in that the HTML and HTTP standards address the exchange of only plain, textual data—all other data types must be handled via MIME support.

Apache boasts rich, highly configurable MIME support. Indeed, in the stock configuration that we suggested you build at the beginning of this chapter, Apache's MIME support is sufficient for the vast majority of Web server installations. This section briefly explains what MIME is, elaborates on Apache's default MIME configuration, and shows you how to extend and customize the default configuration to fit your needs and preferences.

Teaching Apache to MIME

Three Apache modules handle the majority of its MIME processing:

- mod_mime determines document types based on filename extensions.
- mod_mime_magic enables Apache to determine document types using so-called "magic numbers."
- mod_negotiation handles Apache's content-negotiation functionality.

These MIME-related modules provide the functionality beneath Apache's configuration directives that control its MIME processing capabilities. Table 15.4 lists most of the directives that each module provides and briefly describes their purpose. Some of these directives have already been mentioned (see Tables 15.1—5.3) but are included here for the sake of completeness.

TABLE 15.4 Apache MIME Configuration Directives

Directive	Description
mod_mime	
AddCharset	Maps a character set to a filename extension
AddEncoding	Maps a MIME encoding type to a filename extension
AddHandler	Maps a handler, typically a program or Apache module, to a filename extension
AddLanguage	Maps a language to a filename extension
AddType	Maps a MIME type to a filename extension
DefaultLanguage	Specifies the default language for all files that lack an explicit language extension as defined by AddLanguage directives

TABLE 15.4 continued

Directive	Description
mod_mime	
RemoveEncoding	Removes the association between a MIME encoding (see AddEncoding) and a specified filename extension
RemoveHandler	Removes the association between a MIME handler (see AddHandler) and a specified filename extension
RemoveType	Removes the association between a MIME type (see AddType) and a specified filename extension
TypesConfig	Sets the location of the MIME types configuration file (*server_root*/conf/mime.types, by default)
mod_mime_magic	
MimeMagicFile	Sets the location of the MIME magic number file (*server_root*/conf/magic by default) that mod_mime_magic uses to determine file types
mod_negotiation	
CacheNegotiatedDocs	If set, permits proxy servers to cache content-negotiated documents
LanguagePriority	Sets the precedence in decreasing order of the language used when serving documents available in multiple languages to clients that do not express a language preference

As you might surmise from Table 15.4, Apache's MIME handling is driven almost entirely by filename extensions. Although it is not the most elegant way to determine the content of a file, it is very efficient and works surprisingly well.

You have already seen AddHandler and AddType in action in the section "Server-Side Includes." The directives were as follows:

```
AddType text/html .shtml
AddHandler server-parsed .shtml
```

The AddType directive maps the MIME type text/html to the filename extension .shtml. The next statement associates a handler, server-parsed, with the .shtml filename extension. Together, as explained earlier, these two directives tell Apache the MIME type of filenames (documents) ending with .shtml and tell how to process such documents (in this case, by parsing the document for SSI directives and evaluating those statements before serving the resulting document to the requesting client.

15

BASIC WEB SERVICES

TypesConfig defines the file that contains a comprehensive list of MIME types mappings, sort of a mega-AddType statement. The default TypesConfig file is /etc/mime.types. Instead of editing /etc/mime.types, the recommended way to add MIME type mappings is to use the AddType directive.

DefaultType sets a default content type for the Web server to use for documents whose MIME types cannot be determined. By default, Apache assumes that any document that has an indeterminate content type is a plain text file.

CGI Scripts

The Common Gateway Interface (CGI) establishes the means by which the Apache Web server can communicate with external programs, known as *CGI scripts* or *CGI programs*. While CGI scripts are widely used for on-the-fly content creation, they also can be used for authentication, to create a user interface on a Web page, and, within limits, in any situation in which a Web-based interface is used to execute programs and display the results in a near–real-time environment. This section explains how to configure Apache to enable CGI scripts and discusses some of the security issues that CGI scripts raise. Chapter 20 covers the security concerns in greater detail.

Enabling CGI

Naturally, the first thing to do is configure Apache to permit CGI script execution. Recall from Table 15.2 that the ScriptAlias directive associates a directory name with a filesystem path, which means that Apache will treat every file in that directory as a script. If not present, add the following directive to httpd.conf:

```
ScriptAlias /cgi-bin/ /usr/local/apache/cgi-bin/
```

This directive allows any URL beginning with /cgi-bin/ to be served out of /usr/local/apache/cgi-bin/. So, http://localhost/cgi-bin/herscript.pl and http://www.webbeast.com/cgi-bin/scriptdir/hisscript.pl will result in Apache reading and executing the scripts /usr/local/apache/cgi-bin/herscript.pl and /usr/local/apache/cgi-bin/scriptdir/hisscript.pl, respectively.

Alternatively, you can use the ExecCGI option inside a <Directory></Directory> block to specifically enable CGI execution in that directory. The format would resemble the following:

```
<Directory /home/*/public_html/cgi-bin>
    Options +ExecCGI
    SetHandler cgi-script
</Directory>
```

This directive allows CGI scripts in user directories (specified using UserDir public_html). In this case, you would also have to use an AddHandler directive to tell Apache what it should treat as a CGI script. To allow Perl scripts to be treated as CGI scripts, for example, the AddHandler directive to add to httpd.conf would be as follows:

```
AddHandler cgi-script pl
```

After making these changes, restart Apache as shown previously, and then test the configuration.

Testing the Configuration

Use the script in Listing 15.4 to test the configuration. In this case, we modified the configuration file (httpd.conf) to allow execution of CGI scripts in user directories, as just shown.

LISTING 15.4   A CGI Configuration Test Script

```perl
#!/usr/bin/perl
print "Content-type: text/html\r\n\r\n";
$now_string = gmtime;
print "Current time is $now_string";
```

Save this script as cgitest.pl, make it executable (chmod a+x cgitest.pl), and put it in the $HOME/public_html/cgi-bin directory. Then open the URL to the script in your browser using the URL http://*your.server.name*/~*username*/cgi-bin/cgitest.pl. Replace *your.server.name* with the name of your Web server, and replace *username* with the user account name. Figure 15.3 shows example output from the cgitest.pl script.

FIGURE 15.3

The output of the CGI test script.

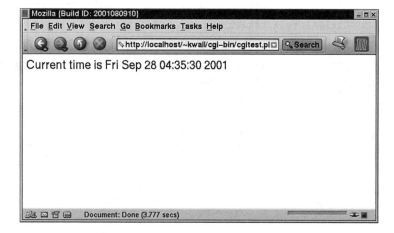

Current time is Fri Sep 28 04:35:30 2001

15

BASIC WEB
SERVICES

If you see similar output, the CGI configuration that *you tested* works. Make sure to test all the CGI configurations that you need to use.

Adding Features with Apache Modules

One of Apache's most appealing features is its modularity. You can add and remove features and functionality using Apache modules. And, if configured at compile time to support it, Apache itself will load and unload modules dynamically at runtime, making its overall memory footprint and CPU demands smaller. This section examines Apache modules in greater depth, looks at the configuration directives for using them, and surveys the range of functionality available in the modules shipped in the standard distribution and the modules available separately.

What Are Apache Modules?

Apache is a modular server, and only the most basic functionality is included in the core server. Most features are available in modules that can be loaded into Apache at runtime. By default, a base set of modules (see Table 15.5) is included in the server at compile time, but the server can be compiled to use dynamically loaded modules. Then modules can be compiled separately and added at any time using the `LoadModule` directive. Otherwise, Apache must be recompiled to add or remove modules. Configuration directives may be included conditional on a presence of a particular module by enclosing them in an `<IfModule>` block (see the section titled "Module Configuration Directives" for more information about `LoadModule` and `IfModule`).

Standard Modules

Apache modules come in two flavors, standard and add-on. *Standard modules* are modules that ship as part of the Apache distribution. *Add-on modules* are modules available separately that are *not* part of the standard distribution. Table 15.5 lists and briefly describes the standard modules.

TABLE 15.5 Standard Apache Modules

Module	Description
Core	
core	Provides core Apache functionality

TABLE 15.5   continued

Module	Description
Environment Creation	
mod_env	Enables Apache to modify the environment that is passed to CGI scripts and SSI pages
mod_setenvif	Enables Apache to set environment variables based upon the attributes of the client request
mod_unique_id	Provides an environment variable that gives a unique identifier to each request
Content Type Decisions	
mod_mime	Allows Apache to determine file types based on filenames and to associate handlers with files
mod_mime_magic	Enables Apache to determine the MIME type of a file by looking at the first few bytes of its contents
mod_negotiation	Gives Apache the capability to select the content that best matches the client's capabilities from one of several available documents
URL Mapping	
mod_alias	Provides the functionality to map parts of the host filesystem to arbitrary locations in the document tree and to redirect URLs
mod_rewrite	Gives Apache the capability to rewrite requested URLs dynamically
mod_userdir	Supports user-specific Web page directories
mod_speling	Corrects misspelled URLs that users have entered by ignoring capitalization and allowing up to one misspelling
mod_vhost_alias	Provides support for easy use of a huge number of virtual hosts with similar configurations
Directory Handling	
mod_dir	Enables Apache to perform basic directory handling and to serve directory index files
mod_autoindex	Allows Apache to index directories automatically
Access Control	
mod_access	Provides access control based on a client's hostname, IP address, or other characteristics
mod_auth	Enables user authentication using text files

15

BASIC WEB SERVICES

TABLE 15.5 continued

Module	Description
Access Control	
mod_auth_dbm	Enables user authentication using DBM files
mod_auth_db	Enables user authentication using Berkeley DB files
mod_auth_anon	Allows anonymous user access to authenticated areas
mod_auth_digest	Enables user authentication using MD5 message digests
HTTP Response	
mod_headers	Supports creation of customized HTTP response headers
mod_cern_meta	Provides Apache's support for HTTP header metafiles
mod_expires	Enables Apache to generate HTTP Expires: headers based on user-defined criteria
mod_asis	Allows Apache to serve documents that contain their own HTTP headers "as is"
Dynamic Content	
mod_include	Provides Apache's support for server-side includes (SSI)
mod_cgi	Allows Apache to execute CGI scripts
mod_actions	Enables Apache to execute CGI scripts based on the media type or the request method
Internal Content Handlers	
mod_status	Supports displaying on server activity and performance
mod_info	Enables Apache to display an overview of its configuration and loaded modules
Logging	
mod_log_config	Enables Apache's request login using either the Common Log Format or a user-defined format
mod_usertrack	Creates cookies that provide a log of user activity on a site
Miscellaneous	
mod_imap	Allows Apache to process for server-side image maps
mod_proxy	Enables Apache to function as an HTTP/1.0 caching proxy server
mod_so	Provides Apache's dynamic shared object (DSO) and module support
mod_mmap_static	Supports in-core caching of a statically configured list of frequently requested but static Web pages

Add-on Modules

Add-on or third-party modules further extend Apache's capabilities. Far too many exist to describe them all in this space, so interested readers should visit the Apache Module Registry on the Web at `http://modules.apache.org/` for the complete list. As this book went to the printer, there were more than 170 modules, from mod_auth_any to mod_z_auth.

Module Configuration Directives

The configuration directives for working with modules include the following:

- AddModule
- AddModuleInfo
- ClearModuleList
- IfModule
- LoadModule

When you build Apache, certain modules are built into the server rather than loaded at runtime using LoadModule and AddModule. To see the list of built-in modules, execute the command httpd -l, as shown in the following:

```
$ /usr/local/apache/bin/httpd -l
http_core.c
mod_so.c
suexec: enabled; valid wrapper /usr/local/apache/bin/suexec
```

The output of this command shows that only the core Apache module, http_core, and the module that provides module loading support, mod_so, are built into the server. In fact, these modules *must* be and always are compiled into the server for it to work. The last line indicates whether Apache's suEXEC feature has been enabled (see the section titled "CGI Scripts" for more information about suEXEC).

To load a module not compiled into the server, use the LoadModule directive, followed by the AddModule directive and, if you want, the AddModuleInfo directive for the same module. Despite their seeming similarity, LoadModule and AddModule serve two different purposes. AddModule activates compiled modules that are not currently used and modules that have been loaded with LoadModule.

The LoadModule directive, on the other hand, links a module into the running server. For example, to load the mod_mime module, first use the LoadModule directive, as shown in the following:

```
LoadModule mime_module modules/mod_mime.so
```

15

BASIC WEB
SERVICES

Next, to activate mod_mime, use the following `AddModule` directive:

```
AddModule mod_mime.c
```

Optionally, you can use the `AddModuleInfo` directive to associate a descriptive string with a module name that can be displayed. The syntax is quite simple:

```
AddModuleInfo module_name string
```

For example, add the following directive below the last `AddModule` directive in httpd.conf:

```
AddModuleInfo mod_mime.c "Determines file types using filename extensions"
```

Next, uncomment the following lines in httpd.conf, or add them if they are not present, and then restart the server as shown earlier in the chapter:

```
LoadModule info_module libexec/mod_info.so
AddModule mod_info.c
SetHandler server-info
```

If loaded, mod_info displays information about the running server when you point a Web browser at the server using the server-info URL—that is, `http://your.web.server/server-info`. So, point your Web browser at this URL and you should see a page resembling Figure 15.4.

FIGURE 15.4

The server information page created by mod_info.

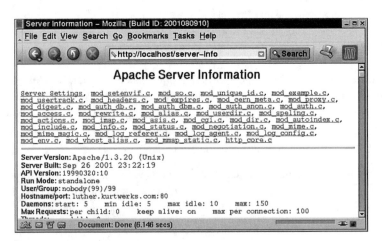

Click the link for mod_mime.c, and then scroll down to the Additional Information section. You will see the description screen that you added (see Figure 15.5).

FIGURE 15.5

The mod_mime.c description string displayed by mod_info.

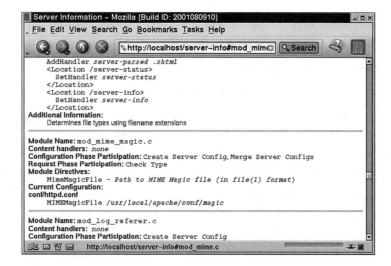

Do not use mod_info on a production server! As you can see in Figures 15.4 and 15.5, it displays a great deal of information about the running Web server, information that can be used to attack and possibly compromise the Web server itself or the system on which it is running.

Running a chrooted Web Server

As discussed in Chapter 7, "Securing a System for Rollout," running services in a chroot jail can significantly increase the overall security of a system. In this respect, Apache's overall security can be enhanced by running it in a chroot jail. This section explains the general procedure for running a chrooted Web server, but, due to space restrictions, it does not cover the details. The "References" section at the end of this chapter provides links to information that cover running a chrooted Web server in detail.

Why Run a chrooted Server?

The most important reason to run a chrooted Apache server is to provide another layer of security for your system on top of Apache's own internal security model and the network- and host-based security measures that you have implemented. If a blackhat somehow manages to compromise the Web server, a chrooted Web environment, in theory, should limit any damage done to the chrooted directory

15

**BASIC WEB
SERVICES**

Setting Up the chroot Environment

To create a chroot Web environment, the general procedure is as follows:

1. Create the chroot tree.

2. Create a user and group for the chroot tree.

3. chroot Apache's server root to that tree.

4. Create a miniature file system in the chroot tree.

Assuming that the user and group apache will own the chroot tree and that the chrooted directory will be /webroot, the following steps create the initial chroot environment:

1. Create the chroot directory:

   ```
   # mkdir /webroot
   ```

2. Set the user and group ownership of /webroot to the apache user and group:

   ```
   # chown apache.apache /webroot
   ```

3. Set the user and group permissions:

   ```
   # chmod -R 775 /webroot
   ```

4. Create the needed filesystem under /webroot and populate the filesystem as necessary. At a bare minimum, you will need a /bin that contains statically linked versions of mv, ls, grep, cat, cp, and so forth.

5. Issue the chroot command to chroot the directory:

   ```
   # chroot /webroot /usr/local/apache/bin/httpd
   ```

Properly creating a chroot Web environment can be tricky, so have a look at the following resources:

- Web Server Setup: http://csel.cs.colorado.edu/udp/admin/apache.html— Describes setting up a restricted, not chrooted, Web server environment

- How to chroot an Apache Tree with Linux and Solaris: http://penguin.epfl.ch/chroot.html—Describes the process of setting up a chrooted Apache Web server in detail

References

Considering Apache's popularity, there is no shortage of information about it on the Internet. This section lists a small subset of such resources, accessibly in many cases directly from Apache's home pages.

Web pages:

- The Apache Software Foundation: `http://www.apache.org/`
- The Apache Project Home Page: `http://httpd.apache.org/`
- The Apache Module Registry: `http://modules.apache.org/`
- Apache Week: `http://www.apacheweek.com/`

Mailing lists and newsgroups:

- News and announcements: `http://www.apache.org/announcelist.html`
- Development: `http://dev.apache.org/mailing-lists/`
- Usage and general support: news://comp.infosystems.www.servers.unix/

Publications:

- *Apache Server Unleashed*, by Rich Bowen, et al. (Sams Publishing, 2000)
- *Apache Pocket Reference*, by Andrew Ford (O'Reilly & Associates, 2000)
- *Apache: The Definitive Guide, 2nd Edition*, by Ben Laurie and Peter Laurie (O'Reilly & Associates, 1999)

Best Practices

- Determine the configuration of the Web services that you want to provide.
- Identify which elements of your site's security policy apply to your Web server's configuration.
- Install the server as a test server, perform any configuration of services (such as CGI or SSI) necessary for your site, and test both those services and the server's compliance to the site security policy.
- Reconfigure the server as a primary server, and put it into service.
- Regularly review the server log files to performance and security information.
- Review the configuration file, and remove or comment out all directives, particularly `AddModule` and `LoadModule` directives, that support features that your site does not need or that conflict with the site security policy.

## CHAPTER 16

Backups

by Carolyn J. Sienkiewicz

IN THIS CHAPTER

Introduction

Backups are, without a doubt, the single most important task you will ever be responsible for as a sysadmin. Yet at the same time, the topic has no glamour, and most people find it tedious and boring. This dichotomy stems from the fact that although backups are extremely important, the work, the planning, the monitoring, and the documenting are unending, even if they're not particularly difficult. The most difficult part of doing backups well is not giving in to complacency or carelessness.

The act of creating a copy of all the information on your system's hard disk drives is called "backing up" or "backups." With this copy, you should be able to recover from a number of categories of misfortune that your system might experience. If your system has two hard drives and one fails, you can replace the drive and restore the failed disk's data from your backup. If electronic intruders damage your system, you can restore files from your backup to put the system back the way it was before the intrusion. And if a user of the system needs to go back to a copy of something he was doing last week, you can restore it for him from backups.

The bottom line is that you can restore it only if you've backed it up. Let's consider the potential value of the bits stored on a system's hard drive. At the operating system level, we could say that there isn't much to be gained in performing regular backups of operating system–level files. You can always reinstall them from your install media. However, if you (or someone else) have done a lot of special system configuration such as the following, it can really simplify your life to know that you have everything backed up, preferably at consistent intervals of time:

- Kernel tweaking
- Special device-driver installation or configuration
- Large user base creation (passwd, group, maybe NIS)

At the database level, there is no argument that backups are a necessity. If the system is housing a database, it's important to someone and, therefore, worth backing up. At the user file level, whether the files are letters to Mom or your employer's corporate trade secrets, again, you'll want to back up everything. Or, there might be machines on which only some data really needs to be backed up. Every organization also might have some number of servers that are considered so unimportant (or expendable) that no backup is done. The key in those cases is that everyone who uses the server must know that the server is never backed up. The users then know that anything they store there is not guaranteed. You can help keep this information at the forefront of your users' thinking by adding a reminder in /etc/motd to that effect.

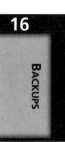

Many things must be considered when thinking about backups. If you don't already have backups in place, before you spend money or implement anything, spend some time analyzing what you really need. If your organization's backups are already set up but are new to you, you'll want to take time now to investigate the current procedures or processes and find out where they diverge from what your organization really needs. If you're a pro at backups, you'll already have experienced the need to review backup policies and procedures annually (at a minimum) because of the quickly changing nature of your computing environment. In the next section, we'll discuss some of the topics that you should examine when making decisions about backups.

Before we continue, it should be mentioned that the terms *backup*, *snapshot*, *copy*, and *image* will be used interchangeably in this chapter. The term *full or full backup* specifically refers to a complete backup of every file on the machine. The term *incremental* or *incremental backup* specifically refers to a backup of every file on the machine that has changed since the last backup was taken.

Components and Criteria for a Backup

As an introduction to criteria to be considered when deciding on a backup strategy, it is helpful to understand the traditional UNIX backup. Backup strategies historically were designed to exploit the tools available. If a backup solution—for example, dump—is based on a particular concept, then that concept defines the framework that you must use to design your backups. So, one important point is that the tool directly determines how you can do backups. Another important point is that some tools, and many sysadmins' point of reference, have been shaped specifically by history—the history of what tool was available and how sysadmins used those tools. Understanding this historical perspective can provide you insight into backup strategy design considerations as well as a vocabulary and frame of reference with which to communicate with other sysadmins regarding the topic of backups. You'll need this frame of reference not only with other sysadmins, but also in many cases with users, developers, and DBAs.

From a historical perspective, the traditional UNIX backup started off with dump and restore. These were the standard utilities. They historically operated on a per-filesystem basis and had different levels of backup consisting of levels 0 through 9.

A Level 0 backup is a backup of everything. A Level 1 backup is a backup of everything that has changed since the last Level 0 backup. A Level 2 backup is a backup of everything that has changed since the last Level 1 backup, and so on through Level 9. Most sysadmins never used 10 levels of backups but were likely to use three or four levels (although not consecutive levels, as we'll talk about shortly).

A typical backup scenario based on these levels would involve the use of Level 0 as a *yearly* backup, Level 1 as a *monthly* backup, Level 5 as a weekly backup, and Level 9 as a *daily* or *incremental* backup. The Level 0 backup typically was referred to as a *full* backup because it captured all files. Monthly, weekly, and daily backups do not have to be levels 1, 5, and 9. They could as easily have been 1, 2, and 3, but there was enough documentation out there (in the late 1970s and early 1980s) to show samples with levels 0, 1, 5, and 9 that it became engrained in the sysadmin culture.

This type of backup scenario requires that you have different sets of tapes to rotate: a yearly set, monthly set, weekly set, and daily set. The number of tapes in each set would vary depending on how far back you wanted to be able to restore. Let's look at a sample backup schedule (see Table 16.1) and tape organization scheme (see Table 16.2) based on a traditional scenario involving a business that operates Monday through Friday.

TABLE 16.1 Sample Backup Schedule—January and February

Sun	Mon	Tues	Wed	Thurs	Fri	Sat
					Full Level 0 Tape Y1	
	Daily Level 9 Tape D1	Daily Level 9 Tape D2	Daily Level 9 Tape D3	Daily Level 9 Tape D4	Weekly Level 5 Tape W1	
	Daily Level 9 Tape D5	Daily Level 9 Tape D6	Daily Level 9 Tape D7	Daily Level 9 Tape D8	Weekly Level 5 Tape W2	
	Daily Level 9 Tape D9	Daily Level 9 Tape D10	Daily Level 9 Tape D11	Daily Level 9 Tape D12	Weekly Level 5 Tape W3	
	Daily Level 9 Tape D13	Daily Level 9 Tape D14	Daily Level 9 Tape D15	Daily Level 9 Tape D16	Monthly Level 5 Tape M1	
	Daily Level 9 Tape D1	Daily Level 9 Tape D2	Daily Level 9 Tape D3	Daily Level 9 Tape D4	Weekly Level 5 Tape W1	
	Daily Level 9 Tape D5	Daily Level 9 Tape D6	Daily Level 9 Tape D7	Daily Level 9 Tape D8	Weekly Level 5 Tape W2	

TABLE 16.1 continued

Sun	Mon	Tues	Wed	Thurs	Fri	Sat
	Daily	Daily	Daily	Daily	Daily	
	Level 9	Level 9	Level 9	Level 9	Level 5	
	Tape D9	Tape D10	Tape D11	Tape D12	Tape W3	
	Daily	Daily	Daily	Daily	Daily	
	Level 9	Level 9	Level 9	Level 9	Level 5	
	Tape D13	Tape D14	Tape D15	Tape D16	Tape M2	

Table 16.1 shows a schedule for two months. If you extend this schedule for the year, you would need sets of tapes as shown in Table 16.2.

TABLE 16.2 Tape Sets Required for a Full Year

Yearly	Monthly	Weekly	Daily
Y1	M1	W1	D1
Y2	M2	W2	D2
	M2	W3	D1
	M3		D3
	M4		D4
	M5		D5
	M6		D6
	M7		D7
	M8		D8
	M9		D9
	M10		D10
	M11		D11
			D12
			D13
			D14
			D15
			D16

It would not be unusual for a restore from this kind of solution to involve building from several tapes. If your system died and you had to do a full system restore from these tapes (let's assume that you have been backing up the whole system), you would need to do the following:

- Do enough of an initial operating system install, to where you'd get a kernel running and have the restore program back on the system
- Start restoring all files by reading back the most recent yearly tape, then each successive monthly tape since that yearly tape, then each successive weekly tape since the last monthly and each daily tape since the last weekly tape

As an example, the tapes that you would need to restore to March 15 would be as follows (depending on exactly how the calendar falls and how you set up your schedule):

Y 1: Full from beginning of the year

M1: From the end of January

M2: From the end of February

W1: From the end of the first week of March

W2: From the end of the second week of March

D 9: From March 15

One thing to keep in mind is that this tradition dates back to an era when UNIX systems in businesses were much more a Monday–Friday, 9–5 kind of thing. Filesystems typically were unmounted before backup, and dump was run on the raw device for each filesystem. Unmounting the filesystem meant that the filesystem was never in use while it was being backed up. This ensured filesystem integrity because a file wouldn't be changing in the middle of being backed up. You knew that you had a cohesive file on tape. At the end of the backup, filesystems were remounted and applications were restarted in preparation for use the following business day.

The real world hasn't been that way for a long time now. But, unfortunately, that was the world in which dump and restore were conceived and created, and they bear the indelible mark of that time. They have not been changed to keep up with the realities of today's pressures to back up so much data on a daily basis—and do it without impacting application availability. Today, if you suggested that you wanted to unmount a filesystem to get a good backup, you would be laughed out of the room. At this time, users everywhere demand and expect their applications to be available to them at any time of the day or night. It can be a real challenge to get good reliable backups in these circumstances.

Now that we've completed our whirlwind tour of the history and tradition of backups, it's time to discuss the criteria to be considered when deciding on a backup strategy. We will discuss the following:

- Budget
- Criticality of the system or the data
- The types of restores you're likely to encounter

- How to back things up
- Speed of recovery
- Retention
- Off-site storage
- Central dedicated backup server
- Fitting it all in—the backup window and other constraints
- Selection of backup media
- Importance of monitoring
- Restore/recovery testing
- Accompanying system-configuration documentation
- Establishment of a backup schedule
- A written backup policy
- Evolving systems

Budget

The budget that you have to implement backups could be your most limiting criteria. Choices in commercial products are much more numerous in recent years as the market demand has increased for reliable, high-capacity solutions. You can spend huge amounts of money for commercial products, tapes, tape libraries, tape silos, or tape robots. The budget that you have at your disposal for system administration will vary greatly from a small startup business, to a university, to a huge corporation. But, without a doubt, that budget is what will determine whether you can afford anything but a free solution and a minimal set of tapes that you rotate by hand.

Criticality of the System or the Data

The use of the term *critical* in this section refers to a number of system characteristics. It frequently is used in the systems administration world in reference to the importance of data to an organization, or a system that is relied on by many other systems or that has a special place in the revenue stream. It is really anything that makes a system or its data vital to the continued operation of a business or organization.

When considering how critical any of your systems or their data are, you need to ask yourself a number of questions:

- How easily replaced are the systems for which you are responsible?

  If the systems are test boxes that can be quickly rebuilt, the best answer could be to do no backup at all. If the systems are test boxes that have valuable development code on them but otherwise are quickly rebuilt when it comes to the operating system, perhaps the answer is to not back up the operating system but to just take occasional snapshots of the filesystems (or portions thereof) containing the code.

- How often does the information on the system change?

  If new users are being added, modified, or deleted frequently, you'll really want to have a backup image made each day. A rule of thumb is that a system with very static data needn't be backed up as often as a system with very dynamic data. The same goes for filesystems. Try to organize your filesystems to keep static data together and separated from dynamic data. For example, a database usually involves a set of static stuff such as database executables and libraries. The database data, however, might be changing constantly. If you store the database data in separate filesystems from the database package (the executables and libraries), then you might need only a single copy of the database package filesystem (to capture some database-configuration information). This way, you can save your tape resources to use when backing up the database data that is changing every day.

- Does your company go out of business or face financial ramifications if data is lost?

  Some companies have data that is so valuable that they keep redundant systems running that are updating identical data in parallel—on different coasts, no less—to ensure that they will always have the data accessible. Make it your business to understand how critical the data in your care is.

Restoring versus Reinstalling

If you have a server farm of 100 identically functioning systems, performing backups would be a waste of money. This is a case in which you'd most likely set up a standard install image for setting up the 100 servers initially, and then use that same install image to reinstall a replacement after a system failure. This is a very clear case of when it makes more sense to reinstall than to restore (thus eliminating the need for backups of the 100 systems). You will want to explore this option mostly for systems with these characteristics:

- Extremely static in disk content
- Extremely unimportant
- Very numerous and identical (or nearly so)

Understanding the Types of Restores You're Likely to Encounter

You need to do backups to prepare for the eventual failures or disasters that we all encounter. How can you know that you are prepared for what you might face? It's helpful to consider the kinds of situations that you are likely to experience. Which ones are applicable to you or your business? How well will the backup solution that you choose perform in these different scenarios?

Full Restore

Let's pretend that you support a system that contains your company's accounting software. Let's also pretend that this system contains a single disk drive and that this disk drive has just failed (maybe there's a whining or grinding noise, or smoke coming from the general vicinity of the disk drive) and the system no longer can be booted. Everything that was on the system is now unavailable (unless you go to a disk recovery service). This situation calls for a *full restore.*

This is the most common scenario that people who do backups plan for. It's probably the least common type of restore that people do (except for folks who work for companies that sell disaster-recovery services or sysadmins who support systems that live outside firewalls). Nevertheless, it is the worst-case scenario and, therefore, one that you have to be prepared for.

Anything that has changed on the system since your last *good* backup is lost (unless you hire a disk-recovery service). This is not a pleasant thought, but if you're playing your cards right and ensuring that you get a legitimate backup every night, you never stand to lose more than one day's work. There are extra expensive solutions that can save you from nearly any kind of data loss. The motto goes something like, "We can solve *any* problem—how much money do you have?" These extra expensive solutions typically involve implementing one or more of the following:

- Mirroring
- High availability
- Full system redundancy
- Database replication
- Transaction logging to tape

If you need to be able to perform a full restore, you will need, at a minimum, these backup materials:

- Bootable recovery tape created from your system (or, optionally, install media)
- Your full backup tapes, plus all incrementals since the full

Point-in-Time Recovery

Continuing with our "let's pretend" game, let's pretend that you are supporting a system that a development team is slaving away on writing a software package. Users already are using this software package—it's an order-taking system for a mail-order catalog. The developers are planning to add a new feature tonight at midnight. At 2:00 in the morning (or, as we like to say, *'o dark thirty*), they page you and inform you that they have messed up the database (and who knows what else). The order-takers are expecting to be online again at 6:00 a.m. The developers request that you perform a point-in-time recovery back to 11:30 p.m. last night.

This is a big can of worms. Make it a point when working on any project to come to a clear understanding of the potential need for point-in-time recovery. If it will be needed, you'll need a backup product that will provide you this capability without twisting yourself into a pretzel. Special considerations also have to be given in advance by the database administrator (which might or might not be you) so that you can roll back to a specific point.

Whole Filesystems

Let's pretend that you have a system with 15 different disks and 1, 2, or 3 separate filesystems on each disk. One disk dies (not the boot disk). After replacing the dead drive, you need to perform a number of whole filesystem restores to replace those that were on the dead disk. This is a pretty common type of restore.

If you need to be able to perform whole filesystem restores, you will need, at a minimum, backup materials of your last full backup of that filesystem, plus all incrementals since the full backup.

Restoring Specific Files

Let's pretend that you just received a call from a panicked developer. She says that she has just accidentally deleted her project source code, and she doesn't have a copy saved anywhere. This is probably the most common type of restore you'll be asked to do. Fortunately for her, the source code is on an area that is being backed up each night, so you can be a hero and give her back what she had as of last night. There's always disappointment at losing the work you did today, but it's nothing compared with the thought of having *nothing* and having to start all over. If she has the misfortune of having kept her code in an area where there is no agreement to back up, then she'll have learned the valuable but painful lesson that she needs to make keeping copies a part of her programming routine. Over the course of your career, you'll find that you are requested to perform restores most often because of user error.

To perform specific file restores, you will need, at a minimum, backup materials of the incremental tape for the filesystem in question from the last known good date (for instance, last night).

Understanding How to Back Things Up

Part of the challenge of making backups is understanding the nature of the thing that you are backing up and how to make an image of it in such a way that the image can give you back what you started with. One example of this is the base operating system. Doing a backup of the filesystems that hold all the operating system files usually isn't enough. After all, you need a functioning system to be capable of running software to invoke a restore and to be capable of receiving the restoring files via either tape or other means. To get the system running first, you'll need either the original operating system install media or need a bootable recovery tape that you made from the specific system that you need to restore. Some vendors supply a utility for creating a bootable recovery tape. This is often also referred to as a bare-metal recovery.

We recommend that you make these recovery tapes of your systems on a regular basis. Also, plan to perform full backups with some regularity and incremental backups daily. Between using a recent recovery tape and applying a number of your last incrementals, your operating system should be back intact.

Neither Linux nor Solaris offers a built-in bare-metal recovery utility. You can either reinstall a minimal piece of the operating system and then restore your backups, or you can boot from alternate media (such as a crash, rescue, or recovery floppy or tape), reformat the drives, and then restore your backups.

How Often Is Often Enough?

For making full backups and special bootable recovery tapes, whenever you need to know the answer to the question "How often is often enough?", do the following:

1. Pick a time interval that you think might be often enough (let's hypothetically say every three months).

2. Create a scenario in your head based on the premise that the system will fail and require restoring the day before you would take your next bootable recovery tape or full backup.

3. Given this worst-case timing of the system failure, exactly what steps will you have to take to fully restore the system?

4. Now repeat this process with different time intervals—maybe monthly and then weekly—and see what differences there in your list of steps.

Beyond the operating system, you also might have other non–operating system filesystems. For these filesystems, assess how static the contents are. If the contents of a particular filesystem are an application package, the contents might never change until the application gets upgraded. For those cases, you might choose to do a single full backup, or you might opt to just keep the application install media as your backup. For filesystems that have dynamic contents, you'll need to do incremental backups on a daily basis.

Databases are a special case in and of themselves. Each database vendor usually supplies its own utilities to back up its product. It is important that you understand and use these utilities. Be sure that you follow the vendor's directions for use of its utilities. If you don't, the vendor won't be able to provide support when you need to do a restore.

The last type of data that you might need to backup is non–filesystem space, sometimes called raw data. Typical backup solutions work only on files and filesystems. Often when you come across raw data, it will be part of a database. If this is the case, again, use the vendor's backup utilities.

Note

If you have a partition of some other type of raw data, you can use the dd command to make a copy of the contents to a tape. We'll look at how to use dd a little later.

Speed of Recovery

How critical is the length of time that it would take you to restore a system, a filesystem, or a file? If you are responsible for supplying backups to a group of flight dynamic engineers at NASA and they need to provide critical flight data for a shuttle launch tonight, then the amount of time that it takes to get back a few files that they've worked on for the launch could be pretty crucial. The importance of speed of recovery is directly related to how critical the data is. When it comes to speed, there is the speed of the backup software, the speed of the restore media, and the speed of the media handler (for example, maybe a tape jukebox or a tape silo). If you're in the market for a backup solution, this is a vital area to test the vendors on (especially if they have any hand in selling you hardware for the solution). Be sure to ask for comparisons of restore times with different media options. On the other hand, if you need a cheap and quick solution, making copies of important files to a different system at regular intervals will give the quickest restore time.

Retention

Another consideration is retention. How long do you need to keep a tape around before you can reuse it? Will you have to keep it permanently? And, depending on how long it has been sitting around, will you be able to read it?

In many environments, you will have legal requirements of how long data must be retained. In these cases, ask your management to verify the time requirements and to clarify precisely *what data* is covered by this requirement. There could be a seven-year retention requirement for certain customer data, but it's unlikely that anyone other than you cares how long you keep your operating system backups. As a precaution, be sure that your organization's legal department is made aware of the retention policies that you decide to use for backups where they have not dictated a retention time to you.

The trade-off in making retention decisions is cost. The longer you keep tapes around without overwriting them, the more tapes you have to purchase and find storage for.

Off-Site Storage

We are big believers in off-site storage. If you can afford it, use a professional vaulting service, which comes to your company and takes your tapes off-site each day.

If you can't afford that, you should buy a small fireproof safe to store your most current tapes in. Entrust the next most current to someone's safe-keeping, to take home every night so that *something* will be off-site in the event of a disaster. You'll typically want to keep your most recent backups on-site because they most likely will be needed for some quickie file restore. The irony here, of course, is that, at the same time, they are your most up-to-date backup and, therefore, your most valuable. It could be argued that they should be off-site if you are going to take anything off-site. Still, as with all things, it's really the balance between prudence and efficacy. If Joe needs his program files back right now, it's going to really slow things down if someone has to drive home and back to retrieve the tape first.

Central Dedicated Backup Server

If the resources are available, it's really nice to have a machine that can act as a dedicated backup server. This can greatly simplify things by centralizing the collection point for tapes, the configuration and control point for the backups, and the monitoring. A dedicated backup server begins to be a must for anything more than a dozen machines.

A backup server can be used to back up other systems through either a client/server connection (typical with commercial products) or by using remote commands. In environments where security is a serious concern, using remote commands might not be allowed at all.

Fitting It All in—the Backup Window and Other Constraints

Sometimes the decisions of how much to back up and how often are severely limited by constraints. Constraints can come from different sources. Let's say that you have a very important application that has a database underlying it, and this database needs to be backed up every night. This database has to be brought down to get a backup, and, of course, everyone wants this database to be up all the time. This time constraint is an *availability* constraint. The application is not available when it is being backed up. (By the way, in this case, you should work closely with the DBA to find the quickest way to back up this database—preferably what we call a *hot* backup, where you can still get a good backup without stopping the application.)

Other examples of constraints that you're likely to encounter include these:

- Too many machines to back up to a single backup server in the preferred time window (which is usually the time outside your business's core office hours)
- Too many machines trying to back up to a tape library in the preferred time window (every form of media has its limitation of how much it can write in a certain length of time)
- Too many machines trying to back up across a network at once
- Too much data to fit on a single tape, and no operations staff to change tapes in the middle of the night

As you encounter these types of constraints, you might have to compromise and back up less data, or do backups less often than you would like. Be aware of the issue of application availability and also the potential for running out of resources when you try to schedule more backup work at a given time than your resources can handle.

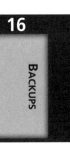

Selecting Backup Media

It's worth mentioning again that a hard disk (on a separate system) is a wonderful choice of backup media. It's quick to restore from, and you can see exactly what files you have from what date and time. It's just not practical cost-wise as a backup solution for everything. Still, it does have its place and is worth keeping in mind for special cases.

It is not uncommon in many environments to use a disk as an intermediate backup device. A backup can be quickly done to a disk; later in the day, the data can be moved from the disk to a tape.

The most common medium used is tape. Tape technology is always changing, so any recommendation made here will be instantly dated. The primary qualities that you'll want in tape technology are high speed (reading and writing), high capacity, and reliability. And, of course, it has to be something that you can afford. A practical consideration that can be helpful in a very small shop is one of multiple devices. If you are making your system backups on a DLT drive, for example, you need to have more than one DLT drive. This is not optional. If you have only one drive and it breaks down, then you can't restore and you can't keep up with your incrementals.

Whether you are looking at DLT, 8 mm, DAT or 1/4-inch cartridge tape, buy the fastest, highest-capacity tape you can afford.

Importance of Monitoring

When you are performing backups on a regular schedule, it's of great importance that someone checks to see that the backups actually succeed every day. There are a couple of reasons why this is imperative. First of all, if there is a problem preventing your backups from completing or being successful, the problem needs to be resolved—and it needs to be resolved as soon as possible. The reasons for failure can be numerous, from network congestion to the existence of a full filesystem somewhere, or even a hardware component beginning to flake out. These problems rarely, if ever, heal themselves, so your best course of action is to get on them pronto. Second, in some cases, if a backup fails, you might need to try to rerun the backup as soon as possible to avoid missing a daily incremental—for example, in the case of a critical database. The only way that you'll know about any of this is if someone checks the status of the backups every day.

The variety of ways to monitor your backups is pretty much infinite. Sticking with something simple, such as an email to all sysadmin staff containing the status of the overnight backup run, is usually sufficient. It is important, however, that the message is going to more than one person. When you're out sick or on vacation, someone still needs to check up on the status of the backups and take corrective action, if necessary.

By the way, whenever you are tempted to let things slide in this area, think how you'll feel when you get a desperate phone call to restore something and you don't have the backup from the day in question because you didn't check to see if the backup really completed successfully that day.

Restore/Recovery Testing

When considering purchasing a backup solution, an important part of your choice of tool must be how easy or difficult it is to use for a restore. If you are doing actual product or tool evaluations, write yourself a small test suite that includes some basic backups and restores. Pay close attention to how the restore portion works. Take the amount that the restore part of the tool irks you and multiply it by 10. That is a closer approximation to how much you will really hate it when the chips are down—you know, when a user (oh, let's say the company president) has a really critical and really specific set of criteria ("Give me all the files that changed on the 15th on host A in /home, and restore them to /tmp on host B—oh, and if I don't have them in 15 minutes, the world is going to end").

When you have decided on a backup tool, or if one is already in place where you work, get to know the restore or recovery portion of your tool well. In particular, learn it like the back of your hand before you ever need to use it for a real-life restore event. Take the time to learn its idiosyncrasies. This is also an excellent time to jump on the Web and look for user groups or newsgroups that are using this tool. These can lead you to a valuable pool of users who have probably already experienced the same issues that you will encounter.

For practice, perform mock restores based on the four basic types of restores mentioned earlier:

- Full restore
- Point-in-time restore
- Whole filesystem restore
- Specific file(s) restore

Doing this will give you a much better feel for the strengths and weaknesses of the backup solution that you have to work with. It also will give you a reasonably complete exercise of the capabilities of the restore portion of the tool. In addition to practicing the restores, use this opportunity to perform some application testing from a user perspective. This is necessary to see if the machine really functions as expected after the various types of restores. This can be an important learning process. What have you missed? Are kernel parameters all back to correct? If not, why not?

While practicing, take the opportunity to document the steps performed when doing each of these types of backup. In practicing, you've got the steps down. They are fresh in your mind now. In six months, it'll be a foggy haze. But if you take the time to document it now while it's fresh, at least you'll have a good guideline to go by six months from now. Also, your documentation can serve as a wonderful starting point for any new sysadmin joining your organization. Imagine a sysadmin's joy in finding documented procedures on how to restore from your backups. Imagine your joy at not having to hold that person's hand every little step of the way.

After using practice cases to refine your backup processes (and to find holes that might exist), exercise the procedures at least every six months to do the following:

- Stave off staleness
- Validate procedures
- Review for correctness

This last one is especially important. The systems and applications likely will be changing all the time, and a procedure that worked last year is not guaranteed to cover everything that you might have on a system now.

Accompanying System-Configuration Documentation

It is very useful to keep a paper copy of some basic system-configuration information (see Chapter 3, "Filesystem Administration") for times when things are going awry with a restore. This system documentation can serve as a bit of an insurance policy and potentially make the restore struggle a little cleaner sometimes. For example, let's say that you're restoring a full system from a disk crash. If you have no bare-metal recovery tool, you're probably starting your restore from basic install media. One of the first things that you'll want to know is what filesystems you had on the system and what size they were. Without this information, you can get the operating system back to a useful point and then start restoring filesystems from backup; the next thing you know, the restore might be failing because you didn't make the filesystems big enough. Having this basic information can make your life a little easier. At a minimum, we recommend that you keep paper listings of the following information about each system, specifically for potential restore situations:

- Volume group and logical volume information (if you are utilizing a logical volume manager)
- Filesystem device names and mount point names

- Filesystem sizes
- Kernel parameter settings

> **Note**
>
> A utility that you can use to gather most of this information is SysAudit. Originally written by Robert Erp, it is available at `http://www.backupcentral.com`.

Establishing a Backup Schedule

As you're going along considering all of these criteria, eventually you'll be ready to put together a backup schedule that will be reasonable for the organization's needs. You will have to find that balance between too much and not enough. Doing a full backup of every machine every night is perfectly doable in an extremely small shop. In a large environment, there wouldn't be enough hours in a day to write all your bits to tape before the next backup window rolled around. Work with your company's management to help figure out what the company can afford, both in terms of investing in a commercial solution and in terms of the risk involved in maybe shooting too low for a solution. Determine a reasonable backup schedule to keep your operating system, other filesystem data, database data, and raw data spaces safe. Above all, document it. Documenting in detail the decision processes that have led to the conclusions is of vital importance. Be sure that all people who have had a hand in the decision process review this documentation, and preferably have them sign off on it.

Written Backup Policy

So far we've already mentioned documenting several areas. First, document the criteria that have been considered in making decisions about backups. Second, document the backup procedures and restore procedures. Third, at a minimum, document the system-configuration information described previously. Finally, it's time to talk about managing user expectations. The most effective way to do this is to document and publish a backup policy.

The audience that you're trying to inform with a backup policy is anyone who has an interest in storing data on the systems and who might be intending to rely on its storage. The backup policy also can act as an agreement between the sysadmin staff and the user community, serving to document what will be backed up, how often it will be backed up, and how long it will be stored.

The backup policy is best presented in a simple format and in a place where it is readily available. As two simple examples, the policy might be displayed on an internal Web

page where it is accessible only by corporate employees, or the schedule might be displayed as part of the message of the day (/etc/motd) that a user sees after logging onto a system. It is easiest to maintain the policy as a single document on a Web page.

We recommend that the following information be included in the backup policy document:

HOST	Data Area	Frequency, Time of Day, Type, Tool, Retention
Guido	/, /usr, /var, /opt, /home, /oracle	Daily, 01:00, incremental, dump, 3 weeks
	Note: /u1 and /u2 are NOT backed up.	
	Oracle instance: snorkel	Daily, 02:00, hot backup, SQL BackTrack, 7 versions on local hard disk plus 14 versions on tape
	Oracle instance: diver	Daily, 04:00, cold backup, SQL BackTrack, 7 versions direct to tape

This gives the user community a good reference and helps users to understand what is getting backed up and what isn't. Provide this URL to new users when giving them their new system ID. You'll want to include definitions of your terminology and perhaps a brief tutorial on your procedures for the user's edification.

Other helpful points to document include these:

- Any requirements that you have of other users or sysadmins (such as, "Be sure to leave your system powered on").
- Software installation/deinstallation policies
- Who is responsible for monitoring backup status
- How to request a restore (include a guideline of how long it will take to complete)

The backup policy should be reviewed on an annual basis. Use this time to verify that backups truly are being done as advertised in the policy. Re-evaluate the usefulness of the current schedules and retention policies. Is there a way to back up less and still keep the same level of effectiveness when it comes time to restore? Also use this time to check for areas not being backed up that do need it.

Evolving Systems

Many of your systems might be quite volatile in terms of filesystems. Most often, new ones will be added. Existing ones go away less often. We recommend that you make the question of whether to back up the new filesystem a part of the new filesystem creation process. Address the issue with the user requesting the space. Come to an agreement, implement the agreement, and update the backup policy to reflect the agreement.

Backup and Restore

You've seen that a lot of planning and thought needs to go into creating a backup strategy. Now you're ready to learn about some available tools or solutions and focus on their relative merits.

The backup tools that we'll survey fall into three categories. We'll refer to the commands that are included as a standard component of nearly any UNIX operating system as *commonly included*. We'll use the term *freely available* to describe a category of tools that are available at no cost but that will not usually be found on the operating system install media. Finally, the remaining category is *commercial products*.

Many tools are available. The remainder of this chapter concentrates on those that are most popular in usage (and, therefore, most likely to be encountered).

> **Note**
>
> It's a very good practice, when backing up to removable media, to make setting the "write protect" latch on the media part of the media-removing process. It's also very important, when inserting media that is being rotated, to check the label on the media (to be sure that it's correct one) and unset the "write protect" latch so that the next backup does not fail trying to write to a write-protected tape.

Commonly Included Tools

We'll go into the most detail on the commonly included tools. If you are somewhat new to doing backups on UNIX, we can assure you that you will have ready access to these tools. Anything else you will have to either purchase or locate and build for yourself. These are also the tools that typically are used for standalone backups, in which a system is being backed up to its own tape drive. The tools in this category are not typically associated with network backups or with the use of a dedicated server for backups.

The terms *incremental* and *incremental backup* specifically refer to a backup of every file on the system that has changed since the last backup was taken. It is important to understand that most of these built-in tools are not natively incremental-aware. This issue will be covered in the case of each commonly included tool so that you are aware of the existing native capability versus what you really want or need.

The issue of *relative pathname* versus *absolute pathname* is extremely important at this juncture. When using the tools in this section, you dictate whether the files going to tape are stored as relative or absolute pathnames. If you have written files to a tape with absolute pathnames, when the tape table of contents is listed, the filenames will all begin with "/". If you have written files to a tape with relative pathnames, when the tape table of contents is listed, the filenames will all begin with ".". Here's a sample listing of a backup tape with absolute pathname files:

```
/home/cjs
/home/cjs/.cshrc
/home/cjs/.login
/home/cjs/stuff
/home/cjs/stuff/IMPORTANT
/home/cjs/stuff/managesna
/home/cjs/stuff/startsna
/home/cjs/stuff/startsnad
/home/cjs/sortedIPSonly
/home/cjs/mmfkh4_all
/home/cjs/source
/home/cjs/source/menu
/home/cjs/source/stuff
```

And here's how the tape listing would appear if the files had been backed up with relative pathname names:

```
./home/cjs
./home/cjs/.cshrc
./home/cjs/.login
./home/cjs/stuff
./home/cjs/stuff/IMPORTANT
./home/cjs/stuff/managesna
./home/cjs/stuff/startsna
./home/cjs/stuff/startsnad
./home/cjs/sortedIPSonly
./home/cjs/mmfkh4_all
./home/cjs/source
./home/cjs/source/menu
./home/cjs/source/stuff
```

The relative pathname backup is what we call *relocateable.* This is a good thing because it means that when you want to read some files off a backup tape, you can restore them under *any* directory. With absolute pathname backups, files can be restored *only* where they originally came from.

For example, if you want to restore the file home/cjs/stuff/IMPORTANT from the tape that you wrote with absolute pathnames, you can restore it only to the location /home/cjs/stuff/IMPORTANT. If you restore from a tape that you've written with relative pathnames, it can be restored virtually anywhere. For example, if you really wanted to stick it under /tmp, from a relativel pathname backup tape, you can restore it to /tmp and then it would be accessed by the pathname /tmp/home/cjs/stuff/IMPORTANT.

From a purely logical standpoint, the superiority of the relative pathname backup is evident. It offers flexibility. Absolute pathname backups offer none. Nevertheless, junior admins often deprive themselves of this flexibility because they've never thought about it or they don't know the difference. If they do know the difference, they'll still too frequently deprive themselves of this flexibility because, frankly, it requires a tad more thought to create a relative pathname backup. If you take only one thing to heart from this chapter, it should be this: Do your backups as relative pathnames every time. Make it a habit, make it an automatic part of your thought process, and make it a religion. If you don't, the day will come when you will regret it. That will be the day when you become a convert to this simple premise. That being said, now that GNU versions of these common tools exist, you can dig yourself out of an absolute path hole by using the GNU version of a tool that will let you remove leading slashes. Still, you are better served being aware of what you are doing rather than receiving an unfortunate surprise at what could be the worst possible moment.

> **Note**
>
> As we examine each of the commonly included backup tools, all examples given will be illustrated with relative paths.

> **Note**
>
> As an additional note, in the discussion of each utility, not all options or arguments to each command will be discussed or covered. Instead, we'll be recommending and covering the arguments that are most common to different operating system versions of these commands. The idea is that you can learn a single set of arguments initially that should work for you just about anywhere. For additional arguments and options, consult your specific man pages.

Backup and Restore with tar

tar is a very commonly used utility for storing and retrieving files to and from tape. It is not commonly used as a backup tool for everyday backups. This is mostly because doing backups is not what it was designed for. It was really designed more as a very general-purpose tape archive utility. You want some files on a tape? Use tar to put them there. It's relatively quick, easy, and painless. Those are also the qualities that make it a tool that you'll want to have in your "moving files from place to place" arsenal.

The basic options of tar are listed here:

- **c**—Create (write) an archive image
- **t**—Read the table of contents of an archive image
- **x**—Extract (restore) archive image
- **v**—Turn on verbose mode, to list all files being written or read
- **f device**—Specify an output device other than the system's default tape device (can be a filename, a tape device name, and so on)

The command to create a backup of the /usr filesystem would be as follows:

```
# cd /usr; tar cvf /dev/rmt/0 .
```

or

```
# cd /; tar cvf /dev/rmt/0 ./usr
```

The first example would produce a tape with a table of contents that reads as follows:

```
r-xr-xr-x   2/2      0 Oct 13 09:59 2000 ./
rwxr-xr-x   0/0      0 Dec 21 06:47 1998 ./lost+found/
rw-------   0/4      0 Dec 21 06:47 1998 ./lost+found/.fsadm
rwxrwxrwt   0/3      0 Nov  3 07:59 1998 ./adm symbolic link to /var/adm
r-xr-xr-x   2/2      0 May 30 12:46 2001 ./bin/
```

The second example would produce a tape with a table of contents with usr at the beginning of each name entry:

```
r-xr-xr-x   2/2      0 Oct 13 09:59 2000 ./usr/
rwxr-xr-x   0/0      0 Dec 21 06:47 1998 ./usr/lost+found/
rw-------   0/4      0 Dec 21 06:47 1998 ./usr/lost+found/.fsadm
rwxrwxrwt   0/3      0 Nov  3 07:59 1998 ./usr/adm symbolic link to /var/adm
r-xr-xr-x   2/2      0 May 30 12:46 2001 ./usr/bin/
```

Generally, we recommend the second form because the tape readily shows you what filesystem is on the tape.

You'll notice that these commands have produced relative pathname backups. If you've inherited a tar tape with absolute paths and you need to restore it elsewhere, you can use GNU tar to remove the leading "/".

You can view the table of contents of what files are on the tape now with this line:

```
# tar tvf /dev/rmt/0 | more
```

To restore from this tar image, `cd` to the directory where you want the files to go, and then issue the command:

```
# tar xvf /dev/rmt/0
```

If you want to restore a number of files and don't know their exact names or paths, do this:

```
# tar tvf /dev/rmt/0 > filename
```

Then use grep to find the files you are looking for. This way, you'll also be able to see how the directory names are formed on the tape, and you'll know whether to request "./home," "/home," or "home." You have to exactly match the entire name the way it appears in the tape's table of contents. By the way, to get the full table of contents of the tape, tar has to read the entire tar image from the tape. It doesn't write any index to the tape anywhere.

A gotcha that seems to occur frequently enough with the use of tar is that an admin will insert a tape previously written with tar and go to extract from the tape, but he will use the c option instead of the x option. This is probably because we all use tar to create tapes more than we use them to restore, so it seems to be a bit of a reflex to type in `tar c`. Unfortunately, even if you Ctrl+C out, it's too late and you can now no longer read whatever you previously had put on the tape. If you use tar often enough, you eventually will do this to yourself. If the tape has any serious value to you, after you've completed writing it, be sure to write-protect it to prevent this type of accident.

Some behaviors of tar to be aware of include these:

- With tar, you write to tape exactly what you specify. Specifying * as the starting point of a backup will miss all files in the current directory that start with a ".". Your best bet is to be in the directory above and to specify `./directory_name`.
- tar doesn't preserve the access time of files being backed up.
- tar does not support wildcards when restoring. However, you specify a directory name to restore, and all files from that directory down will be restored.
- Normally, tar does its work silently. If you want to see what's happening, be sure to use the v option.
- tar has no inherent incremental capability.

Before leaving the topic of tar behind, here is one great little hint that everyone can use. When you want to copy a set of directories and files from one place to another on a machine, do the following:

```
cd fromdir; tar cf - . | (cd todir; tar xf -i)
```

Back Up and Restore with cpio

cpio is a more flexible tool than tar, and yet it's not as popular because it's more complicated to use. (Of course, you can't have more flexibility without being more complicated.) cpio stands for "copy file archives in and out." You use `cpio -o` to write
something out, or `cpio -i` to read something in. Let's start with writing out.

`cpio -o` reads from stdin for the files to be backed up. Usually `find` is used to produce
the list of files, which are then piped to cpio. Here is an example of backing up /home
(Solaris):

```
# cd /home; find . -print | cpio -o > /dev/rmt/0
```

or

```
# cd /; find ./home -print | cpio -o > /dev/rmt/0
```

Both of these examples of `find` provide a list of filenames of the form ./home/cjs...,
./home/joe..., and so on.

This gives you the relative pathnames that you want. The list gets piped to cpio, and then
cpio accesses these files through the filesystem mechanisms and sends the output (the
backup image) to stdout. Because stdout just spews to the screen, you should redirect the
output to a tape device. You also can redirect to a file, if you want (assuming that you
have room somewhere in a filesystem).

```
# find . -print | cpio -o > /tmp/home.TAR
```

There are many options to cpio. For writing out, use the following options:

```
# find . -print | cpio -oacBv > /dev/rmt/0
```

- **a**—Use this to keep the cpio command from altering each file's access time.
- **c**—Use this option to specify the ASCII header format. This is the most readily
  portable header format available and will make life easiest.
- **B**—This option specifies using a blocking factor of 5120 bytes rather than 512
  bytes. This option is available in all versions of cpio.
- **v**—This option specifies verbose mode. Use it if you want to see where you are in
  the backup process or if you want a listing of what's on the tape for some reason.

When using cpio as a primary backup tool it's best to back up a system by doing each
filesystem as a separate cpio image. When you are ready to restore, if you're looking for
a couple of files from /usr, restoring from a tape that contains only /usr and not /usr as
part of a whole system backed up under /, you'll be able to locate the files faster.

You also can do multiple separate filesystem backups to a single tape (depending on the size of the filesystems).

Here's how you would back up /usr and /home to a single tape:

```
# cd /usr; find . -print | cpio -oacBv > /dev/rmt/0n
# cd /home; find . -print | cpio -oacBv > /dev/rmt/0n
# mt -f /dev/rmt/0 rew
```

This creates a tape with two cpio images, as represented in Figure 16.1.

FIGURE 16.1
Multiple cpio images on a single tape.

If you want to store multiple images like this on a single tape (usually to save on tape expenses), be sure to place a label on the outside of the tape or case and list what order the filesystems are stored on the tape. Restoring from this kind of tape also can be quicker because, instead of reading through a full system tape to get to the /home files, you can pop this tape in and get right to the /home part of the tape with this command:

```
# mt -f /dev/rmt/0n fsf 1
```

This is a good time to talk briefly about the mt command. mt stands for magnetic tape, and is a little utility to manipulate a tape inside a tape drive. In the previous example, -f /dev/rmt/0n specifies which tape device to operate upon; specifically, the 0n says to operate upon the first tape drive, in no-rewind mode. The fsf 1 says to fast-forward one tape mark. Check out the man page for mt, and play with writing and reading multiple tape images to a single tape. You'll find that it's a nifty little tool.

The previous command fast-forwards one tape mark and then does not rewind the tape, so the tape is positioned at the second image. Now you can read the /home files (but you still have to use no-rewind device):

```
# cd /
# cpio -icdBvum < /dev/rmt/0n
```

It can be a little tricky getting to know when to use a no-rewind tape device name versus the normal tape device name. It takes experimentation and practice to get the hang of it. After you've done it for a while, it will be second nature. Just be patient with yourself.

This entire concept also translates to the use of tar. You can have multiple tar images on a tape and manipulate them this same way by using no-rewind tape device names as appropriate.

For a restore from a tape that has a single image use, do this:

```
# cpio -icdBvum < /dev/rmt/0
```

If you need to specify a specific file or subset of files to restore, you can use pattern matching:

```
# cpio -icdBvum "pattern_to_match"
```

On the read in the previous example, a lot of options were used besides -i, which indicates read:

- **c**—Specifies to read the header as the ASCII header format.
- **d**—Permits directories to be made as needed.
- **B**—Specifies using a blocking factor of 5120 bytes rather than 512 bytes. Because you'll want to write tapes with this blocking factor, you'll also need to read them with this same factor.
- **v**—Specifies verbose mode. Use it if you want to see how the restore is coming along.
- **u**—Specifies to copy unconditionally. If you're doing a complete filesystem restore or a point-in-time restore, you'll want to overwrite existing files on the system even if the existing files are newer.
- **m**—Retains previous file-modification times. This option does not affect directories that are being copied.

Be aware of what directory you are in when you start your restore and what the relative pathnames are on the tape. cpio will restore whatever you're asking for, starting in your current working directory. Make sure that you know where you are and what you're going to get, or you can end up with a big mess on your hands.

A good way to check yourself before restoring is to get a partial listing of the tape's table of contents or to run the command that you're planning to use, but with the t option, and make sure that what you see is what you wanted. The t option is used along with the i option to just read the contents of the tape without restoring anything. To get a table of contents, cpio must read the whole tape (just like tar). This is how to do it:

```
# cpio -ictBv < /dev/rmt/0
```

If you're about to do a restore of a subset of files, use this command with the t option first, along with your pattern(s), and verify that you're going to get what you want before you use the command without the t. You can save yourself some nasty little messes by always confirming the following before you proceed:

- To what directory are you about to restore the files?
- What set of files are you going to end up with?

cpio also has no awareness of the concept of incrementals. However, because it's typically used in conjunction with find, it's pretty easy to put together your own little multi-level backup system.

To initiate a full and incremental system of backups for a filesystem—let's say, /home—do the following:

```
# cd /home
# touch cpio_home_full
# find . -print | cpio -oacBv > /dev/rmt/0
```

The next day, for the first incremental backup, do this:

```
# cd /home
# touch cpio_home_incr
# find . -newer cpio_home_full -print | cpio -oacBv > /dev/rmt/0
```

To continue doing incrementals from that point, do this:

```
# cd /home
# touch cpio_home_incr
# find . -newer cpio_home_incr -print | cpio -oacBv > /dev/rmt/0
```

If you are backing up your filesystems as separate cpio images, you also will want to keep them properly separated in cases where the system has nested filesystems. For example, you might have separate filesystems such as /usr and /usr/local, where /usr/local is mounted under /usr. When using find to feed a list of filenames to cpio, find will start at the starting point that you give it and then descend through the directory structure, which means that when you run find from /usr, the file list also includes all of /usr/local. To keep the filesystems separated out in backup images, use the -mount option of find (on some versions of UNIX, the option is -xdev). This will prevent find from crossing into different mount points when descending a directory structure.

If you run a backup starting from / like this, you will back up every file on the entire system (and possibly be prompted for multiple tapes):

```
# cd /;  find . -print | cpio -oacBv > /dev/rmt/0
```

If what you really want is to just get the files in the root filesystem, -mount will keep find from crossing over any other mount points and make a backup that consists only of the files and directories that are in the root filesystem.

```
# cd /;  find . -mount -print | cpio -oacBv > /dev/rmt/0
```

To write a cpio backup of a filesystem from host guido to a remote tape drive, you can do the following from the machine with the tape drive:

```
# rsh guido "find . -print | cpio -oacBv" > /dev/rmt/0
```

And now, before leaving the topic of cpio behind, here again is a great little hint that everyone can use. When you want to copy a set of directories and files from one place to another on a machine, do the following:

```
cd fromdir; find . -depth -print | cpio -pd todir
```

Back Up and Restore with dump and restore

dump (on Solaris, it's ufsdump) and restore are probably the most popular noncommercial backup utilities. Because dump and restore are designed specifically for performing backups, they have features built into them that you would typically want. dump is certainly incremental-aware. It allows you 10 levels of backups, and it writes the index of contents at the beginning of the dump image on the tape. It also creates all backup images as relative pathnames. The restore utility provides an interactive facility that can greatly facilitate restores.

The Truth About dump

It's time for a full disclosure about dump. It can write its index at the beginning of the image because it generates its list of files to back up before it starts writing anything. It also generates what it believes to be the list of all the inodes to back up to get these files. This utility originally was conceived and designed to back up unmounted filesystems. In that scenario, putting together the file list and inode list first makes sense. Unfortunately, in a mounted filesystem, files could be changing all the time. In a very active system, chances are pretty high that between the time dump generates its lists and eventually completes writing out all file data to tape, *something* will have changed in that filesystem. The results can be varied, from files not getting onto the tape, files being corrupted, and files being readable but having a different file's contents.

That being said, if you use dump at the most inactive time of day for your system, that's the best you can do to decrease your risk of data loss if you choose to use this utility. In all honesty, chances are good that you can go merrily along your way for any number of years backing everything up this way without encountering a problem when it comes time to restore.

Of course, this is what we refer to as "luck." I never feel that lucky. When I understood the difference between how cpio writes a backup and how dump writes a backup, I stopped using dump and converted to cpio. You'll have to decide what tool you want to use based on how much uncertainty you are comfortable with.

By the way, tar and cpio both work via the filesystem structure. They back up each file one by one. They can miss a file that came into existence after the command was issued. They also can become confused and can try to back up a file that existed when the command was issued but that no longer exists by the time they get to backing it up. But they have a pretty narrow window of opportunity to actually write a file as corrupted. When it comes time to write file_a to tape, the file gets opened at that time and the inodes for the file are followed. The inodes are current. With dump, the inode list might have been generated an hour ago when the command was issued—and now it gets to where it's time to back up file_a (after 5,000 other files) and that inode list was correct an hour ago. Is it now?

Let's begin by looking at the syntax and arguments of ufsdump for Solaris. We'll start with an example of a full dump (or Level 0) of a root filesystem on disk c0t3d0 to a local drive named /dev/rmt/0. The stdout of the command is included here as well:

```
# ufsdump 0unbdsf 126 141000 11500 /dev/rmt/0 /dev/rdsk/c0t3d0s0
  DUMP: Writing 63 Kilobyte records
  DUMP: Date of this level 0 dump: Sun Aug 26 12:09:21 2001
  DUMP: Date of last level 0 dump: the epoch
  DUMP: Dumping /dev/rdsk/c0t0d0s0 (ensis.ucs.umbc.edu:/) to /dev/rmt/0.
  DUMP: Mapping (Pass I) [regular files]
  DUMP: Mapping (Pass II) [directories]
  DUMP: Estimated 6444902 blocks (3146.92MB) on 0.61 tapes.
  DUMP: Dumping (Pass III) [directories]
  DUMP: Dumping (Pass IV) [regular files]

Message from the dump program to all operators at 12:09 ...

DUMP IS DONE
  DUMP: Level 0 dump on Sun Aug 26 12:09:21 2001
```

Before reviewing the main options of dump, observe the last string on the command line. dump and ufsdump take the filesystem specification as the name of the raw disk device. The r before the dsk in the string /dev/rdsk/c0t3d0s5 is what indicates to dump that the device is the raw device (character special) rather than the cooked device (block special). Now on to the options:

- **0-9**—Specifies the level of backup to perform. Level 0 always is a full backup. A Level 1 backup gets everything that has changed since the timestamp of the most recent Level 0. A Level 2 backup gets everything that has changed since the time-stamp of the most recent Level 1 backup, and so forth.

- **u**—Specifies that the /etc/dumpdates file should be updated to record this activity. The raw device file being backed up and the date are recorded.

- **n**—Specifies that all members of the operator group be notified when the command completes.

- **b factor**—From the man page: Blocking factor. Specifies the blocking factor for tape writes. The default is 20 blocks per write for tapes of density less than 6250BPI (bytes per inch). The default blocking factor for tapes of density 6250BPI and greater is 64. The default blocking factor for cartridge tapes (c option) is 126. The highest blocking factor available with most tape drives is 126. *Note:* The blocking factor is specified in terms of 512-byte blocks, for compatibility with tar(1).

- **d bpi**—From the man page: Tape density. Not normally required because ufsdump can detect end of media. This parameter can be used to keep a running tab on the amount of tape used per reel. The default density is 6250BPI, except when the c option is used for cartridge tape, in which case it is assumed to be 1000BPI per track.

- **s size**—Specifies the size of the volume being dumped to. ufsdump interprets the specified size as the length in feet for tapes and cartridges, and as the number of 1024-byte blocks for disks.

- **f dump-file**—Dump file. Use dump_file as the file to dump to instead of /dev/rmt/0 (which is the default for Solaris). If dump_file is specified as -, dump to standard output.

The dump command syntax is constructed with all the options run together. Next, the options' arguments must follow in the same sequence that the options appeared (but with spaces between the arguments). Figure 16.2 provides an illustration.

FIGURE 16.2
Keep dump option arguments in the same order.

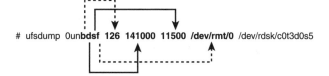

Making a Level 5 dump of the same filesystem would be done like this, for example:

```
# ufsdump 5unbdsf 126 141000 11500 /dev/rmt/0 /dev/rdsk/c0t3d0s5
  DUMP: Writing 63 Kilobyte records
  DUMP: Date of this level 5 dump: Mon Aug 27 14:18:25 2001
```

```
DUMP: Date of last level 0 dump: Mon Aug 27 12:09:21 2001
DUMP: Dumping /dev/rdsk/c0t3d0s5 (ensis.ucs.umbc.edu:/usr/easm) to /dev/rmt/0.
DUMP: Mapping (Pass I) [regular files]
DUMP: Mapping (Pass II) [directories]
DUMP: Estimated 144 blocks (72KB) on 0.00 tapes.
DUMP: Dumping (Pass III) [directories]
DUMP: Dumping (Pass IV) [regular files]
DUMP: 124 blocks (62KB) on 1 volume at 1512 KB/sec
DUMP: DUMP IS DONE

Message from the dump program to all operators at 14:18 ...

DUMP IS DONE
   DUMP: Level 5 dump on Mon Aug 27 14:18:25 2001
```

After this Level 0 and Level 5, backup the contents of /etc/dumpdates look like this:

```
/dev/rdsk/c0t3d0s5                  0 Sun Aug 26 12:09:21 2001
/dev/rdsk/c0t3d0s5                  5 Mon Aug 27 14:18:25 2001
```

This is the set of timestamps that ufsdump uses to determine which files need to be backed up, depending on which backup level you specify.

Turning to the `restore` command now (ufsrestore for Solaris), we can examine a table of contents of a ufsdump tape by using this command:

```
# ufsrestore tbsfy 126 11500 /dev/rmt/0
```

The options used here that are new are as follows:

- **t**—Specifies to read the index and provide a table of contents
- **y**—Specifies to continue even if errors are encountered

The b, s, and f options are the same as before.

restore and ufsrestore have a nice interactive option that can make doing restores a little more user-friendly. When you need to do a restore, first you'll cd to the directory that you want to restore to. Next you can invoke ufsrestore with the interactive option, by specifying i for interactive.

```
# ufsrestore ifvy /dev/rmt/0
Verify volume and initialize maps
Media block size is 126
Dump    date: Sun Aug 26 15:24:00 2001
Dumped from: the epoch
Level 0 dump of / on ensis.ucs.umd.edu:/dev/dsk/c0t0d0s0
Label: none
Extract directories from tape
Initialize symbol table.
ufsrestore >
```

At this point, you are in a pseudoshell and can use a few regular shell commands such as ls, cd, and pwd to assist you in looking for files.

```
ufsrestore > ls
.:
     2 *./               258  apps/        36891  nsmail/
     2 *../               13  bin         176331  opt/
   275  .Xauthority      216  cdrom/       24342  platform/
    61  .cpr_config   468181  dev/           253  prefs_v3
109680  .dt/            97299  devices/    182414  proc/
   218  .dtprofile     352640  etc/        188498  sbin/
   251  .kshrc            197  export/     194581  tmp/
 49414  .netscape/       6259  home/        42560  usr/
   193  .new           121612  kernel/       6080  var/
   252  .profile           15  lib         456157  vol/
   428  .rhosts             3  lost+found/ 383301  xfn/
   361  .sh_history    170251  mnt/        468586  y2k/
407802  .ssh2/         371063  net/
304419  TT_DB/             41  nohup.out
```

```
ufsrestore > cd sbin
ufsrestore > ls
./sbin:
188498  ./          188505  ifconfig   188513  rc3       188517  sulogin
     2 *../         188506  init       188510  rc5       188518  swapadd
188500  autopush    188507  jsh        188510  rc6       188519  sync
188543  bpgetfile   188508  mount      188514  rcS       188520  uadmin
188501  dhcpagent   188509  mountall   188507  sh        188521  umount
188502  dhcpinfo    188510  rc0        188515  soconfig  188522  umountall
188503  fdisk       188511  rc1        188499  su        188523  uname
188504  hostconfig  188512  rc2        188516  su.static
```

To specify that you want to restore the file dhcpinfo in this listing, tell ufsrestore to add it to its list of files that you want restored:

```
ufsrestore > add dhcpinfo
```

Now when you do an ls again, you'll see an asterisk next to dhcpinfo.

```
ufsrestore > ls
./sbin:
188498 *./          188505  ifconfig   188513  rc3       188517  sulogin
     2 *../         188506  init       188510  rc5       188518  swapadd
188500  autopush    188507  jsh        188510  rc6       188519  sync
188543  bpgetfile   188508  mount      188514  rcS       188520  uadmin
188501  dhcpagent   188509  mountall   188507  sh        188521  umount
188502 *dhcpinfo    188510  rc0        188515  soconfig  188522  umountall
188503  fdisk       188511  rc1        188499  su        188523  uname
188504  hostconfig  188512  rc2        188516  su.static
```

You now can add other files as needed. Shell wildcards also can be used. So, you might say add rc* to get all the files and directories beginning with "rc." To remove a file from the list of files to be restored, just specify remove filename.

```
ufsrestore > extract
Extract requested files
You have not read any volumes yet.
Unless you know which volume your file(s) are on you should start
with the last volume and work towards the first.
Specify next volume #:
```

Go ahead and specify volume 1.

```
Specify next volume #: 1
extract file ./sbin/dhcpinfo
Add links
Set directory mode, owner, and times.
set owner/mode for '.'? [yn]
```

At this prompt, if you've been restoring an entire filesystem, say yes. If you've just been restoring a subset of files as in this case, say no. Saying no will leave your current working directory permissions unchanged. Saying yes will cause the restore to set the current working directory permissions to what they were on the backup tape when the backup tape was created.

You can leave the interactive session with a q:

```
# ufsrestore > q
```

To restore an entire filesystem, specify the r option (for recursive):

```
# ufsrestore rvfy /dev/rmt/0n
```

You need to do this command starting with your last Level 0 backup and then repeat the command with each intervening incremental to get everything back.

dump and ufsdump also can write to a tape on a remote host by specifying the f option and qualifying the tape device name with the name of the host to which it's attached:

```
# ufsdump 0unbdsf 126 141000 11500 otherhost.umd.edu:/dev/rmt/0
/dev/rdsk/c0t3d0s5
```

This requires that otherhost.umd.edu trust your system via the /.rhosts file. Many sites do not allow .rhosts entries because of the potential security risks. If you need to do remote backups of this nature and can't use rhosts, you can use ssh (see Chapter 8, "Securing a System for Rollout").

Back Up and Restore with dd

dd is a command that performs a byte-by-byte copy from a source that you specify to a target that you specify. It is particularly well suited to backing up one special kind of data: raw data. Raw data is data that is located on disk space that a raw device points to, but where no filesystem structure has been built. Because there is no filesystem, there are no separate files within this space. It's all one big continuous space. dd is about the only thing you can use to make a copy of this type of disk space. Here is an example of its use:

```
# dd if=/dev/rdsk/c0t3d0s1 of=/dev/rmt/0
```

- **if**—This stands for "input file," or where to read from. Specify the raw device name of the space that you are backing up.

- **of**—This stands for "output file," or where to write to. Specify the name of your tape device here (although, of course, you could specify some other raw disk space on your system and then you'd have another exact copy of this space on your system).

You'll probably want to specify a block size of at least 10KB, to help make the tape writing process more efficient. Just add bs=10k to the command.

To read this back, you just reverse the if and the of:

```
# dd if=/dev/rmt/0 of=/dev/rdsk/c0t3d0s1 bs=10k
```

Rather than making backups, dd is most often used to make disk copies and for forensics work. You can use dd to read a mystery disk or tape and determine what OS (and its revision number) is on the medium.

In Closing

As a final note, whatever utility you choose to use to write files to tape, do yourself and whoever might follow you a favor: Affix a label to the tape and note what is on the tape, the hostname the files are from, the date of creation, and the command and options used to create it. It takes only a minute and can save you precious time when the chips are down.

Freely Available

A number of freely available utilities can be used for backups. A tool that works on most operating systems is hostdump.sh available, at `http://www.backupcentral.com`. Another tool that is available and that is quite popular is AMANDA, the Advanced Maryland Automated Network Disk Archiver.

AMANDA

AMANDA was created at the University of Maryland and is a public-domain utility. It is available at `http://www.amanda.org`. The AMANDA Web page describes it like this:

> AMANDA is a backup system that allows the administrator of a LAN to set up a single master backup server to back up multiple hosts to a single large capacity tape drive. AMANDA uses native dump and/or GNU tar facilities and can back up a large number of workstations running multiple versions of UNIX. Recent versions can also use SAMBA to back up Microsoft Windows 95/NT hosts.

The primary features of AMANDA are listed here:

- It's free!
- It can be used as a central backup server.
- It can back up many different operating systems.

To use AMANDA, you'll need a system to use as a dedicated backup server. The server will need to be attached to a reasonably large tape device, preferably a tape library or jukebox so that it can load tapes for itself as needed.

The details of installing and configuring AMANDA are outside the scope of this chapter, but, to provide a high-level view, you'll need to perform the following steps:

- Download the software to your backup server.
- Build the software (here you might find that there are other public domain packages that, although optional, you want to install to enhance your implementation).
- Configure the AMANDA server.
- Configure the backup clients.

This is a great tool with a lot of flexibility and features that is well worth the time you'll spend getting acquainted with it.

Commercial Products

More commercial products for backups are available every day. The dramatic increase in products over the last 10 years has been due to the increase in the use of computers, and the market demand for backups has followed right along. Because the market is so fluid, with new products appearing all the time and older products disappearing or changing their names as companies get bought out, we will not go into any amount of detail on what is available in the market right now or the features of these products. We will mention very briefly a few products that are particularly popular at this time because these are the products that you most likely will encounter. All of these products are based on

the concept of a dedicated backup server. We'll wrap up this section with a summary of characteristics to look for when evaluating which commercial product could be right for you.

Legato Networker has a long track record in the UNIX community. A lot of people out there are using it because it has been around so long and it's relatively inexpensive (emphasis on relatively). If you buy Networker or inherit it at your place of employment, be aware of the vulnerability of its database. As with most big backup packages, there is a database of information gathered on files, tapes, dates, and so on as you do your backups. Networker's database is more prone to corruption than any other package of this league. When the database gets corrupted, you have to do a lot of tape reading to get it rebuilt. This can put a real crimp in your capability to restore in a hurry. It's not a show-stopper, by any means, and many sysadmins have many happy years of Networker usage with no database corruption. Let's just say that this is a word to the wise: Any precautions that Legato mentions regarding avoiding database corruption should be well heeded.

VERITAS NetBackup is taking the largest data centers of the country by storm. This is a great package that demonstrates tremendous scalability. VERITAS packages back up solutions to fit all different size enterprises.

Alexandria is an older solution. It was very popular about five years ago but has not been keeping up in market share with newer products like those from VERITAS. Alexandria's GUI is not the most intuitive or the easiest to navigate. We've not encountered tales of serious problems with this package, but, then, we've probably lead a sheltered life.

Tivoli Storage Manager (formerly ADSM) is now owned by IBM and has been shoe-horned into the Tivoli product line. It is a reasonably capable package as a whole, targeted at the data center audience and providing great flexibility. If you ever run into it where you work, you can expect good reliability from it. It does have some serious annoyances, though. An unfortunate amount of the code appears to have been written with the philosophy of, "Oh, this function fails; let's quit." For example, in using a tape silo with a number of tape drives available, the software will determine what the next drive is to use in an apparent round-robin cycle when backing up. If the tape cannot be mounted on the drive for some reason, the entire backup for the host being backed up (which might have written to any number of tapes so far) will abort, and the host's backup will be reported as "missed" or "failed." Never mind that there are other tape drives sitting there unused and ready to go. For the price and complexity of setup, it seems reasonable to ask that this software be smarter.

We spent the first half of this chapter covering issues that need to be considered in planning backups. In addition to all of those concerns, when evaluating the purchase of commercial products, there are still more criteria to examine. Here are some other things to look at:

- Which products can be used to back up the largest percentage of your platforms?
- How scalable is the product? If the amount of systems that you have quadruples in the next year, will the product be capable of handling it?
- How good is the product's support? You might want to lurk on some mailing lists of the product's users and see what problems they have and what they complain about.
- How stable is the company? Will they be around and supporting this product for a long time to come?
- How easy or difficult is it to take care of the product's database? How painful is a database recovery?
- How easy is the product to use when the time comes to restore data? Remember, this is when the pressure will be on.

Best Practices

Planning

- Examine relevant backup criteria and constraints for the environment.
- Reach agreement with the user community regarding what needs to be backed up.
- Evaluate backup tools to use in the environment.
- Make decisions of tools to use.
- Decide on backup policies and schedules.
- Document decisions and publish them.
- Create and publish a backup implementation schedule.

Implementation

- Configure backups.
- Test backups and restores.
- Document and publish a backup policy.
- Use relative pathnames to back up filesystems.
- Write-protect tapes after the backup is complete.
- Keep tapes write-protected during a restore or retrieval operation.

Production

- When bringing new systems or disk space online, be sure to add to the backup schedule and policy.

- Monitor backups to verify that they complete each day.

- Perform troubleshooting of any missed or failed backups in a timely manner.

- Perform an annual review of the backup policy.

- Perform tests of all major types of restore no less than biannually.

Online Resources

Documenting system configuration: http://www.backupcentral.com

Alternative tar and cpio: http://www.gnu.org

Resources and references for backups: http://www.backupcentral.com

Summary

This concludes our whirlwind tour of the world of backups. There is much to know and much to learn. Systems are changing all the time. The way we use computers is forever evolving. Nevertheless, there are at least three immutable laws of backups:

1. To the extent appropriate for your environment, they've got to be done—consistently.

2. Someone has to be responsible for monitoring every day to see that they have completed successfully and to promptly and thoroughly troubleshoot when they fail.

3. Test your recoveries and document the procedures.

We wish you fair winds and happy backups.

Applications and Tools

PART

III

IN THIS PART

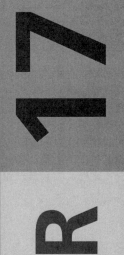

Open Source Software Management

by Robert Banz

IN THIS CHAPTER

Introduction

Managing third-party software is one of the most common tasks given to a UNIX system administrator, but it's one of the least covered in the textbook—and some of the best third-party software is "free," available in source-code format, ready to be compiled and help you meet your software needs. If you're already a pro at finding and building free software, you'll find the beginning of this chapter old news. However, even the most experienced software builder always has new tips and tricks to learn! This chapter is for the novice software builder, who might have struggled through building Emacs once or twice. As for the UNIX system administrator who has been working for years and has never found, compiled, or used free software, how can you live like that?[1]

A Bit More About Free Software

We use the terms 'Free' and 'Open Source' almost interchangeably in this chapter. Though most Open Source software is free (as in cost), to some the 'Free' is not defined on the basis of cost. For more information on this debate, please see `http://www.gnu.org` and `http://www.opensource.org`.

Free software is available for just about anything. There are free SQL database servers, mail transport agents, Web servers, operating systems, mp3 encoders, image manipulators—you name it, it's out there. However, just because there is a free, or Open Source, alternative, doesn't mean that it's the best choice for you. For example, OpenLDAP is an impressive, stable LDAP server. In fact, most commercial LDAP servers were developed from the same code base. However, the commercial servers typically have better performance, better management tools, and someone to yell at when something doesn't work—that is very important if your LDAP server is a key to the functionality of your entire enterprise. If your LDAP server's job is just to route email and provide whitepages lookup, the free alternative might be what you're looking for, especially at the price. You should choose free software just as you would when evaluating commercial software options, considering the following:

- Price
- Performance
- Support
- Product maturity

Just as you would be wary of any commercial product's claims when choosing to plop down the bucks for a license, be just as wary of the claims of free software. Some "zealots" out there make a case for "Open Source" or "free" software just because it's free or because the only alternative is to fork over cash to some megamonopoly software company. The big surprise to these people is that sometimes the software from the mega-monopoly software company *is* the best fit for your business needs. But at the same time, if one of the busiest internet root nameservers (`http://www.isc.org/services/public/F-root-server.html`) runs on the "free" ISC BIND nameserver software, it's a pretty good case for your nameservers to do so also.

Now it's disclaimer time: Just because statements are made in this chapter like the previous one regarding ISC BIND, that does not mean that the following points are necessarily true:

- The specified software package is the right choice for *you*.
- The software package will or will not cause your business to fail.
- The software package has no bugs.
- The software package actually *is* better than another software package.

Reading this chapter is *not a replacement* for testing and evaluating these software packages on your own. Just because it's mentioned here doesn't mean that it's the best, that it will work for you, or that it even works at all. What free software to choose, how to build it, and how to configure it are areas of system administration that are full of opinions. You are reading only one opinion here, and you're expected to form your own.

Some Basic Free Software

Here are examples of some "basic" free software, ranging from a simple utility to complex network services software.

- **GNU Zip**—GNU zip is a command-line utility used for compressing and uncompressing .gz files, which are used to package many Open Source/free software products. It is very easy to build and is available (in uncompressed form, of course) from `ftp://ftp.gnu.org/pub/gnu/gzip`. Many operating system vendors have begun including gzip as part of their standard software installs.
- **GNU Emacs**—GNU Emacs is one of the most popular text editors used by UNIX users. Highly configurable, lots of features, and really big as far as "free" software tends to go. It's available from `ftp://ftp.gnu.org/pub/gnu/emacs`.
- **sendmail**—sendmail is one of the oldest "Open Source" projects around. If you send email to someone, chances are good that it'll go through a machine running sendmail at some point during its travels. That's not to say that sendmail is the only choice for mail transport; there are many good alternatives, both free and otherwise.[2]
- **Apache**—Apache is a very popular, capable, and, best of all, free Web server for UNIX- and Windows-based systems. It's available from `ftp://ftp.apache.org/`.

Where to Find Free and Open Source Software

You can find free software all over the Internet—you do have an Internet connection, right? Some of the best places to look for free software are listed here:

- **Freshmeat (`http://www.freshmeat.net`)**—Freshmeat is a "clearinghouse" for information on Open Source and some commercial software products. It includes some nice search features and a function that will send you mail when the entry for a software package that you have some interest in is updated. Although most "respectable" Open Source/freeware projects are represented here, many unrespectable ones are, too. If you read up on the package, you'll quickly be able to eliminate the junk from the good stuff.

- **GNU / Free Software Foundation (`http://www.gnu.org/`)**—The Free Software Foundation GNU project has been a source of high-quality, free software projects since 1984. Searching the GNU.org Web site, you can find links to software projects such as GNU Emacs, GCC (the GNU compiler set, better than many commercial compilers), and pointers to other free software that has been placed under the GNU Public License (GPL).

- **Sourceforge (`http://www.sourceforge.net`)**—Sourceforge is a system to assist developers in managing Open Source projects. Many projects have their home pages here, as well as the latest and beta versions of their software, bug-tracking information, documentation, and discussions.

- **Your favorite search engine**—Searching around the Web, you might just run into what you're looking for.

Vendor-Provided "Free" Software

Many commercial UNIX vendors have been relying on free software for some time to implement crucial components of their operating environments. Programs such as sendmail and ISC BIND (named) have been included in most commercial UNIX variants since their inception. Recently, it has become popular for vendors to include or make available for download builds of popular Open Source software packages, typically in the vendor's native software packaging format.

"Free" Software Bundled with the Operating System

As mentioned previously, some vendor-provided software is just a build of Open Source software (such as sendmail) included in the operating system. Some vendors make extensive modifications to their included sources (Sun was known to make some major

Open Source Software Management

CHAPTER 17

721

17
OPEN SOURCE
SOFTWARE
MANAGEMENT

changes to sendmail, to make it "perform better" on SunOS and Solaris). Many times, running the vendor-provided port of an Open Source package might suit your needs quite well. However, it is important to note that these vendor-applied modifications might confuse someone who uses these applications on multiple platforms with different operating systems. In addition, vendors are typically "one step behind" when it comes to providing new versions of Open Source programs such as BIND and sendmail. The "latest and greatest" versions of these programs usually contain security fixes and feature upgrades that add value to them. For these reasons, at least with the two applications mentioned previously, we have found it to be good operating procedure to upgrade to the latest versions of these programs when installing a new system.

The "Free Software" CD

Popular UNIX vendors, such as SGI, have been making "freeware" distributions for the past few years. Some operating systems, such as RedHat Linux, are made up completely of freeware, so the concept of separate freeware distribution is kind of strange. However, even Red Hat Linux has a separate distribution of "more stuff" that's distinct from the operating system (the Power Tools CD), as well as most other Linux distributions; even FreeBSD has its "Ports" collection. The following is a list of some major UNIX distributions and a Web site that contains, or contains pointers to, operating system–specific builds of various freeware packages.

- Silicon Graphics IRIX: `http://freeware.sgi.com`
- SUN Solaris: `http://www.sun.com/bigadmin/downloads/indexFree.html` and `http://www.sunfreeware.com`
- HPUX: `http://hpux.connect.org.uk/`
- Red Hat Linux: `http://www.redhat.com/apps/download`
- Debian Linux: `http://www.debian.org/distrib/packages`

Should I Choose Source or Binary?

If you've caught on to the general theme by now, you know that this really depends on your specific needs, skill level, and time requirements. Pulling down a binary distribution of a package can be the quick-and-easy way to get up and running. However, your needs might require the package to be configured with different options or to be installed in a different location than the builder of the binary package chose. Binary packages also carry some inherent risk: You must ask yourself whether you trust the person/people who built this package with root on your system—in some sense, this is what you are doing when installing a third-party package. (The other side to this argument is, do you actually read through the source of a source code distribution?)

Installing Binary Distributions

Binary distributions usually come in one of two forms:

- A vendor-specific package format
- A "tarball," including the application and hopefully some installation scripts or instructions

Because this book is focused primarily on Red Hat Linux and Solaris, we'll take a look at these vendor-specific installation steps. Installing packages for other environments, such as FreeBSD, IRIX, or HPUX, usually can be found either in the vendor-supplied documentation or at the site where the binary package was downloaded.

Red Hat RPMs

Here's the "super-super quick" version:

1. Download the package.
2. Run the following command as root: `rpm –i <filename>`.

If no errors were returned, the package (probably) was installed successfully. Of course, as these things go, you're probably going to see a few errors. A common problem when installing an RPM is a missing prerequisite, usually a package or shared library that is used by the package that you are installing. For example, while trying to install the xsane package, an application that allows you to access a scanner device, we received the following error:

```
[root@tyler /]# rpm -i xsane-gimp-0.62-4.i386.rpm
error: failed dependencies:
        sane >= 1.0 is needed by xsane-gimp-0.62-4
        libgimp-1.1.so.25 is needed by xsane-gimp-0.62-4
        libsane-dll.so.1 is needed by xsane-gimp-0.62-4
```

The first line mentions that the RPM package sane, of at least version 1.0 or greater, is required for this package to work. The other two files mentioned are specific versions of shared libraries that also are required by this package, which might or might not be provided by the RPM requirements. The next step is to track down the sane package. The first place to check is the Red Hat distribution CD or `ftp.redhat.com`, wherever you find the RPM packages for your particular OS version and platform. When you've found the prerequisite package, install it:

```
[root@tyler /tmp]# rpm -i sane-1.0.3-10.i386.rpm
error: failed dependencies:
        libgimp-1.2.so.0   is needed by sane-1.0.3-10
```

Just our luck, this always happens: It seems that the prerequisite package has a prerequisite of its own, and we haven't gotten a package name either—just the name of a file. By the name of the file, it would be a good guess that it's from the imaging application called gimp. But, if you don't know where it comes from, go to the redhat.com downloads site and choose Advanced Search. Choose to search on Provided Packages, and place the name of the package that you're looking for in the search box—in this case, libgimp-1.2. Unfortunately, our search turned up negative on Red Hat's site (Figure 17.1).

FIGURE 17.1

Searching Red Hat's packages.

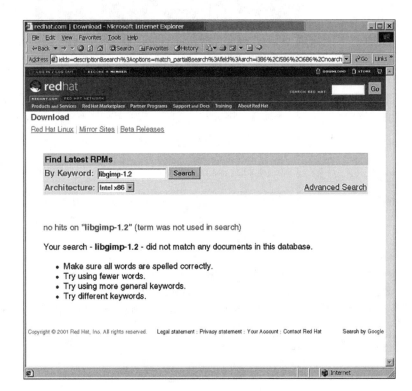

However, all is not lost. The next resource to use on our quest is http://www.rpmfind. net, a larger database of RPM-format distributions. Searching for libgimp-1.2 on rpmfind gives much more positive results.

We're looking for something to run on Red Hat 7.1 on the i386 architecture, so gimp-1.2.1-5.i386 looks like what we're looking for (see Figure 17.2).

FIGURE 17.2

gimp-1.2.1-5.i386.

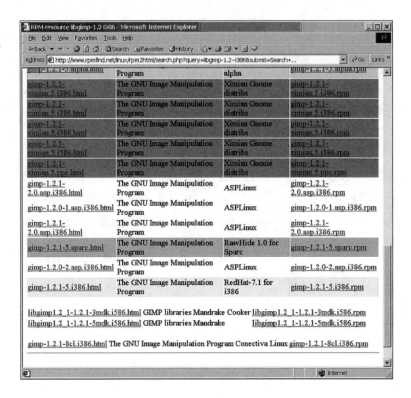

For those of you who said, "Hold on there—doesn't Red Hat Linux come with Gimp?" a little while ago, you were right. However, it seems that this version of sane that we've found ourselves installing seems to require a different version of the Gimp than what was included in the Red Hat distribution. Now that we've downloaded the newer Gimp, we'll install it and finally install sane and then xsane.

```
[root@tyler /tmp]# rpm -i ~banz/gimp-1.2.1-5.i386.rpm
[root@tyler /tmp]# rpm -i sane-1.0.3-10.i386.rpm
[root@tyler /tmp]# rpm -i ~banz/xsane-gimp-0.61-3.i386.rpm
```

That was a tricky piece of software to install—most packages that you will find online will not take as much effort.

The Red Hat RPM packaging system is a very powerful software- and system-maintenance tool, much too complicated to cover in depth in this chapter. For further information, we recommend these references:

- "The Red Hat RPM How-To," at
  `http://rpm.redhat.com/RPM-HOWTO`
- *Maximum RPM*, by Ed Bailey (published by Sams Publishing)

Solaris Packages

On Solaris, the native package-management system is the UNIX System V (SYSV) package manager—most Solaris administrators simply refer to this as pkgadd. It is available on most all SYSV-derived operating systems, including Solaris, IRIX, and SCO. Although it might be available on all of these systems, such as IRIX, it is not always the packaging system used by the operating system. SYSV packages can come in different formats—datastream and filesystem.

The datastream format is similar to RPM in that it's a single file that contains the entire package. Unlike RPM format however, the datastream format is not compressed to save space. Package files typically are distributed compressed with gzip (.gz) or compress (.Z). Both of these can be uncompressed with gunzip. The filesystem format stores the contents of the package in a standard UNIX directory. The files contained in the package, including the files containing metadata and auxiliary installation scripts, are located in a directory whose name is the same as the package name. This format makes it easy to poke around in a package and see what's there without installing it.

The `pkgtrans` command allows you to translate a package from filesystem to datastream format, and vice versa. See the man page for further information.

A couple things should be noted when comparing the SYSV package format to RPM. The SYSV package format knows nothing of prerequisites. In a situation like that encountered when trying to install the scanner package under Red Hat Linux, there is no "automated" way of discovering what prerequisites (if any) are needed and whether they are installed on the target. This makes it important to read the appropriate installation documentation that accompanies the package.

As an example for Solaris, we'll be installing GCC, the GNU Compiler Collection, on a SPARC-based machine running Solaris 8. To find a prebuilt package for GCC, we've visited the `http://www.sunfreeware.com` Web site and found it in the index (see Figure 17.3).

After you've downloaded the package, it's as simple as running the command `pkgadd` to install the package:

```
bfs1[1]# pkgadd -d gcc-3.0.1-sol8-sparc-local.gz
pkgadd: ERROR: attempt to process datastream failed
    - bad format in datastream table-of-contents
pkgadd: ERROR: could not process datastream from </usr/var/tmp/gcc-3.0.1-sol8-
➥sparc-local.gz>
```

17

OPEN SOURCE SOFTWARE MANAGEMENT

FIGURE **17.3**

Finding a Prebuilt Package for GCC at http://www. sunfreeware.com.

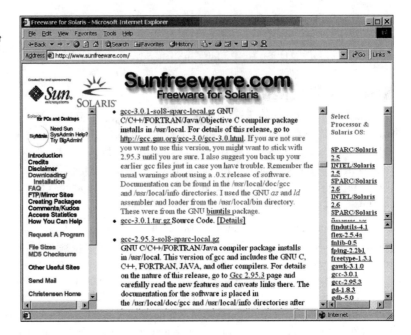

That didn't work too well. As mentioned earlier, most of these packages come compressed (the .gz extension) and need to be uncompressed before pkgadd can process the file.

```
bfs1[2]# gunzip gcc-3.0.1-sol8-sparc-local.gz
bfs1[3]# pkgadd -d gcc-3.0.1-sol8-sparc-local

The following packages are available:
  1  SMCgcc301     gcc
                   (sparc) 3.0.1

Select package(s) you wish to process (or 'all' to process
all packages). (default: all) [?,??,q]: 1

Processing package instance <SMCgcc301> from </usr/var/tmp/gcc-3.0.1-sol8-sparc-
➥local>

gcc
(sparc) 3.0.1
Free Software Foundation

The selected base directory </usr/local> must exist before
installation is attempted.
Do you want this directory created now [y,n,?,q] y
Using </usr/local> as the package base directory.
```

```
## Processing package information.
## Processing system information.
## Verifying disk space requirements.
## Checking for conflicts with packages already installed.
## Checking for setuid/setgid programs.

Installing gcc as <SMCgcc301>

## Installing part 1 of 1.
/usr/local/bin/addr2name.awk
/usr/local/bin/c++
/usr/local/bin/c++filt
/usr/local/bin/cpp
/usr/local/bin/g77
/usr/local/bin/gcc
/usr/local/bin/gccbug
/usr/local/bin/gcj
/usr/local/bin/gcjh
/usr/local/bin/gcov
...
/usr/local/man/man1/gcov.1
/usr/local/share/libgcj.jar
[ verifying class <none> ]
/usr/local/bin/g++ <linked pathname>
/usr/local/bin/sparc-sun-solaris2.8-c++ <linked pathname>
/usr/local/bin/sparc-sun-solaris2.8-g++ <linked pathname>
/usr/local/bin/sparc-sun-solaris2.8-gcc <linked pathname>

Installation of <SMCgcc301> was successful.

bfs1[4]#
```

Apparently, this correctly installed the package, and you can begin using the GNU
Compiler Collection on your Solaris system. There's not very much more to say when it
comes to using the SYSV package system for installations. The Sun Freeware site, where
this package was downloaded, contains a good how-to on building SYSV packages at
`http://www.sunfreeware.com/pkgadd.html`.

Tarballs and Other Distributions

Not all binary packages are available in a "vendor-native" format, such as a SYSV package or RPM. Often you will find packages in compressed or uncompressed tar files or
zip archives. If the file type is not familiar to you, a quick look at the package's installation instructions should clear things up. These packages usually consist of a directory (or
directories) containing the installation script and package contents, and typically installation instructions usually in a file named README or INSTALL. The first step in the

installation is to unpack these files—if you're unfamiliar with the procedure, the following sections give you direction in unpacking the most common file formats.

.tar files

The most common archive format that you'll find UNIX software distributed in is a compressed tar archive. The term *tar* refers to "tape archiver" because it uses a sequential format that originally was created for storing data on magnetic tape. To get started, however, we'll look at using the tar command to unpack and view uncompressed archives. Any modern UNIX system is sure to come with a workable tar command. We'll be using the tar-packaged distribution of GNU Tar during our examples. To view the contents of a .tar file, use tar, as seen here. The t option instructs tar to display the contents of the archive, and the f option instructs it to read from the file's name that follows. By default, tar tries to read from a local magnetic tape device.

```
tyler[3]# tar -tf tar-1.13.tar
tar-1.13/
tar-1.13/README
tar-1.13/stamp-h.in
tar-1.13/ABOUT-NLS
tar-1.13/AUTHORS
tar-1.13/BACKLOG
tar-1.13/COPYING
tar-1.13/ChangeLog
tar-1.13/INSTALL
tar-1.13/Makefile.am
tar-1.13/Makefile.in
tar-1.13/NEWS
tar-1.13/THANKS
tar-1.13/TODO
…
```

This shows that the archive file contains a bunch of stuff that seems to all be in a directory named tar-1.13. It's important to check the contents of an archive before unpacking it. Although it is bad practice, some archives are created using absolute pathnames (paths beginning with a "/"), and, without special treatment, they most likely will not unpack where you intend them to go. You also should take care to not unpack tar files from "untrusted sources" as root. Bad guys might have mixed an /.rhosts, /etc/hosts.equiv, or /etc/passwd into the archive, unknowingly giving them access to your system—not to mention the potential for a "corrupt" tar archive exploiting an unknown buffer overflow in a tar implementation and giving someone root access. We're not trying to make you paranoid, but this serves as yet another reminder to follow good practice and use root only when absolutely necessary.

If you run across a tar archive that was encoded using absolute pathnames, don't panic. Most vendor implementations of the `tar` command allow you to force an absolute pathname–encoded archive to unpack relative to your current directory. GNU Tar, which is distributed with Linux systems, defaults to this behavior. Solaris's tar happily tries to extract tar archives with absolute pathnames using the absolute paths contained in the file, and it has no way of switching to the safer behavior. If you encounter one of these tar files on a Solaris system, your best bet is to download and install GNU Tar and use it for your tarring and untarring needs.

To do the actual extraction of a tar archive, use `tar` with the x (for "extract") option.

```
tyler[7]# tar -xf tar-1.13.tar
tyler[8]#
```

This silently extracts the archive. To have a better idea of what `tar` is doing, you might want to use it in verbose mode, using the v option, which will display the contents of the archive as it is extracted.

```
tyler[9]# tar -xvf ~banz/tar-1.13.tar
tar-1.13/
tar-1.13/README
tar-1.13/stamp-h.in
tar-1.13/ABOUT-NLS
tar-1.13/AUTHORS
tar-1.13/BACKLOG
tar-1.13/COPYING
tar-1.13/ChangeLog
tar-1.13/INSTALL
tar-1.13/Makefile.am
tar-1.13/Makefile.in
tar-1.13/NEWS
tar-1.13/THANKS
tar-1.13/TODO
tar-1.13/acconfig.h
tar-1.13/acinclude.m4
…
```

.tar.gz and .tar.Z Files

The next thing after tar files comes compressed tar files. The most common forms of compression are GNU Zip (.gz) and UNIX Compress (.Z). Depending on the flavor of UNIX and tar that you are using, dealing with these files can be a one- or two-step process. We'll start with the two-step process so that you can get a good idea of what's going on behind the scenes. You may also find files ending in .tgz, which is increasingly being used in place of .tar.gz by some software authors.

The first thing to note before going on is that, although `tar` can read from a file, it also can be told to take its input from stdin, in place of the filename. So, the following two command lines are functionally equivalent:

```
tyler[10]# cat tar-1.13.tar | tar -xf -
```

```
tyler[11]# tar -xf tar-1.13.tar
```

If your system has GNU Zip installed, you can uncompress and unpack a .gz or .Z file with the command line:

```
tyler[12]# gunzip -c tar-1.13.tar.gz | tar -xf -
```

The –c argument to `gunzip` instructs it to send the uncompressed file to stdout, allowing it to be piped directly into `tar`.

Your system might not have GNU Zip installed, either because it didn't ship with your chosen operating system or because you haven't installed it yet. Either way, you can decompress .Z files with the UNIX utility uncompress. Like gunzip, uncompress uses the –c command line argument to instruct it to send its output to stdout. You can uncompress and unpack a .tar.Z file like this:

```
tyler[12]# uncompress -c tar-1.13.tar.Z | tar -xf -
```

Most, if not all, installations of compress and GNU Zip include another command that, without arguments, will decompress a file to stdout. For GNU Zip, this command is gzcat; for compress, it is zcat.

Some versions of `tar` give you an even simpler method of uncompressing and unpacking these files in one command. GNU Tar uses `gunzip` automagically when you use the –z command-line argument. This processes both .Z and .gz files.

```
tyler[96]# tar -xzf tar-1.13.tar.gz
```

.zip Files

The .zip file format has been popular in the Windows/DOS realm for quite some time, but it is quite uncommon to find software distributions archived with it on UNIX. However, you could very well run into ZIP-compressed files in your travels. It is both a compression and archival utility, therefore one utility is used to both un-compress and extract the contents. If your system does not already have the unzip utility installed, you can get it from http://www.info-zip.org, where you can find detailed documentation on its use.

Other Packaging and Compression Formats

We've covered most of what you're going to see already. However, you're bound to run into other compression and packaging file formats. The FAQ for the Usenet newsgroup comp.compression is an invaluable resource for identifying these file formats and finding the appropriate utility to extract data from them. This FAQ can be found at `http://www.faqs.org/faqs/compression-faq/`.

Building Source Distributions

We've covered the basics of finding and installing prebuilt software. Now we're going to move into the realm of configuring, compiling, and installing software packages distributed in source-code format. With all the software that's available in precompiled form, why would you want to compile a package from source to begin with? Let's look at some reasons for building a package from source:

- The package that you are building is not available in binary form or is not available prebuilt for your operating system and hardware combination.

- Desirable (or undesirable) optional features of the package were disabled (or enabled) in the binary version of the package.

- You require the package to be installed in a different location than the binary package was configured for.

- Other software that the software relies on was installed on your system in a different location or is a different version than the binary package is expecting.

- Administrative decisions at your site require you to build software in accordance with certain specifications, to provide commonality across your systems' environments. (See Managing your Software Installations for more on this topic.)

- You may have an interest in learning how the software works (or why it doesn't work the way you expect it to) by looking at the source code. You might even want to change some behavior by doctoring the code.

- You trust your own actions slightly more than those of some nameless stranger when building software packages.

- Security. Even if you don't plan to review the source code line-by-line for security holes before compiling and installing it, there is a high value to having binaries that are compiled from a known source code base, when available. If/when concerns about security of the software arise, it will give you the edge in determining whether your systems are vulnerable if you know exactly which source code revision was built on your system. Likewise, if a patch is released for the source, you

17

OPEN SOURCE
SOFTWARE
MANAGEMENT

will be able to patch and recompile instead of depending on your compiled-binary source (that may or may not be in that business at that point in the future) to do it for your version of the operating system and hardware platform.

Requirements

Building Open Source software requires some basic skills and tools. Finding the tools is usually pretty straightforward, but finding the skills may require a bit more. Some skills you'll find covered elsewhere in this book, however, some come more from experience.

Skills

Building third-party software from scratch is a task that can be accomplished by even beginning system administrators or UNIX users. However, the more skills you have in your corner, the fewer problems you'll have. Here's a run down of some skill sets and how they come in handy:

- **Shell Scripting**—A basic knowledge of shell scripting, typically Bourne Shell, can help you through many software-building problems. You may be required to edit a shell script that configures the software package, or trace its execution to discover why it is failing.

- **Makefile Syntax**—Though a bit more on this is covered later in this chapter, a basic knowledge using the make utility, and their corresponding Makefiles can help you out.

- **C (and/or C++) programming**—Most Open Source software is written in C, and some is written in C++. When you run into a tight spot, be it finding a simple syntax error in someone's code, replacing a library function that doesn't exist on your particular system, or adding a feature to the program that it didn't have, knowing the language is a big win. Knowing it well will set you apart from the crowd.

- **UNIX systems programming**—This isn't language-specific, but it involves knowing how to program in the UNIX environment. It's important to be aware of how the bits of the UNIX system, such as pipes, sockets, and shared memory, work. The differences in implementation of features such as those that exist between UNIX variants can cause uncountable problems when using various pieces of Open Source software on different platforms. (A good book to read up on this topic is *Advanced Programming in the UNIX Environment*, by W. Richard Stevens (published by Addison-Wesley).

Software

In order to successfully build software from source code, your system will need certain tools installed. These turn the 'human readable' source code into executable machine code.

- **Compiler**—A compiler is a piece of software that takes source code (C, C++, Pascal, Fortran, and so on) and generates assembly language code (a mnemonic representation of your processor's machine code).

- **Assembler**—An assembler is a piece of software that, given assembly language code, generates a machine code object file from the assembly generated by the compiler.

- **Linker**—The linker is a piece of software that takes one or more pieces of object code and resolves references that they may make between one another and referenced function libraries.

- **make**—make is a utility that is used to manage the build process, by ensuring that compiles and links happen in the right order, with the right arguments, and so on.

These are the basics—in fact, a plethora of other smaller tools are part of the UNIX software-development environment. If you don't have a development environment on your system, continue reading the following sections; we'll discuss setting one up under Red Hat Linux 7.1 and SUN Solaris 8.

As far as setting up the development environment on Linux goes, the best way is to simply install a "development workstation," or something similar, at the time of first installation because all the development tools are available with the base operating system and require no special licenses. However, if you didn't install your system's development environment, check the Red Hat documentation to learn how to add these packages to your system.

You can set up a development environment under Solaris 8 in two ways. The first involves installing and purchasing a license for the Sun Forte developer kit. The Sun compilers are very capable and probably well worth the money. However, the GNU Compiler Collection for Solaris will serve most purposes related to building Open Source software found on the Net.

Before installing the GNU Compiler Collection, you need to make sure that your system also has the appropriate support tools installed, including the linker, header files, and so on. To do this, you should have installed your system with Developer System Support, Entire Distribution, or Entire Distribution Plus OEM Support. If your system was not installed with either of these software distributions, you will not be able to successfully

17

OPEN SOURCE
SOFTWARE
MANAGEMENT

compile programs, even using the GNU Compiler Collection, because it will be missing the critical support tools, header files, and libraries necessary for compilation. Refer to the Solaris documentation to install these packages on your system if they are not there already.

If these packages are on your system, you should have files such as /usr/ccs/bin/make, /usr/ccs/bin/ld, and /usr/ccs/bin/ar installed.

When you have all the appropriate packages installed, you may need to need to modify your environment slightly. For some reason, Solaris has tools such as make and ld located in the directory /usr/ccs/bin. For compiles to run successfully, this directory should be in your shell's **PATH**, **path**, or other variable that your shell has chosen to place its execution path in. In addition, you might want to verify that /usr/local/bin is also in the path because the GNU Compiler Collection will be installing itself there.

To install the GNU Compiler Collection, see the previous section, Installing Binary Packages, where the GCC package was used as an example. When it comes to choosing what version of GCC to use, you'll have to use your judgment: Read the release notes and act appropriately. The last thing that you want is to have difficulty building packages because the compiler had some nifty new feature or bug that caused your builds to fail or the program you built to malfunction in some hideous way.

Building a Software Package: OpenSSH

SSH is a tool that a Unix user or system administrator should be very familiar with. It is used to provide secure transport and authentication to other networked Unix systems. Here, we will build an Open Source variant of the tool as an example software build procedure.

Getting Started

Building software starts with getting the source code for it from "somewhere." This is sometimes a Web page and sometimes an FTP site—hopefully, it's only a quick Web search away. Earlier in this chapter, we mentioned some tools to help you find Open Source software, such as Freshmeat and Sourceforge. Quite a bit of software that's helpful is part of the GNU project, which you can always find at `ftp.gnu.org/pub/gnu` or one of the many mirrors of this site. Searching the Web for the project's main Web site is also a good way to find where to download the source, to check on the state of development of the project, and to find helpful hints regarding compilation and getting the program working on your system.

Our example project to build, compile, and install will be OpenSSH. OpenSSH is an Open Source implementation of the SSH protocol, used for remote access to UNIX machines. We've chosen OpenSSH for this example for two reasons. First, although it is a relatively complex piece of software, the build process is quite simple. Second, SSH is an important tool to use, and it should be the part of any UNIX system's software install. We'll be walking through building this on a Sun UltraSPARC-based system running Solaris 8 using the GNU Compiler Collection as our compiler. We'll assume that the system and environment have been prepared appropriately, with the compilers and appropriate Solaris development packages installed, and that the user's path has been modified to include the locations of the compilers and tools.

Getting and Unpacking the Software

First, we must get the source code. From doing some very simple research with a search engine—or by trying some random URLs on the browser—we can deduce that the project homepage for OpenSSH is http://www.openssh.org. After browsing the Web site and downloading the tarball from the most convenient FTP site, we're ready to go. First, unpack the software as described in the previous section dealing with tarballs, and enter the directory that it creates for itself:

LISTING **17.1** Unpacking OpenSSH

```
bfs1[8]$ gunzip -dc openssh-2.9p2.tar.gz | tar -xvf -
x openssh-2.9p2, 0 bytes, 0 tape blocks
x openssh-2.9p2/contrib, 0 bytes, 0 tape blocks
x openssh-2.9p2/contrib/SecurID.diff, 148757 bytes, 291 tape blocks
x openssh-2.9p2/contrib/README, 1983 bytes, 4 tape blocks
x openssh-2.9p2/contrib/caldera, 0 bytes, 0 tape blocks
x openssh-2.9p2/contrib/caldera/openssh.spec, 8487 bytes, 17 tape blocks
x openssh-2.9p2/contrib/caldera/ssh-host-keygen, 1210 bytes, 3 tape blocks
x openssh-2.9p2/contrib/caldera/sshd.init, 2923 bytes, 6 tape blocks
x openssh-2.9p2/contrib/caldera/sshd.pam, 410 bytes, 1 tape blocks
x openssh-2.9p2/contrib/chroot.diff, 1654 bytes, 4 tape blocks
x openssh-2.9p2/contrib/gnome-ssh-askpass.c, 4585 bytes, 9 tape blocks
x openssh-2.9p2/contrib/ssh-copy-id, 1144 bytes, 3 tape blocks
x openssh-2.9p2/contrib/ssh-copy-id.1, 2136 bytes, 5 tape blocks
x openssh-2.9p2/contrib/sshd.pam.freebsd, 183 bytes, 1 tape blocks
x openssh-2.9p2/contrib/sshd.pam.generic, 410 bytes, 1 tape blocks
x openssh-2.9p2/contrib/cygwin, 0 bytes, 0 tape blocks
x openssh-2.9p2/contrib/cygwin/README, 6355 bytes, 13 tape blocks
x openssh-2.9p2/contrib/cygwin/ssh-host-config, 11170 bytes, 22 tape blocks
x openssh-2.9p2/contrib/cygwin/ssh-user-config, 4657 bytes, 10 tape blocks
x openssh-2.9p2/contrib/hpux, 0 bytes, 0 tape blocks
x openssh-2.9p2/contrib/hpux/README, 1140 bytes, 3 tape blocks
x openssh-2.9p2/contrib/hpux/egd, 389 bytes, 1 tape blocks
x openssh-2.9p2/contrib/hpux/egd.rc, 2215 bytes, 5 tape blocks
x openssh-2.9p2/contrib/hpux/sshd, 123 bytes, 1 tape blocks
```

17

OPEN SOURCE
SOFTWARE
MANAGEMENT

```
x openssh-2.9p2/contrib/hpux/sshd.rc, 1974 bytes, 4 tape blocks
x openssh-2.9p2/contrib/redhat, 0 bytes, 0 tape blocks
x openssh-2.9p2/contrib/redhat/openssh.spec, 11353 bytes, 23 tape blocks
...
x openssh-2.9p2/ssh-agent.0, 4627 bytes, 10 tape blocks
x openssh-2.9p2/ssh-keygen.0, 8264 bytes, 17 tape blocks
x openssh-2.9p2/ssh-keyscan.0, 2766 bytes, 6 tape blocks
x openssh-2.9p2/ssh.0, 46145 bytes, 91 tape blocks
x openssh-2.9p2/sshd.0, 43873 bytes, 86 tape blocks
x openssh-2.9p2/sftp-server.0, 819 bytes, 2 tape blocks
x openssh-2.9p2/sftp.0, 4351 bytes, 9 tape blocks
bfs1[9]$ cd openssh-2.9p2
```

After entering the directory, we're going to check around and see if there's a README file or some other file that obviously might contain installation instructions, and we'll read them with our favorite text viewer. After reading the INSTALL file, we know that we also need to have working copies of OpenSSL and zlib installed. The configuration script will notify you if these libraries aren't installed. If you don't have them, you've got two choices at this point: Search the Sun Freeware site for binary packages, or visit the Web sites listed in the INSTALL file and build them yourself.

Configuring the Source Tree

The next step in building the package is to run the configuration script. A great percentage of the packages that you will run into use GNU Autoconf to assist the builder in configuring the makefiles, headers, and other such files for the specifics of their system. In addition, the script takes arguments to adjust specifics about the package, such as where it is to be installed or what special features will be enabled. Although these also are documented in OpenSSL's INSTALL file, a --help argument to configure displays each option, including a brief description. Let's run that now:

LISTING 17.2 Getting Help from OpenSSH's Configuration Script

```
bfs1[10]$ ./configure --help
Usage: configure [options] [host]
Options: [defaults in brackets after descriptions]
Configuration:
  --cache-file=FILE      cache test results in FILE
  --help                 print this message
  --no-create            do not create output files
  --quiet, --silent      do not print 'checking...' messages
  --version              print the version of autoconf that created configure
Directory and file names:
  --prefix=PREFIX        install architecture-independent files in PREFIX
                         [/usr/local]
  --exec-prefix=EPREFIX  install architecture-dependent files in EPREFIX
                         [same as prefix]
```

```
    --bindir=DIR              user executables in DIR [EPREFIX/bin]
    --sbindir=DIR             system admin executables in DIR [EPREFIX/sbin]
    --libexecdir=DIR          program executables in DIR [EPREFIX/libexec]
    --datadir=DIR             read-only architecture-independent data in DIR
                              [PREFIX/share]
    --sysconfdir=DIR          read-only single-machine data in DIR [PREFIX/etc]
    --sharedstatedir=DIR      modifiable architecture-independent data in DIR
                              [PREFIX/com]
    --localstatedir=DIR       modifiable single-machine data in DIR [PREFIX/var]
    --libdir=DIR              object code libraries in DIR [EPREFIX/lib]
    --includedir=DIR          C header files in DIR [PREFIX/include]
    --oldincludedir=DIR       C header files for non-gcc in DIR [/usr/include]
    --infodir=DIR             info documentation in DIR [PREFIX/info]
    --mandir=DIR              man documentation in DIR [PREFIX/man]
    --srcdir=DIR              find the sources in DIR [configure dir or ..]
    --program-prefix=PREFIX   prepend PREFIX to installed program names
    --program-suffix=SUFFIX   append SUFFIX to installed program names
    --program-transform-name=PROGRAM
                              run sed PROGRAM on installed program names
Host type:
    --build=BUILD             configure for building on BUILD [BUILD=HOST]
    --host=HOST               configure for HOST [guessed]
    --target=TARGET           configure for TARGET [TARGET=HOST]
Features and packages:
    --disable-FEATURE         do not include FEATURE (same as --enable-FEATURE=no)
    --enable-FEATURE[=ARG]    include FEATURE [ARG=yes]
    --with-PACKAGE[=ARG]      use PACKAGE [ARG=yes]
    --without-PACKAGE         do not use PACKAGE (same as --with-PACKAGE=no)
    --x-includes=DIR          X include files are in DIR
    --x-libraries=DIR         X library files are in DIR
--enable and --with options recognized:
    --with-osfsia             Enable Digital Unix SIA
    --with-cflags             Specify additional flags to pass to compiler
    --with-cppflags           Specify additional flags to pass to preprocessor
    --with-ldflags            Specify additional flags to pass to linker
    --with-libs               Specify additional libraries to link with
    --with-pcre               Override built in regex library with pcre
    --with-skey=PATH           Enable S/Key support
    --with-tcp-wrappers       Enable tcpwrappers support
    --with-pam                Enable PAM support
    --with-ssl-dir=PATH       Specify path to OpenSSL installation
    --with-kerberos4=PATH     Enable Kerberos 4 support
    --with-afs=PATH           Enable AFS support
    --with-rsh=PATH           Specify path to remote shell program
    --with-xauth=PATH         Specify path to xauth program
    --with-random=FILE        read entropy from FILE (default=/dev/urandom)
    --with-prngd-port=PORT    read entropy from PRNGD/EGD localhost:PORT
    --with-prngd-socket=FILE  read entropy from PRNGD/EGD socket FILE
(default=/var/run/egd-pool)
    --with-mantype=man|cat|doc  Set man page type
    --with-md5-passwords      Enable use of MD5 passwords
```

17

OPEN SOURCE
SOFTWARE
MANAGEMENT

```
--without-shadow        Disable shadow password support
--with-ipaddr-display   Use ip address instead of hostname in $DISPLAY
--with-default-path=PATH Specify default $PATH environment for server
--with-ipv4-default     Use IPv4 by connections unless '-6' specified
--with-4in6             Check for and convert IPv4 in IPv6 mapped addresses
--with-bsd-auth         Enable BSD auth support
--enable-suid-ssh       Install ssh as suid root (default)
--disable-suid-ssh      Install ssh without suid bit
--with-pid-dir=PATH     Specify location of ssh.pid file
--disable-lastlog       disable use of lastlog even if detected [no]
--disable-utmp          disable use of utmp even if detected [no]
--disable-utmpx         disable use of utmpx even if detected [no]
--disable-wtmp          disable use of wtmp even if detected [no]
--disable-wtmpx         disable use of wtmpx even if detected [no]
--disable-libutil       disable use of libutil (login() etc.) [no]
--disable-pututline     disable use of pututline() etc. ([uw]tmp) [no]
--disable-pututxline    disable use of pututxline() etc. ([uw]tmpx) [no]
--with-lastlog=FILE|DIR specify lastlog location [common locations]
--with-entropy-timeout  Specify entropy gathering command timeout (msec)
```

As you can see, the configuration script takes quite a few options. Later in this chapter, we'll look at some of the more commonly modified options; however, for now, one looks particularly interesting to us. `--with-pam` enables support of Pluggable Authentication Modules under Solaris, which you might have read about elsewhere in this book. We'll assume that we can take advantage of these on our system, and we'll begin to run configure with these enabled:

LISTING 17.3 Running OpenSSH's Configuration Script

```
bfs1[11]$ ./configure --with-pam
creating cache ./config.cache
checking for gcc... gcc
checking whether the C compiler (gcc  ) works... yes
checking whether the C compiler (gcc  ) is a cross-compiler... no
checking whether we are using GNU C... yes
checking whether gcc accepts -g... yes
checking host system type... sparc-sun-solaris2.8
checking whether byte ordering is bigendian... yes
checking how to run the C preprocessor... gcc -E
checking for ranlib... ranlib
checking for a BSD compatible install... ./install-sh -c
checking for ar... /usr/ccs/bin/ar
checking for perl5... no
checking for perl... /usr/local/bin/perl
checking for ent... no
checking for filepriv... no
checking for bash... no
checking for ksh... /usr/bin/ksh
checking for sh... (cached) /usr/bin/ksh
```

Open Source Software Management

CHAPTER 17

739

17

OPEN SOURCE
SOFTWARE
MANAGEMENT

```
checking for login... /usr/bin/login
checking for inline... inline
checking for obsolete utmp and wtmp in solaris2.x... yes
checking for yp_match in -lnsl... yes
checking for main in -lsocket... yes
checking for innetgr in -lrpc... no
checking for getspnam in -lgen... yes
checking for deflate in -lz... no
configure: error: *** zlib missing - please install first or check config.log
***
bfs1[12]$
```

Looks like there's a problem! Did you really make sure that you had zlib installed?

We created this error on purpose so that you can see how the GNU configuration script tends to report errors. We've fixed the problem, and we'll try again.

LISTING 17.4 Running OpenSSH's Configuration Script, Again

```
bfs1[12]$ ./configure --with-pam
loading cache ./config.cache
checking for gcc... gcc
checking whether the C compiler (gcc  ) works... yes
checking whether the C compiler (gcc  ) is a cross-compiler... no
checking whether we are using GNU C... yes
checking whether gcc accepts -g... yes
checking host system type... sparc-sun-solaris2.8
checking whether byte ordering is bigendian... yes
checking how to run the C preprocessor... gcc -E
checking for ranlib... ranlib
checking for a BSD compatible install... ./install-sh -c
[Lots of configure output deleted]
creating ./config.status
creating Makefile
creating openbsd-compat/Makefile
creating ssh_prng_cmds
creating config.h

OpenSSH has been configured with the following options:
               User binaries: /usr/local/bin
             System binaries: /usr/local/sbin
          Configuration files: /usr/local/etc
            Askpass program: /usr/local/libexec/ssh-askpass
               Manual pages: /usr/local/man/manX
                   PID file: /var/run
      sshd default user PATH: /usr/bin:/bin:/usr/sbin:/sbin:/usr/local/bin
   Random number collection: Builtin (timeout 200)
             Manpage format: man
                PAM support: yes
           KerberosIV support: no
```

```
             AFS support: no
           S/KEY support: no
    TCP Wrappers support: no
    MD5 password support: no
IP address in $DISPLAY hack: no
   Use IPv4 by default hack: no
     Translate v4 in v6 hack: no

             Host: sparc-sun-solaris2.8
         Compiler: gcc
   Compiler flags: -g -O2 -Wall
Preprocessor flags:  -I/usr/local/include
     Linker flags:  -L/usr/local/lib -R/usr/local/lib
        Libraries: -lpam -ldl -lz -lsocket -lnsl  -lgen -lcrypto
```

PAM is enabled. You may need to install a PAM control file for sshd, otherwise password authentication may fail. Example PAM control files can be found in the contrib/ subdirectory

WARNING: you are using the builtin random number collection service. Please read WARNING.RNG and request that your OS vendor includes /dev/random in future versions of their OS.

Building the Software

You're now ready to type make to build the package:

bfs1[24]$ make

Quite a bit of output is generated while make runs—too much for us to include it all here. This particular invocation of it finished up with this output:

LISTING 17.5 The End of a Successful Build of OpenSSH

```
gcc -g -O2 -Wall -I. -I.  -I/usr/local/include -DETCDIR=\"/usr/local/etc\"  -
D_PATH_SSH_PROGRAM=\"/usr/local/bin/ssh\"  -
D_PATH_SSH_ASKPASS_DEFAULT=\"/usr/local/libexec/ssh-askpass\"  -
D_PATH_SFTP_SERVER=\"/usr/local/libexec/sftp-server\"  -
D_PATH_SSH_PIDDIR=\"/var/run\" -DHAVE_CONFIG_H -c sftp-int.c
gcc -g -O2 -Wall -I. -I.  -I/usr/local/include -DETCDIR=\"/usr/local/etc\"  -
D_PATH_SSH_PROGRAM=\"/usr/local/bin/ssh\"  -
D_PATH_SSH_ASKPASS_DEFAULT=\"/usr/local/libexec/ssh-askpass\"  -
D_PATH_SFTP_SERVER=\"/usr/local/libexec/sftp-server\"  -
D_PATH_SSH_PIDDIR=\"/var/run\" -DHAVE_CONFIG_H -c sftp-glob.c
gcc -o sftp sftp.o sftp-client.o sftp-common.o sftp-int.o sftp-glob.o scp-
common.o -L. -Lopenbsd-compat/  -L/usr/local/lib -R/usr/local/lib -lssh -
lopenbsd-compat -lpam -ldl -lz -lsocket -lnsl  -lgen -lcrypto
bfs1[24]$
```

If it had finished up with an error, however, we'd have to do some further troubleshooting, which we'll cover later in this chapter. Some packages also have a test suite that is

documented in their INSTALL or README file, which you can run to verify that the
compilation process produced a workable application or library.

Installing the Software

Now we install OpenSSH. To do this, you probably will have to use su (or sudo) to get
root privileges so that it can be installed to the appropriate place in your filesystem. (You
weren't building this package as root, right?).

To install OpenSSH, we run make install:

LISTING 17.6 Installing OpenSSH

```
bfs1[3]# make install
./mkinstalldirs /usr/local/bin
./mkinstalldirs /usr/local/sbin
./mkinstalldirs /usr/local/man
./mkinstalldirs /usr/local/man/man1
./mkinstalldirs /usr/local/man/man8
mkdir /usr/local/man/man8
./mkinstalldirs /usr/local/libexec
mkdir /usr/local/libexec
./install-sh -c -m 04711 -s ssh /usr/local/bin/ssh
./install-sh -c -m 0755 -s scp /usr/local/bin/scp
./install-sh -c -m 0755 -s ssh-add /usr/local/bin/ssh-add
[output snipped]
        if [ -f /usr/local/etc/ssh_host_rsa_key ] ; then \
                echo "/usr/local/etc/ssh_host_rsa_key already exists, skipping."
➥; \
        else \
                ./ssh-keygen -t rsa -f /usr/local/etc/ssh_host_rsa_key -N "" ; \
        fi ; \
fi ;
Generating public/private rsa1 key pair.
Your identification has been saved in /usr/local/etc/ssh_host_key.
Your public key has been saved in /usr/local/etc/ssh_host_key.pub.
The key fingerprint is:
93:52:93:7c:bf:5a:51:75:bf:17:39:b1:3b:c7:83:50 root@bfs1.afs.umbc.edu
Generating public/private dsa key pair.
Your identification has been saved in /usr/local/etc/ssh_host_dsa_key.
Your public key has been saved in /usr/local/etc/ssh_host_dsa_key.pub.
The key fingerprint is:
29:23:50:0e:55:18:31:ee:86:39:88:df:a2:9c:17:73 root@bfs1.afs.umbc.edu
Generating public/private rsa key pair.
Your identification has been saved in /usr/local/etc/ssh_host_rsa_key.
Your public key has been saved in /usr/local/etc/ssh_host_rsa_key.pub.
The key fingerprint is:
21:4d:33:ce:36:ed:a0:c0:3a:b1:37:2a:3c:c7:9c:e0 root@bfs1.afs.umbc.edu
bfs1[4]#
```

17

**OPEN SOURCE
SOFTWARE
MANAGEMENT**

OpenSSH has now been configured, built, and installed. Now all that's left to do is use it!

Advanced Software Configuration

Building OpenSSH looked relatively easy, didn't it? If your operating environment tends to be "standard," you'll find that a good percentage of the software packages will be as easy as ./configure; make; make install, which, in many respects is almost as easy as finding and downloading a prebuilt version of a package. It takes a little longer, but it feels good knowing that you did something yourself. However, if you're one of those people who wishes to build software from scratch, you're probably going to be making some changes to the default configuration, and the following section will help guide you in this. We'll cover the ins and outs of configuring software that uses GNU configure, and we'll also touch base with some other software configuration methods that you might run into, such as editing makefiles by hand and dealing with imakefiles and xmkmf, usually found in X Window software packages.

Configuration with GNU Configure

The configure scripts that you see on most software packages today are generated by another software package called GNU AutoConf (`http://www.gnu.org/software/autoconf/autoconf.html`). Autoconf is, without a doubt, the single most helpful tool that has been developed for managing the build configuration of Open Source software. Editing makefiles and C header files before building software was standard practice until GNU Autoconf was integrated into many of the popular software packages in the mid-1990s. Some applications, such as Perl and Elm, were known to have well-thought-out "automatic" configuration scripts, but this was the exception and not the rule. Today, all that has changed.

Standard GNU Configure Options

Almost all, if not all, configure scripts generated with AutoConf take some standard options. Here are just a few that are commonly used:

TABLE 17.1   Standard GNU Configure Options

`--prefix=<path>` and `--exec-prefix=<path>`	These set the prefix to the path where architecture-independent and architecture-dependent files are to be installed. If you set prefix without setting exec-prefix, exec-prefix will be set to your setting for prefix. Usually both of these are set to /usr/local, so files are installed in /usr/local/bin, /usr/local/lib, and so on. Running configure with ./configure -prefix=/opt places files in /opt/bin, /opt/lib, and so on.

TABLE 17.1 continued

`--sysconfdir=<path>`	This sets the directory where system-specific configuration files are stored. If you share the location of your third-party software via NFS or some other method, the default of placing these in <prefix>/etc (such as /usr/local/etc) might not be to your liking.
`-x-libraries=<path>` and `-x-includes=<path>`	These tell configure where to look for your X Window System libraries and include files, respectively. configure is pretty good at finding these on most systems without help, but if it can't find them, or if you want to build your package against a different build of the X Window System, use these options.
Various `--with-<option>` and `--with-<option>=<path>` options	These enable or disable use of features within a package. The `--with` options tend to refer to features that require linking with some other package, the path to which can be optionally specified. You should read the documentation that came with the package on the specifics of how to use these options.
Various `--enable-<option>` and `--disable-<option>` options	These turn on or off various features of a package.

When configuring packages that require other installed packages, you might find that it cannot detect their location without some hints. These hints might be provided using a `–with-<package>=` option.

Using Environment Variables

configure also responds to the setting of some key environment variables. In most instances, they can be used for assisting configure in finding key libraries, such as those that might not be installed in a regular place. For example, a site might have its Kerberos 5 install located in a directory other than /usr/local—say, /usr/k5. Although a correctly behaved configure script should take this information in a `--with-kerberos5=` argument, some do not. You can suggest that configure set the flags and linker, compiler, and pre-processor use by setting LDFLAGS, CFLAGS, and CPPFLAGS, respectively. If you are using csh or a derivative and you want to use the Kerberos in /usr/k5, you could do this:

17

OPEN SOURCE SOFTWARE MANAGEMENT

```
bfs1[364]$ setenv CFLAGS -I/usr/k5/include
bfs1[365]$ setenv CPPFLAGS -I/usr/k5/include
bfs1[367]$ setenv LDFLAGS -L/usr/k5/lib
```

If the package that you're doing this for uses shared libraries, you also might want to instruct the linker to prepend the location of these libraries to the runtime library path. For Solaris, you would use this:

```
bfs1[368]$ setenv LDFLAGS "-L/usr/k5/lib -R/usr/k5/lib"
```

For Linux, using the GNU compiler and linker to set the LDFLAGS setting is slightly different:

```
tyler[369]$ setenv LDFLAGS "-L/usr/k5/lib -Wl,-rpath /usr/k5/lib"
```

If the package that you're compiling uses C++, the variable CXXFLAGS might need to be set, usually to the same setting as CFLAGS.

Environment variables also can be used to specify which compiler is used to build the package. In most cases, configure will seek out the "nearest" copy of the GNU Compiler Collection and use it for all builds. Usually, this is fine. However, in a few situations this might not be the best course of action. Some packages are known to have "issues" with the GNU compilers, so using your vendor's provided compilers (usually called cc and c++ for the C and C++ compilers, respectively) might be desirable. To do so, use the CC and CXX environment variables, like this:

```
bfs1[420]$ setenv CC cc
bfs2[421]$ setenv CXX c++
```

Another instance in which you might want to use these same variables is to select a specific instance or version of a compiler. Red Hat Linux, for example, comes with a version of GCC already installed. But, consider that you've built the latest and greatest version in your /usr/local tree and are just itching to try it out. So, you set your variables to use your build of GCC like this:

```
tyler[110]$ setenv CC /usr/local/bin/gcc
tyler[111]$ setenv CXX /usr/local/bin/g++
```

> **NOTE**
>
> These variables should be set before running configure for the first time. If you set them after running configure once, run 'make distclean' to clear any files that have been configured without the environment variables set.

Troubleshooting

If you still can't get your configure to run properly, it's time for some troubleshooting.
Here are a few helpful tips:

- **Read the instructions**—Nobody seems to do this, myself included. I could have
  saved countless hours if I just did what the authors told me to do.

- **Check the package's FAQ**—Most packages have a frequently asked questions list.
  The solution to your problem (or potential lack thereof) might be listed there, plain
  as day. In addition, you may wish to do a general Web search, or look for mailing
  list archives about the package. Most of the time, someone else has had your problem too.

- **If you're trying to use special features, don't**—If you've enabled nondefault
  options when running configure, try it without them. A requirement of that feature
  might not be installed correctly, or it might not work right on your platform.

- **Check the config.log file**—As configure runs, it keeps a record of its output in the
  file config.log. Any errors that configure encounters while "doing its thing," which
  usually consists of doing compiles of sample programs to verify whether a library
  or function exists on your system, will be logged here. You'll see not only the
  error, but also what it was trying. This might direct you to alter your configure
  options or add flags to the compilers using the environment variables discussed
  previously.

- **Remove the config.cache**—configure "caches" the results of its tests in a file
  named config.cache. If you have added environment variables or installed other
  packages between configure attempts, your changes might not be getting picked
  up. Just delete this file, and configure will re-create it when run again. Running
  'make distclean' accomplishes this, along with cleaning up other files that may
  have been left behind.

- **Start from scratch**—If you just can't get it to work, deleting the package's source
  tree and starting from scratch might help. Maybe some file was deleted accidentally, or a configure run might have left some badness in the source tree.
  Sometimes just starting from scratch can get everything moving for you again.

- **Mail the author**—When you've exhausted all your other options, seek help.
  This should be covered on the package's home page, README file, or other documentation.

Edit the Makefile

Although it's less common today than in years past, still quite a few packages are being distributed which have you edit certain files, such as their makefile or header files, to get them to build on your operating system or to enable certain features. Authors tend to document the changes that you need to make in a makefile or header file quite well. However, before jumping in and editing, you should have a few pointers.

The make program is a picky beast, at best. One of it's oddities is that it treats tab characters and spaces differently; yes, the meaning of one blank empty chunk of a line could be different than another. This makes cutting and pasting in certain editors a bit difficult. At some time, everyone will make a mistake and put a tab/space where a space/tab should have been in a makefile, and the error you get will be similar to this

```
make: file 'Makefile' line 192: Must be a separator (: or ::) for rules (bu39)
```

or even something like this:

```
make: Fatal error in reader: Makefile, line 195: Unexpected end of line seen
```

GNU Make (which is shipped with Red Hat Linux) seems to be less picky than the make program distributed with most UNIX variants.

Another gotcha with make is that it looks for multiple files when looking for direction. Although most people create makefiles named Makefile, make also looks for makefiles named makefile (lowercase *M*) and, in fact, actually picks the lowercase-M makefile before the uppercase-M Makefile. This can be amazingly annoying if you've been editing a file called Makefile and you can't seem to figure out why none of your changes ever get made because make is happily processing makefile.

One of make's jobs is to keep track of dependencies and recompile something if a file that it depends on changes. This can bite you because many programmers do not make the makefile itself a dependency on its targets.[3] This causes a problem when you interrupt a build, make a change to the makefile, and then restart the build. If the makefile itself is not listed as a dependency, objects compiled before the edit might have been built differently than objects afterward, causing your program not to compile or, worse, to malfunction after installation. The same goes for header files that contain configuration information. The trick to learn here is to run a make clean after making any such changes; this will delete any objects that have been compiled so far.[4]

Using xmkmf: Imakefiles

The basics: xmkmf is a tool used to turn an imakefile into a makefile, which can then be used in conjunction with make to build the project.

Let's take one step back. xmkmf is a shell script that runs the program imake, which processes certain configuration and template files in addition to the imakefile and generates a file that can be processed with make. The configuration files that imake uses describe, using C preprocessor syntax, the build environment of the machine, including compilers used, libraries to be linked to, and directories to be used. The imake template files are used to provide a basis for the makefile that is to be generated. Finally, the imakefile describes the components that make up the build and how elements of the templates and configuration files are to be utilized. Although imake was designed to be a tool to help with software portability, its most popular use is as part of the X Window System and other X-based applications. The script, xmkmf, is specific to using imake in conjunction with the X Window System because it directs imake to use the template and configuration files installed along with your system's X installation.

Commonly, xmkmf is used with the -a option. After it has used imake to build the makefile in the current directory, -a causes xmkmf to do the following:

```
make Makefiles
make includes
make depend
```

This should put the build tree in a state in which an invocation of make will build your application.

Some applications have editable options in their imakefiles. The same precautions in editing a makefile pertain to an imakefile. Here is an example session building the application xkeycaps on a Red Hat 7.1 system:

After running 'xmkmf', the build process is started by running 'make'.

LISTING 17.7: Configuring and building xkeycaps

```
tyler[310]% xmkmf -a

imake -DUseInstalled -I/usr/X11R6/lib/X11/config
make Makefiles
make: Nothing to be done for `Makefiles'.
make includes
make: Nothing to be done for `includes'.
make depend
gccmakedep -- -I./kbds  -I/usr/X11R6/include  -Dlinux -D__i386__ -
➡D_POSIX_C_SOURCE=199309L -D_POSIX_SOURCE -D_XOPEN_SOURCE -D_BSD_SOURCE -
➡D_SVID_SOURCE     -DFUNCPROTO=15 -DNARROWPROTO    --
./xkeycaps.c  /KbdWidget.c  ./KeyWidget.c ./info.c  ./actions.c
./commands.c ./guess.c ./all-kbds.c  ./sunOS.c  ./hpux.c  ./xtrap.c
tyler[311]% make
```

```
gcc -O2 -march=i386 -mcpu=i686    -I./kbds   -I/usr/X11R6/include   -Dlinux -
➥D__i386__  -
D_POSIX_C_SOURCE=199309L -D_POSIX_SOURCE -D_XOPEN_SOURCE -D_BSD_SOURCE -
➥D_SVID_SOURCE            -
DFUNCPROTO=15 -DNARROWPROTO         -c -o xkeycaps.o xkeycaps.c
gcc -O2 -march=i386 -mcpu=i686    -I./kbds   -I/usr/X11R6/include   -Dlinux -
➥D__i386__  -D_POSIX_C_SOURCE=199309L -
D_POSIX_SOURCE -D_XOPEN_SOURCE -D_BSD_SOURCE -D_SVID_SOURCE        -
DFUNCPROTO=15 -DNARROWPROTO         -c -o KbdWidget.o KbdWidget.c
[ output trimmed … ]
gcc -O2 -march=i386 -mcpu=i686    -I./kbds   -I/usr/X11R6/include   -Dlinux -
➥D__i386__  -
D_POSIX_C_SOURCE=199309L -D_POSIX_SOURCE -D_XOPEN_SOURCE -D_BSD_SOURCE -
➥D_SVID_SOURCE            -
DFUNCPROTO=15 -DNARROWPROTO         -c -o all-kbds.o all-kbds.c
rm -f xkeycaps
gcc -o xkeycaps -O2 -march=i386 -mcpu=i686      -L/usr/X11R6/lib ./xkeycaps.o
➥./KbdWidget.o
./KeyWidget.o ./info.o       ./actions.o ./commands.o        ./guess.o ./all-
kbds.o                 -lXaw -lXt -lSM -lICE  -lXmu -lXt -lSM -lICE -lXext -
lX11 -lXext -lX11
tyler[312]%
```

Managing Multiplatform Builds

If you manage multiple types of machines—differing operating systems, operating system versions, or architectures—and need to keep the same software packages built on each, this is for you. Building software for different platforms from the same source tree has quite a few advantages—most obviously, the savings in disk space. However, it becomes even more beneficial to build against a common source tree when local modifications or customizations are made directly to the source code or configuration files.

Using GNU Make/GNU Configure

When using GNU Make and GNU Configure, many packages can be configured and built in a separate directory from where the source code lives. In this mode, configure generates a directory structure that mirrors the source tree's structure, placing makefiles and other configuration related files in their appropriate places without writing to the actual source tree. When the build process takes place, the VPATH feature of GNU Make is relied upon to "find" the needed files in the source tree.

Here's an example of how it all works. First, we're going to build GNU Tar (which we've built before) under Red Hat Linux, and then we'll build it for Solaris 8 from the same source tree. The directory where we are building this is available on both our Linux system and our Solaris system via NFS (other network-aware filesystems such as AFS would work, too).

```
tyler[9]% gunzip -dc tar-1.13.tar.gz | tar -xf -
```

Next, we'll make a directory to build the package for Linux, and we'll make it our current directory:

```
tyler[10]% mkdir tar-1.13.linux
tyler[11]% cd tar-1.13.linux
```

Now we run configure. We need to run the configure script from the directory that we unpacked the distribution into:

LISTING 17.8 Configuring GNU Tar

```
tyler[12]% ../tar-1.13/configure

creating cache ./config.cache
checking host system type... i686-pc-linux-gnu
checking for a BSD compatible install... /usr/bin/install -c
checking whether build environment is sane... yes
checking whether make sets ${MAKE}... yes
checking for working aclocal... found
checking for working autoconf... found
checking for working automake... found
checking for working autoheader... found
checking for working makeinfo... found
checking for gcc... gcc
checking whether the C compiler (gcc  ) works... yes
checking whether the C compiler (gcc  ) is a cross-compiler... no
checking whether we are using GNU C... yes
checking whether gcc accepts -g... yes
...
creating lib/Makefile
creating m4/Makefile
creating po/Makefile.in
creating scripts/Makefile
creating src/Makefile
creating tests/Makefile
creating tests/preset
creating config.h
```

Now we can run make. You need to make sure that you're running GNU Make, or things will probably not work right. Because we're building on Linux, that's what we've got.

```
tyler[13]% make
```

Our program should build.

LISTING 17.9 Compiling GNU Tar

```
gmake  all-recursive
make[1]: Entering directory `/home/banz/book/tar-1.13.linux'
Making all in doc
```

17

OPEN SOURCE
SOFTWARE
MANAGEMENT

```
make[2]: Entering directory `/home/banz/book/tar-1.13.linux/doc'
make[2]: Leaving directory `/home/banz/book/tar-1.13.linux/doc'
Making all in lib
make[2]: Entering directory `/home/banz/book/tar-1.13.linux/lib'
gcc -DHAVE_CONFIG_H -I. -I../../tar-1.13/lib -I.. -I.. -I../../tar-1.13/lib -
➥I../intl     -g -O2 -c
../../tar-1.13/lib/addext.c
gcc -DHAVE_CONFIG_H -I. -I../../tar-1.13/lib -I.. -I.. -I../../tar-1.13/lib -
➥I../intl     -g -O2 -c
../../tar-1.13/lib/argmatch.c
gcc -DHAVE_CONFIG_H -I. -I../../tar-1.13/lib -I.. -I.. -I../../tar-1.13/lib -
➥I../intl     -g -O2 -c
../../tar-1.13/lib/backupfile.c
gcc -DHAVE_CONFIG_H -I. -I../../tar-1.13/lib -I.. -I.. -I../../tar-1.13/lib -
➥I../intl     -g -O2 -c
../../tar-1.13/lib/basename.c
gcc -DHAVE_CONFIG_H -I. -I../../tar-1.13/lib -I.. -I.. -I../../tar-1.13/lib -
➥I../intl     -g -O2 -c
../../tar-1.13/lib/error.c
gcc -DHAVE_CONFIG_H -I. -I../../tar-1.13/lib -I.. -I.. -I../../tar-1.13/lib -
➥I../intl     -g -O2 -c
../../tar-1.13/lib/exclude.c
gcc -DHAVE_CONFIG_H -I. -I../../tar-1.13/lib -I.. -I.. -I../../tar-1.13/lib -
➥I../intl     -g -O2 -c
../../tar-1.13/lib/full-write.c
gcc -DHAVE_CONFIG_H -I. -I../../tar-1.13/lib -I.. -I.. -I../../tar-1.13/lib -
➥I../intl     -g -O2 -c
../../tar-1.13/lib/getdate.c
gcc -DHAVE_CONFIG_H -I. -I../../tar-1.13/lib -I.. -I.. -I../../tar-1.13/lib -
➥I../intl     -g -O2 -c
../../tar-1.13/lib/getopt.c
gcc -DHAVE_CONFIG_H -I. -I../../tar-1.13/lib -I.. -I.. -I../../tar-1.13/lib -
➥I../intl     -g -O2 -c
../../tar-1.13/lib/getopt1.c
gcc -DHAVE_CONFIG_H -I. -I../../tar-1.13/lib -I.. -I.. -I../../tar-1.13/lib -
➥I../intl     -g -O2 -c
../../tar-1.13/lib/modechange.c
gcc -DHAVE_CONFIG_H -I. -I../../tar-1.13/lib -I.. -I.. -I../../tar-1.13/lib -
➥I../intl     -g -O2 -c
../../tar-1.13/lib/msleep.c
gcc -DHAVE_CONFIG_H -I. -I../../tar-1.13/lib -I.. -I.. -I../../tar-1.13/lib -
➥I../intl     -g -O2 -c
../../tar-1.13/lib/quotearg.c
gcc -DHAVE_CONFIG_H -I. -I../../tar-1.13/lib -I.. -I.. -I../../tar-1.13/lib -
➥I../intl     -g -O2 -c
../../tar-1.13/lib/safe-read.c
gcc -DHAVE_CONFIG_H -I. -I../../tar-1.13/lib -I.. -I.. -I../../tar-1.13/lib -
➥I../intl     -g -O2 -c
../../tar-1.13/lib/xgetcwd.c
gcc -DHAVE_CONFIG_H -I. -I../../tar-1.13/lib -I.. -I.. -I../../tar-1.13/lib -
➥I../intl     -g -O2 -c
```

Open Source Software Management

CHAPTER 17

751

17

OPEN SOURCE
SOFTWARE
MANAGEMENT

```
../../tar-1.13/lib/xmalloc.c
gcc -DHAVE_CONFIG_H -I. -I../../tar-1.13/lib -I.. -I.. -I../../tar-1.13/lib -
➥I../intl    -g -O2 -c
../../tar-1.13/lib/xstrdup.c
gcc -DHAVE_CONFIG_H -I. -I../../tar-1.13/lib -I.. -I.. -I../../tar-1.13/lib -
➥I../intl    -g -O2 -c
../../tar-1.13/lib/xstrtol.c
gcc -DHAVE_CONFIG_H -I. -I../../tar-1.13/lib -I.. -I.. -I../../tar-1.13/lib -
➥I../intl    -g -O2 -c
../../tar-1.13/lib/xstrtoul.c
gcc -DHAVE_CONFIG_H -I. -I../../tar-1.13/lib -I.. -I.. -I../../tar-1.13/lib -
➥I../intl    -g -O2 -c
../../tar-1.13/lib/xstrtoumax.c
rm -f libtar.a
ar cru libtar.a addext.o argmatch.o backupfile.o basename.o error.o exclude.o
full-write.o getdate.o getopt.o getopt1.o modechange.o msleep.o quotearg.o safe-
read.o xgetcwd.o xmalloc.o xstrdup.o xstrtol.o xstrtoul.o xstrtoumax.o
ranlib libtar.a
make[2]: Leaving directory `/home/banz/book/tar-1.13.linux/lib'
Making all in intl
make[2]: Entering directory `/home/banz/book/tar-1.13.linux/intl'
make[2]: Nothing to be done for `all'.
make[2]: Leaving directory `/home/banz/book/tar-1.13.linux/intl'
Making all in m4
make[2]: Entering directory `/home/banz/book/tar-1.13.linux/m4'
make[2]: Nothing to be done for `all'.
make[2]: Leaving directory `/home/banz/book/tar-1.13.linux/m4'
Making all in src
make[2]: Entering directory `/home/banz/book/tar-1.13.linux/src'
gcc -DLOCALEDIR=\"/usr/local/share/locale\" -DHAVE_CONFIG_H -I.. -I../intl -
➥I../../tar-1.13/lib    -g -O2 -c ../../tar-1.13/src/arith.c
gcc -DLOCALEDIR=\"/usr/local/share/locale\" -DHAVE_CONFIG_H -I.. -I../intl -
➥I../../tar-1.13/lib    -g -O2 -c ../../tar-1.13/src/buffer.c
gcc -DLOCALEDIR=\"/usr/local/share/locale\" -DHAVE_CONFIG_H -I.. -I../intl -
➥I../../tar-1.13/lib    -g -O2 -c ../../tar-1.13/src/compare.c
gcc -DLOCALEDIR=\"/usr/local/share/locale\" -DHAVE_CONFIG_H -I.. -I../intl -
➥I../../tar-1.13/lib    -g -O2 -c ../../tar-1.13/src/create.c
gcc -DLOCALEDIR=\"/usr/local/share/locale\" -DHAVE_CONFIG_H -I.. -I../intl -
➥I../../tar-1.13/lib    -g -O2 -c ../../tar-1.13/src/delete.c
gcc -DLOCALEDIR=\"/usr/local/share/locale\" -DHAVE_CONFIG_H -I.. -I../intl -
➥I../../tar-1.13/lib    -g -O2 -c ../../tar-1.13/src/extract.c
gcc -DLOCALEDIR=\"/usr/local/share/locale\" -DHAVE_CONFIG_H -I.. -I../intl -
➥I../../tar-1.13/lib    -g -O2 -c ../../tar-1.13/src/incremen.c
gcc -DLOCALEDIR=\"/usr/local/share/locale\" -DHAVE_CONFIG_H -I.. -I../intl -
➥I../../tar-1.13/lib    -g -O2 -c ../../tar-1.13/src/list.c
gcc -DLOCALEDIR=\"/usr/local/share/locale\" -DHAVE_CONFIG_H -I.. -I../intl -
➥I../../tar-1.13/lib    -g -O2 -c ../../tar-1.13/src/mangle.c
gcc -DLOCALEDIR=\"/usr/local/share/locale\" -DHAVE_CONFIG_H -I.. -I../intl -
➥I../../tar-1.13/lib    -g -O2 -c ../../tar-1.13/src/misc.c
gcc -DLOCALEDIR=\"/usr/local/share/locale\" -DHAVE_CONFIG_H -I.. -I../intl -
➥I../../tar-1.13/lib    -g -O2 -c ../../tar-1.13/src/names.c
```

```
gcc -DLOCALEDIR=\"/usr/local/share/locale\" -DHAVE_CONFIG_H -I.. -I../intl -
➡I../../tar-1.13/lib    -g -02 -c ../../tar-1.13/src/open3.c
gcc -DLOCALEDIR=\"/usr/local/share/locale\" -DHAVE_CONFIG_H -I.. -I../intl -
➡I../../tar-1.13/lib    -g -02 -c ../../tar-1.13/src/rtapelib.c
gcc -DLOCALEDIR=\"/usr/local/share/locale\" -DHAVE_CONFIG_H -I.. -I../intl -
➡I../../tar-1.13/lib    -g -02 -c ../../tar-1.13/src/tar.c
gcc -DLOCALEDIR=\"/usr/local/share/locale\" -DHAVE_CONFIG_H -I.. -I../intl -
➡I../../tar-1.13/lib    -g -02 -c ../../tar-1.13/src/update.c
gcc  -g -02  -o tar  arith.o buffer.o compare.o create.o delete.o extract.o
➡incremen.o list.o mangle.o misc.o names.o open3.o rtapelib.o tar.o update.o
➡../lib/libtar.a
gcc -DLOCALEDIR=\"/usr/local/share/locale\" -DHAVE_CONFIG_H -I.. -I../intl -
➡I../../tar-1.13/lib    -g -02 -c ../../tar-1.13/src/rmt.c
gcc  -g -02  -o rmt  rmt.o ../lib/libtar.a
make[2]: Leaving directory `/home/banz/book/tar-1.13.linux/src'
Making all in scripts
make[2]: Entering directory `/home/banz/book/tar-1.13.linux/scripts'
make[2]: Nothing to be done for `all'.
make[2]: Leaving directory `/home/banz/book/tar-1.13.linux/scripts'
Making all in po
make[2]: Entering directory `/home/banz/book/tar-1.13.linux/po'
make[2]: Leaving directory `/home/banz/book/tar-1.13.linux/po'
Making all in tests
make[2]: Entering directory `/home/banz/book/tar-1.13.linux/tests'
make[2]: Nothing to be done for `all'.
make[2]: Leaving directory `/home/banz/book/tar-1.13.linux/tests'
make[2]: Entering directory `/home/banz/book/tar-1.13.linux'
make[2]: Leaving directory `/home/banz/book/tar-1.13.linux'
make[1]: Leaving directory `/home/banz/book/tar-1.13.linux'
tyler[14]%
```

Using lndir

Applications that don't take advantage of GNU Configure (and even some that do) aren't compatible with this method of compiling. For these, we can use the tool lndir, which typically comes as part of the X Window System distribution. lndir can be used to make a tree of symbolic links, echoing the contents of the original source tree, which then can be used to build the target application. As an example of how to use lndir, we'll look at building xkeycaps, the application that we previously used to demonstrate using xmkmf.

We start out by unpacking the distribution. As when using configure previously, we'll create a directory to build the application in and change into it:

```
tyler[5]% gzip -dc xkeycaps-2.46.tar.Z | tar -xf -

tyler[6]% mkdir xkeyacaps-2.46.linux

tyler[7]% cd xkeycaps-2.46.linux
```

After making the build directory the working directory, we run lndir, specifying the path to the directory structure that we'll be replicating. We can pass either a relative or an absolute path, but a relative path is usually recommended.

```
tyler[8]% lndir ../xkeycaps-2.46

../xkeycaps-2.46/kbds:
```

The only output that lndir gives is a list of the subdirectories that it encounters while creating the link tree. After it runs, the contents of the resulting directory can be seen, with a symbolic link for each file pointing to the real location of the file. If you need to make any *platform-specific* edits to the tree, you should rename the symbolic link pertaining to the file and then copy the contents back to the original filename. Otherwise, you'll edit the file that's in the original source tree.

```
tyler[9]% ls -l

total 12
lrwxrwxrwx    1 user     wheel              26 Sep 14 21:58 actions.c ->
../xkeycaps-2.46/actions.c
lrwxrwxrwx    1 user     wheel              27 Sep 14 21:58 all-kbds.c ->
../xkeycaps-2.46/all-kbds.c
lrwxrwxrwx    1 user     wheel              29 Sep 14 21:58 build-map.sh ->
../xkeycaps-2.46/build-map.sh
lrwxrwxrwx    1 user     wheel              27 Sep 14 21:58 commands.c ->
../xkeycaps-2.46/commands.c
lrwxrwxrwx    1 user     wheel              29 Sep 14 21:58 defining.txt ->
../xkeycaps-2.46/defining.txt
lrwxrwxrwx    1 user     wheel              24 Sep 14 21:58 guess.c -> ../xkeycaps-
2.46/guess.c
lrwxrwxrwx    1 user     wheel              30 Sep 14 21:58 hierarchy.txt ->
../xkeycaps-2.46/hierarchy.txt
lrwxrwxrwx    1 user     wheel              23 Sep 14 21:58 hpux.c -> ../xkeycaps-
2.46/hpux.c
lrwxrwxrwx    1 user     wheel              26 Sep 14 21:58 Imakefile ->
../xkeycaps-2.46/Imakefile
...
```

Afterward, you can build the package as usual.

Although they're few and far between, some packages unfortunately resist being configured and build in a "shared-source-tree" manner. These tend to have skeleton configuration files already in place; instead of moving these aside and re-creating these files, they directly overwrite them, causing the symbolic link to be followed and overwriting the file in the original source tree. In these instances, you're probably best off simply unpacking the source once for each architecture.

Managing Your Software Installations

Developing a software-management system for your site requires solving certain problems:

- How the software is to be organized
- How the software is to be compiled (for Open Source software)
- How the software is to be "provided" to the end system

We'll look first at solving the problems related to organizing and providing the software to your end systems, and why you might want to develop a system to do so, by looking at various software-management methodologies.

Software-Management Systems

So far, we've discussed only building and compiling Open Source software because this is the bulk of the work that's done when dealing with third-party software on UNIX. For some not-so-complicated sites, compiling software and doing its default "make install" is enough to get the job done. However, managing your software installs in some way could be desirable for larger sites. Here are some problems that a comprehensive software-management system for your site can help you solve:

1. **Consistency of software availability**—As you move among different systems at a site, having the same software available on each can be a time saver. Imagine the time saved if the software collections available for developers to use in their development environment were sure to always be available on the production environment. Or, consider the time saved from help-desk calls from frustrated users wondering why different systems have different applications.

2. **Elimination of repetitive work**—Building and installing software on one machine is productive work; repeating it is a waste of time. Having an infrastructure as part of your environment that is dedicated to managing software can take the pain out of the delivery of the software throughout your organization.

3. **Elimination of missing dependencies**—Remember earlier, when we talked about dealing with a software product with multiple dependencies? How can you be sure that these dependencies will be installed on all the systems that other packages will need?

4. **Release control**—A system also should provide an environment to "test" a new package in before it's released into your production environment. In addition, you

should have the capability to "roll back" a release of a package if it causes problems or for other reasons.

5. **Availability**—Software-management systems work by managing "local installations" of software so that your software availability is not hampered by other service outages, such as those that could occur if you were NFS-mounting a /usr/local or such from a network server.

Determining Your Needs

You might not need all of these "features" in your software-management system. Building and installing your packages in a directory tree and then sharing that directory tree via NFS or some other method might suffice for you. Some network filesystems, such as AFS, allow the replication of "read-only" data, such as software collections, lessening the impact of a single server failure. Even when using such systems, you might need to be able to ensure that software is available on a machine even without network availability. Choosing a system for management allows the management of software to be installed locally and software resident through the network for other, less critical systems to use.

We'll look first at methods of making software available to the systems in your environment and some tools that take different methodologies of managing the software. Then we'll take a look at the configuration of an actual site that uses a mix of these tools in production.

Distribution of Software

Now that you've built or installed your open-source software, you'll have to find a way to get it to your end systems, and finally to your users. Here we talk about some tools and methods to accomplish these tasks.

Store Remotely, Install Locally

For the highest availability of your software distributions, there's nothing better than having the software installed locally on every machine in your environment. Doing so keeps your network IO to a minimum and eliminates the reliability on points of failure such as network routers and fileservers. However, now you must engineer a solution to install the software on each server, remove it when necessary, and potentially check it for alteration periodically. To automate the management of such a system, look at a tool such as depot or, as an alternative, a script to manage the periodic installation of operating-system "packages" from a network-based repository. In addition, creating "packages" of software can be complicated, depending on your chosen methodology—it's not as simple as a "make install," in most cases. Let's summarize the pros and cons of this type of arrangement.

Pros	Cons
High reliability	Complicated to manage on a site-wide basis
High performance—no network access required	"Wasted" disk space due to replication of data
Customized software installs on a per-machine level. This also allows "testing" of software releases on specific machines	Potentially difficult to create "packages" for distribution

Store and Run Remotely

The opposite of the previous methodology is to install your software products into a remote repository that is made available to your site's systems via a network-accessible filesystem such as NFS. Software installs can be as simple as running `make install` on a system and then exporting that system's third-party software tree (such as /usr/local) to the rest of your enterprise. However, even if you are utilizing a network filesystem such as AFS, which supports the replication of data across multiple servers and transparent failover, you've now at least added one point of failure to your system: the network. Because you also are sharing the "same" software tree among some—and potentially all—of your systems of the same type, you also lose the capability to configure each one's software collections individually. If you're going for homogeneity, this won't exactly be a problem. Let's look at the pros and cons for this methodology.

Pros	Cons
Easy software installs	Added reliance on network and fileservers
Single point of management	No support for testing software releases on "some" machines
Homogeneous environment	Inability to customize the software distributions on a per-machine level
Disk space used on only one or a few fileservers	

Of course, these are two extremes of a managed software environment. Later, we'll discuss using some software tools to allow the creation of environments that are hybrids of the following two methodologies, giving you greater flexibility.

Using Operating-System Tools

One way to handle software distribution is to create software packages in your operating system's native format, and distribute and install these individually on your systems. As mentioned before, this gives you the ultimate in flexibility and reliability—of course, it also can be relatively difficult to manage. We'll take a look at the basics of creating "packages" using Red Hat's RPM package manager for Linux and the SYSV package system that is used on Solaris.

Red Hat RPM

RPM is a very capable package-management system developed by Red Hat for use in its Linux distribution. On one hand, it provides basic installation management functionality, including tracing package dependencies. On the other hand, it is a complete software build–management system.

Two types of RPMs exist: "binary" RPMs, which contain an installation image of a software package, and a "source" RPM, which contains the source code to the software package, any packages or scripts needed to customize the code before building, and a description of the work needed to be done to build the package and create the binary RPM.

As an example of how to create an RPM, we'll look at building an RPM for a simple package such as GNU Make. We're running RPM on a Red Hat Linux system, so there is a directory structure set up for creating and building RPMs in /usr/src/redhat. There are five directories in this tree:

- **BUILD**—This is the directory where the "work" is done, where packages are untarred, configured, and built.
- **RPMS**—When binary RPMs are created, they're placed in this directory.
- **SOURCES**—This is where the components (tarballs, patches, and so on) used to create the unpacked sources in the BUILD directory are placed.
- **SPECS**—This is where the spec files that describe the RPM creation process are kept.
- **SRPMS**—When source RPM files are created, this is where they are placed.

It all starts by creating a spec file for your package. This file gets placed in the SPECS directory. It includes basic information, such as version numbers, the name of the package, a basic description, information required to build and configure the package, and further information on how and what bits of it to install.

Our build of GNU make will be configured to be installed as gmake, so it will not be confused with the binary called make that is installed with the base operating system; it will be installed in /usr/local. Here's our sample spec file, gmake.spec, which we've annotated describing the meaning of different sections.

```
Summary: GNU Make
Name: gmake
Version: 3.79.1
Release: 1
```

This describes some basic information about the package—these fields are basically self-explanatory.

17

OPEN SOURCE
SOFTWARE
MANAGEMENT

```
Group: Local/Development
```

This is used to organize the package called type. It's optional to use, but it's required to be there.

```
License: GPL
```

This should describe the license that the package for which you're building the RPM is bound by. Yet again, it's optional for you to care about this field, but it has to be there.

```
Source: ftp://ftp.gnu.org/gnu/make/make-%{version}.tar.gz
```

This is either a URL that can be used to "fetch" the package from a remote location or the path to the package in the local filesystem.

```
Prefix: /usr/local
```

This is the assumed prefix that the package will be installed to when it is built.

```
Buildroot: %{_tmppath}/%{name}-root
```

When the package is built and "installed" as part of the package-creation process, this is where the work will be done.

```
%description
GNU Make is used to build stuff.
```

This is a long text description of the package. It can be quite long, but we've left it to one line for brevity.

```
%prep
%setup -q -n make-3.79.1
```

The %prep section describes things that are to be done to the source tree before configuring it. In this case, the setup clause tells rpm that the sources are in the make-3.79-1 directory. You'd also put other information here regarding patches and such.

```
%build
%configure
make
```

This describes the build process. %configure is a macro that executes the GNU Configure program with the standard options, and make is simply the shell command that builds the package.

```
%install
rm -rf ${RPM_BUILD_ROOT}

%makeinstall

{ cd ${RPM_BUILD_ROOT}
  mv .%{_bindir}/make .%{_bindir}/gmake
```

```
  mv .%{_mandir}/man1/make.1 .%{_mandir}/man1/gmake.1
}
```

The %install section describes what is to be done to create the directory tree that the binary RPM will be created from. It's basically a list of shell commands, with the exception of %makeinstall, which is a macro that is executing a "make install" with other options to cause the install to occur into the RPM_BUILD_ROOT directory. The rest are shell commands that rename "make" to "gmake" in the appropriate directories.

```
%clean
rm -rf ${RPM_BUILD_ROOT}
```
These are instructions to "clean up" after the RPM build.
```
%post

%preun

%files
%defattr(-,root,root)
%doc NEWS README
%{_bindir}/gmake
%{_mandir}/man1/gmake.1
%{_infodir}/*.info*
```

These are a list of files that will be included in the binary RPM.

```
%changelog
```

After creating the spec file, to build a binary RPM file for your package, you run rpm—and the magic happens. It unpacks, configures, builds, and creates the binary RPM with no interaction.

LISTING 17.10 Building an RPM Package

```
tyler[99]% rpm -bb SPECS/gmake.spec
Executing(%prep): /bin/sh -e /var/tmp/rpm-tmp.26575
+ umask 022
+ cd /usr/src/redhat/BUILD
+ cd /usr/src/redhat/BUILD
+ rm -rf make-3.79.1
+ tar -xf -
+ /bin/gzip -dc /usr/src/redhat/SOURCES/make-3.79.1.tar.gz
+ STATUS=0
+ '[' 0 -ne 0 ']'
+ cd make-3.79.1
++ /usr/bin/id -u
+ '[' 0 = 0 ']'
+ /bin/chown -Rhf root .
++ /usr/bin/id -u
+ '[' 0 = 0 ']'
+ /bin/chgrp -Rhf root .
```

17

OPEN SOURCE
SOFTWARE
MANAGEMENT

```
+ /bin/chmod -Rf a+rX,g-w,o-w .
+ exit 0
Executing(%build): /bin/sh -e /var/tmp/rpm-tmp.26575
+ umask 022
+ cd /usr/src/redhat/BUILD
+ cd make-3.79.1
+ CFLAGS=-O2 -march=i386 -mcpu=i686
+ export CFLAGS
+ CXXFLAGS=-O2 -march=i386 -mcpu=i686
+ export CXXFLAGS
+ FFLAGS=-O2 -march=i386 -mcpu=i686
+ export FFLAGS
+ '[' -f configure.in ']'
+ libtoolize --copy --force
Remember to add `AM_PROG_LIBTOOL' to `configure.in'.
Using `AC_PROG_RANLIB' is rendered obsolete by `AM_PROG_LIBTOOL'
You should update your `aclocal.m4' by running aclocal.
+ ./configure i386-redhat-linux --prefix=/usr --exec-prefix=/usr --
bindir=/usr/bin --sbindir=/usr/sbin --sysconfdir=/etc --datadir=/usr/share --
includedir=/usr/include --libdir=/usr/lib --libexecdir=/usr/libexec --
localstatedir=/var --sharedstatedir=/usr/com --mandir=/usr/share/man --
infodir=/usr/share/info
creating cache ./config.cache
checking for a BSD compatible install... /usr/bin/install -c
checking whether build environment is sane... yes
checking whether make sets ${MAKE}... yes
checking for working aclocal... found
[output from configure cropped]
+ make
make  all-recursive
make[1]: Entering directory `/usr/src/redhat/BUILD/make-3.79.1'
Making all in i18n
make[2]: Entering directory `/usr/src/redhat/BUILD/make-3.79.1/i18n'
make[2]: Nothing to be done for `all'.
make[2]: Leaving directory `/usr/src/redhat/BUILD/make-3.79.1/i18n'
make[2]: Entering directory `/usr/src/redhat/BUILD/make-3.79.1'
gcc -DALIASPATH=\"/usr/share/locale:.\" -DLOCALEDIR=\"/usr/share/locale\" -
DLIBDIR=\"/usr/lib\" -DINCLUDEDIR=\"/usr/include\" -DHAVE_CONFIG_H -I. –
[remaining output truncated]
```

You will be left with a binary RPM in the RPMS directory that you can then install.

This was a very simple example of how to create an RPM, and the tool has many more features than what we've touched on here. Check out the books and Web references mentioned previously on the subject for more information on using it.

SYSV Package

Alas, the UNIX SYSV packaging system is not at all as powerful as RPM, but it does its simple tasks very well. The most basic package that you can make with it requires two files—one describing the package and a second describing the file contents of that package. These files, as well as the other files used to build the package, are placed in their own directory. We'll be building GNU Zip, a simple package, that has been compiled and the files placed under the files subdirectory of the package directory.

The first file is named pkginfo. As the name suggests, this is the informational part of the package, which contains a set of attribute/value pairs that describe the package. Here's an example of a basic one:

LISTING **17.11** pkginfo File for GNU Zip

```
PKG=GNUgzip
VERSION=1.2.4
NAME=GNU gzip compression programs
ARCH=sparc
CATEGORY=utilities
```

PKG, VERSION, and NAME are as self-explanatory as they come. ARCH describes the machine architecture—in this case, a Sun SPARC. CATEGORY is required and basically informational.

The second file, prototype, contains the actual "contents" of the package. The first line calls out a file (pkginfo) that is part of the installation package and that is not to be installed. The search line and the lines thereafter specify where to find files, where to place them in the directory tree, and with what permissions, respectively.

LISTING **17.12** Prototype File for GNU Zip

```
i pkginfo
!search files/usr/local/bin
d none /usr/local 0755 root sys
d none /usr/local/bin 0755 root sys
f none /usr/local/bin/gzip 0755 root sys
s none /usr/local/bin/gzunzip=gzip
s none /usr/local/bin/zcat=gzip
f none /usr/local/bin/zcmp 0755 root sys
s none /usr/local/bin/zdiff=zcmp
f none /usr/local/bin/gzexe 0755 root sys
f none /usr/local/bin/zforce 0755 root sys
f none /usr/local/bin/zgrep 0755 root sys
f none /usr/local/bin/zmore 0755 root sys
f none /usr/local/bin/znew 0755 root sys
!search files/usr/local/info
d none /usr/local/info 0755 root sys
f none /usr/local/info/gzip.info 0644 root sys
d none /usr/local/man 0755 root sys
d none /usr/local/man/man1 0755 root sys
!search files/usr/local/man/man1
f none /usr/local/man/man1/gzip.1 0644 root sys
```

```
s none /usr/local/man/man1/gunzip.1=gzip.1
s none /usr/local/man/man1/zcat.1=gzip.1
f none /usr/local/man/man1/gzexe.1 0644 root sys
f none /usr/local/man/man1/zcmp.1 0644 root sys
s none /usr/local/man/man1/zdiff.1=zcmp.1
f none /usr/local/man/man1/zforce.1 0644 root sys
f none /usr/local/man/man1/zgrep.1 0644 root sys
f none /usr/local/man/man1/zmore.1 0644 root sys
f none /usr/local/man/man1/znew.1 0644 root sys
```

To "build" the package, simply run `pkgmk` in this directory, specifying a place to put the package with the `-d` option. We'll make a directory called `package` for the data to go to:

LISTING 17.13 Building the GNU Zip Package

```
bfs1[99]% pkgmk -d package
## Building pkgmap from package prototype file.
## Processing pkginfo file.
WARNING: missing directory entry for </usr>
WARNING: parameter <PSTAMP> set to "bfs1.membrain.com15224757"
WARNING: parameter <CLASSES> set to "none"
## Attempting to volumize 26 entries in pkgmap.
part   1 -- 310 blocks, 25 entries
## Packaging one part.
/usr/src/pkg/gzip/package/GNUzip/pkgmap
/usr/src/pkg/gzip/package/GNUzip/pkginfo
/usr/src/pkg/gzip/package/GNUzip/root/usr/local/bin/gzexe
/usr/src/pkg/gzip/package/GNUzip/root/usr/local/bin/gzip
/usr/src/pkg/gzip/package/GNUzip/root/usr/local/bin/zcmp
/usr/src/pkg/gzip/package/GNUzip/root/usr/local/bin/zforce
/usr/src/pkg/gzip/package/GNUzip/root/usr/local/bin/zgrep
/usr/src/pkg/gzip/package/GNUzip/root/usr/local/bin/zmore
/usr/src/pkg/gzip/package/GNUzip/root/usr/local/bin/znew
/usr/src/pkg/gzip/package/GNUzip/root/usr/local/info/gzip.info
/usr/src/pkg/gzip/package/GNUzip/root/usr/local/man/man1/gzexe.1
/usr/src/pkg/gzip/package/GNUzip/root/usr/local/man/man1/gzip.1
/usr/src/pkg/gzip/package/GNUzip/root/usr/local/man/man1/zcmp.1
/usr/src/pkg/gzip/package/GNUzip/root/usr/local/man/man1/zforce.1
/usr/src/pkg/gzip/package/GNUzip/root/usr/local/man/man1/zgrep.1
/usr/src/pkg/gzip/package/GNUzip/root/usr/local/man/man1/zmore.1
/usr/src/pkg/gzip/package/GNUzip/root/usr/local/man/man1/znew.1
## Validating control scripts.
## Packaging complete.
```

Afterward, we can install our package with `pkgadd`, as discussed earlier.

Other Tools

We've covered a couple of packaging systems. The second two packages that we'll be looking at are a couple of systems that tackle the automation of the management of our software packages. The first is a package out of Carnegie-Mellon University called Depot, which uses symbolic links to create a single software tree, a combination of individual software trees. Modules is a package that allows software packages to be managed at a user level by manipulating the user's execution path.

Depot

Depot is a software package that was developed at CMU as part of its Andrew computing environment. As mentioned before, it manages your software collections area by populating it with either symbolic links to or copies of files that make up the collections of software that you have made available on your systems. That sounds confusing, so let's look at an example of how it works.

A *collection* is a term used by depot to refer to a software package—a collection of files. A collection exists as a directory tree that represents what the contents of your software tree would look like if this were the only package installed. You place these collection directories in a location accessible from all your systems, and you configure depot to build your software tree from the contents of those collections and update them periodically. On a collection-by-collection basis, you can configure depot to copy or symbolic-link the files, as your requirements dictate. For example, you might want to have your SSH copied locally, but you might not need your TeX distribution copied to every workstation in your enterprise.

Depot is available from Carnegie-Mellon University, at `http://asg.web.cmu.edu/depot/depot.html`. Other packages have similar functionality to depot; some of these are Stow (`http://www.gnu.ai.mit.edu/software/stow`) and Opt Depot (`http://www.arlut.utexas.edu/csd/opt_depot`).

Modules

Modules is less a software-management system than a user environment–management system. As mentioned in the introduction, it works by modifying the user's environment to make accessible software packages that are installed either locally or remotely. Modules doesn't solve problems regarding software distribution, but it does add a great flexibility to allow for user-level software version selection. You can find the Modules package at `http://www.modules.org`.

Endnotes

[1] *Okay, I know that some companies, for various reasons, don't allow the use of "free" software. I hope you're being compensated appropriately.*

[2] *Don't send me email saying, "But my mailer is better—why didn't you choose mine as an example?"*

[3] *A "target" is either a component or the result of the process that make is managing.*

[4] *Assuming that the author of the makefile configured a "clean" target. Most do, however.*

Databases

by Michael Wessler

IN THIS CHAPTER

Introduction

In this chapter, we examine databases from the system administrator's perspective.

First, we will look at databases in general. Although each vendor's database is different, all share similar characteristics. We will focus on needs and system characteristics common to any Relational Database Management System (RDBMS). We will explain databases at a high level and show why they are indeed large consumers of memory and disk. Additionally, we will show you what your DBA needs to do his job and how you, as a system administrator, can help.

After we have examined databases in general, we will look at two specific RDBMS. From the large system perspective, we will look at Oracle. We will examine Oracle-specific installation and configuration issues, daily management procedures, and how to take valid backups. At the other end of the spectrum, we will examine MySQL, a popular free database that is common on smaller systems.

Databases in General

Information technology, formerly called data processing, exists to serve or provide a business function. At the core of these functions is the need to enter, process, store, and retrieve data of some sort. As a result, most applications require the use of a data store of some type. Typically, this data store comes in the form of a database.

What Is a Database?

A database is a persistent structure to store data. This data typically is organized into substructures called *tables* relating to the object that they represent. For example, here we have a table EMP used to represent employees for a company:

```
SQL> describe emp
 Name                 Null?    Type
 ------------------   -------- ----------------
 EMPNO                NOT NULL NUMBER(4)
 ENAME                         VARCHAR2(10)
 JOB                           VARCHAR2(9)
 MGR                           NUMBER(4)
 HIREDATE                      DATE
 SAL                           NUMBER(7,2)
 COMM                          NUMBER(7,2)
 DEPTNO                        NUMBER(2)
```

This shows a table EMP that stores rows of data for each individual employee. Each row is divided into columns containing employee number (EMPNO), name (ENAME), job title (JOB), and so on. Each column has a data type such as number, date, or variable-length character (varchar) as specified in the table definition. This set of columns together form a row, or record, of information corresponding to each employee.

It is important to note that there is only one row for each individual employee. This rule is enforced by a constraint called a *primary key*. The column EMPNO is the primary key for the EMP table. It states that each row must have a value for this column, which is indicated by the NOT NULL comment in the table description. Other columns, such as commission amount (COMM), can be empty (NULL), but a primary key column cannot. Additionally, each value in a primary key column must be unique. Often primary key values are generated by sequence number generators, which automatically insert a new, unique value every time a new row is inserted into a table.

Additionally, tables may be related to each other. In fact, most tables are related to other tables. For example, the EMP table has a column department number (DEPTNO). This column is a link to another table called DEPT.

```
SQL> describe dept
 Name                Null?    Type
 ----------------    -------- --------------
 DEPTNO              NOT NULL NUMBER(2)
 DNAME                        VARCHAR2(14)
 LOC                          VARCHAR2(13)
```

As we can see here, DEPTNO is the primary key for the DEPT table. The corresponding DEPTNO column in the EMP table is referred to as a *foreign key* because it acts to link two tables. This relationship is shown in Figure 18.1.

Here we have two tables, joined by the foreign key EMP.DEPTNO to the primary key DEPT.DEPTNO. The rules regarding this relationship can be seen by examining the crow's feet notation. As we can see, the DEPT table is the *parent* table, and EMP is the *child* table. This means that every row (department) in DEPT has zero, one, or many children, which happen to be employees. Also, each employee (row in EMP) belongs to exactly one department. This relationship is referred to as *referential integrity*.

Databases supporting large applications often exceed hundreds of tables. Designing the tables and the relationships between them is a task usually done by data modelers and systems designers. The maintenance of the actual database itself usually falls to the database administrator (DBA).

18

DATABASES

> **Note**
>
> For more information regarding database design and best practices, a good book is *Database Design*, by Ryan Stevens and Ron Plew (Sams Publishing, 2001, ISBN 0-672-31758-3). It provides valuable insights on how to optimally design a database application.

FIGURE 18.1

Parent/child table relationships.

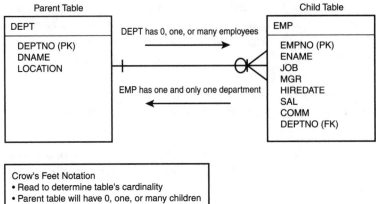

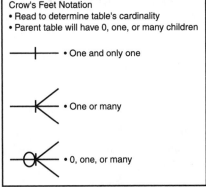

The application or program reads, writes, and deletes data in these tables depending on the program code. This code accesses the database via a language called Structured Query Language (SQL). SQL, pronounced "sequel," is used to select, insert, update, and delete rows of data. For example, the following command will select all the rows of data from DEPT:

```
SQL> select deptno, dname, loc from dept;

    DEPTNO DNAME          LOC
---------- -------------- -------------
        10 ACCOUNTING     NEW YORK
        20 RESEARCH       DALLAS
        30 SALES          CHICAGO
        40 OPERATIONS     BOSTON

4 rows selected.

SQL>
```

This query returns all the rows from the table DEPT. In this case, the table contains only four rows, but tables often contain thousands and even millions of rows.

Rows of data also can be inserted into tables via the SQL INSERT statement. After they have been inserted, they can be updated or deleted. This insert, update, and delete functionality of SQL is classified as Data Manipulation Language (DML). This is an example of an SQL INSERT statement:

```
SQL> insert into dept values (50, 'MIS', 'INDIANAPOLIS');

1 row created.

SQL> commit;

Commit complete.

SQL>
```

The first statement inserts a new role of data into DEPT. The second statement, COMMIT, makes the change permanent inside the database. Had we wanted to undo our INSERT statement, we could have issued a ROLLBACK statement instead of COMMIT.

System Architecture

It is important to plan and understand how the overall system will be implemented. In most modern computer systems, there are at least four components: application code, Web interface, database, and network. By breaking a system into these components, load balancing, tuning, and troubleshooting are simplified. Although this information could seem obvious to an experienced administrator, it is important to diagram your architecture so that everyone can understand the "big picture."

From a DBA's perspective, he wants to understand where his database exists in relation to the application code, Web server, and network. From a sysadmin's perspective, you want to know what each of your boxes is doing from a system standpoint so that you can monitor and allocate your resources appropriately. It should be noted that this everyone should have this information *before* the system is actually implemented.

The application program code that issues the SQL to the database can exist in many different locations. It can be within the database in the form of stored SQL or PL/SQL (when dealing with Oracle databases), in a program outside the database such as C or Visual Basic accessing the database via Open Database Connectivity (ODBC), or in a Java program via Java Database Connectivity (JDBC). This code is created and maintained by application developers/programmers, and it may exist on servers away from the database. In fact, it is common to separate the database onto a different server to reduce resource contention. You can see that separation in Figure 18.2.

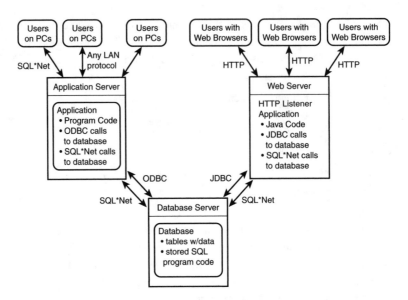

FIGURE 18.2
Sample application architecture.

Here we have a sample system with program code located in the Web server, the application server, and the database server. Although the specifics will vary depending on the system, this layout is typical. By isolating the resource-intensive database on its own box, performance is improved because of reduced resource contention. In this example, we also separated the Web and application servers. If necessary we could have placed the Web and application servers on the same box because that would be preferable to placing either one on the database server.

The key for the sysadmin is to understand which boxes do what. There will be different uptime, performance, and backup and recovery requirements, depending on the server's purpose. For example, impact on the total system will be different depending on whether the Web server crashes versus if the database server crashes. Load balancing and system layout also are impacted. For example, you might want to allocate your Linux server as the Web server and leave your robust Sun box as your database server.

Databases Are Operating Systems

Although at its roots a database is a collection of tables, the most accurate way to visualize modern databases is as operating systems. That's right—modern databases are closer to being operating systems than simple applications.

Databases need to be started, they have different run levels and architectures, they have users owning objects, and they have specific tuning and backup and recovery considerations. The following sections discuss the features that most databases have, corresponding to many aspects of an operating system.

Database File Types

A database contains files to store the data tables. However, most databases separate files into the following categories including these:

- **Data**—Obviously, a database must have files to store the data tables. Additionally, for every data table, there are usually one or more indexes associated with it to act as pointers to specific rows of data. These indexes also are stored in files. Typically, a data or index file can range from several megabytes to well over the old 2GB limit.

- **Control**—Most databases have a data dictionary used to store metadata. This is information about the database, such as database name, file composition, status, and so on. This information is separate from data or index data, so it often is stored separately.

- **Transaction log**—Many databases write a sequential history of every INSERT, UPDATE, or DELETE to one or more transaction logs. There are several reasons for this. First, in case of a database crash and recovery, these logs are used to reconstruct the database to a point in time. Also, many vendors provide products that are used to review these logs to provide auditing or tuning information. These transaction logs often are saved as archive logs for long-term storage in case they need to be used to restore a database to a specific point in time.

- **Configuration**—Just as UNIX has an /etc/hosts or /etc/passwd file, databases have similar configuration files. These files are usually vendor-specific, and it is up to the DBA to know what they are. However, you, as a sysadmin, should be familiar with them in case you need to restore them. Most of the these files relate to networking connectivity with the database, who can log in as a DBA, what databases and versions are installed, and what to do with the database during machine reboot. Also note that many of these files are indeed text files, so many people write shell scripts that use these files.

Keep in mind that each of these files needs to be backed up. Your DBA should know what each file is and its location. Additionally, except for the configuration files, these files are usually binary, so don't attempt to open or read them.

Memory Structures and Background Processes

Just as the UNIX system has memory structures and background processes, modern databases have the same. Databases attempt to cache rows of data in memory. The amount of memory used is usually a tunable parameter and is determined by the DBA. This can range from around 50MB to more than 1GB. The DBA should work with you to strike a balance between the needs of the database and the needs of other applications. Be careful not to allocate so much memory that the machine begins to swap or thrash.

Background processes exist to support the database and follow the same rules as any other UNIX process. The number and type of background processes depend on the specific database, but generally they fall into these categories:

- **User processes**—These are the processes spawned by individual users logging into the database. These sessions typically last as long as the login session. The number and amount of CPU time consumed by these can be used to gauge database usage.

- **Process monitor**—This process is used to clean up failed or terminated user processes. This process also can be split into a system monitor process to monitor the health of the entire database.

- **Database writer**—This process is used to manage reads and writes from memory to the data files on disk. Often vendors develop complex least recently used algorithms to improve caching rows in memory to reduce disk I/O. This caching comes in addition to normal UNIX caching.

- **Transaction log writer**—Sometimes a separate process is used to manage writes to the transaction log. Additionally, if the transaction logs are saved to archive logs, a background process may manage this process.

When a database is running, you should be able to check its status with your normal tools such as ps and top. Many shell scripts are written to check for these background processes to determine whether a database is up or down. Work with your DBA to know what the background processes are and what is expected behavior.

Database Users

Databases have users that need to be managed just as any other UNIX user. Each database has a list of users with the following characteristics:

- **Purpose**—Some users are database-generated to perform some specific purpose. Other users correspond to specific humans that actually log into the database to do work. Group accounts often are created and shared to perform tasks such as testing or administration.

- **Passwords**—Just as you must reset user passwords to log into the box, the DBA must do the same for his users. Most databases allow different options requiring password complexity, expire time, and account locking.

- **Privileges**—Each user has a set of permissions within the database. Some users may start and stop the database, while others may only log in. Furthermore, some users may create data tables and indexes, while others may only read these tables.

- **Objects**—Users within the database can own tables, indexes, and other structures, just as a UNIX user can own files. These database objects have size, timestamps, permissions, and other attributes.

Managing database users can be just as big of a headache as can be managing UNIX users. In fact, often a UNIX user will have one or more corresponding database accounts. Some databases have authentication schemes that check the OS account permission to allow the user to log into the database. Because users on UNIX and in databases are similar, many of the GUI tools used for database users will look familiar to you. At some shops, user account management for both the database and the UNIX server are handled by the same people. However, because roles and privileges inside the database can be complex, we recommend separating these duties between DBAs and sysadmins after the account initially is created.

Security

Security within the database can be just as complex as network or server security. For that reason, it should be approached as a team effort by the SAs, DBAs, and networking people. The following are just some of the ways that security is achieved at the database level:

- **Password policies**—Just as UNIX users have password policies regarding complexity and locking, these usually can be implemented at the database level. Also, most databases have a set of default passwords for system accounts, such as DBA. Make sure that these are changed after the database is created. This is a common mistake.

- **Database permissions**—Equivalent to the root user in UNIX is a DBA user in most databases. This user can start, stop, modify, and potentially destroy a database. Control over the DBA password and permissions should be just a stringent as with root. Within normal database users, there are a plethora of rights and privileges regarding database access, object creation, resource consumption, and access to other users' objects. These are database-specific and are managed by the DBA.

- **Data**—Data in tables can be encrypted, and access can be restricted. This is done both within the database itself and via the application accessing the database.

- **Auditing**—Database access and activity within the database can be audited. The level of complexity depends on the vendor and the characteristics of the system. Keep in mind that auditing often comes at the expense of performance and management overhead.

- **Network**—Just like any computer system, users communicate to their databases over networks. Modern databases allow various levels of encryption and protection at the network level, if it is implemented. However, the levels offered depend on the vendor and often require additional license fees.

- **Applications**—Make sure that appropriate security features exist in the applications accessing the database. Because many database applications are homegrown, there is a possibility for security holes. These holes can be within flashy graphical applications that allow read/write access to any data, or it could simply be a shell script with an embedded password.

Common Security Holes in UNIX

We've seen two security holes regarding database and UNIX numerous times at multiple sites. One is passwords embedded in shell scripts and the other is passwords visible with the `ps -ef` command.

Many DBAs rightfully implement database-maintenance tasks via cron and shell scripts. However, a common mistake is to write a shell script that logs into a database with username/password. This represents a problem if the script is group-readable, and especially if it is world-readable. Anyone savvy with databases and UNIX quickly can find and view all the shell scripts owned by the database group to find embedded passwords. This problem is even worse because often the DBA password (equivalent to root) is embedded. Ask your DBA to verify that this isn't the case in his scripts. You can verify it by searching for whatever connect string is used for your database in each shell script. There are ways for DBAs to log into most databases without embedding passwords; at the minimum, the shell scripts should be 700 or 750.

Another common problem is to log into the database with username/password from the UNIX command line. Depending on the version of UNIX that you are running, this connect string is visible with `ps -ef`. Typically, you can log in specifying a username and then let the database application prompt you for a password so that it is not visible.

Those are the basics of database security. Obviously, much of it falls to the DBA to implement. However, as a sysadmin, you have the right to demand and verify that database security is up to par on your boxes.

Networking

Networking connectivity depends on the database vendor and your needs. This can range from setting a few configuration files to navigating a complex, full-time job. Databases can be accessed either with or without specific client and server software installed and configured. Obviously, ODBC and JDBC are popular open methods to connect, but more security and options are available if you install the vendor's networking software. Options such as encryption, load balancing, connection pooling, and failover severs are usually available if you are willing to pay for the additional cost.

Backup and Recovery

Backup and recovery of databases is a special task and is *not* simply a matter of making a copy of each OS file. I cannot stress that enough: You *must* understand how to correctly back up and restore your specific databases, or you *will* lose them.

Databases typically cannot simply be copied to tape at any given time because they are extremely sensitive to timestamps and internal system change numbers (SCN). When a database is up and running, those files are open and the database processes and data dictionary is tracking the status of every insert, update, and delete within the database. During that time, the database is in a state of flux, and any backup taken during that time likely will be invalid. If the database is running and you back it up and then try to restore it, the database likely will not start because it is "confused" about its current state. This is a common problem, and many database support personnel have stories about how systems were lost because supposedly "valid" backups were really unusable.

Work with the DBA to come up with a solid backup and recovery strategy. Many databases allow you to take special backups while the database is running, *if* you set it up correctly. Also, you can often recover a database to any given point in time *if* it is set up properly. This is vendor-specific information that the DBA should know, and he should be willing to discuss the backup and recovery options with you. Also, many databases have hooks into established UNIX backup utility products, so your help likely will be needed.

Are you starting to view databases as more complex systems then you previously thought? Do many of the areas seem similar to the UNIX-related tasks that you deal with? We have covered the basic characteristics of databases, but we haven't even discussed their hooks into Web/application servers or development tools. Database vendors know that more functionality is available, and performance can be improved if they structure their databases like operating systems. This increase in complexity likely will continue as vendors increase the functionality of their products.

Why Databases Are Resource Hogs

Many system administrators are surprised to see just how resource-intensive a database can be. Some initially think that the DBA must have incorrectly set a parameter, but in

18

DATABASES

reality the database is running as it is supposed to. Often entire servers are dedicated as database servers.

Managing database servers isn't any more difficult than managing any other type of box. In fact, if the only applications on a server are database applications, many aspects of management are simplified. Also, because it is common to dedicate a server for database usage, many database and operating system vendors are working together to fix bugs and promote best practices. We highly recommend that you familiarize yourself with material from both your database vendor and your operating system vendor in this regard.

Because most system administrators look at a box in terms of memory, disk, and CPU, we will examine the impact that databases have on these categories.

Memory Usage

Databases can consume large amounts of memory. The primary reason is that because memory access is so much faster than disk, a good DBA will try to force the database to cache as much frequently accessed data in memory as possible. Indeed, this caching can make or break a system in terms of performance. Generally, the DBA will try to keep the hit ratios of finding data in memory versus disk at 95% or higher. This is very good for the database, but it could require memory allocations of hundreds of megabytes. As of this writing, we have one database that uses more than 700MB of memory. Although that might seem excessive to some people, the reality is that large systems with many users require large servers and resources.

What can you, as a system administrator, do regarding memory usage and databases? First, when initially sizing a server, work with your DBA to determine the needs of the database. Most DBAs will want you to max out the memory on a machine long before they ask for more/faster processors. Next, make sure that you truly understand how memory is allocated on your particular machine. It never ceases to amaze me how many sysadmins really don't understand shared memory, semaphores, swap allocation, and Intimate Shared Memory (ISM). It's not enough to just understand the basics; if you plan to support large database servers, you really need to read literature for your specific platform as well as for your database.

Use your system-monitoring tools to examine paging and swapping on your machine during normal times. You should have a baseline of what to expect for when problems do occur. If you receive reports of poor performance and see large amounts of memory allocated, you might be led to believe that swapping is occurring. However, had you done your homework about how your system handles swap and how the database uses memory, you might find that memory is not the culprit.

Finally, know how to clear out shared memory segments and semaphores. Sometimes when a database crashes suddenly, these memory structures still will be allocated. This poses a problem because the database cannot be restarted until they are removed. Because rebooting the box is not always an option, using ipcs and ipcrm could be your only options. The issue here is that if you have to remove the correct memory and semaphores, this can be tricky if you have more than one database running. If you remove the wrong ones, you will end up crashing another database. Work with your DBA so that both of you can identify and remove these segments.

Disk Usage

The next most used resource regarding databases is disk. Software installations usually take between 1GB and 3GB per release, which really isn't too excessive. What really takes the space is the data files and archived transaction logs.

DBAs generally try to allocate enough disk space for the database to grow unattended for about a year. That means that a database must be created or modified to have X amount of space to grow into, even if it currently is not being used. If a large data load is occurring and a table cannot expand, an error will be generated, that data load will fail, and the entire load might have to be redone. Considering that these loads can take hours or even days, DBAs try to avoid running out of space like the plague.

Another reason that DBAs size databases so large is that accurate estimates for the volume of data are extremely difficult to obtain. It is indeed a rare day that a DBA knows exactly how much space a database will take. Much of this depends on how the developers require the data and business issues outside the DBA's control. For that reason, DBAs are taught to size big.

Another consumer of disk space is archived transaction logs. These log files are a critical component in many backup and recovery situations. Because the number and size of these logs is proportional to the amount of activity in the database, they can be generated frequently. This has the ill affect of filling up entire filesystems if they are not compressed and moved off to tape regularly. This poses an additional problem; depending on your particular database, all insert, update, and delete activity in the database could be halted until there is space to write the archived transaction logs. This a potential show-stopper because it will prevent the database from functioning normally. Most DBAs and sysadmins have cron jobs to monitor these filesystems and send pages when they reach 90% or 95% full.

As a sysadmin, you should make sure that the DBAs are wisely using the disk space that you give to them. Usually they will use whatever you give to them, whether they need it or not. We're not happy about admitting it, but, unfortunately, many DBAs are quite

18

DATABASES

wasteful regarding disk space. The two most common problems are not sizing the database properly and not removing unnecessary files after a reasonable amount of time.

Regarding database sizing, your only real option is encourage your DBA to size his database(s) reasonably. Determining how big to make certain data, index, and metadata files really is a DBA issue, not a sysadmin issue. Depending on the database vendor and the application, moderately sized databases easily can run around 30GB. Larger production databases often reach into hundreds of gigabytes, while even your smallest databases could hover around 2GB or 3GB. If the DBA has a production system to support, don't give him grief over his requests for disk space because his needs are probably legitimate. These systems are hard to size for because much of the growth is outside the DBA's control, and he usually doesn't have accurate figures anyway. Considering the potentially severe ramifications of running out of disk space, it is usually best to make sure that the DBA has enough space for growing databases.

Where the sysadmin can force better space management is making sure that unneeded files are deleted regularly. DBAs, like most people, tend to not want to delete files unless they have to. Although actual data and index files usually cannot be deleted, archived transaction logs, data export files, and log files usually can be compressed and deleted after a period of time. We recommend working with the DBA to establish how long these files need to be maintained on the server, have a job to move them to tape, and then have a cron job to remove the files after a certain number of days.

This is one area in which system administrators might need to be proactive and ask the tough questions such as, "Do you really need log files for six months, even after we move them to tape?" Sometimes the DBA won't understand what gets backed up to tape and will be hesitant to remove anything that might be needed later. Also, the DBA might not have ever considered how long he really needs to retain files, so those files will never be deleted. Finally, some DBAs are not strong UNIX people, so they might not yet have the skills write a cron job to remove their old files. Although most of these reasons are embarrassing for the DBA, they do happen, and the end result is excessive disk usage.

Notice that we discussed disk space usage considerably, but not I/O? Part of the reason is that I/O monitoring should be done by both the DBA and the sysadmin. The sysadmin should know which filesystems correspond to which disks and how much they are being accessed. The DBA should know which tables are being hit heavily and are not being found in memory resulting in disk I/O. By working together, the DBA should know which tables and SQL to tune, and the sysadmin should know how to spread I/O over as many disks as possible.

RAID is discussed in other sections of this book, and no doubt the system administrator will be familiar with it. In terms of databases, most DBAs obviously want RAID 0+1.

Because recovering a database due to media failure will impose system downtime, DBAs will want their datafiles mirrored. Because most databases are considered mission-critical, they should receive this level of protection. If necessary, RAID 5 can be used, but most DBAs fear the performance hit associated with it.

CPU Utilization

Databases generally consume more memory and disk than CPU, but this CPU time can be an issue. Obviously, you want to be working on a multiprocessor machine, if possible, because many databases can take advantage of multiple processors. Aside from that, one of the most common ways that a database will hog a CPU is with a long-running user process.

When a database user issues a long-running SQL statement, it can take hours or even days to execute. Sometimes these queries are valid and take so long just because of the complexity and sheer volume of data accessed. Other times the query is poorly tuned and is running for hours when it could be tuned to run in seconds. This sounds amazing, but we've seen it happen.

Regardless of the reason for the query, it can consume a single CPU and accumulate hundreds of minutes of CPU time. This usually is identified by complaints of poor performance followed by someone checking system load via uptime and then using top to notice a CPU with near 100% utilization.

Fortunately, if a user process is hogging a CPU, that usually can be traced back to a database login and even the individual SQL statement causing the problem. These are DBA responsibilities, but as a sysadmin, you have every right to have your DBA find out who is consuming the CPU and what that person is doing. At that point, the DBA might not yet know whether the query is a valid process or a runaway, but it is a place to start investigating. However, because a long-running query could be valid, you should resist the urge to `kill -9` any database job without permission from the DBA.

18

DATABASES

> **Note**
>
> This shouldn't have to be stated, but some system administrators are tempted to kill database processes that seem to be runaways. In reality, these could well be critical jobs running to create a report or do some other resource-intensive function. What might be excessive to you might well be expected behavior for a given database job.
>
> Work with the DBA to identify usual behavior for database processes. Also make sure that you can identify a database background process versus any

other background process. As a general rule, only the DBA should kill database processes. He will know whether killing a process will impact only one user or whether it will crash an entire database (which is sometimes necessary).

Those are how databases commonly impact server memory, disk, and CPU usage. As you can see, databases can be expected to take large amounts of memory and disk. This is normal. However, this should not be allowed to force the server into swapping and filling up filesystems. High levels of CPU usage might very well be normal, but they should be investigated.

How to Work with the DBA

It seems that, in many shops, DBAs and sysadmins are at odds, at least initially until they learn how to work with each other. This is unfortunate and is not necessary. Both parties are administrators, and both are responsible for their respective systems. Obviously, personality conflicts can occur anywhere, but most problems occur because both parties feel the other is "stepping on his toes."

As the system administrator, you should do the following regarding the DBA:

- Include the DBA when sizing a new database server. The DBA has a valid reason to be included in discussions regarding memory, CPU, disk layout, and RAID levels.

- Schedule any system maintenance and downtime with the DBA before you do it. Anything that you do regarding the box could impact the databases, its users, and any running database jobs. Nothing is more frustrating for a DBA and the user population than to have a box rebooted (crashing a database) without warning because the sysadmin didn't think it necessary to let people know. This isn't just a courtesy issue; databases might need to be recovered, and failed jobs can be difficult to fix when a server goes down.

- Explain to the DBA what you are doing regarding maintenance. Changes to patch levels, networking/firewalls, kernel parameters, and hardware can prevent a perfectly good database from running properly. The DBA needs time to determine whether your changes will impact his system and users.

- Explain the backup procedures for the machine and actually practice recoveries with the DBA. Both parties should clearly understand how backups and recoveries will be performed. Again, the procedures used for regular OS files are radically different than those for database files, and both sides need to understand what needs to be done. Also, notify the DBA of any changes to these procedures and also whether backups have failed.

- Provide the DBA with the same system-monitoring tools that you use, including top, sar, glance, and any third-party tools. The DBA needs these to examine what his database is doing in relation to the machine. Many databases are tightly integrated with the operating system, so the DBA has a valid reason to have these tools. Additionally, many database problems require the use of these tools.

- Don't get upset when the DBA asks questions and wants explanations regarding server performance, uptime, and backup and recovery procedures. It is his job to ask these questions; if he isn't asking them, then he isn't doing his job very well. The welfare of his database and applications are dependent on the server, so he has a duty to stay informed.

Just as you are expected to provide certain information and considerations for the DBAs, you should expect the following from your DBAs:

- A solid, working proficiency with UNIX. This includes using cron, vi, tar, com-press, file permissions, and basic shell scripting. These skills are necessary for the DBA because so much of the database is tied to the operating system. Whether it is scheduling a job to delete files, using tar to move applications, or using compress to shrink huge data files, these are DBA tasks when they involve database files. The sysadmin should be willing to help answer UNIX questions, but the DBA is responsible for learning these skills.

- The DBA should tell you exactly what database files and filesystems to back up and how to do so. The sysadmin should understand at a high level how the databases are backed up, but the detailed planning and ultimate responsibility falls on the DBA.

- Special needs of the database and any caveats should be documented and explained to the sysadmin. For example, it's not your job to intrinsically know that a database will hang if the transaction logs fill up the filesystem. The DBA needs to inform you of important details such as this. However, when he does, it becomes your responsibility to jointly monitor for this type of condition. This sort of education and cross-training reduces the likelihood of mistakes and misunderstandings.

- The DBA should know what database processes are running on the box and whether they are within normal thresholds. If a runaway database job is consuming CPU, the DBA should investigate and kill the job accordingly.

- Expect the DBA to use system resources prudently. He shouldn't take up disk space and memory just because it is available. Although nothing is gained by not

18

DATABASES

using unused memory or disk, the DBA needs to tune his database, not just throw memory at it.

- The DBA should not just create database after database (consuming disk and memory) without regard for system resources. Also, he should take time to plan what databases will be created, how large they will be, and how the box can support them. This type of capacity planning is a joint effort between the DBAs and the SAs.

- Clean out old, unneeded files on a regular basis. Also, accidentally filling up filesystems to 100% is bad and normally can be avoided with proper monitoring.

Note

Some system administrators will happily give their root passwords to the DBAs, while others consider this policy unthinkable. We have worked in both types of environments, and here are our thoughts.

Sometimes the database needs someone with a root password to perform a task. In some cases, these are not time-sensitive issues, so they can wait for the system administrator. Other times, root actions are needed to keep the database running/accessible.

Assuming that the DBA is experienced, knowledgeable, and responsible, he should have the root password for emergency use. This is especially true in small shops in which the sysadmin isn't always available. Ideally, the DBA should be so well versed in the UNIX operating system that he can serve as a backup system administrator. In fact, as time permits, the sysadmin should be trained as a backup DBA. This makes sense because the core responsibilities are so similar. This ultimately makes for a much more skilled, valuable, and marketable administrator.

Those are key points of contention that we've noticed between DBAs and sysadmins. Both parties are skilled, technical administrators, but, unfortunately, there are often conflicts. Some of these are unavoidable, and others are even healthy. At the end of the day, though, it is the computer system which must be the ultimate winner. Management doesn't care whether the DBA or the sysadmin is "right" about an issue or policy; they care only that the database is available, secure, and meeting the business needs. As long as the DBA and sysadmin camps work together to meet this goal, success is easier to achieve.

Choosing a Database Vendor

When designing a system, many vendor-related choices need to be made regarding platform, application, Web server, database, and others. Many factors impact the decision: some technical, some market/industry driven, economical, and others political.

The following factors should be considered when choosing a database vendor, although these factors largely are applicable to the system.

Platform Selection

See what platform the database will run on. For example, what if the database runs only on NT and you are a UNIX shop? Sure, you *could* buy an NT server for it, but adding different platforms adds complexity to your system. Also, make sure that the vendor is committed to your platform in the long term. Some shops that use more exotic versions of Linux or UNIX often find themselves in this situation. They purchase a product for a platform and then find in a year or two that it no longer is supported.

Supporting Large versus Small Systems

Some RDBMS have a proven track record of supporting very large systems, while others are considered to be little more than toys. Oracle and DB2 are two examples of databases that can support large systems. If your project is expected to be large and has a large enough budget, one of these two vendors seriously should be considered. Few things are as disastrous as building an expensive system and going "live," only to find it too underpowered to do the job. This failure in system sizing and capacity planning ultimately results in more costs and downtime than if the system had been built right in the first place.

At the other end of the spectrum, not every application needs a mammoth RDBMS. Many small, in-house systems or Rapid Application Development (RAD) experiments use Microsoft Access in the Windows world. In the UNIX world, smaller, inexpensive systems such as MySQL fit the bill. Reasons for this often include price of the RDBMS, availability, and complexity. In many cases, these small systems are supported by the application developer, who usually isn't a full-time DBA. Also, if a system is used by only a handful of users, a highly tuned and robust RDBMS seems to be overkill.

So, what if your system lies somewhere in between large and small? Given that choice, we recommend scaling for the large system. You don't want to have to build the same system twice. Nor do you want to reach a point at which the performance demands exceed the capabilities of your database. Therefore, when in doubt, scale big.

Performance and Complexity

When you have narrowed the scope to a few vendors, take a detailed look at the capabilities of each database. Meet with the vendors and talk to both their salespeople and their technical people. Also find other customers in other shops who have the database, and ask about their experiences. Here are some of the factors to consider:

- **Locking**—All databases impose locks when a user updates a row. The question is whether the RDBMS is "smart" enough to lock only the row being changed or whether it locks the entire table. If you plan to support anything more than a few users, table-level locking will be a big performance hit. Oracle was one of the first databases to use row-level locking; other vendors have been hurrying to catch up. Check with your perspective vendor and get the solid answers in writing.

- **Size limits**—Just as some UNIX systems now are overcoming the 2GB file limit, database vendors are in the same situation. Check to see if the database still has 2GB file or table limits. If you plan to support large systems, this could be a factor.

- **Backup and recovery**—All databases can be backed up and recovered, but how easily and to what point in time? If you can shut down your database only once a week for OS file copy and can recover only to that time, you risk losing up to a week's worth of data. More complex databases allow you to apply transaction logs to recover to any given point in time. Depending on your business requirements, this could be a factor.

- **Parallel processing**—Some databases can take advantage of multiple CPUs to run long queries and DML statements. This is especially useful in large data warehouse situations.

When looking at the RDBMS, look for these specifics. Also make sure that when the salesperson says, "Yes we support X," he is willing to back it up in writing. Be certain that the features advertised are directly applicable to your system without any additional setup. For example, a database might support parallel processing of SQL statements, but if you are a small OPTP database, you won't notice any benefits.

Support and Interfaces

Some databases, particularly well-established RDBMS, easily can be integrated with other products, have a wide range of supporting tools, and have large number of technical people already trained for it. If you are building a large, expensive, mission-critical system, this is the type of RDBMS that you want. Many databases are designed to be integrated with specific Web/application servers, backup utilities, and programming languages and development tools. These factors need to be considered when designing a total system.

In other cases, all you want is just a database without the Web/application servers, integrated development environments, and other fancy bells and whistles. All you might want are a few tables in a simple database that you can access via ODBC. If so, there is no reason to get a large, complex system. Luckily, there are databases that fit that requirement as well.

Price and Vendor Availability

Some databases can be very expensive. Yearly license renewals can easily exceed $100,000 for a medium-size shop and millions for large organizations. Obviously, you want to get the specific details of what a license will cost for your system before you make the final decision. Be prepared to deal with "sticker shock," complex pricing algorithms, and expensive add-ons when dealing with vendors.

Your vendor should be established and should be expected to be in business for the foreseeable future. You need to do your homework on this. Currently, some vendors might not make it and likely will be bought out soon or will go under. You don't want to build a system and then have to convert to a new database because of this. Also see what kind of support services are offered because they will be needed no matter how good your DBA is.

If the vendor is obscure or the technology is highly advanced, finding skilled people to support it can be difficult. It does no good to own a system that is either too complex to manage or so obscure that no one knows it. Make sure that your system is "popular" enough that you can find a DBA to support it. We have seen cases in which DBAs will leave companies rather than learn certain database systems. The reason is often not because they don't want to learn a new technology, but rather because they can make more money being a DBA for X database rather than Y database. Also, if the system is too complex for your in-house people, you will need to either get them trained or hire new employees/consultants. These issues should not be underestimated because we have seen them adversely impact some shops.

Those are some of the factors involved when selecting a particular database. We will now look at two vendors at opposite ends of the spectrum: Oracle for large systems and MySQL for small systems.

Oracle Database Overview

Oracle Corporation has quite possibly the finest database systems that money can buy. When building large, mission-critical systems on the UNIX platform, Oracle is the

18

DATABASES

choice for most businesses and government agencies. Oracle also runs on Linux and NT, but this discussion will be focused on UNIX.

Oracle's databases are Object-Relational Database Management Systems (ORDBMS) starting with Oracle version 8. These are essentially RDBMS, but with support for some object-oriented features. Currently most systems are supporting Oracle versions 7, 8, and 8i. However, as of this writing, Oracle 9i is being released and no doubt will be as successful as 8i.

Oracle's databases offer the following features:

- **High performance**—Oracle transaction speeds benchmark very well against the competition. However, don't get overly focused on this because speed alone is not the only critical factor.
- **Row-level locking**—Oracle has supported row-level locking for many years now. If you have tens or hundreds of users, this is a requirement. Furthermore, each release of Oracle improves its locking algorithms to be more efficient.
- **Point-in-time recovery**—When properly set up, an Oracle database can be recovered to any given point in time. Additionally, each release of Oracle improves the database reliability and makes it easier and faster to recover a database.
- **Size limits**—Current versions of Oracle no longer have any file size limitations.
- **Parallel processing**—Oracle can be configured to automatically take advantage of multiple processors. This is especially useful in large systems and data warehouses.
- **Clustering**—UNIX clusters can be used to advantage with Oracle databases. Oracle Parallel Server (OPS), now named Real Application Clusters (RAC), allows databases to exist on clusters to improve fault tolerance.

Those are some of the features of interest to system administrators, but there are other benefits as well. An Oracle proprietary SQL-based programming language called PL/SQL is a very common way to write applications for the database. Multiple Oracle design, development, and reporting tools are available and are fully supported. Oracle has tightly embraced the idea of integrating the database with Java and the Web. This has come in the form of enhancing the database itself as well as marketing Web/application servers such as Oracle Application Server (OAS) and now Internet Application Server (iAS).

All of these database tools usually fall under control of the DBA to install, configure, and administrate. Not only is the DBA responsible for the database, but he also is responsible for the design tools (Oracle Designer), developer tools (Oracle Forms and Reports, Developer 6i), and Web/application tools (WebDB/Oracle Portal, OAS, and iAS). Clearly, this becomes a full-time job very quickly!

Although entire books have been written on the subject of Oracle databases, we will cover those points most critical for the sysadmin to understand.

Machine Setup

Oracle databases should be segregated on their own machines (database servers). It is not uncommon to purchase new servers dedicated solely for Oracle. We've even seen Sun E10000s dedicated solely for Oracle databases, so don't try to fit your entire Web, application, and database on one box unless it is truly small.

Users and Groups

It is standard to create a user oracle and primary group dba. All Oracle files (both database and installation) will be owned by the user oracle. Individual user accounts for DBAs should be placed in the group dba. Do not place the user root in dba, nor should oracle be in root.

Some Oracle documentation discusses a group oinstall, but this is *not* necessary and will only add complexity to your system, so you should ignore it.

Many DBAs prefer the Korn shell, but that is largely a DBA preference. Also, give the oracle account his own .profile (not linked to a master file) because he will need to customize it with his own settings. Also make sure that the account has permission to use cron and access to tools such as top.

The oracle home directory can be in a location such as /home/oracle, like any other user. However, the actual Oracle software and database files will need to be on their own filesystems, which we discuss in a later section. Finally, the DBA will need to create some Oracle files in /etc and /var/opt/oracle (for Solaris), so be prepared to fulfill these requests during the software installation.

Memory Sizing and Configuration

When sizing your server initially, try to get as much memory as possible. Oracle operates in one large memory area, referred to as the System Global Area or Shared Global Area (SGA). This DBA-configured memory structure is where Oracle caches data blocks used by SQL and DML. Oracle has efficient caching algorithms, but performance is largely at the mercy of the amount of memory available and how well tuned the SQL code is.

The SGA is composed of multiple memory pools, and your DBA knows how to size these. What he needs is the maximum amount of memory available to work with. Each individual Oracle database needs from 75MB up to nearly 1GB of memory. As for the efficiency of the SQL code, make sure that your DBA is working with the application

18

DATABASES

developers to tune their code because this is an area that can dramatically improve system performance.

Oracle works with shared memory. Specifically, the SGA is one or more large shared memory segments that are attached to and accessed by individual Oracle child processes. Each of these processes represents a user logged into the database. As the user issues SQL statements, Oracle background processes search the SGA for the data blocks needed to fulfill the request. If they are resident in memory, they are returned to the user. Otherwise, calls are made to read from the data files. This can result in a physical read from the disk or from the UNIX disk cache. Regardless, because this was not found in the SGA, it represents a performance hit for the user.

When a user process issues a DML (insert, update, or delete) statement, it writes the change to the row in memory. This is why Oracle must use shared memory, because each user process needs to be capable of writing to this memory area.

The use of such a large amount of shared memory is one area that the sysadmin needs to be concerned with. The sysadmin needs to modify the /etc/system file and bounce the server to make sure that enough shared memory is available for Oracle. The following is an excerpt from a /etc/system on a Solaris machine that we worked on:

```
$ more /etc/system
...
set shmsys:shminfo_shmmax=805306368
set shmsys:shminfo_shmmin=200
set shmsys:shminfo_shmmni=200
set shmsys:shminfo_shmseg=200
set semsys:seminfo_semmni=4096
set semsys:seminfo_semmsl=500
set semsys:seminfo_semmns=4096
set semsys:seminfo_semopm=100
set semsys:seminfo_semvmx=32767
```

Here is a description of some of the key values:

```
set shmsys:shminfo_shmmax=805306368
```

SHMMAX is the maximum allowable size (in bytes) of an individual shared-memory segment. Ideally, this should be larger than any single SGA on your box so that each SGA will have its own single contiguous memory segment. Otherwise, it will be broken into several smaller segments, which is not as good from a performance standpoint.

```
set shmsys:shminfo_shmmin=200
```

`SHMMIN` is the boundary for the smallest allowable size (in bytes) for an individual shared memory segment.

```
set shmsys:shminfo_shmmni=200
```

`SHMMNI` is the total maximum number of shared memory segments on the box at any given time.

```
set shmsys:shminfo_shmseg=200
```

`SHMSEG` is the total maximum number of shared memory segments of any one individual process.

How large should you size your parameters? First, you should remember that when you set these shared-memory parameters, you are *not* saying that they will be automatically allocated at this level. These parameters are simply upper limits and do not cause swapping. As for a good starting point, refer to the Oracle Installation and Configuration Guide (ICG) for your specific platform and database version.

Semaphores are another issue when configuring a box for Oracle. These normally are not a problem unless Oracle cannot acquire them. These are the settings for semaphores that you need to configure:

```
set semsys:seminfo_semmns=4096
```

`SEMMNS` is the maximum number of semaphore identifiers for the system at any one time. This value should exceed the sum of the Oracle `init.ora` parameter `PROCESSES` for every simultaneously running database on your server. It should exceed this value because other processes on the box might need semaphores, and Oracle needs additional semaphores during instance startup.

```
set semsys:seminfo_semopm=100
```

`SEMOPM` is the maximum number of operations per `semop` call.

```
set semsys:seminfo_semvmx=32767
```

`SEMVMX` is the maximum value of a semaphore.

If you are working on Sun Solaris and are running greater than Solaris 2.6 and Oracle 7.3, you should enable intimate shared memory. This locks the SGA into real memory and allows processes to share the same page table entry. Both of these improve performance. Starting with Oracle 8i and Solaris 2.6, this is enabled by default.

Finally, make sure that you understand how your particular operating system handles swap. Some operating systems require a backing space of swap for allocated memory. Some administrators see this and jump to the conclusion that their machines are actively

18

DATABASES

swapping, which they are not. Especially if the sysadmin is already suspect of the seemingly large SGA(s), blaming Oracle and saying that it is causing swapping is a very common scapegoat when unexplained system problems occur.

Filesystems and Disks

Oracle is set to install and run optimally on four or more mount points, usually referred to as /u01, /u02, ... /u0X. The following is a sample of a typical Oracle installation:

```
$ df -k
Filesystem              kbytes     used   avail capacity  Mounted on
/dev/vx/dsk/rootvol    2056211    92440 1902085     5%    /
/dev/vx/dsk/usr        4032142  1047918 2943903    27%    /usr
/proc                        0        0       0     0%    /proc
fd                           0        0       0     0%    /dev/fd
mnttab                       0        0       0     0%    /etc/mnttab
/dev/vx/dsk/var        3933982    46614 3848029     2%    /var
swap                   3386832        0 3386832     0%    /var/run
/dev/vx/dsk/opt        3009327   397623 2551518    14%    /opt
/dev/vx/dsk/u01        5235898  3660752 1522788    71%    /u01
/dev/vx/dsk/u02        5235898  3169993 2013547    62%    /u02
/dev/vx/dsk/u04        5235898  4310880  872660    84%    /u04
swap                   3387200      368 3386832     1%    /tmp
/dev/vx/dsk/u03        5235898  4132592 1050948    80%    /u03
/dev/vx/dsk/ubackup    6251986  2727554 3461913    45%    /ubackup
/dev/vx/dsk/home       4131866  3690144  400404    91%    /export/home
```

Here we have a server with four mount points (/u01 ... /u04) dedicated to Oracle. Following Oracle Corporation's established Optimal Flexible Architecture guidelines, we structure our filesystems like this:

> **/u01**—Oracle installation software only
>
> **/u02**—Oracle database, control, online redo log files
>
> **/u03**—Oracle database, control, online redo log files
>
> **/u04**—Oracle database, control, online redo log files
>
> **/u0X**—Oracle database, control, online redo log files

Specific OFA guidelines exist for the subdirectory structure, such as /u01/app/oracle and oradata, but these will be managed by the DBA. Your job is to make sure that these are available to the DBA and that no other user or application tries to use these Oracle filesystems.

Notice that we also made a /ubackup directory, That is not required, but a location like this is helpful. The Oracle database needs a location to dump its archive log files (saved transaction logs) and export .dmp files (data dumps). It is imperative that this filesystem never becomes full if Oracle automatically is archiving log files to this location. If it does, your databases will hang. We strongly recommend that a cron job monitor this location and send email or pager alerts when it reaches a certain level (as in, 1GB left).

Make sure that the user oracle (in group dba) has write permission to each filesystem. This is a common mistake that almost every sysadmin makes. They create the user oracle and the filesystems, and turn them over to the DBA, only to have the DBA come back 5 minutes later saying that he needs rwx permissions on the directories. It's not a big deal, but it happens all the time.

As for mirroring, RAID 0+1 is preferred for the database. If necessary, RAID 5 can be used for data files and control files, but the transaction logs (online redo logs) really should be on your fastest disks because they continually are written to. Unless you are using OPS or RAC, there is no need to use raw partitions; doing so will only complicate matters for both you and the DBA.

Ideally, you will have your filesystems striped across different disks so that your DBA can segregate his different Oracle files the way he is trained to. Make sure that you provide this information to the DBA. Also make sure that these disks are reserved for Oracle use only. The database should not have to contend with other applications for disk I/O or disk space.

Architecture

An Oracle system can be broken down into the following components: files, memory, and processes. The memory and process components then comprise a database *instance*.

Oracle Files

Two main types of files exist: installation/configuration and database files.

Installation/configuration files are installed with the software from the CD-ROM. The software files almost exclusively should be located on the /u01 filesystem, with only a very few files in /etc and /var/opt/oracle. Some are binary, and others are text files. The DBA can use a text editor such as vi to modify them, or more recent versions of Oracle have GUI assistants that can be used. These files are normal UNIX files and are not subject to the rigorous timestamp and status checking used by Oracle database files. Therefore, you can use normal UNIX backup procedures to back up and restore these installation and configuration files.

Database files are those that compose an actual database. They are different than the installation/configuration files previously discussed. These should be separated from any other files (both Oracle and non-Oracle) on filesystems /u02 ... /u0X. Keep in mind that these are the files that are subject to status and timestamp checking; we will discuss their backup procedures in a later section.

An Oracle database is composed of the following types of files: data, control, and online redo logs.

- **Data files**—These are the files containing the actual data tables and indexes for the database. These files compose the bulk of your database. You usually can expect at least 6 of these files and up to more than 100, depending on the size of the database. Sizes also vary widely from a few megabytes to over the 2GB level. The I/O activity should be low to moderate because Oracle hopefully doesn't need to access them frequently.

- **Control files**—Information about the database structure, timestamp, and status is stored in the control file(s). These are relatively small (a few megabytes) binary files used to store control information about the database. Because these files are so important and so small, it is common to have Oracle automatically maintain several copies of these. The DBA should insist on this and should place them on separate disks. The I/O activity on these should be relatively low because they are accessed only during database startup and shutdown, and periodically during database checkpoints.

- **Online redo log files**—These files represent the database's transaction log. Every change to the database, such as an insert, update, or delete, as well as any structural modification, is written to a these files. These files are used to recover the database in the event of a crash, and new versions of Oracle allow the DBA to review these logs. These files are extremely important, so they should be mirrored on separate, fast disks. Additionally, for fault tolerance and performance reasons, most DBAs have multiple groups of these files multiplexed (Oracle mirroring) in addition to normal disk mirroring. Expect a high level of activity on these files because every change to the database is written to them.

Two other types of important files do not cleanly fit into either of our classifications: database log/trace files and archive log files.

- **Log and trace files**—These files are generated by each individual database and are written to the /u01/app/oracle/admin/*databasename* subdirectories. They are reviewed by the DBA to detect and diagnose database errors. These files can be deleted or compressed as necessary and can be backed up using normal methods with the other Oracle installation/configuration files.

- **Archived redo log files**—Oracle has an option to save off each online redo log file as a means of extending the backup and recovery options available for a database.

When Oracle is done writing each online redo log file, it makes a copy to one or more file locations in the form of archived redo log files. Work with the DBA to place these files on a large, mirrored filesystem. Each of these files usually is 100MB or less (the DBA determines this), but an active database can generate one every few minutes. These files can be compressed, but if the filesystem fills up and Oracle can't write to it, your database will hang.

Oracle Memory

We previously mentioned that each Oracle database has a large shared memory area referred to as the SGA. Depending on the size of the database (in terms of files and concurrent users), this area could be quiet large. However, it should not be so large that it causes swapping or thrashing. The DBA can resize the SGA, but, unless you are using Oracle 9i, it requires restarting the database. Obviously, this isn't always possible if there are a large number of users on the database.

Oracle Processes

Just as UNIX has separate background processes to perform database tasks, each individual database has its own processes. Each running Oracle database has two kinds of processes: background processes and user processes.

Background processes are those supporting processes that do the work for the actual database. They start up when the database is started and terminate when it is shut down. Some are required, and others are configured by the DBA. The following is a list of the most common background processes that you will see:

- **PMON**—Process Monitor (PMON) is required for each Oracle database. It cleans up terminated processes.
- **SMON**—System Monitor (SMON) is required for each Oracle database. It performs instance recovery after database crashes and coalesces segments on disks.
- **DBWR**—Database Writer (DBWR) is required for each Oracle database. It performs writes from the SGA to the data files on disk.
- **LGWR**—Log Writer (LGWR) is required for each Oracle database. It performs writes from the SGA to the online redo log files.
- **CKPT**—Checkpoint (CKPT) is required for Oracle 8 and above. Periodically, it forces a flush of the memory buffers in the SGA and updates header information in each database file.
- **ARCH**—Archiver (ARC0 or ARCH, depending on version) is optional. If you configure Oracle to save off each online redo log file to an archive log file, you should see this process running.

18

DATABASES

Just like any UNIX process, you can see these processes via `top` or `ps -ef`. The name of the database is part of the process name, so you can associate processes with specific databases. For example, here we see all the processes for the database demo:

```
$ ps -ef | grep demo
oracle     897    1  0 20:35 ?        00:00:00 ora_pmon_demo
oracle     899    1  0 20:35 ?        00:00:00 ora_dbw0_demo
oracle     901    1  0 20:35 ?        00:00:00 ora_lgwr_demo
oracle     903    1  0 20:35 ?        00:00:00 ora_ckpt_demo
oracle     905    1  0 20:35 ?        00:00:00 ora_smon_demo
oracle     907    1  0 20:35 ?        00:00:00 ora_reco_demo
oracle     909    1  0 20:35 ?        00:00:00 ora_s000_demo
oracle     911    1  0 20:35 ?        00:00:00 ora_d000_demo
oracle     913    1  0 20:35 ?        00:00:00 ora_d001_demo
oracle     915    1  0 20:35 ?        00:00:00 ora_d002_demo
$
```

Do not kill any database background process unless the database already is crashed and you are performing cleanup. If you kill any of the five required processes (PMON, SMON, LGWR, DBWR, or CKPT), your database *will* crash. Because these processes are required, many DBAs and sysadmins `grep` for the PMON process to check whether a database is up or down. In fact, many shell scripts check for a PMON process before they attempt to do work on a database. Here we see a listing of all the databases currently running.

In this case, we can see that demo and rh1dev1 are the only two databases running on the machine:

```
$ ps -ef | grep pmon
oracle     897    1    0 20:35 ?        00:00:00 ora_pmon_demo
oracle     962    1    0 20:36 ?        00:00:00 ora_pmon_rh1dev1
oracle     991  919    0 20:38 pts/0    00:00:00 grep pmon
$
```

The other type of Oracle process that you will see is user processes. These represent users logged onto the database doing work. Just like the Oracle background processes, we can see these user processes. Here we see that there are three database logins, two for rh1dev1 and one for demo:

```
$ ps -ef | grep -i descrip
oracle     993   992  0 20:38 ?        00:00:00 oraclerh1dev1 (DESCRIPTION=(LOCA
oracle    1011  1010  0 20:38 ?        00:00:00 oraclerh1dev1 (DESCRIPTION=(LOCA
oracle    1037  1036  0 20:40 ?        00:00:00 oracledemo (DESCRIPTION=(LOCAL=Y
oracle    1045  1012  0 20:41 pts/0    00:00:00 grep -i descrip
$
```

We searched for the string `descrip` because this indicates whether the connection into the database is local or remote. We could just as easily have searched for the string `oracle`, but we also would have received the Oracle background processes.

Another good tool to use is `top`. If you find Oracle user processes hogging a CPU or with large amounts of CPU time, ask the DBA to investigate. He can use SQL scripts to tie a UNIX PID to a specific database session. At that point, he can determine whether the process is normal or is a runaway. Always let the DBA kill these processes within the database, if possible. This allows for cleaner rollback and recovery of the user's transactions. However, if necessary, these user processes can be killed at the UNIX level without crashing the database.

Database Instance

DBAs typically talk of databases as instances. An instance is the set of memory structures and background (not user) processes that compose a running Oracle database. Technically, a "database" is just the collection of data, control, and online redo log files on disk for a particular database. By definition, it takes a database (files) and a corresponding instance (memory and processes) to be accessed by the users. Therefore, when a DBA talks about starting or stopping a database, he really means the *instance*, not the actual data files.

DBAs often refer to Oracle databases as SIDs. These refer the term system identifier, which is the actual name for a database. For example, when we saw the database instance demo running, it also could be referred to as the demo SID.

Installation Process

Oracle database installation really is a job for the DBA. Enough factors are involved that the sysadmin should set up the machine and let the DBA do the install. However, here is an overview of the process and common issues encountered.

Before any Oracle software installation, the DBA needs to read the Installation and Configuration Guide (ICG) and search online support services for known bugs. Most problems with installations are related to not reading and complying with the ICG. Additionally, support services such as MetaLink (`http://www.oracle.metalink.com`) and Technet (`http://www.technet.oracle.com`) provide sometimes essential tips, procedures, and software patches needed for installs. The DBA should review all of these sources before he begins. MetaLink is for paying Oracle support customers and has good advice and patches. Technet is free to anyone and has all the Oracle documentation, ICG, free software, and discussion boards (especially useful for Linux users).

18

DATABASES

After the DBA has read the ICG and reviewed the online support services, he will be able to tell you exactly what needs to be created/modified in terms of Oracle users, groups, filesystems, and shared memory parameters. When these are established on a machine, they seldom change greatly between Oracle versions, but minor changes sometimes are needed.

Since Oracle 7.3, each Oracle software tree must be installed in a separate location ($ORACLE_HOME). These trees are located off the $ORACLE_HOME/product subdirectory. For example, here we have different software trees for the databases Oracle 8.1.6 (8i) and 9.0.1 (9i) and the Web server iAS:

```
$ cd $ORACLE_BASE
$ pwd
/u01/app/oracle
$ ls
admin  doc  jre  local  oradata  oraInventory  oui  product
$ ls product
8.1.6  9.0.1  ias10210
$
```

This separation is necessary. Oracle is sensitive to which version of software is used to start each database, and it cannot distinguish between executables. Therefore, you must set your environment variables correctly, as covered in a later section.

Modern releases of Oracle now use a Java-based installer called the Oracle Universal Installer (OUI). This provides the same look and feel across clients and servers. However, it mandates that you launch a graphical tool to install Oracle. Therefore, you need X Windows to be configured because regular telnet won't work.

This shouldn't be an issue for sysadmins, but some DBAs have difficulty getting the OUI to launch when they connect to the server. The most common problem is that they forgot to set their DISPLAY variable:

```
$ echo $DISPLAY
192.168.1.11:0.0
$
```

Obviously, this needs to be set to the IP of their local machine, followed by :0.0. This is a frequent mistake. After the environment is set, the OUI should start up with the following command:

```
$ cd /mnt/cdrom
$ ls
doc  index.htm  install  rr_moved  runInstaller  stage  starterdb
$ ./runInstaller
```

After a few seconds the screen shown in Figure 18.3 will appear.

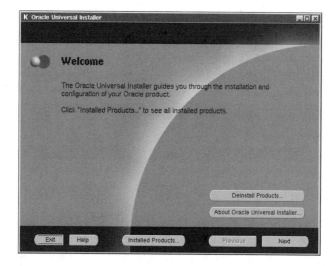

FIGURE 18.3

Oracle Universal Installer.

When the DBA gets to this point, he should be able to follow the directions and install the software.

At the end of the installation process, the DBA will be prompted to run an Oracle pro-vided script called `root.sh`. If the DBA has root, he can run it himself with no problem. Otherwise, you will need to run it for him, but it is a simple script and it takes only sec-onds to run.

There are various post-install actions, such as database verification, patching, and envi-ronment setup. However, these are really DBA functions; when you (as the sysadmin) have set up oracle in accordance with the ICG and have executed the `root.sh` script, the DBA should be mostly self-sufficient.

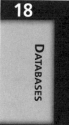

Database Environment and File Configuration

Most of the configuration of the database environment should be done by the DBA, but the sysadmin should understand a few environment variables, files, and processes.

ORACLE_SID

ORACLE_SID is the environment variable that defines which database you are connecting to. By setting this variable to a specific database, you are defining where any utility that you start will be issued against. Here we set our ORACLE_SID to the demo database:

```
$ export $ORACLE_SID=demo
$ echo $ORACLE_SID
demo
$
```

Remember to always verify your Oracle SID before undertaking any type of maintenance operation. It is very easy to get pointed to the wrong database if you don't.

ORACLE_BASE

The ORACLE_BASE variable is a starting point for your database path. It doesn't indicate any particular database SID or version, but it does identify where much of the software is located.

```
$ echo $ORACLE_BASE
/u01/app/oracle
$ ls $ORACLE_BASE
admin  doc  jre  local  oradata  oraInventory  oui  product
$
```

Underneath the admin subdirectory are the logging, trace, and configuration files for each database. Under the oradata subdirectory are any actual database data, control, and online redo log files, although this breaks with the standard of not having these files on /u01. The product subdirectory contains the software tree for each release of Oracle.

ORACLE_HOME

The ORACLE_HOME variable identifies which set of executables will be used against the database identified by $ORACLE_SID. Set the ORACLE_HOME variable to be the $ORACLE_BASE/product/*version* for the database. For example, if we want to access the demo database which is Oracle 9i, we need to have the following ORACLE_HOME variable set:

```
$ echo $ORACLE_HOME
/u01/app/oracle/product/9.0.1
$
```

This will force the use of 9.0.1 executables to be used. It is a good policy to verify your ORACLE_HOME before starting utilities against a database. This is particularly important when starting, recovering, doing other maintenance tasks with the database.

oratab

The /etc/oratab file is a text file that lists each database SID, its $ORACLE_HOME, and whether it should be automatically started when the server is started. Because the $ORACLE_HOME indicates the database version for each database, this file is a good way to quickly identify which databases are on a machine. The following is a sample oratab file:

```
$ more /etc/oratab
demo:/u01/app/oracle/product/9.0.1:N
```

```
rh1dev1:/u01/app/oracle/product/8.1.6:N
ias1021:/u01/app/oracle/product/ias10210:N
$
```

Here we see three databases, named `demo`, `rh1dev1`, and `ias1021`, and the corresponding software version for each.

`oratab` is updated by some Oracle tools and the DBA when databases are created. This file is read by some Oracle utilities to set up environments and networking. Additionally, many DBAs reference this file in their shell scripts to get database information for a machine.

tnsnames.ora

To connect to an Oracle database on another server, you need a tnsnames.ora file in either `/etc` or `/var/opt/oracle` (on Solaris). If the file isn't located in either location, it can be placed in the `$ORACLE_HOME/network/admin` directory, but this method is not preferred.

This text file contains the name of each database, the server it's located on, and the port number (usually 1521) to connect to. This file also is located in the `$ORACLE_HOME/network/admin` subdirectories for each product installed on Windows PCs. The following is an sample tnsnames.ora file:

```
$ more /etc/tnsnames.ora
# TNSNAMES.ORA Configuration File:/u01/app/oracle/product/8.1.6/network/admin/tn
snames.ora
# Generated by Oracle configuration tools.

RH1DEV1.MIKE.COM =
  (DESCRIPTION =
    (ADDRESS_LIST =
      (ADDRESS = (PROTOCOL = TCP)(HOST = mikehat.mike.com)(PORT = 1521))
    )
    (CONNECT_DATA =
      (SERVICE_NAME = rh1dev1.mike.com)
    )
  )

DEMO.MIKE.COM =
  (DESCRIPTION =
    (ADDRESS_LIST =
      (ADDRESS = (PROTOCOL = TCP)(HOST = mikehat.mike.com)(PORT = 1521))
    )
    (CONNECT_DATA =
      (SERVICE_NAME = demo.mike.com)
    )
  )
```

18

DATABASES

This file usually is initially created by Oracle network configuration tools as a template. The DBA then updates it manually to reflect new and deleted databases.

If users are having difficulty connecting to a database, make sure that they have the latest copy of this file and that it is in the correct locations their PCs. Many problems occur because someone didn't get a current copy, made a typo when editing the file, or doesn't have it in the correct $ORACLE_HOME/network/admin directory.

listener.ora

A server hosting a database needs to have a listener process running to receive outside connection requests and route them to the correct database. This Oracle listener process is managed by the lsnrctl utility and configured by the listener.ora file.

The listener.ora file is located in the same locations as tnsnames.ora: /etc, /var/opt/oracle (Solaris), or $ORACLE_HOME/network/admin. This file contains the name of each database on the server, its version, and the port that it expects to receive requests on. The following is a sample listener.ora file:

```
$  more /etc/listener.ora
# LISTENER.ORA Configuration File:/u01/app/oracle/product/9.0.1/network/admin/li
stener.ora
LISTENER =
  (DESCRIPTION_LIST =
    (DESCRIPTION =
      (ADDRESS_LIST =
        (ADDRESS = (PROTOCOL = TCP)(HOST = mikehat.mike.com)(PORT = 1521))
      )
      (ADDRESS_LIST =
        (ADDRESS = (PROTOCOL = IPC)(KEY = EXTPROC))
      )
    )
  )
SID_LIST_LISTENER =
  (SID_LIST =
    (SID_DESC =
      (SID_NAME = PLSExtProc)
      (ORACLE_HOME = /u01/app/oracle/product/8.1.6)
      (PROGRAM = extproc)
    )
    (SID_DESC =
      (GLOBAL_DBNAME = rh1dev1.mike.com)
      (ORACLE_HOME = /u01/app/oracle/product/8.1.6)
      (SID_NAME = rh1dev1)
    )
(SID_DESC =
      (GLOBAL_DBNAME = demo.mike.com)
```

```
      (ORACLE_HOME = /u01/app/oracle/product/9.0.1)
      (SID_NAME = demo)
    )

  )
```

Here we can see that the `listener.ora` file is configured for receiving requests for the rh1dev1 and demo databases on port 1521.

The listener process needs to be running for the databases to receive external connections. To start the listener process, set your `$ORACLE_HOME` for the highest version of the database and execute the following:

```
$ lsnrctl start
```

To stop the listener process, issue this command:

```
$ lsnrctl stop
```

If changes are made to the listener.ora file, you can stop and restart the listener using the previous commands, or you can issue the following command:

```
$ lsnrctl reload
```

Always check that the listener process is running when connectivity problems are reported. DBAs sometimes start their databases but forget to start the listener processes. This can be done either by checking for the listener's background process or with the lnsrctl utility:

```
$ lsnrctl status
```

If a listener process has been running a while or has been reloaded, it might become "confused." In cases like this, it is best to completely stop the process with `lsrnctl`, kill any lingering listener UNIX processes, and then restart it.

init*SID*.ora

Each database has a configuration file that determines the parameters for the database. The sizes of each pool within the SGA and many other parameters are stored in this text file. This file exists in the `$ORACLE_BASE`/admin/*databasename*/bdump directory as a soft link from `$ORACLE_HOME`/dbs.

```
$ ls -l $ORACLE_HOME/dbs
total 64
lrwxrwxrwx    1 oracle    dba               47 Jul  8 07:26 initdemo.ora ->
/u01/app/oracle/admin/demo/pfile/initdemo.ora
-rw-r--r--    1 oracle    dba            12920 May 10 18:05 initdw.ora
-rw-r--r--    1 oracle    dba             8385 May 10 18:05 init.ora
-rw-rw----    1 oracle    dba               24 Sep 30 20:35 lkDEMO
```

As a system administrator, you should not modify this file. This absolutely is DBA territory.

Backups

Developing effective backup and recovery policies needs to be done with the input of the DBA. The DBA understands the different ways that an Oracle database can and cannot be backed up. This is important because Oracle database files are extremely sensitive to internal timestamps and status. Sure, you can back up any file, but if Oracle doesn't think that the restored file is valid, your recovery *will* fail. The problem is that, unless you actually test your backup and recoveries, you won't know whether there is a problem until you need to recover a database for real.

Your DBA will get the database files to a consistent state where you can safely copy the files off to tape as normal. He needs you to provide a method to copy those files to another disk or tape at a given time. The DBA will be able to provide you with two types of backup methods, during which time you can copy the files off like you would for any given file. These two methods are cold and hot backups.

Cold Backups

Cold backups (also called offline backups) consist of cleanly shutting down the database instance. When the database is successfully closed, all the database file headers have the same consistent, shutdown state. At this point, you can copy all of the files off to tape.

Cold backups come at the obvious drawback of requiring the database to be shut down during the backup. The benefit is that they are conceptually simple to implement. The only rules are these:

1. The database must be cleanly shut down while each file is backed up.

2. If the database is in NOARCHIVELOG mode, in which online redo log files are *not* being copied off to archive log files, then you back up *all* database files: data, control, and online redo log files. During the restore, you copy back *all* of these files to their original locations. Oracle will expect to see all of these files with the same timestamp for the recovery.

3. If the database is in ARCHIVELOG mode, in which online redo log files are being copied off to archive log files, then you back up *only* the data and control files. Do not back up and restore the online redo log files if the database is in ARCHIVELOG mode. During the restore and recovery, you also will need the archive log files, so have these available.

One final note about cold backups: Make sure that your DBA supplies with you an updated list of every file to be backed up. A common mistake is to specify *X* files or *Y* filesystem to be backed up. Then the DBA will add another data file but will forget to update the backup procedures. This "missing" file will cause problems during the recovery.

Hot Backups

If the database is in ARCHIVELOG mode (with online redo log files being archived), the DBA can alter the database so that individual data files have consistent internal time-stamps. This allows those files to be copied off to tape in a piecemeal fashion. This has the obvious benefit of allowing the database to be running during backups.

The only two requirements are that the archive log files be available during recovery and that the DBA correctly set up the database so the backed-up files are in a consistent state. Fortunately, many established scripts are available that the DBA can use to put a database into hot backup mode, so this should not be a problem.

Most DBAs prefer a mix of cold and hot backups to make sure that they get everything. A common practice is to take a cold backup on Sunday nights and hot backups every evening. The idea here is that if a few files are damaged, recovery time is minimized because there is a recent copy of each file available.

In addition to database files, make sure you that also take backups of database installation and configuration files (`/u01`), files in `/etc` or `/var/opt/oracle`, and all of your archive log files. Finally, remember to document and actually test your backup and recovery procedures with the DBA before the system becomes production.

In this section, we covered Oracle from a system administrator's perspective. Although it is assumed that someone will be acting in the role of a DBA, the system administrator does need to know certain things to successfully support Oracle. This will improve not only the system, but also the working relationship between the sysadmin and DBA.

18

DATABASES

Note

For more in-depth coverage on this topic, see the book *Oracle DBA on UNIX and Linux*, by Michael Wessler (Sams Publishing, 2002, ISBN 0-672-32158-0). This book provides detailed coverage of Oracle database administration on the UNIX and Linux platforms.

MySQL Overview

Although Oracle is a solid choice for large systems, it can be overkill for smaller systems. If you need only a basic database to store and access some data, a smaller database such as MySQL might be a good choice.

MySQL is a "free" relational database that runs on multiple flavors of UNIX, Linux, and Windows. It comes included with several Linux distributions, or it may be downloaded from `http://www.mysql.com`.

When we say "free," we mean that you generally do not have to pay to use it. That is because it is available via the GNU General Public License (GPL). The exceptions to this are if you want to package and resell it or if you want to run it on Windows. This inexpensive aspect makes it look very attractive, especially in comparison to some of the larger RDBMS vendors that charge thousands of dollars.

Aside from it being free, why would you want to use MySQL? The following are a few reasons:

- It provides fast, simple RDBMS accessible by ANSI SQL92 SQL.
- Size and overhead are relatively small.
- Administration and management is less complex than with other larger RDBMS.
- It's available on a variety of platforms.
- Applications can be written in Perl and PHP, and it supports ODBC.
- It supports database users, passwords, and table-level security.
- It can execute stored SQL code.

These features make MySQL very popular for straightforward applications such as in-house maintenance programs or for just "tinkering." However, it should be noted that much of the transactional control, extensive integrity and business rule checking, and table/row–locking features found in more complex databases are not yet available in MySQL.

Installation Options

You can download MySQL from `http://www.mysql.com`. The current release is MySQL 3.23. You have three choices regarding installation methods:

- **Source**—You can download and compile the source code.
- **Binary**—The binary files can be downloaded, uncompressed, and untared.
- **RPM packages**—Linux users can download, or they already might have available the packages necessary to install.

MySQL installs in different locations, depending on what method you use. Typically, MySQL can be found in a subdirectory under /usr/local. Given a choice between source code and precompiled (binary or RPM) code, most people choose the precompiled option. The reasoning is that it is simpler to install and is more customized/optimized for a specific platform.

Users and groups commonly used are mysql and mysqladm. After the installation process, be sure to chown and chmod the files to be owned by mysql.

When the product is installed, you need to run a configuration script to initialize the data dictionary tables. This is done only once after a new installation. These tables contain the metadata about the databases, users, and tables. The script to execute is mysql_install_db and is shown here:

```
$ id
uid=1003(mysql) gid=1004(mysql) groups=1004(mysql)
$ pwd
/usr/bin
$ ./mysql_install_db
Preparing db table
Preparing host table
Preparing user table
Preparing func table
Preparing tables_priv table
Preparing columns_priv table
Installing all prepared tables

To start mysqld at boot time you have to copy support-files/mysql.server
to the right place for your system

PLEASE REMEMBER TO SET A PASSWORD FOR THE MySQL root USER !
This is done with:
/usr/bin/mysqladmin -u root -p password 'new-password'
/usr/bin/mysqladmin -u root -h mikehat.mike.com -p password 'new-password'
See the manual for more instructions.

You can start the MySQL daemon with:
cd /usr ; /usr/bin/safe_mysqld &

You can test the MySQL daemon with the benchmarks in the 'sql-bench' directory:
cd sql-bench ; run-all-tests

Please report any problems with the /usr/bin/mysqlbug script!

The latest information about MySQL is available on the web at
http://www.mysql.com
Support MySQL by buying support/licenses at https://order.mysql.com

$
```

18

DATABASES

At this stage, MySQL is installed. It can be started in the background by root as the user mysql.

```
# which safe_mysqld
/usr/bin/safe_mysqld
# safe_mysqld --user=mysql &
[1] 3189
# Starting mysqld daemon with databases from /var/lib/mysql

#
```

The database server is now running, and logs can be found in /var/log/mysqld.log.

```
$ ls -l /var/log/mysqld.log
-rw-r--r--   1 mysql    root       75 Oct  3 07:11 /var/log/mysqld.log
$ more /var/log/mysqld.log
011003 07:11:38  mysqld started
/usr/libexec/mysqld: ready for connections
$
```

Processes and Tools

MySQL runs in the background as the mysqld server. This is what the DBA/sysadmin actually starts and stops. From under this structure, the DBA creates separate databases containing tables accessible by users. In this way, MySQL exists as a mysqld process acting as an "instance," supplying access to one or many databases. This is similar to Oracle in that you generally have a database instance supplying access to a database.

To see if the database server is running, you can grep for the background process:

```
$ ps -ef | grep -i mysqld
root      3189     1  0 07:11 pts/4    00:00:00 /bin/sh /usr/bin/safe_mysqld --u
mysql     3215  3189  0 07:11 pts/4    00:00:00 /usr/libexec/mysqld --basedir=/u
mysql     3217  3215  0 07:11 pts/4    00:00:00 /usr/libexec/mysqld --basedir=/u
mysql     3218  3217  0 07:11 pts/4    00:00:00 /usr/libexec/mysqld --basedir=/u
mysql     3219  3217  0 07:11 pts/4    00:00:00 /usr/libexec/mysqld --basedir=/u
mysql     3228  3047  0 07:17 pts/4    00:00:00 grep -i mysqld
$
```

Executables for MySQL are located in /usr/bin, as seen here:

```
$ pwd
/usr/bin
$ ls *mysql*
msql2mysql      mysql_convert_table_format  mysqlimport
mysql           mysqld_multi                mysql_install_db
mysqlaccess     mysqldump                   mysql_setpermission
mysqladmin      mysqldumpslow               mysqlshow
mysqlbinlog     mysql_find_rows             mysqltest
mysqlbug        mysql_fix_privilege_tables  mysql_zap
mysql_config    mysqlhotcopy                safe_mysqld
```

The following tools in particular are used in conjunction with MySQL:

- **mysqladmin**—This tool is used to administrate the database. Use it to start up, shut down, create and drop databases, and collect status information.
- **safe_mysqld**—This is a script that can be used to start the database and restart it if it goes down.
- **mysql**—This is the command-line interface to interactively issue SQL commands directly to the database and receive output. You also can create users, tables, and issue grants from this tool.
- **mysqldump**—Use this utility to make backups in the form of script files and then restore them, if necessary.
- **mysqlimport**—This is a data-loading utility. It is used to bulk-load data from files outside the database into its tables.
- **isamchk and myisamchk**—These tools are used to tune tables with indexes and repair them, if they are damaged.

Notice that these are command-line tools. MySQL isn't at the level of larger databases that come with a suite of fancy GUI tools to manage the entire system. We consider this a benefit because it cuts down on the level of complexity involved in running the system. However, for those who prefer a GUI, third-party tools do exist.

Taking Backups

Backups of the MySQL database are more straightforward than in other systems. Your two basic options are to take a dump of the database or make a copy of the operating system files.

Database Dump

Use the mysqldump utility to create a dump of the database. This creates a text file containing all the code to rebuild the tables and the data. This script can be used to move the database from one location to another (a common DBA task). mysqldump also is used to restore the script file into the database.

MySQL allows logging to be turned on as well. Options are to create an auditing log and a separate log of DML activity. This second log can be applied to restore a database to a point in time.

These methods are good because they can be executed with the database up and running. This imposes no downtime for the system. However, because the database actually must be rebuilt from the script, the total recovery time could be longer.

18

DATABASES

Operating System Copy

Making an operating system–level copy of the data files allows for a faster recovery, but there is a catch. If the database tables are being used while you make the copy, your backup is useless. Just like most databases, MySQL is sensitive to the internal state of its tables.

We recommend taking operating system–level backups of the MySQL files, but make sure that you have shut down the databases first. This should be done in addition to database dumps with mysqldump and transaction logging. Finally, just as with any database, test and document your backup procedures before you actually need them.

Those are the main features of MySQL. There is not as much to its setup or administration as Oracle, which is a good thing. This allows more time using the database to support new applications rather than spending all your time managing the database.

Conclusion

In this chapter, we covered databases at a high level and then examined two specific database vendors: Oracle and MySQL. First we covered what a database was and how it fits in relation to the overall system. We showed that the primary unit of storage is the data table, which contains raw data. You then can use the Structured Query Language (SQL) to access the data and the Data Manipulation Language (DML) to insert, update, or delete data. We saw that databases are complex subsystems that also have users, security, and backup and recovery issues much like an operating system. In addition, we outlined the generic architecture of databases and explained why they take up so much memory and disk space. Finally, we identified what to expect from your DBA and what he expects from you.

Next we covered Oracle databases. We explained how Oracle products are more than just databases; they include Web/application servers, design, and development products as well. Next we showed how to set up the machine in terms of users, groups, disk, memory, and kernel parameters. We discussed how Oracle requires the use of shared memory so that each user process can write to the SGA. This was followed by sections covering Oracle architecture, installation, configuration, and backup and recovery.

In the next section, we discussed the MySQL database. This database is better suited for smaller systems than Oracle. It is a free database, installs easily, and can be used easily.

Automation

by Kevin Lyda and David Ressman

IN THIS CHAPTER

CHAPTER 19

Introduction

Automation enlists a machine to perform jobs. What gives this definition life, however (and the true subject of this chapter), is *attitude*. The most important step that you can take in understanding mechanisms of automation under UNIX is to adopt the attitude that the computer works for you. This chapter offers more than a dozen examples of how small, understandable automation initiatives make an immediate difference. Play with these examples, modify them, experiment with them, and then try writing your own based on what you have discovered.

Scripting

Scripting is the fundamental tool of your automation arsenal. A script consists of a series of commands that perform various tasks. The sysadmin usually identifies these tasks after performing them personally several times without significant variation.

> **Tip**
>
> If you perform a task more than twice, write a script to automate it. Chances are good that you will have to do it again....

Performing simple, regular, repetitive work is a computer's strong suit. Various scripting languages exist that allow sysadmins to turn such work entirely over to the computer.

Interpreted versus Compiled Languages

Shell scripts, and scripts in general, are part of the class of "interpreted" languages. Languages such as C, C++, and FORTRAN are among the "compiled" languages. When a computer executes an interpreted language, it reads each logical line, interprets the meaning of the line, and performs the directed actions. It does this pretty much one line at a time. The advantage of this approach is that the programmer making changes needs only to change the contents of the program file and run it again. Shell scripts, in their simplest form, are actually just lists of the same commands that you could type at the keyboard and execute one at a time. They are interpreted by the specified (or default) shell and are executed. In fact, your interactive UNIX session at the keyboard works the same way. When you log into a UNIX system, your session is actually the interaction of the commands that you type with the interactive shell assigned to interpret them.

When working with a compiled language, the programmer writes the "source code" in the selected language. That code then is "compiled," translated into machine language using a separate program called a compiler. The resulting machine language is very fast in comparison with an interpreted language because the compiler does all the "interpretation" of the code. The resulting machine code is simply a raw set of instructions to the computer. The disadvantage to compiled languages is the inconvenience of recompiling the program each time that it is changed. In addition, compiled languages tend to consist of relatively few, simple directives and have fairly rigid syntax to make the compiler's job easier. As a result, the programmer must invest more time planning and designing the program at the start to create an efficient finished product.

Most sysadmins don't need the kind of performance that a well-designed, compiled program delivers. Sysadmins just want to avoid typing commands and evaluating results that the computer can handle just as well. Many sysadmins rarely, if ever, write compiled code. We have yet to meet an experienced sysadmin, however, who is not conversant with at least one interpreted scripting language.

In the sections that follow, we will look at some examples of interpreted scripts that are often useful in day-to-day operation.

Example: Automating Database Entry

The following example actually arose the day before we started to write this chapter. It illustrates the advantages of using automation to perform even simple tasks.

A client wanted to enhance an online catalog to include thumbnail pictures of the merchandise. After a bit of confusion about what this really meant, we realized that we needed to update a simple database table of products to include a new column (or attribute or value) that would specify the filenames of the thumbnails. The database-management system had a couple of interactive front ends, and for a swift typist, it probably is quickest to point and click my way through the 200 picture updates. Did we do that? Of course not—what happened later proved the wisdom of this decision. Instead, we wrote a shell script to automate the update, which is shown in Listing 19.1.

19

AUTOMATION

> **Note**
>
> Whenever you complete a one-time, detail-oriented task, someone will ask you to do it again. If you take the time to script it the first time that you do it, you'll be ahead of the game when someone wants you to do it again.

LISTING **19.1**   Shell Script That Updates a Database

```
# picture names seem to look like {$DIR/137-13p.jpg,$DIR/201-942f.jpg,...}
# The corresponding products appear to be {137-13P, 201-942F, ...}
DIR=/particular/directory/for/my/client
```

LISTING 19.1 continued

```
:       # Will we use .gif-s, also, eventually?  I don't know.
for F in $DIR/*.jpg
do
        # BASE will have values {137-13p,201-942f, ...}
BASE=`basename $F .jpg`
        # The only suffixes I've encountered are 'p' and 'f', so I'll simply
        #     transform those two.
        # Example values for PRODUCT:  {137-13P, 201-942F, ...}
  PRODUCT=`echo $BASE | tr pf PF`
      # one_command is a shell script that passes a line of SQL to the DBMS.
  one_command update catalog set Picture = "'$DIR/$BASE.jpg'"
➥where Product = "'$PRODUCT'"
 done
```

As it turned out, the team decided within a couple days that the pictures needed to be in a different directory, so it was only a few seconds' work to update the penultimate line of the script, add a comment such as this, and rerun it:

```
    ...
        # Do *not* include a directory specification in Picture;
➥ that will be known
        #     only at the time the data are retrieved.
    one_command update catalog set Picture = "'$BASE.jpg'" where Product =
➥ "'$PRODUCT'"
done
```

It's inevitable that you'll someday have more pictures to add to the database or that you'll want reports on orphaned pictures (those that haven't been connected yet to any product). Then this same script, or a close derivative of it, will come into play again.

Analysis of the Script

Now work through the example in Listing 19.1 in detail to practice the automation mentality. Do you understand how the script in Listing 19.1 works?

You can always learn more by reading any of the fine books available on shell programming. The most certain way to learn, of course, is to experiment on your own. For example, if you have any question about what man tr means by "translation," it's a simple matter to experiment, such as with this:

```
# tr pf PF <<HERE
abcopqOPQ
FfpPab
HERE
```

You can conclude that you're on the right track when you see the following:

```
abcoPqOPQ
FFPPab
```

This is part of the charm of relying on shells for automation; it's easy to bounce between interaction and automation, which shapes a powerful didactic perspective and a check on understanding.

The sample product catalog script in Listing 19.1 is written for `sh` (Bourne shell) processing. We strongly recommend this be your target for scripts, rather than ksh, csh, or bash. We prefer any of the latter for interactive command-line use. In automating, however, when we're often connecting to different types of hosts, availability and esoteric security issues have convinced us to code using constructs that sh—and, therefore, all the shells—recognize. (Default Red Hat Linux installations use a link named /bin/sh that points to /bin/bash.) All the work in this chapter is written so that the scripts will function properly no matter what the details are of your host's configuration. Did we really include the inline comments, the lines that begin with #, when we first wrote the script in Listing 19.1? Yes. We've made this level of source-code documentation a habit, and it's one that we recommend to you. If your life is at all like ours, telephones ring, co-workers chat, and power supplies fail; we find it easier to type this much detail as we're thinking about it, rather than risk having to re-create our thoughts in case of an interruption. It's also much easier to pick up the work again days or weeks later. Writing for human readability eases the transition when you pass your work on to others as well.

Listing 19.1 begins by assigning a shell variable `DIR` in the third line. It's good practice to make such an assignment, even for a variable (apparently) used only once. It contributes to self-documentation and generally enhances maintainability; it's easy to look at the top of the script and see immediately on what magic words or configuration in the outside environment (`/particular/directory/for/my/client` in this case—see the third line down) the script depends.

Many of the jobs that you'll want to accomplish involve a quantifier: "change all...," "correct every...," and so on. The shell's looping constructs, `for` and `while`, are your friends. You'll make almost daily use of them.

`basename` and `tr` are universally available and widely used. `tr`, like many UNIX utilities, expects to read standard input. If you have information in shell variables, you can feed `tr` the information that you want, either through a pipe from `echo`, as in the example, or an equivalent:

```
echo $VARIABLE | tr [a-z] [A-Z]
```

You also can do it with a so-called HERE document, such as this one:

```
tr [a-z] [A-Z] <<HERE
$VARIABLE
HERE
```

You could perhaps do it by creating a temporary file:

```
echo $VARIABLE >$TMPFILE
tr [a-z] [A-Z] $TMPFILE
```

one_command is a two-line shell script written earlier in the day to process SQL commands. Why not inline the body of that script here? Although it's technically feasible, we have a strong preference for small, simple programs that are easy to understand and correspondingly easy to implement correctly. one_command already has been verified to do one small job reliably, so the script lets it do that job. This fits with the UNIX tradition that counsels combining robust toolkit pieces to construct grander works.

In fact, notice that the example in Listing 19.1 shows the shell's nature as a "glue" language. There's a small amount of processing within the shell in manipulating filenames, and then most of the work is handed off to other commands; the shell just glues together results. This is typical and is a correct style that you should adopt for your own scripting.

Certainly, it was pleasant when the filenames changed and we realized that we could rework one word of the script rather than having to retype the 200 entries. As satisfying as this was, the total benefit of automation is still more profound. Even greater than time savings are the improvements in quality, traceability, and reusability this affords. With the script, we control the data entering the database at a higher level and eliminate whole categories of error: mistyping, accidentally pushing a wrong button in a graphical user interface, and so on. Also, the script in Listing 19.1 records our procedure, in case it's later useful to audit the data. Suppose, for example, that next year it's decided that we shouldn't have inserted any of these references to the database's Picture attribute. How many will have to be backed out? Useful answers—at most, the count of $DIR/*.jpg— can be read directly from the script; there's no need to rely on memory or speculation.

Example: Changing Strings in Files

Users who maintain source code, client lists, and other records often want to launch a find-and-replace operation from the command line. It's useful to have a variant of chstr on UNIX hosts. Listing 19.2 gives one example.

LISTING 19.2   chstr—A Simple Find-and-Replace Operation

```
########
#
# See usage() definition, below, for more details.
```

LISTING 19.2   continued

```
#
# This implementation doesn't do well with complicated escape
#     sequences. That has been no more than a minor problem in
#     the real world.
#
########
usage() {
    echo \
"chstr BEFORE AFTER <filenames>
    changes the first instance of BEFORE to AFTER in each line of
➥ <filenames>,
    and reports on the differences.
Examples:
    chstr TX Texas */addresses.*
    chstr ii counter2 *.c"
    exit 0
}

case $1 in
    -h|-help)    usage;;
esac

if test $# -lt 3
then
    usage
fi

TMPDIR=/tmp
    # It's OK if more than one instance of chstr is run simultaneously.
    #    The TMPFILE names are specific to each invocation, so there's
    #    no conflict.
TMPFILE=$TMPDIR/chstr.$$

BEFORE=$1
AFTER=$2

    # Toss the BEFORE and AFTER arguments out of the argument list.
shift;shift

for FILE in $*
do
    sed -e "s/$BEFORE/$AFTER/" $FILE >$TMPFILE
    echo "$FILE:"
    diff $FILE $TMPFILE
    echo ""
    mv $TMPFILE $FILE
done
```

19

AUTOMATION

The preceding `chstr` script takes its first two arguments as the string to look for and the string to put in its place, respectively. In the script, they're in the `BEFORE` and `AFTER` variables. The two shift commands move those strings aside from the list of arguments, and the rest of the arguments are treated as files. Each file is run through `sed` to replace `$BEFORE` with `$AFTER` and is placed in a temporary file. The file then is moved back into place.

Most interactive editors permit a form of global search-and-replace, and some even make it easy to operate on more than one file. Perhaps that's a superior automation strategy for your needs. If not, `chstr` is a minimal command-line alternative that is maximally simple to use.

> **Note**
>
> Of course, experienced Perl hackers might find Listing 19.2 a bit longer than necessary when nearly the same changes can be accomplished from the command line, like this:
>
> ```
> # perl -p -i.tmp -e s/beforestr/afterstr/g file(s)
> ```
>
> For more information on Perl, see the Perl man pages on your system. A good starting point is the `perltoc(1)` (table of contents) man page.

Example: Web Page Content Retrieval

A question that arises frequently is how to automate retrieval of pages from the World Wide Web. This section shows the simplest of many techniques.

For an HTTP interaction, let the Lynx browser do the bulk of the work. Lynx is adequate for all but the most specialized purposes. You can obtain the latest version at `http://lynx.browser.org`. Although most Lynx users think of Lynx as an interactive browser, it's also handy for dropping a copy of the latest headlines, with live links, in a friend's mailbox with this:

```
# lynx -source http://www.cnn.com | mail someone@somewhere.com
```

To create a primitive news update service, script the following and launch it in the background (using the ampersand, &):

```
NEW=/tmp/news.new
OLD=/tmp/news.old
URL=http://www.cnn.com
while true
do
```

```
    mv $NEW $OLD
    lynx -dump -nolist $URL >$NEW
    diff $NEW $OLD
        # Wait ten minutes before starting the next comparison.
    sleep 600
done
```

Any changes in the appearance of CNN's home page will appear onscreen every 10 minutes. This simple approach is less practical than you might first expect because CNN periodically shuffles the content without changing the information. It's an instructive example, however, and a starting point from which you can elaborate your own scripts.

A Final Word About Shell Programming

Shells are glue; if there's a way to get an application to perform an action from the command line, there's almost certainly a way to wrap it in a shell script that gives you power over argument validation, iteration, and input-output redirection. These are powerful techniques and are well worth the few minutes of study and practice that it takes to begin learning them.

Even small automations pay off. Our personal rule of thumb is to write tiny disposable one-line shell scripts when we expect to use a sequence even twice during a session. For example, although we have a sophisticated set of reporting commands for analyzing World Wide Web server logs, we also find ourselves going to the trouble of editing a disposable script such as /tmp/r9 to do quick, ad hoc queries on recent hit patterns:

Recycling Scripts

You will probably end up reusing parts of almost every script that you write. Keep copies of them someplace where you can refer back to them later (don't reinvent the wheel). Remember that /tmp disappears after every reboot.

grep claird `ls -t /usr/cern/log/* | head -1` | grep -v $1 | wc -l

This particular example reports on the number of requests for pages that include the string claird and exclude the first argument to /tmp/r9, in the most recent log.

Other Scripting Languages: Expect, Perl, and More

Are you ready to move beyond the constraints of the UNIX shell? Several alternative technologies are free, easy to install, easy to learn, and more powerful—that is, with

19

AUTOMATION

richer capabilities and more structured syntax—than the shell. A few examples will suggest what they have to offer.

Expect

Expect, by Don Libes, is a scripting language that works with many different programs and that can be used as a powerful software tool for automation. Why? Expect automates interactions, particularly those involving terminal control and time delays. Many command-line applications have the reputation of being unscriptable because they involve password entry and refuse to accept redirection of standard input for this purpose. Expect was designed to solve that problem. Under Red Hat Linux, Expect is installed under the /usr/bin directory, and you'll find documentation in its manual page.

Create a script hold with the contents of Listing 19.3.

LISTING 19.3 hold: A "Keepalive" Written in Expect

```
#!/usr/bin/expect

# Usage:   "hold HOST USER PASS".
# Action:  login to node HOST as USER.  Offer a shell prompt for
#     normal usage, and also print to the screen the word HELD
#     every five seconds, to exercise the connection periodically.
#     This is useful for testing and using WANs with short time-outs.
#     You can walk away from the keyboard, and never lose your
#     connection through a time-out.
# WARNING:  the security hazard of passing a password through the
#     command line makes this example only illustrative.  Modify to
#     a particular security situation as appropriate.
set hostname [lindex $argv 0]
set username [lindex $argv 1]
set password [lindex $argv 2]

    # There's trouble if $username's prompt is not set to "...} ".
    #     A more sophisticated manager knows how to look for different
    #     prompts on different hosts.
set prompt_sequence "} "

spawn telnet $hostname

expect "login: "
send "$username\r"
expect "Password:"
send "$password\r"

    # Some hosts don't inquire about TERM.  That's another
    #     complexification to consider before widespread use
    #     of this application is practical.
```

LISTING 19.3   continued

```
        # Note use of global [gl] pattern matching to parse "*"
        #     as a wildcard.
expect -gl "TERM = (*)"
send "\r"
expect $prompt_sequence
send "sh -c 'while true; do echo HELD; sleep 5; done'\r"
interact
```

This script starts a telnet session and then keeps the connection open by sending the string `"HELD"` every 5 seconds. We work with several telephone lines that are used with short timeouts, as a check on out-of-pocket expenses. We use a variant of the script in Listing 19.3 daily because we often need that to hold one of the connections open.

> **Tip**
>
> Expect is an extension to tcl, so it is fully programmable with tcl capabilities. For information about tcl and tk from its author, Dr. John Ousterhout, visit http:// www.sun.com/960710/cover/ousterhout.html. For more information about Expect, visit http://expect.nist.gov/.

> **Tip**
>
> You'll also find the autoexpect command included with Red Hat Linux. This command watches an interactive session at the console and then creates an executable program to execute the console session. See Chapter 11, "Name Service (DNS) for an example of how to use autoexpect to automate an FTP session.

Perl

Some people consider Perl the most popular scripting language for UNIX, apart from the shell. Its power and brevity take on particular value in automation contexts.

> **Note**
>
> For more information about Perl, or to get the latest release, browse http:// www.perl.com or http://www.perl.org.

For example, assume that /usr/local/bin/modified_directories.pl contains this code:

```
#!/usr/bin/perl
# Usage:  "modified_directories.pl DIR1 DIR2 ... DIRN"
```

19

AUTOMATION

```
# Output:  a list of all directories in the file systems under
#     DIR1 ... DIRN, collectively.  They appear, sorted by the
#     interval since their last activity, that is, since a file
#     within them was last created, deleted, or renamed.
# Randal Schwartz wrote a related program from which this is
#     descended.
use File::Find;
@directory_list = @ARGV;
# "-M" abbreviates "time since last modification", while
#     "-d" "... is a directory."

find ( sub {
$modification_lapse{$File::Find::name} = -M if -d },
@directory_list );

for ( sort {
$modification_lapse{$a} <=> $modification_lapse{$b}} keys
%modification_lapse ) {

    # Tabulate the results in nice columns.
    printf "%5d:  %s\n", $modification_lapse{$_}, $_;
}
```

Also assume that you adjoin an entry such as this to your crontab:

```
20 2 * * * /usr/local/bin/modified_directories.pl /
```

In this case, each morning you'll receive an email report on the date that each directory on your host was last modified. This can be useful both for spotting security issues when read-only directories have been changed (they'll appear unexpectedly at the top of the list) and for identifying dormant domains in the filesystem (at the bottom of the list) that might be liberated for better uses. In the next example, a Perl script is used to provide automatic warning of a filesystem running out of space. The programming style in the script is very simple and straightforward, to allow the user unfamiliar with Perl to follow its logic.

```
#!/usr/bin/perl

# Definitions
$SYSTEM_NAME = `uname -n`;
chop ($SYSTEM_NAME);
$SCRIPT_NAME = "fsfullchk";
$SUBJECT_STRING = join (" ",$SCRIPT_NAME,"-",$SYSTEM_NAME);
$MAIL = "/usr/bin/Mail";

$NOTIFY_MAIL_LIST = "andy\@univ.edu";

$ROOT = "/";
$ROOT_THRESHHOLD = 93;
$USR = "/usr";
$USR_THRESHHOLD = 95;
```

```
$PACKETS = "/usr/packets";
$PACKETS_THRESHHOLD = 95;

$status = "";

open (DF, "/bin/df -k|") || ($status = "fsfullchk - Can't open df.\n");
if (!$status) {

        while (<DF>)    {
                if (/(\S+)\s+(\d+)\s+(\d+)\s+(\d+)\s+(\d+)%\s+(\S+).*/) {
                        $fs = $1;
                        $space = $2;
                        $used = $3;
                        $avail = $4;
                        $capacity = $5;
                        $mntpt = $6;
                        if (($mntpt eq $ROOT)&&($capacity>$ROOT_THRESHHOLD))  {
                                $status = join ("",$status,
                                join (" ",$mntpt,"is at",($capacity."%"),
                                        "capacity","\n"));
                        }
                        if (($mntpt eq $USR)&&($capacity>$USR_THRESHHOLD))    {
                                $status = join ("",$status,
                                join (" ",$mntpt,"is at",($capacity."%"),
                                        "capacity","\n"));
                        }
                        if (($mntpt eq $PACKETS)&&($capacity>$PACKETS_
➥THRESHHOLD)){
                                $status = join ("",$status,
                                join (" ",$mntpt,"is at",($capacity."%"),
                                        "capacity","\n"));
                        }
                }
        }
}
close DF;
if ($status) {
        $mail_status = $status;
        open (MAIL, "|$MAIL -s \"$SUBJECT_STRING\" $NOTIFY_MAIL_LIST");
        print MAIL $mail_status;
        close (MAIL);
}
```

Notice that definition of the important variables used by the script is all in one place at the beginning of the script listing. This makes them easier to find and to modify. Of course, while writing the script, you probably will want to create variables as you go along. Perl lends itself to this sort of programming. Even so, we strongly recommend either putting the new variables at the front of the script or going through the finished product, collecting important variables, and grouping them at the beginning.

Eventually, you will find that most of your scripts use the same variables. At this point, it will be easy to collect them and place them in a separate file that all your scripts can use through the `require` command.

The `open` command defines a *filehandle*, DF, that will be used to access the output of the `df -k` command. The `while` command cycles through the output read from DF one line at a time. Lines matching the pattern in the `if` statement are parsed into variables and tested against the threshold sizes established at the beginning of the script.

If any filesystem is filled past the threshold value, a warning message is appended to the text stored in the `$status` variable.

After the output from the DF filehandle has been processed, the `$status` variable is tested for content. If it is not empty, a filehandle into the `mail` command is created and the contents of the `$status` variable are printed to that filehandle.

Python

Python is object-oriented, modern, clean, portable, and particularly easy to maintain. If you are a full-time system administrator looking for a scripting language that will grow with you, consider Python. The official home page for Python is `http://www.python.org`.

Ruby

Ruby is the new programming kid on the block. Although it is still making its way to fame and acceptance, those sysadmins who know and use it say that it rivals Perl in their affections. Like Python, Ruby is object-oriented, high-level, and flexible. The official home page for Ruby is http://www.rubycentral.com.

Scheduled and Periodic Processes

at: One-time Scheduling for Future Events

Suppose that you write an electronic weekly column on financial cycles in the material world, which you deliver by email. To simplify legal ramifications involving financial markets, you make a point of delivering it at 5:00 Friday afternoon. It's Wednesday now, you've finished your analysis, and you're almost finished packing for the vacation you're starting tonight. How do you do right by your subscribers? It takes only three lines of at scripting:

```
# at 17:00 Friday << COMMAND
   mail -s "This week's CYCLES report." mailing_list
```

```
➥ < analysis.already_written
```
COMMAND

This schedules the `mail` command for later processing. You can log off from your session, and your host will still send the mail at 17:00 Friday, just as you instructed. In fact, you even can shut down your machine after commanding it `at ...`; as long as it's rebooted in time, your scheduled task still will be launched on the schedule that you dictated.

cron: Periodic Scheduling

The crond daemon is started at boot time. This daemon checks your system's /etc/crontab file and /var/spool/cron directory every minute, looking for assigned tasks at assigned times. As a system administrator, you'll schedule system tasks in /etc/crontab. This file initially contains four entries:

```
01 * * * * root run-parts /etc/cron.hourly
02 4 * * * root run-parts /etc/cron.daily
22 4 * * 0 root run-parts /etc/cron.weekly
42 4 1 * * root run-parts /etc/cron.monthly
```

Scripts set to run on an hourly, daily, weekly, or monthly basis will be found under the /etc directory, as shown. Personal cron tasks, created by using the `crontab` command, are saved under the /var/spool/cron directory. Personal at jobs are saved under the /var/spool/at directory and have group and file ownership of the creator, like this:

```
-rwx------  1 bball    bball       1093 Apr 19 17:47 a0000200eb209c
```

> **Note**
>
> The cron directory structure may be different on different operating system variants. Wherever they are, don't edit the files directly; use the `crontab` command with the appropriate options.

There are three `crontab` command options for modifying crontab entries under current implementations of Red Hat and Solaris:

1. `crontab -l`

   The `-l` option lists the crontab entries of the current userid to standard output.

19

AUTOMATION

2. `crontab -e`

   The `-e` option invokes the default editor to edit the crontab entries. To specify your preferred editor as the default, set the one of the environment variables EDITOR or VISUAL to the pathname of editor. Exiting the editor in the usual manner saves the modifications to the crontab entries.

3. `crontab -r`

   The `-r` option removes all the entries from the crontab of the current userid.

The modern `crontab` will also accept a filename as an argument.

`crontab <filename>`

If the referenced file contains correctly formatted crontab entries, the file becomes the new crontab.

Under Red Hat, the crontab command requires an argument or options. Under Solaris, the `crontab` command without arguments or options will expect to read a new crontab file from standard input.

Read the Manual First!

Read the cron and crontab man pages on your system before using crontab. The syntax and the metadata can be very system-specific and you can do damage if you use the wrong syntax for a system.

On many older systems, for instance, the crontab command reads in the crontab from standard input. In contrast, newer implementations open an editor. A sysadmin, expecting the newer version, could type "crontab –e". When "nothing happens" and the sysadmin types Ctrl-D to end the process, the existing system crontab has been erased. Eeek!

The difference between crontab and at is that crontab should be used to schedule and run periodic, repetitive tasks on a regular basis, whereas at jobs are usually meant to run once at a future time.

Note

The /etc/cron.allow and /etc/cron.deny files control who may use the `crontab` command on your system. For details, see the `crontab` man page. You also can control who can use the at command on your system with the /etc/at.allow and /etc/at. deny files. By default, Red Hat Linux lets anyone use the at and `crontab` commands.

anacron: Interruptible Periodic Scheduling

The weakness of cron and at is that they assume the system will always be up. This isn't true for Linux laptop systems, for instance. So, by default, anacron is installed and set to run at boot time and when apmd resumes (see /etc/sysconfig/apm-scripts/resume for how that's done). anacron is controlled by the /etc/anacrontab file and is installed to look at the jobs run from the /etc/cron.daily, /etc/cron.weekly, and /etc/cron.monthly directories. So, it looks like this:

```
# /etc/anacrontab: configuration file for anacron

# See anacron(8) and anacrontab(5) for details.

SHELL=/bin/sh
PATH=/usr/local/sbin:/usr/local/bin:/sbin:/usr/sbin:/usr/bin

# These entries are useful for a Red Hat Linux system.
1       5       cron.daily      run-parts /etc/cron.daily
7       10      cron.weekly     run-parts /etc/cron.weekly
30      15      cron.monthly    run-parts /etc/cron.monthly
```

This makes sure that the cron.daily scripts are run once every day (and that they're run 5 minutes after anacron is run). The cron.weekly scripts are run 10 minutes after anacron starts if they haven't been run in more than a week, and the cron.weekly scripts are run 15 minutes after anacron starts if they haven't been run in 30 days. anacron gets help in determining when a script was last run, thanks to the 0anacron script in each of the cron directories. You'll really notice this if you're a laptop user and always had to update your slocate database by hand!

Examples with cron

One eternal reality of system administration is that there's not enough disk space. The following sections offer a couple of expedients recommended for keeping on top of what's happening with your system.

Tracking System Core Files

cron use always involves a bit of setup. We'll go carefully through an example that helps track down core clutter.

You need at least one external file to start using the cron facility. Practice cron concepts by commanding this first:

```
# echo "0,5,10,15,20,25,30,35,40,45,50,55 * * * * date > `tty`"
➥>/tmp/experiment
```

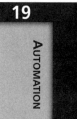

Then invoke `crontab` as follows:

```
# crontab /tmp/experiment
```

Finally, enter the command:

```
# crontab -l
```

The last of these gives you a result that looks something like the following:

```
0,5,10,15,20,25,30,35,40,45,50,55 * * * * date > /dev/ttyxx
```

The current time will appear every 5 minutes in the window from which you launched this experiment.

For a more useful example, create a file named /tmp/entry with this single line:

```
0 2 * * * find / -name "core*" -exec ls -l {} \;
```

Next, use this command:

```
# crontab /tmp/entry
```

The result is that, each morning at 2:00, cron launches the core-searching job and emails you the results. This is quite useful because UNIX systems create files named core under certain error conditions. These core images are often large and easily can fill up a distressing amount of space on your disk. With the preceding sequence, you'll have a report in your email inbox each morning, listing exactly the locations and sizes of a collection of files that are likely doing you no good.

Monitoring User Space

Suppose that you've experimented a bit and accumulated an inventory of cron jobs to monitor the health of your system. Along with your other jobs, you want your system to tell you every Monday morning at 2:10 which 10 users have the biggest home directory trees (`/home/*`). First, enter this to capture all the jobs that you've scheduled:

```
# crontab -l >/tmp/entries
```

Append this line to the bottom of /tmp/entries:

```
10 2 * * 1 du -s /home/* | sort -nr | head -10
```

Make this request, and cron will email the reports that you seek:

```
# crontab /tmp/entries
```

> **Note**
>
> Comments in the crontab files may save your job. Certainly, they will make it easier. You may not look at your crontabs for months or years if no problems arise. It can be hard to remember just why you (or someone else) created a specific entry. A short descriptive comment may mean that you won't have to locate and examine the scripts invoked by each entry. If you're in a hurry to figure out why something is breaking, reverse-engineering the cron jobs can be especially frustrating.

Automated Configuration Management with cfengine

Most of the routine tasks that sysadmins must perform involve some aspect of system configuration. When you have a small site, you can manage new installations and updates by hand, using checklists to ensure consistency and completeness. But once you have more than ten machines in your domain, automation becomes a necessity, not just a nicety—especially if you have to support more than one Operating System.

Mark Burgess designed cfengine with this need in mind. It takes the form of a high-level, platform-independent scripting language that allows sysadmins to state with very few words how they want their UNIX systems to be configured. Many of the most common tasks you routinely perform on a system are actually built-in commands.

Here's how cfengine works:

1. You construct a centralized system profile that defines what a given system should look like. Note that this may span multiple files.

2. You write a local configuration file telling cfengine how to find and process that centralized system profile created in Step 1.

3. When cfengine runs on the target system, it reads in both the local and central configuration files and compares their parameters to the system's current configuration. Any deviation is corrected by cfengine (according to the rules you entered in the configuration files).

Note that if your system is already configured according to the configuration file, cfengine does nothing. Whenever the system deviates from the desired configuration, cfengine brings it back into conformance with the configuration files.

19

AUTOMATION

cfengine – Not Just for root Anymore

In the cfengine tutorial (available at http://www.cfengine.org/docs/cfdocs.html), Mark Burgess says the following:

"Originally cfengine was conceived of as a tool only for the superuser, but during the course of its development it has become clear that it can also be used as a scripting language by ordinary users. It is a handy tool for tidying your old junk files and for making 'watchdog' scripts to manage the access rights and permissions on your files when collaborating with other users. As a bonus it contains a text editing language which can be used to perform controlled edits of line-based text files."

The most common (and best) way to run cfengine is through cron. How often it runs depends entirely on the requirements of the sysadmin. Most sysadmins run cfengine once an hour, but some run it every 10 minutes, and still others run it once a day. Consider the nature and frequency of system changes at your site when choosing an initial interval. After a few days of testing, you'll get a pretty good feel for whether you need to run cfengine more or less often.

The Bare Essentials

Before we go into any detail, it's best to get a broad idea of what kind of configurations cfengine requires and what kinds of tasks it can perform.

The local file controlling cfengine's behavior is named `cfengine.conf` and contains a list of declarations and directives. There are a few syntax rules that you should keep in mind:

- Comments begin with a # mark.
- Excess Tabs and Spaces are not harmful (so you can use them to organize sections).
- Parentheses should have a Space both before and after (to avoid confusing the cfengine parser)
- *Sections* are denoted by a keyword followed by a colon (an example is `control:`)
- *Classes* are denoted by a keyword followed by two colons (an example is `solaris::`)
- Variables are assigned values with the = operator. The value(s) being assigned must appear inside parentheses separated by Spaces. An example is
`actionsequence = ( value1 value2 value3 …)`

At a minimum, you must define an `actionsequence` (the order in which things should be done) and some command directives (the things cfengine should do).

Here is a brief list of cfengine's most useful *section keywords* or *commands*:

- **acl:**—The `acl:` command sets and maintains filesystem access control lists.
- **broadcast:**—The `broadcast:` command provides information about the broadcast address of the network that the host is on. This information also can be provided with the `interfaces:` command. We recommend that you provide it there instead and not use `broadcast:`.
- **classes:**—The `classes:` command is used to include one or more hosts in a single logical unit to which certain actions can be uniformly applied.
- **control:**—The `control:` command lies at the heart of cfengine and is the only mandatory command in any cfengine configuration file. Simply put, the `control:` directive gives cfengine the information that it needs to start running the rest of your input files. You can use it to define variables, set the default behavior for some of cfengine's other commands, define the order in which cfengine will run its commands, and configure a number of other items.
- **copy:**—The `copy:` command is used to copy files and directories locally or from a cfengine server running on a remote host.
- **defaultroute:**—The `defaultroute:` command is used to configure the default route on a host. It's unlikely that sysadmins will be using cfengine on a system before it's networked. This command is generally not useful.
- **disable:**—The `disable:` command moves unwanted files out of the way.
- **editfiles:**—The `editfiles:` command is used to change and examine the content of files. It's most useful for text files, but it can be used in a limited capacity on binary files.
- **files:**—The `files:` command creates files and is used to set and maintain some of their important filesystem attributes.
- **filters:**—The `filters:` command narrows `files:` and `processes:` searches based on more parameters than just a simple file or process name.
- **ignore:**—The `ignore:` command is used in to specify a directory or file pattern to be excluded from any other command that copies or searches through recursive directories.
- **import:**—The `import:` command allows you to split up your configuration files into smaller, more manageable files.

- **interfaces:**—The `interfaces:` command is used to configure one or more network interfaces on a host. For the same reason as the `defaultroute:` command, this command is generally not useful.

- **links:**—The `links:` command is used to create and maintain symbolic and hard file links.

- **processes:**—The `processes:` "command searches" is used for performing a wide variety of actions based on information in the host's process table. It can be used to search for specific process names, send signals to processes, and restart daemons.

- **required:**—The `required:` command is used to examine a list files or filesystems and make sure that they exist and are in a somewhat reasonable state.

- **resolve:**—The `resolve:` command is used to maintain the host's nameservice configuration.

- **shellcommands:**—The `shellcommands:` command is used to run arbitrary programs from within cfengine.

- **tidy:**—The `tidy:` command is used to clean up directories by deleting files based on certain criteria.

Again, notice that all these command directives are followed with a colon (:). This is an important convention that you will see used in the sample files in the next section.

Using the Network to Distribute cfengine's Configuration Files

In its most simple application, cfengine is a program that starts locally on a host (whether run by hand or by cron), reads a local copy of its configuration file, and configures the host according to the instructions in the configuration file.

In most cases, sysadmins use cfengine because they have a large number of networked hosts that they want to configure centrally with one set of configuration files. The hassle involved in manually copying cfengine configuration files to new systems or to all of their existing systems when the configuration changes can be nearly as great as configuring them by hand in the first place. Clearly, some mechanism is needed for getting cfengine's configuration files onto the target system.

There are a number of approaches you can take to accomplish the transfer. You can manually copy the file in place (using scp or some related utility). You can use NFS or some other file sharing mechanism to make a central repository available over the network. Or you could write a brief script to push the cfengine configuration file(s) out from the central repository onto the remote systems.

A cfengine Command Example: `tidy:`

Now let's look a little more closely at how cfengine's commands work. We'll use `tidy:` as our example directive.

As we already mentioned, `tidy:` deletes unwanted files from specified directories. In one of its simpler incarnations, the `tidy` section of a cfengine.conf file might look like this:

```
tidy:

    /tmp
            pat=*
            age=30
            recurse=inf
            rmdirs=sub
```

Here's how cfengine interprets it: The target directory of the tidy action is /tmp. The qualifiers on the following lines are restricted to acting on files and subdirectories under /tmp.

The refining qualifiers specify that if any file or directory matches all of the previous criteria (that is, if its name patches the pattern *, has not been accessed for 30 days or more, is in any subdirectory of /tmp, and is not actually /tmp), it will be deleted from the host. One problem with this particular `tidy:` action is that some UNIX software (such as X Windows) will keep important system files in /tmp/ or any of its subdirectories. We need a way to tell `tidy:` not to delete these files, even if they match all the criteria of a `tidy:` action. Intuitively enough, cfengine has such a mechanism in the `ignore:` command.

As we mentioned previously, `ignore:` does not have to be declared in `actionsequence` because it doesn't actually do anything. It just instructs `tidy:` not to examine files in certain directories. Add this `ignore:` section to your cfengine.conf:

```
ignore:

    /tmp/.X11-unix/

linux::
    /tmp/.X0.lock
    /tmp/.X1.lock
    /tmp/.X2.lock
    /tmp/.X3.lock

solaris::
    /tmp/.X11-pipe
```

It doesn't particularly matter where the ignore section is inserted, but we find that it is most readable near the beginning of the cfengine.conf (above any commands that are listed in `actionsequence`). `tidy:` will now pass right over /tmp/.X11-unix without peeking inside to see if any files in that directory are subject to deletion. Any file in /tmp matching the pattern X*.lock will also be exempt from deletion.

> **Caution**
>
> Using * in `ignore:` patterns in publicly writeable directories can lead to problems. If you specify `ignore:` items such as `/tmp/.X*.lock`, problem users can create files such as `/tmp/.X_Im_smarter_than_the_sysadmin.lock` that will be exempt from `tidy:` deletion. When using `ignore:` to alter `tidy:` usage in public areas, it's always a good idea to be as specific as possible. Don't use wildcards in tmp directories!

If we wanted to get more complex, we could tell cfengine to only clean up /var/tmp if we were running low on space. To do this, we would use `required:` to activate a class that we could check for in another `tidy:` statement. To do this, first add `required` to the action sequence before `tidy:`, and then add this `required:` statement to your cfengine.conf:

```
required:

        /var
                freespace=50mb
                # This option tells required: that /var must have at least 50
                # megabytes of free space.

                define=tidyvartmp
                # If /var does not meet the free space requirement, cfengine
will
                # activate the "tidyvartmp" class.
```

Now that we've defined a class if /var falls below 50MB of free space, we'll write a `tidy:` action to clear out /var/tmp:

```
 tidyvartmp::
        /var/tmp
                pat=*
                age=30
                recurse=inf
                rmdirs=sub
```

This is just the tip of the cfengine iceberg. There are scores of commands and options that we just don't have the space to discuss here. We hope that this section has aroused your interest in cfengine as an automated system administration tool. cfengine is scalable and easy to configure once you get the hang of the syntax, and it saves an enormous amount of time.

This section is neither intended to be a complete cfengine tutorial nor a comprehensive reference. Entire books can be (and have been) written about cfengine, so it is simply too complicated a program to fully describe in this text. The complete reference manual can be found on the cfengine Web site, `http://www.cfengine.org/`.

Sample cfengine.conf File

Listing 19.4 is a complete cfengine.conf file. This should give you a better idea of how the cfengine language flows.

LISTING 19.4 cfengine.conf

```
control:

    access      = ( root )
    domain      = ( mysite.com )
    sysadm      = ( root@mysite.com )
    syslog      = ( on )
    actionsequence   = ( copy editfiles processes required tidy )

    classes:

            custom_motd = ( myhost otherhost anotherhost )

ignore:

    /tmp/.X11-unix/

linux::
    /tmp/.X0.lock
    /tmp/.X1.lock
    /tmp/.X2.lock
    /tmp/.X3.lock

solaris::
    /tmp/.X11-pipe

copy:

    /usr/local/share/cfengine/cfengine.preconf
        dest=/usr/local/etc/cfengine/cfengine.preconf
        type=sum
        owner=0 group=0 mode=644
        server=yourserver
```

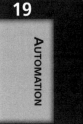

19

AUTOMATION

LISTING 19.4   continued

```
        solaris.custom_motd.Tuesday.Hr03::
   /usr/local/share/cfengine/motd
      dest=/etc/motd
      type=sum
      owner=0 group=0 mode=644
      server=yourserver

    linux.custom_motd.Tuesday.Hr03::
   /usr/local/share/cfengine/motd
      dest=/etc/motd
      type=sum
      owner=0 group=0 mode=644
      server=yourserver

editfiles:

   solaris::
         { /etc/inet/inetd.conf
         SetCommentStart "# "
         HashCommentLinesContaining "in.telnetd"
         DefineClasses "inetd"
         }

processes:

  solaris.inetd::
         "inetd -s"
         action=signal
         signal=hup

required:

         /var
    freespace=50mb
    define=tidyvartmp

tidy:

      /tmp
               pat=*
               age=30
               recurse=inf
               rmdirs=sub

   tidyvartmp::
      /var/tmp
               pat=*
               age=30
               recurse=inf
               rmdirs=sub
```

Tips for Improving Automation Techniques

You're in charge of your career in automation. Along with everything else this chapter advises, you'll go furthest if you do the following:

- Improve your automation technique.
- Engineer well.

These tips have specific meaning in the rest of this chapter. Look for ways to apply them in all that follows.

Continuing Education

There are three important ways to improve your skill with automation techniques, which apply equally well whether you're using sh, Perl, or any other scripting language:

- Scan the documentation.
- Read good scripts.
- Practice writing scripts.

These techniques are applicable whether you are running from the command line or from cron.

Documentation has the reputation of being dry and even unreadable. It's important that you learn how to employ it. All the tools presented here have man pages, which you need to be comfortable using. Read these documents and then reread them. Authors of the tools faced many of the challenges you do. Often, reading through the lists of options or keywords, you'll realize that particular capabilities apply exactly to your situation. Study the documentation with this in mind; look for the ideas that you can use. Give particular attention to commands that you don't recognize. If some of them—cu or od—are largely superannuated, you'll realize in reading about others—such as `tput`, `ulimit`, `bc`, `nice`, or `wait`—that earlier users were confronted with just the situations that confound your own work. Stand on their shoulders and see farther.

19

AUTOMATION

> **Note**
>
> We often find that an initial scan of the documentation, followed by attempts to *modify* good scripts, is an excellent way to learn to *write* scripts yourself.

It's important to read good programming. Aspiring literary authors find inspiration in Pushkin and Pynchon, not grammar primers; similarly, you'll go furthest when you read the best work of the best programmers. Look in the columns of computer magazines and, most importantly, the archives of software with freely available source code. Good examples of coding occasionally turn up in Usenet discussions. Prize these; read them and learn from the masters.

All the examples in this chapter are written for easy use. They typically do one small task completely; this is one of the best ways to demonstrate a new concept. Although exception handling—and argument validation, in particular—is important, covering it is beyond the scope of this chapter.

Crystallize your learning by writing your own scripts. All the documents that you read will make more sense after you put the knowledge in place with your own experience.

Test FIRST!

We can't overemphasize the importance of testing your scripts carefully before running them against production data. We also recommended that you save a "before" copy of the production dataset in case something goes horribly wrong. Testing should be done in a safe environment, with data that resembles the real thing in size and type.

A colleague has related his own cautionary tale to illustrate this advice. He once worked far-too-late into the night on a Perl program to automate processing of an incoming file spool. He finally completed his edits at 2 AM (backups had run at 11:30) and ran the script. Due to a logic error, the script promptly deleted itself, the only existing copy, and then ended.

The moral of the story is always to test with a copy ... copy of the data, copy of the script, copy of the production system. Also, it's very good to test network scripts on a system that you can walk to in case something goes wrong and the system must be reconnected to the network. Otherwise, if the script hangs up the whole system somebody may have to drive over to reboot it.

Good Engineering

The other advice for those pursuing automation is to practice good engineering. This always starts with a clear, well-defined goal. Automation isn't an absolute good; it's only a method for achieving human goals. Part of what you'll learn in working through this chapter is how much—and how little—to automate.

When your goal is set, move as close to it as you can with components that are already written. "Glue" existing programs together with small, understandable scripting modules. Choose meaningful variable names. Define interfaces carefully. Write comments.

Explaining the Value of Automation

You've become knowledgeable and experienced in scripting your computer so that it best serves you. You know how to improve your skills in script writing. You've practiced different approaches enough to know how to solve problems efficiently. The final challenge in your automation career is this: How do you explain how good you have become?

This is a serious problem, and, as usual, the solution begins with attitude. You no longer pound at the keyboard to bludgeon technical tasks into submission; you now operate in a more refined way and achieve correspondingly grander results. As an employee, you're much more valuable than the system administrators and programmers who reinvent wheels every day. In your recreational or personal use of UNIX, the computer is working for you—not the other way around, as it might have been when you started. Your attitude needs to adjust to the reality that you've created by improving your productivity. Invest in yourself, whether by attending technical conferences where you can further promote your skills, negotiating a higher salary, or simply taking the time in your computer work to get things right. It's easy in organizations to give attention to crises and reward those visibly coping with emergencies. It takes true leadership to plan ahead, organize work so that emergencies don't happen, and use techniques of automation to achieve predictable and manageable results on schedule.

One of the most effective tools that you have in taking up this challenge is *quantification*. Keep simple records to demonstrate how much time you put into setting up backups before you learned about cron, or run a simple experiment to compare two ways of approaching an elementary database-maintenance operation. Find out how much of your online time goes just to the login process, and decide whether scripting that is justified. Chart a class of mistakes that you make, and see whether your precision improves as you apply automation ideas.

In all cases, keep in mind that you are efficient, perhaps extraordinarily efficient, because of the knowledge that you apply. Automation feels good!

19

AUTOMATION

Best Practices

- Anything you do more than twice should become a script.

- Test your scripts using copies of the script, data, and if possible, a copy of the production system.

- Do not test scripts running with root privileges (unless you can access the machine physically to reboot it).

- Comment, comment, comment. Add comments as though a complete stranger will have to understand the script based on comments alone.

- Maintain a central repository of scripts—you will be reusing your code.

- If the scripting language supports modular elements (such as subroutines), take advantage of them. They're much easier to reuse.

- Read the man page for `cron` and `crontab` on your local system to check on specific syntax *before* you run commands.

Online References

`cfengine`
`http://www.cfengine.org`

`Python`
`http://www.python.org`

`Ruby`
`http://www.rubycentral.com`

`Perl`

- Perl Mongers: `http://www.perl.org`

- O'Reilly Perl site: `http://www.perl.com`

- Comprehensive Perl Archive Network: `http://www.cpan.org/`

- The Perl Journal online: `http://www.sysadminmag.com/tpj/`

- Pierce, Clinton. *Teach Yourself Perl in 24 Hours, Second Edition.* SAMS Publishing, 2001.

- O'Reilly Perl Books: `http://perl.oreilly.com/`

Advanced Web Services

by Sandy and Emma Antunes

IN THIS CHAPTER

Providing Advanced Web Services

A Web site is more than a server and some pages. It is an integrated and lively place, full of content and utility, often a place where readers and the site builder work together to make a dynamic creation. In this chapter, we talk about how to plan and execute a more advanced site. Starting with a focus, you can decide on coding, implement secure and well-documented functionality, and encourage growth, step by step.

Dynamic versus Static Sites

It would be nice to easily define content as either "dynamic" (pages as code, in which the content is flexible and changes) or "static" (pages that are typed and put on the site and that do not change).

Static sites are simply text files or image files or binary files, things that you could put on a CD-ROM and give to someone. Articles, documents, image libraries, code archives—they all fit the definition of "static content" because they don't change quickly.

If your articles include an attached discussion forum for discussing details, then you have "quasistatic" content: one part is unchanging, while the other part changes frequently. Another quasistatic case exists when an entire site's contents are stored in a database and regenerated when that database is updated.

And even static content evolves on some time scale. Articles that update frequently are well served by dynamic indexes. Likewise, your image library can use a script that automatically builds its index by listing the files in a given directory, rather than requiring creation of a "static" page (even if the time scale for changes to this file are very long).

If you're smart (or lazy) and don't want to have to ever edit HTML, you can add new stuff via a Web form or a browser tool. Your site is "dynamic" because the contents are determined by tools and automated helpers rather than being a collection of flat files.

So, a dynamic site is simply a site that does any of the following:

1. Changes according to each reader (example: MyPortalDuJour)
2. Creates transient pages based on reader input (example: a search engine)
3. Serves fixed data based on reader queries (example: a science data archive)
4. Accepts reader input to make new content (example: a survey)
5. Has frequently updating content (example: forums)
6. Has regular content that automatically gets served (example: a knowledge base)

In short, a dynamic site is any site where all the content isn't in place before you build the site. Using this definition, most sites are dynamic—it's just a question of implementation and time scales. For anything past infrequent trivial updates, it is worth looking into automating your dynamic site.

Enter server-side languages, to make this easier. A server-side language is simply code running on your machine, to distinguish it from client-side languages (code running on each individual reader's browser).

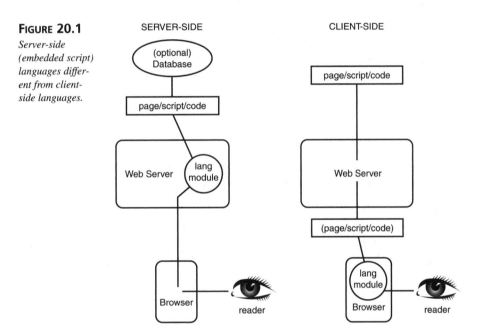

FIGURE 20.1

Server-side (embedded script) languages different from client-side languages.

Essentially, server-side languages parse any code within your Web server and then deliver ordinary HTML to your readers. Client-side languages pass the code unparsed to the readers and hope that the reader's browser is equipped to deal with it. At first glance, you also might note that databases are much easier to incorporate with server-side languages, simply because the language is the way for the server to talk to the database.

The risk of client-side languages is that they require a reader to have a specific browser capability. Failure to have that browser means that one or more of the pages, data, or content will be inaccessible, and utility is reduced.

Either the reader will see that there is a capability there but not be capable of using it (as with JavaScript-based menus), or the reader will never know that there is missing capability (such as JavaScript image maps that fail to load). Both have their downsides, in terms of public relations.

20

ADVANCED WEB SERVICES

With server-side languages, because you control your own server, you can ensure that it has the necessary capabilities. The downside is that the code is running on your server and, therefore, is taking up memory and CPU cycles. Efficient database design and good coding practices are required.

Within this chapter, we will compare and contrast Perl, PHP, Java, ASP, and JavaScript. Factors in choosing a programming language include these (in any order):

- Cross-platform or choice of platform issues
- Feature requirements
- Developer skill set and learning curve
- Code base and COTS
- Performance
- Cost (up-front and total)

Software for Your Site

One initial question for building your site is whether to use standalone pieces or buy an integrated suite that handles the bulk of your functionality.

Standalone development allows you to pick the best packages for each function and to (in general) slowly grow your site as new needs become apparent. The downside is that a large portion of your time will be spent initially on integrating the components and then in adding new ones to the existing structure. Thus, even free software will end up costing you, in integration time (and, thus, costs). Administrative tools and maintenance also will require more time and training because there will not be a single uniform interface for such.

Using a suite—either using a commercial off-the-shelf (COTS) product or hiring a contractor to provide a system—typically has a higher "sticker price." However, integration is already resolved, so the total setup investment can be cheaper than the cost of integrating your own kit.

In addition, any suite worth its salt will include unified administrative tools for maintaining the site. The downside of suites is that you are limited to a single support avenue—the vendor—for fixes and new functionality. You also must be wary of licensing issues because that can involve recurrent costs past the initial setup that, in the long run, could become expensive or limit growth (especially if licenses charge per-reader or per-use fees rather than as a flat rate).

In any case, any software that you get will have five main parts:

1. **The code**—Libraries, code pages and snippets, and HTML pages
2. **The back end**—Any database or file storage systems for containing dynamic data, where dynamic data is simply the information that changes after the site launches
3. **The pages**—HTML pages and code snippets to insert in your existing pages
4. **The admin tools**—A set of Web-based or other method for maintaining, moderating, updating, and editing your site
5. **Documentation and the Advanced Programmer Interface (API)**—Detailed specifications on how everything works and, thus, how to modify or add new functionality to the system

The Code

Here is where you can choose your language. Perl, PHP, C, ASP, and others are all viable choices and are covered in the next section.

The Back End

Here is where our earlier discussion of database-driven sites returns. The short answer is: if your back end is a database, ultimately you have a single point of control that lets you more easily update, add to, or manage your site.

You also have a single point of failure if the database crashes. Frankly, though, Web sites are littered with single points of failure, and databases are among the more reliable items out there. Your site could die because of nameserver issues, disk space filling up, file permission problems, bad memory in the computers, or many other factors. A 24×7 "seven 9s" site (uptime of 99.99999%, which would be down only 3 seconds a year) is tremendously difficult; we will discuss reliability and uptime later.

The effects of a database crash can be minimized by effective caching. That is, any well-written database application can (and probably should, in our opinion) have a text file cache that it accesses if the database does not respond. This text file is simply the page as last produced by the working database. In particular, for pages that refresh on long time scales, this is essential.

A long time scale is relative to the traffic that you get, and roughly breaks down to the fact that, if a dozen readers see it before it changes, it should be cached. Got a "What's New" page that updates every hour? Have a cache. If your database dies, you've just bought yourself up to 59 minutes of time to get it fixed before any reader knows otherwise.

Similar to caching, any database-driven application should have a graceful fallback mode. Software for posting should inform readers, "The database is down, please resubmit later," not, "Error 54, could not connect." The latter not only says nothing, but it makes it look like you don't even know when your own system is not working.

So, databases are not a risk, but an asset. They are robust and can have fallbacks that allow for brief downtime. And because databases are easy to back up, your entire site's content can be easily backed up and safely stored offsite, in case of disaster.

Service Bureau–Based, or Application Service Providers (ASPs)

An ASP is simply an organization that provides the Web services for your site, so you do not need to install or run them yourself. A common ASP service is chat: By accessing a customized chat run on the chat company's machine, you don't directly have to deal with chat software, bandwidth issues, or customer support. Instead, you pay a sum (flat or based on usage) to the ASP for the functionality.

Another common ASP item is e-commerce, in particular shopping carts with credit card processing. Still another area is groupware and intranets. All are just cases of the same concept: Someone else runs it for you.

The advantage of ASPs is quick setup time (no need to get your own code onto your site) and typically good support. The downside is that costs usually scale with usage, as opposed to a "pay now and recover costs later" model for installing your own.

The primary disadvantages of ASPs include these:

1. **Branding**—In many cases, the ASP can incorporate your site colors and logo into its tool, but you are relinquishing some of your brand to use an ASP. How much you relinquish depends on the specific ASP that you are dealing with. Some co-brand—that is, provide their service to your visitors in return for declaring both site identities ("provided by X and Y"). Others can hide their brand everywhere except in the actual URL ("page is X, even though it says www.Y.com"). Others take over your brand ("processing courtesy of Y"). So, this disadvantage is not cut-and-dried, but it must be evaluated for each service.

2. **Future considerations**—If the ASP goes out of business, you lose not only the functionality, but also any legacy information or data contained on it. At best, you have that data and must put it into a new set of tools. At worst, it becomes truly lost, and your archival value for your site is crippled.

The best advice for evaluating an ASP is to do a cost/benefit analysis for three cases:

1. Costs to handle your estimated traffic for two years (versus building and operating the function yourself)
2. Costs assuming that you grow by a factor of 10 within one year, over three years
3. Costs assuming the ASP goes out of business after one year

If all three totals show an advantage of using an ASP (in terms of start-up costs, operating expenses, staffing, and risk), it's a clear decision. If either scenario shows higher costs, you need to make a judgment call on taking this path.

Pages and Code Snippets

Good pages can be broken up into pieces:

- Standard layout, frequently using SSIs to include standard headers, footers, columns, menus, logos, and other items shared by all pages to give a uniform look and feel. Frequently, all pages follow a template to ensure this uniformity.

- Static content, appropriately formatted in HTML.

- Code snippets that provide any necessary dynamic content.

- Interactive coding, including JavaScript or java apps, that let the reader do something on the site (the client side). We separate this from templates and static content (even if every page has them) and from code snippets (even if it ultimately feeds back into your back end) because, frankly, interactive coding is typically the first thing to break in a visitor's browser.

For example, having a Java paint program means that the reader can make a pretty picture, and it doesn't care what your back end is doing. Likewise, JavaScript rollovers for menus are a neat bit of coding that could be considered a template or static content but that require a bit more proofing when building a page. And it is very important to realize that, unlike static HTML (which is well defined) or your code snippets and back end (which the reader never sees), interactive coding can appear very different (or not appear at all) to different readers based on the operating system on their computers and their choices in Web browser and version.

This leads to an important testing mantra: Always test your site using (at the very least) the top two browsers, plus Lynx (a text-only browser, useful for ensuring that folks using devices that assist the disabled with Web browsing will be able to use your site).

Operating a site includes regular maintenance (backups, security checks, system resource usage checks, and log file analysis). It also involves content updating, whether that means moderating and approving items or actually adding new files and reports and sections to the content. And you need good tools for this.

There are two ways to access tools. One is to have standalone tools (custom GUIs, command-line interfaces, and scripts) so that authorized readers who can get onto the system directly can do the work. The other is to have Web-based tools, which is exactly like the standalone tools except that they share the commonality that they are all accessed by authorized readers via the Web browser.

In general, Web-based tools using a secure authentication scheme are an ideal method for doing regular (and content-related) updates. Standalone tools that require logging into the machine frequently are useful for system-wide tasks such as backups—things that might involve services beyond just the Web pages.

Staff costs are the single largest expense in operating any Web site, so admin tools that automate many procedures and reduce the workload necessary to update and maintain a site are crucial. Alas, they often are neglected. A good admin tool first must be easily accessed by the admin but must not be available to the reader. Ideally, authentication is secure but quick, and need not be repeated for each operation with that tool. The tool also must (like any piece of software) be well laid out, with most-used operations listed first.

If you are using a variety of packages, each with their own admin tool, at the very least make sure that you provide your Web master with a single "admin index page" that links to each tool (and handles authentication, if possible) so that he doesn't have to look up anything. Prioritize this index by frequency of use, and have the index generate any required information if some tools are required on an as-needed basis.

Bad admin:

"Go to mysite/forums/admin if you need to fix the forums, with reader name frog and password X. Go to mysite/links when you have to approve new link submissions, with readername wombat and password Y. You can send out email via mysite/sendtostaff with the same reader name."

Good admin:

index.html requires authentication, with these links (given as bracketed terms, for the purposes of this example) and labels (in parentheses):

1. [Link admin] (There are three links awaiting approval.)
2. [Forum admin] (The forums currently are functioning.)
3. [Staff emailer] (Use when you have to send email to all staff.)

In the good case, we've neatly provided the Web master with a single page by which he can access the admin tools and that also contains information on whether any given tool needs to be accessed. The list is ordered in the approximately frequency of use that he will need to act on.

Documentation and the API

Any system requires documentation so that you can fix stuff that breaks, understand how things work for training new sysadmins, and add in new stuff as needed. Good software documentation helps in understanding and repair work, and a good API allows for expansion.

Documentation is frequently abysmal, and giving general guidelines here is beyond the scope of this book. But testing it is easy. The best test of documentation is to give it to a "guest Web master" for an afternoon and see if that person can understand things. The best test of the API specifications is to write a short "Hello World" application (perhaps one that does a simple Web form) to ensure that at least trivial new routines are easily done.

Uptime, Reliability, and Risk

Uptime is the first tier of a site. If the site is not, as a whole, up and on the Web, there's not much that you can do. Typically reasons for site downtime include hardware failures, DNS issues, denial-of-service attacks, overwhelming usage and bandwidth issues, and poor back-end design. Thus, uptime involves your chosen platform and your chosen back end.

Reliability is making sure that things work as expected. If the site is up but the Web forms all fail, that's a reliability issue. Reliability is usually a function of how well the site's code is written. It also can be affected by back-end issues or overall reliability problems: For example, if transactions are lost due to server load, that's a reliability issue. Reliability, therefore, includes responsiveness and issues such as server load and bandwidth saturation—issues that can negatively impact the reader experience of the site.

Risk includes issues of reliability and of security. Issues of risk that we touch on here include whether site failures provide sufficient information to the readers, whether the site can survive downtime for any period of time without losing its audience, and whether reliability issues influence the archival history of the site.

You minimize the risk of losing your audience if your software is capable of informing readers when reliability problems occur. For example, a site error of "404 file not found" during an e-commerce transaction could mean anything, from "This transaction could not be processed, please resubmit later" to "This transaction was processed, but we cannot confirm at this time; please await an email confirmation." So, informative error messages again are necessary to keep your audience involved with your site.

Taking a bigger step back, you need to ensure that your site is robust enough to provide you with the necessary uptime and reliability. If you can shut down for an hour each night for repairs and simply have a "Backups in Progress" page, uptime isn't a priority. If you are handling stock market transactions 24×7, uptime is critical. Everything else falls somewhere in between. Similarly, if your site keeps slowing down to a crawl at noon each day due to lunchtime readers, well, you need to improve your performance so that you don't lose readers.

Use Readers as Testers

One important thing to immediately implement is a way for readers to report problems. Either a Web form for submitting trouble tickets by email or an open forum for such things is essential. If you have an easy-to-use, standard method for reporting bugs and problems, your readers will be your strongest resource for handling crises. These good "whistle-blowers" will let you know even the most minor of page problems—something that, for a very large site, you cannot always check regularly. You also get bonus public relations points for being responsive.

Email for these matters is easy to do, and you should have an autoresponder that immediately sends a "Report received, thanks, we'll get on it!" reply. Trouble-ticket software has the advantage of letting you easily track bugs and (typically) send an automated "solved!" email so that whistle-blowers know they were heard.

Trouble-ticket forums (in which problem reports are visible to all) have the additional advantage of minimizing multiple reports. People who see that "News is down" was reported will refrain from flooding your email box with trouble tickets and will give you time to fix it. The downside of the forum approach is privacy concerns, but this can be easily resolved by simply not publishing whistle-blower names in the forum.

In all cases, you need a method for reporting problems, and you need to have a link to that method on (at least) every major page, and conceivably on every page. Your readers are then a helpful resource.

Integration and System-Wide Settings

By the time you've installed your third COTS or OS Web project, you might well be tired of redundancy. If each tool requires you to enter the database name and password, the Web master email, the top-level directory, and other site-wide values, you might want to consider making a standard "include" file.

Ideally, your many tools are in one—or, at most, two—languages. Using a different programming language for each tool might save you in development time, but it does lead to maintenance hassles.

On the other hand, if you use one site-wide programming language (such as PHP, Perl, or ASP), issues such as maintenance, integration, and speed in adding new functionality are greatly eased. Pick a standard and stick with it.

Then make a general access-identity-configuration file. Any system setting (password, file location, email address, and so on) that a Web program uses should be defined in this one file. This is so that future changes, updates, switches in contact personnel, and security requests can be implemented in one place and then applied to your entire code base. For each Web program, you can include this general file and, if needed, translate to the local values.

So, if your general file lists the database password as $gen-dbpassword (and we suggest that you use a nontrivial naming scheme such as appending gen- to the front of all variables, to prevent overwriting poorly named local variables in other people's code) and your COTS Web forum packages wants you to hand-enter the database password as variable $dbPass, just use something like:

```
include "location/to/general.php";
$dbPass=$gen-dbpssword;
```

You are set—and more easily maintained. Again, now you need to reflect system changes in only your one general file, and you don't have to hunt for each instance of each call in the event of a password change, a filesystem shuffle, or another fairly common maintenance/upgrade activity.

Costs (and Making the Case to Management)

Putting up a Web "thing" has six distinct steps:

1. Design.

2. Implementation. This includes acquiring any needed tools and then coding. At the end of coding, your concept should be (in theory) fully functioning.

3. Deployment. This step involves actually putting the code onto the site, either in a development "clone" of the site or on the live site. In this stage, everything that you wrote is up in the exact environment where it will be used.

4. Integration. This is ensuring that the new stuff fits into the existing live site. This means making the new stuff talk to and mingle with any existing code and pages.

5. Testing. In this step, you ensure that what is there does what was required and does not do things that are bad.

For example, say that the project is to add birthday greetings for all registered readers. The design phase involves choosing a language, mapping out the problem, and stating how it will interface with the existing registration system. Then you write the code specification.

Implementation involves coding it, taking advantage of any existing libraries or code bases. After the code compiles and runs without bugs, it's time to deploy it.

In deployment, you put the code on the site (live or copy) and ensure that it works. The integration phase then kicks in. In that phase, you must ensure that the deployed code works with any existing Web bits that it needs (the database, a reader registry, and so on). You also must verify that the necessary information (birthdays) is available already, or that a tool exists to create and store that information as part of the existing reader registry. Output is needed so that the birthday results easily can be inserted into the relevant site pages.

The testing stage then checks everything from reader issues (can readers easily enter and update the necessary information, and are their entries validated?) to security (do erroneous reader birthdays throw off any other calculations, such as adult verification?) and even simple integration nuances (such as, do all error emails go to the proper contact person—and can this easily be changed, or does it have to be done on a per-script basis?).

Whether it is in the choice of a Web server or a programming language, admins often have to justify their choices (in nontechnical terms) to management. In such cases, feature sets or code subtleties sometimes are undervalued.

The best way to justify an approach is in terms of time, labor, support, and money—frequently in that order. Often business terms such as total cost of ownership (TCO) and return on investment (ROI) are used.

To management, all projects are just a deadline, a TCO, and an ROI. You can figure these out from time + labor + support + money, and it's actually a short and useful exercise to do for any project that will take more than a few days.

Time simply means quantifying how your recommended approach will get things running faster than X and will take less maintenance time as well. X can be anything from what is in place now to what the manager suggested or even (alas) what that trade mag suggested or what some salesman told the manager.

So, you need to know your development, deployment, and integration times, plus what management might have suggested. Good management gives you target "metrics" and dates to aim for; bad management requires mind reading. In both cases, you still have to do your calculations.

Next comes labor, which really also factors into time. The main issue here is the skill sets required by the project, both for creation and for maintenance. In general, short-term projects should be done with hardware and software that the existing staff have.

Long-term projects can require learning a new language if that greatly saves time. For example, if spending two weeks learning PHP means that you can use an existing OS solution instead of doing three months of coding in Pascal, go for the new language approach! But be honest here. The fun of learning a new language can be tempting (and has relevance as a job perk), but it is important to really look at which languages you and your staff are competent in. (Of course, if you have coders and interns sitting idle, by all means break these rules. Set them to work learning new stuff. But if you have idle staff, you likely have some management trouble somewhere already!)

Support means two things. To staff, it means, "Where can we get answers?" and "Can anyone here but me fix this at 11 p.m. at night?" Beware the "guru" projects—brilliant bits that, unfortunately, rely on a single staffer remaining employed. Instead, you want work that is well documented and, ideally, has a support group or Web site when problems happen.

To management, support equals "blame," as in, "When this fails, who do we yell at?" This is why managers might favor a seemingly expensive COTS or outside vendor system. If it fails, it becomes someone else's problem.

So this really ties in with the staff's concept of support. If you do it in-house and it later has a problem, are you likely to have staff, documentation, and other support necessary to handle that? If you can reassure your management that you have considered this, they can approve your plan. Remember, software responsibility does not end when the code is delivered; it ends only when the last reader is dead, so have a support plan.

It all comes down to money. Buying software costs money. Paying staff to develop it in-house costs money. Maintaining it costs staff time as well support expenses, in either staff time or in straight cash paid to support contracts or outside contractors. All this creates TCO—the total tab, from initial idea to end of use.

One thing to remember about money is that your time is valuable. If you get paid $30 per hour as a sysadmin and have a choice of paying $600 for a COTS solution or working one week to make it yourself, well, one week is $1,200 to your employer—just buy the darn software and be done with it!

Ah, but if only life was that simple. More often the choice is to buy it for $600 and then spend two days installing it and six days trying to get it to do what it promised, instead of spending one week coding it yourself and then one week fixing bugs—but, hey, you learned a lot!

ROI addresses the question, "How much will (or did) this project earn the company?" All ROI for sysadmins really boils down to is making sure that you're not spending lots of your time on projects that don't matter much.

With a deadline, a TCO figure, and ROI, a good manager instantly can decide on a project. Although admins might not be privy to the process, it is useful to understand it so that you have greater success in having your projects done in the fashion that *you* know is best.

So, all you need to do is the following:

1. Define what you want to do and when you need it done by.
2. Estimate how useful it is (in bringing in revenue or in saving you time, or even in intangibles such as job satisfaction or PR).
3. Figure out how much in resources (time, staffing, cash) is worth tossing at it.

If it makes sense after that, go for it!

Blogs

Content for a Web site includes original content, metacontent, and indexes. Content is just stuff created or edited by the site operators and site visitors for reading. Metacontent includes excepts from other sites and links and forums; it simply refers to any content compiled but not created by the site operators or site visitors. For example, indexes and excerpts are external metacontent, while reader forums are internal metacontent.

Blogging and Web Ads

A popular form of Web site is the blog, or Web log. The idea is that the site owner puts up content or metacontent, to which readers then can append comments, analysis, and critique. Thus, reader feedback is fully half of the site's content.

The most famous blog is likely /., a.k.a. slashdot.org. There, the editors of the site post either unique essays and reviews (content) or short summations plus links to social and tech articles of interest (metacontent). Readers then visit the material (if offsite) and provide additional commentary on the issue. This has lead to the "Slashdot Effect," wherein a /. reference to a site can cause that site to experience server overload as hundreds of thousands of /. readers visit within a few minutes of the blog posting time.

Blogs are an ideal form for metacontent because the burden of content creation is upon the readers. This does mean that readership maturity and morality—factors very hard to control—are crucial to long-term success. Most blogs use some form of moderation to ensure that reader input is ranked according to quality.

Accessibility: What Is It, and Why Should You Care?

"The power of the Web is in its universality. Access by everyone regardless of disability is an essential aspect."

—Tim Berners-Lee

Web accessibility means more than just being able to connect to a Web site. It means that users with disabilities don't have barriers to navigating or using the information on your site. When we say "users with disabilities," we're referring to three main types:

1. Visual impairment
2. Hearing impairment
3. Mobility impairment

This means that you might need to accommodate users who can't see, hear, or use a mouse. If you work in e-commerce, accommodating users with disabilities means more sales. If you work with the U.S. government, it's the law. We believe that it's simply the right thing to do.

Making sites accessible doesn't have to mean ugly, text-only sites. In fact, the accessibility community hates text-only pages because they're usually created once and forgotten, and they are rarely as up-to-date as the main pages. (Unless you generate all your text-only pages on the fly from a back-end database, it's best to avoid these.) It's quite possible to make sites that read well in Lynx (a text-based Web client—see `http://lynx.browser.org/`) and still look slick in Internet Explorer.

Accessibility isn't just for users with disabilities, either. It's also for those with slow modems, or shell-only connections. It's for users browsing the Web with cell phones, PDAs, and other nonstandard clients as well.

Universal design is the key. If you follow the guidelines provided by the World Wide Web Consortium's Web Accessibility Initiative (WAI), you'll end up with good-looking sites that work for almost everyone.

The W3C divides its WAI guidelines into three priority levels:

- Priority 1 checkpoints *must* be implemented for the Web site to be used at all.
- Priority 2 checkpoints *should* be implemented to remove significant barriers to accessing the Web site.
- Priority 3 checkpoints *may* be implemented to improve accessibility for specific groups.

Section 508 of the Rehabilitation Act, Amendments of 1998, requires that federal employees and members of the public have comparable access to electronic information.

The requirements for Section 508, though similar to the checkpoints for Priority 1, differ slightly from the WAI guidelines. You'll need to follow the 508-specific rules if you want to be compliant with the law (see `http://www.access-board.gov/sec508/508standards.htm`).

In general, if you follow the Priority 1 checkpoints or the Section 508 requirements, you'll be doing the minimum that will satisfy most users.

Here are the main things to remember when designing with accessibility in mind:

- Always use meaningful alt tags.
- Specify alt text for areas in client-side image maps.

- Provide redundant text links for server-side image maps.
- Tables for layout are okay if they flow logically.
- Data tables now require new HTML tags to relate items in rows to specific columns.
- Use meaningful names for frames (such as navigation, content, and so on).
- Pages must work with JavaScript, Java applets, and other scripts turned off.
- Don't rely solely on color to convey information.
- Make sure that style sheets degrade gracefully.
- Multimedia must be captioned.
- Avoid flickering images.

How do you verify that a Web site is accessible? One of the easiest ways is to view it in Lynx. If it makes sense in Lynx, it's probably okay. Other tools include these:

- Bobby, a free tool offered by the Center for Applied Special Technology (CAST): `http://www.cast.org/bobby/`
- 508 Accessibility Suite, a free extension for Macromedia Dreamweaver by UsableNet, Inc.: `http://www.macromedia.com/exchange/dreamweaver/`

References:

W3C's WAI: `http://www.w3.org/WAI/`

Section 508: "The Road to Accessibility": `http://www.section508.gov/`

The Access Board: a federal agency committed to accessible design: `http://www.access-board.gov/`

When Sharing Is Bad: The Case for Dedicated Servers

So, where are you running your Web server? Far too often, it is on a machine that also has reader accounts, handles email, and is used for development work. So, let's rephrase this.

For security, stability, and peace of mind, you should always have your Web services run from a dedicated computer. Although this box naturally will be on your network, it should handle only Web things.

One reason is security. Web stuff is inherently hackable because you are inviting anonymous readers to access part of your box. Any vulnerabilities, therefore, can give an ill-intentioned reader access to everything else also run on that box. Therefore, if no non-Web items are running, you've limited the damage that can be done.

But talking about limiting damage is negative. Let's look at the positive side. Your Web server will perform best because it will have full access to the system resources on a standalone setup. And any local readers or programmers will be pleased that their important work on their development machine isn't slowed down by the random fluxes of outside visitors looking at your Web pages.

Web worms—bits of code that get into a server and then infect all readers, spitting out malicious email—are currently popular. Naturally, if your Web server isn't handling email or readers, you're more protected. Furthermore, having email (in particular) on a separate box is very useful because email is very, very important for a functioning company, university, research site, or home site. It's the Internet's "killer app." Bundling it with the Web server's machine just seems to be a bit risky, and much of what we're covering in good Web development is maximizing productivity (and fun) while minimizing risk.

Finally, in terms of maintenance, you are easily isolating performance and upgrade needs, as well as reducing the risk of failure in one section (say, Web server overload) and negatively affecting totally different areas (say, programmers). Hardware is cheap—do it. Enough said.

Scripting Languages

As shown in Table 20.1, different programming languages have different advantages and approaches for Web use. Whether you are implementing "call-and-fetch" CGI use or more dynamic server-side programming, there isn't one "perfect language" for all jobs—but there is a best language for your project at hand. Beginning with a look at the programming approaches, you can then move into a selection of specific languages based on feature sets and your own programming team talents.

Scripting Languages Versus CGI

The Common Gateway Interface (CGI) is the default language for doing page operations in HTML. It allows for form variables to be set so that submission causes the subsequent target page to receive those values.

Really, CGI is the standard for passing Web variables, and languages are built around handling CGI. This is because data that is acceptable to CGI can be easily passed as Web links (URLs) or within forms.

The most common use of CGI is form variables. These can be entered as part of the URL (a `GET`):

```
url.html?MyVariableA=whatever&MyVariableA=anotherthing
```

Thus, they can be sent as a `get` request, or entered from a form (a `POST`):

```
<form action=url.html>
<input type=text name=MyVariableA>
<input type=text name=MyVariableB>
<input action=submit>
</form>
```

With the exception of JavaScript and Java (which have their own extra input mechanisms), CGI is the standard for reader data input into any Web page. Thus, CGI can be seen as a way to get reader input into whatever languages will then do useful work, and all languages either support CGI directly or have libraries to translate CGI variables into programming variables.

In addition to variables that you may define, the following variables are defined in the HTTP standard and are accessible to all pages. We list the first three as the most likely to be used, and then we list several of the more standard ones after that, in alphabetical order:

- **QUERY_STRING**—All the useful CGI data. (That is, everything after the ?.)
- **CONTENT_TYPE**—Usually text, or an image type such as JPEG or GIF, or a document type such as PDF.
- **REMOTE_READER**—If authentication is on, the validated reader name entered by the reader.
- **AUTH_TYPE**—If server authentication is on, which method is being used.
- **CONTENT_LENGTH**—How big the page will be.
- **GATEWAY_INTERFACE**—CGI/revision.
- **PATH_INFO**—Any extra information passed to the server by a previous page.
- **PATH_TRANSLATED**—Server-translated version of PATH_INFO.
- **REMOTE_ADDR**—The IP address of the reader's host.
- **REMOTE_HOST**—If known, the reader's host.
- **REMOTE_IDENT**—If RFC 931 identification is enabled, a fetched ID.

20

ADVANCED WEB SERVICES

- **REQUEST_METHOD**—GET, HEAD, POST, and so on.
- **SCRIPT_NAME**—Self-reference.
- **SERVER_NAME**—Hostname, DNS alias, or IP address.
- **SERVER_PORT**—Port number.
- **SERVER_PROTOCOL**—Protocol/revision.
- **SERVER_SOFTWARE**—Name/version.
- **HTTP_[any header line provided by the client]**—HTTP_ACCEPT lists MIME types that the client can handle. HTTP_READER_AGENT describes the reader's browser and so on.

In Table 20.1 we look at our sample languages: PHP, Perl, JavaScript, Java, and ASP.

Module and library support refers to how well the language is supported with "rich" feature sets such as database integration, advanced HTML and string handling, and other coding necessities.

"Session variables" refers to whether the language supports state or session variables that persist across different pages (for any single reader).

TABLE 20.1   Sample Languages

Language	Platform	Design	Module Support	Cost	State Variables
PHP	Any OS	Structured	Good	Free	Yes (if enabled)
Perl	Any OS	Structured or OO	Excellent	Free	mod_perl only
JavaScript					
Server-side	Any OS (requires iPlanet server)	Structured and OO	Fair	$$	Yes
Client-side	Any OS	Structured and OO	Weak	Free	No*
ASP	MS, UNIX	OO	Good	$$$	Yes
Java	Any OS	OO	Fair	Free or $$	Yes

* = Client-side JavaScript offers URL encoding in a somewhat automated fashion, as opposed to true intrinsic state variables that remain across sessions.

$$ = costs to use, $$$ = expensive

Notes:

CGI versus server-side versus client-side

- Perl is generally CGI (although mod_perl adds server-side).
- PHP and ASP are server-side.
- JavaScript is client-side.

Open platform:

- Perl, PHP, and JavaScript are open standards, have large Open Source code bases, and work under many OSs (Win*, *nix, Linux, SGI, and so on).
- ASP is a closed platform and interface, with databases often proprietary. It also is bound to one OS (Win*). An Apache module does exist, in an early form.

Domains:

- JavaScript allows interactive pages without requiring a reload.
- ASP has integration within a dedicated MS worksite.
- ASP has Active-X client-side capabilities.
- Perl and PHP are highly portable across systems, servers, and OSes.

The JavaScript distinction is crucial. You can do PHP or Perl pages with embedded JavaScript; they are by no means mutually exclusive.

Note that we differentiate between structured programming (a.k.a. "C-like") and object-oriented design (a.k.a. "C++–like"), although several languages are open to both approaches.

Similar languages are easier to learn, and, of course, the difficulty in learning a language differs for each individual. Using the previous comparisons, however, language similarities can give insight. For example, learning PHP can be described in several ways:

If you know Perl, it is trivial.

If you know C or Fortran, it is easy.

If you know JavaScript, it's not dissimilar and more forgiving.

If you work in Java, C++, or other OOP, you might get frustrated.

If you don't yet program, it has simple syntax, is fairly forgiving, and has useful error messages.

Differences in Server-Side Include (SSI) Implementations

Not all implementations of server-side includes (SSIs) are alike. For example, iPlanet (formerly known as Netscape Enterprise) calls them "server-parsed HTML." But it's not just the name that's different. With Apache, include files are incorporated into the file to be served, and then any SSIs are parsed. With iPlanet, the include files are parsed *first* and then are incorporated into the file to be served.

Why is this significant? Say that you have a footer file that includes the standard information that you'd like to have on your pages, such as contact information and the date that the page was last modified. If you put "Last Updated: `<!—#echo var="LAST_MODIFIED"—>`" in your footer file, Apache will give you the last modified date of the file that referenced the footer, the expected behavior. iPlanet, on the other hand, will give you the last modified date of the *footer file*. Admins who understand these differences can avoid a lot of frustration.

Common Mistakes in Implementation and Coding

The bulk of errors are simply from programmer mistakes. Failing to print an HTML header (such as "Content-type") often means that you get zero output and a page error, making further debugging difficult until you realize this mistake.

Permission issues are endemic in Web programming. If you are writing any files, you need to ensure that the Web server has permission to do so. Thus, writeable directories must include the Web server "owner" as having write permission, or (as a very poor second choice) must be world-writeable.

When doing CGI script work, GET and POST need to be enabled for the cgi-bin directory in your Apache configuration, and scripts must be marked as executable. Most of these issues appear when you write your first script; after the first one, you'll be on track for many future successful scripts.

Databases

Why databases? There are many reasons that databases now rule the Web:

1. They are an effective method for storing regularized data—that is, data that always follows a consistent format and forms complete sets.

2. Most Web pages involve easily described, finite data.

3. Databases are searchable (and can be systematically altered).

4. Databases can be updated, and the result can be made instantly available to all subsequent queries.

5. Databases ease file management and file control (good DBMS).

6. Good Web-based editing tools exist for databases (vs. static live files).

7. Databases can be secured more easily than Web-writeable directories.

8. Databases are easily duplicated and backed up.

9. Databases separate content management from Web mastering and HTML coding; content and look can be done by different people.

Two modes of operation exist for a database-driven site. In the first, the database is the page content, perhaps with some pages being cached (local copies made on the fly). The database must be operating for the site to function. As an advantage, changes to the data instantly are reflected on all site pages.

In the second mode, batch generation of pages from a database occurs at some regular interval. For this, the database generates the pages, but the Web server serves static pages. So, if the database has problems, the Web site is unaffected. The downside is that any changes to the data will not show until the next update/regeneration of pages.

SQL, ODBC, and DBI Interactions

Most serious database work is done in SQL. The older style of Berkeley DBM (a flat-file database standard) is still used in places, and many other flat-file "databases" exist. A flat-file database is just a text file (similar to a spreadsheet) that is accessed by the system as if it were a query-and-return database.

SQL is the Structured Query Language of databases, and it is semiportable. The basic set of SQL commands (select, insert, drop) usually is implemented in all databases. However, sometimes syntax varies, and, in other cases, additional functions or keywords might be offered. Therefore, when writing SQL code, it is important to reference the documentation of the specific database that you are using.

Open Database Connectivity (ODBC) is an application programming interface (API) for database access that tries to escape the hassles of understanding each different vendor's implementation of SQL. It uses SQL as its underlying database language and provides a higher-level way to specify operations.

At its core, ODBC is just a standard so that coders can write for ODBC and then use their code with any ODBC-capable database (such as Oracle, Ingres, and many others). In short, it's a portable database specification.

Technically, ODBC works like this:

- You write a program in ODBC.
- Your server machine has an ODBC driver.
- That driver talks to your database.

PHP abstracts this further, providing a set of "unified ODBC" functions. If you have ODBC code, you can use it under PHP with your database using the database's native (not ODBC) drivers.

In a related manner, Perl introduced DBI as a database interface module, which allows you to write Perl code in a generalized way and then apply it to any database for which a DBI driver exists (including ODBC). Perl DBI even can handle DBM and other flat-file databases. In pragmatic terms, this means that you don't have to install a database server when building or testing Perl DBI code—but if you later install an SQL database, your code will work as written by simply changing a single definition statement (DBI to MySql or such). This code portability is tremendously useful because projects often migrate to different platforms and database vendors over time.

Ultimately, this means that development for a database can be done using either SQL directly (although each database differs slightly in implementation of SQL and in feature sets offered), in ODBC (which sits over SQL) for ODBC-capable databases, in language-specific database abstraction specifications such as DBI or unified ODBC, and finally in language-specific implementations of specific databases (such as the MySql or MSql function sets provided in PHP or Perl).

In practice, it is best to define the top SQL queries needed for a project during the design state. Coding (in ODBC, DBI, or any specific specification) then can proceed, but having the core SQL structure is helpful both for documenting what is happening, and as a reference document if bugs or changes are required.

Database Transactions and Rollbacks

Until recently, transactions and rollbacks were not common in the free databases used, such as MySql. Fortunately, this capability is being added, bringing free DBs up to par relative to such reputable products as Oracle.

A transaction is simply defining a set of database operations as being together. Doing so, a transaction (set) can than be evaluated according to whether it succeeds or fails as a set.

For example, a transaction set might consist of "Remove $5 from account A and put it into account B." Clearly, there is a problem if only one of the two operations succeeds: either money will be lost or falsely gained. In a transactional database, no operation in a defined transaction will occur if any of the operations failed, thus ensuring data continuity. With the previous example, either the money is transferred properly or it is not, with no risk of a partial transaction.

In the absence of a transactional database, the programmers have to code extensive error validation for all such operations. So, a transactional DBS saves programming effort while improving reliability.

Rollback is simply the capability to roll back an entire transaction, setting things back to the original state. For the previous example, say that the completed transaction results in a negative balance: A simple rollback neatly cancels the operation (and your Web page then can inform the reader).

Without rollback, you would have to manually perform the transaction steps in reverse (verifying that each succeeded). So, like transactions, rollbacks are a way to ensure that database operations perform sequences and complex actions in a safe and consistent fashion.

Languages

PHP

We will use PHP as our example language for much of this chapter. In terms of syntax, PHP is nearly identical to Perl and C, and is similar to most structured programming languages. The other type of language, object-oriented, is illustrated primarily in the JavaScript sections of this chapter.

PHP is a server-side, cross-platform embedded scripting that has been quietly sneaking onto millions of sites to provide embedded scripting/programming for Web pages. It's especially useful for dynamic, data-driven Web sites.

Factoids:

- PHP is a recursive acronym for "PHP: Hypertext Preprocessor."
- PHP is a server-side, cross-platform, embedded scripting language.
- PHP is a C- or Perl-like language that is easy to stick in pages and that has good database hooks and a lot of existing code.
- PHP is available from php.net or zend.com.

- PHP was invented in 1994, and php3 was released June 1998.
- Its growth rate (courtesy of ZEnd) is 15% per month, and it is in use for more than five million sites.

PHP currently is maintained by ZEnd, and Zend.com has some good resources for making the business case to managers. The main PHP site is php.net, and there's a handy list of some high profile sites running PHP at `http://www.php.net/sites.php`.

PHP is a server-side language. This means that you can add PHP code into HTML pages, and the code gets interpreted by the Web server into "just more HTML" and passed along to the reader. Thus, PHP lets you make dynamic (defined after the page was first written) content.

Here is an example of server-side coding.

1. Have an HTML file (.phtml, .php):

```
<HTML> <BODY>
<h1>Hello, World!</h1>

<h1>Goodbye, World!</h1>
```

2. Indicate that there is script language with <?php ... ?>.

```
<HTML> <BODY>
<h1>Hello, World!</h1>

<?php
# code will go here, and comments are indicated with a
'#'
?>

<h1>Goodbye, World!</h1>
```

3. Write code.

```
<HTML> <BODY>
<h1>Hello, World!</h1>

<?php
# code will go here, and comments are indicated with a
'#'
echo "Hello, World! Oops, I said that already.\n";
echo "Look, I can count to ten!<ol>\n";
for ($i=0;$i<10;++$i) {
echo "<li>Number = $i</li>\n";
}
echo "</ol>\n";
?>

<h1>Goodbye, World!</h1>
```

4. Look at results in your browser.

```
Hello, World!

Hello, World! Oops, I said that already. Look, I can
count to ten!

 1. 0
 2. 1
 3. 2
 4. 3
 5. 4
 6. 5
 7. 6
 8. 7
 9. 8
10. 9

Goodbye, World!
```

5. Now pick up a book on programming.

- You can do loops.

- You can print with `echo`, escaping any necessary quotes.

- You can include HTML in your `echo`/`print` statements.

- You can create variables on the fly without defining types.

- (*Not shown*) You can put `<?php>` ... `<?>` code snippets in and around your straight HTML at will. All will run and share variables within that page.

What else you can do? Read the PHP manual for a full feature set. In a similar manner, perl.org has the full Perl function set, and there are many good books by publishers (such as this book's publisher).

To learn PHP, visit php.net. Under "Links" are many reference sites in several languages. The site PHPBuilder.com has nice specific articles as well as code, including advanced material such as PDFLib (a library for PDF handling) and other extended functionalities.

A nuance with PHP: It must be compiled into your server. In fact, all server-side languages require this. A useful reference is DevShed.com's "The Soothingly Seamless Setup of Apache, SSL, MySQL, and PHP," by Israel Denis Jr., revised by Eugene Otto (June 7, 2000).

You can use other people's code as well. Several existing freeware code bases include the following"

1. PX: PHP Code Exchange, at `http://px.sklar.com/`.

2. SourceForge.net—browse by language.

   PHP, 1021 projects: vs. Python (549), Perl (1299), JavaScript (74), Java (1463), C (3076), C++ (2456), CF (10), ASP (46), and so on. Note bias.

3. PHPWizard, at http://www.phpwizard.net/

4. PHP.net and Zope.com, of course.

5. ResourceIndex.com, at `http://php.resourceindex.com/`, with 795 PHP resources (456 scripts, 97 classes, and 197 documentations). It's perhaps my favorite in terms of searchability/utility/browsing, with a nice map (also cached here).

Typical DB PHP code (for MySql) looks like this:

```
#       Create your SQL query
$query = "select Content from HTML_Talk where Slide_No='7'";
#       Make a persistent connection to the database
$dbc = mysql_pconnect("localhost","dbreader","dbpassword");

if ($dbc) {
#       Actually run your query
$result = mysql_db_query("db_name",$query);

if (!$result) {
#       oops, it failed — hide the error as a comment so the developer can
➥learn why
echo "\n\n";

} else {

#       yay, it worked! Get the row (the result).
$r=mysql_fetch_row($result);

}

#       Show it to the reader or otherwise manipulate it.
echo "$r \n";

}
```

Note

This is an example of PHP "out of the box." In actual Web site practice, it's advised to use an Open Source or custom library that (as discussed earlier, especially with DBI) provides better abstraction and higher ease of use.

Slow Tryout: Sprinkling PHP into Existing Sites

If you want to ease into trying server-side programming, PHP (and mod_perl) is ideal because you can work with existing HTML. The steps are simple:

1. Get PHP (from php.net) and compile into your Web server (especially Apache).

2. If desired, get a database running on your system so that the Web server "sees" it.

3. Have the Web server recognize a .phtml, .php, php3, (.html), or similar file as a PHP-enabled file (usually in the httpd.conf or similar configuration file).

4. Rename the .html pages that you want to play with to .phtml* files (eek, could be a tedious task!) so that the server can "see" them as potentially containing parseable code.

5. Liberally insert code into your .phtml pages. View in your browser. Have fun.

6. Systematically redesign your entire site to take advantage of having dynamic, DB-driven stuff (optional).

Zope

Zope (zope.com) essentially created an enhanced and faster rewrite of PHP, bundled it with support software, integrated it into a preconfigured Apache, added object-oriented aspects, took over lead development for the language Python, and then offered support. As a potent server-side language, it can be useful for sites looking for an "all in one" Open Source setup with support. This is a useful case study of how Open Source solutions (PHP, Python, Apache) can be integrated into a COTS package.

Perl

In many ways, Perl was the original Web language for CGI (form and script) use. First off, Perl is available for any system, from PDA through desktop and server, ranging up to supercomputer clusters. In addition to supporting nearly all platforms, Perl has excellent library and module support. It is hard to conceive of a programming function for which there is not a module, in fact. The CPAN project (http://www.cpan.org) has a full list of released modules, and Perl includes an automatic update function: If a program requires a module and you've enabled automatic updates, it will fetch and install that module automatically.

Perl, as is, serves well for the CGI form action gateway for both POST and GET methods, and, of course, it handles all the different form objects that you can throw at it, from text boxes to pop-up menus. It can send headers as well as HTML body text, so it can be used to generate the entire HTML page (cookies and all) as well as do system intercommunication and process handling.

Much sample code and many good online tutorials are available at several sites. To learn Perl, Randal Schwartz's *Learning Perl*, from O'Reilly Publishing (http://www.ora.com) is still the best reference we have found. After reading it, you have a selection of more advanced texts for further Perl knowledge.

Perl is fast. For server use, data fetches (reading and writing data) will take longer than any Perl execution time. This is fairly standard for all Web work, actually: Input and output are the main bottleneck. Perl is notable because scripting carries an ill-earned reputation for being slower. As a plus, the mod_perl routine and ActivePerl's PerlIS ISAPI mode for Windows (with some support for ActiveX) both provide even more of a speed-up and allow for server-side Perl.

The main design downside for Perl is that its "throw-lots-of-memory-at-a-problem" architecture could make scaling for large problems tricky. For most Web projects, however, large data operations are more properly handled within the chosen database (rather than internally within the language), so good design easily makes this "flaw" relatively insignificant for all but the rarest cases.

Perl operates as scripts and also can be invoked on the command line, which helps in offline debugging. Essentially, you can test your Perl Web scripts directly, without having to go through the Web server (to better catch error messages during debugging).

Although Perl originally was a structured language, CGI.pm includes OO support for its functions. OO in Perl uses the new() constructor—for example, in the CGI.pm module, $currentRequest = CGI->new() will create the local currentRequest containing all the CGI object contents and methods (form parameters and so on).

In short, Perl is strong, easy to learn, and very well supported.

CGI.pm

CGI.pm is the Perl module for CGI and Web work. Of course, CGI.pm must be installed into your Perl distribution (later distributions already include it).

Simply putting use CGI; at the start of your code loads this module—and greatly simplifies any Web work by providing many useful functions. For example, the single function print header will print all the required HTML headers, from Content-type: on.

Starting the Web body requires print start_html(TITLE);. Forms can be started with print start_form; (and ended with print end_form;), so the creation of Web pages dynamically is quick and hard to mess up. Form values are stored in a single global array, param(), and are accessed by name (as in param(MYVARIABLE)); strong detainting also is available. Discussed further in our security section, *detainting* is simply processing form input to remove "dangerous" (system-disrupting, database-munging, and hack-risky) reader inputs before allowing processing.

Pseudoreferences are provided for HTML markup tags, with <h1>TEXT</h1> being easily handled in CGI.pm as simply a call to h1(TEXT);.

Different parameters determine what is imported into your code. The most common (and useful) is use CGI qw(:standard), which provides support for HTML 2.0, forms, and CGI input using POST and GET. CGI.pm is well documented and, with its strong abstraction of HTML functionality, speeds Web development.

mod_perl

mod_perl is the server-side version of Perl. This is a module that you can compile into Apache to enable embedded Perl in your Web pages. Thus, instead of "fetch-and-deliver" script processing, in which a Web page calls a form to put up a new Web page, the Web page can be self-generated with mod_perl.

Learning mod_perl starts at http://perl.apache.org/guide/ and http://www.modperl.com/, and several chapters of the *Writing Apache Modules with Perl and C* book are devoted to it.

One caveat is that earlier versions of mod_perl and mod_php tended not to co-exist well; if both were enabled, the server could crash. This has been fixed, and because you should be using the latest (and most secure) releases, this is a nonissue. If you have this trouble, simply update.

Java

First, we should point out that Java is totally distinct from JavaScript. JavaScript originally was called LiveScript, but Netscape changed the name to capitalize on the notoriety of Java. The two are completely different, though. That said, Java is an object-oriented programming language, developed by Sun Microsystems and then opened up for general use. It is designed to be cross-platform, not just as code but also with byte-code, an intermediate compiled step. The real meaning of this is that it runs anywhere that there is a Java interpreter or Java Virtual Machine, with no compilers required by the reader.

Java's oft-cited motto is, "Write Once, Run Anywhere," and that is frequently true. We say *frequently* because there are still a number of cross-browser and OS issues being worked out, so sometimes the promise of Java is greater than the reality. However, Java is highly portable and allows full interaction through the browser. Typically, it is used for games or chat. It lets you add graphics and reader interaction to any Web feature, and the burden of processing is done on the reader's PC, not your poor, overloaded server.

Unlike the other languages that we've discussed, however, Java does require compilation. Perl, PHP, ASP, JavaScript—for all these, you simply embed the code into the HTML page. With Java, you write code, compile it into portable bytecode, and then run it.

Java work often is described as making either a Java application (or a standalone routine that might not even require a browser to use) or a Java applet, which runs within the browser and has only limited access to the system.

Here, read *limited* as a good thing. The technique is called sandboxing and means limiting the capability of the Java applet to write or read system files or alter the reader's system. In practice, you can toggle different levels of security/safety.

So, Java means writing full-featured programs that just happen to run through the reader's Web browser, so they also can communicate with your Web server.

Many good books as well as online references are available for Java. The slightly outdated FAQ on comp.lang.java (archived at `http://www.ibiblio.org/javafaq/javafaq.html`) is useful for an independent view on Java, and the canonical site for all things Java is `java.sun.com`.

Here is an example of the classic "Hello World" in Java:

```
// Comments are defined with either double slashes or /** within these */
// First, define the object Class

class HelloWorld {
 // now, within this Class, declare any variables or functions

 public void printMe(String somethingToPrint) {
   // this little function prints out the argument string
   System.out.println(somethingToPrint);
 }

 // the 'main' is what will actually get run, i.e. what calls functions
 // Here we simply are forcing this entire class to simply print "Hello World"
 public static void main(String[] args) {
   printMe("Hello World");
 }

}
```

After you compile this, you simply add the following call to your Web page:

```
<APPLET CODE="HelloWorld.class"></APPLET>
```

(Or, you can add `width=` and `height=` tags to the applet invocation.)

That's it. Although the previous code is slightly more complicated than required just to echo "Hello World," it hopefully gives you a good idea of how functions quickly are defined and thus how flexible code is created.

JSP

JavaServer Pages (JSP) neatly separate presentation from content, the goal of pretty much all Web languages. JSP uses Java as a server-side language (rather than our earlier discussion of pure client-side Java applets). JSP also uses XML tags that work with the JSP "scriptlets" (like applets).

JavaBeans

JavaBeans is a catchy name for little Java scriptlets that work in a Java or Active-X environment. Remember that "Write once, run anywhere" motto? Note that, when you require Active-X functionality, you've effectively removed the "run anywhere" part and limited yourself to Windows readers. So, the first lesson in extending Java is that it also might limit the portability aspects.

JavaBeans work within a builder utility, thus they are part applet/scriptlet and part modular software component and building block. Mostly, they are a development tool for Java work. The strength of JavaBeans is the development environment; however, that is balanced by the fact that it does focus on only one platform, limiting the interoperability nature of the Web.

Some useful resources include the canonical source, `http://java.sun.com/products/javabeans/`, and jGuru (`http://www.jguru.com`), with several good FAQs and articles on JSP. The JSP Resource Index at jspin.com is very handy, with several good tutorials.

ASP

Active Server Pages (ASP) is a Microsoft (MS) product for Windows running either MS IIS or Personal Web Server. This sets perhaps the main limitation of ASP: It is limited to only a handful of Web servers and does not use the most common Open Source server (Apache). Fortunately, a UNIX version is available for purchase from ChiliASP (from

ChiliSoft.com). In either case, however, ASP is expensive, so the decision to use it is usually out of a sysadmin's hands: Either management has bought it or has not.

ASP uses VBScript (Visual Basic Script), JScript (Microsoft's JavaScript), or Active Scripting languages (such as new versions of ActivePerl) to dynamically create its pages and handle all system processes.

Although ASP (like any programming language) can be used as a CGI gateway (for form processing and such), the primary use is to dynamically generate Web pages. ASP code thus is embedded into the HTML files, as in our other examples of server-side programming. ASP applications also can maintain state variables across the reader's session with the Session object.

ASP uses templates well, in that you can create templates with directives for ASP to operate on. It is generally easy to write, and a reasonable amount of sample code and many COTS packages are available. Templates are HTML, rather than script-like, and ASP supports all the standard form objects.

ASP's main advantages are that it is blazingly fast, and (if you are running an MS shop) it interacts well with other MS programs (such as MS Transaction Server). It also supports Active-X and thus can control reader's machines (if readers are browsing with Explorer on a Windows machine). Any Active-X control available to the Internet guest account can be used using the variable = New <control programmatic id> syntax.

This leads into the risk of ASP; besides its inherent security holes, the capability to control aspects of a reader's machine can lead to risky Web behavior. Much as with Java, having access to some privileges on a reader's system brings benefits (to the Web programmer) but also risks (in terms of potential security issues). Again, you cannot always guarantee that your readers are using an appropriate browser or have configured the browser with the permissions that you expect. Therefore, reliance on browser-specific functionality always should be optional.

VBScript (ASP Example)

VBScript has an inherent set of objects. Script code is enclosed in <% %>, and HTML is written using Response.Write TEXT. Headers are created with Response.AddHeader NAME, VALUE, redirects are done with Response.Redirect URL, and cookies are handled with Response.Cookie collection or Request.Cookie collection. Form POSTs are read with Request.Form(NAME), while GET data is handled with Response.QueryString(NAME) or (because these are collections) by index.

JavaScript

JavaScript is a scripting language developed by Netscape Corporation. JavaScript is extremely useful for developing Web-based applications. It allows targeting of different browser windows and frames. Because it is client-side (meaning that it runs on the user's browser), it can provide immediate, event-driven user feedback (without the lag of a server call, such as with a CGI or other server-side script). Thus, it allows for the design of a more fully featured user interface.

Netscape invented JavaScript, and then the European Computer Manufacturers Association (working with Netscape) released a standard, ECMAScript, so that any company or third party can implement JavaScript as desired. This standard also is called ISO-16262. The World Wide Web Consortium (W3C) standardized the Document Object Model as well. Put simply, anyone can use it or write a browser or Web server that supports it.

The JavaScript documentation is available at
`http://developer.netscape.com/docs/manuals/javascript.html`. One of the best FAQ sites for JavaScript is IRT.org's JavaScript FAQ Knowledge Base, at `http://developer.irt.org/script/script.htm`. Good tutorials for learning JavaScript are available at Webmonkey, at `http://www.webmonkey.com/`.

JavaScript's Document Object Model (DOM) is a way to describe all the elements of a page. Using the DOM, you can access these elements in your script, whether you named them or not.

On the Web, JavaScript mostly is used for rollovers, navbars, jump menus, and form validation. In addition, Web pages still need to function when JavaScript is turned off. This might be less important for intranet applications, but it's crucial for those with a wider audience so that everyone can see and use the application.

JavaScript is much easier for nonprogrammers to use than other client-side languages such as Java. It's often built into Web pages automatically by the newer generation of WYSYWIG tools (such as Macromedia Dreamweaver, which has become one of the standard tools of the Web design industry). This is not a bad thing, but it does mean that Web designers in your group might be writing or using code that they don't completely understand.

JavaScript Security Concerns

Most other issues with JavaScript are for visiting other Web sites, not having users visit your own. Remember, with any information that you expect from the Web browser, you can't trust the client! JavaScript validation is helpful for the UI, but you still have to do it again on the back end.

Difference Between Client-Side and Server-Side JavaScript

JavaScript is also available as a server-side language, with extended functionality, when you have the Netscape server installed. (Now called the iPlanet Web Server, it's available from `http://www.iplanet.com`.) Formerly known as LiveWire, Server-Side JavaScript (SSJS) allows for back-end/server functions similar to the other scripting languages covered in this chapter. It can connect to a database, do LDAP queries, generate dynamic Web pages, and so on. As with client-side JavaScript, it's particularly suited to Web use. For example, to access the contents of a GET or a PUSH, you simply use the `request` object. The data would be available as `request.fieldname`. All the CGI environmental variables are available through the `request` object as well. You can maintain state with the `client` object, using cookies, or with the `project` object, on the server.

To print the IP address of the client, you use something like this in the body of your HTML page:

```
Your IP address is <server>write(request.ip);</server>
```

More sophisticated examples are available in the SSJS documentation, available at `http://docs.iplanet.com/docs/manuals/ssjs.html`.

Configuring Server-Side JavaScript for iPlanet

Configuring SSJS isn't that difficult. You just have to make sure that it's turned on:

1. In the iPlanet server administrator, go to Programs and select Server-Side JavaScript.

2. At the prompt "Activate the JavaScript application environment?", choose Yes and click OK.

To add a new application, launch the application manager and click on Add Application. The documentation explains how to write and compile applications, and it includes sample code. One thing to note about SSJS is that you must compile all of the application's files into a single .web file. Make sure that you restrict access to this file—it should not be accessible by users.

Why use Server-Side JavaScript instead of the other scripting languages listed in this chapter? See Table 20.2.

TABLE 20.2 Pros and Cons of Using SSJS

Pros	Cons
It's easy to learn.	Not a lot of support exists (small developer community).
It's very easy to manipulate form data and create HTML on the fly.	Regular expression matching is not as robust as in Perl.
You might have legacy systems that you want to continue to support.	Everything has to be written by hand.
It's good for working with multitable databases because it understands SQL and can handle complex joins and queries.	Few built-in database functions exist (as in ColdFusion).
You can do almost anything because everything has to be written by hand.	

One of us wrote a Yahoo!-like directory for an intranet in 1997 using SSJS. If she had to do it today, she'd use Perl (because she knows it and because the code base of free scripts is vast) or ColdFusion (because it's well supported in her office and has many prebuilt database functions). For simply displaying database data, though, SSJS can be a fast, simple solution if the iPlanet Web server already is installed (for example, a page that lists open tickets or specific reports from a non–Web-based database application).

Authentication, State Preservation, and Cookies

There are two main reasons to have some form of authentication of your readers. One is simply so that the reader can customize his experience. The other is to ensure that only allowed readers can do certain operations. For the former, you don't necessarily have to know who the reader is in a personal sense; you just need to have a way to preserve any settings choices that the reader might make through your Web site tools. For the latter, you typically will want personal details so that you can set the appropriate access level, whether that be authenticating the user as a member of site or having right to debit personal accounts.

In all cases, readers arriving at the site will have to log in. Then you have to somehow track their existence in every subsequent Web page that they visit. The three methods available are cookies, server authentication, and state variables.

Cookies

Many sites use cookies, an effective but not perfect method for retaining state information across pages on a per-user basis. Cookies are little variables your server sets that are stored on the reader's machine. They are effectively invisible and persist past any one browsing session. In fact, you get to set how long you want each cookie to last. On the downside, cookies cannot be trusted—remember, they are saved on the reader's machine, and the reader has (in theory) full control over it. Therefore, a malicious reader can "fake" any cookie value, making it hard for you to verify whether that value truly was issued from your site.

Also, not all readers allow cookies to be set, so requiring cookies could alienate part of your reader base. These days, cookies are ubiquitous enough that this is, at most, a minor concern.

Because of the trust issue, cookies are best for tracking noncritical things. Short-term, nonbinding things such as items in a shopping cart are common usage: The cookies are just tallies before a final cookie-less checkout, so bad cookies are not a risk.

Cookies are also fine for long-term storage of trivial information. Color preferences, Web-filtering criteria, or other dynamic or mutable browsing preferences that you allow for your site can use cookies to easily retain reader preferences. No site ever lost money because a hacker made its fonts look red—because only that hacker saw it!

Cookies should not be used for password storage, authentication, or identity issues. Many people use them that way anyway. The appeal is that a cookie can be set when the reader logs in. Then as long as the reader uses that same machine for browsing, he won't have to relogin all week! However, the downside is that anyone who uses that machine will appear as that reader, instantly. Very risky.

It is good policy to ensure that any cookies that you set have appropriate expiration dates. Trivial cookies can be set to last forever, important ones should expire in no more than a month after their last site visit, and temporary ones (such as a shopping cart) might last only minutes or hours.

The process of setting a cookie is easy and depends on which language you use (including, in this case, HTML as a language). Cookies are set and read by the browser (not the server) *before* any HTML headers are sent. That's part of the HTML specification. So, all cookie work must occur before the <html> and <head> tags are sent.

Also, cookies are not instant. They must be set before they are available, so you cannot both set and use a single cookie value within the same page: It must be reloaded for the new value to be in effect.

Here is how to set a cookie in several sample languages: HTML (the main specification), PHP, Perl, and JavaScript. Note that we neglect error checking here for the sake of conciseness; proper use of cookies always should check whether the given cookie truly exists.

Here's how to set a cookie to the value `Copyright2001`:

- In the HTML header:

  ```
  Set-Cookie: HandyNameToStoreItUnder="Copyright2001";
  ```

  The full specification is `Set-Cookie: name=value; expires=date; path=pathname; domain=domainname; secure`. Up to 400 cookies of 4KB in size generally can be stored across all sites that the reader might visit.

- In PHP:

  ```
  setcookie ("HandyNameToStoreItUnder","Copyright2001",time()+86400);
  ```

  `HandyNameToStoreItUnder` is the variable name, `$value` tells what to set it to, and `time()+86400` is the expiration date (here, expiring in one day [in seconds]). Additional variables are allowed; see the documentation for more complete example.

- In Perl:

  ```
  print "Set-Cookie: name=HandyNameToStoreItUnder; value="Copyright2001"\n";
  ```

- In JavaScript:

  ```
  document.cookie = "HandyNameToStoreItUnder=Copyright2001";
  ```

To delete a cookie in general, just set it to nothing with a time value in the past to ensure that the reader's browser flushes it:

- In the HTML header:

  ```
  Set-Cookie: HandyNameToStoreItUnder="";expires="Sat Nov 04 12:02:33 EST
  1989";
  ```

  Here we arbitrarily choose a date in the past to ensure that it is flushed.

- In PHP:

  ```
  print "Set-Cookie: name=HandyNameToStoreItUnder; value="Copyright2001";
  expire="04-Nov-89 00:00:00 GMT";\n";
  ```

- In Perl:

  ```
  &setCookie("HandyNameToStoreItUnder","","04-Nov-89 00:00:00 GMT");
  ```

- In JavaScript:

  ```
  document.cookie = "HandyNameToStoreItUnder=; expires=" +
  date.setTime(date.getTime() - 1000);
  ```

Here's how to read and use a cookie:

- In the HTML header:

```
Cookie: HandyNameToStoreItUnder="Copyright2001"
```

- In PHP:

```
echo $HTTP_COOKIE_VARS["HandyNameToStoreItUnder"];
```

- In Perl:

```
%allcookies=split(/;/,$ENV{'HTTP_COOKIE'});
foreach (@allcookies) {($key,$value)=split(/=/,$_);
$mycookies{$key}=$value;}
# $mycookies{HandyNameToStoreItUnder} now holds the desired value!
```

- In JavaScript:

```
alert(document.cookie); // shows the value for it
```

More accurately, to use the cookie, you need to find the index in the document. cookies object and then reference that index.

Server Authentication

Server authentication is a much more efficient way to track a reader. In this case, it does not save values, but instead it lets you assign a unique reader name (and password) to each reader and have that name available for any subsequent Web page (on that same Web site) that cares to know.

By following the reader, any page can access a database (using that reader name) to store and fetch values. Shopping lists, page preferences, and feature authorization (such as whether that reader is allowed access to features within a Web page or a program) easily can be figured out with a simple fetch-and-check.

FIGURE 20.2

Diagram of authentication flow.

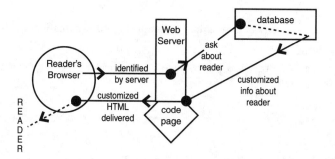

Such authentication requires a point of entry, usually a login page, form, or pop-up box. After he is authenticated, the reader is "valid" for the duration of his browsing or until you provide him with a log-off "deauthentication" function.

Authentication is not saved across sessions; even a browser crash can require a reader to log back in. This is why some sites let readers set a cookie, to avoid them having to type their password each session (that is, after every reboot or after logging off their main system). As explained earlier, this is bad for security and high for convenience, and it is reasonable only when the risk (of someone being able to masquerade as the reader despite not knowing the password) has no significant repercussions and affects only trivial functionalities.

Note that, for authentication, you need to have a system ready to support the following:

- Reader registration (at a minimum, reader name and password)
- Login with that reader name and password
- Use of that information (via Web coding and, likely, a database)

At its simplest, the Apache server has a built-in method called `htaccess` that handles logging in. You simply follow these steps:

1. Create a file named .htaccess in the directory at (and below) the one where all the protected (authorized reader only) files reside.
2. Keep a reader name/password file in a protected or offline area that can be accessed by the Web server.
3. Have some way of adding (and removing and changing) reader name/password sets within that file.

A sample .htaccess file is shown here, with explanations. This is a highly restrictive one—it allows no one access to a given directory.

```
AuthReaderFile /dev/null
AuthGroupFile /dev/null
AuthName "Protected Area"
AuthType Basic
<Limit GET POST>
require reader service
</Limit>
```

A more useful one appears next. It specifies a file of authorized readers (with this file being off the main Web tree), specifies that all readers must be in that authorized reader file (that also contains password information), and titles the authentication pop-up message as Member's Only Area. It does not specify any group authorization at this time.

```
AuthReaderFile /var/spool/offline/zfiles/htlist_of_people
AuthName "Member's Only Area"
AuthType Basic
require valid-reader
```

The full specification for .htaccess files comes from the folks who invented it (http://hoohoo.ncsa.uiuc.edu/docs/setup/access/Overview) or the folks who keep it up (http://httpd.apache.org/docs/configuring.html). There's a good article on user authentication at ApacheWeek, http://www.apacheweek.com/features/userauth.

The reader name/password file is built by tools, often in Linux with the htaccess command from the shell, or in PHP and Perl with htaccess functions in the appropriate add-on modules. Next we'll cover a sample in PHP and Perl for adding or updating an existing reader.

You do not need to use the .htaccess approach to make use of server authentication. One advantage of using a programming language instead of the .htaccess method is more precise control of access. Using PHP as an example, you can just have a standard header for all your files that queries, as needed, for access permission. Thus, instead of a rigid list of protected files stored in .htaccess, each Web file can declare by itself whether it restricts access.

In addition, using such a language (combined with fetches from a database of reader profiles), you can have multiple access levels for a site. The server authentication just tells you the reader's identity, allowing you to code any level of access that you need. So, you could invent a scheme by which reader Suzy can be stored as code Red and reader Fred can be stored as code Blue. Individual pages then choose how much information to give up under the scheme you've created.

Such fine-tuned access control is a very helpful. Fine access control also lets you implement reader tracking and targeted responses. For example, if reader Suzy said that she liked golf in her profile, your software could ensure that Suzy always had golf ads on her pages. Essentially, reader authentication allows for great customization of the site, both by reader request and by targeting output on your part.

State Variables

Often it is desirable to retain a value across different Web pages. To the client and server, each page is isolated and exists only by itself. We have illustrated two methods for passing information across pages—cookies (easy but unsafe) and reader authentication (reliable but complex). It is possible with some languages (and occasionally the need to recompile your server) to have state variables. These are variables associated with a given browsing session (and thus tied to a given reader) without any actual verification of that reader's identity required. We will illustrate this with PHP.

In PHP, you compile it to allow for state variables with —allow_state. Then you can set or access them as any other variable. Think of this as a good mechanism for a cookie-free shopping cart or any situation in which it is handy to retain temporary variables across pages (for a game, perhaps).

JavaScript lets you have state variables, but, as noted in the "JavaScript" section, you cannot guarantee that a given reader has or permits JavaScript.

Security

Security has seven aspects, as defined by Saltzer and Schroeder (Proc. IEEE, September 1975):

1. Least privilege (access granted only as needed)
2. Economy of mechanism (simple systems are easier to verify)
3. Complete mediation (each access checked for authorization)
4. Open design (avoid "security by obscurity")
5. Separation of privilege (sandboxing)
6. Least common mechanism (each reader is separate from other readers)
7. Psychology acceptability (making it easy so that people follow it)

All of these items are significant for adding Web apps and handling long-term operations of a site. You want to ensure that only people authorized to do something are indeed the only ones capable of doing it. Authentication should be simple in coding but should apply to each transaction. Security should not rely on hidden URLs or ignorance of the system. Each Web task should be separate, without a single global "superreader" status. The system also should be easy enough to use at all levels of authentication so that people are not encouraged to find workarounds or avoid authentication when that is necessary.

Furthermore, authentication details should be handled by the server and not included as part of a page. Hidden form variables, URL variables, cookies, HTTP headers, and other data that is part of the reader's page are not "secret" or secure. Therefore, authentication must not rely on trusting the client's browser, but instead should set security and authentication at the server end and should use the server to track access appropriately.

Loosely, we can look at system security and content accuracy. System security is simply ensuring that only the authorized people have access to the appropriate functions that they can use. Content security involves inappropriate or malicious use of the legitimate access that a reader is allowed.

For example, a cracker deleting your site is a violation of system security. A Web visitor using a tech forum to post pornographic images is an example of a content violation: The access means was authorized, but how the visitor chose to use it resulted in corruption of the site. Clearly, these two areas require different approaches to prevent abuse.

System Security

Many times, you will be installing Open Source or COTS packages: In other cases, you will be writing your own routines and scripts. The principles are the same. These are factors to consider when installing software, whatever its origins.

Thus, even installing a well-supported package does not remove the need for verifying its security. We will focus on issues of access control, Web-writeable areas, and system calls.

Web access control has two levels to worry about: reader and admin. Both provide sandboxes (to use a common analogy) restricting the "play" possible after access has been granted. You need to ensure that only properly authorized people gain access and that the sandbox that they entered gives them access to only the tools and capabilities that you intended.

Access: Who gets It and Where

Open or public access is common for Web forms, open forums and bulletin boards, chats, and many forms of reader-contributed content, as well as Web email gateways. The Web page says, "Type your stuff here" and then passes what the reader types for either republishing on the Web (as in forums) or processing and storage elsewhere (as in Web shopping carts). The two main areas of concern here are Web-writeable areas and system calls, or tainting.

Web-writeable areas imply that the reader content is stored on the Web server for viewing. It also includes software installations where the Web server writes files, such as a hidden log file to keep track of transaction IDs or other bookkeeping.

The simple answer is that you should never have any directories or files that are writeable by the Web server. This is not always practical, though. Your software might provide no choice, you might be storing large amounts of content that isn't easily managed by a formal database structure, or you simply might need to allow readers to submit flat files. In such a case, though, you can still improve the security profile of such risky behavior.

The main behavior to prevent is allowing readers to submit content that contains scripting or subversion. Scripting would be reader-submitted pages including code that can compromise the basic physical security of your system. A Web page including code and a page that references a cross-site script (so that, once on your site, that script is run as if by your Web server) are examples where reader-written content will gain permission to run on your system (as the same reader that the Web server runs under). This is a malicious attack that requires some technical competence on the part of the reader.

Subversion involves readers who submit content that is counterproductive to your site's goals. Without review, such content would appear and ruin your image, and also possibly open you up to liability. Such subversion can be malicious intent (a reader seeking to diminish your site's reputation) or simply the result of clueless user (a reader not understanding what your site is about). Both require proofing or vetting of all submitted material by an editor before allowing the material to go onto the site.

If we had to reduce basic security practices down to three handy tips, they would be as follows:

1. Make Web-writeable areas offline, not Web-readable. Just place those directories and files in an area that your Web server will not serve. If material must appear on the Web site itself, you can approve or dismiss it from this offline area using admin tools before it becomes public (Web-live).

2. Have access restrictions in place for the writeable areas. If they must be in Web-live space, lock them down and do filtering.

3. Do rigorous sandboxing and content checking before allowing the information to be written. This means that both authentication and detainting come into play.

Tainting

You need to check all values provided by any site visitor through any Web form or Web application. This is to avoid tainted items, or reader input that has hidden and unexpected side effects. In short, you cannot trust that your readers will actually give you correct input and safe input.

Correct input simply means that readers entered what was required. If you have a field for email addresses, you should verify that the reader entered a valid email address and not just gibberish.

Safe input ensures that no malicious side effects will happen. If you have a Web form requesting email addresses and that form gets processed to send an email, a possible security flaw exists. A common taint is to give system commands in the variable.

Imagine that your form on your UNIX system just does a system call to `/usr/mail $email` to send the email, and `$email` is the form variable input by the site visitor. A clever reader could give the email as `me@whatever ; rm -rf *`. In execution, your form would execute `/usr/mail me@whatever ; rm -rf *`, and the semicolon means that it actually executes the mail command then the `rm` (remove) command. As a result, the command deletes all the Web files.

The solution is, again, to validate the data. Also detaint it—that is, remove any system or metacharacters. The common UNIX/Linux metacharacters are semicolons, backticks, and exclamation marks, among others. You don't need to filter these everywhere, but you do need to filter anything that is acted upon by the system.

Tainting also includes metacharacters for system-specific aspects. If you are inserting data into databases, single and double quotes often must be "escaped," or must have a backslash added before adding the data; otherwise, the database will not parse it correctly.

There is another level of untainting that isn't "character-based," per se. Much as metacharacters or the use of unfiltered quotes can cause errors, code constructs (HTML, language-specific code blocks, and other parseable entities) should be filtered out of user-provided input. A blog implementation, for example, allows user-entered data to be integrated with canned HTML to display the user's data. The input parser must be especially careful to deal with input that is meaningful within the language of the reformatting system, whether that is HTML, PHP, or something else.

Allowing users to add URLs and HTML markup in their text to manipulate the appearance is harmless and often is a desirable feature. Allowing them to add HTML that would turn your Web site into a malicious attack site (such as including active content that attacks the readers' browser) is a risk that needs to be considered when designing and implementing the application and the tainting mechanism.

Also, when working with programming languages embedded within HTML, it's crucial to know when the input data is available to the programming language and whether the language interpreter control flow can be changed by the input data. For example, if HTML is allowed for a page that is handled by PHP, the risk of user-contributed PHP scripting in the HTML has to be blocked. Otherwise, the user can write his own scripts, as PHP + HTML, and thus gain access to your server. You cannot assume that the standard "shell-tainting characters" are consistent regardless of their application or programming language—this is how hackable Web apps get built. Instead, you have to look at what user-contributed data you want and also what malicious data structures could be hiding in such user-contributed data.

Fortunately, data detaining and metacharacter handling is part of most Web programming languages. Check the language specifications for your platform and make sure that all variables are suitably checked. It's a tedious task, but it's essential for both system integrity (such as preventing hacking) and data integrity (such as ensuring processing and content reliability). The tools are out there, so it's a winnable battle.

After the Fact

Now that you have a secure and smoothly running site, you can just sit back, right? At this point, you need to regularly check your Web logs. Primarily, you want to do the following:

1. Spot errors, especially missing pages
2. Curb abuses and spot possible hack attempts
3. Optimize the site based on usage and traffic pattern

Web servers have a limited number of items that they can track. Without custom software, for example, you cannot track individual readers. Instead, you can see only general traffic patterns and aggregate statistics. What you can track includes this:

1. 404s (missing pages and bad links) and other error codes
2. Trending and aggregate statistics

From this, you can derive some data, including reader tracking; the capability to spot hacks, drop sites, and denial-of-service attempts; and stat-running of pages (such as voting cheats and ad banner revenue pumping).

What Web logs record is basically just "hits," with a hit being any item (page, image, or script call) that the Web server serves. Hits need to be translated into meaningful information, such as page views. Sometimes a hit is just a hit—breaking down raw hits into meaningful counts of visitors and then trying to track them through your pages is a tricky problem.

All hits are not created equal. In fact, raw hits are rarely useful. They have value only when aggregated or trended. There are two uses for logs: load issues (for sysadmins) and people/pages (for marketing and content management).

People/Pages

You must translate hits into pages visited. Acquiring some statistics on visitors (unique readers) can be done by checking machine/IP addresses, although that provides only an approximation. Trending involves looking at which pages are popular and when peak visiting hours occur.

To provide an example, knowing that your humor page is visited most often between noon and 3 p.m. local time (EST) provides three interpretive results:

1. Many people are visiting during lunch.

2. Most of your readers are in the United States (because the time zones for lunch are clustered around your local noon).

3. Thus, updating your humor pages before 11 a.m. means that the bulk of your readers will be satisfied.

As you can see, interpreting Web results involves a bit of guesswork and hand waving. Additional bits of information can support such conclusions, though. For example, the country of each visitor can be guessed by much Web-tracking software by correlating the domain name.

One prime bit of information that log software directly can provide is which pages are most visited. This is your content, where customers are going. From this, you can focus your effort on what the customers want.

A more complete list of the types of information logs provide includes the following:

- Raw hits
- Bandwidth
- Pages accessed (number, frequency/popularity, time profiles)
- Visitors (count, tracking paths)
- Depth, time spent (most useful, hardest to tell)
- Domains
- Browser used
- OS used
- Referring page
- Errors

Trending

We will cover three statistical approaches and show what they allow a Web master to do:

1. Time sampling, for tracking visits

2. Depth sampling, for tracking interest

3. Traffic tracking, for tracking flow

Time tracking lets you know when peaks and lulls occur. You can look at the following:

- Time-of-day variations
- Post–press release/announcement spike
- Regular visitor peaks (for example, if a monthly column peaks each month)
- The academic cycle (versus semesters or finals)
- Random fluctuations (some are just random)

As mentioned, tracking readers further requires either server-side modifications (to set cookies, for example, or to use other software allowing for individual reader profiles to be generated). Out of the box, most servers simple collect individual hits and leave correlation to the Web master.

Depth sampling expands reader tracking into looking at how many pages a given reader follows and what path he took to get to a given page. This can be done with "out-of-the-box" Web server logs (see also the upcoming section "Noise"). Depth measures either the value of your site or flaws in its design. If visitors are going deep into your site, this means that you have held their attention for a long time.

Depth is good if the readers continually are accessing content. However, if readers are required to go through many pages simply to access the one bit of content that they want, that is an indication of a site flaw. So, accessing many content pages is good. Accessing four indexes to get to one bit of content is bad.

Load Issues

If you are a sysadmin, much of the previous people/pages information is useful. But, to a large degree, you will be focusing on the time trends for bandwidth and page accesses. A balanced system is one that is operating at less than saturated capacity at all times. If there are peak usage periods, this means that the readers have been behaviorally conditioned to visit in some manner. You then have two choices.

You can add more servers to handle the peak load, or you can modify their behavior. For example, one Web site had a steady stream of traffic at most times, but that jumped to four times as much every Tuesday. Why Tuesday? That was when the site had the update of its main feature (game reviews). So, visitors were conditioned to always check on Tuesday to see what was new. By shifting review publications across a three-day span, the site could reduce the peak load; visitors then could visit early (if they wanted to see the first few new things) or later (if they wanted to see everything), and there was no one "ideal time" to read all of the material. As can be expected, overall traffic increased (from avid readers visiting frequently to catch the multiple publishing dates), but the crucial need—to reduce the peak usage—was achieved.

In addition, a sysadmin can look at the error pages to weed out problems with the site. "404" and other missing page errors are important to fix. In many cases, these can be due to typographical error by readers. If frequent enough, you can consider just cloning the proper page under the often-requested wrong spelling. In a way, 404 errors let readers debug your site for you, tell you what people think is on your site, and tell you what you've named or labeled poorly or awkwardly.

Redesign and Rewards

You can use traffic tracking to redesign your site flow. Simply putting the most visited pages closer to your front page is an excellent way to improve the visitor's experience and reduce server load (that is currently being consumed by readers hunting through intermediate pages). In short, find out where the readers are going and then build a better path there. You get happier readers and less wasted server load per reader.

You also can compile a list of referral URLs, sites that were known to provide visitors to your site. These are ideal sites to partner with (or at least ensure that your link remains active with).

Noise Versus Accurate User Data

Using standard log information to produce detailed demographic and trending results has inherent errors, as described previously. You aren't tracking unique readers; instead, you are statistically creating likely reader profiles.

Noise refers to things that degrade your estimates. This includes first screening out self-hits, where your administrative checks and proofing generated false interest in pages that actual site visitors might not be visiting. Also included are automated site-checking codes and bots and spiders (see the next section, "Robots and Spiders") that are sent by search engines and robots to catalog your site. All generate "hits" that do not correspond to actual readers.

Caches can ruin statistics. In caching, a large provider, ISP, or gateway keeps a local copy of your pages for serving its readers (to save on bandwidth usage), thus throwing off your counts for static pages. It's just another factor to consider—you generally can tell caches because they are fetched by site robots (as listed in your log file).

Robots and Spiders

A robot (or bot), in its simplest form, is a script that fetches a page from your Web site. It's a type of user agent, like a browser but vastly scaled down and tuned to different tasks. Robots are used by search engines (and others) to get information from your Web site. A spider is a type of robot that follows all the links in your site. For example, if you followed a link off your front page and clicked through all the links on all the returned pages, you would have "spidered" your site, You can tell that a robot has visited your site by looking in your access logs for requests for robots.txt or by reviewing the user_agent log.

What is robots.txt? It's a file that you can put in your root Web directory that lets you control the behavior of robots—well, the ones that follow the rules, anyway. Evil robots (as well as poorly coded ones) simply ignore it.

A robots.txt file looks like this:

```
# Exclude all robots from this site, but allow our intranet robot
User-agent: localbot  # Internal Search
Disallow:
User-agent: *
Disallow: /
```

For more information on robots and robots.txt, visit the Web Robots Pages, at `http://www.robotstxt.org/wc/robots.html`.

Visualization and Usage

Log files can be analyzed in real time or as batched processes. In general, aggregate statistics require that you collect the log information over time, so batch processing (whenever you need a report) is efficient. "Rolling reports," compiled at regular intervals by software, are another possibility and have an advantage because you often can back up and then delete the often-large log files.

You can view the output in tabular or graphical format, depending on your choice of log analysis tool. Be careful of overanalysis or overload. Overanalyzing log data—including reports that neglect the problems with aggregate statistics and lack of accurate per-reader tracking—can lead to wrong conclusions. On the other hand, you want to make sure that the raw data is distilled enough that you aren't overwhelmed with many numbers or too much information presented. In general, some data is best served as a tabular format (a list of most popular pages, for example), while other data is more easily understood in graphical format (such as during peak bandwidth times).

Note also that reports can be Web-based, sent by email, or printed for meetings. The actual log files need to be backed up regularly (in case you want to reanalyze the data) because these files can grow quite huge. At one line per hit and any given page often being three or more hits (due to images as well as content), a million page views in a month will create a three-million line file. Over time, the log files quickly can fill up disk space unless routinely handled.

Analog, billing itself as "the most popular logfile analyzer in the world," is available (for free) at `http://www.statslab.cam.ac.uk/~sret1/analog/index.html` and is *very* well documented.

The still-excellent WWW-FAQ includes current links for several tools, even though it is dated 1996. The FAQ, in general, is available at `http://www.boutell.com/faq/old-faq/index.html`, and that boutell.com site in general is a useful place to browse for quirky looks at the current state of the Web and Web programming. It includes an online class on Java programming, a CGI FAQ, a link to its own Web log-analysis package, and other useful resources.

It is worth mentioning privacy issues, specifically log access and retention policy. Some Web logs, especially the ones that acquire personally identifying information, can be sensitive to the privacy of your readers. It is important to have a clear, well-documented log-retention policy that specifically states how long the logs will be kept, whether and how they will be backed up, who is allowed access to them, and to whom the data will be released under what circumstances. Otherwise, as the Web master, you're going to spend a lot of time extracting log data for requests from law-enforcement agencies, especially if you run a site that allows readers to generate actions such as sending email to the White House.

Web Ads

Web ads are an often-required utility that involves many of the concepts covered here, so they are worth looking at as an extended example.

A Web ad can be simply a banner at the top of the page. Done as an image tag, this can be statically coded as follows:

```
<img src="banner.gif" alt="Enjoy this ad">
```

It is more likely that you'll have many banners that you want to run. So, instead of using the previous line, perhaps you'll use an SSI on each page to call your CGI ad script:

```
<!--#include vitualal="/cgi/ad.cgi">
```

Let's say that this CGI is written in Perl. It looks through the list of possible banners, chooses a random one, and then generates an appropriate IMG tag for it. Now you have rotating banners!

It's likely that you'll want each ad, when clicked on, to lead the reader to the appropriate client's site. So, let's embed that image tag into a link:

```
<a href="clientside.whatever"><img src="/images/bannerA1.gif" alt="ad for
company A1"></a>
```

But if you are selling ad space, your clients will want to know how successful their ads were. You can run a log analysis to see how any times any given banner image was loaded—this gives them their ad view rate. Or, because your banner rotation script already is choosing each banner, you can just have it update a database table to reflect which banner it served. A simple table with two fields, `Banner ID` and `Count`, will do this.

At this point you could be doing the script as an included CGI, as shown earlier. Or, especially if your pages are dynamically created or use a standard header with coding, you could use a simple server-side code routine. The result is the same.

Ad companies will want to know how many readers clicked on the ad, too. So, instead of sending them directly to the company's site, you can have an interstitial script. This is just a little script that doesn't print anything itself. Instead, it first updates your ad tally database (adding a new field called `clickthru`). Then it sends a browser redirect to the company's side, using the HTML specification or language-specific function.

Finally, if you want to get fancy, imagine that you have authenticated readers with detailed profiles. You can make your "random banner" script more sophisticated, delivering targeted ads based on profiles. Golf fans get more golf ads, and car fans get car ads. It's all just data handling.

Thus, you can capture the click to tally it and then send the reader on his way. The back-end database keeps track of hits and click-throughs, and the CGI or server-side code makes it all work automatically. To top it off, you probably didn't have to write any of the ad script yourself. You just picked up a reliable Open Source version from sourceforge.net or some other trustworthy site and then installed and integrated it into your site (saving you hours of coding time).

Congratulations, you are now an advanced Web master!

Towards Better Sysadmin

PART

IV

Security

by Jon Lasser

Introduction

We long debated the idea of having a separate chapter for Unix security: If you haven't been considering the security implications of your actions throughout the previous chapters, start again at Chapter 1, "Startup and Shutdown." (No, on second thought, finish this chapter first and then start over again on the first page.) Security is important in all respects, but it's still a secondary aspect of computing: Nobody without an existing computer infrastructure would put one together solely for purposes of computer security. Nobody puts together any general-purpose computer to secure it. In one crucial respect, however, computer security is a primary aspect of computing, or at least computing on a network: Without adequate attention paid to the topic, all computer resources could be unavailable or worthless.

Therefore, computer security is the protection of computer resources so that they may be used by authorized individuals—and by only those individuals—for their appointed task. It is not an end in itself. To confuse the means of computer security with the ends of computing is to succumb to confusion over who our end users are and to then fail to serve them properly. Users want computers that allow them to communicate with others, to perform calculations, and so on; this is their objective. Computer security is generally an abstraction, one with which they have no desire to become familiar. To be sure, there is room in the profession for system administrators who specialize in computer security, but for most of us, that's only part of the job.

After discussing the reasons that system administrators need to worry about security, we will discuss the risks of complex systems and how to develop a threat model. Next we will return to the philosophy of security, the difficulty of doing the job well, and how policy can help. Finally, we'll discuss the ethical implications of computer security work.

Why Worry?

Some system administrators fail to see security as at all relevant to the job and thus widely deploy services—programs that run on the system to serve users' needs—in an insecure fashion. The usual excuse is that to implement a particular service securely might require additional software to be purchased, would take more time and care, would require retraining staff members, and would fail to serve the organization's needs. (Again, we have computers for particular purposes. Users don't care if the print server is secure: They care only that printing works.) "Nobody cares about that system," one administrator might say, "so why waste time securing it?" In short, security is treated as overhead rather than a necessary part of infrastructure.

The answer is simple: An insecure system puts other systems on the same network at risk and can be used as a platform to launch other attacks both outside and within that network. At the time of this writing, numerous computer worms have been spreading across unsecured Linux systems that, once compromised, search for and compromise other insecure Linux systems. These attacks can go on for days if they're not detected and reported, and no human involvement is required. Some of these worms mail the IP address of the compromised system to a mail drop and also install back doors that the worm's launcher can use to enter the system.

Another answer commonly uttered by system administrators who might not have the time or energy to worry about security is, "That system is protected by a firewall, so I don't need to worry about it." This attitude is distressingly common. Firewalls can be subverted through any number of means, even assuming that they are correctly configured and have no security holes of their own. For example, many firewalls are configured to allow all outgoing connections; this allows people to use almost any software without too much hassle. Let's say that somebody has a PC running a common desktop operating system, and that person opens an email with an executable attachment. That attachment might start a program that remains resident and connects to an Internet Relay Chat server. Once connected, the computer can be controlled via messages sent over IRC; those messages might include network commands used to probe and possibly compromise other systems on your network. If you think this is far-fetched, it isn't: All these tools exist today and are used, at the very least, as part of distributed denial-of-service attacks. The tools also exist for intruders to take control of PCs who have simply visited a particular Web site, an activity notoriously difficult to control.

This also suggests, by the way, that you should be concerned not only with the risk to your own systems, but also with the risks that your systems pose to others on the Internet. You might not be legally obligated to do so, but being a good netizen has a healthy impact on your personal reputation. Appropriate security netiquette also means implementing egress filters so that your network will not pass packets that claim to originate somewhere other than your network to the outside world, to prevent your complicity in distributed denial-of-service attacks.

Dangers Presented by Complex Systems

This scenario illustrates a danger presented by complex systems: Often, each part of the system is well understood and has a limited set of risks associated with it, but the parts interact in such a way that they magnify the risks.

Here's a hypothetical example: You have a firewall configured to allow all outgoing connections but to block inbound connections except to a small group of machines that offer publicly available services, such as your Web server. It's a low-maintenance solution that, when properly configured, prevents most casual scans of the network and presents a fairly high barrier to entry. This is a good first line of security, to be sure, but you might be tempted to think that you can be lazy about patching systems. You can't be. The system is still vulnerable to machines within your network being used to attack systems on other networks, but you trust the people at your site, so this isn't an obvious problem.

You might have an email server that permits attachments. Despite the risks of allowing arbitrary email attachments, these attachments are useful—even indispensable—for most businesses because they can send contracts and negotiate proposals via documents attached to messages. A virus scanner might be configured to prevent known-dangerous attachments from passing through to users, but not all threatening programs will be recognized by the scanner because they're too new or because they somehow were concealed from the virus detector. The email server is not in itself compromised by the rogue program, but it also fails to stop it.

You also might have an email reader that accepts attachments. If you haven't patched your mail client, it might open attachments without asking, even if you instructed it not to open them at all. Depending on the kind of attachment, an additional program, such as a word processor, might be necessary; for most attachments, however, no other program is needed. If a Trojan is really clever, you won't even know that it's opened itself and run.

Now the Trojan, which is running without your knowledge, opens a connection to a remote server somewhere on the Internet. This server, possibly compromised as well, is used to coordinate the activities of all the copies of the Trojan infecting other computers. You allow outgoing connections—you almost certainly don't even log them—so your computer can contact its master without you noticing. Now that the connection is established, the master system can send commands to your system and use it to exploit other systems on your network. Because you felt protected by the firewall, you might not have patched your systems as diligently as you should have, so they could be vulnerable to a variety of exploits. Furthermore, your belief that nobody inside of your network would do anything malicious turns out to have been incorrect—you were wrong about who could access your internal systems. There's a large gap between what we believe we have protected ourselves against and what we are actually protected against. This is a recurring theme in computer security: You must test your security and see if it matches your beliefs about your security.

Even without compromising other systems, the Trojan can install a sniffer that captures traffic sent over the network and stores it in a secret file that is periodically sent to the attacker. This traffic would contain, among other things, any passwords sent over the network.

Perhaps the compromised computer is a workstation configured to check email from a Unix server via the POP3 protocol. Each time it does this, the email password is sent in clear text to the server. If the attacker can use this same password to log onto the mail server, he might be able to compromise that system and acquire all users' passwords. Even if your system is on a switched network (one where network traffic passes only to systems that it is intended for rather than to all systems on the network), the sniffer on a single port results in the compromise of a shared resource and ultimately all the clients. The cracker might use a local root exploit to give his user-level account full root privileges, after which he would typically install a rootkit that hides his presence on the system. (We'll talk more about rootkits later.)

This is a fairly simple scenario, requiring only vulnerabilities that are present in widely used applications. In fact, this scenario is fairly typical. Many systems don't even have the firewall, and, after this compromise, the mail server could be connected to directly, making it a very attractive platform for launching further attacks. Now suppose that the compromise of the mail server is discovered first. How will you determine the source of the initial compromise? More importantly, how will you close the holes that resulted in the compromise? How can you predict what avenues future attacks will exploit?

To answer these questions, you must develop a "portrait" of the ways in which your systems may be threatened.

Building a Threat Model

Building a threat model is not incredibly difficult: You must decide what you're trying to protect and who you're worried about.

Attackers typically are divided into four types, listed in increasing difficulty of preventing or resolving these attacks

- "Hackers" on the Internet who will break into whatever systems are the easiest (opportunistic attacks).

- People outside your organization who are interested in information that you have. These can include criminals, competitors, or employees let go after a corporate restructuring (targeted attacks).

- People inside your organization who are not as trustworthy as you might have believed (internal attacks).

- Attackers from government agencies who will stop at nothing to destroy you (omnipotent attacks). (Although this formulation is intended in good humor, you might actually be concerned with very sophisticated, focused attackers who have considerable resources to use against your network. These attackers are quite difficult to repel.)

What are you trying to defend from these attackers? "Everything" is not a particularly useful answer. Start with availability of systems and services: How much money does it cost your company when your Web site goes down? If your users can't receive email, how much does this impact their jobs? Be as specific as possible when putting together the list of services that you need to protect; it will be helpful later if you note which are internal services used by employees and which are external services used by customers.

After availability, consider what data you are trying to protect and what you are trying to protect that data from. Usually you are trying to keep unauthorized individuals from reading the data (protecting its confidentiality), or you are trying to protect unauthorized individuals from modifying the data (protecting its integrity). You might want to protect both the confidentiality and the integrity of some data. For example, you probably don't want anybody outside the payroll department to be able to read employee salaries from the database. And you certainly don't want anyone outside that department to change those salaries! Each employee is authorized to read or alter only the email in his mailbox. Likewise, everyone might be allowed to look at your presentations, but only you are allowed to alter them. Make a list of particular kinds of data, where they should be located, and who is allowed to read or modify them. Prioritize which resources need the most protection and the most monitoring so that adequate attention can be paid to their defense. For example, systems that store customer credit card information usually deserve enhanced protection and monitoring.

The Security Tripod

Availability, confidentiality, and integrity are the three traditional goals of computer security. Expressed as attributes of a secure system, confidentiality and integrity also can be broken down as integrity, authentication, and authorization, each of which we discuss later.

Integrity involves the data's state: Is the data that you have the data that you are supposed to have? Is it intact? Can you tell whether it has been altered? If it has been altered, can you tell who has altered it?

Authentication means that you can tell that the user is who he or she claims to be, that the person behind the keyboard is the person whose username is logged onto the system. This is notoriously difficult to prove; the best authentication systems rely on something you have (a token or a key, or perhaps a fingerprint) and something you know (generally a password). Even these may be considered moderately unreliable: Can you tell whether the person simply forgot to log out of the system and somebody else just walked up to the keyboard? On most Unix systems, authentication is limited to a password.

Authorization is simpler: Assuming that this person has been authenticated, is he allowed to perform the requested action? Can he look at this file? Can he change this document? On most Unix flavors, this is done primarily through standard Unix permissions, although access control lists (ACLs) might substitute for this on some systems; either of these may be supplemented with application-level controls.

For some, a fourth concern is reputation. Failures of computer security can be harmful not only to you directly, but also indirectly through others' changed opinions of you. Most serious financial losses from computer crime commonly go unreported because companies feel that the damage to their reputations outweighs the actual fiscal costs of the incident. You might want to include reputation as an asset to be protected when thinking about your threat model.

Security Philosophy

Thinking about a threat model is a special case of thinking about the problem of computer security in general. Threat models are designed with certain assumptions in mind; one of the tasks of a computer security professional is to explicitly examine the assumptions embedded in any security system and to measure them in relation to the best practices of computer security.

We're Doomed

The central tenet of our security philosophy is simple: "We're doomed." That is, we believe that whatever we do, some systems nominally under our control will be compromised. Why do we think this? Pure statistics. Let's assume that your threat model consists solely of opportunistic attacks from others on the Internet, and you are trying to protect the resources of a single computer attached to the Internet. Even with this minimal threat model, more people are trying to break into our system than there are people trying to protect the system. Given the sheer number of attempted intrusions into the typical system, at least some of the hackers are bound to be smarter than you are. Finally, because the majority of opportunistic attackers are students, they also have a whole lot more free time than we do. Taken together, the sheer scale of this means that you won't always win. In addition, complex systems always have potential behaviors that nobody can anticipate.

Because we can't stop them—and you probably won't catch them—what can you do to protect yourself? You should design your systems to minimize the damage of a single compromise. You should design your systems to provide early warning of both attempts against your system and of successful intrusions. And you should know how to respond when a successful attack is discovered.

Bruce Schneier, a well-known cryptographer and computer security consultant, stresses that security is not a product, but a process. This means, in part, that there is no such thing as a completely secure system: New holes will be found, and old holes will manifest themselves in new ways. There will always be another round of patches to install and a new group of employees who will need safe computing practices explained. And there will always be an old group of employees bent on revenge.

Two Philosophies of Security

Two philosophies of security have competed for longer than computer security has been an issue in the public mind. These philosophies are known as "security through obscurity" and "defense in depth." The former is fervently adhered to by people who have not thought the problem through and who have little practical experience, but the latter is practiced by seasoned professionals. The two differ only slightly, but those differences are critical. These philosophies are also not mutually exclusive; we contrast them in this section because they are easily confused and should both be understood.

Security Through Obscurity

Security through obscurity is the belief that if you can keep the details of how your system functions a secret, your security will be greatly improved. Hallmarks of a solution involving security through obscurity are "secret" or "proprietary" software packages, nonstandard or in-house encryption systems, and the belief that keeping the variety of Web server that you run a secret will protect you from attack.

The phrase "security through obscurity" has been carried over from cryptography research. It is a truism of cryptography that the security of a message can't be protected by keeping the cipher used a secret: The statistical techniques most often used to defeat the encryption of a particular message often can be applied without knowledge of the cipher system. Through open discussion of cipher systems, flaws can be uncovered and the systems can be strengthened.

If the attacker knows the cryptographic system, how can the messages be protected? A good cryptographic system depends on a key that remains secret and can be changed in the event of compromise without necessitating a change in cipher systems. This principle was laid out in the nineteenth century by Auguste Kerckhoffs, who came up with six principles regarding the security of military ciphers that are still widely regarded as crucial to the discipline.

In the most widely cited code-breaking feat in military history, the Allies in World War II managed to defeat the German Enigma cipher machine. Even after determining the nature of the machine, however, hundreds of workers were necessary to divine each

cipher key, which changed daily. Not all messages encrypted with Enigma were broken—months passed during which the Allies successfully decrypted only a few messages, and many ships were sunk as a result of this failure. If the security of the system had relied on the secrecy of the machine itself, all German traffic would have laid itself open to the Allies.

How does this philosophy apply to the much younger science of computer security? It suggests that you cannot expect to keep the system architecture a secret: More elaborate reconnaissance techniques will be used by attackers to map networks and discover which versions of which applications are being run. This is an arms race that you cannot win, although you certainly don't expect to stop fighting. Obscurity is not necessarily a negative trait; it's merely one that you can't count on. Instead, you should place your faith in strong authentication techniques that are not vulnerable to snooping or replay attacks. You should encrypt your traffic with virtually unbreakable cipher systems. You should pay much more attention to bolting the doors and less to camouflaging them. And you should implement defense in depth.

Defense in Depth

Defense in depth is another term that has carried over from the military. It describes a system in which multiple defenses are implemented to protect a resource. The principle dates back centuries: A castle with a moat and a high stone wall is more secure than a castle with only one or the other. Likewise, a castle with a moat, a high stone wall, archers, and a dragon is safer from siege than a castle with only some of these protections. (All right, the dragon was a relatively uncommon defense, but it is difficult to argue that a dragon would not improve the security of a castle.)

In computer security, the theory is roughly that vulnerabilities run in families: A firewall based on the BSD TCP/IP stack is likely to have roughly the same security flaws as a traditional Unix implementation whose TCP/IP stack is based on the same original source. It is always better to have your system protected by two independently developed TCP/IP stacks than one stack or two variations on the same stack.

It's impossible to predict what the next vulnerability will affect: Will your firewall pass traffic on a particular port? Will your TCP/IP stack pass packets with a source port of zero? Will there be a buffer overflow in your SMTP proxy? Having multiple layers of protection helps to insulate you from flaws in any one system even when you are unable to predict the precise nature of future flaws.

Consider each aspect of your security, and assume that it will fail. What should be backing it up?

Security Is Boring

If the price of liberty is eternal vigilance, then security is twice as expensive. If you do your job correctly, nothing should happen. The adrenaline rush of security work—tracking down a hacker with a live connection to your system and slamming doors as quickly as he can open them—is a miniscule fraction of the work that computer security requires. If you lock your doors in the first place, few hackers ever get past rattling the doorknobs. Dusting doorknobs for fingerprints is boring work, especially if you do it every day.

After formulating policy, which we'll come back to, the big steps for computer security are guaranteeing reliable backups, hardening your systems and keeping them patched, reading your logs, and responding to incidents that you uncover while reading the log files. If you do these five things every day, you can almost entirely eliminate successful opportunistic attacks against your systems. Although that might not sound like an adequate payoff, realize that if your systems are on the Internet, they are probably being scanned several times a day for vulnerabilities that can be exploited opportunistically. Without doing these five things, your systems will almost certainly be compromised— and rapidly.

Backups

Most people don't consider backups to be an essential part of security; they're an essential part of system administration, to be sure, but not specifically security. They're wrong. Although backups might be important for other areas of system administration, the most important reasons to back up your systems are to verify the integrity of your data and to restore your data after a security incident. (Given the lifetime of your modern hard drive, you're several times likelier to restore data lost due to a security incident than you are to restore data lost due to a dead hard drive.)

What's involved in backing up properly? We prefer a centralized backup server for a network of Unix systems. This reduces the number of tapes that need to be changed, reduces the number of hardware components that can break, allows you to spend money on more reliable hardware, and allows you to secure the backup media. Securing backup media is often overlooked, but if a competitor can walk off with a tape full of proprietary information, that's as much of a security incident as if he'd broken in through your Web server.

Backups are covered in Chapter 16, "Backups," so we will not dwell on them here. It is sufficient to note that you must read logs to verify that backups are completed successfully, and you occasionally should restore data from an arbitrary backup to ensure that the media remains readable. Tapes do go bad and need to be rotated out regularly; failure to budget for and purchase new tapes for your backup system is a serious security risk that often goes unrecognized.

Hardening Your Systems

The sad fact is that most hacked systems were hacked through a service that was not even being used and certainly need not have been open to the outside world. Many administrators run every service on each system because they are worried about what might break if any service was disabled. The secure approach is the opposite: Turn off all services, and then turn on only those you need. If you find that a necessary application breaks because you disabled a service, you can turn it back on then. This is covered in more detail in Chapter 8, "Securing a System for Rollout."

Simple Services

The "simple services" provided internally by inetd and xinetd should never be enabled except perhaps while you are actively debugging a networking problem. echo, chargen, and other services have no valid daily use, and they are a prime tool for constructing denial-of-service attacks. They also might have security holes; it has happened in the past, and it's difficult to demonstrate that they have been successfully and completely secured. Unless you have multiple users on your system connecting to services such as IRC, disable identd. If you're not receiving email on a system, run sendmail to clear the queue every 15 minutes, but there's little point in having it listen. The list goes on and on. If you're not using it, turn it off.

The Three Least Wanted

Some services are critical, but running them willy-nilly is just asking for trouble. These are the services that your organization might need but that you should run on dedicated servers, to keep them as far removed from your other systems as possible. They are, in no particular order, name servers, Web servers, and FTP servers. Not that everything else is safe—it's just that these are the worst offenders.

First, we recommend running as few name servers as possible and disabling all caching name servers if at all possible. Not only is the performance benefit modest, but name servers are among the riskiest services in the first place. (As with all other recommendations in this chapter, there is no reason to believe that this recommendation is compatible with your environment. Consider the effects of the change and, when possible, test it before implementing it in a production environment.) In our view, it is best to segregate name services on dedicated servers. Name servers can and should run under a separate user account, although many administrators allow them to run as root. It also might be beneficial to chroot the name server, although the additional security conferred by chrooting is minimal. chroot was designed not as a security tool, but as a way to simplify system installation. All the security benefits of chroot were incidental to its design. Remember that chrooting a process running as root is essentially the same as not chrooting it at all, so don't waste your time.

Although mainstream Unix Web server daemons tend to be reasonably secure (although they still have security flaws), the scripts that generate the dynamic content that most sites depend on are not. Much of the CGI scripts that run the embedded Perl and PHP code in Web pages are not written by people who are security-conscious. The sample scripts that developers work from are often riddled with holes. A huge percentage of scripts that, for example, generate printer-ready versions of Web pages can be induced to generate printer-ready versions of any file on the system, including the password file. If you've configured your system properly, at least the shadow file will be inaccessible to the intruder. No code should be placed on a Web site until at least two programmers look at it; the auditor should be highly security-conscious. Where possible, segregate Web servers from other systems on your network. It's best to place Web servers in a DMZ so that you can SSH into the systems and so that they can talk to the back-end databases. However, the Web servers will be otherwise prevented from talking to systems within the network.

A countervailing opinion holds that although most decent Web server daemons can be made reasonably secure, the default installation of most Web servers is a security nightmare. Also, separation of spaces should be a basic design principle for any secure Web server: Pages should not be served from a place where other Web processes dynamically write data. Configuration data for executable server-side code should not be in a place where the Web pages are served from or where dynamic data can be written. This reduces the chance that a bug in the code that produces dynamic data can be abused to obtain access to the server. When possible, different applications run by the Web server should use Unix permissions and setuid/setuid bits to segregate the data space that each can impact—especially if you have little control over the application code being installed. Any back-end applications should validate the identity of the requestor's IP address, restricting its execution to that on the appropriate Web server, and also should verify the validity of the request because it's very likely that the programmer who wrote the Web code didn't write the back-end code. It doesn't do any good to stick the credit card database far behind the firewall if a badly programmed Web application allows anyone on the Internet to make arbitrary SQL queries into the database through the Web.

FTP servers should be avoided wherever possible. This is another service with a long history of serious security vulnerabilities. FTP almost always runs as root. It uses clear-text passwords. The data being passed can be modified with ease by a clever attacker and can be read by even a stupid one. FTP should be replaced with SCP. You can find freely available graphical clients for SCP on Windows and Macintosh systems, so the only barrier to acceptance is user education. Disable named FTP entirely, and segregate any anonymous FTP servers that you have. (Of course, Web servers can be used to serve arbitrary files; they often can be used to replace anonymous FTP.) If people need to see them from the outside, put them in your DMZ; if they are restricted to internal use, block all connections from the outside.

Here's a special bonus service: Many systems have the portmapper turned on. This is unavoidable if you're running NFS, but if you're not running NFS or other software that depends on remote procedure calls, disable it. (If you really care about security, replace NFS or restrict its use as much as possible. It is inherently insecure.) Portmapper and the services running behind it are responsible for an immense number of break-ins. If you do run these services, make sure that you protect them with TCP Wrappers. There is also a secure portmapper replacement available from Weitse Venema, the author of TCP Wrappers; both packages are available from his Web site at `http://www.porcupine.org`.

Access Control

TCP Wrappers and other host-based firewall rules are both excellent tools that you should deploy widely. Every system has a different set of tools for configuring firewall rules. Linux uses either IP chains or IP tables, depending on the version of the kernel you run. Red Hat and most other distributions ship with appropriate tools. For Solaris, the most popular package is Darren Reed's IP Filter, available online at http://coombs.anu.edu.au/~avalon/ip-filter.html. In the case of portmapper, it is unlikely that more than two or three systems will ever need to connect to the portmapper, so restrict access to port 111 to those hosts only. If only two people are authorized to log into a system, allow SSH connections only from their workstations. Wherever you can restrict access, do so. It's like turning off services: You can always open it wider later. Make changes when you can handle downtime, or at least when you can access the console after you lock yourself out.

Configuring Services

It's often possible for an outsider to extract information from a system when there is no need to allow external access to that information. For example, most systems are configured to allow remote users to expand sendmail aliases: The SMTP command `EXPN root` will provide the list of users who receive mail addressed to the root user. Combined with the `finger` command, an attacker can perform reconnaissance and determine whether your system administrators are in the office. Not only should you have disabled the finger daemon, but you also should have disabled the `EXPN` (and, for that matter, the `VRFY`) command on your SMTP server. You might wish to configure your name servers to provide different names within and outside your network: Even the names of your systems might give an attacker information that he could not otherwise obtain. This information is covered in more detail in Chapter 12, "Mail."

Patching Systems

Along with disabling unused services, keeping your patches up-to-date is the single most important thing you can do for your system security. Although patches will not necessarily address every vulnerability on your system—some vendors are better about this than others—they will protect you from the most common exploits available.

An unpatched system might as well be a hacked system. Hackers are continually conducting scans to look for vulnerable versions of particular packages; we see hundreds of name server version requests every single day. Although some of these are legitimate, many are hackers scanning for exploitable systems. The scans are automated and can scan thousands of systems an hour if the attacker isn't cautious. More often than not, an attempt to exploit vulnerable servers is also automated: The software scans and compromises systems, where possible, installs a back door, and notifies the hacker of the compromised system.

Whatever else you do, patching systems is crucial for keeping outsiders out. (Keeping insiders out is much more difficult, of course, as we've discussed.) Although you might suffer the least direct financial harm from these opportunistic attacks, they are incredibly common, they take an incredible amount of time and energy to clean up with a good degree of certainty, and, if they involve Web site defacement, they can be highly embarrassing as well. Moreover, the effort needed to patch systems should be minimal: Full patching should be done before initial rollout of the system. After that point, all you need do is read the vendor's security mailing list, which will inform you of new security-relevant patches and install those announced for your system. If you are in charge of a number of systems, you might want to look at systems to automate patch installation. As long as you keep up-to-date, though, the time and energy involved should average no more than two or three hours a week, at most. Some mailing list suggestions will be listed in Appendix G, "Reference Collection." Also, if you use an integrity check, such as Tripwire, you will need to verify your signatures before patching and then update them after patching. As always, test any changes before implementing them on a production server: "Security" patches have been known to break things worse than they were broken before! Many UNIX flavors have automated patch installation programs that allow the patches to be backed out, but in the case of security patches, this is often a disaster waiting to happen because the old, broken versions are kept intact, with original executable permissions, in a directory elsewhere on the system; in the worst case, a malicious user could locate and execute those original versions of vulnerable software. Often a vendor will release upgraded versions of patches later without a security bulletin; these upgraded patches might fix the real problem rather than the symptom fixed by the earlier patch, and the wise administrator will track these as well.

Reading Logs

It should go without saying that reading system logs is crucial to maintaining system security, but an unbelievable number of system administrators read logs only when debugging a known problem or not at all. Although logs are invaluable for resolving configuration issues, the role that they play in security is even more important.

An opportunity frequently ignored by system administrators is the logging of the actions taken by their own scripts. Using the `'logger'` command or Perl's syslog module, scripts can generate their own syslog entries for particular events. These can be used, for example, by an automatic patching script to log the patches added to a given system on a particular run, or by a firewall-management script to log the blocking and unblocking of addresses.

Looking for security violations almost always comes down to recognizing deviation from the pattern of regular use. If you read logs, you will come to recognize the IP addresses from which your users typically read their email. You will know when they read their email, and you will know which users log onto which machines and when. Internalizing these patterns will make you more attuned to spotting variations in them: Why is Mike logging onto the print server? Why is someone in Croatia attempting to read mail via IMAP? That's certainly an odd username to connect with! All—or none—of these variations could indicate an attempt to compromise one of your servers. Your ability to pick these out from hundreds or thousands of lines of log files is crucial to your ability to rapidly detect and respond to attacks.

For this reason, we suggest a central log server, to which all of your other servers send their log messages. We recommend keeping logs for a substantial length of time, at a minimum of several weeks. With several weeks' worth of logs, you might have supporting evidence to help determine when and how a system was initially compromised. We also recommend having different log files for different syslog facilities to simplify the process of separating the wheat from the chaff. For best effect, read your log files every day. Feel free to use a tool such as Psionic's logcheck to strip out some of the more common status messages.

Detecting Problems

Consider each odd detection an incident. Group incidents by time and source/destination IP pairs. Where possible, correlate syslog-based logs with logs from your intrusion-detection system: Was abnormal network traffic detected that corresponds to the abnormal syslog entries? After the attempt, was abnormal traffic detected leaving from your network? Correlation? Yes!

Examine your router logs as well. Look at the traffic rejected not only by your ingress filters, but also by the egress filters: Is something within your network impersonating a host on the outside? That's probably part of a denial-of-service attack, and you should track down the system; it might just be an errant laptop configured for a different network, but it is cause for suspicion.

Log onto the targeted system and examine the systems for abnormal behavior: Are strange processes running? Have configuration files changed? Are all open network ports accounted for? Do all commands output the expected information with the correct format? One of the most common signs of a system that has had a rootkit installed is that some commands provide incorrectly formatted output or have stopped accepting some of the command-line options. A deep familiarity with the system is the best way to detect these sorts of changes. It helps to be familiar with all the hidden files on a standard install of your operating system, a list of all setuid and setgid applications, and so forth, but there is simply no substitute for experience here.

A Word on Rootkits

What is a rootkit? A rootkit is a package of binary applications installed by someone who has cracked a system, used to hide the presence of that intruder from other users of the system—up to and including the system administrator. Typically, a rootkit will included modified versions of `ps`, `ls`, `netstat`, and as many as two dozen other binaries. More advanced rootkits will include modified versions of check summing utilities that might be used to determine that particular binaries have been compromised. Crackers use these tools to hid their presence on a system: For example, if `ps` does not show processes run by the intruders, it is substantially more difficult to track down and deal with them.

Recently, a new variety of rootkit has become common: the kernel module rootkit, which is known to exist at least for Linux and Solaris, and probably other operating systems as well. A kernel module rootkit takes advantage of the API used to load device drivers and other kernel-level add-ons. It often installs itself and then hides, providing a means for the hacker to hide files or open ports at the system level and protecting him from the standard tools without requiring him to modify them.

The only way to detect a rootkit with certainty is to put the hard drive in a system that is known to be secure and that has the same set of patches installed. Then you can compare each binary on the system using a known good check summing utility and look for hidden or setuid/setgid files. This process is incredibly time-consuming, but, with enough experience, you will become adept at detecting rootkits. Of course, it's virtually impossible to disprove the existence of a rootkit on a particular system, which is why we have emphasized positive signs of rootkits. One last positive sign of a rootkit is that the list of ports that the system reports as open is missing services reported on an nmap probe of the system. Again, deep familiarity with the systems in question can greatly save time and energy. A root shell bound to port 60,000 and not requiring a password to log in is another certain sign of a compromised system.

Keep a bootable CD-ROM or floppy disk handy; the ability to quickly and accurately verify the binaries on your system is crucial for rapid identification of compromised systems. You will need to keep a list of checksums for critical binaries, and you will need to update this list each time you patch your system. Tripwire and AIDE are two programs that can automate this process; if you use them, make sure that you can run them from your boot media.

What Now?

If you find that a system has unquestionably been compromised, take it offline immediately. Not only are hacked systems vulnerable to theft of data, but they also are the most common platform for launching further attacks against other systems both within and outside your network. The data on hacked systems might be destroyed on a moment's notice by a hacker who believes that he has been caught. As long as that system is online, the hacker might be covertly copying your network traffic to a remote site.

On the other hand, "Take it offline immediately" is not always the correct response. In fact, for investigations that will be pursued seriously, it is often best to get a snapshot of the system (ps and netstat) using known good binaries and then isolate the system from the Internet—the traces of connections into the system might tell you if your other systems are compromised. Also, if there are plans to pursue a legal investigation, every step must be documented in detail. Pulling the network cable and then poking around randomly on the disk is a good way to taint any evidence that exists if a legal case is pursued later.

Once you have pulled the system offline, you can examine the hard drive on another system at your leisure. Do not allow the system on an insecure network, in case you inadvertently activate one of the hacker's reporting tools. Do not boot off the compromised system's drive, in case it has been booby-trapped to self-destruct if the system is booted without a network as a probable indication of detection.

Note any IP addresses or hostnames that you uncover, and report the compromise to the site administrators both at your site (if there is one) and at the site of the source IPs. Similarly, even when a system is not successfully compromised, it is best to report hacking attempts to the site administrator as reported by whois. Although your system might not have been compromised successfully, it is quite likely that the same attacker compromised other systems at other sites, and it is quite likely that the attack platform is a compromised system whose administrator is not yet aware that the system in question was hacked or is hacking outbound. A similar notification from elsewhere could be your first clue that you have a problem.

In the rare case that the system is knowingly being used to hack, informing the administrator lets him know that you're on top of the situation. This is fairly rare; however, much more common is the case of an administrator who is too clueless or busy to respond. Expect that your message will be ignored, and be prepared to block the offending system or network at the firewall if the attack is persistent. Still, if you diligently respond to all attempts on your network, a notable proportion of system administrators will thank you for helping them to discover a hacked system on your network. That said, not everything that at first appears to be an attack is an attack, and not all attacks are malicious: A customer might be checking the security of his own server, for example. It's best to keep a cool head and verify your suspicions before pulling the plug.

If this occasional praise is not enough incentive to do the boring work of log file reading and analysis, we suggest making a game out of it: You will find that a disproportionate number of attacks come from smaller countries that are just now getting Internet access and where experienced system administrators are in short supply. Keep a list of ISO country codes on your desk, and mark them off as you are attacked by systems from those countries. At the time of this writing, we are seeing many attacks from Brazil, Korea, China, and Taiwan; we also have been on the receiving end of attacks from countries including Colombia, Venezuela, Morocco, Egypt, Algeria, Kuwait, Turkey, Thailand, and Nepal. Keeping our ever-growing list provides at least one small enticement to do the boring, slow, necessary work of reading log files to uncover incidents.

Configuration Management

As with backups, the conventional wisdom does not consider configuration management to be an aspect of security. In fact, the ability to determine the status of a given configuration file, to know who modified it, how, and when, is crucial for both security and more general sorts of accountability.

Three classes of configuration-management solutions exist: security-specific file auditing, general source-control solutions, and large-scale automatic system administration solutions that necessarily must implement some sort of configuration management. If you can see when something incorrect or dangerous has been inserted into your configuration, you will want to restore things to the correct state. This requires some sort of configuration-management tool. In fact, it is very useful to have some sort of configuration management when installing new systems because it greatly reduces the time that it takes to bring a newly installed system into line with your existing configuration.

A very common sort of configuration-management, security-specific file auditing tools (including AIDE and Tripwire) produce checksums of system binaries and configuration files. These can be used to report when these files have been modified. This is a good start and, without other tools, is a useful technique for uncovering hacked systems. Unfortunately, these tools often do not have mechanisms for determining when changes were introduced into a system, who introduced the changes, or what the reasoning is behind the changes. None of these is necessary for determining that a system is compromised, but all of them might be necessary to determine when a system was compromised, who compromised the system, and whether it was intentional or an innocent misconfiguration.

Source code-management solutions help to address these problems. Of the systems in wide use today, two tools appropriate to managing Unix system configuration files are Revision Control System (RVS) and its big brother, Concurrent Versioning System (CVS). Either of these systems is based on the same premise: You can check out files from a central repository, make changes to those files, and check them back in. The system will keep track of what lines in the file changed, who made the changes, and when the changes were made. When checking the files back into the system, you also are prompted for a log file entry describing the purpose of your changes.

Used consistently, these systems enable you to track changes in system configuration over time. This is important not only for tracking down unauthorized changes but, if you operate at a site with multiple system administrators, it also assists in the process of blame allocation when something does go wrong. Generally, we recommend CVS for more complex sets of configuration files or those maintained by more than two or three administrators. RCS, on the other hand, works for simple sets of configuration files maintained by a small number of administrators, but some people prefer CVS for all of their configuration files. In most cases, either solution works acceptably well.

Automated configuration control solutions that actually implement changes ultimately will reduce the amount of work needed to administer systems. They also will improve security, although there is a lot of up-front work with initial configuration of these systems. Either homegrown Perl or shell scripts or comprehensive solutions such as CFEngine can allow you to manage configurations and thus improve accountability and security. (Even in the case of these solutions, you can generally keep the configuration files or the body of the scripts in a standard source code-management solution such as CVS or RCS.) If you use an automated configuration tool, its control files must be kept well protected and must be audited regularly to ensure that no malicious changes have been inserted. After all, such changes would affect all of your systems!

Policy

Up until now, we have carefully walked around a basic question: What are you trying to accomplish, and how do you expect to accomplish this? Answering this question requires examining your threat model and your security philosophy, which together describe your goals with regard to security. After you've set your goals, you need to describe how you hope to attain those goals. That's the job of the security policy. As with everything else, policy breaks down into theory and practice. The theory is also called policy, but the practice is called procedure. Both are important: The document that defines what ports should be closed and which should be open on your firewall is a policy; the document that specifies how to configure the firewall in this way is a procedure.

The Theory of Policy

Policy defines your goals and can be used to delineate chains of authority and areas of responsibility. The standard place to look when thinking about security policy is the "Site Security Handbook" (RFC 2196). At the very least, your policy should define authorized and unauthorized access and should define penalties for violations. You must be able to enforce your policies: If your department head or human resources department will not stand behind your penalties, they are virtually worthless. Therefore, these policies must be developed alongside your supervisor and the human resources department, along with anyone else who might be called upon to enforce elements of the policy.

Firewall Policy

If you have a firewall, you should have a policy that describes its configuration. In essence, a firewall is a tool that makes concrete a network access policy: If you have a firewall but you do not have an explicit network policy, you have an implicit policy that you should probably make concrete. At most sites, mail may be sent from outside the network to one or mail hosts on the network, and one or more systems on the network may be used to send mail elsewhere on the Internet. Without a firewall set of rule that explicitly restricts SMTP, the implicit policy is that any host may send or receive mail from the Internet. Although this might be acceptable for some organizations, other organizations will want all mail sent and received via centrally administered mail servers so that use and abuse of the service can be audited, and to minimize the security exposure of other systems on the network. The policy at most sites should specify what incoming traffic is allowed: HTTP traffic to the Web server, SMTP traffic to the mail server, and so on.

As a general rule, we recommend that each of an organization's Internet services be provided through one or more systems dedicated to that service. For instance, one or more dedicated mail servers would service the mail, dedicated web servers would provide web hosting for the whole organization, and so forth. These dedicated systems will be much easier to secure and maintain than multiple servers scattered throughout the network.

Larger organizations might not be capable of implementing this level of centralized control without a firewall ruleset that explicitly blocks unauthorized traffic to unauthorized systems. However, this is a blunt instrument at best; many organizations will be better served by a policy requiring the registration of departmental servers and services with a central group, combined with a policy that is essentially a checklist for installation and maintenance of such servers.

Password Policy

Almost every site has a password policy that defines good and bad passwords, describes how frequently they should be altered, and so on. Valid passwords vary from system to system. Traditional Unix systems limit passwords to eight characters, but modern password systems based on LDAP, Kerberos, or MD5 password hashing are not so restricted. Your policy should describe what defines a valid password on your system, specify a minimum length for a good password (at least eight characters, or more on systems without an eight-character restriction), disallow the use of common English words as passwords, disallow the use of passwords that are used on other systems and accounts (work-related or otherwise), and so on. If possible, specify the use of a version of the passwd command that checks passwords for compliance with a policy. Besides the quality of the passwords, a password policy should define what may and may not be done with those passwords. Passwords should never be emailed, and attempts to grab other users' passwords should be forbidden. More information regarding proper use of passwords is in Chapter 7, "Authentication," and those guidelines should be integrated with your password policy.

"Hacker Tools" and System Administration

In the course of system or network administration, you will inevitably want to use tools that might be described as "hacker" tools. These include network traffic-monitoring software, including intrusion-detection systems and simple packet dumpers, to detect malicious traffic and debug network problems; password file crackers, to test compliance with your password policy; and portscanners and vulnerability assessment tools, to evaluate the security of your systems. These tools have valid applications to computer security. You should have a policy specifying who can use which tools on which systems and networks, and under what conditions.

From your perspective, this policy is the most important: Specify individuals and systems by name in the policy, and get a copy signed by your manager. (It could be more effective to have individuals named in a memo that is not part of the formal policy.) If possible, get a copy signed by your manager's manager. Follow this policy to the letter. Doing so could be the only thing that stands between doing your job and breaking the law. There have been several cases of people getting in trouble with the law for doing what they believed to be their job; the case of Randal Schwartz is widely cited in this context. More information regarding the Randal Schwartz case can be found at
`http://www. lightlink.com/spacenka/fors/`.

To use these tools without protecting yourself puts you at risk. Although you have a responsibility to your employer, you have a responsibility to yourself as well. Set rules, document them, get approval, and follow those rules both in letter and in spirit. If things go wrong, it's best to have followed established procedure.

Procedure

We are big fans of procedures. Procedures can range from checklists for system installation and auditing to forgotten-password replacement requests. There is not a whole lot to be said about procedures, except to be as explicit as possible. That allows you to delegate and to explain how your environment works. As your organization grows, well-written procedures allow you to delegate and to spread good practices to new groups.

The big difficulty with both procedures and policies is that they tend to go out-of-date very rapidly, and they are rarely updated in a timely fashion. If your organization already has a system to review policies and procedures on a regular basis, we suggest that you follow it in regard to these procedures and policies as well. If your organization has no such system, we recommend that you develop one in-house and stick to it closely. Procedures should be tested regularly to ensure that they are still correct and that they work with the latest version of whatever is present. A system administrator must plan for continuity of operations in his absence due to illness or a change of employment; accurate, well-written procedures are necessary and are a sign of true professionalism.

Management Buy-In

Of course, none of these procedures or policies is worth anything if any employee can avoid having to follow them simply by complaining to someone in upper management. Without genuine management buy-in, all the documentation that you provide is just a worthless pile of paper. All the policies and procedures in the world count for nothing when they are ignored so that an executive can use the online message service of his choice without regard to the security implications of this decision, or when one group is allowed to manage its own workstations and can ignore your password policy. At least get your own suggestions on record and send "memos of understanding" when exceptions are forced on you. Anything that you can reasonably do to protect yourself when your organization acts against your recommendations is probably a good idea.

Ethics

As a system administrator, especially one who deals with computer security, you will come into contact with material that people believe to be secret or private. Some of it might be confidential company information; some of it will be personal information that people have stored in their accounts or shared via email. When this happens, you need to know where you stand with respect to the law, to the company, and to yourself.

Developing an Ethical Model

As with any other activity of system administration, it is helpful to model your ethical system. Because ethics are so personal, this system is simply one possible framework. Your ethical system might differ entirely, but as long as you are able to make the relevant decisions, that's good enough.

Our system is layered: There are outer layers that are more universal and less flexible, and inner layers that are both more personal and potentially more flexible. The layers in our system correspond roughly to people or ideas to whom one must answer. They are, from the outside, laws of nature, laws of man, generally held cultural ethical standards, professional responsibility, corporate standards, and personal ethics.

The order of these layers might vary somewhat. In intensely loyal corporations, it is not uncommon for corporate standards to trump the culture's ethical standards or even the law. If your personal ethics are the result of deep moral conviction, they, too, can trump the laws of man. The important thing is that you understand the ethical order as it applies to you because this will substantially reduce the amount of time and energy that it takes to decide upon your course of action.

Laws of Nature

It is not unusual for a system administrator to be asked to perform tasks that are simply not possible. Reporting of data that was never recorded in the first place is a common impossible task: You might be asked to report the contents of all deleted emails from a particular user's mailbox. Unless your mail system stores deleted mail indefinitely, and few do, this is simply a task that you will not be able to perform. One classic Dilbert cartoon involves Dilbert's boss and his request to report unanticipated outages in advance. Dilbert responds by providing a list that includes future system outages, along with fires, earthquakes, hurricanes, and volcanic eruptions that have not yet occurred. Although Dilbert is perhaps somewhat extreme, it might be reasonable to send a memorandum of understanding to your supervisor explaining why the request cannot be fulfilled.

Laws of Man

Laws relevant to system administration include privacy laws such as the Electronic Communications Privacy Act (ECPA), which relates to the privacy of electronic communications in general, and the Health Insurance Portability and Accountability Act (HIPAA), which relates to privacy of medical records.

We are not lawyers, and we generally refrain from interpreting the law, but it is worth noting that the ECPA prevents employers from reading employee email—unless the employees have been notified in advance. A written statement to the effect that all computer files, email, and other network transmissions are the property of the company and are subject to interception and decoding at the whim of the organization will help protect you legally. As always, consult your company's counsel before crafting such a statement.

Cultural Standards and Professional Responsibility

Beyond the law, certain standards of behavior are generally followed: You say "please" and "thank you," although no law demands it. People who play along with the cultural standards tend to get along with other people and be more successful in the world than those who ignore these behaviors and go their own way. It is not wrong or incorrect to act outside these societal norms, but to do so has consequences. You ignore those consequences at your peril, although to bow to social pressure has consequences as well.

System administration is not like becoming a lawyer or a doctor: Members of those professions are certified and, as part of that process, agree to abide by certain ethical standards. The absence of an explicit code of moral conduct for system administrators, however, does not imply the total absence of such a code. In fact, the larger system administration community has a wide body of accepted practice that new admins learn as part of the informal apprenticeship system by which they are typically trained. The

Association for Computing Machinery (ACM) has a code of ethics and professional conduct, as does the System Administrators Guild (SAGE). Although you might not endorse every aspect of every rule put together by these professional organizations, they are at the very least worth a look.

System administration community standards might be strange and arbitrary, but they are firmly held. Recently we witnessed a days-long flame war on a local system administrators group mailing list regarding one list member's use of a different email quoting convention. The issue was not that the community was right and the individual was wrong; the issue was that the individual in question wantonly and arbitrarily flouted the conventions of the community. As always, there are consequences for violating the prevailing standards, but, at this level, you generally risk neither life nor limb. Hopefully, however, your interest in and respect for the profession is great enough that you will generally abide by professional standards.

Because most system administrators start out by working under a more experienced admin, many system administrators feel a responsibility to the community in the same way that doctors and lawyers feel loyal to their alma mater. This devotion is most often expressed through a willingness to train new system administrators (by allowing them to work as junior administrators or as interns) and a desire to help other system administrators by sharing knowledge. This most often takes places through local mailing lists or groups for sysadmins, but it also might be through presentations and by networking at conferences. Many administrators are members of the national System Administrators Guild (SAGE) group and appropriate regional or local groups. We strongly encourage participation in these groups as a means of returning to the community, as a way to learn how to better perform as a system administrator, and as a means of building your career. Personally, we consider such active participation as an ethical obligation, although we respect those who feel otherwise.

Many conferences about security or system administration include a session regarding the ethical obligations of system administrators. We highly recommend attending these sessions, to help develop an accurate impression about ethical standards in the system administration community.

Corporate Standards

Most large organizations have codes of conduct, both written and unspoken. Even smaller organizations have such codes, although they often amount to an "us versus them" mentality. As at every other level, administrators who act within these standards are better-liked and better-respected than those who do not.

This issue is more fundamental, however: As a system administrator, you are hired specifically to serve the needs of the company. Those needs are expected to trump your own, at least during the working day. You are hired to do a job, and you are obligated to perform as requested to the best of your abilities, regardless of your personal standards for conduct.

Summary

The best security is preparedness: If you have already acted to minimize both the chances of a security violation and the consequences of such a violation, then your job will be much simpler. Security is not a static state of being, but it's a state of mind that synthesizes your security goals and threat model with policies and procedures to respond to those threats. Security is a state of preparedness, both technological, through backups and appropriate system configurations, and psychological, by knowing what to expect and how you will react. If you are lucky, the paranoia typically induced by security work will be unwarranted; if you are unlucky, your paranoia could be all that stands between you and the loss of your corporate secrets.

Best Practices

- Understand what you are trying to protect and from whom you are trying to protect it.
- Write policies with teeth.
- Write a policy that permits you to use network-monitoring software and "hacker tools" in the course of your job.
- Patch your systems religiously.
- Back up your systems regularly. Verify your backups.
- Harden systems by disabling unused applications and turning off unnecessary features. Use TCP Wrappers and other access control methods such as host-based firewalls.
- Read logs; respond to incidents rapidly but politely.
- Write down all policies in a known place.
- Make sure that everyone affected by a policy can get to it and read it.
- Define mechanisms for changes and updates into the policies at the beginning.

Resources

- *Secrets and Lies: Digital Security in a Networked World*, by Bruce Schneier. (John Wiley and Sons, 2000). Schneier, a well-known and widely respected computer security consultant, discusses security as idea and as process. It's well worth the read for those unfamiliar with the practice of computer security.

- RFC 2196, "Site Security Handbook." http://www.faqs.org/rfcs/rfc2196.html. The standard guide to developing security policies for Internet-connected sites. It's a dry read, but it's full of relevant information.

- "Computer Policy and Law." http://www.cornell.edu/CPL. Cornell's Computer Policy and Law program's Web site is, among other things, a repository for real-world computer security policies. It's an excellent resource when developing your organization's policies.

- SecurityFocus.com. http://www.securityfocus.com/. SecurityFocus is home to a number of security resources, including the widely regarded BugTraq mailing list. Also available are news pieces about current security issues and opinion pieces regarding security.

- Computer Emergency Response Team (CERT). http://www.cert.org/. CERT is one of the oldest active computer security organizations. It specializes in releasing alerts regarding current security threats. Many believe that the team is slow and relatively unresponsive, but it is worth keeping an eye on current alerts.

- System Administrators Guild (SAGE). http://www.sage.org/. SAGE is dedicated to the promotion of system administration as a profession, and it is an excellent resource for those concerned with their professional responsibilities.

Intrusion Detection

by Andy Johnston

IN THIS CHAPTER

CHAPTER 22

Introduction

One of the themes emphasized in this book is that there is no "magic bullet" that will secure your systems for you. The best security plan integrates a variety of measures that function in different facets of your network and system configurations. One broad class of such measures is described as *Intrusion Detection Systems* (IDS). This class is usually divided into Host-based IDS (HIDS) and Network-based IDS (NIDS).

While Intrusion Detection Systems are a valuable component of any security strategy, it is important to understand their underlying functions, capabilities and limitations in order to utilize them effectively. One of the most important points to understand is that Intrusion Detection Systems do not literally detect intrusions; they detect events. Whether or not a given event is an intrusion attempt is often a question of intent. Ten failed login attempts to a user's account in two minutes may indicate a hacker trying ten possible passwords or a frustrated user who has forgotten the real one.

IDS's are useful because intrusion attempts often display event patterns detectable in network traffic or in system activity. Certain patterns are specific to known types of intrusion, and detection of these patterns points unambiguously to a potential threat. Other patterns are characteristic of one or more types of intrusion but may also be generated by benign activity. The recognition and interpretation of such event patterns by the administrator of the IDS is the heart of intrusion detection.

This chapter introduces NIDS by expanding on some of the TCP/IP networking concepts introduced in Chapter 5, "Getting on the Network," in order to describe some of the threats that a NIDS can address. We will then explore some of the detectable patterns these threats create in the TCP/IP traffic that transmits them. Finally, the chapter describes the design and implementation of a simple, script-based NIDS that can be installed and experimented with by a system administrator.

The Network as a Threat Vector

In the early to mid-1990s, access to the Internet began to spread beyond the relatively small number of universities, research sites, and government contractors that had accounted for most of its traffic. As the number of users grew and Web services, in particular, became more sophisticated, it seemed that the dream of global access to ideas and instantaneous communication would become reality.

As of this writing (2001) it seems that the dream has indeed become reality. It also seems that a large fraction of those enjoying this new reality are con artists, ideologues, and assorted nuts trying to leap through the screen into our wallets, minds, and collective sanity. Beyond these, there is a group of people, loosely defined as "hackers," who put forth considerable effort to undermine the authentication and authorization mechanisms in computer systems for various combinations of fun, malice, and profit. The first group of irritants gets more attention at most sites because the users are the ones who get irritated. The second group generally tries to avoid any notice at all, but they can do far more damage and create far more recovery work for the sysadmin.

Network Intrusion Detection Systems can often detect activity that other security measures may miss and alert the sysadmin to a potential problem. The *N* in NIDS might suggest that the networking staff is responsible for any NIDS at your site. This is not usually the case, however. The networking staff generally has its hands full just making sure that network communications keep working without sifting those communications for "evil" transmissions. In addition, the UNIX sysadmin is often in the best position to know what constitutes "evil" for a particular Unix system.

Network Protocol Concepts

Chapter 5 described the organization of network communications through MAC and IP addressing. Data was assumed to travel in discrete chunks that had certain addressing information associated with them. To design a NIDS and interpret its results, you must understand the principles that underlie the actual structure of those discrete chunks, and how that structure contributes to the communication of the data.

> **Note**
>
> This section presents material that may already be familiar to the reader with grounding in the TCP/IP protocol. Such a reader is advised to go directly to the next section, "Exploiting the TCP/IP protocol."

Encapsulation

Using a railroad system as an analogy for network communication was useful in Chapter 5. We will stretch that analogy a little further here to illustrate the crucial concept of *encapsulation*.

Our system of interconnected railroads had to allow for the possibility that rail traffic, in passing from one local railroad to another, might have to move over track of different gauges requiring different types of rail car. At a gateway between two such different railroads, the cargo of any given car would have to be transferred to a different kind of car capable of traveling the different local railroad. The lack of a standard track complicates matters, but it must be addressed. There might be good reasons why some of the local railroads chose to use a certain type of rail. A local railroad might be dominated by certain types of cargo or might pass through unusual terrain and would have adopted standards best suited to those conditions.

Still, it would be preferable to put cargo on a train and not have to unload it until it has reached its final destination. If all cargo is packed in standard containers, the local railroads can add cars specifically designed to carry those containers. Cargo shipped between two stations on the same local railroad can simply be loaded into containers at one end and taken off at the other. Cargo destined for a station on a different railroad also will be loaded into containers and then will travel to a switchyard connecting two local railroads. Rather than unloading and reloading the cargo to transfer it to cars on the next railroad, the containers are transferred directly without even being opened. Every switchyard would use exactly the same type of equipment for handling the standard containers.

This concept can be extended beyond just railroads. For instance, ships and shipyards also can adopt standardized containers. Cargo can be transferred from a ship directly to a rail car.

The trick here is that, no matter what the containers hold—tapioca, turmeric, or titanium—all of the actual transport mechanisms deal only with the containers, never with the cargo. Because the containers are standardized, they can be dealt with by standardized mechanisms and procedures, no matter where they are going or what they hold.

The same approach is used to transfer data over the Internet. Data travels in very different ways over different local networks, so it is placed in a data "container" that adheres to standards accepted throughout the Internet. Data is "contained" by adding *header* data immediately before it and *trailer* data immediately following it. This process of adding a standard header and a trailer is called *encapsulation*.

Layering

Another important concept is inherent in our railroad analogy. As noted, it doesn't matter what cargo is in the containers. The transportation and handling systems manage all containers the same way. People operating these systems also needn't know or care what is in the containers. As soon as cargo is loaded and sealed into a container, the nature of the cargo becomes irrelevant until it is unpacked. By the same token, the producers, packers, unpackers, and final users of the cargo needn't know or care how the cargo was actually transported. As far as they are concerned, the cargo might as well have been handed directly from the packers to the unpackers in an adjoining room. The establishment of these independent contexts through encapsulation is called *layering* and is illustrated in Figure 22.1.

FIGURE 22.1

Illustration of two layers in cargo transport.

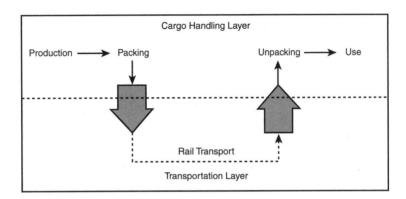

The manner in which a given layer performs its function is not relevant to the layer above or below it. From the point of view of those who pack and unpack the cargo from the containers, they are in direct communication with each other. The specific transport process in the Transportation Layer is completely irrelevant to the packers and could easily be replaced by another process that has the same result.

From a global point of view, the cargo is produced and packed at the top layer and then is encapsulated, passed to the bottom layer, transported, de-encapsulated, and then passed up to the top layer again for unpacking and use. From a purely *logical* point of view, we also can consider the producers and users to be in *direct* communication with each other. What the producers make is what the users eventually receive. The transport mechanisms in between are completely independent and, thus, in a sense, invisible.

If we consider a process involving multiple layers, it is possible to consider any layer in isolation from the others and to consider the sender and the receiver to be (logically) in direct communication at that layer.

When a layer receives newly encapsulated data from the next higher layer, it treats the entire encapsulation, header and trailer included, as data that it will then encapsulate. Encapsulated data is called *payload*. Each level's complete encapsulation is just the payload for the next level down, as illustrated in Figure 22.2.

As in the rail transport example, issues of network transport can also be separated into independent layers. Also as in that example, encapsulation is used to "pack" and "unpack" information payloads at each layer. Each layer encapsulates the payload received from the layer above for transmission to the next layer down. Similarly, the unpacking or "de-encapsulation" of data takes place moving up one layer at a time. Moving "down" through the layers means moving in the direction of successive encapsulations.

FIGURE 22.2

*One layer's
encapsulation is
the next layer's
payload.*

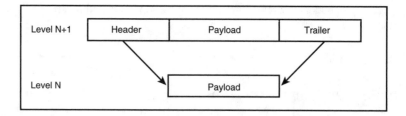

Returning to our analogy, suppose that a container has reached its destination and must now be unpacked. The container might hold gravel, diamonds, or kumquats, each requiring a different type of handling. In fact, you probably wouldn't even want to unpack gravel, diamonds, and kumquats in the same place. Rather than have every container opened at the railroad station to determine its contents, each container could have a contents list attached to simplify its routing to the appropriate unpacking service.

Note that no one involved in the rail transport of the container needs to look at the list of contents. No one at the destination railroad station needs to know how the container got there, nor do they need to unpack it. They simply look at the contents list and send the container to the correct unpacking service. Finally, the unpacking service needn't care about the rail transportation *or* the list of contents. Their workers simply unpack the containers as they arrive, assuming that all the previous systems have delivered the right containers to the right place.

This is a three-layered system. The problems of transporting cargo are organized into three independent categories. Each category can be dealt with independently of the others. The original payload, kumquats for instance, is encapsulated by the addition of the list of contents. The kumquats, together with the list, are encapsulated by the addition of the destination address for the container. The railroad looks only at the destination address. The destination railroad station looks only at the list of contents. The unpacking service looks only at the actual cumquats.

Stacks

A "stack" is a particular way of breaking up the issues of network data transport into layers. The TCP/IP stack is the standard for all Internet data transactions and is the focus of this chapter. We will briefly consider the ISO OSI stack as well, since it is often used as a reference model against which other stacks are described.

The ISO OSI Seven-Layer Model

In this section, we will look at a very refined layering system developed by the International Standards Organization (ISO) to address data transport in an idealized way. Although this does not represent the protocol actually used by the Internet, it provides a framework against which different protocols can be examined and discussed.

The International Standards Organization (ISO) developed the Open System Interconnection (OSI) model as the basis for a standard that would allow any two systems adhering to the standard to communicate over the Internet.

The standard issues of data communication were organized into seven independent groups, called layers. A separate layer of processing is associated with each group. Data that originates at the seventh, or top, layer is first encapsulated with the relevant information from that layer and then is presented to the next layer down for further encapsulation and hand-off down the chain, and so forth.

The final recipient gets the original, top-level data layered inside seven encapsulations and passes it up through successive layers of de-encapsulation to retrieve the payload contents.

The seven layers of the ISO OSI protocol are described in Table 22.1.

TABLE 22.1   The Seven Layers of the ISO OSI Protocol

Layer Number	Layer	Issues Addressed
1	Physical	Actual representation of binary data over physical communications medium
		Physical transmission and reception of binary data
2	Data	Organization of bits from the physical layer into meaningful packets
		Delivery of data from one network device to another over the same network
3	Network	Delivery of data across different networks
		Network traffic control
4	Transport	Delivery of data from a specific user or process on the sending system to an appropriate recipient user or process on the receiving system
5	Session	Establishment, management, and removal of longer-term interactions ("sessions") between users or processes on different systems

TABLE 22.1 continued

Layer Number	Layer	Issues Addressed
6	Presentation	Transformation of data between high-level formats (terminal displays, encryption/decryption, and so on)
7	Application	Direct interaction with the user
		Concealment of any activity in Layers 1–6 from the user

The OSI model is elegant, and Table 22.1 provides only a very rough sketch of the detailed definitions and interactions of which it consists. This refinement, though, makes the model very difficult to implement in a responsive, practical way for real-world use.

The TCP/IP Model

The standard protocol for all Internet communication is the Transmission Control Protocol/Internet Protocol (TCP/IP). In this section, we look at the successive encapsulations of Internet data and see how each layer of encapsulation addresses a communications issue. We will also see that the idealized concepts of layering and encapsulation have been weakened somewhat in this protocol to accommodate various practical concerns.

For our purposes, consider a *packet* to be the result of one or more encapsulations.

Like the ISO OSI model, TCP/IP takes advantage of layering and encapsulation. The most obvious difference is that TCP/IP uses only four layers. The OSI physical and data layers roughly are combined into the TCP/IP Link layer, and the OSI session, presentation, and application layers are combined into the TCP/IP application layer.

The four layers of the TCP/IP protocol are described in Table 22.2.

TABLE 22.2 The Four Layers of the TCP/IP Protocol

Layer Number	Layer	Issues Addressed
1	Link	Actual representation of binary data over a physical communications medium
		Physical transmission and reception of binary data
		Interpretation of binary data into packets
		Hardware addressing of network devices within the local network

TABLE 22.2 continued

Layer Number	Layer	Issues Addressed
2	Network	Delivery of data across different networks
		Network traffic control
		Accommodation of packet size restrictions on the local network
3	Transport	Communication between specific users or processes on different systems
		Connection management (TCP)
4	Application	End-user applications (which might have their own encapsulation protocols)

Computers and other networked systems use specific types of hardware to connect to a network. These are referred to generically as *network devices*. Communications between computers are actually between network devices attached to the computers. The most common devices are network interface cards (NICs). This is particularly important to note if a computer has more than one network device. For readability, the text will continue to refer to communication between computers, except where the distinction is essential to understanding.

The TCP/IP Packet

Because the purpose of this chapter, in part, is to prepare you to deal with network-based intrusion detection systems, we will concentrate on the structure of TCP/IP packets themselves and the interpretation of their contents, rather than discuss the TCP/IP protocol in the abstract. We will refer frequently to listings of individual packets and of short sequences of packets. Such listings are called *packet dumps*.

An example of such a packet dump is shown in Listing 22.1.

LISTING 22.1 A TCP/IP Packet

```
Frame 1 (74 on wire, 74 captured)
    Arrival Time: Jun 20, 2001 16:27:49.5329
    Time delta from previous packet: 0.000000 seconds
    Time relative to first packet: 0.000000 seconds
    Frame Number: 1
    Packet Length: 74 bytes
    Capture Length: 74 bytes
Ethernet II
```

LISTING 22.1   continued

```
    Destination: 00:d0:d3:33:8b:58 (00:d0:d3:33:8b:58)
    Source: 00:a0:24:80:52:44 (00:a0:24:80:52:44)
    Type: IP (0x0800)
Internet Protocol
    Version: 4
    Header length: 20 bytes
    Differentiated Services Field: 0x10 (DSCP 0x04: Unknown DSCP; ECN: 0x00)
        0001 00.. = Differentiated Services Codepoint: Unknown (0x04)
        .... ..0. = ECN-Capable Transport (ECT): 0
        .... ...0 = ECN-CE: 0
    Total Length: 60
    Identification: 0x1294
    Flags: 0x00
        .0.. = Don't fragment: Not set
        ..0. = More fragments: Not set
    Fragment offset: 0
    Time to live: 64
    Protocol: TCP (0x06)
    Header checksum: 0x605a (correct)
    Source: phil.unet.edu (20.100.253.12)
    Destination: unet7.unet.edu (20.100.6.7)
Transmission Control Protocol, Src Port: 8425 (8425), Dst Port: telnet (23),
Seq: 3708375094, Ack: 0
    Source port: 8425 (8425)
    Destination port: telnet (23)
    Sequence number: 3708375094
    Header length: 40 bytes
    Flags: 0x0002 (SYN)
        0... .... = Congestion Window Reduced (CWR): Not set
        .0.. .... = ECN-Echo: Not set
        ..0. .... = Urgent: Not set
        ...0 .... = Acknowledgment: Not set
        .... 0... = Push: Not set
        .... .0.. = Reset: Not set
        .... ..1. = Syn: Set
        .... ...0 = Fin: Not set
    Window size: 16384
    Checksum: 0xccf7 (correct)
    Options: (20 bytes)
        Maximum segment size: 512 bytes
        NOP
        Window scale: 0 bytes
        NOP
        NOP
        Time stamp: tsval 2288547, tsecr 0

  0  00d0 d333 8b58 00a0 2480 5244 0800 4510    ...3.X..$.RD..E.
 10  003c 1294 0000 4006 605a 1464 fd0c 1464    .<....@.`Z.U...U
```

LISTING 22.1   continued

```
20   0607 20e9 0017 dd09 5036 0000 0000 a002    .. .....P6......
30   4000 ccf7 0000 0204 0200 0103 0300 0101    @..............
40   080a 0022 eba3 0000 0000                    ..."......
```

This packet dump was produced with a network packet analysis package called Ethereal. Ethereal is freeware, runs on Microsoft Windows and UNIX systems, and can be found at `http://www.ethereal.com`. I recommend it to anyone who needs to study and interpret network packets.

Listing 22.1 illustrates a packet initiating a telnet session. All four layers of encapsulation are represented. We will focus on Layers 2, 3, and 4 in this chapter. Layer 1 cannot really be examined directly without specialized equipment and is more the purview of the electrical engineer than the systems or network administrator.

The Link Layer—Ethernet

The header for this layer is represented by the section of the packet labeled "Ethernet II" in Listing 22.1. This is the name of the link protocol used by the local network that carried this particular packet. Ethernet is the dominant link protocol over networks in the Internet. The Ethernet II header contains three important pieces of information: a source address, a destination address, and the type of Network layer packet that the link layer encapsulates. This last piece of information, a prewarning of the contents of the link layer encapsulation, is something of an information leak from a higher layer to a lower one. It is one of the places that the TCP/IP compromises abstract design to produce a useful result; strictly speaking, the the Link layer should require no information about the nature of its payload beyond, perhaps, its size. In practice, it is often useful to know what is in the encapsulated package before it is opened.

Ethernet Communication

In the railroad analogy, the standardized containers were taken from station to station by rail car. When changing railroads, they would go to a switchyard with spurs from two different railroads. The containers would be transferred from cars on the first railroad to cars on the next.

Link-Layer Addressing Ethernet functions in much the same way. Transfer of data along a local network is always from one network device to another. The data travels from one network to another via a *gateway*, a system that has a network device in both networks. As illustrated in Figure 22.3, the data leaves a system through a network device with address 1, travels along network A, and arrives at a network device with address 2 that attaches to a gateway. The gateway then retransmits the data from the network device with address 3 along network B to a network device with address 4 (on another gateway), and so on to the final destination attached to a network device with address 6.

FIGURE 22.3

A gateway is a system that has a network device in both networks.

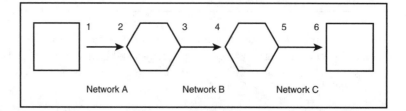

Because the Link layer encapsulation contains the addresses of the source and destination network device, then along network A it contains the addresses 1 and 2, along network B it contains addresses 3 and 4, and along network C it contains addresses 5 and 6. This is because the gateway devices de-encapsulate Layer 2 and then re-encapsulate it with addressing appropriate for the next network that the packet needs to traverse to reach its goal. Just as our containers were moved from one type of rail car to another when switching railroads, the data is moved from one Layer 2 encapsulation to another when switching networks.

The most common Link layer protocol is Ethernet. An Ethernet address consists of 6 bytes, expressed in hexadecimal notation and separated by colons. The address actually is assigned directly to the network device during manufacture and sometimes is called the "hardware" address. It is the responsibility of each manufacturer to ensure that no two devices are ever assigned the same address. To make sure that two different manufacturers don't assign the same address to different devices, each manufacturer is assigned a range of possible addresses for its exclusive use.

The Network Layer

The section of the packet dump labeled "Internet Protocol" displays the Network layer header. The Internet Protocol (IP) is the Network Layer protocol in the TCP/IP stack. This is the layer that is used to route data from one system on the Internet to another so that it must contain, among other things, the source and destination IP addresses (the source address is needed in case delivery fails and the protocol requires the sending system to be notified). The two addresses can be seen at the end of the IP header.

Packet Fragmentation

Different networks will have different properties and will impose different constraints on data transmission. One of the most basic constraints is the maximum size allowed any packet on a network. If a large packet originates from a system on a network that allows large packets and is destined for a system on a network with much stricter size constraints, then the large packet may be broken into smaller chunks or *fragmented* at the gateway to the more restrictive network. It is the job of the destination system to reconstruct the original data.

Setting the Don't Fragment flag in the IP header indicates that this packet is not to be fragmented. If fragmentation is required, the transmission will be allowed to fail. The More Fragments flag (when set) indicates both that the packet contains a data fragment and that it is *not* the last fragment in the series. The Fragment Offset value indicates the position of the fragment in the original packet, starting from 0.

A *flag* is a single binary bit that can have a value of either 0 or 1. The flag is *set* if it has the value of 1. The flag is *not set* or *unset* if it has the value of 0.

Time-To-Live

The Internet is big, and fate is fickle. Certain confluences of network mismanagement will cause a packet to get routed into an endless loop without ever reaching a destination. To keep the Internet from filling up with immortal packets wandering endlessly to and fro, the Network layer header specifies a finite lifetime for the packet. Every time the packet passes through a gateway, this *TTL* value is decremented by one. When the TTL reaches 0, no gateway will pass the packet on and its transmission fails.

The Transport Layer

The job of the Network layer is to see that a packet gets delivered to the destination IP address. After delivery, there is still the problem of what to do with it. Most networked devices are multiprocessing computers, and data in the packet might be intended for one of many possible processes. Worse, there could be many "conversations" consisting of streams of packets going back and forth between the destination system and other networked systems. In fact, there could well be more than one such stream going back and forth between the source and destination IP addresses of this particular packet. The Transport layer ensures that the packet does not end up in the wrong "conversation." In the previous packet dump, the Transport Layer header is marked "Transmission Control Protocol." There are two Transport layer protocols used by the TCP/IP stack:

Transmission Control Protocol (TCP) and User Datagram Protocol (UDP). These protocols will be discussed in more detail later in this section.

Ports

The fields marked Source Port and Destination Port indicate the ports associated with the respective source and destination IP addresses in the IP header.

In our packet dump, the source port is 8425 and the destination port is 23. Port 23 is reserved by convention for the telnet service. That means that any telnet session must start with an initial packet directed to port 23. Any process that listens for a request that way is called a *daemon* or *listener* and the function it serves is called a *service*. Your /etc/services file lists the ports assigned to several of the most common services.

> **Note**
>
> The /etc/services file is a reference list used by the system to provide a name to a service at a given port. It exists primarily as a convenience, since most daemons don't refer to it at all and will run whether or not the ports they use are listed.
>
> Record keeping is a virtue in the sysadmin, though, so if you install some new service on a system, give it a name that does not conflict with the existing list of services, and update /etc/services on all systems running that service.

Table 22.3 provides quick reference to some common services and their default ports.

TABLE 22.3   Assigned Ports of Common Services

Port	Service
21/tcp	FTP
22/tcp	SSH
23/tcp	telnet
25/tcp	SMTP mail
53/tcp	DNS
53/ucp	DNS
69/tcp	tftp
69/udp	tftp
80/tcp	WWW

TABLE 22.3   continued

Port	Service
111/tcp	RPC portmapper
111/udp	RPC portmapper
515/tcp	Printer
6000-6063/tcp	X Window System
6000-6063/udp	X Window System

Reserved Ports

It's a TCP/IP convention to restrict access to ports 1 through 1023 to the super-user. The idea was that each common service would be assigned a standard port throughout the Internet. The telnet server, for instance, would always be listening at port 23 if it was present at all. Non-superusers would be unable to use those ports, so that traffic involving port 23 at one end could be assumed to be a telnet communication.

Unfortunately, the prevalence of single-user PC's on the Internet has weakened this convention considerably. Many PC operating systems do not distinguish a particular administrative identity. Of those that do, the owner of the PC frequently has access to that identity. As a result, you can't be certain that traffic involving a well-known port actually implies that a particular service is being used. In particular, when a NIDS labels a particular thread of network traffic as "mail" based on port assignments, you can only be certain that the NIDS has detected traffic involving port 25.

TCP Wrappers

Many common services are offered through an intermediary listening process, inetd, which listens on various ports assigned to other services. If a request is detected at a port, inetd forwards that request to the service associated with that port. The configuration file that specifies which services inetd is to invoke for which ports is /etc/inetd.conf.

Normally, this is of interest only when the sysadmin implements a new service mediated by inetd, but the /etc/inetd.conf file is a core component of a long-standing security package called TCP Wrappers.

TCP Wrappers is available as of this writing (August 2001) from `ftp://ftp.porcupine.org/pub/security/tcp_wrappers_7.6.tar.gz`

The package, developed by Wietse Venema, substitutes an intermediary process in the inetd.conf file. When inetd receives a packet for one of its services, the intermediary process examines the packet before passing it to the appropriate service. Configuration files, usually /etc/hosts.allow and /etc/hosts.deny, specify that packets from certain IP addresses be rejected or responded to in various ways. All transactions are loggeds in the system log as well.

We *strongly* recommend that you consider using this package. Even if you are not in a position to deny any access to your system at all, the logs of the accesses can be extremely informative.

Connection-Oriented versus Connectionless Protocols

When you send a message on a postcard, you know that you are taking a chance that the message will arrive smudged or torn. In addition, the postal system will not send it back to you if it cannot be delivered. There's no way to discover whether the delivery was even successful. You might hope that the recipient will mention it to you someday if they receive it, but that is not part of the postal delivery system.

You still send postcards, though, because they are cheap and they require no envelopes to be stuffed and sealed. You write on them, stamp them, and send them off to their fate. In other words, there is little overhead work involved in their transmission, just as there is minimal effort by the delivery system to ensure their delivery.

Of course, if you have a long or very important message, you send it in an envelope. In fact, you can send it certified mail with a return receipt. To do this, you write the message, seal it in an envelope, stamp the envelope, pick up two small forms at the post office, fill them out, wait in line, and finally pay a couple of dollars or so beyond the cost of the stamp. In return, the postal delivery system tracks the delivery of the message, gets a signature to confirm a successful delivery, and sends you the signed delivery confirmation by return mail. You incur overhead labor and expense in return for the extra transmission mechanisms that provide a robust delivery service. The extra overhead is worthwhile because of the importance of the message.

Network protocol terminology makes a similar distinction between *connectionless* and *connection-oriented* communication protocols. A connectionless protocol simply transmits data to its destination without any mechanism to ensure that the data arrives intact or at all. A connection-oriented protocol, in contrast, requires that both the source and destination of the transmission communicate extensively back and forth about the state of the transmission itself. If a data packet fails to reach the destination, then the source must be notified and the packet must be retransmitted.

As with the postal example, you would expect connectionless protocols to be used when the data packet is relatively unimportant or, more often, when there is little risk that it won't arrive. Conversely, connection-oriented protocols are used when successful transmission is very important or when successful delivery is at higher risk. Communications that normally would take place within a local network, such as DNS resolution requests and NFS access, tend to use a connectionless protocol. Transmissions that normally would be routed out of a local network across the Internet, such as telnet, ftp, and DNS zone transfers, are likely to use a connection-oriented protocol.

> **Note**
>
> It is important to consider the previous paragraph in the context of the "layering" of the TCP/IP stack. A connectionless protocol can function above or below a connection-oriented protocol. For instance, while NFS uses a connectionless protocol at the Transport layer, the NFS software using the stack keeps track of data sequencing, transmission success, etc.

In the TCP/IP protocol suite, the two protocols are distinguished from each other in the transport layer. The connectionless protocol in the suite is called the User Datagram Protocol (UDP). The connection-oriented protocol is called the Transmission Control Protocol (TCP). Listing 22.1 shows an example of a TCP packet, while listing 22.2 illustrates a UDP packet.

LISTING 22.2   A UDP Packet

```
Frame 3 (126 on wire, 126 captured)
    Arrival Time: Jun 18, 2001 20:08:47.8952
    Time delta from previous packet: 0.000128 seconds
    Time relative to first packet: 0.001372 seconds
    Frame Number: 3
    Packet Length: 126 bytes
    Capture Length: 126 bytes
Ethernet II
    Destination: 00:60:3e:9a:9c:a0 (00:60:3e:9a:9c:a0)
    Source: 00:d0:d3:33:8b:58 (00:d0:d3:33:8b:58)
    Type: IP (0x0800)
Internet Protocol
    Version: 4
    Header length: 20 bytes
```

22

INTRUSION
DETECTION

LISTING 22.2   continued

```
        Differentiated Services Field: 0x00 (DSCP 0x00: Default; ECN: 0x00)
            0000 00.. = Differentiated Services Codepoint: Default (0x00)
            .... ..0. = ECN-Capable Transport (ECT): 0
            .... ...0 = ECN-CE: 0
        Total Length: 112
        Identification: 0xc527
        Flags: 0x00
            .0.. = Don't fragment: Not set
            ..0. = More fragments: Not set
        Fragment offset: 0
        Time to live: 126
        Protocol: UDP (0x11)
        Header checksum: 0x0ab0 (correct)
        Source: 20.100.97.204 (20.100.97.204)
        Destination: 211.117.181.14 (211.117.181.14)
User Datagram Protocol
        Source port: 1139 (1139)
        Destination port: 17162 (17162)
        Length: 92
        Checksum: 0x1299 (correct)
Data (84 bytes)

    0   0060 3e9a 9ca0 00d0 d333 8b58 0800 4500    .`>......3.X..E.
   10   0070 c527 0000 7e11 0ab0 1464 61cc d375    .p.'..~....Ua..u
   20   b50e 0473 430a 005c 1299 8004 d03b 4ae8    ...sC..\.....;J.
   30   295a fb6d d079 9c7e f578 913b 1123 bcf9    )Z.m.y.~.x.;.#..
   40   838f d0c2 ad57 0574 5694 b304 9f16 b02e    .....W.tV.......
   50   f4d4 a9a3 8a63 ae6f e343 0acb 1c5f e5cb    .....c.o.C..._..
   60   164b aa18 1f0f a402 f4c4 692c 20a4 c163    .K........i, ..c
   70   932a 32ca a316 2826 1e99 fcfc 1f07         .*2...(&......
```

Compare the Transport layer header in the packet that we have been looking at in Listing 22.1 to that of the packet in Listing 22.2. The header in Listing 22.2, the UDP packet, contains source and destination ports, a checksum, and information about the size of the encapsulated data. The corresponding header of the TCP packet in Figure 22.1 contains a variety of numeric values, flags, and options as well. This extra information is used by the various mechanisms that make this connection-oriented protocol robust. Some of these mechanisms will be described in the next several sections.

The Triple Handshake—Establishing a Connection

Before any data is exchanged using TCP, a *connection* must be established. The source of the data to be transmitted sends a TCP packet containing no data and with only the SYN flag set. The destination system responds with another TCP packet with no data and with the SYN and ACK flags set. Finally, the source system sends a packet, still with no data, that has only the ACK flag set. An example of such an exchange is shown in Listing 22.3.

LISTING 22.3   The Triple Handshake Frame 1 (74 on wire, 74 captured)

```
    Arrival Time: Jun 20, 2001 16:27:49.5329
    Time delta from previous packet: 0.000000 seconds
    Time relative to first packet: 0.000000 seconds
    Frame Number: 1
    Packet Length: 74 bytes
    Capture Length: 74 bytes
Ethernet II
    Destination: 00:d0:d3:33:8b:58 (00:d0:d3:33:8b:58)
    Source: 00:a0:24:80:52:44 (00:a0:24:80:52:44)
    Type: IP (0x0800)
Internet Protocol
    Version: 4
    Header length: 20 bytes
    Differentiated Services Field: 0x10 (DSCP 0x04: Unknown DSCP; ECN: 0x00)
        0001 00.. = Differentiated Services Codepoint: Unknown (0x04)
        .... ..0. = ECN-Capable Transport (ECT): 0
        .... ...0 = ECN-CE: 0
    Total Length: 60
    Identification: 0x1294
    Flags: 0x00
        .0.. = Don't fragment: Not set
        ..0. = More fragments: Not set
    Fragment offset: 0
    Time to live: 64
    Protocol: TCP (0x06)
    Header checksum: 0x605a (correct)
    Source: phil.unet.edu (20.100.253.12)
    Destination: unet7.unet.edu (20.100.6.7)
Transmission Control Protocol, Src Port: 8425 (8425), Dst Port: telnet (23),
Seq: 3708375094, Ack: 0
    Source port: 8425 (8425)
    Destination port: telnet (23)
    Sequence number: 3708375094
    Header length: 40 bytes
    Flags: 0x0002 (SYN)
        0... .... = Congestion Window Reduced (CWR): Not set
        .0.. .... = ECN-Echo: Not set
        ..0. .... = Urgent: Not set
        ...0 .... = Acknowledgment: Not set
        .... 0... = Push: Not set
        .... .0.. = Reset: Not set
        .... ..1. = Syn: Set
        .... ...0 = Fin: Not set
    Window size: 16384
    Checksum: 0xccf7 (correct)
```

22

INTRUSION
DETECTION

LISTING 22.3   continued

```
    Options: (20 bytes)
        Maximum segment size: 512 bytes
        NOP
        Window scale: 0 bytes
        NOP
        NOP
        Time stamp: tsval 2288547, tsecr 0

 0    00d0 d333 8b58 00a0 2480 5244 0800 4510    ...3.X..$.RD..E.
10    003c 1294 0000 4006 605a 1464 fd0c 1464    .<....@.`Z.U...U
20    0607 20e9 0017 dd09 5036 0000 0000 a002    .. .....P6......
30    4000 ccf7 0000 0204 0200 0103 0300 0101    @..............
40    080a 0022 eba3 0000 0000                   ..."......

Frame 2 (78 on wire, 78 captured)
    Arrival Time: Jun 20, 2001 16:27:49.5337
    Time delta from previous packet: 0.000801 seconds
    Time relative to first packet: 0.000801 seconds
    Frame Number: 2
    Packet Length: 78 bytes
    Capture Length: 78 bytes
Ethernet II
    Destination: 00:a0:24:80:52:44 (00:a0:24:80:52:44)
    Source: 00:d0:d3:33:8b:58 (00:d0:d3:33:8b:58)
    Type: IP (0x0800)
Internet Protocol
    Version: 4
    ·Header length: 20 bytes
    Differentiated Services Field: 0x00 (DSCP 0x00: Default; ECN: 0x00)
        0000 00.. = Differentiated Services Codepoint: Default (0x00)
        .... ..0. = ECN-Capable Transport (ECT): 0
        .... ...0 = ECN-CE: 0
    Total Length: 64
    Identification: 0x4f82
    Flags: 0x00
        .0.. = Don't fragment: Not set
        ..0. = More fragments: Not set
    Fragment offset: 0
    Time to live: 59
    Protocol: TCP (0x06)
    Header checksum: 0x2878 (correct)
    Source: unet7.unet.edu (20.100.6.7)
    Destination: phil.unet.edu (20.100.253.12)
Transmission Control Protocol, Src Port: telnet (23), Dst Port: 8425 (8425),
Seq: 1517696112, Ack: 3708375095
    Source port: telnet (23)
    Destination port: 8425 (8425)
    Sequence number: 1517696112
    Acknowledgement number: 3708375095
```

LISTING 22.3   continued

```
     Header length: 44 bytes
     Flags: 0x0012 (SYN, ACK)
          0... .... = Congestion Window Reduced (CWR): Not set
          .0.. .... = ECN-Echo: Not set
          ..0. .... = Urgent: Not set
          ...1 .... = Acknowledgment: Set
          .... 0... = Push: Not set
          .... .0.. = Reset: Not set
          .... ..1. = Syn: Set
          .... ...0 = Fin: Not set
     Window size: 49152
     Checksum: 0x3fd9 (correct)
     Options: (24 bytes)
          Maximum segment size: 1460 bytes
          NOP
          Window scale: 0 bytes
          NOP
          NOP
          Time stamp: tsval 3499318, tsecr 2288547
          NOP
          NOP
          SACK permitted

  0    00a0 2480 5244 00d0 d333 8b58 0800 4500    ..$.RD...3.X..E.
 10    0040 4f82 0000 3b06 2878 1464 0607 1464    .@O...;.(x.U...U
 20    fd0c 0017 20e9 5a76 3470 dd09 5037 b012    .... .Zv4p..P7..
 30    c000 3fd9 0000 0204 05b4 0103 0300 0101    ..?............
 40    080a 0035 6536 0022 eba3 0101 0402         ...5e6."......

Frame 3 (66 on wire, 66 captured)
     Arrival Time: Jun 20, 2001 16:27:49.5339
     Time delta from previous packet: 0.000176 seconds
     Time relative to first packet: 0.000977 seconds
     Frame Number: 3
     Packet Length: 66 bytes
     Capture Length: 66 bytes
Ethernet II
     Destination: 00:d0:d3:33:8b:58 (00:d0:d3:33:8b:58)
     Source: 00:a0:24:80:52:44 (00:a0:24:80:52:44)
     Type: IP (0x0800)
Internet Protocol
     Version: 4
     Header length: 20 bytes
     Differentiated Services Field: 0x10 (DSCP 0x04: Unknown DSCP; ECN: 0x00)
          0001 00.. = Differentiated Services Codepoint: Unknown (0x04)
          .... ..0. = ECN-Capable Transport (ECT): 0
          .... ...0 = ECN-CE: 0
     Total Length: 52
     Identification: 0x2943
```

22

INTRUSION
DETECTION

LISTING 22.3   continued

```
    Flags: 0x00
        .0.. = Don't fragment: Not set
        ..0. = More fragments: Not set
    Fragment offset: 0
    Time to live: 64
    Protocol: TCP (0x06)
    Header checksum: 0x49b3 (correct)
    Source: phil.unet.edu (20.100.253.12)
    Destination: unet7.unet.edu (20.100.6.7)
Transmission Control Protocol, Src Port: 8425 (8425), Dst Port: telnet (23),
Seq: 3708375095, Ack: 1517696113
    Source port: 8425 (8425)
    Destination port: telnet (23)
    Sequence number: 3708375095
    Acknowledgement number: 1517696113
    Header length: 32 bytes
    Flags: 0x0010 (ACK)
        0... .... = Congestion Window Reduced (CWR): Not set
        .0.. .... = ECN-Echo: Not set
        ..0. .... = Urgent: Not set
        ...1 .... = Acknowledgment: Set
        .... 0... = Push: Not set
        .... .0.. = Reset: Not set
        .... ..0. = Syn: Not set
        .... ...0 = Fin: Not set
    Window size: 16500
    Checksum: 0x0031 (correct)
    Options: (12 bytes)
        NOP
        NOP
        Time stamp: tsval 2288547, tsecr 3499318

 0   00d0 d333 8b58 00a0 2480 5244 0800 4510    ...3.X..$.RD..E.
10   0034 2943 0000 4006 49b3 1464 fd0c 1464    .4)C..@.I..U...U
20   0607 20e9 0017 dd09 5037 5a76 3471 8010    .. .....P7Zv4q..
30   4074 0031 0000 0101 080a 0022 eba3 0035    @t.1......."...5
40   6536                                       e6
```

This exchange is called the *Triple Handshake* and is used to establish the readiness of
both ends of the exchange to communicate. It also establishes the *sequence and acknowledgement numbers* that will be used to maintain the order of transmitted packets and
guard against the insertion of third-party packets into the exchange.

The Triple Handshake and Address Spoofing

It is possible to generate TCP/IP packets with a "forged" source IP address in order to mask the packet's origin. This practice is called "spoofing" the address. The TCP protocol, however, requires that the 3-way handshake be completed successfully before any data can start flowing. The 3-way handshake involves the first recipient (the server) to respond to the sender with a SYN-ACK packet, and the sender must respond with an ACK to the SYN-ACK to establish the connection. If the IP address of either host is forged, it is unlikely that this can succeed. Conversely, a connectionless server has no way to verify that the source address in the transport protocol level is actually that of the sender of the packet. This is very important to keep in mind when doing IDS data analysis.

Sequence and Acknowledgement Numbers

The first packet in Listing 22.3 has the sequence number 3708375094. The second packet responds with an acknowledgement number of 3708375095, one more than the sequence number of the packet that it is acknowledging. The sequence number of the second packet is 1517696112, and it is acknowledged in the third packet with acknowledgement number 1517696113. Note also that the sequence number of the third packet is the same as the acknowledgement number of the second. We won't go through the details of the rules by which these numbers are generated and incremented, but this example illustrates how the source of the data can tell which packets have been received by the destination by the acknowledgement numbers that it receives in return.

Tearing Down a Connection (FIN, ACK)

As might be expected after the work involved in establishing a connection, there is extra work involved in ending a connection as well. Listing 22.4 illustrates the mechanism.

LISTING 22.4 Tearing Down a Connection

```
Frame 81 (66 on wire, 66 captured)
    Arrival Time: Jun 20, 2001 16:28:02.9521
    Time delta from previous packet: 3.346538 seconds
    Time relative to first packet: 13.419182 seconds
    Frame Number: 81
    Packet Length: 66 bytes
    Capture Length: 66 bytes
Ethernet II
    Destination: 00:d0:d3:33:8b:58 (00:d0:d3:33:8b:58)
    Source: 00:a0:24:80:52:44 (00:a0:24:80:52:44)
    Type: IP (0x0800)
```

LISTING 22.4 continued

```
Internet Protocol
    Version: 4
    Header length: 20 bytes
    Differentiated Services Field: 0x10 (DSCP 0x04: Unknown DSCP; ECN: 0x00)
        0001 00.. = Differentiated Services Codepoint: Unknown (0x04)
        .... ..0. = ECN-Capable Transport (ECT): 0
        .... ...0 = ECN-CE: 0
    Total Length: 52
    Identification: 0x18d9
    Flags: 0x00
        .0.. = Don't fragment: Not set
        ..0. = More fragments: Not set
    Fragment offset: 0
    Time to live: 64
    Protocol: TCP (0x06)
    Header checksum: 0x5a1d (correct)
    Source: phil.unet.edu (20.100.253.12)
    Destination: unet7.unet.edu (20.100.6.7)
Transmission Control Protocol, Src Port: 8425 (8425), Dst Port: telnet (23),
Seq: 3708375188, Ack: 1517697435
    Source port: 8425 (8425)
    Destination port: telnet (23)
    Sequence number: 3708375188
    Acknowledgement number: 1517697435
    Header length: 32 bytes
    Flags: 0x0011 (FIN, ACK)
        0... .... = Congestion Window Reduced (CWR): Not set
        .0.. .... = ECN-Echo: Not set
        ..0. .... = Urgent: Not set
        ...1 .... = Acknowledgment: Set
        .... 0... = Push: Not set
        .... .0.. = Reset: Not set
        .... ..0. = Syn: Not set
        .... ...1 = Fin: Set
    Window size: 16500
    Checksum: 0xfa7a (correct)
    Options: (12 bytes)
        NOP
        NOP
        Time stamp: tsval 2288574, tsecr 3499337

 0   00d0 d333 8b58 00a0 2480 5244 0800 4510    ...3.X..$.RD..E.
10   0034 18d9 0000 4006 5a1d 1464 fd0c 1464    .4....@.Z..U...U
20   0607 20e9 0017 dd09 5094 5a76 399b 8011    .. .....P.Zv9...
30   4074 fa7a 0000 0101 080a 0022 ebbe 0035    @t.z......."...5
40   6549                                       eI

Frame 82 (66 on wire, 66 captured)
    Arrival Time: Jun 20, 2001 16:28:02.9530
```

LISTING 22.4   continued

```
    Time delta from previous packet: 0.000954 seconds
    Time relative to first packet: 13.420136 seconds
    Frame Number: 82
    Packet Length: 66 bytes
    Capture Length: 66 bytes
Ethernet II
    Destination: 00:a0:24:80:52:44 (00:a0:24:80:52:44)
    Source: 00:d0:d3:33:8b:58 (00:d0:d3:33:8b:58)
    Type: IP (0x0800)
Internet Protocol
    Version: 4
    Header length: 20 bytes
    Differentiated Services Field: 0x10 (DSCP 0x04: Unknown DSCP; ECN: 0x00)
        0001 00.. = Differentiated Services Codepoint: Unknown (0x04)
        .... ..0. = ECN-Capable Transport (ECT): 0
        .... ...0 = ECN-CE: 0
    Total Length: 52
    Identification: 0x57fa
    Flags: 0x00
        .0.. = Don't fragment: Not set
        ..0. = More fragments: Not set
    Fragment offset: 0
    Time to live: 59
    Protocol: TCP (0x06)
    Header checksum: 0x1ffc (correct)
    Source: unet7.unet.edu (20.100.6.7)
    Destination: phil.unet.edu (20.100.253.12)
Transmission Control Protocol, Src Port: telnet (23), Dst Port: 8425 (8425),
Seq: 1517697435, Ack: 3708375189
    Source port: telnet (23)
    Destination port: 8425 (8425)
    Sequence number: 1517697435
    Acknowledgement number: 3708375189
    Header length: 32 bytes
    Flags: 0x0010 (ACK)
        0... .... = Congestion Window Reduced (CWR): Not set
        .0.. .... = ECN-Echo: Not set
        ..0. .... = Urgent: Not set
        ...1 .... = Acknowledgment: Set
        .... 0... = Push: Not set
        .... .0.. = Reset: Not set
        .... ..0. = Syn: Not set
        .... ...0 = Fin: Not set
    Window size: 49152
    Checksum: 0x7ae7 (correct)
    Options: (12 bytes)
        NOP
        NOP
        Time stamp: tsval 3499344, tsecr 2288574
```

22

INTRUSION
DETECTION

Listing 22.4   continued

```
 0   00a0 2480 5244 00d0 d333 8b58 0800 4510    ..$.RD...3.X..E.
10   0034 57fa 0000 3b06 1ffc 1464 0607 1464    .4W...;....U...U
20   fd0c 0017 20e9 5a76 399b dd09 5095 8010    .... .Zv9...P...
30   c000 7ae7 0000 0101 080a 0035 6550 0022    ..z........5eP."
40   ebbe                                       ..
```

```
Frame 83 (66 on wire, 66 captured)
    Arrival Time: Jun 20, 2001 16:28:02.9557
    Time delta from previous packet: 0.002672 seconds
    Time relative to first packet: 13.422808 seconds
    Frame Number: 83
    Packet Length: 66 bytes
    Capture Length: 66 bytes
Ethernet II
    Destination: 00:a0:24:80:52:44 (00:a0:24:80:52:44)
    Source: 00:d0:d3:33:8b:58 (00:d0:d3:33:8b:58)
    Type: IP (0x0800)
Internet Protocol
    Version: 4
    Header length: 20 bytes
    Differentiated Services Field: 0x10 (DSCP 0x04: Unknown DSCP; ECN: 0x00)
        0001 00.. = Differentiated Services Codepoint: Unknown (0x04)
        .... ..0. = ECN-Capable Transport (ECT): 0
        .... ...0 = ECN-CE: 0
    Total Length: 52
    Identification: 0x57fb
    Flags: 0x00
        .0.. = Don't fragment: Not set
        ..0. = More fragments: Not set
    Fragment offset: 0
    Time to live: 59
    Protocol: TCP (0x06)
    Header checksum: 0x1ffb (correct)
    Source: unet7.unet.edu (20.100.6.7)
    Destination: phil.unet.edu (20.100.253.12)
Transmission Control Protocol, Src Port: telnet (23), Dst Port: 8425 (8425),
Seq: 1517697435, Ack: 3708375189
    Source port: telnet (23)
    Destination port: 8425 (8425)
    Sequence number: 1517697435
    Acknowledgement number: 3708375189
    Header length: 32 bytes
    Flags: 0x0011 (FIN, ACK)
        0... .... = Congestion Window Reduced (CWR): Not set
        .0.. .... = ECN-Echo: Not set
        ..0. .... = Urgent: Not set
        ...1 .... = Acknowledgment: Set
        .... 0... = Push: Not set
        .... .0.. = Reset: Not set
```

LISTING 22.4   continued

```
        .... ..0. = Syn: Not set
        .... ...1 = Fin: Set
    Window size: 49152
    Checksum: 0x7ae6 (correct)
    Options: (12 bytes)
        NOP
        NOP
        Time stamp: tsval 3499344, tsecr 2288574

 0   00a0 2480 5244 00d0 d333 8b58 0800 4510    ..$.RD...3.X..E.
10   0034 57fb 0000 3b06 1ffb 1464 0607 1464    .4W...;....U...U
20   fd0c 0017 20e9 5a76 399b dd09 5095 8011    .... .Zv9...P...
30   c000 7ae6 0000 0101 080a 0035 6550 0022    ..z........5eP."
40   ebbe                                       ..
```

```
Frame 84 (66 on wire, 66 captured)
    Arrival Time: Jun 20, 2001 16:28:02.9559
    Time delta from previous packet: 0.000171 seconds
    Time relative to first packet: 13.422979 seconds
    Frame Number: 84
    Packet Length: 66 bytes
    Capture Length: 66 bytes
Ethernet II
    Destination: 00:d0:d3:33:8b:58 (00:d0:d3:33:8b:58)
    Source: 00:a0:24:80:52:44 (00:a0:24:80:52:44)
    Type: IP (0x0800)
Internet Protocol
    Version: 4
    Header length: 20 bytes
    Differentiated Services Field: 0x10 (DSCP 0x04: Unknown DSCP; ECN: 0x00)
        0001 00.. = Differentiated Services Codepoint: Unknown (0x04)
        .... ..0. = ECN-Capable Transport (ECT): 0
        .... ...0 = ECN-CE: 0
    Total Length: 52
    Identification: 0x5d81
    Flags: 0x00
        .0.. = Don't fragment: Not set
        ..0. = More fragments: Not set
    Fragment offset: 0
    Time to live: 64
    Protocol: TCP (0x06)
    Header checksum: 0x1575 (correct)
    Source: phil.unet.edu (20.100.253.12)
    Destination: unet7.unet.edu (20.100.6.7)
Transmission Control Protocol, Src Port: 8425 (8425), Dst Port: telnet (23),
Seq: 3708375189, Ack: 1517697436
    Source port: 8425 (8425)
    Destination port: telnet (23)
    Sequence number: 3708375189
```

22

INTRUSION
DETECTION

LISTING 22.4   continued

```
Acknowledgement number: 1517697436
Header length: 32 bytes
Flags: 0x0010 (ACK)
        0... .... = Congestion Window Reduced (CWR): Not set
        .0.. .... = ECN-Echo: Not set
        ..0. .... = Urgent: Not set
        ...1 .... = Acknowledgment: Set
        .... 0... = Push: Not set
        .... .0.. = Reset: Not set
        .... ..0. = Syn: Not set
        .... ...0 = Fin: Not set
Window size: 16499
Checksum: 0xfa73 (correct)
Options: (12 bytes)
        NOP
        NOP
        Time stamp: tsval 2288574, tsecr 3499344

 0   00d0 d333 8b58 00a0 2480 5244 0800 4510    ...3.X..$.RD..E.
10   0034 5d81 0000 4006 1575 1464 fd0c 1464    .4]...@..u.U...U
20   0607 20e9 0017 dd09 5095 5a76 399c 8010    .. .....P.Zv9...
30   4073 fa73 0000 0101 080a 0022 ebbe 0035    @s.s......."...5
40   6550                                       eP
```

When either side of the exchange is finished transmitting data, it sends a packet with the FIN flag set. The ACK flag also is set to acknowledge the receipt of some previous packet from the other end. Note that this packet may carry data. The FIN flag indicates that the data in this packet is the last that will be transmitted. In response, the recipient of the FIN packet sends a packet with the ACK flag set and with an acknowledgement number corresponding to the sequence number of the FIN packet.

At this point, the connection is called *half-closed*. One side has signaled that it has finished transmitting data, but the other side still might have data to transmit. In this case, though, the other side signals the end of its transmission with a FIN flag in the last packet, and an ACK packet is sent in response. The connection has been *torn down* and is now considered *closed*. The respective ports that each system had allocated for the connection are now free for reallocation.

The RST Flag

Another flag worth noting here is the reset, or RST, flag. Receipt of this flag is a signal that something has gone very wrong and that the connection no longer exists.

Exploiting the TCP/IP Protocol

The rules of the TCP/IP protocol are designed to ensure flexible, robust, reliable communication—as long as everyone follows the rules. Sadly, as noted at the beginning of this chapter, not everyone using the Internet is motivated by the highest of principles. This section describes a few of the more common abuses of the protocol and the services that depend on it, to illustrate the sort of things that a NIDS can watch for.

Buffer Overflows

Go to the network security site of your choice, and look at the most recent five exploits. At least three, and quite possibly all five of them will involve *buffer overflows*. These actually result from errors in the original program code from which the various network services such as telnet, ftp, portmapper, and sendmail are built. Suppose that you are filling out a form on the World Wide Web. You enter your name, Andy. Each character in that name uses a byte of memory for a total of 4 bytes. Somewhere there is a program that accepts that string of 4 bytes to process the form. That program, implicitly or explicitly, has set aside a certain amount of memory—say, 20 bytes—to store the bytes of the name for processing.

Suppose that instead of using the name Andy, we enter PhilippusAureolusTheophrastusBombastusvonHohenheim. This exceeds the allocated 20 bytes. A good program will, in effect, realize that too many bytes have come in and truncate or otherwise deal with the excess. Such checking requires extra effort and extra time from the programmers who often are being driven by deadlines imposed by a marketing department. If the entire name is stored in memory, then it must exceed the allocated 20 bytes. It might end up occupying memory that was meant to store some other data entirely.

Depending on the way the code is written and the way the particular operating system manages memory, it might be possible to provide a network service with a string so long that it overwrites not just the stored data, but the program and other things in the memory as well. Computers are controlled by the contents of their memories. It is sometimes possible to "overflow" an allocated segment of memory by a precise amount, to overwrite another segment with instructions that result in the attacker gaining access to or control of the computer.

These attacks are quite common. As of this writing, Code Red Versions 1 and 2 are still very much extant. These worms enter target systems through a buffer overflow attack.

Port Scanning

Buffer overflow attacks, like many others, are specific to particular services on particular operating systems. As of this writing, for example, many Red Hat Linux systems are still vulnerable to a buffer overflow attack on the RPC statd service.

To exploit a particular service, a hacker must find a computer offering that service. To attack a specific computer, a list of the services that it is offering will be the first order of business. In both cases, the hacker will want to collect intelligence through *port scanning*, to plan an effective approach.

As noted earlier, specific services are associated with specific ports. A hacker wanting to know whether a computer offers telnet service can try to establish a connection to port 23 on that computer. A hacker wanting to use a telnet exploit on any available computer on a subnet can try to establish a connection to port 23 at each IP address in turn. This will provide a "map" of that subnet for telnet service.

Establishing a connection by the rules means a triple handshake to set it up and a four-packet FIN-ACK exchange to tear it down. The systems involved might log these attempts. Happily for the hacker, the TCP/IP protocol provides a loophole that both speeds the probe and helps hide it from detection.

Consider the Triple Handshake. It is initiated by a SYN packet, which elicits a SYN-ACK packet in response, which, in turn, is acknowledged by an ACK packet. That said, suppose that you send a SYN packet to port 23 on a target computer. If it offers telnet service, it responds with a SYN-ACK. If not, it responds with the RST packet described earlier. If it responds with the SYN-ACK, the system has a telnet server. There is now no use for the actual connection, so there is no reason to finish establishing one with that final ACK packet. Eventually (in seconds or minutes) the target computer will stop waiting for that packet and will go about its business without any record of a telnet connection being established.

Because it involves an exchange of only two packets and leaves no records on most systems, the *SYN scan* is the most popular probe used on the Internet.

By the way, the target system's wait for that final ACK packet will indeed time out harmlessly, as stated earlier. Suppose, however, that instead of one SYN packet, several thousand such packets are transmitted at once. Until they all time out, all the resources allocated for network communications on the target system would be tied up, all without any record of a connection. For all intents and purposes, that system would be cut off from the Internet for the duration of the timeout interval. This is called the *SYN flood* attack.

Positive Signatures

Whether or not the target systems record the buffer overflow attacks or the SYN probes, these events are usually clearly discernible by examining the network traffic.

The buffer overflow attack generates a large packet with a payload that is mostly "filler" to overwrite a precise amount of memory. The remainder of the payload consists of the machine code intended to overwrite that particular part of memory and give control to the attacker. Because the machine code must be precisely located in the packet payload, examination of packets for that specific string of code in the particular location in the payload will reveal that attempt. (Note that this assumes that the attack is known and that the string of code previously was identified—this normally happens within a day of a new attack.)

SYN packets are a common feature of any traffic on the Internet. However, you generally don't see 20 or more of them from the same source in a couple of seconds. If the SYN packets are being used to map all the ports on a single target, you will see a stream of packets coming from one source and going to one destination.

Negative Signatures

NIDS don't actually detect intrusions. They detect events. Specifically, they detect the events that they are told to look for. Although there is research into "adaptive" NIDS that decide for themselves what to look for, most of the NIDS on the market (and for free) work from rules specifying specific signatures.

There is a huge database of rules for Snort, the network sniffer used to build the NIDS described later in this chapter. These rules target known exploits as specifically as possible by their known characteristics. When designing NIDS rules, however, be sure to include rules to detect what *shouldn't be there*.

Suppose that you have a single, well-secured FTP server on your local network. A rule that simply detects any traffic to port 21 on any system *other* than your server could well reveal that some of your other systems are providing MP3s to the Internet at large (this happens more than you might think).

If you have a firewall blocking all telnet traffic into your network, a rule that detects any SYN packet to port 23 with a source IP outside your network suggests a problem if it is triggered inside the firewall.

Although it takes more imagination to create negative signatures than positive ones, the effort is generally worthwhile for anyone concerned with securing a network and systems.

Note

False positives will occur. Transmitting a file with the text contents of this chapter, for example, could trigger a positive detection from several rules of an IDS.

A Word About Firewalls

Firewalls deserve a book of their own, and many books have been written on this topic. For our purposes, a firewall is a device that, like a gateway, sits between a local network or subnet and the rest of the Internet. Unlike a gateway, it decides what traffic to pass in either direction, based on a set of rules. A rule for the situation with one official ftp server might be that incoming TCP packets with destination port 21 can pass only if their destination IP is the official ftp server. More complex firewalls not only apply rules but also can act as intermediaries to network communication. Such a firewall, might accept a packet from the Internet destined for the ftp server and generate *another* packet internally to send to the ftp server. The ftp server will then respond to the firewall, which then generates a separate response packet to the external requestor. In such a system, every connection from the Internet appears to be with the firewall. A smart firewall, for instance, might be designed to limit the rate of SYN packets that it generates internally. A SYN flood from the Internet might isolate the firewall (and the subnet that it serves) temporarily, but systems inside the firewall still would communicate on their own networks.

Bottom line: When a policy has been established about what sort of traffic will and won't be allowed in or out of a network, a firewall is the device that implements that policy.

Moral: Because your firewall is a device to implement policy, no firewall can be more effective than the policy that it implements.

Note that the moral leaves open the possibility that a firewall might not even be as good as the policy that it implements. If the firewall allows only ftp connections to the ftp server, but someone inside the firewall dials into an ISP through a dial-up PPP connection, then that PPP connection can be a second way into the local network from the Internet, completely bypassing the firewall and its restrictions.

> **Note**
>
> Demilitarized zone (DMZ) is a term used in various ways, but it commonly refers to the part of a local network that lies outside the firewall but inside the gateway. In other words, it is on the local network but is not protected by the firewall. It is fairly common practice to put servers that exist for widespread use, such as Web servers and domain name servers, outside the firewall on hosts that get extra care and scrutiny to maintain their security, while placing systems exclusively dedicated for internal use inside the firewall. In such cases, the firewall might allow a few select systems on the inside to communicate with the systems in the DMZ. The theory is that security efforts can be focused on the servers in the DMZ while the firewall protects the internal systems.

22

INTRUSION DETECTION

Snort

If you want to monitor the traffic on your network for free, try Snort. If your organization mandates the use of commercial software, try Snort anyway; there is a commercial, Snort-based IDS available from Sourcefire (http://www.sourcefire.com). Snort originally was developed by Marty Roesch as a network traffic monitor for a honeypot. Since then, Marty and others have enhanced it until it can function as a host-based intrusion-detection system, a network traffic sensor gathering packet data, an analysis engine to examine collected data, and, still, a honeypot monitor. In fact, Snort is capable of doing all of these at the same time, but it probably won't do them very well unless it is either hosted on a very fast computer or situated on a very slow network.

> **Note**
>
> A honeypot is a system designed to be attacked so that you can see how it's being done.

The power of Snort comes from its *rulesets*. The rules in the rulesets are written using a simple, flexible syntax that allows it to detect a very wide range of network events. It also is designed to accept modular pre- and post-processors that can extend Snort's capability to detect, analyze, and report on patterns in network traffic.

This section does not examine every feature of Snort. The most fundamental features are described to allow you to invoke Snort for simple network monitoring and to provide the context for Snort in a larger, distributed NIDS.

Installing Snort

Before you can build Snort, you must install the libpcap library. This library is available from `http://www.tcpdump.org` in its latest version as libpcap.tar.Z. An edited libpcap installation session under Solaris is shown in Listing 22.5.

Snort can be downloaded from `http://www.snort.org`. To compile it, download the compressed tar file and then follow Open Source build and install procedures. A Solaris installation using defaults is illustrated in Listing 22.6.

LISTING 22.5   Libpcap Installation

```
[1]# pwd

/usr/local/src
[2]# zcat libpcap.tar.Z | tar xvf -

x libpcap-0.4/CHANGES, 8874 bytes, 18 tape blocks
x libpcap-0.4/FILES, 588 bytes, 2 tape blocks
x libpcap-0.4/INSTALL, 13689 bytes, 27 tape blocks
x libpcap-0.4/Makefile.in, 4825 bytes, 10 tape blocks
.
.
.
x libpcap-0.4/savefile.c, 9309 bytes, 19 tape blocks
x libpcap-0.4/scanner.l, 4436 bytes, 9 tape blocks
[3]# cd libpcap-0.4/

[4]# ./configure
creating cache ./config.cache
.
.
.
checking for a BSD compatible install... ./install-sh -c
updating cache ./config.cache
creating ./config.status
creating Makefile
[5]# make

gcc -O2 -I.  -DHAVE_MALLOC_H=1 -DHAVE_SYS_IOCCOM_H=1 -DHAVE_SYS_SOCKIO_H=1 -
DHAVE_STRERROR=1 -DHAVE_SYS_BUFMOD_H=1 -DHAVE_SOLARIS=1 -DLBL_ALIGN=1   -c
./pcap-dlpi.c
```

LISTING 22.5 continued

```
gcc -O2 -I.  -DHAVE_MALLOC_H=1 -DHAVE_SYS_IOCCOM_H=1 -DHAVE_SYS_SOCKIO_H=1 -
DHAVE_STRERROR=1 -DHAVE_SYS_BUFMOD_H=1 -DHAVE_SOLARIS=1 -DLBL_ALIGN=1  -c
./pcap.c
.
.

.
ar rc libpcap.a pcap-dlpi.o pcap.o inet.o gencode.o optimize.o nametoaddr.o
etherent.o savefile.o bpf_filter.o bpf_image.o scanner.o grammar.o version.o
ranlib libpcap.a
[6]# make install

./install-sh -c -m 444 -o bin -g bin libpcap.a /usr/local/lib/libpcap.a
ranlib /usr/local/lib/libpcap.a
[7]#
```

LISTING 22.6 Snort Installation

```
[1]# pwd
[2]# gzip -dc snort-1.7.tar.gz | tar xvf -

x snort-1.7/contrib/ACID-0.9.5b9.tar.gz, 48550 bytes, 95 tape blocks
x snort-1.7/contrib/SnortSnarf-111500.1.tar.gz, 73745 bytes, 145 tape blocks
.
.

.
x snort-1.7/LICENSE, 17989 bytes, 36 tape blocks
x snort-1.7/cdefs.h, 3615 bytes, 8 tape blocks
[3]# cd snort-1.7

[4]#./configure
creating cache ./config.cache
checking for a BSD compatible install... ./install-sh -c
.
.

.
checking for a BSD compatible install... ./install-sh -c
updating cache ./config.cache
creating ./config.status
creating Makefile
creating config.h
[5]# make

gcc -DHAVE_CONFIG_H -I. -I. -I.    -DBSD_COMP -I/usr/local/ssl/include -
DENABLE_SSL  -g -O2 -Wall  -c snort.c
gcc -DHAVE_CONFIG_H -I. -I. -I.    -DBSD_COMP -I/usr/local/ssl/include -
DENABLE_SSL  -g -O2 -Wall  -c log.c
.
.

.
```

LISTING 22.6   continued

```
gcc -DHAVE_CONFIG_H -I. -I. -I.   -DBSD_COMP -I/usr/local/ssl/include -
DENABLE_SSL  -g -O2 -Wall  -c spp_anomsensor.c
gcc  -g -O2 -Wall  -L/usr/local/ssl/lib -o snort  snort.o log.o decode.o
mstring.o rules.o plugbase.o sp_pattern_match.o sp_tcp_flag_check.o
sp_icmp_type_check.o sp_icmp_code_check.o sp_ttl_check.o sp_ip_id_check.o
sp_tcp_ack_check.o sp_tcp_seq_check.o sp_dsize_check.o spp_http_decode.o
spp_minfrag.o spp_portscan.o sp_ipoption_check.o sp_rpc_check.o
sp_icmp_id_check.o sp_icmp_seq_check.o sp_respond.o spo_alert_syslog.o
spo_log_tcpdump.o spo_database.o sp_session.o spp_defrag.o parser.o
spo_alert_fast.o spo_alert_full.o spo_alert_smb.o spo_alert_unixsock.o
sp_react.o spo_xml.o sp_ip_tos_check.o spp_tcp_stream.o snprintf.o checksum.o
sp_reference.o sp_ip_fragbits.o spp_anomsensor.o  -lpcap -lm -lsocket -lnsl -
lssl -lcrypto
[6]# make install

make[1]: Entering directory `/usr/local/src/snort-1.7'
/bin/sh ./mkinstalldirs /usr/local/bin
  ./install-sh -c  snort /usr/local/bin/snort
make  install-man8
make[2]: Entering directory `/usr/local/src/snort-1.7'
/bin/sh ./mkinstalldirs /usr/local/man/man8
mkdir /usr/local/man
mkdir /usr/local/man/man8
  ./install-sh -c -m 644 ./snort.8 /usr/local/man/man8/snort.8
make[2]: Leaving directory `/usr/local/src/snort-1.7'
make[1]: Leaving directory `/usr/local/src/snort-1.7'
[7]#
```

Trying Out Snort

On most systems, you will need root privileges to run Snort on the network interface, sniffing live traffic. Secure those privileges and type the following:

```
snort -i <if> -vd
```

Here, `<if>` is the name of your network interface—eth0, hme1, or whatever it happens to be. (You can get a list by typing `netstat -i`.)

If the output streams by too quickly, hit Ctrl+C to stop and pipe the output through more. Listing 22.7 provides a sample of Snort output.

LISTING 22.7   Snort Output

```
05/27-21:33:30.538316 192.168.40.3:3157 -> 10.200.43.5:28
TCP TTL:64 TOS:0x0 ID:4267 IpLen:20 DgmLen:60 DF
******S* Seq: 0x28EDAF85 Ack: 0x0 Win: 0x7960 TcpLen: 40
TCP Options (5) => MSS: 3884 SackOK TS: 969751 0 NOP WS: 0
```

LISTING 22.7   continued

```
=+=+=+=+=+=+=+=+=+=+=+=+=+=+=+=+=+=+=+=+=+=+=+=+=+=+=+=+=+=+=+=+=+=+=+
05/27-21:33:30.538349 10.200.43.5:28 -> 192.168.40.3:3157
TCP TTL:255 TOS:0x0 ID:4268 IpLen:20 DgmLen:40
***A*R** Seq: 0x0 Ack: 0x28EDAF86 Win: 0x0 TcpLen: 20
=+=+=+=+=+=+=+=+=+=+=+=+=+=+=+=+=+=+=+=+=+=+=+=+=+=+=+=+=+=+=+=+=+=+=+
05/27-21:33:30.539381 192.168.40.3:3158 -> 10.200.43.5:27
TCP TTL:64 TOS:0x0 ID:4269 IpLen:20 DgmLen:60 DF
******S* Seq: 0x288DABD8 Ack: 0x0 Win: 0x7960 TcpLen: 40
TCP Options (5) => MSS: 3884 SackOK TS: 969751 0 NOP WS: 0
=+=+=+=+=+=+=+=+=+=+=+=+=+=+=+=+=+=+=+=+=+=+=+=+=+=+=+=+=+=+=+=+=+=+=+
05/27-21:33:30.539414 10.200.43.5:27 -> 192.168.40.3:3158
TCP TTL:255 TOS:0x0 ID:4270 IpLen:20 DgmLen:40
***A*R** Seq: 0x0 Ack: 0x288DABD9 Win: 0x0 TcpLen: 20
=+=+=+=+=+=+=+=+=+=+=+=+=+=+=+=+=+=+=+=+=+=+=+=+=+=+=+=+=+=+=+=+=+=+=+
05/27-21:52:41.379216 192.168.40.3:3220 -> 10.200.43.5:26
TCP TTL:64 TOS:0x0 ID:4271 IpLen:20 DgmLen:60 DF
******S* Seq: 0x70CA68C4 Ack: 0x0 Win: 0x7960 TcpLen: 40
TCP Options (5) => MSS: 3884 SackOK TS: 1084835 0 NOP WS: 0
=+=+=+=+=+=+=+=+=+=+=+=+=+=+=+=+=+=+=+=+=+=+=+=+=+=+=+=+=+=+=+=+=+=+=+
05/27-21:52:41.379250 10.200.43.5:26 -> 192.168.40.3:3220
TCP TTL:64 TOS:0x0 ID:4272 IpLen:20 DgmLen:60 DF
***A**S* Seq: 0x703F081A Ack: 0x70CA68C5 Win: 0x7960 TcpLen: 40
TCP Options (5) => MSS: 3884 SackOK TS: 1084835 1084835 NOP WS: 0
=+=+=+=+=+=+=+=+=+=+=+=+=+=+=+=+=+=+=+=+=+=+=+=+=+=+=+=+=+=+=+=+=+=+=+
05/27-21:33:30.542380 192.168.40.3:3160 -> 10.200.43.5:25
TCP TTL:64 TOS:0x0 ID:4273 IpLen:20 DgmLen:60 DF
******S* Seq: 0x292D252F Ack: 0x0 Win: 0x7960 TcpLen: 40
TCP Options (5) => MSS: 3884 SackOK TS: 969751 0 NOP WS: 0
=+=+=+=+=+=+=+=+=+=+=+=+=+=+=+=+=+=+=+=+=+=+=+=+=+=+=+=+=+=+=+=+=+=+=+
05/27-21:33:30.542418 10.200.43.5:25 -> 192.168.40.3:3160
TCP TTL:255 TOS:0x0 ID:4274 IpLen:20 DgmLen:40
***A*R** Seq: 0x0 Ack: 0x292D2530 Win: 0x0 TcpLen: 20
=+=+=+=+=+=+=+=+=+=+=+=+=+=+=+=+=+=+=+=+=+=+=+=+=+=+=+=+=+=+=+=+=+=+=+
05/27-21:33:30.543456 192.168.40.3:3161 -> 10.200.43.5:24
TCP TTL:64 TOS:0x0 ID:4275 IpLen:20 DgmLen:60 DF
******S* Seq: 0x29008DB9 Ack: 0x0 Win: 0x7960 TcpLen: 40
TCP Options (5) => MSS: 3884 SackOK TS: 969751 0 NOP WS: 0
=+=+=+=+=+=+=+=+=+=+=+=+=+=+=+=+=+=+=+=+=+=+=+=+=+=+=+=+=+=+=+=+=+=+=+
05/27-21:33:30.543488 10.200.43.5:24 -> 192.168.40.3:3161  ·
TCP TTL:255 TOS:0x0 ID:4276 IpLen:20 DgmLen:40
***A*R** Seq: 0x0 Ack: 0x29008DBA Win: 0x0 TcpLen: 20
=+=+=+=+=+=+=+=+=+=+=+=+=+=+=+=+=+=+=+=+=+=+=+=+=+=+=+=+=+=+=+=+=+=+=+
```

The output clearly displays the basic information about each packet: source and destination ports and IPs, protocol, flags (if TCP), sequence and acknowledgement numbers, TTL, and so on.

22

INTRUSION
DETECTION

Now pick a system on your network and enter this command:

```
snort –i <if> -v host <IP of system>
```

You will see output similar to that in Listing 22.7, except that every packet displayed has the IP that you specified as either its source or its destination. This is an example of a BPF filter rule. Snort accepts these rules as command-line arguments after all options are specified, or from a file of filters.

You will find simple example commands like these in the snort README files. Try them out to get a feel for the way that the various options interact.

Figure 22.4 gives a schematic view of Snort processing basics, along with some of the options that control different aspects of processing.

FIGURE 22.4

Snort schematic.

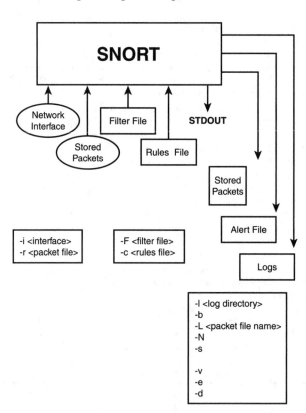

Snort will accept input live from a network interface or from a file containing a binary dump of network packets. The interface is specified with the `-i` option; the binary file is specified with the `-r` option. The `-r` option with a dash (`-`) for the filename tells Snort to accept raw packet data from standard input:

```
gzip -dc compresseddata.gz | snort -r - -vd | more
```

Here, a gzipped file of binary packet data is uncompressed and piped directly into Snort for examination.

Filters can specify or restrict the packets that Snort will process, as with the previous example in which only packets involving a specific IP were processed. Filters can be read in from a file specified with the `-F` options.

Rules must be read from files. The syntax for rules includes a command that allows one file to chain others into one logical set. The initial file in the chain must be specified with the `-c` option. (More later on the specification of rules.)

Snort prints packet data to standard output with the `-v` option. The `-d` option adds packet payloads, and the `-e` option adds Ethernet (MAC) headers.

The `-l` option specifies the directory in which Snort will write logs and several other things.

The `-b` option tells Snort to write packets in a binary file (of the sort that the `-r` option can read) in the log directory.

The `-L` option specifies the name of the binary file in the `-b` option.

The `-N` option tells snort *not* to log packets. It will still do anything else that it is told to do either in the rules or in the command line.

22

INTRUSION
DETECTION

Note

By default, Snort will log the packets that it processes. This means that they are sorted into subdirectories of the log directory. The subdirectories are named after either the source or the destination IP of each packet. They each contain files named after the protocol and the source and destination ports of each packet in them. This is a holdover from the honeypot origins of Snort, and it can generate a lot of logs that are not terribly useful on a busy network. We recommend liberal use of the `-N` option.

The -s option tells Snort to log "alerts" to syslog. Alerts will be discussed later in the context of rules.

It should be noted that, without at least one of the three options -b, -c, or -v, Snort will not execute. It instead prints its usage specifications and asks to be told to do something.

The -D option tells Snort to execute as a daemon.

Our recommendation is to create a directory to be used as a "base" for your familiarization with Snort. It should have the following subdirectories:

- **filters**—Containing filter files
- **rules**—Containing rule files
- **log**—For outputting log files, alerts, and so on
- **packets**—Containing raw packet data for input
- **scans**—For scan output from the portscan preprocessor (specified in the rules)

This will help keep different types of files sorted out as you experiment. It, or something like it, also forms the basis of the "analyst" portion of the NIDS.

Rules

The documentation of rules and rulesets at `http://www.snort.org` is very informative, but the fundamental syntax will be described in this section:

```
<type> <proto> <srcip> <srcport> -> <dstip> <dstport> (options)
```

or

```
<type> <proto> <ip> <port> <> <ip> <port> (options)
```

Rules specify a pattern and one or more actions. The actions will be applied to any packet matching the pattern of the rule.

There are now five or six kinds of rules, but we focus here on the original three: alert, pass, and log. The type of rule determines at least some of the actions that may be taken.

Log rules direct snort to log packets, as described previously. Pass rules direct Snort to ignore packets.

Alert rules direct Snort to enter the packet data, along with a descriptive message, into an "alert" file located in the log directory (or into the system log, if the -s option was used). The descriptive message is specified in the body of the rule.

For the NIDS, we will concentrate on "alert" rules. Because alerts are written to a single file, they are very handy for examination and script processing.

After the rule type, the protocol is specified: tcp, udp or icmp. Then the source and destination IP addresses and port are specified using the -> syntax, or two pairs of IP addresses and ports are specified using the <> bidirectional syntax. The keyword any is a wildcard that will match any port or IP address.

Options follow inside one set of parentheses, using this syntax:

```
(option:argument;option:argument;…)
```

For instance, an alert rule might look like this:

```
alert   tcp 192.134.3.6 any -> 20.100.0.0/16 21 (msg:"FTP connect attempt from
known villain";flags:S;)
```

This rule will match any SYN packet coming from any port on 192.134.3.6 directed to port 21 on any system on the 20.100.0.0 network. (See Chapter 5 for CIDR notation.) Any match will produce an alert message tagged "FTP connect attempt from known villain," followed by packet data. Note that a SYN-ACK packet that otherwise matches the description will be ignored.

Rulesets also allow for variable names. In particular, it's very useful to enter a line specifying your home network so that Snort can tell what's local and what's from outside. Snort uses CIDR notation, so we could say this

```
var $HOME_NET 20.100.0.0/16
```

and rewrite the previous rule as follows:

```
alert   tcp 192.134.3.6 any -> $HOME_NET 21 (msg:"FTP connect attempt from known
villain";flags:S;)
```

The Snort home Web site offers a large collection of rulesets for a variety of applications. Try downloading them into your rules subdirectory, and then run Snort with -c ./rules/<filename> and see if they generate alerts for your network traffic.

Snort as a One-Line NIDS

Get some rules into the rules subdirectory and pick one file of rules that you want to try (see README files with the Snort distribution for the syntax that chains different files into one ruleset). For this example, assume that the network interface is hme0. Don't forget to specify your home network in the ruleset. (You also can use the command-line option -h <home net>, but it's less tidy.)

Now type this:

```
snort -i <if> -N -l ./logs -c ./rules/<filename>
```

Bring up another window to your Snort directory and type the following to see if your ruleset catches anything:

```
tail -f ./logs/alerts
```

NIDS

Earlier we suggested that, although Snort has several uses, they should not all be invoked at the same time. The design of this system has two parts. In one part, Snort is used to collect network data into a sequence of binary files. In the other part, another invocation of Snort reads in these files and writes reports to various output files.

Overall, it looks like Figure 22.5:

FIGURE 22.5

NIDS schematic.

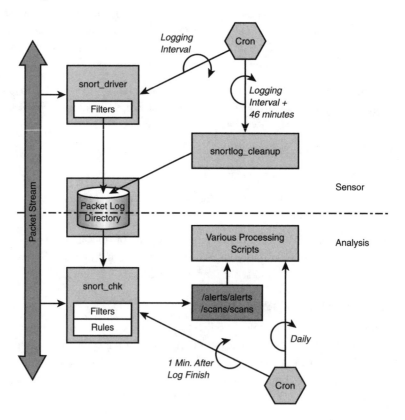

The data collection or "sensor" side runs a script, snort_driver, every 15 minutes that starts a Snort process and kills the previous process. It takes advantage of the file that

Snort writes at invocation containing the process ID. This results in a series of binary files, each containing 15 minutes of binary packet data. Another script, snortlog_cleanup, also runs every 15 minutes and deletes the binary file created 45 minutes previously to keep the storage directory from filling up. Both processes are run under the root crontab. The result is that, most of the time, there are three binary files in the storage directory: two complete files and one being written.

The scripts mentioned in this section are shown in Listings 22.8 through 22.13. You are encouraged to look at them and to try them out *with the permission of the owner of the network*. The best way to start learning network traffic analysis is to start doing it.

The analysis side of the NIDS might be on the same system or on a different one. The script snort_chk in Listing 22.12 is designed for use on the same system as the sensor. A mechanism for the secure transfer of files between systems using SSH is described in Appendix E, "Cryptography in Unix."

22

INTRUSION DETECTION

> **Note**
>
> The systems running Snort to monitor network traffic should be maintained as securely as your most sensitive systems. Remember that the data Snort collects contains *all* network communications, including files being accessed through NFS, mail going in and out of your site, and passwords typed into insecure web applications.

> **Note**
>
> The NIDS presented here is contained on a single platform, though its sensor and analysis components could be implemented on separate platforms very easily. A much more complex system could include several sensor platforms distributed throughout your network, all reporting to a powerful analysis platform which correlates the disparate data.
>
> To implement such a system, you need to have a thorough understanding of your network and the way that traffic moves through it. For instance, if a packet destined for system 3 is detected at sensor A, would that packet normally be detected by sensor B? To answer this, you must know whether sensor B is on a subnet that carries packets destined for system 3. The situation becomes more complicated if traffic on subnets is filtered according to destination port or some other criterion.

snort_chk is quite short. Its job is simply to run a Snort process on the most recent packet log (the name of the file is determined by a call to snort_lastraw, shown in Listing 22.13). The key to the analysis side is the directory structure. It runs in an account called analyst with the following subdirectories:

- **filters**—Containing filter files
- **rules**—Containing rule files
- **log**—For outputting log files, alerts, and so on
- **packets**—Containing raw packet data for input
- **scans**—For scan output from the portscan preprocessor (specified in the rules)
- **bin**—Containing local utilities
- **cronscripts**—Containing scripts run by analyst crontab, including snort_chk and daily report generation

> **Note**
>
> The portscan plug-in should be included in any Snort-based NIDS. There are examples in the Snort distribution, but it comes down to including a couple of lines like these in the rules file.

There are examples in the Snort distribution, but it comes down to including a couple of lines like these:

```
preprocessor portscan: 20.100.0.0/16 4 3 /usr/home/analyst/scans/scans
preprocessor portscan-ignorehosts: 200.10.190.81 200.10.37.63
```

This preprocessor logs the start and finish of a scan to the alert log and provides information about the actual scan packets to /usr/home/analyst/scans/scans. A scan is defined here as at least four packets in 3 seconds from the same source IP address and destined for any address on the 20.100.0.0 subnet.

Some systems might appear to be scanning or to be the target of scans as a side effect of their normal use (some busy mail servers might trip the alarm). These can be entered on the second line to tell the scan detector to ignore them.

If you specify the subnet 0.0.0.0/0, Snort will detect all scans, whether incoming or outgoing. It can be very useful to know which systems on your network are performing port scans that you have not initiated yourself. The result of all this is that the Snort process that analyst runs every 15 minutes will concatenate its findings to the end of the files ~analyst/alert/alert and ~analyst/scans/scans. We recommend compressing and archiving these files each day around midnight for future reference.

The snort_driver in Listing 22.8 does most of the work in controlling the sensor side of the NIDS. It kills the running Snort process and starts a new one. Most of the code is there to handle error conditions. The $report variable is used for debugging.

LISTING 22.8 snort_driver

```perl
#!/usr/bin/perl
#
#       snort_driver

# These are the external variables we need
require "/usr/local/include/sensor.pl";

if ( -s $SNORT_PIDFILE)         # Check for existing pid file
{
        $pid = `cat $SNORT_PIDFILE`;
        $pid =~ s/\n//g;
        $report = join ("\n",$report,
                "Snort pid file detected.",
                "pid: $pid",
                "****");


        $status = ($kill_count = kill (9, $pid)) ?
         "successful":"unsuccessful";

        $status || ($report = join ("\n",$report, "WARNING:"));

        $report = join ("\n",$report,
         "Process $pid kill signal $status",
         "****");

}
else
{
        $report = join ("\n",$report,
                "WARNING: No Snort pid file detected.",
                "****");

        open (PS, "ps -ef |") ||         ($report = join ("\n",$report,
                                          "WARNING: Cannot use ps command",
                                          "****"));

        while (<PS>)             # Search for process to match pid from file
        {
                ($pid, $command) =
                (/\s*\S+\s+(\S+).*(snort.*)\n/);

                        # Kill matching process
```

LISTING 22.8 continued

```perl
                    if ($command =~ /snort.*\-D.*/)
                    {
                            $status = ($kill_count = kill (9, $pid)) ?
                             "successful":"unsuccessful";

                            $status || ($report = join ("\n",$report, "WARNING:"));

                            $report = join ("\n",$report,
                             "Matching Snort process pid detected (pid = $pid)",
                             "Process kill signal $status",
                             "****");
                            last;
                    }
            }
    }

    if ($kill_count)        # Report process killed
    {
            $report = join ("\n",$report,
             "Process $pid detected and killed.",
             "****");
    }
    else
    {
            $report = join ("\n",$report,
             "WARNING: No processes killed.",
             "****");
    }

    #################### Start new Snort process #######################

    $report = join ("\n",$report,
            "Starting new Snort process",
            "****");

    $status = system ($SNORT_CMD);

    sleep 1;        # Give Snort a chance to write a pid file

    if ( -s $SNORT_PIDFILE)          # Check for existing pid file
    {
            $pid = `cat $SNORT_PIDFILE`;
            $pid =~ s/\n//g;
            $report = join ("\n",$report,
                    "Snort pid file detected.",
                    "New Snort pid: $pid",
                    "****");
    }
    else
```

LISTING 22.8 continued

```perl
{
        $report = join ("\n",$report,
                "WARNING: Snort pid file: $SNORT_PIDFILE not detected",
                "****");
}


$MOST_RECENT_LOG = `$SNORT_LASTRAW 0`;
chmod 0644, $MOST_RECENT_LOG;


exit 0;
```

The sensor collects data in fixed "chunks" of time of size $CHUNK_SIZE_IN_
MINUTES minutes. To keep the sensor from filling up, these chunks have a fixed lifetime, $CHUNK_LIFETIME_IN_MINUTES minutes, after which they are deleted. Listing
22.9 shows snortlog_cleanup, the script that deletes chunks when their time is up.

LISTING 22.9 snortlog_cleanup

```perl
#!/usr/bin/perl
#
#        snortlog_cleanup

# These are the external variables we need
require "/usr/local/include/sensor.pl";

##################### Check filesystems - page out if too full ##############
$pageout = 0;
open (DF, "$DF -k|");
while ($line = <DF>)
{

        if (($capacity, $mntpt)
                = ($line =~ /\s*\S+\s+\S+\s+\S+\s+\S+\s+(\d+)\%\s+(\S+)/))
        {
                if ($capacity >= $FILESYSTEM_TOO_FULL)
                {
                        $pageout = 1;
                        $report = join("\n",$report,
                         "$mntpt at $cap\%");
                }
        }
}
close DF;
```

LISTING 22.9   continued

```
#################### Delete Old Snort Log File #######################

# Build name of old log file (based on time $CHUNK_LIFETIME_IN_MINUTES minutes
ago)

$SNORT_LOG = `$SNORT_LASTRAW $CHUNK_LIFETIME_IN_MINUTES`;

if (-e "$SNORT_LOG")
{
        $cmd = "$RM -f $SNORT_LOG";
        $status = `$cmd`;
}
else
{
        $report = join("\n",$report,
          "WARNING: $SNORT_LOG does not exist");

}
exit 0;
```

Listing 22.10 shows the variable definitions in the fields `Sensor.pl` and `Analyst.pl`.
The sensor scripts require the file `Sensor.pl`, which defines the variables needed on the
sensor side of the NIDS. The analyst scripts require `Analyst.pl`, which includes all of
`Sensor.pl` as well as some other information.

LISTING 22.10   Sensor.pl; Analyst.pl

```
Sensor.pl

#
#       Snort configuration and Snort-based Utilities
$NETWORK_INTERFACE = "hme1";
#
$SNORT = "/usr/local/bin/snort";
$SNORT_PIDFILE = "/var/run/snort_$NETWORK_INTERFACE.pid";
$SNORT_LOGDIR = "/nids/special/snort";
$SNORT_CMD = "/usr/local/bin/snort -i $NETWORK_INTERFACE -q -D -b -l
$SNORT_LOGDIR > /dev/null";
$SNORT_LASTRAW = "/usr/local/bin/snort_lastraw";
$NIDS_ADMINS = "andy\@unet.edu";
#
#       Common Utilities
#
$GZIP = "/usr/local/bin/gzip";
$RM = "/usr/bin/rm";
$MAIL = "/usr/ucb/Mail";
$DF = "/usr/ucb/df";
#
```

LISTING 22.10 continued

```
#       Test and Control Values
#
$FILESYSTEM_TOO_FULL = 99;
#
#       Timing and Coordination
#
$CHUNK_SIZE_IN_MINUTES = 15;
$CHUNK_LIFETIME_IN_MINUTES = 45;
#


Analyst.pl

# Get Sensor Definitions
require "/usr/local/include/sensor.pl";

# Handy Programs
$SSH = "/usr/local/bin/ssh";                        # SSH
$SCP = "/usr/local/bin//scp -q";                    # SCP (quiet mode)
$SANITIZE = "/usr/home/analyst/bin/sanitize";       # Delete Local Refs
$CLEAN = "/usr/home/analyst/bin/report_clean";      # Clean out cruft
$DATESTAMP = "/usr/local/bin/datestamp";            # Return ddmmyy

# Variable Definition
$SNORT_ALERTDIR = "/usr/home/analyst/alert";        # Alert directory
$SNORT_SCANDIR = "/usr/home/analyst/scans";         # Scans directory
$SNORT_RULES = "/usr/home/analyst/rules";           # SNORT rules
$SNORT_FILTERS = "/usr/home/analyst/filters";       # BPF-type filters
$SNORT_ALERT_REPORT = "$SNORT_ALERTDIR/alert";      # Output: Alert report
$SNORT_SCAN_REPORT = "$SNORT_SCANDIR/scans";        # Output: Scans report

$PUBLIC_ACCOUNT = "andy\@unet7";
$PUBLIC_ACCESS_DIR = "$PUBLIC_ACCOUNT:./www/";      # Web directory for
                                                    # public access
```

Sensor and analyst scripts are driven by crontab. The crontabs used for the analyst scripts and the sensor scripts, respectively are shown in Listing 22.11.

LISTING 22.11 crontabs

```
Analyst crontab

1,16,31,46 * * * * /usr/home/analyst/cronscripts/snort_chk
55 23 * * * /usr/home/analyst/cronscripts/alerts_scan_report <
/usr/home/analyst/alert/alert | /usr/home/analyst/bin/sanitize | /usr/ucb/mail -
s "[UNET NIDS] Alert Summary (basilisk)" andy@unet.edu
5 0 * * * /usr/home/analyst/cronscripts/update_alerts
10 0 * * * /usr/home/analyst/cronscripts/update_scans
```

LISTING 22.11   continued

```
56 23 * * * /usr/home/analyst/bin/arachnids_upd -q -o
/usr/home/analyst/rules/vision.rules | /usr/ucb/mail -s "Arachnids Rules Update
(basilisk)" andy@unet.edu


Sensor (root) crontab

0,15,30,45 * * * * /usr/local/cronscripts/snort_driver
1,16,31,46 * * * * /usr/local/cronscripts/snortlog_cleanup
```

The script in Listing 22.12, snort_chk, doesn't look like it does much. In fact, all it does is figure out the name of the last chunk completed by the sensor and start a Snort process using the chunk as input. The script is simple because Snort is so versatile. The Snort process that analyzes the data chunk uses some filters and an extensive set of rules. It generates an `alert` file over a 24-hour period that records everything the alert rules detect. We also use the `portscan` directive to generate a separate file recording scanning activity over the same period. These files can also be monitored by a utility such as `Swatch`, described in Chapter 6, "Logging," to provide real-time notification of important events.

LISTING 22.12   snort_chk

```perl
#!/usr/bin/perl
#
#       snort_chk

# Variable Definition
require "/usr/home/analyst/include/analyst.pl";

$SNORT_LATEST_LOG = `$SNORT_LASTRAW $CHUNK_SIZE_IN_MINUTES`;    # return lastet
raw log

# SNORT command
$SNORT_CMD = "$SNORT -q -N -A fast -l $SNORT_ALERTDIR -F
$SNORT_FILTERS/filter.websurf -c $SNORT_RULES/ids -r $SNORT_LATEST_LO
G > /dev/null";


##################  Run Snort #######################

$status = system ($SNORT_CMD);

#################### Send report and finish #######################


exit 0;
```

Many of the scripts in the NIDS require the name of files containing previously completed chunks of data. Listing 22.13 shows snort_lastraw, which takes an argument in minutes and returns the name of the oldest chunk that had been completed that many minutes previously.

LISTING 22.13 snort_lastraw

```perl
#!/usr/bin/perl
#
#        snort_lastraw

# These are the external variables we need

require "/usr/local/include/sensor.pl";

##############  Determine Name of last Snort Log File #################

($#ARGV == 0) || exit(0) ;

$MINUTES_BACK = shift @ARGV;

# Build name of completed log file (based on time $MINUTES_BACK minutes ago)

($sec,$min,$hour,$mday,$mon,$year,$wday,$yday,$isdst)
 = localtime(time - 60*$MINUTES_BACK);

$year = sprintf ("%02d",$year);
$mon++;
$mon = sprintf ("%02d",$mon);
$day = sprintf ("%02d",$mday);
$hour = sprintf ("%02d",$hour);
# Compute last log start time based on interval
$min = $min - ($min % $CHUNK_SIZE_IN_MINUTES);
$min = sprintf ("%02d",$min);
$sec = sprintf ("%02d",$sec);

$SNORT_LOG = join ("","snort-",$mon,$day,"\@",$hour,$min,"\.log");

print STDOUT "$SNORT_LOGDIR/$SNORT_LOG";

exit 0;
```

Scanning Reports—A Case Study

An excerpt from a daily scanning summary is shown in listing 22.14 to illustrate the usefulness of monitoring scans entering *and* leaving your network. The summary report is generated from the contents of the "scans" file generated daily by the simple NIDS described in this chapter.

The report shows that a system on our network (20.100.0.0/16) had been SYN scanning outside. Scans to 45 hosts had been detected. Even without knowing the system's function, there was certainly no valid reason for this system to perform a SYN scan on external IP addresses. Subsequent investigation proved that the system with IP address 20.100.70.197 had been compromised.

LISTING 22.14   Scanning Summary Report

```
========================================================================
===

                    Scanners by Number of Target IP Addresses
                    --------------------------------------------

Scanner IP              # Targets           Ports               Type
-----------------       -------------       -----------         -------
---
20.100.70.197           45                  1214                SYN


-------------------------------------------------------------------------
---
Log Excerpts:
Jul  8 12:16:55 20.100.70.197:1134 -> 25.114.32.141:1214 SYN ******S*
Jul  8 12:16:56 20.100.70.197:1135 -> 170.149.195.57:1214 SYN ******S*
Jul  8 12:16:57 20.100.70.197:1137 -> 74.44.136.138:1214 SYN ******S*
Jul  8 12:16:57 20.100.70.197:1133 -> 34.48.116.56:1214 SYN ******S*
Jul  8 12:16:57 20.100.70.197:1131 -> 107.18.187.190:1214 SYN ******S*
Jul  8 12:16:57 20.100.70.197:1138 -> 71.2.98.128:1214 SYN ******S*
Jul  8 12:16:57 20.100.70.197:1139 -> 45.141.132.221:1214 SYN ******S*
Jul  8 12:16:59 20.100.70.197:1140 -> 54.28.208.107:1214 SYN ******S*
Jul  8 12:16:58 20.100.70.197:1141 -> 56.16.163.157:1214 SYN ******S*
Jul  8 12:17:00 20.100.70.197:1138 -> 78.2.98.128:1214 SYN ******S*
Jul  8 12:17:00 20.100.70.197:1147 -> 92.200.119.87:1214 SYN ******S*


-------------------------------------------------------------------------
---
```

Best Practices

- Remember that a NIDS is an event detector. You must define the events that interest you.
- Configure the NIDS to detect events indicating a definite problem. (For example, buffer overflows.)

- Configure the NIDS to detect events that shouldn't happen. (For example, traffic to and from port 80 on a system that shouldn't offer Web service.)
- If you have a firewall, or otherwise filter network traffic, use the filtering rules to define NIDS rules. The NIDS should detect any failure of the network filters.
- A NIDS is much more powerful in coordination with other event recorders, such as system or Web logs. In so far as possible, correlate events detected by the NIDS with other information from your network and systems.

Online References

Snort Home Page: `http://www.snort.org`

Tcpdump and Libpcap Home Page: `http://www.tcpdump.org`

NSWC SHADOW INDEX: `http://www.nswc.navy.mil/ISSEC/CID/`

Michael Sobirey's Intrusion Detection Systems page: `http://www-rnks.informatik.tu-cottbus.de/~sobirey/ids.html`

FAQ: Network Intrusion Detection Systems: `http://www.robertgraham.com/pubs/network-intrusion-detection.html`

Cisco Secure IDS (Formerly NetRanger):
`http://www.cisco.com/univercd/cc/td/doc/pcat/nerg.htm`

NFR Network Intrusion Detection (NFR NID): `http://www.nfr.net/products/NID/`

Sourceforge: `http://www.sourceforge.com`

Printed References

Network Intrusion Detection: An Analyst's Handbook, 2nd Ed., Stephen Northcutt, Judy Novak, Donald McLachlan, New Riders, 2000

Intrusion Signatures and Analysis, Stephen Northcutt, Karen Frederick, New Riders, 2001

22

INTRUSION DETECTION

Requirements Analysis and Performance Monitoring

by Kurt Wall

This chapter discusses requirements analysis and performance monitoring. The first part of the chapter covers requirements analysis, matching hardware and software needs to a problem specification. As the name suggests, performance monitoring refers to maintaining optimal system performance using a variety of tools that monitor CPU utilization, memory usage, disk I/O throughput, and network traffic. Of course, monitoring and identifying a problem is pointless if you take no measures to solve it, so the second half of this chapter discusses these issues.

This chapter addresses the following points:

- Requirements analysis
- Performance monitoring
- Capacity projection and planning

Requirements Analysis

Requirements analysis (RA) is the process of identifying all of the resources that can be applied to solve a problem and also the process of refining everyone's understanding of the problem itself. As a system administrator, it is natural for you to think first and foremost of systems and their features and characteristics when someone mentions RA, but it is sometimes just as vital to take into account the administrators and other people who are involved in or will be affected by the project.

What, then, is a requirement? Broadly stated, a *requirement* is any item that is necessary or an explicit criterion that must be met to solve a problem. Requirements typically are stated using terms such as *shall*, *must*, *should*, or *will*. During the RA process, requirements are grouped into some logical order, followed by tentative first attempts to define a design that satisfies those. This is where the "resources" begin to come in.

For example, requirements for a database server might be stated in one of the following ways:

- The database server shall be available 18 hours per day.
- Disk space usage must not exceed 75% of available space.
- Swap utilization will remain below 60% between 8:00 A.M. and 5:00 P.M.

Note

To simplify the following discussion, this section assumes that the project is building a database server. Although the particulars for another project, such as a Web server or dial-in server, might differ, the general procedure will vary little.

Moreover, some requirements will be mandatory and others will be optional. The three requirements just listed are worded as being mandatory. They *must* be met to meet the project specifications. Optional requirements, on the other hand, express criteria that are desirable or that should be implemented if possible.

Usually, system administrators are given a project specification and asked to establish baseline requirements for the underlying hardware and operating system software. As a result, you will work closely with the system architects, application programmers, database administrators, end users, management, and other people who understand the problem domain. System architects provide input regarding the current and anticipated work levels that the server is expected to handle and the overall breadth of the project. Application programmers will best understand the tools that they need to develop, debug, and maintain the programs that use the server. The database administrators know the database requirements and will be able to identify the database's needs for RAM, CPU horsepower, disk layout, filesystem design, and the rate at which the database is expected to grow. We mention end users because they are always key stakeholders in a project, but their concern is usually at the application level. Management, naturally, will be most concerned with getting the greatest possible benefit from the smallest possible resource expenditure (that is, doing more with less).

Your mission, should you decide to accept it, is to distill all this information into a set of requirements to identify the needed resources. Although it seems a daunting task at first glance, it really is not so complicated because you are responsible for only a small subset of those resources and you are defining them at a fairly high level.

Of course, depending on the size of the operation in question or the visibility and importance of the project, system administrators might wear multiple hats and function as the system architect, the application or system programmer, the database manager, and even the manager. In such cases, it is even more important to go through the process of defining and redefining the problem and solution space than it is when the functional roles are filled by different people.

23

RA AND
PERFORMANCE
MONITORING

Resources

In the context of requirements analysis, a *resource* is any feature that contributes to solving a problem or to meeting a requirement. If you look at the three requirements for a database server listed a moment ago, the second point identifies disk space as a resource, and the third point suggests that both disk space (configured as swap space) and RAM are resources. However, the definition of resources that we gave includes much more than merely hardware and software. Network infrastructure, system usage and security policies, support needs, and personnel also must be considered as resources.

Each resource can be further decomposed. Hardware resources, for example, might be broken down to the component level, such as the number and speed of the system CPUs; and amount and physical configuration of installed RAM; the size, speed, and interface protocol of disk drives; or the type and speed of the network interfaces and their cabling requirements. System usage and security policies define who may use the system, when, and how. Support needs can include onsite, first-line support (system operators, help-desk technicians, and, of course, system administrators) and also hardware and software maintenance contracts that define service levels and vendor response times.

Not only must you consider which of these and other resources translate into requirements that meet the project specifications, but you also must bear in mind that they are resources that you (and others) must manage, maintain, and monitor.

The Scope of the Job

Identifying requirements starts with the project's perceived scope. The *perceived scope* refers to apparent business problem and the hardware and software products considered acceptable to solve that problem. Unfortunately, the perceived problem might or might not be the real problem. Alternatively, the problem might not be completely understood. Identifying a project's scope also serves to define its ultimate deliverable, the hardware system, the software application, the procedure, the people, or, more likely, some combination of silicon, logic, process, and personnel that solves the problem. Although it might seem self-evident, a clearly expressed problem domain, solution, and deliverable also represent the *end* of a project. Finally, fully and properly apprehending the full scope of a project will help prevent project creep, the tendency of a project to become more ambitious than originally intended and, as a result, lose focus on its initial purpose and the problem that it was first intended to solve.

For example, the basic need might be expressed as, "We need a new database server because the current server is too slow." After some analysis, you find that the real issue is indeed a need for a faster server, but you discover that part of the problem is that other applications share the database server. So, one requirement becomes restricting the new database server solely to applications that need the database. Isolating such subtleties is a challenge, but it is necessary to avoid creating a so-called solution that solves nothing because it is too small or does not address the problem's root causes. In other cases, a solution might be too big, too complex, or too costly. It is vital to use the requirements-gathering process to investigate the expected project scope. The point here is that project stakeholders frequently say "We need" when they *really* mean "I want." Your job is to separate the "we need" wheat from the "I want" chaff.

Worth keeping in mind during the RA process is the value—or perhaps the necessity—of diplomacy and tact. Customers or stakeholders typically come to the RA process with preconceived notions not only of the problem, but also of how to solve it. These notions can be very hard to correct or even to dislodge. However, you must politely, tactfully, and diplomatically press the point that, although the database server might simply need to be replaced, the project's goals and the organization's goals are best served by looking at the problem from all vantage points and considering all the reasonable solutions.

Requirements Analysis Drives Design

Too often, projects fail because one or more vocal and persuasive stakeholders come to the table with a design or solution in mind that does not reflect the nature of the real problem. Rather than letting RA determine the design, the process works in reverse—that is, the preconceived design drives the RA process and determines the "requirements." When a design is chosen before the problem is analyzed, the resulting solution inevitably ignores crucial aspects of the problem. When this happens, the solution too often exacerbates the problem.

It is easy to see how the "I want/we need" fallacy mentioned earlier results in a design-driven RA process. Unfortunately, project stakeholders who know just enough about a problem and its possible solutions can also cause design to drive analysis rather than allowing analysis to drive design. This danger is subtle because such a stakeholder, even though well-intentioned, will camouflage a design approach as a requirement or part of a requirement. Such design elements masquerading as analytic points come from those project stakeholders who know just enough to be dangerous and from those who know a lot, especially about the way that things have worked for the last 20 years. As one of us noted while writing this book, these 20-year veterans are the ones who end up with "requirements" for things such as extra RA81 drives on the VAX cluster. Again, you must diplomatically but persistently focus on analysis and let the real needs surface before focusing on design.

Requirements Analysis Dos and Don'ts

- Do talk to all the stakeholders. Don't rely on any one person for all key information about the problem domain. Talk to as many people as possible or practical who are involved with the current process.
- Don't recommend a product. Do recommend a technology, or at least a class of products. Recommending a specific product prematurely closes the door to alternative products that better meet the requirements. Likewise, provide several alternative choices to prevent prematurely narrowing the range of possible solutions.

- Do consider where technology will be in five years. Don't focus solely on current capabilities. Failing to take into account (or at least attempting to consider) technological advancement might result in a system that is obsolete sooner than anticipated or that is difficult to upgrade as new technologies emerge.

- Don't make the problem bigger than it is. Do maintain focus on the identified problem. Like software projects, feature creep in a hardware upgrade or a new installation can run up the cost and complexity of the project and can result in a system that satisfies no one and annoys everyone.

- Do keep scalability and maintainability in mind. Don't lock yourself into a limited system. A system with limited growth room quickly becomes a maintenance nightmare and must be upgraded or replaced sooner than anticipated. Conversely, avoid the temptation to *overspecify*—that is, to recommend more machine than is required. Unused resources are equivalent to wasted money.

- Don't neglect compatibility with existing systems. Do maintain a sane, consistent computing environment. The luster of the latest gee-whiz gadget quickly fades when you have to use a crowbar to fit it into your existing computing infrastructure and when maintaining it becomes a nightmare because it does not interoperate smoothly with existing equipment.

- Do maintain reasonable expectations. Don't succumb to the Silver Bullet Syndrome. When planning and installing a new system, it is easy to slip into the mode of thinking that it will solve all the problems. If the new system, whether hardware, software, or both, is properly specified, it should adequately address the problem domain, but it will not solve related problems. There is no such thing as a magic bullet.

- Don't generalize. Do clearly define responsibilities and associate them with specific people. By explicitly linking well-defined responsibilities with specific people, or at least with specific job descriptions, you reduce the likelihood of coming to the end of a project and then realizing that one crucial element fell through the cracks because everyone thought that someone else would take care of it.

- Do create a written analysis. Don't assume that verbal agreement is sufficient. Having a written analysis with the signatures of key stakeholders serves as evidence that everyone agreed to the requirements that it contains *and* uses it as a reference point during the design phase.

- Don't forget verification. Do create a checklist of goals and make sure that each one is met. Creating a checklist of goals and requirements, again, serves as a reference point during the project's design, implementation, and postmortem phases and acts as a reality check for making sure that the end product really does meet the goals identified six months ago.

- Do map requirements to recommendations. Don't have unmet requirements or extraneous recommendations. For each requirement, indicate what elements in your final recommendation address that requirement. Then reverse the process and show how each component of your recommendation corresponds to at least one of the original requirements.

Performance Monitoring

From the perspective of a system administrator, especially a junior administrator, the key point to keep in mind is that performance monitoring, like system security, is a continual process rather than a final goal obtained once and never revisited. The requirements analysis and system specification processes should have addressed basic performance issues at the beginning of a system's service life—if not, something went wrong at the very beginning. Once basic performance concerns are addressed, a regular performance-monitoring regimen should be put in place to maintain the best possible performance and identify potential trouble spots *before* they degrade performance.

In most IT shops, Murphy's Law is alive and well. When performance begins to erode, perhaps inevitably, you will need to have some tools that enable you to quickly differentiate between real and perceived performance problems and to solve, or at least isolate and begin closer investigation of, genuine performance problems. In general, these tools fall into two broad categories: high-level, general tools that impose a negligible performance hit, and low-level tools that offer considerable detail at the cost of significant performance degradation. There is room and justification for both in the performance-monitoring spectrum, as you will see the following paragraphs.

This section proceeds from the general to the specific, looking first at the process to follow when analyzing system performance. Next, it shows you how to take a quick snapshot of a system's overall performance and how to drill down into each of the major subsystems. You will learn which tools to use to obtain detailed information about running processes, memory utilization, disk usage and I/O throughput, network traffic, and CPU saturation. You will also learn how to tune the kernel to address particular performance problems. The final sections look at routine maintenance issues that can help alleviate or minimize major problems.

Finding Bottlenecks

As just suggested, performance monitoring is a process. So, this section describes a method (but not "The Method" because every administrator varies it somewhat) that you can follow to track down performance problems to monitor. Briefly, the general procedure is to determine the overall status of the system and then to examine specific subsystems. Sometimes the overall status might give you a hint about which subsystem to evaluate, but, more often than not, you will need to look at each of the major subsystems (disk, memory, network, and CPU) until you find the real problem. As you develop experience using the procedure described here, you will likely modify it to suit your needs. Over time, you *will* develop an intuitive sense of where to look when an apparent performance problem emerges.

Note that little word, *apparent*. Some perceived performance problems are not problems at all, but they're predictable and highly transient bottlenecks. They reflect normal usage and are not worth troubling yourself over. For example, I used to maintain an electronic data interchange (EDI) system for a large insurance company. Its main features were a number of busy dialup lines for data transmission, an enormous database actively and constantly used, and about two dozen power users. Every morning at 8:00 A.M., we all arrived at work, got our coffee, and logged in. By 8:05, the system, named wine, would slow to a crawl, only to recover within 10 or 15 minutes, at most.

Was this a performance problem? Yes, in that wine's response time slowed; no, in that wine's business purpose was not impaired, no revenue was lost, and all users were able to continue working. The slowdown was totally predictable, transient, and, although inconvenient, not worth the effort to solve. It was totally predictable because, at approximately the same time, 25 people were logging in, starting the same applications (a mail client, a couple of database sessions, an IRC client, and maybe a Web browser), and reviewing the same set of reports spewed out by the claims processing system. It was transient in that wine's sluggish response lasted perhaps 15 minutes.

The problem was not worth the effort to solve. Twenty-five people almost simultaneously accessing the same files on a system already heavily loaded with data processing invariably translated into a temporary performance hit on both the system itself and across our little piece of the corporate network. I am still convinced that other traffic on wine's network segment (primarily login sessions by users of other systems on the same subnet) aggravated the problem.

The point is that you need to be aware of the context in which a *perceived* problem occurs and take into account a system's normal usage patterns before deciding that something is a problem that needs to be fixed. Had the slow response lasted longer, impaired wine's business function, or prevented people from working, it *would* have posed a significant problem. There were steps we could have taken, such as using NIS for authentication, mounting home directories from a dedicated NFS server, begging the IT department to change the network segmentation to reduce traffic on our subnet, or adjusting processing times for the database (a large data load started at 7:30 A.M. each day), but these were significant changes the circumstances did not warrant. Fortunately, no one was alert enough at that hour to call and complain—at 8:05 A.M., I certainly was in no mood to deal with grumpy users complaining about not being able to read the morning's email jokes at breakneck speed!

This is just one example of a predictable bottleneck that, while inconvenient, does not represent a performance problem. Slow application startup times are another example. Certain applications, such as emacs, X, most large database management systems (DBMSes), accounting packages, and financial analysis suites, are notoriously slow to start. From a user's point of view, slow start times are a performance problem, but not from the system administrator's point of view. Short of fixing the code, there is very little an administrator can do in this case.

Overall System Status

To get some sense of the system's overall performance status, the most common command is uptime. It displays a one-line report that shows how long the system is up, how many users are logged in, and the load averages over the last 1, 5, and 15 minutes. The *load average* expresses the number of jobs waiting in the run queue—that is, ready to run but not running. The following shows uptime's output on shellbeast, an ISP's shell server system:

```
shellbeast> uptime
  9:31pm  up 44 day(s), 10:04,  40 users,  load average: 2.21, 1.52, 1.28
```

As you can see, the load average is 2.21 over the last minute, 1.52 during the last five minutes, and 1.28 during the last quarter hour. Before you start taking dramatic steps when *your* system's load averages start climbing, however, you need to baseline it. *Baselining* refers to performing basic monitoring to establish a system's normal usage profile. For example, you can create a cron job that runs uptime every 15 minutes and appends the output to a text file. After a week, you would have a good idea of that system's typical usage.

Keep in mind, though, that one week's worth of data might not cover all processing cycles. An accounting server, for example, is likely to be more heavily used at the end of standard accounting cycles, such as the end of the pay period, the month, the quarter, and the fiscal year. A back-end server for a point-of-sale (POS) system, however, will routinely experience its heaviest usage at the end of the business day, when sales are tallied and summarized. The point is that you have to spend some time developing an accurate picture of a system's normal usage before you can reasonably distinguish between heavy usage and a real performance problem.

Note, however, that uptime does not distinguish between high-priority jobs, such as interactive processes (a shell session, for example), and low-priority jobs, such as daemons or database servers. Moreover, `uptime` takes only a snapshot at a given moment, and usage can vary wildly. Consider `uptime`'s report on shellbeast's load average 18 minutes after the first execution:

```
shellbeast> uptime
  9:49pm  up 44 day(s), 10:22,  37 users,  load average: 0.42, 0.52, 0.74
```

Because `uptime` is such a blunt tool, it is best used for obtaining an immediate snapshot of system performance and for trending the load average over a period of time as part of developing a comprehensive system-usage profile.

The `sar` (system activity reporter) command can be a bit more informative because it shows CPU utilization a specific number of times over an interval defined in seconds. The exact invocation is as follows:

```
sar -u secs count
```

`sar` might not be available on your system, and it must be configured before it can be used. The "Online References" section at the end of the chapter includes a link to an open source version of `sar` and related commands. If you run the `sar` command and get output resembling the following, you will need to configure it before proceeding:

```
% sar
sar: can't open /var/adm/sa/sa18
No such file or directory
```

Configuring `sar` is simple enough. `sar` reads data from a log file (/var/adm/sa/sa*dd*, by default, where *dd* is the current day). /usr/lib/sa/sadc, the system activity data collector, creates and maintains these log files. However, most `sar` implementations include two shell scripts, /usr/lib/sa/sa1 and /usr/lib/sa/sa2, that front-end `sadc`. The simplest way to configure `sar`'s data files is to create a system cron entry that calls `sa1`. For example, the following crontab entry runs `sa1` every 10 minutes and appends its output to the `sar` data file:

```
0,10,20,30,40,50 * * * * /usr/lib/sa/sa1
```

`sa1` collects and stores data in a binary file format that `sar` reads. Bear in mind that the log files can grow quite large and that `sadc` can impose a noticeable performance impact depending on the command-line options with which it is invoked.

secs is the number of seconds between samples, and *count* indicates the number of samples to take. For example, the following `sar` invocation shows CPU usage sampled five times in 5 seconds:

```
shellbeast> sar -u 5 5

SunOS shellbeast 5.7 Generic_106541-08 sun4m    08/08/01
```

03:18:27	%usr	%sys	%wio	%idle
03:18:32	2	3	0	96
03:18:37	1	1	0	98
03:18:42	0	1	0	98
03:18:47	1	1	0	98
03:18:52	1	3	1	96
Average	1	2	0	97

`%usr` indicates the percentage of time that the CPU spends executing user mode code (typically, application programs), `%sys` indicates the time spent executing kernel code (system calls), `%wio` shows how much time the CPU spins while waiting for I/O operations to complete, and `%idle` shows how much time the CPU is not doing anything. As you can see, shellbeast is remarkably quiet right now (perhaps because only authors are awake at 3:18 A.M.) because the CPU is almost entirely idle.

As a general rule, if `%sys` is high, application programs might be using system calls (kernel mode code) inappropriately. If `%wio` is high, look at disk performance (see the section "Disk Usage and Performance," later in this chapter, to learn how to identify disk I/O problems) and possibly network traffic that is interfering with NFS reads and writes over the network. If `%idle` is high yet the load average as reported by `uptime` is significant (say, over 5), this suggests either an I/O problem or memory saturation (see the upcoming section titled "Memory Utilization" for tips on how to identify memory saturation); the CPU is idle because jobs are sitting in the run queue waiting for I/O to complete or for memory to be swapped back in from disk.

If you want, you can use a graphical monitor to track the system's load status. perfmeter, part of the OpenWindows GUI toolkit, is one such program, but it is not available on all systems. xload, however, should be available on any system with X11R6, which is any modern Unix system. Figure 23.1 shows a sample xload display.

FIGURE 23.1

xload shows the system load with a graphical interface.

xload's most useful options are listed here:

- **-scale** *count*—The minimum number of lines displayed on the screen. Each line represents a load average value of 1.

- **-update** *seconds*—The number of seconds between each update.

- **-bg** *color*—The color of the graph's background.

- **-fg** *color*—The color of the graph foreground.

- **-hl** *color*—The color of any text and the scale lines.

Figure 23.1, for example, was invoked using the command xload -scale 10 -update 1 -fg darkgreen -hl black. You can see the 10 scale lines, but, unfortunately, not the dark green color of the graph. The graph itself updated every second. The system was lightly loaded—the graph shows a load average just over 3, which corresponds to the load average reported by uptime:

```
shellbeast> uptime
  9:58pm  up 44 days, 10:31,  18 users,  load average: 3.22, 2.61, 1.12
```

Although xload is visually appealing, it is, like uptime, a rather blunt tool that does not provide much detail.

Process Monitoring

The ps command is the weapon of choice for examining running processes. In terms of performance monitoring, the most useful set of command options to use is -ecl—that is, ps -ecl. Why -ecl? As you might recall from Chapter 9, "Day-to-Day System Management," the -e option lists information on every running process, the -c option shows each process's scheduling class, and the -l option generates a long listing that displays information pertinent to performance monitoring and tuning (see Table 23.1). The following short listing illustrates the output of ps -ecl on shellbeast:

```
shellbeast> ps -ecl
 F S   UID   PID  PPID  CLS PRI    ADDR    SZ   WCHAN TTY       TIME CMD
 8 S 17143 21719 21716  TS  52 f72971d0 1017 f72973f8 ?         0:09 perl
 8 S  1504 18384 18382  TS  33 f7a56010  559 f7a56238 pts/47    0:01 tcsh
 8 S 20694 13918 13807  TS  58 f6d0dc20  678 f639a9be pts/4     0:00 bash
 8 S     0  3915   157  TS  58 f75f0028 1014 f6ecc1d2 ?         0:06 smbd
 8 S 17129 14365 12043  TS  13 f77dac98  246 f61645b8 pts/36    0:00 tail
 8 S  7872 14412 14390  TS  43 f75f7870  604 f62136c2 pts/25    1:16 wmbiff
 8 S     0 13413   157  TS  38 f70d9380  586 f74a4196 ?         0:00 nohttp
 8 S     0 24291   343  TS  58 f72963c0  958 f5bb7bba ?         0:04 sshd2
```

The output was severely truncated to conserve space (230 or more lines was overkill). Table 23.1 describes most of the fields shown in the listing.

TABLE 23.1 ps Fields Relevant to Performance Monitoring

Field	Description
F	Contains a value consisting of the sum of one or more hexadecimal values that describes the process's current status

TABLE 23.1 continued

Field	Description
S	Shows the process's current state (running, sleeping, and so forth)
UID	Lists the numeric user ID (UID) of the user who owns the process
PID	Lists the process's process ID (PID)
PPID	Lists the PID of the parent process
CLS	Identifies the process's scheduling class
PRI	States the process's priority (higher numbers mean higher priority)
SZ	Lists how much swap space (virtual memory) the process requires
TTY	Names the terminal on which the process started (also known as the *controlling terminal*)
TIME	Summarizes the total CPU time (in hours and minutes) that the process has consumed
CMD	Displays the command that initiated the process

Note

If you omit -c, CLS is replaced with C, the CPU utilization for the process-scheduling class, and you will also see NI, the process's nice value, which modifies the process's priority relative to other processes in the same scheduling class.

As a refresher, recall that the S field takes one of the following values:

- **O**—The process is currently executing on a CPU.
- **S**—The process is sleeping, waiting for another event to complete.
- **R**—The process is in the run queue (runnable) and is waiting to run.
- **Z**—The process is a zombie (it terminated, but the parent has not reaped its exits status).
- **T**—The process is stopped.

23

RA AND
PERFORMANCE
MONITORING

Rather than rehash the material in Chapter 8, "Securing a System for Rollout," here are some tips that will help you correlate the output of the ps command with particular problems:

- Examine the CLS field for processes running in an unreasonable scheduling class (most processes should be in the TS, or time sharing, class). Real-time (RT) processes can bring a system to its knees and crowd out all other processes.

- Examine the PRI field (and the NI fields, if you omit -c) for processes that can run at lower priorities, and then use the nice or renice commands to modify their priorities. Alternatively, see if long-lived (long-running) or CPU-intensive processes can be scheduled to run at a time when the system is quiescent.

- Processes that remain stopped for long periods of time (a T in the S field) should be investigated and possibly killed.

- Similarly, long-running processes (see the TIME field) that consume significant CPU resources should be investigated, but bear in mind that they might simply require considerable computing horsepower. In the latter case, consider moving them to off-peak times, if possible.

- Processes consuming a great deal of memory, particularly swap space (see the SZ field), might have memory leaks and, when being swapped in and out, will adversely impact performance.

- Sleeping processes (those with an S in the S field) might have I/O problems, or the I/O subsystem itself might be impaired. (See "Disk Usage and Performance," later in the chapter, for ways to diagnose and treat I/O problems.)

The ps command really serves two purposes in performance monitoring and tuning. First, it provides clues about what process (or processes) might be causing the problem, which, in turn, will suggest possible measures to alleviate the problem. Second, ps enables you to see whether the action you took solved the problem. After taking steps to discipline a wayward process, use ps -ecl again and evaluate the results. If the corrective measure worked, you have at least temporarily solved the problem. If not, try another tactic.

> **Note**
>
> The ps -ecl command produces different results when executed on Linux systems.

Memory Utilization

Inadequate amounts of physical RAM and the corresponding problem, heavy swapping activity, can have a profoundly adverse impact on system performance. The previous section suggested examining the amount of virtual memory (the value of the SZ field) that a process requires when diagnosing a system performance problem. The issue is that a process not currently running is not immediately accessible to the CPU. In some cases, its memory image is stored in RAM while other processes execute, so a short delay occurs when it is woken up to run. In other cases, especially on a busy system, either individual pages of the process's memory image or the entire process will be swapped to disk, resulting in a significant delay when the process image is read back into RAM and prepared to run—disk I/O is almost always the weakest link in the system performance chain. The larger the amount of swap that is required, the greater the performance hit will be.

Use the vmstat command to examine the virtual memory subsystem and isolate problems. vmstat reports a variety of statistics about the virtual memory subsystem, CPU load, and disk and CPU activity. Its general format is as follows:

```
vmstat [options] [count [secs]]
```

vmstat takes a total of *count* samples every *secs* seconds and displays its output to stdout (standard output, the screen). *options* controls the type of information that vmstat reports. For diagnosing paging and swapping problems, the options of most value are -p, which displays detailed information on paging activity, and -S, which reports on swap activity rather than paging. The following example uses -p to show paging details.

23

RA AND
PERFORMANCE
MONITORING

Note

The vmstat syntax discussed in this section applies to SunOS 8. The syntax is different for earlier versions of SunOS and also for other Unix variants. Similarly, the output might vary among vmstat versions, so check the vmstat man page for the available options and calling format.

```
shellbeast> vmstat -p 5 5
     memory           page          executable      anonymous       filesystem
   swap   free  re  mf  fr  de  sr  epi  epo  epf  api  apo  apf  fpi  fpo  fpf
 1036152 35552   2   6   2   0   0    1    0    0    0    0    0   16    0    1
 1043768 46344   0   0   0   0   0    0    0    0    0    0    0    0    0    0
 1043768 46344   0   0   0   0   0    0    0    0    0    0    0    0    0    0
 1043768 46344   0   0   0   0   0    0    0    0    0    0    0    0    0    0
 1043768 46344   0   0   0   0   0    0    0    0    0    0    0    0    0    0
```

Looks incomprehensible, eh? Admittedly, the headers are a tad obscure, but the information itself is far too useful to disregard. The first line of any vmstat report shows only summary information. Subsequent lines show the information that you use to track down memory problems. Before proceeding, though, look at Table 23.2 for an explanation of vmstat's output fields.

TABLE 23.2   vmstat Paging Statistics Output Fields

Field	Description
memory	
swap	Shows the amount of available swap space
free	Shows the size of the unallocated memory store
page	
re	Shows the number of pages reclaimed from the free list
mf	Shows the number of minor page faults (pages read from RAM)
fr	Shows the amount of RAM freed (in kilobytes)
de	Shows the estimated RAM shortfall that will need to be made up using paging or swapping
sr	Shows the number of pages scanned
executable	
epi	Shows the number of executable page-ins
epo	Shows the number of executable page-outs
epf	Shows the number of executable page faults
anonymous	
api	Shows the number of anonymous page-ins
apo	Shows the number of anonymous page-outs
apf	Shows the number of anonymous page faults
filesystem	
fpi	Shows the number of filesystem page-ins
fpo	Shows the number of filesystem page-outs
fpf	Shows the number of filesystem page faults

Of the fields listed in Table 23.2, by far the most important are the five columns under the page header because they show the system's paging activity. As pages expire, they are returned to the free page list, so on a smoothly functioning system, the values under fr and re should be high. On the other hand, when values in the mf (minor faults) column are high, the CPU is being forced to read pages in from RAM too often, which can indicate a performance problem. When the number of minor page faults is high, turn to ps, as discussed in the previous section, to identify processes that require significant amounts of virtual memory (as shown in the SZ column of ps's output).

Similarly, when the amount of available swap space (shown in the swap column and displayed in kilobyte units) is low, this is an indication that the system is swapping heavily and likely is performing poorly. Again, use ps to identify the process or processes making heavy use of swap. In some cases, you might be able to tune the application itself to address the issue, but, more often than not, the permanent solution is adding RAM to the system.

On systems that support it, the free command shows memory utilization, including swap usage and capacity. For example, the following command shows the output of the free command on a lightly loaded Linux system:

```
advent> free
              total      used       free     shared    buffers     cached
Mem:         126708    103888      22820          0       6144      68860
-/+ buffers/cache:      28884      97824
Swap:        136512        20     136492
```

At a glance, free gives you an informative snapshot of system memory usage. The first line following the header shows physical memory information (all information is in kilobytes), including the total amount of installed RAM, how much of it the kernel has allocated (but not necessarily used), how much RAM is free, how much RAM is configured as shared memory, and how much RAM is used for buffering and cache.

The second line shows memory usage adjusted for buffering. That is, free subtracts the amount of memory used for buffering and caching from the used column and adds it to the free column so that you get a more accurate picture of actual RAM usage as opposed to the kernel's allocation of RAM, which changes according to system usage and the load average. Note, for example, that if you subtract the buffers and cached values from the used value on the first line, you get 28,884 (10,3888 3 6144 3 68860 = 28,884) and that adding buffers and cached to free yields precisely 97,824 (22,820 + 6144 + 68,860 = 97,824).

The third line, finally, shows the amounts of swap space available, used, and free. As you can see, swap usage on this system was fairly low at the time the snapshot was taken.

If you prefer a graphical display, consider xosview, a program licensed under the GNU General Public License that is more configurable and offers greater detail than xload, as you can see in Figure 23.2. xosview is also a real-time monitor, so it can impose a

23

RA AND
PERFORMANCE
MONITORING

performance penalty on the system that it is monitoring. The "Online References" section at the end of this chapter includes a URL for downloading xosview.

FIGURE 23.2

xosview's graphical performance information is more complete than xload's.

As you can see in Figure 23.2, xosview shows the load average, CPU utilization, RAM and swap usage, CPU paging activity, disk reads and writes, and the number of interrupts. In fact, xosview's display is almost a verbatim translation of the output of vmstat's -S option, shown in the following listing:

```
shellbeast> vmstat -S 5 5
   procs       memory            page              disk          faults       cpu
 r  b  w    swap   free  si  so pi po fr de sr dd -- -- --    in   sy   cs us sy id
 0  0  4 1034400 34856   0   0 27  1  2  0  0  0  0  0  0   341  175   69  1  1 99
 0  0 12  999192 26728   0   0  0  0  0  0  0  0  0  0  0   316   15   36  0  0 100
 0  0 12  999192 26728   0   0  0  0  0  0  0  0  0  0  0   312   13   37  1  0 99
 0  0 12  999192 26728   0   0  0  0  0  0  0  0  0  0  0   314   14   39  0  0 100
 0  0 12  999192 26728   0   0  0  0  0  0  0  0  0  0  0   313   16   37  0  0 100
```

The key differences between vmstat's –p and –S options are that –S shows swap statistics (the si and so columns) and replaces the executable, anonymous, and filesystem paging information with statistics about disk reads (not used in the example), page faults, and system CPU usage. The new fields are described in Table 23.3.

TABLE 23.3   vmstat's Swap and Resource Utilization Output Fields

Field	Description
procs	
r	Number of processes ready to run (in the run queue)
b	Number of processes blocked while waiting for some resources
w	Number of processes swapped out while waiting for some resource
page	
si	Number of pages swapped in from disk
so	Number of pages swapped out to disk

TABLE 23.3 vmstat's Swap and Resource Utilization Output Fields

Field	Description
page	
pi	Number of kilobytes paged in
po	Number of kilobytes paged out
faults	
in	Device interrupts
sy	System faults per second
cpu	
cs	The number of CPU context switches (between processes)
us	Percentage of CPU time spent executing user code
sy	Percentage of CPU time spent executing system/kernel code
id	Percentage of time that the CPU has been idle

If the w column is nonzero and the so and si columns indicate continuous swapping, start looking for processes consuming memory, particularly those with large virtual memory requirements. Similarly, if the po column consistently contains large or high values, you can be reasonably sure that the system is experiencing some sort of memory resource saturation and, as a result, performance is degraded. Watching the r and b columns over a period of time will enable you to get some sense of how fast processes are moving through the queue. Except for long-running processes (easily identified using ps), the values in the r and b columns should stay low.

Disk Usage and Performance

Disk usage is straightforward to monitor using the df and du commands. df reports the amount of disk space that is available, and du reports the amount that is used. Use df's -k option to see disk usage in kilobytes—for example:

```
shellbeast> df -k
Filesystem           kbytes     used    avail capacity  Mounted on
/proc                     0        0        0     0%     /proc
/dev/dsk/c0t3d0s0    143875    30198    99290    24%     /
/dev/dsk/c0t3d0s6    623341   472809    94432    84%     /usr
fd                        0        0        0     0%     /dev/fd
/dev/dsk/c0t3d0s5    201275   102719    78429    57%     /var
/dev/dsk/c0t1d0s7   2560515  1563977   945328    63%     /space1
/dev/dsk/c0t1d0s6   1016375   858749    96644    90%     /usr/local
swap                 760560     7776   752784     2%     /tmp
```

```
nfs.someisp.com:/home
                  209715200 158007620 51707580     76%      /home
mail.someisp.com:/var/mail
                  26457208 6412412 18711404     26%      /var/mail
lists.someisp.com:/var/maillists
                   963333   377133   528401     42%      /var/maillists
```

The output is a little less chaotic if you omit -k. If you use the -l option, you will list only the disk space that is physically located on the your own system, not NFS mounts and other remotely accessible disk drives.

Although it is a little jumbled, the report makes how much space is available on each filesystem. Clearly, /usr and /usr/local are nearing capacity (84% and 90% full, respectively), but, on this system, they are mounted read-only and static, so the capacity issue is not crucial. The last three filesystems are NFS mounts from other hosts. /home is getting rather full, could become a problem, and should be monitored carefully to make sure that it does not suddenly fill up, which would cause all sorts of dismay (actually, the system administrator for these systems uses disk quotas to make sure that a thoughtless user does not fill up /home).

To see how much disk space is in use, use the du command. Its basic syntax is as follows:

```
du [options] file
```

file can be a filesystem, a device, a directory, or even a file. Useful values for *options* are -k, which reports usage in KB units; -s, which reports only summary values; and -d, which limits the report to the specified filesystem. The default report, if no options are specified, shows usage statistics for each directory at or beneath *file*. For example, the following command shows du's default output:

```
shellbeast> du /tmp
8        /tmp/screens
17336    /tmp
```

The next command just shows a summary report for disk usage in /tmp:

```
shellbeast> du -s /tmp
17344    /tmp
```

The last command shows the summary report but uses the –k option to display units of kilobytes instead of 512-byte blocks (the default):

```
shellbeast> du -sk /tmp
8672     /tmp
```

Without a doubt, the weakest link in the performance chain is disk I/O. RAM and CPU speeds are hundreds of times faster than the fastest SCSI disks and Fibre Channel disk arrays. Fortunately, Unix kernels and disk hardware take various measures, largely in terms of software and hardware caches and delayed writes, to work around the enormous speed differential. However, as a system administrator, you still need to know how to identify and address disk I/O problems.

First, however, you will need to be familiar with the following terms, commonly used in performance-tuning circles and literature:

- **Queuing delay**—The delay that occurs while a disk controller identifies where on a disk to locate data to read or write

- **Seek latency**—The delay that occurs while the disk's read/write head moves to the proper cylinder location over the disk

- **Rotational latency**—The delay that occurs while the disk spins into position underneath the read/write head (measured in revolutions per minute [RPMs])

- **Seek time**—The time it takes to move the read/write head from one disk track to another

- **Minimum seek time**—The seek time between two adjacent tracks

- **Maximum seek time**—The seek time between the two tracks that are farthest apart on a disk

- **Average seek time**—An estimate measure of how long an average seek operation takes

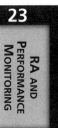

The command most commonly used for drilling down on I/O performance problems is iostat. You can also use the sar command with its -d option. Like vmstat, iostat's simplest invocation is this:

```
iostat [seconds [count]]
```

seconds defines the interval between reports, and *count* specifies the number of reports. For example, the following command generates the default iostat report for shellbeast, the shell server used throughout this chapter, taking five samples at 5-second intervals:

```
shellbeast> iostat 5 5
        tty          sd1            sd3            nfs2           nfs745            cpu
 tin tout kps tps serv  kps tps serv  kps tps serv  kps tps serv  us sy wt id
 151  779   7   1   56   19   3   39   35   5   15    4   1    6  20 10  1 69
   6  740   0   0    0    2   1    3  394  52    4   82  11    6  44 27  0 30
   5  523   0   0    0    1   0    4  430  54    5    0   0    1  43 16  0 41
   6  897  14   2   49   29   4  108  414  52   17    0   0    0  45 16  0 39
   0  279   0   0    0    4   1    5  398  50   11    0   0    0  45 27  0 28
```

As with many of the other utilities you have looked at in this chapter (notably, sar and vmstat), the first line presents summary data since the system's most recent boot.

Subsequent lines show snapshots taken at the end of each interval specified on the command line (5 seconds, in this case).

The default report shows I/O statistics for the terminal (tty), fixed disks (sd1 and sd3), and, in this case, NFS exports (nfs2 and nfs745). This section is concerned with disk I/O, so it focuses on the fixed disks and briefly on the NFS exports. For each of the disks, iostat displays three fields. The final field of interest is the I/O wait field, wt, under the cpu heading. Table 23.4 describes these fields in iostat's output.

TABLE 23.4 iostat Output Fields

Field	Description
kps	The kilobytes per second written to and read from the device
tps	The numbers of transfers (or I/O requests) per second sent to the disk
serv	The average length of time, measured in milliseconds, required to service I/O requests to the disk
wt	The percentage of time that the CPU spends waiting for I/O to complete

With the information in Table 23.4 in mind, return to the iostat report shown a moment ago. The disk nfs2, which, in this case is an NFS export that stores home directories, is the most active, averaging more than 50 transfers (I/O requests) per second and transferring more than 400KB of data per second. I/O wait time is 0, so, all in all, shellbeast's I/O performance is quite satisfactory.

How should you interpret iostat's output? Ideally, over time and, depending on the system's purpose, you want to see disk activity distributed roughly evenly across all the disks so that no single disk or controller is forced to handle the majority of I/O, a situation called an I/O *hot spot*. If you do identify such a hot spot, you may be able to resolve it by attaching the disk concerned to a different controller or moving all or part of the filesystem in question to another disk or perhaps both. When I/O waits (see the wt field) start to climb and stay consistently high, resort to ps or vmstat to identify where the block is occurring and why.

If you want to dig deeper into disk I/O performance, use the option -x with iostat. -x reports the I/O performance of all disks in a tabular format. This listing shows a sample iostat report using the -x option:

```
shellbeast> iostat -x 5 2
                            extended device statistics
device   r/s  w/s   kr/s   kw/s wait actv  svc_t  %w  %b
sd1      0.5  0.2    3.2    3.4  0.0  0.0   55.7   0   0
sd3      0.6  2.8    3.2   16.1  0.0  0.1   38.6   0   3
nfs2     2.0  3.0   13.0   22.2  0.0  0.0   15.0   0   2
nfs745   0.5  0.1    2.9    0.7  0.0  0.0    6.4   0   0
nfs1222  0.1  0.0    0.4    0.0  0.0  0.0   23.0   0   0
nfs1224  0.0  0.0    0.0    0.0  0.0  0.0    2.4   0   0
                            extended device statistics
device   r/s  w/s   kr/s   kw/s wait actv  svc_t  %w  %b
sd1      0.0  0.0    0.0    0.0  0.0  0.0    0.0   0   0
sd3      0.0  1.0    0.0    6.8  0.0  0.0   23.4   0   1
nfs2    10.0  0.6    9.1    0.1  0.0  0.0    1.1   0   1
nfs745   0.0  0.0    0.0    0.0  0.0  0.0    0.0   0   0
nfs1222  0.0  0.0    0.0    0.0  0.0  0.0    0.0   0   0
nfs1224  0.0  0.0    0.0    0.0  0.0  0.0    0.0   0   0
```

Table 23.5 describes the meaning of each field, again ignoring the `tty` and `cpu` categories.

TABLE 23.5   iostat Extended Device Statistics Output Fields

Field	Description
r/s	The number of disk reads per second
w/s	The number of disk writes per second
kr/s	The number of kilobytes read per second
kw/s	The number of kilobytes written per second
wait	The average number of I/O requests waiting to be serviced
actv	The average number of I/O requests actively being serviced
svc_t request	The average time, in milliseconds, of each I/O service

Again, the goal with the `-x` option is to ensure that all the disks are sharing the I/O load more or less equally.

Note

If you are using a Linux system, iostat is part of the sysstat package maintained by Sebastien Godard. The "Online References" section includes a URL for the sysstat package.

Network Traffic

In an increasingly internetworked computing environment (*ubiquitous networking*, if you will), network bottlenecks are highly visible. Moreover, the nature of a network makes troubleshooting performance problems rather difficult because potentially any number of failure or bottleneck points could exist: network cards, cabling, bridges, routers, gateways, and firewalls. Worse still, on a TCP/IP Ethernet, everyone notices a network performance problem. To quote the first edition of this book, "When the [network's] capacity is used up, EtherNet [sic] is very democratic. If it has a capacity problem, all users suffer equally." From the administrator's point of view, this just means more grumpy users demanding a solution right now.

The first thing to check is raw packet traffic, which you can see using the `netstat` command and its `-i` option, which shows the TCP/IP traffic on all active network interfaces—for example:

```
shellbeast> netstat -i
Name Mtu  Net/Dest    Address       Ipkts    Ierrs Opkts   Oerrs Collis Queue
lo0  8232 loopback    localhost     2365937  0     2365937 0     0      0
hme0 1500 shellbeast.someisp.com shellbeast.someisp.com 302163029 10 290454583
➥0    0    0
```

The output shows basic TCP/IP packet traffic for two interfaces, the loopback interface (lo0), and the Internet device (hme0). Table 23.6 describes the fields.

TABLE 23.6 netstat –i Output Fields

Field	Description
Name	The name of the network interface
Mtu	The maximum transmission unit, or packet size, of the interface
Net/Dest	The name of the network to which the interface is connected
Address	The Internet address of the interface (use –n to see numeric rather than symbolic addresses)
Ipkts	The number of incoming (received) packets since the interface was started
Ierrs	The number of errors on incoming packets
Opkts	The number of outbound (sent) packets transmitted since the interface was started

TABLE 23.6 continued

Field	Description
Oerrs	The number of errors on outbound packages since the interface was last started
Collis	The number of packet collisions

Ideally, the number of packets with errors (malformed, incomplete, or garbled packets) should be less than 1%. In the example output, 10 inbound errors out of more than 302 million received packets amounts to perfect; the outbound traffic is precisely perfect. When outbound error rates increase, some sort of problem is occurring on your system; on the other hand, inbound errors, while problematic, rarely indicate problems on your system. That is, the problem is "out there." Packet collisions are inevitable because everyone is using the network simultaneously.

To get a better idea of network saturation, use `netstat` without any options, as shown in the following example:

```
shellbeast> netstat

TCP
    Local Address        Remote Address       Swind Send-Q Rwind Recv-Q  State
    ------------------   ------------------   ----- ------ ----- ------  -------
    shellbeast.http      someplace.1788       17520      0  8760      0 ESTABLISHED
    shellbeast.22        anotherplace.39432    8760      0  8760      0 ESTABLISHED
    shellbeast.22        anotherplace.39434    8760      0  8760      0 ESTABLISHED
    shellbeast.35062     shellbeast.6005      32768      0 32768      0 ESTABLISHED
    shellbeast.6005      shellbeast.35062     32768      0 32768      0 ESTABLISHED
```

A bare `netstat` command shows all active Internet connections. The data that you are looking for here is nonzero values in the Send -Q column. If several connections have nonzero values in this column and the values are increasing, the network is saturated.

To check basic network connectivity, use the `ping` command. First, `ping` localhost by name (ping localhost) and by IP address (ping 127.0.0.1). Next, `ping` your host by hostname and IP address. If these work, networking is at least running on the local system. If you can `ping` your own host by IP address but not by its name, make sure that you have the correct entry in /etc/hosts. Next, `ping` another system on your network, again by both name and IP address. Generally, if you can successfully `ping` any remote system by IP but not by name, you have a name server problem. Finally, `ping` a system on another network (yes, by name and IP address). Successful `ping`s of remote systems not on your network mean that you can at least reach the Internet. If a given remote system is inaccessible, it might not be up. If you cannot `ping` remote systems, make sure

23

RA AND
PERFORMANCE
MONITORING

that you have a properly functioning name server and gateway, and make sure that the interface that you want to use is up and running. Similarly, `netstat -nr` checks both the kernel's routing tables and highlights invalid or incorrect DNS entries.

Before discussing maintenance contracts, consider these final thoughts. Do *not* apply the tuning tips suggested in this chapter based on a single observation or on a small set of observations taken over a short period of time. Instead, endure user complaints about performance and management pressure to solve the problem long enough to develop a more comprehensive picture of the problem. Combining the data that you get from `sar`, `vmstat`, `iostat`, `ps`, and `uptime` yields a more accurate picture of overall system status and the problem domain, and thereby reduces the likelihood that you are chasing a red herring or that tuning one subsystem will adversely affect another.

Similarly, rather than waiting until your end users or your managers are breathing down your neck, take advantage of cron and the command invocations that you have seen in this section to start creating a system usage profile.

Doing so before a crisis develops yields several advantages. First, as you will learn in the section "Capacity Projection and Planning," at the end of the chapter, this sort of routine, regular, and automated monitoring makes it fairly simple to identify upward trends in usage and schedule component upgrades or replacements before degraded performance becomes acute. Second, reviewing these reports gives you additional insight into how the system is used, which *will* make you a better administrator and will help you anticipate problems before they occur. Finally, intimate familiarity with how the system *usually* behaves will cause extraordinary behavior, such as a sudden spike in memory consumption or a sharp increase in disk activity, crystal clear, again giving you time to address a performance problem before it becomes acute and your telephone starts ringing.

Maintenance Contracts

In large installations and when mission-critical, enterprise-level systems are involved, conventional wisdom (and vendors, of course!) recommends maintenance contracts for at least the key components, such as servers and major applications. As a rule, we concur with conventional wisdom in this regard. There are advantages and disadvantages to maintenance contracts, and the issues to consider vary somewhat between hardware and software maintenance.

Advantages and Disadvantages

The advantages of maintenance contracts include these:

- Access to expert resources and for solving hardware and software problems
- Depending on the contract, guaranteed minimum or maximum service levels and response times

- Early access to patches and upgrades
- Free or deeply discounted replacement parts
- Reduced requirements for in-house support and maintenance staff
- Access to vendor-supported forums and other resources restricted to customers
- Input into the next generation of a product
- Peace of mind

Maintenance contracts also have distinct disadvantages, such as these:

- The cost for adequate support is sometimes prohibitive. Ordinarily, contracts must be renewed on a yearly basis, significantly increasing the total cost over the system's lifetime.
- "Expert resources" might prove less than satisfactory.
- Vendor support is time-consuming because fewer vendors take the time to become familiar with your site and its needs. Similarly, outside support personnel are rarely as knowledgeable about any given site as in-house staff.
- Reliance on external support sources creates a potentially unhealthy dependence on a vendor, discouraging in-house staff from learning how to support a product

These disadvantages notwithstanding, and depending on local conditions, maintenance contracts are usually good insurance.

Software Maintenance

Software maintenance contracts provide several key benefits: quick access to security patches and bug fixes, early access to upgrades and point releases, input into product revisions, and a ready pool of people who know more about the product than you do. It is also becoming more common to purchase software for trivial amounts of money, to buy licenses for more money, and then to pay possibly exorbitant prices for annual support contracts. If you have to choose between software and hardware maintenance contracts, we recommend hardware maintenance—it is much easier to locate help with software problems than it is to obtain replacement parts or installation assistance for typically proprietary hardware.

Hardware Maintenance

Unless you are purchasing commodity, off-the-shelf Intel PC hardware, hardware maintenance contracts are essential. Vendors are the best source for replacement parts, and most maintenance contracts include some provision for free or discounted replacement parts. In addition, hardware support can include regular service visits. Increasingly, hardware also is smart enough to phone home when problems are detected during self-diagnostics. Many vendors also have the capability to dial in, depending on the sort of system, of course, to diagnose hardware problems and recommend a course of action. Finally, hardware maintenance contracts turn the vendor into a partner of sorts and can be written so that the vendor forfeits money when problems are not solved in a set amount of time or to the customer's satisfaction.

Capacity Projection and Planning

Capacity projection and planning allow you to plan ahead for component and system upgrades and replacements. Requirements analysis enables you to identify the fundamental characteristics of the system installed and to make sure that it adequately meets the basic needs of the problem or situation that it was designed to address. Performance monitoring, similarly, allows you to make sure that the system continues to meet those needs, to address performance issues before they become critical, and to take measures to solve performance problems that emerge without warning.

At some point, however, system usage, at least on a successful system, exceeds the capabilities of its original design. Memory utilization might max out, CPU saturation might exceed a previously identified threshold, or disk usage might exhaust available capacity. Capacity planning and projection allow you to anticipate such situations, plan ahead for them, and take corrective action proactively. This section outlines the capacity planning and projection process and, hopefully, helps you avoid unpleasant surprises.

Capacity planning and projection synthesize requirements analysis and performance monitoring, incorporating elements of both. How so? The analysis phase identifies the key system components, such as disk space needs, network traffic, or memory requirements that have the greatest impact on the system's success or failure. In a successful system, use of key resources always increases, sometimes slowly and sometimes rapidly. The analytic element of capacity planning and projection involves establishing resource usage growth rates, extending them into the future, identifying approximately when anticipated growth will exceed existing capacity, and scheduling upgrades or replacements of the key system resources to minimize service interruptions.

Establishing Schedules

Unfortunately, or perhaps predictably, reality is not as neat and clean as planners would like. Growth rates can vary, sometimes wildly. Initial estimates might be too conservative or too aggressive. This is where monitoring applies to capacity planning and projection. Performance monitoring maintains the system's overall efficiency, paying particular attention to the critical resources. Fluke deviations from anticipated usage patterns must be noted but might not require any other response. Consistent deviations, however, must be addressed. Growth more rapid than originally estimated necessarily speeds up the upgrade or replacement schedule and, in extreme cases, might render the system obsolete sooner than expected. The key is to *use* performance-monitoring statistics proactively. Do not simply accumulate and ignore them. Review them regularly, compare them to initial estimates and to recent trends, and take appropriate action.

Specifying Replacements

Specifying replace components goes back to the topic that opened this chapter: requirements analysis. There are two considerations to keep in mind here. First, upgrade and replacement hardware components and software should suit the current and projected needs. So, plan ahead for upgrades and replacements, making sure, when possible, that the necessary components will be available over the anticipated (designed) lifetime of the system.

Second, recognize that upgrades eventually reach a point of diminishing returns. This point highlights our earlier suggestion to keep maintainability and scalability in mind during the RA process. At some point, the personnel and resource costs involved and frequent downtime for system upgrades exceed the cost savings that upgrades represent. Similarly, when demands for ongoing maintenance begin to tax the time and tempers of the administrative staff, a system replacement could be in order. Constant CPU saturation can be resolved by upgrading system CPUs to faster processors, but, at some point, upgrading a uniprocessor system ceases to be cost-effective when upgrading to a multiprocessor system can spread the computing load across more processors *and* provide a longer system lifetime. In short, sometimes replacing a system makes a lot more sense than upgrading it.

Maintaining Flexibility

One of the responsibilities of system administrators is to understand the tasks that given systems must perform and to grasp the overall computing environment in which individual systems are situated. The better you understand the overall environment, the more options you have to allocate resources in the environment. Rather than upgrades or replacements, you can shift resources (both systems and personnel) among computing requirements. In this regard, the performance-monitoring statistics that you accumulate can serve you. For example, when neither upgrades nor replacements are possible, use your performance-management data to tell management, "We can support functions X and Y now. If we want to add Z, then we need the following items...." Alternatively, the conversation might be, "No one is using system X right now, and it takes up Y time to maintain. We can shift these resources to system Z, which needs a boost." The point here is that, with good information—that is, performance-monitoring data with which you are familiar—this can work for you and allow you to be more responsive and flexible.

Best Practices

- Take time to refine the statement and understand the problem.
- Involve all project stakeholders or their representatives in the requirements analysis phase.
- Clearly and specifically define and fine-tune the project scope to maintain focus and prevent project creep.
- Complete the requirements analysis process for beginning the design process, to avoid allowing design to drive analysis.
- Take the time to establish system usage profiling before attempting to diagnose or solve apparent performance problems.
- Use both high-level, low-impact performance-monitoring tools and low-level, high-impact performance-monitoring tools to develop a fuller system usage profile and specific information about the performance problem being analyzed.
- Remember that performance monitoring is an ongoing process, not a one-time stop-gap measure.
- Consider purchasing software or hardware maintenance contracts, being careful to provide adequate, ongoing training for in-house staff.
- Develop and adhere to maintenance and upgrade schedules, to avoid unanticipated capacity management problems and to head off performance issues.

Online References

Solaris performance monitoring: `http://docs.sun.com/ab2/coll.47.11/SYSADV2/@Ab2PageView/43443?Ab2Lang=C&Ab2Enc=iso-8859-1`

sar and iostat for Linux: `http://perso.wanadoo.fr/sebastien.godard`

xosview: `http://freshmeat.net/projects/xosview/`

Reference

Carling, M., et al. *Linux System Administration*. New Riders Publishing, 1999.

CHAPTER 24

Working with People

by Robin Miller

IN THIS CHAPTER

Getting Respect

You have specialized knowledge that your coworkers don't. Computers are essential to the business's operation, and if you don't keep the systems going, the whole place will come apart. This gives you an awesome level of power, one that you can use either for good or for evil. It is easy to fall into the Bastard Operator From Hell (http://www.bofh.org) routine, where you are constantly getting over on your bosses and everyone else—and gloating about it. The only problem with this attitude is that, sooner or later, times will get tough, and there will be other people just as skilled as you looking for work. If you are nasty, a UNIX sysadmin with a solid resume and a pleasant smile eventually will apply for your job, and you will be gone.

An essential but rarely discussed part of being an effective sysadmin is what we might call your deskside manner. Think of yourself as a doctor and your users as patients. Sure, you're there to take care of the machines, not the people, but the machines are there to serve the people, not the other way around. In the end, you are solving problems for people, and those problems just happen to be with their computers. Treating those people right will get them to respect you. Think of doctors you have gone to in your life. You are probably not qualified to judge their medical credentials, but it is easy to judge their bedside manner. Given a choice, are you going to pick a surly doctor who looks down on you, or one who treats you with respect and a bit of courtesy? Would you rather have a doctor who grunts at you and tells you little or nothing about what is going on inside your body without being prodded, or one who takes the time to tell you what's wrong, how the drugs or other treatments work, and what you can do to help yourself get well?

Now pretend that you are the doctor and your users are your patients. Treat your "patients" with respect, and you will get respect in return. Remember, true respect is earned, not given freely, so it might take days or weeks, possibly even months, to ramp up the level of respect that your users have for you to an acceptable level. If you (or a previous sysadmin) were surly and contemptuous toward users in the past, it will take even longer because there is damage to undo. But undo that damage you must, and you must build as much respect as you can—in the end, it will make your job easier and more pleasant.

This same habit of mutual respect should take over all your dealings at work—not just with users, but also with other sysadmins, bosses, and with coworkers you don't deal with regularly. It is a good to get into the habit of being at least minimally cordial to everyone in the place on general principles, even when you are busy or lost in thought. In return, they will gradually start being more pleasant to you.

You don't suddenly have to become Johnny Sunshine, mind you; if you are in the middle of solving a tough problem. your brow will probably furrow and you might not be receptive to chatter. But it takes only a second to say (politely), "I, like, have to concentrate on this right now if I'm going to get this working right. Can we talk later?" A bit of a smile when you say this helps. Besides, the smile will relax your facial muscles and relieve some of your own tension, and that is always good—for you.

What Users Want

Users want their computers to work without fuss. They have jobs to do that probably aren't directly related to computers, and time they devote to learning about or messing around with their computers takes them away from their primary tasks. Complaining about "clueless users" is silly. If all the users knew everything you know, you'd be out of a job, just as surgeons would all be standing on street corners carrying "Will Cut You Open For Food" signs if everyone knew how to perform surgery on themselves.

> **Note**
>
> Remember that you are not getting paid to support UNIX systems just because people admire the way you do it. Organizations have goals. The computers are there to help the organization achieve those goals. The users might well be the people who do the actual achieving. Somewhere, someone is authorizing *your* paycheck to make sure that *the users* can get their jobs done.

Your "deskside manner" needs to become as reassuring and as authoritative as a doctor's bedside manner. When you start thinking of yourself as a computer doctor who is trying to keep users' computers in good health and those users happy, it is easier to treat those users with compassion than when you are thinking of them as people who should be looked down upon because they don't share your arcane knowledge. This does not mean that you need to be servile; a good doctor takes care of his patients from a position of strength based on confidence in his knowledge of medicine. Your patients—I mean, users—whether external clients or coworkers, like to see that same confidence in you. When you stand straight and answer their questions forthrightly, in language they can understand, and (over time) when you prove that you can solve their problems rapidly and smoothly, they will respect you more than if you come across as a keeper of arcane secrets that they are too stupid to ever learn.

The reality is that most of the users you help are smart enough to learn enough to take care of their own computers, software, and networking problems, but that they're too busy to put in the time it takes to learn how to do it, just as you are probably too busy to learn enough about how your car's transmission works to service or rebuild it competently. Like your doctor, you are likely to turn to a skilled mechanic when these tasks need to be performed.

Think about your own experiences with doctors and mechanics. You don't like to be kept waiting. If you have a 2:00 appointment with your doctor, you expect to be seen at 2:00 (or at least 2:30, and 3:00 at the latest). If a mechanic tells you that your car will be ready Thursday and it's not done by Friday, you are going to be upset.

There will be days when things screw up and you fall behind in your work. This is inevitable. Your users expect this to happen now and then (their jobs aren't always easy, either), but they expect you to let them know what's going on. If you are going to be late or a task is going to take longer than you expected, speak up immediately!

Don't wait until you are already late to tell the people who depend on you that things are going more slowly than anticipated. Call or email the second you know you are going to be delayed. You don't need to make up bogus excuses.

Tell them the truth, even if that truth is, "I made a mistake configuring sendmail and now I have to redo everything." Everyone makes mistakes. You're allowed to make your share. When you admit that you're human, you will gain more respect than you can possibly lose by revealing that you are not perfect. (A sneaky side effect of admitting that things don't always go perfectly in your line of work is that it will impress on users that your job is hard and that you don't spend all your time sitting around, sucking up caffeine, and surfing Slashdot. This will add to their respect for you!)

The essence of the preceding paragraphs boils down to two things: compassion and communication. When your users have problems or need advice, you must treat them with the same level of compassion you would like to get from a doctor. You also must communicate information about their problem and how you are going to solve it as thoroughly as you'd like a mechanic to tell you what's going on with your car.

Being a Proactive Administrator

Okay, doc, remember that a large part of your job isn't just making sick systems healthy, but keeping healthy ones from getting sick in the first place. Nirvana for your users and bosses (and you) is having everything work all the time, with all upgrades and maintenance done on a prepublished schedule so that everyone can plan their work around system outages instead of having to take forced breaks when they are least prepared for them.

Preventative medicine should be a large part of your job. Make those hard drives quit smoking! Tell those bloated filesystems to lose weight! Offer "computer health" education to your customers, not so much in formal classes as in casual sessions where you help them learn neat things about their computers in tiny, easy-to-digest bits. If you have clueless users and clueless bosses, who could be better than you to give them a clue?

Most people basically enjoy learning if you make it fun for them. With your help—and plenty of patience—today's least computer-grokking clerical worker could be tomorrow's accurate bug-reporter who saves you hours of frustration tracking down a subtle problem.

Teaching Users

Teaching is an important but often overlooked sysadmin task. Teaching isn't particularly hard, as long as you exercise patience and try to understand that different people come to you with different levels of knowledge and that it's up to you to give them information they need at a pace they can handle.

The easiest way to develop your own teaching skills is to think back to your own time in school. You had good teachers, and you had ineffective ones. You have a good memory and excellent analytical skills (or you wouldn't be a sysadmin, right?), so it shouldn't be tough for you to figure out why one teacher made you want to learn and what made others make you want to put your head down and take a nap.

Passion is often the key to effective teaching. If you are truly in love with your subject matter, your students will pick up on your enthusiasm and will want to learn from you even if they start out without any particular interest in what you are trying to show them.

Empowerment

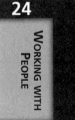

Another trick is what some call "empowerment" but I prefer to call "sharing the keys to the castle." It's very human to want to know things that others don't; multinational businesses have built around sharing celebrity "secrets" (as a trip through almost any supermarket checkout line will show), and gossip is and always has been one of humanity's favorite pastimes. Now here you are, bursting with secrets about how essential working tools (computers) operate, and you are willing to share those secrets with a select few. Come from this angle, even if you ham it up a little, and you will get rapt attention from a bookkeeper to whom you are trying to teach the mysteries of a shared file system. The payoff? For the bookkeeper, less need to call you for help and a sense of being in charge. For you? Fewer trouble calls from that person about file system problems, and those calls that you *do* get will have better descriptions of the problem.

Teaching, in this case, probably doesn't mean standing up in front of a group and giving formal lectures. You are more likely to have few teaching opportunities every day, and each one might last only a few minutes, but that's all it might take to show someone a basic function. Basic functions, of course, are what you should concentrate on when teaching users; it would be nice to have everyone understand the reasons everything works and what TCP/IP means and all that, but it is not essential. (If you find someone who really wants to know, loan her books and go from there.)

Your main assignment, and the one that will do the most immediate good for users, is to teach them simple cause-and-effect relationships involved in their computer use. What your users need to know more than anything else is the answer to the question, "To get result X, which key or keys do I push?" Very few manuals are designed to give them an answer to this question quickly and easily, so the traditional Bastard Operator From Hell's "Read the flooping manual!" reply doesn't cut it. It's better for both you and the user if you simply answer the question. Better yet, show the user how to use that command and what happens when it is invoked, then have the user do it while you watch, possibly two or three times until you're sure he has it right—and has made notes on how to do it when you're not around to give step-by-step instructions.

This is where patience comes in. Sure, this is all basic stuff to you, hardly worth a second's thought. Now put yourself in the shoes of a 42-year-old woman who got married young and stayed home to raise children until she was forced to go back to work eight months ago because her husband got laid off from his factory job. Now she's suddenly Ms. Workerbee, customer service rep, on the phone with strangers all day, worried that if she can't figure out all this computer stuff, she'll get fired and that her family will lose the house if she loses this job. Yes, Ms. Workerbee is a clueless user; her only previous computer experience was logging onto AOL and exchanging email with her daughter who's away at college. You are going to have to take it slow with her. You can't just say "function key" and expect her to know it's the one that says "Fn" on it. No, you have to spell it out for her—in detail. You need to show her how to hold down the Control key (and that it's the one that says "Ctrl") while she pushes the other key in a Ctrl+[X] command sequence instead of pressing the two keys one at a time. You can't just tell her that she can "tab" between screens; you need to show her how to do it and make sure she understands.

But, at the same time, you shouldn't talk down to the hypothetical Ms. Workerbee. She can cook a mouth-watering Chicken Kiev. Several of her paintings have won awards in local art shows. She can change a car tire at night in the rain and hang wallpaper straight. She is, in short, an intelligent, creative person who took this job because it paid better than anything else she could find within a reasonable commuting distance, not because she has any great love for it or any desire to get promoted into management right away. And Ms. Workerbee is more than a little afraid of computers. She remembers the time she did something (she's still not sure what) to the one they have at home, and her 14-year-old son told her she was stupid and had messed things up so bad that he had to reinstall Windows because of her stupidity and had to stay up late now to get his homework done, and if he didn't get his report in tomorrow it was all her fault.

Is it any wonder that Ms. Workerbee, a perfectly nice person, is flustered and more than a little afraid when the computer on her desk does something she doesn't understand?

What Ms. Workerbee needs less than anything in the world right now is a snotty geek in an old T-shirt mumbling strange words at her and muttering about "clueless users." She needs reassurance. If she wants to be treated like a moron, she can go home to her teenage children. She needs you to give her a clear explanation of what happened, why it happened, and how to keep it from happening again. At the same time, she is probably a little worried (remember, she really needs this job) that if she reveals how little she knows, she'll get fired, so she's likely to nod and say "I understand" even if she doesn't, especially if you are younger than she is.

This is when a few words from you, like, "We all started out knowing nothing a computers and had to learn all this stuff the hard way, so don't worry, you'll figure it out," can make all the difference in the world. That bit of compassion can be more important in both the job context and the larger sense than solving a knotty networking problem faster than anyone else. Aside from the direct knowledge you impart while taking care of Ms. Workerbee's immediate computer worry, you give her a sense that this is not a great mystery, but merely a series of skills—like cooking—that she can master with a little time and effort.

Getting users comfortable with you pays off in another way, too. Often users will notice potential problems before you do. After all, there are more of them than there are of you. You're much more likely to find out about problems that they encounter if they feel comfortable stopping off to say "hi."

Once you've given Ms. Workerbee that confidence, the hardest part of your teaching task is done. Now she'll ask questions, you can answer those questions, and in a few months she will hardly have any problems and will page you only if her hardware dies—or if she brings food from home and wants to share some with you.

Of course, there is no reason why you can't ask to hold informal computer knowledge classes. No company training program in the world has ever done a truly good job of getting workers truly familiar with the systems that company uses. A weekly, voluntary "computer question and answer" lunch session can be a great tool for spreading knowledge among your coworkers. Sure, you'll get questions about people's home systems during these sessions, but don't shove them off. Take them as compliments, and answer them (briefly) as well as you can, or at least suggest diagnostic steps and books that might help. You will be amazed at how much respect you will get just by being accessible and helpful.

Teaching Bosses

True story: Five vice presidents of a major multinational bank based in New York City once got together and paid a consultant $3,000 out of their own pockets to spend two days teaching them basic UNIX terminology and a little about the Internet's structure. These guys had plenty of UNIX sysadmins and a few programmers working for them, but they didn't want to admit how little they knew in front of people who reported to them. One of the vice presidents—the one in charge of security for the company's new online banking initiative—went so far as to install Linux on his home computer so that he could become more familiar with a UNIX-style command-line interface and so that he could do a little hacking and cracking himself to see what he was dealing with. It turned out that he picked up a new hobby along the way and got more than a little proficient at it, but that's not the point of this tale; the main moral is that bosses are often afraid to reveal just how little they know to people who work "under" them, even when curing that ignorance would be good for everyone involved.

You might report to a senior systems administrator or IT manager who is technically hip. If so, dealing with noncomputer management is not your direct problem—in theory. But in real life, especially in a small company (or in a small IT department in a large company), you will need to interact at least a little with managers who are technically your superiors but who don't really know much about the systems or networks that make the company run efficiently. This is a touchy situation, not so much for you as for them.

Teaching a boss requires great tact. Sneering or acting superior is exactly the wrong thing to do in this situation. "Would you like me to show you how ___ works?" is generally a better approach. An even better one is to say, "Take a look at ____," and then explain what is being displayed. You don't need to be servile or slave-like. You are a highly skilled, intelligent person, and you deserve to be treated as the professional you are. But the boss you're talking to is also (one hopes) an intelligent person with strong skills of one sort or another. Setting up a climate of mutual respect is important, and it's not all that hard to do.

A basic secret of dealing with people on all levels, and one that works especially well with bosses, is to ask questions—not questions designed to make the person you're talking to feel foolish, but ones that he can answer competently. Even a basic, "How's your email behaving for you these days?" question can be good, especially if the company has had email problems recently.

There are always bosses who simply don't want to be bothered with IT matters, to whom the computers and the network and the servers are uninteresting tools that either work or don't. When they don't, this type of boss just wants you to get them going again as fast as possible and to otherwise stay in your corner and keep quiet. This is not a good boss unless he, in return, gives you complete purchasing authority and general IT decision-making power, in which case this can be the best kind of boss you can possibly have. Unfortunately, bosses—like systems administrators—are individuals, not mass-produced items, so each one takes different handling.

This goes right back to the same "compassion and communication" concept that can help you get along with users. Listening is good. Do it a lot (and ask a question now and then), and you will get a better idea of what your bosses expect from you and how you should treat them. And once you figure out their needs, it is good to go at least halfway toward meeting them. If you work within a rigid bureaucratic structure where all proposals are supposed to be in writing, then put everything in writing—and ask everyone who gets a copy to initial whatever you wrote after they've had a chance to read it. If casual hallway conversations are the company's style, hang out in the hallways. IRC, email, telephone—try to conform to the way things are normally done in your workplace as much as you can, even if you think you know better ways to communicate.

None of this means that you have to be conformist to the point of sheeplikeness; it's just that when it's easier to go along to get along on unimportant issues, you might as well smile and nod, and save disagreements for important matters. Although, if you generally get a reputation as being a sensible, helpful person, you are unlikely to have many people disagree with you unless you make totally outlandish requests, like for a $700 Aeron chair when everybody else in the company—including your boss—is sitting on a $99 Office Depot special, and the company is struggling to show the first quarterly profit in its history. (This sort of thing can blow off a lot of the credibility that you build up by being an otherwise amenable employee if you push it too hard.)

Is your boss teachable? Does your boss want to learn? These are questions that no words in a book can answer for you. You are the person on the spot, and only you can answer them. But teaching your boss about what it takes to do your job and how the network runs, why you need some tools and not others, why you advise buying one router instead of a different model, and how you make your software choices is the main thing. It's also

24

WORKING WITH
PEOPLE

important to show that, in general, without anyone sitting on your shoulder and reminding you, you take a rational, caring, cost-conscious approach to your job. When you've got that information drummed in, specifics will come later.

If not, you'll go someplace else where you will be more appreciated, won't you?

Proactive Maintenance

One hundred percent uptime is a myth found only in marketing blurbs. In real life, people trip over cables, hard drives stop working, software borks in unanticipated ways, power systems fail, and thousands of other things go wrong sooner or later. Part of being a proactive administrator is to anticipate potential failures and try to prevent them before they happen.

Visual cable and wire inspection is a simple tactic. It's easy to do: Get a clipboard and walk around looking for ugly or dangling wires. This not only helps you prevent accidents that can injure either the network or the people who use it, but it also gives you an opportunity to take what marketing people would call a customer satisfaction survey. All this means, in this context, is that you ask people if their computers or terminals are working properly.

You can make a little form for this, if you like; it will certainly impress your boss that you have gone to that much trouble, even though it needs to be only a very simple checklist that takes no more than a few minutes to create and print. But the few minutes making that form, and the minutes or hours spent walking around making sure everything is good, are more than worthwhile, both for you and for your employers. If Ms. Workerbee's hard drive is making a funny noise, isn't it better to back up all the data on it and install a new one before it dies, at your leisure, instead of performing a rush repair when the thing dies—as electronics tend to—just as your shift is ending and you're going to go away for a long weekend?

The same applies to software and network problems. It's easy to ignore small problems and glitches, but some of them might turn into large, work-stopping problems if left alone. Which ones? That's hard to say. Some are going to be inherent hardware or software bugs that can't be cured by you, but others will be things that you can correct with a little research and head-scratching. If nothing else, you will get to know your systems and network (and the people who use them) better by delving into its intricacies whenever you have a chance.

The big secret here is not technical, but human. By solving as many problems as you can on a schedule that you choose, instead of waiting until everything grinds to a halt and only then flying into action, you will make life calmer for yourself and for everyone else around you. A calm sysadim is a confident sysadmin, and a confident sysadmin helps keep all the computer users in his area of responsibility calm and happy so that they can concentrate on their jobs instead of worrying about whether their computers are about to screw up.

Dress for Success

No, we're not talking about a three-piece pinstripe suit. Would you trust a sysadmin in that costume? Hah! "Clean and neat" are the main watchwords for sysadmin clothing.

During the great dotcom explosion of 1995–2000, it became fashionable for people in some parts of the computer world to dress as badly and let their grooming go as much as possible. They apparently wanted everyone around them to believe that they were working so many hours and were so fixated on their jobs, that they had no time for mundane tasks such as bathing, washing clothes, or getting haircuts.

Sleeping with your dog in your work cubicle is no longer hip. Working 16-hour days is rarely necessary, unless by "work" we mean spending half your time playing Quake or similar games.

Most of the companies where playtime and worktime got confused have gone broke. "Old economy" rules are back in fashion, and that means you will be looked on more favorably by bosses and coworkers if you show up on time, wearing long pants, socks, and shoes, than you will if you wander in two hours late in sandals and a swimsuit. *The Nudist on the Late Shift* made a great book title for author Po Bronson, but this isn't what most employers expect in a recession-wary 21st century.

The traditional advice to young people looking for their first job was always, "Show up dressed to do the work." That is, if they were trying to get on with a bank, they should wear a conservative, dark blue suit; if they were talking to tugboat captains about becoming a deckhand, they should wear rugged jeans and waterproof boots.

Even today, there is no hard-and-fast rule for sysadmin dress either during an interview or on the job itself. An admin who works in a stuffy corporation's New York headquarters might be required to wear, if not a tie, a formal shirt, slacks with sharp creases in them, and hard office-type shoes. One who works for a cohosting facility in Texas might fit in better wearing a (clean) T-shirt, faded (but clean) khakis, and running shoes new enough not to have holes in them.

Note on Interviews

If you don't know what the dress standards are for the job you are interviewing for, wear whatever passes for business-formal clothes in your region. If you *do* know, dress slightly more formally for the interview than you would expect to for the job. Slightly conservative dress in an interviewee insults no one and will be taken by some as a sign of respect and serious intent. That's the side to err on.

Hair and grooming standards are just as variable. Only a few employers still think that men should look like they just got out of the military or that women should look like they just finished teaching a Sunday school class, but whatever one chooses for a personal style, it should look as if a little pride is being taken in it. A beard on a man? Sure, even a big, full one—but neatly trimmed, especially around the mouth. And, please: no dangling bits of food after lunch. Midriff-baring clothes on women work well if they're cocktail waitresses, but they probably aren't a good idea in a more professional job environment.

Political or religious slogans on T-shirts are generally not a good idea; some employers might even prohibit them. Like it or not, they have the right to do this in a private workplace. T-shirts themselves are a bad idea for interviews.

Even if working on hardware isn't in your nominal job description, you might want to adhere to the old tech safety rules of keeping hands, wrists, and fingers free of all jewelry, and of avoiding large necklaces or other accessories that could accidentally connect you to a live circuit.

But other than the safety rules, the best choice of clothing and personal style depends on your place of employment. The one thing that holds true everywhere is that keeping yourself odor-free, brushing your teeth regularly, and generally taking care of yourself and your appearance will make it clear to coworkers that you respect yourself—and expect them to respect you, too.

Working with Other Admins

Let's start with a radical thought: You are your own boss.

No one knows your capabilities and skills as well as you do. No one else can supervise your every move and keystroke every moment you're at work. No one else knows as much about your health and mood at any given moment as you. Because of all this, you are the world's best-qualified supervisor for [your name here].

Congratulations on your promotion, even if it's all in your own head—for the moment! (You can even go out and celebrate, if you like.)

But now that you are a supervisor, you have duties and responsibilities that you wouldn't have if you were a mere peon. One of the biggest of these is making sure that your team of 1 works well with other teams that might be composed of anywhere from 1 to 100 other individuals. This is not quite the same as "being a team player," a management bromide that assumes you are taking most or all of your direction from a coach or manager. Instead, it means that you are an independent, self-motivated entity that must work in association with other entities to accomplish a set of goals.

Here are some basic differences between workers and supervisors:

- Workers are told how to do things, often in great detail. Supervisors are told what needs to be done and are expected to figure out the "how" on their own.

- Workers need a supervisor looking over their shoulder all the time to make sure they are "being productive" instead of screwing around when they're supposed to be working. Supervisors are expected to work hard even when no one is checking up on them.

- Workers are (all too often) expected to keep rigid schedules and are measured by how well they adhere to those schedules. Supervisors are judged by how much they accomplish and can be trusted to set their own schedules.

- Workers are expected to do exactly what they are told, no more and no less. Supervisors are expected to suggest better ways to do things —and, if given the go-ahead to put their plans in motion, to follow through and carry out those plans without being prodded from behind.

- Workers don't ask questions. Supervisors are not only allowed to ask questions, but they are encouraged to do so.

- Workers follow. Supervisors lead.

Which would you rather be? A worker or a supervisor?

In some ways, it's easier to be a mere worker and let others take responsibility for your actions. But there is little satisfaction in being a lowly drudge, and there's no room in that role for the creativity and love of learning and problem-solving that led you to learn UNIX and become a systems administrator in the first place.

24

WORKING WITH PEOPLE

Let's face it: You're a supervisor at heart, a boss.

Don't panic, just deal with it. And because you're a boss (whether you like it or not), you might as well be a good one.

Mentoring

One of a boss sysadmin's main responsibilities is teaching; not only teaching users and non–computer-hip big bosses, as previously discussed, but also mentoring sysadmin trainees.

There's a lot to teach that trainee, too. The introduction describes the System Administrator's Guild, SAGE, which works to establish professional standards for sysadmins. Here's the "official" SAGE job description, quoted from the `http://www. usenix. org` Web site:

> Systems administration is a widely varied task. The best systems administrators are generalists: they can wire and repair cables, install new software, repair bugs, train users, offer tips for increased productivity across areas from word processing to CAD tools, evaluate new hardware and software, automate a myriad of mundane tasks, and increase work flow at their site. In general, systems administrators enable people to exploit computers at a level which gains leverage for the entire organization.

Another paragraph says:

> Employers frequently fail to understand the background that systems administrators bring to their task. Because systems administration draws on knowledge from many fields, and because it has only recently begun to be taught at a few institutions of higher learning, systems administrators may come from a wide range of academic backgrounds. Most get their skills through on-the-job training by apprenticing themselves to a more experienced mentor. Although the system of informal education by apprenticeship has been extremely effective in producing skilled systems administrators, it is poorly understood by employers and hiring managers, who tend to focus on credentials to the exclusion of other factors when making personnel decisions.

In the end, in other words, systems administrators learn on the job. Isn't that really how you learned?

Now it's time for you to pass along your knowledge. At the same time, you can do some learning yourself. Your trainee might know things you don't, and if you are confident in your skills there is nothing wrong with reversing roles and being the student now and then. If anything, this will increase the bond between you and your new colleague.

One of the hardest things about teaching a new colleague is putting up with his mistakes. It is a huge temptation, when you see someone screwing up, to jump in and do the job yourself instead of watching the work get botched. The big problem with this technique, and the reason it should never be used except in major emergencies, is that it teaches nothing. The next time a similar problem comes up, you will once again be doing the hands-on work while your trainee looks on, and so on into the future, until your trainee either quits in disgust or decides to take the easy way out and becomes a "worker" who shows no initiative and doesn't make a single move unless you first directly order it (and then stand there and make sure that he follows your instructions to the letter). This might do wonders for your ego, but it is bad management practice and, in the long run, will wear you out. It is better to overcome your urge to do the thing yourself and help your trainee do it, even if this takes four or five times as long at first.

> **Tip**
>
> Your first duty on any new job, project, or assignment is to pick your replacement and start training him. You might want the work because it's challenging and exciting, but that won't last forever. Eventually you will want to move on. Your employer, of course, is happy to see you challenged and excited, but he really needs someone to do that work and might be reluctant to let you go. Make sure that, by the time you want to do something else, there is someone else "one step back" who can come in and take over. Remember that training others is an investment in your own progress.

"At first" is the key. With practice, your trainee will get better and faster at every task he performs under your supervision. Before long, you will find that you don't need to stand there and watch very often. This is when your training efforts start paying off. Suddenly you will start having more time to work on things like making more automation scripts for routine functions, doing those "walkarounds" we talked about earlier, and doing your job better overall instead of simply reacting to crises.

You don't need to be overbearing during this training process. If anything, it is better to be overly humble, as long as you are willing to gain your trainee's attention and hold it. Openness is important. You must be willing to answer questions and, just as important, be willing to admit that you don't have all the answers. Indeed, sharing your sources of information, including favorite IRC channels, email lists, Web sites, and contacts in vendors' organizations, is an important part of your training duty.

Many years ago, mechanical engineers used to say, "It is not as important to memorize all the numbers and calculations as it is to know how to find the books where you can look them up." The same holds true in systems administration. You can't possibly know everything. Even if you know almost everything about the systems that you work with daily, it seems that there is a new piece of hardware or software or a new problem coming at you almost every day. Passing on this sense that learning is a constant process is possibly the most important part of mentoring a newbie.

Notes for Trainee Admins

Not everyone reading this book is a seasoned sysadmin. For instance, you might be reading it and trying to learn all you can either because you want to become a systems administrator someday. Or, you might already doing lightweight sysadmin work and are trying to upgrade yourself beyond being what famous Bell Labs sysadmin Tom Limoncelli once called a "systems clerk," who does nothing but routine tasks such as add new users to the network and install user-selected software on workstation hard drives.

If you're serious about learning, and if you work around senior admins, they are obviously the best people to turn to for advice and knowledge. Some will be willing teachers, and some will seem like they are afraid to share any information with you, possibly because they are afraid you will eventually take their jobs. Yet others would like to teach but aren't as competent at dealing with people as they are at dealing with machines. Another problem in some workplaces is that everyone is killer-busy all the time, to the point where on-the-job training is something everyone "means to get around to" but never really does.

The solution to all these situations: Ask as many questions as you can, as often as you can, without making a total pest of yourself.

You might find that coworkers who seem standoffish at first are really just shy and that when you approach them directly, they will happily help you learn. You also might notice another interesting phenomenon: People who guard information most jealously have the least information to share, and those who help you the most (after making allowance for shyness factors) are the most secure in their abilities.

As you move toward greater responsibility, you might want to reflect heavily on your experiences while first getting hired and learning your job. Keeping your eyes open now not only to the technical side of things, but toward the human dealings involved in being a sysadmin, will help you become better at your work as you move into a more senior position. And always remember that systems administrators don't suddenly know every-thing they need to know after a set period of instruction. The learning goes on forever.

Conferences and Associations

You should go to at least a few conferences every year, and you should join at least one professional association, preferably one that has regular chapter meetings near you. Go to those meetings as often as you can.

Many systems administrators request paid attendance at three or four conferences every year as a condition of employment, right along with medical and life insurance and sev-eral weeks of vacation time. Some employers willingly go along with this request or even offer regular conference attendance without being asked. Some might be less enthu-siastic about the idea, but will go along with it if you give them reasons why it is good for them, not just for you, to have your knowledge kept up-to-date. An employer who refuses to pay your way to conferences is probably one that considers a sysadmin a clerk or low-level mechanic, not a professional.

If other job alternatives are available, you should avoid employers with this attitude. If a job with one of these is all you can get, then take it—but keep your resume updated and handy because you won't want to stay with this one for long.

The point of conference attendance is not to run around the show floor collecting "booth swag" such as T-shirts and fancy pens. You should pick conferences based on the semi-nars they offer, and you spend most of your time in seminars or "Birds of a Feather" sessions. Here some examples of papers presented at a Usenix Symposium on Internet Technologies and Systems held in March 2001:

- "Measurement and Analysis of a Streaming Media Workload"
- "CSP: A Novel System Architecture for Scalable Internet and Communication Services"
- "Dynamic Host Configuration for Managing Mobility Between Public and Private Networks"
- "Measuring Client-Perceived Response Time on the WWW"
- "Fine-Grained Failover Using Connection Migration"
- "End-to-End WAN Service Availability"

> **Note**
>
> At professional conferences, some attendees have common interests not shared with the conference as a whole. Some sysadmins, for instance, have a particular interest in security; others are interested in mass storage facilities, and still others might share experiences working in a classified installation. After a day's scheduled proceedings, conferences provide rooms for attendees to organize informal "birds of a feather" sessions, or "BoFs" (the more informally informal sessions might meet in a hotel room). These sessions are often the best places to get to know your colleagues and pick up useful information.
>
> If you have an interesting topic, try proposing a BoF yourself. It's a good way to start establishing yourself in the professional community.

The full text of these papers, and all other papers presented at this symposium, is available to registered conferences attendees. Presenters are usually available later to answer follow-up questions by email. Publishers, notably O'Reilly, hold useful conferences. Hardware and software vendors and Open Source groups all hold conferences of some sort. Some are big, some are small, some are regional, and some are national. Some focus on one small topic (a particular vendor-specific UNIX), and some are huge and wide-ranging. There is no "one size fits all" advice that a book can give you about which conferences to attend and avoid. However, we will say that Usenix conferences tend to be some of the best-organized and best-attended around, and they generally offer some of the highest-level presenters and the widest range of offerings you are likely to find. As a sysadmin, you should make a particular effort to attend the Usenix LISA conferences. LISA stands for "Large Installation System Administration," and it is devoted specifically to UNIX systems administration.

But again, your choices depend on your specific job duties, the nature of your employer's business, the equipment and software that you use, your location, and your work schedule. Although conference attendance can be important for professional development, you don't want to be too far out of town for too long during a critical period or when you are too short-staffed to have someone cover you while you are gone.

Joining Usenix and SAGE

Yes, you should join Usenix. Not "maybe." You should. Usenix (http://www.usenix.org), a.k.a. the Advanced Computing Systems Association, is the teradaddy of professional-level computer users' groups. It has been around since 1975 and actively works to educate members and help set standards by participating in ISO, IEEE, the

Open Group, and other internationally recognized industry bodies. Usenix publishes a bimonthly magazine for members, *;login:* which has more useful information in it than a dozen of the ad-filled free trade magazines you seem to get whether or not you want them or signed up for a subscription. Usenix members also have access to all papers presented at all Usenix conferences and access to several "members only" email groups that can be fine sources of problem-solving advice from peers (which is something we all need now and then, whether or not we like to admit it).

There is another point to Usenix membership that is more subtle but that is just as important to your career as the technical knowledge it will help you gain: It looks good on paper.

Human Resources people and nontechnical bosses love to see association memberships on resumes. Given two job candidates with generally equal combinations of education and work experience, one who can boast of membership in Usenix, the Advanced Computing Systems Association, is likely to be the one who gets the thumbs-up. Even better is, "Member of Usenix, the Advanced Computing Systems Association, since [date]," assuming that the date is four or five years back.

The cost of an individual Usenix membership (at this writing) is $95 per year. Corporate memberships cost $400. Even if your employer is a corporate member, you might want to consider individual membership. Your employer will probably pay for it; most consider professional association memberships to be legitimate job-related expenses. The IRS certainly does, so if your employer balks at paying, you can still deduct your membership fee if you itemize your return.

Corporate Usenix memberships allow only one individual from each company to get a discount on conference attendance and goodies such as software and books, but each individual member also gets these benefits. The cost of your individual membership will be repaid if you attend even one conference a year. If someone else at your company is already "the" conference attendance person under the corporate membership, as an individual member, you will be able to point out that you get the same discount and are just as worthy of attendance, so why not send two people? (Yes, this is a sneaky political trick, but that's often how it is when dealing with humans—and it is the need-to-know tricks like this that made this chapter necessary in what is otherwise a hard-core technical book.)

A student membership in Usenix costs (at this writing) only $25 per year. If you are a student—or know one who wants to become a professional sysadmin after graduation—it's a good idea to join now instead of waiting, if only so that the "member since [date]" line on the resume right after graduation shows a date at least two years back. Again, it's a sneaky trick designed to impress potential employers. But a student membership is also

24

Working with People

an excellent learning tool, a chance to "sit in" on professional discussions and learn what the job is all about by listening to people already in the field discuss their problems.

Fine. You're a professional systems administrator, an aspirant or a student, and you've joined Usenix. Now it's time to join SAGE, the Systems Administrators Guild. At time of writing, SAGE membership costs $30 per year ($15 for students). You must be a Usenix member to sign up because SAGE is a "Special Technical Group" section of Usenix. Now you get to go to LISA, the annual Usenix-sponsored Systems Administration Conference, as both a Usenix member and a SAGE member. This is obviously the single most-targeted conference there is for sysadmins. If you get to go to only one industry-wide, national-level conference per year, this is probably the one you should choose. LISA is a nice-sized conference. About 2,000 people show up every year, which is enough to support a wide range of relevant technical sessions and fill a hall with interesting exhibits, but not so many that it becomes a swarm where you get lost in the crowd.

> **Note**
>
> At this writing, the relationship between SAGE and USENIX is under consideration by both organizations. See http://www.usenix.org/sage/restructuring.

Of course, if you are at "guru-level" sysadmin status, you should consider presenting papers at LISA and other conferences. It's fun—and talk about resume-building! What could be more impressive than having a list of "papers presented" to show a potential employer?

Casual Encounters with Peers

So far, we've talked about conference attendance and association memberships in a boss-pleasing and career-enhancing context. That's all good, but don't forget about the social side of life. A conference full of geeks is fun. If you haven't ever been to one, it's time to go. If you've heard that the most important part of most conventions is party time after the day's sessions are over, you heard right. Sysadmins are thin on the ground in most companies, a small minority who are far out of the company's mainstream activities in a way that often extends to social events. Imagine being in the same building with 500 to 3,000 people whose interests are similar to yours. Think what you might say to each other over a beer or 10.

A lot of after-hours talk at geek gatherings tends to be technical. Even at company-sponsored parties that have live music and a dance floor, at least half the people tend to be talking to each other instead of paying attention to the music, often drawing this or that on notepads or PDAs or cocktail napkins. But some of the talk is about jobs in general, especially finding them. Hip employers know this, and it's a big reason they worry about sending too many admins to conferences. From the opposite perspective—yours—meeting people who might hire you for a better job is a big reason to go. The same holds true for local SAGE meetings.

It's common for local sysadmin and other professional-level computer user groups to have "resume exchanges" at meetings. It's also common for people to meet at bars or restaurants after the formal meetings. These are good opportunities for a little job-hunting or, if your company is in need, recruiting. If you've read any of the (jokingly estimated) 72 million books about job seeking that are on store shelves or available through online booksellers, you've picked up on the fact that networking is the most effective way to find a job. It's also the most effective way to recruit, and, sooner or later, you're going to need to find either a job or other people to work with you. Why not start your search in either direction with friends? And what better place to find sysadmin friends than at a SAGE chapter meeting?

Indeed, if there is not already an active chapter where you live, you might want to consider starting one. Perhaps you can get your employer to sponsor it as a way to get "first crack" at sysadmins looking for work. In a help-short technical work area, this is good for your bosses—and good for you, too, because as computers and networks become increasingly necessary to businesses of all types, the need for people like you is increasing at such a rapid rate that even a serious recession is likely to only slow the rate of growth rather than cut the need for sysadmins, at least for the foreseeable future.

Note

If you decide to start a local SAGE group, plan to start small. Many local chapters have begun with only four or five people, often working for the same employer. You can announce your group through the SAGE mailing list and in *;login* magazine. Beyond that, use your own creativity to advertise. As people in your original group change employers, they will meet other sysadmins who might be interested as well.

Every local SAGE group operates in its own way. Some have formal dues and elections for officers; others just announce a meeting and see who shows up. Some suggestions:

- Meet at regular intervals in a comfortable place, conveniently located with respect to places you think sysadmins might work.

- Establish a mailing list so that people who can't get to the meetings can participate—or so that those who get to the meetings can communicate the rest of the time.
- Establish a Web site with lots of keywords so that people searching for your group can find it with any good search engine.
- Get a speaker to present an interesting topic for each meeting. At the start, this could mean you.

Some local SAGE groups in at least two cities have found that many people like to socialize after the meetings. In fact, one group made this an agenda item. You might want to meet in or near pleasant restaurants, brew pubs, or other similar venues.

Documentation Is Good

Remember that patch you wrote two years ago that solved a little display problem on a couple of monitors? Of course not. You've done 3,000 things since then. Now one of your coworkers is faced with a similar situation and has to write new code. Too bad he can't look at what you did two years back.

Now let's take a look at the system wiring for that row of server racks the guy who had this job before you installed. Damn! Total spaghetti! It's going to take you at least a day to get it all traced. Why didn't he mark all the cables at both ends and make even a simple, hand-scrawled schematic? Sure, *he* knew where everything went because he wired it, but didn't he take a second to think that he might not always be working here and that someone else might have to figure out what he did?

Before you decide to live without documentation, you must meet three criteria:

1. You must have a perfect memory.
2. You work by yourself and always will.
3. You will never leave your job, get sick, or take a vacation, and you must be available 24 hours a day, 7 days a week, instead of working a reasonable schedule.

Anyone who doesn't qualify on all three counts must keep accurate records of all physical wiring and equipment modifications, all software installations and code changes, and all basic procedures that keep the place running. This includes simple things that nontechnical people can try to do to get things going again in case of failure (such as "reboot server X by following the these steps…") before they haul an admin (you) out of bed at a weird time to perform a simple little task that they could have dealt with on their own if you had given them instructions on how to do it.

The most basic, most essential form of documentation is an accurate equipment inventory. Annual inventories for tax reasons are almost universal in the corporate world, but they don't necessarily provide the information that you need to do your job most efficiently. In a tax inventory, "parts is parts." A hard drive is a hard drive, and a power supply is a power supply. For you, each part is a distinct item with a specific purpose. You need to know not just that you have X number of 2U servers, but you need to have component lists for them. If you are doing your own hardware repairs, you need to know what parts stock you have on your shelves. Having essential equipment down while you wait for parts to arrive by overnight shipping is not good. It is almost always better to cannibalize a spare unit than to have this happen—as long as you immediately order the appropriate parts for the spare unit and put it back into working order as soon as you can.

This last step is often forgotten. You've seen (we've all seen) equipment cages full of gutted or half-assembled servers and workstations, some of them so old that they are useless. They're probably still hanging around because no one really wants to admit that each one of them represents a mistake, and throwing them out would be admitting error. Sooner or later, though, it's time to come clean and admit that you are hoarding equipment that will never be used again. Many people who end up as sysadmins seem to be natural equipment hoarders, so this might not be easy to do emotionally, but it can and should be done at some point. That's when you take your "true" inventory. From that point forward, you must maintain it accurately enough that you have a good idea of what is in stock at any moment, why you have it, and, for the accounting people, how much it's worth.

Nobody likes taking and maintaining an inventory, but it's an essential part of your documentation and one of the most basic, scut-level management responsibilities there is. If you want to be (and have others treat you as) a management-level professional, you must keep an accurate inventory—without being asked.

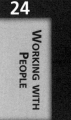

Now you have a hardware inventory. Next is a software inventory. If you have proprietary software from companies such as Microsoft and others that enjoy doing "software audits," you have no choice about knowing not only what software you have on what machines where, but also where to find the licenses for each single program or, if you are running under a site license, documentation that proves you are operating within the terms of that license. A single failure to provide accurate software licensing documentation upon request can cost your employer many times your annual salary in penalties and legal fees, and it can easily get you fired. Maintaining a software inventory is a complete pain (worse than maintaining a hardware inventory), but it is just as essential. Make sure that yours is complete and up-to-date, not just right after you read this, but always.

Now we come to true "operating" documentation. Start with wiring diagrams. These don't have to be fancy, but they must cover the basics. Start with electrical load. Your hardware inventory—the one you keep for yourself, not the one you give to the accountants—ought to include reasonably accurate current requirements for each piece of equipment in the place. Each outlet and each breaker should have its capacity clearly labeled. No outlet or breaker-controlled circuit should ever be at (or, for safety's sake, within 30% of) its maximum load under "normal" operating conditions. The only way to know for sure that it isn't is to know exactly what devices are drawing power from each one. You need at least a basic diagram to keep track. Or, you might choose to use a simple list that shows which devices are on which circuits, with each device clearly labeled not only by function but also with its current requirements.

Now think of a kicker: Just because you understand your schematic and labeling scheme doesn't mean that everyone else will. You need to "test" it on others to make sure that they find it as understandable as you do so that they can figure it all out if you're not around.

Here's a second kicker: Your wiring scheme is a continuing process, not a one-time project. If you add hard drives, you must change the scheme to reflect the new additions as soon as you add the drives instead of waiting until you "have time." You have time now. Make that time! All you have to do is screw up once and cause a fire or an electrical problem that creates downtime, and all the time you "saved" by not documenting your electrical needs will suddenly be eaten up many times over.

Now go apply the same thought process to nonpower wiring. Again, what hooks to what? Can you tell at a glance? Could someone else (with appropriate basic skills) come along and understand what's going on behind the racks or under the equipment tables in a minute or two? If so, congratulations! You are doing this part of your job. If not, you still have work to do.

> **Note**
>
> Depending on your organization, the electricity, networking, temperature control, and so forth might be someone else's responsibility. In this case, it will pay to go out of your way to get on comfortable terms with whoever *is* responsible for them. Your systems depend on the support that these people provide.

Finally, we come to operational documentation—your change log, if you will. If you keep your hardware and software inventories and your wiring scheme up-to-date, you have two-thirds of it done already. The rest is essentially bug fixes that you have made and patches that you have written over the months and years.

One method of keeping this vital, obviously organic metadocument in order is to record each "fix" or change as a short "article" in text format, and use one of the many Open Source search utilities out there as your primary data-retrieval method. You could use CVS (`http://www.cvshome.org`) for this purpose, but a simple flat database would probably do just as well, especially if you are careful to include equipment or software identifiers and dates when you made whatever modifications in all "articles," to make future searches simple. If you have not kept this sort of maintenance log before—and that's really what this is, a maintenance log—you will be surprised at how useful a tool it can become after it has six months or more of information in it. Aside from saving time by showing changes that you have made to your systems (including code that you have written), it can help you identify problem hardware or software—and even problem users—so that you can make changes that will help you avoid repetitive failures in the future.

Your maintenance log can perform several vital functions:

- It's a teaching tool for new coworkers. You can sit a new hire down with it to see what you do, when you do it, and what he can expect to do himself. Knowing what changes and fixes you have made, along with up-to-date hardware and software information, will allow a new person to get up-to-speed many times faster than if he has to come to you with a string of questions about almost every task that you ask him to perform.

- Accurate records of failures and fixes can help you decide what equipment and software needs upgrading, and whether those upgrades makes sense. Is one make of hard drive breaking down often, while other brands are holding up well under their daily loads? Obviously, you will want to consider replacing the flaky ones. Are you seeing a high enough percentage of a particular kind of power supply is failing after (hypothetically) two years that you want to make its replacement after 24 months a routine maintenance task instead of waiting for breakdowns? Have you deployed a software package on some workstations or in some of your servers that is causing you more grief than a previous version you have installed on other machines? If so, do you really want to keep using that package, or should you look for a different one? Is there a later version that you can try that might not have the same problems? Conversely, is it that later version that has the problems, and should you consider dropping back to the previous one? Accurate records can help you answer all of these questions.

24

WORKING WITH PEOPLE

- Certain users seem to have higher failure rates than others. Do they do something with their terminals or workstations that others don't as part of their jobs? Do they simply need more training? Is there another factor at work? Again, good records help you decide what to do.

- Good records also help you judge how long a project will take and help you detail the tasks. This makes them a valuable tool for forward planning. In addition, the same information will be very useful when it comes time to bid out maintenance contracts or to bid on new work.

- Many organizations require regular employee evaluations. No one likes giving or getting these. Your records also can be read as your work log, or as least part of it. They might save you *and* your supervisor the trouble of remembering your glorious accomplishments at review time.

Preparing and maintaining documentation is a tedious task. Few people like to do it. If you can get clerical help with it or shove the task off on a junior admin you are training, that's fine. But if you can't get help, you must still do it. If nothing else, an accurate log can be used to prove to upper management that you really are as overworked as you always claim and that you really do deserve the additional staff you have been requesting all along.

Management Decisions

Earlier we discussed the qualities of a good supervisor. Here we address what it takes to be a good manager. Before going on, we need to clarify the difference.

By *supervisor*, we mean a "first among equals." The supervisor is assumed to function primarily as a senior sysadmin, with appropriate responsibilities. At the same time, the supervisor is responsible for mentoring the more junior staff and monitoring the technical aspects of that staff's work. In some organizations, the supervisor also might schedule the work. In general, the supervisor does not have budgetary authority (the authority to decide how to spend some of the organization's money).

We use the term *manager* to refer to someone who makes hiring and budgetary decisions. The manager probably does not do technical work. Obviously, it helps the manager to understand something of what the staff is doing, but detailed technical oversight is the supervisor's job. The manager's main responsibilities are to allocate resources (staff, equipment, money) to get work done efficiently, to "run interference" for the technical staff by trying to remove nontechnical obstacles and distractions that might interfere with their work, and to report up the management chain on the status of work being done and resources being used.

There are always gray areas, of course, but we are using these descriptions as rough guidelines.

Requesting and getting people, hardware, and software from upper management is an art in itself. You might have spotted a new piece of eye-catching equipment at show and would like to buy it. If it's within your purchasing authority, you might be tempted to go out and get one based on nothing but your own lust for that gear. Not smart. If you do this sort of thing once too often, you might find your purchasing authority limited or even removed entirely. As a manager, whether in charge of a whole corps of sysadmins and technicians or just in charge of yourself, part of your responsibility is to make wise, rational decisions about what you need to do your job, not decisions based on personal desires.

"Wise" and "rational" choices are not always the cheapest ones. Sometimes they might be, but, in many cases, paying extra for higher quality or superior support will pay off. Inventory and personnel controls also need a little juggling and decision-making. Sure, you want to keep your hardware budget under control, but if you have so few spares that you end up with extra downtime while you wait for a $75 item to be shipped overnight (at a shipping cost of $30), you are no hero. Staffing your department at a level that theoretically keeps everybody working at a reasonable pace most of the time is good, but what about crisis moments? What about vacations and sick leave? What if someone quits unexpectedly and things suddenly come apart? Suddenly your decision to run with minimum staff to keep your budget looking good doesn't seem so fine.

Management is an art, not a science. In many ways, it is harder than it looks. One reason it is good to practice "managing yourself" even in the lowest-level job is that it prepares you to manage others if and when that comes to pass; in a volatile and fast-growing field, management opportunities often come quickly—and when you least expect them.

We went over this before: The main difference between a worker and a manager is that a worker does what he is told, while a manager is told what needs to be done and then takes responsibility for doing it. Quality management, at least in technical fields, is not determined by clothes (as long as they're clean and neat), by an imposing presence, or by most other externals. In the end, it comes down to being reliable and trustworthy, and getting your job done competently, rapidly, at the lowest reasonable cost. If you are in charge of others, leadership is part of the equation, too; without cooperation from the people who work for you, your failure is assured.

24

WORKING WITH PEOPLE

Leadership

Leadership and management are separate things. The good manager decides what needs to be done and how to do it. The good leader makes people want to do what needs to be done and to do it as it should be done.

Leadership is starting to walk in a particular direction, saying "Follow me!" to the people you are leading, and knowing that they are following you without having to look back and check. This doesn't mean that you are trying to get blind obedience. More realistically, it means that by the time you say, "Follow me!", you have explained clearly why you have chosen one direction over another, have listened to others who wanted to go north instead of south, and have gotten them to realize that south is a better choice—or at least that they might as well go along and see what happens, which is sometimes the best you can hope for in a typical "herding cats" sysadmin management situation.

Effective leaders rarely issue orders blindly. Indeed, before you say, "Follow me!", you might want to get input from your loyal followers. You might not even know which direction to go before you get this input; you can admit this, if you like, but you don't necessarily have to. "Which way should we go now?" is a fine question to ask all by itself. If everybody has the same answer and, after listening to their reasons, you agree with them, then it's time to give the order. It will be obeyed. This is often called "following from the front," but it can be an effective tactic. What about when the crowd wants to go one way and you want to go another? When you're dealing with sysadmins who are just as bright as you, "Because I said so," is not a good reason. You need to have good reasons for your decisions at all times, even if those reasons are not popular. (It's also just possible that you are wrong, so pay attention!)

> **Note**
>
> Remember that the worst mistake you can make with a group of intelligent, skilled professionals is to pretend to have knowledge that you don't have. If some or all of the staff have expertise that you lack, you show your respect for them by drawing on that expertise before making a decision.
>
> Your staff might be inclined to judge you by your technical abilities because that is the measure that they know and respect. Make it clear that, as a manager, you are not responsible for doing the work, but for seeing that it gets done. Your primary functions are to give your staff as much direction as it needs (no more!) and then trying to make it as easy as possible for them to do their jobs. If you do some of the work yourself, then you are wearing two hats: supervisor and staff. Keep them separate. As a manager, any technical skills that you possess simply assist you in making management decisions.

Sometimes, as a manager, you might have a broader set of goals or a better grasp of the financial controls placed on you from above than the people who work for you do. So don't keep them in the dark! Explain to them, clearly and honestly, why you have one choice and not another. You might not gain love by making unpopular decisions, but if you explain your reasoning openly, you will get respect, and leadership is largely about respect.

> **Tip**
>
> The more respect people have for you, the less they will question your judgment.

Respect is earned. The Army has a saying, "Salute the shirt, not the man," that it uses to explain the reason troops should touch their caps for all officers, not just for the ones they like. But a salute is just an empty gesture, and some officers get none beyond it. Officers who can say, "Follow me!" and know that the troops will obey that order without hesitation have built up a store of respect by their previous actions. They have shown that they care for the people who work for them in tangible ways, including getting promotions for those who obviously deserve them without being asked, making sure the chow hall puts out decent meals, and showing in every way that they consider the troops' welfare more important than their own.

Like the military officer, your success as a manager is ultimately in the hands of the people you supervise. Anything you do that improves their performance will make you look better. The only "success" that you can have will be the product of their efforts. *Unlike* the military, your staff can leave easily. Remember that there are more openings for sysadmins than there are for sysadmin managers.

You're smart, so you can come up with your own civilian analogies for these military situations.

One important military ritual that is often misunderstood by civilians is the "in ranks" inspection, where the officer passes among masses rows of enlisted personnel and looks closely at their uniforms, haircuts, and equipment. What doesn't show from the outside is that before the officer inspects the troops, the highest-ranking enlisted person present inspects the officer and has the right to refuse permission to conduct the inspection. Then, more importantly, while the officer looks at each soldier, each soldier has a chance to look the officer directly in the eyes. A few words are usually exchanged, too, especially in smaller units.

The inspection goes both ways, in other words.

In civilian life, the department or company meeting is the closest thing there is to a military inspection. It serves many of the same purposes. Bosses say what needs to be done and why. Subordinates talk about what they're doing and why. But more importantly, everyone gets to look everyone else in the face and decide who is and is not worthy of respect. This purpose for a meeting is almost never stated in words, but it is always there.

Leading meetings competently is an important part of leadership, and one in which few people get any formal training before moving into management positions.

Here are several rules that will help you run effective meetings:

1. Set an agenda. Say in advance what the meeting is about, and stick to that topic. If you can, hand out a written agenda or something else that will serve as a focus to keep everyone on track.

2. Set a time limit—and keep it short! No company meeting in history that lasted more than four hours has ever accomplished anything. Two hours is better. One is adequate for most single-topic discussions. If you have multiple topics, you should take an hourly break of 10 minutes or so. People will feel more comfortable.

3. Keep your own presentation short. Say what you have to say in the fewest possible words, and then ask for comments and questions. If you're working with good people, the comments and questions could be the most valuable part of the meeting. Take notes!

4. Maintain order. You're leading the meeting, so you decide who speaks when. Try to make sure that everyone has a chance to say their piece and that no one person dominates. Ask people not to interrupt. "You'll have your turn," is a good remonstration. If a discussion starts among a small group of people and strays from the point of the meeting, suggest that they continue after the meeting is over, or tell them that you will schedule another meeting to address their issues.

5. Draw people out. If "Any questions?" is met with a wall of silence, point out an individual person and ask for his opinion. Keep doing this, if necessary, until you've gone around the whole room. If this doesn't work, ask meeting participants what they would like to discuss. Sysadmins and computer people will always think of something. Before a small meeting closes, go around the table and ask each person if there are any final issues to bring up. These issues should be on-topic and probably will be dealt with "offline" or at a later meeting. This wrap-up should be part of the agenda to make sure that the meeting doesn't last too long. The room contains several bright, detail-oriented people. You should use them to make sure that you keep track of important items.

6. Don't sneer at complaints. This is as bad as sneering at users. What might seem unimportant to you can be important to someone else. We are not all the same.

7. Be ready to call a halt at the appointed time, and don't hesitate to break up early if you cover your material faster than you thought you would. You can use "extra" time to discuss things other than work, if you like. Sometimes this can be more valuable than the formal meeting itself, but you must still be willing to cut off discussion at some point and get everyone back to work—or at least out of the meeting room—before things start to drag.

You don't have to be a great public speaker to hold a meeting. In fact, it's better for everyone if you keep your part short and concentrate on listening. When the people to whom you're talking are coworkers you see every day, they already know most of your bad habits. You might be nervous the first few times. Fine. Tell your people you're nervous. There is no reason to be ashamed. Most of them probably like you or would like to like you, if you are all just starting to get to know each other. This is just like dealing with users; when people know you're human, they will end up with more respect for you than if they think you are trying to do a lifelong Mr. Spock impersonation.

Come to think of it, Spock was at his best when he showed his human side, wasn't he?

Setting Policy

As a manager, you set policies. You are the one who decides how things should be done because you are responsible for making sure that everything goes smoothly. "Setting policy" is a mouthful, but it is really simple. It means making sure that certain simple rules are followed—not just once in a while, but always. We're talking about rules such as making sure that incoming equipment gets added to your inventory and religiously recording all fixes, patches, and changes in the maintenance log correctly.

Your policies do not need to be mechanically rigid. If someone else suggests a way to do something that is better than the way you were using, by all means make it part of your policy manual. But make sure, no matter what, that your policies are in writing and that everyone who works with you reads them, understands them, and even signs that they have done so. If certain checks or tests should be carried out once per shift, that is a policy, and each shift-working person must carry out those tests. If you do a system backup every night at a specific time, that is a policy. Ditto recording software installed on workstations or checking software that users want to install before they try to do it themselves.

You might want to have a policy that some users are allowed to install their own software and others aren't, or that no users are allowed to make their own modifications, or that all can because you're not doing any network file sharing from workstations.

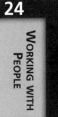

24

WORKING WITH PEOPLE

It's your policy manual, not ours. You're the one who must not only write it, but also follow it and make sure that others do. We can't tell you exactly what to put in it; we can just make suggestions.

Do you have server room security procedures? They go in the policy manual. What about corporate-mandated energy-saving procedures of some sort? They go there, too. Special parking places? That might be going a little too far. Becoming rule-bound can be worse than working in a state of total anarchy.

A policy manual is an ever-evolving work that changes with your needs. It is better to have a few well-enforced, important rules than a bunch of petty regulations that have little or no effect on efficiency, so start your policy manual small and let it grow (but not too large). Major changes make a perfect discussion topic for meetings; policies that most employees agree in advance are useful have a greater chance of being followed voluntarily than rules imposed arbitrarily from above.

Finally, unless you are in charge of the whole organization, get your policies approved (this means *signed*) by as many levels above you as you can. If you *are* in charge, get the approval from your lawyers. This gives the policies more juice, gives your boss(es) a chance to tell you why they might be a bad idea in the larger context, and ensures that if something horrible happens, you are not standing all alone waving your unsigned policy at your boss, a federal judge, or a rampaging mob.

Obtaining Needed Resources

Above every manager there is another manager. Even a CEO has bosses: the board of directors and the shareholders. Even a self-employed sole proprietor has bosses. They're called customers.

Outside of a few poorly managed dotcom companies that flared up briefly between 1995 and 2000, corporate resources have always been limited. X amount of revenue comes in, and there is Y amount of capital on hand, and the top management needs to decide how to allocate it. So much goes to sales and marketing, so much goes to R&D, so much goes to manufacturing, so much goes to customer services, and so much goes to IT or DP systems or network operations, or whatever they call your department.

Yes, your department will come last or be tied for last with facilities management. Unless you work for a systems consulting firm, you are a service to the rest of the company, and the resources that you need will be determined by how much computer and networking "muscle" they need to carry out their part of the company's overall task—which is, of course, to generate the maximum possible return for shareholders. (If you *do* work for a systems consulting firm, you serve the same service for *someone else's* shareholders.) From a purely financial standpoint, if the company could get along without you and your coworkers and your big salaries, and could stop spending money on all those boxes and the electricity to feed them, it would.

From a pure investor's viewpoint, the ideal corporation is one that has no equipment, employees, or customers, and one that offers no services or products but that just sits there and generates reams of money out of thin air. Sadly (for investors), the bottom line depends on having a top line of some sort, and this means hiring people and going through the motions of making goods or providing services and selling them. As an outgrowth of this mess, it becomes desirable to spend as small a percentage of the goods' or services' sale price actually providing them because this is how profits are maximized. The next step in this train of thinking goes, "There are many tasks a computer can perform faster/better/cheaper than people, so if we have a bunch of computers, we can increase productivity big-time without a lot of hiring."

This is where you come in. You are necessary to keep the computers running. You and your staff and all the hardware and software cost R dollars per year, and you save Q dollars that it would otherwise cost to have rows of desks filled with abacus-equipped clerks. Or, if your company is big on e-commerce, Q might be the cost of selling by direct-mail catalogs instead of online. As long as R is lower than Q, you or someone like you will have a job. And as long as R continues to beat Q in new sections of the global business culture, the employment marketplace for people like you, and the rate of computerization in general, will continue to grow.

But never forget, even for one second, that what management wants out of life is to keep R as low as possible, both in gross terms and as a percentage of S, gross sales income. If the company could run all its computerized operations efficiently on a single 486 administered remotely by a teenager in Bangladesh through a dialup modem, it would. When you want new equipment or new staff, you must show very good reasons—with numbers—why the changes you want to make are worth their cost because they will either increase the company's income, lower expenses, or both.

Let's go back to that maintenance log for a moment. It is your key document. Aside from being a useful technical journal for you and your fellow sysadmins, it's a major sales tool for dealing with top management. You can use it to show that one particular type of unit in your inventory is breaking down too often, which is why you want to replace all those units with something different and better. You can show how many "trouble tickets" you and your people handle each day or week; if that number has been increasing for the last year but you still have the same number of bodies, you have a case for adding staff that makes much more sense to an accounting-oriented MBA than you standing there and

24

saying, "We are kind of overworked, you know? Can we maybe hire somebody else? Like this guy I know from SAGE meetings who just got laid off and...."

Another place that maintenance log comes in handy is estimating equipment and personnel requirements for new tasks that are laid on you and your people. Sales, administrative, customer service, and manufacturing executives will come up with plenty of new, wonderful ways to use new software and hardware to improve their departments' productivity. (They go to conventions and read trade magazines too, you know.) Who's going to be asked to implement all their bright ideas? You! And this means you're the one who is going to have to make sure that all the hardware and software behind other people's bright concepts does its job on time and within budget. Your maintenance log can serve as at least a rough guide to additional human time that you will need for the additional workload, based on additional number of boxes, additional code to maintain, and so on.

Your memberships in SAGE, Usenix, and other groups can be important here, too. You might not personally have dealt with whatever equipment or software is being considered by your employers, but chances are good that someone else in the organization has. Before you go back to your bosses with hard numbers, hit those email lists. Make calls. Try to get information from others with experience who can guide you. You'd do it for them, right? Perhaps you already have. This is a large part of why belonging to industry groups is good: They represent a huge knowledge base that, as a member, is yours to draw upon (and contribute to, of course).

You might even come up with alternatives to the original proposal, either through your own research or through suggestions from fellow SAGE members. Software and system sales are competitive, and almost every one has more than one vendor in it. Who knows? Perhaps you will find free, GPLed software that will do the job as well as the expensive commercial package whose publisher's ad caught your marketing VP's eye in the latest edition of *SalesTigers Weekly*. This is a chance for you to be a hero. Go ahead and suggest that alternative! Whether it's GPLed and free or simply a lower-cost commercial program package than the one originally proposed, if it works as well (or, if the price difference is great enough, almost as well), you will have done your job as a manager the best way it can be done, which will get you respect. On the other hand, if your alternative fails, you won't look so hot, so don't just be a contrarian. If you think there's a better way to do something, you must have good reasons for why your way is better—and hopefully some input from others elsewhere who have told you of their experiences, both good and bad, so that you have a fighting chance to make "your way" work with maximum efficiency and least effort.

Note

The term *GPL* refers to the GNU Public License, also known as copyleft. The term is defined at `http://gnu.org/copyleft`. Software under GPL is distributed without constraints on its use, other than that all distributions of the original or modified software must include the source code for that software. However, you should read the copyleft agreement at this site before relying on any other description of the agreement. Beyond that, you are advised to consult a copyright attorney for additional details.

The Formal Presentation

When dealing with upper-upper management, you might want to be a tad less casual than when chatting with fellow sysadmins and techies. This is especially true when you are asking for resources such as equipment and personnel. It might seem like sucking up to prepare a formal presentation in advance, but it's the easiest way to explain technical matters to nontechnical people. There's a thin line between being too simplistic and getting too complicated, and there is no way a single chapter in a single book can tell you where it is for your management. The only overall advice on this subject that means anything is to always err on the side of simplicity, with footnotes for those who want to go beyond the basics.

Simple or complex, a presentation must answer the basic question, "What's in it for the company?" Here is a basic page-by-page layout that that you can use to organize your presentation:

- **Title page**—Use only a few words.
- **Intro**—Tell the main points that you intend to cover.
- **Body pages**—Cover each point in less than 100 words. Graphs or illustrations help. If you are proposing an equipment buy, pictures of the gear can help make it "real" in your audience's minds. For software, graphs showing increased personnel efficiency, less total cost of ownership, how the change will (positively) impact the bottom line, or other management-appealing information is probably best. In any case, make a case for what you want to do in a logical manner.

Note

For a nontechnical audience, each page (or slide) should be devoted to a single idea, which will be the page's title. The idea should be supported by no more than three relevant comments on the same page. If you must use more than three, break down the single idea further.

- **Conclusion**—This is your last page. Use it to sum up everything you already said in as few words as possible.

This outline is an instance of the teaching adage, "Tell them what you are going to tell them. Then tell them. Then tell them what you told them."

Make sure that your supervisor has a copy of this presentation before the meeting. One of the fundamental guidelines in any field is, "*Never* surprise the boss in front of witnesses."

The best way to see whether you're talking on the right level for a nontechnical management audience is to have a nontechnical friend or coworker (or two or three) read your presentation. Rehearse the vocal part, please, even if you do it in front of a mirror. You don't need to be a great public speaker to get a point across, but knowing what you're going to say and how you're going to say it helps. Don't get into a lot of politician-like practiced hand gestures; just make sure you've read your own notes aloud a few times so that you're comfortable with their contents. And that old advice about using jokes to loosen up an audience? Forget it! You are there to talk business, not to be an entertainer.

You can do a slide show, if you like, but it's often more effective to make paper copies and hand them out to everyone at the meeting where you are doing your presentation. This way, they can make notes as you speak, they can refer to those notes if they have questions for you after you finish your prepared remarks (which should closely follow your handouts), and they have something that they can take back to their offices and mull over later. In fact, although a slide show with hard-copy handouts might seem redundant, it is much better than either alone.

Good Syadmins Are Good Humans

Being a systems administrator does not make you a god. Yes, you can use the position to make life miserable for coworkers, but that is the same sort of pettiness that we all hate when we run into a clerk at the Motor Vehicle Administration who seems to delight in making our experience there as unpleasant as possible. Do you really want people you work with every day to see you as having a lot in common with a minor bureaucrat whose greatest pleasure in life is being an irritation?

One question raised by a professional sysadmin while this chapter was being written was, "What about unreasonable requests? What about the people who want to Telnet into the company servers from their AOL accounts at home and who won't believe me when I tell them they can't do this? Why won't they believe me when I tell them this won't work, no matter what I do?"

This is exactly why cultivating that doctor-like "deskside manner" is so important. When you learn to speak with authority and have a reputation among people in your workplace for answering questions in a straightforward manner, people will listen to you.

The sysadmin who was having trouble getting people to believe him was one of the crowd who, despite being a decent person (and a good friend of the author's), tends to slip into a Bastard Operator from Hell mentality when he's at work. He refers to users as "lusers," not only behind their backs but also to their faces, and he rarely takes the trouble to explain what he is doing or why he is doing it "because they wouldn't understand a word [he] said anyway." Maybe they would, maybe they wouldn't, but making a small effort will show your respect for them and will help them respect you—and the more respect they have for you, the more likely they are to take your word when you say that something really can't be done and that there's nothing you can do about it.

Another problem raised by the same sysadim was, "People are always popping their heads in the door with requests. There are too many of them for me to train one-on-one. Besides, a lot of them seem to be here one week and gone the next. How can I develop relationships with people who are always coming and going?"

Hmmm. Sounds like a crummy place to work. Maybe this guy should find another job if the turnover's that high, eh? But let's assume for the moment that he's going to stick around because he's basically happy and the pay and working conditions are good—at least for him. This is where holding informal meetings comes in. Chances are, a lot of the questions he gets asked are asked frequently, as in FAQ. Aside from spending a little time typing up some of the most obvious answers to some of the most obvious questions, if he answers a question in front of a group in a clear manner, other people in that group are less likely to ask the same question either right then or in future sessions.

You Can't Please Everyone...

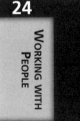

No matter how hard you try or how helpful you are by nature, you will get requests that you just can't fulfill. We ran into someone not long ago who simply had to have an IRC server up and running in the next 20 minutes. Three skilled sysadmins and several hangers-on told him that this was not only not possible, but all he really needed for his 20 or so users was a password-protected channel on any one of the world's many pre-existing IRC networks or servers. But he wouldn't take "no" for an answer. He kept insisting that he needed his very own IRC server, under his own control.

Now, this was a person who did not even know what IRC was. Apparently, as near as we could dope out, he thought that it was some sort of Web-based utility. And he was insistent that nothing but an "IRC server" would do what he needed done. What do you do in a case like that? Eventually, even the most even-tempered sysadmin, confronted with someone who refuses to listen at all, is going to slip into BOFH mode. There are limits, after all. And you are human, even if you try hard to deny it!

In the face of all the adversity, no matter how hard you try to please all the humans who sometimes seem to exist only to make your life harder than it needs to be, you must always remember these watchwords, which we first heard from a friend who is a sysadmin for one of the U.S. government's most computer-dependent agencies:

"My number one priority is the *system*. I am a *system* administrator. It is my job to make certain that the computer systems are in top shape, fully efficient, and well cared for. The systems have no other advocate but me."

Yes, this advice seems to contradict half of what this entire chapter has said to you. No one said life is easy, and no one has ever claimed that dealing with humans is any-where near as easy as dealing with computers. In fact, it is often the hardest part of a sysadmin's job, and the only way to become truly proficient at it is to do your best and learn from your mistakes as you go along.

> **Note**
>
> In the last section, we described a manager as someone who keeps unnecessary problems from bothering the staff. In the case cited here, the user looks like a good candidate for such a problem. Your manager should hear about issues like this from you *first*, before the user decides to escalate past you.

Appendixes

PART
V

In This Part

High-Level Installation Steps

by Timothy M. Champ

APPENDIX A

Before You Begin to Install a Machine

This installation is suitable for a workstation machine. The instructions can be modified to install a server but should not be used exclusively for that purpose. Before you begin to install either a client or a server, you should consider the following things:

- Check the site where the machine will be physically located. The place should have surge-protected power, proper ventilation, a network line for the machine, along with all the peripherals needed to install the machine. Also, if you have a machine onto which you can download all appropriate patches to before starting the install, do so. If, during the install, you are pulled away or otherwise have to suspend it, disconnect the network line, leave a note on the keyboard informing anyone who comes by that you are installing this machine and to leave it alone. Also, marking down where you are in the steps is a good idea.

- Verify whether you are using DHCP for your network or whether you have a static IP. Consult your network administrator and inform him of the MAC address (also called the Ethernet address) of the machine. The network administrator will need this information to add your machine to the table of DHCP machines. Also inform him that this is a Unix machine and that it will need a permanent IP, not a revolving one, as is usually assigned with DHCP. If you cannot find your MAC address, check your documentation or attempt to start the installation just for the purpose of reading the MAC address. If all else fails, contact the manufacturer.

- If you are using DHCP, make sure that your network administrator has your machine in the DHCP database.

- If you are using a static IP, you need to know your DNS servers, your static route, and your hostname.

  IP Address

  Hostname of Machine

  Netmask

  DNS Server(s) IP(s)

  Default Route(Static Route)

Step-by-Step Solaris 8 Installation

1. For the Solaris installation, a CD-ROM will need to be attached to the Sun machine. If one is attached, put the first CD in the drive and turn on the machine.

2. When the machine starts to boot, hit the key combination Stop+A to bring the machine into its PROM. The "OK" prompt should appear. At this prompt, type **boot cdrom** and then hit Enter.

3. When the CD boots, it might ask if you want an initial install or an upgrade install. These instructions assume that you want an initial install. This will delete the contents of your hard drive, so if any data is on it, make sure that you have backups.

4. The installation program should ask you if you want to format your disks. When it does, answer yes by typing "yes" and hitting enter. The program will delete all the data on the drive and prepare it. Accept the default size of swap presented, and allow the program to put the swap space at the beginning of the drive for speed. When the program asks if this is okay, type **yes** and hit Enter.

5. When the program is finished formatting and copying data to the disk, the machine will reboot and start up in graphical install mode. Click Next at the first window.

6. If your machine is networked, click Networked and then click Next. If it is not networked, click Not Networked and then click Next. If your machine is not networked, you can skip steps 7 and 8 and ignore the text in which the installer refers to networking.

7. If you are using DHCP (consult your network admin), click Yes for Use DHCP. If not, click No. Click "next" and continue through the sub-steps for non-DHCP machines. If you are using DHCP, skip to Step 8.

    A. If you are using the non-DHCP option, the next screen will ask for your machine's hostname. Enter it and click Next.

    B. Now enter the IP address and click Next.

    C. Enter the netmask and click Next.

    D. Do not enable IPv6 unless you know that you need it. Click No and then click Next.

    E. Click DNS as your name service and click Next. Enter your domain part of the hostname (example: Machine name: foo Domain: yahoo.com, which would give foo.yahoo.com as a complete hostname). Click Next.

    F. Enter the DNS server(s) IP address(es) and click Next. Enter nothing on the DNS Search List, and click Next.

    G. When asked about a default route, click Specify One and click Next. Enter the default route and then click Next; skip to Step 9.

8. DHCP-enabled machines have shorter instructions for network configuration.

   A. Choose DNS as your name service and click Next. Enter the domain part of the hostname (example: Machine name: foo Domain: yahoo.com, which would give foo.yahoo.com as a complete hostname).

   B. Enter the IP address(es) of the DNS server(s) and click Next. Enter nothing in the DNS Search List, and click Next.

   C. When asked about a default route, click Specify One and click Next. Enter the default route and then click Next.

9. Specify your time zone by geographic region and click Next. Choose the time zone that you are in from the list, and click Next.

10. Set the root password. For more information on passwords, turn to Chapter 7, "Authentication." Click Next.

11. Unless you are connected to the Internet via a proxy, click Direct Connection to the Internet and then click Next.

12. Check all the settings then click Confirm. The Solaris Web Start interface will start. After it loads, click Next.

13. You will be using the CD as your installation medium. Click CD and then click Next. Insert the Solaris 8 software CD (one of two) and click OK. Choose Default Install and click Next. Click Install now.

14. The installation summary pops up when the installation is complete. Click Next and repeat the same steps on the next two CDs that you followed for the first. At the end of this, the Reboot Now button appears. Click Reboot Now and wait for the machine to reboot.

15. Upon reboot, log in as root. Open a console window and edit /etc/hosts to enter the full name of your machine, as well as the short name. (example: 192.168.1.1 foo.yahoo.com foo loghost). We recommend using `vi` as your editor, but use whatever is comfortable. Save the file after the changes.

16. Edit /etc/nsswitch.conf. At the line for `hosts`, add `dns` before `files`. If `dns` is already there, ignore this step.

17. Edit /etc/resolv.conf to add your DNS information, if it is not listed. It should be in the following format:

domain my.domain.com

nameserver 192.168.1.1

search domain.com

If you have trouble with this step, take a look at another Solaris machine. This should not be necessary, but because of some problems in the installation of Solaris, we are including it here.

18. Reboot and wait for the machine to come back up. When it does, log in as root again. Edit /etc/passwd with `vi`, and enter a line as follows: `user1::12001:20:User account for install:/bin/csh:/`. Save the file and exit. Now type **passwd user1** and set a password for the user. Log out and then log back in as user1.

19. Open Netscape by typing **netscape&** in a console window. When Netscape starts, go to `http://www.sun.com/bigadmin` and click Patches. Open a Console Window or Xterm, type **su root**, and enter the root password. In this window, create the directory /usr/site with the command `mkdir /usr/site`. Then change the owner of this directory to user1 with the command `chown -R user1 /usr/site`. Download the patches for Solaris 8 into /usr/site. As soon as the patches are downloaded, close Netscape and disconnect the network line for the machine.

20. Change the directory to /usr/site and type **unzip *name_of_patches*.zip**. This will create the patches directory. `cd` to this directory and then type **./install_cluster**.

21. When the patcher is finished, reboot the machine. When the machine comes back up, log back in as user1. Open a Console, `su` to root, and edit /etc/inetd.conf to comment out every line in the file by inserting a # in the first column. Unless you are absolutely sure that you need something, do not leave it uncommented. Reboot and reconnect the network line. Log back in as user1.

22. Open Netscape again, go to `http://www.sunfreeware.com`, and download the latest version of OpenSSH and OpenSSL for Solaris 8. You also might need to download some extra libraries that will be listed in the short description for the packages. When you have downloaded all you need, install the libraries, then OpenSSL, and finally OpenSSH. These should be in Solaris package form, which means that all you need to do to install them is to use `pkgadd -d name_of_pack-age`. Make sure that you are in the directory where you downloaded the packages—we recommend /usr/site. Also make sure that you have su'ed to root. After this is all done, reboot.

23. Lastly, you should create a user account (refer to Appendix B, "From Disk to Filesystem") because of the security problems associated with logging in as root. After you have done this, you can enjoy Solaris 8!

Step-by-Step Red Hat Linux 7.1 Installation

1. Put the CD in the drive and reboot the computer. You will need a computer with a bootable CDROM to do this. If you don't have a bootable CDROM, you will need to make a boot floppy, which can be done using instructions on the Red Hat site.

2. When the CD boots, the Installation window appears. Press F1 for the graphical install and then allow the installer to load.

3. After the installer loads, choose your language—in this case, English—from the list and click Next.

4. Your keyboard should be autodetected by the installer. If you are *certain* that the installer is wrong, choose your keyboard from the list. After this, click Next.

5. Your mouse should be autodetected by the installer. If you are *certain* that the installer is wrong, choose your mouse from the list. After this, click Next.

6. The Welcome screen from Red Hat comes up. Feel free to read this and then click Next.

7. For the purposes of this installation, you will be doing a workstation install. Click Workstation and then click Next.

8. Partitioning is covered in depth in Chapter 3, "Filesystem Administration." For this installation, click Automatic Partitioning. (*Please realize that this will delete all the data on your hard drive.*) After the selection, click Next.

9. If your network administrator has provided DHCP support for your machine, leave Configure Using DHCP checked and click Next. If not, deselect it and fill in the blanks on the screen with the information asked for in each blank. If you are unsure of any of the information, talk to your network admin. When you have finished filling in the blanks, click Next.

10. Choose Medium Security for the firewall rules. Also click Customize and then click both SSH and DHCP. This allows incoming connections of both types. After you do this, click Next. Do not set the level to No Security unless you are planning to install another firewall program. Refer to Chapter 8, "Securing a System for Rollout," for more information on security.

11. For this installation, you are not adding other languages. Click Next when the screen appears.

12. Choose your time zone from the list and then click Next.

13. Create and enter your root password. Refer to Chapter 7, "Authentication", for good password practices. Also create a user account that you will use for normal logins. Make this password different from your root password, and be sure to remember both. After you add the user account, click Next.

14. Install GNOME as the window manager. You can choose to install KDE, but this installation assumes that you are using GNOME. Click Next.

15. Your video card should be autodetected by the installer. If it is not, or if you *know* that the installer is wrong, choose your video card from the list. Click Next.

16. Your monitor should be autodetected, but the list will appear if you want to choose from it. We recommend being very careful in changing this because it can keep X from working. Click Next.

17. Choose the color depth that you prefer. We recommend 16-bit color. Then choose the resolution that you prefer and click Test. If the box comes up and asks if you can see it, click Yes, which means that the test was successful. If the test was successful, click the Graphical Login option and then click Next. If the test was unsuccessful, try a lower resolution or color depth until it succeeds.

18. Now you are ready to install. Click Next and wait for the install to complete. You will have to insert the second disk when the installer asks for it.

19. When the installation is complete, the installer will ask to create a boot disk. We *highly* recommend doing this in case of future problems. Insert one writeable floppy and click Next.

20. Before allowing the machine to reboot, pull out the floppy. Then click Exit and allow the machine to reboot.

21. Upon first bootup, kudzu might start. kudzu is a program that Linux uses to provide some plug-and-play support. It will detect new hardware and configure it. Allow it to configure, by default, any hardware that it recognizes.

22. When the login screen appears, log in to the user account that you created.

23. Click the Terminal button at the bottom to open a local terminal.

24. Double-click the Red Hat Network icon on the desktop. You are asked for the root password. Enter it and continue. You will be registering with Red Hat to use its free upgrade service. If you choose not to register, you can download all the patches from `http://www.redhat.com/errata` and `rpm` them in manually.

25. After you register with the Red Hat network, open a Web browser and go to `http://www.redhat.com/network`. Log in with the username and password that you created. Red Hat allows all registering persons to have one machine that can use the Software Manager service free of charge. That free machine will be used in the next step.

26. When you are logged in, click Assign Service Level and use your one free machine as the box that you are installing. Set the service level to Software Manager. Then open a terminal window, su to root, and type **up2date**.

27. The Update agent pops up. Allow it to run all updates by clicking Install All Packages. Then continue to click Next until the updating starts.

28. When the updating is complete, click Finish and then reboot the computer.

29. After the machine has rebooted and you have logged back in, open your Web browser, go to `http://www.bastille-linux.org`, and follow the instructions for downloading and installing Bastille Linux.

30. When the Bastille installation is complete, open a terminal window, su to root, and type **InteractiveBastille**. InteractiveBastille is located in /usr/sbin with a typical install.

31. For the purposes of this installation, accept all defaults unless you know of something that must be done differently for your machine. For more detailed security measures, refer to Chapter 8, "Securing a System for Rollout."

32. Reboot the machine and enjoy Red Hat Linux 7.1!

From Disk to Filesystem

by Robin Anderson

IN THIS APPENDIX

Logical View of a Disk

The physical layout of a disk does not necessarily impose any particular constraints on how it is viewed logically. In fact, the logical structure of a disk is very simple, as Figure B.1 shows.

FIGURE B.1

Logical structure of a partitioned disk.

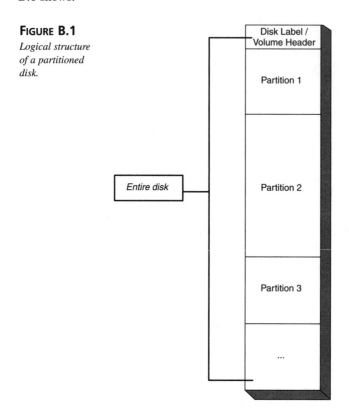

There must always be a disk label or volume header; otherwise, the disk will have no self-identifying statistics. Beyond that, there may be as few as one partition or as many as your OS will recognize.

Note that not all partitions must be in use at any given time. Also note that not all space on a disk need be allocated or partitioned at any given time.

Logical View of a Partition

Now let's step down into a partition that has a filesystem on it. This is a critical qualifier; none of the structures in Figure B.2 actually is created until the filesystem is initialized (except for the boot block, which is created at partition time).

FIGURE B.2

Logical structure of an individual partition.

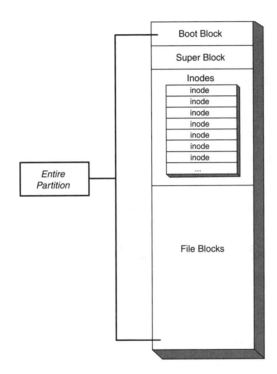

The key to understanding these structures is that everything is created in advance; all structures are put in place before use. This means that allocations and space reservations are done ahead of time, resulting in time savings and insurance that the space will be there when required.

The boot block, created by the system's partitioning program, is created even if the partition is not currently bootable. This is so that the partition can be converted at will. Again, it is a matter of preallocating any space that might be called into use later.

> **Note**
>
> The superblock is discussed in more detail in the next section.

The area marked "Inodes" is reserved at filesystem creation time. The inode structures themselves are instantiated in their most minimal configurations at that time as well. So, even when unused, the inodes are there and available. The corollary, though, is that you can't add any more inodes *after* filesystem creation. Of course, you have a finite amount of space on the partition—the more you set aside for inodes, the less you have for files. Conversely, if you run out of inodes, you can't store any more files, even if you have free data blocks, because you won't be able to reference them. All in all, inodes take up little enough space that it's better to have more than you likely will need.

The area marked "File Blocks" is the remainder of the partition's space and contains files of all kinds, including directories. Although sequential block arrangements are most efficient, the unpredictable nature of file additions and deletions (and even modifications) makes this hard to do well. Thus, the file blocks are often noncontiguous, and one file might be scattered across multiple physical locations.

The job of the filesystem is to provide the organizational structure used by the operating system to interpret the information in the inode list, free block list, and superblock. Once given a structure, the operating system can order data I/O and manage all metainformation, including free block and inode lists and superblock information.

Logical View of a Superblock

As we go on, you might notice that the complex filesystem is actually made up of very simple elements. This is key to the philosophy of Unix: to create intricate structures from atomic elements put together in a clear way.

The superblock holds the keys to the kingdom. Without its indexes and lists, the filesystem would just be so much garbage. The operating system uses the superblock to determine which blocks of the partition containing the filesystem are in use and which are available for writing new data. This is why many filesystems have backup superblocks. If corruption or failure occurs, the backup superblock can be used to manage the filesystem.

Figure B.3 represents some of the more common and critical elements of a superblock.

You often will see messages about superblocks when a system boots after an "unclean" shutdown (usually a sudden loss of power). These messages are generated by fsck and usually deal with the free list being inaccurate and the superblock being marked "dirty" (by the modification flag). Another time fsck might complain is when the various numbers don't add up. The superblock is used to keep track of the total filesystem size, overhead, free space, and used space. If the last three don't sum to the first, then there's a problem.

FIGURE B.3

Logical structure of a superblock.

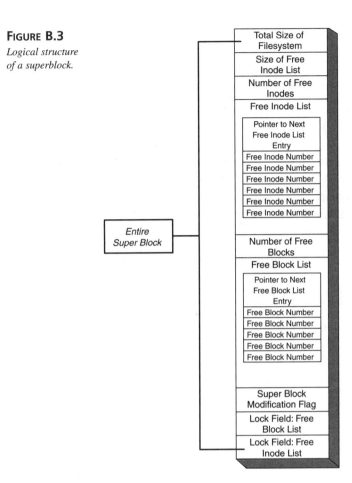

Notice that most of the superblock is dedicated to the free inode and block lists. Why maintain such lists and pointers to the next free structure in them? Because it would be inefficient to have to search the entire filesystem looking for a hole every time a new inode or data block needs to be allocated. In fact, fsck checks that these lists are in agreement with the actual filesystem for this very reason.

The lock flags exist to prevent race conditions. Inodes must be manipulated by exactly one process at any given time. Locks prevent multiple processes from modifying the filesystem or the data in the inode simultaneously. Without locks, one process might lay claim to an inode but get pre-empted in favor of another process that claimed and wrote to the inode before the first came back to perform its writes. This would result in either total data loss for one of the processes or data corruption for both.

When a user invokes rm, the data blocks and inode are simply added back into the free list. Their contents are unaltered and could presumably be recovered until they are overwritten, but on a multiuser system, they are quite likely to be overwritten before you could even type a recover command.

The rm command also must deal with the parent directory entry associated with the deleted file. Under Solaris and Red Hat, the directory entry is marked "unused," indicating that the original entry may be overwritten by a new directory entry. Under RH Linux 7.1, the original contents of that directory location now are inaccessible through standard system tools. Under Solaris 8, the contents of that location can be viewed using the strings command. In principle, the original entry could be reconstructed and the deleted file could be recovered on a Solaris system as long as none of the blocks or inodes used by the deleted file has been overwritten.

Some filesystems have tools for recovering deleted files under some circumstances.

Logical View of a Directory

Remember that a directory is just a specialized file. The particular function of a directory is to store and associate inode numbers with the names of all files (special and regular) for which it acts as a container. This information is stored in the directory's data blocks; the rest of a directory's inode is standard issue.

As you might surmise, users are not allowed to write to directory files. Directory manipulations must be done through system commands such as cp, rm, or mv.

Figure B.4 shows a logical view of a directory and its component structures.

The entry location list indicates which locations currently are filled in the next segment. This is an internal-use structure similar to the free inode list that improves efficiency in storage and retrieval times.

The directory entries are the real key to the directory file's function. Figure B.5 provides a closer look at the more interesting components of the actual directory entries.

Note that although our example shows all locations filled, they can be nonsequential (this is a result of files being moved or deleted). The first entry is always ".", the self-referent that allows a relative path within (and "below"[1]) the directory. The second entry is always "..", the parent referent that allows a relative path "above" the current directory. There is no necessary ordering to the remaining entries (that is, they are not sorted by inode number or filename).

FIGURE B.4

Logical structure of a directory file.

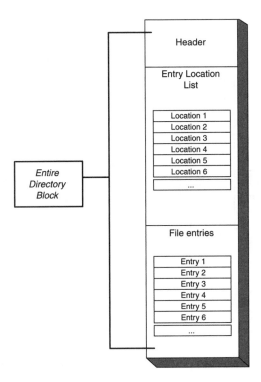

FIGURE B.5

Logical structure of directory file entries.

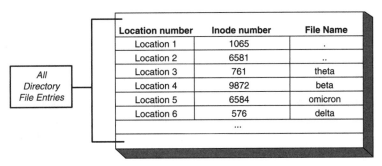

Logical View of an Inode (Regular File)

Finally, Figure B.6 offers a glimpse into the world of the inode itself.

More complex than any of the other filesystem structures, an inode is still a simple structure. File attributes are old friends, usually displayed through some variant of ls. The physical addressing scheme is where some confusion might arise.

FIGURE B.6

Logical structure of an inode.

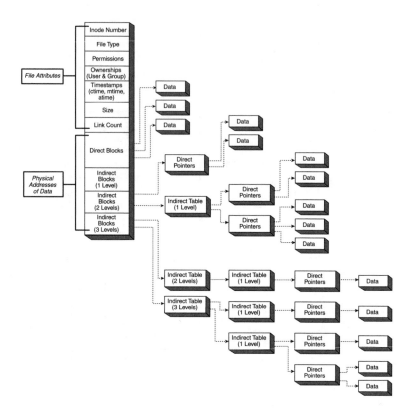

If a file is small enough, its addresses could be few enough to be handled by the *direct blocks* that were preallocated when the inode was created. Direct blocks are pointers to physical disk locations where the literal bits of the file are stored.

If a file grows beyond the size that direct blocks can accommodate, the filesystem resorts to *indirect addressing*. This means that the next group of block pointers actually points to a lookup table rather than disk locations. In a *single-indirect* block, the lookup table actually contains the physical disk location pointers.

If the file grows even larger, *double-indirect addressing* might have to be used. This means that the lookup table actually points to another set of lookup tables, which, in turn, point to physical disk locations.

Not all filesystems support *triple-indirection*, but if they do, it just adds another layer of lookup tables. It's quite a bit to keep track of, but the mechanisms are straightforward.

Using the Filesystem: Command Internals

Now it's time to put all this together and present a few example scenarios.

Let's begin with an axiom: Every file on a system must be uniquely identified.[2] Also, every file that exists on a system does so within a filesystem. Thus, the filesystem is the first part of the file's unique identifier, much like the street name in a postal address.[3]

The inode number is the second piece of a file's unique identifier, just like a house number. It points to the inode, which actually holds physical location and other information about the file.

This is why you can't create a hard link across filesystems: Directories don't have any way to represent another filesystem name internally. For symbolic links, or *symlinks*, the directory name is part of the actual filename. Symlinks rely on name, not inode number. Hard links simply point to another local inode. Note that symlinks also can point to a nonexistent file, whereas hard links cannot.

Now, let's start with a simple example.

Example 1: Listing a Filename

What happens when a user types `ls /space/aa/myfile`?

1. Traverse the absolute path specified.
    - A. Verify that / contains a valid entry for space.
    - B. Retrieve space's inode number.
    - C. Retrieve space's inode.
    - D. Verify that space is a directory.
    - E. Verify that the user is allowed to access subdirectories of space.
        - I. Retrieve owner, group, and permission bits from the inode.
        - II. Check that at least one directory traversal (execute) bit applying to the user is set.
    - F. Verify that space contains a valid entry for aa.
        - I. Retrieve aa's inode number.
        - II. Retrieve aa's inode.
        - III. Verify that aa is a directory.

G. Verify that the user is allowed to list the contents of aa.

    I. Retrieve owner, group, and permission bits from the inode.

    II. Check that at least one read bit applying to the user is set.

H. Verify that aa contains a valid entry for myfile.

2. Report the information stored in myfile's entry in aa.

Note that, at a minimum, directory traversal permission (specified by the execute bit) is required to `cd` into a subdirectory, and directory read permission (specified by the read bit) is required to obtain a directory listing.

> **Note**
>
> When we refer to permission bits applying to a user, we refer to one of the three "triplets" of permission bits: user, group, and other. Specifically, we mean that the user has the necessary permissions based on the user's user ID ("user" bits), the user's group ID ("group" bits), and default "world" privileges ("other" bits). Chapter 3, "Filesystem Administration," contains a detailed description of a file's permission bits.

All in all, this was a simple example, so let's look at something more interesting.

Example 2: Changing a Filename

What happens when a user types `mv myfile newname`?

1. Traverse the relative path specified. (Note that relative path is implied even without the ./)

    A. Verify that . contains a valid entry for myfile.

    B. Retrieve myfile's inode number.

    C. Retrieve myfile's inode.

2. Verify that the user is allowed to access myfile.

    A. Retrieve owner, group, and permission bits from the inode.

    B. Check that at least one read bit and one write bit applying to the user are set.

3. Verify that the user is allowed to write to ..

    A. Retrieve the . inode number.

    B. Retrieve the . inode.

      C. Retrieve owner, group, and permission bits from the inode.

      D. Check that at least one write bit applying to the user is set.

4. Change the filename for the stored inode number associated with myfile in ".".

> **Note**
>
> The previous example illustrates the mv command's operation when both the source and the destination of the move are in the same filesystem (in this case, the same directory as well). The original inode number of the file does not change as a result of the move.
>
> When the source and destination of the move are on *different* filesystems, the operation is more complex. Inodes are created and maintained internally by filesystems, so there is no relationship between the inodes of one filesystem and those of another. Moving a file across filesystems therefore requires the creation of a new inode entry (and inode number) in the destination filesystem, as well as the deletion of the original inode entry in the source filesystem.

Hmmm, looks like this was straightforward as well. Want more?

Example 3: Printing the Contents of a File

What happens when you type cat newname?

1. Traverse the relative path specified.

      A. Verify that . contains a valid entry for newname.

      B. Retrieve newname's inode number.

      C. Retrieve newname's inode.

2. Verify that the user is allowed to read newname.

      A. Retrieve owner, group, and permission bits from the inode.

      B. Check that at least one read bit applying to the user is set.

3. Get direct block data.

      A. Examine the first direct block.

      B. Retrieve the physical data location.

      C. Retrieve stored data from the specified location and print to the screen.

      D. Check to see if there are more direct blocks.

          I. If yes, examine the next direct block and repeat retrieval steps 3/B–D.

          II. If no, continue.

  4. Check to see if there are indirect blocks.

      A. If no, stop.

      B. If yes, follow the indirect block's pointer to the indicated direct lookup table.

          I. Examine the first direct block.

          II. Retrieve the physical data location.

          III. Retrieve stored data from the specified location and print to the screen.

          IV. Check if there are more direct blocks specified in the lookup table.

              a. If yes, examine the next direct block and repeat retrieval steps 4/II–IV.

              b. If no, continue.

      C. Check to see if there are more indirect blocks.

          I. If yes, return to 4/B for retrieval steps.

          II. If no, stop.

When I Tried cat /bin/ls, It Printed Garbage to My Screen! What Happened?

The cat command does *not* check whether the file that you are attempting to print to screen is a non–binary/printable file. The cat command, like most primitives that live in /bin, is very simple and has no safeguards or controls. If you want a backstop, use more or less.

That was more complex but still a fairly repetitive and mechanical operation. Take a look at one final example that crosses filesystem boundaries.

Example 4: Copying a File from One Filesystem to Another

What happens when you type `cp newname /space2/finito`?

1. Traverse the relative path specified.
   A. Verify that . contains a valid entry for newname.
   B. Retrieve newname's inode number.
   C. Retrieve newname's inode.

2. Verify that the user is allowed to access newname.
   A. Retrieve owner, group, and permission bits from the inode.
   B. Check that at least one read bit applying to the user is set.

3. Traverse the absolute path to the destination specified.
   A. Verify that / contains a valid entry for space2.
   B. Retrieve space2's inode number.
   C. Retrieve space2's inode.
   D. Verify that space2 is a directory.

4. Verify that the user is allowed to write to space2.
   A. Retrieve owner, group, and permission bits from the inode.
   B. Check that at least one write bit applying to the user is set.
   C. Check to see if there is a directory entry called finito in /space2 (assume that there is not, for this example).

5. Allocate a new inode in /space2.

6. Set file attributes based on standard defaults and current environment settings, including user and group ownership, permission bits, and so on.

7. Recurse through the direct and indirect block pointers of the original inode to retrieve the file data.

8. Save the file data through direct and indirect block pointers as necessary in the new inode.

B

FROM DISK TO FILESYSTEM

Online References

Books

Stevens, W. Richard. *Advanced Programming in the UNIX Environment.* Addison Wesley, 1992.

Bach, Maurice J. *Design of the Unix Operating System.* Prentice Hall, 1987.

Vahalia, Uresh. *UNIX Internals: The New Frontiers.* Prentice Hall, 1995.

Web Sites

Disk and filesystem structures

- http://www.angelfire.com/myband/binusoman/Unix.html
- http://tractor.mcs.kent.edu/~walker/classes/coal.f98/lectures/L14.pdf

Linux filesystems: http://www.linuxdoc.org/LDP/tlk/fs/filesystem.html

Solaris filesystems:
http://www.computerbooksonline.com/chapters/solarischap.htm

Inodes

- http://www.algonquincollege.com/~alleni/dat2330/01s/unix/inodes.htm
- http://morpheus.hartford.edu/~fmaddix/CS451/Lec5Res/inodes.gif

File Recovery Techniques

Files Wanted, Dead or Alive, Wietse Venema, Dr. Dobb's Journal, December 2000
(http://www.ddj.com/articles/2000/0012/0012h/0012h.htm)

Endnotes

[1] *Note that we are using "above" and "below" in the inverted-tree hierarchy used in Chapter 3. If root is at the top, then subdirectories fan out toward the bottom.*

[2] *Imagine the terrifying confusion that would ensue if you could have non-unique files.*

[3] *The analogy actually holds pretty well going upward as well: system=zip code, subnet=city, and so on, but that's beyond the scope of our discussion.*

User Creation Checklist

by Robin Anderson

Fast Facts

Does your site use NIS?   **Yes**   **No**

Server name:

_____

Home Directory Server

Hostname: _____

Skeleton/Config Files Location

Hostname: _____

Directory: _____

Quota Policy (by Filesystem)

Home Directory: _____   _____MB

Mail Directory: _____   _____MB

Other Directories: _____   _____MB

                            _____   _____MB

                            _____   _____MB

Checklist

Step 1

❑ Allocate a unique UID: _____

   ❑ Verify that the UID is not reserved.

   ❑ Verify that the UID is not already in use.

   ❑ Verify that the UID is not colliding with a pre-existing UID on remote server(s).

Step 2

❑ Choose a default GID: _____

❑ Extra group names: _____

_____

_____

_____

❑ Netgroup names: _____

_____

Step 3

❑ Allocate a unique username: _____

   ❑ Verify that the username is not reserved.

   ❑ Verify that the username is not already in use.

Step 4

❑ Full path to home directory: _____

   ❑ Verify that sufficient space exists on the device.

Step 5

❑ Full path to login shell: _____

❑ Verify existence of the shell.

❑ Verify that the shell is listed in /etc/shells.

Step 6

❏ Create the /etc/passwd entry.

    ❏ Run ypmake to update and push out the map, if you're running NIS.

❏ Set a strong password for the new user.

Step 7

❏ Modify /etc/group as necessary.

❏ Modify /etc/netgroups as necessary.

    ❏ Run ypmake to update and push out the map, if you're running NIS.

Step 8

❏ Use mkdir to create the home directory.

Step 9

❏ Copy local configuration files into the new user's home directory.

Step 10

❏ Use edquota to set quotas for the new user on each applicable filesystem.

Step 11

❏ Use chown -Rh to set user and group ownership on the user's home directory.

Step 12

❏ Test—log in as the user, in the user's intended environment (where possible).

Binary–Hex Notation Summary

by Andy Johnston

IN THIS APPENDIX

APPENDIX D

Representation

It has been my experience that sysadmins are almost never lukewarm on the subject of mathematics. As a rule, sysadmins either love math or hate it. Assuming that this is true of the reader as well, a treatise on place-value notation with detailed instruction on the conversion of one integer base to another is either unnecessary or unwelcome. In fact, much of it is irrelevant as well. The emphasis often placed on base conversion obscures the far more useful aspects of binary representation and manipulation. This appendix stresses the significant aspects of binary, decimal, and hexadecimal notation in their most common applications, IP address configuration and file permission specification.

> **Note**
>
> Of course, there is an almost endless supply of hexadecimal/decimal/binary conversion utilities on calculators, PDAs, and assorted GUI tools, so if you *do* need to do some converting between different bases, there is still no reason to do it by hand. In fact, we will introduce you to a standard UNIX utility, bc, that will convert bases as well.

Computers operate using only ones and zeros internally. Anyone working with computers and delving into their internal functions must eventually face this fact. Computers must represent everything—numbers, words, commands, internal storage locations, Internet addresses, and anything else they need—using the same two symbols, ones and zeros. This means that when you look at a string of ones and zeros, you must know the *context* in which it is used so that you can interpret what it represents. The string 01100001 might represent the number 97, the letter *a*, or the choices no-yes-yes-no-no-no-no-yes, depending on its context as a number, an ASCII character, or a set of flags applied to eight options, respectively. Knowing which of these possible interpretations to use usually depends on where you found that string. Inside a text file, for instance, it will mean *a*. If it is one of the quads in an IP address, it should be read as 97.

Collective Nouns

Endless cascades of ones and zeros are hard to face with any equanimity, so the strings are broken into groups of standard sizes. A single 1 or 0 in a string is called a *bit*. A string of 8 bits is a *byte*. (A string of 4 bits is a *nybble*, just to be cute.) A 32-bit string (4 bytes) is called a *word*.

> **Note**
>
> The definition of *word* can be somewhat fluid and might depend on a computer's hardware. Some contexts define 16-bit or 64-bit words. One older (non-Unix) operating system used an implicit 36-bit word. The 32-bit word, however, is commonly used, so we will stick with it here.
>
> Bytes, words, and so forth are not just a convenience for the reader. These groupings are used to organize the computer's operations at the most fundamental levels. Different operating systems use different methods to store this information in memory. When looking at a binary string, it is also of key importance to know where the byte and word boundaries *start*. For instance, 101000101000101000... could be grouped into bytes as 10100010,10001010,... or as ...10,10001010,00101000,...
>
> To interpret the string correctly, the reader must know how the computer groups the bits, whether to read the bits and bytes right to left, or vice versa, and so on.
>
> A detailed discussion of these issues is beyond the scope of this book. In general, they are in the realm of system programming and the sysadmin will rarely have to deal with them directly.

Decimal Representation

> **Note**
>
> In case you don't remember your early math classes, we use a "place-value" system of representing numbers. The number 181, for instance, actually represents the sum of 1, eight 10s, and 100, or one 10-to-the-zero-power, eight 10s-to-the-first-power and one 10-squared.
>
> $$181 = (1 \times 10^0) + (8 \times 10^1) + (1 \times 10^2)$$
>
> Because everything refers to powers of 10, this is called *base-10* notation. There is nothing special about the choice of 10 as a base. Any integer from 2 on up can be used.

A byte—say, 10110101—is an awkward thing to write and to remember. A more compact representation is commonly used. Specifically, the 8 bits can be read as a number expressed in base-2 notation and then expressed in base-10. The byte 10110101 would be represented as the decimal number 181. You don't believe it? Well, here is the math:

$$(1 \times 2^0) + (0 \times 2^1) + (1 \times 2^2) + (0 \times 2^3) + (1 \times 2^4) + (1 \times 2^5) + (0 \times 2^6) +$$
$$(1 \times 2^7) =$$
$$1 + 0 + 4 + 0 + 16 + 32 + 0 + 128$$
$$= 181$$
$$= (1 \times 10^0) + (8 \times 10^1) + (1 \times 10^2)$$

Note that the base-2 value of a binary byte (8 bits) can range from 00000000 through 11111111, or 0 through 255 in base-10 representation.

Operating on Binary Strings

Context is important. The byte 01100001 in a text file is the ASCII representation for the character *a*, though it can also be represented in base-10 notation as 97. There is a rather subtle distinction here. You see two squiggles of ink; one looks like 9 and the other looks like 7. Together, in this context, they represent the character *a*. The same squiggles may be used elsewhere to represent a numeric value that is half of 194 or the square root of 9409. Here, because they are representing a byte in a text file, they are interpreted as the character *a*.

Even though binary bytes can be represented as numbers, they are not manipulated with the usual arithmetic operations of addition, subtraction, multiplication, and division. Instead, binary information is processed using *binary* operations.

Programmers and computer scientists recognize several binary operations for binary strings. You will get by with two of them: NOT and AND.

NOT is pretty straightforward:

> NOT 1 = 0
> NOT 0 = 1
> NOT 10110101 = 01001010

Note that when NOT is applied to a string of bits, it is applied to each bit in the string. Technically, this is called the bitwise NOT. This distinguishes it from the logical NOT used in programming.

AND is also pretty simple. Note that, unlike NOT, AND operates on two binary strings:

> 0 AND 0 = 0
> 0 AND 1 = 1
> 1 AND 0 = 1
> 1 AND 1 = 1

The rest of the examples are easier to follow vertically (see Table D.1):

TABLE D.1   Binary Operations

	10110101		10110101		10110101		10110101
AND	11111111	AND	11111100	AND	11110000	AND	00001111
	----------		------------		------------		------------
	10110101		10110100		10110000		00000101

Subnets, Netmasks, and CIDR

As noted before, IP addresses are represented in the computer as 32-bit words and to humans as decimal dotted-quads. The way IP addresses are assigned as groups to local networks or *subnets* is defined by operations on the binary representation. The most common notation used to describe these subnets is called *classless interdomain routing (CIDR)* (pronounced "*sigh*-der," as in apple cider) notation. It works as follows:

An organization requests (or rents or buys) IP address space and is assigned 133.46.96.0/19.

The number after the slash is used to define a 32-bit *subnet mask*. In this case, the first 19 bits of the mask (read left to right) are ones, and the remainder are zeros.

To determine whether an IP address is in the assigned IP space, apply the subnet mask to the address in question and to 133.46.96.0. If the results match, the IP address is in the assigned space; otherwise, it is not. This process is demonstrated in the following example.

The binary representation of 133.46.96.0 is:

    10000101 00101110 01100100 00000000

And now, apply the subnet mask:

	10000101	00101110	01100100	00000000
AND	11111111	11111111	11100000	00000000
	----------	--------	--------	--------
	10000101	00101110	01100000	00000000

The effect of the subnet mask is to leave the first 19 bits of the address unchanged and zero out the remaining 13 bits. This result is the key to defining the assigned address space.

The address space consists of all 32-bit addresses that give the same result when the net-mask is applied to them.

For instance, applying the subnet mask to 133.46.102.143 yields this computation:

```
    10000101 00101110 01100110 10001111
AND 11111111 11111111 11100000 00000000
    _____
    10000101 00101110 01100000 00000000
```

This matches the result of applying the subnet mask to 133.46.96.0, so 133.46.102.143 is in the address space 133.46.96.0/19.

When a computer determines whether another IP address belongs to the same local network or whether the other address must be reached through a gateway, it applies the subnet mask as shown previously to its own IP address and to the other address. The decision process is described algorithmically as follows:

If ((MY_IP_ADDRESS AND NETMASK) equals (OTHER_IP_ADDRESS AND NETMASK))

Then

OTHER_IP_ADDRESS is on local network

Else

OTHER_IP_ADDRESS is not on local network

End

The sysadmin usually is assigned the subnet mask, but for testing network configuration, it's often useful to be able to determine whether another IP address is on the same local network.

In fact, in this example, any address in which the first 19 bits are 10000101 00101110 011 is in the address space. The remaining 13 bits can be any combination of ones or zeros.

Hexadecimal Notation

Decimal notation is comfortable for people but masks the structure of what is happening in applications such as IP addressing. Binary notation displays that structure but is very unwieldy, given the length of the strings. Hexadecimal (base 16) notation is a compromise between the two in that it closely reflects the binary structure but represents it in about the same amount of space as decimal notation does (actually, a little less space on average).

Table D.2 illustrates all three forms:

Table D.2   Binary/Decimal/Hexadecimal Equivalents

Binary	Decimal	Hexadecimal
0000	0	0
0001	1	1
0010	2	2
0011	3	3
0100	4	4
0101	5	5
0110	6	6
0111	7	7
1000	8	8
1001	9	9
1010	10	A
1011	11	B
1100	12	C
1101	13	D
1110	14	E
1111	15	F

If you're not familiar with hexadecimal, you might be a bit shaken by the use of the letters A through F to represent the numbers 10 through 15. It's really worth the trouble of getting used to in the long run.

Notice that the table lists binary numbers with 4 bits, even when the leading bits are zeros. This is meant to illustrate the relationship between binary and hexadecimal notation. There are 16 possible binary strings of 4 bits or nybbles (it's not just a cute name, after all). Each of the possible nybbles corresponds to a single, unique hexadecimal symbol.

Consider the earlier address 133.46.102.143. It's easy to remember, but the subnet structure based on the first 19 bits of the 32-bit binary representation is not evident. That structure, 10000101 00101110 01100000 00000000, is easy to derive from the representation 10000101 00101110 01100110 10001111, but the four words in base-2 notation are awkward even to write down, let alone remember.

There is yet another notation, called *hexadecimal* that can be converted easily to and from the base-2 notation, yet it is compact enough to take in at a glance. Hexadecimal (hex, for short) notation is simply the place-value representation of numbers using 16 as a base.

Break the binary representation into nybbles:

1000 0101 0010 1110 0110 0110 1000 1111

You can see from Table D.2 that each nybble corresponds to a single hexadecimal symbol:

8   5   2   E   6   6   8   F

You write this as follows:

85 2E 66 8F

It is standard practice to write the hexadecimal symbols in pairs so that the first and last symbol in each pair represents the first and last 4 bits in a byte, respectively.

Like decimal notation, hexadecimal is compact. Although subnet structures are not as clear as in binary notation, the translation between binary and hexadecimal representation can be done using a simple 16-line table like Table D.2. With a little practice, you don't even need the table. As an additional benefit, each pair of hexadecimal symbols corresponds to a binary byte. At the beginning of this appendix, the decimal number 97 was said to represent the letter *a* in certain contexts. Because each ASCII character is represented within the computer as a unique byte, ASCII definitions are often represented as a pair of hexadecimal symbols. The binary representation of decimal 97 is 01100001, which is 61 in hexadecimal notation (check Table D.2 for the hexadecimal equivalents of 0110 and 0001). This is the ASCII code for the character *a*.

Note

To illustrate the way hexadecimal notation works, let's double-check the previous example.

In base-16, we read 61 as:

$(1 \times 16^0) + (6 \times 16^1) =$

$1 + 96$

$= 97$

$= (7 \times 10^0) + (9 \times 10^1)$

As another example, take the base-16 representation, A5C9. We read this as:

$(9 \times 16^0) + (12 \times 16^1) + (5 \times 16^2) + (10 \times 16^3)$

$= 9 + 192 + 1280 + 40960$

$= 42441$

$= (1 \times 10^0) + (4 \times 10^1) + (4 \times 10^2) + (2 \times 10^3) + (4 \times 10^4)$

The Tool at Your Fingertips: bc

Unix has a built-in calculator program called bc. It works through command-line entry—there is no GUI. Even so, it is always there when you need it to do simple arithmetic or convert between different base representations.

When you type **bc**, you can enter arithmetic expressions and the results will appear beneath them—for example:

```
%bc
8*7
56
quit
%
```

You can specify the base in which input is to be interpreted with the `ibase` variable, and you can specify the base in which output is to be displayed with the `obase` variable. The following examples in Listings D.1 and D.2 illustrate conversion between base-10 and base-16.

LISTING D.1   Base Conversions Using bc

To do hex-to-decimal conversion, use the following:

```
%bc
obase=10
ibase=16
A4
164
2924
10532
quit
```

To do decimal-to-hex conversion, use the following:

```
%bc
ibase=10
obase=16
10532
2924
164
A4
quit
```

In this example, the hex representation of the IP address 3F560277 is converted to dotted-quad format.

LISTING D.2   Converting an IP Address to Dotted-Quad Format

```
%bc
obase=10
ibase=16
3F
63
56
86
02
2
77
119
quit
```

So, in dotted-quad format, the IP address is 63.86.2.119.

Note

Another instance in which alternative base arithmetic in Unix is in the representation of file permission bits or *permbits*. Standard Unix has three classes of file permission—user, group, and other. Each class includes three types of permission, read (r), write (w) and execute (x). The permbits rwxr-xr-- indicate that the user owning the file has read, write, and execute permissions. Members of the user's group may read and execute the file but not write to it. Others may read it but not write to it or execute it.

Because the bits always appear in the same order, we could represent the previous permbits by the 9-bit binary string 111101100. This string does not lend itself to compression into hexadecimal because it can't be separated into chunks of 4 bits each. It can, however, be separated into three chunks of 3 bits each, 111 101 100. These 3-bit chunks, or *triplets*, can easily be converted between binary and *octal* called base-8 notation using the relationships shown in Table D.3.

TABLE D.3   Binary/Decimal/Octal Equivalents

Binary	Decimal	Octal
0000	0	0
0001	1	1
0010	2	2
0011	3	3
0100	4	4

TABLE D.3 continued

Binary	Decimal	Octal
0101	5	5
0110	6	6
0111	7	7

The umask command is used to specify the default permbits for file creation. Rather than specify which bits will be set, however, the argument to umask specifies which bits will *not* be set. For instance, a common umask setting is 022. This is the octal representation of the binary string 000010010.

An executable file with all permissions set has permbits 111111111. The default permbits are determined through this computation:

(NOT 000010010) AND 111111111

= 111101101 AND 111111111

= 111101101

representing the permbits rwxr-xr-x.

Similarly, a nonexecutable file with all permissions set has permbits 110110110. A similar computation yields this:

(NOT 000010010) AND 110110110

= 111101101 AND 110110110

= 110100100

or rw-r--r--

Cryptography in UNIX

IN THIS APPENDIX

Introduction

This appendix is by no means an attempt to introduce you to either the theory or the practice of cryptography. We believe, in fact, that a "deep" theoretical understanding of cryptography is not truly essential to the UNIX sysadmin (although we still encourage the interested reader to investigate the references at the end of this appendix). That stated, there are common UNIX applications that use cryptographic methods to establish and enhance the security of the UNIX operating system. In many cases, a grasp of fundamental concepts and methods can be of great benefit to the sysadmin configuring and troubleshooting such applications.

Cryptographic Elements

Applied cryptography can be viewed as the combination of basic cryptographic methods into more advanced algorithms, each intended for a specific security task, such as user authentication or assurance of data integrity. These algorithms are then combined and implemented as cryptographic security applications. In this section, we describe three fundamental elements of cryptographic applications. These elements are supported themselves by a strongly mathematical body of theory, which is addressed in the references.

Hashes

The term *cryptography* is almost synonymous in the public mind with keeping secrets. To most people, the primary or even sole purpose of the field is to conceal information from all except the intended recipient. In fact, the most common use of cryptography is to provide authentication of information rather than confidentiality. This is frequently done through one of several procedures that computes a number, the *hash*, from various details of a message in such a way that:

- The same procedure applied to the same message always yields the same hash.
- Any change in the original message will almost certainly produce a different number.

A procedure that produces a hash is called a *hash function*.

The two properties listed here do *not* provide a sufficient definition of a hash. They also describe another class of numbers, called *checksums*, which are computed from messages. We will build a working definition of hashes in the subsections that follow.

Checksums vs. Hashes

Consider the phrase "My dog is gray." Suppose that you transmitted this message but were afraid that it might accidentally become corrupted, perhaps through keyboard errors, before reaching its destination. For instance, it could become "Mt dog ks grqy." To guard against this, you could advertise some very small but useful bit of information about the message that could be used to evaluate it automatically upon receipt. For instance, if it were known that the original phrase contained five vowels, then it would be obvious that the message "Mt dog ks grqy" has been corrupted. (We grant *y* permanent status as a vowel, for simplicity.)

A checksum is a simply computed value that is very likely to change whenever the message that it was generated from is accidentally corrupted. Because messages, files, and everything else on a computer ultimately are represented as strings of ones and zeros, real checksums are produced through binary operations performed on the ones and zeros of the message. The final checksum is itself a binary number.

Suppose now that someone *deliberately* tampers with your message and it becomes "My dog is green." There are still five vowels, so the checksum remains the same. Given a message, it is usually easy to determine what changes in that message will produce other messages with the same checksum.

The hash is used to guard against deliberate tampering. In practice, a hash function operates on the binary representation of a message in a *much* more complex and involved way than would produce a checksum. In the previous example, it was obvious that the substitution of any two-vowel word for "gray" would leave the checksum unchanged. It wasn't even necessary to count the vowels in the corrupted phrase to know that the checksums hadn't changed.

One of the defining properties of a hash function is that it is *impossible* to know how any change in the original message will affect the original hash other than by making the change and computing the new hash.

> **Note**
>
> It should be noted that, in this appendix, *impossible* means "computationally infeasible." This means that it would take a *very* long time (a few billion years is considered a good margin), even taking advances in computer technology into account.

The Hash Space

The *hash space* is the set of all the values that the hash can have. If the hash were a two-digit decimal number, for instance, the hash would have 100 possible values, from 00 through 99.

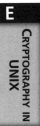

Suppose, in this case, that a given message produced a hash of 34. If someone computed that hash for variations of that message, then, on average, a variation that produced that same hash could be found after 100 attempts.

Clearly, this hash space is too small to be practical. In practice, most hashes are 128-bit numbers, belonging to hash spaces with 2^{128} possible values. Given a message and its hash, the trial-and-error method described previously, checking one million variations per second, would be expected to produce a message with the same hash about every 10,000,000,000,000,000,000,000,000 years. Note that there is no guarantee that this new message would actually make any sense; it just would have the same hash.

Characteristics of a Hash

To the extent that a hash displays the following qualities, it is called a "strong" hash:

- A hash should be easy to compute for any given message.

- It should be impossible to determine a message that would yield any given hash (other than by trial and error).

- Any change in a message should produce unpredictable changes in the message hash.

- The hash space should be large enough to make trial and error infeasible.

Symmetric Key Cryptography

This is the sort of cryptographic system that seems to dominate the popular perception of cryptography. The sender wanting to conceal the contents of a message uses some piece of information called the *key* and an encryption procedure to produce a second message that appears meaningless. (The original message is called the *plaintext*, and the result of the encryption is called the *ciphertext*.) The second message is transmitted to the recipient, who uses the same key along with an associated decryption procedure to reproduce the original plaintext from the ciphertext.

A very simple example of this type of cryptography is the simple substitution for each letter of the message with the third letter following it in the alphabet. The key is 3, and the plaintext, "Alice," becomes the ciphertext "Dolfh." The recipient uses the same key and the corresponding decryption procedure (going three letters backward in the alphabet) to decrypt "Dolfh" back into "Alice."

Like the hashes described previously, modern symmetric key cryptosystems operate through binary operations on the binary representations of messages, "scrambling" the bits. Thus, like hashes, symmetric key methods tend to be quite fast.

An inherent problem with this type of cryptosystem is that it requires the sender and the recipient to have the same key. This means that some secure means must be found for transmission of the key. If such a secure means exists, though, you might ask why we are encrypting the message in the first place.

A related problem arises when there are more than two parties to an interaction. Either all of the computers involved must be supplied with the same key, or every two computers must share a unique key used only for communication between those two. The first option multiplies the risk of compromising the key through multiple copies, while the second creates a key management headache on a large network.

Characteristics of a Symmetric Key Cryptosystem

A "strong" symmetric key cryptosystem has the following characteristics:

- Given the ciphertext alone, it is impossible to determine the original plaintext.
- Given the original plaintext *and* the resulting ciphertext, it is impossible to determine the key used to produce the ciphertext.
- The previous property holds even if the attacker is allowed to *choose* the plaintext used to produce the ciphertext.

Asymmetric Key Cryptography

Asymmetric key cryptography is simple to describe, subtle in its application, and has made an enormous contribution to the secure transmission of information through the Internet.

As with symmetric key cryptography, plaintext messages are encrypted with a key according to a known procedure to produce ciphertext. The ciphertext is transmitted to the recipient, who then recovers the original plaintext using a key and an associated decryption procedure. The "asymmetry" comes from the fact that the key used to encrypt the message is *different* than the key used to decrypt it.

The two keys are created at the same time. They constitute a matched set called a *keypair*. Either key can be used to encrypt a message. A message encrypted by one key can be decrypted *only* by the *other* key. One key is designated the *public* key and can be advertised to everyone interested in secure communications. The other key is the *private* key and should be treated with the same or more care than the single key in the symmetric key cryptosystem. It doesn't matter which key of the pair is chosen for which use, but once either key is public the choice cannot be changed.

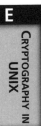

E

CRYPTOGRAPHY IN UNIX

Like hashes and symmetric key cryptosystems, asymmetric key cryptosystems treat messages as binary strings of ones and zeros. Unlike them, asymmetric key cryptosystems do *not* perform binary operations to "scramble" bits. Instead, the binary strings are treated as binary representations of *very* large numbers. The encryption and decryption procedures are based on fairly sophisticated mathematics.

To get some very rough idea of these procedures, consider a 12-hour clock. Suppose that you want to arrange a meeting a four o'clock. The two keys used to encrypt and decrypt the time of the meeting will be 5 and 7. To encrypt the time, move five hours ahead to nine o'clock, and let that be your "encrypted" message. To decode the message, move the time an extra seven hours ahead, and the time comes back around to four o'clock.

In all asymmetric key procedures popular as of this writing (September 2001), the keys are both large numbers with the property of "canceling" each other through the mathematics underlying their cryptosystem, just as moving around the hour hand of a clock five hours and then seven more takes you back where you started.

Of course, anyone who understood the earlier clock system could subtract your public key (7) from 12 to get your private key (5). That's because subtraction is easy. In practice, the computations involved in unraveling the value of the private key from the public key are impossible (in the sense used in this appendix) to perform. This leads us to the characteristics of the asymmetric key cryptosystem.

Characteristics of an Asymmetric Key Cryptosystem

A "strong" asymmetric key cryptosystem has the following characteristics:

- Given the ciphertext alone, it is impossible to determine the original plaintext.
- Given the original plaintext *and* the resulting ciphertext, it is impossible to determine the private key used to produce the ciphertext.
- The previous property holds even if the attacker is allowed to *choose* the plaintext used to produce the ciphertext.
- Given the public key of a keypair *and* the plaintext *and* the ciphertext produced using that key, it is impossible to determine the value of the private key.

Security Through Obscurity

The phrase "security through obscurity" refers to the strategy of maintaining security by keeping the details of your security mechanisms a secret. Although there is certainly no reason to publish such details, it is extremely bad practice to *depend* on secrecy for your security.

Characteristics of "strong" cryptosystems have been described for hashes and symmetric and asymmetric systems. Another characteristic applies to all cryptographic systems: The security of the cryptosystem is not compromised to any degree by publication of the cryptosystem's mechanisms.

In fact, a cryptosystem is not considered "strong" in practice until it has been published and professional cryptanalysts (and everyone else) have had a chance to find weaknesses.

Applications such as SSH are respected in large part because both the algorithms and the source code have been publicly available for years. Users are constantly checking and evaluating the code. When weaknesses have been found, they have been publicized both as a warning to other users and to enlist developers in the effort to develop a fix.

Cryptographic Methods

This section illustrates how the different types of cryptographic tools described in the previous section are used in different procedures to provide security. As we have noted, hashes, symmetric key cryptosystems, and asymmetric key cryptosystems are basic building blocks. These blocks combine in different ways to form the cryptographic protocols that provide information security.

Secure Communication

By tradition, the two parties involved in the description of a secure communication are named Alice and Bob. The opponent, if any, trying to intercept their communication is named Oscar. Tradition will be respected here.

Alice and Bob both agree upon an asymmetric key cryptosystem. Each generates a key-pair. Each selects one key of their pair to be the public key and makes it available to the other (and to anyone else interested).

Alice uses Bob's public key to encrypt a message and sends the ciphertext to Bob. Because the message was encrypted with Bob's public key, only Bob's private key can decrypt it. Even Alice cannot decrypt the encrypted message because only Bob has his private key. This is why the private key must be kept secure.

Bob then encrypts his reply with Alice's public key and transmits the ciphertext to Alice. Alice decrypts the reply with her private key.

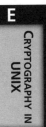

Signatures

Bob wants to send a message to Alice securely *and* wants her to be sure that the message came from him. Before encrypting the message with Alice's public key, he encrypts the phrase "Bob wrote this" using his *private* key and appends the result to the end of the message. Then he encrypts the whole message using Alice's public key and transmits it.

Alice decrypts the message with her private key and sees the appended ciphertext. She decrypts this ciphertext with Bob's *public* key. Because it is decrypted with Bob's public key, it *must* have been encrypted with his *private* key that only Bob has. Thus, Bob *must* have put it there, effectively *signing* the main message. In fact, Bob could have encrypted the phrase "Bob dances with the wildebeest" just as well because it's the successful decryption of the message with his public key that matters, not the contents of the signature.

Notice that the private key must be guarded not just for privacy, but to prevent others from using *your* signature!

Signatures and Hashes

Suppose, in the previous example, that Bob had used neither "Bob wrote this" nor "Bob dances with the wildebeest" as the appended signature encrypted with his private key. Instead, he could compute the hash of the original message, encrypt *that*, and append the encrypted hash to the original before encrypting the whole thing with Alice's public key.

Alice decrypts the whole message using her private key, thus receiving it securely.

Alice decrypts the appended ciphertext with Bob's public key, ensuring that the message was actually signed by Bob.

Alice then computes the hash of the original message (without the appended ciphertext) and compares it to the hash decrypted from the appended ciphertext. If the hashes match, she can be sure that the message wasn't modified or corrupted in any way because Bob computed the hash for use in his signature.

Asymmetric Key Challenge

Suppose that Alice has contacted Bob, but Bob will not converse with Alice until she proves that she really *is* Alice.

Bob can generate a random message, store a copy of the message, encrypt the message with Alice's public key, and transmit the encrypted message to Alice. This encrypted message is the "challenge" referred to in the section title.

Alice, if she really *is* Alice, can decrypt the message with her private key, then re-encrypt it with Bob's public key, and transmit the re-encrypted message to Bob.

Bob can then decrypt the re-encrypted message with his private key and check it against the stored copy. Because the message was chosen at random and only Alice could have decrypted it successfully before re-encrypting it, Alice has proven her identity to Bob.

Verifying the Public Key

Suppose that Alice receives a public key through email. It is attached to a message (not encrypted) that identifies the key as Bob's. Oscar could have spoofed this email. Oscar might have generated a keypair and could now be claiming that the public key is really Bob's. If anyone used this key to encrypt a message to Bob, Oscar could read it. Oscar also could sign documents using the private key of the keypair, and the public key would authenticate the signature. As long as the public key was believed to be Bob's, Oscar would be able to act in Bob's name.

There are two common approaches to this problem: key fingerprints and trusted signatures.

Key Fingerprints

When Bob generates a keypair and distributes a public key, he can also compute the hash of the new key, encrypt it with the private key from his *last* keypair, and make that encrypted hash publicly available. Because only Bob's last public key can decrypt the hash, the hash can be trusted insofar as anyone believes that Bob's *last* private/public keypair was really his. The hash, of course, matches the hash of the new key to verify it with the same degree of certainty.

Alternately, because the hash is 128 bits (16 bytes) long, it is short enough to fit on a business card or other item that Bob can hand Alice personally or sign in the traditional manner.

In both options, the hash can be used to verify that the new public key is Bob's—at least as far as you believe that the hash is Bob's as well.

Trusted Signature

If Alice and Bob have a mutual friend, Chuck, then Bob can give the new public key to Chuck in person so that Chuck can be *sure* that the key is Bob's. Chuck can then sign the key as he would a message, using his private key. Bob can then send the key to Alice with Chuck's signature attached.

Alice can then trust that the key is Bob's, insofar as she has faith in Chuck's honesty *and* sense.

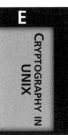

Certificate Authorities

Alice and Bob might not have a mutual friend. Even if neither of them knows Chuck at all, though, Chuck has an opportunity to help. Chuck can start his own business as a signer of public keys. He can develop rigorous procedures to be used to verify the identity of a person or an organization. Those procedures will be published so that everyone knows what Chuck is doing to verify his customers before signing their keys. In fact, Chuck could have several levels of verification corresponding to increasingly rigorous procedures. Chuck would charge his customers for signing their keys, of course; the more rigorous the verification procedure, the more he would charge.

Anyone seeing Chuck's signature on a signed key certifying a certain level of verification could look up the verification procedure for that level. Chuck's signature asserts that the key went through the verificatin procedure.

Of course, this means that instead of Chuck's friends needing to trust his honesty and sense, Chuck's market must trust his business ethics and practices. Other types of business, such as insurance, are based on trust to a great extent, so there is some precedent.

Chuck's business has the basic components of a *Certificate Authority* (CA). In fact, he provides his customers not only with a signature, but with an electronic "certificate" that contains the public key, signature, timestamp, expiration date, and other information in a standard format used throughout the Internet.

Pseudo–Random-Number Generators

The cryptographic procedures described here and in Chapter 7, "Authentication," often require the generation of random information, such as random numbers or random bitstrings. The RSA key challenge, for instance, doesn't work if the opponent can guess the random message that has been encrypted for the challenge. The challenge is significantly weakened if an opponent can even determine that certain challenge messages are more likely than others.

Randomness is difficult to define formally. Intuitively, we expect randomness to be somehow unpredictable. We will follow this intuition and say that, given a sequence of *randomly* generated information, the sequence provides no clue to help predict what information will be generated next. More precisely, a process that produces a sequence $x_1, x_2, x_3, \ldots, x_n$ is *random* if knowing the first n values in the sequence tells you nothing about the value of x_{n+1}.

Physical phenomena, such as coin flipping, can be a pretty good source of randomness. Operating systems, however, normally don't have access to the physical world, but have to generate random information from programmed algorithms. These algorithms usually work by generating a number and then using that number as input to generate a new number, and so on to generate as many numbers as are required. The algorithm takes x_1 and produces x_2, then uses x_2 to produce x_3, and so forth.

Such algorithms must be fast and must demonstrate no "pattern" that would allow an observer to predict what output is likely to be produced from a given input. Because the algorithms are deterministic—that is, the same input will always produce the same output—they are not considered to be *really* random. They are called *pseudorandom* algorithms.

The study of such algorithms, called *pseudo–random-number generators,* or PRNGs, is a profession in itself and won't be discussed further here. Assuming that you have such an algorithm available, though, there is still a problem. The PRNG uses each output number subsequently as input to generate the next output number, but it must be provided with some number to use as input the first time that it is applied. This number is called the *seed.*

Because the algorithm is deterministic, a given seed always produces the same sequence of numbers. Using the same seed all the time, producing the same sequence, is almost as bad as using sequence that repeats the same number (42, 42, 42, 42, …), so it's important to pick a new, random seed whenever a new random sequence (or even a single random number) is produced.

You can't get the random seed from a PRNG because you need a seed to *start* the PRNG. It takes randomness to make randomness. In fact, it takes good randomness to make good randomness. The more random your choice of seeds is, the more random the output of your PRNG will be. Unfortunately, real quality randomness is surprisingly hard to find.

Programs find initial randomness for the seed in various ways. Many programs use bits from the system time. The encryption program, PGP, asks the user to type things at random and uses the time intervals between keystrokes to seed the random generation of asymmetric keys. In some cases, special hardware that monitors a random physical process is connected to the computer as a source of randomness.

Another method, outlined in Chapter 7, takes advantage of the properties of a strong hash function to generate an unpredictable seed from volatile data. This system is probably the best compromise between convenience and randomness available to most sysadmins.

Cryptographic Applications

Having established some of the building blocks of cryptography and seen how they combine into protocols for specific tasks, we will examine some of the common implementations of these procedures into UNIX. We will pay particular attention to SSH, both because of its importance in securing information channels and because of the variety of protocols that it employs to do this.

The Password File

It is often assumed that the password field of the /etc/passwd file contains the user's encrypted password and that the computer either encrypts the user's entry or decrypts the contents of the password field at login time. In fact, the field is a hash of the password. When a user enters a password, the password is hashed and the result is compared to that in the password field. If the two match, the user is logged on.

Note that true encryption would require a key hidden somewhere in the system *and* would have the potential to produce ciphertext larger than the password field will allow. Hashes, however, require no key and have a fixed range of output values and thus of sizes.

SSH

Suppose that Alice is using a communication utility such as telnet or ftp to connect to a remote system. She will type in her password, and the password will be hashed and authenticated (if she typed it correctly); Alice will have access to the remote system. Both telnet and ftp, however, will transmit the password that Alice types through the network, byte by byte. Oscar, monitoring network traffic, will be able to "sniff" Alice's password and use it at will. The standard UNIX communications utilities depend solely on a password (at most!) for authentication and make no attempt to conceal that password during transmission.

SSH provides an excellent substitute for telnet, ftp, rlogin, rcp, and other communications packages that provide unencrypted communication. SSH is designed to provide authentication of the user and of the server; establish a secure, encrypted channel of communication between the two; provide an encrypted "tunnel" through which other communications such as X Windows might pass, and do it all without any noticeable impact on performance.

Currently, two versions of SSH are in use, version 1 and version 2 (SSH1 and SSH2, respectively). The two versions are incompatible—that is, an SSH1 client cannot establish a secure connection with an SSH2 server, and vice versa. The SSH2 server installation, however, supports the option of installing the SSH1 server as well. If the SSH2 server detects a connection attempt by an SSH1 client, the SSH2 server passes the attempt to the SSH1 server to continue the connection.

In addition, OpenSSH, a free implementation of SSH under the OpenBSD license, is available. OpenSSH supports both SSH1 and SSH2 protocols under one installation and has been ported to a variety of UNIX types. It does not support the complete, combined feature sets of SSH1 and SSH2, but it is developing rapidly.

This section looks at the cryptographic methods used by the SSH1 and SSH2 protocols. This can be useful to the sysadmin in configuring and debugging SSH implementations.

SSH1

This list outlines the operation of SSH1 and illustrates the use of various protocols to provide secure communication:

1. When the SSH1 server daemon is installed, it generates a keypair for itself on the host machine. The public key in this pair is called the *host key* and is used to identify the SSH server's host to connection clients. In addition, a keypair is regenerated by the daemon every hour. The public key of this pair is called the *server key*.

2. When an SSH1 client connects to an SSH1 server, the two exchange version information. The server then sends its host key and current server key to the client.

3. The SSH1 client compares the host key to host keys maintained in a specific file, normally ~/.ssh/known_hosts. If there is no entry with the name of the host that sent the key, the key is added to the file. If an entry exists under that hostname and the keys themselves match, the connection proceeds. If an entry exists under that hostname and the keys *don't* match, the client aborts the connection. (The client normally is configured to ask the user before either accepting a new key or aborting the connection.)

4. The SSH1 client generates a key called the *session key*. This key is intended for use in symmetric cryptography. When the SSH1 server has this key, the client and server can use the speed of symmetric cryptography to communicate both securely *and* without undue delays. The client (asymmetrically) encrypts the session key with the host key provided by the server. It then encrypts the resulting encryption again, this time with the server key. Now the doubly encrypted session key is sent to the SSH1 server. The server decrypts the session key using the private server and private host key, in order. Note that, even if the host private key should be compromised, the server key is changed every hour. Because the server private key must be used *before* the host private key, the doubly encrypted session key cannot be determined even if Oscar the attacker has the host private key.

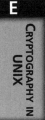

5. After all this, it's the user's turn to authenticate the client side and get access to the server's host computer. This can be done in several ways. The most common is to authenticate the user as would be done in the absence of SSH. SSH is compatible with /etc/passwd, /etc/shadow, NIS, and other common authentication schemes (some of which are extremely insecure themselves). Alternatively, the user can configure a personal asymmetric key challenge.

- Before making the connection, the user runs ssh-keygen on the client. This produces a keypair. One key is in the file ~/.ssh/identity.pub and is stored in ASCII format with information identifying the user and the user's client. The other key is stored in binary form in the file ~/.ssh/identity. During execution, ssh-keygen asks for a passphrase with which to encrypt the private key before storing it in ~/.ssh/ identity.

- The user adds the contents of the file ~/.ssh/identity.pub in the user's client account to the file ~/.ssh/authorized_keys in the user's accounts on all servers to which the user wants to connect.

- When the server requests authentication of the client, the client requests a challenge. The server checks in ~/.ssh/authorized_keys to see if there is a key matching the userid and client name. If so, it generates a random bit string, encrypts it with the client's key, and sends it to the client.

- The client needs its private key to decrypt the challenge. The client asks the user to supply the passphrase with which it can decrypt the private key. The private key is used, in turn, to decrypt the challenge. Alternatively, the user might already have loaded the private key into memory using ssh-agent and ssh-add. In this case, the passphrase is needed only once to decrypt and load the key into memory, and then the key is used automatically to answer the challenge.

Note

If the request for a passphrase by ssh-keygen was answered by a blank (just a carriage return), then the private key is automatically loaded every time it is requested, whether or not ssh-agent and ssh-add has been used. This method can be used to automate scripted file transfers and other interaction by using an unencrypted private key in the client account where scripts execute. This method is used to transfer files between sensor and analysis systems in the network intrusion-detection system, described in Chapter 22, "Intrusion Detection."

- The client decrypts the challenge and appends other identifying information to the bit string. It then hashes the result and returns the hash value to the server.

- The server uses its copy of the original bit string and other information to verify the hash from the client, thus completing the challenge.

6. The authenticated user is given access to the user's account on the server's host system.

SSH2

Although the implementation and installation details of SSH2 differ considerably from those of SSH1, as do the available selections of cryptographic algorithms, its underlying use of cryptographic methods is very similar. The primary difference lies in the use of the Diffie-Hellman algorithm in SSH2 for generation of a session key shared by both client and server.

The Diffie-Hellman algorithm was not described earlier because it is not a hash, nor is it an encryption system. Instead, the algorithm uses the same underlying mathematics as asymmetric key cryptography to establish a symmetric key to be used by both sides of the exchange.

- To attempt to illustrate this, we will let Alice and Bob agree to a base number— say, 21. Oscar can have this number, too.

- Now both Alice and Bob choose secret numbers at random. Say that Alice chooses 42 and Bob chooses 17. Neither of them will ever share these numbers with any-one, including each other.

- Alice computes $21 + 42 = 63$. Alice sends the number 63 to Bob. Oscar might see this number.

- Bob computes $21 + 17 = 38$. Bob sends the number 38 to Alice. Oscar might see this number.

- Alice adds 42 to the number that Bob sent, $38 + 42 = 80$.

- Bob adds 17 to the number that Alice sent, $63 + 17 = 80$.

- Bob and Alice now both share the number 80, even though that number was never transmitted. That number can now be used as the key in a symmetric system.

Of course, all Oscar needs to do is subtract 21 from the numbers transmitted by both Alice and Bob. This will give him their "secret numbers," and he can then compute the key himself. As in an earlier example, Oscar can do this because subtraction is easy. Reversing the math that actually is used for the Diffie-Hellman exchange is not easy.

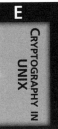

E

CRYPTOGRAPHY IN UNIX

For all intents and purposes, it is impossible barring some spectacular and *very* unexpected breakthrough in several branches of math at once.

> **Note**
>
> An example installation of OpenSSH can be found in Chapter 17, "Third-Party Software."

SSL

Secure Socket Layer (SSL), commonly is used to authenticate and secure communication between Web browsers and servers. Two versions are in use, SSL version 2 and SSL version 3 (SSL2 and SSL3, respectively).

The authentication mechanisms used in both versions are similar. This section describes the *SSL handshake* that establishes the connection between the client and server.

SSL Handshake

When a client (perhaps a Web browser) connects to an SSL-enabled server and requests a secure connection, the client and server first exchange some basic version information to allow communication. The server also provides the client with its certificate. This certificate is normally provided by a Certificate Authority, or CA, as described previously, and consists of a public key and information identifying the server and the CA. The certificate also contains a cryptographic signature from the CA, validating the server's public key.

1. The client checks the CA named in the certificate against a database of known CAs. SSL-enabled clients normally install with such a database. If the CA is recognized, the transaction continues. If the CA is not recognized, the client notifies the user of the problem. The user can abort the connection or continue. Also, the client can be directed to add the new CA to its database.

2. The client generates a random bitstring, asymmetrically encrypts it using the server's public key from the certificate, and sends the result to the server.

3. The server decrypts the encrypted bitstring with its private key.

4. The client and server perform a series of identical operations on the bitstring, producing the same result. This result is called the *master key* for this particular session.

5. The shared master key is used to compute symmetric keys to be used to encrypt communications between the client and the server.

Although this exchange is common for SSL implementations, the protocol supports a variety of options, including the use of Diffie-Hellman key generation to replace steps 2–4.

Online References

Cryptography FAQ

- http://www.faqs.org/faqs/cryptography-faq
- http://www.employees.org/~satch/ssh/faq

Cryptography: The Study of Encryption by Franz Littero: http://world.std.com/~franl/crypto.html

SSH.COM

- http://www.ssh.com
- http://www.ssh.com/tech/crypto

OpenSSH home page: http://www.openssh.com

SSH FAQ: http://www.faqs.org/faqs/computer-security/ssh-faq/

SSH, The Secure Shell: The Definitive Guide, from O'Reilly: http://www.snailbook.com/

SSH Reference Pages

- http://www.cs.toronto.edu/~djast/ssh.html
- http://www.boran.com/security/ssh_stuff.html

SANS Library: An Introduction to SSH Secure Shell, by Damian Zwamborn: http://www.sans.org/infosecFAQ/encryption/intro_SSH.htm

SANS Library: Open Source Implementations of SSL: Why and How by Jeff Dickens: http://www.sans.org/infosecFAQ/encryption/open_source.htm

SANS Library: Digital Certificates: A Secure Method for Digital Transfers by Stephen N. Williams: http://www.sans.org/infosecFAQ/encryption/digicert.htm

Iplanet: Introduction to SSL: http://www.iplanet.com/developer/docs/articles/security/ssl.html

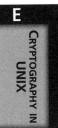

Books

Bhattacharya, P.B., S.K. Jain, and S.R. Nagpaul. *Basic Abstract Algebra 2nd Ed.* Cambridge University Press: 1994.

Schneier, Bruce. *Applied Cryptography 2nd Ed.* John Wiley & Sons, 1996.

Stinson, Douglas. *Cryptography Theory and Practice.* CRC Press: 1996.

Barrett, Daniel J., and Richard Silverman. *SSH, The Secure Shell: The Definitive Guide.* O'Reilly: 2001.

Handy Commands

Andy Johnston

IN THIS APPENDIX

Handy Command List

One of the most popular features of Unix through the years has been its powerful command set. Using features such as standard input and output, pipes, and redirection, the user can combine simple commands into tools to perform specific and seemingly complex tasks. To facilitate the creation of such tools, Unix also supports a variety of "text processing" commands such as `cat`, `cut`, `paste`, `head`, `tail`, `sort`, and `grep`. Quite a lot can still be done directly from the command line and from very short and simple scripts.

Over time, most sysadmins develop a personal "toolbox" of these commands. Some of these tools are used for troubleshooting, others might appear in crontab files, where they monitor and report on specific system features at regular intervals. In all cases, they save time, trouble, and typing.

The authors of this book were asked to contribute some of their favorite command tips and tricks. We pass these "recipes" along to you here, organized by contributor. If you like them, use them. In any case, we suggest that you examine them because careful study of their construction will help you develop your own.

From Robin Anderson

- These are some handy settings that you can add to your .cshrc file:

  - Set the prompt to look like `myhost[1]%`.

    ```
    set prompt = "`hostname | sed 's/\..*//'`[\!]% "
    ```

  - Source typical system .cshrc files *before* adding your own stuff.
    ```
    if ( -e /usr/site/etc/system.cshrc ) source
    /usr/site/etc/system.cshrc
    if ( -e /usr/local/etc/system.cshrc ) source
    /usr/local/etc/system.cshrc
    ```

  - New files get permission 700.
    ```
    umask 077
    ```

  - Enable file completion (Escape key) and no auto-overwrite.
    ```
    set filec noclobber
    ```

- Here are some handy command aliases that you can add to your .cshrc file:

  - Keep your xterms from showing up in process listings.
    ```
    alias xterm    'xterm -ut'
    ```

  - As with whoami, query the system:
    ```
    alias whereami 'printenv HOST'
    ```

- Manually set your DISPLAY variable.

```
alias setdis 'set tty=`tty | & sed 's,/dev/tty,,'` ; setenv DISPLAY
`w | perl -n
 -e "if(s/^${USER}\s+${tty}\s+([^\.]+)\..*\n/\1/) { print };"`:0.0 ;
unset tty'
```

- Check the header on a tape (modify the tape device).

```
alias check-tape-contents "dd if=/dev/mt/tps0d6ns ibs=1024 count=1"
```

- Check for multiple users on a system.

```
alias find-folks "w | egrep '(robin|andy|root)'"
```

- These are some handy settings that you can add to your .tcshrc file:

  - Remember to merge in your .cshrc file settings.

    ```
    if (-e ~/.cshrc ) source ~/.cshrc
    ```

  - If your current effective UID is the same as your login name, make the prompt look like [myhost:1 ~]. If you've switched to another user (with su or sudo), reflect that username in the prompt, as in [myhost:1 root ~].

    ```
    if ("`whoami`" == "robin") then
    set prompt = "[%B%m%b:%h %~] "
    else
    set prompt = "[%B%m%b:%h `whoami` %~] "
    endif
    ```

- Retrieve a user's GECOS information:

  - From NIS: ypmatch robin passwd | awk -F: '{print $5}'
  - From local: grep robin /etc/passwd | awk -F: '{print $5}'

- Delete /etc/cron.d/cron.deny to disallow all cron.

- Solaris kernel information

  - Get a listing of possible variables.

    ```
    nm /kernel/genunix/*
    ```

  - Get a listing of *all* current settings.

    ```
    sysdef -i
    ```

- To disable Solaris keyboard combinations to drop to firmware (including Stop+A, L1+A, and Break):

  ```
  kbd -a disable
  ```

  To re-enable this, use kbd -a enable.

- To find a remote machine's MAC address:

  ```
  ping hostname; arp -a | grep hostname
  ```

- Use the `tar` command to back up /usr using relative pathnames onto a remote machine:

```
find ./usr -mount -print | xargs tar cvfb - 512 | rsh remotehost /sbin/dd
of=/dev/tape obs=512b
```

- List local filesystems in increasing order of fullness:

```
df -kl | sort -n -k6
```

- For a long listing of cwd in increasing order of file size:

```
ls -la | sort -n -k5
```

From Jay Beale

- Show a list of all SUID programs:

```
find . -type f -perm -04000 -print
```

- Show a list of all SGID programs:

```
find . -type f -perm -02000 -print
```

- Show a list of all SUID root programs:

```
find . -type f -perm 04000 -uid 0 -print
```

- Show a list of all SGID root programs:

```
find . -type f -perm 02000 -uid 0 -print
```

- Use the "safe" way to zero out a log:

```
cat /dev/null > /var/log/foo
```

- Query the target_nameserver for the BIND version:

```
dig @target_nameserver target_nameserver txt chaos version.bind
```

- Query the target_nameserver for a zone dump of an entire zone:

```
dig @target_nameserver target_nameservers_zone axfr
```

- Show the third column of file, based on space separation:

```
awk '{print $3}'  < file
```

- Tell tail to watch the messages log file and print each new line, from now on, as it is written to the file:

```
tail -f /var/adm/messages
```

From Matt Bishop

- Here's a list of C-shell aliases:

```
alias   addr    echo \!\* "|" nslookup
alias   cname   "(" echo set q=CNAME ";" echo \!\* ")" "|" nslookup
alias   mx      "(" echo set q=MX ";" echo \!\* ")" "|" nslookup
```

```
alias   hinfo   "(" echo set q=HINFO ";" echo \!\* ")" "|" nslookup
alias   ns      "(" echo set q=NS ";" echo \!\* ")" "|" nslookup
alias   any     "(" echo set q=ANY ";" echo \!\* ")" "|" nslookup
alias   soa     "(" echo set q=SOA ";" echo \!\* ")" "|" nslookup
alias   ptr     "(" echo set q=PTR ";" echo
\\!\$:e.\!\$:r:e.\!\$:r:r:e.\!\$:r:r:r.in-addr.arpa ")" "|" nslookup
```

So, if you want to know the host whose IP address is 127.0.0.1, type this:

```
ptr 127.0.0.1
```

You get this (here, at least):

```
Default Server:  regnant6.cs.ucdavis.edu
Address:  169.237.6.10

Server:  regnant6.cs.ucdavis.edu
Address:  169.237.6.10

1.0.0.127.in-addr.arpa  name = localhost
0.0.127.in-addr.arpa    nameserver = regnant6.cs.ucdavis.edu
regnant6.cs.ucdavis.edu internet address = 169.237.6.10
so it's "localhost".
```

From Rob Jenson

- Show all filenames with non-printable characters displayed as ?s or in quoted C form. It helps you figure out what to do about "undeletable" files:

```
ls -aq
ls -aQ
```

- Get rid of a file that contains flag characters like '-' in its name:

```
rm './filename with unprintable characters'
```

- Show long listings of the most recently modified files (it's good when you don't have a working TTY to page stuff):

```
ls -lart | tail [-n]
```

- This command shows a long listing of all files in order of inode modification time (ctime). This can tell you what files have been backed up most recently and when because ctime is changed by any well-behaved backup program when it reads a file (to avoid permanently changing utime). This command also tells you when files have been installed or modified using a tarball, a rootkit, or some other means that sets the file modification time to something other than "right now." Remember, mtime and utime can be changed by any program/person with write access to the directory and the inode. Changes to mtime or utime without affecting ctime can only be effected by changing either the system clock first (which, hopefully, results in a log discrepancy) or changing the `ctime` (or performing an update of the raw filesystem structure outside the Unix operating system).

```
ls -lact  [directory name]
```

- This command displays the top *n* (default of 10) disk space hogs in a directory, in descending order. It should be run as root and might take a while on large disks:

```
du -sk * | sort -rn | head [-n]
```

- If your network or your DNS (or both) is hosed, many of the troubleshooting commands that you will use also will gum up because they are expecting to look up the names for the network numbers.

```
ping -n[other flags]
ifconfig -n[other flags]
netstat -n[other flags]
traceroute -n[other flags]
```

- This command starts a continuous display showing `vmstat` values calculated over a sampling period of *n* seconds. It allows you to run an inexpensive real-time profile of system load and resources. The argument n is the number of seconds between samples.

```
vmstat n
```

- The following short script was cooked up just for this book. The script monitors a system continuously with timestamps. It should roll itself daily so that older versions can be pruned when they're not needed.

```
#!/bin/sh
#
# Simple monitoring scriptlet using vmstat

LOGDIR=/var/tmp/monstat # Where you want the logs to go (directory)
VMSTATFLAGS="-n"        # Dont show extra header lines
VMSTATDLY=15            # Sample every 15 seconds
VMSTATCNT=40            # Stop sampling and put datestamp every 40 samples
                        # (every 10 minutes)

# You can probably leave the rest alone from here
FNAMEPREFIX="monstat"
FILEDATEFMT="+%Y%m%d"
DISPHEADER="+TIMESTAMP: %s UTC = %Y/%m/%d %H:%M:%S %z %Z"

# No more user-serviceable parts beyond here
mkdir -p ${LOGDIR}

while [ 1 ]
do
  logfile=${LOGDIR}/${FNAMEPREFIX}.`date ${FILEDATEFMT}`
```

```
    date "${DISPHEADER}" 2>&1 >> ${logfile}
    vmstat ${VMSTATFLAGS} ${VMSTATDLY} ${VMSTATCNT} 2>&1 >> ${logfile}
done
```

From Andy Johnston

- As noted elsewhere in the book, name resolution can slow down commands such as netstat and traceroute, so we recommend using the -n option to disable DNS lookups while running them. If you run regular cron jobs to generate reports with IP addresses in them, you might like the option of regenerating the same document with the IP addresses resolved wherever they can be.

  The following script accepts any file as standard input and checks for anything in dotted-quad format. If found, and if the dotted-quad can be resolved, it is replaced in the text with the resolved name.

  Note that unresolved addresses are marked internally by appending the suffix ".UNRESOLVED" to the IP address. That suffix is stripped off in the final output, but that is a matter of personal preference.

```perl
#!/usr/bin/perl

use Socket;
$: = " \n\.";

while ($line = <STDIN>)
{
        while (($ip) = ($line =~ /(\d+\.\d+\.\d+\.\d+)(?![\.\w])/))
        {
                if (exists $resolved{$ip})
                {
                        $hostname = $resolved{$ip};
                }
                else
                {
                        @ipoctets = split(/\./, $ip);
                        $binip =
                                pack "c4",$ipoctets[0],$ipoctets[1],
                                $ipoctets[2],$ipoctets[3];
                        @hostdata = gethostbyaddr ($binip, 2);
                        $hostname = $hostdata[0];
                        if ($hostname)
                        {
                                $resolved{$ip} = $hostname;
                        }
                        else
                        {
                                $resolved{$ip} =
                        join (".",$ip,"UNRESOLVED");
```

```
                                }
                        }

                        $line =~ s/$ip/$hostname/g if ($hostname);
                }
                $line =~ s/.UNRESOLVED//g;
                print $line;
        }
```

- During the summer of 2001, several computer worms appeared that infected Microsoft IIS servers through their Web ports. The worms tried to infect any system offering a service at port 80. An examination of the access logs on a Unix Web server will often produce failed infection attempts along with the IP addresses from which they came.

  The following command string selects access log entries containing the string `cmd.exe`, indicative of a NIMDA attack. The `cut` command selects the first field of each record, containing the IP address of the probe. The `sort` command operates on the four numeric fields of the dotted-quad, recognizing the dots as separators. The `-n` option of `sort` specifies numeric sorting, and the `-u` option makes each address sorted appear only once in the output. Finally, the whole thing is run through name resolution.

  ```
  % grep cmd access_log | cut -d" " -f 1 | sort -t"." -nu | ./bin/resolv_name
  ```

  For a more complete report, the next command string selects the same record, extracts the IP address and timestamp from each record, removes the distracting left square bracket from the time stamp, and prints the source IP address and time of each probe.

  ```
  % grep cmd access_log | cut -d" " -f 1,4 | sed -e 's/\[//'
  ```

From Scott Orr

- This command that I use occasionally is buried in the `tar` man pages. We always referred to it as a "super `tar`" because it is used to copy a directory tree structure from one location to another while preserving file/directory ownership and permissions.

  ```
  cd fromdir; tar cf - . | (cd todir; tar xfBp -)
  ```

  Note that if you want to see the list of files as they are being copied, you also need to add the v switch to the first `tar` command line.

From Andrew Senft

- The following commands in your .cshrc file will set the prompt to display the host-name and current directory for C-shell.

```
set hostname = `uname -n`
    alias cd 'chdir \!*;set prompt="${hostname}-$cwd "'
set prompt="${hostname}-$cwd "
```

From Mike Wessler

- This command lists all Oracle databases that are running. Each Oracle database instance requires the Process Monitor (PMON) background process, so this is a handy way to check their status.

```
ps -ef | grep pmon
```

References

Periodicals

Dr. Dobb's Software Tools for the Professional Programmer: http://www.ddj.com/

Linux Journal: http://www.linuxjournal.com

Linux Magazine: http://www.linux-mag.com

;login, The Magazine of USENIX and SAGE

- http://www.usenix.org/publications/login/login.html
- http://www.usenix.org/

Sysadmin, The Journal for UNIX System Administrators:

- http://www.sysadminmag.com/

Mailing Lists

Apache Web Server Mailing Lists:

- News and announcements: http://www.apache.org/announcelist.html
- Development: http://dev.apache.org/mailing-lists/
- Usage and general support: news://comp.infosystems.www.servers.unix/

BIND Users: http://www.isc.org/ml-archives/bind-users

Bugtraq: http://www.securityfocus.com (Click on Bugtraq. This is a full-disclosure mailing list that generally represents the very first public release of vital information about vulnerabilities in your operating system and software.)

CERT-Advisory: Send email to majordomo@cert.org with a message body of "subscribe <listname> [<optional address>]". (This is a mailing list run by CERT/CC [CERT Coordination Center, Carnegie Mellon].)

LogAnalysis: Send email to loganalysis-subscribe@securityfocus.com. (This is a mailing list dedicated to log analysis issues of all kinds, run by Security Focus.)

SANS Lists:

- All SANS lists: http://www.sans.org/aboutsans.htm
- SANS NewsBites: http://www.sans.org/newlook/digests/newsbites.htm
  (This is a weekly summary of important published news stories concerning information security.)

- SANS Security Alert Consensus: `https://server2.sans.org/sansnews` (This is a weekly summary of new security alerts and countermeasures, produced in collaboration with *Network Computing* magazine.)

Vulnwatch: `http://www.vulnwatch.org` (This new mailing list begun this year has a similar purpose to BugTraq but was begun as a completely noncommercial community resource.)

Professional Organizations

FIRST, Forum of Incident Response and Security Teams: `http://www.first.org/` ("...the Forum of Incident Response and Security Teams (FIRST), brings together a variety of computer security incident response teams from government, commercial, and academic organizations. FIRST aims to foster cooperation and coordination in incident prevention, to prompt rapid reaction to incidents, and to promote information sharing among members and the community at large. Currently FIRST has more than 100 members." Many organizations across the country have a FIRST team, so FIRST is where you can find out in whose constituency you are. Many of the organizations that participate in FIRST have useful Web sites; if you are interested in security information, browse FIRST's members/contacts list to find them.)

CERT, Computer Emergency Response Team: `http://www.cert.org/` (CERT is one of the oldest active computer security organizations. It specializes in releasing alerts regarding current security threats.)

CIAC, Computer Incident Advisory Capability, DOE: `http://www.ciac.org/ciac/`

SAGE, The System Administrators' Guild:

- International: `http://www.sage.org/`
- U.S.: `http://www.usenix.org/sage/`
- Local SAGE groups: `http://www.usenix.org/sage/locals/sage-localgroups.html`

USENIX, The Advanced Computing Systems Association: `http://www.usenix.org/` ("USENIX is the Advanced Computing Systems Association. Since 1975 the USENIX Association has brought together the community of engineers, system administrators, scientists, and technicians working on the cutting edge of the computing world. ... The USENIX Association and its members are dedicated to: problem-solving with a practical bias, fostering innovation and research that works, communicating rapidly the results of both research and innovation, providing a neutral forum for the exercise of critical thought and the airing of technical issues.")

G

REFERENCES

URLs

The authors have collated something like 35 pages of reference URLs to supplement the material in this book. Because of the transient nature of online information and the volatility of URL names, SAMS Publishing will be hosting a Web site for general information, errata, and current/updated references. To access the site, just go to `http://www.samspublishing.com` and enter this book's ISBN or title in the "Search" box.

Here are our top ten URLs (in no particular order) that you should have handy when approaching a sysadmin task:

- **Whatis.com**: `http://whatis.techtarget.com` (This is a database of thousands of IT-related terms, buzzwords, and more.)

- **Internet FAQ Archives**: `http://www.faqs.org` (Here you'll find frequently asked questions of all types: Internet RFCs, Usenet [newsgroup] FAQs, and others.)

- **Unix Guru Universe (UGU)**: `http://www.ugu.com` (This is an amazing collection of tips, tricks, and information for admins of every level.)

- **SecurityFocus.com**: `http://www.securityfocus.com/` (SecurityFocus is home to a number of security resources, including the widely-regarded BugTraq mailing list. Also available are news pieces about current security issues and opinion pieces regarding security.)

- **SANS Institute Online**: `http://www.sans.org/` ("The SANS [System Administration, Networking, and Security] Institute is a cooperative research and education organization through which more than 96,000 system administrators, security professionals, and network administrators share the lessons they are learning and find solutions to the challenges they face. SANS was founded in 1989." This page has a link to the top Internet Security Vulnerabilities identified by SANS in conjunction with the FBI, along with other information about system security.)

- **Red Hat:**
  Main site: `http://www.redhat.com`

  Patch site: errata page (versions 4.0 to 7.0): `http://www.redhat.com/support/errata/`

  Support page (updates, more errata, and advisories): `http://www.redhat.com/apps/support/updates.html`

- **Linux.com:** `http://www.linux.com` ("Linux.com is a volunteer-supported site created for and by the Linux and Open Source communities. Our mission is to educate, inform, and entertain.")

- **Linux Documentation Project:** `http://www.linuxdoc.org`
- **Sun Microsystems, Inc**: Main site: `http://www.sun.com/`

  Main Sun support and patch site: SunSolve: `http://sunsolve.sun.com/`

  Docs and searchable information: `http://docs.sun.com/`

  Sun Security Coordination Team: `http://sunsolve.sun.com/pub-cgi/show.pl?target=security/sec`

  Sun's BigAdmin: `http://www.sun.com/bigadmin`
- **CERT Security Improvement Modules:** `http://www.cert.org/security-improvement/` ("Each CERT Security Improvement module addresses an important but narrowly defined problem in network security. It provides guidance to help organizations improve the security of their networked computer systems. Each module page links to a series of practices and implementations. Practices describe the choices and issues that must be addressed to solve a network security problem. Implementations describe tasks that implement recommendations described in the practices.")

Books

General System Administration

- Frisch, Aeleen. *Essential System Administration.* (Nutshell Handbook.) O'Reilly & Associates, 1996.
- Nemeth, Evi, Garth Snyder, Scott Seebass, and Trent R. Hein. *UNIX System Administration Handbook.* Prentice Hall PTR, 2000.

Red Hat-Specific

- Bailey, Ed. *Maximum RPM.* Sams, 1997.
- Carling, M., and James Dennis. *Linux System Administration.* (The Landmark Series). New Riders Publishing, 2000.

UNIX Operating System Internals

- Bach, Maurice J. *Design of the Unix Operating System.* Prentice Hall, 1987.
- Vahalia, Uresh. *UNIX Internals: The New Frontiers.* Prentice Hall, 1995.

General System Security

- Mann, Scott, and Ellen L. Mitchell. *Linux System Security: The Administrator's Guide to Open Source Security Tools.* Prentice Hall PTR, 1999.

Subsystems and Specific Tools

Apache

- Bowen, Rich, et al. *Apache Server Unleashed.* Sams Publishing, 2000.
- Ford, Andrew. *Apache Pocket Reference.* O'Reilly & Associates, 2000.
- Laurie, Ben, and Peter Laurie. *Apache: The Definitive Guide, 2nd Edition.* O'Reilly & Associates, 1999.
- Stein, Lincoln, Doug MacEachern, and Linda Mui (editors). *Writing Apache Modules with Perl and C: The Apache API and mod_perl.* (O'Reilly Nutshell.) O'Reilly & Associates, 1999.

NIS

- Stern, Hal, Mike Eisler, and Ricardo Labiaga. *Managing NFS and NIS, 2nd Edition.* (O'Reilly System Administration Series.) O'Reilly & Associates, 2001.

SSH

- Barrett, Daniel J., and Richard Silverman. *SSH, The Secure Shell: The Definitive Guide.* O'Reilly & Associates, 2001.

X Windows

- *The Definitive Guides to the X Window System, volumes 0-8.* O'Reilly and Associates. See `http://unix.oreilly.com/`.

Miscellaneous References

- Lasser, Jon. *Think Unix.* Que, 2000.
- Stevens, W. Richard. *Advanced Programming in the UNIX Environment.* Addison Wesley, 1992.

Cryptography

- Schneier, Bruce. *Applied Cryptography: Protocols, Algorithms, and Source Code in C, 2nd Edition.* John Wiley & Sons, 1996.

- Schneier, Bruce. *Secrets and Lies: Digital Security in a Networked World.* John Wiley and Sons, 2000. (Schneier, a well-known and widely respected computer security consultant, discusses security as idea and as process. This is well worth the read for those unfamiliar with the practice of computer security.)

- Stinson, Douglas. *Cryptography Theory and Practice.* CRC Press, 1996.

SCSI

- Field, Gary et al. *The Book of SCSI, 2nd edition.* No Starch Press, 2000.

G

REFERENCES

INDEX

SYMBOL

/ (slash) directory in, 113–114, 132

A

absolute pathname, 105, 695–696
access control, 413
  Apache module for, 667-668
  login problems and, 415-417
  in securing a system for rollout, 353
access rights, user administration and, 199
account security module, Bastille, 382
accounts. *See also* **entity; user administration**
  Bastille security applied to, 382
  creating, 194-204, 213, 421
  locking, 207-208, 212
  management of, 421
  removing, 204-212
  troubleshooting problems with, 416-417
adapters, 57
adding/removing disks and devices, 84-90
  best practices in, 90-92
  buses for, 85
  cables and, 85-87
  compatibility issues, 85
  connectors and terminators, 85

documenting changes in, 84
filesystem creation in, 89
hot swapping and, 89
initialization, 88
kernel support, 85
partitioning of disks in, 89
physical addition, steps in, 86-87
power supplies, 86
removing devices in, 89-92
self test in, 88
test-all command, 88-89
testing after physical addition of device in, 88-90

address resolution protocol (ARP), 232-237
address space, in IP addressing, 226-227
adduser, 201
AfterStep window manager in, 450
air conditioning, 412
alerting via logging, 290-293
Alexandria, 711
aliases, user administration and, 199
AMANDA backup, 245, 246, 709-710
American National Standards Institute (ANSI), 55
Andrew File System (AFS), 134, 549
anonymous FTP, 246
ansi-terminal, 18

Apache and Web services, 368, 548, 639-673, 720
  access control module for, 667-668
  add on modules for, 669
  adding feature modules in, 666-671
  alias directives, 655
  Bastille security applied to, 384
  best practices for, 673
  building using make command, 644
  chrooted Web server for, 671-672
  Common Gateway Interface (CGI) scripts and, 664-666
  configuration files for, 647-648
  configuring source code for, 643-644
  configuring, 647-658
  content type decision module for, 667
  directives in, 647
  directory handling module for, 667
  dynamic content Apache module for, 668
  environment creation module for, 667
  global configuration directives for, 648-651
  HTTP and httpd daemon in, 641-642
  HTTP response Apache module for, 668
  internal content handler Apache module for, 668
  introduction to, 641-642